A HISTORY OF ANTIOCH IN SYRIA
FROM SELEUCUS TO THE ARAB CONQUEST

A HISTORY OF ANTIOCH IN SYRIA

from Seleucus
to the Arab Conquest

BY GLANVILLE DOWNEY

PRINCETON, NEW JERSEY
PRINCETON UNIVERSITY PRESS

1961

Publication of this book has been aided
by the Ford Foundation program to support publication,
through university presses,
of works in the humanities and social sciences.

Glanville Downey is Professor of Byzantine Literature
at the Dumbarton Oaks Research Library and Collection,
Washington, D.C. and Member of the Faculty
of Arts and Sciences, Harvard University.

Printed in the United States of America
by Princeton University Press, Princeton, N.J.

In *Memory* of
Charles Rufus Morey

PREFACE

THE writing of this book has grown out of the opportunity given me by the Committee for the Excavation of Antioch and its Vicinity to become a member of the excavation staff during the first season of work, in 1932. For this opportunity, and for continued encouragement, advice, and support in research then initiated on the history of Antioch, I am indebted to the late Professor Charles Rufus Morey of Princeton University. Those who knew the kindness and generosity of Professor Morey will understand how deeply I regret that the book could not have been published before he died in 1955.

A work of this kind necessarily owes much to those who have written on Antioch in the past. The names of the many scholars on whose writings I have freely and gratefully drawn appear in the List of Abbreviations and the Bibliography; but I must record here my respect for the memory of Carl Otfried Müller, whose pioneer work on Antioch, published in 1839, formed the point of departure for my own research.

Other support and assistance has come from many quarters. At Dumbarton Oaks I have been fortunate to enjoy a freedom that has greatly advanced the work. As guest professor during two years in the Princeton Theological Seminary I enjoyed associations that contributed much to my researches. The John Simon Guggenheim Memorial Foundation awarded me a fellowship that enabled me to complete much of the latter part of the book. The Institute for Advanced Study, in Princeton, twice offered me memberships that provided leisure for research and writing, and hospitality during my tenure of the Guggenheim Fellowship. Those whose good fortune it has been to enjoy the incomparable facilities of the Institute will know how much my work profited from membership in it. Princeton University awarded me a Procter Fellowship which enabled me to spend a year collecting material.

Many friends and associates have helped in many ways, and to all these I offer thanks. Here my greatest debts are to the R. P. René Mouterde, S. J., of the Université Saint Joseph, Beirut, for his unfailing generosity and friendly advice; to Professors A. R. Bellinger and C. B. Welles, of Yale University, and Professor Richard Stillwell, of Princeton University, who generously read the manuscript, and thereby saved me from many errors; to Dr. Carl H. Kraeling, Director of the Oriental

Institute at the University of Chicago, whose reading of the chapter on the early Christian community at Antioch left it much less imperfect than it might have been; and to the Reverend Dr. Albert C. Outler, of Southern Methodist University, who made many generous suggestions concerning the later chapters. Both Dumbarton Oaks and the Committee for the Excavation of Antioch and its Vicinity, through Professor Richard Stillwell, generously furnished photographs.

My early study of the history of Antioch was guided by teachers in Princeton University whose patience and generosity I must especially acknowledge. In addition to Professor Morey, these were: Professor G. W. Elderkin, the late A. C. Johnson, David Magie, W. K. Prentice, the late E. Baldwin Smith, and the late D. R. Stuart.

Other friends whose assistance contributed to many parts of the work are Professor Sterling Dow of Harvard University, Professor W. J. Oates of Princeton University, Mr. Marvin C. Ross of Washington, M. Henry Seyrig, Director of the Institut Français d'Archéologie, Beirut; and Dr. D. N. Wilber of Princeton.

I am deeply grateful to the Princeton University Press for accepting my work for publication, and I must record here my appreciation of the assistance of Miss Harriet Anderson of the staff of the Press, whose careful editing of the manuscript was responsible for the introduction of many improvements. I must also express here my thanks for the financial aid toward the cost of publication which has come from the program of the Ford Foundation in support of the publications of university presses; from the Committee on Publications of Dumbarton Oaks; and from the William L. Bryant Foundation, which provided a grant-in-aid to meet the cost of the preparation of some of the illustrations.

Acknowledgement must also be made of the permission of the Princeton University Press to draw on my paper on the Emperor Julian which appeared in *Studies in Roman Economic and Social History in Honor of Allan Chester Johnson*, published by the Press in 1951, and of the authorization of M. Jean Lassus, Director of the Antiquities Service in Algeria, and of the Librairie Orientaliste Paul Geuthner, Paris, to make use of the drawing by M. Lassus in J. Sauvaget, *Alep* (1941), on which Fig. 10 is based. Scholars anticipate with keen interest M. Lassus' forthcoming study of the main street at Antioch.

A word needs to be said about the way in which some of the material has been arranged. In order to avoid overloading the text and the footnotes with repetitions, cross references, and discussions of problems of the sources, I have made use of the Excursus to collect and record material not easy to accommodate in the text or dealing with matters in which the evidence is of a difficult or debatable character. However, in order to permit the reader to pick up at a point of special interest to him and read the material consecutively as narrative, it has seemed useful to repeat in some cases rather than to send the reader to cross-references. For example, reference to the winter torrent Parmenius recurs in many different contexts and data relevant to the particular context are repeated.

This book is not intended to be a compendium of everything that is known about Antioch. The attempt to prepare such a volume would have postponed almost indefinitely the publication of a work already too long delayed. If readily available monographs treat special aspects of the history of Antioch in a detail that would be disproportionate in the present volume, it has seemed sufficient to limit the accounts given here to essentials. Such an instance is provided by the important new researches on Libanius of Professor Paul Petit, of the University at Grenoble. His two books, published after my own work was substantially completed, treat the career of Libanius and the Antioch of his time on a scale far beyond what would be appropriate to the present work. I gratefully acknowledge the assistance I have received from his studies. My purpose has been to assemble the essential information concerning the history of the city as a whole, and while I am sure that there must be details that have escaped me, I hope that the work may serve as a guide and a source of information on which others may build.

Dumbarton Oaks, Washington, D.C.
November 1958

CONTENTS

Contents

Contents

Contents

Contents

Contents

APPENDICES

HISTORICAL EXCURSUS

TOPOGRAPHICAL EXCURSUS

Contents

ILLUSTRATIONS

(Following the Index)

A HISTORY OF ANTIOCH IN SYRIA
FROM SELEUCUS TO THE ARAB CONQUEST

INTRODUCTION

THE great monograph of Carl Otfried Müller (1797-1840), *Antiquitates Antiochenae*, was published at Göttingen in 1839, the year before he died of a fever in Greece at the age of forty-three.[1] It was no coincidence that this monograph was written by one of the leading classical philologists of the day, and that it appeared among the earliest of the special studies of ancient cities that the scholarship of the nineteenth century recognized as one of the most important bases upon which our knowledge of ancient and mediaeval history is to be built. Ancient cities, as the epitomes and custodians of civilization, have continued to be natural centers around which modern scholars have often found that their studies can be most fruitfully developed.

Among the great centers of the Hellenistic, Roman, and Early Byzantine worlds, Antioch came to occupy a rather special position, both in the Middle Ages and in the program of modern scholarship. While it was in its day to be listed among the foremost cities in the Graeco-Roman world, its fate was quite different from that of Alexandria, Constantinople, and Rome. With the Moslem conquest of Syria in the seventh century, Antioch soon ceased to be a major city and, while it did take on a temporary and romantic role as a frontier fortress in later Byzantine times and as a famous principality during the Crusades it returned to obscurity under the Turkish regime; the Patriarch of Antioch had his residence in Damascus. Modern Antakiya has in recent years regained a measure of commercial importance, but it is still a relatively small town, occupying only a portion of the ancient site. The monuments that remained above ground before the beginning of the excavations in 1932 were far from numerous—parts of the city walls, the ruins of the Frankish citadel on the top of the mountain, the mysterious rock carving known as the Charonion, some remains of the hippodrome and the aqueducts, and one ancient bridge over the Orontes which is still in use.

Thus, while Rome, Alexandria, and Constantinople, as well as such cities as Athens and Jerusalem, have had a continuous tradition and have been more or less accessible to travelers and scholars since the close of the Middle Ages, Antioch by comparison virtually disappeared from the direct knowledge of European students. Carl Otfried Müller,

---

[1] See the List of Abbreviations under Müller's name for further details concerning this work.

for example, was able to travel in Greece, but a visit to Antioch, difficult and dangerous for any traveler in those times, would have been
impossible without resources that he did not command, and his monograph had to be prepared entirely from such written sources as were
available.

The supply of sources is in fact another respect in which Antioch is
set apart from the other great cities. In the case of Constantinople and
Rome, for example, the ancient texts that have been preserved, along
with the monuments, are considerable. For Antioch the documentation
is notably uneven. For the Seleucid epoch we possess relatively few texts.
With the coming of the Roman regime in Syria in 64 B.C., our preserved information begins to increase, but it is never abundant until
the fourth century of our era, and in the fifth and sixth centuries there
are once more great gaps in our knowledge. The result is that while
Du Cange in the 1680's could produce monumental studies of the history and antiquities of Constantinople, and while at the same period
the historians of the city of Rome had at their disposal the material
for even more detailed treatises, Müller's book in 1839 was the first
monographic study of the antiquities of Antioch, and it is by no means
a large volume.

In these circumstances it was natural that although the history of
Antioch was related to many aspects of ancient civilization, it seemed
more rewarding for scholars to devote themselves to special studies of
various aspects of the city's history, rather than to attempt to expand
and continue Müller's study, which was in fact so thoroughly carried
out that it remained the principal treatise on the subject for many years.
As travel in Syria became easier, an increasing number of scholarly
visitors went to Antioch, including E. G. Rey (1859) and E. Renan
(1860-1861).[2] Even so, it was not until the last decade of the nineteenth
century that any scholar went to the city for the express purpose of
obtaining material for a comprehensive study of the site. The first such
visitor was Richard Förster (1843-1922), whose preparation of the
Teubner edition of the works of Libanius had given him a special
interest in Antioch and a greater command of the ancient and mediaeval sources than any scholar since Müller had possessed. Förster was
in the city for twelve days (March 18-29) in 1896, and in the following
years he published three important articles embodying the results of his

[2] For the records of these and other travelers to Antioch, see below, Excursus 19,
under date of visit.

visit.[3] As was to be expected, Förster was able to make a number of additions to Müller's study. He included in his publication a selection of views of the city made by travelers in the eighteenth and nineteenth centuries, and this formed the first such collection of material readily available to scholars. He also printed an improved version of the Baedeker map of the city.[4]

Eleven years after Förster's visit, the learned industry of Dom H. Leclercq produced an expanded account of the city in the *Dictionnaire d'archéologie chrétienne et de liturgie*,[5] which provided scholars with a convenient survey of the history of Antioch, pagan and Christian, though Müller's work remained the basic work on the subject. Dom Leclercq's article was followed by the books of E. S. Bouchier and V. Schultze,[6] which were intended for the general public; and continued study of the history of Syria as a whole, as well as of special episodes in the history of Antioch, began to broaden our picture of the city considerably.

The excavation of Antioch had long been a dream of archaeologists,[7] but while other great cities had long since been excavated, the plan to explore Antioch was not realized until, on the initiative of the late Professor Charles Rufus Morey (1877-1955) of Princeton University, the Committee for the Excavation of Antioch and its Vicinity began work in 1932.[8] Representing the Musées Nationaux of France and a group of American universities, museums, and private donors, this Committee carried on excavations annually in Antioch, the suburb Daphne, and the seaport Seleucia Pieria until 1939, when the outbreak of war in Europe made further campaigns impossible. The publication of the excavation reports,[9] and particularly of the numerous fine mosaic floors that were discovered, immediately stimulated the study of all aspects of the history and antiquities of the city.

[3] "Antiochia am Orontes," *Jahrbuch des k. deutschen Archäologischen Instituts* 12 (1897) 103-149; "Skulpturen von Antiochia," *ibid.* 13 (1898) 177-191; "Zu den Skulpturen und Inschriften von Antiochia," *ibid.* 16 (1901) 39-55.

[4] On the maps of Antioch, see below, Excursus 8-9.

[5] Vol. 1 (1907) cols. 2359-2427.

[6] E. S. Bouchier, *A Short History of Antioch* (Oxford 1921) (this book is to be used with caution); V. Schultze, *Antiochia* (Gütersloh 1930), in the series *Altchristliche Städte und Landschaften*, vol. 3.

[7] Paul Perdrizet visited Antioch in 1896 to make a survey of the possibilities of excavating the site; see Excursus 19.

[8] On the organization and history of the excavations, see the Foreword of Morey's *The Mosaics of Antioch* (New York 1938) v-vi, and the Forewords to the three volumes of the excavation reports, *Antioch-on-the-Orontes* 1-3 (Princeton 1934-1941).

[9] Mentioned in the preceding note; see also the preliminary reports by W. A. Campbell published in *AJA*, listed below in the Bibliography.

The excavations brought the city back to life in a way which no mere study of the literary sources could do. Circumstances prevented a complete exploration of Antioch, but it was possible nevertheless to recover important evidence for the topography of the city, and a comparison of the reconstructed map of Antioch as it can now be drawn (Fig. 11) with C. O. Müller's hypothetical map, based solely on the literary texts and the reports of travelers (Fig. 9), will show how much we have learned and how extraordinarily careful and accurate Müller's work was, within the limits of information available to him.

Thus our knowledge of ancient Antioch today enables us to appreciate more fully the role of the city in the ancient world and to understand in particular its contributions to the mediaeval world. We still, however, lack certain kinds of information, and while there are many aspects of the city's history about which we may expect to learn more as specialized studies continue to be made, it is not likely that we shall ever know as much about the Syrian metropolis as we do about Constantinople and Rome.

Both the problems and the recent gains illustrate the significance of the history of the city. Almost the greatest gap in our knowledge is on subjects about which we learn elsewhere in the ancient world from epigraphic sources. Relatively few Greek and Latin inscriptions of importance have been recovered at Antioch. The chief reason for this seems to be that on several occasions in antiquity the city had to be more or less extensively rebuilt after earthquakes and fires, and that it has been continuously occupied since, so that ancient stones were re-used for building purposes in ancient, mediaeval and modern times, or were burned for lime.[10] Whether complete excavation of the site, which was hardly possible in the years 1932-1939, would add materially to our epigraphical testimonia is doubtful, since the areas that were excavated did not produce any impressive number of texts.

The resulting lacunae in our knowledge will be at once apparent. For the Seleucid period, for which literary texts are themselves scanty, we have little epigraphic evidence for the local administration and the municipal life of the city, or for its administrative, military, and economic role as the Seleucid capital. Information about cults, festivals, and dedications at this period is limited for the same reason.

In the early Roman Imperial period, Antioch furnishes virtually

---

[10] As has been the case at other sites, the excavators at Antioch found lime kilns which had been built inside the ruins of the ancient buildings for the more convenient burning of the marble; see for example *Antioch-on-the-Orontes* 1.25.

nothing of the evidence for municipal life and imperial administration that is supplied by inscriptions elsewhere in the eastern provinces, and it is not until we have the extensive material found in the writings of Libanius, in the latter half of the fourth century, that we become familiar in any detail with the administration as well as the social and intellectual life of Antioch.

There are other areas as well in which, through the accidents of preservation of our literary texts, we lack highly desirable information. One of these subjects is the history of the early Christian community at Antioch, in the period before Constantine the Great in general, and in particular in apostolic and sub-apostolic times. Because of the importance of this whole epoch in the development of the early church, the history of the early Christian community at Antioch has received more attention—and from a greater number of scholars—than any other similar aspect of the history of the city. The texts we do possess are sufficient to demonstrate the vital significance of the role of Antioch as the center of the mission to the Gentiles and as a place in which important features of church polity developed. Yet the information available is necessarily so limited that many questions remain unanswered, and here again it is not until we reach the latter part of the third century that we begin to have any kind of detailed and continuous information.

Considering the general scarcity of literary texts concerning the early church, the limitations of our knowledge of this phase of the history of Antioch are perhaps not surprising. In another area, however, it seems less easy to account for our lack of information. This is the intellectual history of the city. In the Seleucid period, it is puzzling that we do not hear more of literary, philosophical, and scientific activity at Antioch. The libraries and the scholarly programs of the Attalids and the Ptolemies, as well as the philosophical studies at Athens, are relatively well known, and we can assess the intellectual atmosphere of Pergamum and Alexandria far better than we can that of the Seleucid capital. We do from time to time have texts that record some of the intellectual activities of Antioch under the Seleucids and in the earlier part of the Roman period. We know of at least one public library at Antioch in Seleucid times, and we hear the names of some scholars and men of letters at the royal court, as well as the names —often the names alone—of natives of Antioch who pursued their careers elsewhere; but the sum of our information is in no way comparable to what we know of elsewhere in the Hellenistic world. While it is difficult to base any conclusion upon such meager evidence as we have, it seems a question whether Antioch may not have been less of a literary and scientific center than the other Hellenistic capitals and Athens.

For the earlier part of the Roman period, the situation seems somewhat the same. Here again we have the names—again, little more than the names in most cases—of literary figures connected with the city. There is, however, a new kind of evidence which may serve to some degree as a corrective of the picture suggested by the literary texts. A series of mosaic floors, the earliest from about the time of Trajan, illustrate a variety of themes of classical literature and mythology.[11] These certainly show that the citizens of Antioch who could afford such floors had at least as much interest in such subjects as is indicated by the over-all literary activity of the Graeco-Roman world of that day. When we come to the fourth century, the career of Libanius—and of the immediate predecessors whom he mentions—shows that Antioch was one of the leading academic centers of the day. Whether, before the fourth century, there was comparable activity at Antioch, which has perished almost without a trace, we cannot at present determine. What does seem striking is that in the fifth and sixth centuries, after Libanius' brilliant career had ended, we hear little further about Antioch as a literary center. It is perhaps suggestive that what we do know indicates a notable survival of pagan thought at Antioch;[12] and we know that the literary school of Gaza in Palestine in the late fifth and sixth centuries achieved distinction as a center of scholarship and teaching in the new tradition of Christian-Hellenic culture at a time when we know of nothing comparable at Antioch. It would seem that Antioch, like Athens in its later period, was unable or unwilling to adjust itself to the new tradition of Christian learning, transforming and adapting the classical tradition, which was developed so successfully at Gaza and Constantinople.[13]

But if our knowledge of Antioch is irregular and deficient in some areas, there are other aspects of the city's history and creative activity for which we have much more abundant testimony. One subject that has long been familiar to scholars because the documentation is relatively ample is the ecclesiastical history and the theological and exegetical

[11] See the list of dated mosaics in Levi, *Antioch Mosaic Pavements* 1.625-626.

[12] See below, Ch. 17, nn. 40-41; Ch. 19, § 1 (on episodes of paganism in fifth and sixth centuries).

[13] See the study of G. Downey, "The Christian Schools of Palestine: A Chapter in Literary History," *Harvard Library Bulletin* 12 (1958) 297-319.

activity of the city during the fourth, fifth, and sixth centuries. Here the material has long engaged the attention of scholars and it continues to furnish a rich field for study. This part of the history of Antioch is known in so much detail that it has almost seemed to develop into a special topic, parallel with the secular history of the city. We are still gaining important new understanding of a number of departments of the activities of the church at Antioch, and we are learning more about the influence that radiated from it, not only in theological thought, but in scholarship on the text of the Greek Bible, and in the development of the liturgy of the church. The ecclesiastical history of the city has already been so thoroughly investigated that it seems sufficient to limit the account of church history given here to a presentation of the essential developments.[14]

Another phase of the history of the city for which we have by good fortune exceptional documentation is the social, economic, cultural, and administrative life of Antioch in the latter half of the fourth century, which we know in some detail from the voluminous writings of Libanius, supplemented in important respects by those of St. John Chrysostom, the Emperor Julian, and Ammianus Marcellinus. This is in fact the only period in the history of the city during which we have extensive and detailed information about numbers of the major figures in Antioch, so that we can sometimes follow the daily events in the city, especially during such episodes as the great riot of A.D. 387. The abundance of the material available here has naturally attracted many scholars, and while the texts are by no means exhausted, we have at our disposal a number of detailed modern studies from which we know more about Antioch at this period than we do about any other city of the eastern part of the Graeco-Roman world at this time. It would be both impractical and unnecessary to review all the known material in the present volume, and the treatment here takes up only the major events and developments.

The great discovery of the excavations of 1932-1939 was the mosaic floors. While the excavators had, of course, hoped to find some evidence for the role of Antioch in the history of classical and Christian art, the quantity of the mosaics found in the excavations exceeded expectations, and art historians found themselves presented with a corpus of material that filled one of the gaps in the history of ancient art and

[14] A notion of the richness of the material available may be gained from the fact that the most detailed history of the Church at Antioch, that of Chrysostom A. Papadopoulos, Ἱστορία τῆς ἐκκλησίας Ἀντιοχείας (Alexandria 1951), comprises 1048 pages, though even this work does not undertake to be exhaustive.

provided material of inestimable value for the history of culture in all its aspects, as well as new and impressive testimony to the place of Antioch in the intellectual and artistic world of antiquity.

The mosaics immediately supplied one of the missing chapters in the history of ancient painting. From the frescoes of Pompeii we knew painting at the beginning of our era, and the earliest illuminated manuscripts and the famous mosaics preserved in churches in Italy showed the way in which this art had developed in the fifth and sixth centuries, but the evidence for painting in the second, third, and fourth centuries remained very scanty. From the splendid collection of floors recovered at Antioch we learned how the "Alexandrian" style, as it had previously been known, must have been common to the great cities founded in the Near East by Alexander the Great and his successors. C. R. Morey, the pioneer in the interpretation of the new material, showed how the early "Alexandrian" manner, now attested at Antioch, followed a line of development there under the influence of the Neo-Attic style characteristic of Asia Minor.[15] At the same time, the Antioch floors showed the influence, increasingly as time went by, of Persia, with which Antioch, of all the great cities of the Graeco-Roman world, was naturally in closest contact. Our new and growing knowledge of the developments that took place in all aspects of the mosaic-makers' art—subject matter, composition, ornament, and such special characteristics as the Iranian interest in animals as ornament—not only shows us how artistic interests and techniques developed at Antioch as a result of the special local factors but also allows us to see, more clearly than ever before, the features of early Byzantine art that reflect the influence radiating from Antioch in the Christian Byzantine Empire.

We are now able to appreciate, in this new field as well as in others with which we have been familiar, the characteristic differences between Antioch and Alexandria, the two great cities which, founded at the same time, developed so differently along the lines determined by their geographical position, the composition of their populations, and the distinctive academic traditions that grew up in each of them. The characteristic trends of the two cities with which we were already familiar in theology, literature, and science, reappear in their artistic

[15] Morey's first evaluation of the new evidence was published in his *Mosaics of Antioch* in 1938, to be followed by more detailed studies represented in his comprehensive work *Early Christian Art*, the second edition of which (Princeton 1953) was published not long before his death. Studies along the lines pointed out by Morey have been carried on by a number of scholars, including A. M. Friend, Jr., K. Weitzmann, D. N. Wilber, D. Levi, and E. Kitzinger (see their studies listed in the Bibliography).

interests and techniques, and we can appreciate from another point of view the diversity of the factors that entered into the transmission of the classical heritage to the Byzantine world.

We have also been coming to a new understanding, through recent discoveries and continued study, of the work of the Antiochene silversmiths, who carried on in the Christian era a tradition of distinguished craftsmanship in precious metals that dated back to the early Seleucid history of Antioch. The recovery of Syrian liturgical silver and our new insights into the origin and diffusion of this work have given us a heightened appreciation of the role of Antioch not only in this phase of its contribution to the development of late antique and Byzantine art but in the manufacture of sacred vessels, which constituted an essential element in the liturgical and devotional life of Greek Christianity.

CONCLUSION

While our knowledge of classical and Byzantine Antioch is uneven in some respects, the total significance of what we know is becoming more and more clear. Four generations after Carl Otfried Müller gave us our first scholarly picture of the ancient city, our whole understanding of the Graeco-Roman and Byzantine world has immeasurably increased, and we have come to a fuller realization of the extent to which we are debtors to the ancient world. The revival of interest in classical antiquity in recent years has been a heartening sign to those who see in the present the continuity of the past, and connected with this is the very remarkable increase of interest in Byzantium. Antioch constituted one of the essential links between classical antiquity and Byzantium, and it is as a custodian and a transmitter and creator that we must think of the city.

At all periods in the nine hundred years of its history Antioch shows us several faces. While it was intended by its founders to serve as a center of Greek civilization on the oriental frontiers, it was never purely a Greek city, and its population included from the first an oriental element.

While it began as a Graeco-Macedonian *polis*, its geographical position and the historical development of the ancient world made Antioch into a city of highly marked individuality. A number of factors— mixed population, strategic position, wide commercial connections, especially with the East, and political importance as first a Seleucid and then a Roman administrative center—all combined to make

Antioch a natural focus for both the collection and the diffusion of ideas. Perhaps the most important single result of this was that it came to be uniquely qualified to serve as the first major center of Christianity outside of Jerusalem, and the base for the mission to the Gentiles. It was at about the same time that the Romans, realizing its potentialities, began to develop Antioch as one of the two chief centers of their power in the Eastern Mediterranean, the other center being Alexandria, as the capital of Egypt. As the power of Persia grew and the eastern frontier became more and more important for the defense of the Empire, Antioch took on increasing responsibility as a military center, and the establishment of Constantinople as the eastern capital did not diminish the military and economic importance of Antioch. To the Persians, at the same time, Antioch represented the power and wealth of the Roman Empire and was the natural target of their raids.

The founding of Constantinople coincided with, if it did not serve to bring out, the increasing manifestations of the nationalist tendencies that had always existed in Syria and Egypt, as they had in other parts of the Roman Empire. Always conscious of their own traditions and their special position, both Antioch and Alexandria now began a new phase of their individualistic careers. The theological differences and rivalries that developed in time only increased in each a sense of independence, and they both came to look upon themselves as something rather different both from each other and from the new imperial capital. While Constantinople now represented a central government that was closer to them than Rome had been, the people of Antioch were still conscious of their own independent origin—recalled in the splendid encomium of the city by Libanius, the *Antiochikos*—and they did not hesitate to give the Emperor Julian a lively reception or to respond to a law of the Emperor Theodosius with the worst riot in the history of the city, in A.D. 387. This was also, we must remember, the period of the maximum size and influence of Antioch, and probably one of its greatest periods of prosperity.

In the world of that time, nationalist tendencies, once rooted, could not be reversed, and when the Monophysite question arose, Antioch, like Alexandria, finally isolated itself from Constantinople. Here we see Antioch not only as an ancient Graeco-Roman metropolis, but as the rallying point of the Syrian people who now felt, as did the Egyptians, that the government in Constantinople was their enemy.

And this is how the history of Antioch came to an end. An extraordinary series of calamities within seventeen years in the time of Justinian

Introduction

—a major fire, two earthquakes (one catastrophic), a sack by the
Persians, and a plague (all between A.D. 525 and 542)—left the city in
a permanently reduced condition. A century later the Moslem conquest of Syria ended the story. The history of Antioch is that of a
Greek *polis*, founded on non-Greek soil, which absorbed much from
its new environment. It was as a *polis* that Antioch played its destined
role, and it was through the various stages of its development as a city—
Hellenistic, East Roman, Byzantine, pagan, and then Christian—that
Antioch achieved its characteristic stamp and made its own special
contribution to the history of civilization. Younger than Athens and
Rome, of about the same age as Alexandria, and older than Constantinople, Antioch played a distinctive part in the process which brought
together the traditions of Athens and Jerusalem and worked them into
a new form that was eventually to be preserved by Constantinople
alone.[16]

[16] In 1959 the annual Symposium of the Dumbarton Oaks Research Library and Collection was devoted to the topic of "Antioch in the Byzantine Period," presented under
the direction of the present writer. The papers read on this occasion (which will be
published elsewhere) either expanded the treatment of the subjects given in the present
volume, or dealt with topics which lie outside the scope of this work. The papers read
were as follows: H. Seyrig, "Antioch in the Road-System of Syria"; A. R. Bellinger,
"The Mint of Antioch"; R. Stillwell, "Tradition and Change in Antiochene Houses";
M. H. Shepherd, Jr., "Formation and Influence of the Antiochene Liturgy"; B. M.
Metzger, "The Antiochian Text of the Greek Bible, its Formation and Influence";
M. C. Ross, "Byzantine Silver: Antioch and Constantinople"; A. C. Outler, "The Affair
of the Three Chapters: An Anticlimax in the History of the School of Antioch."

CHAPTER 1

THE PHYSICAL RESOURCES OF ANTIOCH

COMMUNICATIONS, CLIMATE, WATER SUPPLY,
NATURAL PRODUCTS

Antioch lies at the southwestern corner of the Amuk plain, at the point where the Orontes river, after flowing along the southern edge of the plain, cuts through the mountains to continue its journey to the sea. Because of its position, the city controls the network of roads, supplemented by the Orontes river, which from earliest times has made this part of Syria the route by which land traffic passes between Anatolia and the countries to the South, and between the Mediterranean and the upper Euphrates (Fig. 3).[1]

The site of Antioch is spectacular.[2] The mountains that follow the left bank of the river all the way from the sea terminate at Antioch in the magnificent Mount Silpius, which rises to 506 meters (about 1660 feet) above sea level, the Orontes itself being at this point about 90 meters above sea level. When it reaches Antioch, the Orontes flows from northeast to southwest past the city, which in antiquity was almost entirely built on the left bank of the river and on an island that was formed in the river at the northern part of the city.[3] The right bank,

[1] The strategic and economic importance of the site of Antioch, and the reasons for the choice of the site, are discussed more fully below. For a list of maps of the site (in addition to those reproduced below, Figs. 3-5, 6-9, 11), see Excursus 8. On the road system in northern Syria, in Roman times, see R. Mouterde and A. Poidebard, *Le limes de Chalcis* (Paris 1945), with excellent maps. On the commercial routes see M. P. Charlesworth, *Trade Routes and Commerce of the Roman Empire*[2] (Cambridge, Eng. 1926) 37-40; E. H. Warmington, *The Commerce between the Roman Empire and India* (Cambridge, Eng. 1928) 18-19, 35-36, 86, 100; M. Rostovtzeff, *Caravan Cities* (Oxford 1932) 94-95, with map on p. 2; C. G. Seligman, "The Roman Orient and the Far East," *Antiquity* 11 (1937) 5-30 (on trade routes); M. Cary, *The Geographic Background of Greek and Roman History* (Oxford 1949) 169-172; H. H. von der Osten, "Anatolische Wege," *Eranos* 49 (1951) 65-83, with map on p. 66.

[2] The description of the city given here is not intended to be exhaustive, but is designed chiefly to put before the reader (with the assistance of the maps and photographs) the features of the topography that have a bearing on the history of the city. For a detailed description of the site see Weulersse, *Antioche*, with numerous photographs and drawings; reference may also be made to the second volume of Jacquot, *Antioche*. Other modern views of the city are reproduced in the excavation reports in *Antioch-on-the-Orontes* 1-3. For reproductions of old views, as well as modern photographs, see Förster, "Antiochia" and Schultze, *Antiocheia*.

[3] One of the curiosities of the history of Antioch is the confusion that prevailed in ancient times and that has persisted until quite recently concerning the points of the compass at Antioch. There appears to have been a convention (or confusion?) by which the long axis of the city was spoken of as east-west, whereas in reality it is northeast-southwest. Many modern travelers were unable to take accurate compass observations,

to the northwest and west of the city, was a flat plain that does not seem to have been systematically settled; it was not brought within the walls in antiquity, and in the fourth century A.D. part of it served as a Campus Martius.[4] Two of Antioch's principal roads crossed this plain and entered the city by bridges, one of which occupied the site of the modern bridge, which incorporates some ancient masonry in its foundation. One of the roads that ended at this bridge came from the south, from Seleucia Pieria, the seaport of Antioch; this road ran along the right bank of the river since the left bank is in many places mountainous and would not accommodate a road. The other road came from the north, from the Beilan Pass, Alexandretta, Cilicia, and the remainder of Anatolia.

The main part of the city, on the left bank of the Orontes, was built on relatively level ground between the river and the mountain. It formed an irregular oblong rectangle varying in size and in shape at different periods of the city's history, since the city was developed by a series of quarters founded by the Seleucid kings and then by building operations of the Romans (Fig. 11). Mount Silpius, running roughly parallel to the river, confines the city on one of its long sides, as the river does on the other.[5] At the short ends of the city, at northeast and southwest, are the termini of two of the principal roads that provided communication between the city and other parts of Syria. One was the road to Beroea (modern Aleppo) at the northeastern end of the city; along this road, outside the gate, were built baths and churches, and, doubtless, villas.[6] The other road, at the southern end, led to the famous suburb Daphne and over the mountains to Laodicea-ad-Mare. The termini of these two roads served to define the ends of the long axis of the city, and in the time of Augustus and Tiberius a straight

---

and some of the modern published maps are incorrectly oriented. This confusion and its results are discussed in detail below in Excursus 9.

[4] The important cruciform church of Kaoussié (Ch. 15, §1) was found on the plain across the river (see J. Lassus, "L'Église cruciforme de Kaoussié," *Antioch-on-the-Orontes* 2.5-44), and a Roman villa was excavated some distance beyond this. The suburbs of the city are discussed below.

[5] Jacquot, *Antioche* 2.358-359, provides a useful panoramic sketch of the mountain. The name *Staurin* is sometimes applied to the northern part; this name came into use after an earthquake in the sixth century, when a vision of the Cross was seen over the mountain (see Ch. 18, §5).

[6] A church has been found at Machouka, on this road (Levi, *Antioch Mosaic Pavements* 1.368-369), and a bath at Narlidja, farther along the road (*ibid.* 304-306). A tomb was excavated at Kara-Bourk, near Narlidja (*ibid.* 225-226). These were all chance finds. It happens that no houses were excavated, but their presence is suggested by the bath and the church.

colonnaded street was built along this axis, connecting the northeastern (Beroea) gate and the southwestern (Daphne) gate (Figs. 6-9, 11).

Another entrance to the city, less used in antiquity, was at the Iron Gate, the Bab el-Hadid (Fig. 17), described below, which stood at the ravine that divides Mount Silpius into two sections. Here there was a smaller and for some purposes shorter road which led to Apamea and to eastern and southern Syria, but this was not much used in antiquity since it was narrow and made a difficult entrance and exit, over pre-cipitous ground, in contrast to the broad and level road that left the city at the northern end.[7]

Towering above the city is Mount Silpius, with its ancient walls and citadel. On the side toward the city, the lowest slopes of the moun-tain are gradual; in antiquity, they were sometimes terraced to provide sites for villas and public baths which commanded a magnificent view. After the first slopes, however, there is a steep rise, giving the mountain the appearance of a huge wall. On the side away from the city, the slope is more gentle and can be ascended without great effort. The result is that a hostile force can reach the top of the mountain over-looking the city without difficulty; and if the walls and fortifications along the top of the mountain were breached, the city lay at the mercy of the attacker. Antioch was captured in just this way on at least two occasions in antiquity,[8] and in fact we hear of no assault on the city which was unsuccessful.

The mountain is broken at one point, toward the northeastern part of the city, by the ravine through which ran the road to Apamea, which has been mentioned. Here a winter torrent of great strength, called Parmenius or Onopnictes ("Donkey-drowner"), rushed down the slope to empty into the Orontes. This ravine was closed and secured by a dam designed to control the water by means of sluice gates. This wall, which is still well preserved, is known as the Bab el-Hadid, or Iron Gate (Fig. 17).[9] At other places the contours of the mountain led to the formation of other torrents that flowed in the rainy season.

A special problem of drainage was created by the combination of the effects of the location of the city below Mount Silpius and of the rains sometimes of torrential proportions (often cloudbursts) during the

---

[7] This road is shown in *La Syrie antique et médiévale illustrée* pl. 66. A trace of it appears on the map of the Forces Françaises du Levant 1:200,000 (see the list of maps below, Excursus 8).

[8] By the Persians, in the third and in the sixth centuries.

[9] Photographs in Jacquot, *Antioche* 2.360, 380; Förster, "Antiochia" 135-137.

winter rainy season, which lasts from November to March or April.[10] These rains are not infrequently so heavy that the enormous quantity of water precipitated in a few minutes cannot be carried off the slope of the mountain by the various streams and ravines that run down the side of Mount Silpius and empty into the river. The result is a heavy wash of loose stones, soil, and debris carried down and deposited on the level part of the site between the mountain and the river. The deposit brought down by one rainstorm can be considerable, and the constant recurrence of this phenomenon explains the fact that in some parts of the site, where the reduction in size of the city in mediaeval and modern times has removed the barriers and channels provided by house-walls and streets, the remains of the Hellenistic period lie buried to a depth of ten meters.[11]

While the Orontes is not navigable today between Antioch and the sea, several ancient sources declare that at least at certain periods in antiquity it was navigable,[12] and the traffic on the river is said to have played a major part in the commercial life of the city in the fourth century of our era. The original agora at Antioch lay on the bank of the river, and we hear of building materials for the original settlement being brought down the river on flat barges. In addition to the deposit of silt from Mount Silpius, earthquake action, which is recurrent in the region of Antioch, has filled the river since the Middle Ages with the debris of the city walls that toppled into the stream, and it appears that the bed of the stream has also been raised by the effect of the earthquakes. In addition, the arm of the river that ran between the island and the city proper has been filled up, apparently since the time of the Crusades.[13]

[10] The rainy season is described by C. Combier, "La climatologie de la Syrie et du Liban," *Revue de géographie physique et de géologie dynamique* 6 (1933) 319-346.
[11] See the observations of J. Lassus in *Antioch-on-the-Orontes* 1.100, and W. A. Campbell's valuable description of the effects of a torrential rain which he witnessed during the excavations of 1938, with a photograph of the resulting flood in parts of the ancient city (*Antioch-on-the-Orontes* 3.5-6); see also the observations on the evidence for similar occurrences that were found in the excavations (*ibid.* 14, 15-18). On the depth of the burial of the ancient city, see the observations of Förster ("Antiochia" 106, n. 12, based on information furnished by the engineer Toselli, who lived in Antioch at the time of Förster's visit) and of Weber (*Studien* 52).
[12] Strabo 16.2.7, 751 C; Pausanias 8.29.3; Libanius *Or.* 11.262, cf. 265. On the Gourob papyrus as evidence for the navigability of the Orontes in 246 B.C., see Ch. 5, n. 13.
[13] Förster, "Antiochia" 132. This arm can be traced by the contours of the ground and by the remains of bridges and of the city walls along the river. A photograph taken from Mount Silpius, on which the course of the east branch of the river and the outline of the island have been indicated, is published by C. R. Morey, "The Excavation of Antioch-on-the-Orontes," *Proceedings of the American Philosophical Society* 76 (1936) pl. 1.

In antiquity, the suburb Daphne was as famous as Antioch, and the city was sometimes called "Antioch near Daphne." The plateau of Daphne lies at a higher level than Antioch—the ancient texts speak of "going up to Daphne"—and the road between them was lined with villas, gardens, inns and all manner of pleasant places. Daphne itself was a picturesque garden spot, overlooking the Orontes, about eight kilometers (or five miles) south of the city. It was made fertile and beautiful by numerous natural springs, which not only provided an ample supply of water for the villas, baths, and gardens of Daphne, but furnished Antioch itself with a large part of its water through aqueducts that skirted the lower slopes of the mountain. This abundant supply of water, still utilized today, was one of the reasons that determined Seleucus to build his city at Antioch (Daphne itself is too small for a city).[14]

Libanius, writing in the second half of the fourth century A.D. describes flourishing suburbs all about the city, in addition to Daphne; and villas, baths, and churches have been excavated at various points without the walls, and sometimes relatively far from them.[15] We hear how the villas outside the walls were plundered and burned by the Persians when they captured and sacked the city in A.D. 540.[16]

The terrain about Antioch and Daphne is varied, from low hills and the slopes of the mountains to occasional plateaus and the flat plains of the Amuk region. In antiquity the hills and mountain sides were thickly wooded,[17] and the Amuk plain itself seems to have been forested

[14] For descriptions of Daphne, see Bazantay, *Le Plateau de Daphne*, and D. N. Wilber, "The Plateau of Daphne," *Antioch-on-the-Orontes* 2.49-56. The classic ancient description of Daphne is that of Libanius in his *Antiochikos, Or.* 11.234-243. See also Procopius of Gaza *Epist.* 66 (Hercher, *Epistolographi Graeci* p. 556). For the name "Antioch at Daphne," see the inscription of a bronze statuette, *IGLS* 1072, and Strabo 15.1.73 (719), 16.2.4 (749). For the Latin usage (Epi Daphnes, Epidaphne) cf. Pliny *Nat. hist.* 5.18 (79). Strabo (750) gives the distance between Antioch and Daphne as 40 stades (about five miles). Sozomen (*Hist. eccl.* 5.19, PG 67.1276) gives the same figure, while the *Artemii Passio* 55 (Philostorgius, p. 92.13-14 ed. Parmentier) states that the distance is "more than 50 stades." Presumably these figures represent reckonings made from different points. In the same way, Strabo (751) gives the distance between Antioch and Seleucia Pieria as 120 stades, while Procopius (*Bell. Pers.* 2.11.1) gives it as 130 stades. This difference may mean that the road had been altered between the time of Strabo and that of Procopius.

[15] Libanius *Or.* 11.231. A Roman villa was excavated at Jekmejeh village, 2.5 km. west of the city, on the rising ground at the edge of the Amuk plain; Levi, *Antioch Mosaic Pavements* 1.28-34, 219. This was a chance find; doubtless more villas of the same kind could be found in many places in the neighborhood of Antioch if systematic search were made. The sites excavated along the Aleppo road have been mentioned above, n. 6.

[16] See Ch. 18, §7.

[17] This is plain from Libanius *Or.* 11.19; later in the same oration (§25) he speaks of

at least in part.[18] Natural springs abounded, as a result of the presence underground of fissured calcareous rock that stored water, which then found outlets at places where weak points in the rock allowed the formation of springs, as at Daphne.[19] In this Mediterranean climate the wet winter was followed by a long, hot, and completely dry summer, and the regular water supply available the year round from Daphne and from the springs in and near the city was one of the principal advantages of the site of Antioch. Spring and autumn are brief.[20] The average annual temperature in the region of Antioch today varies between 15 and 20 degrees Centigrade (59 and 68 degrees Fahrenheit), and the average annual precipitation today is 1181 mm. (about 46 inches).[21]

A distinctive feature of the climate, in antiquity as well as today, is the wind that blows from the west or southwest, up the valley of the Orontes, from May to mid-October. Often the wind begins at noon and blows during the afternoon, evening, and night. By lowering the temperature and dissipating the humidity, this wind not only makes life much more agreeable but favors the development of summer crops by preventing them from being parched and scorched.[22] Our evidence all indicates that the climate of Antioch and its vicinity has not changed since antiquity.[23]

---

ample supplies of wood for building being available near Antioch. See further Honigmann, "Syria" 1559-1560; L. Woolley in *AJ* 17 (1937) 2-3; Braidwood, *Mounds in the Plain of Antioch* 9.

[18] Dio Cassius 40.29.1-2, speaking of the middle of the first century B.C., mentions that the neighborhood of Antigonia, up the Orontes from Antioch, on the southern edge of the Amuk plain, was thickly wooded; see Ch. 7, n. 37.

[19] On the geology of the region around Antioch, see L. Dubertret, in *La géologie et les mines de la France d'outre-mer* (Paris 1932; Publications du Bureau d'études géologiques et minières coloniales) 362, 377; idem, "La carte géologique au millionième de la Syrie et du Liban," *Revue de géographie physique et de géologie dynamique* 6 (1933) 303; idem, "L'Hydrologie et aperçu sur l'hydrographie de la Syrie et du Liban dans leurs relations avec la géologie," *ibid.* 357.

[20] See Libanius' description of the seasons at Antioch, *Or.* 11.29-33. On the characteristics of the Mediterranean climate, see E. Huntington, F. E. Williams, and S. van Valkenburg, *Economic and Social Geography* (New York 1933) 274-282.

[21] See C. Combier, "La Climatologie de la Syrie et du Liban," *Revue de géographie physique et de géologie dynamique* 6 (1933) 319-346; idem, *Aperçu sur les climats de la Syrie et du Liban, avec carte au millionième des pluies et vents* (Beirut 1945).

[22] Libanius devotes loving attention to his description of the breezes at Antioch, *Or.* 11.222-226. On the wind there today, see Jacquot, *Antioche* 2.349.

[23] See Honigmann, "Syria" 1558. E. Huntington's theory of a change in the climate of Syria since antiquity (*Palestine and its Transformation* [Boston 1911] 283-302, summarized in the same author's *Civilization and Climate*[3] [New Haven 1924] 344-345) seems exaggerated. Huntington knew nothing, for example, of the evidence to be found in Libanius. On the evidence of the now deserted parts of northern Syria (the "dead cities" between Antioch and Aleppo) for the climate in antiquity, see (as a corrective to Huntington's statements) Tchalenko, *Villages antiques de la Syrie du Nord* 1.62-65.

The immediate neighborhood of Antioch, including the lower Orontes valley and the Amuk plain, were unusually fertile, thanks to the favorable natural conditions, and these regions, together with the suburban farms and truck gardens around the city, supplied Antioch with a variety of excellent products, though not in sufficient quantity to fill all the needs of the city.[24] The cereal crops were wheat[25] and barley; the latter was regarded as an inferior grain, and in Antioch bread made from barley was eaten by the poor.[26] The sowing took place between the end of November and the end of December, as soon as the land (baked hard by the summer drought and heat) could be worked after the rains had begun; and the harvest took place in May and June.[27] In the fourth century after Christ, at least, enough grain was grown to satisfy local needs; but a crop failure due to a drought could cause a local famine.[28] Olives and olive oil and wine were produced in abundance.[29] In such fertile ground, garden vegetables flourished. We are told that Antioch produced the best cucumber ($\sigma\iota\kappa\nu\acute{o}\nu$),[30] and we hear of $\lambda\acute{a}\chi\alpha\nu\alpha$, the green vegetables, and of the squash-like $\kappa o\lambda o\kappa\acute{v}\nu\theta\iota\alpha$, which were common throughout the East.[31] Pulse, the edible seeds of peas, beans, etc., likewise is mentioned.[32] The lilies of Antioch and of its sister city Laodicea were famous, and the oil of lilies (also called "Syrian oil" in antiquity), which was in demand for medical use, was exported from Antioch.[33] Antioch produced the next to the best

[24] Tchalenko, *Villages antiques de la Syrie du Nord* 1.422, n. 3.

[25] Libanius *Or.* 11.19, 23; Julian *Misopogon* 350 B.

[26] Libanius *Or.* 1.8. The present description is confined to natural products specifically associated with Antioch and its vicinity by the ancient texts and monuments. There are other products which are spoken of more generally as "Syrian," or are associated with other parts of Syria. Some or all of these were doubtless cultivated at Antioch as well, but since adequate lists of them are available, they are not enumerated here. On the products of Syria, in addition to the study of Tchalenko cited above, see West, *Commercial Syria*; Heichelheim, *Syria* 127-157; Honigmann, "Syria" 1561-1564.

[27] Ammianus Marcellinus 22.13.4; Libanius *Or.* 18.195.

[28] The famine of A.D. 362, in the reign of Julian the Apostate was in part the result of a crop failure caused by a drought in the early part of the winter. This episode, which will be described below (Ch. 13, §1), provides useful information concerning agricultural conditions around Antioch.

[29] Libanius *Or.* 11.20, 23; Julian *Misopogon* 369 A.

[30] Athenaeus 2.59 b, quoting Diocles.

[31] In a graffito in plaster found at Antioch (*Antioch-on-the-Orontes* 3, pp. 93-94, no. 156). On the garden vegetables of Syria see Heichelheim, "Syria" 133. Various items of food, such as pig's feet, artichokes, celery, olives, fish (sculpin or porgy) appear in a mosaic found at Antioch which represents the components of an elaborate meal (Levi, *Antioch Mosaic Pavements* 1.132-136). These items would not be uncommon anywhere in the ancient Mediterranean world.

[32] Julian *Misopogon* 350 C.

[33] Pliny *Nat. hist.* 21.24, 23.95.

grade of oenanthe, picked from the wild vine, which was used for medical purposes.[34]

At a greater distance there were other sources of supplies, of different types, which came from the large domains of the upper Orontes valley and the plains of Beroea and Chalcis, as well as from the mountain region of the Belus, which specialized in the production of olive oil, one of the principal products and exports of Syria.[35] Antioch partly consumed and partly assisted in the exportation of the products of these regions.

Wood for building and for fuel, both for domestic use and for bakeries and baths, was taken from the thick forests around Antioch.[36] The cypresses of Daphne were famous since the wood, which was grown throughout Syria, was highly prized, especially for building.[37] The laurel ($\delta\acute{\alpha}\phi\nu\eta$) was also grown at Daphne; the very tree into which the nymph Daphne was transformed was shown there.[38] A representation of what looks like the plane tree that grows in Antioch today appears in the mosaic of Yakto.[39]

Building stone, the basalt and limestone characteristic of this part of Syria, was quarried near Antioch,[40] but the finer marbles had to be imported. Metal working (especially gold- and silver-smithing) was so important an industry at Antioch that one would expect the metals to be readily available in the neighborhood, but there is no direct evidence that the metals were found near Antioch.[41]

Various domestic animals are mentioned, such as poultry,[42] geese,[43] pigs,[44] sheep,[45] and goats.[46] A particular source of both enjoyment and

[34] Pliny *Nat. hist.* 12.132-133.
[35] Tchalenko, *Villages antiques de la Syrie du Nord* 1.394-395, 422-424.
[36] Libanius *Or.* 11.19, 25, 254.
[37] Among the many references to the cypresses of Daphne the most important are Libanius *Or.* 11.236-238; Malalas 204.10ff.; Procopius *Wars* 2.14.5; Paulus Silentiarius *Ekphrasis of St. Sophia* 524; cf. Müller, *Antiq. Antioch.* 46. There are two laws protecting the cypresses of the sacred grove, of Arcadius and Honorius, and of Theodosius and Valentinian (*CJ* 11.78).
[38] Eustathius' commentary on Dionysius Periegetes 916 (C. Müller. *Geogr. graeci minores* 4, p. 378).
[39] *Antioch-on-the-Orontes* 1, p. 141, no. 27.　　[40] Libanius *Or.* 11.25.
[41] Libanius *Or.* 11.267; Athenaeus 5.193 d, quoting Polybius 26.1.2. (on Antiochus Epiphanes' interest in metal work; see below).
[42] Julian *Misopogon* 350 B. The catching of game birds is depicted on some of the mosaics found in the excavations, e.g. Levi, *Antioch Mosaic Pavements* 2, pl. 23.
[43] Julian *Misopogon* 362 B.　　[44] Julian *Misopogon* 350 C.
[45] Julian *Misopogon* 350 C; Libanius *Or.* 11.26. It is difficult to know whether the pastoral scenes of the mosaics of a villa at Daphne (Levi, *Antioch Mosaic Pavements* 2, pl. 59) are idyllic and decorative, or whether they were intended to depict the activities of the farms around Antioch.
[46] Libanius *Or.* 11.26.

pride was the variety and abundance of the fish and shell fish available in the lake of Antioch (in the Amuk plain), in the river and in the sea; sea food apparently formed a major part of the diet of those who could afford it.[47] The work animals of which we hear were the horse,[48] the camel[49] and the donkey.[50] Race horses were bred at Antioch, where racing was a popular pastime.[51] As late as the fourth century after Christ there were still wild animals in the mountains around Antioch, such as the lion, the tiger, and the fallow deer; and the ostrich and the humped ox are attested.[52]

In antiquity, as today, there were scorpions and gnats. The famous wonder-worker Apollonius of Tyana set up a talisman which drove them out of the city.[53]

[47] Libanius *Or.* 11.258-260; Julian *Misopogon* 350 B-C. A notably large number of the mosaics found in the excavations depict fish and shell fish of many kinds; see Levi, *Antioch Mosaic Pavements* 2, pls. 6, 31, 39, 41, 44, 50, 51, 62, 75, 152, 163, 182, 183. Levi justly points out (*op.cit.* 1.596) that the popularity throughout the Greco-Roman world of fish and sea food in mosaics is to be explained by the circumstance that pools were often paved with mosaic, and that scenes of fish and sea food would be especially appropriate in such cases. This is certainly true; but the literary texts (which Levi does not seem to have taken into consideration in this connection) also show that sea food was a favored item in the diet of Antioch.

[48] Libanius *Or.* 50.32. It is not certain whether the passage in Julian *Misopogon* 371 A refers to race horses or work horses. Saddle horses appear in the Yakto mosaic: *Antioch-on-the-Orontes* I, p. 131, n. 7; p. 152, nos. 53 and 55.

[49] Julian *Misopogon* 355 B.

[50] *Ibid.*

[51] Libanius mentions the local breeding of race horses in *Or.* 49.10; cf. also above n. 48. Race horses would have been of particular importance for the local Olympic games and the other races held in the city; see below.

[52] Libanius, writing in the fourth century, alludes (*Epist.* 113 W. = v. 10.112.18 F.) to the local procurement of wild beasts for the various shows and combats presented at Antioch. Many of the mosaics found at Antioch depict various kinds of wild beasts, and Doro Levi rightly points out (*Antioch Mosaic Pavements* 1.365, n. 4) that these cannot be taken as evidence for the local occurrence of the animals shown, since hunting scenes in particular were popular throughout the Roman world at that time. However, there is at least one case (concerning which Doro Levi seems overly cautious) in which it can be shown that most of the identifiable animals in a mosaic are known from other sources to have existed in Syria, and in some cases in the vicinity of Antioch; and the variety and wildness of the country around Antioch (as the author of the study in question points out) made the region a particularly favorable one for wild beasts; see Dorothea M. A. Bate, "Note on an Animal Mosaic from Antioch-on-the-Orontes," *Honolulu Academy of Arts, Annual Bulletin* I (1939) 26-31.

[53] Malalas 264.6ff.; cf. Honigmann, "Syria" 1564, and see below.

CHAPTER 2

THE SOURCES FOR THE HISTORY
OF ANTIOCH

As HAS been pointed out in the Introduction, the sources for the history of Antioch in the Seleucid period are scanty, much scantier indeed than the material available for the histories of some other Hellenistic capitals; only one public inscription of the Seleucid period has been found at Antioch and Daphne. By contrast, parts of the history of the city during the Roman period are relatively well known, and for certain decades, and certain episodes, we possess special sources which provide abundant information. As a consequence of such differences, a history of Antioch must vary markedly in scale, and in the amount of detail with which events are treated, at different periods.

As is the case with some other ancient cities, there are, in addition to the literary sources of a general nature, certain sources of a special character that are of immediate interest for the history and antiquities of Antioch. Antioch in fact produced some of the best known examples of the literary work of the later Roman period, namely, the works of Libanius, the celebrated pagan teacher and man of letters of the fourth century; the satire *Misopogon* of the Emperor Julian; the writings and sermons of Libanius' pupil St. John Chrysostom, one of the most celebrated Christian preachers and pastors; the world-chronicle of Ioannes Malalas, in the sixth century, the earliest and most important specimen of the popular Byzantine chronicle; and the *Ecclesiastical History* of Evagrius, written at the end of the sixth century, a notable example of this type of work, and the chief source for the history of Antioch in the second half of the sixth century. We have lost many details of the intellectual history of the city—we know little, for example, about its libraries—but these authors, covering a variety of literary and historical interests, give us precious information about the history of the city and the life of its people.

In addition, we have the evidence of the local coins and inscriptions, and the archaeological evidence, both from the few surviving monuments and from those recovered by the excavations of 1932-1939.

1. INSCRIPTIONS

The surviving inscriptions discovered and excavated at Antioch and its vicinity are mostly Greek and Latin; a few are Kufic. Both in number and content the inscriptions are for the most part disappointing. For example, as has been mentioned above, only one significant inscription of the Seleucid period has survived (*IGLS* No. 992), in striking contrast to the much greater epigraphical evidence found at other Hellenistic cities; and no official inscription of the Roman Imperial period has survived. Apparently Antioch has suffered too much damage, both from human destruction and from earthquakes, for the survival of inscriptions, particularly large ones. Many of the inscriptions on marble probably were destroyed in lime kilns (the excavators found kilns that had been built for greater convenience inside the ruins of the ancient buildings), and the re-use of ancient stones in modern buildings has doubtless deposited at least some ancient texts within the walls and floors of modern houses, whence some of them may some day be recovered. It seems doubtful that excavation of the Hellenistic level, which as a rule was not possible in the excavations of 1932-1939, would produce any larger proportion of inscriptions than has been found in the past. Among the inscriptions found, some of the most interesting and valuable are the Greek building inscriptions in mosaic, of the Roman period.

The Greek and Latin inscriptions of Antioch, Daphne, and the immediate vicinity have been collected and edited by the RR. PP. Louis Jalabert, S.J. (+1943) and René Mouterde, S.J., in the third volume of their *Inscriptions grecques et latines de la Syrie* (Paris 1950-1953). This corpus, with its careful criticism of the texts and its valuable commentary, is definitive. Since the reproduction of facsimiles and the development of a detailed commentary is not in all instances a part of the plan of this collection, the reader will sometimes wish to consult also the publications from which the editors of the *IGLS* have drawn their material,[1] except, of course, in the case of the inscriptions that are published for the first time in the *IGLS*.

The Greek and Latin inscriptions found elsewhere which have a bear-

---

[1] The Greek and Latin inscriptions found in the excavations, or purchased by or presented to the expedition, are published in the first, second, and third volumes of the excavation reports. Some of the mosaic inscriptions are republished in Levi, *Antioch Mosaic Pavements*. For useful comment on the inscriptions, see the "Bulletin épigraphique" of R. Flacelière, J. and L. Robert, *REG* 51 (1938) p. 473; the "Bulletins épigraphiques" of J. and L. Robert, *REG* 59/60 (1946-1947) pp. 353-356; 64 (1951) pp. 196-199; and of F. Halkin in *Anal. Boll.* 70 (1952) 381-382. On *IGLS* No. 932 see Delehaye, *Origines du culte*[2] 157. On *IGLS* No. 869 see F. Halkin, "Inscriptions grecques relatives à l'hagiographie," *Anal. Boll.* 67 (1949) 95 (*Mélanges P. Peeters* 1). *IGLS* No. 832 is also published by Th. Preger, *Inscriptiones graecae metricae ex scriptoribus praeter Anthologiam collectae* (Leipzig 1891) No. 11.

ing on the history of Antioch are cited below in the text where pertinent. Of these the most celebrated is the *Res gestae divi Saporis*.[2]

The eighteen Kufic inscriptions found in the excavations are mostly tombstones. Some of them date apparently from the middle ninth to the middle tenth centuries of the Christian era and would thus be among the earliest of their kind found in Syria.[3]

2. Coins

The Greek and Latin coins of the mints of Antioch have been published in several catalogues, most recently Mrs. Waagé's catalogue of the Greek, Roman, Byzantine, and Crusader coins found in the excavations; and a number of monographs and special studies have been devoted to the coins. In some cases, when other evidence is lacking, the coins supply information of the first importance, and in many instances they furnish evidence obtainable from no other source.[4]

3. Other Archaeological Evidence

In addition to the coins and inscriptions, archaeological evidence is provided by the extant monuments and by the results of the excavations of 1932-1939.

a. *Travelers' Reports.* A number of European and American travelers have visited Antioch since the Middle Ages and have written accounts of what they saw, and in this way a certain amount of useful evidence has been preserved concerning monuments that are no longer extant or that have deteriorated since they were mentioned. Some of the travelers copied inscriptions, and others sketched, drew, or photo-

---

[2] On the inscription of Sapor, see below, Excursus 5.

[3] The Kufic inscriptions are published by P. K. Hitti in *Antioch-on-the-Orontes* 1.54-57 and by N. A. Faris in *Antioch-on-the-Orontes* 2.166-169.

[4] Among the catalogues and monographs should be mentioned: *British Museum, Catalogue of Greek Coins, Seleucid Kings of Syria*, by Percy Gardner (1878); in the same series, *Galatia, Cappadocia and Syria*, by Warwick Wroth (1899); E. Babelon *Les Rois de Syrie, d'Arménie et de Commagène* (Paris 1890; Catalogue des monnaies grecques de la Bibliothèque nationale); E. T. Newell *The Seleucid Mint of Antioch* (New York 1918, reprinted from *American Journal of Numismatics*, 51); idem, *The Coinage of the Western Seleucid Mints from Seleucus I to Antiochus III* (New York 1941; American Numismatic Society, Numismatic Studies 4); H. Mattingly and E. A. Sydenham *Roman Imperial Coinage* (London 1923—in progress); *Coins of the Roman Empire in the British Museum*, by H. Mattingly (1923—in progress); *Catalogue of the Imperial Byzantine Coins in the British Museum*, by W. Wroth (1908); *Excavations at Dura-Europos, Final Report* 6: A. R. Bellinger *The Coins* (New Haven 1949); G. C. Miles, "Islamic Coins," in *Antioch-on-the-Orontes* 4, pt. 1 (Princeton 1948) 109-124; Dorothy B. Waagé, "Greek, Roman, Byzantine and Crusaders' Coins," in *Antioch-on-the-Orontes* 4, pt. 2 (Princeton 1952). Special studies based on the coins, among which the articles of A. R. Bellinger and H. Seyrig are notable, will be cited below.

graphed monuments. The gradual destruction and dismemberment of many of the monuments, and the use of the ancient stones for lime or for modern building purposes, can be traced through these accounts.[5]

b. *Views of Surviving Monuments.* Beginning with the handsome engravings of the French artist Cassas, made in the latter part of the eighteenth century (Figs. 18-21), several artists made views of scenes at Antioch, some of which show ancient monuments.[6] In the middle of the nineteenth century E. G. Rey[7] made the first scientific drawings of the extant walls and fortifications, and later travelers photographed various monuments.[8] The excavation reports (described in greater detail below) contain, in addition to photographs of the excavations, views of some of the monuments that were extant before the excavations began.

c. *Survival of the Ancient City Plan.* The ancient walls are in fairly good condition on the top of the mountain and can be traced in most other places; in some instances, in the modern town, they have been incorporated in modern buildings. The ancient island no longer exists as such since the branch of the river that ran between the island and the main part of the city was filled up in the Middle Ages, but this branch can be traced by the contours of the ground, by remains of the city walls that bordered it, and by remains of bridges. A photograph made from the air by the French military authorities (Fig. 6) shows in many places distinct traces of the ancient streets, and sometimes even seems to suggest outlines of buildings (the photograph does not include the fortifications along the top of Mount Silpius). The evidence for the survival of the ancient plan was made the subject of a careful and illuminating study by Weulersse, "Antioche: essai de geographie urbaine." Valuable information on this subject was also contributed by Sauvaget, "Plan de Laodicée-sur-mer."

[5] Inscriptions have been recorded both by travelers who left written accounts (listed below, Excursus 19) and by other visitors who did not have occasion to publish reports. For the recording of inscriptions prior to the excavations, we are indebted to Crofts, Ainsworth, Renan, Perdrizet, Fossey, Mouterde, Chapot, Seyrig, Cagnat, Tracol, Toselli, Merlat, Vos, Chammas, Renard, Uspensky, Virolleaud, Pococke, Drummond, Ronzevalle, Seetzen, Poche, Khoury, Morgan.

[6] See (Excursus 19) under the names of Ainsworth, Bartlett, Buckingham, Cassas, Chantre, Chesney, Drummond, Laborde, Niebuhr (plan drawn in 1766), Parsons, Pococke (plan and views, 1738), Taylor.

[7] See Excursus 19 under the name of Rey.

[8] See Excursus 19 under the names of Gertrude Bell, Lammens, and Perdrizet; also Förster, "Antiochia," Jacquot, *Antioche,* and Schultze, *Antiocheia.* The three last named works also contain convenient reproductions of some of the older engravings. The photographic archive of the excavations of 1932-1939 is deposited at Princeton University.

d. *The Excavations of 1932-1939.* In 1930 the Committee for the Excavation of Antioch and its Vicinity was formed, under the chairmanship of the late Professor C. R. Morey of Princeton University. The Committee represented several American institutions and individuals and the Musées Nationaux de France; Princeton University was made responsible for the direction of the expeditions and the publications of the results.[9] Excavations began in the spring of 1932 and were continued annually until the season of 1939, when the outbreak of war in Europe made further work impossible.

The excavations were conducted in Antioch and its immediate vicinity; in Daphne, the famous ancient suburb of Antioch; and in the seaport Seleucia Pieria. The size of the sites, the circumstance that part of the site of ancient Antioch is occupied by the modern town, and the existence in many parts of the sites of valuable orchards, meant that systematic topographic investigations could not be carried out except on a limited scale. Distractions occurred when local farmers and builders discovered mosaic floors by chance and these had to be excavated and raised in order to save them from destruction.[10] In some instances work was hampered by the unusual depth (often ten meters) to which the ancient remains have been buried by the earth washed down from Mount Silpius by the heavy winter rains.[11] Nevertheless results of great value were achieved in the reconstruction of the topography of the city and in the discovery of individual buildings and mosaics.

Four volumes of excavation reports covering the seasons of 1932-1939 have been published (1934-1952; see the List of Abbreviations under *Antioch-on-the-Orontes*). The mosaics have been published by Doro Levi *Antioch Mosaic Pavements* (Princeton 1947).

e. *The Topography of Antioch.* Among the most important topographical results of the excavations and of the study of the surface remains was the establishment of the course of the great colonnaded main street, one of the celebrated thoroughfares of antiquity, which ran through the city from the northeast to the southwest. The existence of this street, and its importance in the plan and in the life of the city, had already been known from literary sources (notably the chronicle of Malalas and the oration in praise of Antioch of Libanius) and from the accounts of some of the travelers who visited the site in post-classical

[9] For the composition of the Committee, and its history, see the Forewords to the first three volumes of the excavation reports.
[10] The history of each season of work may be found in the Forewords to the first three volumes of the excavation reports.
[11] On the effects of the wash from the mountain, see further below, Ch. 4, §2.

times; and from the route of the street as it can be traced on the aerial photograph of the city. The discovery of parts of the street in the excavations confirmed and extended all this knowledge and provided a point of reference for other topographical study of the site.[12]

The study of the main street resulted in determining the approximate limits of the original Seleucid settlement and the location, in the modern *souk* or market area, of the Seleucid agora.[13]

In the other direction, the excavation of the vicinity of the main street at the point where it crosses the torrent Parmenius gave precise evidence for the location of the "basilica" of Julius Caesar and of the buildings connected with it, which subsequently developed into the Forum of Valens.[14]

For the island also we possessed valuable information from Libanius' oration in praise of Antioch, in which the palace of Diocletian, which stood on the island, is described. The ancient size and shape of the island have in recent years been a matter of some uncertainty, since the branch of the Orontes river that flowed around it has long been dry, being partially filled with earth and debris of the ancient walls. Study of the surface remains now shows the size and course of the channel, which flowed between the island and the principal part of the city; and the abutments of the bridges which served the island have been found. The palace was not located in the excavations, but the major features of the plan of the island, including the noteworthy hippodrome, can be restored.[15] The investigation of the area of the palace and the hippodrome at Antioch is of interest in connection with study of the contemporary palaces at Salona, Constantinople, and elsewhere.

f. *The Topography of Daphne.* The plan and the monuments of Daphne have never been as well known from the ancient sources as those of Antioch, for two reasons. First, as is not unnatural, the literary sources concerning the suburb are not as abundant as those that relate to the city. Second, it was not possible, during the excavations, to make systematic exploration of Daphne because the excavators were con-

---

[12] On the construction of the main street, its successive enlargements, and its relation with the history of the city, see below, Ch. 8, §2. The restored plan of the street is shown in Fig. 11.

[13] See below, Ch. 4, §3.

[14] On the work of Julius Caesar, see below, Ch. 7, §2. The Forum of Valens is described in Excursus 12.

[15] On the settlement and development of the island, see below, Ch. 5, §§3-4. The construction of the hippodrome is described below, Ch. 6, §3. For the restored plan of the island see Fig. 11. Diocletian's palace is described below, Ch. 12, §2.

stantly distracted by the necessity of raising mosaic floors accidentally discovered by the inhabitants and requiring immediate attention to save them from destruction. Through these very distractions, however, we have gained a considerable knowledge of the domestic architecture of the suburb, and of its development as a residential area over a considerable period of time. The only major public building excavated was the theater, which had been known from literary sources, though its location had not been certain.[16] The famous springs, which are still functioning, can be located,[17] and the site of the famous Temple of Apollo must be somewhere near them.[18] The location of the Olympic stadium, however, and of the temples associated with it, still has not been determined. Other features of the topography of Daphne are known from the topographical border of the Yakto mosaic, which will be discussed presently.

One of the major sources of information concerning the ancient life of Antioch, in which the literary and archaeological sources can be combined, with valuable results, is the water system of Antioch and Daphne, with the springs, aqueducts, and reservoirs, which provided one of the best supplies of water of any ancient city. The main features of this system were known in general before the excavations were begun; archaeological information now enables us to date parts of the system more accurately, and to relate its development to the history of the city.[19]

g. *The Yakto Mosaic.* The most unusual of the archaeological sources for the topography and antiquities of Antioch and Daphne is the remarkable topographical border of the mosaic of *Megalopsychia*, found in a villa in Yakto, a section of Daphne.[20] This mosaic, which is dated by internal evidence and by its style at about the middle of the fifth century after Christ, consists of a central medallion containing a per-

[16] D. N. Wilber, "The Theatre at Daphne," *Antioch-on-the-Orontes* 2.57-94.
[17] On the location and present condition of the springs, see Bazantay, *Le Plateau de Daphne*, whose map is reproduced below (Fig. 15). On the history of the springs and their relation to the water supply of Antioch, see Downey, "Water Supply," and D. N. Wilber, "The Plateau of Daphne: The Springs and the Water System Leading to Antioch," *Antioch-on-the-Orontes* 2.49-56. The presence of the water supply at Daphne must have been a major consideration in the choice of the site of Antioch; see below, Ch. 4, §2.
[18] See below, Ch. 4, §5.
[19] See the studies cited above in n. 17. The relation of the water system to the growth of the city is described below, Ch. 4, §§3-5; Ch. 7, §2; Ch. 9, §§5, 7.
[20] This mosaic, now in the Museum at Antioch, was first published by J. Lassus, "La mosaïque de Yakto," *Antioch-on-the-Orontes* 1.114-156; it was later republished by Doro Levi, *Antioch Mosaic Pavements* 1.323-345, with plates 76-80. Doro Levi cites the various discussions of the mosaic which appeared following Lassus' publication of it.

sonification of *Megalopsychia*, surrounded by hunting scenes;[21] and
framing the whole is a border depicting both buildings and scenes of
everyday life which is one of the most precious documents of its kind
which we possess. Scholars have differed as to whether the border
depicts an itinerary of Antioch and Daphne, or merely shows characteristic groups of buildings and genre scenes. One of the principal
students of the Antioch mosaics, Doro Levi, believes that there is no
orderly progression of buildings and that there is not even any certainty that the border shows buildings outside Daphne itself.[22] On the
contrary, J. Lassus, who originally published the mosaic, believed that
the border depicted an itinerary, in which the spectator, following
the scenes in order, made an imaginery journey through Daphne and
then through Antioch. It seems to the present writer that the border
does depict an itinerary (as is suggested, for example, by the representations of travelers and of bridges within the city), but that the
route followed begins at the northeastern end of the city, at the gate
on the road which led from Beroea, proceeds through the main part
of the city to the island, then returns from the island to the main part
of the city and goes once more through the city to the road leading to
Daphne; and at Daphne the journey ends at the famous springs. The
stages of this route can be easily traced in the mosaic, and it is exactly
the same itinerary as that adopted by Libanius in his oration in praise
of Antioch, dated in A.D. 360.[23] This route has the advantage, for both
literary and artistic purposes, of having the journey end at the springs
of Daphne, which could be made (as indeed they deserved to be) the
grand climax of the encomium or of the mosaic. That this was the
route followed in the mosaic is also indicated by the circumstance
that in such an itinerary the scenes would succeed each other from left

[21] The representation of *Megalopsychia* and the hunting scenes will be discussed below in the treatment of the other mosaics found at Antioch. The date of the floor is
indicated by the presence in the border of a representation of a private bath belonging
to Ardaburius, who was *magister militum per Orientem* under Marcianus (A.D. 450-
457) and until A.D. 464, and was in Antioch for at least part of this time; cf. Evagrius
1.13; Seeck, "Ardabur," no. 3, *RE* 2 (1896) 610.

[22] Doro Levi, *op.cit.* 326. One reason, perhaps the chief one, why the distinguished
Italian scholar believes that the mosaic contains no itinerary from Daphne to Antioch
is that he found no "representations of walls, long colonnaded roads and conspicuous
groups of imposing structures." It is true that in this respect the Yakto mosaic differs
from, for example, the Madaba mosaic (illustrated by Doro Levi, *op.cit.* 618). The
Madaba mosaic, however, is a central composition, not a thin border, and it is intended
to represent a city in one general view. The Yakto mosaic, on the other hand, seems
not to be intended as a centralized evocation of a city, and its strip form calls for a
representative technique different from that used in the Madaba floor. Moreover, the
Yakto mosaic does represent, though briefly, colonnaded streets and imposing buildings.

[23] See the detailed discussion of the itinerary of the mosaic, Excursus 18.

to right, the normal direction of reading for a Greek-speaking person, whereas Lassus' hypothesis of a route from Daphne through Antioch would require that the scenes be read from right to left. In any case the border is a priceless source of knowledge both for buildings and places in Antioch and Daphne, and it gives us vivid pictures of the daily life of the people there.[24]

h. *Other Mosaic Floors.* The Yakto mosaic is only one of the most notable of the large and remarkable collection of mosaic floors of the first to the sixth centuries after Christ[25] recovered in the excavations in Antioch, Daphne, Seleucia Pieria, and the vicinity. This unexpected treasury has formed one of the most important groups of ancient mosaics found, and they furnish us with precious evidence concerning many aspects of ancient life. Their over-all contribution to the history of Mediterranean art, in showing both the development of the Hellen-istic tradition and the influence upon it of Oriental, particularly Persian, factors, lies beyond the scope of the present book, and the reader who wishes to trace this phase of the artistic development of ancient Antioch may consult the discussions, readily available elsewhere, of the new chapter the mosaics have made necessary in the history of art.[26] In

[24] See the charming and original study of J. Lassus, "Dans les rues d'Antioche," *Institut Français de Damas, Bulletin d'Études Orientales* 5 (1935) 121-124, in which panels from the mosaic and snapshots made in the modern streets of Antioch are set side by side.

[25] The earlier limit was determined by the circumstance that the condition of the burial of the ancient levels, and the size of the area in which excavations were con-ducted, brought it about that levels earlier than the first century of the Empire were reached only in unusual cases. The later limit is fixed by the decline of the city's prosperity following the earthquakes and the invasion of the Persians in Justinian's time. For a chronological table of the mosaics, see Levi, *Antioch Mosaic Pavements* 1.625-626.

[26] The mosaics are published with detailed commentary and discussion by Doro Levi, *Antioch Mosaic Pavements* (one volume of text, one volume of plates). In the text volume may be found (p. xxi) a list of the collections in Europe and the United States in which the mosaics are preserved, in addition to the floors (including many of the finest) in the Museum at Antioch. An excellent general survey and introduction to the subject is provided by Morey, *Mosaics of Antioch.* Doro Levi in his book provides references to the discussions of the mosaics that had appeared before his book went to press (March 1945). Among studies published since that time may be mentioned the valuable reviews of Doro Levi's book by Clark Hopkins, "Antioch Mosaic Pavements," *Journal of Near Eastern Studies* 7 (1948) 91-97 and by G.-Ch. Picard, "Autour des mosaïques d'Antioche," *RA* ser. 6, vol. 34 (1949) 145-150; and the studies of G. Brett, "The Brooklyn Textiles and the Great Palace Mosaic," *Coptic Studies in Honor of Walter Crum* (Boston 1950) 433-441; G. M. A. Hanfmann, "Socrates and Christ," *Harvard Studies in Classical Philology* 60 (1951) 205-233; idem, *The Season Sarcopha-gus in Dumbarton Oaks* (Cambridge 1951); E. Kitzinger, "The Horse and Lion Tap-estry at Dumbarton Oaks," *Dumbarton Oaks Papers* 3 (1946) 1-72; idem, "Mosaic Pavements in the Greek East and the Question of a 'Renaissance' under Justinian," *Actes du VI*e *Congrès international d'Études byzantines, Paris 1948* (Paris 1951) 2.209-

these discussions one may see how the Antioch floors for the first time make it possible to develop a history of mosaic art by means of a large series of floors, many of which can be dated by archaeological evidence, in a single site. Antioch alone offers a continuous series of floors, not only for the period before Constantine, for which comparative material exists elsewhere, but for the period after Constantine, for which comparative material elsewhere is more scarce.

Other contributions of these mosaics are of no less importance. The floors show, for one thing, that the standard of living in the city was relatively high, for no private house that made the smallest pretence to comfort seems to have been wholly lacking in mosaic floors.[27] This is in fact the first time that such common use of mosaics has been made evident in a large site covering a considerable span of time.[28]

The mosaics have also added to our knowledge of the intellectual history of the city.[29] In all this large collection of figured mosaics there is, outside the floors found in churches, only one plainly exhibiting Christian motifs in its composition—the mosaic of "Philia" found at Daphne, which illustrates the description of the Golden Age in Isaiah 11, "The wolf will lodge with the lamb, and the leopard will lie down with the kid. . . ."[30] Another could be Jewish or Christian, but is more probably Jewish—the inscription of welcome in the phraseology of 1 Sam. 16:4 ("Peace be your coming in").[31] This discovery has been

233; D. Schlumberger, "Deux fresques Omeyyades," *Syria* 25 (1946-48) 99-102; J. M. C. Toynbee, "Some Notes on Artists in the Roman World, III: Painters," *Latomus* 9 (1950) 182. Other studies will be mentioned in the following notes.

[27] This is pointed out by Levi in his opening remarks in *Antioch Mosaic Pavements* 1.1.

[28] While the discovery of the floors was in many cases determined by chance, and while it was not possible to carry out the same amount of excavation at all chronological levels, it is of interest to note that Levi's chronological table of the mosaics found (*Antioch Mosaic Pavements* 1.625-626) suggests that new mosaics were laid in approximately the same numbers at all periods of the city's history between the first and the sixth centuries of our era.

[29] For the study of this aspect of the mosaics, see the papers by the present writer, "Personifications of Abstract Ideas in the Antioch Mosaics," *TAPA* 69 (1938) 349-363; "Ethical Themes in the Antioch Mosaics," *Church History* 10 (1941) 367-376; "The Pagan Virtue of *Megalopsychia* in Byzantine Syria," *TAPA* 76 (1945) 279-286. See also Levi, *Antioch Mosaic Pavements* 1.337ff.

[30] The mosaic of "Philia," which dates from the middle of the fifth century, was found in a building at Daphne; it is published by Levi, *Antioch Mosaic Pavements* 1.317-319.

[31] The inscription, which is probably to be dated in the sixth century after Christ, is published in *Antioch-on-the-Orontes* 3, pp. 83-84, no. 111 and republished, with an important commentary, in *IGLS* No. 770. Doro Levi describes the mosaic briefly (*Antioch Mosaic Pavements* 1.320) without committing himself as to its Jewish or Christian character. A personification of *Ananeosis* was found in the same area as the mosaic containing the Biblical quotation, but it is not certain that this was in the same building.

most instructive in showing that even in a great center of Christianity the Hellenic tradition persisted in the floor decorations of houses, some of which at least must have been owned by Christians. Equally instructive is the presence in many of the mosaics of personifications of pagan virtues and abstract ideas representing some of the major concepts of ancient philosophy and ethics, such as *Megalopsychia* or Greatness of Soul, *Chresis* or Service, *Bios* or Life, *Dynamis* or Power, *Soteria* or Salvation (or Healing), coupled with *Apolausis* or Enjoyment, and others.[32] These floors—particularly that exhibiting *Megalopsychia*, the virtue so important in Aristotle's system,[33] and perhaps one of the chief rivals to the Christian virtues[34]—raise questions of fundamental importance as to the nature and strength of the Hellenic tradition, which clearly persisted at Antioch down to the reign of Justinian. It has sometimes been assumed, perhaps too easily, that paganism persisted longest among the wealthier people. The mosaics of Antioch may be taken as at least partial confirmation of this, joining other "documents of dying paganism"[35] preserved by chance to show the lingering strength of the "opposition" that Christianity in part overcame, in part absorbed. A number of floors that illustrate scenes of classical literature give testimony to the active interest taken at Antioch in the ancient authors.[36]

One more lesson offered by the mosaics is the significant testimony they provide to the interest Antioch showed in Persia throughout the period of the Roman Empire. The influence of Persia on Roman thought has long been recognized in certain instances, such as in Diocletian's borrowing of certain features of Sassanian court ceremonial,[37] and it has recently been shown that Persian influence, or at least interest in Persian ideas and in the political power and influence of Persia, can be traced in local political developments within Antioch, notably during the third century of our era.[38] The mosaics, a noticeable number of

---

[32] See above, n. 29. [33] *Nicom. Ethics* 1123 b 1 (4.6).

[34] See my study of the mosaic of *Megalopsychia* cited above, n. 29.

[35] The phrase is borrowed from the title of the book by P. Friedländer, *Documents of Dying Paganism: Textiles of Late Antiquity in Washington, New York and Leningrad* (Berkeley 1945).

[36] See K. Weitzmann, "Euripides Scenes in Byzantine Art," *Hesperia* 18 (1949) 159ff.; idem, "Illustrations of Euripides and Homer in the Mosaics of Antioch, *Antioch-on-the-Orontes* 3.233-247; A. M. Friend, Jr., "Menander and Glykera in the Mosaics of Antioch," *ibid.* 248-251. On mosaics representing the stories of Ninus and Semiramis, and of Metiochus and Parthenope, which plainly reflect literary sources, see Levi, *Antioch Mosaic Pavements* 1.117-119, and on a mosaic showing a scene from *Iphigeneia in Aulis*, see the same monograph 1.119-126.

[37] See W. Ensslin in *CAH* 12.387.

[38] See below, Ch. 10, §8. The pioneer study of this subject is the article of J. Gagé,

which contain Persian motifs, both decorative and symbolic, add to this growing body of testimony to the connections between Rome and Persia, which, as more and more evidence is found or is recognized in our existing stock of information, should lead to the rewriting of this chapter of ancient history.[39] The oriental type of house plan found at Antioch also reflects this influence.

4. THE ANCIENT HISTORIANS OF ANTIOCH

The *polis* played such a vital role in the development and preservation of all aspects of civilization in Graeco-Roman times that treatises on cities, including accounts of their foundation and descriptions of their beauties, formed an important literary genre. While not a great deal of this type of literature is preserved in its entirety, we possess a certain amount of knowledge about it from the quotations and allusions of later authors who used these works.[40]

a. *Accounts of the Founding of Antioch*. Since the founding of a city was an event of special importance an individual founder, such as a Hellenistic king, would be careful to see that an official record was made of an enterprise that would form a significant part of the record of his accomplishments. We are told that when Seleucus founded Antioch he appointed three men, Attaeus, Perittas, and Anaxicrates, as "supervisors of the buildings," and that they wrote accounts of the foundation of the city.[41] These descriptions have not been preserved, but we may

---

"Les Perses à Antioche et les courses de l'hippodrome au milieu du IIIe siècle, à propos du 'transfuge' syrien Mariades," *Bulletin de la Faculté des lettres de Strasbourg* 31 (1953) 301-324.

[39] See for example the mosaic of the beribboned lion (Levi, *Antioch Mosaic Pavements* 1.313-315), that of the beribboned parrots (*ibid.* 1.358), and the heraldic rams' heads (*ibid.* 1.478-479), all of which are Persian symbols of royal power. The subject is discussed by D. N. Wilber, "Iranian Motifs in Syrian Art," *Bulletin of the American Institute for Iranian Art and Archaeology* 5 (1937) 22-26, and by Morey, *Mosaics of Antioch* 41-45, 47; see also C. Hopkins' observations, in his review cited above, n. 26. Doro Levi, who does not seem to have taken into account the historical evidence for the relations between Rome and Persia, and appears to have looked at the subject only from the point of view of the history of art, concludes (*Antioch Mosaic Pavements* 1.479) that the Persian elements in the Antioch mosaics are purely decorative, introduced early to the Hellenistic world, and that they do not reflect contemporary influence from Persia. A new study of the relations between Rome and Persia, taking into account the archaeological and the literary material, including texts which have not yet been utilized in this connection, such as the references to Persian matters in the orations of Themistius, would modify the views most scholars today hold.

[40] On this type of literary production see Christ-Schmid-Stählin, *Gesch. d. gr. Lit.*[6] 2, pt. 2, pp. 1039-1041, with the references given there, also G. Downey, "Ekphrasis," *Reallexikon für Antike u. Christentum* 4. 921-944.

[41] Tzetzes *Chiliades* 7.118, v. 176-180.

gain some idea of their contents from the description of the founding of Antioch by Malalas, whose information may be in part derived from these accounts.[42] It has been pointed out that the literary tradition concerning the founding of Antioch shows affinities with the tradition of the founding of Alexandria in Egypt.[43]

The best known ancient account of the foundation of Antioch is the lost 'Αντιοχείας κτίσις of Pausanias, which was used and mentioned by later writers.[44] The quotations seem to suggest that Pausanias' work included a history of Antioch, whether as a part of the *Ktisis* or as a separate composition is not clear. There were a number of writers named Pausanias in antiquity, and modern scholars were for some time uncertain whether the Pausanias who wrote on Antioch was to be identified with the much better known Pausanias the *periegete*, whose work is preserved. The evidence seemed to most students to indicate that these two writers named Pausanias were not identical, but then the question arose as to whether the writer on Antioch was the Pausanias who was called Pausanias of Damascus. Opinion on this question varied, and indeed the evidence is very slender.[45] A recent study by Aubrey Diller of the whole problem of the authors named Pausanias, based on a much better collection of material than was previously assembled, has shown that the writer on Antioch is to be separated from Pausanias of Damascus, and that he is not to be identified with the other writers so named who are known in other connections.[46] While

[42] Malalas' description is discussed and analyzed below in Ch. 4.
[43] See A. Ausfeld, "Zur Topographie von Alexandria und Pseudo-Kallisthenes I 31-33," *Rh. Mus.* 55 (1900) 348-384, esp. 381; A. Ippel, "Ein Sarapisrelief in Hildesheim," *Archäol. Anz.* 1921, 8-9; M. Erdmann, *Zur Kunde der hellenistische Städtegründungen* (Progr. Strassburg 1883) 23-30, and cf. Förster, "Antiochia" 109-110.
[44] For the fragments of Pausanias, see *FHG* 4.467-471; Tzetzes *Chiliades* 7.118, v. 167 speaks of the work and gives its title; cf. also Stephanus Byz. *s.v. Seleukobelos.* Malalas quotes Pausanias (38.15; 197.17; 203.22; 204.2, 8; 248.15), as he does many other writers, but this does not necessarily mean that Malalas used Pausanias directly; Malalas may have taken the information from an intermediate source, while giving the impression that he was making a direct quotation (on Malalas' literary technique see further below). Förster, "Antiochia" 110 cites passages which, he states, prove that Libanius made use of Pausanias' work in writing his oration in praise of Antioch, the *Antiochikos* (which is discussed below). It is likely that Libanius did derive some of his material from Pausanias, whether directly or indirectly; but the passages cited by Förster are of such a generalized character that it may be doubted whether they are by themselves as convincing as Förster believed.
[45] See Förster, "Antiochia" 109-110, and the same scholar's study "De Libanio, Pausania, templo Apollinis Delphico," *Album gratulatorium in honorem H. van Herwerden* (Utrecht 1902) 45-54; Christ-Schmid-Stählin *Gesch. d. gr. Lit.*[6] 2, pt. 2, pp. 759, 993, 1039, 1041; Honigmann, "Syria" 1684-1685; O. Seel, "Pausanias," no. 15, *RE* 18.2402-2404 (on the question of Pausanias of Damascus as the historian of Antioch).
[46] A. Diller, "The Authors Named Pausanias," *TAPA* 86 (1955) 268-279.

the evidence is not extensive, it appears that Pausanias' work on Antioch is to be dated either in the second or the fourth century after Christ.

b. *Other Lost Works on Antioch or Syria.* In the preserved literature we encounter traces of several other books concerned with Antioch or Syria. One of the early works is the ἱστορικὰ ὑπομνήματα of Euphorion of Chalcis (born ca. 275 B.C.), who was a librarian of the royal library at Antioch under Antiochus the Great (224-187 B.C.); this apparently dealt with the history of Antioch and the Seleucid kings.[47] Euphorion's work seems to have been a forerunner of the great history of Posidonius of Apamea, in fifty-two books (now lost), which was a source of material (including information about Antioch) for the geographer Strabo.[48] Another great historical work in which Antioch played a part was the compilation of Nicolaus of Damascus.[49] In the time of Antiochus IV (176-146 B.C.) Protagorides of Cyzicus wrote a treatise "On the Festivals in Daphne."[50] The work of Athenaeus of Naucratis "On the Kings of Syria" doubtless contained material on Antioch.[51]

c. *The Sources of Malalas*; *The* acta urbis. The sixth-century chronicler Ioannes Malalas, whose work will be discussed below, cites among his sources the names of four writers, all of whose works are lost, namely Pausanias (already discussed), Domninus, Timotheus, Theophilus. Our information concerning these writers is very scanty; according to the citations in Malalas, Domninus, and Pausanias each wrote a chronicle that was largely or primarily concerned with Antioch, while the others seem to have composed world-chronicles in which Antioch was mentioned. Malalas' citations sound as though he used these sources directly, but it is possible that he drew upon them only at second hand. Malalas also quotes the *acta urbis* (τὰ ἄκτα τῆς πόλεως, 443.20) as a source of his information concerning the earthquake of A.D. 528, and it is clear in any case that some of his information could well have come from local official records, though we are not sure precisely how the information would have reached him.[52] We have not

[47] See Christ-Schmid-Stählin, *Gesch. d. gr. Lit.*[6] 2, pt. 1, pp. 148-150; and cf. below Ch. 5, §4.

[48] On Strabo's account of the foundation of Antioch, in which material from Posidonius is used, see below, Ch. 4, §4.

[49] See W. Crönert, "Die Epikureer in Syrien," *Jahreshefte d. Oesterreich. Archäol. Inst.* 10 (1907) 151-152.

[50] On Protagorides' work περὶ τῶν ἐν Δάφνῃ πανηγυρέων, see Christ-Schmid-Stählin, *Gesch. d. gr. Lit.*[6] 2, pt. 1, p. 299; and cf. R. Mouterde, "Pierides Musae," *MUSJ* 25 (1942-3) 8. The work is mentioned in Athenaeus 4.176A = *FHG* 4.484.

[51] Cf. *FHG* 4.656, with Introd., 1, p. ix.

[52] See the discussion of Malalas' work and his use of his sources in the following paragraph.

enough information to know whether there were *acta urbis* at Antioch
for the whole of the Roman period, and we do not know what kind of
official records of local events might have been kept during the Seleucid
period.[53]

d. *The World-Chronicle of Ioannes Malalas.* This chronicle, the
earliest and in some ways the most characteristic of the popular annal-
istic histories so much in demand in Byzantine times, is also a source of
special importance for the history and monuments of Antioch.[54] A large
part of the work was evidently compiled in Antioch while the author
was living there, and it also seems plain that the information concerning Antioch comes from local sources, including official records and
the *acta urbis* (which, as has been noted, he cites, 443.20). In addition,
for the period of the chronicler's own life, he must have used local oral
tradition. The work as we have it suffers from several limitations. The
author appears to have had a poor knowledge of history, to have used
his sources uncritically, and to have been credulous of material that he
ought not to have accepted. He cites his sources in such a way as to
give the impression that he has used them at first hand, whereas it is
clear—often from the chronicler's own childish mistakes—that he has
obtained his citations through intermediate sources. Finally, Malalas'
own style—the earliest extensive text in colloquial Greek—is on occasion quite ambiguous (sometimes as a result of the writer's ignorance).
Moreover, the Greek text, preserved in a unique manuscript in Oxford,
represents a condensation of the original version; the original (or at
least an earlier) form is represented by fragments preserved in excerpts
that were made before the text was edited, and especially in the Church
Slavonic version, which was translated before the Greek text was abbreviated.[55] In spite of all these limitations, the work of Malalas re-

[53] On the record offices of the Seleucids, see Rostovtzeff, *Soc. Econ. Hist. Hellenistic World* 1.440, with n. 241 in 3.1429, also Bikerman, *Institutions des Séleucides* 190-197.

[54] So much study has been devoted to Malalas that it would be neither possible nor useful to attempt a survey of the literature in this place. See K. Krumbacher, *Gesch. d. byz. Litteratur*[2] (Munich 1897) 325-334; K. Wolf, "Ioannes Malalas," No. 22, *RE* 9.1795-1799; G. Moravcsik, *Byzantinoturcica* 1: *Die byz. Quellen der Geschichte der Türkvölker* (Budapest 1942) 184-189. Moravcsik lists the bibliography published through 1938. Important studies dealing with Malalas published since that time are: A. Frolow, "La dédicace de Constantinople," *Revue de l'histoire des religions* 127 (1944) 61ff.; F. A. Lepper, *Trajan's Parthian War* (Oxford 1948), with the valuable review by M. I. Henderson in *Journal of Roman Studies* 39 (1949) 121-132; and E. Bikerman, "Les Maccabées de Malalas," *Byzantion* 21 (1951) 63-83.

[55] On the fragments of the Greek text of Malalas see Moravcsik, *op.cit.* (above, n. 54) 186. The parts of the Church Slavonic version that deal with Greek and Roman history have been utilized by Stauffenberg in his edition of the Greek text (*Die röm. Kaisergeschichte bei Malalas; griech. Text der Bücher IX-XII und Untersuchungen*

mains one of the major sources for the history of Antioch, and gives us valuable information concerning events and monuments in the city. The work covers both the Seleucid period (including the mythical dwellers on the site and the foundation of the city) and the Roman period. Beginning with the Roman occupation of Syria in 64 B.C., Malalas' information becomes much more detailed and it is apparent that beginning at this time his sources were much better than they were for the Seleucid period. All of this material must be used with due caution, for in spite of the impressive list of sources he mentions— Pausanias, Domninus, Theophilus, Timotheus, the *acta urbis*—we cannot be sure that he had these in a reliable form, and he certainly seems to have been incapable of a consistently judicious use of them.[56] Malalas lived in Antioch, evidently in the reigns of Justinus I and Justinian. After the capture of Antioch by the Persians in A.D. 540 (479.23ff. Bonn ed.), the information about Antioch in Malalas' work—which had been very full, for example, for the years A.D. 528-531 (442-470 Bonn ed.)— comes to an abrupt end, and it is supposed that Malalas (like many people) may have left Antioch at this time to live at Constantinople. It has also been suggested that the remaining parts of the chronicle, in which Constantinople, rather than Antioch, is the center of interest, were written by a continuator (perhaps the patriarch of Constantinople, John III Antiocheus, A.D. 565-577).[57] A special feature of Malalas' chronicle, for other cities as well as for Antioch, is his interest in imperial visits to cities and imperial building activities in them. The building activities and the visits are often associated in Malalas' presentation, when we can be reasonably sure that there was no connection between them. This interest, which gives the work one of its special values for us, is a typical reflection of the ancient conception of building as one

---

[Stuttgart 1931]) and have been translated into English: *Chronicle of John Malalas, Books VIII-XVIII, translated from the Church Slavonic by Matthew Spinka in collaboration with Glanville Downey* (Chicago 1940); for the bibliography of the Church Slavonic text, see the introduction to this translation, 1-10.

[56] Malalas' methods of using his sources seem on occasion so baffling that in spite of the large amount of study devoted to the problem, we really know very little about either his procedures or the contents of the sources. A good summary of the research on the subject is provided by Wolf, *op.cit.* (above, n. 54). Stauffenberg in his edition of Books IX-XII (cited above, n. 55) undertook a new investigation of the problem, though his conclusions do not always inspire confidence; see the important review of Stauffenberg's book by W. Ensslin, *Philologische Wochenschrift* 53 (1933) 769-789.

[57] For the various hypotheses concerning the composition of the later parts of Malalas' chronicle, see Wolf, *op.cit.* (above, n. 54). Because of the similarity of the names and of the subjects they treat, there has sometimes been confusion of Ioannes Malalas and Ioannes Antiocheus (Moravcsik, *op.cit.* [above, n. 54] 171-174).

of the characteristics of the royal office; and in Antioch, this material would certainly have come from local official records.[58]

5. OTHER LOCAL LITERARY SOURCES[59]

a. *Libanius.* One of the best known, and also one of the most characteristic of the authors connected with Antioch is the orator and teacher Libanius, who was born at Antioch in A.D. 314. After studying at Athens and teaching for a time at Constantinople and at Nicomedia, he settled in Antioch in A.D. 354 and spent the remainder of his career there (he died probably in A.D. 393). His preserved works, which are among the most voluminous writings of a Greek author to have survived from antiquity, give us an enormous amount of information concerning all aspects of life at Antioch. The value of these writings—local speeches, pamphlets, addresses to the throne, a quantity of private letters —may be judged from the series of important studies, written by a number of scholars, which are based on parts or the whole of Libanius' work.[60] Every feature of life in Antioch—political, social, intellectual,

[58] Special attention was devoted to this by Stauffenberg (note also the important observations of Ensslin in his review cited above, n. 56). For a further study, see G. Downey, "Imperial Building Records in Malalas," *BZ* 38 (1938) 1-15, 299-311.

[59] The work of Ammianus Marcellinus is not included in this survey of the principal local sources in spite of the fact that Ammianus was a native of Antioch and well acquainted with the city: his style and purpose were such that Antioch does not play a leading role in his history, though of course we do gain from his book a very vivid picture of life in the city, and information that would not otherwise be known to us.

[60] The most recent, and indeed the most impressive of these, are the monographs of Paul Petit, *Libanius et la vie municipale à Antioche au IV⁰ siècle après J.-C.* (1955) and *Les Etudiants de Libanius: Un professeur de Faculté et ses élèves au Bas Empire* (1956). The former is vol. 62 of the "Bibliothèque Archéologique et Historique" of the Institut Français d'archéologie de Beyrouth, while the latter is a "complementary thesis." See the important reviews by A. F. Norman, *Journal of Roman Studies* 47 (1957) 236-240, W. Ensslin, *Gnomon* 6 (1957) 374-378, and R. Pack, *AJP* 79 (1958) 219-221. Since Petit gives an exhaustive bibliography of modern works of all kinds concerned with Libanius, it will be sufficient here to mention only some of the most characteristic studies, and those of special interest for Antioch, namely G. R. Sievers, *Das Leben des Libanius* (Berlin 1868); O. Seeck, *Die Briefe des Libanius zeitlich geordnet* (Leipzig 1906; *Texte und Untersuchungen zur Geschichte der altchristlichen Literatur* 30, pt. 1-2); J. W. H. Walden, *The Universities of Ancient Greece* (New York 1909); Christ-Schmid-Stählin, *Gesch. d. gr. Lit.*[6] 2,² (Munich 1924), pp. 987-1000; R. Förster and K. Münscher, "Libanios," *RE* 12 (1925), 2485-2551; C. Bonner, "Witchcraft in the Lecture Room of Libanius," *TAPA* 63 (1932) 34-44; R. A. Pack, *Studies in Libanius and Antiochene Society under Theodosius* (Dissertation, University of Michigan 1935); P. Wolf, *Vom Schulwesen der Spätantike: Studien zu Libanius* (Baden-Baden 1952); A. D. Nock, "The Praises of Antioch," *Journal of Egyptian Archaeology* 40 (1954) 76-82. A statue of the late fourth century, found at Antioch and first published by R. Förster, *Jahrbuch des k. deutschen Archäologischen Instituts* 13 (1898) 184-185, has been identified as either Libanius or Ammianus Marcellinus. To the present writer it seems more likely that the statue might represent Libanius.

economic—is touched upon in Libanius' writings, and all the important figures of the day in Antioch, and also a number of the high officials in Constantinople, are mentioned. Some of the material on administration and economic problems that Libanius gives us is unique, and some of this still awaits detailed study. In addition, Libanius' works preserve special information of the most precious kind. Along with his pupil Chrysostom he gives a very detailed account (in a series of orations and pamphlets) of the great riot of A.D. 387, one of the best known episodes in the history of Antioch.[61] Libanius' autobiography is also of great historical importance. His best known work on Antioch is his encomium of the city, the *Antiochikos* (*Oration* 11), which was written in A.D. 356 or 360 for delivery at the local Olympic Games. The work is a unique source for the history of Antioch before Libanius' time (especially for the legends of the colonization of the site) and for the plan and appearance of the city in his own day. It is one of the best of the preserved encomia of ancient cities and from it we can gain valuable insight into the importance of the city's role at this time as a center of Graeco-Roman civilization. The work also shows us the real depth and intensity of the enthusiasm and loyalty its citizens felt for Antioch.[62] One could expect Libanius to be learned in the antiquities of his beloved home. Thus it is disappointing—though not surprising—to find that he speaks of his written sources only as "the histories" (αἱ συγγραφαί).[63] Indeed it would not have suited his style to give the names of the historians, and (as has been pointed out) his hearers were familiar with the local sources anyway.[64] One of the special features of the work is its *periegesis* or tour of the city and Daphne. It is curious to note that the route that seems to be indicated in the topographical border of the Yakto mosaic (described above) corre-

---

[61] See below, Ch. 15, §2.

[62] A translation of Libanius' eleventh oration, with introduction and commentary, has been published by the present writer in the *Proceedings of the American Philosophical Society* 103 (1959) 652-686. For a valuable study of the antiquarian background of such an oration, see the investigation by Nock cited above (n. 60). The corresponding pride in the Roman Empire is illustrated by the monograph of James H. Oliver, *The Ruling Power: A Study of the Roman Empire in the Second Century after Christ Through the Roman Oration of Aelius Aristides* (*Transactions of the American Philosophical Society*, N.S. 43, pt. 4, 1953). The *Antiochikos* was enormously popular in antiquity. Nikolaos Mesarites borrowed extensive passages from it; see Mesarites' *Description of the Church of the Holy Apostles at Constantinople*, edited by G. Downey (*Transactions of the American Philosophical Society*, N.S. 47 [1957]) p. 862.

[63] *Or.* 11, 43 and 107.

[64] See Hugi, *Der Antiochikos*, p. 146, commentary on §107. Presumably Libanius had access to the sources named above, especially the works of Pausanias and the other writers named by Malalas.

sponds with the route over which Libanius takes his audience in imagination.

b. *The Emperor Julian.* One of the best known of the literary sources associated with Antioch is the *Misopogon* or "Beard-Hater," the satire on the people of Antioch written by the Emperor Julian the Philosopher (January, A.D. 363) during his stay in the city. This work, together with the letters and decrees of Julian which date from the same period, gives us a considerable amount of information on both the background and the events of Julian's experiences and activities at Antioch, and recent study of the famine which occurred during the emperor's visit has given us further understanding of the motivation of the satire.[65] It should be remembered, however, that the *Misopogon* is something of a literary curiosity and tour de force, and that while it undoubtedly tells us a great deal about the special characteristics of the people at Antioch, it must not be read today as a serious and trustworthy description of the population of Antioch as a whole. The vivid style and the imperial authorship of the piece, which make it one of the most remarkable works of its kind, have sometimes had the effect of giving it more weight as a historical source than it deserves. As much as anything, it should be read as a commentary on the highly complex character of its author.

c. *St. John Chrysostom.* One of the most respected and influential figures in Antioch in his day (he was born in Antioch in the 340's and lived there until A.D. 398, when he became Patriarch of Constantinople) was Libanius' pupil Chrysostom, whose sermons give us a valuable picture of life in Antioch at this time, as well as of the problems of a spiritual leader in ministering to a city congregation in a place like Antioch. As another facet of the picture we find in the writings of Libanius and Julian, Chrysostom's works complete our knowledge of Antioch at this time as much by the background they supply indirectly as by the specific facts they mention. Of special interest are the homilies on the local martyrs—notably St. Babylas—which supply details about the local cults and also about churches and *martyria.* Many valuable historical details are furnished by the series of homilies, "On the Statues," preached at the time of the great riot of A.D. 387, in which the imperial statues were destroyed. Chrysostom's greatest significance for us, in the study of ancient Antioch, is the illustration he provides of the way in which the best elements of Greek literature and philosophy were absorbed in the new Christian culture of the fourth century.

[65] See the account of Julian's reign, below, Ch. 13.

Owing to the activity of Libanius and his colleagues, Antioch was at this time still one of the places where a student could get the best training in the Greek tradition, and Chrysostom's career—along with those of his contemporaries and coworkers, the Cappadocian fathers— gives us an impressive demonstration of the real practical value of the traditional Greek *paideia* in both the training and the active ministry of one of the most gifted of the Christian clergy of the day.[66]

d. *Evagrius.* The *Ecclesiastical History* of Evagrius Scholasticus is the principal source of our knowledge of the history of Antioch between A.D. 540 (the end of the period covered by Malalas) and A.D. 593, when Evagrius closed his work. Evagrius was born in Epiphania in Syria about A.D. 536, and spent his career as a lawyer in Antioch. As legal adviser and assistant to the Patriarch Gregory (A.D. 570-593) he was in close touch with both secular and ecclesiastical affairs and was in a position to have access to documents and official records. Evagrius was a man of scholarly habits, and he compiled a volume of documents— copies of speeches, official reports, minutes of conferences, letters—to serve as a companion to his history. This volume unfortunately is lost. He was also much interested in the earlier history of Antioch. In his account (1.20) of the visit of the Empress Eudocia to Antioch, he re- calls the compliment she offered to the citizens in reminding them that she came from Athens, which had sent colonists to Antioch, and then he remarks, "If any one wishes to know about these colonies, an account is given by Strabo the geographer, by Phlegon and by Diodorus of Sicily, as well as by Arrian and Peisander the poet, and, besides, by the most distinguished sophists Ulpian and Libanius and Julian." Of these accounts of the colonizing of Antioch, only those of Strabo and Libanius are preserved. For us, one of the special interests of Evagrius' work is that it gives us a picture of the way in which normal life and activities continued in Antioch during the latter years of the sixth century when the city was already declining and would soon pass into the possession of the Arabs (A.D. 637-38). Evagrius was to some extent aware that Antioch had lost some of its earlier greatness, but his account of the normal continuation of the city's life serves to remind us that the disastrous earthquakes of A.D. 526 and 528 and the sack by the Per- sians in A.D. 540 did not bring the city's activities wholly to an end. A particularly valuable part of Evagrius' work is his account of the career

---

[66] The first volume of the study of P. Chrysostomus Baur, *Der heilige Johannes Chrysostomus und seine Zeit* (Munich 1929-1930), deals with Chrysostom's life and work in Antioch.

of the Patriarch Gregory, which shows, in greater detail than our other sources, the hazards to which local hostility exposed a patriarch of Antioch.

6. MODERN STUDIES OF ANTIOCH

Though the modern studies of Antioch do not fall within the category of sources, it seems appropriate to close this chapter with a brief account of the work of the scholars of the nineteenth and twentieth centuries who studied various aspects of the history and antiquities of Antioch prior to the excavations of 1932-1939.

Here, of course, the greatest name is that of Carl Otfried Müller (1797-1840), whose *Antiquitates Antiochenae* (Göttingen 1839), the first modern study of the city, and one of the earliest and best of the monographs on ancient cities, represented an astonishing achievement.[67] Müller had never visited the site, which was difficult and dangerous of access in those days, but he succeeded, by a careful study of the ancient texts and of the travelers' accounts, in reconstructing a plan of the city (reproduced here, Fig. 9) that is not at all far from the truth. Müller's collection of texts represented, in his day, an enormous amount of patient collecting of material, and his work has been, and remains, basic to all research on the subject, and all scholars who deal with any aspect of the history of Antioch will always be in his debt.

In 1896, from March 18 to 29, Richard Förster of Breslau visited Antioch, examined the site carefully, and made photographs of such inscriptions, sculpture, and other antiquities as he could find. His long article "Antiochia am Orontes," dedicated to the memory of C. O. Müller,[68] serves as an expansion and continuation of Müller's book, and provides a wealth of information and acute observation. Förster's interest in Antioch had had its origin in his preparations for a new edition of the works of Libanius, which began to appear in 1903; and by providing this edition, Förster put all students of Antioch in his debt.

Some time before 1927 Wilhelm Weber visited the site and as a result published a study of various problems connected with the chronicle

[67] Müller's work, which is generally met with in its separate publication in book form, was officially published as a part of the *Commentationes societatis regiae scientiarum Gottingenses recentiores*, 8 (1832-1837, published 1842), *classis historicae et philologicae*, 205-278, 279-334. Valuable "reviews" of his own work, containing additions and corrections, were published by Müller in the *Göttingische Gelehrte Anzeigen*, 1834, Stück 109-111, and 1839, Stück 101-104 (= *Kleine deutsche Schriften*, hrsg. v. Eduard Müller [a brother], 1 (Breslau 1847) 90-102, 110-129.

[68] *Jahrbuch des k. deutschen Archäol. Instituts* 12 (1897) 103-149. Förster's study is completed by a second article, "Zu den Skulpturen und Inschriften von Antiochia," in the same publication, 16 (1901) 39-55.

of Malalas.[69] This study bore fruit in the edition of Books ix-xii of Malalas published by Weber's pupil Alexander Schenk Graf von Stauffenberg in 1931.[70]

Finally, it is appropriate to mention the work of Lt.-Col. Paul Jacquot, *Antioche, Centre de Tourisme*, published at Antioch in 1931, in which a large amount of material, including illustrations, sketches, and maps, is brought together in convenient form. The work covers Antioch and its vicinity and is a useful source of practical information, based on intimate acquaintance gained during the author's military duty there.

[69] "Studien zur Chronik des Malalas," *Festgabe für Adolf Deissmann zum 60. Geburtstag* (Tübingen 1927) 20-66.

[70] See above, n. 55.

CHAPTER 3

ANTIOCH AND THE REGION IN
PRE-MACEDONIAN TIMES

IN the geography of northwestern Syria one of the principal features
from the point of view of military and economic communication
is the Amuk plain.[1] Through it must pass all land traffic between
southern Anatolia and the coastal or western part of Syria and Palestine,
and all traffic between the northern part of Mesopotamia and the
Mediterranean Sea (Figs. 3, 4).[2] Fertile, well watered, and enjoying a
favorable climate, the plain early attracted both nomadic and settled
inhabitants, and in time it became densely inhabited and wealthy: it
is today dotted with mounds that represent ancient settlements. Commercial traffic through the plain flourished, and the successive powers
that ruled this part of Syria established military controls there.[3] The
foundation of Antioch, in 300 B.C., followed logically upon a long development of the region, and the primary significance of the site of
Antioch is that it stands at the southwestern gateway of the Amuk
plain, and at the head of navigation of the Orontes river which, with
its valley, forms the principal highway between the Amuk region and
the sea.

While implements of the Stone Age have been found in the neighborhood,[4] there is, at least thus far, no archaeological evidence for any

[1] The best descriptions of the plain are those of Braidwood, *Mounds in the Plain
of Antioch* and of L. Woolley, *A Forgotten Kingdom* (Penguin Books 1953); see also
Jacquot, *Antioche* 1.161ff. I use the modern spelling Amuk for the sake of euphony,
and because it has become familiar in English, though the second vowel is intrusive.
See Braidwood, *op.cit.* 1, n. 1.

[2] For the roads of the region, see, in addition to Fig. 4 Braidwood, *Mounds in the
Plain of Antioch* 139, map 9; Honigmann, "Syria" 1555-1556, and H. H. von der
Osten, "Anatolische Wege," *Eranos* 49 (1951) 65-83, with map on p. 66.

[3] I have not attempted to relate the pre-Macedonian history of the region in detail
because the material is readily available in Honigmann, "Syria" 1572ff., in the reports
of Braidwood, and in Woolley's monograph (cited above, n. 1), as well as in the general
survey of Hitti, *History of Syria* 17ff. For an excellent summary of the commercial
relations between Syria and Greek lands in the fifth and fourth centuries see Rostovtzeff,
Soc. Econ. Hist. Hellenistic World 1.84-88, with notes in 3.1324-1326. See also P. J. Riis,
"The Syrian Astarte Plaques and their Western Connections," *Berytus* 9 (1949) 89-90.
On the chronology, see G. M. A. Hanfmann, "The Bronze Age in the Near East,"
AJA 55 (1951) 355-365, and 56 (1952) 27-38, especially vol. 55, 360, with nn. 36-37,
and vol. 56, 27. For the early history of the region to the east of the Amuk plain, see
Sauvaget, *Alep* 22ff.

[4] See Isambert in the *Syrie, Palestine* of the Guides-Joanne (Paris 1882) 3.731, and
(for the journey of Chantre, cited by Isambert) E. Chantre, "De Beyrouth à Tiflis,"
Le Tour du Monde, nouveau journal de voyages 58 (1889) 273-304.

pre-Macedonian settlement on the site of Antioch, and the local Anti-ochene tradition of earlier Greek settlements on the site is not unim-peachable. There is, however, archaeological testimony to other settle-ments in the Amuk plain and at the mouth of the Orontes, and through these settlements can be traced the history of the region and the development of the factors that led to the foundation of Antioch and its development into one of the principal cities of the Graeco-Roman world.

It is characteristic that one of the earliest records of the inhabitation of this area is the evidence of pottery, which shows a movement of peoples from Anatolia to Palestine via the Amuk route in the third millennium B.C.[5] This movement followed the north-south route linking Egypt and Anatolia, which has been called the "international high-way,"[6] a route which Antioch in later times was destined both to profit from and to control.

There is more evidence for the important traffic that passed between east and west across the Amuk plain. This has come in large part from the recent excavations at al-Mina and Sabouni at the mouth of the Orontes and at Tell Atchana (ancient Alalakh) and other sites in the Amuk plain.[7] Al-Mina was the harbor of the town of Sabouni; the two stood in much the same relationship as the Peiraeus and Athens. Tell Atchana stood on the road that led to and from al-Mina-Sabouni. The archaeological evidence indicates that these three places were all founded about 2000 B.C., if not indeed earlier, and that Greek merchants lived at al-Mina-Sabouni from an early period. At this time northern

---

[5] Ruth B. K. Amiran, "Connections between Anatolia and Palestine in the Early Bronze Age," *Israel Exploration Journal* 2 (1952) 89-103, especially 102; Braidwood, *Mounds in the Plain of Antioch* 7. On the earlier period see M. Pervès, "La préhistoire de la Syrie et du Liban," *Syria* 25 (1946-48) 109-129, and R. de Vaux, "La préhistoire de la Syrie et de la Palestine d'après les recherches récentes," *Rev. bibl.* 53 (1946) 99-124.

[6] On this "highway" see for example Hitti, *History of Syria* 60.

[7] See Woolley, *A Forgotten Kingdom* (cited above, n. 1). Previously published re-ports were: L. Woolley, "Excavations near Antioch in 1936," *AJ* 17 (1937) 1-15, on the excavations of al Mina, Sabouni, and Tell Atchana, with map, pl. 1, opposite p. 2, showing the location of the excavation sites; "Excavations at al Mina, Suedia," *JHS* 58 (1938) 1-30, 133-170; "Excavations at Tal Atchana, 1937," *AJ* 18 (1938) 1-28; "Exca-vations at Atchana-Alalakh, 1938," *AJ* 19 (1939) 1-37; "The Date of al Mina," *JHS* 68 (1948) 148. For the final report on Alalakh, see L. Woolley, *Alalakh: An Account of the Excavations at Tell Atchana in the Hatay 1937-1949* (London 1955, Society of Antiquaries; Reports of the Research Committee, 18). Reference should also be made to C. W. McEwan, "The Syrian Expedition of the Oriental Institute of the University of Chicago," *AJA* 41 (1937) 8-13. On the chronology, see C. F. A. Schaeffer, *Strati-graphie comparée et chronologie de l'Asie occidentale* 1 (Oxford 1948) 98-107. On the finds of pottery, see C. Clairmont, "Greek Pottery from the Near East," *Berytus* 11 (1955) 85-141.

Syria was occupied successively by Amorites, Assyrians, and Egyptians, then by Hurrians and Hittites. A very early Hittite building is a fourteenth century palace found at Tell Atchana. During all this period important trade was carried on with the west; Mycenaean and Cypriote Bronze Age pottery is common both at al-Mina-Sabouni and in the villages and towns of the Amuk plain, including Tell Atchana, and the products of Greece and the Greek islands continued to pass along this route until the Macedonian conquest. At first al-Mina-Sabouni was largely dependent upon trade with Cyprus and the trade with this island, which lay only sixty miles from Syria, must have been brisk; Mount Casius, at the mouth of the Orontes, is visible from Cyprus, so that navigation along this route would be favored. In the seventh and sixth centuries trade was chiefly with Corinth and Rhodes, and then Athens played the chief role.

The Aramaeans who overran northern Syria in the fourteenth and thirteenth centuries swamped the Amorites, Hurrians, and Hittites, and after the twelfth century Tell Atchana was deserted. However, al-Mina-Sabouni continued to flourish, and trade with Greece and the Greek islands was vigorous. Local legends of Antioch would put the arrival of certain Greeks, Cypriotes, and Cretans at the site of Antioch at about this period, but discussion of these must be postponed for the moment. Historically, the next great change in the region is its passing under the domination of the Assyrians, beginning in the ninth century. Here again a local Antiochene legend appears in Libanius' story that Semiramis built a temple at the place later called Meroë, five miles east of Antioch, in honor of Artemis, i.e. the Assyrian deity, probably Anaitis, whom the Greeks would identify with Artemis.[8] The Semiramis of the Greeks was a legendary figure, famous as the builder of Babylon; she represents, almost certainly, the Assyrian queen Sammuramat (844-782 B.C.), wife of Shamsi-Adad V, who after her husband's death acted as regent (810-805 B.C.) during the minority of her son Adad-Nirari III.[9] The story of her temple near Antioch appears

---

[8] Libanius *Or.* 5.42ff. (Appendices, Translation of Documents); *Or.* 11.59. The location of Meroë is shown not only by Libanius but by Stephanus of Byzantium, *s.v.*, and in the life of St. Symeon the Elder by Antonius, ed. H. Lietzmann, *Texte u. Untersuchungen* 32, 4 (1908) pp. 74.2, 178.30. See Honigmann, "Topographie" pt. 2, 18 (*s.v.* Meroë).

[9] See T. Lenschau, "Semiramis," *RE* Suppl. 7.1204-1212; Hugi's commentary on the passage in Libanius, in his translation of part of the *Antiochikos*, pp. 115-116; and M. Braun, *History and Romance in Graeco-Oriental Literature* (Oxford 1938) 6-13. On the Assyrian rule in this region see also Ellen C. Semple, *The Geography of the Mediterranean Region* (New York 1931) 204.

only in Libanius, and we have no way of confirming it; there is no evidence that the queen ever visited the neighborhood of Antioch, but she might well have done so. For the present, Libanius' story must be looked upon as an aetiological legend, designed to provide an illustrious origin for the cult of his own day, as described in his *Oration* 5; but it might well prove some day that the story has some foundation in fact.

Another relic of Assyrian rule near Antioch may be the place name Βητάγων or Βηθδάγων, which might have been named for the Assyrian god Dagan.[10]

Jewish tradition, seeking to establish the antiquity of the Jewish community at Antioch, placed the meeting of Nebuchadnezzar and the Great Sanhedrin at Daphne, and attempted to identify Hamath and Riblah of the Old Testament with the site of Antioch.[11] There is, so far as we know, no real basis for either of these traditions.

Under Cyrus, Syria became a Persian satrapy and remained so until the Macedonian conquest.[12] Libanius, after telling the story of Semiramis, goes on to describe the visit to the site of Antioch of the Persian king Cambyses (529-522 B.C.), who, accompanied by his wife Meroë, encamped there in the course of his campaign against Egypt (525 B.C.).[13] The queen (who, Libanius says, gave her name to the place called Meroë) found that Semiramis' temple was in ruins, and she persuaded the king to restore it and increase its height, and she herself presented it with treasure. A festival in honor of Meroë was established, with resident priestesses, and in Libanius' day (fourth century A.D.) the temple was still standing, in a suburb to the east of the city.[14] A place named Marua appears in a list of Syrian cities subject to the Assyrians, and this might be the Meroë of Libanius.[15] What basis there was for the story of Cambyses and his queen we do not know; it would be easy for such a legend to arise on the basis of the place named Meroë or Marua and in connection with a temple of Artemis that could actually have been built at a much later date.

Much more attention is devoted by Libanius and Malalas to the

---

[10] Honigmann, "Syria" 1579.

[11] Kraeling, "Jewish Community at Antioch" 131-132.

[12] Honigmann, "Syria" 1602. See K. Galling, "Syrien in der Politik der Achaemeniden bis zum Aufstand des Megabyzos 448 v. Chr.," *Der Alte Orient* 36 (1937) pts. 3-4.

[13] Libanius *Or.* 11.59-68. In his fifth oration Libanius describes the cult of Artemis at Antioch. He mentions that Artemis saved Meroë's eyes.

[14] Libanius *Or.* 5.42. See E. Honigmann, "Meroë," no. 2, *RE* 15.1048; Lehmann-Haupt, "Kambyses," no. 3, *RE* 10.1812-1813.

[15] Honigmann, "Syria" 1599.

traditions of the early Greek settlements on the site of Antioch. According to the local legends, Io the daughter of Inachus, when she was driven from home, came to Mount Silpius in her wanderings and died there. Inachus sent his Argives (led by Triptolemus) to search for her, and though they did not find her, they settled on Mount Silpius and founded Iopolis.[16] According to Libanius, they abandoned their search and settled in this spot because of its attractions. The next settlers came to the site when Kasos was moved by divine impulse to leave Crete and to bring the noblest of the Cretans with him to the region of the future city, where they were gladly received by the Argives, and founded Kasiotis, at the acropolis on Mount Silpius. In time Kasos married Amyke the daughter of Salaminus, king of Cyprus, and the bride brought with her many of her people, who formed an important addition to the Argives and Cretans already settled on the spot. According to the legend as it appears in Malalas, Amyke when she died was buried 100 stadia from Kasiotis, for which reason, the chronicler says, the place was called Amyke. Of course the name of the Amuk region (a Semitic word meaning "hollow," "depth") is older than this legend; but it is interesting to see that tradition connected the Amuk plain with a Cypriote princess who ruled on Mount Silpius. Again, when some of the Herakleidae were driven into exile by Eurysthes and wandered in search of a home all through Europe and Asia, accompanied by many Eleans, they finally chose the region of Antioch for their home, and founded Herakleia, near the site which later became the famous suburb Daphne.[17]

Finally, Malalas records that Perseus visited the Argives in Iopolis and built for them a temple of Zeus Keraunios.[18]

[16] The accounts of the foundation of Iopolis given by Malalas (28-30) and by Libanius (*Or.* 11.44-52) differ somewhat; Libanius' is the more detailed, and is better designed for the glorification of Antioch. Malalas' account also appears in *Chron. Pasch.* 1.74-76 Bonn. On a comparable difference between Libanius' and Malalas' accounts of the founding of Antioch, see below, Ch. 4, §2. The local legend of Io is treated by Cook, *Zeus* 1.236-237; see also K. O. Müller, *Kunstarchäologische Werke* 5 (1873) 23-24. Strabo (16.2.5, p. 750) also mentions Triptolemus' settlement at the site of Antioch. A mosaic showing Io guarded by Argos (an earlier point in the story) was found in a house at Daphne: Levi, *Antioch Mosaic Pavements* 1.75-80, cf. 210.

[17] Libanius *Or.* 11.52-56. The location of Kasos' settlement, and the story of Amyke, are given by Malalas 201.19ff.

[18] Malalas' garbled account (37.17-38.16) makes of Perseus the king of the Persians, and (by confusion with Persian fire-worship) states that the temple he built was dedicated to "undying fire." However, the context of Malalas' own account (see 38.5) shows that the temple in question was that which he later (199.13-14) says was supposed to have been dedicated to Zeus Keraunios by Perseus. Seleucus set up a statue to Zeus Keraunios which may have stood in this temple (Malalas 212.2-4; see below, Ch. 4, §3, with n. 97). Coins of Seleucus I bearing the Medusa head seem to refer to the temple

According to these legends, then, there were three Greek settlements in the region of the future Antioch. Iopolis (also called Ione) is spoken of as a *polis*, and it seems to have stood on Mount Silpius, though its precise position on the mountain is not recorded.[19] This settlement is said to have possessed a temple to Io and a temple to Kronos, both built by the inhabitants;[20] a temple built by Triptolemus to Nemean Zeus, whose dedication was later changed to Zeus Epikarpios (Fruitbringer);[21] and the temple to Zeus Keraunios attributed to Perseus, which has been mentioned. The other two settlements were Herakleia, near the site of Daphne,[22] and Kasiotis at the acropolis on Mount Silpius. No temples in these two places are recorded.

These stories, typical of the legends of wandering heroes which became associated with the foundations of cities,[23] may be only aetiological tales, designed to provide the people of Antioch with an illustrious descent. As we shall see, the foundation of Seleucus Nicator was made even more illustrious by the story (which might actually be true) that the site had been chosen by Alexander the Great himself; and a tradition of original settlement by Argives, Cretans, Cyprians, Heraclids, and Eleans would only add luster to the city's ancient history. The legends might have arisen in part in connection with temples that could have come to be identified with those supposed to have been built at Iopolis, and the annual commemoration of the search for Io, which Malalas says the people of Antioch later observed, might have grown out of an oriental rite that came to be associated with the commemoration of Io's wandering.[24] It is also possible that the existence

---

of Zeus supposed to have been built by Perseus: Newell, *West. Sel. Mints* 100-101. On a sarcophagus found at Daphne which is decorated with the Medusa head and the head of Perseus, see R. Mouterde, "Antiquités et inscriptions (Syrie, Liban)," *MUSJ* 26 (1944-46) 40-41.

[19] The name of Iopolis appears in Malalas *locc.citt.*; Libanius (*Or.* 11.61) calls the settlement Ione. Malalas (29.16) writes of the settlement as being εἰς τὸ Σίλπιον ὄρος, and when he tells how Seleucus, when founding Antioch, transferred the previous inhabitants from Iopolis and Kasiotis to the new city, he uses the verb *katagein*, meaning that Seleucus "led them down" to the new city (201.18, 202.4). Libanius (*Or.* 11.47) speaks of the early settlers going ἐπὶ τὸ ὄρος, which should mean "up on the mountain," but in another passage (*ibid.* 51) he writes of Ione as ὑπὸ τῷ ὄρει. Libanius' whole account of the early history of the site has a literary flavor, and his inconsistency as to the location of Iopolis not only suggests that his information was vague, but may itself be an indication of the legendary character of the settlement. On the location of Iopolis with relation to Seleucus' city, see below, Ch. 4, §3.

[20] Malalas 29.15-16, 30.2-3.

[21] Libanius *Or.* 11.51. On Zeus Epikarpios, see Cook, *Zeus* 2, p. 1186, no. 7 (on p. 1187).

[22] Libanius *Or.* 11.56.   [23] For other examples see Jones, *Greek City* 49-50.

[24] Malalas 29.18-21; cf. *Chron. Pasch.* 2.76.2-5 Bonn, and see Müller, *Antiq. Antioch.* 19.

of a village or a quarter of the city that bore a name such as Io or Ione could have suggested the origin of the legend. It may be significant that Malalas[25] mentions that according to some authorities Io died in Egypt, and so did not go to Syria at all.

Stories of this kind are so common, and often so transparently legendary, that scholars in the past have understandably been dubious about any such early Greek settlements at Antioch.[26] The new archaeological evidence, however, suggests that there may be some basis for these tales. The excavations have shown that there were Greek traders established at al-Mina and Sabouni at an early date, and that this trading center had a close connection with Tell Atchana in the Amuk region, so that the Greeks at al-Mina-Sabouni found it easy to carry on trade with the wealthy and closely populated Amuk plain; and this trade, of course, all had to pass by the site of Antioch. Moreover, it has plausibly been argued that al-Mina-Sabouni (taken as a unit) is to be identified with Posidium, which Herodotus describes as a Greek city founded by Amphilochus.[27] Herodotus' account makes it clear that the Posidium which he mentions was flourishing in the fifth century B.C. Whether or not this is the correct identification of al-Mina-Sabouni, it is certain that Greek merchants were active at the mouth of the Orontes from Mycenaean times to the Macedonian conquest, just as there were Greek traders farther down the coast, at Ras Shamra-Ugarit; and while one might expect that as a rule Greek traders would remain in coastal towns through the pre-Macedonian period, it seems by no means impossible that some Greek merchants might have pushed on beyond al-Mina-Sabouni and established themselves on the future site of Antioch at some time before Alexander's conquest. There were several reasons why they might have done this. Antioch was a day's journey by river from the sea;[28] and it was here that goods coming from the east could be put into boats or on rafts to be carried down the river to al-Mina. Also the site of Antioch was an easy journey on foot

---

[25] 29.5; cf. *Chron. Pasch.* 2.75.10 Bonn.

[26] See Müller, *Antiq. Antioch.* 17ff. and Cook, *Zeus* 2.981, 1186ff.

[27] Herodotus 3.91. Woolley in *JHS* 58 (1938) 28-30 (cf. *A Forgotten Kingdom* 179) convincingly argues in favor of the identification, and the reference to Posidium and Seleucia Pieria in the Gurob papyrus (col. II, line 20) is consistent with this identification; see Holleaux, "Le papyrus de Gourob," 285, 293, with n. 3. Before Woolley's discoveries, Posidium had been identified with Ras el Basit, further south on the coast: Dussaud, *Topographie* 418-422; Honigmann, "Syria" 1604.

[28] Strabo 16.2.7 p. 751; Pausanias 8.29.3 (describing Roman operations to improve the harbor at Seleucia Pieria, Pausanias indicates that the Orontes was navigable as far up as Antioch before the improvements in the harbor were carried out); Libanius *Or.* 11.262, 265. See also Ch. 5, n. 13.

for travelers going upstream; a messenger on foot, traveling rapidly, could make the round trip between Antioch and the sea in one morning.[29] Finally, the site of Antioch is approximately half way between al-Mina-Sabouni and the towns of the eastern part of the Amuk plain. Thus it does not seem difficult to believe that a Greek trading post and rest stop might have been established on the future site of Antioch. To this extent there might be some truth in the stories of the early settlements which we find in Libanius and Malalas. The tale of the Cypriote princess Amyke dwelling on Mount Silpius and then, after her death, being buried 100 stadia away, in "Amyke," especially suggests the connection between the site of Antioch and the plain. The tradition of the Greek settlers also appears in the story that Libanius tells of how Cambyses, on the visit already mentioned to the site of Antioch, had an interview with the Greeks who dwelt in Ione, in which the king showed favor to these subjects of his, gave them gifts, and allowed them to remain at peace within the realm. On the same occasion, the Sun-god appeared to Cambyses in a dream and told him that a city of the Macedonians would be built on the spot; and Cambyses built a temple to the Sun, near that of Artemis.[30] Much of this story must be embroidery; but the presence of the Greek settlements at al-Mina-Sabouni and at Ras Shamra-Ugarit indicates that it may contain some kernel of truth.

No evidence is preserved for the pre-Macedonian connections between Egypt and the settlements around the future site of Antioch. However, there is reason to believe that Strabo's story concerning Typhon at Antioch, in connection with the name of the Orontes, is not of Greek origin, but is Phoenician or Egyptian.[31]

After the various events, legendary and historical, described above, we hear nothing further concerning the future site of Antioch until the Macedonian conquest. There were still Greeks at least in the neighborhood, for we know that al-Mina-Sabouni continued to prosper during the fifth and fourth centuries before Christ, and it was only when Seleucus Nicator founded Seleucia Pieria that the ancient port ceased to exist.

[29] Libanius *Or.* 11.41 says that a messenger setting out from Antioch at dawn could go to Seleucia and return to Antioch by noon. He gives the distance between the cities as 120 stadia. In the reign of Diocletian, a body of rebellious troops took a day to march from Seleucia to Antioch, stopping occasionally to plunder en route (Libanius *Or.* 11.158-162); on the incident see below, Ch. 12, §4.

[30] Libanius *Or.* 11.61-68.

[31] See G. Seippel, *Der Typhonmythus* (Greifswald 1939; Greifswalder Beiträge zur Literatur und Stilforschung 24).

CHAPTER 4

THE FOUNDATION OF ANTIOCH AND THE
REIGN OF SELEUCUS I

1. Alexander the Great and the
Foundation of the City

ANTIOCH was one of the four "sister cities" of the Seleukis described by Strabo—Antioch, Seleucia Pieria, Apamea, and Laodicea-on-the-Sea. The establishment of these four cities (each seaport linked with an inland city) evidently represented a concerted plan, and archaeological evidence, cited below,[1] suggests that at least two of the cities, Antioch and Laodicea, either were laid out by the same architect or followed the same general specifications in their design. Seleucia Pieria originally was the Seleucid royal headquarters and capital city in northwestern Syria, but before long Antioch eclipsed it and the other cities of the tetrapolis.[2] When these four cities were built they formed a part of the practical Seleucid plan of colonization for military purposes, by which the establishment of cities inhabited by Macedonians and Greeks was to assure the domination of the Macedonian power in the conquered territory; and in this plan the four cities of northwestern Syria played a vital role.[3]

According to Libanius, however, the plan for the foundation of Antioch did not originate with Seleucus Nicator, but with Alexander the Great himself. After defeating Darius at the battle of Issus (October 333 B.C.), Alexander moved on to Phoenicia.[4] En route (Libanius says) he stopped at a spot east of the future site of Antioch where there was a spring of remarkably sweet water beside the mountain. Drinking this, he exclaimed that it was like his mother's milk, and gave her name, Olympias, to the spring and built a fountain there. Perceiving the beauty of the site, Libanius goes on, Alexander desired to build a city there, but was prevented from doing so by the necessity of continuing his campaign. However, he made a start by founding a temple of Zeus Bottiaios, named for the Bottiaei who lived in the region called Emathia,

---

[1] See below, §§2-3.   [2] See below, Ch. 5, §1.

[3] See the excellent discussion of the Seleucid policy in the foundation of cities by Sauvaget, *Alep* 34-36, with map (36) of the new Seleucid cities in northern Syria. The Macedonian character of the Seleucid realm has been made clear by Charles Edson, "*Imperium Macedonicum*: The Seleucid Empire and the Literary Evidence," *CP* 53 (1958) 153-170.

[4] Arrian *Anab.* 2.13.7—2.14.1.

Alexander's homeland, in Thrace, and by establishing a citadel (*akra*) which was itself named Emathia.[5] Malalas mentions a village (*kome*) named Bottia which was in the plain, near the Orontes, "opposite Iopolis," this he says was the site on which Seleucus later founded Antioch.[6] Emathia was probably a fortification on the spur of the mountain.[7]

Whether Alexander actually visited and stopped at the neighborhood of the future city of Antioch is debatable. The tradition of his visit and of his plan for the foundation of the city could well represent an etiological legend, designed to cast glory on the origin of Antioch, much like the legend of the colonization of Iopolis, which is patently a local invention;[8] in particular, there is reason to believe that the temple of Zeus which Alexander is supposed to have founded was actually built by Seleucus Nicator at the foundation of the city.[9] Moreover, Antioch would wish to have as great a claim to glory as those cities officially founded by Alexander, and a legend of this kind could easily be invented; every city in Syria would have been glad to boast of a visit from Alexander. Nevertheless, the region of Antioch lay on a route which he may easily have followed in his march from Issus to Phoenicia, and the planting of a small colony and garrison of Macedonians in such a strategic spot would be consistent with his actions in similar circumstances elsewhere. As to his plan to build a city there and make it his capital after the completion of his campaigns, we have only the word of Libanius, who may well have been overly enthusiastic on this point.[10]

[5] Libanius *Or.* 11.72-77, 87, 250. Malalas (234.11-16) mentions the visit of Alexander but does not speak of the plan to found a city. Libanius says that in his own day the spring was converted into a shrine (*hieron*). Malalas mentions that Tiberius built a public bath near it (see below, Ch. 8, §2). An anonymous epigram in the *Greek Anthology* (9.699) purports to be an inscription set up at the spring to record Alexander's naming of it. On the temple of Zeus Bottiaios, see below, §3.

[6] Malalas 200.11-14; see further below, §3.

[7] On the legendary origins of these pre-Macedonian settlements, see above, Ch. 3.

[8] This is the opinion of Honigmann, "Syria" 1609.

[9] See below, §3.

[10] Honigmann, "Syria" 1609, considers the story of Alexander's visit to the site of Antioch very doubtful. On Alexander's activities in colonization, see Rostovtzeff, *Soc. Econ. Hist. Hellenistic World* 1.130-134, 158, 472, and Jones, *Cities of the East. Rom. Prov.* 238-239. Alexander's colonies in Syria were military garrisons rather than real city foundations. Antigonus was the first Greek ruler to found a real city in Syria. Much exaggeration in the accounts grew up concerning Alexander's establishment of cities, and many of the foundations attributed to him are fictitious; see W. W. Tarn, *Alexander the Great* (Cambridge 1948) 2.232-259. Tarn does not mention Alexander's supposed visit to Antioch. The region of Antioch is not mentioned specifically by the historians of Alexander; see C. A. Robinson, *The Ephemerides of Alexander's Expedition* (Providence 1932) 21.

A History of Antioch

2. Traditions Concerning the Foundation;
Choice of the Site;
Antigonia and Seleucia Pieria

Concerning the actual foundation of Antioch there are varying traditions. The fullest extant accounts are those of Libanius and Malalas, which, in view of the fact that the writers were themselves Antiochenes, may be taken to represent the local "official" tradition of the origin of the city. Malalas' account appears in his *Chronicle*, written in the sixth century after Christ, in which the history of Antioch plays a large part. The chronicler's information concerning his beloved city is ultimately derived in large part from local official records, and thus has great value in spite of the fact that Malalas used his sources carelessly, sometimes without understanding them.[11] Libanius' account is given in the famous oration in praise of Antioch (*Or.* 11, *Antiochikos*) which he wrote in A.D. 356 or 360 for delivery at the local Olympic games.[12] The tradition repeated by these writers differs in important respects, however, from information that Diodorus gives in the brief passage in his *History* in which he has occasion to mention the foundation of Antigonia, which Antigonus established as his capital in 307/6 B.C. on a site not far from the future location of Antioch. Furthermore, numismatic evidence recently examined in this connection throws additional light on the origin of Antioch. The testimony of Diodorus (who wrote in the middle of the first century B.C., long before the time of Libanius and Malalas) and of the coins shows that the tradition reproduced by Libanius and Malalas is simply a story designed to increase the prestige of the city by the easy suppression of certain details that, since they gave a place of honor to the foundation of Seleucia Pieria, would detract from the luster of the origin of Antioch.

The details of the foundation will be treated fully below; here only the principal events will be described, especially as they affect the relations between Antioch, Antigonia, and Seleucia Pieria. The essential facts of the foundation, according to Malalas,[13] are that after defeating Antigonus at the battle of Ipsus in August, 301 B.C.,[14] Seleucus, wishing

---

[11] On Malalas' sources and methods, see above, Ch. 2, §4.

[12] On Libanius and his work, see above, Ch. 2, §5.

[13] 198.23ff.; note that the Church Slavonic version of Malalas (p. 13 transl. Spinka) after the words "small city" (199.3 Bonn ed.), adds "which he heard was called Palaeopolis."

[14] On the date, see Beloch, *Griech. Gesch.*[2] 4, pt. 1, 167, and Olmstead, "Hellenistic Chronology" 5-6. On Seleucus' situation after the battle of Ipsus, see Bevan, *House of Seleucus* 1.61ff.

to found cities, made his first foundation on the coast of Syria, where on 23 Xanthikos (April 300 B.C.) he established Seleucia Pieria, which he named for himself. He then went to Iopolis and celebrated a festival to Zeus Keraunios on the first day of the following month, Artemisios.[15] Next he went to Antigonia, the city previously founded by his enemy (Malalas in fact makes the ridiculous statement that the war between Antigonus and Seleucus was occasioned by the latter's objection to the establishment of Antigonia),[16] and prayed to Zeus for a sign to show him whether to occupy this city, changing its name, or to build a new city elsewhere. The sign was given, and it bade him build on the site of the future Antioch, which was not far away. The new city, like fifteen others founded by Seleucus, was named in honor of Seleucus' father, Antiochus.[17] The ceremony of the foundation of Antioch took place on 22 Artemisios, in the twelfth year of Seleucus' reign (May 300 B.C.), almost exactly a month after the foundation of Seleucia.[18] Seleucus destroyed Antigonia completely and used the salvaged material in the construction of Antioch. He also transferred the inhabitants of Antigonia to his new city.

Libanius' information is less full.[19] He does not mention the establishment of Seleucia or Seleucus' question whether he should occupy Antigonia or found a new city elsewhere. Libanius describes the sacrifice to Zeus performed at Antigonia, and the omen that directed the king to build on the site of Antioch; and he records the destruction of Antigonia and the removal of its inhabitants to Antioch. Finally, he says expressly that Seleucus made Antioch his capital. The absence from this version of the foundation of Seleucia and of the question concerning the possible occupation of Antigonia shows that this tradition was designed to emphasize the primacy of Antioch among Seleucus' cities. Malalas' version, in which the foundation of Seleucia takes precedence over that of Antioch, had been less carefully edited in this respect.

In reality the course of events was quite different. It seems clear that Seleucus' original intention was to make Seleucia Pieria his capital, and there is good reason to believe that the city remained the Seleucid capital in western Syria, at least in name, during his reign.[20] A passage

[15] Zeus and Apollo were the protectors and founders of the Seleucid Dynasty; see below, §3.
[16] Malalas 198.2-4; Church Slavonic version, p. 12 transl. Spinka.
[17] On the naming of Antioch, see below, Excursus 1.
[18] On the date, see below, n. 59.   [19] *Or.* 11.85ff., 104.
[20] This was first recognized by Honigmann, "Seleukeia" 1185f. On the various forms of the name of Seleucia, see M. Holleaux, *Etudes d'épigraphie et d'histoire grecques*, 3: *Lagides et Séleucides* (Paris 1942) 212-213.

in Plutarch indicates that the city which preceded Seleucia Pieria on the same site had been founded by Antigonus between 315 and 313 B.C.[21] That Seleucus intended his foundation here to be his capital is indicated by a number of circumstances, first of all by the fact that he named it for himself. The other Successors of Alexander named their capitals for themselves (e.g. Lysimachia; Cassandria; Seleucus' earlier capital, Seleucia on the Tigris),[22] and if Seleucus, immediately after his success at the battle of Ipsus, named a city for himself, we must conclude (in the absence of good reason to believe the contrary) that he intended to make it a new capital. Also it is to be noted that Malalas says expressly that Seleucia was the first of Seleucus' foundations after his victory over Antigonus, and it is reasonable to suppose that this honor would be reserved for his new capital. Significant evidence is also provided by the output of the mints of Seleucia Pieria and Antioch during the reign of Seleucus I. In the first place, the coins struck at Seleucia Pieria show that Seleucus moved the mint of Antigonia (both personnel and equipment) direct to Seleucia. Finding a mint already in operation in his defeated enemy's capital, it would be natural for him to install this mint in his own new capital. Since Antioch was founded only a month after Seleucia, it would seem likely that the mint would have been taken there instead of to the seaport (especially since Antioch was closer to Antigonia) if it had been Seleucus' plan to make Antioch the new capital. Moreover, the mint of Seleucia Pieria issued more varieties than the mint of Antioch during the reign of Seleucus I, and the output of silver at Seleucia Pieria was greater than that of Antioch until 285 B.C.[23] Again, in keeping with the custom by which a ruler, no matter where he died, was buried in his capital, Seleucus was buried at Seleucia Pieria, in a temple (the "Nikatoreion") built in his honor by his son.[24] Finally, there is a suggestive passage in Polybius in which an official who was born in Seleucia Pieria is reported to have remarked, in 219

[21] Plutarch *Demetr.* 17; see Honigmann, *loc.cit.* The passage formerly was thought to refer to Antigonia, but it is much more reasonable, as Honigmann points out, to believe that it refers to the seaport. See Rostovtzeff, *Soc. Econ. Hist. Hellenistic World* 157, 1350.

[22] See Honigmann, *loc.cit.*

[23] For the coins of Seleucia Pieria and Antioch during the reign of Seleucus I, see Newell, *West. Sel. Mints* 86-103, and D. B. Waagé, "Coins" 3-4. See also Lacroix, "Copies de statues sur les monnaies des Séleucides" 164. The output of the two mints indicates that the capital was transferred to Antioch beginning with the reign of Antiochus I; see below in this chapter, also Ch. 5, §1.

[24] Appian *Syr.* 63. For other examples of the burial of rulers in their capitals, see Tscherikower, "Hellenistischen Städtegründüngen" 132.

B.C., that Seleucia Pieria was the "chief city (ἀρχηγέτις) and, one might almost say, the sacred hearth" of the Seleucid Empire.[25]

All this evidence is supported by the testimony of Diodorus (20.47.5-6), who, in his brief account of the foundation of Antigonus' capital Antigonia (Ol.118, 2 = 307/6 B.C.), writes that "it did not happen that the city lasted long, for Seleucus destroyed it and transferred the inhabitants to the city built by him which he named Seleucia for himself." Since this statement disagrees with the accounts of Libanius and Malalas, who write that Seleucus settled the inhabitants of Antigonia in Antioch, scholars have supposed that there is a confusion in Diodorus' information, and his editors have emended the text to make it agree with the tradition of the Antiochene authors. Yet there is nothing incredible in Diodorus' words.[26] If Seleucia was the earlier foundation and was intended to be the capital, it would be most natural for Seleucus to transfer the inhabitants of his defeated enemy's capital to his own new one rather than to Antioch. It is possible to believe that some of the people of Antigonia were taken to Seleucia and some (as Libanius and Malalas say) to Antioch; but in any case the fact that Diodorus, who had no *parti pris* in the matter, knew only of the transfer to Seleucia, shows that according to the knowledge available to him the seaport was Seleucus' new capital.

It is easy to see why nothing of this appears in the works of the Antiochene writers. They were, in fact, not quite guilty of direct untruth so far as Seleucia was concerned, but only of discreet omission of information that, from a patriotic point of view, did not really concern Antioch. Besides, Seleucia in their day was merely the seaport

---

[25] Polybius 5.58.4. In a letter addressed to Seleucia in the summer of 109 B.C. by either Antiochus VIII or Antiochus IX, the royal author speaks of the city as his πατρίς (Michel, *Recueil* no. 49 = *OGIS* no. 257 = Welles, *Royal Correspondence* no. 71, line 15). As Welles points out in his commentary (p. 293, cf. p. 270, note on line 6), the king could speak thus of the city because it had been his lifelong residence. It may be, however, that the use of the term here has more significance, and that the king, who was attempting to win the support of Seleucia Pieria, employed the word as an allusion to the city's having been the original capital and family seat of his dynasty. There is some reason to believe that the statue of Seleucus made by Bryaxis (Pliny *Nat. Hist.* 34.83) stood in Seleucia, and if this were the case, the placing of so important a statue in this city would be one more indication of its being the capital. There is, however, no text which shows conclusively where the statue stood; see Reinach, *Cultes, mythes et religions*[2] 2.351.

[26] As Honigmann points out, "Seleukeia" 1185f. Müller (*Antiq. Antioch.* 28, n. 6) rejects Diodorus' account. The misunderstanding of the relationship between Antigonia and Antioch which could have arisen in antiquity is illustrated by the statement of Cedrenus (1.292.8-11 Bonn) that Seleucus built Antioch on the site of Antigonia.

of Antioch, occupying a relatively insignificant position, and its original primacy could safely be disregarded. Libanius' categorical statement that Seleucus made Antioch his capital would have been challenged by no one at Antioch, and the orator evidently thought it safe
to ignore the feelings of Seleucia.[27]

Our sources, in their effort to magnify the importance of Seleucus'
activity, are guilty of misrepresentation in another point as well. Antigonia cannot have been literally destroyed, for a passage in Dio Cassius (40.29) shows that it was in existence in 51 B.C. There are other
instances in which a city, absorbed by or replaced by a new foundation,
was said to be "destroyed," when actually it was not physically demolished, but was merely degraded to the status of a *kome* of the new *polis*.
Evidently this is what happened in the case of Antigonia.[28]

It is illuminating to review the reasons for the foundation of Antigonia and of Antioch, and their relation with Seleucia Pieria. Although Antigonus founded a seaport in the region of Seleucia Pieria
between 315 and 313 B.C., some years before he built Antigonia (307/6
B.C.), it is clear from the name of the city that he intended Antigonia
to be his capital.[29] The city lay about 8 km. (about 5 miles) northeast
of the site of Antioch, in a secure situation in a triangle of land,
bounded on the north by the lake later called the Lake of Antioch,
on the south and east by the winding course of the Orontes river, and
on the west by the Arceutha river (also called Iaphtha, modern Kara
Su) which flowed out of the lake into the Orontes. Here there is an
oblong plateau, roughly 4 km. in length by 3 km. in width, which
runs from one river to the other. The average elevation is 100 m. above
sea level, though at one point a height of 158 m. is reached. This puts
the plateau well above the level of the rivers and of the surrounding
plain, which here is less than 50 m. above sea level. This site is ad-

---

[27] *Or.* 11.104.

[28] On this significance of a "destruction" of a city, see Tscherikower, "Hellenistische
Städtegründungen" 61, 118. Müller (*Antiq. Antioch.* 27) thinks that the evidence of
Dio Cassius, cited above, shows that Antigonia (literally destroyed by Seleucus, Müller
supposes) was refounded at some time before 51 B.C. However, as Tscherikower points
out, if the city had been refounded, it would have been given a new name. The degradation of Antigonia to a *kome* would account for the absence of other references to it
in ancient literature, except on the occasion (mentioned by Dio Cassius) when it was
of importance for military reasons.

[29] On the date at which Antigonus founded a city at the mouth of the Orontes, see
Honigmann, "Seleukeia" 1185. On Antigonia, see Malalas 199.16-20, 201.3-4; Diodorus
20.47; Strabo 16.2.4, p. 750 (cf. 16.2.8, p. 751); Syncellus 519.9-10, 520.5-6 Bonn ed.;
also Müller, *Antiq. Antioch.* 23; Benzinger, "Antigoneia," no. 1, *RE* 1.2404; Dussaud,
Topographie 426, 439; Honigmann, "Syria" 1610; *Griech. Gesch.*[2] 4, pt. 1, 135-136.

mirably suited for defense, and conveniently situated with respect to the Orontes.[30]

The site which Antigonus chose was centrally located in his vast kingdom. Adapted for efficient communication equally with all parts of the realm, it would also serve as a base of possible operations against Egypt, the lands along the Euphrates, or Greece. It is noteworthy that Antigonus did not decide to use the seaport at the mouth of the Orontes for his headquarters, but preferred a site about 30 km. inland, though still on the river.

When Antigonus was defeated at Ipsus, his kingdom was divided between Lysimachus and Seleucus I. Seleucus, who already controlled Babylonia, now gained Syria and Mesopotamia, thus coming to rule a heterogeneous as well as a widespread kingdom. The recent course of events and the condition of Aegean politics made it plain that his headquarters should be in the western part of his new kingdom, where Antigonus also had had his capital. The Macedonian element was naturally stronger along the coast of Syria than in the interior, and the Greek heritage could best be preserved there and propagated from that region. All these factors would influence Seleucus to abandon Seleucia on the Tigris, where he had made his headquarters before Ipsus, and set up his new capital in the northwestern corner of Syria, renouncing the alternative of establishing his new capital in Mesopotamia, where he would lose much of the value of his Greek and Macedonian resources and become primarily a successor of the Persian kings.[31]

Seleucus' principal reasons for choosing the site of Seleucia Pieria as his new capital probably were, first, that this site was superior for purposes of communication and commerce in that it lay directly on

---

[30] See the schematic map of the site of Antigonia and its vicinity in Jacquot, *Antioche* 2.192, and the excellent detailed map of the area in Weulersse, *L'Oronte* p. 79, fig. 35. So far as the circumference of the elevation can be measured on maps, it is approximately 12 km., which agrees closely with the statement of Diodorus (20.47) that Antigonia was 70 stadia in circumference; and the situation, of course, corresponds exactly with Malalas' description of it (199.18-20). This site has been accepted as that of Antigonia by Dussaud, *Topographie* 426, 439, and by Jacquot, *Antioche* 2.192, 214, 439. Traces of ancient buildings were found on the site in 1738 by Richard Pococke (*A Description of the East, and Some Other Countries*, 2. pt. 1 [London 1745] 188). Since Pococke's time the site has been cleared very thoroughly for agricultural purposes, for R. J. Braidwood reports (*Mounds in the Plain of Antioch* [Chicago 1937] 38, n. 2) that in a search for the location of Antigonia he "has gone over all of this area very thoroughly and is convinced that it contains no cultural debris." The military importance of the site is attested by the reference to it in Dio Cassius (40.29).

[31] The reasons for Seleucus' decision are to be inferred from the later course of Seleucid policy; see M. Rostovtzeff in *CAH* 7.155ff. and *Soc. Econ. Hist. Hellenistic World* 1.422ff.

the sea (it had one of the best harbors in the eastern Mediterranean), and second, that the acropolis on the site was virtually impregnable.[32] At the same time, however, Seleucia Pieria would obviously be unable to fulfill the optimum requirements of a Seleucid capital. The control of the land routes that met in the neighborhood of the Lake of Antioch and connected Asia Minor, the Euphrates, and southern and central Syria, was a matter of prime importance, and Seleucia Pieria could not serve for this purpose. Hence it would seem necessary to establish a second city, farther inland, which would play a subsidiary role, as a kind of outpost of the capital, Seleucia Pieria.

It was doubtless with this in mind that Seleucus decided to found a city on the site of Antioch. The example of Antigonus in establishing Antigonia as his capital would only have served to emphasize the importance of the country around the Lake of Antioch; but the decision to build on the site of Antioch, rather than take over Antigonia, was not an altogether happy one—in some respects, indeed, it proved to be a major error.

The motives that led Seleucus to build a new city, instead of occupying Antigonia, are fairly clear.[33] The foundation of a new capital would give Seleucus a prestige that the occupation of his defeated enemy's capital would not, and the destruction of Antigonia would be a gesture of power and of magnificence that could hardly fail to impress both his subjects and his rivals. As the victor he probably also felt that he could as a matter of course make an improvement over his predecessor's choice. In addition there were practical considerations, among which the unrivaled water supply may well have been the most prominent. While we do not know how well Antigonia was situated in this respect, the supply available at the springs of Daphne, 6 km. south of Antioch, was superb and was very likely superior to anything accessible to Antigonia. While Daphne itself was not a good site for a city, the abundance and purity of its water would have led a thoughtful planner to try to place a new city in the nearest suitable spot, which of course is the site of Antioch.[34] The fertility and mag-

[32] On the security of Seleucia Pieria, see below, Ch. 5, §3. Seleucia Pieria replaced an earlier Greek trading settlement in the same neighborhood, modern al Mina and modern Sabouni. There is evidence that Seleucus, when he founded Seleucia Pieria, forcibly transferred the inhabitants of al-Mina-Sabouni to the new town, just as he forcibly transferred the inhabitants of Antigonia to Antioch; for further detail, see above, n. 23.

[33] Malalas (199.16ff.) and Libanius (*Or.* 11.85-88) attribute the rejection of Antigonia and the choice of the site of Antioch simply to divine intervention.

[34] On the water supply of Antioch, see above, Ch. 1.

nificent beauty of the immediate surroundings of Antioch, and especially Daphne, which form a recurrent theme of the ancient writers,
may also have been taken into account.[35] Also, this location was probably considered more desirable, in relation to the Orontes river and
the distance from the sea, than Antigonia. Antigonia was about 30
km. from the sea, Antioch about 22 km.[36] The journey upstream from
the sea to Antioch required about one day.[37] It was still, however, far
enough from the coast for security.[38] A messenger traveling rapidly
could make the round trip between Antioch and Seleucia Pieria in
a morning,[39] while a body of troops required nearly a day to move
from Seleucia Pieria to Antioch, where they arrived in the evening.[40]
Thus there would have been ample warning of the approach of a hostile force from the sea.

There are, however, two conditions which make the site of Antioch
unfavorable. Whether these were appreciated by Seleucus and his advisers and how far they were taken into consideration, along with
the attractions of the site, we of course have no way of knowing. For
one thing, the city would be found to suffer from the effects of the
torrential winter rains, which, falling steadily from October to April,
wash quantities of soil down the slope of the mountain and sometimes
flood the level portions of the area which lie along the river.[41] The
seriousness of this wash from the mountain can be measured by the
surprising depth to which the remains of the ancient buildings are
now buried; in places it is necessary to excavate 10 m. of soil before
reaching ancient remains.[42] The torrent, which was given the name
Parmenius, running down the mountain side, carried off a large quan-

---

[35] On the region, see above, Ch. 1.

[36] Strabo (16.2.7, p. 751 C) and Libanius (*Or.* 11.41) reckon the distance of Antioch
from the sea as 120 stadia, while Procopius (*Wars* 2.11.1) gives the distance as 130
stadia. The difference probably reflects the choice of different points on the coast as
termini of the reckoning.

[37] See Ch. 1, n. 12.   [38] Libanius *Or.* 11.35-41.   [39] Libanius *Or.* 11.41.

[40] Libanius *Or.* 11.158-162. This information appears in Libanius' account of the
revolt of Eugenius under Diocletian.

[41] Malalas says that Seleucus founded his city on the level part of the site, near the
river, through fear of the flow of water from Mount Silpius and the winter torrents
which came down from it and caused floods (200.10-11; 233.11-12). This sounds more
like an explanation offered by a chronicler than an actual motive of Seleucus. Occupation of the upper part of the slope of the mountain would expose buildings to
danger from the effects of erosion on their foundations, but occupation of the flat
ground along the river would not free the city from the danger of floods or from
the effect of the wash.

[42] See for example the report on excavations near the main street of the city in
Antioch-on-the-Orontes 3.17-18. A report of the effect of a torrential rain in 1938 (*ibid.*
5-6, 14) shows how serious the problem must have been in antiquity.

tity of water, but it had to be carefully channeled and restrained to prevent it from flooding the city; the excavations disclosed the remains of two large masonry vaults built over this stream, possibly in Hellenistic times, at about the point where the main street of the city crossed it.[43] Other engineering measures, and constant attention, must have been necessary to protect the city from this inescapable nuisance.

But the more serious drawback to the site is that the structure of Mount Silpius made Antioch extremely difficult to fortify and defend; it was captured, apparently fairly easily, by the Persians on several occasions.[44] The source of the difficulty is that the side of the mountain which faces toward the city is rough and precipitous, while the other side, which faces away from the city, has a relatively gentle grade which can easily be ascended.[45] In the Seleucid period, apparently, the city was walled only in the districts that lay along the river.[46] The transport of stones was a difficult and expensive business, and it was evidently decided to risk having the top of the mountain outside the fortifications. There must have been a citadel on the top of the mountain;[47] but this would have been so difficult of access, and so far away from the city proper, that it can hardly have served as a refuge during a siege as the citadel at Beroea did. An enemy who gained control of the top of the mountain would be able to dominate the city, even

[43] On these vaults, see *Antioch-on-the-Orontes* 3.13. Procopius describes in detail the measures taken for the control of Parmenius in Justinian's time; see below, Ch. 18, §8.
[44] In the middle of the third century after Christ and in A.D. 540.
[45] An impression of the steepness of the slope of the side of Mount Silpius toward the city can be gained from Figs. 1 and 2 below, as well as from photographs printed in *Antioch-on-the-Orontes* 2, pp. 2 and 6, and in Jacquot, *Antioche* 2, facing p. 216. The ascent to the top of the mountain from the city at the present time, when the roads and paths of access have not been maintained, is exceedingly difficult (see Jacquot, *Antioche* 2.384-385). Procopius (*De aed.* 2.10.13) mentions roads built in the time of Justinian to maintain communication between the city and the top of the mountain (which must have actually been repair or rebuilding of existing roads), but these must have been artificially built, and no traces of them, apparently, remain. On the character of the side of the mountain away from the city, see Jacquot, *Antioche* 2.385. The relatively easy nature of the ascent here is illustrated by Jacquot's observation that on this side it would be easy to build and maintain an automobile road leading to the summit.
[46] Malalas states that Tiberius was the first to include the mountain within the city wall (see below, Ch. 8, §2), and this agrees with the chronicler's account of the foundation of the city, in which it is said that Seleucus built a wall about one quarter which he founded, and no reference is made to a wall on the mountain. The anonymous Arabic description of Antioch (Guidi, "Descrizione araba" 152) states that Seleucus for security reasons included the mountain within his wall. However, this account exhibits so many legendary characteristics, and is so obviously calculated to exaggerate the size and magnificence of the city, that it seems hazardous to rely upon it for such a question as the course of the wall.
[47] See below, §3, with n. 78.

without capturing the citadel. The Romans extended the wall so that it ran along the top of the mountain, and while this had the effect of securing the top of the mountain, it also added enormously to the length of wall, which had to be manned.

In its disadvantageous situation below Mount Silpius, Antioch was not unlike Priene, which also lay below a high mountain. The site of Priene, like that of Antioch, is spectacular, but the defense of the city made it necessary to construct a wall of tremendous length, and even with this the city was subject to grave danger because it was impossible to wall off all the heights that dominate the city.[48] Since Priene was rebuilt in the fourth century B.C. on the site of an unimportant town, its situation, like that of Antioch, founded on the site of an indigenous village or villages, represents, to some degree, deliberate choice, and we can only conclude that the planners of these two cities were so anxious to utilize the sites that they were willing to risk the disadvantages which they entailed.

It is difficult to understand why Antioch was not placed in the flat plain across the river from the actual site. In this situation, it could have been provided with adequate walls which need not by their extent have imposed an undue burden on the defenders. Water could have been brought in aqueducts from the mountains to the north and west; there are in fact traces of aqueducts which supplied this area.[49] Possibly this site was rejected because it was across the river from Daphne and such a position would have necessitated extending the aqueducts over water.

All these considerations (though some of them represent wisdom after the event) make it seem difficult to understand why Seleucus rejected Antigonia, although incomparably superior in situation, and chose instead to build a new city at Antioch.[50] Space was not a consideration because the site of Antigonia is larger than the area of

---

[48] On the military disadvantages of the situation of Priene, see Th. Wiegand and H. Schrader, *Priene* (Berlin 1904) 35-39 and Fabricius, "Städtebau (der Griechen)," *RE* 3A (1929) 2015. A map of Priene and its vicinity is printed by Gerkan, *Griech. Städteanlagen* Abb. 9. The situation of the city of Samos is not unlike that of Antioch (*Gerkan op.cit.* Abb. 5).

[49] D. N. Wilber in *Antioch-on-the-Orontes* 2.51, n. 6.

[50] The writer does not agree with Tscherikower's opinion ("Hellenistischen Städtegründungen" 169) that the only value of the site of Antigonia was military, and that the site had no value for purposes of commerce and transportation. While it did not lie on the main routes, as Antioch did, it was certainly sufficiently close to them to enjoy nearly all the advantages that Antioch possessed in this respect. The evidence for commercial activity in this region in pre-Macedonian times (see above Ch. 3) is ample proof of the importance of the site of Antigonia.

the original Seleucid settlement at Antioch,[51] and it would have been possible to expand Antigonia to a fairly large size by utilizing the lower ground around the plateau, as was done in many Greek cities. Perhaps the answer to all these questions is to be found in the astonishing number of the cities that Seleucus founded or re-founded in his new realm—seventy-five according to Pausanias of Damascus, fifty-nine according to Appian.[52] When so many cities were to be planned and built, it was perhaps inevitable that in some instances careful study was not given to the site before a decision was made. Moreover, we must bear in mind that the site of Seleucia Pieria, chosen by Seleucus, was far superior to the locations of the two Greek trading settlements that had previously existed at the mouth of the Orontes (the modern al Mina and Sabouni; possibly the ancient Posidium). The archaeological evidence indicates that when Seleucus founded Seleucia Pieria he transported the residents of al Mina-Sabouni to the new town.[53]

After the death of Seleucus, Seleucia was given up as the capital and Antioch took its place. As has been noted, Seleucus' burial in Seleucia indicates that the seaport was still regarded as the capital at the time of his death. The activity of the mints of Seleucia Pieria and Antioch suggests that the transfer of the capital was made by Antiochus I (280/1-261 B.C.). During the reign of Seleucus I, as has been seen above, the mint of Seleucia Pieria had issued more varieties of coins than the mint of Antioch, and its output of silver was greater than that of Antioch until at least 285 B.C. Beginning with the reign of Antiochus I the situation was reversed, and the output of Antioch became much more important, while the mint of Seleucia Pieria was reduced to a minor role. Enough coins have been found to make it reasonably certain, on the basis of this evidence, that it was at this time that Antioch became the capital.[54] The move was judicious for Seleucus had no fleet, and Seleucia, as the capital, would have been unduly exposed to attack from the sea.

[51] See below, §3.

[52] Pausanias, frag. 4, *FHG* 4.470, preserved in Malalas 203.22; Appian *Syr.* 57. To the traditional list of the cities founded by Seleucus may now be added Dura-Europus, which according to the evidence of the coins found in the excavations was founded about 300 B.C.: *Dura Final Rep.* 6: Bellinger, *The Coins* 196. The figure given by Pausanias may be a round number, while Appian's list appears to contain some inaccuracies. Nevertheless, Seleucus' activity must have been impressive. For discussion of his foundations, see Tscherikower, "Hellenistische Städtegründungen" 165-170, 174, and Stähelin, "Seleukos (I)," *RE* 2A (1923) 1228-1230.

[53] Woolley, "Al Mina." On the identification of al Mina-Sabouni with Posidium, see above, Ch. 3.

[54] See above, n. 23.

3. The Founding of Antioch;
The City of Seleucus

The local version of the ceremonies of the foundation of Antioch is carefully recorded, as has been seen, by Malalas and Libanius,[55] and there is in addition an anonymous Arabic account of the foundation and construction of the new city which, though it contains many of the conventional exaggerations and legendary tales characteristic of such accounts, may be based ultimately on a factual account.[56] According to Malalas, Seleucus went to the site of Seleucia Pieria and on 23 Xanthikos (April 300 B.C.) made a sacrifice to Zeus on Mount Casius, asking where he should found his city. The sacrificial meat was seized by an eagle, which carried it to the site of the "old city" and thus indicated the place upon which Seleucia Pieria should be founded. After founding and naming the city, Seleucus went to Iopolis to give thanks, and three days later, on the first of Artemisios (May), he performed a sacrifice to Zeus Keraunios in the temple of that deity in Iopolis.[57]

Following this, Malalas continues, Seleucus went to Antigonia to sacrifice to Zeus on the altars built by Antigonus; and with the priest Amphion he asked for a sign, to tell him whether to occupy Antigonia,

[55] Tzetzes *Chiliades* 7.118, v. 176, says that Seleucus appointed Attaeus, Perittas, and Anaxicrates as "supervisors of the buildings" (κτισμάτων ἐπιστάτας), and that they wrote accounts of the foundation of the city. Malalas' narrative presumably is based on local official records (see above, Ch. 2, §4). Libanius' account is of a literary character and does not contain certain details preserved by Malalas. The foundation of Antioch is represented on a sculptured pilaster capital (now in the Museum at Beirut) found about 20 km. north of Laodicea on what seems to have been the site of the seaport Paseria. The sculpture is assigned on stylistic grounds to the beginning or middle of the fourth century after Christ. The scene, skillfully interpreted by H. Seyrig ("Scène historique sur un chapiteau du Musée de Beyrouth," *Mél. G. Radet = REA* 42 [1940] 340-344), shows a sacrificial altar on one side of which stands the Tyche of Antioch, holding on her arm a small figure representing the Apollo of Daphne. On the other side of the altar stands Seleucus Nicator, preparing to sacrifice a bull. A Victory crowns Seleucus, and the eagle of Zeus appears above the Victory's head. The traditional version of the foundation of Antioch is in some details modeled on the tradition of the founding of Alexandria; see A. Ausfeld, "Zur Topographie von Alexandria und Pseudo-kallisthenes I 31-33," *Rh. Mus.* 55 (1900) 348-384, esp. 381, and A. Ippel, "Ein Sarapisrelief in Hildesheim," *Archäol. Anz.* 1921, 8-9, and M. Erdmann, *Zur Kunde der hellenistische Städtegründungen* (Progr., Strasbourg 1883) 23-30.

[56] Guidi, "Descrizione araba." A new edition has been prepared by William F. Stinespring (Diss., Yale, unpublished).

[57] Malalas 199.2ff.; the Church Slavonic version (p. 13, transl. Spinka) after "Xanthikos" adds "April." On the cult of Zeus Casius in Syria, see A. Salac, "ΖΕΥΣ ΚΑΣΙΟΣ," *BCH* 46 (1922) 176-180, and Cook, *Zeus* 2.981-983. For characteristic local references to the cult, see Ammianus Marcellinus 22.14.4-5; Julian *Misopogon* 361 D; Libanius *Or.* 11.116ff., *Or.* 18.172; Malalas 327.6-7 with Church Slavonic version, p. 5 transl. Spinka. Rostovtzeff points out (*Soc. Econ. Hist. Hellenistic World* 437-438) Seleucus' special care to sacrifice to the local gods.

changing its name, or to build another city in another place. Again an eagle carried off the sacrificial meat, this time to Bottia, and thus revealed that it was the divine will that the new city should be built on this spot.[58] So Seleucus on 22 Artemisios (May),[59] in the twelfth year of his reign, at the first hour of the day, as the sun was rising, performed a sacrifice, with the priest Amphion, and laid the foundations of the walls at Bottia, "opposite Iopolis," which stood on Mount Silpius.[60] He named the city for his father Antiochus,[61] and at once began the construction of a temple to Zeus Bottios (or Bottiaios).[62]

The foundation of Antioch (like that of Seleucia) was carried out under the auspices of Zeus because this deity was regarded as one of the two founders of the Seleucid dynasty. The other tutelary deity, Apollo, who was reputed to be the father of Seleucus, was honored by the dedication to him of the famous sanctuary in the suburb of Daphne.[63]

[58] On the eagle, see below, 76, with n. 100. Beginning at this point we have the accounts of both Libanius (*Or.* 11.85ff.) and Malalas (199.16ff.); Libanius does not describe the foundation of Seleucia, presumably because he does not wish to detract from the glory of Antioch. On the foundation of Antioch, Libanius and Malalas differ in some details. Libanius, for example, is careful to note that the foundation of the city was really the fulfillment of Alexander's wish, a point which Malalas does not mention, though he knows of Alexander's visit to the spring of Olympias (234.11-16).

[59] Eusebius *Chron.* 2.116-117 ed. Schoene; Malalas 200.17; cf. Syncellus 519.9-10, 520.5-6 Bonn. For a list of the modern discussions of the event, see references given by Downey, *AJA* 42 (1938) 108, n. 2. On the date given by Malalas, see also Olmstead, "Hellenistic Chronology" 6-7. Müller (*Antiq. Antioch.* 27) by a slip of the pen gives the day of the month as the 24th.

[60] Amphion was commemorated in a statue; see below. On the sacrifice of a maiden which Malalas says (200.15-16) formed a part of this ceremony, see further below.

[61] See below, Excursus 1.

[62] Malalas 200.18-20. Libanius states (*Or.* 11.76) that Alexander had founded a temple of Zeus Bottiaios on the site (see above, §1). Malalas, though he knows of Alexander's supposed visit to the site (234.11-16), does not mention this visit in connection with the founding of the city, and does not say (as Libanius does) that the original plan for the establishment of the city was Alexander's. This would suggest that the temple in question was really founded by Seleucus and that in later days a tradition grew up that it had been founded by Alexander. Müller (*Antiq. Antioch.* 35) supposes that the temple was founded by Alexander and that Malalas' account of its construction by Seleucus refers to an enlargement of the shrine. Müller feels no hesitation in accepting Libanius' account of Alexander's visit and establishment of the temple, but there is, as has been seen (above, §1), reason to think that the tradition of Alexander's activities at the site of Antioch may be at least in part legendary. Cook, *Zeus* 2.1187-1188, makes a distinction between the Zeus Bottios of Malalas and the Zeus Bottiaios of Libanius, but he does not seem to have taken into account the considerations mentioned above which indicate that the cults were identical.

[63] On Zeus and Apollo as the protectors and ἀρχηγέται of the Seleucids, see A. D. Nock, "Notes on Ruler-cult, 4: Zeus Seleukios," *JHS* 48 (1928) 38-41; Welles, *Royal Correspondence* pp. 108, 159, 183; Rostovtzeff, "Progonoi" 56-66; idem, *Le Gad de Doura* 281-295; Tondriau, "Souverains et souveraines Séleucides en divinités" 173-174; idem, "Comparisons and Identifications of Rulers with Divinities"; idem, "Bibliogra-

Seleucus' city was built, Malalas writes (200.10-15), on the site of the village of Bottia, "on the level part of the valley, opposite the mountain, near . . . the river." Seleucus, the chronicler records, chose this location in order to avoid the wash from Mount Silpius and the winter torrents that flowed down from it. Seleucus' settlement appears to have stood, in general, on the northern part of the area of the present city, and to have lain along the bank of the river. It would be natural to begin the building of the city on the bank of the stream that was to form one of the city's principal links with Seleucia Pieria and with the cities of the interior; and the location of Seleucus' agora may with great plausibility be taken to be the market area or souks of the present city. One would expect the area of major commercial activity of the original city to remain unchanged in location so long as there was any continuity of such activity, and the continuance in such use of the original agora areas of Dura, Aleppo, and Damascus indicates that the modern souks along the river occupy the site of Seleucus' market place.[64] An idea of the size of the agora at Antioch may perhaps be gained from the known size of the agora at Dura, which was founded at about the same time as the agora at Antioch: the agora at Dura measured 159.79 m. by 147.13 m., covering 23,510 sq. m., which comprised approximately five per cent of the total area of the city, not counting the citadel.[65] By the time of Antiochus IV Epiphanes (175-164 B.C.) either the original agora was found inadequate or a shift in the center of commercial and municipal life took place, for Epiphania, the new quarter of the city founded by this king, seems to be have contained a new agora.[66]

---

phie du culte des souverains hellénistiques et romains," *Bulletin de l'Association Guillaume Budé*, N.S. no. 5 (1948) 106-125. On the epithet Δαΐτται, applied to Apollo and Artemis, which may have some significance as to the Macedonian origin of the cult, see F. Cumont, *Comptes rendus, Acad. des inscr. et belles-lettres* 1931, 282-284 and Welles, *Royal Correspondence* p. 183. On coins of Seleucus I bearing the head of Zeus, see Newell, *West. Sel. Mints* 90, 96, with n. 22a.

[64] The modern souk area at Antioch is indicated on the maps of Weulersse, "Antioche" 39, 41. On the relationship between the position of modern souks and ancient commercial quarters, see Sauvaget, "Plan de Laodicée-sur-mer" 99. On the market places of Aleppo and Damascus, see Sauvaget *Alep* 47-48.

[65] On the agora at Dura, see F. E. Brown in *Excavations at Dura-Europus, Preliminary Report of the Ninth Season of Work, 1935-1936* (New Haven 1944) 23. Brown points out that the agora at Dura was only slightly smaller than that at Magnesia-on-the-Meander and the south agora at Miletus. The market place at Dura, he observes, was four times the size of that at Priene, and shows the practical thought that was given to the possible future expansion of the colony.

[66] See below, Ch. 5, §6.

The architect in charge of the building of the walls was Xenarius.[67] Libanius gives a conventional picture of the laying out of the plan of the city, with elephants stationed to mark the sites of towers in the city wall, and the streets outlined with wheat.[68] Traces of the course of the ancient streets, clearly preserved in the plan of the modern town, show that the city was originally laid out on the gridiron plan associated with the name of Hippodamus of Miletus which was employed in many of the cities founded or refounded after the time of Alexander.[69] The arrangement of the streets closely agrees with the Hellenistic plans, which have recently been established with some precision, of Beroea (Aleppo), Dura-Europus, Damascus, Apamea, and Laodicea, all of which were either Seleucid foundations or Seleucid colonies refounded on the site of older cities.[70] It is of particular interest to find that the *insulae* at Antioch (112 x 58 m.) are almost exactly the same size as those of Laodicea-ad-mare (112 x 57 m.),[71] which was founded by Seleucus I, and, according to Malalas (202.21ff.), was created after Antioch. The difference of one meter in one dimension may have been caused by differences in the size and shape of the sites. The direction of the streets at Antioch (Figs. 6, 10) indicates that care

[67] The Greek text of Chilmead and Hody, reprinted without revision or correction in the Bonn edition, gives the name Xenaius (200.21), but the MS has the name Xenarius: see the collation of the MS published by Bury, "Malalas: the Cod. Barocc.," 225. The Latin translation printed in the Bonn edition, which was made by Chilmead from the MS, gives the correct form of the name. Müller, who did not consult the Latin version at this point, gives the incorrect form (*Antiq. Antioch.* 27). There seems to be no other evidence for this architect. Tzetzes (cited above, note 55) gives the names of three "supervisors of the buildings," who were presumably Xenarius' assistants.

[68] *Or.* 11.90. This traditional account of the founding of the city is modeled in some respects upon the account of the foundation of Alexandria (see above, n. 55).

[69] Figs. 6-8, 11, also Weulersse, "Antioche" 47. On the survival in modern times of the lines of ancient streets and other topographical features, see also the studies of J. Sauvaget, cited in the following note, and the observations of E. Oberhummer, "Constantinopolis," *RE* 4 (1900) 986-987, on the survival in modern Istanbul of the ancient plan. The *insulae* at Antioch are apparently mentioned in a Greek inscription found at Antioch which records the construction of a canal connected with the Orontes in A.D. 73/4. The canal is said to have been made κατὰ πλινθεῖα, the term *plintheion* apparently meaning *insula*. On the inscription see below, Ch. 9, n. 31.

[70] Sauvaget, "Plan de Laodicée-sur-mer" 81-114, with schematic plans of the cities in question. See Sauvaget's further observations in *Bull. d'études orientales* (*Inst. franç. de Damas*) 6 (1936) 51-52, and the same scholar's study "Le plan antique de Damas," *Syria* 26 (1949) 339-345, 356-357. For the Hellenistic plan of Beroea, see the same scholar's monograph *Alep* 41. On Hellenistic city planning, see Rostovtzeff, *Soc. Econ. Hist. Hellenistic World* 3, p. 1587, n. 19; also P. Lavedan, *Histoire de l'urbanisme: antiquité, moyen age* (Paris 1926) 123ff.

[71] See the table of measurements of *insulae* in Sauvaget, "Plan de Laodicée-sur-mer" 94. While the measurements are necessarily approximate, they are sufficiently accurate to be valuable for comparison among the various cities.

was taken to orient them according to the sun in both summer and winter, and the prevailing breeze in the summer, which blew from the sea up the valley of the Orontes and helped to keep the city relatively cool and pleasant in the hot season.[72]

As has been mentioned, Strabo's account[73] of the foundation of the tetrapolis indicates that their construction represented a plan to link seaports with inland cities.[74] Furthermore, the agreement between the sizes of the *insulae* at Antioch and Laodicea suggests that these two cities, at least, were laid out by the same architect (figures for Apamea are incomplete, and there are none available for Seleucia Pieria). In any case, Antioch was a typical example of what has been called "the mass-production of new Hellenistic cities which took place under Alexander and his successors."[75]

The evidence for the transformation of the city which took place (Malalas says) in the reign of Tiberius, combined with the evidence from the excavations, indicates that the inner (eastern) wall of Seleucus' settlement ran along the course of the thoroughfare which, when paved and lined with monumental colonnades in the Roman period, became the main street of the city. The Hellenistic pottery found along the course of this thoroughfare indicates that in Seleucid times this was a slum area.[76] Our knowledge of the plans of other Seleucid foundations indicates that they were built, when possible, with rectilinear city walls,[77] and it seems safe to conclude that this was true of Antioch.

A citadel on the top of Mount Silpius must have been an important feature of Seleucus' foundation. There is no specific literary or archaeological evidence for such a citadel, but the presence of citadels in the other major Seleucid foundations makes it seem almost beyond question that there was one at Antioch.[78]

[72] Libanius in his description of Antioch (*Or.* 11.222-226) speaks of the local breezes as one of the chief sources of the city's pride. Vitruvius (1.6.12) gives rules for the orientation of the streets of a city with respect to the winds. The orientation of the streets of Antioch, which do not point toward any major point of the compass, may be in part responsible for the curious confusion over the points of the compass which prevailed at Antioch in antiquity and has lasted until quite recent times; see below, Excursus 9.

[73] 16.2.4, pp. 749 750 C.

[74] See Weulersse, *L'Oronte* 5.

[75] Wycherley, *How the Greeks Built Cities* 35.

[76] The evidence for this is cited in the account of the construction of the main street and the accompanying transformation of the city plan; see below, Ch. 8, §2.

[77] See Sauvaget, *Alep* 43-44.

[78] On Seleucid citadels, see Sauvaget, *Alep* 44.

The principal public buildings erected by Seleucus would have been grouped about the agora; and it may be assumed that the temple of Zeus Bottios (or Bottiaios), which Malalas says Seleucus founded when he established the city,[79] stood on the agora. Our sources, which are rather scanty for this period, happen to be of such a nature that they do not mention other public buildings, but on the analogy of other Hellenistic foundations for which plans have been wholly or partly recovered it may be assumed that Seleucus planned other temples, baths, and the necessary administrative and military installations. A palace in the generally accepted sense of the word would not have been built, since the royal residence, in the Hellenistic period, was not a distinct type of building, specifically designed for the use of the ruler and his court, but was merely a private dwelling of the then usual type, enlarged and developed perhaps but not otherwise distinguished from other houses.[80] Whether Seleucus built a bouleuterion we do not know.

The anonymous Arabic description of the foundation of the city states that Seleucus built two grain elevators, raised on arches, to assure the city's grain supply.[81] There is no reference in our scanty sources to a theater at Antioch at the time of its foundation, but it seems difficult to believe that the builders of the city could have failed to provide one. It would presumably have been built outside the area of Seleucus' city, on the slope of the mountain, which provided several excellent sites.[82] There is no reference in our sources to the water supply of the original foundation. There were springs on the side of the mountain which could have been utilized, and reservoirs could have been constructed there. Moreover, it is likely that Seleucus' engineers built an aqueduct to bring the famous water of Daphne to the city.[83] There was a sewage system which emptied into the Orontes.[84]

[79] Malalas 200.20; above n. 62.

[80] See Gerkan, *Griech. Städteanlagen* 108-109, and T. Fyfe, *Hellenistic Architecture* (Cambridge, Eng., 1936) 154-155.

[81] Guidi, "Descrizione araba" 156; cf. Welles, *Royal Correspondence* 29, n. 21.

[82] Förster ("Antiochia" 106) believed that he had found the site of the theater, but whatever traces he saw have since disappeared, and the site which he identified cannot now be located.

[83] The anonymous Arabic description of Antioch (Guidi, "Descrizione araba" 155) states that Seleucus I built an aqueduct to bring water to the city, though it is not clear from what source the water was led. This account is late, and the statement might simply represent an inference based on the supposition that a city such as Antioch must have possessed aqueducts from the beginning. Libanius (*Or.* 11.125) in his account of the development of the city in the Hellenistic period writes only that various rulers built aqueducts. See Downey, "Water Supply" 175-176.

[84] Polybius 5.58.

Foundation and Reign of Seleucus I

As to whether a stadium was built at Antioch by Seleucus or his immediate successors we have no specific evidence. It might be supposed that a city of Antioch's aspirations would of necessity be provided with a stadium or hippodrome. However, the earliest such structure of which we hear is the circus on the island in the Orontes, which seems to have been built by Q. Marcius Rex in 67 B.C.; and if this really was the first circus at Antioch, the stadium at Daphne, apparently in existence in 195 B.C., would have been the only such structure available before the close of the Seleucid period.[85]

Though we have no record to that effect it is to be presumed that Seleucus, in addition to bearing the cost of the public buildings, granted the new settlers financial assistance for the construction of their houses, as well as providing them with building lots.[86]

A number of statues set up by Seleucus are recorded. Of these the best-known is that of the Tyche of the city, made for Antioch by Eutychides of Sicyon, a pupil of Lysippus, which may have been set up during the years 296-293 B.C.[87] The statue, which was of bronze, showed the robed goddess seated on a rock representing Mount Silpius; with her left hand she supported herself on the rock, in her right she held a sheaf of wheat. On her head a turreted crown represented the city wall, and at her feet the body of a youth or river god symbolized the Orontes.[88] Tyche, when associated with a city, was regarded

[85] On the circus of Marcius Rex, see below, Ch. 6, §3; on the stadium at Daphne, see below, Ch. 12, §3.

[86] Similar assistance on the occasion of a synoecism or physical joining of two cities into one is described in two letters of Antigonus to Teos concerning the synoecism with Lebedus, written about 303 B.C. (*Michel, Recueil* no. 34 = Dittenberger *Syll.*³ no. 344 = Welles, *Royal Correspondence* nos. 3-4.

[87] The statue is described by Malalas, 201.1-2, 276.6-9. Pausanias writes (6.2.7): "This Eutychides made for the Syrians on the Orontes an image of Fortune, which is highly valued by the natives" (transl. of W. H. S. Jones, Loeb Classical Library). The date is suggested by the circumstance that in his chronological list of sculptors, Pliny (*Nat. hist.* 34.51) places Eutychides in *Ol.* 121 = 296-293 B.C.; that this date was chosen because it represented the completion and erection of the sculptor's most famous statue is suggested by Robert, "Eutychides" 1532-1533, followed by Waser, "Tyche in bildlicher Darstellung" in Roscher, *Lexikon* 5.1362 (where the date given, *Ol.* 120, is a typographical error).

[88] In Malalas' description of the statue, Förster ("Antiochia" 145) proposes, very plausibly, to restore καθημένην to the text before the words ὑπεράνω τοῦ ποταμοῦ (201.2), on the analogy of the phraseology of Malalas' subsequent description (276.7) of the copy set up by Trajan. On the form of the work of Eutychides, and on its later copies and imitations, the most convenient and most complete sources of information are P. Gardner, "The *Antioch* of Eutychides," *New Chapters in Greek Art* (Oxford 1926) 216-268; Toynbee, *Hadrianic School* 131-133, and Herzog-Hauser, "Tyche" 1679, 1684-1685; see also Müller, *Antiq. Antioch.* 36-38; Förster, "Antiochia" 145-149; Waser in Roscher, *Lexikon* 5.1362-1366; Richter, *Sculpture and Sculptors of the Greeks*³ 295;

[73]

as the city's protector, and the addition of the symbols of Mount Silpius and of the Orontes served to make the goddess also a personification of Antioch.[89] Tyche was also thought of as the guardian of the king, and in this aspect also the goddess would be regarded as protector of the city.[90] The conception of Tyche as embodied by Eutychides became popular among the cities of the Hellenized East, in great part because she united, with the attributes of success associated with the Greek figures of Tyche, the attributes of fertility and prosperity associated with the corresponding oriental mother-goddess (Ba'alat).[91]

The marble statuette in the Vatican is probably the closest extant copy of the work of Eutychides.[92] While there is no direct evidence to show the fashion in which the statue was set up, it seems likely that it was placed in a *tetrakionion*, as was the statue of the Tyche of An-

---

Bosch, *Kleinasiatischen Münzen*, Teil 2, Bd. 1, 1. Hälfte, 253-258; Rostovtzeff, "Le Gad de Doura et Seleucus Nicator" 292, with bibliography in n. 1; Levi, *Antioch Mosaic Pavements* 1.57-59; H. Seyrig, "Cachets d'archives publiques de quelques villes de la Syrie romaine," *MUSJ* 23 (1940) 87. The figure of Cilicia in a mosaic of Seleucia Pieria is derived from the Tyche of Eutychides; see Levi, *op.cit.* 1.58, with pl. 9 d. Somewhat surprisingly, a figure of Tyche does not appear on coins of Antioch until the reign of Demetrius I (162-150 B.C.), and then it is a figure seated on a throne, nude to the waist, and not the type of the statue of Eutychides: Newell, *Seleucid Mint of Antioch* 34-37; D. B. Waagé, "Coins" 13. Demetrius presumably placed the figure on his coins because he represented the restoration of the legitimate branch of the Seleucid house. Even more surprisingly, the Tyche of Eutychides is not represented on coins of Antioch until the regime of Tigranes, who occupied Syria from 83 to 69 B.C. (see below, Ch. 6, §3); see Lacroix, "Copies de statues sur les monnaies des Séleucides" 175. The Tyche of Eutychides appears on Roman coins of Antioch beginning with the time of Augustus (Bosch, *loc.cit.* and below, n. 93). On the Tyche of Antigonia which was set up at Antioch, see below, n. 93.

[89] L. Ruhl, "Tyche" in Roscher, *Lexikon* 5.1334. Malalas states (200.15-16) that the ceremony of founding the city and dedicating the statue of Tyche included the sacrifice of a maiden named Aimathe. The sacrifice of a maiden is a motif that frequently appears in Malalas' accounts of the foundations of cities; see 31.8-12; 37.5-6; 139.13-21; 192.4-7; 203.9-10, 13-14; 221.21-22; 268.8-10; 320.17-21. Sometimes the construction of a building is accompanied by the sacrifice of a maiden; see 235.1-2; 275.19-21; 276.4ff. These supposed sacrifices, which are most often associated with the erection of statues of Tyche, evidently represent a motif invented by Christian writers in an effort to cast discredit on the cult of the goddess; see Müller, *Antiq. Antioch.* 27 n. 2, 71 n. 6; Stauffenberg, *Malalas* 157-159, 216-217, 469-470; Weber, "Studien" 48, n. 5; Schultze, *Antiocheia* 6, n. 2; K. Krumbacher, *Gesch. der byz. Lit.*[2] (Munich 1897) 326; Ruhl *op.cit.* 1355. Bosch, *Kleinasiatischen Münzen*, Teil 2, Bd. 1, 1. Hälfte, 258, n. 194, thinks that the regular recurrence of the legend of the sacrifice of a maiden at the foundation of a city, shows that originally such sacrifices actually took place, and he supposes that such sacrifices still took place in the time of Seleucus I. This can hardly be true.

[90] See Lily Ross Taylor, *The Divinity of the Roman Emperor* (Middletown 1931) 32.

[91] See Rostovtzeff, "Le Gad de Doura" 292 and the list of cities that placed the Tyche on their coins, compiled by Bosch, *Kleinasiatischen Münzen* Teil 2, Bd. 1, 1. Hälfte 254-257.

[92] See Toynbee, *Hadrianic School* 131-133.

tigonia which Seleucus also set up in the city.[93] As to the size of the statue we have no specific indication.[94] Figures of Tyche were manufactured as souvenirs for sale to visitors to the city.[95]

Zeus and Apollo were the founders and protectors of the Seleucid dynasty; Apollo was reputed to be the father of Seleucus I, and Seleucus was officially identified with Zeus, while his son Antiochus was identified with Apollo.[96] In Antioch Seleucus is said to have set up a statue of Zeus Keraunios.[97] This may have been placed in the temple of Zeus Keraunios in Iopolis, which was supposed to have been built by Perseus, in which Seleucus made a sacrifice before the foundation of Antioch.[98] The temple itself may well have been built by Seleucus, and the legend of its construction by Perseus, and of Seleucus' sacrifice

[93] Coins of Antioch from the reign of Trajan (A.D. 98-117) through the reign of Valerian (A.D. 253-260) shows the Tyche of the city, represented in the type of the statue of Eutychides within a tetrastyle shrine, holding a sheaf; *BMC Galatia etc.*, pp. 222, 225, 226, 229, 231, 232; Bosch, *Kleinasiatischen Münzen*, Teil 2, Bd. 1, 1. Hälfte 254; Wruck, *Syrische Provinzialprägung*, catalogue (pp. 178ff.) nos. 2ff., 98-99, 104, 113, 153, 157, 160, 163, 166, 169, 174, 179; Toynbee, *Hadrianic School* 131-133. While these coins are of relatively late date, it is likely that they represent the original setting of the statue, especially since Malalas, though he happens to say nothing as to the location of the statue of the Tyche of Antioch, does say (201.6-8) that the statue of the Tyche of Antigonia, which Seleucus brought to Antioch, was placed in a *tetrakionion*. Elsewhere Malalas relates that Trajan, when he completed the theater at Antioch, set up in it, in the middle of the nymphaeum of the proscenium, "above four columns" (ὑπεράνω τεσσάρων κιόνων), a statue of the Tyche of the city, seated above the Orontes, and crowned by Seleucus and Antiochus (276.3-9; on the theater, see below, 216). Müller (*Antiq. Antioch.* 38-40) takes this passage to mean that the original Tyche was set up in a *tetrakionion*, and that Trajan transferred the statue, along with its *tetrakionion*, to the theater. This inference seems unwarranted, especially since the statue set up by Trajan is described as being different, in that Tyche was depicted being crowned by the Seleucid kings. It seems much more plausible to suppose, with Toynbee (*Hadrianic School* 131-133), Förster ("Antiochia" 146), Robert ("Eutychides" 1532-1533), Maass (*Tagesgötter* 57), and Rostovtzeff ("Le Gad de Doura" 288), that Trajan's statue was a copy of the original. Müller (*Antiq. Antioch.* 39-40) appears to think that the original statue of Tyche was set up over the river ("supra fluvium") and evidently supposes that a *tetrakionion* was built to straddle the stream. This can hardly be right. Müller must have been misled by the words ὑπεράνω τοῦ ποταμοῦ in Malalas' account of the dedication of the statue (201.2). This phrase must mean that the figure of the goddess was seated above that of the personification of the Orontes (cf. Malalas' description of the Tyche set up by Trajan, καθημένην ἐπάνω τοῦ Ὀρόντου ποταμοῦ, 276.7), but the words could unthinkingly be construed to refer to the location of the whole group, and this is, indeed, the interpretation adopted in the Latin translation of Malalas. The Tyche seated on a throne, nude to the waist, which appears on coins of Demetrius I, might or might not represent the Tyche of Antigonia; see above, n. 88.

[94] Robert, "Eutychides" 1532-1533, writes that it was of colossal size, but cites no evidence for this statement, and the present writer has been able to find none. Perhaps Robert's supposition was based on Müller's mistaken belief (see preceding note) that the statue was set up over the river. Robert's assertion is accepted by Herzog-Hauser, "Tyche" 1684, but not by Toynbee, *Hadrianic School* 131-133.

[95] Herzog-Hauser, "Tyche" 1685.   [96] See above, n. 63.
[97] Malalas 212.2-4.   [98] Malalas 199.12-16; see above, n. 18.

there before the founding of the city, are legends such as would have been invented at a later date. A statue of Zeus Keraunios, which was presumably the one set up by Seleucus, was sent from Antioch to Rome (along with a statue of Athena, mentioned below) while M. Calpurnius Bibulus was governor of Syria (51-50 B.C.).[99]

Two other statues commemorated events in the foundation of the city. One was a stone figure set up outside the city in honor of the eagle of Zeus, which had shown Seleucus the site on which the city was to be built.[100] The other was a marble statue of the priest Amphion who had assisted Seleucus in the sacrifices; this was placed outside the gate that was later called the Romanesian Gate.[101]

To commemorate the destruction of his enemy's capital and, at the same time, as a gesture of friendship for the inhabitants of Antigonia whom he had brought to Antioch, Seleucus set up in Antioch a bronze statue of the Tyche of Antigonia, who was shown holding the horn of Amalthia before her. This statue, Malalas says, was placed in a *tetrakionion*, "on high," and had a lofty altar in front of it.[102]

Likewise, in order to provide for the religious needs of the Athenians whom he had brought from Antigonia, Seleucus set up a great bronze statue of Athena.[103] This statue was sent to Rome (together with a statue of Zeus Keraunios, already mentioned) while M. Calpurnius

---

[99] See below, Ch. 7, nn. 40-41.

[100] Malalas 202.6-7; see above, nn. 57-58. In commemoration of this episode of the foundation, an eagle frequently appears on the coins of Antioch: see A. Dieudonné, "L'Aigle d'Antioche," *Rev. num.*, ser. 4, vol. 13 (1904) 458-480.

[101] Malalas 202.19-21; on the role of Amphion, see Malalas 199.22, 200.15 (cf. above, n. 58).

[102] Malalas 201.5-11. The chronicler does not say whether this was a new statue, or was brought from Antigonia; it seems likely (as Müller believes, *Antiq. Antioch.* 40) that the latter was the case. Malalas adds that after the death of Seleucus, Demetrius Poliorcetes took the statue to the city of Rhosus in Cilicia. This, as Müller points out (40, n. 10), cannot be true, for Demetrius, who surrendered to Seleucus in 285 B.C., died in 283/2 B.C., before Seleucus' death (Kaerst, "Demetrios," no. 33, *RE* 4.2791-2792). Müller suggests that it was Demetrius Soter (162-150 B.C.) who took the statue to Rhosus, and that Malalas confused the two Demetrii.

[103] Malalas 201.16-18; he calls the statue ἀνδριάντα χαλκοῦν φοβερὸν τῆς ᾽Αθήνης. Athena Promachus, in fighting attitude, appears on coins of Seleucus I struck at Antioch: Newell, *West Sel. Mints* 96-97. Lacroix, "Copies de statues sur les monnaies des Seleucides" 168, understands φοβερός in the sense of "terrifying," and suggests that Malalas' description of Seleucus' statue shows that it depicted Athena in warlike attitude. This interpretation is hazardous because Malalas elsewhere uses φοβερός in the Byzantine and modern Greek sense of δεινός, θαυμαστός, "wonderful, remarkable, extraordinary," (278.10, 395.8, 83.1, 91.11, 225.19, 200.21; see also E. A. Sophocles, *Greek Lexicon of the Roman and Byzantine Periods, s.v.*). Thus, while it is conceivable that Malalas meant that the statue was of terrifying aspect, his usage of φοβερός elsewhere (with which Lacroix is evidently not acquainted) suggests that he meant simply that the statue was an imposing one (this is the sense in which Newell inter-

Bibulus was governor of Syria (51-50 B.C.).[104] The people who had
come from Antigonia in their turn erected a bronze statue of Seleucus,
with bull's horns added to the head, alluding to the king's famous feat
of strength in restraining a wild bull.[105] As a symbol of the union that
had been effected between the people of Antigonia, who worshiped
Athena, and the subjects of Seleucus, who were protected by Zeus and
Apollo, some of the coins issued at Antioch by Seleucus I show Athena
and Apollo on the two sides of the same coin.[106]

Another episode in Seleucus' career was recalled by a statue that he
placed outside the city across the Orontes, showing a horse's head, with
a gilded helmet near it. The group, Malalas says, bore the inscription
"On this Seleucus fled Antigonus, and was saved; and returning and
conquering him, he destroyed him."[107] The statue may have been set
up at the place later called Hippocephalum, three miles from Antioch.[108]

4. Size, Plan, Population, and Government
of Seleucus' City

According to the testimony of Malalas, Seleucus built his original
settlement on the level part of the site, near the river.[109] This location

prets the passage, *op.cit.* 96, n. 23a; Müller, *Antiq. Antioch.* 41, n. 1, quotes the epithet
in Greek without committing himself as to its significance). That this was Malalas'
meaning is suggested by the manner in which he refers to the statue again in the account which he subsequently gives of its being sent to Rome as a gift in 51 or 50 B.C.,
along with the statue of Zeus Keraunios which had also been erected by Seleucus I.
Malalas describes the statues (212.2-4) as τὸ ἄγαλμα τῆς Ἀθήνης τὸ παρὰ Σελεύκου
γενόμενον, φοβερὸν ὄντα, καὶ τὸ ἄγαλμα τοῦ Κεραυνίου Διός, παρὰ τοῦ αὐτοῦ Σελεύκου
γενόμενον, καὶ αὐτὸ φοβερόν. The way in which φοβερός is employed here indicates that
at least in this passage it means "imposing" rather than "terrifying."

[104] See below, Ch. 7, n. 40.
[105] Libanius *Or.* 11.92. The episode is described e.g. by Appian *Syr.* 57: "He [Se-
leucus] was of such a large and powerful frame that once when a wild bull was brought
for sacrifice to Alexander and broke loose from his ropes, Seleucus held him alone,
with nothing but his hands, for which reason his statues are ornamented with horns"
(transl. of H. White, Loeb Classical Library). For coins of Seleucus from the mint of
Antioch which commemorate this exploit, see Newell, *West. Sel. Mints* 101. On the
Seleucid dynastic cult, see W. S. Ferguson in *CAH* 7.16, 19-20; Rostovtzeff, *ibid.* 162;
idem, "Progonoi" *JHS* 55 (1935) 59 n. 10, and above, n. 63. The bull's horns on the
statue of Seleucus may have had religious significance.
[106] D. B. Waagé, "Coins" 3, nos. 1-7.
[107] Malalas 202.17-19. The text printed in the Bonn edition by mistake omits νικήσας
before ἀνεῖλεν; see Bury, "Malalas: the Cod. Barocc." 225. The horned horse's head
appears as a counterstamp on coins of Seleucus: Newell, *West. Sel. Mints* 97.
[108] Ammianus Marcellinus 21.15.2; Church Slavonic Malalas, p. 111 transl. Spinka;
cf. Honigmann, "Syria" 1699. There seems to be no trace of the possible assimilation
of Seleucus to Dionysus, mentioned by Tondriau, "Souverains et souveraines Séleucides
en divinités" 174.
[109] Malalas 200.10-11; 233.11-12. See above, §3.

is what we should expect, since it would be natural to place the city on the bank of the Orontes in order to make use of the river both as a means of transportation and as an element in the fortification of the city. As has already been noted, the existence of the modern souk area on the bank of the river suggests that this was the position of the agora. In some other cities of Syria the souks are known to represent the sites of the ancient market places, and it would be natural of course to locate the agora on the river.[110]

Strabo's account of Antioch indicates that Seleucus' original settlement consisted of a walled quarter for the European settlers with another quarter (which may or may not have been walled) for the native Syrians.[111] The European quarter, as has been seen, must have lain along the river; and that the Syrian quarter likewise was on the river is shown not only by the statement of Malalas quoted above, but by the circumstance that the additions later made to the city, first by Seleucus II (246-226 B.C.) and Antiochus III (223-187 B.C.), then by Antiochus IV (175-164 B.C.) and finally by the Romans, all were built either on the island in the Orontes or on the slope of the mountain,[112] which indicates that the section along the river was already fully built up.

The approximate boundaries of Seleucus' settlement can be determined fairly satisfactorily (Fig. 11). It seems unlikely that the settlements extended north or south beyond the wall of Tiberius, the course of which, at these points, is known from preserved remains. The eastern limit would seem to be indicated by the course of the thoroughfare which later became the colonnaded main street of the city. This avenue, when it was paved in the time of Augustus, was described as lying "outside the city," which would appear to mean that it ran outside the walled part of the city.[113] Moreover, the street runs just along the line where the first slopes of Mount Silpius begin to rise from the flat ground along the river.

The outer limits of Seleucus' settlement can thus be established with a fair degree of reliability. For the division between the walled quarter of the Europeans and the quarter of the natives, there is no specific evidence. It seems, however, possible that this division was indicated by the course of the colonnaded street which (we know from Libanius)

[110] See above, n. 64.
[111] Strabo 16.2.4, p. 750 C; see Downey, "Strabo on Antioch" and cf. further below.
[112] On these expansions of the city, see below, Ch. 5, §§3-4, 6; Ch. 8, §2.
[113] On the construction of the colonnades of the main street, and on the role which the new avenue played in the city plan under the Romans, see below, Ch. 8, §2.

later ran between the main street and the river (Fig. 11). Such a division would give a walled quarter for the European settlers approximately 5 km. in circumference, containing about 370 acres (150 hectares), and a native quarter about 2.5 km. in circumference, containing about 185 acres (75 hectares). The two quarters together would be ca. 7.5 km. in circumference, containing about 555 acres (225 hectares) (640 acres = 1 sq. mi.). This area compares quite significantly with the areas of two other members of the tetrapolis of "sister cities" (Antioch, Seleucia Pieria, Apamea, and Laodicea) described by Strabo (16.2.4, pp. 749-750). At Antioch and Laodicea, as we have seen, the *insulae* were practically of the same dimensions, which suggests that the cities were laid out by the same architect or from the same general specifications. Thus the boundaries and measurements of the Seleucid foundation at Antioch suggested here seem to find confirmation in the fact that Apamea covered 250 hectares or about 260 acres and that Laodicea had an area of 220 hectares or about 543 acres.[114] These areas, it may be noted, were relatively large.[115] It is of considerable interest to find that the area of the site of Antigonia, Seleucus' enemy's capital, which he destroyed, was much greater than that of Antioch, the circumference of Antigonus' capital being about 12 km., enclosing about 889 acres (about 360 hectares). These figures can be only approximate since the irregular shape of the site makes calculation from a map difficult.

The inhabitants of Seleucus' city were gathered from various sources; among the settlers are listed Athenians, Macedonians;[116] retired soldiers of Seleucus;[117] some of the Cretans, Cypriotes, Argives, and Heraclids who had previously settled on Mount Silpius;[118] inhabitants of Antigonia (described as Athenians) whom Seleucus resettled in his new city;[119] and a number of Jews, some of whom were presumably retired

[114] On the *insulae* of Antioch and Laodicea, see above, n. 71. For the area of Apamea, see F. Mayence, "Les fouilles d'Apamée," *Acad. roy. de Belgique, Bull. de la cl. des lettres et des sciences morales et politiques*, ser. 5, vol. 25 (1939) 333, and for that of Laodicea, Sauvaget, "Plan de Laodicée-sur-mer" 111. Sauvaget gives the size of Apamea as 205 hectares, but the figure of M. Mayence, the director of the excavations, is preferred here, M. Sauvaget's figure presumably being a typographical error.

[115] See Sauvaget, "Plan de Laodicée-sur-mer" 111 and Tscherikower, "Hellenistischen Städtegründungen" 136, who collects evidence for the size of other Greek cities.

[116] Malalas 201.16; see further below.

[117] Libanius *Or.* 11.91.

[118] Malalas 201.18-202.6; Libanius *loc.cit.* However, some of the descendants of the original settlers on the mountain are said to have continued to live at the acropolis at least until the time of Julius Caesar (Malalas 346.21—347.5).

[119] Malalas 201.12-18; Libanius *Or.* 11.92. Other inhabitants of Antigonia, according to Diodorus (20.47), were resettled in Seleucia Pieria.

mercenaries of Seleucus' army. The historian Josephus, who writes of the Jews at Antioch, claims that they were granted citizenship and special privileges by Seleucus Nicator, but this is probably an exaggeration, and it is more likely that individual Jews, as ex-soldiers, were privileged to be enrolled, if they chose, in the citizen lists. Jews could not have been given the privileges of full citizenship wholesale because this would have meant worship of the city gods, which to a Jew would have been apostasy, and many at least would not have taken this step. Instead, the Jews at Antioch, like those of Alexandria, doubtless lived in their own community, with their own religious and political chiefs; and they may have enjoyed a form of isopolity or potential citizenship, meaning that a Jew could become a citizen on demand.[120]

In addition, the population seems to have included a group of indigenous Syrians which did not form a part of the *demos*. Either this group was assigned by Seleucus (as has been noted) to a separate walled area adjoining the principal foundation, or its members settled outside Seleucus' foundation in an area which was originally unwalled but was later enclosed by a wall that joined the wall of the original foundation, forming the second of the four quarters of which the city ultimately consisted.[121]

Thus, in its ethnic composition Antioch was, at the time of its foundation, a typical example of the Seleucid policy of settling Macedonians and Greeks at strategic points in the newly conquered territory in order to assure the security of the new regime.[122] In later times the people of Antioch seem to have taken even more pride in their descent from their Athenian forebears (the original settlers of Antigonia, who had been transplanted to Antioch) than in their Macedonian origins.[123]

[120] Josephus *Contra Apionem* 2.39; *Ant.* 12.119; *Bell.* 7.43ff. There is a considerable literature on the status of the Jews at Antioch, in some of which Josephus' patently false claims are followed. See Kraeling, "Jewish Community at Antioch" 137-139; R. Marcus in Appendix C in the seventh volume (1943) of the Loeb Classical Library edition of Josephus; Tarn-Griffith, *Hellenistic Civilization*³ 221; W. Ruppel, "Politeuma," *Philologus* 82 (1927) 268ff., 434ff.

[121] On the four quarters of the city, see Strabo 16.2.4, p. 750; on the native Syrian quarter, see Müller, *Antiq. Antioch.* 28-29; Jones, *Cities of the East. Rom. Prov.* 244; Downey, "Strabo on Antioch" 85-96. On the composition and status of the native elements in the Hellenistic foundations, see also Tscherikower, "Hellenistischen Städtegründungen" 190ff.

[122] See the excellent survey of Seleucid colonization by Sauvaget, *Alep* 34-36, with map (36) of the new foundations in northern Syria. See also the valuable treatment of the subject by M. Launey, *Recherches sur les armées hellénistiques* (Paris 1946) 331ff.

[123] Malalas 211.19; Evagrius 1.20. The significance of the pride of the people of

As to the size of this population we have no clear evidence. Malalas (201.12-16) gives the number of Athenians whom Seleucus transferred from Antigonia to Antioch, and of the Macedonians whom Seleucus settled in Antioch, with the phrase τοὺς πάντας ἄνδρας ,ετ΄. Whether this figure, 5,300, represents the total of the inhabitants of Antioch who were of Athenian and Macedonian stock, or only the total of the adult male citizens of this group, is not, from the phrase itself, certain.[124] Malalas' use of the word ἀνήρ in such contexts does not allow us to be sure whether he used it in the present passage to mean "man" or "person";[125] it is likely in fact that the chronicler simply reproduced the phrase verbatim from his source. It seems possible, however, that the figure 5,300 represents the number of the adult male citizens who

Antioch in their Macedonian descent is brought out by C. Edson, *"Imperium Macedonicum*: The Seleucid Empire and the Literary Evidence," *CP* 53 (1958) 153-170.

[124] Müller (*Antiq. Antioch.* 28, n. 6) seems to think that the figure 5,300 is supposed to represent the entire population of Antigonia, and concludes that the numerals must be corrupt, since Antigonia (which according to Diodorus 20.47 had a circumference of 70 stadia = about 14 km.) must have had a larger population. However, Müller did not understand that Seleucia Pieria, not Antioch, was almost certainly Seleucus' capital, and that there is no good reason to reject the statement of Diodorus (*loc.cit.*) that the inhabitants of Antigonia were settled in Seleucia (see above, n. 119). Since Antioch was apparently at first intended to be secondary in importance to Seleucia, it would be by no means surprising that only a relatively small number of the inhabitants of Antigonia were sent to Antioch. Jones (*Cities of the East. Rom. Prov.* 239) believes that the number 5,300 represents the European portion of the population of Antigonia. The views of both scholars, that the figure applies to Antigonia, are based upon a misunderstanding of the language of Malalas' account (201.12-16). Although Malalas' sentence structure is involved, it seems clear that he meant the number 5,300 to be the total of the two separate groups, (1) the Athenians who were transferred from Antigonia to Antioch, and (2) others, who were Macedonians, whom Seleucus also settled at Antioch. That Malalas (or his source) meant this is shown not only by the sentence structure, but by the use of the word πάντας in connection with the figure; this meaning is clearly brought out in the Church Slavonic version of Malalas (p. 14 transl. Spinka), which presumably was not available to Müller and Jones. Moreover, that only Athenians were brought from Antigonia to Antioch is suggested by the circumstance, which Malalas next records (201.16-18), that Seleucus erected a statue of Athena for the Athenians whom he moved from Antigonia to his new capital. If Macedonians likewise had come from Antigonia, we might expect to hear of some similar provision made for them.

[125] The writer has collected the following examples of the use of ἀνήρ by Malalas: *a man* (*a person*): 34.6, 41.6, 42.3, 55.16, 57.10, 63.12, 69.21, 71.3, 78.11, 81.16, 83.21, 89.21, 114.22, 115.12, 118.19-20 (*bis*), 168.2, 181.13, 256.18, 390.10, 394.20, 395.6, 399.8, 422.3; *a man* (opp. to *woman*): 40.9 435.13-14 ("men, women, and children"); *husband*: 24.9, 97.6, 101.6, 178.7, 378.2; *soldier*: 44.4, 329.14. In speaking of the "people" (men?) who were killed in the sack of a city, Malalas writes ἄνδρας (101.1). In two instances in which it is clear from the context that a total of men, women, and children is meant, ψυχαί is used (260.10, 417.15-16), but in another such passage (476.19-20) only οἱ σφαγέντες is written. Ἄνθρωπος is used in the sense of *mankind* or *man*: 3.1, 3.3 (Adam the first *anthropos*), 6.3, 7.7, 10.4, 35.10, 57.2, 57.5, 74.20, 75.6, 163.15, 202.10; *man* (opp. to *woman*) 66.10; this word is not used in passages in which numbers are given.

formed the original settlement at Antioch. The figure approximates that which Plato gives, 5,040, for the number of landholders and heads of households in the ideal city (*Laws* 737 E, 740 D-E); and the uniformity observed in the size and plan of a number of the Seleucid settlements in Syria suggests that in this wholesale founding of new cities there was a certain standardization of the size of population, modeled on Plato's doctrine, as well as in the size and arrangement of the streets and *insulae*.[126] The figure preserved by Malalas also seems comparable with the figure 6,000 given by Polybius (5.61.1) for the *eleutheroi* (that is, presumably, the adult male citizens) of Seleucia Pieria in 220 B.C.[127] Depending on the view one adopts as to the proportional relationship between the number of adult male citizens and the number of women and children, the total free population of Antioch, if there were 5,300 adult male citizens, would have been from about 17,000 to about 25,000 (plus slaves, who were not counted). This seems to be a large number for a foundation such as Antioch.[128]

For the government and organization of the city at this period there is little direct evidence and we are dependent upon analogy and inference, which in this instance may be quite hazardous. The city may have been governed by an *epistates*, as royal governor with both civil and military powers; and it may have been organized, not like a Greek *polis*, governed by citizens and council, but on the Macedonian model, which may have meant that there was a *gerousia* or council of elders.[129]

5. The Foundation of Daphne; Its Cults

As to the legendary origin of the famous suburb Daphne, the local authorities differed. Malalas writes that Herakles in person founded, near Antioch, a place named for himself which was later called Daphne.[130] Libanius speaks of a place which he calls both Herakleis

---

[126] For a masterly study of Plato's conception of the founding of a *polis*, and of the methods and purposes, in relation to this, of the founders of Hellenistic cities, see C. Bradford Welles, "The Greek City," *Studi in onore di A. Calderini e R. Paribeni* (Milan 1956) 81-99.

[127] On this meaning of *eleutheroi*, see Beloch, *Bevölkerung* 245.

[128] See Beloch, *Bevölkerung* 54. We are not well informed as to the size of the population of the cities of Syria at this time. For a study of the evidence (which does not, however, include Malalas' figure for Antioch), see Tscherikower, "Hellenistischen Städtegründungen" 199-200. Tscherikower concludes that it would seem likely that cities such as Antioch did not possess more than 10,000 free citizens at the time of their foundation.

[129] See in further detail Ch. 5, §8, on the organization and administration of the city in the Hellenistic period.

[130] 204.9-16. Eustathius in his commentary on Dionysius Periegetes 916 writes that Daphne was once called Herakleias.

and Herakleia, which had been founded by the Herakleidae when they were driven into exile by Eurysthes, but he seems to understand that this place was distinct from Daphne and that it lay on the road between Antioch and Daphne; and in his account of Seleucus' undertakings at Daphne, he does not speak of Herakleia.[131] This apparent contradiction suggests that the localities, originally distinct, grew until they became contiguous, and that when they were no longer separate, the tales of their origins became consolidated.[132]

Libanius writes that it was Seleucus who dedicated Daphne to Apollo, who was, like Zeus, regarded as a tutelary deity of the Seleucid dynasty, reputed to be the father of Seleucus;[133] and our evidence for the temples and statues set up in the two places indicates that Antioch was thought of as sacred to Zeus, while Daphne was considered sacred to Apollo. Apollo's pursuit of the maiden Daphne was supposed to have taken place at this spot and the very laurel (Greek *daphne*) into which Daphne was transformed was shown.[134] The god, in his grief at the loss of the maiden, shot all his arrows, and the tip of one, with the god's name inscribed on it, was buried in the earth and was preserved as an omen for Seleucus. Then, one day, when the king was hunting, his horse pawed the earth and revealed the arrowhead, and Seleucus perceived from the inscription on it that the spot was to be made into a shrine of Apollo. He laid out an enclosure, planted the famous grove of cypress trees, built a temple, and held the place in great honor.[135] The temple stood near the spring

[131] *Or.* 11.56, 94-99, 233-236.

[132] This is Müller's conclusion, *Antiq. Antioch.* 44, n. 14. Stauffenberg (*Malalas* 456; cf. 465) prefers to follow Libanius and concludes that Herakleia was a suburb on the road from Antioch to Daphne. Palladius, *Dial. de vita S. Ioannis Chrysostomi*, 96.8-9 ed. Coleman-Norton (Cambridge, Eng., 1928), writes of the games held at Daphne in his time as "Heraklian games, called Olympics." The earliest extant examples of the use of the name Daphne for the suburb are found in the inscription of 189 B.C. discovered at Daphne relating to the cults of Apollo and Artemis (*IGLS* 992; see below, Ch. 4, n. 29), and in Polybius (31.3.1), Livy (33.49.6) and Strabo (16.2.4, p. 749).

[133] Libanius *Or.* 11.94; Justinus 15.4. On Apollo and Zeus as the tutelary deities of the Seleucids, see above, n. 63. The building of the temple of Apollo at Daphne is attributed to Antiochus IV or Antiochus XI by some sources, but these references would appear to be to supplementary work carried out by Seleucus' successors; see below, n. 135. Seleucus would scarcely have dedicated a grove to his tutelary deity without likewise building, or at least founding, a temple there.

[134] Libanius *Or.* 11.94; Philostratus *Life of Apollonius* 1.16, Eustathius, Commentary on Dionysius Periegetes 916. The pursuit is depicted on a mosaic of the Roman period found in a house at Daphne: Levi, *Antioch Mosaic Pavements* 1.211-214, with pl. 47 a-b. The story of Apollo and Daphne as told at Antioch differed from the versions that were told elsewhere (cf. Pausanias 8.20.2).

[135] Libanius *Or.* 11.94-99. Sozomen (5.19 = *PG* 67.1273) also says that Seleucus built the temple of Apollo at Daphne. Malalas (204.9-16) merely records that Seleucus planted

Castalia, in which an oracle of Apollo was considered to reside,[136] and the water from the spring flowed along either side of the temple.[137]

Other legends were likewise attached to the spot. A stream at Daphne was named for Ladon, the father of Daphne, who was supposed to have been the deity inhabiting the stream.[138] The cypress trees, famous throughout antiquity, were connected with the story of the youth Cyparissus, who was so saddened when he accidentally killed a pet stag that the gods in pity changed him into a mourning tree.[139] There was a local legend that Daphne had been chosen on account of its beauty as the spot at which the Judgment of Paris took place.[140] And there were legends of the Nymphs who dwelt in the famous springs, which were one of the chief beauties of the place.[141]

---

the cypress trees near the temple of Apollo, Herakles having previously planted trees there. Herakleia, he notes, was itself outside the grove, near the temple of Athena. As to the builders of these two temples, the chronicler says nothing. It is possible that he mentions the temple of Athena merely as a point of reference for the location of Herakleia, and that he does not mean that this temple existed at the time of which he wrote. The circumstance that this cypress grove later came to have a special fame of its own, quite independently of the temple (Müller, *Antiq. Antioch.* 46, n. 2) may have been responsible for Malalas' neglect, in recording the planting of the grove, to mention the building of the temple. On the history of the temple, and on the literary sources for it, see, in greater detail, Förster, "De Libanio, Pausania. . . ." Malalas (234.3-8) reports that Antiochus XI Philadelphus, who reigned for a short time in 93 B.C., "built two temples in Daphne of Apollo and Artemis." This cannot mean that these temples were built for the first time in 93 B.C., for we have epigraphic evidence from the reign of Antiochus III for the existence of the Temple of Apollo in 189 B.C. (see below, Ch. 4, n. 29). The passage in Malalas doubtless refers to repair or restoration of the buildings (see further below, Ch. 6, nn. 56-57). Ammianus Marcellinus says that the Temple of Apollo was built by Antiochus IV, but this can hardly be true; see below, Ch. 5, n. 91.

[136] For the history of the oracle of Apollo at Daphne, see A. Bouché-Leclercq, *Histoire de la divination dans l'antiquité* (Paris 1879-1882) 3.266ff. The celebrated oracle given to the Emperor Julian the Philosopher at Daphne is described below, Ch. 13, n. 41.

[137] Libanius *Or.* 11.242. In the fourth century after Christ the body of the famous Christian bishop of Antioch, St. Babylas, was placed near the Temple of Apollo, and its presence had the effect of inhibiting the prophetic spring of Castalia; the episode is described below, Ch. 12, §10, with nn. 217-218.

[138] Philostratus *Life of Apollonius* 1.16. A personification of Ladon appears on a mosaic of the Roman period in a house found at Daphne: Levi, *Antioch Mosaic Pavements* 1.205, 212-213.

[139] Philostratus *loc.cit.*

[140] Libanius *Or.* 11.241. A fine mosaic showing the Judgment (now in the Louvre) has been found at Antioch: Levi, *Antioch Mosaic Pavements* 1.15-21. G. M. A. Hanfmann has published (*Archaeology* 9 [1956] 3-7) a painted glass bowl showing the Judgment of Paris, which the owner of the bowl, Ray Winfield Smith, suggests was made in Antioch. The style places the bowl at about the time of Constantine the Great. In the same study Hanfmann illustates a painted glass jug, probably made in Syria, which shows Daphne being transformed into a tree.

[141] Libanius *Or.* 11.241.

Seleucus' temple of Apollo contained a colossal acrolithic statue of the god which was attributed to the Athenian sculptor Bryaxis, who is also supposed to have executed a portrait of Seleucus.[142] Apollo was shown playing and singing, with lyre in one hand and bowl in the other, wearing a high-girdled chiton, which was gilded. The god's hair and laurel crown were also gilded and his eyes were formed of two enormous violet stones;[143] it was said that the statue was the equal in size of the statue of Zeus by Phidias at Olympia.[144]

[142] The attribution of the statue to Bryaxis is based on a passage in Cedrenus (1.536.11 Bonn ed.), where the name given, Bryxis, is obviously an error for that of the famous sculptor. Since Bryaxis is known to have been at work on the Mausoleum at Halicarnassus about 350 B.C., some scholars have supposed that he could not have lived long enough to have made the statue for the temple at Daphne fifty years later, and it has been suggested that the statue at Daphne was made by a younger sculptor of the same name. It is, however, not at all impossible that Bryaxis enjoyed an unusually long career, and there seems to be no good reason to disbelieve the attribution; see C. Robert, "Bryaxis" *RE* 3.916-920, and Richter, *Sculpture and Sculptors of the Greeks*[3] 281-283. As one way of obviating the supposed chronological difficulty, Robert suggests that the statue was originally made for Antigonia and transported by Seleucus to Daphne. This suggestion, of course, shortens the sculptor's career by only a few years. The portrait of Seleucus, a bronze statue, is mentioned by Pliny *Nat. hist.* 34.73.

[143] The statue is described by Libanius in his *Monody on the Temple of Apollo at Daphne* (*Or.* 60.9-11), which was written soon after the destruction of the temple in 362, and by Philostorgius *Hist. eccl.* 7.8, pp. 87, 19ff. ed. Bidez. Further details are supplied by Theodoret *Hist. eccl.* 3.6 = *PG* 82.1100 A, and the statue is mentioned by Cedrenus *loc.cit.*, in pseudo-Chrysostom, *Hom. de S. Babyla contra Iulianum et gentiles* 20 = *PG* 50.565 (quoting Libanius), and by Julian *Misop.* 361 C. Malalas (234.4-8) speaks of statues of Apollo and Artemis in temples of these gods which he says Antiochus XI Epiphanes Philadelphus (reigned 92 B.C.) built at Daphne. Malalas probably misunderstood his source, which actually referred to repair or rebuilding of the temples (on his procedures in this respect, see above, Ch. 2, §4). On representations of the statue on coins, see Förster's commentary on Libanius *Or.* 60 (v. 4, p. 317 of his edition); Richter *op.cit.* 281, with figs. 731-732; L. Lacroix, *Les reproductions de statues sur les monnaies grecques: la statuaire archaïque et classique* (Liège 1949) 319-320; idem, "Copies de statues sur les monnaies des Séleucides," 174. On the form of the statue, see also Müller, *Antiq. Antioch.* 47-49; Th. Reinach, "Apollo: Statue trouvée à Magnésie du Sipyle," *Mon. Piot* 3 (1896) 161; A. J. B. Wace, "Apollo Seated on the Omphalos," *Annual of the British School at Athens* 9 (1902-1903) 217-220; and Reinach, *Cultes, mythes et religions*[2] 2.351-352.

[144] This statement, which does not appear in the other sources, is made by Ammianus Marcellinus (22.13.1). Ammianus says that the temple was built by Antiochus IV Epiphanes (175-163 B.C.). This is at variance with the testimony of the other sources (see Müller, *Antiq. Antioch.* 63); it seems that Antiochus only repaired or embellished the temple, and that Ammianus (or his source) misunderstood a tradition to this effect, thinking wrongly that Antiochus built the temple for the first time. The phraseology of Ammianus' reference to the statue has been misunderstood, and some scholars have supposed that Antiochus IV (or Seleucus I) set up a statue of Zeus in the Temple of Apollo at Daphne, but this was almost certainly not the case (see Lacroix, "Copies de statues sur les monnaies des Séleucides" 164-165). Apparently the Seleucids thought of Antioch as sacred to Zeus and Daphne as sacred to Apollo, so that a statue of Zeus in the Temple of Apollo at Daphne might have been looked upon as inappropriate.

An inscription of Antiochus III dated 189 B.C. shows that the chief shrine of Daphne at that period was dedicated jointly to Apollo and Artemis Daittae.[145] As to whether the temple bore this dedication from its foundation we have no specific evidence; no cult of Artemis at Daphne is mentioned in our sources for the period of Seleucus I and his immediate successors.

There is no certain record of other activities of Seleucus at Daphne. It is likely that he constructed an aqueduct to carry water from the celebrated springs of Daphne to Antioch.[146] He may also have built the temple of Artemis that some sources mention as standing at a later date within the enclosure which contained the temple of Apollo.[147] In any case it seems likely that in the reign of Seleucus Daphne began to develop as the luxurious and beautiful suburb that in time became one of the chief glories of Antioch.

Of the size and plan of Daphne at the time of its foundation we have, at least as yet, no knowledge. At some time in the Hellenistic or early Roman period, Daphne became a regular town, laid out on a quadrated plan; but how early we do not know.[148]

[145] Waddington, no. 2713A = *OGIS* no. 244 = Welles, *Royal Correspondence* no. 44.
[146] See above, n. 83.
[147] See above, n. 143.
[148] *Antioch-on-the-Orontes* 3.28.

CHAPTER 5

FROM ANTIOCHUS I TO ANTIOCHUS IV,
281/0-163 B.C.

1. ANTIOCHUS I SOTER, 281/0-261 B.C.

WHEN SELEUCUS I died in 281/0 B.C., he was buried at Seleucia Pieria, and this choice of the place of burial indicates that Seleucia Pieria was still regarded as the capital at that time.[1] The increased activity of the mint of Antioch beginning with the reign of Antiochus I, matched by a decline in the importance of the mint of Seleucia Pieria, indicated that the capital was transferred from Seleucia Pieria to Antioch at this time.[2] One reason for the change may have been that Antioch was much safer from attack by sea than Seleucia Pieria.

Antiochus I entertained at his court, from ca. 274 to ca. 272 B.C., the famous poet Aratus of Soli, author of the astronomical poem *Phaenomena*, who left the Macedonian court when Antigonus Gonatas was attacked by Pyrrhus. While he was at Antioch, Aratus, at the king's request, prepared an edition of the *Odyssey*, and planned an edition of the *Iliad*, which seems never to have been executed. Concerning other intellectual activity at the court at this time our scanty sources give no information.[3]

2. ANTIOCHUS II THEOS, 261-247/6 B.C.

In the reign of Antiochus II both Antioch and Ephesus served as royal residences and headquarters, and this king evidently had no occasion to promote the Syrian city to a position of preeminence.[4]

Antiochus for political purposes put aside his first wife Laodice and married Berenice, the daughter of Ptolemy Philadelphus, king of Egypt, evidently with the understanding that Berenice's issue should inherit the Seleucid throne. This marriage, which took place in 252 B.C., was the beginning of a period during which Egyptian influence was strong in Antioch. Libanius—by way of citing proof that Antioch

---

[1] See the preceding chapter, §2.

[2] For the numismatic evidence, see the preceding chapter, n. 23. On the reign of Antiochus I, see Bevan, *House of Seleucus* 1.127-170, and Bouché-Leclercq, *Hist. des Séleucides* 1.52-75.

[3] See Knaack, "Aratos," no. 6, *RE* 2 (1896) 391-399.

[4] On the reign of Antiochus II, see Bevan, *House of Seleucus* 1.171-180, and Bouché-Leclerq, *Hist. des Séleucides* 1.76-94.

was so lovely that the gods themselves were eager to dwell in it—
writes that when Ptolemy, Antiochus' father-in-law, visited the city
he was smitten with the beauty of the city's statue of Artemis[5]—presumably the one that according to tradition had been set up by the
Persian Queen Meroë[6]—and carried it off to Egypt.[7] The goddess,
however, visited Ptolemy's wife with disease, and warned her that the
statue must be returned to Antioch. This was done, and the goddess
was restored to her old temple.[8] Because of this episode, Libanius writes,
the goddess' name was changed and she was henceforth called Eleusinia.[9]

The second incident of this kind related by Libanius concerns "the
gods of Cyprus."[10] These deities, being anxious to migrate to Antioch,
"impelled the city to seek a response from the Pythian oracle, and
persuaded Apollo to declare that there was only one solution for the
city's difficulties," which was the migration of the gods of Cyprus to
Antioch. What the city's difficulties or adversities were, Libanius does
not mention. Antiochus sent to Cyprus envoys who succeeded in ef-
fecting the gods' journey. This they accomplished by pretending to
make exact replicas of the island gods. The replicas were so exact
that when completed they were easily substituted for the originals,
which were carried off to Syria. We may not be prepared to accept
this story literally; but if it is an invention or an exaggeration, it certainly points to the introduction at Antioch of Cypriote cults, as a
sequel to the migration to Antioch of a group of Cypriotes in the pre-
Macedonian period, which has already been described.[11] Libanius does
not mention the gods by name because his readers would have known

[5] *Or.* 11.108-109.
[6] Libanius *Or.* 11.59ff.; see above, Ch. 3, n. 13.
[7] A similar story is told of a statue of Serapis which Ptolemy III took from Seleucia Pieria; see Honigmann, "Seleukeia" 1187.
[8] Müller (*Antiq. Antioch.* 49) writes that Antiochus built a temple for the statue when it was returned. There appears to be no evidence to this effect (unless we are to assume that Antiochus would have taken this occasion to build a new temple), and on the contrary Libanius expressly states that the statue was replaced in its old shrine. Müller appears to have overlooked the tradition recorded by Libanius of the erection by Meroë of the temple and statue of Artemis.
[9] Hugi points out in his note on this passage in Libanius (*Der Antiochikos* p. 149) that the new name was designed to suggest the similarity between this incident and the episode of Persephone, who was carried off to Hades and then returned to Eleusis at the wish of Demeter. Artemis was called Eleusinia in Laconia and Sicily. One might detect in this episode a certain parallelism with the stories of how Ptolemy III took back to Egypt from his campaign in the Seleucid kingdom (245 B.C.) images of Egyptian gods which had been carried off by Cambyses and the Persians; see Grace H. Macurdy, *Hellenistic Queens* (Baltimore 1932) 89-90.
[10] *Or.* 11.110-113.
[11] See above, Ch. 3, n. 17.

who they were. It is significant that the type of Apollo seated on the omphalos which appears on the coins of the Syrian kings resembles the type that appears on coins of Nicocles, king of Cyprus, struck between 320 and 310 B.C., so that it would seem fairly clear that this type of Apollo at Antioch represents a borrowing from Cyprus, possibly in connection with the oracle of Apollo established at Daphne.[12]

3. SELEUCUS II CALLINICUS, 246-226 B.C.

The death of Antiochus II in 247/6 B.C. was followed by a struggle for the succession to the throne. Antiochus' first wife Laodice, who had been put away in favor of the Egyptian princess Berenice, hoped to crown her son, the future Seleucus II, while Berenice hoped to secure the succession for her small son. Laodice, who had gone to Ephesus when put away by her husband, had powerful supporters in Asia Minor, while Berenice, who had lived in Antioch, had her own circle of supporters there.

When Antiochus died, an Egyptian naval force was dispatched to uphold the claims of Berenice for her son (246 B.C.). The squadron occupied Seleucia Pieria without difficulty, the seaport perhaps having proclaimed its sympathies with the Egyptians. Thence the Egyptian force proceeded to Antioch, where it was given an elaborate reception described in an official report, preserved in a papyrus and perhaps written by Ptolemy III himself.[13] The Egyptians arriving probably

---

[12] See Reinach, *Cultes, mythes et religions*[2] 2.354, n. 1; Babelon, *Rois de Syrie* pp. xlvii-xlviii; Lacroix, "Copies de statues sur les monnaies des Séleucides" 169-175. On the establishment of the cult of Apollo at Daphne, see above, Ch. 4, §5. Antiochus I Soter was officially assimilated to Apollo Soter, and Antiochus II may have been assimilated to Apollo, who was one of the legendary founders of the Seleucid dynasty (see above, Ch. 4, no. 63); see Tondriau, "Souverains et souveraines Séleucides en divinités" 173-175. Lacroix is perhaps too severe in his criticism of the hypothesis of Babelon that a statue of Apollo, or a copy of it, was taken from Cyprus to Antioch. Babelon's suggestion is expressed with all the reserve proper to such a theory. Antioch took pride in the tradition (see above, Ch. 3, n. 17) that a party of Cypriotes had been among the early settlers of the site of Antioch in the pre-Macedonian days. This tradition, which appears to have escaped both Babelon and Lacroix, would seem to be quite sufficient to account for the borrowing of the coin type in the historical period.

[13] The celebrated Gourob papyrus has been published several times, notably by L. Mitteis and U. Wilcken, *Grundzüge und Chrestomathie der Papyruskunde* I. *Historische Teil*, pt. 2, *Chrest.* (Leipzig 1912) no. 1, and by Holleaux, "Le papyrus de Gourob." For a bibliography by L. Robert of the texts and commentaries on the papyrus, see Holleaux, *op.cit.* 309, n. 7. The history of this period is obscure in many respects and a number of problems connected with the papyrus and with the other sources, which are meager and unsatisfactory, have not yet been solved to the satisfaction of all scholars. A thorough exposition of the difficulties and of the various solutions will be found in Holleaux's study. The present summary follows what seems at present to be the most plausible reconstruction of the sequence of events, which in the main corre-

outside the Daphne gate, at the southern end of the city, were astonished by the size of the crowd that met them outside the gate, led
by satraps, generals, priests of the official cults, other high officials and
the youths of the gymnasium, all wearing crowns. Sacrifices were
offered on the road outside the gate, and the newcomers were greeted
with glad cries.[14] The succession thus seemed assured for Berenice's
son. However, Laodice contrived to have Berenice and her son murdered in Daphne, by two men named Eikadion and Kaineus, who are
described by a later writer as *principes Antiochiae*.[15] Berenice's devoted
women buried her body secretly, and by concealing one of themselves
in the queen's bed, they kept up a pretence that Berenice had only
been wounded. This they managed to maintain until Ptolemy III, to
whom word had been sent, came to Antioch a second time with an
army, not as a foreign invader, but to support the rightful heir to the
throne.[16]

Ptolemy proceeded to occupy all of Syria and to collect a considerable
amount of plunder. Many of the Greek cities, however, joined forces
to drive the Egyptians out, and Seleucus II succeeded in occupying
Antioch in 244 b.c., making the city his headquarters for his operations
against the Egyptians, which met with only a limited success.[17] Seleucia
Pieria remained in Egyptian possession until 219 b.c.[18]

---

sponds to that of W. W. Tarn in *CAH* 7.715ff. It should be noted that the papyrus as
preserved does not state that the Egyptian force reached Antioch by river, though
Holleaux restores it in this sense. On the navigability of the river, see Ch. 1, n. 12.

[14] The reception is described in the Gourob papyrus, col. 3, lines 16-25; see also col. 4,
lines 16-25. The description of the reception, including the sacrifices offered on the road
outside the gate, indicates that the Daphne gate was meant, for this would be the only
point at which there would be room outside a city gate for an elaborate reception
accompanied by a sacrifice. There was a landing available at the site of the agora,
within the city, but this would not be a dignified setting and probably would not
furnish enough room. On the part taken in the reception by the students of the gymnasium, see C. A. Forbes, *NEOI: A Contribution to the Study of Greek Associations*
(Middletown 1933; American Philological Association, Philological Monographs, 2) 11,
61, 63, and M. P. Nilsson, *Die hellenistische Schule* (Munich 1955) 73-74.

[15] Polyaenus 8.50; Justinus 27.1; Jerome, Commentary on Daniel 11.6 = *PL* 25.560;
Valerius Maximus 9.10 ext. 1, 9.14 ext. 1; Pliny *Nat. hist.* 7.53.

[16] Polyaenus and Justinus, *loc.cit.*

[17] Justinus 27.2. The coins known to Newell (*West. Sel. Mints* 121) indicate that the
mint of Antioch did not issue coins between 246 and 244 b.c. D. B. Waagé ("Coins," 7)
suggests that a coin of this period found in the excavations, which was previously
assigned to the mint of Apamea (Newell, *West. Sel. Mints*, p. 163, no. 1145) may actually have been struck at Antioch; but this coin seems so clearly connected with other
issues of Apamea (*West. Sel. Mints* 162-163) that at least in the absence of further evidence its attribution to Antioch does not seem certain. The evidence of provenance
has to be taken into account, but in this case it does not seem by itself conclusive. In
the same way Mrs. Waagé (*loc.cit.*) suggests that the mint of Antioch, between 244
and 232 b.c., may be the source of a large series of bronze coins which was formerly

Since the eastern parts of the Seleucid domains had already been lost, Seleucus II now found himself forced to abandon Asia Minor, which, after he had made it over to his younger brother Antiochus Hierax (236 B.C.), finally became a part of the Attalid kingdom. That Antioch, as a result of these developments, now began to take on added importance in the Seleucid realm, is indicated by the fact that Seleucus Callinicus added a new quarter to the city. This quarter, located on the island that lay in the Orontes abreast of the original settlement of Seleucus Nicator, was evidently designed to accommodate the increase in the population that followed upon Antioch's growth in military and political importance.[19] We are told that the island was surrounded by a wall, and bridges must have been built; but there is no indication of what public buildings may have been built there.

About 228 B.C. Seleucus II made an attempt to recover Parthia, which had broken away from the Seleucid Empire in the time of Antiochus II.[20] About 227 B.C., however, a plot was made by Stratonice, the daughter of Antiochus I and sister of Antiochus II. Divorced by Demetrius II of Macedonia, she was living in Antioch. Stratonice schemed with her nephew Antiochus Hierax, the younger brother of Seleucus II, to overthrow Seleucus and seize the whole kingdom. For this purpose, Stratonice raised a rebellion in Antioch and Antiochus invaded Mesopotamia in order to harass Seleucus in Parthia. Seleucus withdrew from Parthia and forced Antiochus out of Mesopotamia; he then recovered Antioch and executed Stratonice, who had fled to Seleucia Pieria.[21]

The migrations of gods to Antioch in the reign of Antiochus II, as recorded by Libanius, were followed, according to the same author, by the migration of Isis to the city.[22] This migration took place peacefully, with Seleucus, warned in a dream, sending for the deity from

---

attributed to the mint of Apamea (Newell, *West. Sel. Mints*, 166-170). Here again the connection of the coins with other issues of Apamea suggests that, in the absence of further evidence, the change in attribution may not be entirely certain.

[18] Polybius 5.58.

[19] Strabo (16.2.5, p. 750 C) says that Seleucus Callinicus was the founder of the island quarter, while Libanius (*Or.* 11.119) declares that it was Antiochus the Great who added this quarter to the city. This apparently means that Antiochus finished the work inaugurated by Seleucus; if the successor completed an undertaking which had been begun by his predecessor, each could have been given the title of "founder" of the quarter. See Downey, "Seleucid Chronology" 109, and "Strabo on Antioch" 85-91.

[20] Debevoise, *Hist. of Parthia* 9ff.

[21] Agatharcides in Joseph. *Contra Apion.* 1.206 = *FHG* III p. 196, fr. 19. See Bouché-Leclerq, *Hist. des Séleucides* 109-118; Tarn in *CAH* 7.722; Bevan, *House of Seleucus* 1.289, with n. 4; Debevoise, *Hist. of Parthia* 13.

[22] *Or.* 11.114.

Memphis, and the king of Egypt making a ready gift of the goddess. Libanius' story, however, has been regarded as suspect, and there is no other evidence for the introduction of Egyptian cults at Antioch at such an early period as this.[23]

4. ANTIOCHUS III, THE GREAT, 223-187 B.C.

Seleucus II Callinicus' son, Seleucus III Soter, reigned for only a few years (226-223 B.C.), during which he seems to have made no noteworthy contribution to Antioch, and nothing of the city's history is known during this period. He was succeeded by his younger brother Antiochus III, the second son of Seleucus II. It fell to Antiochus III to occupy the throne during the period when friction between Rome and the Seleucid Empire came to a head.[24] Antiochus declared his intentions by giving protection to the arch-enemy of Rome, Hannibal, who visited Antioch in the summer of 195 B.C. to try to stir up war against the Romans.[25] In the inevitable clash, the new power in the West was victorious (192-189 B.C.). It was as a result of his defeat that Antiochus III completed the construction of the new quarter of the city on the island which had been founded by his father Seleucus II Callinicus (246-226 B.C.). The traditions which attach the names of both Seleucus II Callinicus and Antiochus II to this new part of the city apparently mean that the quarter was established by Seleucus II and completed by Antiochus III.

As settlers for the new quarter, Libanius says,[26] Antiochus III "brought in Hellenic stock, Aetolians and Cretans and Euboeans." Libanius, of course, was trying here (as elsewhere) to supply the noblest possible ancestry for his fellow citizens. His words seem designed to imply that Antiochus, wishing to strengthen the noble stock of his city, sent to Greece for colonists. In reality the Greek settlers must have been veterans of Antiochus' campaigns in his war with Rome

[23] See P. Roussel, "Décret des Péliganes de Laodicée-sur-mer," *Syria* 23 (1942-1943) 27. Isis seems to appear for the first time on coins of Antioch in the reign of Antiochus IV, ca. 168 B.C. and later: see D. B. Waagé, "Coins" p. 11, no. 12. In the Roman period Isis was popular at Antioch and important mosaics depicting her cult have been found there; see D. Levi, "The Allegories of the Months in Classical Art," *Art Bulletin* 23 (1941) 258-259, 270-271; idem, *Antioch Mosaic Pavements* 1.49-50, 163-166.
[24] On the reign of Antiochus III, see Bevan, *House of Seleucus* 1.300-2.114; Bouché-Leclerq, *Hist. des Séleucides* 1.123-226.
[25] Livy 33.49. Antiochus was in Asia Minor when Hannibal reached Antioch and the king's son received the visitor and entertained him at the games at Daphne (see below). Hannibal then journeyed to Ephesus to meet the king. On Hannibal's visit to Antioch, see M. Holleaux, *Études d'épigraphie et d'histoire grecques* 5 (Paris 1957) 181-183.
[26] *Or.* 11.119.

(192-189 B.C.), and others of his adherents in Greece, who after the Roman victory chose to establish themselves in exile in Antioch in preference to remaining in their homeland to suffer retaliations from the Romans.[27] These settlers are the last Greek immigrants into Syria of whom we hear; after the defeat of Antiochus III at Magnesia (190 B.C.) and the treaty of Apamea (188 B.C.), the Seleucid Empire was cut off from the Aegean, and no more Greek colonists seem to have gone to Syria.[28] One of the most famous of the relatively few inscriptions found at Antioch preserves a letter of Antiochus III, dated 12 October 189 B.C., on the appointment, as chief priest to Apollo and Artemis at Daphne and to the other sanctuaries at Daphne, of a retired officer, no longer in good health, who had served under Seleucus III.[29] The office was an important one since the sanctuaries at Daphne were large and wealthy, requiring capable financial administration, and since they attracted throngs of visitors from all over the ancient world, so that there would on occasion have been serious problems in the maintenance of order if disputes arose affecting patriotic or religious sentiments.[30] Antiochus III must have had to supply many other similar appointments for his veterans.[31]

As to the development of the island we have only meager information. Specifically, Antiochus III is said to have provided it with a wall, which suggests that the work of development had not been completed by Seleucus II Callinicus. It is to be presumed that the two kings were responsible for the regular plan of the streets on the island (a continuation of the plan of the older part of the city on the mainland) which Libanius describes in the fourth century after Christ.[32]

Not only did Antiochus complete the new quarter on the island, but (Libanius writes) he used the booty of his early successes to adorn the

[27] See Müller, *Antiq. Antioch.* 51, and Mommsen, *Röm. Gesch.*[4] 5 (Berlin 1894) 456. A different view, which seems less plausible to the present writer, is taken by H. Dessau, *Gesch. der röm. Kaiserzeit* 2, pt. 2 (Berlin 1930) 659-660, who believes that the Aetolians, Cretans, and Euboeans, who were settled in Antioch were veterans of Antiochus' war with Ptolemy Philopator (217 B.C.). Dessau's view seems to be weakened by the circumstance that there would have been less reason for Antiochus to provide refuge for his veterans after the Egyptian war than after the Roman war; after the Egyptian war the mercenaries could have returned to their homes, while they might have been unable or unwilling to do so after the war with Rome.

[28] See Jones, *Cities of the East. Rom. Prov.* 248; idem, *Greek City* 16.

[29] Waddington no. 2713a = *OGIS* no. 244 = Welles, *Royal Correspondence* no. 44, cf. pp. xlviii-xlix.

[30] See Welles' commentary on the inscription, *Royal Correspondence* pp. 182-183.

[31] See further in the chapter on the organization and administration of the city in the Hellenistic period, below, §8. On Antiochus III as the reorganizer of the dynastic cult in the Seleucid Empire, see M. Rostovtzeff in *JHS* 55 (1935) 59 n. 10.

[32] See below, Ch. 12, §2.

city.[33] What these adornments were, we do not know; but it is likely that the king did everything possible for the beautification of the city that had now become the principal metropolis of the Seleucid realm. From the account of Hannibal's visit to Antioch in the summer of 195 B.C., we learn of games celebrated at Daphne by the king's son, the future Antiochus IV.[34] An increase in the prosperity of the city during the reign of Antiochus III may be indicated by the fact that the coins of this monarch found in the excavations were by far more numerous than those of any other Seleucid king.[35]

It is in the reign of Antiochus that we have our earliest reference to a library in Antioch. The king appointed Euphorion of Chalcis in Euboea, a distinguished poet, to be librarian of the "public library" of the city.[36] As to the nature of the library itself, or the building in which it was housed, we have no evidence. It is to be presumed, however, that a city such as Antioch would have possessed a library at an early period in its history. Hegesianax, a poet, historian, and grammarian, was one of the king's "Friends" (φίλοι), and Apollophanes of Antioch, a Stoic philosopher, probably was active at this time.[37]

5. Seleucus IV Philopator, 187-175 B.C.

The defeat of Antiochus III by the Romans and Eumenes of Pergamum at the battle of Magnesia (190 B.C.), and the terms of the treaty of peace of Apamea (188 B.C.), according to which the Seleucid Empire lost its military power and had to assume the burden of heavy tribute to the Romans, mark a turning point in the history of the Seleucid dynasty and thus also of the history of Antioch.[38]

[33] Libanius *Or.* 11.121.

[34] Livy 33.49. Whether these games were periodic or occasional is not known. The most famous games held at Antioch in the Seleucid period of which we hear are those celebrated by Antiochus IV ca. 167 B.C., described below.

[35] D. B. Waagé, "Coins," chart on p. 173.

[36] Suidas *s.v.* Εὐφορίων; see Müller, *Antiq. Antioch.* 107. According to Suidas, some writers stated that Euphorion was buried in Antioch, while others gave his place of burial as Apamea. On the life and works of Euphorion, see F. Skutsch, "Euphorion," no. 4, *RE* 6.1174-1190, and (with more recent information) E. A. Barber, "Euphorion," no. 2, *OCD* 346. On ancient libraries, see C. Callmer, "Die antiken Bibliotheken," *Opuscula Archeologica* 3 (1944) 145-193.

[37] See Stähelin and F. Jacoby, "Hegesianax," no. 1, *RE* 7.2602-2606; von Arnim, "Apollophanes," no. 13, *RE* 2.165; E. Zeller, *Die Philosophie der Griechen,*[5] ed. by E. Wellmann (Leipzig 1920-1923) 3, pt. 1, p. 36, n. 2. Apollophanes' date is indicated by the fact that he was a pupil of Ariston of Chios, who flourished ca. 250 B.C.

[38] The consequences of the defeat of Antiochus III have been well set forth by Jansen, "Politik Antiochos' des IV" 17ff., 28ff.

Antiochus the Great's son, the future Seleucus IV Philopator, was
made co-ruler with his father in the spring of 188 B.C., and succeeded
him in 187 B.C., reigning until 175 B.C.[39] During his brief career he was
preoccupied with the reorganization of the reduced territory that he
had inherited and with the strengthening of his financial resources,
for prudence was necessary if the indemnity imposed on his father by
Rome was to be met.[40] Thus we find, as we should expect, no major
work at Antioch recorded in the reign of this king. Had he lived
longer (he was assassinated at the age of about forty-two, after a reign
of about twelve years) he might well have been able to carry on his
father's work in the enlargement and beautification of the capital; but
the continuance of this work was reserved for his brother Antiochus IV,
who succeeded him. The Epicurean philosopher Philonides may have
been active in Antioch toward the end of the reign of Seleucus IV.[41]

6. ANTIOCHUS IV EPIPHANES, 175-163 B.C.

The reign of Antiochus Epiphanes, one of the most remarkable
members of the dynasty, marks an epoch in the history of Antioch.[42]
Possessed of a dazzlingly brilliant mind, the king seems at times to have
behaved as though he were insane; certainly his humor was sometimes
remarkable. More active as a builder than any of his predecessors save
perhaps Seleucus I Nicator (at least so far as our sources tell us),
Antiochus IV brought his capital to a point of luxury and magnificence

[39] On the reign of Seleucus IV, see Bevan, *House of Seleucus* 2.120-125; Bouché-
Leclerq, *Hist. des Séleucides* 1.227-243.

[40] Evidence of Seleucus' efforts to reestablish public credit is given by his increasing
the weight of his bronze currency; see A. R. Bellinger, "The Bronze Standards of
Antiochus III, Seleucus IV, and Antiochus IV," *Num. Rev.* 2, no. 2 (Oct. 1944) 5-6.

[41] See R. Philippson, "Philonides," no. 5, *RE* 20 (1941) 65-66 and W. Crönert, "Die
Epikureer in Syrien," *Jahreshefte oesterr. Archäol. Inst.* 10 (1907) 145ff.

[42] On the reign of Antiochus IV, see Bevan, *House of Seleucus* 2.126-177, and Bouché-
Leclerq, *Hist. des Séleucides* 1.244-306. On the circumstances of his accession, see M.
Holleaux, "Un prétendu décret d'Antioche sur l'Oronte," *REG* 13 (1900) 258-280,
reprinted with additions by L. Robert in Holleaux, *Etudes d'épigraphie et d'histoire
grecques* 2 (Paris 1938) 127-147. The inscription (Fränkel, *Inschr. v. Pergamon* no.
160 B = Michel, *Recueil* no. 550), which Holleaux republishes and discusses, is a
fragmentary decree in honor of King Eumenes of Pergamum and of members of his
family who had assisted Antiochus to obtain the throne after the assassination of
Seleucus IV had left the succession to be disputed between Demetrius, the infant son
of Seleucus IV, and Antiochus, the dead king's brother. This text, when it was discovered at Pergamum, was thought by its original editor, Fränkel, and by other
scholars, to be a decree of the senate and people of Antioch. If this interpretation were
correct, this text would be the only decree of Antioch thus far recovered. Holleaux
plausibly argues, however, that the decree was issued by Athens, and his interpretation
is accepted by Bevan (*House of Seleucus* 2.151, n. 1) and by Dittenberger, who places
the inscription among the decrees of Athens (*OGIS* no. 428).

that placed it among the foremost cities of antiquity, even though at this time the Seleucid power was in reality declining, as the ultimate result of the defeat of Antiochus the Great by the Romans.

Antiochus IV's activities at his capital city are to be viewed against the background of the political situation of the Seleucid Empire as he found it on his accession. Antiochus tried to redeem the diminution of the Seleucid territory, the loss of military power, and the economic dependence on Rome, by a vigorous effort to unify his people by political, religious, and cultural means.[43] This he sought to accomplish by strengthening the Hellenic religion and the ruler cult, by eliminating the separatist tendencies promoted by the Jewish religion, and by confiscating the property of temples that could be used (as in the case of the temple at Jerusalem) to finance opposition or revolt.[44] Antiochus regarded the ruler cult more seriously than any of his predecessors on account of its importance for his political program, and he spent much energy and treasure on the enhancement of the cult of Zeus Olympius, with whom he identified himself;[45] his title Epiphanes, though broad in meaning, ranging from "distinguished" to "god showing himself," could have been utilized in impressive fashion for religious purposes.[46] It is in the light of these factors that we must view Antiochus' enlargement and adornment of his capital, an undertaking which would well serve to enhance the prestige of his dynasty and to win him additional support among the people by whom he was immediately surrounded, by solidifying the various elements within the city itself.[47] It may be indicative of this effort that under Antiochus IV the coins minted at

[43] On the evidence of the coins for economic recovery under Antiochus IV, see *Dura Final Rep.* 6: Bellinger, *The Coins*, p. 199.

[44] The worship of Zeus, as a unifying factor, was brought to bear in Antiochus' efforts to integrate the Jews into his state, when the Temple at Jerusalem was converted into a shrine of Olympian Zeus (2 Macc. 6.2). On Antiochus' political and religious policy with respect to the Jews, see further below.

[45] See the original study of Antiochus' identification with Zeus Olympius, by E. R. Bevan, "A Note on Antiochos Epiphanes," *JHS* 20 (1900) 26-30, and the more complete information of Tondriau, "Souverains et souveraines Séleucides en divinités," 175-176; and cf. Tarn-Griffith, *Hellenistic Civilization*³ 49ff. and Rostovtzeff, "Le Gad de Doura" 293. On Zeus on the coins of Antiochus, see Müller, *Antiq. Antioch.* 63; *BMC Seleucid Kings of Syria* p. 42, nos. 86-87; Newell, *Seleucid Mint of Antioch* p. 28; Lacroix, "Copies de statues sur les monnaies des Séleucides" 164-165. One consequence of the added importance given to the cult of Zeus was the diminution of the cult of Apollo: Newell, *Seleucid Mint of Antioch* p. 37. It is possible that Antiochus was also identified officially with Apollo, Dionysus, and Herakles (Tondriau *loc.cit.*).

[46] See A. D. Nock, "Notes on Ruler-Cult, III: Ptolemy Epiphanes," *JHS* 48 (1928) 38-41; Newell, *Seleucid Mint of Antioch* p. 23.

[47] On Antiochus' policy of improving urban life as a means of amalgamating and consolidating the diverse elements in his realm, see Rostovtzeff, *Soc. Econ. Hist. Hellenistic World* 64.

Antioch bear for the first time both the name of the city and that of the king.[48]

This "second founder" of Antioch had as a youth been a hostage in Rome, and later had lived in Athens, so that he was well acquainted with the art and culture of those two cities. When he became king, he took pleasure in introducing Roman art and customs (including gladiatorial shows) into his domains.[49] He loved pageantry and display. His character and conduct were paradoxical and erratic and he was sometimes called "Antiochus the Mad";[50] yet, as Livy writes,[51] "in two great and important respects his soul was truly royal—in his benefactions to cities and in the honors paid to the gods." The lavishness of his outlay has become almost proverbial through the magnificence of the games that he celebrated at Daphne ca. 167 B.C.; the awestricken accounts of the wealth displayed show the impression which the spectacle must have made on contemporaries.[52] The procession included eight hundred ephebes wearing gold crowns, innumerable sacred images,[53] six hundred royal pages bearing gold vessels, two

[48] See Babelon, *Rois de Syrie* pp. 79-81, nos. 624-644; Newell, *Seleucid Mint of Antioch* p. 24; Dieudonné, "Monnaies grecques de Syrie" 12.

[49] Polybius (26.1) describes Antiochus as playing at the forms of Roman government. This passage is not to be taken literally, as it has been by some scholars. Polybius expressly cites the king's conduct in this respect as an example of his reputed madness and says that his behavior puzzled people. For a detailed discussion of the passage and its interpretation, see below, §8.

[50] The classic description of the king's character is found in the two fragments of the twenty-sixth book of Polybius, preserved in Athenaeus 5.193 d, 10.439 a. See also Livy 41.20, who tells how the gladiatorial shows that Antiochus introduced at Antioch, importing gladiators from Rome at great expense, were at first not well received by the population, though they eventually became popular (see L. Robert, *Les gladiateurs dans l'Orient grec* [Paris 1940] 263-264). Athenaeus (2.45 c) quotes from Heliodorus (frag. 6, *FHG* 4.425) a tale of the king mixing wine with the water in a well at Antioch.

[51] 41.20.5, transl. of E. T. Sage in the Loeb Classical Library.

[52] Athenaeus (5.194, 10.439) preserves the account of Polybius (30.25-27); cf. Diodorus 31, frag. 16.2 (*Excerpta de virtutibus et vitiis*, pt. 1, §281, pp. 282-283 ed. Büttner-Wobst), and see Müller, *Antiq. Antioch.* 64-65 and M. P. Nilsson, *Die hellenistische Schule* (Munich 1955) 79. On the literary technique of the description of the procession, see P. Friedländer, *Johannes von Gaza und Paulus Silentiarius* (Berlin 1912) 42-43. Newell has suggested (*Seleucid Mint at Antioch* pp. 28ff.) that certain coins of Antiochus bearing a head of Zeus were struck in commemoration of the games at Daphne. It is not clear whether the lost work of Protagorides of Cyzicus, Περὶ τῶν ἐν Δάφνῃ πανηγύρεων (Athenaeus 4.150 c, 176 a, 183 f = *FHG* 4.484) was concerned with the special games of Antiochus IV, or described all the festivals celebrated at Daphne. On this work see Christ-Schmid Stählin, *Gesch. d. gr. Lit.*[6] 2, pt. 1, p. 299, and Mouterde, "Pierides Musae" 8.

[53] It is evident from the description of the procession that it was designed to include all the gods; K. Ziegler ("Pantheion," *RE* 18 [1949] 713-714) points out the significance of the procession in this respect. There must, as Ziegler observes, have been a Pantheon at Antioch dating from early Seleucid times; we know of the restoration of a Pantheon there by Julius Caesar (see below, Ch. 7, §2). On the ephebes, see C. A. Forbes, *NEOI:*

hundred women sprinkling scented oils from gold vessels, and countless other displays of luxury. These games were unusually magnificent
because the Seleucid king seems to have wished, in presenting them,
to offset the impression produced by the victory of Aemilius Paullus
over the Macedonians at the battle of Pydna (168 B.C.),[54] following
which the Roman general had presented magnificent games.[55] However, even when allowance is made for the additional outlay planned
for a special occasion, Antiochus IV must have been accustomed to
indulge in public display on a remarkable scale, and we must not be
misled, by the celebrated account of the games of ca. 167 B.C., into
thinking that these were the only noteworthy games that Antiochus
produced.[56] The funds that made these spectacles possible came from
the booty Antiochus took from his enemies and from the temples he
plundered.[57] Antiochus IV's reign must have given a notable impulse
to the artistic activities of Antioch, and the territories it influenced,
both because the king's acquisitive habits doubtless brought many art
treasures to his capital and because he himself took a lively interest in
the work of the artists of Antioch and must have given them splendid
commissions. In particular, the comments on the king's interests in
these matters show us that there already existed at this period the tradition of craftsmanship in gold and silver work for which Antioch was
famous in later times.[58] The wealth of Antiochus' court is suggested

---

A Contribution to the Study of Greek Associations (Middletown 1933; American
Philological Association, Philological Monographs, 2) 67.

[54] This is the motivation of the spectacle according to Polybius' account; on this
"retort" of Antiochus "to the Roman triumphs over the humiliated Hellenistic world,"
see Rostovtzeff, *Soc. Econ. Hist. Hellenistic World,* 699.

[55] Described by Livy 45.32-33.

[56] A decree in honor of Eumenes of Pergamum dated 175 or 174 B.C., apparently
passed by the city of Athens, provides that the honors bestowed on the Pergamene king
shall be published at the festivals of Athens and of Pergamum and "in those which
King Antiochus will celebrate ([θ]ήσει) at Daphne" (*Inschr. v. Perg.* no. 160 B, line 50,
with other editions and studies cited above, n. 42). There seems to be no specific record
of a national festival of Antioch celebrated regularly by games at this period, but it is
difficult to believe that a city like Antioch can have been without such a festival. The
so-called Olympic games of Antioch were apparently not instituted until the Roman
period, though it is possible that our sources here (as elsewhere) describe as an innovation of the Romans what was really only a reorganization of a Hellenistic institution
(see below, Ch. 8, n. 31). On the history of the stadium at Daphne, see below, n. 89.

[57] Polybius 30.26.9 *apud* Athen. 5.195 f.

[58] "He would sometimes slip out of the palace without the knowledge of his attendants, and would appear wandering about in some quarter of the city with one or two
companions; usually he was found near the shops of the silversmiths and goldsmiths
talking glibly, and airing his views on art before the workmen engaged in making
reliefs [or molders: τορευτάς] as well as before other artisans" Athen. 5.193 d (transl. of
C. B. Gulick in the Loeb Classical Library) quoting Polyb. 26.1.2. Cf. Bikerman, *Inst.
des Séleucides* 223, n. 3.

by the statement that the secretary (*epistolographos*) in charge of his chancery, Dionysius, was represented in the procession at the games of ca. 167 B.C. by one thousand slaves carrying silver vessels none of which weighed less than a thousand drachmas (about eleven and a half pounds).[59]

Antiochus IV's gifts to cities outside his realm—Megalopolis in Arcadia, Tegea, Cyzicus, Rhodes, Athens, Delos—are described as magnificent;[60] and his benefactions to his own capital must have been even more splendid.[61] Nevertheless he left many of his undertakings unfinished,[62] either because they were too ambitious for even his energy and copious resources, or because his reign was relatively brief (he came to the throne at about forty, in 175 B.C., and died in 163, at about fifty-two).

His greatest benefaction to Antioch was the foundation of a new quarter, called Epiphania, which brought the city to what was to be, substantially, its final physical form.[63] This quarter lay on the slope of Mount Silpius, adjacent to the original settlement of Seleucus Nicator which stood on the level ground along the river.[64] Evidently the new quarter was needed in order to provide for an increase in the population of the city. When such expansion might have begun, we do not know; possibly the city had begun to grow soon after the time of Seleucus I. Seleucus II Callinicus (246-226 B.C.) and Antiochus III, the Great (223-187 B.C.) had founded a new quarter (that on the island)

[59] Polybius 30.25.16 *apud* Athen. 5.195 b; cf. Rostovtzeff, *Soc. Econ. Hist. Hellenistic World* 518. On the office of *epistolographos* in Syria, see Welles, *Royal Correspondence* p. xxxviii.

[60] Livy 41.20.6-9.

[61] As Müller points out, *Antiq. Antioch.* 53.

[62] Livy 41.20.9.

[63] Strabo 16.2.4, p. 750 C. On the interpretation of the passage, see Downey, "Strabo on Antioch" 85-95. U. Köhler, "Zwei Inschriften aus der Zeit Antiochos' IV. Epiphanes," *Sitzungsberichte der k. Preussischen Akademie der Wissenschaft zu Berlin* 1900, 1100-1106, published a fragmentary Greek inscription in Berlin which he believed came from Antioch, although the evidence connected with its acquisition indicated that it has been found at Babylon. The text mentions χαριστήρια, which Köhler took to be games instituted by the people of Antioch in gratitude for the foundation of Epiphania by Antiochus Epiphanes. The inscription seems to allude to a new city era which, according to Köhler's hypothesis, would be dated from the foundation of Epiphania, but the two references to this era in the inscription present an apparently insoluble puzzle, and there is no other testimony for the existence of such an era. B. Haussoullier, *Revue de philologie* N.S. 24 (1901) 40-42, with better evidence than Köhler had for the place of discovery of the stone, and with improved readings of the text, shows that the stone came from the region of Babylon, and does not refer to affairs in Antioch. R. Philippson, "Philonides," no. 5, *RE* 20 (1941) 67 n., adopts Köhler's interpretation.

[64] The location is specified by Malalas 205.14-22, 233.23ff. The excavations of houses on the slope of the mountain have revealed thick Hellenistic retaining walls; see Doro Levi, *Antioch Mosaic Pavements* 34, 36, 40, 45.

which was peopled at least in part with Aetolians, Cretans, and Euboeans, who were veterans of Antiochus the Great's wars with Rome
(192-189 B.C.).[65] The construction of Epiphania suggests either that the
island had not proved sufficient to accommodate the settlers brought
in by Antiochus the Great, or that there had been a further influx since
his time. Possibly the growth of Roman power in the East had impelled
some Greeks to leave the lands now under Roman influence and seek
out a city still free from the new power.

There is, unfortunately, not a great deal of literary evidence for the
plan of Epiphania and its principal buildings. Malalas says only that
Antiochus IV built a bouleuterion and "various temples" in his new
quarter.[66] From Livy we know that the king also built, but may not
have finished, a magnificent temple to Jupiter Capitolinus,[67] evidently an
imitation of the one in Rome; not only did it have a ceiling paneled
with gold, but its walls were covered with gilt plates. This temple was
of special importance for Antiochus because in the official ruler cult
he identified himself with Zeus Olympius.[68] Our sources do not happen
to specify the location of this temple, but it seems likely that it stood
in the area which Antiochus IV developed as his new quarter.[69] The
temple, left unfinished, appears to have been completed by Tiberius.[70]

A new agora seems to have been one of the features of Epiphania.
Its existence is indicated by the notice in Malalas of Antiochus IV's
construction of a bouleuterion and by his report of a fire in the reign
of Tiberius which destroyed "the greater part of the agora and the
bouleuterion and the shrine of the Muses."[71] If we are to assume that
the bouleuterion is the same (and we have no evidence for more
than one bouleuterion at Antioch until the fourth century after Christ),
then it would appear that Antiochus, in planning his new quarter,

[65] See above, §4.
[66] 205.14-19, 234.2-3. Libanius (*Or.* 11.125) mentions that a bouleuterion was built by a Seleucid king whom he does not happen to name.
[67] Livy 41.20.9.
[68] See above n. 45.
[69] In the reign of Tiberius, a building program included the completion or improvement of Epiphania and Malalas records the "construction" by Tiberius of a temple to
Jupiter Capitolinus (see below, Ch. 8, §2). In the chronicler's usage, this might actually
mean that Tiberius rebuilt or renovated an existing building (see above, Ch. 2, §4);
Malalas did not, it will be recalled, mention the founding of Antiochus IV's temple to
Jupiter, of which we know only from Livy. Thus it seems quite likely that Antiochus'
great temple stood in his new quarter.
[70] See the preceding note, and cf. A. D. Nock, "The Roman Army and the Roman
Religious Year," *HTR* 45 (1952) 210, n. 85, who is perhaps unduly cautious on the
point. On Tiberius' work, see below, Ch. 8, §2.
[71] Malalas 205.14-19, 234.2-3, 235.17ff. On the fire, see below, Ch. 8, §3.

took the occasion to provide the city with a new agora, which would of course have been the natural location for a bouleuterion if one were to be built at this time. We know of at least two agoras at Antioch. In addition to that mentioned in the account of the fire under Tiberius, there was a "tetragonal agora" which was burned in the course of disorders in A.D. 69 or 70; here stood the *grammatophylakion* or archives.[72] It seems clear that an agora would only be called "tetragonal" in order to distinguish it from another agora (or other agoras) of another shape (e.g. of the "horseshoe" type). Whether the "tetragonal" agora and that in Epiphania were the same, we cannot tell; neither is there any evidence whether the "tetragonal agora" could have been that of Seleucus' original settlement along the river. It is of importance, however, to find that Antiochus IV's plans for the expansion of the city should have included the construction of a new agora. The original agora of Seleucus I probably lay close to the river, which would have been an important means of transportation when the city was built.[73] In any case, a new agora might well have been needed by the time of Antiochus IV, for it might have been difficult for an agora to be expanded in keeping with the marked growth of the city. In addition, the foundation of Epiphania may have been either the cause or the result of a shift in the center of commercial and municipal activity at Antioch, and the establishment of a new agora would have been a natural concomitant of such a shift. Antioch would thus have come to resemble Miletus, Pergamum, and the Peiraeus in possessing two agoras.[74] Possibly when there were two agoras at Antioch, they served different purposes, in keeping with Aristotle's recommendation that a city should have two agoras, located in different places, one a "free agora," kept clear of all merchandise and devoted to political and educational activities, the other an "agora for merchandise" devoted to commercial activity and located in the most convenient position for the purpose.[75] If such a division of functions were carried out in Antioch, the new agora of Epiphanes, with the bouleuterion, would have been the "free agora," while the old

---

[72] Josephus *Bell.* 7.55, 60-61; on the burning of this agora, see below, Ch. 9, §1.

[73] On the original agora, see above, Ch. 4, §3.

[74] On the agoras of Miletus and Pergamum, see Gerkan, *Griech. Städteanlagen* 98-99, and Wycherley, *How the Greeks Built Cities* 69-73, 78-80. The two agoras at the Peiraeus are mentioned by Pausanias 1.2.3; one lay near the harbor, the other further inland. Roman towns often had several forums, some of which were designed for special purposes: K. Lehmann-Hartleben, "Städtebau," *RE* 3A (1929) 2063, 2115.

[75] *Politics* 7.9.1-3, p. 1331 a-b; see Gerkan, *Griech. Städteanlagen* 103-104, and Wycherley, *How the Greeks Built Cities* 67.

market place of Seleucus would have served as the agora for merchandise.

Whether Antiochus IV built a wall about his new quarter became a
matter of dispute in antiquity. Strabo indicates that he did, while
Malalas declares that he did not.[76] It might be thought that the king
would not have added a new quarter to the city, containing magnificent
public buildings, without taking the elementary precaution of enclosing it within a wall. Nevertheless, Antiochus IV's conduct was so
erratic and his outlay was so lavish that it seems possible that he may
have begun the work on his new quarter with the buildings rather
than with the wall, intending to construct the wall (which would
have been expensive, and much less interesting than the new buildings) at a later time; and then his money may have been exhausted,
or he may have died before the wall could be built, and his successors
may have had no funds with which to finish the work. It must be
remembered that Sparta and Elis remained unwalled in classical
times, and that Palmyra had no wall until the time of Odenath and
Zenobia, in the middle of the third century after Christ.[77] However,
too much weight cannot be placed on the testimony of Malalas, for
though the chronicler's evidence suggests that Antiochus did not build
a wall about his new quarter, we must bear in mind that Malalas'
sources for the history of Antioch under the Romans were more
extensive than his sources for the Seleucid period, and that his sources
for the Roman period might well have shown a tendency to give credit
to the Romans for work which was in reality done by the Seleucids.[78]

For at least some of his construction projects at Antioch, Antiochus
IV employed the Roman architect Cossutius, a man "of great skill and
scientific attainments" (Vitruvius writes) who was in charge of the
Syrian king's work on the temple of Olympian Zeus at Athens, which
had been begun by Pisistratus but was left unfinished at the time of
his death.[79] The Seleucid ruler undertook to complete the great temple
but was unable to do so (presumably because he died before the work

[76] Strabo 16.2.4, p. 750 C; Malalas 205.21, 233.22. The question is discussed in detail
by Downey, "Strabo on Antioch" 91-93.
[77] See C. Watzinger, "Palmyra," *RE* 18 (1949) 270.
[78] Malalas states that Tiberius was the first to build a wall about Epiphania, and
while this might be true, it might also mean only that Tiberius repaired, strengthened,
or extended an existing wall; see below, Ch. 8, §2.
[79] Vitruvius 7 *praef.* 15. On Cossutius' career, see J. M. C. Toynbee, "Some Notes on
Artists in the Roman World," *Latomus* 8 (1949) 310, reprinted in the volume by the
same author, bearing the same title (Brussels 1951), p. 9 (*Collection Latomus*, vol. 6).
A Roman citizen by birth, he might have been of Campano-Greek stock.

could be finished).[80] At Antioch, Cossutius' name has been found scratched twice in the cement wall of the channel of an aqueduct running along the slope of the mountain above the city, which is, on the basis of archaeological evidence, dated by the excavators in the second century B.C.[81] Since the aqueduct is independently dated in this period, the coincidence of the rather unusual name makes it seem certain that the Roman architect who was employed by Antiochus IV at Athens was also active at Antioch, and it is tempting to suppose that, having been in charge of the work on the temple of Olympian Zeus at Athens, he also designed the temple of Jupiter Capitolinus at Antioch, if not other of Antiochus' buildings there as well. The aqueduct in which Cossutius' name is inscribed was designed to tap the lively winter torrent Onopnictes ("Donkey-drowner") which flows down from the mountain through the city and into the Orontes; the water diverted by the aqueduct during the rainy season would have been brought to cisterns along the terraced slope of the mountain. Evidently this channel was constructed during the creation of Epiphania. It happens to be the earliest dated portion of the water system of Antioch which has thus far been found, though it seems difficult to believe that the springs of Daphne had not been utilized before this time to bring water to the city.

One of Antiochus IV's monuments, the rock-hewn bust traditionally called the Charonion (Fig. 16), is still visible on the mountain-side above the city.[82] During his reign, Antioch was visited by a plague

[80] Livy 41.20.8; Vitruv. loc.cit.; Pausanias 1.18.6. The work was finished by Hadrian. Cf. P. Graindor, Athènes sous Hadrien (Cairo 1934) 218-225.

[81] Antioch-on-the-Orontes 2, "Greek and Latin Inscriptions" 160-161, no. 90 = IGLS no. 825; cf. W. A. Campbell in AJA 42 (1938) 205-206. For the location, see the quadrated map of the city in Antioch-on-the-Orontes 2.215. The inscription was not necessarily made by Cossutius himself, but may have been made by a workman as a construction mark, or perhaps as a form of compliment to the master.

[82] The monument has been studied in detail by G. W. Elderkin, who has published a report on it and on excavations carried out in its vicinity in 1932: "The Charonion," Antioch-on-the-Orontes 1.83-84. Elderkin's conclusions are reproduced here. See also the earlier discussion by R. Perdrizet and Ch. Fossey, "Voyage dans la Syrie du Nord," BCH 21 (1897) 79-82, with an excellent photograph (pl. ii), which is superior to that published by Elderkin; Müller, Antiq. Antioch. 62; Förster, "Antiochia" 107-108. With Förster, "Skulpturen von Antiochia" 177, this writer cannot accept the suggestion put forward by Perdrizet and Fossey, loc.cit., that the sculpture is of the Roman period and that it represents Attis or Mithras; and that Malalas' account represents a Christian legend designed to account for the sculpture. Perdrizet and Fossey themselves recognize that their hypothesis is fragile, and conclude that perhaps after all one ought to accept the account of Malalas. It is worth noting that F. Cumont (Textes et monuments figurés relatifs aux mystères de Mithra [Brussels 1896-1898]) and F. Saxl (Mithras [Berlin 1931]) do not mention the sculpture as a possible Mithraic monument.

in which many people perished.[83] The story is that a seer named Leios[84] commanded that a great mask (προσωπεῖον) be carved out of the mountain overlooking the city; "and inscribing something on it (Malalas writes) he put an end to the pestilential death."[85] This mask the people of the city called "the Charonion." What the inscription was, Malalas does not say; no writing is visible on the preserved sculpture, but, as Elderkin points out, an inscription might have been destroyed, for the face of the bust has been badly battered and a portion of the chest is missing. Possibly the word was something like παυσίνοσος or παυσίκακος. The bust, which was never finished (possibly because the plague had ceased before the carving was completed), shows a veiled head. On the right shoulder stands a smaller draped figure (now much weathered) which appears to wear on its head a calathus or basket. The name Charonion appears to mean that the bust was thought to represent a chthonic deity "who [Elderkin suggests] had been appeased and brought to an end the affliction which sent many souls to Charon." The deity, Elderkin thinks, represents the Syrian goddess of Hierapolis. At a later time a similar apotropaic image was set up at Antioch by the seer Debborius to protect the city from earthquakes.[86]

Another monument set up in the reign of Antiochus IV was a bronze statue of the king taming a bull. This was dedicated by the people of Cilicia in gratitude for the king's suppression of a band of robbers who had been active in the Taurus mountains, the bull being a punning representation of the mountains of the same name.[87]

The construction of a temple to Jupiter Capitolinus in Antioch, reflecting the king's development of the cult of Zeus as a means of unifying his subjects, has been mentioned.[88] The magnificent games in honor of Zeus held at Daphne about 167 B.C. have also been described.[89]

---

[83] The episode is described by Malalas 205.8-13 and (in slightly different terms) by Tzetzes *Chil.* 2, *hist.* 59, 920-924 and *Chil.* 4, *epist.* 527, also in the scholia on Tzetzes' allegory of the *Iliad* in *Anec. Oxon.* 3.379 (cf. *Tzetzae Allegoriae Iliadis*, ed. J. F. Boissonade [Paris 1851] p. 70, note on verse 65).

[84] This diviner appears to be otherwise unknown. In the MS of Malalas the name is written Λήιος (a name which appears to be otherwise unattested), while in the other sources it is given as the commoner name Λάιος or Λάϊος. It seems more likely that Tzetzes altered the seer's name to conform to the better-known one than that the unusual form given in Malalas is an error. Elderkin, however, adopts the form Laius.

[85] Malalas 205.8-13. The inscription is not mentioned in the other accounts.

[86] Malalas 265.8 ff.; see below, Ch. 8, §4.

[87] Libanius *Or.* 11.123. Müller (*Antiq. Antioch.* 62, n. 2) suggests that the statue was associated with the Porta Tauriana (for which see below, Ch. 8, n. 90, and Excursus 10).

[88] See above, n. 67.

[89] See above, nn. 26-29. The presentation of Antiochus IV's games presupposes the

Antiochus probably set up a statue of Zeus Nikephoros in the Temple of Zeus at Antioch.[90] Although the evidence is not clear, there seems to have been a tradition that Antiochus IV adorned or embellished the Temple of Apollo at Daphne built by Seleucus I. Possibly, Antiochus executed this work in order to match his construction of a temple to Jupiter Capitolinus in Antioch itself.[91]

One final monument remains to be discussed, namely the bouleuterion which Antiochus is said to have built at Antioch.[92] There is no specific evidence for either the plan or the location of the building but it seems possible that it resembled the bouleuterion built at Miletus in honor of Antiochus IV by Timarchus and Heracleides, two wealthy Milesians who were influential ministers of the king. The bouleuterion at Miletus must have been built with the king's knowledge and approval, and it has been suggested that the bouleuterion at Miletus was a copy of that at Antioch, or vice versa.[93] Malalas' words, though not

---

existence of a stadium at Daphne, though one is not mentioned in our sources until the time of Diocletian. Malalas (307.5-17) states that Diocletian "built" the stadium at Daphne for use in the Olympic games, and that in this stadium he constructed temples of Olympian Zeus and of Nemesis, the latter being in the *sphendone* or curved end of the stadium. The same emperor, the chronicler adds, restored the temple of Apollo at Daphne. Müller (*Antiq. Antioch.* 62, 96) concluded that here (as elsewhere) Malalas misunderstood his sources, and mistakenly attributed to Diocletian work actually done by Antiochus IV; for, as Müller points out, there must have been a stadium available at Daphne for the celebration of the games of Antiochus IV which Polybius describes. Further study of the evidence has shown, however, that the construction of a stadium that Malalas attributes to Diocletian was probably only a renovation of an existing stadium that had been in disuse, and that, moreover, the work was probably done by Caracalla; see Downey, "Antioch under Severus and Caracalla." It remains possible, of course, that Antiochus IV built a new stadium for his games, but there is no real evidence to this effect, and it seems more likely that the stadium had been built by an earlier king (see above, n. 56).

[90] This would be the statue despoiled by Alexander Zabinas; see below, Ch. 6, §2, with n. 41.

[91] Ammianus Marcellinus (22.13.1), in his account of the burning of the Temple of Apollo at Daphne on 22 October A.D. 362, states that Antiochus had built the temple. It is difficult, however, to accept this tradition, which appears nowhere else. Sozomen and Libanius say that the Temple of Apollo at Daphne was the work of Seleucus I (see above, Ch. 4, n. 135), and this must be right; since Apollo was a tutelary deity of Seleucus I, it is difficult to believe that the founder of the Seleucid dynasty, in dedicating Daphne to Apollo, would have failed to build a temple to the god there. On Ammianus' allusion to the statue in the Temple of Apollo, see below, Excursus 6. The evidence, there discussed, seems to indicate that Antiochus did not set up a statue of Zeus in the Temple of Apollo at Daphne, as some scholars have supposed. Antiochus' work of repair or embellishment may have been so extensive that some persons, like Ammianus, could believe that he had actually built it.

[92] The building of the bouleuterion is recorded by Malalas 205.14-16.

[93] This suggestion is made by H. Knackfuss in *Milet* 1, pt. 2 (Berlin 1908) 99. On the building of the bouleuterion at Miletus, see Bikerman, *Inst. des Séleucides* 123, n. 9, and Rostovtzeff, *Soc. Econ. Hist. Hellenistic World* 668-669, with note on 1482. As these

perfectly clear, could be taken to mean that Antiochus IV was the first ruler to build a bouleuterion at Antioch,[94] and indeed we hear of no earlier bouleuterion. This raises the question whether no council existed at Antioch before the time of Antiochus IV.[95] This bouleuterion may have been erected when Antiochus IV built his new agora in Epiphania to replace an older building that had stood on the original agora of Seleucus I. Antiochus IV may have built his bouleuterion not to provide the city with its first council-chamber but simply because it was part of his plan to shift the civic center from the old agora to the new one. Malalas' notice need not mean that Antiochus IV was the first ruler to build a bouleuterion at Antioch, but simply that this was the king's first building operation in Epiphania.[96] In any case the construction of the bouleuterion, whether it was a new building or a replacement, is indicative of the relations between Antiochus IV and the municipality. It has been well suggested that the construction of the building shows that Antiochus was willing to grant wider powers to the municipal authorities,[97] and this fits with the fact that Antiochus IV instituted a municipal coinage in bronze, bearing both his portrait and the name of the city, which indicates

---

scholars point out, it is incorrect to attribute the building of the bouleuterion at Miletus to Antiochus himself; the building inscription makes it clear that it was created in his honor. W. B. Dinsmoor in his *Architecture of Ancient Greece* (London 1950) writes (297) that "the inscription on [the bouleuterion] at Miletus records that Antiochus IV simultaneously built another like it at Antioch," but this writer has been unable to find evidence in support of this statement.

[94] Malalas writes (205.14-16) Ἀντίοχος . . . ἔκτισε πρῶτον ἐν Ἀντιοχείᾳ . . . τὸ λεγόμενον βουλευτήριον. . . This use of πρῶτον is an excellent example of the kind of difficulty created by Malalas' ignorance and slovenly way of writing. Ἀντίοχος πρῶτος or τὸ πρῶτον βουλευτήριον would be clear. However, if πρῶτον modifies ἔκτισε (which apparently is what Malalas meant), it could mean either that Antiochus was the first to build a bouleuterion in Antioch, or that this was the first thing that he built in Epiphania. It is always possible, of course, that Malalas' information came ultimately from a source that was anxious to magnify Antiochus' act by suggesting that it had a significance that it did not really possess.

[95] For the discussion of the organization and administration of Antioch in the Seleucid period, see below, §8.

[96] See n. 94. Malalas (211.18) records the repair of "the bouleuterion" at Antioch by Pompey; see below, Ch. 7, §1. His reference to "the bouleuterion" need not be taken to mean that there was only one such building in the city, for the chronicler was not interested in such points (on his methods, see above, Ch. 2, §4).

[97] See Jones, *Cities of the East. Rom. Prov.* 250-251. The passage in Polybius 26.1 does not show that Antioch enjoyed autonomous government under Antiochus Epiphanes, as some scholars have supposed; see §8 below. An inscription found at Pergamum has been thought to record a decree of the senate and the people of Antioch, but Holleaux has argued plausibly that the decree was issued by Athens; see above, n. 42.

that the king was willing to share with his cities the profits resulting from the issuing of the coins.[98]

There was a tradition that Antiochus IV built the famous colonnaded street that ran through the length of Antioch, parallel to the river, and this for a time was believed by some modern scholars. However, the literary evidence indicates that in reality this work was done by Herod and Tiberius,[99] and since there is no other good monumental or literary evidence for the existence of such streets in the East before the close of the Hellenistic age,[100] it is necessary to deprive Antiochus IV of the credit for this work.

7. THE JEWISH COMMUNITY AT ANTIOCH
UNDER ANTIOCHUS IV

The Jewish community at Antioch comes into prominence in connection with the policy that Antiochus IV pursued toward the Jews.[101] Under Seleucus I Jews who were presumably retired mercenaries settled at Antioch. Probably they were granted individually isopolity, that is, the right to be enrolled as citizens, provided, of course, that they apostatized and worshiped the city gods. Whether they were also given special privileges at this time, as Josephus claims, seems very doubtful. Probably those Jews who preferred to retain their faith (and these must have been the majority) were organized in a *politeuma* which made them a quasi-autonomous unit within the Greek community, enjoying certain rights, such as being judged by their own judges according to their own law. This status was enjoyed by the Jews who lived at Alexandria and in other Hellenistic cities, and though we happen to have no specific evidence in the case of Antioch at this period, it seems safe to assume that the Jews there enjoyed this

[98] Bellinger, "Early Coinage of Roman Syria" 61-62; cf. Dieudonné, "Monnaies grecques de Syrie" 12.

[99] See below, and cf. Downey, "Building Records in Malalas" 301-311. Müller (*Antiq. Antioch.* 56 ff.) supposed that Antiochus IV must have built the colonnaded street because the construction of the new quarter Epiphania, and the concomitant completion of a wall enclosing the entire city, would necessarily have entailed the building of the street, which would, architecturally, have been an integral part of the king's work. Müller, however, had not studied the literary tradition in detail, and did not realize that the evidence favors a later date for the street.

[100] See Robertson, *Greek and Roman Architecture*[2] 291.

[101] Since the history of the community has already been studied by Kraeling, "Jewish Community at Antioch," no attempt need be made here to repeat the complete history of Antiochene Jewry. Only the essential facts will be presented here, and the reader is referred to Kraeling's study for further details.

dispensation.[102] What the size of the community may have been at this early period, we do not know; but the references to Antioch in later Jewish tradition make it plain that the city, under the first Seleucid kings, attracted Jews and was considered by them to be an important center.[103]

When the Seleucid government and the Jews were brought into conflict in the time of Antiochus IV, it was inevitable that Antioch, as the capital, should become closely involved with the developments affecting the Jews. Judaea, previously under Egyptian rule, had come into Seleucid possession under Antiochus III in 200 B.C.[104] The Jews there were already divided into two camps, those who maintained strict observance of Jewish law and customs, and the "liberal" Hellenizers, who were willing to conform at least in some outward matters (such as Greek athletic exercises) to the practices of the alien culture that now dominated them. When Antiochus IV came to the throne, he found himself involved in a series of troubles that had originated before his time among the Jews themselves. First there was a purely domestic quarrel in progress between two rival factions, the Oniads and the Tobiads, who were both Hellenizers. Then, in addition to the struggle between the Hellenizing and the "strict" Jews, there was a point of friction between the Jews who favored the Ptolemies and those who thought that their best interest lay in support of the Seleucids. In its revolt, Palestine was also seeking to take advantage of the weak position to which the Seleucid Empire had fallen after the defeat of Antiochus III by the Romans. The rebellious Jews doubtless had the moral support of Rome, though no material assistance was given them. The situation in Palestine presented a special problem in the effort which Antiochus IV was making to overcome his father's defeat by Rome; the Seleucid Empire must be unified, materially and politically, and the separatist tendencies inherent in the orthodox Jewish religion must be overcome.[105]

[102] On the privileges and status of the Jews, see above, Ch. 4, n. 120.

[103] Kraeling, "Jewish Community at Antioch" 131 ff. He cites, among other evidence, the tradition in the Jerusalem Talmud according to which Nebuchadnezzar and the Great Sanhedrin had met at Daphne, several centuries, of course, before the foundation of Antioch and Daphne.

[104] Joseph. *Antiq.* 12.131ff. For the background of the relationships between the Jews and Hellenism, which is sketched here very briefly, the reader may consult E. R. Bevan's chapter (16) in *CAH* 8, with the appropriate bibliography, and the useful chapter "Hellenism and the Jews" in Tarn-Griffith, *Hellenistic Civilization*³ 210-238, with references to the principal modern studies (210, n. 1).

[105] See Jansen, "Politik Antiochos' des IV."

Antiochus IV finally found himself forced into an outright attack on the Jewish religion itself. He plundered the Temple in Jerusalem, carrying off the sacred vessels and materials to Antioch, and rededicated the shrine to Zeus Olympius.[106] Warfare between government forces and nationalist bands led by Judas Maccabaeus continued until after the death of Antiochus IV, whose forces were too weak to defeat the rebels, and the king's attempt to integrate the Jews into a unified Hellenic state came to nothing.

During these struggles the Jews who lived at Antioch doubtless found themselves in an invidious position. The non-Jewish majority in the city can hardly have remained on friendly terms with the local co-religionists of the rebels in Judaea.[107] Some of the Jews taken captive by the government forces were probably sent to Antioch, and their presence cannot have improved the standing of the resident Jews.[108] Antioch, as the capital of the persecutor, would be bound to play a large part in the tradition that established a third "captivity" (following those of Egypt and Babylon) under Antiochus Epiphanes.[109]

The Antiochene Jews of this period (who lived in a neighborhood of their own) were probably settled somewhere near the southwestern end of the city, where there is known to have been at a later period a synagogue, the Kenesheth Hashmunith, which contained the sepulcher of the Maccabean martyrs.[110] There may also have been a settlement near Daphne, the presence of which is suggested by the circumstances of the death of the former Jewish High Priest Onias III. Onias

[106] I Macc. 1.23-24. Josephus (*Bell.* 7.44) states that "Antiochus' successors" presented the bronze vessels from the Temple to the Jews of Antioch, who placed them in their synagogue. T. W. Davies, "Temple," Hastings, *Dictionary of the Bible* 4 (1902) 711, citing the passage in Josephus, states that Antiochus Epiphanes himself gave the bronze vessels to "sympathizing Jews" at Antioch. It is not clear what the authority may be for this statement. Josephus goes on to make what sounds like an exaggerated claim concerning the granting of citizen rights to the Jews by Antiochus' successors (on the impossibility of such claims, see above) and one wonders whether his statement concerning the bronze vessels from the Temple is not to be taken *cum grano salis*. Bikerman, "Les Maccabées de Malalas" 82, suggests that it was Demetrius I who presented the bronze objects from the Temple to the synagogue at Antioch. Cf. Kraeling, "Jewish Community at Antioch" 146.

[107] See Kraeling, "Jewish Community at Antioch" 146. T. W. Davies (see preceding note) supposes that there were Jews at Antioch who were in sympathy with Antiochus' purposes, but it seems difficult to believe this.

[108] The destination of the captives is not mentioned (I Macc. 1:32; Josephus *Antiq.* 12.251), but some of them at least must have been sent to the capital. Josephus says that ten thousand persons were made captive. See Kraeling, "Jewish Community at Antioch" 134, 146.

[109] The "third captivity" under Antiochus IV is mentioned by Chrysostom, *Orat. adv. Jud.* 6.2 = *PG* 48.905. See Kraeling, "Jewish Community at Antioch" 134.

[110] On this synagogue, see further below.

lived at Antioch, presumably after he had been supplanted by his brother and rival Jason; and in the course of a quarrel with Menelaus, a member of the faction that opposed his own, he took refuge in the "sanctuary of Daphne" (presumably the Temple of Apollo, the only one at Daphne sufficiently famous to be so described).[111] He was treacherously induced to leave the sanctuary and killed as soon as he had come outside. The episode implies that Onias lived in or near Daphne; had he lived in Antioch itself, we should expect that he would have sought refuge in one of the temples there.[112]

How intimately the city became bound up, in tradition, with the course of events at this time is illustrated by the development of the story of the martyrdoms of the priest Eleazer and the seven Maccabean brothers and their mother, who were executed by Antiochus IV for refusal to abandon their religion.[113] The accounts of the martyrdoms in 2 Maccabees and 4 Maccabees[114] indicate that the executions took place in Jerusalem, but these sources are not wholly reliable.[115] There existed at Antioch the synagogue already mentioned, the Kenesheth Hashmunith, named for the mother of the Maccabees, which was supposed to contain the tombs of the mother and sons and, according to some sources, that of the high priest Eleazer.[116] This synagogue was built on the mountainside, in the southern part of the city; one source mentions that it was the first synagogue to be built after the destruction

[111] 2 Macc. 4:33-48; cf. Bevan in *CAH* 8.504.

[112] See Kraeling, "Jewish Community at Antioch" 141.

[113] The Maccabees became so famous in both Jewish and Christian tradition that there are numerous studies of the accounts of their martyrdoms, including detailed investigations of the conflicting accounts of their places of burial. A repetition of all this material would go far beyond the limits of this history, and only the salient points are given here. See F.-M. Abel, *Les Livres des Maccabées* (Paris 1949), *Excursus 6: Les sept frères Maccabées dans la tradition*; Obermann, "Sepulchre of the Maccabean Martyrs"; Bikerman, "Les Maccabées de Malalas." Cardinal Rampolla da Tindaro's study will be noticed below.

[114] 2 Macc. 6-7; 4 Macc. 5-18.

[115] See Townshend's note on 4 Macc. 5:1 in *Apocrypha and Pseudepigrapha of the O.T.*, ed. by R. H. Charles (Oxford, 1913) 2.671. In 4 Macc. 18:5 it is said that the martyrdoms took place at Jerusalem.

[116] See Obermann's and Bikerman's studies cited above, n. 113. The synagogue is mentioned in the Judeo-Arabic Martyrology of Nissim Ibn Shahin of Kairowan, the text of which is discussed by Obermann in his study, 254-259; see also *The Arabic Original of Ibn Shahin's Book of Comfort*, ed. by J. Obermann (New Haven 1933; *Yale Oriental Series* 17) 25-28. It is also mentioned in the anonymous Arabic description of Antioch published by Guidi, "Descrizione araba" 160. Malalas (206.20-22; 207.10-13) states that Antiochus IV brought Eleazer and the Maccabees to Antioch and executed them there, and that a shrine was built for their bodies in the reign of Demetrius I Soter (162-150 B.C.). Bikerman, in his study cited above (n. 113), believes that this represents not a Jewish tradition but a version (whether correct or incorrect) which would have come from the local Antiochene historians of the Seleucid dynasty.

of the Second Temple by Titus in A.D. 70,[117] and in time it became a Christian church.[118] There was some uncertainty in antiquity as to the location of the relics of the Maccabees. St. Jerome, who had seen these relics at Modeim in Palestine, was astonished when he saw them again at Antioch,[119] and St. Augustine seems to hint at the real reason for the presence of the cult at Antioch when he remarks that the church in honor of the Maccabees is reported to be in Antioch, which was the city that bore the name of the king who had put the martyrs to death.[120] As to the presence at Antioch of a synagogue (later a church) dedicated to the Maccabean martyrs there can be little doubt; but it cannot be considered proven that the martyrdoms took place at Antioch.[121]

[117] Ibn Shahin, cited in the preceding note. If Antiochus Epiphanes' desecration of the Temple could be looked upon as a "destruction," then Ibn Shahin's story would fit with the version preserved in Malalas (mentioned in the preceding note) according to which a shrine was built for the Maccabees at Antioch under Demetrius I Soter (162-150 B.C.).

[118] The church is mentioned in the anonymous Arabic account of the city published by Guidi, "Descrizione araba" 160; by Augustine, *Sermo* 300.6 = *PL* 38.1379; and by Jerome, *De situ et nomin. Hebraic., PL* 23.958. The Jewish cult of the Maccabees had an important influence on Christian conceptions of martyrdom and Christian martyrological literature; see O. Perler, "Das vierte Makkabaeerbuch, Ignatius von Antiochien und die ältesten Martyrerberichte" *RAC* 25 (1949) 47-72.

[119] *De situ et nomin. Hebraic., PL* 23.958.

[120] *Sermo* 300.6 = *PL* 38.1379: *Sanctorum Machabaeorum basilica esse in Antiochia praedicatur: in illa scilicet civitate, quae regis ipsius persecutoris nomine vocatur.*

[121] On the Maccabees as Christian saints, see below, Ch. 15, §5. Cardinal Rampolla da Tindaro has argued, with much learning, that Antiochus IV's persecution of the Jews was universal and was not confined to Jerusalem, and that in this case Antioch was the most likely place at which the martyrdoms may have occurred; moreover, the Cardinal believed that the martyrs' relics were buried in the city. See his study, "Del luogo del martirio e del sepolcro dei Maccabei," *Bessarione* 1 (1896-1897) 655-662, 751-763, 853-866; 2 (1897-1898) 9-22, which was reprinted under the same title as a pamphlet, with separate pagination (Rome 1897), and is also published in French translation, "Martyre et sépulture des Macchabées," *Rev. de l'art chrét.* 48 (1899) 290-305, 377-392, 457-465. His theory was accepted by Leclerq, "Antioche (Archéologie)," *DACL* 1.2375-2379; "Macchabées," *ibid.* 10.724-727. It does not, however, seem convincing to Delehaye, who finds himself unable to solve the problem (*Origines du culte*[2] 201-202) or to Obermann, "Sepulchre of the Maccabean Martyrs" 260ff., and the present writer would like to see stronger evidence than the Cardinal is able to adduce. The presence of a church dedicated to the Maccabees at Antioch by no means proves that they were martyred there and that their relics were in possession of the city. These martyrs were widely venerated; and if a church in their honor were built at Antioch simply because it was the capital of their persecutor, it would then be easy for a city of the size and fame of Antioch to claim their martyrdom and their relics. Kraeling suggests ("Jewish Community at Antioch" 148) that 4 Macc. is a product of Antioch, and points out how the author's speculation on the construction of a memorial shrine to the martyrs (4 Macc. 17:7-10) shows a liberal point of view, quite far from the strict Jewish beliefs on such subjects. See also M. Maas, "Die Maccabäer als christliche Heilige," *Monatsschrift für Geschichte u. Wissenschaft des Judenthums* 44 (1900) 145-156; M. Simon, in his study, "La polémique anti-juive de S. Jean Chrysostome et le mouvement judaïsant d'Antioche," *Annuaire de l'Inst. de philologie et d'histoire orientales* (Brussels) 4 (1936) 413-420; J. Jeremias, "Die Makkabäer-Kirche in Antio-

8. The Organization and Administration of Antioch in the Seleucid Period

Since the evidence for the way in which Antioch was governed during the Seleucid period is scanty and in many respects unsatisfactory, at certain important points we must be content with inference and perhaps conjecture. This situation reflects the general paucity of evidence which is a characteristic of the history of the city during Hellenistic times.[122]

Until quite recently scholars have taken for granted that the Seleucid foundations in Syria were organized as Greek *poleis,* governed by the citizens, who elected the council and the magistrates[123]—a form of government that could have been carried on, within certain obvious and well-recognized limits, under an absolute ruler like the Seleucid king. There is, however, some reason to doubt whether this was necessarily the case at Antioch. An inscription of Laodicea published in 1942-1943 shows that that city, which was one of the sister cities founded by Seleucus I along with Antioch,[124] was, at least in 175 B.C., administered according to Macedonian, not Greek, institutions.[125] This is, in fact, what one might expect in a Seleucid foundation. There was an *epistates,* or royal governor, entrusted with both civil and military powers, such as is found in other Seleucid cities, including (at just this same period) Seleucia Pieria.[126] There were also archons, and *peliganes* (πελιγᾶνες). The latter term, defined by Hesychius, *s.v.,* as οἱ ἔνδοξοι · παρὰ δὲ Σύροις οἱ βουλευταί, is declared by Strabo, Book 7, frag. 2,

chia" *ZNTW* 40 (1941) 254-255; O. Perler, "Das vierte Makkabaerbuch, Ignatius von Antiochien und die ältesten Martyrerberichte," *Rivista di archeologia cristiana* 25 (1949) 47-72.

[122] On the sources, see above, Ch. 2.

[123] See for example Bikerman, *Institutions des Séleucides* 157; Jones, *Greek City* 7. M. Holleaux has shown that an inscription of Pergamum, first thought to be a decree of Antioch, almost certainly originated at Athens: "Un prétendu décret d'Antioche sur l'Oronte," *Etudes d'épigraphie et d'histoire grecques* 2 (Paris 1938) 127-147.

[124] The others were Seleucia Pieria, and Apamea: Malalas 199-204 Bonn ed.; Strabo 16.2.4, p. 750 C; see further above, Ch. 4, §2.

[125] The inscription is published by P. Roussel, "Décret des péliganes de Laodicée-sur-mer," *Syria* 23 (1942-1943) 21-32, upon whose valuable commentary the present discussion is based. The text is republished, with new bibliography, in *IGLS* 1261. For a correction of the date of the inscription see Seyrig, "Poids antiques de la Syrie," 67, with n. 3. He points out that there was a miscalculation in the original publication, and that the text was drawn up under Antiochus IV, not under Seleucus IV.

[126] On the *epistates,* see Magie, *Asia Minor* 2, 953, n. 62, and 970-971, n. 1; Bikerman, *Institutions de Séleucides* 163; W. W. Tarn, *The Greeks in Bactria and India* (Cambridge 1938) 24-26; A. Heuss, "Stadt und Herrscher des Hellenismus," *Klio,* Beiheft 39 (1937) 59-61.

to be a Macedonian word meaning "elders." These definitions leave it uncertain whether the *peliganes* of Laodicea formed a *gerousia* or a *boule*. In any case it seems clear from this text that Laodicea was organized by Seleucus Nicator on the Macedonian model and not as a Greek *polis*.[127] Whether we should infer that this was the case with Antioch as well is not clear. There were Macedonians among the original settlers, and Macedonian names were given to localities in and near Antioch; but there were also Athenians among the original settlers in the city, transferred thither by Seleucus from his rival's capital Antigonia, which he demolished;[128] and this might suggest that the city was organized as a Greek *polis*, though it would seem more natural to expect the Macedonian forms of government, at least at first, in spite of the presence of the Athenians. There is a very little evidence (cited below) which suggests that the institutions of the Greek *polis* prevailed later in the Seleucid period.

We have one further glimpse of the early government of the city. Soon after they were founded, both Antioch and Seleucia Pieria issued a small amount of municipal bronze coinage.[129] This is very rare; the coins of Seleucia, which was the capital at this period,[130] are somewhat more numerous than those of Antioch. Soon, however, both issues were apparently superseded by "royal bronze" coins issued on the authority of the king. This very brief appearance of municipal coinage suggests that at first the two new cities possessed certain municipal powers, such as that of coining bronze, which were then soon withdrawn. What else may have been involved in this change we do not know.

The earliest extant document that refers directly to the organization and administration of Antioch is the famous Gurob papyrus, which describes the capture of Seleucia Pieria by the Egyptians in 246 B.C. and the formal entry of the Egyptian forces into Seleucia and Antioch.[131] In Antioch the Egyptians were met by (col. 3, lines 20-22) [οἵ τε] σατράπαι καὶ οἱ ἄλλοι ἡγε / μόν[ες καὶ οἱ στρατιῶ]ται καὶ οἱ ἱερεῖς καὶ αἱ συναρχίαι / καὶ [πάντες οἱ ἀπ]ὸ τοῦ γυμνασίου νεανίσκοι. The

---

[127] On the Macedonian forms of government, which have recently been the subject of renewed study and debate, it will be sufficient here to refer to P. de Francisci, *Arcana imperii* (Milan 1947-1948) 2, 354, n. 5, and 373ff.; A. Aymard, "Sur l'assemblée macédonienne," *REA* 52 (1950) 115-137, especially 128; idem, "L'Organisation de la Macédoine en 167 et le régime réprésentatif dans le monde grec," *CP* 45 (1950) 96-107.

[128] Malalas 199-204; see above, Ch. 4, §2.

[129] Newell, *Western Seleucid Mints*, p. 94, no. 910, cf. pp. 86-88, 96; D. B. Waagé, "Coins" pp. 3-4.

[130] See above, Ch. 4, n. 23.

[131] The papyrus has often been published and discussed; for the best text and commentary, see Holleaux, "Le papyrus de Gourob."

presence of the satraps recalls the fact that in the territorial organization which the Seleucids had taken over from their Persian predecessors, Antioch was the capital of a satrapy.[132] In addition to the satrap resident in Antioch, one or more of his colleagues from other parts of Syria might have been in the city on this occasion. For the rest, the papyrus gives little specific evidence for the administration of the city. The ἄλλοι ἡγεμόν[ες] are presumably military officials. The [στρατιῶ]ται (the restoration seems reasonably certain), or high military officers, might include the commander of the garrison of Antioch and the officers of the mounted militia of the city, if that existed at this time as it did in 167 B.C. (see below). The ἱερεῖς would include the priests of the royal cult and the priests of the other cults; at least later, we know, there was a chief priest for the whole of Daphne.[133] The reference to the συναρχίαι gives us no specific information, for the writer of the papyrus, who was evidently not concerned with drawing up an official list of the dignitaries at the reception, used this comprehensive term to describe all the other holders of offices that were of any consequence. Since the list is so plainly a rather casual one, not concerned with precise titles, it seems unwise to try to discover significance in the absence of any reference to an ἐπιστάτης or to πελιγᾶνες or βουλευταί.

Since, as we have seen, a bouleuterion at Antioch is not mentioned until the time of Antiochus IV Epiphanes (175-163 B.C.), it has been supposed that this was the first council chamber built at Antioch,[134] and that while the city may have had a council before this time, the construction of a bouleuterion was a gesture that indicated greater autonomy to the municipal authorities.[135] The building of a council chamber is in keeping with what we know of Antiochus' policy, since, as we have seen, he instituted a municipal bronze coinage at Antioch.[136] By the time of Octavian, Antioch had acquired the institutions of the Greek *polis*, for we hear of the *boule* and *demos* of the city in an in-

---

[132] Strabo 16.2.4, p. 750 C. On the interpretation of the passage, see Jones, *Cities of the East. Rom. Prov.* 242-243, and Rostovtzeff, *Soc. Econ. Hist. Hellenistic World* 1436, n. 265. On the administration of the satrapies, see Rostovtzeff, *op.cit.* 464, 481.

[133] On the royal cult, see above, Ch. 4, §3. The appointment of a chief priest of Daphne is mentioned below.

[134] By Jones, *Cities of the East. Rom. Prov.* 250-251.

[135] The question of the construction of Antiochus' bouleuterion is discussed more fully above, §6, with nn. 92-98.

[136] See above, n. 98.

scription dated 36-34 B.C., found at Rhosus, on the coast of Syria not far from Antioch.[137]

The citizens were divided into tribes according to the ward of the city in which they lived; by the time of Libanius there were eighteen such tribes, but we do not know their number in the Seleucid period.[138] That the citizens likewise belonged to demes, which were grouped to make up tribes, may be inferred from what is known of the organization of Seleucia Pieria.[139]

The non-Hellenic population of Antioch was probably organized in *politeumata*.[140] These were quasi-political organizations, based on nationality, which were employed to provide political and administrative status for noncitizens of alien race. There was, for example, a *politeuma* of Syrians at Seleucia on the Tigris.[141] The members of a *politeuma* had certain political rights, short of being real citizens, and they had their own magistrates and to some extent their own legal processes; they also managed their own religious affairs. At Antioch, the foundation of Seleucus I had consisted of a walled quarter, of which the king was the "founder," plus a second quarter which, Strabo says, was a "foundation of the multitude of the settlers."[142] The first quarter evidently accommodated the Macedonians and Greeks who were full citizens of the new city. The way in which Strabo describes the second quarter suggests that this was the dwelling place of the native Syrians whom the king had brought to the new site; and everything that we know of such cities elsewhere indicates that these natives would have been organized in *politeumata*.

In addition to the native Syrians, Antioch also possessed a Jewish community, which appears to go back to the time of the founder. Those Jews who preferred to retain their faith probably were organized in a

[137] *IGLS* no. 718, line 7. In the reign of Nero, coins of Antioch show the *boule* of the city dropping a pebble into a voting urn: D. B. Waagé, "Coins" p. 33, nos. 343-344.

[138] Libanius *Or.* 11.245, 19.62, cf. 23.11, 24.26, 33.35-37.

[139] There is no specific evidence for demes and tribes at Antioch in the Seleucid period, but their existence at Seleucia Pieria (attested by an inscription of June, 186 B.C.), makes it seem safe to assume that they existed likewise at Antioch; see M. Holleaux, "Une inscription de Séleucie-de-Piérie," *Études d'épigraphie et d'histoire grecques* 3 (Paris 1942) 199-254, especially 247-250; Welles, *Royal Correspondence* no. 45; Jones, *Greek City* 158-159.

[140] On the *politeuma*, see Rostovtzeff, *Soc. Econ. Hist. Hellenistic World* 1401, n. 137; Tarn-Griffith *Hellenistic Civilization*[3] 157-158; E. Ziebarth, "Politeuma," *RE* 21 (1952) 1401-1402.

[141] Josephus *Antiq.* 18.372, 378.

[142] Strabo 16.2.4, p. 750 C: τὸ δὲ δεύτερον τοῦ πλήθους τῶν οἰκητόρων ἐστὶ κτίσμα. On these quarters, and on Strabo's account of them, see above, Ch. 4, §4, with n. 111.

politeuma, like the Jews of Alexandria, while those who wished to do so could probably become eligible for full citizenship by renouncing their faith and worshiping the city gods.[143]

As to the other details of the organization and administration of the city we have only random information. We hear of what seems to have been a local cavalry militia, three thousand members of which took part in the famous procession organized by Antiochus IV at Daphne ca. 167 B.C.[144] It may have been some such organization that was forcibly disarmed by Demetrius II in 143 B.C. when the people of the city rose in revolt against the excesses of his Cretan mercenaries.[145]

One of our most extensive texts unfortunately provides us with little useful information. Polybius, in a fragment preserved by Athenaeus, lists examples of the erratic conduct that caused Antiochus IV Epiphanes (175-163 B.C.) to be called Epimanes. One specimen of the king's oddness is the way in which "he would frequently put off his royal robes, and, assuming a white toga, go round the market place like a candidate, and, taking some by the hand and embracing others, would beg them to give him their vote, sometimes for the office of ἀγορανόμος and sometimes for that of δήμαρχος. Upon being elected, he would sit upon the ivory curule chair, as the Roman custom is, listening to the lawsuits tried there, and pronouncing judgment with great pains and display of interest. In consequence all respectable men were entirely puzzled about him, some looking upon him as a plain man and others as a madman."[146] It has been thought that this description represents the normal political life of Antioch at the time,[147] and that it shows that the *agoranomos* was an elected official vested with judicial powers. However, it seems difficult to make any such use of the passage. Polybius expressly cites these actions of the king as an example of his eccentricity, and remarks that his conduct in this respect puzzled sober citizens.[148] Antiochus had been deeply impressed by Roman institutions and customs during his early residence as a hostage in Rome, and he expressed gratitude for the treatment which he had

---

[143] See above, §7.

[144] Polybius (30.25.6) calls them ἱππεῖς πολιτικοί. See further above, §6.

[145] Diodorus 33.4.2; on the episode see Willrich, "Demetrios," no. 41, *RE* 4, 2799, and see below, Ch. 6, §1.

[146] Polybius 26.1.5-7 *apud* Athen. 5.193 e-f. I quote the translation of W. R. Paton in his edition of Polybius in the Loeb Classical Library.

[147] By Bikerman, *Institutions de Séleucides,* 157-158.

[148] Bikerman, it must be noted, does not quote Polybius' opening and closing remarks, which he may not have taken into account in this connection.

received there.[149] It seems much more likely that in the scenes which
Polybius describes, Antiochus was pretending to be a Roman candidate, soliciting the offices of aedile and tribune of the people. This
would surely cause astonishment at Antioch; nevertheless the courtiers
would doubtless have fallen in with the king's whimsical humor, and
would have carried through the pretence of election and of the sub-
mitting of legal disputes to the "tribune." Whether these episodes
merely represent harmless fun, or whether they indicated real de-
rangement, is another question.

As the Seleucid capital, Antioch was the center of a vast administrative machine, but we hear only a little of its workings in the city. An
illuminating glimpse of the difficulties encountered by the Seleucids
in the early days of their regime is given in a letter of Antiochus I
written about 275 B.C. to Meleager, governor of the Hellespontic satrapy.
In this letter the king informs the governor that he has presented to
one of his "friends" the fortress or fortified manor-house of Petra in
the Hellespont, "unless it has been given previously to someone else."[150]
There was, then, no reliable record available in Antioch itself of the
ownership and the status of Petra; and from this small phrase it is easy
to imagine the administrative problems that faced the Seleucids when
they took over their territory.[151]

The men at the head of the administrative machinery became on
occasion immensely rich.[152] Hermeias, the prime minister of Antiochus
III, was able, in an emergency during the revolt of Molon, to advance
the funds necessary to cover the arrears of pay of the royal army.[153]
The wealth displayed by the royal *epistolographos* (chief of the chancery) Dionysius on the occasion of the fabulous games of Antiochus IV
has been mentioned.[154]

Within Antioch itself, there must have been a special group of officials
charged with the administration and maintenance of the royal property
and of the temples of the dynastic cult. We happen to possess one
document that illustrates the situation of the city in this respect and
also testifies to the importance of the sanctuaries at Daphne in the life
of Antioch. This is the letter of Antiochus III (dated 12 October 189

149 Livy 42.6; cf. Polybius 30.27, and see above, §6.
150 Michel, *Recueil*, no. 35 = *OGIS*, no. 221 = Welles, *Royal Correspondence*, no. 11.
151 See the commentary of Welles, *Royal Correspondence*, p. 66 (on lines 9-10).
152 Rostovtzeff, *Soc. Econ. Hist. Hellenistic World*, 517-518, 1156.
153 Polybius 5.50.2.
154 See above, §6.

B.C.) on the appointment of a chief priest at Daphne, which was preserved in an inscription found at Daphne in 1858.[155] This document
shows that all the sanctuaries at Daphne (not only the principal
temple, that of Apollo and Artemis Daittae, but all the others as well)
were under the supervision of a single chief priest, who was appointed
by the king. Presumably (though nothing is said to this effect) the
individual sanctuaries would also have their own principal priests. It
is instructive, however, to find that the over-all supervision of the
sanctuaries was placed in the hands of one man, who was a veteran
of the royal service. His duties apparently would not be onerous;
nevertheless the administration was evidently anxious to have the shrines
of Daphne under the supervision of a man who could be trusted to
administer this center, which was of major importance both financially
and for religious purposes, for the best interests of the king's government.

As the capital of the Seleucid realm, Antioch had to support a garrison of the royal troops. Many units of these, of various arms, are
enumerated in the description of the procession organized by Antiochus
IV at Daphne ca. 167 B.C.; infantry armed in the Roman fashion, Mysians, Cilician light infantry, Thracians, Gauls, cavalry from Nisa, the
"companion cavalry," the regiment of "royal friends," mailed cavalry,
corps of chariots and elephants. The mounted militia of Antioch itself,
numbering three thousand, also took part in the procession.[156]

Antioch was not only the royal capital, but, as has been mentioned,
was the capital of a satrapy. We have as yet no knowledge of the extent
of the satrapy which was governed from Antioch, and our only knowledge of the activities of the satraps of Antioch is the reference, which
has been mentioned, to "satraps" (presumably including the satrap of
Antioch) among the dignitaries who welcomed the Egyptians to
Antioch in 246 B.C.

As a city, Antioch also possessed its own "territory," consisting of
cultivated and cultivable land, from which it obtained revenue.[157] No
details of the city's possessions in this respect are known for the Hellenistic period, though we do have evidence as to the city's land in the
fourth century after Christ.[158]

[155] Waddington, no. 2713a = *OGIS*, no. 244 = Welles, *Royal Correspondence*, no. 44.
[156] Polybius 30.25.2-11 *apud* Athen., 5.194.
[157] Rostovtzeff, *Soc. Econ. Hist. Hellenistic World*, 481.
[158] See below, Ch. 13, nn. 55-56.

CHAPTER 6

THE DECLINE OF THE SELEUCID DYNASTY

1. THE SUCCESSORS OF ANTIOCHUS IV, 163-129 B.C.

AFTER the death of Antiochus IV the Seleucid realm was never again to play a part as a world power. Rome was now the dominant nation, and from this time the history of the Seleucid house is one of steady contraction and decline, ending in the occupation of Syria by Tigranes (83 B.C.) and finally in its conquest by the Romans (64 B.C.).

The history of Antioch during this period is a depressing story in which we get only scattered glimpses of the Seleucid capital as a scene of intrigue, revolt, and warfare. Pretenders fought over the city and there was bloodshed and destruction in it.

Antiochus IV Epiphanes left an infant son who reigned briefly (163-162 B.C.) as Antiochus V Eupator, under the guardianship of Antiochus IV's minister Lysias.[1] Lysias found it necessary to conduct an expedition against the nationalist rebels in Palestine, taking the boy king with him. When they returned to Antioch, they found that the city had been occupied by Philip, a minister of Antiochus IV who claimed that the king, when dying in Persia, had named him as his successor and had given him the royal diadem and seal. Lysias attacked Philip and defeated and killed him, regaining control of the capital.[2] Lysias, however, was soon to fall from power on the return to Syria of the legitimate heir, Seleucus IV's son Demetrius (later Demetrius I Soter, 162-150 B.C.), who had been a hostage in Rome. Refused permission by the Roman Senate to return to Syria, Demetrius escaped with the aid of the historian Polybius and reached Tripolis in 162. The population of Syria supported him and he established himself on the throne.[3] He had

---

[1] See Bevan, *House of Seleucus* 2.178-187; Bouché-Leclerq, *Hist. des Séleucides* 1.307-315.

[2] This summary of events follows Bouché-Leclerq, *Hist. des Séleucides* 2.310, n. 2, in preferring the account of Josephus (*Ant.* 12.386) to that of 2 Macc. 9.29, according to which Philip escaped and fled.

[3] See Bevan, *House of Seleucus* 2.188-211; Bouché-Leclerq, *Hist. des Séleucides* 1.316-337. In order to emphasize the restoration, in his person, of the legitimate branch of the Seleucid house, Demetrius removed the effigies of Zeus from the coins of Antioch and made Apollo the predominant figure, and also represented the Tyche on the coins for the first time: Newell, *Seleucid Mint of Antioch* pp. 37-38; D. B. Waagé, "The Coins" p. 13. On Zeus and Apollo as the protectors of the Seleucid house see above,

the misfortune, however, to become unpopular with his subjects, who found him arrogant and unapproachable; he in his turn no doubt considered the Syrians fickle and degenerate. Finally he built himself a fortified country residence (*tetrapyrgion*) not far from Antioch, in which he shut himself up and allowed himself to be seen by no one.[4] Demetrius was converted to Epicureanism by the philosopher Philonides, who founded a school at Antioch during his pupil's reign.[5]

The Pergamene king Attalus discovered a youth named Balas who bore a remarkable resemblance to Antiochus IV Epiphanes. In order to weaken Demetrius' position, Attalus put forward Balas, whom he named Alexander, as claimant to the Seleucid throne. Rome in 153/2 B.C. recognized his claim; some of Demetrius' generals deserted to Balas, and the populace of Antioch finally rose in his favor.[6] Demetrius perished in a battle with his rival, and Alexander I Balas (150-145 B.C.) became king of Syria.[7]

The new ruler, it is said, lacked energy and was unfit for his position; he had a taste for the company of philosophers and for conviviality.[8] The government of Antioch he turned over to two men named Hierax and Diodotus, probably popular leaders who had led the opposition to Demetrius. There is some reason to believe that during Alexander's reign Antioch suffered from an earthquake, which, if it is to be assigned to this period, would be dated in 148 B.C.[9] Malalas

---

Ch. 4, n. 63. On representations of Tyche on the coins of Antioch, see above, Ch. 4, nn. 88, 93.

[4] Josephus *Ant.* 13.35-36; cf. Justinus 35.1.3 and 8. On fortified country houses, see P. Grimal, "Les maisons à tour hellénistiques et romaines," *Mélanges d'archéol. et d'hist., École française de Rome* 56 (1939) 28-59. On the tradition that suggests that Demetrius I presented to the Jews of Antioch the bronze vessels that had been carried away from the Temple at Jerusalem by Antiochus IV, see above, Ch. 5, n. 106.

[5] See W. Crönert, "Die Epikureer in Syrien," *Jahreshefte oesterr. Archäol. Inst.* 10 (1907) 146.

[6] Justinus 35.1.5. In order to make a complete break with the pretensions of his defeated predecessor, Alexander removed from the coins the figure of Apollo, which had been made predominant on the coinage by Demetrius I, and substituted that of Zeus: see Newell, *Seleucid Mint of Antioch* p. 37, and see above, n. 3. After the fall of Alexander Balas, Demetrius II restored Apollo on the coinage. Alexander may have made an effort to identify himself in the official cult with Zeus, thus linking himself personally with one of the fundamental Seleucid cults (see above, Ch. 4, n. 63). The evidence for this, however, is not conclusive; see Tondriau, "Souverains et souveraines Séleucides en divinités" 177.

[7] For a note on a puzzling coin wrongly attributed to the mint of Antioch at this period (the attribution illustrating the numismatic problems created by the complicated succession of the rulers of Syria at this time), see A. R. Bellinger, "King Antiochus in 151/0 B.C.," *Hesperia* 14 (1945) 58-59.

[8] Diodorus 33.3; Athenaeus 5.211; Bouché-Leclerq, *Hist. des Séleucides* 1.339.

[9] The chronology of the account of Malalas (207.17—208.4) is confused and contra-

writes that the city was "entirely restored" and "became better." This account cannot be verified. If it were true, it would indicate that the royal or the local financial resources were still, in spite of the recent disorders, sufficient to undertake the work of restoration.

A brief experience of the reign of Alexander Balas, who seems to have spent most of his time at Ptolemais, where he was closer to the Egyptians who were his patrons,[10] led Antioch to take a significant step, concerning which we unfortunately have only meager information. In 149-147 B.C. there appeared at Antioch and Seleucia Pieria bronze coins inscribed ΑΔΕΛΦΩΝ ΔΗΜΩΝ, representing what was evidently a kind of league of Antioch and Seleucia Pieria.[11] The precise nature and the political basis of this league are not known; the use of the term *demos* suggests that an effort was made to introduce popular rule. It is plain that the two cities, alarmed by the insecurity of their position in the midst of the intrigue and misrule which had prevailed since the death of Antiochus IV, felt it necessary to seek some basis for common protection that should be independent of the weak and untrustworthy royal administration. It may even have been hoped that such a union would have been able to control the succession. This innovation seems, however, to have been unsuccessful, for the coins were discontinued in 147 B.C. only three years after their initial appearance. Evidently the resources of the cities were too weak, and the external pressures were too great, for this attempt at solidarity to succeed.[12]

Possibly one of the factors in the disappearance of the league was the arrival in the kingdom, in 147 B.C., of Demetrius, the elder son of

---

dictory. For a detailed study of the problem, see Downey, "Seleucid Chronology" 106-120. Bevan, *House of Seleucus* 2.218, n. 4, points out that if an earthquake did occur in 148, the consequent hardships suffered by the people would have added to the general discontent with Alexander Balas' rule. A certain part of Malalas' garbled data could be taken to refer to an earthquake which occurred in 130 B.C.: see further below, n. 32.

[10] I Macc. 10:68; cf. Bevan, *House of Seleucus* 2.213.

[11] Babelon, *Rois de Syrie* p. cvii; *BMC Galatia etc.* pp. 151-152; Dieudonné, "Monnaies grecques de Syrie" 5-8; D. B. Waagé, "Coins" p. 69, nos. 720-721. It was formerly supposed that these coins were struck for Antioch, Apamea, Laodicea and Seleucia Pieria, the tetrapolis described by Strabo 16.2.4, p. 750 C. It is pointed out, however, by Bellinger in "End of the Seleucids" 60, n. 6, that H. Seyrig has observed that the coins are common at Antioch and Seleucia, but are never found at Apamea and Laodicea; thus it seems plain that they were not struck for all four cities. Moreover, the coins show two heads representing two *demoi* (Dieudonné, *loc.cit.*). On the disappearance of the league, see Bellinger, *op.cit.* 62, n. 17.

[12] The next attempt at political autonomy of which we hear is revealed by the issue by Antioch of bronze coins struck in the city's own name, beginning in A.D. 91/2; see below, nn. 74-75.

A History of Antioch

Demetrius I. Alexander hastened from Ptolemais to Antioch.[13] However, Ptolemy Philometor, who had been maintaining Alexander Balas on his throne, and at first came to his aid against Demetrius, quarreled with his protégé, and offered his support to the new claimant. At the same time, the people of Antioch, who had come to hate Alexander Balas because of the misdeeds of his minister Ammonius, welcomed the opportunity for a change of rulers,[14] especially since Demetrius could justly claim to be the legitimate representative of the Seleucid Dynasty. Hierax and Diodotus, who were in charge of the government of Antioch, saw their patron's position in the city weakening; and fearing Demetrius because they had headed the local opposition to his father, they led the city to open revolt against Alexander, who was expelled.[15] Ptolemy Philometor came to Antioch, was invested with the diadem, and was invited to become king (he was a Seleucid through his mother). However, he refused, and calling the people of Antioch together to an assembly, he persuaded them to accept Demetrius (145 B.C.).[16] Alexander Balas, who had fled to Cilicia, gathered an army there and descended on the plain of Antioch, which he began to burn and plunder. Ptolemy met him near Antioch, on the banks of the river Oenoparas (presumably one of the streams which flowed into the Lake of Antioch). Ptolemy was victorious. Alexander fled, and was murdered a little later, while the Egyptian king soon died of wounds received in the battle.

Demetrius II's return to Syria had been made with the assistance of a force of Cretan mercenaries commanded by a chief named Lasthenes. When Demetrius was established in power, he took two steps which brought him into trouble: he instituted a persecution of the adherents of Alexander Balas, and on the advice of Lasthenes, whom he had made his prime minister, he dismissed his native troops, thinking in this way to save expense and to do away with a possible center of disaffection, and retained in his service only the Cretan mercenaries. The precise sequence of the events which grew out of these two measures is not entirely clear;[17] the effect, however, was disastrous.

[13] 1 Macc. 10:68; Josephus *Ant.* 13.87.

[14] Josephus *Ant.* 13.108, 112. The restoration of the legitimate line was symbolized in the coins by the return of Apollo to the predominant position on the coinage: Newell, *Seleucid Mint of Antioch* pp. 37-38.

[15] Diodorus 32.9c (*FHG* 2, p. 16, no. 19); Justinus 35.2.3; Livy *Epit.* 52; see Bevan, *House of Seleucus* 2.220.

[16] Josephus *Ant.* 13.113-115.

[17] Our knowledge of these events comes from the accounts of Diodorus (33.4), 1 Macc. (11) and Josephus (*Ant.* 13.129-142). Since each of these texts contains details

The Cretan mercenaries naturally became unpopular both with the former adherents of Alexander Balas upon whom they had to carry out the new king's vengeance, and with the native troops whom they had displaced in the royal service. Many of these native soldiers doubtless lived in and near Antioch, and the civilian population would of course sympathize with them. The populace, indeed, which throughout the city's history was to display a reckless propensity for mocking its rulers, now took to lampooning Demetrius. This indication of the prevailing sentiment against him must have alarmed the king, for he ordered the discharged troops (and no doubt the general public as well) to be disarmed. When those who had weapons in their possession refused to give them up, the Cretans tried to take them by force, and did not scruple to kill even women and children in the process. Thus the city found itself in a state of civil war.

Demetrius, apparently when the disorders began, had appealed for help to the Jewish leader Jonathan, and three thousand picked Jewish troops were sent to Antioch to support the king. Demetrius was forced to barricade himself in the royal residence, and there was fighting in the streets between the populace, which was besieging the king's residence, and the troops, who both fought back from the royal residence and attacked the people in the streets from the flanks and the rear. The Jewish troops were outnumbered and at first were beaten; then they took to the rooftops and set the city on fire. As the houses were close together and mostly of wood, the flames spread quickly, and the civilians, distracted by this new peril, left off fighting and dispersed in an effort to save their homes and possessions. The king's troops then set upon the disorganized mob in the streets and killed so many that the survivors speedily surrendered. The Jewish soldiers, evidently with the king's approval, plundered the city and boasted that they killed 100,000 of the 120,000 Antiochenes who had resisted them. These figures appear in 1 Maccabees; Josephus merely says that the Jewish troops had to fight "many tens of thousands."[18] The Jewish claim of the number slain could well be an exaggeration (especially when there were only three thousand Jewish troops); but it need not follow from this that the other figure, if it represents the number of able-bodied men, is distorted.[19]

---

not given by the others, it is not possible to be perfectly clear, at some points, as to the sequence of events. See Bevan, *House of Seleucus* 2.223-226, and Bouché-Leclerq, *Hist. des Séleucides* 2.349-352.

[18] 1 Macc. 11.45-47; Josephus *Ant.* 13.137.

[19] The only other figure bearing on the population of the city during the Seleucid

The end of the revolt was followed by the punishment of the rebels, in which the new Demetrius showed himself far more cruel than his father, and the confiscation of their goods by the royal treasury. Syria was filled with citizens of Antioch who had fled their city in fear and hatred of the king, and who now sought only an opportunity to strike back.[20] The use of Jewish mercenaries also contributed greatly to the growing unpopularity of the Jewish community at Antioch.[21]

The chance for a blow at Demetrius soon presented itself for Diodotus, one of the former officers of Alexander Balas, who had left Antioch before the revolt against Demetrius II, now saw his opportunity to overthrow the hated ruler. Taking the name Tryphon, he put forward a son of Alexander Balas whom he proclaimed king as Antiochus VI Epiphanes Dionysus (before October 145 B.C.). Antioch, ready after its recent experiences for any change, welcomed the new king.[22] Neither of the rival rulers, however, was strong enough to eliminate the other; and while Tryphon and Antiochus VI occupied Antioch, Demetrius II simply retired to Seleucia Pieria and established his court there.[23]

Tryphon soon did away with the young Antiochus VI (142/1 B.C.) and set himself up as successor to the Seleucids; Antioch would now be the center of a "Macedonian" monarchy, in which the descendants of Alexander's people would be supreme, instead of merely forming a part of a mixed nation.[24] The attempt, however, failed and for a dozen years more Antioch had to witness the contendings of the would-be kings of Syria. Demetrius II, in the midst of his struggle against Tryphon, set out on an unsuccessful eastern campaign which ended by his being taken captive by the Parthians (139 B.C.). In the

period is found in the statement of Malalas that the Athenians and Macedonians whom Seleucus I transferred from Antigonia to Antioch, when he founded the city, numbered 5,300, i.e. presumably, 5,300 adult males, or heads of families. See above, Ch. 4, §4.

[20] Diodorus 33.4.3-4; Josephus *Ant.* 13.142.

[21] See Kraeling, "Jewish Community at Antioch" 146-147.

[22] 1 Macc. 11:56; Josephus *Ant.* 13.144. On the career of Tryphon, and the history of the period, see W. Hoffmann, "Tryphon," no. 1, *RE* 7A (1939) 715-722; E. Cavaignac, "A propos des Monnaies de Tryphon. L'Ambassade de Scipion Emilien," *Rev. Num.*, ser. 5, vol. 13 (1951) 131-138. On the coins of Tryphon, see Newell, *Seleucid Mint of Antioch* 71-73; *Dura Final Rep.* 6: Bellinger, *The Coins* p. 112, no. 84; H. Seyrig, *Notes on Syrian Coins* (New York 1950; *Numismatic Notes and Monographs* no. 119) 12-17. On the significance of his name, see J. Tondriau, "La Tryphé, philosophie royale ptolemaique," *REA* (1948) 49-54.

[23] Livy *Epit.* 52; Josephus *Ant.* 13.145, with Ralph Marcus' note *ad.loc.* in the Loeb Classical Library edition of Josephus. See Bevan, *House of Seleucus* 2.227.

[24] Bevan, *House of Seleucus* 2.230-231.

next year another son of Demetrius I, Antiochus VII Euergetes Sidetes (138-129 B.C.) took his brother's place at Seleucia Pieria.[25] Tryphon, driven out of Antioch, was captured near Apamea, and was allowed to commit suicide (138 B.C.).[26]

Antiochus VII, who was an able man, set out to restore the Seleucid power, and made substantial progress. By the year 130 he considered that he was in a position to undertake the recovery of the Seleucid possessions in the East; indeed, the accounts of his luxurious mode of living, though doubtless exaggerated, suggest that the kingdom now enjoyed some degree of prosperity, as it later did in the early years of Antiochus VIII Grypus.[27] For his eastern expedition, Antiochus was able to raise what seems to have been a very large army. Our sources speak of 80,000 or 100,000 troops and of 200,000 camp followers.[28] These figures of course, in the light of more reliable evidence for the size of ancient armies, must be an exaggeration; nevertheless, it is plain that the size of the force which Antiochus was in a position to collect

[25] 1 Macc. 15:10; Josephus *Ant.* 13.222. On the history of Seleucia Pieria at this period see Welles, *Royal Correspondence* 290-293. On the significance of the *asylia* which the city possessed by 138 B.C., see H. Seyrig, "Les rois Séleucides et les concessions de l'asylie," *Syria* 20 (1939) 35-39.

[26] 1 Macc. *loc.cit.*; Josephus *Ant.* 13.223-224; Strabo 14.5.2, p. 668 C.

[27] A fragment of Posidonius (*FHG* 3, p. 257, frag. 17) preserved by Athenaeus (5.210 d) tells how Antiochus VII daily held receptions for huge crowds, at which vast quantities of luxurious food were consumed or taken home by the feasters. Justinus (38.10) describes the fantastic luxury of the expedition which Antiochus led to the East; the very cooking vessels, he says, were of silver.

[28] The campaign is recorded in Josephus *Ant.* 13.250-253; Livy *Epit.* 59; Justinus 38.10; Appian *Syr.* 68; Euseb. *Chron.* 1, p. 255 ed. Schoene; Diodorus 34.15-17; Orosius, *Hist. adv. paganos* 5.10.8. Justinus mentions 80,000 troops and 200,000 camp followers (300,000 camp followers, according to the inferior MSS). Orosius speaks of 100,000 troops and 200,000 camp followers; Diodorus says that the disaster to Antiochus' army brought the loss of 300,000 men including noncombatants; though he writes ἀπολομένων, this does not necessarily mean that 300,000 were killed, but could mean only that this figure represented the number "lost," in the sense of killed or captured. The number 300,000 may thus be taken to represent Diodorus' information as to the total size of the army, for since the defeat was a total one, Diodorus (or his source) would have assumed that those who were not killed were made captive and enslaved, so that they were lost to their homeland. Debevoise, writing of this expedition in his *Hist. of Parthia* 31, n. 9, is needlessly severe in his censure of the accounts of it. He states that Diodorus wrote that "300,000 exclusive of camp followers were killed," whereas in reality Diodorus (as we have seen) says that 300,000 *including* camp followers were "lost" (one wonders whether Debevoise's error may grow out of the error in the Latin version of the passage in C. Müller's Didot edition of Didorus [Paris, 1842-1844], in which the passage is mistranslated in the sense given by Debevoise). Again, Debevoise criticizes Bevan for writing in one place (*House of Seleucus* 2.242) of an army of 80,000 men, while stating elsewhere (*ibid.* p. 247) that 300,000 men were lost. Debevoise does not realize that in the earlier passage Bevan was reproducing the figure given by Justinus, while in the latter he was citing the statement of Diodorus (a little carelessly, it is true, writing "men" when he ought to have specified "troops and camp followers").

made a great impression at the time, and the magnitude of his under-taking illustrates the degree to which Antiochus had been able to re-store the unity of Syria.[29] Though at first successful in his campaign, Antiochus was defeated by Phraates II and killed (129 B.C.), and his army was slain or made captive; every house in Antioch was filled with mourning.[30] There is some evidence that there was an agreement at this time for coordinated action between the Jews and the Parthians, and a passage in the Talmud may show that the Jews at about this period made an attack on Antioch.[31] There may have been an earth-quake at Antioch in 130 B.C., which would have added to the trials of the city.[32]

2. THE WEAKENING DYNASTY, 129-83 B.C.

The death of Antiochus VII, the last able king of the line, can be taken to mark the end of the Seleucid dynasty as an effective force.[33] From this time until the occupation of Syria by the Romans in 64 B.C., the history of Syria, and thus the history of Antioch, is a confusing and depressing record of growing weakness and dissolution, in which, from our meager sources, we learn little of importance concerning the capital.[34]

Demetrius II, who had been a Parthian captive since his defeat in 139 B.C., had been released while Antiochus VII was campaigning

[29] See Bevan, *House of Seleucus* 2.242.

[30] Diodorus 34.17.

[31] This is suggested by a veiled reference in the Talmud, Sota 33a, p. 281 ed. Goldschmidt. See Debevoise, *Hist. of Parthia* 94.

[32] The evidence for the earthquake consists of a garbled passage in Malalas that could refer to a disaster in 148 B.C., or to one in 130 B.C., or to two earthquakes, one in 148 and one in 130 (see above, n. 9). Malalas' data seem hopelessly confused; but if the earthquake he describes actually occurred in the month of Peritios (Febru-ary), as he says it did (p. 208, 1), it may seem difficult to believe that the event is really to be placed in the year 130 B.C. Antiochus VII would have set out on his eastern campaign in the spring or summer of this year, and it is hard to suppose that he would have gone on such an expedition (even though it had been long before planned and organized) if his capital had recently suffered a major earth-quake. Perhaps, however, the account preserved by Malalas exaggerates the severity of the disaster; and knowing of the confusions which are possible in Malalas' sources and in his use of them, we might even wonder whether the disaster which, in Malalas' chronicle, has come to sound like an earthquake in 130 B.C., might not actually have been originally the defeat of Antiochus VII in the following year, which, with its loss of life, would have struck the city almost as heavily as an earthquake.

[33] See Bevan, *House of Seleucus* 2.246.

[34] This difficult and obscure period has been illuminated by the valuable study of Bellinger, "End of the Seleucids," to which the narrative given here is greatly in-debted. For a more detailed examination of the events treated here, the reader should consult Bellinger's account.

against Phraates II in order to make trouble in Syria in the absence of Antiochus. Demetrius now began his brief second reign (129-126 B.C.). His return can hardly, after the events of his first reign, have been welcome at Antioch.

Demetrius was persuaded by his mother-in-law, the elder Cleopatra, to undertake an expedition to restore her to power in Egypt. He set out, but after his departure both Antioch and Apamea revolted from him.[35] Moreover, Ptolemy arranged to send to Syria a youth named Alexander who was put forward as an adopted son of Antiochus VII Sidetes, though in reality his father was a merchant in Egypt. The people of Antioch, who evidently believed the claim as to Alexander's adoption, and were in fact ready to receive almost any king if they could be free of Demetrius' cruelty, welcomed their new ruler (128 B.C.), who was to reign briefly as Alexander II Zabinas (128-123 B.C.).[36] Alexander made himself popular in Antioch by showing deep filial piety when the body of Antiochus VII was returned to the city, with great honor, by Phraates.[37] In 127/6 B.C. Demetrius was defeated near Damascus, and was later killed on a ship in the harbor of Tyre.[38]

Alexander II Zabinas, once established in Syria, felt secure enough to slight Ptolemy Physcon, who had put him on the throne. The Egyptian king then made an agreement with the elder Cleopatra, and formed an alliance with her son Antiochus (nicknamed Grypus from his enormous nose), who as a son of Demetrius II could be considered to represent the legitimate line. A marriage was arranged between Antiochus Grypus and Cleopatra Tryphaena, and the elder Cleopatra associated him with herself, as joint ruler of Syria. This reign, of Cleopatra and Antiochus VIII Epiphanes Philometor Callinicus, lasted from 125 to 121 B.C.[39]

Alexander's hold on the kingdom could hardly be maintained against this new effort to restore the Seleucid family, and his supporters began to desert him. In 123/2 B.C. he was defeated in battle by the forces of Antiochus VIII and fled to Antioch. There he felt that he would receive no support from the unstable populace, who might be expected to favor the legitimate claimant, especially since he was supported by the power of Egypt; besides Alexander had no funds with which to pay

[35] Justinus 39.1.2-3; cf. Bevan, *House of Seleucus* 2.248; Bellinger, "End of the Seleucids" 62.
[36] Justinus 39.1.5. On the details of Alexander's arrival and position in Antioch, see Bellinger, "End of the Seleucids" 62, n. 17.
[37] Justinus 39.1.6.   [38] Bellinger, "End of the Seleucids" 63-64.
[39] Justinus 39.2.1.

his troops, whose number is given as 40,000.[40] In order to obtain funds with which to maintain himself in power, he took the desperate step of removing from the Temple of Zeus the solid gold image of Victory that the statue of Zeus was holding, excusing the sacrilege by saying jokingly that "Victory had been offered to him by Zeus." There appears to have been no immediate reaction to this; but when a few days later it was discovered that he was secretly attempting to have the huge golden statue of Zeus himself removed from the same temple, the people took violent action. Alexander collected the royal treasure and fled at night toward Seleucia Pieria. The news of his sacrilege having already reached that city, the gates were shut against him, and he then set out along the coast toward Posidium. A great storm happened to come up, his people deserted him, and he fell into the hands of brigands. His captors at once took him to the camp of Antiochus VIII, where he was executed or allowed to commit suicide.[41]

Antiochus VIII, harassed by his mother's intrigues, found himself compelled to murder her in 121/0 B.C., and he reigned alone until 96 B.C. The first years of this reign were tranquil, and permitted some recuperation of the kingdom's resources. Antiochus was able to celebrate games at Daphne with unusual splendor, and the people, Posidonius wrote, were prosperous and lived in comfort, "using the gymnasia as mere baths in which they anointed themselves with expensive oil and perfumes, and living in the *grammateia*—for this is the name by which they called the commons where the diners met—as though they were their private houses."[42] While allowance must be made for exaggeration in the sources, it is important to find that Antioch at this period seems to have enjoyed a relative prosperity, suggested also by the accounts of the luxurious living of Antiochus VII Sidetes.[43]

[40] Justinus 39.2.5; Diodorus 34.28; Josephus *Ant.* 13.269. The location of the battle is not recorded.

[41] Justinus 39.2.5-6; Diodorus 34.28; Josephus *Ant.* 13.269. Eusebius *Chron.* 1, pp. 257-258 ed. Schoene, alone reports the suicide. See Bellinger, "End of the Seleucids" 65, and Jansen, "Politik Antiochos' des IV" 34. The statue of Zeus Nikephoros is presumably one that Antiochus IV seems to have erected; see Lacroix, "Copies de statues sur les monnaies des Séleucides" 166. A somewhat similar story of the purloining of a gold statue is told about Antiochus IX Cyzicenus (114-95 B.C.); see the account of his reign below.

[42] Justinus 39.2.7-9; Appian *Syr.* 69; Posidonius, frag. 31, *FHG* 3, p. 263, preserved by Athenaeus 5.210 e and 12.540 b, and frag. 18, *FHG* 3, p. 258 = *F Gr Hist* 2A, p. 228, 87 F 10, preserved by Athenaeus, 5.210 e-f and 12.540 a-b. The translation of frag. 18 quoted is that of C. B. Gulick in the Loeb Classical Library edition of Athenaeus. On the use of gymnasia for such purposes, see C. A. Forbes, "Expanded Uses of the Greek Gymnasium," *CP* 40 (1945) 39-40.

[43] See above, notes 27, 29.

The somewhat barren history of the city in these days is relieved by a brief reflection of its intellectual life in what we know of the career of the celebrated Greek poet Archias (later to be a client of Cicero), who was born in Antioch probably before the reign of Antiochus VIII. Antioch, at the time when Archias grew up there and gained a distinguished place for himself by his intellectual gifts, was (Cicero writes) "a renowned and populous city, the seat of brilliant scholarship and artistic refinement."[44]

After Antiochus VIII had reigned alone for about seven years, a rival arose in the person of his half-brother Antiochus, the son of his mother Cleopatra Thea by Antiochus VII Sidetes. This Antiochus, who was to be known as Antiochus IX Philopator (114-95 B.C.), had been living in Cyzicus and so was nicknamed Cyzicenus. In 114/3 B.C. Antiochus Cyzicenus collected enough forces to invade Syria from the north and to drive Antiochus Grypus out of Antioch (before October 113 B.C.).[45] Within a year Antiochus Cyzicenus seems to have been in control of the whole Seleucid territory. His position appeared to be further strengthened when an Egyptian princess, Cleopatra, who had been divorced in the course of dynastic intrigues in Egypt, fled to Syria and offered herself to Antiochus Cyzicenus as his wife, bringing as a welcome dowry the army of Cyprus, which she had attached to herself. In spite of this reinforcement, however, the new Antiochus was defeated when he offered battle to Antiochus Grypus (the place of the battle is not recorded), and he was forced to flee, leaving his wife Cleopatra in Antioch. Antiochus Grypus laid siege to the city and took it (summer 112 B.C.).[46] His wife Tryphaena, in spite of his vigorous protests, insisted on the execution of her sister Cleopatra, whom she hated. Tryphaena sent soldiers to bring Cleopatra from the temple in which she had sought sanctuary; and when the men were unable to drag Cleopatra away from the cult statue to which she clung, they brutally cut off her hands and then executed her.[47]

Soon, however, Antiochus Cyzicenus recovered Antioch and had Tryphaena executed in retaliation for her shocking murder of her sister.[48] The city changed hands again when Antiochus Grypus gained possession of it at some time between July and October 111, and then

---

[44] *Pro Archia* 4, transl. of N. H. Watts in the Loeb Classical Library.
[45] For the chronology, see Bellinger, "End of the Seleucids" 66-67, 87-91.
[46] Justinus 39.3.3-5; on the date, see Newell, *Seleucid Mint of Antioch*, 97.
[47] Justinus 39.3.5-11. The name of the temple is not mentioned.
[48] Justinus 39.3.12; Newell, *Seleucid Mint of Antioch* 98.

A History of Antioch

once more lost it to Antiochus Cyzicenus in 110/9 B.C.[49] During the periods when he was forced out of Antioch, Antiochus Grypus seems to have made Seleucia Pieria his capital; his grant of "freedom" to the city, in recognition of its loyal support, is attested in a royal letter dated in September 109 B.C. which is preserved in an inscription of Cyprus.[50] It is indicative of the relative weakness of the rivals that they were able on occasion to maintain their capitals in cities as close as Antioch and Seleucia. The struggle in fact reached a stalemate; Josephus writes that both kings "were in the position of athletes whose strength is exhausted but who are ashamed to yield, and so continue to prolong the contest by periods of inactivity and rest."[51] The dwindling of their power is illustrated by the fact that by 104/3 B.C. the silver coinage of Antiochus Grypus had ceased to be issued by the mints at Antioch and Tarsus, while the silver coins of Antiochus Cyzicenus likewise ceased to be struck; Seleucia Pieria began to issue autonomous coins in 104 B.C. and Antioch in 103 B.C.[52] Antiochus Cyzicenus, according to a report preserved by Diodorus,[53] was mainly interested in actors and such things as mechanical curiosities, while he made no effort to provide himself with essential military supplies; and Antiochus Grypus, at least before the struggle with his half-brother began, took pleasure in presenting lavish games at Daphne.[54]

The details of the struggles of these last Seleucids to maintain themselves in power are for the most part lost; but we do have at this point one further glimpse—apparently a characteristic one—of the shabby expedients to which they were sometimes driven. Clement of Alexandria, writing early in the third century of the Christian era, gives as an example of the worthlessness of pagan belief a story of how Antiochus IX Cyzicenus (114-95 B.C.), when unable to raise money by any other means, had a solid gold statue of Zeus, fifteen cubits in size, melted down and replaced by a gilded image.[55] This act alone would have seemed sufficiently shocking; but there may have been more of

[49] On the chronology and sequence of events, see Bellinger, "End of the Seleucids" 68, 87.
[50] The inscription has been published most recently by Welles, *Royal Correspondence* nos. 71-72, pp. 288-294; see also Bellinger, "End of the Seleucids" 69, with n. 47.
[51] *Ant.* 13.327, transl. of Ralph Marcus in the Loeb Classical Library.
[52] Dieudonné, "Monnaies grecque de Syrie" 13; Newell, *Seleucid Mint of Antioch* 107; idem, *Ake-Ptolemais and Damascus* 76-78; Bellinger, "End of the Seleucids" 71, 87-88. The municipal coin of Antioch of 103 seems to be the only one known. It is not clear whether this is an isolated phenomenon or whether it forms a part of a series with the autonomous coins that appear beginning in 92/1 (see below, n. 74).
[53] 34.34.   [54] See above, n. 42.
[55] *Protrept.* 4.52.3, p. 40, 22-25 ed. O. Stählin (Leipzig, 1936).

the same thing, for Malalas[56] preserves a report that Antiochus XI Philadelphus, who reigned briefly in 93 B.C. as one of the successors of Antiochus IX Cyzicenus (114-95 B.C.), "built two temples in Daphne, of Apollo and Artemis, setting up in them two golden statues, granting to those who took refuge there the privilege of not being ejected from these temples." The statement that Antiochus Philadelphus "built" temples of Apollo and Artemis in Daphne may, in Malalas' usage, mean only that this king repaired or renovated existing buildings.[57] The real significance of the passage seems to be that some predecessor of Antiochus Philadelphus had either removed altogether the golden cult statues of Apollo and Artemis from their temples at Daphne, or had replaced them with images of baser material, so that the function of the temples as sanctuaries seemed either impaired or destroyed. Thus it would appear to have been one of the first acts of the reign of Antiochus Philadelphus to replace the sacred images and to renew the function of the temples as sanctuaries. Whether Antiochus Cyzicenus had seized and melted down these statues in addition to that of Zeus (which presumably was at Antioch or Daphne, though Clement does not specify this detail), or whether some other desperate king had removed them (as Alexander II Zabinas in 123/2 B.C. had tried to seize the solid gold statues of Victory and of Zeus in Antioch),[58] we do not know. Nor do we know how Antiochus Philadelphus could have found the funds to replace the gold images of Apollo and Artemis. But many of the last Seleucids must have been forced to desperate measures; and the rapidity of the appearance and disappearance of one claimant after another is doubtless to be laid in large measure to the slenderness of the resources at their command. But if a king's funds were meager, his rival's might be equally scanty, and so the gamble must often have seemed to promise some hope of success.[59]

---

[56] 234.2-9.

[57] Malalas regularly lumps under the term "to build" building activities of all sorts, whether new work or restoration; see above, Ch. 2, §4.

[58] See above, n. 41.

[59] Newell, *Seleucid Mint of Antioch* 110, suggests that Antiochus Cyzicenus melted down the statue of Zeus at Antioch when he was hard pressed for funds on the appearance of his rival Seleucus VI in 95 (see further below). The suggestion is plausible, though there were of course other moments during Antiochus' career when he might have been driven to such an expedient. Bevan, *House of Seleucus* 2.252, n. 2, suggests that Clement of Alexandria's story about the melting down of the statue of Zeus by Antiochus Cyzicenus may be merely an echo of Alexander II Zabinas' plundering of the Temple of Zeus in Antioch. Bevan, however, does not seem to know the passage in Malalas which suggests that Antiochus XI Philadelphus may have been eager to rectify a misdeed of Antiochus IX Cyzicenus; and the details of the actions of Alexander II Zabinas and Antiochus IX Cyzicenus seem sufficiently different to make it

Most of what we know of the history of Antioch at this period concerns the almost constant struggles between the successive claimants to the throne. One of the few known events not connected with this perpetual warfare is the construction of a museum and library which appears to have taken place either during the reign of Antiochus IX Cyzicenus (114-95 B.C.) or during that of Antiochus X Eusebes (95-92 B.C.). In his account of the reign of Tiberius, Malalas writes that there was a fire that destroyed, among other buildings, "the shrine of the Muses which was built by Antiochus Philopator with the money left in his will by Maron of Antioch, who had emigrated to Athens and had then stipulated that there should be built with his money the shrine of the Muses and a library."⁶⁰ Maron was presumably a merchant who, like other Syrian business men, had settled in Athens and, having made a fortune there, had remembered his native city in his will.⁶¹ It is not possible to determine with any precision the date of Maron's benefaction. Maron himself seems to be otherwise unknown, and Malalas does not make it clear which king carried out the terms of the will. There were three Antiochi who were called Philopator, namely Antiochus IX Philopator Cyzicenus (114-95 B.C.), Antiochus X Eusebes Philopator (95-92 B.C.) and Antiochus XII Dionysus Epiphanes Philopator Callinicus (87-84 B.C.). The last-named cannot have been concerned with Maron's bequest, since he reigned only in Damascus and it seems certain that he never occupied Antioch.⁶² Since Malalas does not mention an Antiochus Philopator elsewhere in his work, we cannot be sure whether he meant Antiochus IX or Antiochus X.⁶³ The museum

---

unnecessary to doubt Clement of Alexandria's account. On the other hand, Müller (*Antiq. Antioch.* 66-67), not knowing the story preserved by Clement of Alexandria, suspects that Malalas' record of the work of Antiochus XI Philadelphus may be garbled or incorrect; but though it is very possible that there is an element of error in Malalas' account, the story preserved by Clement of Alexandria suggests a plausible occasion for the work that Malalas describes.

⁶⁰ Malalas 235.18—236.1. On ancient libraries, see C. Callmer, "Die antiken Bibliotheken," *Opuscula archeologica* 3 (1944) 145-193. On the cult of the Muses in Antioch and its neighborhood, see Mouterde, "Pierides Musae."

⁶¹ Evidence for the foreign population of Athens at this time, and for its commercial activities, is collected by John Day, *An Economic History of Athens under Roman Domination* (New York 1942); see especially 79-81 (Maron, however, is not mentioned).

⁶² Newell, *Ake-Ptolemais and Damascus* 90-92; Bellinger, "End of the Seleucids" 77-78.

⁶³ See the table of Malalas' references to the Seleucid kings in Downey, "Seleucid Chronology" 111-113. Müller, *Antiq. Antioch.* 67-68, supposed that Malalas referred to Antiochus XIII, who reigned briefly after the withdrawal of Tigranes from Syria in 69 B.C. However, the appellations Dionysus Epiphanes Philopator Callinicus which Müller

built with Maron's bequest stood, according to Malalas' accounts, on the agora on which the bouleuterion also stood. This was apparently the Hellenistic agora in Epiphania.[64] The museum was destroyed in the fire that ruined this agora in a.d. 23/24, during the reign of Tiberius.[65]

Finally in 96 b.c. the reign of Antiochus Grypus came to an end when he was murdered by his minister of war, Heracleon of Beroea, who plotted to seize the throne. Antioch, however, was almost immediately occupied by Antiochus Cyzicenus.[66] Two more claimants to the throne soon appeared. Ptolemy Lathyrus now abandoned Antiochus Cyzicenus and in 96/5 b.c. installed Demetrius, the fourth son of Antiochus Grypus, in Damascus, as Demetrius III Theus Philopator Soter (96-88 b.c.).[67] Moreover, the eldest son of Antiochus Grypus, Seleucus VI Epiphanes Nicator (96/5 b.c.), raised an army, evidently on the coast of Cilicia, and set out for Antioch. Antiochus Cyzicenus collected an army in Antioch and went out to meet Seleucus, but was defeated and lost his life. Seleucus then occupied Antioch, apparently during 95 and 94 b.c.[68]

Seleucus was attacked, however, by Antiochus X Eusebes (95-92 b.c.), son of Antiochus IX Cyzicenus, and driven out of Antioch. The city may have welcomed a new claimant because Seleucus, it is said, was violent and tyrannical. Seleucus fled to Cilicia, whence he had originally set out, and there either was murdered or committed suicide.[69] Antiochus X Eusebes reigned in Antioch from 94 to 92 b.c.;[70] but he soon had to contend with two brothers of Seleucus VI, the twins Antiochus XI Epiphanes Philadelphus and Philip I, also surnamed Epiphanes

---

attributes to Antiochus XIII are in reality those of Antiochus XII, whose history had not yet been reconstructed in detail in Müller's time. Why Müller did not take Antiochus IX and Antiochus X into account is not apparent. Stauffenberg (*Malalas* 467) reproduces Malalas' words and does not undertake to decide the question.

[64] See above, Ch. 5, §6.   [65] See below, Ch. 8, §3.

[66] Josephus *Ant.* 13.365; Trogus *Prol.* 39; Posidonius, frag. 36, *FHG* 3, p. 265 preserved by Athenaeus, 4.153 b; Eusebius *Chron.* 1, pp. 259-260 ed. Schoene; cf. Strabo 16.2.7, p. 751 C; Newell, *Seleucid Mint of Antioch* 108-110.

[67] The hitherto mistaken impression of the sequence of events that led to Demetrius' establishment as a claimant to the throne is corrected by Bellinger, "End of the Seleucids" 72, with n. 63.

[68] Josephus *Ant.* 13.366, 368. Josephus says that Seleucus captured and executed Antiochus, while Eusebius (*Chron.* 1, pp. 259-260 ed. Schoene) says that Antiochus killed himself to avoid being captured. See Newell, *Seleucid Mint of Antioch* 111-113 and Bellinger "End of the Seleucids" 72-73.

[69] Josephus *Ant.* 13.367; Appian *Syr.* 69. The conflicting accounts of Seleucus' death are discussed by Bellinger, "End of the Seleucids" 74, n. 70.

[70] Newell, *Seleucid Mint of Antioch* 113-114.

Philadelphus. Antiochus XI drove Antiochus X out of Antioch, and held the city for a time in 93 B.C.[71] Antiochus X, however, made a counterattack, and Antiochus XI was defeated near Antioch and was drowned in the Orontes while fleeing.[72]

Demetrius III, who apparently had taken no part in this struggle, now joined Philip I in attacking Antiochus X Eusebes. Antiochus was killed in a battle with the Parthians, who were threatening Syria, and Demetrius occupied Antioch, where he issued coins ca. 92-89 B.C.[73] At the same time, however, the minting of royal Seleucid bronze ceased, and Antioch issued (92/91 B.C.) municipal bronze coins in its own name, inscribed ANTIOXEΩN THΣ ΜΗΤΡΟΠΟΛΕΩΣ.[74] It is not clear whether these coins represent a new issue or whether they form a series with the municipal coinage issued in 103 B.C. (see above, n. 52). That Antioch undertook or was allowed to issue its own coins, which continued to appear for twenty years, may be taken as an indication of the lessening of the royal authority.[75] Demetrius no doubt had felt it necessary to concede a measure of autonomy to the city in order to win its support, somewhat as Antiochus Grypus had granted "freedom" to Seleucia Pieria in 109 B.C.[76] It is also a sign of the times that Antioch now acted for itself, instead of returning to the "league" with Seleucia Pieria which the two cities had tried unsuccessfully to establish (in 149-147 B.C.) under Alexander I Balas.

While Demetrius III occupied Antioch, Philip I seems to have ceased to act in concert with his brother; by 88 B.C. he had made alliance with Straton, the ruler of Beroea, and had made that city his headquarters. When Demetrius returned to Syria from an expedition into Judaea, he proceeded to besiege Beroea with ten thousand infantry and a thousand

[71] Newell, *Seleucid Mint of Antioch*, 115-117; Bellinger, "End of the Seleucids" 74, 92-94. As Bellinger points out, the numismatic evidence indicates that Antiochus XI was in possession of Antioch for more than the "few weeks" which Newell supposed represented his residence in the city.

[72] Josephus *Ant.* 13.369; Eusebius *Chron.* 1, pp. 261-262 ed. Schoene.

[73] Josephus *Ant.* 13.370-371. On the accounts of the death of Antiochus X, which differ, see Bellinger, "End of the Seleucids" 75, n. 73. On the coins of Demetrius, see Newell, *Seleucid Mint of Antioch* 117-18. A coin suggests that in the interval between the death of Antiochus X and the occupation of Antioch by Demetrius III, Cleopatra Selene, the widow of Antiochus X, set up a regency in the city for her young son, who later became Antiochus XIII; see Bellinger, "Some Coins from Antioch" 53-55.

[74] G. Macdonald, *Cat. of the Greek Coins in the Hunterian Collection* (Glasgow, 1899-1905) 3.143-144; D. B. Waagé, "Coins" p. 24.

[75] For a convenient discussion of the economic and administrative factors involved in the issuance of municipal bronze coins, see A. R. Bellinger in *Dura Prelim. Rep., 7th-8th Seasons*, 405-407, and the same scholar's "Early Coinage of Roman Syria" 61-62.

[76] Newell, *Seleucid Mint of Antioch* 117-118, 124; Bellinger, "End of the Seleucids" 76. On Antiochus Grypus' grant of "freedom" to Seleucia, see above, n. 50.

cavalry. Straton appealed for help to an Arab chieftain named Aziz and to Mithradates Sinaces, a Parthian governor, and they blockaded Demetrius and his troops, who were eventually forced to surrender. Demetrius was sent to honorable captivity in Parthia, and those prisoners who happened to be citizens of Antioch were set free without ransom, a wise and generous measure which doubtless made it easy for Philip to occupy Antioch, which he did at once.[77]

Philip I reigned in Antioch from 88 to 84/3 B.C.[78] He had to contend with his youngest and sole remaining brother, Antiochus XII Dionysus, called Epiphanes Philopator Callinicus (87-84 B.C.), who established himself as king at Damascus in 87/6 B.C.,[79] but Antiochus' activities all seem to have been centered about Damascus, and Antioch during this time seems to have enjoyed a brief period of tranquillity under Philip. The city continued to issue its municipal bronze coins, which indicates that Philip, like Demetrius III, under whom this coinage began, was not considered to have full authority in such matters. Philip's silver coinage is abundant and is found as far east as Dura, which by now was a Parthian city. This may show that Philip was supported by the Parthians; at any rate it suggests that the reign, though brief, was a relatively stable one and that Antioch and its territory enjoyed some measure of economic prosperity.[80]

We have in fact at this time one of our rare glimpses of the contemporary commercial relations between Antioch and the outside world, in the form of a Greek dedication in honor of the city of Antioch set up at Delos, soon after 88 B.C., by one Lucius Granius.[81] It is not clear

[77] Josephus *Ant.* 13.384-386. Bouché-Leclerq, *Hist. des Séleucides* 1.425, n. 2, and Bellinger, "End of the Seleucids" 77, n. 82, point out that the phraseology which Josephus uses of Philip's occupation of Antioch (κατασχὼν αὐτήν, §386) does not, as some students have thought (e.g. Ralph Marcus in his translation of Josephus in the Loeb Classical Library), necessarily mean that Philip had to take the city by force.

[78] Newell, *Seleucid Mint of Antioch* 119-124; on the chronology of his reign, see Bellinger, "End of the Seleucids" 95-97. Malalas (318.4-6) speaks of the demolition of "the public bath of King Philip" in the reign of Constantine to make room for the octagonal Great Church. It is not clear whether this bath was named for Philip I or Philip II.

[79] Josephus *Ant.* 13.387; Newell, *Ake-Ptolemais and Damascus* 82-92. Antiochus X is said by Eusebius (*Chron.* 1, pp. 261-262 ed. Schoene) to have come into collision with Philip, but this account must be mistaken; actually Antiochus X appears to have been killed in a battle with the Parthians in 92 B.C. (Bellinger, "End of the Seleucids" 75, n. 73).

[80] See Bellinger, "End of the Seleucids" 79.

[81] J. Hatzfeld, "Les italiens résidants à Délos," *BCH* 36 (1912) p. 40, no. 6 and pp. 212-214, no. 34 = *Inscriptions de Délos* no. 2355 (cf. no. 2612). On the Roman and Syrian traders at Delos, see Rostovtzeff, *Soc. Econ. Hist. Hell. World* 702, 741-742, 778, 787ff., 791.

whether he was a Roman merchant or a freedman of Syrian origin; but his dedication (consisting of a small altar which bore a statuette, now lost) illustrates the close connections which must have existed between Antioch and the free port of Delos, which for some years had been serving as the principal commercial link between the eastern Mediterranean and Italy. Many Roman and Syrian merchants lived there, and although Granius' dedication (made either because he was a native of Antioch or was bound by close ties to the city) happens to be an isolated document, we may be sure that commercial communication between Antioch and Delos was frequent and close.

3. Tigranes and the Coming of the Romans, 83-64 b.c.

The deaths of Antiochus XII and of Philip I in 84/3 b.c.[82] left three claimants to the Seleucid throne, namely, Philip II, son of Philip I, and two sons of Antiochus X, the elder of whom was later Antiochus XIII Asiaticus, who reigned briefly after the withdrawal of Tigranes in 69 b.c.; the name of the younger is not known. It seems likely that all three claimants were minors.[83] Cleopatra Selene, the widow of Antiochus X, was able to seek support for her son Antiochus Asiaticus.[84] Of Philip's son we hear nothing. The resources of the contesting families must have been exhausted, and it is not surprising to read in Justinus that the people of Syria began to think of turning to outside help, and considered the various kings to whom they might offer their land.[85] The chief candidates were Mithradates of Pontus and Ptolemy Lathyrus. Some of the Syrians favored the one, some the other; but Mithradates was involved in hostilities with Rome, and Ptolemy had shown himself to be fundamentally hostile to Syria. The final choice (of at least a majority of the people of influence) was Tigranes of Armenia.[86] He had the merit of being allied with the Parthians and related by marriage to Mithradates of Pontus, so that it could be hoped that Syria under his tutelage would be safe from at least these two potential enemies.

The accounts of Tigranes' occupation of Syria differ. According to the tradition preserved in Justinus, Tigranes came to Syria peacefully, by invitation, and his reign was tranquil and prosperous. Appian, how-

---

[82] Josephus *Ant.* 13.391; on Philip's end, see Bellinger, "End of the Seleucids" 97.
[83] This is the opinion of Dobiáš, *Hist.* 547.
[84] See Bellinger, "End of the Seleucids" 79, n. 91; 81; idem, "Some Coins from Antioch" 53-55.
[85] 40.1.1-4.
[86] On his career, see F. Geyer, "Tigranes," no. 1, *RE* 6A (1937) 970-978.

ever, and Strabo speak of a conquest by force; Strabo, followed by Eutropius, writes that Seleucia Pieria refused to admit Tigranes.[87] What probably happened was that the oriental elements in the population, plus perhaps those of Greek descent who could no longer tolerate Seleucid rule with its perpetual civil war, summoned and supported the Armenian prince, while he inevitably met opposition, among certain elements of the population, as a foreign usurper. Certainly Tigranes could not have taken over the rule of Syria as he did without the approval of an important part of the population.[88] An indication of the economic condition of Syria just before the arrival of Tigranes is given by the fact that when he occupied the country he found bronze coins forty years old in circulation at Antioch.[89] If the public services had deteriorated to the extent suggested by this condition of the coinage, a radical change in the administration might have been welcome indeed.

Tigranes' viceroy in Syria for the fourteen years during which he ruled the country was his general Magadates, who presumably made

[87] Justinus 40.1.2—2.1; Appian *Syr.* 48; Strabo 11.14.15, p. 523 C, and 16.2.8, p. 751 C; Eutropius 6.14.2. Josephus likewise seems to understand that force was necessary (*Ant.* 13.419). During the political troubles of the Seleucid period, Seleucia Pieria consistently favored the legitimate claimants to the throne (Honigmann, "Seleukeia" 1188-1189). The text of Strabo 16.2.8, p. 751 C is obviously corrupt. Writing of Seleucia Pieria, Strabo says that it is a notable fortress, too strong to be taken by force: ἔρυμα δέ ἐστιν ἀξιόλογον καὶ κρείττων βίας ἡ πόλις. διόπερ καὶ ἐλευθέραν αὐτὴν ἔκρινε Πομπήιος, ἀποκλείσας Τιγράνην. The text as it stands implies that Pompey somehow prevented Tigranes from occupying Seleucia Pieria, and so far as we know there is no occasion on which this could have happened. Moreover, there is no logic in the statement "Seleucia is too strong to be captured; therefore Pompey, when he had shut Tigranes off from it, declared it free." And if the city was too strong to be captured, why should there have been occasion for Pompey to shut Tigranes off from it? Bouché-Leclerq, *Hist. des Séleucides* 1.444, n. 1, comparing the passage with the statement of Eutropius (16.4.2: *et cum venisset* [sc. Pompeius] *in Syriam, Seleuciam vicinam Antiochiae civitatem libertate donavit, quod regem Tigranem non recepisset*), perceived that the clue to the necessary correction of the text of Strabo is given by Eutropius' words. "On se demande [the French scholar writes] si Eutrope n'a pas lu et si on ne devrait pas lire dans Strabon: Σελεύκειαν ἀποκλείσασαν Τιγράνην au lieu de: [Πομπήιος] ἀποκλείσας Τιγράνην." It seems difficult to believe, however, that Bouché-Leclerq meant to delete Pompey's name, for in this case ἔκρινε would be left without a subject, and there is no antecedent from which a subject could be supplied. Evidently Bouché-Leclerq's bracketing of Pompey's name is a lapse; the emendation of ἀποκλείσας to ἀποκλείσασαν is certainly right (it is accepted by Honigmann, "Seleukeia" 1189). Casaubon seems to have perceived that the Greek text as it stood in his time lacked sense, for in his Latin version he eschewed a literal rendering, writing instead *ea insignis munitio est, et urbs inexpugnabilis: quapropter excluso hinc Tigrane, Pompeius eam liberam pro nunciavit.* This was a step in the right direction; but Casaubon did not suggest an emendation. The text as emended (διόπερ καὶ ἐλευθέραν αὐτὴν ἔκρινε Πομπήιος, ἀποκλείσασαν Τιγράνην) gives Strabo's own thought as to the reason why Pompey bestowed *libertas* on Seleucia.

[88] See Bouché-Leclerq, *Hist. des Séleucides* 1.430; Dobiáš, *Hist.* 547 and the same scholar's later study, "Occupation de la Syrie" 215-256.

[89] *Dura Final Rep.* 6: Bellinger, *The Coins* p. 114, nos. 112, 112a.

his headquarters at Antioch.[90] The mint of Antioch began to issue coins in the name of Tigranes as βασιλεύς; later the oriental title βασιλεὺς βασιλέων appears, suggesting that while Tigranes may at first have been careful to present himself as a Hellenic ruler, or as a successor to Hellenic rulers, he came in time to adopt some of the forms of an oriental monarch.[91] The government, however, cannot have been wholly orientalized, for the Tyche of Antioch, as portrayed by Eutychides, the famous symbol that recalled the origin of the city as a Seleucid foundation, appeared on the coins (for the first time in the history of the city)[92]; and the city of Antioch itself continued to issue the municipal coins bearing its own name, ΑΝΤΙΟΧΕΩΝ ΤΗΣ ΜΗΤΡΟΠΟΛΕΩΣ, which it had begun to strike in 92/1 B.C.; these continued to appear until 69 B.C., when Antiochus XIII, on becoming Seleucid ruler with the support of Lucullus, apparently put an end to this issue in order to curtail the powers of the municipality.[93]

During the reign of Tigranes in Syria, we hear little concerning Antioch. At some time before Tigranes' evacuation of Syria in 69 B.C., the whole country suffered from a severe earthquake in which, Justinus says,[94] "170,000 people and many cities perished." This disaster, he continues, was taken to be a portent of coming change; and events bore out the prophecy. The Greek element of the population had come to dislike the rule of Tigranes, who had become "pompous and haughty in the midst of his great prosperity."[95] Antioch had been allowed to retain so much autonomy as permitted the city to issue coins in its own name; but when at the same time the ruler styled himself "King of Kings" in Syria, and observed the ceremonial of an oriental court,[96] many citizens of Syria must have found their situation distasteful. The discontinuance of the autonomous coins of Antioch, which apparently took place in 72 B.C., may show that by this time Tigranes abandoned whatever pretence he may once have made to observe the forms of Hellenic government, and had finally converted his rule to an oriental despotism.

[90] Appian *Syr.* 48-49; Bouché-Leclerq, *Hist. des Séleucides* 1.436.
[91] G. Macdonald, "The Coinage of Tigranes I," *Num. Chron.* ser. 4, vol. 2 (1902) 193-201.
[92] See Lacroix, "Copies de statues sur les Monnaies des Séleucides" 175, and Toynbee, *Hadrianic School* 132, and cf. above, Ch. 4, n. 88.
[93] See H. Seyrig, "Antiquités syriennes, 42: Sur les ères de quelques villes de Syrie," *Syria* 27 (1950) 12-14, 18; cf. Newell, *Seleucid Mint of Antioch* 117-118; Dieudonné, "Monnaies grecques de Syrie" 13-17.
[94] 40.2.1; cf. Downey, "Seleucid Chronology" 106-108, 119, n. 1.
[95] Plutarch *Lucullus*, 21.3.   [96] Plutarch *Lucull.* 21.4-5.

An opportunity for change presented itself. Rome had been at war with Mithradates of Pontus, and in 72 B.C. the Roman commander Lucullus had forced Mithradates to take refuge in Armenia under the protection of his son-in-law and ally Tigranes. In an effort to put an end to the war, Lucullus sent his brother-in-law Appius Clodius Pulcher to Antioch to demand that Tigranes hand Mithradates over to the Romans. Tigranes happened to be absent in Phoenicia engaged in operations against Cleopatra Selene, who was attempting to place her son Antiochus Asiaticus, son of Antiochus X Eusebes, on the throne of Syria. Clodius waited in Antioch for the return of Tigranes, and took the opportunity to intrigue with the dissatisfied element of the population both in Antioch and in other cities, which sent representatives to him secretly. Clodius promised the assistance of Lucullus against Tigranes. Tigranes, when he returned to Antioch, refused to surrender Mithradates.[97] This of course meant war. Tigranes set out to defend Armenia, and the Armenian government and its forces withdrew from Syria. Lucullus invaded Armenia and defeated Tigranes, capturing his capital Tigranocerta (69 B.C.).

When Tigranes left Syria, Antiochus XIII Asiaticus took the opportunity to set himself up as the legitimate Seleucid ruler, with the support of Lucullus and the consent of the people of Antioch, who had come to realize that even a member of the Seleucid house might make a more acceptable ruler than an Armenian prince.[98] Antiochus reigned at Antioch in 69/8 B.C. He issued coins in his own name, and put an end to the minting of bronze by the municipality, a practice that had continued even during Tigranes' occupation of Syria.[99] He was defeated in a battle probably with one of the Arab chieftains who seem to have attempted from time to time to establish principalities for themselves, This defeat provided the occasion for a revolution in Antioch. The king managed to remain in power, but the leaders of the rebellion escaped and joined forces with Philip II Barypous, son of Philip I,

[97] Plutarch *Lucull.* 21.2-7; Josephus *Ant.* 13.419-421. See Bellinger, "End of the Seleucids" 82, with n. 103.

[98] Appian *Syr.* 49; Justinus 40.2.2 (who says that Antiochus XIII was called to the throne by Lucullus). See Newell, *Seleucid Mint of Antioch* 125-128, and Bellinger, "End of the Seleucids" 82-83. The details of the careers of Antiochus XIII and Philip II are set forth in a study of Dobiáš, "Philippos Barypous," the results of which are incorporated in the same scholar's *Hist.* 52ff., with summary in French on pp. 549-550. The account of Antiochus XIII and Philip II given here follows that of Dobiáš.

[99] For tetradrachms of Antiochus XIII issued at Antioch, see Newell, *Seleucid Mint of Antioch* 125-128 and idem, *Ake-Ptolemais and Damascus* 98; cf. Bellinger, "End of the Seleucids" 83. On the municipal bronze and its cessation, see above, n. 93.

and the Arab chieftain Aziz undertook to place Philip II on the throne. Antiochus XIII for his part obtained the support of another Arab chieftain, Sampsigeramus. The two Arabs, however, made a private arrangement to dispose of the two weak Seleucid rivals and divide the kingdom between themselves. Sampsigeramus captured Antiochus, but Philip heard of the plan of Aziz in time to escape to Antioch, where he apparently would be safe.[100]

By this time it must have become clear to the Roman government that the Seleucid princes could not hope to maintain order in the northwestern corner of Syria, around Antioch, which was serving as a refuge for the Cilician pirates, and it was plain that if the pirates were to be suppressed, the Romans must have some control of this region.[101] Apparently the Roman government, hesitating to annex Syria at this time, tried the experiment of supporting the Seleucid ruler as a client king, and it seems to have been in this status that Philip II reigned in Antioch in 67/6 and again in 66/5 B.C.[102] In 67 B.C. Q. Marcius Rex, the proconsul of Cilicia, paid a visit to Philip in the course of which (evidently by order of the Roman government) he made arrangements for building a palace and a circus at Antioch, as a token of Roman support and interest in the city and in an effort to bolster Philip's prestige with his subjects, some of whom at least must have favored Roman intervention at this point. There may already have been a colony of Italians living in Antioch at this time, and Roman commercial circles had interests in Syria.[103] On the same occasion the proconsul asked Philip for a contribution toward the cost of the operations that were then being carried out against the Cilician pirates. Given the internal condition of Syria at this time, the contribution cannot have been a large one, but it would have been politically important as a token of "cooperation" on the part of the Seleucid government.[104]

The circus which Marcius Rex ordered built is evidently the one in

---

[100] Diodorus 40.1a-1b.

[101] For further details, see Dobiáš, "Occupation de la Syrie"; Downey, "Occupation of Syria"; and Bellinger, "Early Coinage of Roman Syria." For the background of conditions in Cilicia, see also R. Syme, "Observations on the Province of Cilicia," *Anatolian Studies Presented to W. H. Buckler* (Manchester 1939) 299-332.

[102] On coins which, according to Bellinger's plausible suggestion, were issued at Antioch by Philip II, see Bellinger, "End of the Seleucids" 93-94.

[103] See Rostovtzeff, *Soc. Econ. Hist. Hellenistic World* 991. On the part played by Roman commercial interests in the annexation of Syria, see below, Ch. 7, §1.

[104] The visit of Marcius Rex to Antioch is described by Malalas 225.7-11. On the significance of Marcius' visit in relation to the Roman policy in Syria at this time, see further in Downey, "Occupation of Syria," the principal conclusions of which are reproduced here.

ruins on the one-time island in the Orontes (Fig. 11). Study of the preserved remains and excavation of the foundations show that this circus, one of the largest and finest in the Roman Empire of which we know, was built probably in the first century B.C., and since the political and financial circumstances of the last Seleucid kings were such that it is difficult to believe that they can have undertaken the construction of a circus of this size, it seems reasonable to suppose that this is the one built by Marcius Rex. There is no evidence for an earlier circus or stadium at Antioch itself, so that before the time of Marcius Rex the only such structure available for the use of the people of Antioch must have been that at Daphne.[105]

The palace (which Malalas calls παλάτιον) might likewise be the first structure at Antioch that could properly be so called. In the Hellenistic period, the residence of the ruler was not a building of distinct type, designed specifically for the use of the king and his court, but was merely a private dwelling of the then usual type, of appropriate size and appointments.[106] It would appear, then, that Marcius Rex, in building such typically Roman structures as a palace and a circus, was attempting to assist the spread of Roman culture and prestige in Syria by introducing Roman buildings in Antioch.[107] As to the location of this palace, we have no specific evidence; it may have stood, like the circus, on the island.[108]

Apparently soon after Marcius' visit to Antioch, Clodius, who had been captured by the Cilician pirates but released by them for fear of Pompey, went to Antioch, where he proceeded to stir up trouble. He declared, Dio Cassius writes,[109] that he would assist the people of Antioch against the Arabs, with whom they were having difficulties; and he stirred up a sedition in which he nearly lost his life. The precise meaning of this episode is not known. Philip had once had the support of the Arab chieftain Aziz, but Aziz had subsequently plotted, in concert with another Arab chieftain, Sampsigeramus, to eliminate

---

[105] See the accounts of the games of Antiochus Epiphanes at Daphne, above, Ch. 5, n. 52.

[106] See Gerkan, *Griech. Städteanlagen* 108-109 and T. Fyfe, *Hellenistic Architecture* (Cambridge, Eng. 1936) 154-155. Malalas, in saying that Marcius Rex built "the old circus" and "the old palace," is writing with reference to his own day, in the sixth century A.D., when they would have been called "old" as distinguished from other, newer, structures.

[107] This process was continued by Pompey, Antony, and Julius Caesar, as well, of course, as by Augustus; see below, Ch. 7, §§1, 3; Ch. 8, §§1-2.

[108] Malalas (318.4-6) speaks of "the public bath of King Philip." It is not clear whether this bath was named for Philip I or Philip II; see above, n. 78.

[109] Dio Cassius 36.17.3.

Philip, along with his rival Antiochus XIII Asiaticus. Ultimately Sampsigeramus, who had been holding Antiochus XIII in captivity, released him and apparently placed him once more on the throne. There is nothing, however, to show what the position with respect to the Arabs was when Clodius came to Antioch, or to suggest what Clodius' plan may have been in undertaking to help the people of Antioch against the Arabs; nor do we know whether it was this undertaking that led to the sedition Dio mentions.[110] It has been conjectured that the disorders for which Clodius was responsible cost Philip his throne, for we hear nothing more of him as claimant to the Seleucid throne.[111] Sampsigeramus, after Clodius' failure and return to Rome, set free his prisoner Antiochus XIII, who again occupied the throne at Antioch during the year 65/4 B.C.[112]

While Antiochus XIII occupied the throne (65/4 B.C.), Pompey defeated Mithradates; and in 64 B.C. the Roman commander came to Antioch to make a settlement of the status of the city. With his arrival a new chapter in the history of Antioch begins.

[110] It may be suggested that when Clodius went to Antioch, he found that Sampsigeramus was plotting to expel Philip and place Antiochus on the throne, and that Clodius then offered his assistance against Sampsigeramus; he might even have offered to obtain Roman military support for Philip. The disorders might then have arisen when a local party that distrusted Rome tried to drive Clodius out of the city. But all this is pure conjecture. It is interesting to speculate whether there may have been some connection, which is no longer apparent, between the visits to Antioch of Marcius Rex and of Clodius, for Marcius was married to a sister of Clodius. See Walter Allen, Jr., "Claudius or Clodius?," *CW* 33 (1937) 107-110.

[111] Dobiáš, *Hist.* 549; Bellinger, "End of the Seleucids" 84.

[112] Appian *Syr.* 70; Dobiáš, "Philippos Barypous" 226-227; Stähelin, "Sampsigeramus," no. 1, *RE* 1A, 2227; Bellinger, "End of the Seleucids" 84, n. 112. On Clodius' return to Rome, see Fröhlich, "Clodius," no. 48, *RE* 4, 82.

CHAPTER 7

ANTIOCH UNDER THE ROMAN REPUBLIC

1. Pompey; The Parthian War

THE ADDITION of Antioch to the territory controlled by Rome was a major epoch both in the history of the city and in the course of Roman colonial expansion. The curiosity of the Romans concerning the city that had now come under their control is exemplified by the visit that Cato the Younger made to it soon after Pompey's defeat of Tigranes.[1] Not only were the political consequences of the change great, but the economic developments that followed were of major importance.

When Pompey found himself faced with the question of how he was to provide for the administration of Syria, two of the principal factors that he had to consider were, first, that the Seleucid kingdom had been gradually breaking up into a weak collection of cities, principalities, and tribes, and second, that it was plain from recent events that it would be impossible to maintain a Seleucid king, even if a competent one were available, as an ally or client of Rome. It became necessary, then, both for reasons of military security and for the protection of Roman commercial interests, to turn Syria into a Roman province;[2] and as for the cities, the basic units of the country, Pompey for the most part simply recognized the existing situation, making only the minimum adjustments necessary to fit the cities into the Roman scheme.

The political situation that Pompey found in Antioch was as follows. During the perpetual warfare between the Seleucid claimants which had filled the hundred years before Pompey's time, Antioch, by virtue of its position as the Seleucid capital, had seen more changes in its rulers, probably, than any city in Syria. The inevitable result of its experience was that the city attempted, with some success, to assert a measure of independence. The first move in this direction of which we hear is the league of Antioch and Seleucia Pieria attested by the issuance of coins inscribed ΑΔΕΛΦΩΝ ΔΗΜΩΝ between 149 and 147 B.C.[3] This effort seems to have failed rather quickly; but what was apparently a firmer position is represented by the appearance in 92/1 B.C. of coins,

---

[1] Plutarch, *Pompey* 40 and *Cato Min.* 13-14.
[2] See the studies of the occupation of Syria by the Romans cited above, Ch. 6, n. 101.
[3] See above, Ch. 6, n. 11.

inscribed ΑΝΤΙΟΧΕΩΝ ΤΗΣ ΜΗΤΡΟΠΟΛΕΩΣ. Thus coins began to be issued in the name of, and by authority of, the city itself. The appearance of this money side by side with the coins issued in the name of the king of the moment (including Tigranes) suggests that while the king was still acknowledged to have a certain authority over the city, the city now possessed some independent powers (whose limits we do not know) of its own.[4]

These autonomous coins ceased to appear at Antioch in 69 B.C., when Antiochus XIII came to the throne. Apparently this ruler, enjoying the support of Lucullus, felt himself strong enough to curtail the powers of the municipality, and during his reign and that of Philip II, which lasted until Pompey's settlement of Syria, the mint of Antioch issued only royal coins, and put out no municipal issues.[5] However, the interval between the disappearance of the autonomous coins (69 B.C.) and the time when Pompey had to decide on a settlement of the status of Antioch (64 B.C.) was short enough, and the intervening years were sufficiently unsettled, to keep alive the memory of whatever measure of independence the city had once claimed.

From the Roman point of view, there could be no question of Antioch's status. Both as the largest and most highly developed city in northwestern Syria and as the Seleucid capital, which before the break-up of the dynasty had been an important military, administrative, and commercial center, Antioch required a position of honor; and it was, of course, the only city worthy to be the capital of the new province of Syria which Pompey organized. Moreover, Pompey (like other Romans) was impressed by the city's beauty. When, therefore, Antiochus XIII requested that he be confirmed as king of Syria by the Romans, Pompey refused him and drove him out of the city. There arose a malicious tale that the people of Antioch had bribed Pompey to dismiss Antiochus.[6]

---

[4] See above, Ch. 6, nn. 74-76.

[5] See above, Ch. 6, n. 99.

[6] Justinus 40.2.3-5; Appian *Syr.* 49 and 70, *Mith.* 106. See Bellinger, "End of the Seleucids" 85, n. 116. According to Porphyrius of Tyre in Eusebius' *Chronicle* 1, pp. 261-262 ed. Schoene = *FHG* 3, p. 716, frag. 26, Pompey first brought Antiochus XIII to Antioch in order to place him in power, but then accepted a bribe from the people of the city to expel Antiochus. Dobiáš, *Hist.* 71-72, demonstrates the spiteful character of the story of the bribe. If Pompey did accept such a bribe, it would seem likely that he must have done so knowing all the time that he had no intention of keeping Antiochus in power. Malalas has a contradictory and garbled account of the transaction which might be related in some way to the story that appears in Eusebius. Malalas first declares (212.9-17) that after the Romans defeated Tigranes, Antiochus XIII went to Pompey and asked that his kingdom be restored to him. Pompey granted

Pompey granted *libertas* to Antioch, as he did to other cities in Syria, including Seleucia Pieria,[7] and it was presumably as a gesture of good will to accompany this act that he repaired the bouleuterion of Antioch, which had been damaged (possibly in the earthquake during Tigranes' regime) or had fallen into disrepair.[8] Precisely what this "freedom" meant for Antioch, we do not know. The "freedom" that Hellenistic kings had on occasion granted to certain cities was not independence but a privileged status, bestowed by the sovereign, which theoretically allowed the city to enjoy its own political constitution, to be free from the presence of a garrison, and to be exempt from the payment of tribute. In reality, few "free" cities in the Hellenistic period possessed all these privileges. The Romans, when they took over the rule of Greek lands, perpetuated the royal concept of "freedom," so that *libertas* meant that a city, far from being independent, enjoyed certain privileges while at the same time it was subject to the suzerainty of Rome.[9] The privileges varied considerably, and there is nothing to show what they were in the case of Antioch.[10] Pompey did allow the mint of Antioch to issue municipal bronze coins, in which the city bore the title of *metropolis*. These coins, which first appear in the year 64/3 B.C., were evidently looked upon as a continuation of the municipal coins that the city had issued down to 69 B.C. when Antiochus XIII put a stop to the practice.[11]

---

the request and then set out from Antioch for Egypt (this latter detail is certainly not correct). Then Malalas goes on after a digression to say (212.20-22) that on his deathbed Antiochus (whom the chronicler calls Ἀντίοχος ὁ Διονίκους) willed his kingdom to the Romans and that Antioch then passed under Roman rule.

[7] The only extant literary source that records Pompey's grant of *libertas* to Antioch is the account of Porphyry of Tyre preserved in the *Chronicle* of Eusebius (see preceding note); and while in other respects this passage betrays a malevolent bias, there is no reason to doubt the grant, which would have been a matter of common knowledge.

[8] The repair of the bouleuterion is recorded by Malalas 211.18. This is presumably the bouleuterion that according to Malalas (205.15, 334.2) was built by Antiochus IV Epiphanes, which may have replaced an earlier building: see above, Ch. 5, §6. The bouleuterion of Libanius' time—which so far as we know was the one restored by Pompey—contained a roofed meeting hall and a court enclosed by four colonnades; vines, fig trees, and vegetables were grown in the court (Libanius *Or.* 22; cf. Pack, *Studies in Libanius* 82-83). On the statement that Pompey "built" the structure, when he may only have repaired or restored it, see the discussion of Malalas' methods, above, Ch. 2, §4.

[9] It seems clear that a Roman governor resident in a city would, if only by reason of the deference paid to his position, exercise an important influence on the "autonomous" affairs of the city even if he tried to abstain from doing so. See the remarks on administrative interference by provincial officials by Grant, *Imperium to Auctoritas* 314-316, 396-397.

[10] The conception of "freedom" is well set forth by Jones, "Civitates liberae et immunes" 103-117. See also the valuable discussion of *libertas* and *civitas* by Grant, *Imperium to Auctoritas* 401-405.

[11] See Seyrig, "Sur les ères de quelques villes de Syrie" 5-15.

As a further sign of the new order, Pompey, in 64/3 B.C., abolished the use in Antioch of the Seleucid era as a means of reckoning dates, and established a new system, the Pompeian era. This was reckoned retrospectively from the autumn of 66 B.C., the date of the surrender of Tigranes to Pompey, in order to show that it was on the day of Tigranes' defeat that the control of Syria had passed into the hands of the Romans.[12]

Other acts of Pompey in Antioch of which we hear are the liberation of hostages, which the city presumably had had to give during the war against Tigranes, and the granting of additional land to the sacred grove of Daphne, which Pompey particularly admired.[13]

Pompey's benefactions doubtless assisted the recovery of the city, which had gone through a number of difficult years, beginning with the earthquake that preceded Tigranes' departure from Syria, and which must have suffered commercially as a result of the anarchy that prevailed during the last years of the Seleucids.[14] Moreover, Roman commercial interests, which had exercised strong influence to procure the annexation of Syria, quickly took advantage of the occupation of the new province, and Roman merchants promptly established themselves at Antioch, where their presence played a part in the economic recovery of the city.[15]

[12] See preceding note.

[13] Eutropius 6.14.2; cf. Festus 16.4. Malalas writes that Pompey "bestowed many things upon the Antiochenes" and that he honored them as being of Athenian stock (211.18-19). Libanius (*Or.* 11.239) remarks particularly upon the impression that Daphne made upon the Romans. Pompey's popularity in the city is attested by a story, ascribed to Damophilus of Bithynia, which is preserved in Plutarch (*Cato min.* 13; *Pomp.* 40) and in Julian (*Misop.* 358 B-C), of how Cato the Younger, when he visited Antioch at about this time, found a magnificent reception committee waiting outside the city, and supposed that the honor was intended for himself, only to discover that he was unknown and that the reception was prepared for Demetrius, a freedman of Pompey. On the incident, see Dobiáš, *Hist.* 70, n. 263, and Honigmann, "Syria" 1622. C. A. Forbes, *Greek Physical Education* (New York 1929) 245 (on the ephebes who are said to have taken part in the reception).

[14] On the decayed economic condition of the cities of Syria at this time, see Rostovtzeff, *Soc. Econ. Hist. Hellenistic World* 981.

[15] The important part played in the annexation of Syria by Roman commercial interests is shown by Dobiáš, "Occupation de la Syrie" 244-256; cf. J. Hatzfeld, *Les trafiquants italiens dans l'Orient hellénique* (Paris 1919) 142, 374-375 (*Bibl. des écoles franç. d'Athènes et de Rome*, fasc. 115). The colony of Roman citizens engaged in business in Antioch was well established and influential by 48 B.C. (Caesar *Bell. civ.* 3.102; see below, n. 43). A portrait head of a young Roman found at Antioch and now in the museum there, may date from about this period: F. Poulsen, "Portrait hellénistique du Musée d'Antioche" *Syria* 19 (1938) 355-361. On Roman business men at Antioch before Pompey's time, see above, Ch. 6, n. 103. Rostovtzeff (*Soc. Econ. Hist. Hellenistic World* 869-870) does not accept Dobiáš' view of the influence which Roman commercial circles brought to bear in favor of the annexation of Syria, but it seems to me that he both

Just what form the Roman administration of Antioch took at this time we do not know. It is recorded, however, that Pompey's freedman Demetrius exercised great influence at Antioch at this period,[16] and it may well be that the work of the administration depended to a considerable extent upon him.

At the same time, it is significant that there are certain steps that Pompey did not take in Antioch. The acquisition of the new territory in Syria presented the Romans with many administrative problems, some of which were avoided as long as possible. The introduction of Roman coinage would have constituted one of the principal tokens of the new power that governed Syria; and it might have been expected to be one of the first steps that the Roman government would take. However, this measure was complicated both by the shortage of silver in Italy at this time and by the difficulty of determining the proper relation between the Roman standard and the Attic standard used in Syria; and so for the time being it was decided that the mint of Antioch should issue no silver, and no Roman coinage of any kind.[17] The silver coinage of the last Seleucid kings, plus the municipal bronze authorized by Pompey, was apparently sufficient for current needs. It is not until 57 B.C. that we find silver coins issued by the Romans at Antioch.

In the years immediately following Pompey's return to Italy (62 B.C.) the government of Syria was carried on in somewhat irregular form.[18] Pompey had left M. Aemilius Scaurus to govern the province.[19] The first regularly appointed governor was the propraetor L. Marcius Philippus, appointed in 59 B.C., who in the following year was succeeded by

underrates the evidence adduced by Dobiáš and neglects to attach sufficient importance to the loss of Delos as an entrepôt when it was captured by the pirates in 64 B.C. In any case it would have been more profitable for the Romans to deal with Antioch directly than to carry on their trade through Delos.

[16] See above, n. 13.

[17] See Bellinger, "Early Coinage of Roman Syria" 63-64 and Seyrig, "Sur les ères de quelques villes de Syrie" 5-15 (it should be noted that Bellinger's article went to press before the publication of Seyrig's; cf. Bellinger 63, n. 23). On the subject of Roman experimentation and adjustment in currency matters in the East, see also *Dura Final Rep.* 6: Bellinger, *The Coins*, p. 190.

[18] The roster of the governors of Syria between the time of Pompey and the principate of Augustus provides an accurate mirror of the political vicissitudes of the province during the civil wars; see the list drawn up by Schürer, *Gesch. d. jüd. Volkes*[3-4] 1.304-316, which is reprinted by Honigmann, "Syria" 1628. It should be noted that the dates of the tenure of some of the officials have been modified by research conducted since the time when Schürer wrote; the necessary corrections may be found in Dobiáš, *Hist.* On the rank and administrative powers of the governors of Syria during the Republican period, see Marquardt, *Staatsverwaltung*[2] 415-416.

[19] Joseph. *Bell.* 1.7.7 = *Ant.* 14.79; cf. von Rohden, "Aemilius," no. 141, *RE* 1.588.

the propraetor Cn. Cornelius Lentulus Marcellinus.[20] Syria was still, however, exposed to danger from the Arabs. In order to provide greater security for the province, it was elevated to proconsular status and in 57 B.C. Aulus Gabinius, who had served Pompey in the East, was appointed governor.[21] The evidence for Gabinius' career gives us our only knowledge of the economic and political condition of Antioch and of Syria at this period. It is in his administration (after the shortage of silver had ceased) that the first administrative sign of Roman sovereignty in Antioch appears in the activity of the mint there; and this took a form that was characteristic of the hesitancy and indecision the Roman authorities seem still to have felt with respect to the government of Syria—perhaps also of their desire not to wound the sensibilities of the local population. The mint in fact did not now begin to issue regular Roman currency, but put out tetradrachms of the type issued by Philip I Philadelphus (93-84 B.C.), which were distinguished from the real coins of that king only by an inconspicuous monogram of Gabinius.[22] Philip's coins had apparently continued to circulate with those of Tigranes, and the Roman administration evidently felt that if it was unwise either to allow Antioch to issue silver coins of its own or to introduce Roman types, the best thing that could be done was to revive the coins of the last Seleucid king before the time of Tigranes; the types of Antiochus XIII and Philip II, it was apparently thought, would revive disagreeable memories of the unpleasant years when these rulers were on the throne. The coins of Philip I were familiar, and were probably still in circulation. The Seleucid rulers now having disappeared completely, no political significance could attach to the apparent continuation of their currency; but there was a distinct advantage, commercially, in leaving the circulating medium so far as possible undisturbed.[23] The types of Philip continued to be issued by Crassus and by Cassius in 53 and 51 B.C. and by Julius Caesar, and it was not until the time of Augustus that a radical change was made in the currency.

Further evidence for conditions at this time in Antioch, as in the other cities of Syria, is provided by the activities of Gabinius in con-

[20] Dobiáš, *Hist.* 96-97 corrects the chronology which is adopted by Münzer, "Cornelius," no. 228, *RE* 4.1389, and "Marcius," no. 76, *RE* 14.1568-1569.

[21] Dobiáš, *Hist.* 98ff., 553.

[22] Newell, "Pre-Imperial Coinage of Rom. Antioch" 87, no. 1, as interpreted by H. Seyrig; cf. Bellinger in *Dura Final Rep. 6: The Coins* p. 202, n. 23; idem, "Early Coinage of Roman Syria" 64-65, with n. 28; and H. Seyrig in *Syria* 27 (1950) 15; also Bellinger, "Some Coins from Roman Antioch" 55-57.

[23] On the preservation of obsolete types of coins for commercial and sentimental reasons, see Rostovtzeff, *Stor. econ. soc. imp. rom.* 108, n. 17, and Grant, *Imperium to Auctoritas* 75.

nection with the *publicani*, who obtained by contract the right of collecting taxes. The system was subject to well-known abuses and it was inevitable that the collectors should extract from the people more than was due to the government. Gabinius sought in every way possible to limit the activities of these collectors, and in many cases arranged for taxes to be paid direct to the treasury of the province. These arrangements may have been accompanied by a certain amount of financial profit to the governor himself, but they may also have done something to help the economic recovery of the province.[24]

Gabinius on the whole administered Syria competently, but through the activities of his personal enemies he was recalled on charges of misconduct in 55 B.C.[25] He was replaced by the triumvir M. Licinius Crassus, who was appointed to serve for five years.[26]

Crassus, in an effort to win power and prestige, launched an attack on the Parthians in 54 B.C., but was disastrously defeated and killed at Carrhae in Mesopotamia in the following year.[27] Crassus' quaestor, C. Cassius, automatically took over the governorship of Syria.[28] We have a glimpse of his administration from coins that show that he continued the compromise by which the silver tetradrachms supplied for use in Syria by the mint of Antioch were merely imitations of those that had been issued by Philip I Philadelphus.[29] The minting of such coins, in the Seleucid period, had been a token of the "free" status of a city, and the same significance must have attached to the practice under the Romans.[30] From 54 to 51 B.C. the mint also issued municipal bronze of the type put out under the Seleucids, but dated by the Pompeian era.[31]

[24] Gabinius' policy with regard to the *publicani* is described by Cicero, *De provinciis consularibus*; for a detailed discussion, with further bibliography, see Rostovtzeff, *Soc. Econ. Hist. Hellenistic World* 981-984, with notes on 1572-1574. Collection of the *stipendium* in Syria is mentioned by Velleius Paterculus 2.37.5.

[25] See Eva M. Sanford, "The Career of Aulus Gabinius," *TAPA* 70 (1939) 64-92. Cicero's accounts of Gabinius' maladministration of Syria are based on personal enmity. It is known from archaeological evidence that Gabinius was active in restoring the damage that the cities of Syria and Palestine had lately suffered; see for example, Crowfoot-Kenyon-Sukenik, *Buildings at Samaria* 31. No evidence that Gabinius carried out such work at Antioch has as yet been discovered.

[26] Dobiáš, *Hist.* 103ff., 553-554.

[27] Dobiáš, *Hist.* 120-130, 554; Debevoise, *Hist. of Parthia* 78-95.

[28] Dobiáš, *Hist.* 130, 554-555.

[29] A. R. Bellinger, "Crassus and Cassius at Antioch," *Num.Chron.* ser. 6, vol. 4 (1944) 59-61; in *Dura Final Rep.* 6: idem, *The Coins* p. 120, no. 182; idem, "Early Coinage of Roman Syria" 65; H. Seyrig in *Syria* 27 (1950) 15.

[30] See Bikerman, *Institutions des Séleucides* 235, and H. Seyrig in *Syria* 28 (1951) 213-214.

[31] *BMC Galatia etc.* p. 155, no. 32; Bellinger, "Early Coinage of Roman Syria" 65, with n. 30.

M. Calpurnius Bibulus was to succeed Crassus as governor, but while
he was still en route from Italy to his new post, the Parthians invaded
Syria and penetrated as far as Antioch (August 51 B.C.).[32] Cassius shut
himself up in the city and the Parthians, who did know how to conduct
a siege,[33] were unable to take it.[34] When the Parthians withdrew from
Antioch, they set out for Antigonia, which lay about 40 stadia (7 or 8
km.) northeast of Antioch. This city had been built by Antigonus as
his capital, but had been destroyed by Seleucus I when he founded
Antioch.[35] Evidently it had subsequently been resettled, and it would
appear to have become sufficiently prosperous to be an attractive prize
in the eyes of the Parthians.[36] They found, however, that the land
about Antigonia was thickly wooded, and since their cavalry could not
operate in a forest, they began to cut down the trees. The task proved
more difficult than they had anticipated; and meanwhile Cassius had
moved out of Antioch and had begun to harass them. The Parthians
decided to abandon their undertaking. Cassius set an ambush on the
road by which they were to depart, and defeated them; his dispatch
reporting the victory was dated 7 October 51 B.C.[37] The Parthians withdrew from the neighborhood, but did not leave Syria.[38]

Shortly after this, Calpurnius Bibulus, the new governor of Syria,
arrived at Antioch. There was still serious danger from the Parthians,
who passed the winter in Syria and in the spring once more threatened

[32] Dobiáš, *Hist.* 234ff., 555; Debevoise, *Hist. of Parthia* 100-101.
[33] Tacitus *Ann.* 12.45; 15.4.
[34] The accounts of what happened at Antioch vary. Dio Cassius (40.29.1) states that
Cassius effectively repulsed the Parthians, who were unable to carry on a siege. Cicero,
in letters written at different times, gave differing versions of the episode. In the earliest
of these (*Ad Fam.* 2.10.2), which was written to M. Caelius Rufus on 14 Nov. 51 B.C.,
five or six weeks after the event, he states that Cassius had driven the enemy back from
Antioch. Writing to Atticus five or six weeks later (*Ad Att.* 5.20), he remarks that it
was the news of the approach of his own forces which caused the Parthians to retreat
from Antioch. Then, on 13 Feb. 50 B.C., he writes again to Atticus (*Ad Att.* 5.21) that
the Parthian withdrawal from Antioch was not due to any military success of the
Romans. It appears that the changes in Cicero's statements reflect an alteration in his
feelings toward his military rival Cassius, which is indicated, for example, in *Ad Att.*
5.21 (see Debevoise, *Hist. of Parthia* 102). Thus it would seem likely that Cicero's
earliest statement, which agrees with that of Dio Cassius, is more nearly right. The
Parthians must in any case have taken the opportunity to plunder the unprotected suburbs of Antioch. It seems plain that Orosius is wrong in stating (*Hist. adv. paganos*
6.13.5) that the Parthians penetrated Antioch itself.
[35] See above, Ch. 4, §2.
[36] There are no extant references to Antigonia between the accounts of its destruction
by Seleucus and Dio Cassius' description of the Parthian attempt upon it. There seems,
however, no reason to doubt the truth of Dio's description, which has been accepted by
Müller, *Antiq. Antioch.* 27; Dobiáš *Hist.* 137; Bouchier, *Antioch* 90, and Debevoise,
Hist. of Parthia 101.
[37] Cicero *Ad Att.* 5.21.
[38] Dio Cassius 40.29.1-3.

Antioch; Cicero and Caesar wrote that Calpurnius Bibulus did not dare leave his capital. The governor did, however, succeed in making trouble among the Parthians, who finally left Syria.[39]

Calpurnius Bibulus' internal administration of his province seems to have been efficient and beneficial. It is said that he obtained from the people of Antioch, as a gift to the Roman people, the statues of Athene and of Zeus Keraunios which had been set up at Antioch by Seleucus I.[40] These were sent to Rome and placed in the Capitolium, with inscriptions recording the gift. Eventually the statue of Zeus, at least, seems to have been returned to Antioch.[41]

Calpurnius Bibulus gave up his office early in October 50 B.C., and left the government of Syria in the hands of his legate Veiento.[42]

2. The Civil War; Caesar at Antioch

The next major event in the history of Antioch arose out of the civil war between Caesar and the Senate which began in 49 B.C. When Caesar

[39] Cicero Ad Fam. 12.19.3, 15.4.7; Ad Att. 5.21, 6.8, 7.2.6; Caesar Bell. civ. 3.31. Calpurnius Bibulus' career, and in particular his administration of Syria, has been misjudged because much of our evidence concerning it comes from Cicero, a personal enemy. A different and more favorable view emerges from the study of Dobiáš, "Syrský prokonsulát M. Calpurnia Bibula," the principal results of which are incorporated in the same scholar's Hist. 141-148, 555-556.

[40] On the setting up of the statues by Seleucus I, see above, Ch. 4, nn. 97, 103.

[41] On the episode, see the study of Calpurnius Bibulus' career by Dobiáš cited above (n. 39) 43-47. Malalas' account of the sending of the statues to Rome (212.1-8) is obscured by the chronicler's (or his source's) misunderstanding of the governor's name (which is given as Byblos), by the impossible statement that this Byblos established the city of the same name in Syria (actually the name was an old Greek one), and of the placing of the account in the passage describing Pompey's activities in Syria. However, as Dobiáš points out, these errors, which are all too characteristic of Malalas, need not be taken to mean that the statement concerning the sending of the statues to Rome is untrue. Malalas' chronology is correct insofar as the governorship of Calpurnius Bibulus is placed between Pompey's defeat of Tigranes and the time of Julius Caesar. Benzinger ("Byblos," RE 3 [1899] 1100) suggests, very plausibly, that Malalas' account, including the supposed establishment of the city of Byblos by "Byblos," is brought into relation with Pompey's activities because Pompey had "liberated" the city by executing Kinyras, the local prince who ruled it (see Dobiáš op.cit. 46). An ostensible quotation of the inscriptions placed on the statues when they were sent to Rome appears in Malalas 212.7-8. Here the Bonn text of Malalas omits τά which appears in the MS before ἀγάλματα (see Bury, "Malalas: the Cod. Barocc." 225); the text, thus corrected, has a flavor of anapaestic verse. The return of the statue of Zeus to Antioch appears to be indicated by Libanius Or. 11.116. Libanius here it is true names Zeus Kasios, but he gives him thunder as an attribute, and as Dobiáš points out, it would have been easy, especially in Libanius' time, to confuse Zeus Keraunios and Zeus Kasios. Malalas' statement (212.6) that the statues "still exist" is ambiguous; the chronicler might mean they still existed at Antioch, but if he was referring to Rome, he might very well have taken the statement from a much earlier source (see G. Downey in TAPA 66 [1935] 65, n. 17).

[42] Dobiáš, Hist. 148, 556. Calpurnius Bibulus' son, L. Calpurnius Bibulus, was governor of Syria 34-32 B.C., dying while in office; see Cichorius, "L. Calpurnius Bibulus," no. 27, RE 3 (1899) 1367.

defeated Pompey at Pharsalus (6 June 48 B.C.), the people of Antioch declared against Pompey, who had taken flight in the direction of Syria; there were by this time Roman citizens engaged in business in Antioch who were doubtless influential in making the decision.[43] Caesar, after spending the winter of 48-47 B.C. in Alexandria, set out in the spring of 47 B.C. on his way to Pontus to put down Pharnaces, one of the client kings who had been profiting by the opportunity to seize power in Asia Minor. On his way through Syria, Caesar paused at various cities to bestow rewards for the support that he had received from them.[44]

While en route to Antioch, Caesar sent the city a letter that contained the announcement of his second appointment as dictator and a declaration of the "freedom" of the city.[45] This letter reached Antioch on 17 June in the unreformed Roman calendar then in use (= 5 April in the Julian calendar). It was not, however, published until 25 June (= 13 April, Julian). Then, on 28 June (= 16 April, Julian), Caesar himself entered the city.[46] Whether by accident or design, his arrival fell on 23 Artemisios (according to the uncorrected lunar calendar in use locally), which was the day following the anniversary of the foundation of the city by Seleucus I.[47] Caesar remained in Antioch for about nine days, and then continued his journey to Pontus.[48] His stopping at Antioch for a number of days during a journey in which speed was important suggests that the material and moral support the city had given him was substantial, and that he wished to assure himself of its further support.

[43] Caesar *Bell. Civ.* 3.102; see Dobiáš, *Hist.* 154, 557, and the same scholar's more detailed study, "Occupation de la Syrie" 253, also Holmes, *Roman Republic* 3.175-176. The people of Antioch were no doubt strengthened in their decision when, shortly afterward, a portent visited them in the form of the noise of an army, which was so convincing that they manned the walls of the city (Caesar *Bell. Civ.* 3.105).

[44] *Bell. Alex.* 65.4; Dobiáš, *Hist.* 160-163.

[45] Malalas 216.7-18; *Chron. Pasch.* 354.17-355.6 Bonn. On the interpretation of the passage in Malalas, see Müller, *Antiq. Antioch.* 75-76 and Stauffenberg, *Malalas* 107-112. Müller is mistaken in saying (76, n. 3) that in the passage in the *Chronicon Paschale* (which is based on Malalas' account) it is stated that the proclamation was published on 22 Artemisios, not on 23 Artemisios as Malalas has it. The Latin translation of the *Chronicon* in the Bonn edition gives the date, by typographical error, as the 22nd; the Greek text has the 23rd.

[46] The three dates are given by Malalas as 12, 20, and 23 Artemisios (approximately May) according to the uncorrected lunar calendar then in use in Antioch; on the correction, see W. Judeich, *Caesar in Orient* (Leipzig 1885) 106-110; Stauffenberg, *Malalas* 111; Dobiáš *Hist.* 162, n. 70; Holmes, *Roman Republic* 3.509-510; Longden, "Parthian Campaigns" 34-35. See also L. E. Lord, "The Date of Julius Caesar's Departure from Egypt," *Classical Studies Presented to Edward Capps* (Princeton 1936) 223ff.

[47] On the foundation on 22 Artemisios, see Mal. 200.17.

[48] The date of Caesar's departure from Antioch is not certain; see Stauffenberg, *Malalas* 111, with n. 84.

Malalas[49] gives the opening words of the decree in which the "freedom" of Antioch was proclaimed: Ἐν Ἀντιοχείᾳ τῇ μητροπόλει ἱερᾷ καὶ ἀσύλῳ καὶ αὐτονόμῳ καὶ ἀρχούσῃ καὶ προκαθημένῃ τῆς ἀνατολῆς Ἰούλιος Γάϊος Καῖσαρ καὶ τὰ λοιπά. This grant of "freedom," establishing the city's dignity in the new regime, must have contained terms at least as generous as those of the similar grant made by Pompey; and it would seem likely that Caesar would have outdone Pompey if this were possible within the limits of his policy. We do not know how much actual autonomy was entailed in either Pompey's or Caesar's grants of *libertas*;[50] the city would at most have been allowed a certain amount of self-government under Roman suzerainty, and the presence of the Roman governor of Syria, who had his residence in the city, would have been a guarantee that the administration of the city would in all essential respects have been firmly under Roman control.

Under Caesar's dispensation, the minting of autonomous bronze coinage was continued, and the city was allowed to inscribe on this a more magnificent title, ΑΝΤΙΟΧΕΩΝ ΤΗΣ ΜΗΤΡΟΠΟΛΕΩΣ ΙΕΡΑΣ ΚΑΙ ΑΣΥΛΟΥ ΚΑΙ ΑΥΤΟΝΟΜΟΥ,[51] which embodies the opening phraseology of the edict of Caesar as quoted by Malalas (see above). It is significant, however, that at the same time there was no radical change in the silver coins, a change that would have been of more importance as a reflection of the official position and authority of the city's mint. No coins were minted which could be taken to constitute, through their types and symbols, either a declaration of the complete autonomy of the city or on the other hand an announcement that Antioch, as represented by its mint, had been deprived of its dignity and completely subjected to Rome. Instead, the silver tetradrachms imitating those of Philip I Philadelphus (93-84 B.C.), which had earlier been adopted as a compromise coinage, were continued; but these were now dated according to the era of Caesar.[52] So far as silver was concerned, Caesar

---

[49] 216.15-17.

[50] On the Roman conception of *libertas*, see above, n. 10. On Caesar's grant to Antioch of the three titles of sacred, inviolable, and autonomous, see H. Seyrig, *Notes on Syrian Coins* (*Numismatic Notes and Monographs*, no. 119; New York 1950) 21, n. 50.

[51] Newell, "Pre-Imperial Coinage of Roman Antioch" 69-113; Seyrig, "Sur les ères de quelques villes de Syrie" 5-15, with a table (13) showing the occurrence of the titles; D. B. Waagé, "Coins" 26-28; cf. Bellinger, "Some Coins from Antioch" 55-57. The former title, ΑΝΤΙΟΧΕΩΝ ΤΗΣ ΜΗΤΡΟΠΟΛΕΩΣ, continues to be used side by side with the more elaborate one.

[52] In addition to the studies of Newell and Seyrig cited above (n. 51), see the supplementary material published by Bellinger in *Dura Final Rep.* 6: *The Coins* p. 120, no. 185, and p. 202. See also Bellinger, "Early Coinage of Roman Syria" 65, and D. B. Waagé, "Coins" 23. On the continuation of the type of tetradrachms issued by Philip, see above, nn. 22-23. The type was also issued by Crassus and by Cassius at Antioch; see above, nn. 29-30.

evidently preferred to maintain the monetary status quo, which in this respect had apparently proved satisfactory.

Caesar continued the notable series of public buildings constructed at Antioch by the Roman government.[53] The most famous of his buildings was the "basilica" called the Kaisarion, which is thought to be the oldest "basilica" in the East for which evidence is preserved.[54] It stood opposite the former Temple of Ares, near the stream called the Parmenius which flowed down from the mountain through the city and into the Orontes. The location must have been a central one, since in the reign of Valens (A.D. 364-378) the Kaisarion was demolished so that its site could be used as a part of a new forum.[55] The "basilica," according to Malalas, contained an open court and a κόγχη or vaulted apse; it may have been similar in plan to the Kaisarion which Caesar built in Alexandria, which was later used as a Christian church.[56] Outside the apse (that is, presumably, in front of it), there stood, we are told, statues of Caesar and of the Tyche of Rome.[57] The setting up of these statues indicates that Caesar, as the statesmanlike, conscious Romanizer of the empire, was consciously preserving, transmuted into a new form, the elements of the Hellenistic ruler cult and of the cult of Dea Roma, already well known in the province of Asia, which were

[53] Caesar's buildings are described by Malalas 216.19-217.4. On the building activities of Marcius and Pompey, see above, Ch. 6, §3; Ch. 7, §1.

[54] See Downey, "Architectural Significance of *stoa* and *basilike*" 194-211, esp. 197-199, and E. Sjöqvist, "Kaisareion: A Study in Architectural Iconography," *Opuscula Romana* 1 (1954) 86-108 (Acta Instituti Romani Regni Sueciae, series in 4°, 18).

[55] Malalas 338.19-339.15.

[56] Strabo 17, p. 794 C; Mal. 217.5-12. On the Kaisarion in Alexandria, see Stauffenberg, *Malalas* 118-119 and H. Leclerq, "Alexandrie (Archéologie)," *DACL* 1.1108-1109.

[57] Malalas 216.19-21; 286.16-287.7; 290.18-20; 338.19-339.15; see Downey, "Architectural Significance of *stoa* and *basilike*" 197-199. The meaning of the word ἐξάερον, which Malalas uses to describe the open court, is shown by a number of passages, some of which have not found their way into the entries for this word in the lexica. See Constantine Porphyrogenitus, *De Cerimoniis* 2.6, p. 533.20; 2.7, p. 538.4; 2.13, pp. 561.18-19 and 563.4 Bonn ed., also 1.1, p. 15.29 ed. A. Vogt, and Theophanes Continuatus, p. 141.12 Bonn ed. The word can also be used to mean *the open country, the open air*: Theophanes, A.M. 6282, p. 464.27-28 ed. De Boor; *Scriptores originum Constantinopolitanarum*, p. 283.12 ed. Preger; Nicephorus, *Vita S. Andreae Sali*, in *PG* 111.740 B (the colloquial form ξίαρον); *Synaxarium ecclesiae Const.* (*Acta SS.*, vol. 63, ed. H. Delehaye), p. 124.5-7. On church buildings in which a hypaethral court served as nave, see A. Grabar, "Les ambons syriens et la fonction liturgique de la nef dans les églises antiques," *Cahiers archéol.* 1 (1945) 133; idem, *Martyrium* (Paris 1943-1946) 1.91, 122ff.; A. M. Schneider, "Basilica Discoperta," *Antiquity* 24 (1950) 131-139. On "basilicas" of this type, see also the examples cited by Stauffenberg, *Malalas* 476, n. 87. For older views on the Kaisarion, see K. Lange, *Haus u. Halle* (Leipzig 1885) 189-191. Malalas characteristically enough does not mention the statue of Caesar (287.3-4) and that of the Tyche of Rome (216.21) in connection with each other, and he does not say that they stood together, but this must have been the case (see the following footnote).

later developed more systematically by Augustus in the cult of Roma and Augustus.[58] In this respect Caesar's example was followed by Antony, who likewise thought of himself as both heir to the Seleucid throne and ruler of the new Roman Empire, and was honored on coins of Antioch as a divine Seleucid ruler.[59] Caesar, however, seems to have given more tangible expression to his position than Antony. That Caesar attached great political and religious importance to the "basilicas" that he built at Alexandria and Antioch is indicated by their being of a novel type, instead of a traditional Roman type, and by the circumstance that Caesar named the buildings after himself, instead of giving them a more conventional and familiar name.[60] The statue of Caesar in his basilica at Antioch doubtless came, in time, to serve in the cult of the Deified Julius,[61] which was recognized under Augustus.

The other measures carried out at Antioch by Caesar's orders included the rebuilding of the Pantheon, which (Malalas says) was about to collapse, the building of a new theater on the slope of the mountain (or the rebuilding of an older one), the construction of an amphitheater (likewise on the slope of the mountain), the building of an aqueduct designed to supply the needs of the people who lived on the upper part of the mountain, and the construction of a public bath on the upper part of the mountain, served by this aqueduct.[62] The planning of this aqueduct, to supply a community high on the mountain which presumably had been dependent upon springs and cisterns since the time of Seleucus I, is characteristic of the Roman interest in public utilities;[63]

[58] See Magie, *Asia Minor* 447-449, 1295-1298, 1613-1614; F. Richter, "Roma," Roscher, *Lexikon* 4.136-137; Grant, *Imperium to Auctoritas* 302-307, 368-375; A. N. Sherwin-White, *The Roman Citizenship* (Oxford 1939) 167, 233. Roma was usually represented in the form of Athena Polias, with long robe, shield, helmet, and spear (F. Richter *op.cit.* 133, 145-161). It is curious to note that Caesar was at Antioch on 21 April (by the corrected Julian calendar), which was celebrated as the birthday of Roma (F. Richter *op.cit.* 134-135). However, the calendar at this period had become so inaccurate that in contemporary reckoning the birthday of Roma did not fall during Caesar's visit to Antioch.

[59] See below, §3.   [60] See Stauffenberg, *Malalas* 118-119.

[61] For the cult of the Deified Julius, see Dio Cassius 51.20.6ff. On this cult in Asia Minor, see Magie, *Asia Minor* 447.

[62] Malalas 216.21-217.4; see Stauffenberg, *Malalas* 468-469, 474, 486. Malalas speaks only of the restoration of the altar of the Pantheon but it seems plain that the whole building is meant. This is the earliest reference to a Pantheon in Antioch, but as K. Ziegler points out ("Pantheion," *RE* 18, pt. 3 [1949] 713 714), there must have been such a temple in Antioch from early Seleucid times.

[63] It is amusing to note that Malalas, in whose chronicle the construction of public baths is a leading motif, writes as though Caesar had the aqueduct built primarily for the service of the bath on the mountain; in reality, of course, the aqueduct must have been constructed in order to serve the general needs of the settlement which existed in that locality, and the building of a public bath, when water had become available, would have been merely an added provision for the health and comfort of the people.

the Seleucids, for all their care to adorn their capital, had apparently never provided an aqueduct to serve this part of the site, and it may well have been that the settlement in the area was not an important one. Characteristic also of the prompt measures taken by the Romans to introduce their way of life into the Greek East is the construction of the amphitheater (which Malalas calls a *monomachion*[64]) designed to accommodate the gladiatorial fights and other brutal sports that the Romans enjoyed. The earliest known Roman amphitheater is that built at Pompeii ca. 80 B.C., and the first permanent building of this character in Italy was set up in 29 B.C.; thus Caesar's structure at Antioch was erected at a time when such buildings were just beginning to become popular.[65] The work done in connection with the theater—whether it was a new building or a reconstruction of an older one we cannot tell—also shows how important Caesar considered the entertainment of the people to be.[66]

The extent and the comprehensive character of the building program that Caesar instituted during his short stay at Antioch indicate, then, that he had fairly precise ideas as to the measures that might be employed in this respect to enhance Roman prestige and to introduce the Roman way of living into a city such as Antioch. It seems clear, also, that Caesar had in his suite Roman technicians (presumably military engineers, who had to possess many talents) capable of instituting building and engineering operations that were characteristically Roman; in particular, the amphitheater that Caesar ordered to be built was a typically Roman building, probably almost unknown in the Greek East. The protection and extension of Roman commercial interests in Syria had been an important factor leading to the annexation of the country as a province by Pompey, and as soon as the territory became Roman there was undoubtedly a marked increase in the number of Romans who lived and traded in Antioch; and it was at

---

[64] Chilmead corrects μονάχιον of the unique MS of Malalas (217.2-3) to μονομάχιον.

[65] On amphitheaters, see Robertson, *Greek and Roman Architecture*[2] 283-289, 351, and I. A. Richmond, "Amphitheatres," *OCD* 45.

[66] Malalas writes (217.2-3) that Caesar "built" a theater, but the chronicler's use of the verb "to build" is so broad that an entry of this kind might mean that Caesar rebuilt, restored, or repaired an older theater. There must have been a theater at Antioch in the Seleucid period, though it does not happen to be mentioned in our meager sources. This might have fallen into such disrepair by Caesar's time that a new one was needed. The ruins of the theater were easily recognizable at the time of Förster's visit in 1896; see his description of the site, "Antiochia" 106-107, and his map (pl. 6) on which the location is shown. Since Förster's time the regular despoiling of ancient buildings for building stone has caused the remains of the theater to disappear so completely that efforts of the excavators to locate it were not successful: *Antioch-on-the-Orontes* 2.3-4.

least in part to provide for their comfort and pleasure that Caesar inaugurated his building program.[67]

One more event connected with Caesar's visit which was of capital importance in the history of Antioch was the replacement of the Seleucid era, by which the city had hitherto reckoned its dates, by the era of Caesar, eventually known as the era of Antioch. This continued in use at Antioch (with a minor interruption[68]) at least until the Arab conquest of Syria. Malalas mentions the introduction of the new era immediately after recording Caesar's death; he writes (217.20-21), "The great Antioch in his honor reckons [its] first year from the same Gaius Julius Caesar." From literary and epigraphic testimony we know that the beginning of the first year of this era was reckoned as 1 October 49 B.C. (Julian calendar), in conformity with the usage of the Seleucid calendar, in which the new year also began on a date corresponding to 1 October.[69] It is not, however, certain why 1 October 49 B.C. was selected as the epoch of the new era. A plausible explanation is that this date was chosen because Caesar was dictator for the first time in 49 B.C. and because it was in this year that the operations of the Civil War began; Malalas' phraseology could be taken to show that at least the source or sources that he used supposed that these were the reasons for the choice of the year 49 B.C. for the beginning of the era.

The decision to introduce the era was, according to the evidence of coins,[70] made either at the time of Caesar's visit to Antioch in the spring of 47 B.C. or very soon after; and it would indeed be natural for the city to seek some way of showing its appreciation of Caesar's benefactions, however hollow its "freedom" and "autonomy" may have been. There are coins dated in the third year of the era (1 October 47 B.C.—30 September 46 B.C.), which make it certain that the era was

[67] On Roman commercial interests in Syria at this time, see Dobiáš, "Occupation de la Syrie" 244-256, esp. 253, and see above, Ch. 6, §3; Ch. 7, §1.

[68] During the Parthian occupation in 40-39 B.C.; see below.

[69] On the evidence for the epoch of the era, see F. K. Ginzel, *Handbuch der math. u. tech. Chronologie* (Leipzig 1906-1914) 3.43-44; *PAES* commentary on no. 1108; *IGLS* commentary on no. 524. The history of the modern study of the era (during which it was for some time not certain what the epoch was) is summarized by Stauffenberg, *Malalas* 108-112. Some scholars (e.g. Ginzel and Stauffenberg), not familiar with the epigraphic evidence, have been uncertain whether the year in the era of Caesar began on 1 September or 1 October (Julian), but inscriptions show that the new year's day was originally 1 October and was changed to 1 September at some time between A.D. 449 and A.D. 483; see *PAES, loc.cit.*; *IGLS, loc.cit.*; Downey, "Calendar Reform at Antioch" 39-48.

[70] Newell, "Pre-Imperial Coinage of Rom. Antioch" 73, 78, 87, 91.

introduced either soon before 1 October 47 B.C. or at some time during
the year 47/6 B.C.; and the legend of one coin might be taken to show
that there was a small issue of coins dated during the second year of
the era, i.e. presumably during the summer of 47 B.C., between Caesar's
visit and 1 October. It appears, then, that although the decision to
adopt an era in honor of Caesar was made in 47 or 47/6 B.C., the epoch
was set as a compliment at 1 October 49 B.C.[71]

3. Cassius and Antony in Syria, 47-41 B.C.; The Parthian Occupation of Antioch, 40-39 B.C.

Caesar, when he left Antioch in the spring of 47 B.C., left behind
him in charge of Syria a young relative, Sextus Julius Caesar.[72] Early
in 46 B.C., Q. Caecilius Bassus, an adherent of Pompey's, engineered a
mutiny among the troops in the course of which Sextus Caesar lost his
life, but a new governor, L. Antistius Vetus, managed to keep Bassus
in check.[73] Struggles continued between Caesar's emissaries and Bassus
until the arrival in Syria at the end of 44 B.C. of Cassius, who had been
forced out of Italy after the assassination of Caesar in March 44 B.C.
Cassius succeeded in winning the support of the people of Syria and
of the troops stationed there. In raising money, he appears to have
seized property of the Jews in Antioch.[74] Finally, he was able to compass the defeat of the legitimate governor, Cornelius Dolabella, who
had reached Syria after him.[75] We have Cicero's accounts of Dolabella's effort, on one occasion in 43 B.C., to dislodge Cassius from
Antioch.[76] By the end of 43 B.C. and the beginning of 42 B.C., no more
of Caesar's adherents remained active in the East, with the exception
of Cleopatra; and Cassius was preparing a campaign against her when
he was called away to assist Brutus against Octavian, the adopted son

---

[71] It should be noted that Malalas does not mention the introduction of the new era
in his account of Caesar's visit to Antioch, but only records it after he has written of
Caesar's death. In the work of a careful historian, this arrangement of material might
be taken to mean that the inauguration of the era was not associated, either directly or
closely, with Caesar's visit to Antioch, but Malalas' procedures are so erratic that it is
not safe to see any significance in a circumstance such as this. Ginzel (above, n. 69)
gives a false impression when he combines, without indicating the considerable extent
of the text which separates them, Malalas' accounts of Caesar's granting of freedom to
Antioch and of the introduction of the era.

[72] Dobiáš, *Hist.* 164-168, 557.

[73] Dobiáš, *Hist.* 168-173, 557-558.

[74] The Jews in Tyre, Sidon, and Aradus also suffered. Josephus (*Ant.* 14.319-323)
quotes the decree by which Antony restored their property to the Jews.

[75] Dobiáš, *Hist.* 180-190, 558.

[76] *Ad fam.* 12.15.7, 12.14.4; cf. Dio Cassius 47.30.2. See Dobiáš, *Hist.* 189-190.

of Caesar, who had undertaken to carry on the dictator's cause. Brutus and Cassius were defeated at Philippi (42 B.C.) and both took their own lives. Antony, who with Lepidus had made common cause with Octavian, set out for the East in 41 B.C. in order to raise money to pay the troops of the new triumvirate.[77] He restored to the Jews of Antioch and other cities property that had been seized by Cassius in his efforts to raise money.[78] In the course of his journey, Antony visited Antioch; and in Daphne he received a deputation of the most influential Jews, who accused Herod and Phasael of usurping the government in Palestine.[79] Antony reorganized the province of Syria, and there may have been a change in the status accorded to Antioch in the new regime, for the coins issued there in the year 42/1 B.C. lack the epithets "Sacred and Inviolate" and bear only the titles "Metropolis" and "Autonomous." We hear that Antony's acts in Syria caused many disturbances,[80] and it is possible that a curtailment of the sovereignty of Antioch was a part of his policy.[81]

From Syria, Antony went to Alexandria, where he became involved with Cleopatra; and the Parthians, taking advantage of this distraction of his interests and of the dissatisfaction with Antony in Syria, determined to invade Syria (spring 40 B.C.). The Parthian army was commanded jointly by Pacorus, son of the Parthian king Orodes, and Labienus, who had been sent by Brutus and Cassius as ambassador to Parthia and had remained there after Philippi;[82] it was he who had persuaded the Parthians to invade Syria. The Parthians defeated Decidius Saxa, Antony's governor of Syria, who fled to Antioch. Labienus pursued Saxa and forced him to flee to Cilicia, where he captured and executed him. Antioch surrendered to the Parthians, who occupied all of Syria and Phoenicia with the exception of Tyre.[83]

The new regime proved popular. The Syrians, Dio Cassius writes,

[77] Plutarch, *Antony* 24; Dobiáš, *Hist.* 204, 559.

[78] See above, n. 74.

[79] Josephus *Bell.* 1.243-245 and *Antiq.* 14.324-326; cf. Dobiáš, *Hist.* 204-205. Josephus mentions that M. Valerius Messalla Corvinus acted on this occasion as defendant for Herod.

[80] Dio Cassius 48.24.3; Plutarch *Antony* 24.

[81] Newell, "Pre-Imperial Coinage of Roman Antioch" 94. While noting that the diminution of the titles on the coins may have political significance, he also suggests that the omission of part of the old legend may simply indicate that it was felt that the long, crowded title was difficult to read and that it was shortened in order to make it more legible and more pleasing in appearance. It may, however, seem difficult to suppose that an official title of this kind, which must have been a matter of pride to the people of Antioch, would be changed for any but political reasons.

[82] Debevoise, *Hist. of Parthia* 108-109.

[83] Dio Cassius 48.24.3, 48.25.3-4; cf. Debevoise, *Hist. of Parthia* 109-111.

"felt unusual affection for Pacorus on account of his justness and mildness, an affection as great as they had felt for the best kings that had ever ruled them."[84] The coins minted at Antioch during this period are of the same general type as the previous issues, showing that the Parthians did not think fit to introduce drastic changes in their administration. There are, however, characteristic signs of Parthian influence. The important title "Autonomous" disappears, and is replaced by "Sacred and Inviolate"; evidently the Parthians did not wish to allow even titular autonomy to the capital of the former Roman province, though there was evidently no objection to the politically less significant epithets "Sacred and Inviolate." A palm-branch, symbolizing the Parthian victory, was added behind the head of Zeus; and the era of Caesar is replaced, in the dates given on the coins, by the Seleucid era, which the Parthians themselves had always used.[85]

The foreign regime lasted until the Parthians were driven out of Syria by Antony's forces in the summer of 39 B.C.[86] A year later, Antony reached Syria and took over from his general Ventidius the task of punishing Antiochus of Commagene, who had aided the Parthians.[87] While Antony was besieging Antiochus in Samosata, Herod, whom Antony had chosen to be client-king of Judaea, came to Antony's assistance, marching by way of Antioch, where he evidently expected to find Antony.[88] After the surrender of Samosata, Antony put Gaius Sosius in charge of Syria and himself left the province.[89] Herod seems to have gone to Antioch at this time, presumably in order to cooperate with Sosius.[90] Sosius and Herod now set out against the Hasmonean Antigonus (Mattathias), who had usurped Herod's place in Jerusalem. Antigonus surrendered Jerusalem in the summer of 37 B.C. Sosius eventually sent the usurper to Antony at Antioch, and there he was put to death.[91]

Antony, after an absence in the West, returned to Syria in the late autumn of 37 B.C. to prepare for the campaign that he was planning

[84] Dio Cassius 49.20.4, transl. E. Cary, Loeb Classical Library; cf. Debevoise, *Hist. of Parthia* 117.
[85] Newell, "Pre-Imperial Coinage of Rom. Antioch" 96-98; Bellinger, "Some Coins from Antioch" 60-63.
[86] Debevoise, *Hist. of Parthia* 111-116.
[87] Debevoise, *Hist. of Parthia* 119.
[88] Josephus *Ant.* 14.439-440.
[89] Josephus *Ant.* 14.447. Josephus says that Antony went to Egypt, Plutarch (*Antony* 34) that he went to Athens; cf. Tarn in *CAH* 10.54, who adopts Plutarch's account.
[90] Josephus *Ant.* 14.448.
[91] Strabo frag. 15, *FHG* 3, p. 494; Plutarch *Antony* 36; Josephus *Ant.* 14.488-490; *Bell.* 1.357; Dio Cassius 49.22.6; cf. Wilcken, "Antigonos," no. 9, *RE* 1.2420.

against the Parthians. He sent Fonteius Capito to bring Cleopatra to Syria, and when she arrived he married her. The wedding, though none of the extant sources happens to say so specifically, presumably took place in Antioch.[92] As a wedding gift, Antony presented Cleopatra with territories in Syria and Palestine, and Cleopatra having brought with her to Antioch the twins whom she had borne in 40 B.C., Antony recognized them as his own and named them Alexander Helios and Cleopatra Selene.[93] While he was at Antioch, Antony, who was now the master of the whole East, bestowed many gifts of titles and of the crowns of tetrarchies and kingdoms, and it was at this time (as has been noted) that, in order to confirm Herod as king of Judaea, he executed Antigonus.

In the spring of 36 B.C. Antony set out on his conquest of Parthia. His elaborate expedition failed, and he was forced to return to Antioch in the autumn with only a handful of his troops.[94] During the next few years, while Antony was still busy with his plans for the reconquest of the eastern possessions of Alexander and the Seleucids, we hear nothing of Antioch, although it is safe to assume that the city served during this time as one of Antony's military bases. When Octavian opened his campaign against Antony, Antioch was the scene of one final, and quite minor, episode in the struggle. A band of gladiators enrolled in Antony's service had been training in Cyzicus; and when they heard of Antony's need for assistance, they tried to make their way to Egypt to join him. When they passed by way of Antioch they were overpowered by Q. Didius, the governor of Syria, with the aid of forces provided by Herod of Judaea, and were made to settle in Daphne.[95]

With Antony's defeat at the battle of Actium (September 31 B.C.),

[92] Plutarch *Antony* 36; cf. Stähelin, "Kleopatra," no. 20, *RE* 11.759; Dobiáš, *Hist.* 250-251. It would seem almost beyond doubt that Antony would have had the marriage celebrated in Antioch, not only because this was the capital of Syria, in which he would have to organize his military preparations, but because Antioch would have been the city in Syria best suited to be the setting for such an event. There is a passage in Servius' commentary on *Aeneid* 7.684 in which it is stated that Antony after his marriage to Cleopatra ordered coins to be struck *in Anagnia*. It has been suggested the *Anagnia* be emended to *Antiochia*, or to *Alexandria* (see Dobiáš, *Hist.* 273, n. 134), but this seems unnecessary (see Grant, *Imperium to Auctoritas* 38). On a coin of Antony and Cleopatra which has been wrongly attributed to Antioch, see T. V. Buttrey, Jr., "*Thea Neotera* on Coins of Antony and Cleopatra," *American Numismatic Society, Museum Notes* 6 (1954) 95-109.
[93] Plutarch *Antony* 36; cf. Stähelin in *RE* 11.760-761; Tarn in *CAH* 10.67.
[94] Florus 2.20.10; Orosius 6.19.1; cf. Dobiáš, *Hist.* 260, n. 87. On the campaign, see Debevoise, *Hist. of Parthia* 123-132.
[95] Dio Cassius 51.7.2-6 and 51.9.1; Josephus *Bell.* 1.392, *Ant.* 5.195, and cf. Dobiáš, *Hist.* 287 and Schürer, *Gesch. d. jüd. Volkes*[3-4] 1.383.

followed by his suicide in Alexandria (30 B.C.), another phase in the history of Antioch comes to an end. Antony had carried on Caesar's policy for the Romanization of Syria by presenting himself both as a Roman magistrate and as a divine heir to the divine Seleucid rulers.[96] It remained for Augustus to carry on the same course among the more stable conditions of the *Pax Augusta*.

[96] *BMC Galatia etc.* p. 157, no. 52; Grant, *Imperium to Auctoritas* 368-375.

CHAPTER 8

ANTIOCH UNDER THE AUGUSTAN EMPIRE,
31 B.C.-A.D. 69

1. Antioch in the Time of Augustus, 31 b.c.-a.d. 14; The Mint; The Olympic Games of Antioch

THE triumph of Octavian, the political heir of Julius Caesar, meant that Antioch, in common with the other cities of the East, was now free of the vicissitudes of political fortune which had beset it almost constantly since the power of the Seleucids began to decline. The dawn of the golden age founded by Octavian brought to the city, with the blessings of peace, a material prosperity that it was to enjoy for many years. The *Pax Augusta* was to unify the Empire as a whole and to reconcile the Greek East to Roman rule. Pompey and Caesar had, it is true, begun the process of fitting Antioch into the Roman scheme by the construction of public buildings that served to embody the preeminent position Antioch was predestined to occupy in the Roman East. Their work, however, was only a beginning, and its significance was inevitably overshadowed by the events of the civil wars. It remained for Augustus,[1] Agrippa, and Tiberius to effect, within the framework of their program for the Greek East, the transformation of the metropolis of Syria.[2]

In point of prestige, the position of the city was elevated as a result of the change made by Augustus in the status of the province of Syria. In the time of the Republic, Syria had been a senatorial province, governed by officials (of rank varying with the prevailing circumstances) who held office for one year each.[3] When Augustus divided the provinces of the Empire into three categories, senatorial, imperial, and procuratorial, Syria, because of its strategic importance, was made an

---

[1] The title was bestowed on Octavian by the Senate in 27 b.c.

[2] It must be borne in mind that beginning with the Roman period our sources for the history of Antioch are much more extensive than they were for the Seleucid period, thanks in great measure to the circumstance that the chronicle of Malalas begins at this point to contain information drawn ultimately from local official sources such as either did not exist for the Seleucid period or were not available either for Malalas himself or for his intermediate sources (see further above, Ch. 2). The inevitable result of this sudden increase in our material is that there appears to be a marked increase in the tempo of life at Antioch as we know it; but while this outward change doubtless reflects more or less accurately the actual course of events, we must remember that much knowledge of the history of the city, particularly during the late Seleucid period, has perished.

[3] See above, Ch. 7.

imperial province, governed by a *legatus Augusti*, of consular or praetorian rank, depending on the circumstances of the time, who was
appointed by the emperor for an indefinite number of years.[4] The post
of legate of Syria was one of the most important in the Empire, and
on occasion the legate acted as supreme commander in the Roman
East.[5] The legate was assisted in his administration of the province by
a *procurator* of equestrian rank, in charge of financial matters, who
was appointed by the emperor and was responsible, not to the legate,
but directly to the emperor.[6] The legate had under his command
legions (originally three, but sometimes four and later sometimes two)
which were permanently stationed in the province. The legate and the
procurator had their headquarters at Antioch.[7] Although the city remained "autonomous," the legate, if only by his mere presence in the
city, must have exerted a considerable influence on the administration
of the internal affairs of the city.[8]

The establishment of the Roman power in Antioch also meant that
the city now came to play a role in international affairs which it had
not known under the later Seleucids. We are told, for example, how
Nicolaus of Damascus, when he was at Antioch, saw ambassadors
from India on their way to visit the Emperor Augustus.[9]

[4] See Marquardt, *Staatsverwaltung*[2] 416-419, 548-550; also von Premerstein, "Legatus," *RE* 12 (1925) 1143-1146.

[5] Th. Mommsen, *Röm. Gesch.*[4] (Berlin 1894) 5.447; cf. R. Besnier, "Les procurateurs provinciaux pendant le règne de Claude," *Rev. belge de philol. et d'hist.* 28 (1950) 455.

[6] Marquardt, *Staatsverwaltung*[2] 556-557; Grant, *Imperium to Auctoritas* 130, 135; P. Horovitz, "Essai sur les pouvoirs des procurateurs-gouverneurs," *Rev. belge de philol. et d'hist.* 17 (1938) 776. On the theory that the procurator of Judaea was subordinate to the legate of Syria, see Horovitz, *op.cit.* 779ff.

[7] For the legions stationed in Syria, see the tables of the distribution of the legions during the reigns of the several emperors in E. Ritterling and W. Kubitschek, "Legio," *RE* 12 (1925) 1362-1367; the evidence for the history of each legion may be found in the same article. See also H. M. D. Parker, *The Roman Legions* (Oxford 1928). Lists of the known governors and procurators of Syria during the imperial period may be found in Marquardt, *Staatsverwaltung*[2] 418; Liebenam, *Legaten* 360; Schürer, *Gesch. d. jüd. Volkes*[3-4] 1.316-337; R. E. Brünnow and A. von Domaszewski, *Die Provicia Arabia* (Strasbourg 1904-1909) 3.300-302; Harrer, *Studies*; idem, "Was Arrian Governor of Syria?," *CP* 11 (1916) 338-339; idem, "Inscriptions of Legati in Syria," *AJA* 36 (1932) 287-289; Honigmann, "Syria" 1628-1631. On the functions and careers of the procurators of Syria, see H. G. Pflaum, *Les procurateurs équestres sous le Haut-Empire romain* (Paris 1950) esp. 6, 52-53. On the career of M. Titius, see T. Corbishley, "A Note on the Date of the Syrian Governorship of M. Titius," *JRS* 24 (1934) 43-49, and Lily Ross Taylor, "M. Titius and the Syrian Command," *JRS* 26 (1936) 161-173. See also Lily Ross Taylor, "Quirinius and the Census of Judaea," *AJP* 54 (1933) 120-133.

[8] This is shown, for example, by the way in which the coins issued by the mint of Antioch are dated by the names of the various legates; see Grant, *Imperium to Auctoritas* 396-397.

[9] Strabo 15.1.73 (719); Dio Cassius 54.9.8.

The reign of Augustus was not only the commencement of a new era in the history of Syria, but it also established the province as the center of two problems that engaged the constant attention of the Roman government. From this time on, it was necessary to look upon Syria both as the frontier (along with Cappadocia) against Parthia, and as the thoroughfare of some of the most important trade routes in the Roman Empire. Roman protection gave the highly developed commercial capabilities of the Syrians the maximum opportunity for expansion.

Our principal knowledge of the history of Antioch during the reign of Augustus comes from the coins of the city's mint and from the accounts by Malalas and other writers of the important building activities carried on in the city at this period.

The coins issued at Antioch are significant because the mint of this city played a more important role in the Augustan currency system than any other peregrine mint,[10] so that Antioch became an important center for the efforts of Augustus to reform the coinage. In order to supply the eastern part of the Empire with an adequate supply of money, it was necessary for the mint of Antioch to be given the function of an imperial mint, playing a role in the over-all program, while at the same time it continued its services to the provincial coinage in supplying money for local needs.[11] The changes, however, were made gradually. The mint of Antioch at first continued to issue much the same types, both the autonomous issues and the silver tetradrachms imitating those of Philip I, dated by the era of Caesar, which were themselves traditional signs of the "free" status of the city.[12] Variations in type and legend suggest fluctuations in the control of the mint and in the procedures by which the city was administered. For example, on the coins first issued after the battle of Actium (September 31 B.C.), Antioch was given only the title of Metropolis. The absence of its other titles (Autonomous, Sacred, Inviolate) suggests, as Newell writes, that the position of the city in the new regime may at first have been not quite

---

[10] See Grant, *Imperium to Auctoritas* 376; C. H. V. Sutherland, *Coinage in Roman Imperial Policy 31 B.C.-A.D. 68* (London 1951) 43, 190.

[11] See H. Mattingly, "Origins of the Imperial Coinage in Republican Times," *Num. Chron.* ser. 4, vol. 19 (1919) 221-234; idem, Introd. to *BMC Rom. Emp.* 1, p. xvii; Wruck, *Syrische Provinzialprägung* 3-41; Dieudonné, "Monnaies grecques de Syrie" 25-34.

[12] See Newell, "Pre-Imperial Coinage of Rom. Antioch" 102-113; A. R. Bellinger's review of Grant, *Imperium to Auctoritas* in *AJA* 51 (1947) 339; Macdonald, "Pseudo-Autonomous Coinage of Antioch" 105ff.; Bikerman, *Institutions des Séleucides* 235; H. Seyrig in *Syria* 28 (1951) 213-214.

assured enough for the city to be given the title of Autonomous.[13]
Soon, however, this title was restored; and the head of Apollo appears
on the coins as a dual allusion to the influence the god exercised at
Antioch and to his role in the winning of the victory at Actium.[14]
Another compliment to the city is made by the use of the figure of
the Tyche of Antioch on the coins, for the first time since the regime
of Tigranes.[15]

While the silver tetradrachms were continued until the year 21/20
B.C.,[16] there appeared also two series of bronze coins, one bearing the
head of Augustus and the letters SC (*senatus consulto*), the other the
inscription AVGVSTVS or CA (*Caesaris auctoritate*). The dates at which
these series began are not definitively established; the years, 27, 23 or
22-19 B.C. have been proposed.[17] The coins show, however, that the mint
of Antioch was now beginning to take its place in the larger monetary
system that Augustus was developing.

In 20 B.C. Augustus visited the city for the second time,[18] and to
commemorate the occasion the mint issued, in place of the well-known
silver tetradrachms of Seleucid type with Philip's portrait, which had
continued in use, a new variety bearing the portrait and title of Augustus, dated, not by the era of Caesar, but by Augustus' regnal year.[19]
The old type of tetradrachm again appears, however, in 17/6 B.C.[20] A
decade later a major change is found, with the issue of both silver and
bronze of Augustus with, for reverse type, the seated Tyche of Antioch.

[13] Newell, "Pre-Imperial Coinage of Rom. Antioch" 103.

[14] *Ibid.,* 105.

[15] *BMC Galatia etc.* p. 166, nos. 131-132; p. 167, no. 137; p. 168, nos. 140, 144, 146; p.
169, nos. 147-149; cf. Bosch, *Kleinasiatischen Münzen* 254, and Toynbee, *Hadrianic
School* 132.

[16] Newell, "Pre-Imperial Coinage of Rom. Antioch" 109-110.

[17] See Grant, *Imperium to Auctoritas* 98-110, with Bellinger's review, cited above (n.
12), and A. R. Bellinger, "Greek Mints under the Roman Empire," *Essays in Roman
Coinage Presented to Harold Mattingly* (Oxford, 1956) 146-147. See also D. B. Waagé,
"Coins" pp. ix, 30ff.

[18] On this visit, see further below in the account of his building activities, §2.

[19] See Newell, "Pre-Imperial Coinage of Rom. Antioch" 110-112. Such coins of
Augustus have been said to be dated by the Actian era, an era that was supposed to
have been inaugurated to commemorate Augustus' victory. Thus it would be necessary
to suppose that the use of the Caesarian era was suspended, at least temporarily (see,
for example, Newell *loc.cit.*). However, it is plain that what is called the Actian era
is merely the system of reckoning by the regnal years of Augustus, which amounted
to the same thing; see B. Pick, "Zur Titulatur der Flavier," *Ztschr. f. Num.* 14 (1887)
311; Macdonald, "Pseudo-Autonomous Coinage of Antioch" 106; and Dobiáš, *Hist.*
284-285. The use of the regnal year in the case of the coins issued at Antioch in 20 B.C.
could thus be taken to be an acknowledgement of Augustus' imperial authority, which
could have been regarded as a further compliment offered on the occasion of his visit
to the city.

[20] Newell, "Pre-Imperial Coinage of Rom. Antioch" 112-113.

These issues were accompanied by pseudo-autonomous small change dated by the names of the governors of Syria.[21] Apparently these issues were intended to commemorate the *vicennium* of Augustus' new regime, which fell in 7 B.C.[22] Moreover, there appears, in 7/6 B.C., an issue of coins of Augustus as high priest of his own cult at Antioch, a series which seems, at least at present, to be unique among city coinages.[23] Evidently this series was intended to celebrate the *quinquennium* of the Roman high priesthood, as well as to give due recognition to the counterpart of this priesthood in Antioch.[24] These changes coincide with the appointment (7/6 B.C.) as governor of Syria of P. Quintilius Varus, of whom it was said "that he was no despiser of money is demonstrated by his governorship of Syria: he entered the rich province a poor man, but left it a rich man and the province poor."[25] It seems likely that the changes in the production of the mint which followed the new governor's arrival resulted somehow in a profit to the governor himself.[26] At any rate the placing of the governors' names on the coins, while it is of course primarily a chronological device, suggests that the governors exercised a fairly close supervision over local finances, the closeness of the control varying from one administration to another.[27] One noteworthy issue, dated in A.D. 5/6, reflects a change in the city's dignity. In this year Herod Archelaus, ethnarch of Judea,

[21] Grant, *Imperium to Auctoritas* 100, 397-400; Macdonald, "Pseudo-Autonomous Coinage of Antioch" 105ff.; *Dura Final Rep.* 6: Bellinger, *The Coins* pp. 147-148, no. 1599.

[22] Grant, *Anniversary Issues* 20, with n. 2.

[23] Grant, *Imperium to Auctoritas* 376-378. As Grant points out (378), "it did not seem anomalous to the ancients that the *princeps* should be high priest of a cult that was largely devoted to his own worship (in combination with Rome); he was in precisely the same situation as *Pontifex Maximus.*" See also Dieudonné, "Monnaies grecques de Syrie" 32-33. Evidence for the cult at Antioch of Augustus, of Roma, and of Roma and Augustus is scanty; comparative material is provided by the evidence for Asia Minor, where the cults are much better known; see Magie, *Asia Minor* 447-449, 1295-1298, 1613-1614.

[24] Grant, *Anniversary Issues* 20, with n. 2.

[25] Velleius Paterculus 2.117.2, transl. of F. W. Shipley, in the Loeb Classical Library. Stauffenberg (*Malalas* 482, n. 10) suggests that a public bath called τὸ Οὐάριον, which Malalas says (244.7) was built in the reign of Caligula, was actually built by Quintilius Varus while legate of Syria; and this suggestion is adopted by Groag, "Lurius Varius" 203, n. 9. There seems, however, to be no good reason to doubt Malalas' account; see further below, §4.

[26] This suggestion is made by Macdonald, "Pseudo-Autonomous Coinage of Antioch" 107. The mint authorities might likewise have profited. In particular it may be suggested that the peculiar archieratic coins, which do not appear after Varus' time in Syria, represent a special issue appealing to local pride and that these were intended to be absorbed, as a novelty, by local patriotic collectors of coins.

[27] Grant, *Imperium to Auctoritas* 396-398. The fluctuations may be seen in Macdonald, "Pseudo-Autonomous Coinage of Antioch."

Samaria, and Idumea, was banished by Augustus to Gaul, and the territory that he had ruled was incorporated into the province of Syria.[28] The coins of Antioch issued in this year omit the name of the Roman legate, and bear instead the title Metropolis, which had fallen into disuse. Evidently the old title was employed again in this year in allusion to Antioch's new position as the capital of an enlarged province.[29]

When Agrippa was in the East, about 14 B.C., there is evidence, in the issues of the mint of Antioch and of other Eastern mints, of a second stage in Augustus' plan for the reform of the Roman coinage. In the case of Antioch, this is marked by the appearance of bronze *dupondii* and *asses* with s·c· within a laurel wreath.[30]

One of the major events in the history of Antioch under Augustus was the foundation of the local games, which in time became the Olympic games of Antioch, one of the most famous festivals of the Roman world. A senator of Antioch named Sosibius, who accompanied Augustus to Rome after one of the *princeps'* visits to Antioch and who died there, bequeathed his property to his native city, with the provision that the income be used to present games every four years for thirty days in the month of Hyperberetaios (October). At first the games were presented regularly. Soon, however, the officials charged with their administration began to abuse their trust, diverting the money from Sosibius' estate into their own pockets, and by the time of Claudius the festival had ceased to be presented. The citizens of Antioch petitioned Claudius for a reorganization of the festival, and this was granted, the games being now called Olympic.[31]

In addition to the Olympic Games, we hear of certain other festivals, such as the "contest of Eucrates," which is said to have included running and flute-playing.[32] During the reign of Antoninus we hear of a

---

[28] Schürer, *Gesch. d. jüd. Volkes*³⁻⁴ 1.453.

[29] See Macdonald, "Pseudo-Autonomous Coinage of Antioch" 110-111.

[30] See M. Grant, "Complex Symbolism and New Mints, c. 14 B.C.," *Num. Chron.* ser. 6, vol. 9 (1949) 22-35.

[31] Malalas 224.22—225.2, 248.5ff. See the chapter "Die antiochenischen Olympien" in Stauffenberg, *Malalas* 412-443. For evidence on the festivals elsewhere in the Empire similar to the Olympic Games, see Rachel S. Robinson, *Sources for the History of Greek Athletics in English Translation* (Cincinnati 1955). There is no indication of the date of Sosibius' journey to Rome; he might have accompanied the *princeps* there after either of his visits to Antioch, which were made in 31-30 and 20 B.C. There is likewise no evidence of the date of Sosibius' death. On this endowment, in comparison with other similar endowments in the Empire, see J. H. Oliver, "The Ruling Power: A Study of the Roman Empire in the Second Century after Christ through the Roman Oration of Aelius Aristides," *Transactions of the American Philosophical Society*, new series, 43, pt. 4 (1953) 969, 971. Whether the games at this time were identical with those of the *Koinon* of Syria, as they seem to have at a later period, is not known.

[32] *Fouilles de Delphes*, vol. 3, pt. 1, no. 550, line 30; *ibid.*, no. 555, line 25; Edhem

victor in flute-playing in a festival at Antioch which does not seem to have been identical with the Olympic Games. There were also festivals named for the Emperor Hadrian and the Emperor Commodus, of which we hear in epigraphical texts.

2. THE BUILDINGS OF AUGUSTUS AND TIBERIUS

Of the magnificent public buildings that throughout the Empire symbolized the peace and prosperity of the Augustan age, Antioch had a notable share. What we know of the building activities carried on in the city during the reign of Augustus indicates that the city at this period was enlarged and beautified to a noteworthy degree; there is evidence, too, that there was an increase in the population. It happens that our sources attribute to King Herod of Judaea and to Agrippa and Tiberius many building undertakings probably carried out during Augustus' reign; and it is unfortunately not possible to determine the precise dates of the operations in question. Nevertheless there are indications that the inception of much of the work is connected with Augustus' visits to Antioch in 31-30 B.C. and 20 B.C. (more likely the latter visit); and in any case the knowledge we do have of the buildings erected at Antioch at this time (which is, indeed, the earliest body of evidence of this kind we possess for the city during the Roman period) is sufficiently valuable in itself to compensate for the chronological uncertainty inherent in it.

Two factors rendered conditions unusually favorable to the present enlargement and adornment of the city. The first was the reorganization of the province of Syria and the restoration of peace and prosperity which followed Augustus' accession. Antioch had been the capital of the province since the time of Pompey (64 B.C.), and its position as political and military headquarters would inevitably have resulted in some increase in economic activity and in some growth of population, along with the stimulation afforded by the more or less constant presence of numbers of government officials and troops in and near the city. Serious efforts had been made by Pompey, Caesar, and Antony

---

Bey, "Fouilles de Tralles," *BCH* 28 (1904) 87-88; L. Robert, *Études anatoliennes* (Paris 1937) 144 (statue base from Smyrna); M. Gough, "Anazarbus," *Anatolian Studies* 2 (1952) 128-129 (inscription found at Anazarbus, possibly of the time of Severus and Caracalla). A Greek inscription dated A.D. 73/4, found at Antioch, contains what seems to be a reference to a locality "of the Στεφανειτῶν," which has been taken to refer to an association of the athletes and musicians who had won contests at various festivals. On the inscription, see below, Ch. 9, n. 31. For the festivals named in honor of Hadrian and Commodus, see below the accounts of their reigns.

both to Romanize the metropolis and to restore it physically to the position of prestige that it had enjoyed under the earlier Seleucids. The years between 64 B.C. and 31 B.C., however, were at the same time troubled by the civil wars and by the inevitable changes of regime in the city. After Actium, peace was restored, and trade could be resumed; and there would naturally have been some influx of visitors and new residents, both from Rome and from the East, who were attracted to the city by the presence of the governor and of the now regularly authorized garrison of Syria. Testimony to this growth is found (as will be seen below) in the foundation of a new quarter of the city by Agrippa and in the enlargements of the theater made successively by Agrippa and (ostensibly) Tiberius.

The second factor conducive to the city's expansion was the appearance, at this juncture, of men in authority who took a notable interest in public building enterprises. Augustus himself gave keen attention to the building and repair of public works, especially during the early part of his reign when he had at his disposal the large sums of treasure he found in Egypt and the booty he took from his opponents.[33] The *princeps* visited Antioch twice, once during the tour of the East which he made in 31-30 B.C. after the battle of Actium (September 31 B.C.), and a second time in 20 B.C., during his stay (22-19 B.C.) in Greece and Asia;[34] on the latter occasion, as has been noted, the mint of Antioch issued a coin in commemoration of his visit.[35] Augustus thus had ample opportunity to know the city. Agrippa, the emperor's son-in-law and trusted coworker, was watchful for the public welfare, and paid close attention to the importance of public buildings; his work, we know, was predominantly practical in character.[36] Herod of Judaea was famous as a munificent builder, and a long and impressive list of his enterprises can be drawn up.[37] He was also an enthusiastic supporter

[33] See Bourne, *Public Works* 16.

[34] *CAH* 10.112-115, 119, 144-145; Dobiáš, *Hist.* 291-292, 316, 562-564; Reinhold, *Marcus Agrippa* 59-60, 84-88.

[35] See above, n. 19.

[36] See Reinhold, *Marcus Agrippa* 162-163. Agrippa built an *odeion* in the agora at Athens ca. 15 B.C.: H. A. Thompson, "The Odeion in the Athenian Agora," *Hesperia* 19 (1950) 31-141 (cf. *ibid.* 21 [1952] 90). Agrippa's interests as reflected in his building activities are well brought out in the study of F. W. Shipley, *Agrippa's Building Activities in Rome* (Washington University Studies, New Series: Language and Literature, no. 4; St. Louis 1933). On Agrippa's unusual technical knowledge of engineering, see Daniel, *M. Vipsanius Agrippa* 41-50.

[37] See the accounts of his building activities given by Schürer, *Gesch. d. jüd. Volkes*[3-4] 1.387-393 and by F.-M. Abel, *Histoire de Palestine* (Paris 1952) 1.363-380. In writing of Herod's work at Antioch (391), Schürer mentions only the account in Josephus' *Antiquities.* For the archaeological evidence for Herod's building activities at Samaria-

of the Roman regime,[38] and Antioch profited from his eagerness to do honor to Augustus. Tiberius does not today enjoy the reputation of having been a great builder, but much work that was done at Antioch (some of it possibly during Augustus' reign) went under his name. Whether this work was actually done by Tiberius is not clear (see further below).

For our knowledge of the building activities of these benefactors we are largely indebted to the chronicler Malalas. In the account he gives of Octavian's settlement of the East after Actium, Malalas states that Octavian and Agrippa visited Antioch, and that Agrippa, pleased with the beauty of the city, commissioned various buildings there. He founded a new quarter of the city, named for himself (ἡ γειτνία Ἀγριππιτῶν), which included a public bath.[39] Outside the city, on or near the slope of the mountain, in a spot where there was a spring to furnish water, he built another public bath, likewise bearing his own name (τὸ Ἀγριππιανόν). At a later period at least, if not indeed originally, the bath stood in a rustic setting, for it came to be called (Malalas says) τὸ Ἀμπελινὸν λουτρόν, "The Bath in the Vineyards." Finally, in order to accommodate an apparent increase in the popula-

---

Sebaste, see Crowfoot-Kenyon-Sukenik, *Buildings at Samaria* 31-34, 39-41, 123-129; and for Tiberias, see M. Avi-Yonah, "The Foundation of Tiberias," *Israel Exploration Journal* 1 (1950-1951) 160-169.

[38] See Schürer, *Gesch. d. jüd. Volkes*[3-4] 1.404-405.

[39] Malalas' record of the construction of this bath is of linguistic interest as being the only instance (at least in the present state of the unique Oxford MS of the chronicle) in which the term βανιάριν (222.20) is used to denote a bath that has already been called a *demosion loutron* (222.17). Since there is some variety in the usage in this respect, which has not always been understood by scholars, it may be useful to collect some typical examples. Malalas uses *demosion* (192.8, with Chilmead's note, p. 546 ed. Bonn; 276.1-3, 19-21; 282.7, 290.20, 292.4, 318.3-6, 346.21, 359.18ff., 363.12, 367.14, 426.2), *demosion loutron* (216.23, 222.17-19, 234.12, 243.16-20, 277.6-7, 278.1, 280.15, 281.7-9, 283.5, 293.16-17, 21; 294.12, 17ff.; 307.1, 322.4-5, 339.16-17, 409.15), and *loutron* (294.19ff., 208.3-5, 397.11, 423.5, *Exc. de insid.*, 35, p. 166.34 ed. De Boor). In four passages he uses both *demosion loutron* and *demosion* of the same structures (244.7-9, 263.12-15, 291.17-21, 321.12-15); in two passages he uses both *demosion loutron* and *loutron* of the same structure (222.17-19, 281.7-9). The compiler of the *Chronicon Paschale* uses *demosion* (534.17-19, 557.11-12, 566.12-13, 580.19ff., 582.5), *demosion loutron* (583.17-18, 609.2-3=Mal. 339.16; 618.20), and *balaneion* (622.11); all of these apparently are public baths. Theophanes uses *loutron and demosion loutron* (cf. De Boor's Index Graecitatis, s.v. *loutron*, II, p. 758, and the heading *loutra* in the entry for Constantinople in the *Index nominum rerumque*, II, p. 651); some of the baths which he calls *loutron* may have been private, but this is not certain. Evagrius uses both *balaneion* (II, 12, pp. 63.32ff.) and *demosion balaneion* in the passage quoted above of public baths (cf. also III, 37, pp. 136.14-15). Joshua the Stylite uses both *demosion* and *balaneion* in Syriac transliteration (chaps. 29, 43, 75), and *demosion* is used in Syriac transliteration in the *Chronicle* of Zachariah of Mitylene to mean both public bath (7.6, 8.1) and latrine (10.16).

tion, he added a second zone of seats to the theater.[40] On a later visit to Antioch, Malalas writes, Agrippa cleared the hippodrome of rubbish with which it had been encumbered as the result of an earthquake, and attended an entertainment that was presented to celebrate the restoration. There is an error in these accounts: Malalas is mistaken in stating that Agrippa accompanied Octavian on the tour that he made after Actium.[41] Agrippa made two visits to the East, the first in 23-21 B.C., when he remained in Mytilene and did not visit Syria,[42] the second in 17/16-13 B.C., when he probably visited Antioch in 15 B.C.[43] If we are to suppose that building operations such as Malalas describes would have been inaugurated by Agrippa in person, then all of them must date from 15 B.C.; but it may have been that Agrippa issued orders from Mytilene for some of the work to be done, and in this case the suburb, the bath, and the addition to the theater would date from 23-21 B.C., the clearing of the hippodrome from 15 B.C.[44]

[40] Mal. 222.15-22. The chronicler says the theater had been "built" by Julius Caesar, but this may mean only that Caesar restored or rebuilt an existing Hellenistic theater not otherwise recorded; see above, Ch. 7, §2. On the location of the *vicus Agrippae* (which Malalas calls γειτνία 'Αγριππιτῶν) see below. According to Bourne, *Public Works* 26, Malalas records (222) that Agrippa led water into Antioch. Malalas says, of the bath, that it was supplied by a spring; and since he says nothing as to the water supply of the new *vicus Agrippae*, the implication is that the existing aqueduct system was used for the supply of the new suburb. Daniel, *M. Vipsanius Agrippa* 44, n. 34, rejects Malalas' account of Agrippa's activities at Antioch simply because the chronicler is a late and untrustworthy source. It is worth noting in this connection that in the note cited Daniel expresses surprise that Müller, in his review of his own book reprinted in his *Kleine deutsche Schriften*, does not mention Agrippa's work at Antioch. Apparently Daniel was not acquainted with Müller's *Antiquitates Antiochenae*. Stauffenberg (*Malalas* 487) writes that the two baths which Malalas says Agrippa built are "doubtless identical." He does not, however, give his reason for this supposition, and there seems to be no cause to doubt Malalas' statements.

[41] Mal. 225.3-11. There is no other record of the earthquake that apparently made the hippodrome useless. Presumably it occurred between the repair or rebuilding of the hippodrome by Marcius Rex in 67 B.C. (see above, Ch. 6, n. 104) and Agrippa's visit to Antioch which seems to have taken place in 15 B.C. (see further below). On Malalas' error see Reinhold, *Marcus Agrippa* 59, n. 63, and Stauffenberg, Malalas 150-151, 164.

[42] Dio Cassius 53.32.1; Josephus *Ant.* 15.439; see D. Magie, "The Mission of Agrippa to the Orient in 23 B.C.," *CP* 3 (1908) 145-152, and Dobiáš *Hist.* 304, 564.

[43] See Reinhold, *Marcus Agrippa* 84, 111, 169; Stauffenberg, *Malalas* 176. Daniel, *M. Vipsanius Agrippa* 44, n. 34, states that the only occasion on which it could be supposed that Agrippa visited Antioch was his sojourn in the East in 23-21 B.C., when (as Daniel points out) it can be proved that Agrippa did not visit Syria (Daniel did not know the study of Agrippa's mission by Magie, cited above, n. 42). Why Agrippa should not have visited Antioch in 15 B.C., Daniel does not say.

[44] Malalas' account of Agrippa's visit in company with Octavian could be a conscious or unconscious invention of Malalas or his source, reflecting a desire to show that the city made such a striking impression on Octavian and Agrippa immediately after Actium that it was at once adorned with important public buildings. Stauffenberg (*Malalas* 164) suggests that Malalas divided Agrippa's building activities between two visits because he considered it inappropriate or unlikely that so much building should

One of the principal events in this period of building activity was the construction of a great colonnaded street, two Roman miles in length, which ran through the city (Figs. 6-11). This street, which formed one of Antioch's claims to fame in antiquity, appears to have been among the earliest monumental thoroughfares of its kind of which we have knowledge; it was roughly contemporary with the colonnaded streets of Olba and Pompeiopolis in Cilicia, which are known from inscriptional evidence to have existed in the time of Augustus and Tiberius,[45] though of course the street of Antioch must have been larger than those of the Cilician cities. According to the testimony of Malalas and Josephus, the construction of the street at Antioch was carried out, ostensibly at two different times, by Herod and Tiberius respectively.[46] Herod, in honor of the new *princeps* whose

---

be inaugurated during one visit. Malalas' source, knowing that Agrippa was in the East in 23-21 B.C., may have made the assumption that he visited Syria at that time, and so may have invented a visit to Antioch, in order to account for the building operations; and this visit may then have been turned into the tour with Octavian following Actium. On Agrippa's official position during his visits to the East, see, in addition to the passages cited above in Reinhold's study, Grant, *Imperium to Auctoritas* 428. On the work of Tiberius and Agrippa in Syria, see also Lily Ross Taylor, "M. Titius and the Syrian Command," *JRS* 26 (1936) 161-173.

[45] See R. Heberdey and A. Wilhelm, "Reisen in Kilikien," *Denkschr. Akad. Wien. Philos.-hist. Kl.* 44, pt. 6 (1896), pp. 84, 87; and Robertson, *Greek and Roman Architecture*[2] 291-292, 359. One of the consoles of the colonnaded street at Olba bears the inscription (Heberdey and Wilhelm, p. 84, n. 160) Αὐτοκράτορα Καίσ[α]ρα Τιβέριον θεοῦ υ[ἰὸν] τὸν κτίστην καὶ σωτῆρα. A list of the known colonnaded streets is collected by K. Lehmann-Hartleben, "Städtebau," *RE* 3 A (1929) 2109-2110. See also J. B. Ward Perkins, "The Art of the Severan Age in the Light of Tripolitanian Discoveries," *Proceedings of the British Academy* 37, p. 297, n. 24. Robertson points out that while it has been assumed that colonnaded streets of this type developed in Asia Minor or Syria during the Hellenistic period, "there is no good literary or monumental evidence for the fully developed type in this area till the close of the Hellenistic period." See also Wycherley, *How the Greeks Built Cities* 32. It is worth noting that the opinion of older scholars who believed that monumental colonnaded streets originated earlier in the Hellenistic age may have been influenced by the theory developed by C. O. Müller that the colonnaded street of Antioch was built by Antiochus Epiphanes. This hypothesis, however, was based entirely upon an interpretation of literary sources which we now (with evidence not available to Müller) can see was mistaken; see Downey, "Building Records in Malalas" 301-302.

[46] The accounts of Malalas and Josephus present certain difficulties of interpretation, and the hypotheses concerning them offered by modern scholars being not only complex but in part vitiated by the fact that until recently accurate maps of Antioch were not available, the problem has become so intricate that it cannot be rehearsed in full here; the reader who wishes the details will find them in Downey, "Building Records in Malalas" 300-311, the results of which are summarized here. Malalas mentions the street twice. First he writes (223.17-19), in his account of the reign of Augustus, that Herod, in honor of Augustus, paved the street because it was difficult to traverse. Then, in his account of the reign of Tiberius, he gives (232.17ff.) the description of Tiberius' work reproduced above. Josephus, in two brief passages (*Bell.* 1.425; *Ant.* 16.148), states that Herod both paved the main street of Antioch with dressed stone (marble is mentioned in *Bell.*) and built roofed colonnades along either side of it. Malalas, whose

favor he was anxious to win, first supplied the paving of the street, which Josephus says was of marble. This work was presumably inaugurated either in 30 B.C., when Herod accompanied Octavian on his journey from Egypt to Antioch,[47] or in 20 B.C., on the occasion of Augustus' second journey to the East, when the emperor again visited Antioch; during this journey Augustus is known to have conferred favors on Herod.[48] Then Tiberius built the roofed colonnades that lined the thoroughfare, and erected tetrapyla at each main cross street,[49] adorning them with mosaic work and marbles; and he ornamented the whole street with bronzes and statues.

Malalas goes on to describe much other work at Antioch which, he says, was done by Tiberius. An error in this account has caused uncertainty as to the time when this work was carried out,[50] and since Tiberius has the reputation of not having been a great builder,[51] there exists some doubt as to whether he did the work at Antioch which Malalas ascribes to him. What we know of Malalas' sources and methods makes it possible to suppose that Tiberius' name, in his chronicle, is wrongly attached to work that was performed under the auspices

---

material goes back ultimately to local contemporary records of official character, must certainly be right in dividing the work between Herod and Tiberius as he does. Either Josephus had vague information that led him to conclude that since Herod was said to be concerned with the building of a colonnaded street at Antioch, he must have done the whole work, or the Jewish historian was anxious to claim as much credit for Herod as possible and so permitted himself a little mistake.

[47] Josephus *Ant.* 15.218; see Schürer, *Gesch. d. jüd. Volkes*[3-4] 1.385.

[48] See Schürer, *Gesch. d. jüd. Volkes*[3-4] 1.369, 404-405. There was a close friendship between Agrippa and Herod, the importance of which is well brought out by Daniel, *M. Vipsanius Agrippa* 31-37. Thus it is possible that the benefactions conferred on Antioch by Agrippa and Herod represent a plan that was concerted between the two friends.

[49] This must certainly be the meaning of the imprecise phrase κατὰ ῥύμην (232.19). It is hard to take the words in their literal sense that a tetrapylon was built at every cross street.

[50] The chronicler lists Tiberius' buildings at Antioch in his account of the emperor's reign, saying (232.13-16) that it was on his return from a campaign against the Parthians that the new emperor visited Antioch and inaugurated his public works there. This is not true, for Tiberius, as emperor, made no such expedition against the Parthians and in fact he never left Italy after becoming emperor (see below, n. 52).

[51] While Malalas, in the conventional characterization which he prefixes to his account of each Roman emperor, calls Tiberius *philoktistes* (232.13), and while Velleius, the unabashed flatterer of Tiberius, writes with enthusiasm of his buildings (2.130.1: *Quanto suo suorumque nomine exstruxit opera!*), what we know from other sources suggests that Tiberius was, in comparison with Augustus at least, of necessity frugal in such matters. He did keep important buildings in repair, and he gave liberal assistance to cities that had suffered from fires and earthquakes; but aside from the work at Antioch ascribed to him, he appears to have inaugurated no new work on a grand scale; see Bourne, *Public Works* 31-37. Suetonius *Tib.* 47, writes: *Princeps neque opera ulla magnifica fecit.*

of someone else. The condition of the evidence is such that these questions cannot be decided with any certainty. Several hypotheses can be offered. One is that the work at Antioch which Malalas attributes to Tiberius was inaugurated, not during Tiberius' reign, but in 20 B.C., when the youthful Tiberius was in the East in command of a mission to Armenia.[52] In this case the work that went under the name of the young prince would have had a close connection, in time, with the similar operations of Herod and Agrippa, which are associated with the dates 30 or 20 B.C., and 15 B.C., and it would be interesting to find that Augustus permitted such major undertakings in one of the chief cities of his empire to be recorded under the names of Agrippa and Tiberius, rather than under his own. There was, however, a fire at Antioch during the reign of Tiberius, in A.D. 23/24, which seems to have caused serious damage, and while Malalas in recording this (235.15-236.1) does not connect it with any building activities of Tiberius, it seems possible that the disaster may have furnished the occasion for some or all of Tiberius' building operations. Another explanation offered is that the work that Malalas attributes to Tiberius was actually carried out by his adopted son Germanicus when the latter was in the East on a special mission with extraordinary powers, in A.D. 17-19.[53] Germanicus' cognomen was Caesar, the same as the emperor's nomen, so that Malalas or his source might have confused the two; and it might be possible that it was Germanicus who carried out the work at Antioch at the orders of Tiberius.

Though these problems seem insoluble, at least at present,[54] it is

---

[52] The expedition was sent by Augustus to Armenia to secure the submission of Parthia and the return of the standards that had been captured from the Romans; see Gelzer, "Iulius (Tiberius)," *RE* 10.481; *CAH* 10.262-263; Debevoise, *Hist. of Parthia* 140-141. On this occasion, Tiberius passed through Syria (Suetonius *Tib.* 14.3); and what we know of Malalas' procedures makes it possible to believe that the chronicler (or his source) made the mistaken assumptions (1) that buildings such as Tiberius erected at Antioch would properly have been inaugurated only while Tiberius was emperor, (2) that such buildings would be fittingly inaugurated by an emperor in person, and (3) that it would be most fitting for the work to be done in the course of a triumphal tour following a victorious campaign against barbarians. It would thus be easy for a chronicler of the caliber of Malalas and his sources to turn the expedition of 20 B.C., when Tiberius was twenty-one years old, into an event that occurred during his reign, and to attach to the triumphal return from this campaign the building activities recorded under Tiberius' name. The chronological problem, and the possible origins and significance of Malalas' errors, are exhaustively discussed by Weber, *Studien* 40-65. See also Downey, "Building Records in Malalas" 300-311; and on this feature of Malalas' methods, see above Ch. 2, §4.

[53] See Weber, *Studien* 61-64; Stauffenberg, *Malalas* 183; Groag, "Lurius Varius" 204, n. 11; Downey, "Building Records in Malalas" 303, 310, n. 1.

[54] Malalas' information on such work at Antioch comes ultimately from a local official source and the information is to be regarded as fundamentally sound, though

plain that the work that has come down under the name of Tiberius was intimately connected, in plan, with the operations carried out under Augustus by Herod and Agrippa.[55] Antioch was, it is plain, undergoing a major transformation at this time.

The operations that went under the name of Tiberius consisted, essentially, of the completion and improvement of the quarter of the city known as Epiphania, which had been established by Antiochus IV Epiphanes (175-163 B.C.), the "second founder" of Antioch.[56] This quarter was situated between the mountain and the original quarter founded by Seleucus I, which lay on the level ground along the river. References to buildings in it suggest that Epiphania extended up the slope of Mount Silpius, but it is not possible to determine how much of the slope was actually occupied.[57] In his new quarter Antiochus IV had built a bouleuterion and "various temples," and, apparently, a new agora.[58] Malalas says expressly that the Seleucid king did not

Malalas and his predecessors may have garbled it in points of detail. It is significant to find that Malalas' account of Tiberius' work at Antioch forms a major part of his account of that emperor's reign, the text of which runs from 232.10 to 243.2. The remainder of the account consists largely of the narrative of the life and passion of Christ (236.3—242.22); and aside from these two main sections, there are only brief notices of other events of the reign, which in fact have to do entirely with building operations in other places than Antioch (235.9-14, 236.1-2). Malalas states that the senate and the people of Antioch set up a statue to Tiberius in the colonnaded main street that the emperor built, and the chronicler's words purport to reproduce the opening words of the inscription: Τιβερίῳ Καίσαρι ἡ βουλὴ καὶ ὁ δῆμος τῶν Ἀντιοχέων (233.4-5). It might be claimed that the erection of the statue constitutes evidence that Tiberius actually carried out the work which Malalas ascribes to him. As Groag points out, however (*loc.cit.* above, n. 53), this is not necessarily the case. Indeed, it is possible that the statue was intended to commemorate some other event, or was merely a routine honor, and that the legend of Tiberius' work took its beginning from a false conclusion drawn from the existence of the statue.

[55] While it does not seem possible to find a thoroughly convincing solution to the problem at present, the present writer feels that the close connection, in scope and purpose, between the work of Herod and Agrippa and the work attributed to Tiberius favors the supposition that the latter operations were carried out when Tiberius was in the East in 20 B.C., at about the time when the work of Herod and Agrippa seems to have been done. It may seem difficult to believe that a building program of such proportions would have been inaugurated by Tiberius as a young man of twenty-one in 20 B.C. (or, if not actually inaugurated by him, planned by others and executed under his name). However, it may seem even more difficult to believe that Tiberius would have instituted such a program after he became emperor. It would seem not at all unnatural that this great transformation of Antioch should date wholly from the reign of Augustus, with the emperor planning or allowing the work to be carried out, not in his own name, but in those of Agrippa and Tiberius.

[56] See above, Ch. 5, §6.

[57] In one place Malalas writes of Epiphania as ἐπὶ τὸ ὄρος (205.22), in another he speaks of it as τὸ παρὰ τὸ ὄρος μέρος τῆς πόλεως (234.1). The statements as to the location of the buildings in it will be noted below as the buildings are discussed. The situation of Seleucus' quarter is known from Mal. 200.10ff., 233.10ff.

[58] Malalas 205.14-19; 234.2-3.

build a wall about his new quarter, but that this was first done by Tiberius.[59] It is very difficult indeed to believe that Antiochus IV can have left his new quarter unwalled, and the categorical tone of Malalas' statements on this point indicates that there was disagreement on this subject in antiquity; Strabo, for example, says that Epiphania was enclosed within a wall when it was first built. It seems likely that Malalas' sources for the Roman period, which were more extensive than those which he had for the Seleucid period, were anxious to give as much credit to the Romans as possible. Thus if the Romans merely repaired or extended an existing wall, it would be in keeping with the procedures of Malalas, and of the sources which he used, to let it be understood that the Romans were the first to build this wall.[60]

This wall, according to Malalas, joined the old city wall built by Seleucus I, and it must have run along the top of the mountain, for the chronicler says that it brought the mountain within the city, enclosing the acropolis and Iopolis.[61]

Since Epiphania lay between Seleucus' original settlement and the mountain, the enclosure of Epiphania within a wall would have meant that the ground occupied by the walled city between the river and the mountain would thereby have been increased by the area of Epiphania. We do not know the size and shape of Seleucus' settlement, but some idea of its situation may be gained from the route of the main street. The line of the ancient principal thoroughfare is followed by that of the modern main street.[62] The street built by Herod and "Tiberius" is said by Malalas (232.17) to have been "outside the city," that is, presumably, it would have been outside the old city of Seleucus at the time that the street was built (though it would of course have been within the area of Epiphania). Furthermore, this ancient main street follows the pattern of the rectangular *insulae* which, in the case of the older settlement near the river, represent the original Hellenistic grid of streets (this grid is repeated, as we should expect, in the area of Epiphania).[63] Thus it seems certain that the street of Herod and

[59] Malalas 205.21; 232.22ff.; 233.22ff.

[60] On the work of Antiochus IV Epiphanes, see above, Ch. 5, §6. On Malalas' procedures, see above, Ch. 2, §4.

[61] Malalas 232.22—233.2. The meaning which the chronicler attached to the verb ἀποκλείω, which might by itself be ambiguous, since it can mean either "include" or "exclude," is made clear by his adding ἔσωθεν.

[62] Traces of the street were found in the excavations, below the modern principal street of the city: see the report of J. Lassus in *AJA* 44 (1940) 417-418, and *Antioch-on-the-Orontes* 3.12-18. The course of the modern street is shown in Figs. 6, 7 below and in the drawings of Weulersse, "Antioche" pp. 39, 41.

[63] The outlines of the ancient *insulae* can be seen clearly on the aerial photograph,

"Tiberius" ran parallel to the wall belonging to this side of Seleucus' quarter. There have been found in the excavations, along the Roman street, traces of "a very heavy wall, over two metres thick," which might be the Seleucid city wall;[64] this would indicate that the street of Herod and "Tiberius" ran along the old Seleucid city wall (which would have been demolished when the street was built), and indeed in many places the main street seems to bisect roughly what must have been the combined areas of Seleucus' settlement and Epiphania.[65] About midway where it crossed the torrent Parmenius, the street altered its direction slightly, and at this point there was a square or plaza with a *nymphaeum*[66] and, probably a statue of Tiberius standing on a column (see further below). This change in the course of the thoroughfare would serve to give a specific vista, instead of a limitless line, to persons walking along either section of the street toward the center of the city, and the point at which the change occurred would likewise emphasize the *nymphaeum* and the statue. The great colonnaded street at Palmyra was planned with a similar shift in direction midway along its course, with a tetrapylon at the point where the change occurred.[67] The street was carried over Parmenius on large vaults.[68] From the square containing the statue and the *nymphaeum* another colonnaded street ran toward the river,[69] connecting at the Orontes with a monumental building that has not been identified.[70]

The pottery and the remains of buildings found in the excavations along the main street show that in the Hellenistic period the thoroughfare, which later became the principal street, was a slum district, lined with poor structures occupied by people who used the simplest kind of pottery.[71] This is what we would expect, for until the paving of this thoroughfare and the construction of its ornamental colonnades in Roman times, this area comprised the outer fringe of Seleucus' original settlement, and so would have been undesirable as a residential area.

At the beginning of the second Christian century, the roadway of the main street was 9.60 m. wide and each of the flanking porticoes

---

with overlay, published by Weulersse, "Antioche" pl. v (facing p. 36) and in the same author's sketch plan, p. 47. See also Figs. 7, 8, 11 below.

[64] *Antioch-on-the-Orontes* 3.15.

[65] See the sketch plans of Weulersse, "Antioche" 39, 41 and Figs. 7, 9, 11 below.

[66] Described by Libanius *Or.* 11.202.

[67] See, for example, the plan in Starcky, *Palmyre*, pl. 3, pp. 24-25.

[68] *Antioch-on-the-Orontes* 3.13-14.

[69] Libanius *Or.* 11.202.

[70] Levi, *Antioch Mosaic Pavements* 1.195.

[71] See *Antioch-on-the-Orontes* 3.15 and the observations of F. O. Waagé in *Antioch-on-the-Orontes* 4, pt. 1, p. 18.

was 10 m. wide.[72] The street of Herod and "Tiberius" was very likely of approximately the same dimensions. Below this street have been found traces of paving dating from the Seleucid period.[73] This indicates that although the old street may have been "difficult to traverse" (as Malalas writes) before Herod provided his paving, it need not have been true that it was shunned because of mud, as Josephus writes, implying that it was unpaved.[74]

The construction of the street, then, provided a main artery along the long axis of the area occupied by Seleucus' settlement and Epiphania, which had formerly been cut off from one another to some extent by Seleucus' wall, which presumably had continued to stand even after the unwalled quarter Epiphania was founded by Antiochus IV Epiphanes. The transverse streets of Seleucus' settlement and of Epiphania met at the main street;[75] and so, when the old wall was demolished, the consolidation of the two quarters was completed.

The improvement of the quarter was accompanied by the construction or reconstruction of three temples and of other buildings. Foremost among these must have been the Temple of Jupiter Capitolinus which Malalas (230.10-11) says Tiberius "built." This must be the temple which Livy (41.20.9) says was built by Antiochus IV Epiphanes (175-163 B.C.), which had a ceiling paneled with gold and walls wholly covered with gilded plates. Presumably the temple stood in Epiphania, the new quarter that Antiochus founded. Evidently Tiberius completed, restored, or redecorated the Seleucid king's building; it seems possible, as Stauffenberg suggests, that the cult statue was a representation of Tiberius himself.[76]

Another temple built at this time was that of Dionysus, which stood "toward the mountain," that is to say, presumably in Epiphania. Before

---

[72] See the reports of Lassus cited above, n. 62. The ancient colonnaded street of Beroea (Aleppo) was 20 to 25 m. in width; see Sauvaget, *Alep* 46.

[73] *Antioch-on-the-Orontes* 3.13-16.

[74] Malalas 223.19; Josephus *Bell.* 1.145.

[75] See Figs. 7-9; 11 and Weulersse, "Antioche" Pl. v.

[76] Stauffenberg, *Malalas* 464. The common opinion is that Antiochus left this temple unfinished and that Tiberius completed it (see above, Ch. 5, nn. 67, 69), and this seems very probable; Livy mentions the temple in a passage in which he emphasizes the Seleucid king's tendency to initiate magnificent building operations and leave them unfinished. However, it must be kept in mind that Livy does not say explicitly that this temple remained incomplete, as he does in the case of some other buildings that he mentions in the same passage; and so it seems possible, as Müller points out (*Antiq. Antioch.* 55-56) that the work that Malalas attributes to Tiberius consisted of a restoration of the temple, which might have been damaged by an earthquake. In any case, it is typical of Malalas to say that a ruler "built" a structure when he actually only completed or restored it (see above, Ch. 2, §4).

A *History of Antioch*

this temple, Malalas states, stood two statues of the Dioscuri, Amphion
and Zethos, the sons of Antiope and Zeus. The placing of the statues
indicates that this temple was built on a podium approached by a flight
of steps, with the statues standing on the flanking walls of the steps.[77]
We hear that in the fourth century one of the local judges, in order to
escape the heat, held the sittings of his court in the portico of the
temple.[78]

The third temple mentioned is that of Pan, which Malalas says
stood "behind the theater." Since the theater was located on the side
of the mountain, above Epiphania, it seems possible that the shrine
of Pan was a cavern or grotto in the slope of the mountain.[79]

The construction of the shrine of Pan may have been connected with
the enlargement of the theater by means of the addition of another
zone of seats, which took place at this time. When the theater was
enlarged, a statue which represented either the heroine Antigone or
the Tyche of Antigonia was placed in it.[80] Caesar had "built" (i.e.,
possibly, rebuilt) the theater at Antioch,[81] and Agrippa had constructed
an additional *zone* of seats because of the increase in the population of
the city.[82] The further addition, which Malalas ascribes to Tiberius,
suggests that the population continued to increase; Trajan was to make
another and final enlargement.[83]

[77] Malalas 234.17-20. The type of temple described is shown on a coin of Tiberius
struck at Rome (*BMC Rom. Emp.* 1, p. 137, no. 116), to which Weber calls attention
(*Studien* 56, n. 3; cf. Stauffenberg, *Malalas* 480).
[78] Libanius Or. 45.26. See the translation and commentary of Pack, *Studies in Libanius*
90, 117.
[79] Malalas 235.6-7. Stauffenberg points out (*Malalas* 480) that Pan was associated
with theaters. The same scholar is mistaken in stating (*Malalas* 480, n. 102) that a
passage in Libanius (*Or.* 15.79 = vol. 2, p. 152.9 ed. Förster, cited by Stauffenberg as
II 132) shows that there was a temple of Pan in Antioch in the Seleucid period. While
there very likely was such a shrine, the passage in Libanius which Stauffenberg adduces
merely attests the worship of Pan in Antioch in the time of Julian the Apostate, and
conveys no implication as to an earlier date.
[80] 234.22—235.3. Malalas relates that Tiberius accompanied his work by the sacrifice
of a maiden named Antigone. The sacrifices of maidens that the chronicler frequently
associated with the foundations of cities or the erection of buildings are, as Stauffenberg
points out (*Malalas* 469-472), Christian tales designed to discredit the acts of pagan
rulers. The story of this Antigone suggests, as Stauffenberg observes, that the theater,
when enlarged by Tiberius, was presented with a statue which represented either the
Tyche of Antigonia or the legendary Antigone who appears in Sophocles' drama. It
would be easy for the presence of such a statue to form the basis, among chroniclers
like Malalas, of the legend of Tiberius' sacrifice.
[81] Malalas 217.2-3; see above, Ch. 7, §2.
[82] Malalas 222.20-22; see above, n. 39.
[83] Malalas 276.3-9. Malalas remarks that Tiberius did not "finish" the theater, and
he speaks of Trajan as completing an unfinished building. However, it seems more
likely that the various additions the chronicler describes were made to take care of

One important part of the program that was being carried out at this time was the provision of some sort of protection against the effects of the washing of soil and debris, regularly brought down from Mount Silpius and deposited in the level part of the site by the torrential rains of winter. The wash is so formidable that in some parts of the site Hellenistic remains are now buried to a depth of ten meters.[84] The precise nature of the work undertaken by the Romans is not clear since the only literary evidence that we have for it is a legendary tale preserved by Malalas of a talisman that protected the city against the winter torrents; this talisman, evidently a product of local folklore, accounted for the effects of storm-drainage and other devices of hydraulic engineering by ascribing the results to the powers of a magical object procured by Tiberius.[85] Precisely what was done, we do not now know; the beds of the mountain streams which ran through the city may have been enlarged and reinforced. How much of such work was original with the Romans, and how much may have been merely the adaptation and extension of arrangements installed by Seleucid engineers, we again do not know.[86] In any case it is plain (as indeed we should expect) that the Romans were careful to make provision for a drainage problem that must have been acute. We hear of elaborate engineering measures carried out in the reign of Justinian to control the floods caused by the winter torrents.

The building that is said to have been executed by Tiberius' orders was not confined to Epiphania. Malalas records that Tiberius built the "Eastern Gate," on top of which stood a stone statue of the she-wolf nursing Romulus and Remus.[87] This statue, the chronicler says,

---

the needs of the moment and were not a part of a plan that was spread over a number of years.

[84] The situation is described in detail above, Ch. 4, §2, with nn. 41-42.

[85] Malalas 233.10ff. The talisman is said to have been provided by the seer and priest Ablakkon. This magical object, to which the credit was given for freeing the city from the wash from the mountain, bears in the name of its supposed maker a trace of its legendary origin, for Ἀβλάκκων is evidently cognate with αὖλαξ which means a furrow or hollow place or course for water (cf. αὖλαξ ὑδροφόρος used of an aqueduct in *IG* 14.453, cited by Liddell-Scott-Jones *s.v.* αὖλαξ). Thus the word used to describe what was built came to be transformed, in local legend, into the name of a mythical seer who produced a talisman held responsible for the effect of the αὖλαξ (or αὖλακες) built by the Romans.

[86] Here, as elsewhere, it is possible that Malalas has described as original work of the Romans operations which were actually only a rebuilding or a continuation of undertakings which were originally the work of the Seleucid period (on the chronicler's procedures in this respect, see above, Ch. 2, §4). The excavations have revealed "two large vaults or culverts, side by side," which carried the principal mountain stream, Parmenius, under the main street of the city. The vaults may have been built as early as the Hellenistic period; see *Antioch-on-the-Orontes* 3.13-14.

[87] Malalas 235.3-6. Actually northeast. See Ch. 1, n. 3 above and Excursus 9.

was intended to signify that the addition of the new wall to the city was a work of the Romans. This explanation, however, must be an invention of Malalas, or of a source of his, for it seems plain that the statue was erected in order to provide the city with a symbol of Roman sovereignty.[88] The name of the gate indicates that it stood at the north-eastern limit of the colonnaded street where the road that led from both Beroea and the southern part of Syria entered the city, so that this gate would be the first monument of the city to be seen by travelers arriving at Antioch from the hinterland of Syria.

In the same region, Tiberius built a public bath near the spring to which Alexander the Great was supposed to have given his mother's name, Olympias. This spring was in the eastern part of the city, on the slope of the mountain, outside the new wall ascribed to Tiberius; some kind of ornamental fountain structure, it was said, had been built by Alexander himself to adorn the spring.[89]

---

[88] On the significance of statues of the she-wolf with Romulus and Remus as a symbol of Roman citizenship, see E. Strong, "Sulle tracce della Lupa Romana," *Scritti in onore di B. Nogara* (Rome 1937) 475-501, with reference to earlier literature; also Friedländer, *Sittengeschichte*[10] 3.22, n. 7; and K. Lehmann-Hartleben, "Städtebau," *RE* 3A (1929) 2082. On the use of Roman city gates and arches at this period to carry statues, see I. A. Richmond, "Commemorative Arches and City-Gates in the Augustan Age," *JRS* 23 (1933) 149-174. Malalas always speaks of "Romus and Remus," e.g. 33.15, 171.1, 13; 172.3, 12, 20; 176-180 passim. Weber suggests (*Studien* 54, n. 1) that the words which Malalas uses in speaking of the gate and the statue, σημαίνων 'Ρωμαῖον εἶναι κτίσμα, preserve some of the phraseology of the inscription that accompanied the monument. Another statue of the she-wolf with Romulus and Remus was placed over the Middle Gate that Trajan built at Antioch; see below, Ch. 9, §5.

[89] Malalas 234.11-17; Liban. *Or.* 11.72-74, 250. Müller correctly locates the spring of Olympias in the eastern part of the city, but he also says that it was in Epiphania (*Antiq. Antioch.* 22, 83), which he himself locates in the western part of the city area (see his map). Moreover, there is no specific evidence that the public bath named for Tiberius was enclosed within the wall, as Müller says it was (83). Malalas states that the spring itself lay outside the wall, and it would seem reasonable to suppose that a bath built near the spring (as Malalas writes) would likewise be outside the wall. Müller (83) finds a difficulty in reconciling, with the evidence of Malalas for the bath, certain passages in the Lives of St. Symeon the Younger and of his mother St. Martha. In the former *Life* there is a description (*Acta SS.* 24 May, tom. 5, 345 C) of how a paralytic, cured by the stylite at his seat on the Miraculous Mountain between Antioch and Seleucia, ran down the mountain for a distance of 22 stadia to a certain bath of Tiberius (παρά τι βαλανεῖον Τιβερῖνον), where he washed. In the *Life of St. Martha* in the same volume (408 D) there is a reference to τὸ λεγόμενον Τιβερίνου χωρίον, distant ἀπὸ σημείων τριῶν from the Miraculous Mountain. The two places must be the same, for 22 stadia is almost exactly three Roman miles. Müller thought that the context of the second passage shows that the "village" of Tiberius, 2 m. p. from the Miraculous Mountain, was close to Daphne, and so he found difficulty in reconciling this evidence with the topographical indications given by Malalas. Müller went astray for lack of precise knowledge of the topography of the region, which indeed was not available in his time. The location of Symeon's sanctuary on the Miraculous Mountain has, in fact, been established only in recent years (see J. Mécérian, "Monastère de Saint-Syméon-Stylite-le-Jeune: Exposé des fouilles," *CRAI* 1948, 323-328). The mountain lies

In gratitude for his benefactions to the city, the senate and people of Antioch erected a bronze statue of Tiberius on a column of Theban stone in the colonnaded street that—according to Malalas—the emperor had constructed.[90] The place in which this statue stood, Malalas writes, was called "the omphalos of the city." Presumably it was an open square; the name omphalos may indicate that it was circular in plan.[91] Malalas' account of the monument preserves a phrase that evidently represents the opening words of the dedicatory inscription that accompanied the statue: Τιβερίῳ Καίσαρι ἡ βουλὴ καὶ ὁ δῆμος τῶν Ἀντιοχέων.

The way in which Malalas mentions the column and its statue shows

on the right bank of the Orontes, roughly midway between Antioch and Seleucia, but rather closer to Seleucia than to Antioch. The distance from Antioch to Seleucia is about 22 km. (Libanius, *Or.* 11.41, gives the distance as 120 stadia). Thus any bath or village named for Tiberius which was located 22 stadia from Symeon's home cannot possibly have been in or near Antioch or Daphne. The bath and village mentioned in the passages of the *Acta SS.* quoted above are presumably identical with the Τιβερινὴ χώρα which is said to be ὑπὸ τῇ γείτονι Σελευκείᾳ κειμένη, which is mentioned in another passage in the same *Life* of Symeon (314 D).

[90] Malalas 233.4-9. In the topographical border of the mosaic found at Yakto, which illustrates scenes and buildings at Antioch and is dated in the late fifth or early sixth centuries after Christ, there is a representation of a column accompanied by a mutilated Greek inscription of which only the letters PIANA remain. It has been suggested that these letters refer to the name of Tiberius, so that the column would be that on which his statue stood. However, it seems more likely that the fragmentary inscription is a part of the name of the Porta Tauriana; see Ch. 5, n. 87, and Excursus 10. Malalas states that the statue existed in his own time, and the Yakto mosaic was made not long before the chronicler lived in Antioch. Statements to this effect by Malalas cannot, however, always be taken at their face value, for, like other ancient chroniclers, he sometimes copied such phrases from his sources, and it can be proved that some monuments concerning which he makes this claim cannot possibly have existed in his own day; see above, Ch. 2, §4.

[91] Malalas solemnly writes that the place in which the statue stood "is called the *omphalos* of the city because it contains a representation of an eye (*ophthalmos*) carved in stone." This absurd etymology is typical of Malalas; an open square like that in question would have been called omphalos either because it was regarded as the center of the city or because it was round, or, in some cases, because it might contain a statue of Apollo seated on the omphalos. What lies behind Malalas' description of the place in which the statue of Tiberius stood is not easy to determine. Müller (*Antiq. Antioch.* 57, n. 10), evidently not being prepared to allow Malalas to perpetrate a characteristically illiterate popular etymology, proposed to emend ΟΦΘΑΛΜΟΥ to ΟΜΦΑΛΟΥ, but this rehabilitation of the chronicler seems unnecessary and only serves to deprive us of a legend that may well have been current in Antioch. If the open space in which Tiberius' column stood were oval in plan, it could easily have been nicknamed "the eye" (*ophthalmos*), and since other public places were on occasion called *omphaloi*, it would be easy for illiterate people at Antioch to confuse the terms. Muller supposes (57-58) that the "omphalos" in which Tiberius' statue stood actually contained a statue of Apollo seated on the omphalos, Apollo being one of the ancestors of the Seleucids (see above, Ch. 4, n. 63). This may of course be true, but it cannot be proved from Malalas' use of the term omphalos. The open space at the center of the island at Antioch, where the transverse main streets of this quarter crossed, was called the omphalos (see the description of Libanius, quoted in Ch. 12, §2).

that he (or his source) believed that the erection of the monument was a natural expression of the gratitude of the people of Antioch for Tiberius' generosity in building the colonnades of the main street; the placing of the column and the statue in a public square located on this street would seem to emphasize the connection between the building of the colonnades and the offering of the statue. Malalas' evidence for the statue might thus be thought to constitute an argument for the theory that Tiberius built the colonnades. However, it seems equally possible that it was from the existence, and indeed the location, of this statue that there arose a mistaken story that it was Tiberius who built the colonnades.[92] A column and statue such as Malalas describes might very well have been erected merely by way of thanks for other benefactions; and of course the only real motive behind the offering might have been flattery.

3. The Reign of Tiberius, A.D. 14-37

One bit of folklore that Malalas includes in his account of the reign of Tiberius is the statement that this emperor changed the name of the river that flowed past Antioch from Drakon to Orentes, which Malalas explains means "eastern" in Latin.[93] This is only one example of the aetiological stories, found in many ancient authors, which were devised in order to accommodate myths concerning the early history of the river, the original name of which is given by various writers as Typhon, Drakon, or Ophites. Actually these early names are all mythical, for the true name of the river must have been very ancient; it was called Arantu by the Assyrians.[94] The ascription to Tiberius of this change in the name of the river, which certainly never actually took place, may be taken as an example of the adulation with which the people of Antioch, at least at a later time, treated Tiberius.[95]

After finishing his account of Tiberius' buildings at Antioch, Malalas

[92] Groag, "Lurius Varius" 204, n. 11, points out that the erection of a column of Tiberius does not necessarily prove that he did the work that Malalas ascribes to him.

[93] 234.20-22. The unique MS of Malalas in Oxford everywhere calls the river Orentes, but this spelling was silently "corrected" to Orontes when the MS was transcribed and published by Chilmead and Hody, and the erroneous readings stand in the Bonn edition; see Bury, "Malalas: The Cod. Baroccianus" 220-221. The correct readings are printed in Stauffenberg's text.

[94] Johanna Schmidt and E. Honigmann, "Orontes," *RE* 18 (1939) 1160-1164; Stauffenberg, *Malalas* 481-482. Schmidt and Honigmann overlooked Bury's information (cited in the preceding note) on the spelling of the name of the river in the MS of Malalas, and they do not seem to have used Stauffenberg's text, in which the correct readings are given.

[95] This is the suggestion of Müller (*Antiq. Antioch.* 82).

goes on to describe other activities of the emperor in other places. Soon, however, he returns to Antioch, to describe (235.15ff.) a fire that occurred in A.D. 23/4. Breaking out at night, and burning for a time before it was discovered,[96] the conflagration destroyed "the greater part of the agora and the bouleuterion and the shrine of the Muses which had been built by Antiochus Philopator[97] with the money left in his will by Maron of Antioch," who had emigrated to Athens and had then stipulated that there should be built with his money "the shrine of the Muses and a library."

The reference to the bouleuterion suggests that this was an old Hellenistic agora, and that it was located in Epiphania.[98] The first bouleuterion of which we hear at Antioch is that which is said to have been built by Antiochus IV Epiphanes (175-163 B.C.)[99]; and, as has been pointed out, it seems reasonable to suppose that a bouleuterion built by this king would have stood in the new quarter (Epiphania) which he founded, and that the new quarter would have contained a new agora.[100] What other buildings may have stood on this agora, we do not know; but since Malalas does not mention them, we must assume that they were not affected by the fire.

Whether this fire may have provided some or all of the impetus for the building program attributed to Tiberius, which evidently was largely centered in Epiphania, is an intriguing question. Malalas it is true records the fire quite independently of his account of the building operations that he attributes to Tiberius, but in a chronicle compiled as mechanically as that of Malalas, this separation of the material need not imply that there was no connection between the fire and the building program. For example, Antiochus IV Epiphanes is said to have built (or at least begun) a Temple of Jupiter Capitolinus which would

---

[96] ἀδήλως (235.17) must mean that much of the damage was done before the fire was discovered.

[97] There were three Antiochi called Philopator, namely Antiochus IX Philopator Cyzicenus (114-95 B.C.), Antiochus X Eusebes Philopator (95-92 B.C.), and Antiochus XII Dionysus Epiphanes Philopator Callinicus (87-84 B.C.). Antiochus XII cannot be meant because he reigned only at Damascus. Which of the others is meant is not certain because Malalas' account of the last Seleucid kings is not clear and he nowhere else mentions an Antiochus Philopator. Since Maron appears to be otherwise unknown, it does not seem possible to determine the date when the buildings were erected.

[98] There was at least one other agora at Antioch, the "tetragonal agora" said by Josephus to have been burned in A.D. 69 or 70 (see below, Ch. 9, §1); and the way in which the Jewish historian distinguishes this agora by a distinctive epithet suggests that it was different from another agora (or other agoras; see Excursus 11).

[99] Malalas 205.14; 234.2. A bouleuterion (presumably that of Antiochus IV) was rebuilt or restored by Pompey (Malalas 211.8); see Ch. 7, §1.

[100] On the building operations of Antiochus IV, see further above, Ch. 5, §6.

have been (in that king's program) a temple of such importance that it might well have stood on his new agora; and if the testimony of Malalas indicates, as we have seen, that Tiberius completed or rebuilt the same temple, there might be reason to believe that Tiberius' building activities were, in part at least, closely connected with this agora, and consequently to suppose that the fire gave the immediate occasion for Tiberius' undertaking. However, the evidence being what it is, we can only speculate on this possibility.

In addition to the fire, only one other untoward event disturbed the tranquil history of Antioch under Tiberius; but this episode, the mysterious death of Germanicus, was sensational indeed. Germanicus, a son of Tiberius' brother Drusus, had been Augustus' favorite grandson, and Tiberius had been forced to adopt him and make him senior, in the family, to his own son Drusus. Germanicus was handsome, affable, and popular, but not conspicuously able, and there was good reason for Tiberius to view his career with some misgivings. In A.D. 17, a complicated political situation had been created in the East by internal disorders in Parthia and Armenia, accompanied by discontent in Syria and Palestine over the size of the tribute imposed on them.[101] Germanicus was sent to the East on a special mission, similar to that of Agrippa, with extraordinary powers[102]; but in order to provide a check on the young man, whom he did not wholly trust, Tiberius also appointed Cn. Piso as legate of Syria in place of Creticus Silanus, whose daughter was betrothed to a son of Germanicus. Piso, a harsh and unyielding man of the old Republican type, might be expected to curb Germanicus' actions if necessary. P. Suillius Rufus, who was a notorious informer in the reign of Claudius, was appointed by Tiberius to be Germanicus' quaestor, and it may be that he was placed in this position in order to spy upon the prince.[103] Germanicus made himself popular everywhere he went, and treated the people of the provinces with signal generosity. However, he was also highly indiscreet in his official conduct, and on his return to Antioch from a vacation in Egypt (A.D. 19), differences of policy between Piso and Germanicus came to a head,

---

[101] On the situation, see *CAH* 10.619; Dobiáš, *Hist.* 359ff., 566; Debevoise, *Hist. of Parthia* 152-155. For an account of Germanicus' career and character, see Charlesworth in *CAH* 10.609-623.

[102] The source and extent of Germanicus' powers are not yet entirely clear; it is evident that he disagreed with Tiberius over his status in Egypt and with Piso over his authority in Syria. On this subject, see Grant, *Principate of Tiberius* 165-166.

[103] Tacitus *Annals* 4.31, 13.42 and *IGLS* 836 as interpreted by A. von Domaszewski, "Eine Inschrift des P. Suillius Rufus," *Rhein. Mus.* 67 (1912) 151-152.

and Germanicus dismissed the legate.[104] Soon after Piso's departure from Antioch, Germanicus became seriously ill. The preserved description of his symptoms indicates a fever; but he was convinced that Piso had poisoned him, and there were those who said that Piso had acted at Tiberius' orders. When Germanicus died (10 Oct. A.D. 19, aged 33) his unclothed body was displayed "in the forum" at Antioch, but there was doubt as to whether signs of poisoning appeared on it. The body was then cremated at Antioch, and the ashes were taken to Rome. A cenotaph was erected at Antioch, presumably in the forum where the body had been exhibited, and a further memorial, apparently in the form of a catafalque, was set up in Daphne, where Germanicus had died.[105]

Among the children of Germanicus who witnessed his death at Antioch was the future emperor Caligula, then seven years old. Caligula's pious respect for the scene of his father's death led him, after he became emperor, to issue at Antioch a series of coins commemorating Germanicus and also to show noteworthy generosity to the city when it was damaged by an earthquake.[106]

Germanicus' sojourn in Antioch brings up once more the question as to the authorship of the building program in the city which Malalas ascribes, perhaps erroneously, to Tiberius. If Malalas is really in error, his mistake can be accounted for through the confusion of Germanicus and Tiberius, which it would be easy for an ignorant or careless chronicler to make, if given the opportunity, since both bore the name Caesar; and the connection of Germanicus' mission with the affairs of Parthia might well be responsible for the garbled story that Malalas tells of how the buildings at Antioch were inaugurated by Tiberius on his triumphal return from a victorious campaign against the Parthians. This question is not easy to settle, and it may be that it could be resolved only through the discovery of an inscription; but it is perfectly possible that it was on the occasion of Germanicus' mission to the East

---

[104] The story of Germanicus' death is told by Tacitus *Ann.* 2.70-73, 83; cf. Suetonius *Caligula* 1.2 and Dio Cassius 57.18.9. See Kroll, "Iulius (Germanicus)," *RE* 10, 455-456.

[105] Tacitus writes (*Ann.* 2.83) *sepulchrum Antiochiae ubi crematus, tribunal Epidaphne quo in loco vitam finierat. Epidaphne,* representing a misunderstanding of the appellation Ἀντιόχεια ἐπὶ Δάφνῃ which was frequently given to Antioch because of the fame of the suburb (see Excursus 1) appears to be unique in Tacitus. On the tribunal as a funerary monument, see V. Chapot, "Tribunal," Daremberg-Saglio, *Dict. des antiq.* 5.418; the usage is not brought out by E. Weiss, "Tribunal," *RE* 6A (1937) 2428-2430. Tacitus, writing simply *in foro Antiochensium* (*Ann.* 2.73), does not make it clear in which forum or agora the body was displayed.

[106] See below, §4.

that Tiberius ordered a major public building program to be carried out in Antioch, and that Germanicus inaugurated the work under the emperor's auspices.[107]

The physical transformation of Antioch by the Romans was typical of their program in Syria as a whole. The history of Damascus, for example, seems to have been much the same in this respect. Although we happen to have much less literary evidence for the development of Damascus after its foundation in the Hellenistic period than we do for that of Antioch, archaeological study has shown that in the imperial period the main street of the city was enlarged and the street leading from the agora to the temple was embellished, and that at the same time the arrangements for the water supply were either reorganized or established for the first time.[108]

As to the remainder of the history of Antioch during Tiberius' reign we have not enough knowledge for a connected story.

The coins issued by Antioch during this period for local use show that the legates of Syria still had to be careful not to allow too great an appearance of local autonomy to be displayed on the currency; the supremacy of Rome was carefully kept to the fore.[109] At the same time, Tiberius allowed the mint of Antioch to issue coins in honor of two governors who happened to be his friends, A. Caecilius Metellus Creticus Silanus, legate A.D. 11-16/7, who was a prospective relative by marriage of the imperial family,[110] and L. Pomponius Flaccus, legate A.D. 32-35 (?).[111] This practice was occasionally adopted in other parts of the Empire.[112]

During this time the city continued to serve as a center in the constant planning and diplomatic activity that attended the difficult and delicate task of maintaining equilibrium in the vassal states on the eastern borders of Syria.[113] Antioch at this period must have been constantly visited by oriental rulers and their agents. Vonones, when forced by the Parthian king Artabanus to abdicate the throne of Armenia (A.D. 15 or 16), found refuge with the governor of Syria, Creticus Silanus,

[107] The view that the building program was carried out by Germanicus on his own initiative is adopted by Groag, "Lurius Varius" 204, n. 11.

[108] See J. Sauvaget, "Le plan antique de Damas," *Syria* 26 (1949) 357-358.

[109] Macdonald, "Pseudo-Autonomous Coinage of Antioch" 113-116.

[110] *BMC Galatia etc.* p. 169, nos. 150-153. He was similarly honored on coins of Seleucia Pieria: *ibid.* p. 273, nos. 33-34.

[111] *BMC Galatia etc.* p. 170, no. 161.

[112] See Grant, *Principate of Tiberius* 59, 162-163.

[113] The complicated story is told by Debevoise, *Hist. of Parthia* 153-164.

who allowed him to live in Antioch with his accustomed luxury and to keep his royal title.[114]

A further glimpse of the cosmopolitan character of the city is afforded by the story of the Babylonian Jewish emir Zamaris, who during the time when C. Sentius Saturninus was governor of Syria (9-6 B.C.) migrated from Babylon to Antioch accompanied by a retinue of one hundred relatives and five hundred mounted bowmen.[115] If the group included the families of the relatives, and attendants for the cavalry, it would have been of substantial size. Evidently Zamaris was a wealthy landowner who found it necessary for some political reason to flee from his home, and it is significant to find that it was Antioch that attracted him. The city's advantages for such a man would have been that it lay in a rich agricultural district, where he might hope to be able to resume his farming activities, that it possessed an important Jewish community, and that as the capital of Syria it offered at once the protection of the Roman government and the possibility that some advantageous political connection might be made with this government, which might easily welcome the services of the emir's private army. Zamaris, Josephus writes, came first to Daphne, but Saturninus (who evidently did not wish to have so large a group of organized and armed foreigners so near the capital) assigned to him, as a place in which to settle, a locality named Οὐαλαθά, which appears to have been a region near Antioch, called Hulta in the Jewish sources, in which there was a Jewish community.[116] Eventually Zamaris left Antioch at the invitation of King Herod, who offered him special inducements to settle in Batanea, in Transjordania.

The establishment of the Christian community at Antioch—where "the disciples were called Christians first" (Acts 11:26)—took place in the last years of the reign of Tiberius or early in the reign of Caligula. This event is described in a separate chapter (Ch. 11, below) in which the history of the Christian community at Antioch from apostolic times to A.D. 284 is brought together.

[114] Tacitus *Ann.* 2.4; Josephus *Ant.* 18.52; see Groag, "Q. Caecilius Metellus Creticus Silanus," no. 90, *RE* 3 (1899) 1212, and Debevoise, *Hist. of Parthia* 153. Tacitus and Josephus do not mention Antioch by name, but the capital is the only city in which Vonones could have lived under the governor's protection in the manner described.

[115] Josephus *Ant.* 17.23-27; Kraeling "Jewish Community at Antioch" 135, 141ff.; Debevoise, *Hist. of Parthia* 145-146.

[116] On the identification and location of this community, which appears to have lain in the valley of the Orontes above and northeast of Antioch, see Kraeling, "Jewish Community at Antioch" 141ff.

4. The Reign of Gaius (Caligula), a.d. 37-41

The history of Antioch, during Gaius' short reign,[117] was eventful. As a member of a family in which domestic affection was strong, the new emperor had a special feeling for the city in which his father Germanicus had died, surrounded by his family, in a.d. 19, when Gaius himself was seven years old.[118] A characteristic expression of Gaius' piety is preserved in the form of an issue of silver tetradrachms commemorating his father which he caused to be issued at the mint of Antioch.[119] A similar series commemorating his mother Agrippina was issued at the same mint in a.d. 39-40,[120] and Germanicus was likewise commemorated by coins issued at Antioch under Claudius.[121]

The principal opportunity, however, for the emperor to show his feelings toward Antioch came when the city suffered an earthquake, in which a part of Daphne also was damaged. This disaster occurred on 9 April a.d. 37, only a few weeks after Gaius had been proclaimed emperor (18 March).[122] The emperor immediately responded with assistance. In this early part of his reign, Gaius had at his disposal the considerable sums left in the treasury by Tiberius,[123] and since he was prodigal by nature, the assistance that he provided for the rebuilding of Antioch must have been substantial.

Three officials were sent from Rome to carry out the work of restoration.[124] One was Salianus (Salvianus?), who seems to have had the

[117] Caligula ("Baby Boots") was a nickname given to Gaius as a child by his father's troops, on account of his being dressed in replicas of military uniform.
[118] Gaius was born 31 Aug. a.d. 12. It has been suggested by Groag ("Lurius Varius" 204, n. 11) that the building activity that Malalas attributes to Tiberius was in reality executed by Germanicus. If this were true, Gaius would of course have all the greater interest in the restoration of the city. On this problem, see above, §2, with n. 53.
[119] See Dieudonné, "Monnaies grecques de Syrie" 37; Grant, *Anniversary Issues* 70.
[120] Dieudonné, "Monnaies grecques de Syrie" 37-38.
[121] See below, §5.
[122] Malalas 243.16ff. Malalas dates the earthquake on 23 Dystros, which corresponds to 9 April; see Stauffenberg, *Malalas* 187. The chronicler describes the earthquake as the second to occur after the end of the Macedonian dynasty. The first in this series is not mentioned in his chronicle, or elsewhere, as such, though it seems to be the one that occurred during the occupation of Syria by Tigranes. The absence of a record of this "first" disaster after the end of the Seleucid dynasty may be connected with a confusion in Malalas' knowledge of Seleucid chronology; see Downey, "Seleucid Chronology" 107, n. 1; 119, n. 2.
[123] Suetonius *Cal.* 37; Dio Cassius 59.2. On Gaius' public buildings in general, see Bourne, *Public Works* 38-41.
[124] There are numerous examples of the remission of the tribute of cities that had suffered from earthquakes or fires, of the appropriation of imperial funds for reconstruction after such disasters, and of the appointment of imperial commissions to supervise the spending of such money; see Liebenam, *Städteverwaltung* 172-173; F. F. Abbott and A. C. Johnson, *Municipal Administration in the Roman Empire* (Princeton

title of *legatus Augusti pro praetore*.[125] He is said to have built a public bath "near the mountain," and "temples," which are not further described, and to have built (or repaired) an aqueduct from Daphne.[126]

The other two were senators, who are described as "very wealthy," Lurius Varius and Pontius.[127] Their mission is said to have been to

---

1926) 147-148; Capelle, "Erdbebenforschung," *RE* Suppl. 4 (1924) 346-356; Prehn, "Ktistes," *RE* 11 (1922) 2086; Friedländer, *Sittengeschichte*[10] 3.29-30. Characteristic texts on the subject are Tacitus *Ann.* 2.41.4-5; 2.47.3-4, 4.13.1, 14.27.1; Strabo 12.8.18, p. 579; *SHA Sev. Alex.* 44.8. Malalas does not mention a remission of tribute at Antioch in connection with the earthquake under Gaius, but the chronicler ordinarily would not mention such a detail, being much more interested in the buildings involved. Many examples of imperial financial aid to cities that had been damaged by earthquakes may be found in Malalas: 246.11; 259.6; 261.19; 267.13; 279.2; 289.8; 360.5; 369.8; 378.14; 385.1; 406.20; 417.17 (a fire at Antioch); 417.20; 418.4; 418.7; 419.1; 422.1; 424.3; 436.21; 443.13; 444.3; 448.4; 448.18.

[125] Malalas gives his name and title in the accusative: Σαλιανὸν ἔπαρχον (243.18), and the form Salianus is used here, although it may not be correct; Stauffenberg points out (*Malalas* 187) that a Flavius Salia, who lived in the middle of the fourth century A.D. is called Salianos by Theodoret (*H.E.*, 2, 8, 54, not §34 as Stauffenberg prints); cf. Stein, article "Salia," no. 1, *RE* 1 A (1920) 1872. The form Salianus is accepted by Müller (*Antiq. Antioch.* 84) and (although with hesitation) by Stein in his article on the official mentioned by Malalas, in *RE* 1 A, 1873. Stauffenberg uses the form Salianus in his index and on pp. 187 and 487 (the latter passage is not cited in his index), but on p. 482 he suggests that the correct form of the name might be Salvianus. *Eparchos* should represent *praefectus*, but Malalas' usage with regard to such titles is often loose; Stauffenberg on p. 187 calls Salianus "Proprätor oder besser Prätorier," and "Prätor" on pp. 482 and 487. The nature of Salianus' mission, and his title, are suggested by Tacitus' account of the relief of twelve cities of Asia which had been damaged by an earthquake under Tiberius (*Ann.* 2.41.4-5): *mittique ex senatu placuit qui praesentia spectaret refoveretque. delectus est M. Ateius e praetoriis, ne consulari obtinente Asiam aemulatio inter pares et exeo impedimentum oreretur.* That Ateius had the rank of *legatus Augusti pro praetore* is shown by Dio's reference to his five fasces (57.17.7).

[126] Malalas, to whom the construction of a public bath seems to have represented a particularly splendid act of imperial liberality, relates that the aqueduct was built by Salianus in order to provide water for the new bath. In reality, of course, the aqueduct would have been intended for much more general use, and the bath would have been added for good measure. There is reason to think that Salianus really did not build a new aqueduct, but repaired an existing one that had been damaged by the earthquake.

[127] Stauffenberg (*Malalas* 187-188) feels some doubt as to whether Pontius and Varius were sent to Antioch in order to repair damage caused by the earthquake, but his hesitation seems unwarranted, especially since Malalas indicates quite clearly (244.2) that this mission was connected with the emperor's plans for restoration. Malalas gives the names of these men in the nominative as Πόντοος καὶ Οὐάριος (244.1) and in the genitive as Ποντόου καὶ Οὐαρίου (245.9); the name of Varius is clear, and the form Pontius is adopted here because it is very probably correct. Förster ("Antiochia" 124) and Groag ("Lurius Varius" 202-205) accept the forms Pontius and Varius, the latter suggesting that Varius may be the consular Lurius Varius mentioned by Tacitus and apparently alluded to by Suetonius. Stauffenberg uses the form Varius (*Malalas*, index, *s.n.*, and 448, 482, 488), but hesitates concerning Pontius: in the index he prints Pontous, on p. 448 Pontius, and on p. 482 Pontous, with Pontius suggested. Malalas often garbles the names of Roman officials; cf., e.g., *Byblos strategos* (211.20, 212.1) for M. Calpurnius Bibulus, proconsul of Syria in 51/50 B.C. (this is pointed out by Dobiáš, "Syrsky prokonsulat M. Calpurnia Bibula"); Pronoios (244.21) for P. Petronius, legate

"protect" the city, to supervise the buildings erected with the emperor's funds, to make gifts to the city out of their own personal fortunes, and to take up residence in it.[128] They are said to have built houses for themselves near the river, and many other buildings, including a public bath called the Thermae Variae,[129] located near their houses, and a Trinymphon adorned with statues, to be used for weddings.[130]

A legend related that after the earthquake a seer named Debborius set up a talisman in the city to protect it against future earthquakes. This consisted of a porphyry column, placed "in the middle of the city," which bore a bust on which was inscribed the phrase "Unshaken, unthrown" (ἄσειστα, ἄπτωτα). At some time before the reign of Domitian, the column is supposed to have been struck by lightning, which consumed the bust but left the shaft standing, though scarred. What foundation in fact this tale might have had, is not clear. It is entirely possible that such a talisman was erected, but the story could well have grown up concerning an empty column which had once borne an imperial statue.[131]

The third year of Gaius' reign (A.D. 40) brought internal disorder in Antioch, unfortunately known to us only from an obscure and confused account. In addition to being an outbreak of factional strife and anti-Semitism (as our account purports), this episode may actually have had some importance in the development of the Christian missionary effort. The incident apparently seemed so minor at the time

---

of Syria under Caligula in 39-41/42 (cf. Dobiáš, *Rivista di Filologia* 53 [1925] 245-246; the identification is made independently by Stauffenberg (*Malalas* 187), who does not know Dobiáš' note); and *Kourion strategos* (222.4) for P. Sulpicius Quirinius, governor of Syria (the identification is suggested by Stauffenberg, *Malalas* 161; he prints Quirinus but the former spelling is to be preferred, cf. Groag, "Sulpicius Quirinius," no. 90, *RE* 4 A, 23).

[128] In similar fashion, Roman senators took part in the restoration of the city after the earthquake in the reign of Trajan (Malalas 278.20ff.; see below, Ch. 9, §5).

[129] Stauffenberg (*Malalas* 482, n. 106), followed by Groag ("Lurius Varius" 203, n. 9), thinks that Malalas is mistaken in attributing the Thermae Variae to Lurius Varius, and that it is more probable (from the name) that this bath was built by P. Quintilius Varus, who was governor of Syria 6-4 B.C. There seems, however, to be no very compelling reason to make this change (Stauffenberg offers no explanation of his opinion). Malalas' account of the origin of this bath is accepted by Müller (*Antiq. Antioch.* 84) and by Maass (*Tagesgötter* 58).

[130] For examples of such buildings, and their use, see Müller, *Antiq. Antioch.* 59, Maass, *Tagesgötter* 58, and Stauffenberg, *Malalas* 482.

[131] It may be significant that Malalas relates this story (265.10-20), not in his account of the earthquake under Gaius, but in his account (quoted from Domninus, 266.10-11) of the visit of Apollonius of Tyana to Antioch in the reign of Domitian (on this see further below, Ch. 9, §2). A column of this sort surmounted by a bust is one of the prototypes of the images of stylite saints which later became popular in Byzantine art; see A. Xyngopoulos in *Epeteris Hetaireias Byzantinon Spoudon* 19 (1949) 127-128.

that the only record of it was preserved in local Antiochene sources, from which it has come down to us in the chronicle of Malalas. The chronicler's account is inadequate and distorted, but it seems possible to recover from it some suggestion of the significance of the events.

Malalas relates (244.15ff.) that in the third year of Gaius' reign the Blue faction of the circus at Antioch began to abuse the Greens in the circus, on an occasion when P. Petronius, the governor of Syria (A.D. 39-41/2) was present. The cry was "Time raises and time brings down; the Greens are lechers."[132]

The outbreak, Malalas says, led to a civil commotion, in which the pagans at Antioch attacked the Jews, killed many of them, and burned their synagogues. According to the chronicler Phineas, the Jewish high priest in Jerusalem, brought a punitive expedition of thirty thousand men to Antioch,[133] and killed many of the people of the city. The emperor punished Pontius and Varius, his special representatives, for allowing this to happen; their property was confiscated and they themselves were arrested and sent to Rome. Phineas was beheaded as a rebel and his head was exhibited on a pike outside Antioch, across the river. The emperor furnished money for the rebuilding of the burned parts of the city.

Such is Malalas' account. The story sounds as though it had grown in transmission, and it is difficult to know at first sight how much of what Malalas says is true. That there was some kind of an outbreak in the circus seems clear. What the pretext may have been is not certain; but that the episode was engineered for political purposes is suggested by the circumstance that the emperor was known to favor the Greens, and that the outbreak occurred in the presence of the governor of Syria, who in theory at least would have shared the emperor's partiality. Whether the original disorder was merely an ordinary manifestation of factional strife,[134] or had some further significance, the events that followed indicate that the strife, spreading, became involved with

---

[132] This translation represents Stauffenberg's emendation of μάχοι of the MS to μάχλοι. The phrase must have given trouble in antiquity, since the Church Slavonic version (p. 53 transl. Spinka) has "soldiers," showing that μάχοι was present in the MS from which this translation was made. In the Oxford and Bonn editions the word is misprinted μάσχοι, though the Latin translation (*pugnae*) shows that translator, who worked directly from the MS, read μάχοι. The phrase might mean either (1) that the Blues had been down, but now it was their turn to be up, or (2) that although the Greens, once down, were now up, they were still μάχλοι.

[133] In the Church Slavonic version (p. 54 transl. Spinka) the figure is 230,000.

[134] The most recent special survey of the circus factions in the Roman Empire, with complete bibliography of earlier treatments of the subject, is the article of Dvornik, "Circus Parties."

further sources of friction. There had been several events that would have put the Jews of Antioch in a belligerent frame of mind. In the summer of A.D. 38 there were disorders in Alexandria during the visit to the city of Agrippa I, to whom Gaius had given the kingdoms of Trachonitis and Ituraea; the Greeks of the city, aided by the governor of Egypt, insulted the Jewish king, and eventually there was a pogrom. Relations between the Jews of Antioch and those of Alexandria were close and constant, in the normal course of commercial intercourse between the two cities,[135] and the attack on the Jews of Alexandria would have made a deep impression on the community at Antioch. Then, in the winter of A.D. 39/40, Gaius provoked the enmity of the Jews by decreeing that a statue of himself be placed in the temple in Jerusalem.[136]

Thus there was good reason for the Jews of Antioch to be alert and restless. There is evidence that in Alexandria, at least, the Jews had been accustomed to take part in, or even provoke, disorders in connection with athletic games and festivals,[137] and the same situation may have existed at Antioch. Hence it seems possible that instead of a factional disorder leading to an outbreak against the Jews, such as Malalas describes, the episode in Antioch may have begun as a circus disorder in which the Jews themselves took part, which subsequently turned into a pogrom.

A final point of interest in the disorders both in Alexandria and Antioch is that they reflect the unrest that would have been provoked by the preaching of Christianity, which began among the Jews at this time.[138] In the case of Antioch, it is significant to find that the disorders came at a time when the Christian mission at Antioch turned from preaching exclusively to the Jews and began to work among the

[135] This is shown by a passage in Claudius' letter to the people of Alexandria in which the Jewish questions are discussed: Bell, *Jews and Christians in Egypt*, p. 25, lines 96-97 (transl. on p. 29).

[136] On Gaius' dealings with the Jews, see the chapter "Gaius and the Jews" in J.P. V. D. Balsdon, *The Emperor Gaius (Caligula)* (Oxford 1934) 111-145 (in which the episodes in Antioch do not appear to be mentioned); M. Gelzer, "Iulius," no. 133, *RE* 10 (1919) 398-399; Charlesworth in *CAH* 10.661-663; and (with special reference to Antioch) Kraeling, "Jewish Community at Antioch" 148-150.

[137] See the letter of Claudius (cited above, n. 135), p. 25, lines 92-93, with Bell's commentary, p. 37, and the comments of H. Grégoire in his review of Bell's volume in *Byzantion* 1 (1924) 644-646, and of G. De Sanctis in *Riv. di Filologia* 53 (1925) 245-246.

[138] See the opinions of S. Reinach and G. De Sanctis cited by H. Grégoire, *loc.cit.* (above, n. 137).

pagans. It would seem that this change was suggested, or motivated, by the anti-Jewish feeling that prevailed in the Syrian metropolis; thus the new faith was set on the road to becoming a world religion.[139]

Malalas' story, which appears to have been frequently overlooked by modern students, thus gives us a glimpse of events in the history of Antioch which, though they seemed relatively unimportant at the time, actually were of real significance. Some details of the chronicler's record are patently incorrect. Malalas' story of the punitive expedition led by Phineas is naturally apocryphal; such a thing could not have happened at this time. It is likewise difficult to believe his story that it was for their negligence in not preventing this disorder that Pontius and Varius were punished by Gaius. We know that Varius, at least, was tried and condemned under the *lex repetundarum*,[140] evidently for peculation with the official funds entrusted to him for the reconstruction of Antioch, and it would seem likely that Malalas or his source invented a connection between this and the anti-Jewish disorders in the city. This detail, along with the story of Phineas' expedition, suggests that some of Malalas' information came from a Jewish or pro-Jewish source.

Gaius was murdered before any final disposition as to the situation in Alexandria could be made and it remained for Claudius, his successor, to issue edicts that put an end to the strife (at least temporarily) between Greeks and Jews in both Alexandria and Antioch.

5. The Reign of Claudius, A.D. 41-54

The three major events at Antioch during the reign of Claudius were a famine, an earthquake, and the reorganization of the pentaeteric festival of the city into its Olympic games, which became celebrated throughout the Roman world.

The famine, caused by failures of crops in Syria, Palestine, and Egypt, affected Antioch for several years. A flood of the Nile caused a shortage of grain in Egypt which extended either from the fall of A.D. 44 to the spring of A.D. 46, or from the fall of A.D. 45 to the spring of A.D. 47. This would have affected the price of grain in Antioch, and might well have produced a shortage. More direct results would have been felt from the shortage of grain which occurred in Judaea and all Syria in

---

[139] This is pointed out by Dobiáš, *Hist.* 568. On the conflict which arose among the missionaries over the preaching to the Gentiles, see Lietzmann, *Beginnings of the Christian Church* 140-143. See further the description of the early Christian community at Antioch, below Ch. 11.

[140] Tacitus *Ann.* 13.32; Suetonius *Otho* 2; see Groag, "Lurius Varius" 203.

A.D. 46 or 47. The Christian community at Antioch sent assistance to Jerusalem to relieve the distress caused by the famine there.[141]

The earthquake (the date of which is not recorded) was one that damaged Ephesus, Smyrna, and many other cities of Asia, as well as Antioch. At Antioch it destroyed the temples of Artemis, Ares, and Herakles, as well as "a number of houses."[142] The Temple of Artemis that was destroyed may have been the one that had existed at least as early as the time of Antiochus I Soter (281-261 B.C.), while the Temple of Herakles was presumably the one built by another Seleucid king whose name is not recorded.[143] The construction of a Temple of Ares is not recorded, but presumably this shrine likewise would have been an old one. It stood near Parmenius, opposite Caesar's basilica, the Kaisarion.[144]

The emperor granted relief to all the cities that had suffered in the earthquake. In the case of Antioch, the relief included the cancelation of a special liturgy. Malalas' account of the transaction is garbled, so that we cannot be sure just what occurred. It would appear that the restoration of the roofed colonnades along the main street, which Malalas says were built by Tiberius, was involved; the chronicler's account might mean that the colonnades were damaged in the earthquake under Claudius, or (more likely) that they had suffered in the earthquake of Gaius' reign and were still being restored when the earthquake in the time of Claudius occurred.[145]

[141] See Acts 11:27-30 and Orosius *Hist.* 7.6.12. The evidence is discussed by K. S. Gapp, "The Universal Famine under Claudius," *HTR* 28 (1935) 258-265.

[142] Malalas 246.9-19.

[143] Libanius *Or.* 11.109, 125. The location of these temples is not known.

[144] The location is shown by several passages in Malalas 216.19-20, 275.15-16, 287.4-5. In another passage in Malalas (285.15-16) it is stated that a joint festival of Ares and Artemis was celebrated. This Müller (*Antiq. Antioch.* 69, n. 4; 77, n. 1) takes to mean that the Temple of Ares was attached to that of Artemis.

[145] Malalas writes (246.16-19) that the emperor "relieved the guilds, that is, trade associations, of Antioch of the liturgy of the hearth-tax (ὑπὲρ καπνοῦ) which they performed for the renewal of the city's roofed colonnades built by Tiberius Caesar." It is plain that the chronicler was transcribing a source that he did not understand, or which was already confused; the hearth-tax of course was not a liturgy (nor was any other tax). The passage as it stands might be taken in two different senses: (1) Claudius excused the members of the guilds from payment of the hearth-tax and directed that instead they were to undertake, as a liturgy, the restoration of the roofed colonnades that had been damaged in the present earthquake; such a measure would probably provide no real relief for the members of the guilds, for instead of paying a tax they would be furnishing (or hiring) labor; or (2) Claudius relieved the guilds of the liturgy they had been performing for the restoration of the colonnades that had been damaged in the earthquake of A.D. 37, in Gaius' reign, and were still in process of being repaired when the earthquake in the reign of Claudius occurred. This interpretation

The Olympic Games of the city were established in A.D. 43/4. The games founded in the reign of Augustus by the bequest of the Antiochene senator Sosibius had fallen into disuse through the maladministration of the funds,[146] and the landowners and citizens of Antioch petitioned Claudius for permission to purchase from the people of Pisa the right to hold Olympic Games.[147] This petition was granted in the year A.D. 43/4. The festival was to consist of scenic and athletic events, including dramatic contests and the events of the hippodrome. The games were to be held in every fifth year, for thirty days beginning with the new moon in the month of Hyperberetaios (October). The games were not, however, celebrated regularly. Pretexts for interruptions were found in wars, earthquakes, fires, and various other public calamities, and the games were celebrated only at intervals of fifteen or twenty years, and on six occasions, until a reorganization took place in the reign of Commodus (A.D. 180-192).

Claudius, like Gaius, issued coins commemorating Germanicus, presumably on the twenty-fifth anniversary of his death in the city.[148]

Other events in the history of Antioch under Claudius may be noted briefly. In A.D. 41 the emperor put an end to the enmity between the Greeks and the Jews in Alexandria, reprimanding the Alexandrians for their intolerance and confirming (but not enlarging) the privileges of the Jews; both parties were exhorted to keep the peace. At the special request of King Agrippa, a copy of the document concerning the privileges of the Jews in Alexandria was (Josephus says) also sent "to Syria," so that the Jews of Antioch, among others, were confirmed in

---

ignores the reference to the hearth-tax, but it seems, of itself, to be much more logical. If Stauffenberg is right (*Malalas* 197, n. 33a) in emending ὑπὲρ καπνοῦ to ὑπὲρ καπηλικοῦ, it would be possible to suppose that the liturgy which Claudius cancelled was a λειτουργία καπηλική, that is, a liturgy performed by the shopkeepers (possibly the association of the tradesmen who had shops in the colonnades) for the restoration of the colonnades. In this case it would be necessary to suppose that this liturgy was one that the shopkeepers had been performing when the earthquake occurred—otherwise its remission would not have been any kind of relief.

[146] Malalas 224.22—225.2, 248.5—249.22.

[147] Malalas says that permission was requested to purchase the games themselves (248.7-10, 249.4-5), but this can hardly have happened; the chronicler's words probably reflect an effort to give greater dignity and importance to the games of Antioch. No other example of the purchase of the right to hold Olympic Games seems to be recorded. It may be that such permission was sold, on imperial authority, as a means of strengthening the finances of the original Olympic Games; see L. Ziehen, "Olympia," *RE* 18 (1939) 48. Local "Olympic Games" were presented in many parts of the Greek world, but they are usually attested only by inscriptions (see list of such festivals compiled by Ziehen, *op.cit.* 47-48). The local games of Antioch are the only ones that are known from literary evidence of any extent.

[148] Grant, *Anniversary Issues* 75-76.

their privilege of observing their customs.[149] Thus the cause for the anti-Jewish disorders which had occurred in Antioch under Gaius was (officially, and at least temporarily) removed.

A change in the condition of the local administration of Antioch at this time may be indicated by the appearance, on the local coins, of the emperor's name and titulature, in Latin, side by side with the name of Antioch and the name of the legate of Syria, both in Greek. This may suggest that the imperial government wished to make clear its authority over the activities of both the legate and the local mint in the matter of issuing local currency.[150]

According to tradition, it was in the early 40's in the reign of Claudius, that the disciples at Antioch first received the name of Christians. The significance of the name, and the manner of its introduction, have been disputed; it seems likely that the designation was adopted by the Roman authorities when they found it necessary to have some way to describe the new sect, which was becoming distinct from Judaism.[151]

6. THE REIGN OF NERO, A.D. 54-68

The principal events of which we hear in the history of Antioch under Nero are those connected with the Jewish rebellion. For a number of years there had been friction between the Jews and the Greeks of Syria, Palestine, and Egypt because of the privileged position of the Jews, who were exempt from military service and were not obliged to worship the emperor in the official imperial cult. The Jews themselves had a serious grievance in the effect of Roman taxation, which made agriculture unprofitable and forced many men to seek a living through brigandage. These conditions, combined with the fact that their religion made the Jews a religious rather than a political community, and with the division within this community between the Sadducees, who favored cooperation with Rome, and the Pharisees, whose religious intolerance generated hostility to Rome, made for a situation which was bound to produce a major crisis.

Under Gaius there had been, as we have seen, an outbreak at Antioch, during the governorship of P. Petronius (A.D. 39-41/2), which had resulted in a pogrom, and although the privileges of the Jews at Antioch

---

[149] See the letter of Claudius to the Alexandrians published by Bell, *Jews and Christians in Egypt* 1-37, and the edict of Claudius quoted by Josephus *Ant.* 19.279-285; cf. Kraeling, "Jewish Community at Antioch" 149-150.

[150] Dieudonné, "Monnaies grecques de Syrie" 38-39.

[151] See Ch. 11, n. 19.

and elsewhere had been confirmed by Claudius in A.D. 41, the basic sources of friction remained. In A.D. 66 massacres at Caesarea and Jerusalem touched off a full-scale national revolt of the Jews, and there were popular attacks on them in other cities of Syria and Palestine.[152] Later in the same year Cestius Gallus, the governor of Syria, went to Palestine with a military force to restore order. Jerusalem was fortified against him, and although he succeeded in capturing the New City, he considered it necessary to withdraw (12 November A.D. 66); and under pressure from the Jews his withdrawal turned into an ignominious rout.[153]

In the winter of A.D. 66/7 Nero, during his tour of Greece, appointed his general Vespasian to the governorship of Judaea, with command of a large army with which he was to suppress the rebellion. Traveling overland via the Hellespont, Vespasian proceeded to Antioch, where he planned to assemble his forces, which were to consist both of Roman troops and native contingents furnished by the vassal kings of the neighboring territories.[154]

The rebellion, and the humiliation of Cestius Gallus, naturally inflamed anti-Jewish feeling in Syria, and only the occasion for an outbreak was wanted. Just after Vespasian's arrival in Syria—which in itself, with the military preparations that were to be set on foot, would have heightened anti-Jewish sentiment—a renegade Jew of Antioch named Antiochus, son of the chief magistrate (*archon*) of the Jews at Antioch, seized the opportunity to stir up an attack on his own people. He entered the theater while a public assembly was being held and accused the Jews of a plot to burn the whole city in one night; he likewise delivered up, as accomplices in the undertaking, some foreign Jews whom the state of public opinion had presumably made it possible for him to have arrested. Feeling was sufficiently strong to make the people of Antioch burn to death on the spot the men who had been handed over to them. They then set out to attack the Jewish community. Antiochus, to demonstrate the completeness of his conversion and his detestation of Jewish customs, suggested that the Jews

[152] At this time, Josephus writes (*Bell.* 2.479), the inhabitants of Antioch, Sidon, and Apamea alone abstained from attacks on the Jews. In this, the Jewish historian says, the Greeks were moved by "pity for men who showed no revolutionary intentions." This, as Kraeling points out ("Jewish Community at Antioch" 150), can hardly be true; it is more probable, at least in the case of Antioch, that disorder was averted through the action of the governor of Syria, Cestius Gallus.

[153] Weynand, "T. Flavius Vespasianus," no. 206, *RE* 6 (1909) 2630.

[154] Josephus *Bell.* 3.8; see Weber, *Josephus und Vespasian* 113-116, who suggests that Vespasian sent Titus by sea to Alexandria to take charge of the troops there.

be compelled to offer pagan sacrifices (including, perhaps, sacrifices for the imperial cult); a few complied but most refused and were massacred. Antiochus then seems to have been given some sort of authority, and a force of troops was placed at his disposal, and he proceeded to compel the Jews to give up their observance of rest on the seventh day.[155] This outbreak was to be followed by another, led by the same Antiochus, after the fall of Jerusalem.

At some time during this period an effort seems to have been made to take away from the Jews, who would not use Gentile oil, the privilege of receiving from the gymnasiarchs a refund of the oil tax so that they might purchase their own kind of oil. However, C. Licinius Mucianus, who had been appointed governor of Syria in A.D. 67, upheld the privilege.[156] There is nothing to show that this attempt on the Jews' special privileges was connected with the outbreak described above. The privilege in question was such a minor one that it is difficult to see how it can have been made a point of issue during the more serious attack instigated by Antiochus.

The only other noteworthy events in the history of Antioch are the death of Evodius, bishop of Antioch, which is said to have occurred when Peter was stopping in the city on his way to Rome, and the choice, as his successor, of Ignatius, who is supposed to have been consecrated by Peter.[157]

As in the preceding reign, the mint of Antioch issued coins bearing the name of the emperor in Latin and the names of the city and of the legate of Syria in Greek.[158] This procedure, it has been suggested, was designed to show the imperial authority over the activities of the legate and of the local mint.[159] On the other hand, the appearance of a type showing the *boule* of Antioch dropping a pebble into a voting urn[160]

---

[155] Josephus *Bell.* 7.46-53; see Dobiáš, *Hist.* 473-474. It may be noted that Josephus contradicts himself as to the manner of Vespasian's journey to Antioch after his appointment to prosecute the war against the Jews. In the present passage he states that Vespasian sailed to Syria, but in *Bell.* 3.8 he writes that Vespasian traveled overland from the Hellespont. The latter statement must be true, since Vespasian's appointment was made in the winter, when journeys by sea, unless unavoidable, were not made because of the chances of delay en route caused by bad weather. The present writer is unable to agree with the view of Kraeling ("Jewish Community at Antioch" 150-151) that Josephus' account of the episode at Antioch is incorrect, and that the main events should be referred to the outbreak against the Jews at Antioch which occurred in November, A.D. 70; for a discussion of the problem, see Excursus 4.

[156] Josephus *Ant.* 12.120.

[157] Malalas 252.8-13. This is the only event that Malalas records in the history of Antioch under Nero.

[158] See Dieudonné, "Monnaies grecques de Syrie" 40-41, 45.

[159] See above, §5, with n. 150.   [160] D. B. Waagé, "Coins" 33, no. 343.

might point to some revival of the forms of municipal government, possibly reflecting Nero's philhellenism. A special issue of coins in the year A.D. 59/60, which bear signs of hasty manufacture, may reflect the need for supplying funds for use in Corbulo's war against the Parthians.[161]

[161] See Dieudonné, "Monnaies grecques de Syrie" 43, 49. The issues of the mint of Antioch present further problems which pass the limits of this study; see D. B. Waagé, "Coins" 33-36. On certain coins of Nero and Divus Claudius, which may represent an anniversary, and may be from Antioch, see Grant, *Anniversary Issues* 83, n. 9. An inscription of Antioch (*IGLS* 867), dated in the second year of Nero's reign (A.D. 55-56), seems to commemorate the introduction, in the city, of a new system of weights, and it has plausibly been suggested that such a change might be connected with a revision of the coinage. On the weights in use at Antioch see, in addition to the material cited in the commentary on *IGLS* 867, Seyrig, "Poids antiques de Syrie." It is of interest to note that *IGLS* 867 may show that the acrophonic numeral system was in use at Antioch at this period, as it was in some other isolated parts of the Graeco-Roman world as late as the second century after Christ; see M. N. Tod, "The Greek Numeral Notation," *Annual of the British School at Athens* 18 (1911-1912) 129 and cf. S. Dow, "Greek Numerals," *AJA* 56 (1952) 22.

CHAPTER 9

FROM THE FLAVIAN DYNASTY TO THE
DEATH OF COMMODUS, A.D. 69-192

1. The Year of the Four Emperors; The Reigns of
Vespasian (a.d. 69-79) and Titus (a.d. 79-81)

ERO'S DEATH (9 June A.D. 68), which brought to an end the Julio-Claudian dynasty, was followed by a year in which the legions (having, as Tacitus says, discovered the fatal secret of the empire, namely that the *princeps* could be nominated elsewhere than in Rome) created in succession four emperors, Galba, Otho, Vitellius, and Vespasian. The first three were in turn overthrown, and Vespasian emerged as the founder of a new dynasty, that of the Flavians. In Vespasian's rise to power, Antioch and the province of Syria played a major part, exemplifying for the first time the importance of the province in the contests for the succession to the imperial power. By reason of the presence in Syria of three or at some periods four legions and a detachment of the fleet stationed at Seleucia Pieria,[1] the legate of the province was the most powerful of the provincial governors, and on repeated occasions the governor of Syria influenced the choice of a new emperor, until Septimius Severus, to put an end to this potential source of danger to the emperor and his succession, divided Syria into Syria Coele and Syria Phoenice.[2]

On the news of Nero's suicide, Vespasian, who had almost ended the Jewish war and was now preparing for the final attack on Jerusalem, decided to suspend operations until his command could be confirmed by Nero's successor.[3] The eastern troops took the oath of allegiance to Galba, Otho, and Vitellius in succession, and Vespasian sent his son Titus to Rome to pay his respects to Galba on his accession and to receive his orders with respect to the Jewish war.[4]

The mint of Antioch struck coins for Galba and Otho but not for

---

[1] On the legions that were stationed in Syria at different times, see Parker, *Roman Legions* 91-92, 119, 126-128, 137-140, 145, 149, 158, 159, 162-163 and Chapot, *Frontière de l'Euphrate* 70-92. On the detachment of the fleet stationed at Seleucia Pieria, see H. Seyrig, "Le cimetière des marins à Séleucie de Piérie," *Mélanges syriens offerts à M. R. Dussaud* (Paris 1938) 1.451-459.

[2] On the division of the province, see Ch. 10, §3. Britain was almost as powerful as Syria in matters affecting the imperial succession.

[3] Tacitus *Hist.* 2.4; 5.10; Josephus *Bell.* 4.497-498; see Weynand, "T. Flavius Vespasianus," no. 206, *RE* 6 (1909) 2633ff.

[4] Tacitus *Hist.* 2.1; Josephus *Bell.* 4.497-498.

A.D. 69-192

Vitellius. A significant innovation in the coins of Galba struck at Antioch is a method of reckoning that appears to be a revival, in a new form, of the era of Actium, which had been used to commemorate the victory of Octavian, and to symbolize the foundation of the Augustan Empire. Galba, in reviving this method of dating on the hundredth anniversary (A.D. 69) of the battle of Actium, would thus present himself officially as the restorer of the empire of Augustus.[5] There are, however, signs on the coins of republican sentiment in Antioch.[6]

Vespasian at first allowed events in the west to take their course, and took no action himself; but with C. Licinius Mucianus, who had been legate of Syria since A.D. 67, he watched the situation, and the two men, who between them controlled a large army, came into close consultation. Vitellius' rule eventually provoked dissatisfaction, and by the summer of A.D. 69 it became apparent that the eastern troops, having watched three emperors created by the western legions, would be willing to put forward a candidate of their own. It was plain that Mucianus or Vespasian might be this candidate.[7] Mucianus had no ambition for the office, and preferred to support Vespasian, whom he considered a stronger candidate.[8]

On 1 July A.D. 69, Vespasian was proclaimed emperor at Alexandria.[9] Mucianus returned from Alexandria to Antioch and administered the oath of allegiance to his own troops there.[10] He then addressed the people of the city, who had hurriedly gathered in the theater to show their loyalty to the new regime. Here Mucianus cleverly put into circulation a rumor that Vitellius intended to transfer the legions of Germany to Syria, where service was easy and life pleasant, and in exchange to send to Germany, with its harsh climate and laborious duties, the legions which were stationed in Syria. This infuriated not only the troops, who had grown fond of Syria, but the civilians who had formed many ties of friendship and marriage with the soldiers. Before 15 July,

---

[5] See B. Pick, "Zur Titulatur der Flavier," *Ztschr. für Numismatik* 14 (1887) 331-340; *BMC Galatia, etc.* 176-177; Wruck, *Syrische Provinzialprägung* 105-106; Grant, *Anniversary Issues* 88. The method of dating (the years being designated with the phrase ETOYΣ NEOY IEPOY) is not used by Galba's enemy Otho, but is employed on the coins struck at Antioch by Vespasian, Titus, Domitian, and Nerva. Trajan abandoned the device, using a regular system of dating by tribunician years. For a coin of this type issued at Antioch immediately after the accession of Trajan, see A. R. Bellinger, "Greek Coins from the Yale Numismatic Collection, II," *Yale Classical Studies* 12 (1951) 263, no. 7.

[6] These indications are found in the fact that the coins of Antioch minted while Galba was in power refrain from giving him the title of Augustus, and also bear the mark PR (Populus Romanus): Dieudonné, "Monnaies grecques de Syrie" 157.

[7] Tacitus *Hist.* 2.4-7, 73-74. [8] Tacitus *Hist.* 1.10; 2.76-77.
[9] Tacitus *Hist.* 2.78. [10] Tacitus *Hist.* 2.78, 80.

all Syria had pledged allegiance to Vespasian, and a grand council was held at Berytus.[11]

In the preparation for war, Antioch as would be expected played a large part. Gold and silver coins were struck at the mint and the city was doubtless one of those in which arms factories were established; fresh troops were enrolled and veterans recalled to service, and Vespasian held conferences in the city.[12] Titus was entrusted with the completion of the war against the Jews, Vespasian went to Egypt, planning, by control of that province and of Africa, to starve Rome into submission, and Mucianus set out at the head of an army to attack Vitellius.[13] By the end of A.D. 69 Vitellius was defeated and Rome occupied.[14]

Titus began his operations against Jerusalem in the spring of A.D. 70, and completed the conquest of the city in late August.[15] After the city and the temple had been razed, Titus was prevented from sailing for Italy by the approach of the winter season. He therefore made a triumphal tour in Palestine, pausing to hold games and spectacles in which Jewish prisoners were killed in various ways. At Caesarea Philippi Titus celebrated the birthday (24 October) of his brother Domitian.[16] He next went to Berytus, where with great magnificence he celebrated his father's birthday (17 November).[17]

While Titus was in Berytus,[18] a great fire broke out in Antioch, destroying the "tetragonal agora," the government administrative offices (ἀρχεῖα), the record office (γραμματοφυλάκιον) and "the basilicas," (βασιλικαί, meaning presumably the law-courts); the flames were prevented only with difficulty from spreading over the whole city. Antiochus, the renegade Jew who had instigated a persecution of his former co-religionists in the winter of A.D. 66/7 by accusing them of a plot to fire the city, now repeated his charges. The people of the city were now even more inclined to believe Antiochus, and rushed against

[11] Tacitus Hist. 2.80-81.
[12] Tacitus Hist. 2.82; Josephus Bell. 4.630; on the coins, see BMC Rom. Emp. 2, pp. lxvii-lxix, 104-109; Mattingly-Sydenham, Rom. Imp. Coinage 2.4, 56-58; Wruck, Syrische Provinzialprägung 104; Dieudonné, "Monnaies grecques de Syrie" 159; BMC Rom. Emp. 2.104-109; Toynbee, Hadrianic School 131; also Dobiáš, Hist. 502, n. 169.
[13] Weynand in RE 6.2638-2639.   [14] Weynand in RE 6.2639-2641.
[15] Josephus Bell. 6.435; see Weynand, "T. Flavius Vespasianus," no. 207, RE 6 (1909) 2700-2705.
[16] Josephus Bell. 7.20-37.   [17] Josephus Bell. 7.39.
[18] Josephus Bell. 7.39, 96. Another indication of the date is that in §63 Josephus writes that it was at this time that Titus received word of the eagerness with which his father was received in Italy and in Rome; and we know that Vespasian reached Rome in the late summer or autumn of A.D. 70; see Weynand in RE 6.2647-2648.

the Jews. They were, however, restrained by Cn. Pompeius Collega, who was acting as governor of Syria pending the arrival of L. Caesennius Paetus, whom Vespasian had appointed to succeed C. Licinius Mucianus when Mucianus left the province in A.D. 69 to prosecute the war against Vitellius.[19] Collega, telling the people that the matter would have to be laid before Titus, made an investigation and determined (Josephus says) that no Jews had any part in the affair, but that the fire had been started by certain men who, being in financial straits, imagined that they could save themselves by burning the public records and so destroying the evidence of their debts.[20]

While these events were taking place in Antioch, Titus remained for some time in Berytus. He then resumed his tour of Syria, exhibiting spectacles, and in due course reached Antioch.[21] Here he was given an enthusiastic reception, men, women, and children streaming out from the city for a distance of thirty stadia (about 6 km. or over 3½ mi.) to meet him. With their greetings and acclamations, Josephus writes, they mingled a running petition to him to expel the Jews from Antioch. To this request Titus made no reply; he stayed in Antioch only a short time, and pushed on to Zeugma on the Euphrates, where he received a deputation from Vologeses, the Parthian king, bringing a gold crown in honor of his victory over the Jews. He then returned to Antioch. The senate and people invited him to visit the theater, where the whole population was assembled to greet him. Again a request was made for the expulsion of the Jews, in reply to which Titus pointed out that they could not be banished to their own country since it had been destroyed,

[19] Collega was doubtless a legate of a legion to whom the governor's powers were temporarily deputed; see Harrer, *Studies* 11, and Dobiáš, *Hist.* 509, with n. 197.

[20] Josephus *Bell.* 7.54-62; see Dobiáš *Hist.* 509-510, 572. A different view of this outbreak, and of that of the winter of A.D. 66/7, is proposed by Kraeling; see Excursus 4. A similar case of the burning of archives in a time of trouble is illustrated by striking archaeological evidence from Palmyra, where excavations have shown that documents were thrown into the agora and burned when the Romans occupied the city in A.D. 272 after the defeat of Zenobia; see H. Seyrig, "Cachets d'archives publiques de quelques villes de la Syrie romaine," *MUSJ* 23 (1940) 103-105.

[21] The route followed by Titus from Berytus to Antioch is discussed by A. Chambalu, "Flaviana, III," *Philologus* 44 (1885) 509-511, who believed that Josephus' statement (*Bell.* 7.96-99) that Titus in the course of his march saw the Sabbatical river, which flows "between Arcea . . . and Raphanea," shows that Titus followed an inland route via Arcea and Raphanea; if he followed this route he must have gone from Raphanea to Apamea (cf. the map of the Roman roads in Syria in Honigmann, "Syria" 1647f.). There is no evidence whether, in this case, he would have proceeded to Antioch by the direct road from Apamea or via Chalcis, but in either case he would enter the city from the north, i.e. following, for at least the last part of his journey, the modern route from Aleppo. Weynand, "T. Flavius Vespasianus," no. 207, *RE* 6.2705, appears to believe that the route followed by Titus from Berytus to Antioch cannot be determined exactly.

and that no other place would receive them. It was then requested that the privileges of the Jews and their rights of citizenship be abolished, and that the bronze tablets on which their privileges were inscribed be taken down. This request Titus likewise refused.[22] However, in order to provide some compensation for these refusals, he did present the people of Antioch (whose good will it was desirable to keep) with a part of the Jewish spoils, which would serve as perpetual memorials in Antioch of the humiliation of the Jews.[23] Outside the city gate on the road that led to Daphne,[24] he set up bronze figures that were supposed to be the Cherubim from the Temple (the Cherubim no longer existed, and these were either an imitation, or winged figures that were called cherubim). On the gate itself Titus set up a bronze figure of the Moon with four bulls, facing Jerusalem. This group was supposed to commemorate the fact that Jerusalem had been captured by moonlight, but in reality it must have been a symbol of Aeternitas.[25] The location of all these figures was in itself an affront to the Jews, since there was a Jewish quarter in this part of the city.[26] The region came to be known as "the Cherubim," and a famous statue of Christ later stood there.[27]

In Daphne, a theater was built (on the site, it is said, of a synagogue which was destroyed to make room for it); this is said to have borne the inscription EX PRAEDA IVDAEA ("From the Jewish spoils") and a statue of Vespasian was placed in it.[28] The theater found during the

[22] Josephus *Bell.* 7.96-111; *Ant.* 12.121-124.

[23] Malalas' account (260.21-261.12) of Titus' gifts to Antioch contains certain inaccurate details, which need not be examined here since they have already been discussed at length in Downey, "Gate of the Cherubim"; see also Stauffenberg, *Malalas* 230-232, 489; Müller, *Antiq. Antioch.* 85-87; Dobiáš *Hist.* 511-512, 572; Weber, *Josephus u. Vespasian* 276-278. It is to be noted that Josephus does not mention these gifts.

[24] The location is shown by passages in Malalas (281.4-5), in the anonymous *Vita S. Symeonis Iunioris* (ch. 9, p. 238, lines 1 and 5, and ch. 126, p. 258, lines 1ff., in Delehaye, *Saints stylites*), and in the *Life* of St. Symeon by Nicephorus Magister of Antioch (*Acta SS.* Maii, tom. 5 [Paris 1866] 313 C, 359 Bff.).

[25] Jerusalem was not taken by night (see Stauffenberg, *Malalas* 231 and Josephus *Bell.* 6.392ff.). On the Moon and Sun as symbols of *Aeternitas* in the imperial symbolism of this period, see Mattingly-Sydenham, *Rom. Imp. Coinage* 2.7, and J. Gagé, "Le 'Templum Urbis' et les origines de l'idée de 'Renovatio,'" *Ann. de l'Inst. de philol. et d'hist. orient. et slaves* 4 (1936) 157 (= *Mél. Cumont* 1).

[26] Malalas 207.10; Guidi, "Descrizione araba" 160; see Kraeling, "Jewish Community at Antioch" 140.

[27] See a recently published section of the *Pratum spirituale* of Johannes Moschus: Th. Nissen, "Unbekannte Erzählungen aus dem Pratum spirituale," *BZ* 38 (1938) 368, lines 11-23. The presence of this statue would be connected with the vision of Christ mentioned in the anonymous biography of St. Symeon the Younger mentioned above (n. 24).

[28] On Malalas' quotation of this inscription, see Downey, "Inscriptions in Malalas,"

excavations at Daphne may, from the archaeological and architectural evidence, have been constructed in the last quarter of the first century after Christ, and so may be that built by Titus. There had previously been found on the site fragments that might have belonged to either one or two imperial statues, and during the excavations parts of two more imperial statues were found.[29] All these fragments are so meager that it is not possible to know whether any of them belonged to a statue of Vespasian.

Other events of which we hear during the reign of Vespasian are the erection in the city of a Tower of the Winds near the theater,[30] and the building (A.D. 73/4) of a canal that was connected with the Orontes.[31] During Titus' brief reign (A.D. 79-81) we hear nothing of the history of Antioch.

2. THE REIGN OF DOMITIAN, A.D. 81-96

Domitian, who took a keen interest in building,[32] presented Antioch

---

and Weber, *Josephus u. Vespasian* 277, no. 3. Kraeling ("Jewish Community at Antioch" 140) doubts that a synagogue was destroyed to make room for the theater (by a slip of the pen he writes "Tiberius" for "Titus").

[29] D. N. Wilber, "The Theatre at Daphne," *Antioch-on-the-Orontes* 2.57-94; V. Chapot in *BCH* 26 (1902) 163-164; "Catalogue of Sculpture" in *Antioch-on-the-Orontes* 2, p. 172, no. 147 and p. 174, no. 173.

[30] Malalas 262.3-4. It has been suggested that the representations of the winds on this monument may be responsible for the unusual way in which they are depicted on an altar at Carnuntum in Pannonia, the style having been carried from Antioch to Carnuntum by soldiers of the XV Legion, which was stationed in Syria in A.D. 62 and transferred to Pannonia in A.D. 71; see H. Steinmetz, *De ventorum descriptionibus apud Graecos Romanosque* (Diss. Göttingen 1907) 78-82; idem, "Windgötter," *Jahrb. d. k. deutschen Archäol. Inst.* 25 (1910) 41, 43; and a note in *Antioch-on-the-Orontes* 2.207, n. 11. An inscription (*Wiener Studien* 54 [1936] 188-192 = *Année épigr.* 1937, no. 174) attests the presence at Carnuntum of a soldier from Antioch. If Steinmetz' hypothesis is correct (and it seems very plausible), the altar at Carnuntum would enable us to visualize the Tower of the Winds at Antioch, which is not preserved. The Tower of the Winds may be identified with the Horologion which stood on or near the Forum of Valens; see the description of the Forum in Excursus 12.

[31] The construction of the canal is mentioned in a Greek inscription found at Antioch which has not yet been published. The text is described and discussed by L. Robert, "Contribution à la topographie de villes de l'Asie Mineure méridionale," *Comptes rendus, Académie des inscriptions et belles lettres*, 1951, 255-256. The canal—which Professor Robert calls "le canal des foulons"—was built under the governor Marcus Ulpius Trajanus, father of the Emperor Trajan. The inscription states that the cost of the work was pro-rated among property owners, presumably those who owned land which the canal served. The text contains the phrase κατὰ πλινθεῖα, used of the construction of the canal, which apparently refers to the city-blocks or *insulae* in the area in which the canal was located, one of which was owned by "Pharnakes, former gymnasiarch." The text also refers to Στεφανειτῶν (genitive plural), evidently an association of athletes and musicians who had won victories in games, and to Εὐεργεσιασταί. The location of the canal and its purpose are not yet known.

[32] See Bourne, *Public Works* 64.

with a public bath originally called τὸ Δομετιανόν, which was built
on the slope of the mountain near the amphitheater of Caesar and the
Temple of Aphrodite. In the same locality the emperor also built a
Temple of Asclepius. When Domitian, for his misdeeds, suffered
damnatio memoriae after his death and his name was everywhere
erased from monuments, the bath began to be known by the name
of Medea, from a celebrated statue of the Colchian princess which
stood in it.[33]

During Domitian's reign, it is said, the city received a visit from
Apollonius of Tyana, the famous Pythagorean philosopher and wonder-
worker.[34] Apollonius presented the city with some of the talismans for
which he was celebrated. One, a protection against the north wind,
was placed on the Eastern Gate; another, against scorpions, consisted
of a bronze scorpion, on top of which was placed a small column,
set up in the middle of the city. The wonder-worker also prescribed
an annual ceremony that would act as a charm against gnats. He saw
the column on which another seer named Debborius had set up a
talisman against earthquakes after the disaster in the reign of Gaius;
and since the talisman itself had been destroyed by lightning, the
people of the city asked Apollonius to provide another. This, however,
he declined to do.[35]

[33] Malalas 263.11-17. Stauffenberg in one place (*Malalas* 243) writes that the bath
was near the gladiatorial school, though elsewhere (488) he speaks correctly of the
amphitheater (on p. 243, by a slip of the pen, he calls the bath Διοκλητιανόν). Müller
(*Antiq. Antioch.* 87) believed that this statue of Medea was described by Libanius in
one of his *ekphraseis* (vol. 4, pp. 1090-1091 ed. Reiske = vol. 8, pp. 516-518 ed. Förster).
Subsequent research, however, has shown that this *ekphrasis*, on the basis of its style
and manuscript tradition, is to be attributed to Nikolaos of Myra, a sophist of the fifth
century after Christ; see Förster's introduction to the *ekphraseis* in vol. 8 of his edition
of Libanius (published 1915) 438-439; Förster and Richtsteig, "Libanios," *RE* 12 (1925)
2521; and W. Stegemann, "Nikolaos," no. 21, *RE* 17 (1937) 424ff. Since Nikolaos was
born in Myra (now Dembre) in Lycia, studied in Athens, and pursued his calling in
Constantinople, and apparently had no intention of trying to present his writings as
works of Libanius, it seems unlikely that the statue described by him is that which stood
in the bath in Antioch. Stauffenberg (*Malalas* 488) was unaware that it had been shown
that the *ekphrasis* is not a work of Libanius, and follows Müller's suggestion. Müller's
further suggestion, that the statue is represented in a copy at Arles, is naturally invalidated by the removal of the *ekphrasis* from the works of Libanius.
[34] Philostratus, *Life of Apollonius* 6.38. On Apollonius' career, see J. Miller, "Apol-
lonios," no. 98, *RE* 2 (1896) 146-148, and H. J. Rose, "Apollonius," no. 14, *OCD* 71-72.
Philostratus states that an earthquake occurred when Apollonius visited Antioch, but
Malalas does not mention such an event in his description of Apollonius' visit, which
he places in his account of the reign of Domitian (264.6—266.11). The nature of the
material concerning the life of Apollonius is such that there would be some justification for the belief that this earthquake is fictitious.
[35] Malalas 264.6—266.11; Cedrenus 1.431.18—432.5 Bonn ed. Malalas' story (262.22—
263.10) of the suburban villa built near Antioch by the dancer Paris, a favorite of Do-

A.D. 69-192

In the time of Domitian we hear for the first time of the games of the *koinon*, or provincial assembly, of "Syria, Cilicia, and Phoenice," celebrated in Antioch.[36] These provincial assemblies, which had existed in various parts of the empire since republican and early imperial times, served as parliaments for the expansion of public opinion, and had come to be closely connected with emperor worship, and they held local games, accompanied by fairs.[37] Very little is known concerning the games of the *koinon* of Syria, and there is some reason to believe that they were later amalgamated with the local Olympic games.[38]

mitian, is wholly fictitious; see Stauffenberg, *Malalas* 239-243, and E. Wüst, "Paris," no. 3, *RE* 18 (1949) 1537-1538, also G. Highet, "The Life of Juvenal," *TAPA* 68 (1937) 490-491. There are several ways in which such a story might have originated. It might, as Müller suggests (*Antiq. Antioch.* 87, n. 4), have grown up around a suburban park called the παράδεισος, which could erroneously have been thought to be "the house of Paris"; compare Stauffenberg's suggested emendation of the passage (*Malalas* 239, n. 63a), which would make necessary (as Stauffenberg apparently did not realize) the further emendation of τὸ λεγόμενον to ὁ λεγόμενος—a rather sweeping change which does not seem either necessary or palaeographically probable. Or the tale might have originated concerning property of another Paris, a celebrated landowner of Antioch of the second century A.D. mentioned by Libanius in *Or.* 64.41; cf. E. Wüst, "Paris," no. 4, *RE* 18 (1949) 1538. This Paris might easily have been confused with the one who lived in the time of Domitian, and a property named for the later Paris could easily have been supposed to have been built by the earlier one. J. V. Francke, *Examen criticum D. Iunci Iuvenalis Vitae* (Altona and Leipzig 1820) 37-40, proposes to emend παράδεισος, the name given by Malalas (263.9) for the supposed establishment of Paris in Antioch, to παρίδειον, which would (Francke suggests) have been the name of a public bath built by a member of one of the circus factions at Antioch, from a mistaken interpretation of which Malalas' story of Domitian and Paris would have arisen; and the name παρίδειον would have been corrupted to παράδεισος. Had Francke known of the existence of the Paris of Antioch, he could have strengthened the basis for his emendation. Finally, the story might have had its origin in the local legend that the Judgment of Paris had taken place at Daphne (Libanius *Or.* 11.241): there might have been at Daphne some monument connected with this legend which somehow came to be known as a "house of Paris" and thus, in turn, came to be thought of as the residence of a dancer of that name.

[36] *Bull. dell' Inst.* 1887, p. 110 = *IG* 14 no. 746 = *IGRR* 1, no. 445. The language of the inscription does not necessarily mean that Cilicia was attached to Syria at the time when Artemidorus won his victory (Phoenice was still a part of Syria and became a separate province only when Syria Coele and Syria Phoenice were divided in the time of Septimius Severus). Most likely the games of the *koinon* had been celebrated in Antioch from the time when Cilicia Campestris was attached to Syria, and after Cilicia became a province in the time of Vespasian, the games continued to be celebrated in Antioch, which was the most attractive place to hold them. In this case it would be natural to mention Cilicia and Phoenice in the title of the games simply as a reminder of the geographical territory which they represented. On the festival of "Syria, Cilicia and Phoenice," see Harrer, *Studies* 72-73; F. Cumont in *CAH* 11.603; Magie, *Asia Minor* 1419-1420, 1439. Dieudonné, "Monnaies grecques de Syrie" 49, takes a local issue of Antioch of A.D. 66-67 to refer to games of the *koinon*, but his interpretation seems forced and there is nothing on the coin itself to make this interpretation necessary. There is, however, no reason to deny the existence of a *koinon* of Syria at this time.

[37] G. H. Stevenson, *Roman Provincial Administration* (Oxford 1949) 112-113.

[38] Beurlier, "*Koinon* de Syrie"; Stauffenberg, *Malalas* 422ff. See further below, n. 151. In contrast to the meagerness of our information concerning the *koinon* of Syria, we

[209]

Pliny the Younger spent a half year or a year in Syria early in Domitian's reign, in A.D. 81 or 82, serving as a military tribune of *Legio III Gallica*, as one of the first steps of his official career.[39] Since that post was merely a part of the *cursus honorum* through which he had to progress, the young man—he was about twenty—doubtless spent no more time on his duties than was necessary, and one may be sure that he was in Antioch as much of the time as was possible.[40] Pliny writes that while he was in Syria he became closely acquainted with the philosophers Artemidorus, the son-in-law of C. Musonius Rufus, and Euphrates of Tyre, the popular Stoic preacher.[41] While Pliny does not mention specifically where he heard these teachers, it seems likely that he would have known them at Antioch. Thanks to Pliny's letters, we know the names of several of his friends and contemporaries who served with him in the army in Syria—Calestrius Tiro,[42] Nymphidius Lupus,[43] and Claudius Pollio, commander of a division of horse, whose accounts Pliny found in admirable order (unlike the accounts of most officers) when he was appointed by the consular legate to inspect the financial affairs of the cavalry and the cohorts.[44]

The Christians were persecuted during Domitian's reign, but nothing is known of the effects of the persecution at Antioch.[45] Probably of greater significance in the history of the church at this period, is the activity of the teachers of Gnosticism, Christianity's rival and enemy, who made Antioch one of their centers of activity. The role of Gnosticism at this time is described more fully below.[46]

3. NERVA, A.D. 96-98; TRAJAN IN SYRIA AS A YOUNG MAN

Domitian's reign, ended by the murder of the hated tyrant, was

---

are much better informed concerning the *koinon* of Asia, clearly described by Magie, *Asia Minor* 447-452.

[39] Pliny *Epistt.* 1.10, 3.11, 7.16, 7.31, 8.14, 10 (*To Trajan*) 87. See T. Mommsen, "Zur Lebensgeschichte des jüngeren Plinius," *Hermes* 3 (1869) 78-79 = *Gesammelte Schriften* 4 (Berlin 1905) 412-413; Chapot, *Frontière de l'Euphrate* 66; M. Schuster, "Plinius," no. 6, *RE* 21 (1951) 439-440.

[40] Pliny writes in *Epist.* 8.14 of the demoralized state of the army and the slack state of discipline which prevailed when he was serving as military tribune.

[41] Nothing more is known about Artemidorus than the information that Pliny gives, *Epist.* 3.11; presumably he taught the Cynic-Stoic doctrine (see von Arnim, "Artemidoros," no. 30, *RE* 2 [1896] 1331). Euphrates of Tyre (Pliny *Epist.* 1.10) was born in the late 30's of the first century and was active in Syria before moving to Rome. The details of his career in Syria are not known. See von Arnim, "Euphrates," no. 4, *RE* 6 (1909) 1216.

[42] *Epist.* 7.16. [43] *Epist.* 10 (*To Trajan*) 87. [44] *Epist.* 7.31.

[45] Grégoire, *Les persécutions* 27-28; J. Zeiller in Fliche-Martin, *Hist. de l'église* 1.301-304. See below.

[46] Ch. 11, §3.

followed by a brief period of *reddita libertas* under Nerva. The new government, however, came to be looked upon as politically unstable, and Pliny speaks of the rumors that were circulating concerning the intentions of the powerful governor of Syria and the large and famous army that he had at his command.[47] What the chances were that another emperor would have come, like Vespasian, from Syria, we do not know. The emperor, in any case, saved his regime from collapse by adopting M. Ulpius Traianus, commander of the army of Upper Germany, and on Nerva's death (25 January A.D. 98), there began the rule of Trajan, the first of the able administrators who made this period of the Empire's history one of its happiest.

Trajan had had an opportunity to become acquainted with Syria and Antioch before becoming emperor. His father M. Ulpius Traianus had commanded *Legio X Fretensis* in the Jewish war (ca. A.D. 67-68), and then had served as legate of Syria from A.D. 76/7 to 79. As a young man (born A.D. 53) the future emperor had served as a military tribune in Syria while his father was governor and he doubtless acquired, both from personal observation and from his father, a good knowledge of the province.[48]

4. Trajan, A.D. 98-117 and Antioch; The Parthian War

The rumors that had emanated from Syria during Nerva's reign called for resolute action on the part of Trajan if he wished to forestall the possible appearance of a rival from that rich and powerful province. As governor of Syria Trajan appointed C. Antius A. Julius Quadratus, a wealthy elderly gentleman who seems previously to have held no military command; such a governor would not be likely to attempt a revolution.[49] In Antioch itself, the temporary disappearance of the municipal bronze coinage early in Trajan's reign suggests that the municipal privileges of the city were curtailed;[50] evidently Trajan felt it desirable to keep the city under closer control than his predecessors had done.

Trajan did not, however, neglect the physical welfare of Antioch,

[47] Pliny *Epist.* 9.13.22. The governor may have been C. Octavius Tidius Tossianus L. Iavolenus Priscus, whose career is described by Harrer, *Studies* 15-16; see R. P. Longden in *CAH* 11.196, n. 1, and Syme, "A governor of Syria under Nerva" 243-244.

[48] See Harrer, *Studies* 12-13; C. H. V. Sutherland, "Trajan," *OCD* (1949) 920-921; idem, "Ulpius Traianus (no. 1)," *ibid.* 932. Pliny, *Paneg.* 14.1, speaks of Trajan's presence in Syria during his father's governorship. On the mint of Antioch under Trajan, see Bellinger, "Some Coins from Antioch" 57-60.

[49] See Syme, "A governor of Syria under Nerva" 244-245.

[50] D. B. Waagé, "Coins" 38-39.

for at some time before the earthquake of A.D. 115 he built an aqueduct to bring water from Daphne to the city.[51] This would indicate that the population of Antioch had grown since the reign of Gaius, when we hear of an aqueduct from Daphne to Antioch being repaired following an earthquake.[52] Malalas records that Trajan built a new public bath, named for himself, in connection with the aqueduct.[53] Hadrian seems to have had something to do with this aqueduct, either completing Trajan's work, or repairing it after the earthquake of A.D. 115.[54]

Antioch plays a prominent part in the history of Trajan's reign since the city served as headquarters for the preparations for the Parthian war, one of the chief glories of the reign, by means of which the boundaries of the Roman Empire were carried to greater limits than they had ever reached.[55] The Parthian king in A.D. 113 broke the peace that had prevailed between Rome and Parthia since the time of Nero, and Trajan, feeling that in any case the situation on the eastern frontier was unsatisfactory, resolved to effect a definitive settlement. Leaving Rome in the autumn of A.D. 113 (possibly on 27 October), Trajan arrived by sea at Seleucia Pieria in December.[56] On his arrival he dedicated to Zeus Kasios, with a prayer for success in the coming cam-

---

[51] Archaeological evidence shows that Trajan's aqueduct was built before the earthquake of A.D. 115: Levi, *Antioch Mosaic Pavements* 1.34. Malalas describes the construction of the aqueduct (276.1ff.) following his account of the earthquake of A.D. 115 (275.11ff.), which will be described below. In a more orderly work than Malalas', this would be taken to mean that the construction of the aqueduct followed the earthquake, and perhaps was occasioned in some way by it. Malalas himself may have supposed that this was the case. However, the circumstance that his primary interest was simply in listing an emperor's buildings (see above, Ch. 2, §4) makes it unsafe to find chronological implications in the arrangement of his material. To the chronicler, the earthquake would be the major event in Trajan's reign, and so would have to be mentioned first.

[52] On the work under Gaius, see Ch. 8, §4. Trajan is also said by Malalas (276.3ff.) to have "completed" the theater at Antioch which had been left unfinished when it was enlarged by Tiberius (Malalas 235.2). Malalas mentions only the execution of a statue in the theater by Trajan (see further below), and we are not told whether the completion involved a further enlargement of the building. If it were certain that the seating capacity was enlarged by Trajan, we should have further evidence for an increase in the population of the city.

[53] Malalas 276.1-3. The construction of a public bath was a fitting concomitant for the building of an aqueduct; for other examples, see above, Ch. 7, §2; Ch. 8, §4, and below, §7.

[54] See below, §7.

[55] The account of the war given here is based upon the study of Lepper, *Trajan's Parthian War*, which, though some problems connected with the war cannot be solved at present, seems to the writer to be the best review of the events which has been made. Reference should also be made to A. R. Bellinger's review of Lepper's monograph in *AJP* 71 (1950) 311-316.

[56] The dates of departure and arrival are given by Malalas 270. 17-23; see Lepper, *Trajan's Parthian War* 29-30.

paign, two engraved silver cups and a gilded auroch's horn, spoils of his campaigns in Dacia (A.D. 101-106). The dedication was commemorated in a Greek epigram by Trajan's ward and nephew by marriage, the future Emperor Hadrian, who had been chosen to act as governor of Syria during the operations against the Parthians.[57]

Trajan entered Antioch on 7 January A.D. 114, and spent the remainder of the winter there, making preparations for his campaign.[58] In the spring he set out for Armenia, which he conquered easily, and then proceeded to annex Mesopotamia, spending the winter of A.D. 114/5 in the field. Late in A.D. 115 he returned to Antioch for the winter, in order to rest and plan further operations.

5. THE EARTHQUAKE OF A.D. 115; TRAJAN'S BUILDINGS IN ANTIOCH

While the emperor was thus passing the winter in Antioch between his campaigns, the city suffered one of the most severe of its many earthquakes. The disaster began at dawn on 13 December A.D. 115.[59]

[57] *Anth. Pal.* 6.332; Suidas *s.v.* Κάσιον ὄρος (Arrian, frag. 36 in *FGrHist* 2, pt. 4, p. 575).
[58] On the date of Trajan's arrival at Antioch (given by Malalas 272.21-22) see Lepper, *Trajan's Parthian War* 71-73, 206. Malalas gives a long and circumstantial account (271.1—273.4) of how, before Trajan's arrival, the Parthians had occupied Antioch; of how the emperor, when he arrived at Seleucia Pieria, incited the people of Antioch to revolt, and of how the Parthians were massacred; finally the emperor made a triumphal entry into the city. This story seems in itself improbable, and there is no confirmation or even hint of it in any other source. One explanation of it is that offered by A. von Gutschmid *apud* J. Dierauer, *Beiträge zu einer kritischen Gesch. Trajans* (in M. Büdinger, *Untersuchungen zur röm. Kaisergesch.* 1 [Leipzig 1868]) note on 157, namely that the episode described is a garbled account, mistakenly referred at a later date to Trajan's reign, of the occupation of Antioch by the Persians in the time of Sapor I in the third century after Christ (on this period see below, Ch. 10, §8). Probably the real basis of Malalas' story, as Gagé suggests ("Les Perses à Antioche" 319-321), on the basis of a briefer suggestion by Stauffenberg (*Malalas* 283-284), is that the episode is based upon a story of a performance of a Persian purification rite, carried out to forestall a threatened epidemic (following the earthquake?); as Gagé points out, Perseus, "the Persian," was one of the legendary early settlers on the site of Antioch (see Ch. 3, n. 18) so that a Persian rite could easily come to be one of the ancient customs of the city. Stauffenberg (*Malalas* 270-284), ever anxious to vindicate Malalas and to prove the importance of his chronicle, holds that this account of the occupation of Antioch is essentially true, though possibly exaggerated, and has a basis in historical fact. His arguments, however, have been thoroughly discredited by Longden, "Parthian Campaigns" 30-34. Elsewhere (*CAH* 11.248-249) Longden discusses the possibility that the invasion of Syria and occupation of Antioch that Malalas describes took place in A.D. 116, during the Parthian counteroffensive. However, as Longden points out, it is difficult to suppose that Malalas' story can be satisfactorily explained in this way.
[59] A vivid description of the catastrophe is preserved in the account of Dio Cassius 68.24-25; Malalas records the disaster more briefly, 275.3-10. A passage in Juvenal, *Sat.* 6.411, appears to refer to this earthquake. The date, which is given by Malalas, has been disputed. Since the day of the week on which Malalas says the disaster occurred does not agree with his other chronological data, scholars have either rejected the whole date, or emended parts of it. However, it seems plain that the weekday is an

Because of the emperor's presence, the city was filled with soldiers and with civilians who had come for business or for pleasure.[60] The shocks continued for several days and nights, and the destruction, both in Antioch and in Daphne, appears to have been considerable. Many people were killed, including M. Pedo Vergilianus, one of the consuls for the year.[61] Trajan himself escaped with a few slight injuries; he had, it was said, been led to safety through a window of the room in which he was staying by a being of supernatural size. During the remainder of the earthquake he lived in the open in the circus.[62] The future Emperor Hadrian, who was then governor of Syria, was likewise in the city when the earthquake occurred.[63] After the disaster, the survivors, in gratitude for their preservation, built a temple to Zeus Soter in Daphne.[64]

addition which was wrongly introduced into the date from another source, and that its inaccuracy need not invalidate the remainder of the chronological data. See the detailed discussion of the problem by Lepper, *Trajan's Parthian War* 54-83, whose conclusion is adopted here. Malalas lists this as the "third" earthquake at Antioch in a series of disasters to which he assigns numbers. Presumably this means that it was the third major disaster, for there is independent evidence for other earthquakes at Antioch which the chronicler either does not mention or does not include in his numbered series; see Downey, "Seleucid Chronology" 107, 119, n. 2.

[60] Beurlier, "*Koinon* de Syrie" 289, followed by Dieudonné, "Monnaies grecques de Syrie" 9, suggests that the crowding that Dio Cassius mentions was caused by the arrival of visitors who had come for the games of the *koinon* of Syria. It seems implausible that such games would be held in the middle of the winter (this consideration may not have occurred to Beurlier and Dieudonné, who speak only of the year of the earthquake and do not mention the month). It seems clear that the presence of the emperor and of his staff and army would have attracted all kinds of people to the city for a variety of reasons. Dio Cassius (68.24.1), giving the reasons why so many people had come to the city, says that some of them had come κατὰ θεωρίαν. Beurlier and Dieudonné take *theoria* to refer to games and spectacles, but the word would equally well be taken to mean "sightseeing," e.g. in connection with the arrival of the emperor. On the games of the *koinon*, see above, n. 36.

[61] Although Dio Cassius 68.25.1 calls Pedo ὁ ὕπατος, it is not clear whether he was acting as consul at the time of his death, or whether he had already ceased to be consul and had become a consular (ὑπατικός). See Lepper, *Trajan's Parthian War* 84-87.

[62] Müller is mistaken in stating (*Antiq. Antioch.* 88) that the circus in which Trajan found refuge was *in campo extra urbem*. The only circus at Antioch for which there is evidence at this period is that on the island (see above, Ch. 6, §3). Trajan's seeking safety there might be taken to mean that the building in which he was staying was on the island, and this might suggest, in turn, that what was called the palace, or the building which emperors occupied on their visits, was located on the island. However, there is no real evidence for the existence of such a building at Antioch before the time of Diocletian (see Ch. 12, §2), and it would be hazardous to find in the circumstances of Trajan's escape evidence for both the existence and the location of a palace.

[63] Malalas 278.20ff.

[64] Malalas (275.9-10) gives an ostensible quotation of the inscription which was placed on it: Οἱ σωθέντες ἀνέστησαν Διὶ Σωτῆρι.

Apparently the Christians were accused of having been responsible for the earthquake, which Malalas calls a *theoménia*, a "sign of divine wrath." Elsewhere is given an account of how Ignatius, the bishop of the city, was arrested, condemned, and sent to Rome, where he was executed by being exposed to wild beasts. Other executions took place in Antioch itself.[65]

Whether most of Trajan's varied building activity in Antioch was occasioned by the damage caused by the earthquake cannot be determined.[66] The restoration of the colonnades along the main street almost certainly followed earthquake damage.[67]

One of the principal works was the Μέση Πύλη, which appears to have been a monumental arch (not a real city gate) bearing the group of the she-wolf suckling Romulus and Remus, traditional symbol of Roman citizenship.[68] This stood near the torrent Parmenios which ran down from the mountain into the Orontes, flowing under the principal street at a point where there was a slight change in the direction of the thoroughfare. The arch is also said to have been near the Temple of Ares and "very close" to the Macellum, which are associated with the basilica of Julius Caesar and with the site that later became the Forum of Valens. These data suggest two possible locations for the arch: astride the principal street at the point where the thoroughfare, crossing Parmenius, changed its course slightly or to one side of the main street, astride the transverse avenue which ran from the main

[65] See the history of the early church at Antioch, below Ch. 11, §4.

[66] Malalas places his description of Trajan's buildings after his account of the earthquake, but this need not be taken to indicate sequence in time; see above, n. 51. One may speculate whether some of Trajan's work at Antioch may have been executed by his famous architect, Apollodorus of Damascus; see the account of his career by Fabricius, "Apollodoros," no. 73, *RE* 1 (1894) 2896.

[67] Malalas (275.21-22) says only that Trajan "raised the two great *emboloi*." These must have been the colonnades along the main street, which were the colonnades *par excellence* at Antioch; we hear of no others which were so important that they could be mentioned thus without more exact description.

[68] Malalas 275.13ff. A statue of the she-wolf with Romulus and Remus had been placed on the Eastern Gate, which was traditionally ascribed to Tiberius; on this gate and on the symbolism of the statue, see Ch. 8, nn. 87-88. Trajan's Middle Gate was presumably not a central city gate because so far as we know there was no city wall in the region where it stood. Stauffenberg (*Malalas* 477-480) is mistaken in supposing that the Middle Gate was at the south of the city and that it was identical with the main gate in the southern wall of the city; the maps of the city which were available to him were not correctly oriented, and it was not until 1931, the year in which Stauffenberg's book was published, that Jacquot's map, the first properly oriented one, was published (see Excursus 8-9).

A History of Antioch

street up toward the mountain, parallel with Parmenius, and past the Temple of Ares and the Macellum.[69]

Another major work of Trajan, apparently not connected with the earthquake, was the completion of the unfinished theater. This theater is presumably the one which had been rebuilt by Julius Caesar. It had been enlarged by Agrippa, in the time of Augustus, because of the increase in the population of the city, and again enlarged under Tiberius, but left incomplete.[70] We are not told precisely what the completion involved, and in particular whether it included an enlargement of the seating capacity.

In the theater, Trajan placed a statue of Calliope.[71] This Muse ranked

[69] The Forum of Valens and the topography of this region will be described below in Excursus 12. Malalas relates that at the construction of the Middle Gate, Trajan sacrificed a maiden. This tale and its significance are discussed below in n. 71.

[70] Malalas describes the completion of the theater, 276.3-9. On the site of the theater and its "building" by Caesar, see Ch. 7, §2. Its enlargements by Agrippa and Tiberius are mentioned above, Ch. 8, §2.

[71] Malalas (275.19-21) states that when Trajan built the Μέση Πύλη he sacrificed a maiden named Calliope, "in expiation and for the purification of the city," and that he made a νυμφαγωγία for her. Later the chronicler records (276.3-9) that the emperor set up in the theater a statue of the slain maiden, in gilded bronze, seated above the Orontes river, being crowned by Seleucus and Antiochus, "in the fashion of the Tyche of the city" (εἰς λόγον Τύχης τῆς αὐτῆς πόλεως). The group stood, Malalas says, "in the middle of the nymphaeum of the proscenium" of the theater. It is impossible, of course, that Trajan should have performed a human sacrifice of this kind. The numerous stories that appear in Malalas of such immolations, accompanying the foundation of cities or the erection of buildings, are Christian legends, designed to cast discredit on pagan practices; see Müller, Antiq. Antioch. 27, n. 2 and 71, n. 6; Weber, Studien 48, n. 5; Stauffenberg, Malalas 158-159, 216-217, 469-470. It is sometimes possible to see, in the name of the victim or in the circumstances of the supposed incident, the origin of the legend. In the present case it seems plain that the story was connected with the statue in the theater. Müller (Antiq. Antioch. 40) believed that the figure Trajan set up in the theater was the original Tyche of the city, which Trajan removed from its original location to the theater. However, it seems more natural to believe, with Stauffenberg (Malalas 471-473), that the statue was of Calliope, represented, as Malalas says, in the guise of the Tyche; certainly (as Stauffenberg points out) there would be more reason to place a statue of Calliope in the theater than to set up a Tyche there. In another place (158-159) Stauffenberg writes that the statue was a Tyche. One must suppose that the opinion which he expresses on pp. 471-473 represents a conclusion reached after he had written pp. 158-159. In his text of Malalas, Stauffenberg is mistaken in placing a comma after Καλλιόπην and omitting a comma after πόλεως (275.20), for according to this punctuation, the sentence would mean (to Stauffenberg) that Trajan "sacrificed . . . Calliope, building a nymphagogia for her for the atonement and purification of the city." Apparently Stauffenberg believes that the meaning is that the nymphagogia was built as an atonement for the sacrifice of Calliope; but it seems more likely that the passage means that Calliope was sacrificed for the atonement and purification of the city after the earthquake, and that the nymphagogia was built in memory or in honor of her. This interpretation is supported by the fact that Malalas says that when Perseus founded Tarsus he sacrificed a maiden named Parthenope εἰς ἀποκαθαρισμὸν τῆς πόλεως (37.5-6), and that when Augustus built walls about Arsinoe and changed its name to Ancyra he sacrificed a maiden named

with Zeus and Apollo as a tutelary deity of the city.[72] Libanius repeatedly speaks of her as presiding over the life of Antioch, and mentions her temple, which was in the central part of the city, as one of the principal shrines of Antioch; he also alludes particularly to the honor that was paid to her in the theater, referring presumably to the rhetorical exhibitions that took place there.[73] Trajan's statue was of gilded bronze and showed the Muse in the guise of the Tyche of Antioch, seated above the Orontes river, being crowned by Seleucus and Antiochus (evidently to symbolize the honor that had been paid to Calliope at Antioch from earliest times).[74] The group was placed, Malalas says, "above four columns in the middle of the nymphaeum of the proscenium." This nymphaeum may have been a deep, semicircular exedra of the type used in other theaters of the Roman period.[75]

It has been supposed that Trajan also built a nymphaeum which was a separate building, not identical with the "nymphaeum" in the theater mentioned, and that this nymphaeum of Trajan stood near a temple of Calliope. The evidence for such a building is, however, far from certain, and it seems more likely that a separate nymphaeum was not built.[76]

Gregoria εἰς ἀποκαθαρισμὸν (221.22). It is necessary therefore to follow the punctuation of Dindorf's edition, in which a comma is placed after πόλεως. *Nymphagogia* here means "bridal procession," not "nymphaeum" or "aqueduct"; see below, n. 76.

[72] Julian *Misop.* 357 C; Libanius *Ep.* 1317 W. = 1182 F.

[73] Libanius *Or.* 1.102; *Or.* 15.152; *Or.* 20.51; *Or.* 31.40; *Or.* 60.13 (location of temple). With reference to the statue in the theater, Stauffenberg (*Malalas* 473) cites a passage in a letter of Libanius (*Epist.* 722 W. = 811 F.) in which there is an allusion to sacrifices offered to Calliope in the theater. Stauffenberg appears to think that this means that actual rites of sacrifice to the Muse were performed in the theater. Libanius' phrase is, however, more probably metaphorical, referring to literary exhibitions presented in the theater during the Olympic games, which would be, symbolically, offerings in honor of the Muse; see further remarks on the same subject in Libanius, *Epist.* 1311 W. = 1175 F. and *Epist.* 1317 W. = 1182 F., and the discussions of the subject by Sievers, *Leben des Libanius* 102-103, 119, and by Seeck, *Briefe des Libanius* 423.

[74] The statue presumably resembled that of Eutychides (on which see above, Ch. 4, nn. 92-94) the difference being, as Stauffenberg points out (*Malalas* 472), that the statue of Calliope, since the Muse was shown being crowned by Seleucus and Antiochus, would have lacked the turreted crown that the Tyche of Eutychides wore. See also Toynbee, *Hadrianic School* 131-133.

[75] On the use in Roman theaters of the nymphaeum as an architectural decoration, see O. Reuther, "Nymphaeum," *RE* 17 (1937) 1517-1524, especially 1522.

[76] Müller (*Antiq. Antioch.* 88, n. 4) and Stauffenberg (*Malalas* 159) take Malalas' statement (275.21) that Trajan made a νυμφαγωγία for Calliope (νυμφαγωγίαν αὐτῇ ποιήσας) to mean that the emperor built a nymphaeum, possibly in the neighborhood of the Temple of Calliope (the evidence for which has been cited above, n. 73). This seems unlikely. In the Latin translation that accompanied the Oxford edition of Malalas, νυμφαγωγία is rendered *Nymphaeum*, and this sense is accepted by Müller and Stauffenberg. However, the word ordinarily means a bridal procession, and the

The final work of Trajan's to be recorded is the construction of a Temple of Artemis at Daphne, mentioned by Malalas. Taken at its face value, the chronicler's notice would mean that the original temple had been destroyed in the earthquake and had to be replaced. However, Malalas' procedures are such that he might describe as a new undertaking work that was only repair of an existing monument. Thus we cannot be sure whether Trajan built a new temple, or repaired the old one.[77]

In addition to the emperor's own contributions toward the restoration of the city after the earthquake, work was carried out by P. Aelius Hadrianus (later the Emperor Hadrian), the emperor's ward and nephew by marriage, who was governor of Syria at the time, and by a number of Roman senators who were in the city with the emperor when the disaster occurred. These were all ordered by the emperor to build houses and baths, presumably with their own money.[78]

In the reign of Trajan we find one of the few pieces of evidence for the *koinon* or provincial assembly of Syria, in the form of a bronze coin among the local municipal issues of the mint.[79]

6. The End of Trajan's Reign

After remaining in Antioch during the winter of A.D. 115/6 (during which, probably, he set on foot the restoration of the damage caused by the earthquake), Trajan set out in the spring of A.D. 116 for the Tigris. After capturing Ctesiphon, the Parthian capital, he descended to the Persian Gulf. Later, however, while he was arranging the administration of the new provinces, the Parthians launched a counteroffensive and a revolt broke out in Mesopotamia. The revolt was suppressed with some difficulty and a political settlement was reached by which southern Mesopotamia was reconstituted as a Parthian client-kingdom. The

---

present writer has been unable to find any instance of its use to mean a building; Reuther, in his collection of material on the nymphaeum cited above (n. 75), cites only νυμφαῖον and νυμφεῖον as designations of the building. In speaking of the setting in which the statue was placed in the theater, Malalas (276.5) writes νυμφαῖον. Thus it seems clear that in writing νυμφαγωγία he was not referring to a building, but to a "bridal procession" which formed a part of the ceremony in which the maiden was sacrificed.

[77] Malalas 277.11. On the chronicler's methods, see above, Ch. 2, §4. On the original Temple of Artemis, see above, Ch. 3, n. 8.

[78] Malalas 278.20-279.2 (in the account of Hadrian's reign).

[79] See D. B. Waagé, "Coins" 38-39; Beurlier, "*Koinon* de Syrie" 288, and Dieudonné, "Monnaies grecques de Syrie" 8-9. On the games of the *Koinon*, which appear in the reign of Domitian, see above, n. 36.

emperor returned to Antioch fatigued and ill.[80] He planned to make a fresh expedition into Mesopotamia, but before he could start he suffered a stroke that left him partly paralyzed and dropsical.[81] In addition to the state of his health, news of troubles elsewhere in the empire, and business that demanded his attention in Rome, induced him to set out for the capital. He began his journey by sea, from Seleucia Pieria, on 3 or 4 August A.D. 117.[82] His illness grew worse, however, and he was put ashore at Selinus (later Trajanopolis) on the coast of Cilicia, where he died suddenly, at some time before 9 August.[83]

7. HADRIAN AS GOVERNOR OF SYRIA; HIS VISITS TO ANTIOCH AS EMPEROR, A.D. 117-138

When Trajan set out from Antioch for Rome in August of A.D. 117, he left in charge of the army in Syria his ward and nephew by marriage, P. Aelius Hadrianus, the governor of the province. On 9 August, word was supposed to have been brought to Hadrian that he had been adopted and made Trajan's successor; then on the 11th the news came of Trajan's sudden death during the journey, at Selinus on the coast of Cilicia, and Hadrian was proclaimed emperor by the troops.[84]

Like Trajan, Hadrian had become familiar with Syria and with Antioch before he became emperor. He had been appointed governor of Syria when Trajan embarked upon the Parthian war,[85] and had apparently made his headquarters in Antioch during the war, for his name is not mentioned in connection with the campaigns.[86] He was in Antioch at the time of the great earthquake of 13 December A.D. 115, and in the course of the reconstruction work that followed, Trajan

---

[80] On the significance of Trajan's Parthian War, and the reason for its failure, see Pflaum, *Procurateurs équestres* 107-109.

[81] Dio Cassius 68.33.

[82] On the date, see Weber, *Hadrianus* 36-37.

[83] Dio Cassius 68.33. The date of Trajan's death is uncertain; see Weber, *Hadrianus* 37-41, and R. P. Longden in *CAH* 11.299-300. On the emperor's medical history and the causes of his death, see Lepper, *Trajan's Parthian War* 198-201.

[84] The question whether Trajan actually adopted Hadrian is not clear; on this problem, and on the chronology of Trajan's journey and death, see Weber, *Hadrianus* 35-42.

[85] Dio Cassius 69.1.1; see Harrer, *Studies* 22-23. Harrer placed the commencement of Hadrian's term of office at the beginning of the Parthian war, in A.D. 115. Subsequent investigation has shown that Trajan left Italy for Syria in October of A.D. 113 and reached Seleucia Pieria in December of that year (see Lepper, *Trajan's Parthian War* 28-30), so that Hadrian's governorship should apparently be dated from A.D. 113. Hadrian composed a Greek epigram to commemorate a dedication which Trajan made to Zeus Kasios on his arrival at Seleucia Pieria; see above, n. 57.

[86] See Harrer, *Studies* 22.

ordered Hadrian and certain Roman senators who were in the city to build houses and baths, presumably with their own money.[87]

After Trajan's death in Selinus, his body was brought back to Seleucia Pieria, where it was formally received by Hadrian. The body was burned and the ashes sent to Rome, and Hadrian returned to Antioch to attend to affairs there before setting out for Rome.[88] It was presumably at this time that he gave orders for the construction in Antioch of a "small and very graceful" temple in honor of the deified Trajan.[89] Hadrian appointed L. Catilius Severus Julianus Claudius Severus as his successor as governor of Syria and set out for Rome, apparently at the beginning of October A.D. 117.[90]

Coming to the throne when the Roman Empire had reached its greatest development, Hadrian devoted his restless energy and remarkable creative ability to the supervision and improvement of the government and the development of the cities of the empire. He traveled in every part of the Roman world for nearly twelve of the twenty-one years of his reign, everywhere observing the functioning of the government and planning new buildings and public works.[91] Antioch was among the many cities which received notable benefits at his hands.[92]

Hadrian visited Antioch three times, first (as has been seen) during the Parthian War, and again in A.D. 123 and in A.D. 129-130. The city would naturally have been of particular interest to him both as a center of Greek culture and as the capital of Syria; in addition, it was an object of his special concern because of the damage that it had suffered in the earthquake of 13 December A.D. 115, during which (together with Trajan) he was present.[93]

[87] Malalas 278.20-279.2.

[88] *SHA Hadrian* 5.9-10; Victor *Epit.* 14.2; see Weber, *Hadrianus* 54.

[89] Suidas *s.v.* 'Ἰοβιανός; John of Antioch fr. 181, in *Excerpta de virtut. et vit.* 1.20 ed. Büttner-Wobst. According to Suidas the temple was turned into a library by Julian the Apostate, and later burned by Jovian.

[90] *SHA Hadrian* 5.10; see Weber, *Hadrianus* 54-56, and Harrer, *Studies* 24-26.

[91] An idea of the importance of Hadrian's travels in the East can be gained from the account of his activities in Asia Minor in Magie, *Asia Minor* 611ff. On Hadrian as a builder, see H. Kähler, *Hadrian u. seine Villa bei Tivoli* (Berlin 1950), and the survey of his public works in B. d'Orgeval, *L'Empereur Hadrien* (Paris 1950) 269-276.

[92] Dio Cassius (69.10.1) speaks of Hadrian's habit of building theaters and holding games in the various cities he visited. While there is no specific evidence for the production of such games in Antioch, it can be assumed that the Syrian capital would have been among the cities that enjoyed the emperor's generosity in this respect. The evidence of the coins, while not wholly clear, might indicate that Hadrian restored to the city some privileges, possibly nominal in character, which had been taken away in Trajan's reign: see D. B. Waagé, "Coins" 38-39; cf. above, n. 50.

[93] There are coins of Antioch showing the Tyche of Antioch which were probably issued to commemorate one of Hadrian's visits to the city, in A.D. 123 or 129-130; see Toynbee, *Hadrianic School* 131-133.

The building projects for which Hadrian was responsible at Antioch—in addition to the houses and baths and the temple of the deified
Trajan, which have been mentioned—were related to the water supply
of the city; some of this work may have been a continuation or completion of work done by Trajan. Malalas records[94] that Hadrian built
an aqueduct and a public bath which were named for him,[95] and that
at Daphne he carried out an elaborate undertaking in connection with
the springs that were one of the major sources of the city's water. The
principal purpose of this operation was evidently the conservation and
control of the water supply. There was constructed what was called
"the *theatron* of the springs of Daphne," evidently a general reservoir
built or decorated to resemble a theater; presumably there was a façade
decorated like that of a theater out of which water flowed.[96] The topographical border of the Yakto mosaic shows a theater-like structure,
next to the springs of Daphne, which appears to be the *theatron* mentioned by Malalas.[97] Into this reservoir (Malalas says) was directed the
water of one of the springs, named Saramanna,[98] which (Malalas' account implies) had not previously been properly controlled. The
reservoir also received other water which formerly had flowed out
through ravines called the Agriae ("the Wilds"), presumably in a
torrent going down through Daphne toward the Orontes; this water
was now brought under control by means of a dike or wall of piles.[99]
The reservoir itself was equipped with a set of five *ajutages* or efflux
pipes of different sizes (called the *pentamodion, tetramodion, tri-
modion, dimodion,* and *modion*)[100] by means of which the rate of flow
through the aqueduct leading to the city could be regulated.[101] There

[94] 277.20-278.19. See Downey, "Water Supply."
[95] Stauffenberg in his text of Malalas prints αὑτοῦ, the reading of the Oxford and
Bonn editions. In his collation of the unique MS of Malalas, made in order to correct
the errors of the Oxford and Bonn texts, J. B. Bury reports the reading αὐτοῦ ("Malalas:
the Cod. Barocc." 227).
[96] On the evidence for the construction and decoration of such structures, see
Müller, *Antiq. Antioch.* 89-90, and Stauffenberg, *Malalas* 491-492, also Dio 68.27; cf.
C. Cichorius, "Altertümer von Hierapolis," *JDAI Ergänzungsheft* 4 (1898) 38. An inscription (*Année épigr.* 1934, no. 133) mentions a *pronaus aqueducti*, and Dio Cassius
(68.27) describes a *theatron* built over a spring which was apparently a kind of gallery
for visitors.
[97] Lassus in *Antioch-on-the-Orontes* 1. 130 and fig. 10; Levi, *Antioch Mosaic Pavements* pl. 79a.
[98] On the name, see H. C. Youtie and C. Bonner, "Two Curse Tablets from Beisan"
TAPA 68 (1937) 49-50.
[99] The text (278.3-4) has πίλας (acc.), evidently representing Lat. *pila*. While piles
might be meant, it seems more likely that *pila* is used here in its sense of "mole."
[100] Cf. Frontinus' description of Roman *ajutages, De aq.* 1.23-34.
[101] This interpretation of Malalas' account represents the view, which seems the most

was also built, apparently at the upper end of the reservoir, at the point where the water from the springs entered it, a Temple of the Nymphs which contained a great seated statue of Hadrian as Zeus, holding the celestial sphere.[102]

Hadrian also rebuilt the installation at another of the springs, named Pallas, which had been damaged (presumably by the earthquake), and constructed (or repaired) a channel for the distribution of its water to Daphne. He closed the spring called Castalia, evidently because it was not active in his time; this was later reopened by the Emperor Julian.[103]

The dedication of the work at Daphne was celebrated by a festival held on 23 June A.D. 129, while Hadrian was visiting Antioch. The festival instituted on this occasion was named in honor of the emperor

plausible one, that the *theatron* and the *theatridion* of which he writes are the same structure, or at least parts of the same structure. If they were different, then there would have been two reservoirs, a large one (the *theatron*) attached to the springs in general, and a smaller one (the *theatridion*) attached to the spring Saramanna. However, the description given of the *theatridion* is that of a principal reservoir. Possibly the use of the diminutive means that the part of the reservoir which was called *theatridion* was so designed (being the point where the outflow was regulated) that it seemed distinct from the major part of the reservoir (the *theatron*). It is plain from the disjointed character of his account that Malalas himself had no clear idea of the disposition and connection of this water system. Müller (*Antiq. Antioch.* 89-90) thought that the *theatron* and the *theatridion* referred to the same structure, which was a cistern and was in Antioch, but there is nothing in the text to indicate that Malalas meant to speak of Antioch, and Stauffenberg, who likewise thinks that the *theatron* and the *theatridion* were the same, rightly places the structure at Daphne. Richard S. Chowen ("The Nature of Hadrian's *Theatron* at Daphne," *AJA* 60 [1956] 275-277) believes that the building at Antioch resembled the structure built by Hadrian as part of the aqueduct taking water from Mount Zaghouan to Carthage, which was extended by Alexander Severus. This was a theater-like building serving as a reservoir.

[102] Malalas (278.8-11) writes that the statue was of Zeus, but it seems likely, as Müller points out (*Antiq. Antioch.* 89), that is was Hadrian who was represented. The statue is said to have been holding a πῶλον, which Chilmead in his Latin translation in the *editio princeps* of Malalas (followed by Müller, *loc.cit.*) takes to mean the eagle of Zeus. However, as Maass points out (*Tagesgötter* 40, n. 100), it seems clear that the reading of the MS must be an error for πόλον, and that the statue was holding the celestial sphere. The description of the image indicates that the *polos* was not the crown which was denoted by the same word; on this use of *polos*, see K. V. Müller, *Der Polos, die griech. Götterkrone* (Diss. Berlin 1915).

[103] The closing and reopening of Castalia are not mentioned by Malalas, but are recorded by Ammianus Marcellinus 22.12.8 and by Sozomen *Hist.eccl.* 5.19 = Migne *PG* 67.1273 C-D. It was reported by Ammianus and Sozomen that Hadrian closed the spring because he had received a prophecy from the oracle there that he would become emperor, and he did not wish similar prophecies to be given to others. Since the oracle is said to have been still working in the time of the Caesar Gallus, it seems likely that the report of Ammianus and Sozomen is a tale invented in connection with Julian's opening of the spring, and that the closing actually was simply a part of Hadrian's reorganization of the hydraulic installations. On the identification of Castalia, see D. N. Wilber, "The Plateau of Daphne: The Springs and the Water System Leading to Antioch," *Antioch-on-the-Orontes* 2.50, n. 4.

and was continued, as we learn from inscriptions of athletes dating from the reign of Commodus of victories won in it.[104]

How much of the work at Daphne was original with Hadrian, and how much of it represented a continuation or conclusion of an operation begun by Trajan, is not clear. Malalas relates that Trajan built a public bath and an aqueduct at Antioch,[105] diverting the water of the springs of Daphne which had flowed out into the Agriae. Since the chronicler also ascribes to Hadrian the controlling of the water which had flowed into the Agriae, as well as the construction of an aqueduct and a public bath, it would look as though in this case, as in others,[106] Malalas was ascribing separately, to two emperors, work which was begun by one and finished by the other. Study of the remains of the aqueducts that run from Daphne to Antioch has shown that there were only two lines. The masonry of one indicates that it was constructed (or reconstructed) at about the time of Gaius, who is said to have "built" such an aqueduct following an earthquake (that is, he may have rebuilt an existing one).[107] Brick stamps and other archaeological evidence indicate that Trajan built an aqueduct at Antioch before the earthquake of A.D. 115.[108] From this it would appear that Hadrian either completed Trajan's work, or repaired damage done to it by the earthquake of A.D. 115.[109]

[104] Malalas (278.16) gives only the month and day of the original celebration of the festival, but as Weber points out (*Hadrianus* 121, 132) the year A.D. 129 must be meant, since the timetable of the emperor's movements shows that Hadrian cannot have been in Antioch as early as 23 June during his visit to the city in A.D. 123. Possibly the work had been planned during the visit of A.D. 123, as Weber suggests, though it does not seem very likely that (as Weber thinks) the work described would take six years to complete. For inscriptions recording victories won in the festival (τὸν Ἀδριάνειον) see Edhem Bey, "Fouilles de Tralles," *BCH* 28 (1904) 87-88, and M. Gough, "Anazarbus," *Anatolian Studies* 2 (1952) 128-129. These inscriptions are not dated, but they mention the festival instituted at Antioch by Commodus (τὸν Κομόδειον) showing that the festival founded by Hadrian continued to be celebrated at least until the time of Commodus. For the festival named in honor of Commodus see below in this chapter, §10.

[105] 276.1-2; see above, §5.

[106] On the chronicler's methods, see above, Ch. 2, §4.

[107] See Wilber in *Antioch-on-the-Orontes* 2.53-54, and Stauffenberg, *Malalas* 491. On Caligula's aqueduct, see above, Ch. 8, §4.

[108] Levi, *Antioch Mosaic Pavements* 1.34; see above, §5.

[109] The biography of Hadrian in the *SHA* (20.5) says that the emperor built aqueducts "without number." There is no reason to accept the statement of this biography (14.1) that "in the course of these travels he [Hadrian] conceived such a hatred for the people of Antioch that he wished to separate Syria from Phoenicia, in order that Antioch might not be called the chief city of so many communities" (transl. of D. Magie in the Loeb Classical Library). As Magie points out in his commentary on the passage, this statement (which is not supported by other evidence) may represent a deduction from the circumstance that Hadrian raised Tyre, Damascus, and Samosata to the rank

A History of Antioch

8. ANTONINUS PIUS, A.D. 138-161

The reign of Antoninus Pius was on the whole tranquil and the provinces were prosperous. In Antioch, the well-being of this period was broken by a fire, which is recorded in the biography of the emperor in the *Historia Augusta* (9.2) as one of three noteworthy conflagrations which occurred during his reign (*et Narbonensis civitas et Antiochense oppidum et Carthaginense forum arsit*). In order to be included in such a list, the disaster must have been a relatively important one. Taken literally, the biographer's words would mean that the whole city burned; but since there is no mention of the fire in any other source, it does not seem certain that this was the case.[110]

There is a record that Antoninus Pius at his own personal expense paved with Theban granite the main colonnaded street and all the other streets of Antioch.[111] The work was commemorated in a stone inscription (now lost) placed on the Gate of the Cherubim, at the southern end of the main street, where the operation was begun.[112] If the report is not exaggerated, and if it is true that all the streets of the city were paved with Theban granite, this was a princely gift indeed, even though the stone could have been transported by the cheapest method, by water, direct to Antioch itself.[113]

Some doubt has been felt as to whether this operation was actually carried out by Antoninus Pius, and it has been suggested that the

of *metropolis*. On the political and administrative aspects of this measure, see Weber, *Hadrianus* 232-234.

[110] Surprisingly, Malalas is silent about the fire.

[111] Malalas 280.20—281.6. The stone used for the paving is described by Malalas as "mill stone" (μυλίτης λίθος) from the Thebais. "Mill stone" could be sandstone, granite, porphyry, basalt, or volcanic stone (F. Ebert, "Molaris lapis," *RE* 15 [1932] 2517-2518), but in the present instance the description of the stone as coming from the Thebais shows that it was granite; see Fiehn, "Steinbruch," *RE* 3A (1929) 2243.

[112] On the location of the Gate of the Cherubim, see above, nn. 24-27. Malalas states that the inscription was still extant, but this does not necessarily prove that the chronicler himself had seen it, since it can be shown that in other cases he makes such statements concerning inscriptions and other monuments that he cannot possibly have seen. Malalas would have taken over such statements, which are characteristic of popular chronicles, from his literary sources; on his methods, see above, Ch. 2, §4.

[113] It might be possible to suppose that Malalas meant that only some of the paving was done with Theban granite. He writes (280.20ff.) that the emperor "made the paving of the street of the great colonnades which had been built by Tiberius, and of all the city, paving it with mill stone, paying out of his own funds for stones from the Thebais and for the other expenses." These words could be taken to mean that Theban granite was not employed everywhere, but only for some parts of the work, e.g. the main street. This interpretation, however, might seem to press the chronicler's meaning too closely. Certainly the natural reading of the sentence is that every street in the city was paved with Theban granite. On the road and street paving activities of Antoninus elsewhere, see Hüttl, *Antoninus Pius* 1. 334-335.

work was done by Caracalla (A.D. 211-217), whose name and activities might have been confused with those of Antoninus Pius. However, there is no conclusive argument against Antoninus' authorship of the project,[114] and such an undertaking would have been characteristic of his noteworthy generosity with his own money.[115] Moreover, it is just such an operation as might well be carried out after a major fire.

During the reign of Antoninus Pius, we have epigraphic testimony from Delphi concerning T. Aelius Aurelianus Theodotus and P. Aelius Aelianus, who had won victories in flute-playing in a festival (or festivals) at Antioch, the name of which is not given.[116] Since the Olympic Games are normally named in records of such victories, it would appear that the inscriptions at Delphi refer to some other festival or festivals at Antioch.

From this reign we also have one of our few surviving records of literary activity in Antioch in this period, in the works of the famous astrologer Vettius Valens. We do not know how much of his activity is to be associated with Antioch, but in the sources he is given the epithet Antiochenus, and it may be supposed that at least some of his writing, which can be dated between A.D. 152 and 162, was done at Antioch.[117]

9. MARCUS AURELIUS (A.D. 161-180) AND LUCIUS VERUS (A.D. 161-169)

Marcus Aurelius on his accession assumed as his imperial colleague L. Aurelius Commodus, the adopted son of the late emperor, thus introducing the principle of collegiality in the imperial office. Marcus

[114] For a detailed treatment of the problem, see Downey, "Building Records in Malalas" 299-300. The principal reason for doubting that Antoninus Pius did this work in Antioch is that Malalas says that he executed it in the course of a journey following a victorious campaign in Egypt. There is no other sound testimony that the emperor made an eastern journey after he came to the throne, and there is reason, from other evidence, to attribute to Caracalla some of the work (other than the operation at Antioch) which Malalas ascribes to Antoninus Pius. However, Malalas, evidently feeling that it was fitting for a major building operation to be inaugurated by an emperor in person, sometimes seems to invent journeys in order to explain building operations. Malalas' citation of an inscription in which the work was recorded is not decisive (see above, n. 112). Antoninus Pius could easily have had the work done at Antioch without visiting the city. Pending the discovery of further evidence, there seems to be no compelling reason to suppose that the paving at Antioch was not done by Antoninus Pius.
[115] On the emperor's liberality (which is often stressed in the biography of him in the SHA), see Hüttl, Antoninus Pius I. 334-338.
[116] Fouilles de Delphes, vol. 3, pt. 6, no. 143, line 5; ibid., no. 547. See also Fouilles de Delphes, vol. 3, pt. 1, no. 551, line 25.
[117] E. Boer, "Vettius Valens," no. 67, RE 8A.1871-1873.

Aurelius on this occasion adopted the name Antoninus for himself and gave his own name, Verus, to his colleague.[118]

The accession of the new Roman emperors seemed to Vologases III, the King of Parthia, to be a suitable opportunity to revive his own plan for an expedition against the Armenians which had been stopped by the intervention (by correspondence) of Antoninus Pius.[119] The Roman governor of Cappadocia marched against Vologases but was beaten and the Parthians then invaded Syria and again defeated the Roman. Marcus dispatched reinforcements to Syria and appointed Verus to supreme command of the war. Verus set out from Rome in March, A.D. 162, and after a leisurely journey by sea, during which he amused himself at various stopping-places, he arrived at Antioch at the end of the season of navigation, in the late autumn of 162.[120]

The success of the Parthians and the Roman reverses had created possibilities of revolution in Syria.[121] Verus when he arrived in the East spent his time in riotous living, moving in turn between Daphne, where he spent the summers, Laodicea, where he spent the winters, and Antioch, where he passed the remainder of his time. He was ridiculed by the people of Antioch, and was on bad terms with Annius Libo, the legate of Syria.[122] Fortunately, however, the three generals to whom he entrusted the conduct of the war (Statius Priscus, Avidius Cassius, and Martius Verus), were able soldiers. Avidius Cassius, a native Syrian who had already achieved eminence as a commander and was famous as an iron disciplinarian, was put in charge of training the Syrian legions, which had become debauched and demoralized and were "given over to the behavior of Daphne."[123]

After campaigns in Armenia and Parthia, the Romans finally defeated Vologases in A.D. 166. During all this time Verus had remained

[118] On the reign of Marcus Aurelius, see H. D. Sedgwick, *Marcus Aurelius* (New Haven 1921).
[119] For an account of Parthian affairs at this time, see Debevoise, *Hist. of Parthia* 244ff.
[120] On the chronology of Verus' journey to Antioch and his stay there, see C. H. Dodd, "Chronology of the Eastern Campaigns of the Emperor Lucius Verus," *Num. Chron.* ser. 4, vol. 11 (1911) 215-216, 256.
[121] *SHA Verus* 6.9.
[122] *SHA Marcus Antoninus* 8.2, *Verus* 7.1-10. It is said that Verus occupied himself with gladiatorial shows and hunting. Annius Libo, a cousin of Marcus, may have been sent to Syria as legate to act as a check on Verus; when he died in office, it was rumored (*SHA Verus* 9.2) that Verus had poisoned him. On his career, see Harrer, *Studies* 31. For a possible allusion in a mutilated inscription to games celebrated when Verus was in Antioch, see L. Robert, *Études anatoliennes* (Paris 1937) 144-146. The possibility, as M. Robert remarks, is slight.
[123] *SHA Avidius Cassius* 3-6; cf. Fronto's letter to Verus 2.1.19.

in Antioch, Daphne, and Laodicea, with the exception of one trip as far as the Euphrates which his staff compelled him to make.[124]

In December A.D. 165,[125] the Roman forces, after the capture of Seleucia on the Tigris, were stricken with an epidemic disease, probably smallpox. Returning to Syria, the troops brought the disease with them; and for fifteen years it ran through the whole Roman world, causing many deaths.[126] It must have been some time before Antioch recovered from the effects of this plague. The city was the first large center of population which the infected army reached, and the loss of life among the civil population may have been considerable.

In the middle of A.D. 166, Verus returned to Rome, and in the autumn both emperors celebrated a triumph.[127] Verus took with him to Rome a number of actors, musicians, and other entertainers from Syria and Egypt, of whom some at least must have been from Antioch.[128]

For almost ten years we hear nothing of the history of the city. Then, in mid-April of A.D. 175, it became one of the two chief centers of the revolt of Avidius Cassius.[129] Cassius had been governor of Syria in A.D. 165 while he was in command of the Parthian war. Later, while continuing to serve as governor of Syria, he was given a *maius imperium* over the *Oriens* (possibly as early as A.D. 166, certainly by A.D. 169); evidently this extraordinary power was conferred upon him in order to ensure the tranquillity and security of the eastern provinces while the emperor was busy with wars in the northern part of the empire. By the spring of A.D. 175 the empire appeared to be in such a state of difficulty that Cassius (perhaps instigated by the empress, who anticipated her husband's early death) judged it opportune to proclaim himself emperor. He had a reputation for harshness, but he had some claim to popularity in Syria, being a native of Cyrrhus, and he controlled Egypt, the granary of the empire, as well as Syria with its important army. What success he might eventually have had we cannot judge, for his revolt was brought to an end, after three months and six days, by his being murdered by two army officers.

The emperor had already set out for the east before Cassius' death.

[124] *SHA Verus* 7.6.
[125] On the date, see Debevoise, *Hist. of Parthia* 251.
[126] *SHA Verus* 8.2-3; Dio Cassius 71.2.4; Ammianus Marcellinus 23.6.24. For a detailed discussion of the epidemic, which was witnessed and described by Galen, see H. Haeser, *Lehrbuch der Gesch. der Medicin u. der epidemischen Krankheiten*[3] (Jena 1875-82) 3.24-33.
[127] See above, n. 118.
[128] *SHA Verus* 8.7-11.
[129] On the career of Avidius Cassius, and his revolt, see Harrer, *Studies* 32-36, 94; and R. Rémondon, "Les dates de la révolte de C. Avidius Cassius," *Chronique d'Egypte* 26 (1951) 364-377.

He appointed as legate of Syria Martius Verus, formerly one of the commanders in the Parthian war, who at the time of Cassius' revolt was governor of Cappadocia. Verus proceeded to Syria and set about restablishing the imperial authority.[130]

When the emperor reached Syria he adopted a policy of clemency toward the rebels, and he pardoned communities that had sided with Cassius, with the exception of Cyrrhus and Antioch, which had been centers of disaffection. He at first refused even to visit Antioch; and he abolished the local games of the city and forbade all public meetings, issuing an edict in which the people of the city were censured. The prohibition of public meetings and the abolition of the games were both necessary precautions against further plotting and revolution; the racing factions in particular, the Greens and the Blues, were active in politics and in the expression of popular discontent, and if the spectacles and races were abolished the factions would have no further opportunity for their dangerous activities.[131] Later, however, the emperor relented and did pay a visit to Antioch; and presumably on this occasion he revoked the penalties that he had imposed upon the city.[132] Marcus' daughter Lucilla, the widow of Verus, was married to Tiberius Claudius Pompeianus, a native of Antioch,[133] who was one of the emperor's most trusted friends, and this connection may have played

[130] Dio Cassius 71.29.2.

[131] *SHA Marcus Antoninus* 25.9-10; *Avidius Cassius* 9.1. In both texts, the word used is *spectacula*, which presumably means all the games and spectacles of the city, including the Olympic games. Malalas records (284.8-9) that the people of Antioch petitioned Commodus for the resumption of the Olympic and other spectacles (on this petition, and on the resumption of the games, see further below, §10). On the role of the circus factions in politics, see the study by Dvornik, "Circus Parties," in which the earlier literature on the subject is cited; and on the prohibition of the games at Antioch by Marcus Aurelius, see Gagé, "Les Perses à Antioche" 310. Parker, *Hist. of the Roman World A.D. 137-337*, 25, writes that Marcus on his arrival in Syria did not visit Antioch because Martius Verus was still engaged in subjecting the city. While this may have been the case, there is, so far as I have been able to discover, no indication to this effect in the sources. Marcus may at first have refused to visit the city in order to show his displeasure, and his later visit was evidently made after he was mollified. It may be significant in this connection that, according to the biography in the *SHA*, Marcus never did visit Cyrrhus, Cassius' birthplace.

[132] *SHA Marcus Antoninus* 25.8 and 12; *Avidius Cassius* 9.1. According to the reading of one MS in the life of Marcus Aurelius in the *Historia Augusta* (*Marc. Ant.* 25.12—26.1), Antioch was the scene of a meeting in which the emperor "conducted many negotiations with kings, and ratified peace with all the kings and satraps of Persia when they came to meet him" (transl. of D. Magie, Loeb Classical Library). This reading of the text, however, is not accepted by all editors, and it does not suit the context; thus it is not certain that such a meeting took place. The tradition of such a meeting is accepted by A. Solari, *L'Impero romano* 3 (Genoa etc. 1945) 197.

[133] *SHA Marcus Antoninus* 20.6-7; see E. Groag in *PIR²* vol. 3, no. C973, p. 234. For later activity of the family at Antioch, see below, n. 144.

some part in the emperor's decision to pardon the city. Then, too, Marcus, one of whose chief interests was the unification of the empire, may have realized that it was not politic to keep a city of the importance of Antioch perpetually in disgrace.

The public buildings of Marcus Aurelius at Antioch are not dated by Malalas, whose record constitutes our only source of knowledge concerning them; thus, it is not known whether they were constructed before the revolt of Avidius Cassius or after the city had been restored to favor following the revolt.[134] The emperor rebuilt a public bath called the Centenarium, which had fallen in the earthquake of Trajan's reign (A.D. 115).[135] *Centenarium* was the technical term for the largest size of water-pipe, which was made of sheets of lead which were one hundred Roman inches in width before they were bent into pipes. This size of pipe was ordinarily used only in aqueducts,[136] and its employment in the construction of a bath, which would mean that the bath had an unusually abundant supply of water, would be sufficiently unusual to cause the establishment to be called by the name of the remarkable pipe that it contained.[137]

The other public structure which Marcus erected at Antioch was a Museum, attached to which was a "sigma-shaped" Nymphaeum which later was called "the Ocean," because of a mosaic showing Ocean which was placed in it by the emperor Probus (A.D. 276-282), who at the same time added adornment to the Museum.[138] The Nymphaeum (presumably shaped like a "lunar" sigma or a "square" sigma) was evidently an ornamental façade placed on the front of the Museum.[139]

10. COMMODUS, A.D. 180-192; THE OLYMPIC GAMES

Commodus, the unworthy son of Marcus Aurelius, was born in

[134] Müller, *Antiq. Antioch.* 90-91, believed that the buildings were erected at the time when Marcus pardoned the city for its support of Cassius.

[135] Malalas 282.8-10. On the earthquake under Trajan, see above, §5.

[136] Vitruvius *De arch.* 8.6.4; see also the life of Pope Nicolaus (A.D. 858-867) in the *Liber Pontificalis* 2.154.9 ed. Duchesne.

[137] For an example of the use of a *centenarium* in a bath in Rome, see the life of Pope Hadrianus (A.D. 772-795) in the *Liber Pontificalis* 1.503.23ff. ed. Duchesne. A less plausible explanation of the use of the term as the name of the bath at Antioch would be that the building was one hundred feet long, or contained a chamber one hundred feet in length. Neither of these features, however, would seem to be sufficiently unusual to warrant the bath being given its name for that reason. On other uses of the term, see Kubitschek, "Centenarium," *RE* 3 (1899) 1926.

[138] Malalas 282.10-11; 302.7-9. On the cult of the Muses in Antioch and its neighborhood, see Mouterde, "Pierides Musae."

[139] On the plan and appearance of such nymphaeums, see Müller, *Antiq. Antioch.* 91, and Maass, *Tagesgötter* 157-160.

A.D. 161, and was made co-emperor with his father in A.D. 177. He became acquainted with Antioch when he visited it in company with his father during the imperial tour in the East in A.D. 175-176,[140] but he was never in the city again, as he did not leave Italy after becoming sole emperor.

Commodus' principal interest was in his own pleasures, and the government was largely conducted by his favorites. It is characteristic of the emperor's devotion to athletics and spectacles of all kinds, in which he himself liked to appear as a performer, that most of what is known of the history of Antioch during his reign is concerned with the Olympic Games and other festivals of the city. In this respect the history of Antioch seems to be characteristic of other eastern cities under Commodus. No major political events are known, but Nicomedia, through the influence of the powerful chamberlain Saoterus, who was originally a slave in that city, obtained the privilege of celebrating certain games and of erecting a temple to Commodus.[141]

The games and spectacles of Antioch, including the Olympic Games, had been abolished by Marcus Aurelius in A.D. 175/176 as a punishment for the city's support of the rebel Cassius.[142] Apparently soon after Commodus became sole emperor, the people of Antioch, knowing his passion for games and spectacles, presented a petition asking for permission to resume the Olympic Games and the other festivals of the city, and requesting as well that the financial arrangements for the games be reorganized.[143] The petition may have been supported by Claudius Pompeianus Quintianus, who was probably the nephew of Tiberius Claudius Pompeianus of Antioch, the son-in-law and trusted friend of Marcus Aurelius. The family, even though partly transplanted to Rome, would have had a special interest in the affairs of Antioch, and it is recorded that when the games were resumed under Commodus, the *grammateus* was a Pompeianus, who may have been Claudius Pompeianus Quintianus.[144] It would be easy to conjecture

[140] *SHA Commodus* 2.3; see the account of the reign of Marcus Aurelius, above, §9. On the reign of Commodus, see Parker, *Hist. of the Roman World A.D. 137-337*, 26ff. and W. Weber in *CAH* 9.376-392.
[141] Dio Cassius 73.12.2. Malalas relates (289.8-12) that Nicomedia suffered an earthquake during the reign of Commodus and that the emperor contributed to the restoration of the city; see Stauffenberg, *Malalas* 328.
[142] See above, n. 131.
[143] Here, as elsewhere in the history of the Olympic Games of Antioch, our knowledge comes largely from Malalas, who gives a detailed account of their reorganization and presentation in the time of Commodus, 283.1—290.2.
[144] The *grammateus* Pompeianus, who is called *quaestor*, is mentioned by Malalas 287.9. On the family, see *PIR*² vol. 3, nos. C 757, 973-975, pp. 163, 234-236. Tiberius

that this office was given to him in recognition of his or his family's
assistance in the reestablishment of the games.

The petition to Commodus was granted, and the Olympic games
were celebrated in the summer of A.D. 181; normally they were held
in Julian leap-years, so that a celebration ought to have been held in
A.D. 180, but there was evidently not time after the accession of Commodus, on 17 March 180, to present the petition, obtain approval, and
prepare for games in that year, so that A.D. 181 was the earliest date
at which they could have been held.[145]

At the same time that approval was given for the reestablishment of
the games, measures were taken (Malalas says) to place them on a
sounder financial basis. The income from the endowment for the upkeep of the games established by Sosibus in the time of Augustus[146]
had been misused by the successive officials of the games, who postponed or omitted celebrations of the festival and diverted the money
into their own pockets. To correct this abuse, the people of Antioch
requested the emperor to transfer the endowment to "the public
treasury" (τὸ δημόσιον), as Malalas says, so that the funds of the
festival might be officially controlled.[147] This request was granted in
the edict which reestablished the games; the decree likewise set forth
the requirements for the production of the games, which were to be
held in every fourth year for forty-five days during July and August.

Malalas gives an account of the principal offices connected with the
games at this time. Apparently the principal official was the Alytarch,
who seems to have been in charge of the actual performances of the
games. During his tenure of office he received divine honors, as the
representative of Zeus, in whose honor the games were held. He did
not sleep under a roof or in a bed, but carried out an ascetic ritual
of sleeping in the open air, in the courtyard of the Kaisarion, on clean
bedding and rush mats which were spread on the ground. He wore
a white robe ornamented with gold, a crown adorned with rubies and
pearls and other precious stones, and white sandals, and carried an
ebony rod. The first incumbent after the reorganization was Afranius,

---

Claudius Pompeianus may have been instrumental in obtaining pardon for the city
from Marcus Aurelius after the revolt of Cassius; see above, n. 133.

[145] A celebration in A.D. 181 is recorded in the *Chronicon Paschale* 490.8-16 Bonn ed.
Malalas' chronology is confused; see Downey, "Antioch under Severus and Caracalla"
146-156. On the celebration of the games in Julian leap years, see the same study, 148,
n. 22.

[146] See above, Ch. 8, n. 31.

[147] Malalas 284.1ff. Precisely what is meant by *to demosion* is not clear. This phrase
could probably be used about as loosely as one would say "the government."

an ex-prefect and citizen of Antioch.[148] The manner of his appointment is not stated.

The *grammateus* or secretary of the games was appointed by the senate and the people of the city; he received the honors paid to Apollo, and wore a white robe and a solid gold crown in the shape of laurel leaves. The first incumbent after reorganization was Pompeianus, of a Roman senatorial family, who, as has been suggested, may have been Claudius Pompeianus Quintianus, nephew of Tiberius Claudius Pompeianus.[149] The *amphithales*, also chosen by the senate and people, wore a white silk robe and a crown woven of laurel leaves, containing a gold bust (medallion?) of Zeus. He received the honors paid to Hermes. The name of the first incumbent after the reorganization is given as Κάσιος Ἰλλούστριος (Cassius Illustris?).[150]

Malalas also mentions the appointment, in the time of Commodus, of a Syriarch or presiding officer of the *koinon* (provincial assembly) of Syria, but the reference is brief and apparently garbled, and it is difficult to know what it really means.[151] This Syriarch, who on another occasion also served as Alytarch of the Olympic games, was named Artabanios (in Persian, Artabanes). It is significant of the importance at Antioch of persons of Persian blood or descent to find that a man with a Persian name was both wealthy enough and sufficiently promi-

---

[148] Malalas 286.12—287.7. There is, however, some reason to think that Afranius held office under Caracalla; see Downey, "Antioch under Severus and Caracalla" 153-154. On the Kaisarion, see above, Ch. 7, nn. 54-61.

[149] Malalas 287.8-12. On the Pompeiani, see above, nn. 133, 144.

[150] Malalas 287.13-18.

[151] In one passage (285.17-19) the chronicler records the appointment as "first Syriarch" of a citizen of Antioch named Artabanios (i.e. Artabanes). There must have been Syriarchs before Artabanes, for the existence of a *koinon* of Syria is attested at least as early as the time of Domitian (see above, nn. 36-38), and the assembly's title appears on a coin of Trajan (see above, n. 79). It may be that there was a reorganization of the *koinon* of Syria, or of its games, in the time of Commodus, and that Artabanes was thus the first of a new series of Syriarchs. Malalas, who never mentions the *koinon* of Syria or its games, might not have understood what happened in the time of Commodus, and he could easily suppose that Artabanes was the first Syriarch ever appointed. Later (289.13ff.) he states that the Alytarch Artabanes, after the completion of the Olympic games in Daphne, gave a free distribution of bread in Daphne. Stauffenberg in his text of Malalas, rashly corrected the title given in the latter passage to Syriarch, though there is no compelling reason to make the change; Artabanes might easily have held both offices on different occasions. The latter passage, even if it be supposed that Artabanes was Syriarch, does not necessarily show that the Syriarch was connected with the Olympic games at this time; Artabanes, a wealthy citizen, who happened to be Syriarch, might have chosen the termination of the Olympic festival as a suitable occasion for his act of magnificence. For a study of the question, see Downey, "Antioch under Severus and Caracalla" 153-154. The study of W. Liebschuetz, "The Syriarch in the Fourth Century," *Historia* 8 (1959) 113-126, appeared after this was written.

nent in the community to hold the offices of Syriarch and Alytarch.[152]

There is nothing to show whether any or all of the offices connected with the games at this period were liturgies, in which wealthy citizens contributed money or services (e.g. by providing performers and horses). In the fourth century the giving of the games was a liturgy, performed sometimes by an individual, sometimes by several persons.[153] In the time of Commodus there may still have been sufficient income from the legacy of Sosibus to provide for the games, and the state may have made a contribution as well. In any case the holding of an office connected with the games gave wealthy citizens an opportunity to display their munificence. Malalas records that when Artabanes was serving as Alytarch of the Olympic games, he gave a free distribution of bread in Daphne, after the completion of a celebration of the games, and established a fund for the future maintenance of the distribution. In gratitude the people of Antioch erected a marble statue of him in Daphne.[154]

To signalize the restoration of the games, various buildings were erected. The most important of these, for the games, was the *Xystos*, a covered running-track. This was of the Greek type, roofed and with a colonnade and seats, so that it could be used by athletes in rainy weather or during excessive heat.[155] It is to be noted that the *Xystos* was built in Antioch, not in Daphne where the principal part of the celebration was held; presumably it was not intended to restrict the use of the *Xystos* to the Olympic Games, and it was located in the city so that it could be employed for other athletic purposes. The *Xystos* was built as a part of an important complex of public buildings which was developed at this time. It stood opposite the temple of Athena, which was restored on the occasion of the building of the *Xystos*; and on the other side of the *Xystos* a public bath named for Commodus was erected. At the lower end of the *Xystos* itself was built a temple to Olympian Zeus, the patron of the games.[156]

---

[152] On the Persian influence at Antioch, see further below, Ch. 10, n. 100.

[153] See Downey, "Olympic Games."

[154] Malalas 289.13-290.2. The generosity of Artabanes is also recorded in the *Chronicon Paschale* 490.8-16 Bonn ed. (where no title is given to him).

[155] Malalas (283.7-8) mentions the colonnade and seats. Müller (*Antiq. Antioch.* 94) believes that the *Xystos* was of the Roman type, which was hypaethral. On the distinction between the types, see Vitruvius 6.7.5; cf. H. Graillot, "Xystos," Daremberg-Saglio, *Dict. des antiq.* 5.1025-1027. The *Xystos* at Olympia was 210.50 m. long and 11.30 m. broad; so far as is known it contained no seats; see G. Fougères, "Gymnasium," Daremberg-Saglio, *Dict. des antiq.* 2.1694. For other such buildings, see elsewhere in Fougères' article.

[156] Malalas 283.4-9. Commodus' biographer in the *Historia Augusta* (17.5-7) says that

Other festivals and entertainments at Antioch were reorganized at the same time. In the decree by which the Olympic Games were re-established, Commodus also made provision (Malalas says) for the payment out of public funds of "certain sums" (the amount is not specified) for the support of several entertainments.[157] Among these, the best known is the Maiouma, presumably a survival of an old Syrian cult, which in the time of Commodus had come to be an orgiastic nocturnal festival honoring (at least in part) Dionysus and Aphrodite; celebrated every three years, in May, it acquired a reputation for licentiousness. Commodus' decree provided for the purchase with public money of lamps, candles, and other supplies and equipment.[158] Another entertainment that became a public charge was the series of horse races which, Malalas says, were held weekly on the day of the Sun. A third appropriation was made for the hunts of wild beasts which were held in connection with the festivals of Ares and Artemis. Apparently provision was now made to assure the supply of animals, which, it seems, were being used up more rapidly than they could be collected; Commodus' decree provided that in each period of four years, hunts were to be held only during forty-two months, while they were to be suspended for six months during which beasts were to be assembled.[159] Finally, the decree provided for the public support of mimes and dancers.[160] In gratitude for all these benefactions, the people of Antioch set up a bronze statue of Commodus.[161]

the emperor left no buildings of his own, though he inscribed his name on the works of others. There is, however, epigraphic evidence from Corinth and Athens which indicates that this accusation is not wholly true, or is at least exaggerated; see R. Scranton, "Two Temples of Commodus at Corinth," *Hesperia* 13 (1944) 315-348, esp. 346-348, and A. E. Raubitschek, "Commodus and Athens," *Hesperia Suppl.* 8 (1949) 290 (*Commemorative Studies in Honor of T. L. Shear*). Since the evidence of Malalas on such matters is not always trustworthy, the record of the buildings at Antioch cannot safely be interpreted as telling for or against the assertion of the *SHA*. It is possible that the people of Antioch initiated and paid for the work and named the bath for the emperor in gratitude for his restoration of the games. The bath of Commodus later became the praetorium of the consularis Syriae (Malalas 338.19ff.; see below Excursus 12).

[157] Malalas 284.18—285.16, 285.20—286.4.

[158] On the Maiouma, see Müller, *Antiq. Antioch.* 33, with n. 6, and Preisendanz, "Maïumas," *RE* 14 (1930) 610-612.

[159] Malalas, 285.12-16. His account might be taken to mean that the hunts were to be held during forty-two successive months, followed by a period of six months without hunts. It would seem, however, that it would have been more practical, as well as more satisfactory to the devotees of the sport, to space several periods of suspension (totaling six months) through the four-year period.

[160] Malalas 285.12-16.

[161] Malalas 286.4-5. The statue is said to have been placed "in the middle of the city," but there is no more precise identification of its location, and no other reference to it appears to have been preserved. Presumably "in the middle of the city" is a way of saying that it was in a prominent place.

We know from several inscriptions[162] that there was a festival at Antioch which was named for the emperor (τὸν Κομόδειον). Whether this was one of the festivals described above, or was a further celebration of which there is no other record, we do not know. In other cities of the East, Commodus' name was added to the titles of existing festivals, as a compliment to the emperor or as a token of appreciation for imperial assistance following misfortunes, especially earthquakes.[163] In the case of Antioch, since the title of the festival as we have it consists only of the emperor's name, it would appear that either an existing festival was renamed or (perhaps less likely) a wholly new one founded. When Commodus' memory was officially condemned by the Senate following his death, his name was removed from the titles of the festivals that had been named for him.

[162] *Fouilles de Delphes* vol. 3, pt. 1, no. 550, line 34 (=Waddington no. 1257); Edhem Bey, "Fouilles de Tralles," *BCH* 28 (1904) 87-88; M. Gough, "Anazarbus," *Anatolian Studies* 2 (1952) 128-129.
[163] For examples see Magie, *Asia Minor* 668, 1538, and T. T. Duke, "The Festival Chronology of Laodicea ad Lycum," *Studies Presented to D. M. Robinson* 2 (St. Louis 1953) 853-854.

CHAPTER 10

FROM THE DEATH OF COMMODUS TO THE ACCESSION OF DIOCLETIAN, A.D. 192-284

1. The Struggle for Power in a.d. 193-194;

The Attempts of Pertinax, Didius Julianus, and Pescennius Niger, and the Success of Septimius Severus

THE DEATH of Commodus without an heir (31 December 192) created a situation not unlike that which followed the assassination of Nero. Two emperors, Pertinax and Didius Julianus, were proclaimed and assassinated in quick succession and a third aspirant, Pescennius Niger, appeared in Syria before the government passed effectively into the hands of Septimius Severus.

Pertinax, so far as we know, had no connection with Antioch during his brief reign (1 January—28 March 193), though he had begun his military career in Syria and had been governor of the province ca. 180-182.[1] However, during the even briefer reign of Didius Julianus (28 March—1 June 193) Antioch, along with the remainder of Syria, played a role in the struggle for power. The proclamation of Didius Julianus as emperor was unpopular with the people of Rome, and they at once began to call for help from the armies, and especially for assistance from Pescennius Niger, the governor of Syria, and his troops.[2] This news would have traveled to Syria quickly, and could have reached Antioch by the middle of April. Pescennius was immediately proclaimed emperor in Antioch by his soldiers, and he proceeded to make the city his headquarters, using the mint there to issue his own coins, and receiving delegations from the rulers of the frontier states to the east.[3] At about the same time, P. Septimius Severus, the governor of Upper Pannonia, was proclaimed emperor by his troops. Didius Julianus, we are told, was not particularly concerned by the action of the Illyrian army, but was very much afraid of Pescennius Niger and

---

[1] *SHA Pertinax* 1.6, 2.1, 2.11; Harrer, *Studies* 38-39; Fluss, "P. Helvius Pertinax," *RE* Suppl. 3 (1918) 895-904.

[2] Dio Cassius—Xiphilinus 74.13.5. Pescennius Niger had been governor of Syria since 190 or 191: Harrer, *Studies* 42; W. Reusch, "C. Pescennius Niger," *RE* 19 (1938) 1092.

[3] Herodian 2.7.9—2.8.8; Reusch in *RE* 19.1088; H. Mattingly, "The Coinage of Septimius Severus and his Times," *Num. Chron.* ser. 5, vol. 12 (1932) 178-180; T. O. Mabbott, "On the Coinage of Pescennius Niger," *Numismatic Review* 3 (1946) 145-150; H. Mattingly in *BMC Rom. Emp.* 5, pp. cvii-cxiv. On Pescennius Niger's activities at Antioch, see further below, n. 10.

his forces, for Syria was a powerful factor at that time, as it had been on other occasions.[4]

It was during the reign of Didius Julianus, according to Malalas,[5] that the Plethrion at Antioch was built to accommodate the wrestling contests in the local Olympic Games. Previously, Malalas says, these wrestling matches had been held "in the theater," but this had presumably come to be considered unsuitable for the purpose, so that (the chronicler relates) the people of Antioch presented a petition to the emperor, and he granted money for the construction of the Plethrion. The building was presumably not an elaborate one. If the archetype of such structures received its name from the measure *plethron*, it would presumably have been either 100 feet long, or 10,000 square feet in area; and Libanius, writing in the first half of the fourth century, speaks of the original Plethrion at Antioch as a structure of modest size, with two rows of stone seats for spectators.[6] According to Malalas, it was located near the Kaisarion, the *Xystos*, and the Bath of Commodus, on ground formerly occupied by the house of a Jewish curialis named Asabinos, which was purchased for the purpose.

Whether the building was actually constructed in the circumstances that Malalas records is not clear. It is, of course, quite possible that, as the chronicler says, the people of Antioch simply addressed a petition to the emperor and that he granted funds as they requested; Didius Julianus is said to have been "very courteous in the matter of petitions."[7] However, there would also seem to be the possibility that the Plethrion was planned as a part of the series of structures for use in the Olympic games inaugurated under Commodus,[8] and that it happened, as the last of this series, to be "built" (i.e. either started or completed) in

---

[4] *SHA Didius Julianus* 5.1; Herodian 2.7.4.

[5] 290-14-20.

[6] In addition to the passage in Malalas, most of our knowledge of the Plethrion at Antioch and its use comes from the oration (10) in which Libanius in A.D. 383/4 protested against its enlargement. (See Appendices, Translation of Documents, 2.) At the time when Libanius wrote, the building was used for trials or preliminary contests of the athletes who came to Antioch intending to enter the Olympic Games. Libanius out of regard for classical usage, calls the building Plethron, not Plethrion. According to Pausanias (6.23.2; see also Lucian, *The Passing of Peregrinus* 31) the Plethrion used in the original Olympic Games was in the gymnasium at Elis; the athletes who wished to enter the wrestling contests went to this Plethrion before the games began, and were there matched by the *hellanodikai* according to age and skill; see J. Wiesner, "Olympia," *RE* 18 (1939) 8. Malalas employs the Byzantine diminutive form: τὸ Πλεθρίν, acc., 290.14-17 (twice) and τοῦ Πλεθρίον, 339.1; on the spelling and meaning of the word cf. Chilmead's note on Malalas 290.14, p. 586 Bonn ed., and Müller, *Antiq. Antioch.* 95, n. 9.

[7] *SHA Didius Julianus* 9.2.   [8] See above, Ch. 9, §10.

the reign of Didius Julianus. One further possibility also occurs, and
that is that Didius Julianus, knowing the pleasure-loving character
of the people of Antioch, presented them with the building in an effort
to win them away from Pescennius Niger. Didius Julianus was, we are
told, anxious to win popularity and support by bestowing favors, and
in addition was himself fond of spectacles;[9] and he may well have hit
upon this rather fatuous method of trying to undermine the pretender.

2. THE DEFEAT OF PESCENNIUS NIGER, A.D. 194

After Didius Julianus was condemned to death by the Senate, and
killed on 1 June 193, it was the first task of the new emperor, Septimius
Severus, to deal with Pescennius Niger, who was collecting strong
support in Syria and was actually more popular in Rome than Severus
himself.[10] Many of Pescennius' troops were from Antioch, and almost
all the young men of the city had joined his forces.[11] Early in July 193,
Severus left Rome and, gaining control of Asia Minor, forced Pescennius to fall back on Antioch, where he collected fresh troops and resources.[12] Here he was distracted by the jealousy and rivalry between
Antioch and Laodicea, which had declared for Severus.[13] The two

[9] Dio Cassius-Xiphilinus 74-14.1. The shortness of the reign of Didius Julianus (28
March—1 June 193) might make it seem unlikely that he initiated the construction of
the Plethrion himself, and he is not known to have had any special interest in Syria or
in Antioch (cf. von Wotawa, "Didius," no. 8, *RE* 5. 412-424). On the other hand he is
said, in the biography of him in the Scriptores Historiae Augustae, to have declared
when he was proclaimed emperor that he would restore the good name of Commodus,
i.e. on monuments and in public records (3. 6); later in the same work it is said that
"in order to win favor with the people, Julianus restored many measures which Commodus had enacted and Pertinax had repealed" (4. 8, transl. of David Magie; cf. von
Wotawa, *op.cit.* 420). Since Commodus restored and reorganized the Olympic Games
of Antioch, it might seem likely that the construction of the Plethrion was planned or
ordered by Commodus (who was murdered 31 Dec. 192), but was carried out or completed by Julianus; Malalas would very probably attribute the building wholly to Julianus
if he found a statement in a source that he completed it, even if the source said at the
same time that it had been begun by Commodus. It is not impossible that Commodus'
name would not be associated with the building in Malalas' source because of the
damnatio memoriae which he suffered.
[10] For a clear account of the revolt of Pescennius, see Magie, *Asia Minor* 669-672.
Herodian declares (2.8.9) that Pescennius Niger, when he was in Antioch after his
proclamation as emperor, was unduly elated and confident, and that he neglected to
make the proper preparations for the coming struggle, giving himself over to luxurious
living and to festivals and spectacles instead. That this account is not only not true, but
is probably invented by Herodian, who liked to give his narrative a romantic tinge, is
demonstrated by the careful study of G. M. Bersanetti, "Sulla guerra fra Settimio
Severo e Pescennio Nigro in Erodiano," *Rivista di Filologia e d'Istruzione classica* 66
(1938) 357-364. Herodian's account is followed faithfully by John of Antioch, frag. 124,
FHG 4, p. 586 = frag. 50, *Excerpta de insidiis* ed. De Boor, p. 91.
[11] Herodian 3.1.4, 3.3.3.   [12] Herodian 3.2.10.
[13] Herodian 3.3.3. On the rivalry between Antioch and Laodicea, see below, n. 27.

armies met in the spring of 194 at Issus, and Pescennius, his forces completely routed, was defeated.[14] Pescennius fled on horseback to Antioch and found the city full of lamentation for its men who had fallen in the battle. Evidently it was clear that Pescennius could expect no more support from Antioch, and his only recourse was to flee, with some of his soldiers. According to some accounts, he was caught and executed in one of the suburbs of the city;[15] and Antioch surrendered to the imperial troops.[16]

3. Antioch in the Reign of Septimius Severus, a.d. 193-211

Septimius, in order to guard against any future attempt by a governor of the powerful province of Syria to make himself emperor, divided the province into two, Syria Coele and Syria Phoenice (late 194 or early 195).[17] Special punishment was devised for Antioch, not only because it had supported Pescennius Niger and had served as his headquarters but because its citizens, always independent in spirit, had seen fit to make fun of Septimius Severus when he was stationed in the city in a.d. 179 in command of the Fourth Legion (Scythica).[18] For the punishment of Antioch, Septimius had at his disposal a peculiarly effective device.[19] Laodicea, which with Antioch was one of the four

[14] The date of the battle has been disputed; the present writer follows the opinion of Magie, *Asia Minor* 1539-1540, n. 20, who reviews the evidence and the various interpretations of it and concludes that the battle took place in May or later. G. A. Harrer, "The Chronology of the Revolt of Pescennius Niger," *JRS* 10 (1920) 162-168 (followed by S. N. Miller in *CAH* 12.6) places the battle in March or April, but this seems too early. On the inscriptional evidence, see Murphy, *The Reign of the Emperor L. Septimius Severus* 2-4. H. Mattingly, in the introduction to *BMC Rom. Emp.* 5 (1950) pp. lxxx-lxxxi, assigns the battle to early 195.

[15] Herodian 3.4.6; Amm. Marc. 26.8.15. According to Dio Cassius—Xiphilinus 75.8.3, Pescennius was taken while in flight toward the Euphrates. See W. Reusch, "Pescennius," *RE* 19 (1938) 1099-1100.

[16] Dio Cassius' words (*loc.cit.*) ἁλούσης δὲ τῆς 'Αντιοχείας do not seem necessarily to indicate or imply that Antioch resisted the imperial troops and had to be captured. It seems more likely that the complete defeat of Pescennius' troops at Issus, with heavy loss of life, would have alienated the people of Antioch, so that they would have offered no resistance to Severus; Dio's words need mean no more than "when Antioch was occupied," i.e. as a result of its surrender.

[17] Harrer, *Studies* 87-90. An inscription of Palmyra shows that the division had taken place at the end of 194 or the beginning of 195: H. Ingholt, "Deux inscriptions bilingues de Palmyre," *Syria* 13 (1932) 282-286. This text has apparently escaped the notice of Murphy, *The Reign of the Emperor L. Septimius Severus* 43-44. On the title Syria Coele, which was a revival of an ancient name, see E. Bikerman, "La Coelé-Syrie: Notes de géographie historique," *Rev. bibl.* 54 (1947) 256-268.

[18] *SHA Severus* 3.6.7, 9.4; see Fluss, "L. Septimius Severus," *RE* 2A (1923) 1945-1946. The reason why the people of Antioch had laughed at Septimius is not specifically stated (*SHA Severus* 9.4), but either his frugality (*ibid.* 17.6, 19.7-8) or his unbending character (Fluss, *op.cit.* 2001) would have been likely to excite their ridicule.

[19] It may be a significant commentary on Septimius' experience at Antioch that his

principal foundations of Seleucus Nicator in northwestern Syria, had
been from the beginning jealous of Antioch,[20] which, originally equal
with Laodicea in rank and size, had soon become the principal city
of Syria, then the capital of the Roman province, and one of the great
cities of the ancient world. The people of Antioch, never noted for
tact or modesty, very likely took no trouble to ease any of the numerous
and varied causes of neighborly friction which formed a regular feature
in the life of the Greek cities.[21] As Dio Chrysostom pointed out in
another connection, a weaker and inferior city always assumed the
air of being the injured party,[22] and in addition Laodicea possessed
many advantages of situation and climate that would have caused its
people to feel that their city could justly be compared with Antioch
and was in fact superior to it in some respects.[23] Laodicea possessed a
better strategic position than Antioch, and the conformation of its site
permitted much better drainage than Antioch enjoyed.[24] The climate
at Laodicea was mild and free from extremes; both cities must have
taken note of the fact that when Verus spent four years in Syria during
his Parthian war (A.D. 162-165), he spent his winters in Laodicea,
though he lived in Daphne in the summers and at Antioch the remainder of the time.[25] Laodicea had a good port (Libanius in his
encomium of Antioch dwells on the dangers and disagreeable features
of life in a seaport),[26] and its fertile territory supplied excellent crops
(the wine of Laodicea was widely exported) as well as abundant
building stone and wood; and pure water was plentiful.[27]

---

biographer in the *SHA* notes (3.7) that when Septimius lived in Athens as a private
citizen in A.D. 180, just after leaving his military post in Syria, he suffered certain wrongs
or affronts (*iniuriae quaedam*) from the Athenians. Again details are not given, and
we can only speculate whether there may have been some particular reason why Septimius should have fallen into disfavor at both Antioch and Athens in succession.

[20] Theodoret *Hist. eccl.* 5.19 = *PG* 82.1240 B.

[21] See Jones, *Greek City* 249.

[22] *Or.* 34.11; on rivalries and disputes between cities, see further in the remainder of
this oration, also *Orations* 38 and 40. Dio Chrysostom also speaks of the rivalry of
Apamea with Antioch (*Or.* 34.48).

[23] The situation and physical advantages of Laodicea are well summed up by Sauvaget, "Plan de Laodicée-sur-mer" 114.

[24] On the disadvantages of the site of Antioch, see above, Ch. 4, §2.

[25] *SHA Verus* 7.3.

[26] *Or.* 11.35ff.

[27] Ammianus Marcellinus (14.8.8) lists Laodicea as one of the most flourishing cities
of Syria after Antioch. E. Honigmann rightly observes ("Laodikeia," *RE* 12 [1925]
715) that Laodicea should never actually have aspired to rival Antioch in rank; but
the considerations pointed out above indicate that it could with some justice have
imagined itself a rival of Antioch in some other ways. Libanius (*Ep.* 1348 W = 1262
F.) speaks with respect of the state of education and learning in Laodicea.

Septimius took full advantage of this situation. Antioch was deprived of its title of metropolis and of its position as the capital of Syria, and was made a *kome* or village of Laodicea, which was given the *ius Italicum* and the title of metropolis and was made the capital of Syria Coele, *ob belli civilis merita*.[28] Septimius conferred many other benefits on Laodicea, and presented it with public buildings, and its mint became the principal eastern mint.[29] Tyre, Sebaste (Samaria), Rhesaena, Nisibis and Zaytha were similarly rewarded for their services in the civil war.[30] As a further humiliation to Antioch, Septimius removed the local Olympic festival from the city and combined it with the games that he instituted at Issus in commemoration of his victory over Niger. This measure was also necessary politically, since the factions of the circus, the Greens and the Blues, were active political parties, serving as focal points for discontent and for opposition to the administration and as potential sources of revolution and disorder.[31] This change was presumably made effective in 196.[32] The necessity of these devices with

[28] *Dig.* 50.15.1.3.

[29] Herodian 3.6.9; *SHA Severus* 9.4; Ulpian *Dig.* 50.15.1.3; Paulus *Dig.* 50.15.8.3; Malalas 293.23ff.; Suidas *s.v.* Σεβῆρος; Waddington no. 1839 = *IGRR* 3, no. 1012; cf. Eckhel, *Doct. Num.* 3.317-319; Marquardt, *Staatsverwaltung*[2] 1.423-430; G. M. Harper, Jr., "Village Administration in the Roman Province of Syria," *Yale Class. Stud.* 1 (1928) 115; E. Kornemann, "Coloniae," *RE* 4 (1901) 552, 581; W. Reusch, "Pescennius," *ibid.* 19 (1938) 1098; J. Hasebroek, *Untersuch. zur Gesch. des Kaisers Sept. Severus* (Heidelberg 1921) 64-68; E. Honigmann, "Laodikeia," *RE* 12 (1925) 715; H. Mattingly in *BMC Rom. Emp.* 5 (1950), pp. cxxii, clxi; idem, "The Coinage of Septimius Severus and his Times," *Num. Chron.* ser. 5, vol. 12 (1932) 177-198. The actual date of the degradation of Antioch is not known; presumably it was effected promptly, probably about the time of the division of the province of Syria. The basis of the statement of Parker, *Hist. of the Roman World A.D. 138-337* 64, that the theaters and buildings of Antioch were razed to the ground, is not clear. Possibly this assertion rests upon Herodian's account (3.6.9) of the treatment of Byzantium. After the riots of A.D. 387 Antioch was again punished by being made a *kome* of Laodicea (see Ch. 15, n. 103).

[30] Murphy, *The Reign of the Emperor L. Septimius Severus* 50-51.

[31] The transfer of the Olympic Games, and their combination with the Severan games at Issus, is shown by coins and by evidence in Malalas, which has been obscured by errors and misunderstanding; see Downey, "Antioch under Severus and Caracalla." For the coins, see W. Kubitschek, *Num. Ztschr.* 27 (1895) 87-100; *BMC Lycaonia* etc. (London 1900), p. xciii; Mionnet, *Descr. de médailles* 3, p. 629, no. 449, p. 635, no. 479, and Suppl. 7, p. 264, no. 428, p. 272, no. 459; Eckhel, *Doct.num.* 3.79; B. V. Head, *Hist. Num.*[2] (Oxford 1911) 733. See also (for coins of Gordian and Valerian with the legend Σευήρεια) Mionnet 3, p. 649, no. 750, and Suppl. 7, p. 283, nos. 514, 516; E. Babelon, *Invent. de la coll. Waddington* (Paris 1898) no. 4672; Eckhel, *Doct. num.* 3.78; cf. Hartmann, "Sebereia," *RE* 2 A (1923) 963, and Magie, *Asia Minor* 1540, n. 21. On the political activities of the circus parties, see the study by Dvornik, "Circus parties," in which references are given to the previous literature on the subject; and on Septimius Severus' measures at Antioch, see Gagé, "Les Perses à Antioche" 311.

[32] Since the Olympic Games were celebrated in Julian leap years (see above, Ch. 9, n. 145), 196 would have been the first year in which the games would have been held after the defeat of Pescennius.

a city such as Antioch is shown by the fact that similar measures had been taken by Marcus Aurelius, who abolished the games and public assemblies of Antioch after the city had supported the rebel Avidius Cassius,[33] while such treatment was again adopted by Theodosius I after the riots of A.D. 387, when Antioch was again made a *kome* of Laodicea.[34]

While Antioch was in disgrace, it served as the headquarters for Septimius' war against the Parthians, which was carried on in A.D. 197 and 198.[35] Eventually, however, Antioch was restored to favor. After his rule was securely established, Septimius adopted a policy of conciliating provincial opinion, in which he showed marked favor to Africa, where he had been born, and to Syria, the native land of his wife, Julia Domna, a member of a Syrian high-priestly family.[36] Late in 201 Septimius went from Egypt, which he had been visiting (A.D. 199-201), to Antioch, in order to show, by visiting the city, that it was no longer in disfavor. While he was there, Septimius invested his son, the future emperor Caracalla, with the *toga virilis* (an important ceremony, which normally would have taken place in Rome), and immediately thereafter, still in Antioch, the two entered upon a joint consulship—a rare event—on 1 January 202.[37] Coins of Antioch issued in A.D. 202 show the Tyche of Antioch, evidently as a token of the rehabilitation of the city.[38] Moreover, Septimius presented Antioch with a large public bath on the slope of the mountain, which was named the Severianum.[39] He likewise ordered the construction of another public bath on the level ground near the river, on a site, purchased for the purpose, which had been occupied by the house, with a bath and a garden, of a lady named Livia. This bath was given the name Livianum because, Malalas says, the magistrates out of jealousy for each other could not agree upon any other name for it. The emperor ordered that

---

[33] See Ch. 9, n. 131.

[34] See Ch. 15, n. 103.

[35] Murphy, *The Reign of the Emperor L. Septimius Severus* 21-27; the epigraphic evidence, which Murphy studies, is more significant than the brief and unsatisfactory accounts of Dio Cassius (75.9-12) and *SHA Severus* (15-16).

[36] Gertrud Herzog, "Iulia Domna," *RE* 10 (1919) 929; Murphy, *The Reign of the Emperor L. Septimius Severus* 46-51.

[37] *SHA Severus* 16.8; cf. P. M. Meyer, "Papyrusbeiträge zur röm. Kaisergesch.," *Klio* 7 (1907) 133; Fluss, "L. Septimius Severus," *RE* 2 A (1923) 1973; Stauffenberg, *Malalas* 350. On the coins with which this joint consulship was celebrated, see H. Mattingly in *BMC Rom. Emp.* 5 (1950) p. cxlvi. This event naturally aroused the resentment of Antioch's ancient enemy Laodicea; see Mattingly *op.cit.* p. clxvii.

[38] Bellinger, *Tetradrachms of Caracalla and Macrinus* 21, see also 6.

[39] Malalas 294.17-19.

its construction be financed from a surplus which had accumulated in the municipal funds allotted for the heating of the public baths; evidently certain baths were no longer in use (Malalas says that they had "fallen," whether because of earthquakes or from disrepair is not clear), and the money set aside for their heating was not being spent.[40] It is said that it was at the intervention of Caracalla that Septimius restored its "old rights" to Antioch. This may represent a device suggested by Septimius, partly in order to advance his son in the public eye, partly to provide an excuse for the revoking of his punishment of Antioch, though it might only be an inference on the part of Caracalla's biographer, based on the favor that he later showed toward Antioch.[41]

The Olympic Games were not restored to Antioch until the accession of Caracalla, presumably because Septimius did not wish to detract from his own games at Issus, possibly also because he did not see fit to effect the complete rehabilitation of Antioch at once.[42]

4. ANTIOCH UNDER CARACALLA, A.D. 211-217

Severus died at York on 4 February 211, and was succeeded by his sons Caracalla, who was twenty-five years old (he was born probably in A.D. 186),[43] and Geta. The brothers, who had recently been joint

[40] Malalas 294.19ff. A comparable order for the disposition of surplus municipal funds is contained in *Cod. Just.* 10.30.4 (A.D. 530). The cost of heating public baths seems to have been one of the principal items in municipal budgets; see Jones, *Greek City* 253, and cf. P. Oxy. 2127; Arcadius Charisius *Dig.* 50.4.18.5; *Cod. Theod.* 15.1.32; *Cod. Just.* 1.4.26; Just., *Edict* 13.14, and *Nov.* 160. Malalas' phrase (294.20) ἐγκαυστικὰ χρήματα does not seem to appear elsewhere (the term is λουτρωνικὰ χρήματα in *Cod. Just.* 1.4.26 and 10.30.4), but the meaning, as L. Dindorf perceived (*s.v.* ἐγκαυστικός, Stephanus, *Thesaur. Graec.*, ed. C. B. Hase, W. and L. Dindorf) seems clear; cf. οἶκοι ἐγκαιόμενοι in Lucian, *Ver. Hist.* 2.11. Müller, *Antiq. Antioch.* 97, who was apparently not familiar with the evidence cited above, took Malalas' words to mean money that was realized from the sale of building materials salvaged from baths destroyed by fire. This interpretation fails to take into account the implication of the word περισσεία ("surplus") which Malalas uses, and likewise does violence to the term χρήματα, which in Malalas always means "money."

[41] *SHA Caracalla* 1.7. Domaszewski, "Personennamen bei den S.H.A." 34, n. 2, is mistaken in stating that Caracalla delivered a speech in the Roman senate on behalf of Antioch and Byzantium. The inscription that he cites in support of this (*Forsch. in Ephesos* 2, pp. 125-126, no. 26) records a communication of Caracalla to the people of Ephesus, conveying his thanks for a *psephisma* of congratulation on the occasion of a victory of Septimius, and discussing a petition addressed to Caracalla on behalf of the temple of Artemis at Ephesus. The inscription shows that Caracalla was friendly toward the Ephesians, but it furnishes no support of Domaszewski's statement with regard to Antioch and Byzantium. Domaszewski's hypothesis is adopted by J. Hasebroek, *Untersuch. zur Gesch. d. Kaisers Sept. Severus* (Heidelberg 1921) 106 and by Reusch, "Caracallavita" 11.

[42] On the restoration of the Olympic Games at Antioch, see below, n. 50.

[43] On the year of his birth, see P. von Rohden, "M. Aurelius Antoninus (Caracalla)," *RE* 2 (1896) 2439.

rulers with their father, had already come to complete disagreement, and had even thought of dividing the empire, Caracalla taking the West and Geta the East; and if this plan had been put into effect, Geta would have chosen either Antioch or Alexandria as his capital.[44] The arrangement, however, was not carried out, and a year after Septimius' death Caracalla murdered Geta (26 February 212) and killed a number of prominent persons, including Papinian, whom he suspected. His reign thus began under the most unfavorable auspices.

Caracalla had been in Antioch several times as a child. He had stayed in the city when he accompanied his father as far as the Syrian capital during Septimius' campaigns against Pescennius (A.D. 194), in Mesopotamia (A.D. 195) and against the Parthians (autumn A.D. 197).[45] Moreover, as has been noted, two major events of his early life took place at Antioch when his father visited the city in the winter of A.D. 201/2.[46] It was on this occasion that Caracalla had received the *toga virilis* and had entered upon a joint consulship with his father.[47] Caracalla, when he became emperor, thus had good reason to be well disposed toward Antioch; and in more general terms, the chief city of Syria would have a claim upon him in that his mother, the brilliant and masterful Julia Domna, was a member of a native royal dynasty of Emesa.[48]

The civil measure by which Caracalla is best known is the promulgation (A.D. 212) of the *Constitutio Antoniniana*, the edict which granted Roman citizenship to all the free inhabitants of the empire, with certain special exceptions. This measure actually only completed a process which was already well advanced (Septimius had followed a policy of political and social leveling); its ulterior significance is that the gesture, made so soon after Caracalla's accession, was plainly an effort to gain the good will of his subjects, who had been revolted by his murder of his brother Geta and of Geta's supposed associates and supporters.[49] These motives suggest a further reason for the generosity that Caracalla displayed toward Antioch. First of all, the emperor not only restored

[44] Herodian 4.3.7.
[45] *SHA Severus* 10.3, 16.3, 16.7; cf. von Rohden in *RE* 2.2440-2441.
[46] For Septimius' punishment of Antioch, see above, n. 28.
[47] *SHA Severus* 16.8. See above, n. 37.
[48] See above, n. 36.
[49] On the *Constitutio Antoniniana*, see now the detailed study by C. Sasse, *Die Constitutio Antoniniana* (Wiesbaden 1958), also the important observations of Magie, *Asia Minor* 687, with n. 48 on p. 1555. As Magie observes, the measure was probably taken by the imperial council rather than by the emperor himself. In either case, the motives would be the same.

to the city its Olympic Games, which his father had transferred to Issus, but did this with noteworthy promptness, so that they could be celebrated in the summer of A.D. 212, which was the first occasion during his reign (and the first occasion after his murder of Geta) on which these games (traditionally held in Julian leap years) could be celebrated.[50]

In addition to returning to the city its chief traditional festival, Caracalla restored the civic pride of Antioch by granting it the title of colony.[51] Politically this title was at this time practically meaningless; it was, however, a coveted distinction,[52] and it had special significance in the circumstances, in placing Antioch nominally on the same level as Laodicea, which had been made a *colonia iuris Italici* by Septimius.[53]

[50] The evidence may be recovered from the chronicle of Malalas, in which it has become obscured; see the study of the problem by Downey, "Antioch under Severus and Caracalla." As has been pointed out, Septimius evidently refrained from returning the Olympic Games to Antioch because he did not wish to detract from the games that he had instituted at Issus in honor of his victory over Pescennius Niger.

[51] Paulus *Dig.* 50.15.8.5: *Divus Antoninus Antiochenses colonos fecit salvis tributis.* Mommsen pointed out ("Die Kaiserbezeichnung bei den röm. Juristen," *Ztschr. f. Rechtsgesch.* 9 [1870] 111 = *Gesam. Schr.* 2.167-168) that the *divus Antoninus* mentioned here must be Caracalla, since the local coins begin to bear the title of colony during his reign; cf. Eckhel, *Doct. num.* 3.302; Mionnet, *Descr. de médailles* 5.205-214, and Suppl. 8.145-147; *BMC Galatia etc.* 205ff.; S. H. Weber, in *Antioch-on-the-Orontes* 1.78-79. For a detailed study of this measure, see Downey, "Political Status of Roman Antioch," adding, to the bibliography cited there, A. H. M. Jones, "Civitates liberae et immunes in the East," *Anatolian Studies Presented to William Hepburn Buckler* (Manchester 1939) 103-117, and W. Schwann, "Tributum," *RE* 7 A (1939) 46. Most scholars follow Mommsen, *Röm. Staatsrecht* (Leipzig 1887-1888) 3, p. 684, n. 1 and p. 807, n. 2, in believing that *salvis tributis* (apparently a unique phrase) means that Antioch had to pay tribute even after it became a colony ("the tribute remaining unimpaired, untouched"); Kornemann alone has dissented ("Coloniae," *RE* 4 [1901] 579), believing that *salvis tributis* means that Caracalla abolished the tribute that Antioch had formerly had to pay. It seems beyond doubt that Mommsen is right; see Downey, *op.cit.* 2-3 and 6. Mommsen believed that Antioch had had to pay tribute from the time of the Roman occupation of Syria, but there is no specific evidence on this point; and other scholars have hesitated to follow Mommsen's opinion; see Downey, *op.cit.* 2. Caracalla introduced new types but did not reform the bronze coinage of Antioch; see D. B. Waagé, "Coins" 51.

[52] Aulus Gellius writes (*Attic Nights* 16.13.3) that there is general ignorance as to what *municipia* are and what rights they have, and how far they differ from colonies, and that it is generally supposed that *coloniae* are better off than *municipia*. He concludes (16.13.9) that the condition of colony, "although it is more exposed to control and less free, is nevertheless thought preferable and superior because of the greatness and majesty of the Roman people, of which these colonies seem to be miniatures, as it were, and in a way copies, and at the same time because the rights of the municipal towns become obscure and invalid, and from ignorance of their existence the townsmen are no longer able to make use of them." (transl. of J. C. Rolfe, Loeb Classical Library).

[53] Ulpian *Dig.* 50.15.1.3. Laodicea continued to have the titles *metropolis* and *colonia*; see Downey, "Political Status of Roman Antioch" 4, n. 3. Domaszewski, "Personennamen bei den S.H.A." 148, followed by Reusch, "Caracallavita" 29, thought that the

Moreover, this was a discreet and appropriate measure for Caracalla to take in that it was neither a reversal nor a criticism of any act of his father's.[54]

There is a possibility, depending upon the interpretation of an error in the chronicle of Malalas, that Caracalla paved the streets at Antioch. The chronicler attributes this work to Antoninus Pius, but some of the activities that Malalas ascribes to that emperor cannot have been carried out by him, while there is reason to attribute some of them to Caracalla, whose name, Antoninus, could easily have been confused with that of Antoninus Pius. In the case of the paving of the streets of Antioch the evidence is indecisive, and pending the discovery of further evidence, there seems to be no reason to suppose that this operation was not carried out under Antoninus Pius. It might, however, eventually prove to be the case that Caracalla did the work.[55]

Caracalla stayed in Antioch twice when he went to the East in an effort to unite the Roman and the Parthian empires.[56] His visit to the city took place in the spring of A.D. 215, at the end of a journey with his army through Pannonia and Asia Minor, during which he spent the winter at Nicomedia. He arrived at Antioch probably in May and was given an enthusiastic reception, in gratitude for his favors to the city.[57] He proceeded to indulge in all the pleasures which Antioch could offer,[58] including no doubt the games and shows for which he

---

grant of the title of colony to Antioch was simply one of the grants of the same title that Caracalla made to other cities in Syria and Palestine, in which grants of the land of wealthy cities were made to Caracalla's veterans. Domaszewski and Reusch, however, did not take into account the special circumstances of the grant of the title to Antioch, and there is no reason to think that the title was given to Antioch for this reason; see Downey, *op.cit.* 5.

[54] There is no specific evidence for the date at which Caracalla granted the title of colony to Antioch. However, since the Olympic games were restored to Antioch before the summer of A.D. 212 (see above, n. 50), it would seem likely that the title of colony was granted at the same time. Reusch, "Caracallavita" 42, states, as though it were a fact, that Caracalla made Antioch a colony on the occasion of his visit in A.D. 215; this is of course a possibility, but there is no extant evidence to support it.

[55] See above, Ch. 9, §8.

[56] See F. W. Drexler, *Caracallas Zug nach dem Orient und der letzte Partherkrieg* (Diss. Halle 1880), and A. Maricq, "Classica et orientalia, 3: La chronologie des dernières années de Caracalla," *Syria* 34 (1957) 297-302.

[57] Herodian 4.8.6. Caracalla celebrated his birthday (4 April) before leaving Nicomedia (Dio Cassius 77.19.3), and then visited Troy and other cities before reaching Antioch, so that if he traveled leisurely, as one might expect he would, his arrival would not have taken place before May.

[58] Dio Cassius 77.20.1. Dio mentions, as a token of the luxuriousness of Caracalla's life at Antioch, that he kept his chin wholly bare. Von Rohden in *RE* 2.2452 takes this to mean that Caracalla's self-indulgence induced an illness which caused his beard to fall out.

had a passion.[59] At this time his health was so undermined that he was in a condition of extreme nervous agitation which unfitted him for business, and his mother, Julia Domna, who accompanied him, took charge of the affairs of state.[60]

Later in the year a sedition in Alexandria, which made the emperor's personal intervention necessary, took Caracalla away from Antioch.[61] He returned late in the same year, A.D. 215, and spent the winter in the city,[62] continuing his plans to gain control of Parthia. We hear of him presiding on 27 May, A.D. 216, at the appeal of a suit connected with the temple of Zeus Hypsistos at Dmeir, in the plain east of Damascus; one of the lawyers participating was the distinguished Egnatius Lollianus.[63] Then, after diplomatic efforts had proved unsuccessful, Caracalla was forced to undertake an invasion of Parthia; he left Antioch in the summer of 216 and conducted a campaign that took him as far as Arbela.[64] He spent the winter of A.D. 216/7 in Edessa making preparations for a further offensive. During this time his mother remained in Antioch, charged with the task of sorting the official communications which arrived for the emperor, so as to prevent a mass of unimportant letters from being sent to him while he was campaigning.[65] On 8 April A.D. 217, while on a journey from Edessa to Carrhae, Caracalla was killed by a soldier on the orders of the praetorian prefect Opellius Macrinus, who feared for his own safety because there had got into circulation a prophecy that he would become emperor.[66]

5. Macrinus, A.D. 217-218

Macrinus was proclaimed emperor by the troops four days after Caracalla's death.[67] He at once sent for his son Diadumenianus, who

---

[59] Cf. e.g. Dio Cassius 77.9.7.

[60] Dio Cassius 77.18.2; see Gertrud Herzog, "Iulia Domna," *RE* 10 (1919) 933.

[61] Herodian 4.8.6.   [62] Herodian 4.9.8.

[63] P. Roussel and F. de Visscher, "Les inscriptions du temple de Dmeir," *Syria* 23 (1942-1943) 173-194; L. Wenger, "Ein Prozess vor Caracalla in Syrien," *Annuaire de l'Inst. de philol. et d'hist. orient. et slaves* 11 (1951) 469-504 (= *Mélanges H. Grégoire* 3). The suit was concerned with the tenure of the priesthood of the temple. On the career of Egnatius Lollianus, for which this inscription provides new evidence, see E. Groag, "L. Egnatius Victor Lollianus (No. 42)," *RE* 5 (1905) 2001-2003; idem, in *PIR²* 3 (1943) pp. 73-74; Magie, *Asia Minor* 1563-1564, n. 18.

[64] Dio Cassius 78.1.2. The preparations for the military campaign are reflected in the great increase in the minting of silver in Syria at this time. See Bellinger, *Tetradrachms of Caracalla and Macrinus.*

[65] Dio Cassius 78.4.2-3.

[66] See von Petrikovits, "M. Opellius Macrinus," *RE* 18 (1939) 543-544.

[67] On the reign of Macrinus, see, in addition to the standard histories, von Petrikovits,

had been staying in Antioch, and had him proclaimed Caesar.[68] Macrinus then returned to Antioch,[69] with his son, and proceeded to consolidate his position. He wrote to the Senate in Rome, and, with his son, distributed a largesse to the people of Antioch.[70] He also found it necessary to guard against hostile action on the part of Caracalla's mother. When the news of her son's murder first reached Julia Domna in Antioch she tried to kill herself, but was unable to carry through the attempt. She then began plotting with the soldiers whom she had about her to make herself sole ruler. As a consequence Macrinus ordered her to leave Antioch; and this time she either killed herself, by starvation, or died from the effects of a disease from which she had long suffered.[71] After her death, her sister Julia Maesa, who had always lived with her at the court, was dismissed by Macrinus, but was allowed to retire to Emesa, her native city, taking her considerable wealth with her.[72]

Normally, Macrinus ought to have gone to Rome at once after becoming emperor, but he was unwilling to leave Syria before the hostilities with Parthia were brought to some conclusion, and so he decided to remain in Antioch for the time being, a step which made him unpopular and contributed to his downfall. The emperor's presence thus turned Antioch into a kind of Eastern capital; the coins issued at this time show that the local mint, in order to meet the new situation, was transformed into a new imperial mint.[73]

"M. Opellius Macrinus," *RE* 18 (1939) 540-558; H. Mattingly, introduction to *BMC Rom. Emp.* 5, pp. ccxiii-ccxxvii; idem, "The Reign of Macrinus," *Studies Presented to D. M. Robinson* 2 (St. Louis 1953) 962-970. Some of the chronology of the reign remains uncertain because of discrepancies and omissions in the sources. The sequence of events given here now seems the most probable.

[68] Dio Cassius 78.19.1.

[69] Herodian 5.1.1. The biography of Macrinus in the *SHA* (2.2, 8.1) might be thought to show that Macrinus took the offensive against the Parthians immediately after Caracalla's death, without returning to Antioch. However, this can hardly have been true (cf. von Petrikovits in *RE* 18.545), for Macrinus can scarcely have dared to leave such powerful persons as Julia Domna and Julia Maesa, with the court, behind him at Antioch.

[70] Mattingly in *BMC Rom. Emp.* 5, p. ccxxiii.

[71] Dio Cassius 78.23.1-5. Her body was sent from Antioch to Rome (*ibid.* 78.24.3).

[72] Herodian 5.3.2.

[73] Herodian 5.2.3.ff.; cf. Mattingly, *BMC Rom. Emp.* 5, pp. ccxiv, ccxx, ccxxii, and Bellinger, *Tetradrachms of Caracalla and Macrinus.* Herodian says that while he was in Antioch Macrinus neglected the affairs of the government and gave himself over to luxurious living, which displeased the troops who were stationed in and around the city. This report, however, is to be viewed with caution, since it sounds like the malicious gossip of soldiers who were dissatisfied with their living conditions. The eventual revolt against Macrinus was made possible largely by the dissatisfaction of the army (cf. Dio Cassius 78.28) but there were graver reasons for this.

In the autumn the Parthians invaded Mesopotamia,[74] and Macrinus
had to take the field against them. After some indecisive fighting, a
peace was patched up by which the Romans, though they gave up no
territory, surrendered the captives and the booty that had been taken by
Caracalla. After the Parthian settlement, in the first part of A.D. 218,
Macrinus returned to Antioch, where he next found himself faced with
a revolt of the troops stationed near the important garrison city of
Emesa. This movement had been set on foot by Julia Maesa, whom
Macrinus had allowed to settle in Emesa, her native city, where she
could take full advantage both of her wealth and of the prestige of
her family, the hereditary priests of the Sun God.[75] Julia Maesa had
two grandsons, Varius Avitus (the future emperor Elagabalus) and
Gessius Bassius Alexianus (the future emperor Severus Alexander).
Elagabalus, as he now began to be called after the sun deity, was a
depraved youth of fourteen who was serving as a priest of the temple
in Emesa. It was given out that he was a natural son of Caracalla,
and on 16 May A.D. 218 he was proclaimed emperor by the troops at
Emesa. When the news of this was brought to Macrinus at Antioch,
he underestimated the seriousness of the danger and sent a force of
troops under the praetorian prefect Julianus to put down the revolt.[76]
Julianus' men deserted and slew their commander. Macrinus himself
now took action and marched on Emesa, taking with him troops that
had been stationed at Apamea. The emperor's forces and those of
Elagabalus met, apparently, somewhere near the boundary between
the provinces of Syria Coele and Syria Phoenice. Macrinus' soldiers
deserted and he was forced to return to Antioch. Elagabalus' forces
now took the offensive and marched on Antioch. Macrinus set out
against them and the armies met on 8 June, probably near the village
of Immae, twenty-four miles from Antioch on the road from Antioch
to Beroea.[77] The fighting was confused, and it seems that Macrinus

[74] On the date and sequence of events, see Mattingly in *BMC Rom. Emp.* 5, pp.
ccxxi-ccxxii.

[75] Gertrud Herzog, "Iulia Maesa," *RE* 10 (1919) 940-944.

[76] Herodian 5.4.1ff.

[77] Our sources are not entirely clear on these last phases of the struggle between
Macrinus and Elagabalus. The sequence given here seems the most plausible (similar
results are reached by Parker, *Hist. of the Roman World A.D. 138-337* 100), though
the evidence has more often been interpreted to mean that there was one battle between the forces of Macrinus and Elagabalus, rather than two, and that this occurred
at a village 24 miles from Antioch on 8 June; see H. J. Bassett, *Macrinus and Diadumenianus* (Diss., Michigan 1920) 66-74; S. N. Miller in *CAH* 12.52; H. von Petrikovits,
"Die Chronologie der Regierung Macrins," *Klio* 31 (1938) 103-107; idem, "M. Opellius
Macrinus," *RE* 18 (1939) 554-556. Herodian (5.4.5ff.) describes only one battle "on

might eventually have won; but he lost courage and fled with a few soldiers to Antioch. On entering the city he pretended that he had won the battle; but when further reports began to arrive, fighting broke out in and around the city as the partisans of Elagabalus (or the enemies of Macrinus) began to attack people who had supported the emperor, and on the same night Macrinus was forced to flee toward Cilicia.[78] He was finally caught and executed.[79]

6. ELAGABALUS, A.D. 218-222

Elagabalus entered Antioch on the day following his victory, after promising his soldiers two thousand sesterces apiece if they would refrain from sacking the city. Part of the money necessary for this payment he collected from the citizens.[80] The new emperor remained in Antioch for several months, until his position was established and his rule recognized by the Senate in Rome.[81] While at Antioch he executed a number of the officers of Macrinus, including Fabius Agrippinus, who had been governor of Syria Coele.[82] He then left for Nicomedia, where he spent the winter of A.D. 218/9, before proceeding to

---

the border" between Syria Coele and Syria Phoenice, in which Macrinus was finally defeated, so that he fled to Antioch and then to Cilicia. The biographer of Macrinus in the *SHA* (10.3) likewise records only one battle. Dio Cassius' narrative is incompletely preserved at this point and has apparently suffered serious disturbance. He describes a final battle (78.37.3ff.) at a village twenty-four miles from Antioch. This cannot have been on the border between Syria Coele and Syria Phoenice, which was much farther from Antioch (see Honigmann, "Syria" 1686). Dio's account also differs from Herodian's in other important respects. There is a trace in Dio's work of an earlier encounter (78.34.5), though in the extant version this does not actually appear as a battle. Herodian appears to have telescoped into one the accounts of two battles and certain features of his description of a single final battle seem to belong to the earlier encounter, which survives in Dio only in the form of a meager reference. Dio's description of the place of the final encounter as "a certain village of Antioch, 180 stadia from the city" (78.37.3) would fit Immae, which is 24 miles (42 km.) from the city, and Honigmann and others have concluded that the battle occurred at Immae (Honigmann *loc.cit.*). Dio says (78.37.3) that the troops of Elagabalus occupied "the pass in front of the village" (τὰ στενὰ τὰ πρὸ τῆς κώμης), and while there are no στενά at Immae itself, there is a secondary road about a mile south of the village which runs through a narrow pass, forming a position of some tactical value. Fifty-four years later Immae was the scene of a victory of Aurelian over Zenobia; see below, n. 162.

[78] Dio Cassius 78.39.1-3.

[79] See von Petrikovits, "M. Opellius Macrinus," *RE* 18 (1939) 557. Macrinus was executed while being conveyed to Antioch, where he was being taken because Elagabalus at first made the city his headquarters (see below).

[80] Dio Cassius 79.1.1. Elagabalus introduced a new, very large bronze at the mint of Antioch, in two denominations, with a seated Tyche on the reverse: *Antioch* 4, pt. 2, p. 54.

[81] Dio Cassius 79.3.1.

[82] Dio Cassius 79.3.4; see Harrer, *Studies* 45-46.

Rome.[83] There, after three years of religious mania and fantastic excesses he was ultimately murdered, along with his mother (March A.D. 222). During these years we hear nothing of the history of Antioch.

7. SEVERUS ALEXANDER, A.D. 222-235

Severus Alexander, who at the age of fourteen succeeded his cousin Elagabalus, was a person of far different character and upbringing.[84] Honest and virtuous, he had been kept away from the influence of Elagabalus and had been carefully educated and trained for the responsibilities of power. During his reign he was constantly under the influence of his mother Julia Mamaea, who was made Augusta.

The first years of Severus Alexander's reign were relatively uneventful and were devoted to reconstruction and to repairing the damage caused by the misrule of Elagabalus. About eight years after his accession, however, he was called upon to deal with a new threat in the East, where the rise of the new Sassanid Empire, succeeding the Parthian rule, presented a challenge which was to bring grave danger to the Roman state. For the next two generations the Roman emperors were to struggle to resist the Persian menace, and in these efforts Antioch was destined to play a major role.

By the year 230 it was plain that war with the Persians was no longer to be avoided. Ardashir (Artaxerxes), the new Persian monarch, was now operating in Mesopotamia, and his forces threatened Cappadocia and Syria.[85] In the spring of A.D. 231 Severus Alexander set out from Rome accompanied by his mother and made his way east,[86] collecting troops on the way. Arriving at Antioch, he began to train the soldiers and to put his forces in readiness.[87] He then sent an embassy to the Persians to try to arrange a peace, but Ardashir not only rejected the embassy but himself sent four hundred richly outfitted Persian nobles to Severus Alexander, with an ultimatum calling for the Romans to evacuate Syria and Asia Minor, as territory which had belonged to the ancient Persian Empire.[88]

At this time riots and mutinies took place among various of the

[83] Herodian 5.5.3; *SHA Elagabalus* 5.1.

[84] See A. Jardé, *Études critiques sur la vie et le règne de Sévère Alexandre* (Paris 1925).

[85] On the rise of the Sassanids, see A. Christensen, *L'Iran sous les Sassanides*[2] (Copenhagen 1944) 85ff., 218.

[86] Cf. the *Profectio* coins of A.D. 231 in H. Cohen, *Description historique des monnaies*[2] (Paris and London 1884) 4, p. 484, no. 18.

[87] Herodian 6.4.3.   [88] Herodian 6.4.4-6.

Roman contingents in the East, including some of the soldiers stationed at Antioch. There, it is said, the troops became demoralized by
the pleasures that had become available to them in Antioch and
Daphne, and they had to be disciplined by the emperor in person.[89] This
episode cannot have increased Alexander's love for Antioch, whose
citizens, ever ready to ridicule their rulers, had on the occasion of a
certain festival taunted him as a "Syrian synagogue chief" and a "high
priest," gibes which were particularly distasteful to the emperor, who
was anxious to bury all recollection of his connection with Elagabalus.[90]

In the spring of A.D. 232 Severus Alexander set out from Antioch
against the Persians, with his army divided into three parts. The expedition was only partly successful. In the winter of A.D. 232/3 the
emperor, himself ill, was forced to withdraw to Antioch. There he at
first began to prepare for another campaign, but then learned that
the Persians themselves had suffered such losses that no further action
on their part was to be expected in the immediate future.[91] At this
time, while Severus Alexander was in Antioch, he received reports
that the Germans had crossed the Rhine and the Danube and were
threatening Illyricum and even the neighboring parts of Italy. On this
news, in the summer of A.D. 233 he left Antioch for Rome, where he
celebrated a triumph for his victory over the Persians.[92] Probably early
in the next year the emperor and his mother left Rome for the Rhine
frontier. Here the troops, dissatisfied with Severus Alexander's conduct, chose as emperor Maximinus, a Thracian officer of outstanding
courage and energy, and Alexander and his mother were murdered
(A.D. 235).

It was probably during Julia Mamaea's stay in Antioch in A.D. 231-233
that the celebrated meeting took place between the empress and the
Christian teacher Origen, which is described elsewhere.[93]

8. ANARCHY AND INVASION, A.D. 235-260; THE TAKING OF ANTIOCH BY SAPOR I

The years following the death of Severus Alexander in 235 were
filled with the struggles for power of the two Maximini (235-238),

[89] Herodian 6.4.7; *SHA Severus Alexander* 53-54. Similar disorders had occurred at
Antioch in the time of Marcus Aurelius, when the troops were unable to resist the
pleasures offered by the city (*SHA Avidius Cassius* 5.5; see above Ch. 9, n. 123).
[90] *SHA Severus Alexander* 28.7.
[91] Herodian 6.6.1-6; *SHA Severus Alexander* 55.1-2.
[92] Herodian 6.7.1.ff.; *SHA Severus Alexander* 56.1; John of Antioch, frag. 141, *FHG*
4, p. 593 = frag. 55, *Excerpta de insidiis* ed. De Boor, p. 100.
[93] See Ch. 11, n. 135.

Pupienus (238), Balbinus (238) and the Gordians (238-244). During this period of strife and uncertainty, events were centered in the West, and little is known of the history of Antioch. However, developments were afoot in Persia which were soon to open a disordered and difficult chapter in the history of Syria and of Antioch.

When Sapor I, who reigned 241-272, came to the throne in Persia, he pressed on with the imperialist plans for conquest of his father Ardashir, who had already, during the reign of Maximinus (235-238), captured Carrhae and Nisibis. In the spring of 242 Syria was invaded and Antioch was seriously threatened.[94] The Roman forces of the youthful Gordian III (238-244), however, succeeded in driving the Persians back. Gordian was murdered in February 244, and was succeeded by Philip the Arabian (244-249), who at once made peace with the Persians. It is at this time that the famous encounter at the church door of Bishop Babylas and the emperor is supposed to have taken place, when the bishop refused to allow Philip to attend a service in the church at Antioch because the emperor had committed murder. The story—a striking parallel to the tale of St. Ambrose and Theodosius —is edifying, but (as is shown elsewhere) everything connected with it indicates that it is fictitious.[95]

In spite of the peace with Persia, affairs in the East were in a far from tranquil state. In order to finance the defense of the empire against the barbarians who successively threatened its various frontiers, heavy taxes had to be exacted, and the levies imposed by Priscus, the emperor's brother and minister, resulted in a revolt in Syria and Cappa-

[94] On the career of Sapor, see Fluss, "Sapor (I)," *RE* 1 A (1920) 2325-2333; and on the circumstances of Sapor's accession, and on Persian policy at the time, see Ensslin in *CAH* 12.86, 130. In the biography of Gordian III in the *SHA* there are two passages (26.5, 27.5) which have been taken by a few scholars to mean that Antioch was captured, not merely threatened, by Sapor in A.D. 242; see Stein, "C. Furius Sabinius Aquila Timesitheus," *RE* 7 (1912) 366; Fluss in *RE* 1 A 2327; K. Pink, "Antioch or Viminacium?", *Num. Chron.* ser. 5, vol. 15 (1935) 94-113. Most scholars, however, feel that these statements are not to be interpreted in this sense, and this view is supported by the important evidence of the coins, which shows that there was no interruption in the activity of the mint of Antioch at this time; see von Rohden, "M. Antonius Gordianus," *RE* 1, 2626; Parker, *Hist. of the Roman World A.D. 138-337* 149; Olmstead, "The Mid-Third Century" 251, n. 1; G. Pugliese Carratelli, "Res gestae divi Saporis," *La parola del Passato* 2 (1947) 218; Magie, *Asia Minor* n. 15 on p. 1562; and especially the convincing discussion by Ensslin, "Zu den Kriegen des Schapur I" 14-15. See also Rostovtzeff, "Res gestae divi Saporis" 22-23. It may well be that a statement that Gordian "saved" Antioch from a threat by the Persians was exaggerated into a tradition that he actually freed the city from Persian occupation.

[95] For a detailed discussion of the story of Babylas and the emperor, see Ch. 11, nn. 140-143.

docia led by a man named Iotapianus, probably early in A.D. 248.[96] This
revolt reflected the local disaffection from the central government
which was appearing in many parts of the empire at this time;[97] a
similar outbreak was to take place in Antioch not many years later.
If, as Olmstead thinks,[98] there is evidence that the Persians again began
hostilities at about this juncture, Antioch would have had further
reason to feel uneasy. One cause of alarm and depression of which
we have certain knowledge was a plague that began to ravage the
Roman Empire about A.D. 251.[99] In addition to this, very serious discontent must have been caused by the difficult economic conditions
and the political uncertainties that prevailed throughout the Roman
world. In Antioch this discontent would have affected all classes, and
if conditions were favorable, it would inevitably have turned people's
thoughts eastward, to Persia. The thought that anything might be
better than the current government had led to the invitation to Tigranes
to occupy Syria in 83 B.C.

As one might expect in such a situation, there were people ready
to turn the state of affairs to their own profit. Although the Persian
government may not have been guilty of actual intrigue in Antioch,
there must have been enough friendly feeling toward Persia in the
city—which counted several Persian figures in its legendary history—
to make possible an attempted coup by a pro-Persian adventurer.[100]
Such a person does in fact appear just at this time, in the person of
Mariades, who has become a famous figure in the history of the city.
Mariades' name represented the Aramaic name Mâryâd'a, "My Lord

[96] See Stein, "Iotapianus," *RE* 9 (1916) 2004-2005; Parker, *Hist. of the Roman World A.D. 138-337* 155-157; Olmstead, "The Mid-Third Century" 261-262; Magie, *Asia Minor* 702 and n. 22 on p. 1565.
[97] Van Sickle, "Particularism in the Roman Empire" 353.
[98] See above, n. 96.
[99] Zosimus 1.37.3; cf. Parker, *Hist. of the Roman World A.D. 138-337* 165, and *CAH* 12.167-168. There is no specific evidence to show when the plague reached Antioch. It is supposed to have run through the Empire for fifteen years.
[100] On the Persian elements in the early history of Antioch, see Ch. 3, nn. 12, 15, 18, as well as Ch. 9, n. 152. Gagé's important study, "Les Perses à Antioche," deals with the subject in more discursive fashion. The subject requires further study, in order to clarify the extent and the significance of the intercourse between Rome and Persia, which, it seems, may have been much more active than has been supposed. The amount of Persian influence apparent in the mosaics of Antioch certainly suggests that an in-terest in Persia and Persian affairs, such as the royal symbols, was by no means un-common at Antioch; see D. N. Wilber, "Iranian Motifs in Syrian Art," *Bulletin of the American Institute for Iranian Art and Archaeology* 5 (1937) 22-26, and Levi, *Antioch Mosaic Pavements* 1.315, 350, 353 n. 12, 453, 478-479, with the valuable ob-servations of Clark Hopkins, "Antioch Mosaic Pavements," *Journal of Near Eastern Studies* 7 (1948) 93-97.

discerns," which was hellenized as Kyriades;[101] thus he belonged to the Semitic stock that would have been particularly liable to be discontented with the Roman rule. Mariades' action in going over to the Persians introduces a calamitous period in the history of Antioch. Our literary sources for this epoch are sometimes unclear and contradictory, and there has been some difficulty in interpreting them. It now seems clear, however, on the basis of the recently found inscription in which Sapor described his victories, and of the evidence of the coins, that Antioch was captured twice by the Persians at this time, once, probably, in A.D. 256, the year in which Dura was taken (though it is possible that the city may have fallen in one of the following years), and again in A.D. 260.[102]

The accounts of Mariades' career differ in some details.[103] He is said to have been wealthy and well-born, and a member of the senatorial class at Antioch. According to one account, Mariades, after living a profligate life, robbed his father of a great quantity of gold and silver and fled to Persia. Another account of his career, which at least sounds more circumstantial, is that while performing the liturgy that required him to furnish horses for the public entertainments, he embezzled official funds and was expelled from the senate, so that he fled the city and went to Sapor, offering to betray Antioch to him. On the basis of this connection with the races, it has recently been suggested, very plausibly, that Mariades was connected with (possibly even head of) one of the circus factions, the Greens and the Blues, which traditionally served as political parties, one loyal to the government, the other in opposition to it.[104] On two former occasions it had been found necessary to suspend the games and spectacles in Antioch in times of political unrest, in order to obviate the possibility of revolutionary activity by the factions,[105] and if Mariades were able to combine the

---

[101] On the name, see Gagé, "Les Perses à Antioche" 307-308.

[102] The evidence for the chronology, which is in some respects uncertain, is discussed in detail in Excursus 5.

[103] The sources are SHA Trig. tyr. 2, Amm. Marc. 23.5.3, Peter Patricius frag. 1 (FHG 4.192), Mal. 295.20-296.10. See Stein, "Mariades," RE 14 (1930) 1744-1745, and Gagé, "Les Perses à Antioche." Libanius, Or. 60.2-3, mentions the capture of the city by treachery, and its burning, but does not (at least in the extant fragments of this oration) speak of Mariades by name. The capture of the city is mentioned also by Zonaras 12.23, p. 630 B.

[104] See Gagé, "Les Perses à Antioche" 309-310. On the potential role of the circus factions, see, in addition to the remarks of Gagé, the study of Dvornik, "Circus parties," in which references may be found to the existing literature on this important subject.

[105] The games were suppressed by Marcus Aurelius and by Septimius Severus; see Ch. 9, n. 131; and above in this chapter, nn. 31-34.

members of his faction with the pro-Persian elements of the population, he might have been able to build up a strong backing.

Almost the only account of Mariades' conduct that does not have a dubious air is a very brief fragment of Peter Patricius' account of the arrival of Sapor at Antioch.[106] According to this fragment, Sapor, when he reached Antioch, accompanied by the traitor, camped twenty stadia from the city, evidently waiting to see what the reaction to his arrival would be. "And the respectable people [Peter writes] fled the city, while the common folk remained, partly because they were friendly toward Mariades, partly because they welcomed a change, as is apt to be the case with ignorant people." Peter's account, which has the ring of truth, suggests that whatever the ostensible cause for Mariades' departure from Antioch may have been, there must have been enough pro-Persian sentiment in the city for him to feel that it would be worthwhile for him to persuade Sapor to try to take the city; and Sapor of course must have had reason to be convinced by Mariades' story. The episode, as Peter Patricius tells it, suggests fairly plainly that Mariades was able to organize a pro-Persian party before he left Antioch. There was a tradition that Mariades led two Persian expeditions into Syria. The first invasion, in which Antioch was not involved, would have taken place in A.D. 251,[107] and if, as the evidence seems to indicate, the first capture of Antioch took place in A.D. 256,[108] Mariades' participation in the earlier invasion would make it seem likely, as Rostovtzeff thinks,[109] that the traitor could count on the support not only of a part of the population of Antioch but of the corresponding segment of the population of Syria as a whole.

As to what precisely happened when Antioch was taken, apparently in A.D. 256, we cannot be sure since most of our literary sources, which are meager to begin with, appear to confuse the two captures of the city, which occurred in A.D. 256 and A.D. 260, and the evidence suggests that Mariades was involved only in the earlier taking of the city.[110] When the Persians came to Antioch in A.D. 256 they did not (according to Peter Patricius) attack the city at once, but waited to see whether it would give itself up to them. What then happened, we do not know.

[106] Frag. 1, *FHG* 4, p. 192.

[107] According to Ensslin's chronology, however, in which Antioch was captured only in A.D. 260 (see Excursus 5), the first invasion on which Mariades could have accompanied the Persians into Syria would have been the expedition of A.D. 253, which did not reach Antioch.

[108] For details, see Excursus 5.   [109] "Res gestae divi Saporis" 45.

[110] See Excursus 5.

Ammianus relates that when the Persians were led to Antioch by Mariades, they took the city by surprise, appearing suddenly on the top of Mount Silpius while the people were sitting in the theater watching a mime.[111] The audience, seated with their backs turned to the mountain, perceived nothing until one of the actors, facing the top of the mountain, cried out "Is it a dream, or are the Persians here?" The audience turned their heads, and then fled from the arrows that the Persians showered upon them; and the invaders proceeded to sack and burn the city, though they spared Daphne.[112] This striking account unfortunately is discredited by several defects. Ammianus relates the episode in his account of the second capture of the city (in A.D. 260), in which, there is reason to believe, Mariades did not take part. Either the episode did occur in A.D. 260, and Ammianus is mistaken in giving Mariades a part in it, or it occurred in A.D. 256, when Mariades was present, and Ammianus is mistaken in dating it in A.D. 260. In the latter case it would appear that Ammianus did not tell the whole truth, and that Sapor, after his wait at a distance from Antioch had proved fruitless, attacked the city and burned it. Certainly it would be difficult to take Ammianus' story at its face value and suppose that the Persians, having made their way through a considerable part of Syria, were able to reach Antioch without any warning of their approach having reached the city, and were then able to occupy the fortifications on the top of Mount Silpius without betraying any sign of their presence to the city below until they were suddenly seen by an actor in the theater. Further reason for suspicion of this detail is that the same scene in a theater, including the shower of arrows, is told by Macrobius of an event at the *ludi Apollinares* in Rome;[113] thus the theater scene might well seem to be merely a literary detail, added to the story by Ammianus or his source. All the sources, however, mention the burning of Antioch and there seems no reason to doubt this.

Whether the Persians, having burned the city, continued to occupy it for a time, we do not know. The evidence of the coins indicates that

---

[111] See above, n. 103.

[112] The burning of the city is mentioned by Ammianus Marcellinus 23.5.3, by Malalas 296.6ff., and by Libanius *Or.* 60.2-3, who says that Apollo stopped Sapor from burning Daphne. Ammianus elsewhere speaks (20.11.11) of a great ram (*aries*) which the Persians had used in demolition operations at Antioch. This was found by Constantius' army in A.D. 360 at Carrhae, where the Persians had abandoned it on their withdrawal from Syria. Libanius (*Or.* 15.16) stated that in his time the effects of the burning of the city by the Persians were still apparent.

[113] Macrobius 1.17.25. The parallel is pointed out by Gagé, "Les Perses à Antioche" 317, n. 1 (where the reference to Macrobius has suffered from a misprint).

the mint of Antioch had been moved to Emesa in A.D. 253, and that
there were interruptions and irregularities in the activity of the mint
between A.D. 253 and 261.[114] This could mean either that the Persians
remained in Antioch for a time, or that the city was so damaged that
even though the Persians withdrew at once, it was not possible to re-
open the mint.[115] On the whole it seems more likely, as Rostovtzeff
believes,[116] that the Persian operations on this occasion merely represented a raid, carried out for purposes of propaganda and plunder, and
that they did not remain in Antioch.

What role Mariades played after this capture of Antioch is not
known, though it is recorded that he came to a violent end. According
to one tradition he was killed by his own followers,[117] and it is quite
possible to believe that his supporters turned against him when the
Persians whom he had brought to Antioch burned the city.[118] According to another report,[119] which may seem less plausible, Sapor executed
Mariades because he had betrayed his own city.[120]

When the Persians withdrew from Antioch, they took with them

[114] A. R. Bellinger, "The Numismatic Evidence from Dura," *Berytus* 8 (1943) 61-64.
See also the results of the studies of Alföldi, cited below, Excursus 5.

[115] F. M. Heichelheim, "Numismatic Comments," *Hesperia* 16 (1947) 277-278, calls
attention to a Roman coin of this period, struck at the mint of Antioch, which bears
overstrikes indicating that it was reissued by the Persians for use in territory they occupied in Syria. Whether the overstriking was done at Antioch, we do not know; if
it was, the Persians would have occupied the city at least long enough to make such
arrangements for the currency.

[116] "Res gestae divi Saporis" 45.

[117] *SHA Trig. tyr.* 2.

[118] It has been suggested (cf. Bouchier, *Antioch* 120) that the uprising said to have
taken place among Mariades' followers was really a massacre of the Persian garrison
of Antioch, and that this episode formed a basis for Malalas' story of a massacre of a
Persian garrison at Antioch in the time of Trajan (see Longden, "Parthian Campaigns"
32, and Lepper, *Trajan's Parthian War* 20-21, 64). The suggestion that the slaying of
Mariades was connected with a rising against the Persians is attractive, but there is no
documentary support for it. On the supposed episode in the time of Trajan, see Ch. 9,
n. 58.

[119] Malalas 296.9-10. Ammianus (23.5.3) writes that Mariades was burned alive, but
does not say by whom. There is some evidence which suggests that Mariades was still
alive, and in the service of Sapor, after A.D. 260, but this is by no means certain; see
Ensslin in *CAH* 12.135; Olmstead, "The Mid-Third Century" 399; Rostovtzeff, "Res
gestae divi Saporis" 40.

[120] There exists a barbarian coin, with a legend composed of a strange mixture of
Greek and Latin letters, which Fr. Lenormant, *La monnaie dans l'antiquité* (Paris
1878-1879) 2.385-387, believes to be a coin struck by Mariades as Roman emperor (this
interpretation is accepted by Bardy, *Paul de Samosate*[2] 240). However, the interpretation of the coin is not entirely certain, and it seems more likely that, as Ch. Lenormant
(*Rev. num.* 1846, 277-280) and V. Langlois (*Numismatique des Arabes avant l'Islam-
isme* [Paris 1869] 103-104) believe, the piece was issued at Palmyra by Odenath, the
Palmyrene prince who later became for a time the effective ruler of the eastern part
of the Roman Empire (see below, §10).

a number of captives, whose technical knowledge and skills Sapor was anxious to utilize.[121] Among those deported was Demetrianus, who had succeeded Fabius as bishop of Antioch at some time in A.D. 252.[122] The captives were settled in Persia, where they were later to be joined by others who were deported after the second capture of Antioch in A.D. 260.[123]

9. THE REIGN OF VALERIAN, A.D. 253-260

In A.D. 253 the joint emperors Gallus and his son Volusianus were overthrown and a new emperor, Valerian, came into power, to be joined shortly as coruler by his son Gallienus. Valerian set out for the East, leaving his son as ruler of the West. The date of his coming to the East is still a matter of discussion. Ensslin favors the year A.D. 255, while Alföldi, Olmstead and, Rostovtzeff place the journey in A.D. 253/4, and Parker believes that the years A.D. 256 or 257 are indicated.[124] These last dates seem to agree best with the remainder of the evidence.

Valerian, finding Antioch in ruins, set about rebuilding it with the help of his newly-appointed praetorian prefect Successianus.[125] The only part of his work for which any evidence is preserved is the laying, on the island, of the foundations upon which Diocletian later built his palace.[126] Malalas, in whose chronicle this report is preserved, does

[121] See W. B. Henning, "The Great Inscription of Sapor I," *Bull. of the School of Oriental Studies* (University of London) 9 (1937-1939) 843.

[122] For further details, see Ch. 11, n. 150.

[123] See further below. The deportation of Demetrianus is recorded in the Arabic Nestorian history called the *Chronicle of Seert* (PO 4.222).

[124] Ensslin, "Zu den Kriegen des Schapur I" 134; Alföldi in *CAH* 12.170; Olmstead, "The Mid-Third Century" 410; Rostovtzeff, "Res gestae divi Saporis" 45; Parker, *Hist. of the Roman World A.D. 138-337* 167; R. Göbl, "Gallienos als Alleinherrscher," *Num. Ztschr.* 75 (1953) 5-34. See also Pugliese Carratelli in *La parola del passato* 2 (1947) 233.

[125] Zosimus 1.32.3. There is nothing in Zosimus to indicate that Valerian had to recapture Antioch from the Persians; Olmstead, however (cited in the preceding note), believes that Valerian had to retake the city.

[126] In his account of the reign of Diocletian, Malalas states that at Antioch the emperor built "a great palace, finding foundations laid by Gallienus Licinnianus" (306.21-22). This account has been accepted at its face value by Müller (*Antiq. Antioch.* 99) and by Stauffenberg (*Malalas* 458-459). These scholars did not take into account that during the whole of Gallienus' sole reign (A.D. 260-268) Antioch was under the control of Palmyra, and that in such circumstances it would seem unlikely that the emperor should undertake the construction of a new palace in the city. Malalas' accounts of the reigns of Valerian and Gallienus show that the chronicler on occasion confused the father and the son; for example, his statement (297.21ff.) that Valerian was killed at Milan appears to represent a misunderstanding of the death of Gallienus, who died in this fashion, while Valerian perished in Persian captivity (see Wickert, "Licinius (Egnatius)," *RE* 13 [1927] 361; for other examples of similar confusion in

not make it clear whether Valerian began to build a palace, or whether the foundations that he laid were those of a fortified *castrum*, later converted by Diocletian to a palace of the type constructed at Salona, whose plan was basically that of a *castrum*. The circumstances of the time, however, make it seem probable that Valerian set out to build a fortification on the island, which geographically was well adapted for the purpose. Recent experience with the Persians had shown that a defensive work of this kind was urgently needed, whereas a palace, at this time, could only have been a matter of luxury and display. Why Valerian's project could not be completed is not known. Presumably it was found that the expense involved in restoration work elsewhere in Syria, combined with the costs of the war against the Persians, would not permit the completion of the undertaking at Antioch.[127]

Not only Antioch but Dura had been captured by the Persians, apparently in A.D. 256 (though Dura may have fallen later).[128] Valerian set about organizing a counteroffensive, and one instructive detail of his arrangements is preserved in the evidence for his establishment of a second mint in Syria, in addition to that of Antioch; eventually, in fact, the work of the Antioch mint was suspended, in A.D. 258/9.[129] Apparently Valerian wished to concentrate the production of money

---

Malalas' material on Valerian and Gallienus, see Stauffenberg, *Malalas* 377-378, whose efforts to vindicate Malalas in this connection cannot entirely explain away the chronicler's misinformation). The names of the two emperors were sufficiently similar for Malalas to confuse them, particularly if, anywhere in his sources, Gallienus were called Publius Licinius Valerianus Gallienus, as he was in Egypt during his father's rule (Wickert, *op.cit.* 351; in Egypt, the two emperors, when named together, were called Valeriani). Therefore, since we know from other evidence that Valerian undertook rebuilding operations at Antioch, it seems practically beyond question that Malalas' statement about the foundations that Diocletian utilized represents a confusion of Gallienus with his father. A possible explanation of Malalas' account is that the foundations that he mentions were laid during Valerian's reign but under the name of Gallienus. Gallienus was left in command of the European provinces when his father set out for the East (Wickert, *op.cit.* 353), and so far as we know he never visited the East. It is possible that Valerian associated his son's name with some of the work that he carried out at Antioch. However, this explanation would not affect the conclusion reached here as to the date or the purpose of the work. It may be noted that Ensslin, in speaking of Diocletian's palace ("Valerius [Diocletianus]," *RE* 7 A 2 [1948] 2475), writes that the emperor used foundations of a "nicht herausgekommener Palast," which indicates that he does not accept Malalas' story.

[127] Evidence of building activity in Valerian's time is preserved by a coin of that emperor which was found adhering to a mosaic in a large house on the island, called "House A" by the excavators: *Antioch-on-the-Orontes* 1.12.

[128] *Dura Final Rep.* 6: Bellinger, *The Coins* 209-210.

[129] A decree (*Cod. Just.* 9.9.18 = 5.3.5) shows that Valerian was in Antioch on 15 May 258; see Ensslin, "Zu den Kriegen des Schapur I" 48-49. On Valerian's problems in the East at this time, see Rostovtzeff, "Res gestae divi Saporis" 45-46.

for the payment of his troops in one spot, closer to his military headquarters and also better protected than Antioch, which would always
be the principal goal of a Persian invasion of Syria. The new mint
seems to have been located at Emesa.[130]

There is a report that at some time during this period the future
emperor Aurelian, who was at this time an army officer, was sent as
an envoy to the Persians, and that when he visited Antioch, in the
course of his journey, various omens foretold his future rule.[131]

Valerian's original success against the Persians did not continue. In
midsummer A.D. 260 sickness and low morale weakened the army, and
the emperor himself was taken prisoner by the Persians—whether in
battle, or by a ruse, is not clear.[132] The Persians then invaded Syria
and once more captured Antioch. Whether Mariades was once more
active in this campaign is not certain.[133]

The deportation of captives to Persia which had followed the earlier
capture of the city was now repeated, and a second group of the
learned and skilled inhabitants of the city were taken to Persia where
the king was anxious to utilize their services.[134] The Christians were
given land and dwellings and proceeded, under the tolerant regime of
the Persians, to build churches and monasteries. Sapor is said to have
rebuilt the city of Gondisapor, which had fallen into ruins, and to have
settled some of the captives there, naming the place Beh-az-Andêw-i-
Šâpûr, which may be translated "Sapor's Better-than-Antioch."[135] The
most famous undertaking of the captives was the construction of a great
irrigation dam at Šôštar (mod. Šûšter), which was still in use in
modern times.[136]

[130] Rostovtzeff, "Res gestae divi Saporis" 47; A. R. Bellinger, "The Numismatic
Evidence from Dura," *Berytus* 8 (1943) 65-67.

[131] *SHA Aurelian* 5.3.6. There is no guarantee of the historicity of the episode; see
Groag, "L. Domitius Aurelianus," *RE* 5 (1905) 1353.

[132] Ensslin in *CAH* 12.135.

[133] See above, n. 119, and Excursus 5. The account of the capture of the city by
Ammianus Marcellinus (23.5.3) ostensibly refers to this occasion, but there is reason
to believe that Ammianus may have been wrong, and that some of the details that he
gives actually belong to the earlier capture of the city (see above).

[134] See above, n. 121.

[135] When Chosroes took Antioch in A.D. 540 he is said to have deported some of the
inhabitants and to have settled them in a city which he built as an exact replica of
Antioch, named "Antioch of Chosroes." See below, Ch. 18, nn. 184-185.

[136] The deportation of Roman captives is mentioned in the *Res gestae divi Saporis*,
lines 34ff. The story of their establishment in Persia is told by Tabari ed. Nöldeke
(32-33, 40-41) and in the Arabic Nestorian history called the *Chronicle of Seert* (*PO*
4.221-222); see Bardy, *Paul de Samosate²* 240-243. This transportation of Christian
prisoners is thought to have marked a major step forward in the foundation of the
Christian community in Persia. On Sapor's policy of religious toleration, see A. Chris-

10. Antioch under the Control of Palmyra;
Paul of Samosata; Aurelian;
Probus; The Usurper Saturninus

The capture of Valerian in midsummer A.D. 260 and the second taking of Antioch by the Persians later in the same year left Syria and the remainder of the East at the mercy of Persia.[137] Gallienus, who had succeeded Valerian, was fully occupied in the West, and could do nothing against the Persians. One of Valerian's generals, Macrianus, with the support of the praetorian prefect Callistus (nicknamed Ballista), took this opportunity to proclaim his sons Macrianus and Quietus emperors, and Ballista succeeded in driving Sapor back to the Euphrates. Macrianus and Quietus were recognized as emperors in Syria, and they issued coins in Antioch.[138] The emperor Gallienus, however, defeated Macrianus and his son when they tried to establish themselves in Europe. Gallienus himself could not go to the East or send troops, but he now gained support from the prince of Palmyra, Odenath.[139]

For some years the Palmyrenes, realizing the weakness of the Romans in Syria, had been trying to establish their independence, and Odenath saw an opportunity in the situation that had developed by A.D. 260. He first approached Sapor, but being rebuffed, he decided to support Rome, and proclaiming himself king of Palmyra he marched against Sapor and inflicted a severe defeat on the Persians. Gallienus in gratitude gave Odenath the title of *dux* and appointed him to the supreme command of the Roman forces in the East. Odenath proceeded to win control of most of the cities of Syria, and defeated Ballista and Quietus, who were killed, late in A.D. 261 or early in 262.[140] Syria was

---

tensen in *CAH* 12.112, 121. The presence of a Greek version in the *Res gestae divi Saporis* shows that Sapor recognized the importance of the Greek-speaking population in his realm; see Rostovtzeff, "Res gestae divi Saporis" 21, and G. Pugliese Carratelli, "Res gestae divi Saporis," *La parola del passato* 2 (1947) 210.

[137] For an account of the history of the East at this period, see Parker, *Hist. of the Roman World A.D. 138-337* 172-175, 188ff.

[138] For their coins, see Mattingly-Sydenham, *Rom. Imp. Coinage* 5, pt. 2 (by P. H. Webb) 580-583.

[139] For the career of Odenath, see A. Alföldi, "Die romische Münzprägung und die historischen Ereignisse im Osten zwischen 260 u. 270 n. Chr.," *Berytus* 5 (1938) 74, n. 3; Magie, *Asia Minor* 709, with n. 32 on pp. 1569-1570; H. Mattingly, "The Palmyrene Princes and the Mints of Antioch and Alexandria," *Num. Chron.*, ser. 5, vol. 16 (1936) 89-114; Van Sickle, "Particularism in the Roman Empire" 353-354. For an excellent general picture of the role of Palmyra at this period, and of the careers of Odenath and Zenobia, see Starcky, *Palmyre* 53-66.

[140] Zonaras 12.24; *SHA Gall.* 3.1-5; *SHA Trig. tyr.* 14.1-2, 15.4-5. See Stein, "T.

thus nominally brought under the control of Gallienus, though Odenath was the actual master of the East, and it was Odenath and the Palmyrenes who saved the eastern Roman Empire from the Persians. In A.D. 262 Odenath invaded Persia with an army composed of Romans and Palmyrenes, and penetrated as far as Ctesiphon. Gallienus then granted him the title of *imperator*. In A.D. 266/7, however, a dynastic plot against Odenath was formed, and he was assassinated. He was succeeded, in the government of Palmyra, by his second wife Zenobia and his infant son Waballath. Gallienus, in an effort to check the power of Palmyra, withheld from Waballath the Roman titles that had been conferred on Odenath, so that in theory Waballath was merely king of Palmyra. Zenobia, however, remained in actual control of Syria.

During this period Antioch was at first for a brief time under the nominal control of the regime of Macrianus, and its mint issued coins for the younger Macrianus and Quietus.[141] After Odenath established himself as master of the East in A.D. 261 and 262, Antioch (with the rest of Syria) came under Palmyrene domination, though it remained nominally under the rule of Gallienus. Coins of Gallienus began to be struck at the mint of Antioch in A.D. 263.[142] At this time the leading figure in the city was its bishop, Paul of Samosata.[143] Paul had been elected bishop in A.D. 260, to succeed Demetrianus, who had been carried into captivity by the Persians when Sapor first took Antioch (apparently in A.D. 256).[144] It seems likely that Paul's election was

---

Fulvius Iunius Macrianus" and "T. Fulvius Iunius Quietus," *RE* 7 (1912) 253-258. According to *SHA Trig. tyr.* 18.7 (which does not, however, agree with the other sources), Ballista was killed on an estate that he had bought for himself "near Daphne" (presumably the suburb of Antioch).

[141] On the coins of Macrianus the Younger and Quietus issued at Antioch, see O. Voetter, "Die Münzen des Kaisers Gallienus u. seiner Familie," *Num. Ztschr.* 33 (1901) 84-85, and Mattingly-Sydenham, *Rom. Imp. Coinage* 5, pt. 2 (by P. H. Webb) pp. 580-583.

[142] See Alföldi in *Berytus* 5 (1938) 48, 76. The evidence of Malalas which has been taken to mean that Gallienus began to build a palace at Antioch is unreliable; Gallienus would hardly wish to build a palace in the city while it was under the control of Palmyra. Malalas' account probably refers actually to work carried out by Valerian, whom the chronicler sometimes confuses with Gallienus; see above, n. 126.

[143] We have so much information concerning Paul's career, in contrast with the meagerness of our sources for the other events of this period, that an adequate description of the bishop's activities in this context would constitute too much of an intrusion on the narrative. Only the essential features of Paul's career—particularly those showing its political significance—are given here. A more detailed account will be found in the treatment of the church at Antioch at this period; see Ch. 11, §6.

[144] On Paul's election, see Bardy, *Paul de Samosate*² 249-250. On the deportation of Demetrianus, see above, n. 122.

influenced by political considerations. Coming as he did from Samosata, he probably represented the Semitic rather than the Graeco-Roman element in the population of Syria;[145] and since he was entrusted with civil as well as ecclesiastical functions, and appears to have enjoyed the support of Palmyra when he was attacked and eventually deposed by his enemies, it seems clear that the bishop served as the principal representative of the Palmyrene regime in Antioch. Our knowledge of his career comes largely from the letter of condemnation by which an ecclesiastical council at Antioch in A.D. 268 deposed him from office;[146] and even when allowance is made for bias in this document, it gives us a picture of the bishop's activities which can readily be believed. According to the letter, Paul professed and taught the heretical doctrine that Christ was in His nature an ordinary man. Not only this, but Paul had made himself wealthy through extortion and the taking of bribes. He clothed himself in worldly honors and "wished to be called *ducenarius*[147] rather than bishop, strutting about in the market-places, reading and dictating letters as he walked in public, and attended by a bodyguard." He also, it is charged, possessed a *secretum*, as the private chamber of a magistrate or judge was called. Paul appears to have been, in fact, what amounted to Palmyrene viceroy in Antioch.[148] In the circumstances, he was bound to have both ardent supporters among the clergy of Antioch and its vicinity,[149] and equally determined enemies in the circles which looked to the political supremacy of Rome.[150] An effort was made to depose Paul in a church council called at Antioch in A.D. 264, but no result was achieved.[151] Four years later a second council did depose Paul, and elected Domnus, son of Paul's predecessor Demetrianus; but Paul, again relying on the support of Palmyra, refused to lay down his office.[152]

At about this time Gallienus was assassinated (March A.D. 268) and after a brief interval Claudius II (A.D. 268-270) established himself as emperor. Claudius at once found himself absorbed with checking the

[145] See Bardy, *Paul de Samosate*[2] 258.

[146] Quoted by Eusebius, *Eccl. Hist.* 7.30.2-17. Translations of this letter quoted below are taken from the edition of Oulton and Lawlor in the Loeb Classical Library.

[147] The *ducenarius* was a *procurator*, called *ducenarius* at the time when the rank or office was instituted because the salary was 200,000 sesterces per annum; see O. Seeck, "Ducenarius," *RE* 5 (1905) 1752-1754.

[148] See Bardy, *Paul de Samosate*[2] 260, n. 1.

[149] *Ibid.*, 315-316.   [150] *Ibid.*, 277.

[151] *Ibid.*, 283.

[152] Eusebius *Eccl. Hist.* 7.30.19. One of the leaders of the fight against Paul was Malchion, a presbyter of Antioch, "a learned man who also was head of a school of rhetoric, one of the Greek educational establishments at Antioch" (Euseb. *op.cit.* 7.29.2).

Goths in the Balkans, and his only known activity in affairs in the East seems to have consisted of a refusal to grant Waballath the titles that Gallienus had given Odenath. Antioch remained outwardly under the control of Claudius; during his reign, the mint struck only coins in his name, though the types of the coins were apparently influenced by Palmyrene ideas.[153] As Mattingly points out,[154] "it suited diplomatists on both sides—Roman and Palmyrene—to pretend that the rule of the Roman Emperor continued unabated." During Claudius' time, the deposed bishop Paul of Antioch, obviously relying on Palmyrene support, continued to refuse to vacate his office.[155]

The situation was altered when Claudius died in Sirmium of the plague in January A.D. 270. For a few months his brother Quintillus was recognized as emperor, but Aurelian, a famous general, quickly displaced him.[156] One of Aurelian's first problems was the question of the spreading power of Palmyra. Whether Aurelian at first, being occupied in Italy, felt that he had to make concessions, at least for the time being, or whether Zenobia took the initiative in an attempt to increase her son's power and dignity, is difficult to decide. All that is known is that with Aurelian's accession, the mint of Antioch began to strike coins bearing on one side the head of Aurelian and on the other that of Waballath, accompanied by the Roman titles that Gallienus had granted Odenath. The design of the coins indicates that Aurelian's head was intended to be on the reverse.[157]

[153] Our knowledge of the sequence of events at this period is deficient, and divergent views have been expressed as to the conduct of Zenobia. J. G. Février, *Essai sur l'histoire politique et économique de Palmyre* (Paris 1931) 105, points out that we know little as to what Zenobia did between A.D. 267 and 269. In the past, some scholars, such as P. Damerau, *Kaiser Claudius II. Gothicus* (Klio Beiheft N. F. 20, 1934) 60-61, and Parker, *Hist. of the Roman World A.D. 138-337* 190-191, took the evidence then available to mean that Zenobia "occupied" Antioch in the winter of A.D. 268/9 and put a stop to the issue of coins in Claudius' name from the mint. Alföldi's more recent study of the coins, however (*Berytus* 5 [1938] 56), has shown that the mint continued to strike in Claudius' name throughout his reign (cf. Alföldi in *CAH* 12.179), though the coins do betray their origin under Palmyrene influence and it is clear that Antioch was dominated by Palmyra; see H. Mattingly, "The Palmyrene Princes and the Mints of Antioch and Alexandria," *Num. Chron.* ser. 5. vol. 16 (1936) 110-111; Henze, "M. Aurelius Claudius Augustus," *RE* 2 (1896) 2460-2461; (Groag, "L. Domitius Aurelianus," *RE* 5 (1905) 1362; L. Homo, *De Claudio Gothico, Romanorum imperatore* (Diss., Paris 1903) 63, n. 1. For lead tokens of Herodian, son of Odenath, which were struck at Antioch, and tokens of Zenobia apparently coming from the same source, see H. Seyrig, "Note sur Hérodien, prince de Palmyre," *Syria* 18 (1937) 1-4.
[154] "The Palmyrene Princes and the Mints of Antioch and Alexandria," *Num. Chron.* ser. 5. vol. 16 (1936) 114.
[155] Bardy, *Paul de Samosate*[2] 353-355.
[156] On Aurelian's accession, see Mattingly in *CAH* 12.297ff. and Groag, "L. Domitius Aurelianus," *RE* 5 (1905) 1354-1355.
[157] Differing interpretations are put on these coins by Alföldi, *CAH* 12.179, and by

A German invasion of Italy, and a rebellion in Rome in A.D. 271[158] suggested to Zenobia that this was a favorable moment to make a final break with the Roman Empire and to assert the complete independence of Palmyra; and at some time between 11 March and 28 August A.D. 271 this was done.[159] Waballath took the title of Augustus and had appropriate coins struck at the mints of Antioch and Alexandria. Simultaneously there appeared coins in which Zenobia was styled Augusta.[160]

Aurelian took action in the summer of A.D. 271, sending the future emperor Probus to reconquer Egypt, which the Palmyrenes had occupied. Later in the same year Aurelian himself proceeded by way of the Danube and Byzantium to Asia Minor, which he reconquered in the early part of A.D. 272. A substantial force of the Palmyrene army under command of the general Zabdas and accompanied by Zenobia herself, was waiting in Antioch,[161] which Aurelian could be expected to make his first objective in Syria.

Aurelian, apparently planning to circle about Antioch and cut the escape route to the south, did not approach the city by the direct Pagrae-Antioch road, but took the route which skirted the eastern side of the Lake of Antioch. From this he would reach (via the road to

---

Mattingly, *ibid.* 301-302. On Aurelian's position, see also Bardy, *Paul de Samosate*² 355-356; Parker, *Hist. of the Roman World A.D. 138-337* 194-195; and Groag in *RE* 5.1364-1366.

[158] This uprising, the *bellum monetariorum*, began as a revolt of the mint officials or employees in Rome, the immediate cause of which is not entirely clear. The revolt was joined by some members of the senatorial order who presumably saw an opportunity to overthrow Aurelian, and something like a civil war ensued. The rising was quelled, it is said, with considerable loss of life. See the accounts of the rebellion by Groag in *RE* 5.1372-1374; Parker, *Hist. of the Roman World A.D. 138-337* 195-196; and Mattingly, *CAH* 12.300. Malalas (301.1-4) records a rising of the mint-workers at Antioch which (as Groag and Mattingly think) may be only a mistaken version of the outbreak in Rome. Stauffenberg, in his desire to vindicate the importance of the material found in Malalas, argues (*Malalas* 387-389) that since the chronicler lived in Antioch and had access to local sources embodied in a city chronicle, his notice of a rising of mint-workers at Antioch must be true. Stauffenberg forgets, however, that at the time when the rising in Rome probably occurred (A.D. 271), the mint of Antioch was under Palmyrene control, and that the factors which caused the disturbance in Rome need not have existed at Antioch. It would be perfectly possible for a careless and unintelligent writer such as Malalas, finding in a source a notice of a rising of mint-workers, the location of which was not specified because it occurred in the imperial capital, to conclude that the rising took place in Antioch, the center of his interest.

[159] See Groag in *RE* 5.1360, 1380; Parker, *Hist. of the Roman World A.D. 138-337* 198; and Mattingly in *CAH* 12.301.

[160] For the coins, see Groag in *RE* 5.1380 and Mattingly-Sydenham, *Rom. Imp. Coinage* 5 (by P. H. Webb) pt. 1, pl. 9, no. 132, and pt. 2, pp. 584-585. See also Mattingly in *CAH* 12.301-302.

[161] Zosimus 1.50.2.

Gindarus) the Antioch-Beroea road, along which he could move on Antioch from the east. Somewhere along the Antioch-Beroea road east of the crossing of the Orontes at Gephyra (mod. Djisr el-Hadid) the Romans encountered a large force of Palmyrene cavalry. This seems to have represented a major part of the Palmyrene forces at Antioch, dispatched by Zabdas when he learned of the Romans' approach.[162]

On learning that he would have to face the Palmyrene cavalry, Aurelian detached his infantry and sent it across the Orontes, presumably because he knew that it could not stand against the Palmyrene horse. He ordered his cavalry, which he knew was inferior to the enemy's, not to offer battle at once, but to simulate withdrawal, so that the Palmyrenes might be worn out with the heat and the weight of their heavy armor. The Romans fell back along the highway toward Immae, a village which lay in the direction of Beroea, and when it was seen that the Palmyrenes were fatigued, the Romans turned on them and won a complete victory. Those of the Palmyrenes who could do so, escaped to Antioch. Zabdas probably realized that the people of the city, on learning of the disaster, would rise in favor of Aurelian, whose clemency during his recovery of Asia Minor had doubtless become known in Antioch; besides, knowledge of the superior power of the Roman army would turn the local population against the Palmyrene regime. Zabdas therefore, in order to gain time and to prevent any attempt by the inhabitants to interfere with his withdrawal, immediately after the battle let it be known that he had defeated and captured Aurelian, and paraded through the streets a man who resembled the emperor. The trick succeeded, and Zabdas and Zenobia

---

[162] On the Romans' first clash with the Palmyrene forces, see Downey, "Aurelian's Victory over Zenobia at Immae, A.D. 272," *TAPA* 81 (1950) 57-68 (with map), where the evidence which leads to the reconstruction of the engagement presented above is discussed. The principal source for the battle is Zosimus (1.50), but his narrative has been misunderstood, particularly since he does not mention Immae in his account of the engagement. Rufius Festus (*Brev.* 24), Syncellus (vol. 1, p. 721 Bonn ed.) Jordanes (*Rom.* 291) and Jerome (*Chron.* an. Abr. 2289) put the decisive battle of this campaign at Immae, but they do not mention the engagement at Emesa, which according to Zosimus (1.52-53) was the decisive battle. It has been supposed that the reference to Immae in the chronicles is a mistake, or the result of a confusion of Immae with Emesa (see Honigmann, "Syria" 1691-1692). However, a new study of Zosimus' account and of the road system around Antioch (cf. Dussaud, *Topographie* 232, and Groag, "L. Domitius Aurelianus," *RE* 5 [1905] 1383-1384) makes it clear that the first battle that Zosimus describes took place at Immae, and that this engagement was not a mere cavalry skirmish, as some scholars have thought, but an important battle; see the map accompanying the study by the present writer mentioned above. Malalas (300.11) and the other chroniclers cited above mistakenly write that Zenobia was captured at Antioch; in reality she was taken later as she was attempting to escape from the siege of Palmyra (Zos. 1.55).

were able to flee from Antioch that same night with the remainder
of their forces, leaving a rear guard behind them. Evidently they went
by the road which led through Daphne to Seleucobelus and then to
Apamea, whence they could have gone via Epiphania to Emesa. Apparently Aurelian had not been able to occupy this road. The Palmyrene rear guard established itself on a height above Daphne, probably
that on the left of the road (as one goes south) which rises above the
valley where the springs are located. Occupation of this position would
slow down, at least, the Roman pursuit of Zenobia and her people.

On the next day, when he learned of Zenobia's flight, Aurelian gave
up his plans for an infantry assault on Antioch and entered the city,
receiving an enthusiastic welcome from the inhabitants. Finding that
many people had fled the city in fear of punishment for their having
sided with Zenobia, the emperor proclaimed an amnesty and had copies
of the proclamation circulated in the surrounding areas, upon which
the refugees returned.[163] It is a tribute to the strength of Aurelian's
military discipline that he was able to keep his troops from plundering
the city.

The Palmyrene rear guard was easily dislodged from its stronghold
at Daphne and annihiliated.[164] Aurelian then issued such orders as
were necessary concerning the internal affairs of the city.[165] It was
doubtless at this time that an appeal was made to him to take action
with regard to the intractable bishop, Paul of Samosata, who though
deposed by a council four years earlier had refused to hand over his
office to his elected successor Domnus. Paul's history as a supporter of
the Palmyrene regime made only one decision possible; he was ejected
from Antioch and disappeared, and Domnus was able to exercise his
proper functions.[166]

[163] According to the biographer of Aurelian in the *SHA* (25.1), Aurelian was moved
to clemency by the appearance to him of the spirit of Apollonius of Tyana, who had
earlier saved the city of Tyana from destruction by appearing to the emperor (24.3).
On Aurelian's treatment of Antioch, see also W. H. Fisher, "The Augustan Vita
Aureliani," *JRS* 19 (1929) 138, 142, 148.
[164] Zosimus 1.52. The biography of Aurelian in the *SHA* (25.1) mistakenly places
this engagement at Daphne, before Aurelian's entry into Antioch, and omits altogether
the battle at Immae.
[165] Zosimus 1.52, p. 36.22 ed. Mendelssohn. On Aurelian's occupation of Antioch, see
L. Homo, *Essai sur le règne de l'empereur Aurélien* (Paris 1904; *Bibl. des Écoles franç.
d'Athenes et de Rome*, fasc. 89) 96-97.
[166] Eusebius *Hist. Eccl.* 7.30.18-19, states that Domnus' claim to the bishopric of Antioch was made to depend upon his being recognized by the bishop of Rome and the
other bishops of Italy. This statement, however, does not seem trustworthy. See Ch. 11,
nn. 175-177.

Aurelian then set out in pursuit of the Palmyrenes. He defeated them at Emesa, and Zenobia and Zabdas withdrew to Palmyra, where the Romans carried out a successful siege. Zenobia escaped from the city before the siege was completed, but was captured as she was crossing the Euphrates.[167] Malalas tells how Zenobia, as she was being taken to Rome, was exhibited as a captive in Antioch.[168]

An invasion of Lower Moesia by the Carpi recalled the emperor to Europe (autumn, A.D. 272). During his absence from the East, Palmyrene rebellions broke out in Palmyra and in Egypt, and the emperor returned from the Danube with such speed that he astonished the people of Antioch by arriving unannounced while a horse-race was in progress (A.D. 273).[169] Aurelian pushed on to Palmyra and Alexandria and subdued the rebels.[170]

Aurelian was assassinated in A.D. 275, while on his way from Rome to carry out another campaign against the Persians.[171] He had succeeded, even during his brief reign, in restoring the political unity and financial stability of the empire. Antioch, which had for more than thirty years suffered repeated Persian conquest, pillage, depopulation, destruction, and finally Palmyrene domination and the civil and ecclesiastical disturbances that rose about Paul of Samosata, had in the last few years of Aurelian's reign enjoyed a brief period of tranquillity.

In the interval between the death of Aurelian and the accession in the following year of Probus, the *pacator orbis* who was to be a fitting successor to Aurelian the *restitutor orbis*, there was an interregnum during which the former senator Tacitus and his half-brother Florianus were emperors. During this period Antioch suffered under the harsh rule of Maximinus, a relative of Tacitus' who had been made governor of Syria. Maximinus was assassinated[172] and his death was followed by that of Tacitus.[173]

---

[167] Parker, *Hist. of the Roman World A.D. 138-337* 201-202.

[168] 300.11-17; cf. Stauffenberg, *Malalas* 385-387.

[169] Zosimus 1.61.1. See Groag in *RE* 5.1389.

[170] Malalas (301.1-4) records a rising of the mint-workers at Antioch under Aurelian, but this may be only a mistaken doublette of the rising that took place in Rome; see above, n. 158.

[171] See Magie, *Asia Minor* 718, with n. 46 on p. 1576.

[172] Zosimus 1.63.2; Zonaras 12.28.

[173] The biography of Tacitus in the *SHA* contains (18.5-6) a copy of a letter that was supposed to have been sent by the Senate in Rome to a number of cities, including Antioch, at the time of Tacitus' accession. The letter was intended to remind the provincials of the authority of the Senate. Apparently in connection with Tacitus' military operations in Asia Minor, the mints of Antioch and Tripolis during his reign issued a large number of a special variety of Antoniniani: K. Pink, "XI, IA und XII auf Antoninianen," *Numismatische Zeitschrift* 74 (1951) 46-49.

A History of Antioch

The accession of Probus opened a reign of six years (A.D. 276-282) devoted to the consolidation of Aurelian's successes and the reorganization of the empire's frontiers. Antioch, having suffered unusual damage, received special assistance. A free distribution of wheat, at public expense, was instituted, though we are not told whether this took the form of only one distribution, or whether a permanent free supply of wheat (or of bread) was established.[174] There was also a building program for the restoration of the physical damage to the city, though here again the paucity of our sources prevents us from knowing how extensive the work was. The only details concerning the work itself which are preserved come from the chronicle of Malalas, in which it is recorded that the Museum was beautified, along with a sigma-shaped Nymphaeum which it contained; the Nymphaeum, which was presumably shaped like a lunar sigma (c), contained a mosaic of Oceanus —a subject which, as we know from the mosaics recovered in the excavations, was popular at Antioch.[175] Nothing is said concerning any

[174] The distribution of wheat (σιτήσεις) is mentioned by Malalas (302.9-11), the obviously corrupt Oxford MS being emended by Stauffenberg in his edition. In the fourth century, in a time of famine, grain and bread were sold at Antioch at fixed prices by order of the emperor Julian; see Downey, "Economic Crisis under Julian," and the chapter on Julian below. On the public control of the distribution of grain in the cities of the Greek East, and on imperial benefactions in this respect, see Jones, *Greek City* 217-219; Magie, *Asia Minor* 1.619 (generosity of Hadrian at Tralles); H. Francotte, "Le pain à bon marché et le pain gratuit dans les cités grecques," *Mélanges Nicole* (Geneva 1905) 153-157. The passage in Malalas had been corrupted into an obviously garbled statement that Probus decreed the *siteseis* so that children in Antioch could be educated free of charge. While it is quite possible that at some time provision was made in Antioch for the free education of children, the passage in Malalas could not have this meaning. See H.-I. Marrou *Histoire de l'éducation dans l'antiquité* (Paris 1948) 562, n. 13 (where the reference to Stauffenberg *Malalas* should be to p. 392).

[175] Malalas 302.6-9. The texts which appear to refer to a restoration or rebuilding of Antioch are Jordanes, *Rom.* 293: *Saturninus magister militum, dum ad restaurationem Antiochenae civitatis missus fuisset . . .* ; Jerome, *Chron.* an. Abr. 2297: *Saturninus magister exercitus novam Antiochiam exorsus est condere . . .* ; Syncellus, vol. 1, p. 723.7 Bonn ed.: Σατορνῖνος στρατοπεδάρχης τὴν καινὴν Ἀντιόχειαν ἤρξατο κτίζειν . . . Harrer, *Studies* 49, not knowing the passage in Jordanes, took the notices in Jerome and Syncellus to mean that "Saturninus tried to found either a new city Antioch, or a new state at Antioch." Such a reading is, literally, possible, but Jordanes' entry suggests that Jerome and Syncellus were merely indulging in hyperbole. A. Stein, "Saturninus," *RE* 2A (1923) 214, realizes that a reconstruction program is meant, but he thinks that it was made necessary by earthquakes. No earthquake at Antioch during this period is recorded, and Stein forgets that Antioch had been pillaged and supposedly destroyed by the Persians a few years previously. Bouchier, *Antioch* 124, writes that Saturninus had prepared to add "a new quarter" at Antioch, but there is no evidence or even suggestion to this effect in the texts, and there is no occasion to think that a new quarter should have been desirable or necessary at this period, while on the other hand there is good reason to think that at least some restoration was called for. Stauffenberg (*Malalas* 459) believes that the island was called the "new city," ἡ νέα, ἡ καινή, because it was brought into being by Saturninus, on the basis of an over-all plan made by Gal-

utilitarian undertakings, though these must have been fairly extensive if the Persians had succeeded in doing any amount of damage in the city. A functionary named Julius Saturninus was placed in charge of the work; whether he was governor of Syria or not, is not clear. In circumstances that are not entirely plain, Saturninus was proclaimed emperor (at Antioch, according to some), and coins of his are preserved which seem to have been struck at Antioch.[176] His career, however, was brief, and he was killed, either by his own or Probus' troops.

Probus may have visited Antioch when he was in the East in A.D. 279 and 280.[177] In A.D. 282 he was assassinated by his own troops when the army in Raetia proclaimed Carus emperor. Carus made associates of his sons Carinus and Numerianus,[178] but the careers of Carus and Numerianus were quickly terminated, and when the army (17 November A.D. 284) chose as emperor Diocles, the commander of the *protectores domestici,* a new phase in the history of the empire was opened.

---

lienus. It may be that the work attributed by Malalas to Gallienus, which actually seems to have been done by Valerian (see above, n. 126), involved changes in the plan of the island, though it would seem improbable that the Roman government at this time should have been able to find the money for any extensive building program at Antioch. In any case, there is no evidence whatever as to the nature of the work planned by Saturninus. It is more likely that the island was called the "new" quarter because it was settled by Seleucus II Callinicus and Antiochus III the Great, as an extension of the original settlement of Seleucus I (see above, Ch. 5, §§3-4). At this time the epithet "new" would have been attached to the settlement on the island, and it would be natural for such an epithet to remain in use through the centuries.

[176] On the varying reports concerning Saturninus' career, see Stein in *RE* 2A, 213-215, and Mattingly in *CAH* 12.315. There is a unique *aureus* of Saturninus, attributed to the mint of Alexandria by E. Babelon, "Le tyran Saturninus," *Rev. num.* 1896, 133-144, reprinted in the same author's *Mélanges numismatiques,* ser. 3, 167-178 (on the sale of the coin, see *Bull. de num.* 3 [1895] 107-108). Mattingly (*loc.cit.*), however, seems inclined to believe that the mint of Antioch is the place of origin. The date of Saturninus' uprising is not certain; on the various dates which have been proposed (A.D. 277, 280, 281/2), none of which can be accepted without question, see Harrer, *Studies* 50.

[177] On his visit see Henze, "M. Aurelius Probus," *RE* 2 (1896) 2521. Little is known of the emperor's movements during this visit, and there is no specific indication that he visited Antioch.

[178] Some ancient sources name Numerianus as the emperor whom Babylas, the bishop of Antioch, rebuked at the church door. However, it seems certain that Babylas was bishop under the Gordians (A.D. 238-244) and Philip the Arab (A.D. 244-249), and it is, besides, doubtful that the famous episode ever really occurred. See Ch. 11, nn. 140-143.

CHAPTER 11

THE CHRISTIAN COMMUNITY AT ANTIOCH, FROM APOSTOLIC TIMES TO A.D. 284

1. THE APOSTOLIC AGE; THE ORIGIN OF THE CHRISTIAN COMMUNITY AT ANTIOCH

IN THE TIME of Christ, there had developed in Antioch, as in other centers in which eastern and western cultures came into contact, a religious situation that was to make the city fertile ground for Christianity. Antioch had shared, with other places in which Hellenic religion and philosophy had flourished, the developments characteristic of the late Hellenistic age, in which the old religious cults and the philosophies were tending to become matters of individual belief, as people independently sought religious satisfaction for their own problems and aspirations.[1] In addition, Antioch, as a meeting point of the Greek and the Oriental civilizations, filled with orientalized Greeks and Hellenized Orientals, of all classes and all degrees of education, had come to contain, as part of its normal daily existence, not only the old established Hellenic cults, of Zeus, Apollo, and the rest of the pantheon, but the Syrian cults of Baal and the mother-goddess—partly assimilated to Zeus and Artemis—as well as the mystery cults with their doctrines of salvation, of death and regeneration, and their promises for the after life. By virtue of its position as one of the three largest cities of the Roman Empire, and one of the great commercial centers of the ancient world, with business connections in all parts of the Empire, Antioch saw the coming and going of peoples of all sorts, bringing news of religious movements everywhere in the Roman world. Another local factor of prime importance was the presence of a large and ancient Jewish community which seems to have felt no great hostility toward the Gentiles, and, in turn, appears not to have been

---

[1] Among the numerous studies of the pagan religious atmosphere at the time of Christ and the factors in this which prepared the way for the coming of Christianity and affected its development, it is sufficient here to refer to A. D. Nock, *Early Gentile Christianity*, 51-156, with the same author's further study of the important question of the relation of the mysteries to Christianity, "Hellenistic Mysteries and Christian Sacraments," *Mnemosyne*, ser. 4, vol. 5 (1952) 177-213; H. R. Willoughby, *Pagan Regeneration* (Chicago, 1929); A. D. Nock, *Conversion* (Oxford, 1933); A.-J. Festugière, *Le monde gréco-romain au temps de Notre-Seigneur*, 2: *Le milieu spirituel* (Paris, 1935); G. Bardy, *La Conversion au Christianisme durant les premiers siècles* (Paris, 1949). In these works the ancient texts and the modern studies of the subject are documented in detail.

looked upon with any marked degree of disfavor by the Gentiles as a whole, at this time. As was the case elsewhere in the Graeco-Roman world,[2] the Jewish community in Antioch attracted to its ceremonies and teachings a number of Gentiles who found in Jewish monotheism and ethics a form of religion which was more satisfying than the pagan beliefs.[3] The fact that they were able to read the Jewish Scriptures in Greek translation undoubtedly promoted the interest that these inquirers felt in the Jewish teachings. Among these Gentiles may have been Nicolaus of Antioch, an early proselyte and one of the seven deacons in Jerusalem.[4] Thus it was that when the religious development of the Graeco-Roman world created a situation in which that world was well prepared for Christianity, Antioch was one of the places that was receptive to the new teaching.

When a persecution broke out in Jerusalem after the execution of Stephen, some of the followers of Jesus fled from the city and traveled as far as Phoenice, Cyprus, and Antioch, preaching to Jews.[5] In Antioch, however, some of the refugees who were Hellenist (Greek-speaking) Jews from Cyprus and Cyrene began to preach to "Greeks" (i.e. Greek-speaking Gentiles, not necessarily Greeks by birth), a new departure.[6] Whether, when persecution occurred, the deacon Nicolaus returned to Antioch with the early missionaries, we are not told, but it is easy to believe that he would have wished to do so, rather than remain in hiding in Jerusalem.[7] He is not, however, named among the men who are listed as being prominent in the Christian community at Antioch along with Barnabas and Paul.[8]

The efforts of the Hellenist Jews in Antioch met with great success,

[2] Acts 10:2, 22, 35; 13:43; 14:1; 16:14; 17:4, 17; 18:7.

[3] Josephus *Bell.* 7.45 records the interest of the "Greeks" of Antioch in Judaism and their attendance at Jewish services. On the importance of the Jewish community in this respect, see Kraeling, "Jewish Community at Antioch" 147, and Knox, *St. Paul and the Church of Jerusalem* 156, with n. on 161.

[4] Acts 6:5.   [5] Acts 11:19.

[6] At this point some MSS of Acts, including the Koine or "Antiochene" text which was developed by Christian scholars at Antioch ca. A.D. 300 and is represented in the Textus Receptus published by Erasmus and Stephanus, say that in Antioch the Greek-speaking Jews preached to "the Hellenists," which would mean either Greek-speaking persons in general or (on the analogy of Acts 6:1) Greek-speaking Jews. However, in the case of Antioch, it seems plain from the context, as well as from subsequent developments, that the writer intends to distinguish between Jews and non-Jews. If "Hellenists" is to be read here, it seems clear that it must be regarded as the equivalent of Hellene. See the detailed study, "The Hellenists," by H. J. Cadbury, in *Beginnings of Christianity* 5 (1933) 59-74.

[7] See Bauer, *Antiochia* 19-20. The establishment of the Nicolaitan heresy is attributed (probably falsely) to this Nicolaus by some sources; see below, §3.

[8] Acts 13:1.

and thus the mission to the Gentiles was firmly established.[9] Some of the early converts were doubtless Gentiles who had already been attracted to Judaism and had some knowledge of it, and the conversion of other Gentiles would follow readily in a large cosmopolitan city such as Antioch where traditional barriers of race, nationality, and formal religion could easily be crossed.[10] For both religious and philosophical needs, the new teaching was unique, and was superior to anything that could be found elsewhere.[11] Practical reasons for the success of the early mission at Antioch may have been that in this city the missionaries had not to fear Jewish fanatics such as they encountered in Jerusalem; also that the city, as the capital of Syria, was governed by a legate, and so enjoyed a greater degree of public order, with less opportunity for mob violence such as had occurred in Jerusalem, where the procurators of Judaea seem (at this period at least) not to have been able to restrain the Jewish fanatics.[12]

When the elders in Jerusalem heard of the encouraging and, in some respects, novel work that was going on in the Syrian capital, they sent Barnabas—a native of Cyprus like some of the early missionaries in Antioch[13]—to inspect the undertaking and report on its success and

[9] The best general account of the early mission at Antioch is that of Knox, *St. Paul and the Church of Jerusalem* 156-198. Good accounts are also provided by Bauer, *Antiochia* and by K. Pieper, "Antiochien am Orontes im apostolischen Zeitalter," *Theologie und Glaube* 22 (1930) 710-728. See also Harnack, *Mission und Ausbreitung*[4] 1.57ff., and the third volume of Meyer, *Ursprung u. Anfänge*. A perceptive account of the early Christian community at Antioch may be found in Philip Carrington's *The Early Christian Church* (Cambridge 1957), which appeared after the present chapter was completed. Special studies are cited below. The celebrated "Chalice of Antioch," now a part of the collection at The Cloisters of the Metropolitan Museum of Art in New York, is supposed to have been found at Antioch about 1910, and some have claimed that it was used in the Last Supper and in time taken to Antioch. Specialists now believe that the Chalice was made at a much later period, though recent studies of the fabric have shown that it was made in antiquity and is not a modern forgery, as has sometimes been asserted. See H. H. Arnason, "The History of the Chalice of Antioch," *Biblical Archaeologist* 4 (1941) 50-64; 5 (1942) 10-16, and J. Rorimer, "The Authenticity of the Chalice of Antioch," *Studies in Art and Literature for Belle Da Costa Greene* (Princeton 1954) 161-168.

[10] On the role of Antioch and other non-Jewish centers in the spread of Christianity, see especially Bauer, *Antiochia* 23-25; D. W. Riddle, "Environment as a Factor in the Achievement of Self-Consciousness in Early Christianity," *JR* 7 (1927) 146-163; M. C. Tenney, "The Influence of Antioch on Apostolic Christianity," *Bibliotheca Sacra* 107 (1950) 298-310.

[11] For an excellent statement of the reasons for the early success of Christianity, see A. D. Nock, "Early Gentile Christianity and its Hellenistic Background," in *Essays on the Trinity and the Incarnation*, ed. by A. E. J. Rawlinson (London 1928) 154-156.

[12] On this important point, see Knox, *St. Paul and the Church of Jerusalem* 156, with n. on 161.

[13] Acts 4:36. Eusebius (*Hist. eccl.* 1.12.1) reports a tradition that Barnabas had been one of the Seventy.

prospects. Barnabas as a Cypriote would have felt quite at home in Antioch, and the people of the city would have recognized him as a member of a neighboring community with which they were familiar. He made further conversions, and seeing that the mission was prospering, he went to Tarsus, where Paul was now living, and asked him to come to Antioch to help in the work. Barnabas and Paul remained in Antioch for a year, teaching.[14] The local tradition, recorded by Malalas, was that they preached in an alley (or street) called Singon or Siagon ("jawbone") near the Pantheon.[15] The chronology of these events is not clear. The death of Stephen seems to have taken place about A.D. 34 or possibly 36,[16] and the mission to Antioch would have begun soon after that. Barnabas was apparently sent there about A.D. 38. The chronology of Paul's conversion (though this is disputed) and of his sojourn in Cilicia following it would put the beginning of the activity of Paul and Barnabas in Antioch at about A.D. 40.[17]

It was in Antioch, in the early 40's that the followers of Christ first came to bear the name of Christians.[18] The word apparently was adopted by the Roman authorities in the city when they found that it was necessary to have some official description of the group or sect, which by now, in Antioch, was becoming distinct from Judaism.[19]

[14] Acts 11:22-26.

[15] Malalas 242.11-12. In the Oxford MS of Malalas the place is described with the words ἐν τῇ ῥύμῃ τῇ πλησίον τοῦ Πανθέου τῇ καλουμένῃ τῶν Σίγγωνος (corrected to Σίγγωνος by all editors). In the *Thesaurus* of Stephanus, ed. by Hase and W. and L. Dindorf, it is suggested *s.v.* Σίγγων, on the basis of this text, that the word is a personal name that had been given to this quarter of the city (τὰ Σίγγωνος). The Church Slavonic version of Malalas (p. 52 transl. Spinka) renders: "in the parts which are formerly near the Pantheon, being named after a jawbone." The Greek word for "jawbone" is σιαγών. It is not easy to determine what the real name of the locality was. The text of Malalas might originally have contained the word σιαγών, which was correctly rendered in the Church Slavonic translation but later became corrupted in the Greek text. However, the Church Slavonic translation might represent a misreading of the proper name Σίγγων for the perhaps more familiar σιαγών. One can suppose that a street or alley might have been called "Jawbone" because of its shape. The location of the Pantheon is not known. The only other reference to it is the notice of its restoration by Julius Caesar (Malalas 217.3). Müller (*Antiq. Antioch.* 85, n. 5) by a slip of the pen writes that Malalas is mistaken in stating that Peter and Barnabas preached near the Pantheon. Actually Malalas names Paul and Barnabas, though he speaks of Peter later in the same sentence.

[16] See *Beginnings of Christianity* 4.86, note on Acts 8.1, and Lake, "The Chronology of Acts," *ibid.* 5.445-474.

[17] On the chronology, see Knox, *St. Paul and the Church of Jerusalem* 160, n. 1.

[18] Acts 11:26.

[19] In this I follow the opinion of R. Paribeni, "Sull'origine del nome Cristiano," *Nuovo bullettino di archeologia cristiana* 19 (1913) 37-41, as developed by E. Peterson, "Christianus," *Miscellanea G. Mercati* 1 (Vatican City 1946) 353-372 (*Studi e Testi* No. 121). There are, however, other explanations of the origin of the word, e.g. that followed by Kidd, *Hist. of the Church* 1.26, who believes that the term was a nickname

Such a designation would be necessary in a place such as Antioch where there were many cults of all kinds.

Concerning the size, composition, and administration of the group of Christians in Antioch at this time, we have not much evidence, and some of the information we do possess is difficult to interpret. It is said that "a great number were converted" and that Barnabas and Paul taught "a large number of people" (ὄχλον ἱκανόν)[20] but this statement is only relative, and we do not know what the basis of measurement was.

There is no indication of the form of government or administration of the community; indeed, there is no indication that there was any formal government at this period, and it is not until the time of Bishop Ignatius, at the beginning of the second century, that we possess any reliable evidence of an established administration in the community at Antioch. In the apostolic period there seem to have been, at Antioch, no titles designating "elders" or chiefs such as the leaders in Jerusalem. Barnabas and Paul doubtless enjoyed a certain personal prestige based upon their personal histories and their known spiritual experiences, as well as upon their manner of life and their eloquence; but we do not hear that they were given titles which would indicate administrative positions. They are in fact listed simply among the five "prophets and teachers" (προφῆται καὶ διδάσκαλοι)—namely Barnabas, Symeon Niger, Lucius of Cyrene, Manaen a "companion" of Herod the Tetrarch, and Saul—who are mentioned (Acts 13:1) as the men who were (it is implied) the most active and the most prominent in the local *ekklesia* (κατὰ τὴν οὖσαν ἐκκλησίαν) in Antioch at the time. The local *ekklesia* (mentioned also in Acts 11.26 and 14.27) appears simply as the general group of the faithful in the city, or as the group when it was gathered for worship. Composing the group are "the brethren" (οἱ ἀδελφοί) who appear in Acts 15:1 and 15:32-33, and the "disciples" (οἱ μαθηταί) who are called Christians (Acts 11:26; cf. 14:28). The Christian community when it is all assembled is called τὸ πλῆθος

---

invented by the people of Antioch, who ridiculed the new sect, and that of E. J. Bickerman, "The Name of Christians," *HTR* 42 (1949) 109-124, who believes that the term was devised by the Christians themselves. See also J. Moreau "Le nom des Chrétiens," *Nouvelle Clio* 1-2 (1949-1950) 190-192, and H. Fuchs, "Tacitus über die Christen," *Vigiliae Christianae* 4 (1950) 69, n. 5. Another suggestion has been put forward by Harold B. Mattingly ("The Origin of the Name Christiani," *JTS*, N.S. 9 [1958] 26-37), who thinks that the term *Christiani* was inspired by the title *Augustiani* which was given to the members of the Emperor Nero's organized claque. This theory does not seem to me to be convincing.

[20] Acts 11:21, 26.

(Acts 15:30); and the same kind of gathered assembly at Antioch (as has been mentioned) is also called ἐκκλησία (Acts 14:27), the word *ekklesia* also being used to describe the whole number of Christians at Antioch when they were not necessarily gathered together (Acts 11:26, 13.1). While the word *ekklesia* was not yet formally established at this time as a technical term, there is nothing in any of the evidence to show that there were elders or any other kind of formal chiefs in the "church" at Antioch at this period. The religious activities of the Christians were probably both at the early period and for some time to come, of an informal character. The tradition preserved by Malalas that Barnabas and Paul preached in an alley or street near the Pantheon has been mentioned. Public preaching probably could not be carried on with any regularity. For the most part, the new converts, and interested or curious friends whom they brought with them, doubtless met, as Jesus and his followers had done, in private houses. The use of houses for such meetings—in which a certain measure of secrecy could be preserved—is amply attested elsewhere, and a private house part of which was arranged for use as a church has been discovered in the excavations at Dura-Europos. A later, and not too reliable, tradition has it that Theophilus, the friend of the evangelist Luke, donated his luxurious house for use as a church at Antioch.[21]

There were very likely at least several different groups among the early Christians of Antioch, and these probably met in different houses for teaching and fellowship, for the breaking of bread, and for prayers, as is described in Acts 2:42 (cf. Acts 2:46). The Jewish Christians and the Gentile Christians presumably met separately, at least in so far as the orthodox Jews observed the Law in the matter of eating with Gentiles; and when Peter visited Antioch, as will be described later, he found different groups (Gal. 2:12). Doubtless these groups had their natural leaders, or prominent members, who in some cases would be the owners of the houses in which the meetings were held. There were

[21] The question of the organization and government of the *ekklesia* at Antioch is a vexed one, with wide ramifications in the later history of Christianity which go beyond the limits of the present study. In addition to the discussions of the early history of the community at Antioch which have been cited in the preceding notes, reference should be made to the lucid summaries of the evidence and its significance by Cadbury, *Beginnings of Christianity* 5.387-389 (on the meaning of *ekklesia, plethos,* etc.) and by Hort, *Ecclesia,* especially 90-91. On the house church at Dura, see *The Excavations at Dura-Europos, Preliminary Report of the Fifth Season of Work, 1931-1932,* ed. by M. I. Rostovtzeff (New Haven 1934), in which the building is described and studied by C. Hopkins, especially 238-253, with plate 39. Hopkins (246) provides a collection of the literary testimonia on the use of private houses as churches. The house at Dura is later in date than the apostolic age, but it may fairly be taken to represent the early custom.

also, no doubt, charismatic teachers who went from house congregation to house congregation.

The subsequent history of the Christians at Antioch in fact suggests—as one might in any case suppose—that there were a number of these congregations, and that the various groups often followed quite different lines in their teaching and worship. The Jewish Christians and the Gentile Christians have been mentioned. Among the latter, there were perhaps some who followed the ideas of salvation and of the sacraments which had been developed by Paul, and others who did not accept these ideas. There were probably also other groups following their own interests in the direction of a blending of the teachings concerning Jesus with certain aspects of the pagan cults, particularly the mysteries, which were current at the time; for in the period before the Gospels as we know them were written down, different kinds of information concerning Jesus and his activities must have been in circulation (as is indicated in the opening sentence of the Gospel according to Luke). Certainly a diversity of this kind in the early period of Christianity at Antioch is indicated, as we shall see, by the appearance in the city, toward the end of the first century of our era, of such different phenomena as the Gnostic movement, with its emphasis upon thaumaturgy, and the mystic concepts of Ignatius. In addition there were almost certainly various kinds of ecstatics and mystics, and devotees of various atonement doctrines. Ignatius' *Epistle to the Trallians* suggests that he had a considerable experience with docetic teachings, against which he inveighs strongly, and this indicates that such teachings had troubled the Christian community at Antioch from early times. The history of the development of the church at Antioch is, indeed, a reflection—which it is often difficult to trace—of the origin and fate of these special movements.

So far as we can tell, the Christians at Antioch were not organized along the lines of the community at Jerusalem, which was governed, in the manner of a synagogue, by a board of elders or presbyters, among whom James, the brother of the Lord, had a leading or presiding position. Since the community at Antioch had been started by refugees from Jerusalem, it may be tempting to speculate whether the difference in the status of the community at Antioch reflects deliberate choice, and whether the refugees, dissatisfied with conditions at Jerusalem, adopted in Antioch a form of fellowship more in keeping with their own views. It has been suggested that this difference may be the

earliest token of the rift between Antioch and Jerusalem which later
became of radical importance.[22]

Whether because of its numbers or because it included some well-
to-do people—such as, perhaps, Menaen the "companion" of Herod—
the community was strong enough by about the year A.D. 46 to send
financial aid to the brethren in Jerusalem, by the hands of Barnabas
and Paul, to relieve the distress caused by a famine that had occurred
in Jerusalem at that time.[23] It was apparently on this same visit to
Jerusalem[24] that the question was discussed between Barnabas and
Paul and the elders of the mother-church of the application of the
Jewish ritual law in the case of the Gentile converts.[25] Titus, a Greek
who had not been circumcised when he joined the new faith, accompanied Barnabas and Paul on this visit (Gal. 2:3), and it was apparently
his presence which brought the problem into the open. Originally,
when the converts had all been Jews, there had been no question as
to their observance of the Law, although some of the Hellenist Jews,
when the new faith began to take on a distinct form, began to dispute
the necessity of preserving the Law.[26] However, when Gentiles like

[22] This possible significance of the difference between the communities of Antioch
and Jerusalem is suggested by Streeter, *Primitive Church* 76-80. The view is opposed by
A. M. Farrer, "The Ministry in the New Testament," in Kirk (ed.) *The Apostolic
Ministry* 126-127, 143-144, 238, n. 8, who believes that there were "elders" in the church
at Antioch, who happen not to be mentioned in the sources. On the relation of the early
community at Antioch to the church at Jerusalem, see also Bauer, *Antiochia* 27-28; P.
Gaechter, "Jerusalem und Antiochia: Ein Beitrag zur urkirchlichen Rechtsentwicklung,"
ZKT 70 (1948) 1-48, and J. Colson, *L'évêque dans les communautés primitives* (Paris
1951) 27ff.

[23] Acts 11:27-30. See K. S. Gapp, "The Universal Famine under Claudius," *HTR* 28
(1935) 260. It is possible, of course, that the contribution was not large and was sent
chiefly as a token of brotherhood.

[24] The sequence of events here is disputed, because of the supposed discrepancies between the narrative in Acts and the account in Gal. 2, which involve the unsettled
questions concerning the compilation and reliability of Acts. There is no need in the
present work to enter into the details of this complicated problem, which has been a
stumbling block since ancient times. The solution followed here is that outlined by
Lake in *Beginnings of Christianity* 5.203; it appears to be the most satisfactory explanation in spite of the difficulties that it still involves. Among other studies of the problem
may be mentioned Knox, *St. Paul and the Church of Jerusalem* 181ff.; idem, *Acts*
40-53; C. H. Buck, Jr., "The Collection for the Saints," *HTR* 43 (1950) 1-29.

[25] A clear summary of the question may be found in Lietzmann, *Beginnings of the
Christian Church* 106-109. For a penetrating study of the conflict and of its ultimate
results, see B. W. Bacon, "Peter's Triumph at Antioch," *JR* 9 (1929) 204-233. Among
detailed studies of the subject may be mentioned D. W. Michaelis, "Judaistische Heiden-
christen," *ZNTW* 30 (1931) 83-89; W. Grundmann, "Das Problem des hellenistischen
Christentums innerhalb der Jerusalemer Urgemeinde," *ibid.* 38 (1939) 45-73; idem,
"Die Apostel zwischen Jerusalem und Antiochia," *ibid.* 39 (1940) 110-137; P. Gaechter,
"Petrus in Antiochia (*Gal.* 2.11-14)," *ZKT* 72 (1950) 177-212.

[26] Acts 6:11-14.

Titus began to be converted, the question became acute, in connection with circumcision and the prescriptions governing foods and the sharing of meals between Gentile and Jewish Christians. Paul maintained that it would not be practical to apply the Law to the Gentiles and that the converts should be exempted from the ceremony of circumcision, which, to the convert, would mean that he became a member of the Jewish nation or race. In Jerusalem, Barnabas and Paul seem to have reached with James, Peter, and John, the conservative leaders there, some agreement (the real details of which we do not know) that the Gentile mission should not have to observe the law strictly.[27] After this, Peter himself visited Antioch, apparently to bring thanks for the famine relief and to inspect the missionary work; and in the course of expressing thanks he ate with the Gentile Christians.[28] However, emissaries (Judas and Silas) were sent to Antioch by James,[29] whether in connection with the question of the Gentiles and the Law or for some other purpose; and these men, representing the traditional point of view, sought to win over the Jewish members of the Christian community to the view that the Law must be enforced on the Gentile Christians. They may have brought with them a letter from the elders in Jerusalem in which the minimum requirements of the Law for the Gentile converts were laid down, but this is not certain.[30] Peter and Barnabas appear to have been impressed by the arguments that born Jews might not disregard the Law, and they broke away from Paul.[31] What the real terms of the settlement of this controversy were, we do not know (as has been remarked), and it is probably impossible to reconstruct the story accurately from the evidence which we have. The problem is an important one because a full and accurate knowledge of it (if it were available) would help us to understand better than we do now the special and characteristic contribution that Antioch made to the successful spread of Christianity in its early days.

The chronology of this controversy is not clear, because of the con-

---

[27] Gal. 2:1-10.

[28] Gal. 2:11-12; cf. Knox, *St. Paul and the Church of Jerusalem* 184, with note on 191.

[29] On James, see among other studies G. Kittel, "Die Stellung des Jakobus zu Judentum und Heidenchristentum," *ZNTW* 30 (1931) 145-157, and W. K. Prentice, "James the Brother of the Lord," *Studies in Honor of A. C. Johnson* 144-151.

[30] Acts 15:22-29; Gal. 2:12. The question of the authenticity and significance of the letter of the "apostles and *presbyteroi*" of Jerusalem to the brethren in Antioch and Syria and Cilicia which is quoted in Acts 15:23-29 has been much disputed. Probably the letter is not an actual document, though some such decree may have been issued. See the discussion of the problem by K. Lake in *Beginnings of Christianity* 5.195-212.

[31] Gal. 2:11ff.

tradictory and incomplete condition of the evidence. For the same reason we cannot be sure of the dates of the systematic and carefully planned missionary journeys that Paul and his colleagues carried out at about this time. The very important fact that financial support for these early journeys was furnished by the brethren at Antioch is implied by the account of the first departure of Barnabas and Paul (Acts 13:1), though no statement to this effect is made (perhaps it was taken for granted by the writer, who thought it unnecessary to mention the point). The date of the first journey of Paul is difficult to determine. The second may have taken place in A.D. 47. On this, Paul did not travel with Barnabas, as before, but took Silas with him.[32] Barnabas also set out on another journey, taking Mark as his companion.[33] After a journey through Asia Minor and Greece, during which he stayed at Corinth for eighteen months, Paul returned to Antioch, probably in A.D. 51 or 52.[34] In A.D. 52 he set out on this third journey, again through Asia Minor and Greece, from which he returned, not to Antioch, but to Jerusalem, in A.D. 55 or 56.[35] This was the end of his connection with the community at Antioch.

In later times Peter was sometimes spoken of as the "founder" of the church at Antioch and as its "first bishop."[36] This tradition has given rise to extensive debate in connection with the claims of the Roman see to primacy, based on the belief in the foundation of the church in Rome by Peter, and in connection with the question which later arose of the respective ranks of the major churches (Rome, Jerusalem, Alexandria, Antioch). One of the essential difficulties is chronological. According to the Roman tradition, Peter was bishop in Rome for twenty-five years, until his martyrdom in A.D. 65, and it has seemed impossible to reconcile this tradition with the other evidence for Peter's activities elsewhere. An episcopate of this length in Rome would, for example, allow no opportunity for Peter's presence in Jerusalem when Paul consulted the elders there at the time of the famine, and it would not allow Peter to be in Antioch when his dispute with Paul occurred

[32] The chronology of the missionary journeys is not easy to settle; see J. Jeremias, "Untersuchungen zum Quellenproblem der Apostelgeschichte: Die Datierung der ersten Missionsreise," *ZNTW* 36 (1937) 220-221.

[33] Acts 15:36-41.

[34] Acts 15:41—18:22. On the chronology, see Lake, "The Chronology of Acts," *Beginnings of Christianity* 5.470-471.

[35] Acts 18:23—21:18.

[36] The principal texts concerning Peter at Antioch are listed below in Excursus 3. A useful summary of the problem of Peter's episcopate in Antioch may be found in F. H. Chase, "Peter (Simon)," in J. Hastings, *Dict. of the Bible* 2 (1900) 768.

(Gal. 2:11). It now seems plain that the tradition that Peter was in Rome for twenty-five years before his death cannot be maintained in its literal sense. The origin of this tradition, as C. H. Turner has pointed out,[37] probably lies, not in papal claims, but in the effort of ancient scholars to draw up a complete sequence of bishops beginning with the Ascension. The most reasonable interpretation of the sources indicates that Peter was in Rome on three occasions, in A.D. 42-45, 55-56 and 63-65.[38] Whether Peter visited Antioch in the early days of the mission there, at some sources claim,[39] we cannot now determine. The evidence for a very early visit is not good, but it is intrinsically likely that the success of the early missionaries in a place as important as Antioch would have led Peter to visit the city in order to see and assist in the work. Peter was certainly in Antioch at the time of the dispute with Paul, which took place probably in A.D. 47, and it seems likely that he was active in the city, and made excursions from it for missionary work, between A.D. 47 and 54.

Independently of the question of the origin of the episcopal office, which will be discussed below, it is not difficult to understand how Peter might have been looked upon as the "founder" of the church at Antioch and as its "first bishop." Peter was, according to all accounts, the first of the Twelve to visit the city, a fact which would have special importance when the major churches later laid claim to apostolic foundation—that at Alexandria being established by Mark, that at Rome by Peter and Paul, or Peter alone, that at Jerusalem by James the brother of the Lord[40]—for the fact that Peter visited Antioch would by itself give rise to the inference that he (officially) "founded" the church there. The church at Antioch in fact looked upon Peter and his teaching with special reverence; Matthew was the gospel which Ignatius, bishop of the city at the end of the first century, knew best,[41] and the contents and doctrine of this Gospel have suggested to some scholars that it was written at Antioch about A.D. 85. This cannot be proved, but whatever the origin of the Gospel may be, Peter takes a leading part in it. The celebrated words attributed to Jesus in Matthew (16:18),

[37] "The Early Episcopal Lists," *JTS* 18 (1916-17) 115.

[38] This is the conclusion reached by G. Edmundson, *The Church at Rome in the First Century* (London 1913) 49-51, 71-78 (cf. 239-240) and accepted by Kidd, *Hist. of the Church* 1.53.

[39] See Excursus 3.

[40] On the early episcopal lists see Harnack, *Chronologie der altchr. Lit.* 1.70ff.; C. H. Turner, "The Early Episcopal Lists," *JTS* 1 (1900) 181-200, 529-553; 18 (1916-17) 103-134.

[41] Cf. Streeter, *Four Gospels* 504-507.

The Christian Community to A.D. 284

"And I tell you, you are Peter (Greek *Petros*) and on this rock (Gr. *petra*) I will build my church," constitute a striking alteration of a scene described in Mark (8:27ff.), in which this statement is not made. Whether or not these words were originally spoken by Jesus, and whatever their original form and meaning may have been, it seems reasonable to suppose that as they appear in Matthew they represent the tradition of Antioch concerning the foundation of the church there.[42] Thus the words in Matthew could form a basis for the claim of the church at Antioch to supremacy over Jerusalem.[43] The local interest in Peter is reflected in a tradition—albeit a late one— that Evodius, who was the first person after Peter to serve as "bishop" of Antioch, wrote an epistle called *Light* ($\phi\hat{\omega}\varsigma$), now lost, in which he described how Christ baptized Peter alone and then Peter began the baptism of the other apostles.[44] The claim of the supremacy of Antioch can also be perceived in the confused and obscure tradition that grew up later to the effect that the first Apostolic Council—the first synod of the Church—was held in Antioch rather than in Jerusalem.[45]

So, whether or not Peter could be said to be literally the founder of the church at Antioch and its first "bishop," it is plain that in local opinion he became a principal figure in the early history of the community. As for his supposed episcopate, the tradition, again, could easily arise from local patriotism; to Jerome, the first writer who actually calls Peter bishop of the city, the term, though it may have been an anachronism, was one that would seem to describe the importance of Peter's activity in the city. Actually of course his work there would most likely have been in the nature of an apostolate, rather than an episcopate. The title of bishop in the apostolic period, at least, was (as will be seen below) a designation of function, indicating the head of a local church, rather than a title of rank and it seems likely

[42] Jackson and Lake in *Beginnings of Christianity* 1.329-330; Streeter, *Four Gospels* 500-527; cf. J. T. Shotwell and L. R. Loomis, *The See of Peter* (New York 1927) 19. The conclusion that the Gospel was composed at Antioch has been contested by B. W. Bacon, *Gospel of the Hellenists* (New York 1933) 14, and by F. C. Grant, *Growth of the Gospels* (New York 1933) 184-185, but their objections do not seem to me to be sufficient to overcome the arguments in favor of Antioch. See further below.

[43] Streeter, *Four Gospels* 514-515. See also H. Strathmann, "Die Stellung des Petrus in der Urkirche: Zur Frühgeschichte des Wortes an Petrus Matthäus 16.17-19," *Ztschr. für systematische Theologie* 20 (1943) 223-282. For a different (and to me less convincing) view see J. Haller, *Das Papsttum*, rev. ed., 1 (Urach 1950) 4-6, with notes on 473-475.

[44] Nicephorus Callistus Xanthopolus, *Hist. eccl.* 2.3 = *PG* 145.757 B.

[45] See Hefele-Leclecq, *Conciles* 1.126, n. 1. It is curious to note how this tradition is stated in Origen, *Contra Celsum* 8.29 in such a way as to make it a plain contradiction of Acts 15:22, according to which the council was held in Jerusalem.

[283]

that Peter was later spoken of as first bishop of Antioch simply because, it was supposed, he had acted as head of the community there,
and also, probably, because he was one of the Twelve. His appearance
in the list of bishops of the city also reflects the effort that was made
later to establish a list of orthodox bishops of the city. That Peter did
not appear originally in the list of the bishops of the city is indicated
by the fact that some sources do not mention his successor Evodius,
but state that Peter appointed Ignatius as his successor at Antioch,
which is manifestly a chronological impossibility. This seems to show
that some authorities ousted Evodius from the list in order to make
room for Peter.[46]

According to the *Pseudo-Clementine Romance*, written in the early
third century, one of the most prominent men in Antioch, named
Theophilus, donated his "huge house" for use as a church, and the
cathedra of Peter was placed in this.[47] Although it is known that private
houses were used as places of worship at an early period, there is no
way of determining whether the tradition of this early church in
Antioch has any real basis.[48] It has been suggested that this Theophilus
is the person to whom the Gospel of Luke and the Acts of the Apostles
were dedicated, but there is no proof of this.[49]

After Peter, the head of the community in Antioch, according to
several later sources, was Evodius (sometimes, apparently incorrectly,
called Euodos), who from his name seems to have been a Gentile, not
a Jewish, Christian. The sources speak of him as having been "bishop"

[46] On this point see Bauer, *Rechtgläubigkeit u. Ketzerei* 119-123. Origen, Chrysostom,
and Theodoret (cited in Excursus 3) state that Ignatius was Peter's immediate successor. On the formation of the early lists see Harnack, *Chronologie der altchr. Lit.*
1.208-218; E. Schwartz's introduction to the third volume of his edition of Eusebius'
Hist. Eccl. (1909) ccxxiff., and Turner's articles (above, n. 40).

[47] Pseudo-Clementine *Recognitiones* 71 = *PG* 1.1453. In one MS of the Syriac *Doctrine
of the Apostles* it is stated that Peter built a church at Antioch (see Excursus 3, p. 583).
The traveler Wilbrand of Oldenburg, who visited Antioch in November 1211, was
shown the church in which Peter presided, which contained his *cathedra* (*Peregrina-
tiones Medii Aevi Quattuor*, ed. J. C. M. Laurent [Leipzig 1864], p. 172, §§13-16).
The festival of the *cathedra* of St. Peter at Antioch was celebrated on 22 February; see
the testimonia collected in the *Acta Sanctorum* under this date. Cf. Cabrol, "Chaire de
S. Pierre à Rome," *DACL* 3. 76-90. A grotto on Mount Silpius has traditionally been
called the grotto of St. Peter, where he is supposed to have preached and baptized, but
there is no satisfactory proof of this association. See the anonymous pamphlet *La Grotte
de St. Pierre à Antioche. Étude par un missionaire Capucin* (*Mission des Capucins en
Syrie et en Mesopotamie*) (Beirut 1934), with the review by M. Van Cutsum in *Anal.
Boll.* 54 (1936) 184. St. Paul's house and table were shown at Antioch in the time of
St. John Chrysostom (*PG* 60.666).

[48] On the early use of houses as churches, see above, n. 21.

[49] Luke 1:3; Acts 1:1. See *Beginnings of Christianity* 2.507 and 4.2.

of the city; Eusebius and Jerome call him "the first bishop" of the city (Malalas anachronistically calls him "first patriarch"), and Eusebius and Malalas state that he was the first incumbent after Peter.[50] How Evodius came to be bishop, we do not know. In the *Apostolic Constitutions*[51] (composed ca. A.D. 380) it is stated that Peter appointed Evodius to the episcopate, and that Paul appointed Ignatius, Evodius' successor. Peter might have appointed Evodius, thus founding the apostolic succession at Antioch, just as the other apostles had appointed overseers of various Christian communities,[52] but it is unsafe to conclude this on the authority of the *Apostolic Constitutions*, a document that has small authority in such matters. Evodius might have been elected by the local clergy, a practice which may have been followed at this time,[53] and the tradition of his appointment by Peter could easily have arisen from the circumstance that he followed Peter, chronologically, and from the local Antiochene pride in Peter's work in the city; and of course it was a matter of importance to assure the existence of the apostolic succession at Antioch. All these possibilities, however, are so obscure that it is difficult to lay any stress upon them.

The date of Evodius' incumbency cannot be accurately determined. Our only safe datum is that his successor Ignatius was martyred during the reign of Trajan (A.D. 98-117).[54] There is also the statement of Syncellus, based on the lost Greek version of the *Chronicle* of Eusebius, that Evodius was bishop of Antioch for twenty-nine years.[55] The Armenian version of Eusebius' chronicle puts his appointment in the fifth year of Claudius, A.D. 45/6,[56] while Jerome's *Chronicle*, based on Eusebius', puts it in A.D. 44.[57] Malalas dates his appointment in A.D. 41.[58] According to these dates, an incumbency of twenty-nine years would

---

[50] Eusebius *Hist. eccl.* 3.22.1 (on the succession see also 3.36.2, where, however, Evodius is not mentioned by name); Eusebius *Chron.*, in the Greek version as preserved by Syncellus 1.628.11-12 Bonn ed., and the Armenian translation, 2.150 ed. Schoene; Jerome *Chron.* p. 179 ed. Helm; Malalas 246.20ff.; *Apostolic Constitutions* 7.26.

[51] *Loc.cit.* (see above, n. 50).

[52] See above, n. 46.

[53] The evidence for the early episcopate is summarized by K. Hilgenreiner, "Bischof," *Lex. f. Theol. u. Kirche* 2.370-375; see also Kidd, *Hist. of the Church* 1.173-175, and Lietzmann, *Beginnings of the Christian Church* 145, 193-194, 247-248. Lietzmann suggests (145) that the titles used in the early churches were modeled on the usage of some leading community, in which case one would expect that the usage of Antioch would be followed. For more detailed discussion see below.

[54] See §4 below.

[55] Syncellus 1.628.12 Bonn ed.

[56] P. 152 ed. Schoene.

[57] P. 179 ed. Helm.

[58] Malalas 246.20ff. places Evodius' accession ten years after the Crucifixion, which he dates (241.8-12) in A.D. 31 (confusing the consuls of 33 with those of 31).

put the termination of Evodius' episcopate in A.D. 70, 73, or 74/5. This would agree roughly with the statement of Jerome in his *Chronicle* that Ignatius became bishop in A.D. 68.[59] However, the sources that give dates for the accession of Evodius are all suspect because they may represent attempts to reach a compromise between irreconcilable statements concerning episcopates of Peter in Antioch and in Rome.[60] Also it has become plain that the dates that Jerome gives in his *Chronicle* for the accessions of the early bishops of Antioch are quite untrustworthy and represent merely the chronicler's efforts to provide a suitable framework for the succession.[61] In reality, as has been mentioned, our evidence suggests that Peter was active in and around Antioch between ca. A.D. 47 and 54 (as well, perhaps, as in earlier years). Whether Evodius would have been called "bishop" during the time when Peter worked in Antioch, we cannot determine. It seems most likely that Evodius would have begun to serve as "bishop" when Peter left Antioch for the last time, not expecting to return.[62] In this case his episcopate would have begun ca. A.D. 54, and, if it lasted for twenty-nine years, would have extended to ca. A.D. 83, at which time Ignatius would have succeeded.[63] Mention has already been made of the lost epistle entitled *Light* in which Evodius is said to have written concerning the apostolic supremacy of Peter, whom the church of Antioch looked upon as its founder.

During the time when Evodius was head of the church at Antioch, the Jewish Christian community in Jerusalem was broken up and driven into exile, first by the persecution initiated by the high priest Ananus in A.D. 62, in which James the brother of the Lord, who was head of the church in Jerusalem, was martyred,[64] and finally in the Jewish War of Vespasian and Titus, which ended in the destruction of Jerusalem in A.D. 70. Most of the Jewish Christians who fled from Jerusalem at this period probably sought refuge to the south and east

[59] P. 186 ed. Helm.
[60] See above, the discussion of the question of Peter's episcopate at Antioch. The sources are collected below in Excursus 3.
[61] See for example n. 81 in this chapter, and Excursus 3.
[62] In the *Apostolic Constitutions* (7.26) it is said that Peter appointed Evodius, while Malalas says that he was elected (τὴν χειροτονίαν . . . ἔλαβεν, 246.23f.). Neither text is a safe authority; Malalas calls Evodius "patriarch," and could easily have inferred from the practice of his own day that Evodius was elected.
[63] On the chronology of Ignatius, see below §4.
[64] The persecution is described, e.g., by Eusebius *Hist. eccl.* 2.23. See Kidd, *Hist. of the Church* 1.46; Schürer, *Gesch. d. jüd. Volkes*[3-4] 1.581-582; Meyer, *Ursprung u. Anfänge* 3.69-77. Schürer seems unnecessarily skeptical in the matter of accepting the date A.D. 62 for the martyrdom of James. On James see above, n. 29.

of the city; it seems unlikely that any considerable number of them would have gone to Antioch, not only the headquarters of the Roman military power that had destroyed Jerusalem but the original seat of Gentile Christianity.[65] It is possible, however, that some Jewish Christians did go to Antioch, and if they did, they may have taken with them their books and their collections of the sayings of Jesus, by means of which the spiritual life of the community of Antioch would have been enriched.[66] We do not, however, possess any real evidence concerning the history and the ultimate fate of the Jewish Christian community at Antioch, and this question remains one of the most important problems in the early history of Christianity at Antioch.

2. CONTRIBUTIONS OF ANTIOCH TO THE DEVELOPMENT OF THE CHURCH

Some of the important ways in which Antioch made its special contribution to the spread of Christianity may be summarized briefly here. It is hardly necessary to repeat that the sources are in many respects deficient or unsatisfactory. Nevertheless there emerge from them certain points that can safely be accepted.

First, the mission to Antioch made possible the spread of Christianity to a substantial number of people, outside of Judaism, of diverse backgrounds; and the success in Antioch of the effort to preach to Gentiles, and the ultimate acceptance of these Gentiles without insistence upon their observance of the Jewish Law, determined the oecumenical character of Christianity.

Second, it is evident that the Christians at Antioch were able to provide financial resources important for the growth of Christianity: famine relief sent to the brethren in Jerusalem and the support of the early missionary journeys that were organized at Antioch. It seems plain that resources of this kind could not have been found in Jerusalem; and without money of this kind the early missions could never have been sent out.

Third, Antioch by virtue of its geographical position as the center of

---

[65] On the flight of the Jewish Christians and their refuges, see S. G. F. Brandon, *The Fall of Jerusalem and the Christian Church: A Study of the Effects of the Jewish Overthrow of A.D. 70 on Christianity* (London 1951) 218-219.

[66] Streeter in his *Primitive Church* 143 and his *Four Gospels* 511ff. supposes that there was a mass exodus from Jerusalem to Antioch, but his hypothesis seems sufficiently refuted by the observations of Brandon, cited in the preceding note. There is, however, no reason to suppose that a few Jewish Christians of Jerusalem may not have found their way to Antioch.

a network of well-established communications radiating in all directions was able to serve efficiently and fruitfully as a focal point for expansion. Paul and his companions traveled on their missions from Antioch to Cyprus, Asia Minor, Greece, and Italy, while there was almost certainly another missionary, now unidentified, who traveled through the inland part of Syria (some scholars believe that some of this missionary work was done by Peter). Antioch rendered valuable service as a central headquarters to which all of the missionaries could return periodically for spiritual and physical rest and replenishment.[67]

Such, in brief, are some of the main contributions of Antioch to the early spread of Christianity. Other contributions of Antioch which are still matters of uncertainty—the development of the monarchical episcopate, the real basis of the settlement of the question of the Gentile concepts and the Law, and the origin of Ignatius' thought—must be postponed for further discussion below. We may now continue to trace some of the concurrent threads of the story which will carry the narrative forward.

3. The End of the Apostolic Age;
The Nicolaitan Heresy; Gnosticism

The closing years of the first century must have been a time of steady activity in the spread of Christianity, and the results can be seen in the time of Bishop Ignatius, in the early years of the second century. However, our sources for this period are very meager, and fail to give us much of the information we desire. Most of what we do know of the history of the community at Antioch in this period concerns the development of the Nicolaitan heresy and of Gnosticism, both of which were separate movements, related to Christianity, which, characteristically for a place such as Antioch, grew up alongside the Christian faith.

When St. Paul had finished his work, the religious situation of Christianity was by no means a unified one. Paul himself had transformed the primitive belief about Jesus, with its Judaistic terms, into a religion of salvation by faith which had to make its way among all

---

[67] It has been suggested that Antioch was also the scene of some of the literary work —the writing of the Gospels and of Acts particularly—which was necessary to provide material for the use of the missionaries who made the city their headquarters. Study of the Gospels and of Acts with this in mind has produced a large number of hypotheses, some very elaborate and some very daring, to the effect that the Gospels and Acts were all written at Antioch. Some of these hypotheses conflict with or contradict others, and some are of the most tenuous description. The present writer considers it impossible to be certain in any of these matters.

kinds of pagan beliefs, representing everything from philosophy to mystery cults. The Epistle to the Ephesians shows the existence of sects and secret cults which claimed to be Christian, and may have had some Christian elements in them, but were of such a character that they could be accused of vile practices.[68] Such cults are not specifically attested for Antioch, but we should expect to find them there.

Something of this sort may have been involved in the Nicolaitan heresy. According to some sources, Nicolaus of Antioch, who had been an early proselyte and one of the seven deacons of Jerusalem,[69] became the originator of an early heresy, which came to be named for him. It seems to have been the purpose of this movement to achieve a compromise between Christianity and the prevailing social usages of the time by reconciling the observance of certain pagan practices with membership in the Christian community. This effort, however, involved the Nicolaitans in what seemed to some Christians to be sensual and idolatrous behavior.[70] Whether the heresy actually originated with Nicolaus the proselyte of Antioch is doubtful, for it seems more likely that the heresy, after it had come into being, falsely laid claim to Nicolaus as its author, hoping to win support from the prestige of his name.[71]

The Nicolaitan heresy was in some respects a forerunner of the much more prominent, and more important, Gnostic movement. Gnosticism represented an effort to find a new formulation of the Christian teaching in terms of the contemporary, "modern" science and philosophy, and it possessed a powerful attraction for people who were searching for a comprehensive speculative religion that would combine the "best" features of Christianity and "enlightened" pagan thought. This system, which seems to have been essentially Christian in origin, flourished in an intellectual and religious atmosphere such as that of Antioch, where the mingling of diverse Greek and Oriental racial and religious groups provided ample opportunity for the study and propagation of new cults and philosophical systems.[72] As a syncretistic system of pagan

[68] On the significance of Ephesians in this respect, see W. L. Knox, *St. Paul and the Church of the Gentiles* (Cambridge, Eng., 1939) 199.

[69] Acts 6:5.   [70] Apoc. 2:6, 15.

[71] Cf. E. Amann, "Nicolaïtes," *DTC* 11 (1931) 499-506; Kidd, *Hist. of the Church* 1.195-196; A. von Harnack, "The Sect of the Nicolaitans and Nicolaus, the Deacon in Jerusalem," *JR* 3 (1923) 413-422; M. Goguel, "Les Nicolaïtes," *Revue de l'histoire des religions* 115 (1937) 5-36.

[72] On Gnosticism, reference may be made to F. C. Burkitt, *Church and Gnosis* (Cambridge, Eng., 1932), and to H. Jonas, *Gnosis und spätantiker Geist*, 1 (Göttingen 1934). A brief survey may be found in Kidd, *Hist. of the Church* 1.190ff. On the tradition in

philosophy and religion which embodied some Christian, some Hellenic, and some Jewish ideas, Gnosticism was in a position to offer serious competition to the existing Christian teachings, springing as it did from the impulse toward speculation that played a part in the development of Christian theology. While Jesus was the central figure, the system promised knowledge (*gnosis*) of the divine scheme of the universe, and salvation, including security against evil forces on earth and a happy life in the hereafter. Starting in the East, Gnosticism spread throughout the Roman Empire. Its variations were innumerable, and the teaching of its individual leaders ranged all the way from systems that were definitely non-Christian to adaptations that took the form of Christian heresies.

The inclination toward a system such as Gnosticism could easily have grown up spontaneously in a city that was as interested in religion and philosophy as Antioch was. Irenaeus, its opponent, who may not have been well informed, says that Gnosticism was brought to Antioch, and that it was descended from the teaching of Simon Magus of Samaria, who in apostolic times preached that there was a Supreme God who gave out powers or emanations, of which Simon himself was one. Simon claimed indeed to be a rival of Jesus Christ, and gave displays of magic which attracted many followers.[73] Whether or not Menander, the next figure we encounter, was really a pupil and successor of Simon Magus, and whether he carried the teaching to Antioch, it seems certain that there was in the city a man of this name who made conversions by means of exhibitions of magic. There is no precise evidence for the date of Menander's activity at Antioch; but it may be inferred from the date of Simon's career and from the career of Menander's supposed pupil Satornilus of Antioch (whose activity is described below) that Menander worked in Antioch in the latter part of the first century, during the time of Bishop Evodius.[74]

The teacher Satornilus (or Saturninus), said to be a native of Antioch,

---

Syria of the mythical Anthropos, of eastern origin, and its connection with Gnostic doctrine, see C. H. Kraeling, *Anthropos and Son of Man* (New York 1927). An important discovery of Gnostic writings has recently been made in Egypt; see H. C. Puech, "Les nouveaux écrits gnostiques découverts en Haute-Egypte (Premier inventaire et essai d'identification)," *Bulletin of the Byzantine Institute* 2 (1950) 91-154 (*Coptic Studies in Honor of W. E. Crum*). A summary of the problems involved in the understanding of Gnosticism is undertaken by R. P. Casey, "The Study of Gnosticism," *JTS* 36 (1935) 45-60.

[73] Acts 8:9-24: Irenaeus, *Adv. haer.* 1.23.1; Justinus *Apol.* 1.26; Eusebius *Hist. eccl.* 2.13-14; cf. R. P. Casey in *Beginnings of Christianity* 5.151-163.

[74] Irenaeus *Adv. haer.* 1.23.5; Justinus *Apol.* 1.26; Eusebius *Hist. eccl.* 3.26.

is identified by Irenaeus as a disciple of Menander, and eventually his successor. In reality, the systems of Satornilus and Menander show little similarity. The teaching of Satornilus did not represent a new religion that contained only some Christian elements; it constituted a real Christian heresy. Satornilus taught that Christ was sent to destroy the forces of evil, and that the Savior was unborn and incorporeal and without figure, and that it was in appearance only that He was seen as a man.[75] Thus Gnosticism, instead of attacking the Church from without, began to adapt Christianity, which caused great confusion in people's minds, especially because Christianity itself was still relatively new. Bishop Ignatius' warnings against this teaching about Christ as a phantom (known as docetism)[76] show that Satornilus had been at work in Antioch before the bishop's arrest and condemnation, which took place ca. A.D. 108/9 or possibly later.[77] These docetic tendencies had earlier roots, in the native Greek and Oriental disposition to credit the appearance of the divine in human form. However, to people who followed this belief, the thought of a real incarnation was incredible.

Another famous religious leader in Antioch at this time was Basilides of Alexandria, who is said by Satornilus (with how much justice is not clear) to have been a pupil of Menander and thus ultimately a follower of Simon Magus. Basilides is supposed, after studying with Menander in Antioch, to have served as the transmitter of Gnosticism to his native city Alexandria, in the time of Hadrian (A.D. 117-138).[78]

One of the best known figures of this time was the Syrian Cerdo (Kerdon), a product of the Gnostic teaching in Antioch, who when he settled in Rome ca. A.D. 138-144 came into contact with Marcion, the founder of a new Gnostic sect that actually developed into a church and attained some importance. Important features of Marcion's teaching, notably on the dual nature of divinity, have been thought to be derived from Cerdo. The Marcionite church became popular in Syria, as well as in other parts of the Roman Empire.[79]

In sum, we have seen that in the closing years of the first century, when Christianity had been established at Antioch for a generation or

---

[75] Irenaeus *Adv. haer.* 1.24.1-2; cf. Eusebius *Hist. eccl.* 4.7.3.
[76] E.g. in his letter to the people of Smyrna, 4ff.
[77] On the date, see below, §4.
[78] Irenaeus *Adv. haer.* 1.24.3ff.; cf. Kidd, *Hist. of the Church* 1.204.ff.
[79] Irenaeus *Adv. haer.* 1.27, 3.4; Hippolytus *Philosophumena* 7.37; Epiphanius *Haer.* 41.2; Tertullian *Adv. Marc.* 1.2. Cf. G. Bareille, "Cerdon," *DTC* 2.2138-2139; Kidd, *Hist. of the Church* 1.214-220; John Knox, *Marcion and the New Testament* (Chicago 1942) 7-8, 13, 17-18; E. C. Blackman, *Marcion and his Influence* (London 1948).

more, there had come to exist in the city a number of different religious systems in which elements of Christianity were present. Oldest in point of time were the Jewish Christians. Their influence was broken when Jerusalem was destroyed in A.D. 70, and while some members of this branch may have lingered on in Antioch, they ceased before long to be a factor of importance. Antioch, as the original center of Gentile Christianity, could in fact never have been a sympathetic environment for the Jewish Christians. There existed, then, the teaching of St. Paul and the syncretistic systems of the Gnostics, plus whatever mystic and ecstatic concepts of Christianity might have grown out of the influence of the pagan mystery cults, popular at Antioch as they were throughout the eastern part of the Graeco-Roman world. The great question was, which of these systems would win at Antioch? The answer is found in the work of the martyr bishop Ignatius.

4. BISHOP IGNATIUS, HIS CAREER
AND WRITINGS; THE OUTBREAK AGAINST THE CHRISTIANS
AT ANTIOCH UNDER TRAJAN

Bishop Ignatius, whose personality and faith are familiar to us from his letters, is the first figure in the history of Christian Antioch at the close of the apostolic age who is at all well known.[80] Even so, details of his life are scanty. The date when he became bishop, succeeding Evodius, is not known with any certainty.[81] According to what is evidently a local source, preserved in the *Chronicle* of Malalas, Ignatius was arrested and condemned at the time of the earthquake which took place at Antioch on 13 December A.D. 115.[82] Malalas says that Trajan

[80] Among recent works on Ignatius may be cited C. C. Richardson, *The Christianity of Ignatius of Antioch* (New York 1935). Streeter's study of Ignatius in his *Primitive Church* 146ff. should also be consulted. For the principal bibliography on Ignatius, see Altaner, *Patrologie*[2] 78-81; more extensive references are given in some of the special studies cited below. To Altaner's bibliography may be added L. H. Gray, "The Armenian Acts of the Martyrdom of S. Ignatius of Antioch," *Armenian Quarterly* 1 (1946) 47-66.

[81] In Eusebius' Chronicle as preserved by Syncellus 1.647.13 Bonn ed., it is stated that Ignatius was bishop of Antioch for thirty years. Jerome's *Chronicle* which is an adaptation of Eusebius', indicates that Ignatius became bishop in A.D. 68 (p. 186 ed. Helm) and that he was martyred in A.D. 108 (p. 194 ed. Helm). This however disagrees with the evidence for the career of Evodius, who seems to have been bishop until A.D. 83 (see above, n. 63); and an episcopate of thirty years for Ignatius, beginning in A.D. 68, would not conform with the evidence that he was martyred in A.D. 107 or 108. There is good evidence in Malalas (cited below) that he was arrested and condemned in A.D. 115 and suffered martyrdom in 116. The chroniclers evidently had no good information and were trying to construct an artificial chronology that would give a satisfactory sequence for the early bishops of Antioch.

[82] Malalas 276.10-11; on the date of the earthquake see Ch. 9, §5.

was angry with Ignatius because the bishop had used improper language concerning him. It also seems likely (although the chronicler does not mention the point) that the populace held the Christians responsible for the earthquake. Malalas speaks of this disaster as a θεομηνία, a "sign of divine anger," and the pagans would have been especially alarmed because the emperor was in the city when the disaster occurred and narrowly escaped death in it.[83] It is easy to believe that there was a popular outbreak of anti-Christian feeling, the first victim of which would have been the head of the Christian community.[84] Ignatius was sent to Rome by way of Asia Minor and was murdered by being exposed to wild beasts, presumably in the Coliseum. His death, after what was apparently an unhurried journey, may have taken place on 20 December A.D. 116.[85] Later his remains were taken back to Antioch and buried in the cemetery outside the Daphnetic Gate.[86]

Other martyrdoms are said to have taken place in Antioch itself. The outbreak apparently was not protracted, for Ignatius' own letters seem to indicate that it lasted only a few weeks.[87]

The only other victim whose name is known is Drosis or Drosina,

[83] On Trajan's escape in the earthquake see Ch. 9, §5. Earthquakes in Pontus and Cappadocia in the third century were blamed on the Christians, according to a letter of Firmilianus, bishop of Caesarea in Cappadocia (*CSEL* 3, pt. 2, p. 816); cf. Kidd, *Hist. of the Church* 1.351-352.

[84] Eusebius (*Hist. eccl.* 3.36) and Jerome (*De vir. ill.* 16; *Chron.* p. 194 ed. Helm) say only that Ignatius was arrested in the course of a persecution that took place at Antioch in the reign of Trajan, and that he was sent to Rome for martyrdom. Jerome gives the date of his death as the eleventh year of Trajan's reign (A.D. 108/9). Allard in his account of the persecutions (*Persécutions* 1.185-202) believes that Ignatius' condemnation took place in A.D. 107, and this date is accepted in the *BHG*² p. 114. Other scholars (e.g. Kidd, *Hist. of the Church* 1.165 and Altaner, *Patrologie*² 78) think it wiser to date his martyrdom only ca. A.D. 110 or ca. A.D. 110-117. These students do not appear to have been acquainted with the account of Malalas which is plausible in itself, and presumably represents a local Antiochene source.

[85] In later years Ignatius' festival was kept on 20 December. We have of course no way of knowing how long he was kept in Antioch after his arrest, and his journey to Rome may have been leisurely—that part of it which took him through Asia Minor was certainly unhurried. Perhaps his execution was timed to fall approximately on the first anniversary of the earthquake. However, the date 20 December may not represent an accurate record of the day of his death, and may instead represent the day of his arrest in Antioch. See Schultze, *Antiocheia* 47-48.

[86] Jerome *De vir. ill.* 16; cf. Chrysostom *In S. Ignatium* 5 = *PG* 50.594. There is no indication of the date of the translation of the relics.

[87] Ignatius' letters refer to the election of his successor which took place while he was still in Asia Minor on his journey; see J. Moffatt, "Ignatius of Antioch; A Study in Personal Religion," *JR* 10 (1930) 169, 173. On Trajan's policy and activities with regard to the Christians, see Kidd, *Hist. of the Church* 1.234-238. Accounts of the period are also given by Allard, *Persécutions* 1.141-202, and by J. Zeiller in Fliche and Martin, *Hist. de l'église* 1.304-308.

mother of three children, who is said to have been burned.[88] "Many others" are reported to have been executed, or to have thrown themselves into the flames, but no details of their martyrdoms are preserved, and these victims may have been imaginary.[89] Five bronze statues in the public bath built by Trajan at Antioch were said to have been cast from metal with which were mingled the ashes of five Christian women who confessed their faith before the emperor in person and were burned. This tale of course has the air of having become attached to public statues that actually had no such origin.[90]

On his journey to Rome through Asia Minor Ignatius wrote seven letters to churches which give a remarkably vivid picture of the popular faith of the early church and of the eager religious life of the times. They also show some of the current practices in the services of the church, particularly with respect to the Eucharist. One of the principal values of the letters is that they show that by Ignatius' time there was, in Antioch at least, a settled three-fold ministry consisting of a monarchical bishop, presbyters, and deacons, to whom the laity were urged, or expected, to give due obedience.[91] This ministry replaced the early conception of the labors of apostles, prophets, and teachers which is the only order or system of ministry which is known in the first years of the Church (see for example Acts 13:1, which records the work of prophets and teachers at Antioch in the time of Barnabas and Paul, and I Cor. 12:28, in which apostles, prophets, and teachers are ranked in that order). How to account for the change from the apostles, prophets, and teachers of the Acts and the Epistles to the bishops possessing supreme authority and to the presbyters and deacons of Ignatius' time is the central and most important problem in the organization and development of the early Church.[92] The time and the place in which the transformation began, the reason for it, and the time when it was completed, are alike uncertain; but the change is of vital importance because of its significance in the future history of the

[88] Her martyrdom is recorded by Malalas, who calls her Drosine (277.9-10), and described by Chrysostom, who calls her Drosis (*Laud. S. mart. Drosidis, PG* 50.683-694). Other references to her are collected by Delehaye, *Origines du culte*[2] 198.

[89] Malalas 277.9-10.

[90] This story apparently occurs only in Malalas 276.10—277.10. The absence from the account of the martyrs' names is a common phenomenon in hagiographic literature; see Delehaye, *Passions des martyrs* 210.

[91] On Ignatius' conception of the episcopate, see, among other studies, C. C. Richardson, "The Church in Ignatius of Antioch," *JR* 17 (1937) 428-443; H. Chadwick, "The Silence of Bishops in Ignatius," *HTR* 43 (1950) 169-172, and G. Dix, "The Ministry in the Early Church," in Kirk (ed.), *The Apostolic Ministry* 250-253.

[92] Cf. C. H. Turner, *Studies in Early Church History* (Oxford 1912) 14.

Church; and since it is at Antioch that the three-fold ministry under the bishop first appears, it is natural to try to discover whether it was some factor in the life of the community at Antioch that brought about the change.

Various explanations of this development have been put forward and have won varying degrees of acceptance. One view was that the Christian offices, both in title and in function, had no divine sanction, but were borrowed from Jewish institutions and from pagan organizations. It is generally felt that this view does considerable violence to the sources.[93] A further development of this theory sought to distinguish between the "charismatic" and "universal" ministry of the apostles, prophets, and teachers and the "ordained" and "local" ministry of the bishops, presbyters, and deacons; the ordained officers, it was supposed, replaced the earlier charismatic missionaries as they died out, and the episcopate is an original creation, made on the local level.[94] There is,

[93] This theory was proposed by Edwin Hatch in the Bampton Lectures for 1880, *The Organization of the Early Christian Churches* (London 1881). For a criticism of the hypothesis, see C. Gore, *The Church and the Ministry*, new ed. revised by C. H. Turner (London 1936) 362ff.

[94] This is the theory of A. Harnack, set forth (after an earlier publication) in his *Entstehung und Entwickelung der Kirchenverfassung und des Kirchenrechts in den zwei ersten Jahrhunderten* (Leipzig 1910), translated into English by F. L. Pogson under the title *The Constitution and Law of the Church in the First Two Centuries* (London 1910). Harnack's study contains an essay attempting to refute the position of R. Sohm, "Wesen und Ursprung des Katholizismus," *Abhandlungen der philol.-histor. Kl. der k. sächischen Gesellsch. der Wiss.* 27, no. 10 (1909) 335-390, who had maintained that the local ministries were regarded as charismatic. Harnack's view is criticized for misreading of the evidence; see for example Hort, *Ecclesia*; C. Gore's volume cited in the preceding note, 362ff.; and G. Dix, "The Ministry in the Early Church," in Kirk (ed.), *The Apostolic Ministry* 239-290. Harnack's view originated in his study in 1884 of the *Didache* or *Teaching of the Twelve Apostles* which he supposed to be an illustration of the development in question. In the *Didache*, the "prophets and teachers" who appear in the New Testament (cf. Acts 13:1) are active alongside a two-fold ministry of bishops and deacons. Warning is given against false prophets, and it is urged that honor and respect be paid to bishops and deacons. The *Didache* has recently been invoked by Streeter in support of his own theory of the ministry. Streeter has argued (*Primitive Church*, 144-152, 279-287) that the *Didache* originated in Antioch ca. A.D. 90 as an instruction sent by the church of Antioch to the smaller communities of Syria in order to encourage the growth of a settled and ordered resident ministry, and to protect the people against charlatans. See also Streeter's article, "The much-belabored Didache," *JTS* 37 (1936) 369-374, and J. M. Creed, "The Didache," *ibid.* 39 (1938) 370-387. This hypothesis has not met with general acceptance, and most scholars are inclined to give a later date to the document, though there are so many problems connected with it that scholars find it difficult to come to general agreement concerning it. It has been thought, for example, that the book represents an attempt, in much later years, to compose an apostolic document, describing the apostles' ordering of the Gentile communities. Thus the work would represent an effort to persuade the church of the author's day to return to the simplicity of apostolic times (see J. A. Robinson, *Barnabas, Hermas and the Didache* [London 1920]). For a review of the modern studies, see F. E. Vokes, *The Riddle of the Didache* (London 1938), and the literature

however, no real evidence known to us for such a two-fold ministry.[95]

It seems plain that there was both latitude and inconsistency in the use of the terms denoting the various functions and offices, and that the words that we think of as technical terms—bishop, presbyter, deacon—were employed to denote function rather than office. The most reasonable conclusion is that since the bishops ultimately exercised the powers that the apostles had possessed, there was a connection between them in the transmission of this function. There are factors in the history of the community at Antioch that may have influenced this development. In the first place there were at Antioch from early times, in the persons of Barnabas and Paul, resident apostolic ministers of the Way, and Antioch was looked upon by other Christian communities as the source from which the Word had reached them; in these other communities the apostolic ministers of the Word were only visitors and supervisors.[96] It is possible to see here the seed of a monarchical episcopate. The story that Peter was first "bishop" of Antioch has been examined above; whether or not Peter had this title, he seems to have exercised some of the functions of the leader who was later called bishop. It has been suggested that Peter's traditional successor Evodius was such a nonentity that he could not well have been invented;[97] and so it would be possible to perceive the origin in Antioch of the monarchical episcopacy as we find it in Ignatius' writings, and to suppose, as many scholars have done, that it was by apostolic authority that this development occurred. But it must be remembered that these views are hypothetical and they rest upon evidence that is far from being trustworthy.[98] The development may not have been such a natural or easy one. It is apparent from the way in which Ignatius writes that the subject of the three-fold ministry has been a source of anxiety to him, and

---

cited by Altaner, *Patrologie*[2] 37-40, especially W. Telfer, "The Didache and the Apostolic Synod of Antioch," *JTS* 40 (1939) 133-146, 258-271, and J. H. Srawley, *The Early History of the Liturgy*[2] (Cambridge, Eng., 1947) 18-19. On Telfer's interpretation, see below. See also Gregory Dix in Kirk (ed.), *The Apostolic Ministry* 239-242.

[95] Another hypothesis (see Farrer in Kirk, ed., *The Apostolic Ministry* 168) is that the origin of the episcopate is to be explained by supposing that "a small committee of leaders called episcopi was allowed to dwindle to a single head."

[96] See Farrer's study in Kirk (ed.), *The Apostolic Ministry* 180, also G. Dix's essay in the same volume, 292.

[97] See G. Dix in Kirk (ed.), *The Apostolic Ministry* 250.

[98] It does seem reasonably clear that some local factor at Antioch had a strong influence on the process of the development of the episcopate; on this point see Harnack's study cited above in note 94 (p. 63 of the German orginal, 86 of the English translation). It is possible to suggest that the monarchical episcopate at Antioch was copied from the monarchical power of James in Jerusalem, but the Antiochene sources are strangely silent about any such borrowing.

that its proper functioning is something for which he has had to struggle. External factors may also have influenced the development of the episcopate, by making it plain that a strong and ordered ministry of this sort was necessary for the protection of Christians both from heresy (notably Gnosticism) and from official persecution.

In addition to the need for a recognized and established organization of its communities, the church by the time of Ignatius seems to have been coming to appreciate the necessity and the value of the leadership of the larger communities. It would be only natural for the smaller congregations in Syria to look to Antioch for leadership and support, not only because of the historic role of the city in the growth of the early Church and because of the prestige that attached to the work there of Paul and of Peter, but because Antioch was the capital of the province and the center of communications and information. It was in this sense that Ignatius in one of his letters (Rom. 2:2) spoke of himself as "bishop of Syria."[99]

Ignatius' personal religion, as it is amply revealed to us in his letters, is the warm and vivid faith of an essentially religious spirit.[100] "Faith and love" are his two guiding stars. To him, the life of Christ was of an immediate reality, and both his teaching and his example were directed toward the imitation of Christ. In his constant seeking to make a real blending of religion and morality, he adopted and frequently quoted the teachings of both Paul and the Fourth Evangelist. It has in fact been suggested that he was a pupil of the author of the Fourth Gospel, who, it has been suggested, may have lived at Antioch for a time and may have completed there a first draft of his Gospel, which was later published at Ephesus.[101] The evidence in support of this suggestion is very tenuous, but it illustrates the relationship that existed.

Of particular interest is the mysticism that formed an essential part

[99] See P. Gaechter, "Jerusalem und Antiochia," *ZKT* 70 (1948) 48; Bauer, *Rechtgläubigkeit u. Ketzerei* 67-69; G. Dix in Kirk (ed.), *The Apostolic Ministry* 264; C. Gore, *The Church and the Ministry*, new ed. revised by C. H. Turner (London 1936) 291, n. 1.

[100] See C. C. Richardson, *The Christianity of Ignatius of Antioch* (New York 1935).

[101] Both the place of composition of the Fourth Gospel, and the question whether Ignatius was acquainted with it, are disputed. The suggestion has been made (see Grant, "The Odes of Solomon" 363-377) that Ignatius, who was probably bilingual, in Greek and Syriac, was familiar with the eastern doctrines contained in the Odes of Solomon, which some scholars believe were composed in Syriac at Edessa. While this hypothesis is of interest, it cannot be accepted without reservations, since there is some ground for the belief that the Odes of Solomon were composed after Ignatius' death, and it has been claimed that their original language was Greek; see J. de Zwaan, "The Edessene Origin of the Odes of Solomon," *Quantulacumque: Studies Presented to Kirsopp Lake* (London 1937) 285-302.

of Ignatius' personal faith, and a very characteristic one. The mystic point of view and the mystic conception of Christianity evident in his thought is in fact so strong that it has been suggested that before he became a Christian, Ignatius was a member of a mystery cult. For Ignatius, there existed a world of divine reality that one might under proper conditions come to understand, as a part of the complete comprehension of the significance of the Christian faith.[102] The question of how far this simple and pure mysticism, which is one of the most attractive aspects of Ignatius' character, took hold upon the Christians of Antioch, is one of the important questions in the history of the early church at Antioch, and the answer has thus far not been found. Certainly nothing of this sort appears in the extant writings of Theophilus, the next figure in the history of the community at Antioch whose thought is known to us to any extent.

A marked poetic strain in his writings, and a number of references to singing as a part of divine worship, show that Ignatius was himself musically inclined. According to a later tradition, it was Ignatius who introduced antiphonal singing into the church, having learned it from a vision of angels singing. Actually, of course, this type of singing came from the Jewish synagogue. The tradition of Ignatius' role does, however, reflect the importance of the churches of Jerusalem and Antioch in the development of church music.[103]

Valuable insight into the development of Christianity in the environment of Antioch is suggested by Ignatius' very personal and individual religion, and particularly by the combination in it of aspects of the prophetic mysticism of St. Paul and of features of the prophetic mysticism of the Syrian mystery cults. The Pauline and Johannine conceptions of the Christian religion, themselves mystic in many respects, had of necessity to undergo the influence of the pagan mysteries and of the Gnostic teachings, and the result, as it is seen in the faith of Ignatius, shows what Christianity made of itself in its efforts to rise above its rivals. Before Ignatius' time, as we have seen, there had been a number of systems in which Christian elements were being used to a greater or less extent—those of the Jewish Christians, the Paulinists, the mystics,

---

[102] See F. A. Schilling, *The Mysticism of Ignatius of Antioch* (Philadelphia 1932; Diss., Univ. of Pennsylvania), and R. Reitzenstein, *Das iranische Erlösungsmysterium* (Bonn 1921) 86, n. 3; 234-236 (for some of the sources of Ignatius' mysticism). Passages in the letters which are especially illustrative of Ignatius' mystic ideas are *Trall.* 5.1; *Rom.* 5 to 7.1-3; *Philad.* 7.1-2; *To Polycarp* 2.1-3.
[103] Socrates *Hist. eccl.* 6.8 = *PG* 67.689 f. See E. Wellesz, *A History of Byzantine Music and Hymnography* (Oxford 1949) 26-28, 35.

and the Gnostics; and the fundamental question facing Christianity had been which would triumph. The achievement of Ignatius reveals the answer, and the results, in both faith and church organization, are shown in the spiritual life, individual and corporate, reflected in the bishop's letters. However, the processes that led to these results are, as we have seen, by no means clear, and there still remain unanswered certain obscure and difficult questions, chief among which is the problem of the steps in the transition from the "apostles, prophets, and teachers" to the monarchical bishop with his presbyters and deacons. There is also the question, which has been mentioned several times above, as to what development lies behind the appearance of Johannine ideas in Ignatius' letters, after the community at Antioch had begun its existence in terms of the teaching of Paul and Barnabas. And again, preceding these questions in point of time, there is the problem of the early controversy, which centered in Antioch, over the Gentile converts and their exemption from observance of the Jewish Law. These questions, though still unanswered, are the fundamental problems in the history of the early Christian community at Antioch. Answers to them would show us the true character of the early community in the city, and would enable us to understand what it was that gave this community its characteristic quality which exercised so important an influence on the development of the new religion. The material at our disposal, however, is so scanty, as we have seen, and in some respects so difficult to interpret, that it is not possible to find answers to these questions that will satisfy all scholars, and so we can determine only in general terms what the special position of Antioch after the end of the apostolic age was. The characteristics of the community appear for the first time, in relatively settled terms, in the work and teaching of Bishop Ignatius, in whose day the Antiochene church appears before us as an entity emerging from a shadowy period, now in possession of certain definite and recognizable characteristics in doctrine and organization.

5. From the Death of Ignatius to the Persecution Under Valerian

Our knowledge of the period following Ignatius' death is scanty; the principal authority, Eusebius, himself had available only a bare list of the bishops of Antioch.[104] The activity of the Gnostics at Antioch

---

[104] On Eusebius' list, see above, n. 40.

seems to have met with considerable success, and the popularity of their teaching, which would have drawn some people away from orthodox Christianity, may in part be responsible for the circumstance that our sources have little to say about the church at Antioch during the first three quarters of the second century.[105]

Ignatius' successor, in A.D. 116, was Heron.[106] Our knowledge of him comes from the corpus of Ignatian writings, which includes a letter to Heron, falsely attributed to Ignatius, and a laudatory prayer which Heron is said to have written in honor of Ignatius while he was still a deacon.[107] Heron was succeeded by Cornelius, concerning whose career we have no reliable evidence. Jerome in his *Chronicle* gives the date of Cornelius' accession as A.D. 128, but Jerome's dates for events of this type are not to be trusted. Cornelius in turn was followed by Eros, of whom, again, we have no knowledge except for the dubious statement of Jerome that he became bishop in A.D. 142.[108]

At about this time there was probably a considered movement on the part of the Jews in Antioch to join the Christian church, as a result of Hadrian's crushing defeat of the revolt of Bar Cochba in Palestine (A.D. 132-135).[109] There was a strong Jewish element in Christian doctrine at Antioch, which, as will be seen, played an important part in the development of the exegetical method that characterized the work of the Christian theologians in the city.

Christians were persecuted fairly widely under Marcus Aurelius (A.D. 161-180), a conscientious emperor who would take pains to see that the laws were enforced; but our sources for the history of Antioch at this period are scanty in the extreme and we hear nothing of persecution there.[110]

Eros was succeeded by Theophilus, in A.D. 169 according to the artifi-

---

[105] See Bauer, *Rechtgläubigkeit u. Ketzerei* 69-71, and Lietzmann, *Founding of the Church Universal* 258-259.

[106] Eusebius *Hist. eccl.* 3.36.15, 4.20.1; Jerome *Chron.* p. 194 ed. Helm (A.D. 108). On Heron's name, which is given in different forms (Heron, Heros, Hero) by various sources, see C. H. Turner's note, *JTS* 18 (1916-17) 110, n. 3. On the date of Ignatius' death, see above, n. 81. Heron was elected some weeks after Ignatius left Antioch for Rome (see above, n. 87), and since Ignatius was arrested after the earthquake of 13 December A.D. 115, Heron must have become bishop some time in A.D. 116.

[107] See Christ-Schmid-Stählin, *Gesch. d. gr. Lit.*[6] 2, pt. 2, 1228.

[108] Eusebius *Hist. eccl.* 4.20.1; Jerome *Chron.*, pp. 199, 202 ed. Helm. It is plain that Jerome's chronology of Theophilus (discussed below) is artificial.

[109] This is pointed out by Grant, "The Problem of Theophilus," 196. On Hadrian's war against the Jews, see Schürer, *Gesch. d. jüd. Volkes*[3-4] 1.670-704.

[110] On Marcus Aurelius' attitude toward the Christians, see J. Zeiller in Fliche-Martin, *Hist. de l'église* 1.311ff., and Grégoire, *Les persécutions* 28-30.

cial chronology of Jerome.[111] The only certain date in connection with Theophilus' career is a reference that shows that he was engaged in writing the third book of his *Ad Autolycum* soon after the death of Marcus Aurelius on 17 March A.D. 180, but there is nothing to show that Theophilus was bishop at this time. He died at some time before A.D. 188, when Maximinus is found in office as bishop.[112] Theophilus was a Syrian by birth, and was well educated; he became a Christian only after he had grown to manhood, and his conversion (as he tells us himself) took place after he had given careful study to the Christian scriptures.[113] Of his writings, which were fairly numerous, only the apology for the Christian faith, *Ad Autolycum*, has survived. His exposition is somewhat unsystematic and in places tends towards rationalism; he did not present clearly either the Christian faith or the Hellenistic philosophies that he contrasted with it.[114] His thought owes so much to Judaism, with which he was familiar because of the presence of the important Jewish community at Antioch, that he seems himself to be more Jewish than Christian, and the fact that a man of his views could become bishop of Antioch is suggestive of a rather unsettled condition of the Christian community there at the time. The distinctions between orthodoxy and heresy, and between Christianity and Judaism, do not seem as yet to have been perfectly clear on all points,[115] and it is characteristic that the Christian liturgy of the period contains many Jewish elements.[116] Modern scholars have come to a variety of conclusions regarding Theophilus' *Ad Autolycum*, most looking upon it as mediocre and confused, if not worse, while it has, on the contrary, been viewed by some as a great apology.[117] In spite of these differences of opinion among scholars, Theophilus occupies a position of great

[111] *Chron.* p. 205 ed. Helm.

[112] *Ad Autolycum* 3.27-28; cf. Harnack, *Chronologie d. altchr. Lit.* 1.210-211. The old view that the apology was not written by the bishop has now been abandoned, and it is agreed that Theophilus the apologist is the same person as Theophilus the bishop.

[113] On the life and writings of Theophilus, see, most recently, Altaner, *Patrologie*[2] 99-101, with bibliography; G. Bardy and J. Sender, *Théophile d'Antioche, Trois Livres à Autolycus* (Paris 1948), introduction; Grant, "The Problem of Theophilus," 179-196, with other important studies by the same scholar cited in n. 1, p. 179; idem, "The Textual Tradition of Theophilus of Antioch," *Vigiliae Christianae* 6 (1952) 146-159. Theophilus' work is described by Eusebius *Hist. eccl.* 4.24; see the notes of Lawlor and Oulton in their edition.

[114] This is the estimate of R. M. Grant, "Theophilus of Antioch to Autolycus," *HTR* 40 (1947) 256.

[115] Cf. Bauer, *Rechtgläubigkeit u. Ketzerei* 22-23, and R. M. Grant in *HTR* 43 (1950) 196.

[116] R. M. Grant, "The Early Antiochene Anaphora," *Anglican Theological Review* 30 (1948) 91-94.

[117] See R. M. Grant in *HTR* 40 (1947) 255-256.

importance in the history of the church at Antioch and in the development of Christianity. He represents an early attempt to formulate a learned theology—he is the first of the apologists to use the term "trinity" in speaking of the Godhead—and his work in this respect is of special significance, since his doctrine reappears three generations later in the work of one of his successors at the head of the church of Antioch, Paul of Samosata, who endeavored to reconcile Jewish and pagan teaching with the Christian doctrine;[118] and Theophilus' literal interpretation of scripture, relying on Jewish exegesis, marks him as a forerunner of the methods that later characterized the theological school of Antioch.

Another important contribution of Theophilus was the teaching that the Evangelists were inspired by the Holy Spirit and that the Gospels and the Pauline Epistles, which formerly had been looked upon merely as "writings of the apostles," were divine books, on the same footing as the works of the Old Testament prophets. Thus these scriptures, as inspired writings, have in themselves the power to convert. Theophilus, as has been claimed, may have been a man of moderate powers. However, he was honest in his belief that there is a necessity for faith, and he was earnest in teaching the superiority of Christianity over paganism from a moral point of view. His simple examples and homely arguments show the reality of his conviction, and the substantial number of his writings (though all but one are now lost) suggests that his methods and his arguments, whatever their success may have been, were often called for by the Christians of Antioch. In the work of Theophilus we may be able to perceive a change in the direction of missionary activity in Antioch itself. Ignatius' mysticism and simple faith had, apparently, done what they could; now Theophilus goes on to appeal to the more sophisticated pagans who possessed the current Hellenic education but were not highly trained in philosophy.

Of other aspects of the history of the church at Antioch in this period we have only glimpses. In Theophilus' time, apparently about A.D. 172, the heretical teachings of Tatian became popular in Antioch, following Tatian's return to the East from Rome. Tatian may indeed have opened a school at Antioch, though the evidence for this is not specific. He was an eclectic, teaching ascetic, dualistic, and docetic doctrines concerning the Creator, Christ, and the Eucharist.[119]

---

[118] On Paul of Samosata, see below, §6, also Ch. 10, §10.
[119] On Tatian's life and teachings see Christ-Schmid-Stählin *Gesch. d. griech. Lit.*[6] 2.pt. 2 1288-1291; Kidd *Hist. of the Church* 1. 199-201; J. Zellinger, "Tatian" *Lex. f.*

Commodus (A.D. 180-192), who came to the throne before Theophilus' death, was more leniently disposed toward the Christians than his father had been; he had a Christian mistress named Marcia, whom he eventually married.[120] However, we have no details on the history of the community at Antioch during this period.[121] Theophilus, writing soon after Commodus' accession, could say that the word Christian was still an "evil name" at Antioch.[122]

At some time during the reign of Commodus, Theophilus was succeeded by Maximinus (incorrectly called Maximus in some sources), who is known to have been bishop between about A.D. 188 and 198 or 199; he may have entered office before A.D. 188.[123] All that we know of Maximinus' activities is that he took part in the paschal controversy, which was being carried on at this time, over the proper date of celebrating Easter.[124]

With Serapion, who succeeded Maximinus, we come once more to a figure who is more than a name.[125] His accession to the bishopric can be dated in A.D. 198 or 199 since the dates of his predecessor Maximinus can be fixed fairly certainly; and the end of his tenure can also be fixed since it is known that his successor Asclepiades became bishop during the first year of Caracalla's reign (A.D. 211/2).[126] Serapion wrote a number of letters, now lost but extant in the time of Eusebius, who

---

Theol. u. Kirche 9 (1937) 1002-1003. Epiphanius *Haeres.* 46.1 = *PG* 41. 840 B writes that his teaching prevailed especially from Antioch in Syria to Cilicia and Pisidia, which could very plausibly be taken to mean that he taught at Antioch.

[120] See Grégoire, *Les persécutions* 30-31, and J. Zeiller in Fliche-Martin *Hist. de l'église* 1.319-320.

[121] According to the hypothesis of W. Telfer, "The *Didache* and the Apostolic Synod of Antioch," *JTS* 40 (1939) 133-146, 258-271, the *Didache* would have been written at Antioch about this time by a man who was a leader of the church there; according to this hypothesis the document was, for propaganda purposes, composed and given out as being an encyclical written by St. Peter to the Gentile believers of Antioch, Syria, and Cilicia.

[122] Theophilus *Ad Autol.* 1.1, κακὸν ὄνομα.

[123] Eusebius *Hist. eccl.* 4.24.1, 5.19.1; *Chron.* p. 207 ed. Helm (where Maximinus' accession is impossibly dated in A.D. 177). In the chronology I follow Harnack, *Chronologie d. altchr. Lit.* 1.211, cf. 126 (Maximinus' accession is dated in A.D. 188 by Julius Africanus).

[124] Maximinus is mentioned by Eutychius of Alexandria (*Annales, PG* 111.989) as being the recipient of a letter from Demetrius of Alexandria concerned with this question. On the paschal controversy, see Hefele-Leclercq, *Conciles* 1.133-151.

[125] On his life and writings see Eusebius *Hist. eccl.* 5.19 and 22; 6.12; Jerome *De vir. ill.* 41; cf. *Acta SS.*, 30 October, vol. 13, p. 248-252 (Paris 1883). See Harnack, *Chronologie d. altchr. Lit.* 1.211-212; H. Leclercq, "Lettres chrétiennes," *DACL* 8.2751ff.; Kidd, *Hist. of the Church* 1.84-85, 272, 279.

[126] Harnack, *loc.cit.* (see above, n. 125).

quotes from them.[127] He dealt with heretical questions, writing of Montanism and Docetism, and advised the church at Rhosos, a coastal town on the Gulf of Issus not far from Antioch, not to read the apocryphal Gospel of Peter, which was docetic. One letter was to a Christian who had fallen away into Judaism.

The history of the Christian community at Edessa during Serapion's bishopric gives us an insight into the influence that Antioch exerted among the Christian churches elsewhere in Syria. Ignatius, it will be recalled, spoke of himself in one of his letters (Rom. 2.2) as "bishop of Syria." Whether or not this was a real title, it indicates (what we should expect in any case) that Antioch, both as the political metropolis of Syria and as the original center of Gentile Christianity, enjoyed special prestige, if not formal and official leadership, among the Syrian Christians. This hegemony is now well illustrated in the case of Edessa, which was the chief city in the eastern part of Syria. Edessa was not a Hellenic city, like Antioch, but remained predominantly Syrian in speech and culture. The circumstances of the arrival of Christianity in the city are, for lack of evidence, not clear, but it does appear that Christianity when it became established in Edessa—far away as it was from the great centers—took on a syncretistic character reflecting the influence of the native Syrian pagan cults. It appears—though again the evidence is not perfectly clear—that Serapion, while bishop of Antioch, undertook to correct this situation in Edessa and that he sent a missionary named Palût to the city in an effort to bring the community there into closer union with the body of the church. Palût was successful in introducing the accepted teachings of the times, and Serapion consecrated him as Bishop of Edessa.[128] This episode may be taken as an example of the way in which the influence of Antioch must have penetrated inland and put an end to the independent (and often irregular) existence of the old Christian communities which had grown up by themselves, from very ancient origins, outside the influences and developments that had shaped Christianity in the Graeco-Roman centers to the west.

[127] *Hist. eccl.* 5.19, 6.12. The fragments are reprinted in *PG* 5.1373-1376.
[128] *Ancient Syriac Documents*, ed. by W. Cureton (London 1864) 23. See H. Leclercq, "Edessa," *DACL* 4.2073f., 2087; F. C. Burkitt, *Early Eastern Christianity* (London 1904) 18-35, 68-78; Kidd, *Hist. of the Church* 1.107; Streeter, *Four Gospels* 72ff.; C. C. Torrey, *Documents of the Primitive Church* (New York 1941) 271ff. Burkitt believes that Palût took with him to Edessa a Syriac translation of the New Testament, made from the Greek text that was in use at Antioch. This, Burkitt thinks, was intended to replace the *Diatessaron* of Tatian, which had previously been in use at Edessa.

It was during Serapion's bishopric that Septimius Severus issued his edict (between A.D. 200 and 202) in which conversions to Judaism and Christianity were forbidden.[129] There appears to have been no real persecution under Septimius Severus. There were martyrdoms, but there is not a great deal of evidence for organized attack. At Antioch, the future bishop Asclepiades distinguished himself as a confessor.[130]

Of the next bishops we know little. The tenure of Serapion's successor, Asclepiades (A.D. 211/2—217/8), apparently coincided closely with the reign of Caracalla (A.D. 211-217). Alexander, the future bishop of Jerusalem, who was in prison at the time of Asclepiades' accession, wrote a letter to the community at Antioch expressing his joy at hearing the news, and sent it by the hand of Clement of Alexandria, who was traveling to Antioch.[131] Asclepiades was succeeded in A.D. 217/8 by Philetus, who seems to have lived until about A.D. 230/31.[132]

Philetus' successor was Zebennus, of whom nothing is known beyond his name; he was bishop under Severus Alexander (A.D. 222-235) but the dates of his accession and death are not clear. His successor Babylas became bishop in the time of the Gordians (A.D. 238-244).[133] The "Syrian emperors" who occupied the throne at this period, and the members of their families, were much interested in religious matters. Elagabalus (A.D. 218-222) tried to establish a syncretistic religion, which would include Christianity, and his cousin Severus Alexander (A.D. 222-235), who succeeded him, was disposed to be tolerant of the Christians, having many of them at his court.[134] His mother, Julia Mamaea, possessed a wide education, like the other women of her family, and a philosophical mind; and if not actually a Christian, she was deeply interested in the religion. While she was living in Antioch between A.D. 231 and 233, she sent for Origen, whose fame as a teacher was then spreading, to come and instruct her in the Christian doctrine. Accompanied by a military escort, which the empress had provided

---

[129] *SHA Sept. Severus* 17.1. On the date of the edict (which is often given as 202) see J. Zeiller in Fliche-Martin, *Hist. de l'église* 2.115, n. 2. On the church under Septimius Severus, see J. Zeiller in Fliche-Martin, *Hist. de église*, 2.113-117; G. Uhlhorn and A. Hauck, "Severus," *PRE*³ 18.257; and Grégoire, *Les persécutions* 31-35. Severus' edict was merely the renewal of existing law.

[130] Eusebius *Hist. eccl.* 6.11.4; *Acta SS.*, 18 Oct., vol. 8, 313-318 (Paris 1870).

[101] Eusebius *Hist. eccl.* 6.11.4-6; on the chronology see Harnack, *Chronologie d. altchr. Lit.* 1.212.

[132] *Eusebius Hist. eccl.* 6.21.2; see W. Ensslin, "Philetos," no. 2, *RE* 19 (1938) 2171; Harnack, *Chronologie d. altchr. Lit.* 1.212.

[133] Eusebius *Hist. eccl.* 6.23.3 (accession of Zebennus), 6.29.4 (accession of Babylas); on the chronology, see Harnack, *Chronologie d. altchr. Lit.* 1.214-215.

[134] See Kidd, *Hist. of the Church* 1.350-351.

for his safety, Origen traveled to Antioch from Caesarea in Palestine, where he was living, and remained at the court, Eusebius says, "for some time," giving instruction to the empress, and doubtless to her friends.[135] Since Julia Mamaea exercised a strong influence over her son, and was in fact the leading figure in the government, her interest in Christianity, and her invitation to Origen, must have given much encouragement to the community at Antioch. At about the same time, the community was distinguished by the activity of the learned presbyter Geminus, whose works are now lost.[136]

A change came, however, when Severus Alexander was succeeded by Maximinus the Thracian (A.D. 235-238). Maximinus was anxious to obliterate all traces of the influence of his predecessor, and since the Christians had been prominent at court, Maximinus thought it desirable to institute a persecution. This was aimed particularly at the bishops.[137] However, we hear of no martyrdoms at Antioch.

Under the Gordians (A.D. 238-244) Babylas became bishop.[138] Babylas is well known because of his supposed encounter with the emperor Philip the Arab (A.D. 244-249) and because of the later adventures of his relics at Antioch under Gallus and Julian; and a church dedicated to him, as his last resting-place, has been found in the excavations, on the right bank of the Orontes, across from the city.[139]

The widely circulated tale of Babylas and the emperor at the church door is plainly fictitious. Babylas, the story goes, refused to allow Philip to attend a service in the church at Antioch, barring his way at the

[135] Eusebius *Hist. eccl.* 6.21.3-4 (followed by Zonaras 12.15); cf. Christ-Schmid-Stählin, *Gesch. d. griech. Lit.*[6] 2, pt. 2 (Munich 1924) 1318. Harnack, *Chronologie d. altchr. Lit.* 2.30, n. 5 puts Origen's visit to Antioch in the reign of Elagabalus (A.D. 218-222) rather than in the reign of Severus Alexander. This creates difficulties in the interpretation of the text of Eusebius, as Harnack recognizes. Actually there is no evidence that Julia Mamaea was in Antioch in the reign of Elagabalus, while we do know that she lived in Antioch for a time during her son's reign.

[136] Jerome *De vir ill.* 64. As a result of confusion and false identifications, there arose a legend of a Hippolytus, bishop of Antioch, who was himself born in the neighborhood of Antioch, who was martyred there in the middle of the third century; see Peter Damian, *Lib.* 1, *Epist.* 9 *ad Nicol.* 2, in *PL* 145.436 C-D. This legend grew out of that of the martyrdom of Hippolytus of Rome, which is supposed to have taken place about A.D. 235; evidently a writer at Antioch discovered local material which he thought indicated that Hippolytus the Roman bishop suffered at Antioch. The martyr of Antioch was commemorated on 30 January. Sometimes there are indications that Hippolytus of Antioch suffered later in the third century, e.g. under Claudius (A.D. 268-270). On the sources and their errors see H. Achelis, *Hippolytstudien* (Leipzig 1897) 37-38, 57-60; and Delehaye, *Origines du culte*[2] 193-195.

[137] Eusebius *Hist. eccl.* 6.28; cf. Kidd, *Hist. of the Church* 1.351-352.

[138] Eusebius *Hist. eccl.* 6.29.4; cf. Harnack, *Chronologie d. altchr. Lit.* 1.214-215.

[139] *Antioch-on-the-Orontes* 2.5-48. See below, Ch. 15, §1.

door, because the emperor had slain his predecessor (or, in some versions, because he had slain a Persian hostage who had been entrusted
to him). There is no contemporary reference to such an episode, which
appears only at a later date, in versions which are sometimes suspi-
ciously different. It is, in fact, unthinkable that the episode can have
occurred as it is related. The bishop's command to the emperor would
have been a blow to the imperial prestige which could not have been
tolerated. Moreover, the sensation caused by Ambrose's excommunica-
tion of Theodosius I, which occurred after Christianity was the recognized state religion, makes it seem certain that if something similar
had occurred in the mid-third century, when Christianity was still an
illicit sect, some trace of it would have been left in contemporary
literature.[140] What the basis for the story may have been is not clear.
Philip seems to have shown some partiality toward the Christians,
though it is not certain whether, as has been supposed, he was a
catechumen or even secretly a Christian.[141] It would be easy for stories
of the bishop's courage and the emperor's obedience to grow up at
Antioch; and then the tale could have been developed (as it is, quite
frankly, in one late version) as a lesson in the preeminence of the
ecclesiastical authority over the civil power.[142] The story of the encounter

[140] Here the argument follows those of E. Stein, "Iulius (Philippus)," no. 386, *RE*
10 (1919) 769-770.

[141] Kidd, *Hist. of the Church* 1.352 and J. Zeiller in Fliche-Martin *Hist. de l'église*
2.121, are not inclined to accept the story. Whether or not Philip belonged to the church
(which has been doubted by scholars), it seems safe to conclude from Eusebius *Hist.
eccl.* 6.41.9 that he was favorably disposed toward the Christians. Grégoire, *Les Persécutions* 11-12, with notes on 90-91, has argued forcefully that Philip was a Christian.

[142] The episode of Babylas and Philip appears first in the *Ecclesiastical History* of
Eusebius (6.34); the author first makes it clear that the story is a report, for which
he does not vouch (κατέχει λόγος, λέγεται). Chrysostom twice mentions the boldness
of Babylas in rebuking a guilty emperor (whom he does not name); the episode of
the church door is not mentioned: *Hom. 9 in Ephes.* 4, §2 = *PG* 62.71; *De S. hieromart.
Babyla, PG* 50.529. In the *Chronicon Paschale* 1.503.11ff. the story of Babylas' rebuke
of the emperor at the church door is given as a story that used to be told by Leontius,
bishop of Antioch in the middle of the fourth century. In some accounts the emperor
becomes Numerian (A.D. 283-284), e.g. in the life of Babylas published by A. Papa-
dopoulos-Kerameus, *Pravoslav. Palestin. Sbornik* 57 (1907) 75, and in the *Chronicle* of
Malalas 303.8-20 (the displacement of the episode to the time of Numerian disagrees
with all the independent evidence for the date of Babylas' career, and of Numerian
we know nothing that would furnish any basis for the story). For other sources in
which the story appears, more obscurely, see P. Peeters, "La passion de S. Basile
d'Epiphanie," *Anal. Boll.* 48 (1930) 302-323. The most revealing account is that which
appears in the *De S. Babyla contra Iulianum et gentiles* (*PG* 50.533ff.) which has been
handed down under the name of St. John Chysostom but is so unlike his work in
style that scholars do not attribute the work to him (see Peeters, *op.cit.* 307-310;
Delehaye, *Origines du culte*[2] 36, n. 3; *BHG*[2] no. 208; G. Downey, "The Shrines of St.
Babylas," *Antioch-on-the-Orontes* 2.47, n. 14: Bauer, *Der hl. Joh. Chrysostomus* 1.24).

of Ambrose and Theodosius, which is also legendary, and appears
in literature for the first time in the fifth century, plainly was put in
circulation for the same reason, and it may not be impossible that the
tale of the encounter of Ambrose and Theodosius was suggested by the
apocryphal tale of Babylas and the emperor.[143]

With Philip's successor Decius (A.D. 249-251) the position of the
Christians was reversed. Wishing to undo the influence of his predecessor in every possible way, Decius instituted a persecution,[144] in the
course of which Babylas died in prison in Antioch, and was succeeded
by Fabius, in A.D. 250 or 251.[145] We know of Fabius chiefly in connection
with the Novatian schism, which was dividing the church at Rome at
that time over the question of the legality of the position of Novatian,
who had set himself up as a rival to Pope Cornelius after the Decian
persecution.[146] Fabius, it seems, was inclined to support Novatian.[147]
A synod at Antioch was planned, at which it was apparently expected
that Novatian's adherents, under the leadership of Fabius, would make
a pronouncement in his favor. However, Fabius died before the synod
could meet.[148] The invitations to it were issued by Helenus, Bishop

---

Here the statement is made explicitly, especially in the closing paragraph (cf. cols.
547, 571) that Babylas by his action demonstrated for future emperors and future
priests that the ecclesiastical power is superior to the emperor's authority, and that
the emperor may not overstep the bounds set for him by God. On the significance of
this kind of propaganda, see the following note.

[143] The story of the encounter of Ambrose and Theodosius in the atrium, which is
supposed to have occurred in A.D. 390, appears for the first time in the *Ecclesiastical
History* of Sozomen (7.25 = PG 67.1493), which was written between A.D. 439 and
450; on its fictitious character and its political meaning, see Dudden, *St. Ambrose*
387-388. The dramatic date of the pseudo-Chrysostom *De S. Babyla contra Iulianum
et gentiles*, in which the story is used for propaganda, is twenty years after the burning
of the temple of Apollo in Daphne, i.e. A.D. 382 (PG 50.567), but there is no real evidence to show when this tract was published. On the resemblances between the episode
of Babylas and Philip and the encounter of Ambrose and Theodosius, see Chrysostomus
Baur, "Zur Ambrosius-Theodosius-Frage," *Theol. Quartalschr.* 90 (1908) 401-409, with
a note by H. Koch in the same volume, 647.

[144] See J. Zeiller in Fliche-Martin, *Hist. de l'église* 2.145-152, who believes that there
was a severe persecution, aimed at the destruction of the church. Grégoire (*Les Persécutions* 44-46) thinks that many of the details that have commonly been attributed to
this persecution are not actually connected with it.

[145] Eusebius *Hist. eccl.* 6.39.4. Babylas was not executed, as Chrysostom says, *De S.
hieromart. Babyla* = PG 50.529; see above, n. 139. On the date of Fabius' accession,
which is not certain, see Harnack, *Chronologie d. altchr. Lit.* 1.215; Kidd, *Hist. of the
Church* 1.453.

[146] Eusebius *Hist. eccl.* 6.43.3; cf. 6.41-42. On the schism of Novatian, see Kidd,
Hist. of the Church 1.450-453.

[147] Eusebius *Hist. eccl.* 6.44.1ff.

[148] Eusebius *Hist. eccl.* 6.46. Schultze *Antiocheia* 64, n. 2, thinks that the synod may
have been planned after Fabius' death.

of Tarsus, acting while the see at Antioch was vacant; and the meeting assembled in A.D. 252 under Fabius' successor Demetrianus. Demetrianus held views different from those of his predecessor, and Novatian was condemned and deposed.[149]

Not long after Demetrianus became bishop, Antioch was captured by the Persians, in A.D. 256. As was their custom on such occasions, the conquerors, when they retired from the city, carried off into exile a number of skilled workmen whose services they desired. Among these there must have been a number of Christians, for one of the captives carried off was Demetrianus; as on other similar occasions, the Persians were careful to take the leader of the Christian community so that he might reconcile his people to their fate and keep order among them.[150] When the exiles were settled in Persia, the bishop served as leader of the exiled community until he died. Evidently it was hoped in Antioch that Demetrianus might some day return, for no successor seems to have been elected before his death, and Demetrianus appears to have been regarded as still bishop of Antioch while in captivity. Other Christians were among the captives carried off by the Persians when they took the city for the second time in A.D. 260, and these were added to the community of the first exiles in Persia. When news of the exiled bishop's death finally came, Paul of Samosata was elected to succeed him, in A.D. 260 or 261.[151] During Demetrianus' absence the community at Antioch was presumably ruled by the senior presbyter of the local clergy. It also appears that when the see of Antioch was vacant, or

[149] On the action of the synod see the *Libellus synodicus*, quoted by Mansi 1.871, and Eusebius *Hist. eccl.* 7.8; cf. Hefele-Leclercq, *Conciles* 1.169 (on the *Libellus*, see the note of Hefele-Leclercq *ibid.* 128, n. 3).

[150] The deportation of Demetrianus is recorded in the Arab Nestorian history called the *Chronicle of Seert, PO* 4.222 (in which his name is written Demetrius). Eusebius (cf. *Hist. eccl.* 7.27.1) appears not to have known of it. On the career of Demetrianus, see P. P(eeters), "Démétrianus, évêque d'Antioche?", *Anal. Boll.* 42 (1924) 288-314, and the study "De S. Demetriano Antiochiae episcopo" by the same scholar in *Acta SS.*, Nov., vol. 4 (1925) 384-391. Peeters in the study first named lists the other occasions on which the Persians carried off skilled artisans, with their spiritual leaders, from cities of the Roman Empire. It should be noted that Père Peeters' chronology was drawn up before the discovery of the *Res gestae divi Saporis* and the more detailed study of the numismatic evidence, from which it appears that Antioch was first taken by the Persians in A.D. 256, rather than in A.D. 253, as Père Peeters supposed (see below, Excursus 5). When Chosroes captured Antioch in A.D. 540, a number of the inhabitants were carried into exile; see Ch. 18, nn. 184-185.

[151] The date of Demetrianus' death in exile is not known; but as Bardy points out (*Paul de Samosate* 249) the news of the exiled bishop's death might not have reached Antioch for some time. Bardy's chronology is now to be revised, as is that of Peeters (see preceding note).

was in dispute, the neighboring Bishop of Tarsus exercised a sort of protective supervision over it.[152]

There is no record of the effect at Antioch of the persecution of Valerian (A.D. 253-260), which lasted from A.D. 257 to 260. This persecution, a severe one, fell in a period when the empire was laboring under grave difficulties and dangers. Barbarian invasions were a serious threat on all the frontiers; and the government was fatally entangled in a policy of deliberate inflation of the currency. It was in fact financial distress that was one of the real causes of the persecution, for the Christian communities by this time were accumulating valuable property, and the government hoped to improve its position by confiscating the wealth of the Christians.[153] At this period Antioch was recovering from the plundering and burning of A.D. 256, when the Persians had captured the city. The sources are scanty and say nothing about the persecution in Antioch at this time; but the emperor either was in Antioch himself, or made it the headquarters of his campaigns against the Persians, for a large part of his reign; and where the emperor was present the measures against the Christians would presumably have been faithfully carried out.[154]

6. PAUL OF SAMOSATA

The persecution under Valerian was only one of the troubles from which Antioch suffered at this period. In A.D. 260 Valerian himself was captured by the Persians, and in the summer of the same year the forces of Sapor again invaded Syria and once more captured Antioch.[155] Roman power and prestige sank; and the rulers of Palmyra took the opportunity to free their kingdom from Roman control and lay the foundations of an independent state. Antioch, though it was nominally still within the Roman state, soon found itself within the spreading Palmyrene sphere of influence.[156]

---

[152] This is suggested by the way in which the Bishop of Tarsus, Helenus, issued the invitations to the synod of A.D. 252 at Antioch after Fabius had died and his successor Demetrianus had not yet been elected (Eusebius *Hist. eccl.* 6.46.3), and by the way in which the Bishop of Tarsus again (the same Helenus, as it happened) presided at the synod of Antioch of A.D. 269 which deposed Paul of Samosata from the bishopric of the city (Eusebius *Hist. eccl.* 7.30.2; *Libellus synodicus*, quoted by Mansi, 1.1099; see Hefele-Leclercq *Conciles* 1.199).

[153] On the persecution of Valerian, see J. Zeiller in Fliche-Martin, *Hist. de l'église* 2.152-157, and Grégoire, *Les Persécutions* 46-54.

[154] Ch. 10, §9. Valerian's arrival in the East, after he became emperor, is variously assigned, by different scholars, to the years A.D. 253/4, 255, 256 or 257.

[155] See above, Ch. 10, §8.

[156] See above, Ch. 10, §10.

In this same year, A.D. 260, Paul of Samosata on the Euphrates became bishop of Antioch. The appearance on the scene at this moment of Paul of Samosata is significant for both political and ecclesiastical reasons.[157] Coming from the eastern frontier, he was a representative of the ancient native territories of Syria that had never become Hellenized; these regions all through Syria, probably even those close to the great cities, at this time were doubtless looking to Palmyra to free them from Rome. There is good evidence that when the Persians invaded Syria and captured Antioch in A.D. 253 and 260, they found an element in the population that was hostile to the Roman administration and looked with favor upon the possibility of Persian domination; there may indeed have been a regular pro-Persian faction that gave assistance to the invaders. The man who may have been the leader of this faction had a Semitic name (Mariades or Kyriades in its Hellenized form), and it is not unreasonable to suppose that it was the people of Semitic stock in and around Antioch who hated the Romans and looked to the East for sympathy and possible rescue.[158] This Semitic element in Antioch and in the country round about would doubtless have welcomed the advent of the Palmyrenes, and would have been glad to serve a man like Paul of Samosata as the enemy of Rome and the representative of the new regime.[159] Paul's position was in fact made very clear, for he was both the bishop of Antioch and the chief fiscal officer (*procurator ducenarius*) in the city.[160] The circumstances of his election to the bishopric and of his appointment to the civil office are not recorded, so that we do not know, for example, whether Paul was already serving in his civil function when he was made bishop. In any case it can be regarded as certain that the Palmyrene regime at least

[157] On the career of Paul, see Loofs *Paulus von Samosata* and Bardy *Paul de Samosate*[2], corrected and supplemented, especially with respect to his doctrine and to the proceedings against him, by Riedmatten, *Procès de Paul de Samosate*, who provides for the first time a reliable collection of the texts concerning Paul (see the valuable review of this work by H. Chadwick, *JTS* N.S. 4 [1953] 91-94). The passage describing Paul's career in the *Ecclesiastical History* of Eusebius, 7.27.1—7.30.19, quotes part of the synodal letter of A.D. 268. On Paul's teaching, see also Sellers, *Two Ancient Christologies* 118ff. On the date of his accession see Loofs, *Paulus von Samosata* 51-52.

[158] On the Persian invasions of Syria at this time and the political events in Antioch connected with them, see above Ch. 10, §8, and Excursus 5.

[159] Paul's popularity with some of the neighboring bishops and their clergy is mentioned in the synodal letter as quoted by Eusebius *Hist. eccl.* 7.30.10; cf. Bardy *Paul de Samosate*[2] 274.

[160] On the function of the procurator, see Jones, *Greek City* 193. The term *ducenarius* is an indication of rank, indicating that the official had a salary of 200,000 sesterces; in the time of Paul of Samosata this was a high rank (see Seeck, "Ducenarius," *RE* 5 [1905] 1752-1754).

approved his combining secular and churchly offices, and it is possible, if not likely, that his appointment to both was influenced by the new government. It is easy to believe that Palmyra took this way (however unusual it may have been at this time) to exercise complete control over the city. Paul is thus one of the earliest examples—if not indeed the earliest—of the type of worldly "political" bishop which becomes more familiar in the later history of the church,[161] and it is characteristic of the mixed population of Antioch, and of the vacillating political role which it often adopted, that Paul was enabled to pursue his remarkable career in the Syrian capital. The accounts of his career also indicate that the Christian community at Antioch had by this time achieved some importance, for Paul's conduct, as it is described by Eusebius, suggests that the bishop of Antioch was regarded, and could consider himself, as a person of some consequence.[162]

Theologically, also, Paul of Samosata is a figure of the first importance. His doctrine, which stressed the unity of God and the manhood of Christ (who according to Paul's teaching had a human soul), paved the way for Arianism and established a tradition in the teachings of the theological school of Antioch.[163] Whether or not this simplified, and to many people attractive, doctrine was to some extent put forward by Paul for political reasons, to please Zenobia the queen of Palmyra, who was supposed to have Jewish sympathies, cannot be demonstrated.[164] Paul's view of the unity and power of God might have been influenced by the strict monotheism of the Jews, but there is no proof of this.[165] The denial or subordination of the divinity of Christ was a view which had arisen very early, as soon as the nature of Christ had been debated, and Antioch by Paul's time was a place in which such a doctrine would find support, just as, in the next century, the city became one of the strongholds of Arianism, which in essence held to the same teaching, though it employed different methods.

While Paul's doctrine, to many of the faithful and of the clergy, seemed blasphemous and perilous, his conduct as a civil official and

---

[161] See Bardy *Paul de Samosate*² 262, who cites examples.

[162] See Bardy *Paul de Samosate*² 213.

[163] On Paul's doctrine, see the studies cited above, n. 157.

[164] Athanasius *Hist. arianorum ad monachos* 71 = *PG* 25.777 B, is the oldest text which speaks of a relation between Paul and Zenobia; the queen is called a Jewess, and a protector of Paul. Zenobia was of Semitic origin, and must have been acquainted with Judaism; but that she belonged to the Jewish faith is not certain. Eusebius and the synodal letter as he quotes it do not speak of any Palmyrene connections of Paul's. See Loofs, *Paulus von Samosata* 18ff.

[165] See Bardy, *Paul de Samosate*² 253-254.

his private life—or what his private life was rumored to be—likewise gave rise to scandal and alarm.[166] As *procurator ducenarius* he was in charge of the collection of taxes in Antioch; he was accused of corruption and greed, and of using every opportunity to turn his office to his own gain. In daily life, it is said, he behaved more like a civil official than a bishop, going about attended by secretaries and a guard. He apparently conducted church services, and preached, in a theatrical fashion; and he was accused of putting a stop to the singing of psalms in honor of Christ and of substituting hymns in honor of himself—and, what was almost worse, it was reported that he had these sung by a chorus of women. He and the clergy of his suite were attended by handsome young women assistants, apparently deaconesses, and this gave rise to gossip.[167]

At length, Paul's teaching came to exercise such a powerful influence at Antioch that to many people in the city and to the bishops of some of the neighboring towns action seemed necessary. Helenus, bishop of Tarsus, evidently acting in his capacity as head of the nearest large church (as he had done a few years before when the see of Antioch was vacant), called a synod that met at Antioch in A.D. 264.[168] This synod was convoked in order to inquire into Paul's doctrine, not into any alleged scandals connected with his personal conduct. That a synod called to examine the doctrine of a bishop should meet in the bishop's own city was no doubt unusual, but the political situation may have made this step necessary. Paul may very likely have indicated that he would refuse to appear before a synod that met in a city outside the Palmyrene sphere of influence, and the bishops may have felt that a verdict reached in the absence of the accused would have carried less weight than a verdict reached in Paul's own city. Circumstances thus favored Paul and made the task of the visiting bishops difficult, for the accused enjoyed not only the favor of the regime and the prestige of his civil office but the support of his own followers among the clergy and the faithful both in the city and in its neighborhood. When the synod met, Paul was able to conceal and disguise his doctrines, and the bishops had to be content with a promise that Paul would change his teaching.

[166] See the extracts from the synodal letter quoted by Eusebius *Hist. eccl.* 7.27.1-7.30.19, on which the present brief account is based.

[167] On the *subintroductae*, Paul's attendants, see Loofs, *Paulus von Samosata* 199-201.

[168] On the council, see Hefele-Leclercq, *Conciles* 1.28, nn. 3-4; 195ff.; Loofs, *Paulus von Samosata* 45-50; Bardy, *Paul de Samosate*[2] 285ff.

Paul's doctrine, however, must have enjoyed such a strong position among the faithful at Antioch (as is evident from the influence that it continued to exercise in the city after his death), that Paul and his followers seem to have considered that there was no need to carry out this promise. In a few years it became plain that Paul was not going to reform his teaching, and a new group of bishops, some of whom were the successors of those who attended the first synod, were convoked for a council that met in A.D. 268.[169] The occasion was looked upon as an important one, and a "large number" of bishops, perhaps eighty, attended.[170] This time the attack was successful. It was led by Malchion, a priest who was head of a school of rhetoric in Antioch; it is not clear whether this was a Christian institution in which classical learning was taught and classical methods of logic and dialectic were followed,[171] or a lay establishment of which Malchion was the head.[172] Malchion evidently possessed both the skill in dialectic and the superior learning that such a task demanded, and he succeeded in forcing Paul to abandon the efforts to conceal his doctrine that had saved him at the earlier synod; and so the heretical nature of Paul's teaching was

[169] See Hefele-Leclercq, *Conciles* 1.198ff.; Loofs, *Paulus von Samosata* 45-50; Bardy, *Paul de Samosate*[2] 295ff.

[170] Eusebius *Hist. eccl.* 7.28.1; cf. Bardy, *Paul de Samosate*[2] 299ff.

[171] Eusebius *Hist. eccl.* 7.29.2; Jerome *De vir. ill.* 71. With J. H. Srawley, "Antiochene Theology" Hastings, *Ency. Rel. Eth.* 1.584; Christ-Schmid-Stählin, *Gesch. d. griech. Lit.*[6] 2, pt. 2, 1349; Kidd, *Hist. of the Church* 1.499; A. Puech, *Hist. de la littérature grecque chrét.* 2 (Paris 1928) 485-486; and Sellers, *Two Ancient Christologies* 107, 202, the present writer takes the passage in Eusebius to mean that Malchion was at the head of a school. The view that Eusebius' words mean only that Malchion was eminent as a teacher (cf. Bardy *Paul de Samosate*[2] 279, with n. 2) seems mistaken. It has been considered remarkable that Malchion should have combined different functions such as the priesthood and the teaching of sophistic. Harnack, *Chronologie d. altchr. Lit.* 1.137-138, proposes to solve this supposed difficulty by believing that Malchion was a teacher of Hellenic culture who was converted to Christianity and continued to teach after his conversion. These scruples and explanations are unnecessary if one supposes (cf. Srawley, *loc.cit.*) that the school in which Malchion taught was a Christian institution in which classical learning and classical logic and dialectic were taught at a necessary part of a Christian education. Whether this should be taken to mean that Antioch at this time possessed a theological school comparable to that at Alexandria is not clear; there is no other evidence for such a school at Antioch at this period (see further below in the discussion of the career of Lucian of Antioch). Or it is perfectly possible to suppose, as Bardy suggested (*Lucien d'Antioche* 38, n. 24) that this was simply a Greek school directed by Malchion. The evidence really is not sufficient for any safe conclusion (cf. Bardy, *Lucien d'Antioche* 42).

[172] An older generation of scholars, notably Kattenbusch, Hort, and Harnack, believed that as a consequence of Paul's heresy there was drawn up at Antioch, presumably by the synod which condemned him, a revision of the old Roman creed which served as the basis for the later Eastern creeds which we know. This theory has now been given up as a result of more recent study, which has indicated that the creeds that are found in the East are of eastern origin. See A. R. Burn, "Creeds and Articles," Hastings, *Enc. Rel. Eth.* 3.237-238, and Kelly, *Early Christian Creeds* 196-197, 201-202.

definitely proved. Paul was excommunicated, and in his place the synod elected Domnus, son of the old bishop Demetrianus, Paul's predecessor, who had died in captivity in Persia. The choice of a native of Antioch as the new bishop is significant in view of the trouble that had attended the career of the "outsider" Paul of Samosata.

Paul, relying on the support of the Palmyrene government and of his own followers, refused to accept the decision of the synod, and continued to exercise the functions of his office. Antioch thus, for the first time, possessed two rival bishops, one orthodox, one heterodox, a situation that was often to recur during the Arian troubles of the following century. Paul's confidence was justified, and he was able to maintain his position until Aurelian defeated Zenobia and drove her and her followers from Antioch in A.D. 272.[173] Paul of Samosata, as a leading figure of the Palmyrene regime in Antioch, must have been ejected from the city soon after it returned to Roman control. One might in fact have expected that Paul would have considered it prudent to leave the city when it was evacuated by the Palmyrene troops, and we can only wonder why he chose to remain and to be expelled with, Eusebius says, "the utmost indignity."[174] Where and when his life came to an end, we do not know. The continuing influence of his teaching, as will be seen in the following chapters, was destined to be for many years a central factor in the religious life of Antioch.

7. From the Deposition of Paul of Samosata to the Accession of Diocletian, A.D. 284

Concerning the decade following the career of Paul of Samosata we have little precise information. Eusebius furnishes a bare skeleton of the succession of the bishops. Something of the theological activity in Antioch at this time can be inferred from the career of Lucian of

[173] On Aurelian's defeat of Zenobia, see Ch. 10, n. 162.

[174] Eusebius *Hist. eccl.* 7.30.18-19 (cf. Bardy, *Paul de Samosate*[2] 358ff.) relates that when Aurelian regained control of Antioch, the orthodox party, basing their claim to the bishopric on the fact that they were in communion with the bishop of Rome, the capital of the empire, appealed to the emperor to confirm them in the possession of the physical property of the church in Antioch, which was being illegally occupied by Paul of Samosata, and that Aurelian granted this appeal and had Paul ejected. That such was the procedure is, however, somewhat doubtful, for there is no reason to believe that Aurelian knew or cared enough about the organization of the Christian church to be impressed by such an appeal (see Loofs, *Paulus von Samosata* 59). There seems no question that when Aurelian's troops occupied Antioch, Paul of Samosata, as the protégé of Palmyra, would have been ejected immediately, without any need for legal process. Eusebius' account is, however, accepted by a number of scholars, most recently Grégoire, *Les persécutions* 60-61.

Antioch (or "of Samosata"), who may have begun to teach at Antioch at about this time; but the circumstances of his career make it necessary to treat it at a later point in the history of the city, under the reigns of Diocletian and Constantine.

In the interval between the deposition of Paul of Samosata and the accession of Diocletian, three bishops of Antioch are recorded by Eusebius. Domnus, as has been seen, was elected bishop in A.D. 268 by the synod which deposed Paul; but Paul refused to vacate his office and had to be driven out of the city when Aurelian defeated Zenobia in A.D. 272. During this period Domnus presumably functioned among his supporters as the orthodox bishop of Antioch.[175] According to the *Chronicle* of Jerome, based on that of Eusebius, Domnus lived for only three years after his election, which would place his death in A.D. 271 or the first part of 272;[176] he may have died before Aurelian, after defeating Zenobia's forces near Antioch in the late spring or early summer of A.D. 272, drove Paul of Samosata out of the city.[177]

Domnus' successor was Timaeus, of whom nothing is known save his name. He is supposed to have served as bishop for nine years, until his death in A.D. 279/80.[178] His successor was Cyril, who held office until A.D. 303. The events of his tenure of office will be taken up in the account of the reign of Diocletian.

[175] Eusebius *Hist. eccl.* 7.30.18.

[176] Eusebius' chronology is represented in Jerome *Chron.* pp. 221-22 ed. Helm and in Syncellus, p. 714.14 Bonn. ed.

[177] Domnus is not mentioned by name in Eusebius' account (see above, n. 174) of Aurelian's expulsion of Paul of Samosata, which might be taken to suggest that Domnus had died and that his successor had not been elected. On Eusebius' chronology of Domnus and his immediate successors, see Harnack, *Chronologie d. altchr. Lit.* 1.216-218.

[178] Eusebius *Hist. eccl.* 7.32.2. The date of his death is indicated by the entry in the *Chronicle* of Jerome, p. 224 ed. Helm, which puts the accession of his successor Cyril in the fourth year of Probus = A.D. 279/80. See Harnack, *loc.cit.*

CHAPTER 12

ANTIOCH UNDER DIOCLETIAN (A.D. 284-305),
CONSTANTINE THE GREAT (A.D. 306-337),
AND CONSTANTIUS (A.D. 337-361)

1. Diocletian's Visits to the City

IOCLETIAN transformed the Roman Empire from a principate into an absolute monarchy. Recent history had shown the need for important changes. Order had to be restored, the civil administration reorganized, taxation and currency stabilized and reformed; the imperial throne and dynastic succession had to be safeguarded and the defense of the frontiers assured. The rise of Christianity posed a problem for which a solution must be found.[1]

It was to be expected that a city such as Antioch should be affected in many ways by the changes that now made themselves felt in every sphere of life in the Roman Empire. In addition, the city, in Diocletian's time, may still have been in need of assistance to repair the damage suffered when it was pillaged and burned by the Persians of Sapor. Probus (A.D. 276-282) appears to have planned the rebuilding of the city, but the circumstances of his reign were such that it may not have been possible to accomplish much in this direction, and some at least of the rehabilitation may well have remained for Diocletian to carry out.[2]

The emperor himself visited Antioch on a number of occasions, and at least three times remained there for substantial sojourns. He may have stopped at Antioch during the journey through the eastern provinces which he made in the spring and summer of A.D. 286; we

---

[1] The extent of the economic and political changes introduced by Diocletian is so great that it would be impossible to give an adequate description of them in the present work. Excellent treatments of the many complex subjects involved are readily available; see for example the chapters on Diocletian by H. Mattingly and W. Ensslin in *CAH* 12 (1939) 324-408; W. Ensslin, "Valerius (Diocletianus)," *RE* 7A (1948) 2419-2495; W. Seston, *Dioclétien et la Tetrarchie*, 1: *Guerres et réformes*, 284-300 (Paris 1946; *Bibl. des Ecoles franç. d'Athènes et de Rome*, fasc. 162), with the important review, containing valuable observations on the subject in general, by W. Ensslin, *Deutsche Literaturzeitung* 1949, 115-124 (see also W. Ensslin's further remarks, "Zum dies imperii des Kaisers Diocletian," *Aegyptus* 28 [1948] 178-194); Rostovtzeff, *Stor. econ. soc. Imp. rom.* 585-619. A valuable study of the Edict on Prices has recently been published by L. C. West, "The Coinage of Diocletian and the Edict on Prices," *Studies in Honor of A. C. Johnson* 290-302.

[2] On the plans of Probus, see Ch. 10, n. 175.

happen to have no specific indication of his presence at Antioch on this tour, but Diocletian had then been emperor for a relatively short time and the tour was an important one, so that it would seem likely that he visited the Syrian capital.[3] Four years later he made a hurried trip through Syria to repel an invasion of the Saracens, and this time we know that he was in Antioch on 6 May A.D. 290 and in Emesa on 10 May.[4] In A.D. 297 the Sassanian king Narses invaded Syria and defeated the caesar Galerius, who had been called from Illyricum to deal with the attack. Diocletian, on his way north after suppressing a revolt in Egypt, met Galerius in Antioch, probably late in the year, and evidently spent the winter of A.D. 297/8 there. In A.D. 298 Galerius mounted a new offensive and defeated the Persians, capturing the king's wives and children, as well as a large amount of booty.[5] The queen, Arsane, was held in honorable captivity in Daphne until she was returned to her husband on the conclusion of peace.[6] Diocletian and Galerius celebrated a triumph in Antioch, apparently depicted on the triumphal arch that Galerius later erected in Thessalonica. By this time, Galerius' arch shows, Diocletian's great palace at Antioch had been built.[7]

Diocletian evidently remained in Antioch after the triumph over the Persians, and spent the winter of A.D. 298/9 there, for it was in Antioch, on 1 January A.D. 299, that he entered on his seventh consulship, and a rescript shows his presence in the city on 5 February A.D. 299.[8] So far as we can tell, he also made Antioch his headquarters in A.D. 300 and 301; he is known to have been in the city on 12 February, 26 March, and 25 June A.D. 300 and on 4 July A.D. 301.[9]

2. THE PALACE

Of the many buildings constructed at Antioch under Diocletian, the most prominent was the great palace, which was (as has been remarked) built at some time before A.D. 298.[10] Libanius, in his panegyric of Antioch, written for the local Olympic games of A.D. 360, describes the palace, and the island on which it stood, as follows (*Or.* 11.203-207):

[3] See Ensslin in *RE* 7A (1948) 2427-2428.
[4] See Ensslin in *RE* 7A, 2431.
[5] Ensslin in *RE* 7A, 2442-2443; Malalas 306.16-21, 308.6-14. Mattingly in *CAH* 12 (1939) 335 puts the original Persian invasion in the summer of A.D. 296, but Ensslin's argument that the invasion took place one year later is convincing.
[6] Malalas 308.10-14; see Stauffenberg, *Malalas* 399-400.
[7] On the triumphal arch and the palace, see further below.
[8] Ensslin in *RE* 7A, 2445.   [9] Ensslin in *RE* 7A, 2446.
[10] On the date, see further below.

"Such then is the form of the old city. The new city stands on the island which the division of the river formed. . . . The form of this new city is round. It lies in the level part of the plain, the whole of it in an exact plan, and an unbroken wall surrounds it like a crown. From four arches which are joined to each other in the form of a rectangle, four pairs of stoas proceed as from an omphalos, stretched toward each quarter of the heaven, as in a statue of the four-handed Apollo. Three of these pairs, running as far as the wall, are joined to its circuit, while the fourth is shorter but is the more beautiful just in proportion as it is shorter, since it runs toward the palace which begins hard by and serves as an approach to it. This palace occupies so much of the island that it constitutes a fourth part of the whole. It reaches to the middle of the island, which we have called an omphalos, and extends to the outer branch of the river, so that where the wall has columns instead of battlements, there is a view worthy of the emperor, with the river flowing below and the suburbs feasting the eyes on all sides. A person who wished to describe this part carefully would have to make it the subject of a discourse, but it cannot be a part of a discourse on another subject. Nevertheless, one should say at least that to the other palaces which exist in every part of the world, some of which are praised for their size and others for their beauty, it is in no way inferior; but it is far superior to many, nowhere surpassed in point of beauty, and in size surpassing all others, divided into so many chambers and stoas and halls that even those who are well accustomed to it become lost as they go from door to door. I believe that if this palace stood by itself in some insignificant city, such as are numerous in Thrace, where a few huts form the cities, it would give the one that possessed it good reason to claim a proud position in the catalogue of cities."[11]

[11] Malalas (306.21-22) merely mentions the construction of the "great palace" (as he calls it) and says nothing as to its location or plan. Libanius, it is true, does not say that the palace he describes was built by Diocletian, but it seems certain that this must have been the case. We have no specific evidence for the Seleucid royal residence that must have existed at Antioch; possibly it became in time the residence of the Roman governor of Syria. There is no evidence whether before Diocletian's time there was also a palace reserved for the use of the emperors. There may well have been such a building, which Diocletian's new palace replaced. However, if there were such an older palace, Libanius would certainly have chosen for description in his panegyric the imperial residence which, in his day, was the most prominent, and this would certainly have been the one built by Diocletian. We hear virtually nothing about the interior of the palace. Ammianus Marcellinus (25.10.1) mentions that there was a statue of Maximian in the vestibule, but we learn nothing else from the sources about the numerous other statues that must have stood in the palace. The palace appears to be represented in the topographical border of the mosaic from Yakto (see below Excursus 18).

The gallery along the river side of the northern front of the palace is mentioned by the church historian Theodoret, who says that there were towers at either end of the portico, and that between the palace and the river there was a road which led from the city gate across a bridge to the suburbs.[12]

The position of the palace on the island can be determined with a fair degree of certainty (Fig. 11). Libanius says that the palace occupied space between the middle of the island and the outer branch of the river, by which he must mean the western branch, which was farthest away from the city. The same location is indicated by the testimony of Libanius and Theodoret that the palace had a gallery along the river from which there was a view of the suburbs. The excavations made on the southwestern part of the island indicate that the palace cannot have stood there.[13] The northwestern part of the island, where no excavations have been made, thus seems indicated, and it is not without interest to find that this quarter of the island would accommodate a palace of approximately the same size as Diocletian's palace at Salona, or even one of greater size.[14]

[12] Theodoret *Hist. eccl.* 4.26.1-2, pp. 264-265 ed. Parmentier. The incident in connection with which Theodoret gives this information occurred during the reign of Valens (A.D. 364-378). Theodoret does not specifically mention the bridge, but its existence is to be inferred from his account. Whether the road between the palace and the river ran along the whole of the portico which faced the river, or along only a part of it, is not clear. Theodoret's account indicates only that a man passing along this road could be seen by the emperor from the portico. Bouchier, *Antioch* 160, states that the north wall of the palace was here carried across the road to the enclosing wall of the island on a series of arches. This is a possible interpretation of the passage in Theodoret, but there is no specific evidence for it in the texts.

[13] No traces of a palace were discovered in the excavations, and the remains that were found (which happened to be baths) indicate that if a palace stood here it must have disappeared completely between A.D. 350-400—a most unlikely occurrence, for which there is no evidence in the sources. Moreover, there seems to have been an east-west thoroughfare running before one of the large baths on the southwestern part of the island (*Antioch-on-the-Orontes* 1.20-21), and this would seem to preclude the existence of a palace in this area. The area is shown on the map of the excavations in *Antioch-on-the-Orontes* 2.215, Plan 1; a map of the area, with plans of the buildings excavated, is published in *Antioch-on-the-Orontes* 1, Pl. 11, facing p. viii. The inner, or eastern branch of the river has become filled in since antiquity, so that its course is indicated, on the map in *Antioch-on-the-Orontes* 2, only by the wall of the mainland part of the city, which the river followed. There are, however, ample indications, in the present contours of the ground, of the course of the eastern branch of the river, and there are also traces of the abutments of the bridges which connected the island and the mainland. The ancient course of the river, and the position of the bridges, are shown on the restored plan of the city printed here (Fig. 11). The excavations on the southwestern portion of the island are described in *Antioch-on-the-Orontes* 1.1-48 and *Antioch-on-the-Orontes* 2.1. A panoramic view of the northern part of the island area appears in *Antioch-on-the-Orontes* 3.6, Fig. 5, and below, Fig. 2.

[14] The palace at Salona measures 179.48 or 175.30 m. by 216 or 215.10 m.: Vulic, "Salona," *RE* 1A (1920) 2005.

The plan of the palace at Antioch can be determined with a fair degree of certainty from several types of evidence. First, Libanius' remark (quoted above) that the side of the palace that lay along the river had a pillared gallery, from which one overlooked the river and the suburbs, recalls the gallery overlooking the sea in the palace at Salona. Second, the triumphal arch of Galerius at Thessalonica, which records the caesar's victory over the Persians, shows Diocletian and Galerius sacrificing at an altar that stands before a colonnade composed of pillars bearing arches of the same kind as those in the peristyle of Diocletian's palace at Salona. Since Galerius' triumph in A.D. 298 was celebrated at Antioch, it seems reasonably certain that the arched colonnade is that of the palace built by Diocletian at Antioch.[15] Incidentally, the construction of the palace at Antioch is thus dated before A.D. 298. A further indication of the plan may be found in the circumstance that the palace was built on foundations laid by Valerian, apparently in A.D. 256.[16] Valerian undertook the restoration of Antioch after the city had been damaged by the Persians when they captured it in A.D. 253. It seems highly unlikely that Valerian should have used his resources at this time in the construction of a palace at Antioch. On the other hand there would be good reason for him to begin the construction of a fortified *castrum* on the island; and if, when this project remained unfinished, Diocletian employed the foundations for a palace, the result would have been a structure of the same type as the palace at Salona.

A further point of interest is that the site of the palace at Antioch is adjacent to the hippodrome, which had stood on the island since the first century B.C.[17] This recalls the arrangement adopted at Constantinople, where Constantine in building his palace chose a site alongside the hippodrome which had been built by Septimius Severus,[18] and at

---

[15] See K.-F. Kinch, *L'arc de triomphe de Salonique* (Paris 1890) 37; F. Weilbach, "Zur Rekonstruktion des Diocletians-Palastes," *Strena Buliciana* (Zagreb-Split 1924) 125; H. von Schoenebeck, "Die zyklische Ordnung der Triumphalreliefs am Galeriusbogen in Saloniki," *BZ* 37 (1937) 361-371; and Ensslin in *RE* 7A (1948) 2445-2446.

[16] Malalas (306.21-22) says that the foundations were laid by Gallienus, but the history of this emperor's reign (during which Antioch was controlled by Palmyra) makes it seem improbable that he did any such work at Antioch. Malalas in other respects confuses Gallienus and Valerian, and since Valerian is known to have undertaken work of restoration at Antioch, it seems clear that the construction of these foundations was done by him. The question is discussed above, Ch. 10, n. 126.

[17] On the history of the hippodrome, see the report of its excavator, W. A. Campbell, in *Antioch-on-the-Orontes* 1.40, and Excursus 14.

[18] On the construction of Constantine's palace at Constantinople, see C. Du Cange, *Constantinopolis Christiana* (Paris 1680), pt. 1, p. 113 (and cf. R. Janin, *Constantinople byzantine* [Paris 1950] 109); on the hippodrome of Septimius Severus, see Oberhummer

Thessalonica, where Galerius, after becoming emperor in A.D. 305, built a palace adjacent to the hippodrome and on its west side (as at Antioch).[19] The ceremonies and spectacles of the hippodrome played an important part in the political and ceremonial life of the emperor, so that it was essential that palace and hippodrome be closely integrated.[20]

The evidence, then, makes it possible to suppose (as some scholars do)[21] that the palace at Antioch served as a model for the palace that was later built at Salona, although a more cautious view would be that the two structures represent a type of plan so common that there would have been no necessary influence of the one on the other.[22] The military tradition that surrounded Diocletian would naturally lead him to build palaces of this type.[23]

The approaches to the palace are occasionally mentioned. Libanius (quoted above) speaks of a short colonnaded street running from the center ("omphalos") of the island to the palace. Julian the Apostate (A.D. 361-363) published his *Misopogon* at the "Tetrapylon of the Elephants" outside the palace, which was presumably a tetrapylon surmounted by a statue showing elephants drawing a triumphal quadriga.[24] An account of Antioch written by a Chinese visitor states

and J. Miller, "Byzantium," *RE* 3 (1899) 1125, 1140, and Janin, *op.cit.* 178. The position of the hippodrome with relation to the palace at Constantinople is shown in the plan published by A. Vogt, *Constantin VII Porphyrogénète, Le Livre des Cérémonies, Commentaire*, vol. 1 (Paris 1935), folding plate at end of volume. The plan of the palace at Constantinople resembled that of the palace at Salona; see K. Lehmann-Hartleben, "Städtebau," *RE* 3A (1929) 2124.

[19] See E. Oberhummer, "Thessalonike," *RE* 6A (1937) 149; O. Tafrali, *Topographie de Thessalonique* (Paris 1913) 131; E. Dyggve, "Kurzer, vorläufiger Bericht über die Ausgrabungen in Palastviertel von Thessaloniki, Frühjahr 1939," *Diss. Pannonicae*, ser. 2, no. 11 (*Laureae Aquincenses* 2), 1941, 63-71.

[20] See Bury, *Later Roman Empire* 1.81-86; Dvornik, "Circus Parties."

[21] See Weilbach, cited above, n. 15.

[22] See Lehmann-Hartleben in *RE* 3A, 2124; E. Dyggve, *History of Salonitan Christianity* (Oslo 1951) 28, with n. 40 (on p. 42).

[23] See G. Rodenwaldt in *CAH* 12 (1939) 567-568. It is curious and instructive to see that there is difference of opinion as to whether the camp-like structure of which traces have been preserved at Palmyra was a permanent camp or a palace of Diocletian; see *Palmyra*, ed. by Th. Wiegand (Berlin 1932) 85, 106-107; C. Watzinger, "Palmyra," *RE* 18 (1949) 270; and Rodenwaldt, *loc.cit.* A building inscription seems to refer to the structure as *castra*, and this has been taken to mean that it was a permanent camp, although the term *castra* was regularly used to denote whatever place the emperor was using for the time being as his residence (see Ensslin in *CAH* 12.386 and in *RE* 7A, 2454). The scholars who have called the structure at Palmyra a palace do not seem to have reckoned with the question whether Diocletian supposed that he or his associates and successors would spend enough time in Palmyra to make the building of a palace there necessary or desirable. It seems to the present writer unlikely that Diocletian, fond of building as he may have been, would have gone to the expense of constructing a palace at Palmyra. The structure is to be dated between A.D. 292 and 304, or between 293 and 303 (see *Palmyra*, ed. Wiegand, 106-107).

[24] See below, Ch. 13, nn. 88-89.

that as one approached the palace there were three gates (presumably standing in succession along the approach), the second of which, on its "upper floor," possessed a clepsydra or water-clock, consisting of a human figure and an arrangement of twelve balls, one of which moved and struck each hour.[25]

The building of the palace at Antioch shows of course that Diocletian appreciated the city's importance for administrative and military purposes, particularly in the vital matter of the defense of the eastern frontier, and that he expected to have to spend a substantial amount of time there—and this, as we have seen, he did. Nicomedia, indeed, proved to be his favorite residence, but Antioch seems to have been not far behind it as a seat for the imperial headquarters. As to whether Diocletian built the palace at Antioch because at one time he thought of making the city his principal residence we can only speculate,[26] and the principle of mobility of the court, which was a necessary element in Diocletian's scheme of government, would have operated against the choice of one particular city as a fixed capital.[27] However, it is clear in any case that with the division of the Empire into areas for which the members of the Tetrarchy—the two Augusti and their junior colleagues the caesars—were responsible, Antioch came to play a new role in the imperial organization.

3. OTHER BUILDINGS OF DIOCLETIAN; THE OLYMPIC GAMES

The administrative and military importance of Antioch was recognized not only in the construction of the palace, but by other structures

[25] The account follows (F. Hirth, *China and the Roman Orient* [Leipzig and Shanghai 1885, reprinted 1939] 213): "Coming from outside to the royal residence there are three large gates beset with all kinds of rare and precious stones. On the upper floor of the second gate they have suspended a large golden scale; twelve golden balls are suspended from the scale-stick by which the twelve hours of the day are shown. A human figure has been made all of gold of the size of a man standing upright, on whose side, whenever an hour has come, one of the balls will drop, the dingling sound of which makes known the divisions of the day without the slightest mistake."

[26] Since there seems to be no evidence to show when the palace at Nicomedia was built (W. Ruge, "Nikomedia," *RE* 17 [1937] 476, 491), while the construction of the palace at Antioch can only be dated at some time before A.D. 298, it is not possible to find in the history of the buildings any suggestion as to whether one city at one time enjoyed preference over the other.

[27] On the mobility of the court, see Ensslin in *CAH* 12 (1939) 385-386. Galerius when he succeeded Diocletian in A.D. 305 chose Thessalonica as his residence and built a palace there (E. Oberhummer, "Thessalonike," *RE* 6A [1937] 149). This illustrates the latitude of choice that was possible in such matters, and also suggests that Galerius may have been trying to demonstrate his new independence and authority, in the gesture of building a new palace instead of occupying one of Diocletian's.

of utilitarian character. For the strengthening of the defense of the eastern frontier, arms factories were built at Antioch, Edessa, and Damascus. There were two at Antioch, one devoted to the production of shields and weapons, the other to the making of coats of mail.[28] Diocletian also built granaries at Antioch in order to assure regular supplies of grain for both civilian and military use, possibly also in order to provide facilities for the storage of cereals received by the government in the payment of taxes in kind.[29] The mint of Antioch was reorganized and took its place in the new system in which all mints throughout the Empire now came under direct imperial control and produced coins of uniform type.[30]

Diocletian's other buildings at Antioch of which we have records were five baths. One was a public bath, named for the emperor τὸ Διοκλητιανόν, on the island near the great circus.[31] There was also a

[28] Malalas 307.20-23; *Notitia Dignitatum*, Orient. 11.18ff.: *Fabricae infrascriptae: . . . scutaria et armorum, Antiochiae; clibanaria, Antiochiae.* See Ensslin in *RE* 7A (1948) 2471. Mattingly, in *CAH* 12 (1939) 336, suggests that the arms factories at Antioch, Damascus, and Edessa were established at the time when Diocletian arrived at Antioch from Egypt to support Galerius in his campaign against the Persians. This is of course quite possible, but there must also be borne in mind the possibility that the construction of the factories was undertaken earlier, as a part of an over-all plan to strengthen the army that was guarding the eastern frontier.

[29] Malalas 307.2-5. In describing these granaries, the chronicler seems to be trying (though not really understanding the matter) to combine (1) a statement that the granaries were designed to assure regular supplies for the civilian population and to prevent the disruption of the civilian supply by its being diverted to use by the army, and (2) an allusion to Diocletian's attempt to fix maximum prices. The need in a place like Antioch for regulation of cereal supplies is illustrated by the famine and price inflation produced by the influx of troops at Antioch during the preparations of Constantius and Julian the Apostate for their Persian campaigns; see below, nn. 221-225, and Ch. 13, §1. The possibility that the *horrea* were also intended for the storing of the *annonariae species* is pointed out by Ensslin, *RE* 7A, 2475.

[30] See Ensslin in *CAH* 12.403-404 and in *RE* 7A, 2468-2469; Stein *Gesch.* 1.112, n. 2; and Mattingly-Sydenham, *Rom. Imp. Coinage* 5, pt. 2 (by P. H. Webb) 205-212, 217-218. Malalas writes (308.1-3) that Diocletian "built a mint in Antioch so that coins could be struck there, for this mint had been destroyed by an earthquake; and it was rebuilt." Since there is no evidence of an interruption of the activity of the mint of Antioch either during Diocletian's reign or before it, and no evidence of an earthquake at Antioch during this period, it would seem that the chronicler's statement represents a misunderstanding of an allusion in a source to the reorganization (which might have been described as a "reopening") of the local mint. It is also possible, of course, that it was found necessary, as a result of the reform of the coinage and of the introduction of the imperial mint-system, to enlarge the existing mint, or even to construct a new building for it. Moreover, Malalas may have been so bent upon magnifying Diocletian's benefactions to Antioch that he unconsciously exaggerated the purely routine measures taken with respect to the mint.

[31] Malalas 306.22-307.2. The chronicler states that this bath was situated "in the plain [or: "level ground"] near the old circus." By πεδιάς, Malalas apparently means the flat part of the city, as distinguished from the section which was built on the slope of Mount Silpius. This term could, by itself, be used to describe either the oldest section

bath called "the senatorial bath," possibly because it was reserved for members of the senatorial order; the location of this is not stated. Three other baths are mentioned, but they are not described or located.[32]

Other activities of Diocletian at Antioch formed a part of his program for religious revival and for the strengthening of the basis upon which was built his Tetrarchy, or division of the administration of the Empire among four rulers. Diocletian put his own dynasty, called the Jovian, under the protection of Jupiter, while that of his colleague Maximianus was placed under the protection of Hercules.[33] The Olympic games of Antioch, held in honor of Zeus, naturally provided Diocletian with an opportunity to find ways in which to pay special honor to his patron deity. To this end he rebuilt or adorned the stadium at Daphne which had been used in the Olympic games.[34] In this stadium he constructed

---

of the city, along the left bank of the river, or the island, or the flat ground across the river from the city, which seems never to have been incorporated within the walls. In the present case the island seems to be meant, for the great circus built in the first century B.C. which has been excavated there is apparently the one which was called "the old circus" as distinguished from the smaller stadium, also on the island, which seems, from the evidence of the excavations, to have been built in the late fifth or early sixth centuries after Christ (see Excursus 14, §A). Thus far there have been discovered no remains of a bath near the "old circus" which could have been built by Diocletian. It is characteristic of Malalas' mechanical manner of writing that while he mentions that Diocletian's public bath "in the πεδιάς" was near the "old circus," and records this bath in a sentence which follows immediately the record of the building of the palace, he does not indicate the location of the palace, and does not mention that the palace, the "old circus," and Diocletian's bath were near each other. Evidently he considered this relationship to be sufficiently well known not to need mentioning.

[32] Malalas 308.3-5. The construction of the palace, and the presence in the city for extended periods of time of the imperial court, must have caused other building activities of various kinds of which we do not hear. One tangible monument of Diocletian's reign survives in the fine porphyry head of a tetrarch which was found at Antioch: *Antioch-on-the-Orontes* 2, pl. 6, no. 136, with description on p. 172; and Morey, *Mosaics of Antioch* 13.

[33] On this aspect of Diocletian's religious program, see Mattingly in *CAH* 12 (1939) 329-330; Ensslin, *ibid.* 387; N. H. Baynes, *ibid.* 661, 668; Ensslin in *RE* 7A (1948) 2479-2482; Parker, *Hist. of the Roman World A.D. 138-337* 234-236; H. Mattingly, "Jovius and Herculius," *HTR* 45 (1952) 131-134.

[34] Malalas 307.5-16. The statement that Diocletian "built" a stadium for use in the Olympic games implies that none existed, which is probably untrue. A stadium existed at Daphne as early as 195 B.C. (see Excursus 14). Malalas, evidently either thinking that Diocletian's work at Daphne was so important that it ought to have entailed the construction of a stadium, or attempting to magnify the emperor's benefactions, turned a record of rebuilding or renovation into a statement of new building, as he does on other occasions (on the chronicler's procedures in this aspect, see Ch. 2, §4). Malalas' statement that Diocletian "built" the stadium at Daphne so that the Olympic victors might be crowned there, instead of going to Quadrigae to be crowned, represents a misunderstanding of the history of the removal of the Olympic games from Antioch by Septimius Severus and their restoration by Caracalla and their reorganization by Commodus; see Ch. 9, §10; Ch. 10, nn. 31-32; Ch. 10, §4; and the detailed study of the problem by Downey, "Antioch under Severus and Caracalla" 141-156.

(or reconstructed) a shrine of Olympian Zeus and built a shrine of Nemesis, the latter being placed in the *sphendone*, where the officials and judges of the games sat; the placing of the shrine of Nemesis thus brought the officials of the games, symbolically, ever under the scrutiny of Justice.[35] He also, on one occasion, as the "Jovian emperor," assumed the office of Alytarch of the Olympic games, this official being the president of the games and being considered, while holding his office, to be the representative of Zeus.[36] Diocletian probably acted as Alytarch in the celebration of the games that took place in July and August of A.D. 300, a year in which he spent much time in Antioch.[37] Diocletian's junior colleague, Galerius, likewise appears once to have served as Alytarch of the Olympic games of Antioch, at a date which cannot be determined.[38]

[35] On the significance and development of the cult of Nemesis in Syria, where the deity seems to have enjoyed unusual popularity, see H. Seyrig, "Antiquités syriennes, 1: Monuments syriens du culte de Nemesis," *Syria* 13 (1932) 50-64. For parallels for the placing of the shrine of Nemesis, see Müller, *Antiq. Antioch.* 62, n. 4. Müller (62) thinks it much more likely that the Temple of Olympian Zeus was originally built by Antiochus IV Epiphanes, and was only rebuilt or adorned by Diocletian. While this is possible, there is no way, given the meager and unsatisfactory condition of the sources, of proving when the shrine was originally built. Diocletian's special interest in the cult of Zeus (which Müller may not have taken into account) might have impelled him to build a wholly new temple, rather than restore an old one; but all this can only be speculation.

[36] Malalas 310.7-311.2. On the Alytarchate, see Ch. 9, nn. 148, 151; and cf. Gagé, "Les Perses à Antioche" 314, n. 2.

[37] Malalas states that the emperor held the Alytarchate on an occasion when he came to Antioch from Egypt. Which journey this was, is not clear; the date that best fits Malalas' account is A.D. 300, since Diocletian (as has been mentioned above) is known from other evidence to have been in Antioch in June of this year (see Stauffenberg, *Malalas* 437-441 and Ensslin in *RE* 7A [1948] 2446, 2487-2488). Malalas' fantastic statement that Diocletian announced his abdication at the Olympic games at which he served as Alytarch must represent either confusion with the celebration of Diocletian's vicennalia in Rome in A.D. 303 (Ensslin, *op.cit.* 2487) or a misguided effort to magnify the importance of Antioch and its Olympic games (see Stauffenberg, *Malalas* 440-443, and Ensslin, *op.cit.* 2490).

[38] Malalas relates (311.12-312.5) that the Emperor Maximianus acted as Alytarch of the Olympic games of Antioch on an occasion when he made war against the Armenians, who were attacking the Romans. There is no evidence that Maximianus ever conducted such a campaign or ever visited Antioch (see Ensslin, "Maximianus (Herculius)" *RE* 14 [1930] 2486-2516), but it would seem quite possible for chroniclers such as Malalas and his sources to confuse the Emperor Maximianus (M. Aurelius Valerius Maximianus), with the Caesar Galerius (C. Galerius Valerius Maximianus), who is ordinarily called simply Maximianus in papyri, and often bears this name alone on coins (Ensslin, "Maximianus (Galerius)," *RE* 14 [1930] 2516). And of course the reference to the Armenian campaign points clearly to a confusion with Galerius, who conducted operations in Armenia. Thus it seems practically certain (as Stauffenberg suggests, *Malalas* 441) that Malalas' account represents the result of such a confusion. The year in which Galerius would have held the Alytarchate is not clear; he may have acted in this capacity while serving as caesar under Diocletian, or after he had succeeded Diocletian as emperor (see Stauffenberg, *Malalas* 441-442). Galerius may have

Other buildings of Diocletian at Daphne were a palace and an underground shrine of Hecate, which was reached by 365 steps; the emperor
also rebuilt or adorned the Temple of Apollo.[39]

4. THE CHURCH AT ANTIOCH UNDER DIOCLETIAN; THE
PERSECUTION; THE REVOLT OF EUGENIUS

The bishop of Antioch during most of Diocletian's reign was Cyril,
who succeeded Timaeus on his death in A.D. 279/80[40] and held office
until he was arrested early in the persecution that began in A.D. 303
(see below). Cyril's tenure of office witnessed the labors of Dorotheus
of Antioch, a learned priest who was a friend of Eusebius', and of
Lucian of Antioch (or "of Samosata"), the celebrated teacher and head
of the theological school at Antioch, who was later to become a martyr.
Lucian's career, by reason of its significance theologically in the history
of the church at Antioch, is best treated later in this chapter.[41] Dorotheus' career was an important one. According to Eusebius,[42] who knew
him, this learned priest was especially distinguished for his knowledge
of Hebrew, which enabled him to read the Scriptures in the original;
Eusebius' description of this ability seems to imply that such knowledge
was rare at the time. Dorotheus was also well trained in classical literature, and Eusebius heard him expound the Scriptures systematically in
church. He may have collaborated with Lucian of Antioch in the
revision of the text of the Bible which Lucian carried out; and in the

---

been in Antioch in the summer of A.D. 296, when preparations for the defense of Syria
against the Persians were being made, and since a celebration of the Olympic games
would have fallen in this year (the festival being held in Julian leap-years), this may
have been the occasion on which he served as Alytarch. Libanius (Or. 11.269) speaks
of an emperor presenting the Olympic games and another emperor appearing as
hellanodikes. He does not name the emperors, but he may have had Diocletian and
Galerius in mind.

[39] Malalas 307.16-20; cf. Müller, Antiq. Antioch. 99, and Stauffenberg, Malalas 489-
490. No further details of this palace are known; Malalas says that none had previously
existed at Daphne, and that the emperors when they visited the suburb had had to
live in tents in the sacred grove. Stauffenberg believes that Malalas' reference to tents
shows that temporary accommodation of this kind was provided for the emperors only
when they visited Daphne at the time of the Olympic games. While emperors who
visited Daphne to witness the games probably did live in tents, there is no reason to
suppose that they did not visit Daphne on other occasions, for purposes of recreation,
and that on these occasions also they lived in tents. Förster ("Antiochia" 107) believed that he found the entrance to the shrine of Hecate.

[40] Eusebius Hist. eccl. 7.32.2-4, records only that Cyril succeeded Timaeus, and that
he was succeeded by Tyrannus. In the Chronicle of Jerome (p. 224 ed. Helm) Cyril's
accession is put in the fourth year of Probus, A.D. 279/80, and the accession of his
successor Tyrannus is placed in the eighteenth year of Diocletian, A.D. 303/4 (Jerome
Chron. p. 227 ed. Helm). See Harnack, Chronologie d. altchr. Lit. 1.216-218.

[41] See below, §6.   [42] Hist. eccl. 7.32.2-4.

same way it is possible that Dorotheus assisted Lucian in his school.[43] Finally Dorotheus' life took a remarkable turn. He attracted the attention of Diocletian, who often visited Antioch,[44] and the emperor liked the priest so well that as a sign of favor he placed him in charge of the dye-works at Tyre, which were state-controlled.[45]

Otherwise, we do not hear of the Christians at Antioch under Diocletian until the outbreak of the great persecution. Inaugurated on 23 February A.D. 303, this is commonly known as Diocletian's although it seems plain that it was instigated by Galerius.[46] The causes of the persecution are obscure—it would seem that Galerius was trying to increase his power—but one factor which played a part was the growing difficulty with Christians (especially among the officers) in the army, who refused to perform the sacrifices required of them for the sake of military discipline.[47]

[43] On Lucian's school and on the revision of the text of the Bible, see below, §6.

[44] See above, §1.

[45] Eusebius' account in *Hist. eccl.* 7.32.2-4 constitutes the earliest evidence that the dye industry at Tyre had been placed under the control of the government; see Eissfeldt, "Tyros," *RE* 7A (1948) 1902. At a later period Dorotheus of Antioch was confused with Dorotheus, bishop of Tyre, to produce a mythical bishop of Tyre, a learned author, who died in exile in Moesia Inferior in the reign of Julian the Apostate, aged 107. This story seems to appear first in Theophanes, a. 5816, p. 24.20-33 ed. De Boor. See J. Zeiller, *Les Origines chrétiennes dans les provinces danubiennes de l'Empire romain* (Paris 1918) 128, and (on the writings attributed to Dorotheus) Christ-Schmid-Stählin, *Gesch. d. gr. Lit.*[6] 2, pt. 2, 1350.

[46] On the persecution, see Baynes in *CAH* 12 (1939) 646-677; Grégoire, *Les persécutions* 65ff.; Ensslin in *RE* 7A (1948) 2484ff.; Kidd, *Hist. of the Church* 1.510ff.; Allard, *Persécution de Dioclétien*[2]; J. Zeiller in Fliche and Martin, *Hist. de l'église* 2.457ff. Allard, *Persécution de Dioclétien*[2] 1.173, writes that the edict was put into effect at Antioch by the closing of the churches on Passion Sunday, 16 April A.D. 303. For this he cites Theodoret, *Hist. eccl.* 5.38, but the chapter cited is concerned with other matters and I have been unable to find the passage Allard mentions.

[47] See H. Delehaye, "La persécution dans l'armée sous Dioclétien," *Acad. roy. de Belgique, Bulletins de la cl. des lettres et des sciences morales et politiques,* 1921, 150-166 (with bibliography, 150, n. 1, of earlier studies of the subject). The immediate occasion of the persecution was an episode that occurred at a public sacrifice attended by Diocletian and Galerius. Christians who were present crossed themselves to ward off demons, and the chief augur declared that the livers of the sacrificial animals yielded no omens because of the presence of profane persons. Diocletian was so angered that he ordered all personnel of the palace to perform sacrifices, and instructed military commanders to require sacrifices by the troops on pain of dismissal. Lactantius, who describes the episode (*De mort. pers.* 10; *Div. inst.* 4.27.4-5) says that it took place *in partibus Orientis.* Allard, *Persécution de Dioclétien*[2] 1.145, n. 1, takes *in partibus Orientis* to mean that the ceremony occurred at Antioch because (he writes) "chez les anciens, le diocèse d'Antioche était désigné spécialement par le mot *Oriens.*" Allard's interpretation is quite unwarranted, since the phrase *in partibus Orientis* was used in a very broad sense to distinguish the eastern division of the Empire from the west (*Occidens*). Allard's statement about the scene of the episode is repeated by Zeiller in Fliche-Martin, *Hist. de l'église* 2.462. It is curious to note that Lactantius gives the name of the chief augur as Tagis. This was the name of the legendary Etruscan in-

At Antioch, the bishop, Cyril, was arrested and condemned to the marble quarries in Pannonia, where he died three years later, in A.D. 306.[48] He was succeeded, as bishop, by Tyrannus; and if the *Chronicle* of Jerome is correct in stating that Tyrannus became bishop in A.D. 303/4, it would appear that Tyrannus was elected as soon as possible after the arrest and deportation of Cyril at the beginning of the persecution in A.D. 303.[49]

Another martyr of Antioch was a deacon named Romanus who about 17 November was condemned to be burned. Galerius was in the city at the time and he stopped the execution, but had the prisoner's tongue cut out instead. Contrary to expectation the man lived, but he was later executed in prison.[50]

There are also accounts of the martyrdom at Antioch at this period of Cyprian, Iustina, and Theoctistus or Theognitus.[51] Cyprian was a legendary wonder-worker whose career as it is described has affinities with the story of Faust.[52] The Empress Eudocia in the fifth century composed an epic poem on his martyrdom.[53]

In addition to martyrs who were executed at Antioch, the bodies of some who were martyred elsewhere were in time brought to Antioch and buried there. Such was St. Julian of Anazarbus, martyred in Cilicia under Diocletian, and buried at Antioch.[54]

---

ventor of haruspicy (S. Weinstock, "Tages," *RE* 4A [1932] 2009-2011); and unless we are to suppose that Diocletian's augur adopted the name as a kind of professional badge, Lactantius would seem to have been guilty of embroidering his account.

[48] Cyril's exile and death are described in the *Passiones* (under 8 Nov.) of the *Quattuor Coronati: Acta SS.*, Nov., tom. 3 (Brussels 1910) 769-770, 778, 781, 784, cf. 751 *b*, 759 *e*, 760 *a-b*; see Delehaye, *Passions des Martyrs* 328-344.

[49] Eusebius *Hist. eccl.* 7.32.4; Jerome *Chron.* p. 227 ed. Helm. Cf. Ensslin, "Tyrannos," no. 4, *RE* 7A (1948) 1847.

[50] Eusebius *De mart. Palest.* 2; Chrysostom, *In S. Roman. mart. PG* 50.605-618; see Delehaye, "St. Romain martyr d'Antioche," *Anal. Boll.* 50 (1932) 241-283; Kidd, *Hist. of the Church* 1.520; Baynes in *CAH* 12 (1939) 667. Ensslin, "Maximianus (Galerius)," *RE* 14 (1930) 2524, doubts that Galerius was present at Antioch, but does not elaborate on his reason for so thinking.

[51] H. Delehaye, "Cyprien d'Antioche et Cyprien de Carthage," *Anal. Boll.* 39 (1921) 314-332; *De sanctis Cypriano, Iustina et Theoctisto seu Theognito martyribus, Acta SS*, Sept., tom. VII, 195-262. The *passio* (cf. Delehaye, p. 319) mentions a *comes Orientis* at Antioch named Eutolmius, but this must be a later addition since the office of *comes Orientis* had not yet been instituted at this time. Fl. Eutolmius Tatianus was *comes Orientis* between A.D. 370 and 374 (Downey, *Comites Orientis* 12), which gives an indication of the date of the composition of the *passio* in the form in which it has reached us.

[52] T. Zahn, *Cyprian von Antiochien und die deutsche Faustsage* (Erlangen 1882); Delehaye, *Légendes hagiographiques*³ 59.

[53] A. Ludwich, *Eudociae Augustae Procli Lycii Claudiani carminum graecorum reliquiae* (Leipzig 1897) 16ff.

[54] See the *Laudatio* by Chrysostom, *PG* 50.665-676.

Soon after the persecution began, there occurred, at Seleucia Pieria and Antioch, a brief and abortive revolt of an army officer named Eugenius.[55] Such an episode at another time might have had little significance, but in the circumstances in which it occurred it had grave consequences for the people of Antioch and Seleucia.

Five hundred soldiers were employed in deepening the mouth of the harbor at Seleucia.[56] The men claimed that they were inadequately fed and that they had to spend their nights foraging for food. Their grievance seems to have driven them to mutiny, and one morning they proclaimed their commander, Eugenius, emperor—against his will, it was said. The band of revolutionaries set out for Antioch, plundering the farmhouses on the way and making themselves drunk on the wine that they found. At sunset they reached the city, which had no garrison, and attempted to seize the palace. The citizens collected what weapons they could find and attacked the troops; even women joined in the fight. The soldiers, who by this time must have been both tired and intoxicated, were routed by the civilians; some were slain, some fled, the rest were captured. The revolution ended in the early part of the night.

Instead of thanking the people of Antioch for putting down the revolt and saving the city, the imperial authorities inflicted severe punishment on both Seleucia Pieria and Antioch; prominent men in both cities were executed and their property confiscated. Some punishment might have been due for laxity in supplying provisions for the troops, but the executions and confiscations seem to have gone far beyond the penalties suitable for such a failure. The severity of the punishment can only mean that the imperial authorities believed (or feared) that the rebellion had been instigated by the Christians, and that strong measures were necessary to prevent the further spread of the movement. The recent difficulties with Christians in the army would naturally make the authorities suspect that any military disorder had a religious basis. Whether the Christians really had any

[55] The revolt is described by Libanius in three passages (*Or.* 11.158-162, *Or.* 19.45-46, and *Or.* 20.18-20). The episode is mentioned briefly by Eusebius (*Hist. eccl.* 8.6.8), who places it not long after the beginning of the persecution, which was officially launched on 23 February A.D. 303 (Ensslin in *RE* 7A [1948] 2484). The revolt is discussed by Sievers, *Leben des Libanius* 2-5, by Seeck, *Gesch. d. Untergangs* 1⁴, 17-18, with notes in *Anhang* 442, and by Allard, *Persécution de Dioclétien²* 1.225-227. Briefer allusions to it are made by Baynes in *CAH* 12 (1939) 666, by Zeiller in Fliche-Martin, *Hist. de l'église* 2.465, and by Kidd, *Hist. of the Church* 1.517.

[56] On the engineering operations which were undertaken at various times for the improvement of the harbor at Seleucia, see Honigmann, "Seleukeia" 1191-1192.

connection with the rising, and whether the question of rations was only a pretext, or an explanation invented later (possibly even an official explanation), we cannot now know;[57] but the episode shows the state of anxiety to which the government had been brought, and of course illustrates the danger to which a city such as Antioch, without a garrison or organized police force, was exposed.

5. FROM THE ABDICATION OF DIOCLETIAN TO THE DEFEAT OF LICINIUS, A.D. 305-324

In the period of almost twenty years between the abdication of Diocletian and the emergence of Constantine as sole ruler of the Roman Empire we have only occasional glimpses of the history of Antioch. Many of the major events in the history of the Empire at this time took place in the West, and the course of life at Antioch, aside from the scattered incidents that have been recorded, must largely be inferred from the developments elsewhere.

Diocletian's retirement placed Galerius, with Maximinus Daia as his caesar, in control of the East. Both Galerius and Maximinus determined to continue with all possible rigor the "Great Persecution" of the Christians which had been inaugurated in February A.D. 303. As one of the greatest cities in the East, which was in addition an old center of Christianity, Antioch witnessed its full share of martyrdoms. The city must often have been the imperial residence, and thus also the headquarters of the persecution.

Some Christians, it is said, were roasted over slow fires; others killed themselves before being taken.[58] In A.D. 306, Domnina, a wealthy lady,

---

[57] Eusebius *Hist. eccl.* 8.6.8, mentions that there was a similar outbreak at about the same time at Melitene, which apparently is not recorded elsewhere. This might have added to the nervousness of the authorities over the episode at Antioch. Eusebius would naturally be silent on the point if these risings were the work of Christians. Libanius' silence concerning any Christian share in the undertaking cannot be taken as proof that there was none. One of his accounts of the revolt occurs in his panegyric of Antioch (*Or.* 11), and here he gives only a few details, all designed to reflect credit on the brave citizens. The other two passages in which he mentions the matter are in orations (19 and 20) addressed to the Emperor Theodosius, in which it would hardly have been tactful for the pagan orator to remind the Christian emperor that the rising for which such severe punishment was inflicted had been organized by Christians. Of course the uprising may have been purely a military one, as Libanius implies it was; Seeck points out (*loc.cit.,* n. 51), that during Diocletian's reign there were six other usurpers in addition to Eugenius.

[58] Eusebius *Hist. eccl.* 8.12.2. Chrysostom also describes in general terms the sufferings of the martyrs, who were sometimes betrayed by members of their own families (*PG* 50. 634-635). The chronology of Eusebius' accounts of the martyrdoms at Antioch is confused and he gives no specific indication of the dates (see the commentary of

fled from Antioch with her daughters Bernice and Prosdoce, but their flight was betrayed by Domnina's husband, who was sent with a band of soldiers to capture them; and on the way back to Antioch the three ladies drowned themselves in a river.[59] The maiden Pelagia, surprised alone in her house by the soldiers sent to fetch her, killed herself by leaping from the roof.[60] Barlaam, who suffered his hand to be consumed by incense and burning coals rather than make the prescribed sacrifice to the emperor, may have been martyred at this time.[61] Other martyrs at Antioch at this period were Tyrannio, bishop of Tyre, and Zenobius, a priest of Sidon.[62]

At some time during the reign of Galerius, Malalas states, the celebrated Neoplatonist philosopher Iamblichus settled in Daphne and taught there until the end of his life (ca. A.D. 330).[63]

On 30 April A.D. 311,[64] Galerius, who had been stricken with an incurable disease and perhaps feared that this was a punishment from the Christian God, issued an edict in which freedom of worship was permitted to Christians, on certain conditions. Shortly after, he died at Serdica (5 May). Licinius, who was at Serdica at the time, was supposed to succeed to Galerius' position, but Maximinus determined to seize his powers for himself. He set out with his army from Syria (probably from Antioch) for Chalcedon, and established his authority

---

H. J. Lawlor and J. E. L. Oulton in their translation of Eusebius *Hist. eccl.* [London 1928] 2.268, note on the preface to Book 8).

[59] Chrysostom *Hom. de SS. Bernice et Prosdoce, PG* 50.629-640; Eusebius *Hist. eccl.* 8.12.3.

[60] Chrysostom *Hom. in S. mart. Pelagiam, PG* 50.579-584; cf. Eusebius *Hist. eccl.* 8.12.2, where her death seems to be mentioned though she is not named. This Pelagia is to be distinguished from a purported martyr of the same name, who was said to have been a penitent courtesan of Antioch. The courtesan Pelagia is not a historical figure, and the accounts of her are fictitious; see Delehaye, *Légendes hagiographiques*[3] 186-195, and A. Zimmermann, "Pelagia," *Lex. f. Theol. u. Kirche* 8.62-63.

[61] Such a martyrdom is said by Eusebius (*Hist. eccl.* 8.12.2) to have taken place at Antioch at this time, though he does not mention the martyr's name, and this date for Barlaam's martyrdom is accepted by Allard, *Persécution de Dioclétien*[2] 2.76, though others, in the absence of more specific evidence, leave the date uncertain; see R. Janin, "Barlaam," *Dict. d'hist. et de géogr. eccl.* 6.812-813. On the accounts of St. Barlaam (which include a homily of Chrysostom, *PG* 50.675-682) see H. Delehaye, "S. Barlaam, martyr à Antioche," *Anal. Boll.* 22 (1903) 129-145.

[62] Eusebius *Hist. eccl.* 8.13.3-4. On the accounts of these martyrdoms see J. Moreau, "Observations sur l'*Hypomnestikon biblion Ioseppou*," *Byzantion* 25-27 (1955-57, published in one vol.) 274.

[63] Malalas 312.11-12. This evidence seems to have escaped the scholars who have written on the life of Iamblichus; cf. e.g. G. Mau in Mau and Kroll, "Iamblichos," no. 3, *RE* 9 (1916) 645-646, and E. Zeller, *Die Philosophie der Griechen*, pt. 3, sec. 2[4] (Leipzig 1923) 736, n. 3. As Stauffenberg points out (*Malalas* 407), there is no reason to doubt Malalas' statement, which must come from a local Antiochene source.

[64] Lactantius *De mortibus persecutorum* 35.1.

over Asia Minor.[65] Maximinus then effected an agreement by which Licinius was to control the European territory that had been under Galerius, while Maximinus was to rule the East as senior Augustus. Thereupon Maximinus returned to Nicomedia,[66] and soon began to issue a series of orders that imposed restrictions upon the Christians. He arranged propaganda that sought to invalidate the Christian teaching, and set up in each city a pagan priesthood organized like the Christian hierarchy.[67] At the same time, he encouraged in every way the revival of the pagan cults and of the cult of the emperor.[68] At some time in the course of this activity he came to Antioch, probably in the late winter or early spring of A.D. 312.[69]

One of the emperor's principal assistants there was Theotecnus, the official auditor (*curator*, λογιστής) of the city of Antioch.[70] This man, a renegade from Christianity to Neoplatonism, was zealous against the Christians, and he no doubt used to the full the great influence that he would have possessed as manager of the property and revenue of the city; Eusebius indeed suggests that he was the orginator of the principal devices employed against the Christians by Maximinus. One of Theotecnus' stratagems was the organization of an embassy to the emperor from the people of Antioch, petitioning that the Christians be banished from the city and its territory; and this device was adopted elsewhere.[71] After hunting down individual Christians in Antioch, Theotecnus erected a statue of Zeus Philios equipped for the delivery

---

[65] Lactantius (*De mort. pers.* 36.1) writes only that Maximinus set out *ab Oriente*, but it seems reasonable to conclude that he was at Antioch when he started; see the note in the edition of Eusebius *Hist. eccl.* by Lawlor and Oulton (cited above, n. 58) 2.287.

[66] Eusebius *Hist. eccl.* 9.9a.4.

[67] Lactantius *De mort. pers.* 36.4; Eusebius *Hist. eccl.* 8.14.9, 9.4.2ff. Cf. Kidd, *Hist. of the Church* 1.526.

[68] For reflections of this in the coins issued at Antioch in this period, see J. Maurice, *Numismatique constantinienne*[3] (Paris 1912) 143ff.

[69] His presence in Antioch is indicated in Eusebius *Hist. eccl.* 9.3 (see further below). On the chronology of this period, see the note by Lawlor and Oulton in their translation of Eusebius *Hist. eccl.* (cited above, n. 58) 2.287-288. Allard, *Persécution de Dioclétien*[2] 2.171, supposes that Maximinus made a general tour of his territory at this time. This is possible, if not indeed likely, but there seems to be no specific evidence for it.

[70] Eusebius *Hist. eccl.* 9.2ff.; Theophanes a. 5794, p. 9.29ff. ed. De Boor; *Passio S. Theodoti* 4, in Ruinart, *Acta martyrum selecta*[2] (Amsterdam 1713) 338; *Acta Sanctorum Maii* tom. 4 (1866) 150 (18 May). Cf. Ensslin, "Theoteknos" no. 1, *RE* 5A (1934) 2253; Allard, *Persécution de Dioclétien*[2] 2.171-173, 181-183; Kidd, *Hist. of the Church* 1.521; A. Bigelmair, "Tekusa," *Lex. f. Theol. u. Kirche* 9.1032. On the office of *curator*, see Jones, *Greek City* 136-138, 242.

[71] Lawlor and Oulton in their edition of Eusebius *Hist. eccl.* 2.288, believe that this petition was presented in April of A.D. 313, some time after Maximinus' arrival in Antioch; see A. J. Lawlor, *Eusebiana* (Oxford 1912) 216ff.

of oracles, which took the form of statements that the Christians were the enemies of the god and must be driven away from Antioch. These oracles, produced in the presence of Maximinus, flattered and pleased him, and furthered the persecution when the officials of other cities, seeing the emperor's satisfaction, hastened to follow Theotecnus' lead. Maximinus was so pleased by Theotecnus' activities that he promoted him to a governorship.[72] Later, however, when Licinius came into power in the East, Theotecnus was executed as a charlatan, along with his collaborators.[73]

One of the celebrated martyrs of this period was the priest Lucian of Antioch (or "of Samosata"), founder of the exegetical school of Antioch (described below), who was executed at Nicomedia on 7 January A.D. 312.[74]

Maximinus' position was altered as a result of Constantine's victory over Maxentius at the Milvian Bridge, outside Rome, on 27 October A.D. 312. Constantine now became senior Augustus, by decree of the Senate, and Maximinus was degraded from this position, which he had held since the death of Galerius. Constantine ordered Maximinus to cease the persecution of the Christians, and Maximinus was constrained to obey.[75] In the following winter the provinces of the Orient were harassed by a plague and a famine,[76] which added to the troubles of Maximinus. After the defeat of Maxentius, Constantine and Licinius had come to an agreement that seemed to threaten the position of Maximinus; and when Constantine was called to the Rhine by a rebellion of the Franks, Maximinus seized the opportunity to strike at Licinius. In the depth of the winter he started out from Syria, probably from Antioch, with a force of 70,000 men, and by forced marches invaded Europe.[77] Licinius moved to meet him. His force was smaller, but in the ensuing battle Maximinus, whose troops must have been exhausted by their march, was defeated. Maximinus retreated into Asia Minor, and Licinius followed him. During his pursuit of Maximinus,

---

[72] Eusebius *Hist. eccl.* 9.11.5. What the governorship was, is not stated; Lawlor and Oulton in their edition of Eusebius, *Hist. eccl.* 2.304, suggest with some plausibility that, having been *curator* of Antioch, Theotecnus was made *praeses* of Syria Coele.

[73] Eusebius *Hist. eccl.* 9.11.6; Theophanes a. 5810, p. 16.27ff. ed. De Boor.

[74] Eusebius *Hist. eccl.* 8.13.2, 9.6.3; Kidd, *Hist. of the Church* 1.527-528. Cf. Allard, *Persécution de Dioclétien*[2] 2.197-199; Altaner, *Patrologie*[2] 159, 178-179.

[75] Cf. Parker, *Hist. of the Roman World A.D. 138-337* 253ff.; Baynes in *CAH* 12.688; J.-R. Palanque in Fliche-Martin, *Hist. de l'église* 3.20ff.

[76] Lactantius *De mort. pers.* 37.4; Eusebius *Hist. eccl.* 9.8.

[77] Lactantius *De mort. pers.* 45. Lactantius writes that Maximinus set out *e Syria*, but it seems reasonable to conclude that he started from Antioch; see Lawlor and Oulton in their edition of Eusebius, *Hist. eccl.* 2.289.

Licinius in June A.D. 313 published a letter at Nicomedia in which freedom of belief was permitted;[78] and confiscated churches were restored to the Christians. Maximinus withdrew to the Taurus mountains and there, hemmed in by the forces of Licinius, he died, at Tarsus, in the autumn of A.D. 313. Licinius captured Maximinus' wife Valeria and his son and daughter; and proceeding to Antioch, he executed them there, Valeria being drowned in the Orontes.[79] Licinius likewise executed Theotecnus, as one of the chief agents of Maximinus in the persecution of the Christians. While he was at Antioch (according to a somewhat distorted entry in the chronicle of Malalas) Licinius incurred the displeasure of the people of the city by failing to distribute the largesse that they expected from a new ruler. Accordingly the populace made uncomplimentary remarks about Licinius on an occasion when he was watching the races in the hippodrome. This so angered the emperor that he ordered his archers to open fire on the people in the hippodrome, and (Malalas says) two thousand of them were killed.[80]

Licinius and Constantine were now the sole rulers of the empire, with Licinius in control of the East. Their joint rule almost at once (A.D. 314) produced a short civil war between them, when Constantine discovered that Licinius planned an attack on his colleague. Constantine's victory in this struggle brought about a new partition of the Empire, by which Licinius was forced to give up all territory in Europe except Thrace. Outward harmony was restored, but there was no real concord between the emperors. At the end of six years, Licinius thought it necessary to alter the official policy of toleration and encouragement of the Christians, who would, for one thing, seem to him to be partisans of Constantine. Christians were dismissed from the court and the civil service.[81] From A.D. 320 it seemed plain that a rupture between Licinius and Constantine must take place. A pretext was offered when Constantine entered the territory of Licinius during an operation against the Goths in A.D. 323, and war between the emperors broke out in the following year. The forces of Licinius were defeated in a series

[78] Baynes in *CAH* 12.689-690.

[79] Lactantius *De mort. pers.* 49-50; Eusebius *Hist. eccl.* 9.11.7; cf. Allard, *Persécution de Dioclétien*² 2.268.

[80] Malalas 314.3-8. The chronicler gives the ruler's name as "Maximus Licinianus" and states that he was the successor of Constantius I (the father of Constantine the Great). There is obviously a confusion here with Maximinus. However, as Stauffenberg points out (*Malalas* 410-411), the episode, with its cruelty, is more consonant with what we know of Licinius' character and conduct than with what is known of Maximinus.

[81] Cf. Baynes in *CAH* 12.694-695.

of engagements that ended with the battle of Chrysopolis (18 September A.D. 324). Licinius was placed in forced retirement, then executed, and Constantine became sole Augustus.

During the early part of Licinius' rule in the East the Christian communities had an opportunity to recuperate, and in Antioch the opportunity was taken to rebuild the "Old Church," which had been destroyed during the earlier persecution. This church, which was also called the "Apostolic Church" because it was supposed to have stood in the old part of the city on the site of a more ancient building that was reputed to date from the time of the apostles, was begun by Vitalis, who became bishop probably in 314, and completed by his successor Philogonius, who was in office from 319 to 20 December A.D. 324.[82]

Our evidence for the economic life of Antioch at this period is very meager, but it does include some documents of unusual interest. There are the papyrus records of Theophanus, an advocate and legal adviser of some high official in Egypt, probably the *augustalis*. Some time between A.D. 317 and 323 Theophanus made an official journey from Egypt during which he visited a number of places in Palestine and Syria, and stayed for two months in Antioch. The preserved documents contain his itinerary, expense accounts, and details of maintenance, including itemized lists, with prices, of the food purchased for himself and his servants while they were in Antioch.[83] As we should expect, these lists show that fruit played an important part in the diet at Antioch. The nature of Theophanus' business in the city is not indicated in the papers that have come down to us.

From the same period there is preserved a brief account of a severe famine that occurred "in the East" in A.D. 324, during which the people in various places, including Antioch and the villages near it, set out

---

[82] Eusebius *Hist. eccl.* 7.32.4; Theodoret *Hist. eccl.* 1.3.1-2, 2.31.11; Chrysostom *In princip. Act.*, hom. 2, title and §1 = *PG* 51.77. On the death of Philogonius, see E. Schwartz, *Nachr. Götting. Gesellsch.* 1905, 268. Eltester's suggestion "Kirchen Antiochias" 272-273, 275, n. 87, that the church was called "old" not because of its age but because it was in the old part of the city is unconvincing, as is his supposition that Constantine's octagonal church, built between A.D. 327 and 341 (see below) was called the "new" church not because of its chronological position but because it was on the island, the "new" part of the city. The "apostolic" church would naturally be called old both because it was, by tradition, on the site of the oldest church in the city, and because it preceded Constantine's in date. Eltester's argument seems invalidated also by the fact that Theodoret (*Hist. eccl.* 4.24.4) calls Constantine's church ἡ νεόδμητος ἐκκλησία, showing clearly that the octagonal Great Church was thought of as newer, in age, than the (old) "apostolic" structure.

[83] *Catalogue of the Greek and Latin Papyri in the John Rylands Library*, vol. 4, ed. by C. H. Roberts and E. G. Turner (Manchester 1952), especially nos. 629-630. See the review by N. Lewis, *CP* 49 (1954) 267-269.

to find grain in other places, and met with resistance when the inhabitants tried to prevent the seizure of their own supplies. There was fighting, and grain depots and warehouses—including presumably stocks of grain stored for the use of the government—were broken into and pillaged. The price of grain rose, and the Emperor Constantine distributed supplies of grain to the churches in the cities and towns affected by the famine for the relief of widows, the poor, persons living in hostels, and the clergy. It is recorded that on this occasion the church at Antioch received 36,000 *modii* of grain.[84]

6. Lucian and the School of Antioch

One of the most significant figures in the history of the church at Antioch during the reign of Diocletian and in the following years was Lucian of Antioch (sometimes called Lucian of Samosata), whose career came to a close with his martyrdom at Nicomedia in A.D. 312. Lucian's work was so important that it must be described here separately from the general account of the period in which he lived.

As a priest famous for the sanctity of his life, a revered martyr, and a celebrated scholar who edited the text of the Bible, Lucian played a prominent role in the history of Christianity. Yet the trustworthy and indisputable evidence concerning his life is scanty, and modern scholars have come to very different conclusions with regard to certain aspects of his activities.[85]

Lucian was born of Christian parents, probably at Antioch, rather than at Samosata, as some sources claim; and it was at Antioch, presumably, that he entered upon the priesthood. The year of his birth is nowhere indicated, and there is no reference to his age at the time of his martyrdom in A.D. 312. Since, at that period, men were usually not ordained until they were of mature years, it seems reasonable to conclude that Lucian did not become a priest before about A.D. 270, and that he was probably ordained at some time after that date.[86]

---

[84] Theophanes *Chron.* a. 5824, p. 29.13-23 ed. De Boor. See Chapot, *Frontière de l'Euphrate* 213.

[85] Lucian's career has attracted wide attention in recent years. The modern studies that should be mentioned (which review the older scholarship and cite specialized investigations) are: Loofs, *Paulus von Samosata*; Bardy, *Lucien d'Antioche*; d'Alès, "Autour de Lucien d'Antioche"; H. Dörrie, "Zur Geschichte der Septuaginta im Jahrhundert Konstantins," *ZNTW* 39 (1940) 57-110; G. Mercati, "Alcuni appunti ad un saggio novissimo di critica testuale dei LXX," in "Nuove note di letteratura biblica e cristiana antica," *Studi e testi* 95 (1941) 135-157.

[86] The *Synaxarium* of Constantinople (ed. Delehaye; *Propylaeum ad Acta SS Novembris*, Brussels 1902) 137.30-141.10 and the *Menologium of Basil*, PG 117.109, both place Lucian's birth and formative years at Antioch, while the anonymous *Vita Con-*

In later times Lucian was looked upon as a glorious martyr and his memory was officially honored by the church. Eusebius spoke of him with praise for his private life and for his learning and St. John Chrysostom delivered an eloquent homily in Antioch on Lucian's festival, 7 January A.D. 387.[87] His recension of the Bible came into general use in the patriarchates of Antioch and Constantinople and is the ancestor of the early modern printed versions.[88] He was one of the earliest of the teachers whose work led to the development of the important and characteristic theological school of Antioch, with its careful training and meticulous Biblical scholarship; in fact the school that he organized may be said to be the beginning of the theological school of Antioch, which rivaled that of Alexandria.[89] At the same time, Lucian of Antioch has been held to be ultimately responsible for the Arian heresy, since he was the teacher of most of the prominent Arians and semi-Arians of the early fourth century, including Arius himself;[90] and he is supposed to have remained out of communion with three bishops of Antioch because of his beliefs.[91] The reconciliation of

---

stantini of the Codex Angelicus (in Philostorgius, ed. Bidez, p. 184.3), Suidas, *s.v.* Λουκιανός, and Symeon Metaphrastes, *Vita Luciani* 1, in Philostorgius, ed. Bidez, p. 184.17-18, cf. *PG* 114.397 D, place his birth at Samosata. As Bardy points out (*Lucien d'Antioche* 33-34, 37-38) the circumstances of his career make it more natural to suppose that he was born and educated at Antioch. This of course renders impossible the hypothesis sometimes put forward (cf. Bardy, *loc.cit.*) that Lucian was an early follower of Paul of Samosata and was taken to Antioch by Paul. On the career of Paul of Samosata, see Ch. 10, §10; Ch. 11, §6. It is possible, as scholars have pointed out, that Lucian the theologian was sometimes called "of Samosata" because of the similarity of his name to that of Lucian the satirist, who was properly called "of Samosata."

[87] Cf. the *Life* of Lucian by Symeon Metaphrastes and the passages in the *Synaxarium* of Constantinople and the *Menologium of Basil*, cited above, n. 86; Eusebius *Hist. eccl.* 8.13.2; Chrysostom *In S. Lucianum martyrem, PG* 50.519-526.

[88] See the studies of Dörrie and Mercati cited above, n. 85; also Streeter, *Four Gospels* 39ff., 112-121; Bardy, *Lucien d'Antioche* 164-182. It has been suggested that Dorotheus, a priest of Antioch noted for his Hebrew learning, who flourished under Bishop Cyril, i.e. A.D. 279/80-303 (Eusebius *Hist. eccl.* 7.32.2-4), assisted Lucian in his school and in his revision of the Septuagint, but there is no specific evidence to this effect; cf. Harnack, *Chronologie d. altchr. Lit.* 2.138, n. 3.

[89] For an excellent account of the origin and development of the exegetical school of Antioch, see Pirot, *Théodore de Mopsueste* 14ff. On the differing christologies of Antioch and Alexandria, which gave the respective schools their characteristic reputations, see Sellers, *Two Ancient Christologies*. As E. R. Hardy has pointed out (*Christian Egypt* [New York 1952] 18), both schools ultimately go back to the approach developed by Origen.

[90] Lucien's pupils are listed by Philostorgius; see further below.

[91] This information appears in a letter of Alexander, bishop of Alexandria, to his colleague Alexander, bishop of Constantinople, which is quoted by Theodoret. In this text, which raises the most difficult of the problems concerning Lucian's career, there is a reference (Theodoret *Hist. eccl.* 1.4.35, pp. 17-18 ed. Parmentier) to a Lucian which appears to connect, or to compare, his teaching with that of Paul of Samosata and with

these disreputable aspects of his career with the esteem in which he was later held by the church presents problems that have vexed scholars since the seventeenth century and have never been solved to general satisfaction. Some students have attempted to clear up the difficulty by supposing that the Lucian who remained out of communion with the church at Antioch for many years was another Lucian than the martyr; the name, indeed, was a not uncommon one. It has been suggested that this Lucian was a follower of Paul of Samosata who was excommunicated along with Paul; and in this same direction another suggestion is that this Lucian was elected by Paul's followers to be their schismatic bishop. Another solution offered, which on the whole has seemed to most scholars the most judicious, is that the Lucian who long remained out of communion at Antioch because of his beliefs is indeed the learned teacher and martyr, and that at some time he was reconciled and restored to communion with his fellow-Christians at Antioch. This explanation makes it possible to suppose that after his reconciliation there was enough time for him to develop his school and to produce the pupils who were later bishops.[92]

Certainly there are confusions and obscurities in the evidence; the sources seem too scanty and difficult to allow an interpretation that will meet with general acceptance, and it may well be that the difficulties will never be completely solved. It is significant, for example, that Eusebius when he writes of Lucian in his *Ecclesiastical History* speaks

---

Arianism; and it is said that Lucian was Paul's "successor" and that he remained "excluded from the church for many years under three bishops." This text has given rise to a number of quite different interpretations, some of which will be mentioned in the following note.

[92] A comparison of the translations given by various scholars of the passage in Alexander's letter is significant in showing how different some of the possible interpretations of it are. The summary given above represents only the main results of the explanations that have been offered; there are actually more hypotheses embodying variations on these explanations, but a complete review of these would fall beyond the scope of the present work. Summaries of these views may be found conveniently in Bardy, *Lucien d'Antioche* 49-56; cf. also Sellers, *Eustathius of Antioch* 9-12. Bardy himself (*Lucien d'Antioche* 58) thinks that Alexander's letter (see above, n. 91) refers to a second Lucian, a real follower of Paul, who is otherwise unknown, and that Lucian the teacher and martyr was never excommunicate. This view is not accepted by d'Alès, "Autour de Lucien d'Antioche," and in fact the various efforts to resolve the difficulties by supposing that there were two Lucians have not as yet gained general acceptance. At present it seems best to adopt the position taken by J. Lebreton (in Fliche-Martin, *Hist. de l'église* 2.350-352), by d'Alès, "Autour de Lucien d'Antioche," and by A. Anwander, "Lucian," *Lex. f. Theol. u. Kirche* 6 (1934) 676-677, who, though they recognize that the difficulties in this view are great, consider that Alexander's letter must refer to Lucian the teacher and martyr. See also Riedmatten, *Procès de Paul de Samosate* 110-111. Lucian's theology, as has often been pointed out, had nothing to do with that of Paul of Samosata.

of him with the greatest reserve, and says nothing about his school or his doctrine. On the whole, however, there is no question as to the importance of the career of Lucian (or of the two Lucians), which betokens the founding of the theological school of Antioch, with its meticulous and literal tradition of exegesis, which was to be a rival of the theological school of Alexandria (where a mystical point of view prevailed) and was to influence the whole development of Christianity in the fourth century; and the Lucianic recension of the Bible had great influence. It is not clear how far Lucian ought to be made responsible for the Arian doctrine of his pupils—we do not really know what he taught—but it does seem plain that Arianism, as exemplified in Lucian's disciples, was of Antiochene origin.[93] Arius himself, as has been noted, was a disciple of Lucian; and while it was from Alexandria that Arius launched his attack, it was at Antioch that he had been a student with those other companions, later united by the strong bond of the memory of their teacher, who when the controversy broke out became Arius' leading protagonists. Eusebius of Nicomedia, Maris of Chalcedon, Theognis of Nicaea, Asterius the Sophist, Athanasius of Anazarbus, and Leontius and Eudoxius of Antioch, all prominent in the struggle, were Lucian's pupils, and there were doubtless less well-known figures whose names have not been preserved.[94]

When these men studied at Antioch, we do not know; the answer would depend somewhat on the questions pointed out above concerning Lucian's career. If he was out of communion with the church at Antioch under three bishops, that would mean that he lived apart under Domnus, Timaeus, and Cyril. This would indicate that he was excommunicate from A.D. 268 to 303 if he remained apart during the whole of Cyril's bishopric; but it has been suggested that he became reconciled soon after Cyril's accession in A.D. 279/80.[95] There is of course the question whether he could have organized a school while he was outside the church of Antioch, or whether he could have begun to

[93] Jerome *De vir. ill.* 77 mentions *"de fide" libelli et breves ad nonnullos epistulae* by Lucian, but these are lost. See further Bardy, *Lucien d'Antioche* 81ff. Lucian is thought to have been the author of one of the creeds that were debated at the synod of Antioch of A.D. 341.

[94] A list of Lucian's pupils was given by Philostorgius *Hist. eccl.* 2.14-15, p. 25 ed. Bidez (preserved in a quotation by Photius), with an additional name (that of Athanasius of Anazarbus) in another passage, 3.15, p. 46.1. Philostorgius does not mention Arius as a pupil of Lucian, but Arius himself makes this claim in a letter to Eusebius which is quoted by Theodoret *Hist. eccl.* 1.5.4, p. 27.7 ed. Parmentier. On Lucian's pupils, see in detail the second part of Bardy's study (*Lucien d'Antioche* 185ff.), which is devoted to this subject.

[95] On the chronology of these bishops, see Ch. 11, §7.

teach only after his reconciliation; if his pupils were bishops in the 320's, his school must have been in operation before about A.D. 300.

The earliest reliable date preserved in connection with Lucian's career is that of the great persecution that broke out in A.D. 303; Lucian was in Nicomedia at the time and while he was there he wrote a letter to the community at Antioch, describing the glorious martyrdom of Anthimus.[96] Lucian may have returned to Antioch after the cessation of the persecution and may have taught at that time. He next appears in the persecution of Maximinus, when he was arrested and conveyed to Nicomedia. There, after making a defense of his faith, he died, on 7 January A.D. 312, after suffering many torments.[97] Lucian is said to have been accompanied to Nicomedia by various companions and pupils, notably his favorite student Antonius, who served as his secretary during his imprisonment.[98] A disciple named Glycerius is recorded as having suffered martyrdom at Antioch at the same time (one account, which is evidently wrong, puts his death at Nicomedia).[99] There were said to have been other companions at Nicomedia, whose names were not recorded; and then the hagiographer names three lady disciples who followed the master to Nicomedia, Eustolion, Dorothea, and Severa. A fourth, Pelagia, remained at home and killed herself by leaping from the roof of her house when soldiers came to arrest her. This part of the account of Lucian's last days is to be treated with great caution. The way in which Glycerius appears in the account of the martyrdom suggests that the story of his having suffered at Nicomedia, at the same time, is merely an ornamental detail later added to the account, and we have no other reason to believe that Glycerius was actually a pupil of Lucian.[100] In the same way it appears that the names of the lady followers had been added (in some cases possibly even invented) in order

[96] The beginning of the letter is quoted in the *Chronicon Paschale*, p. 516.2-5 Bonn ed. = p. 203 in Bidez' edition of Philostorgius. On the effects of this persecution at Antioch, see above, §4.

[97] On the accounts of Lucian's martyrdom, see Delehaye, *Légendes hagiographiques*[3] 182-186, and Bardy, *Lucien d'Antioche* 61-81. On the persecution in Antioch at this time, see above, §4.

[98] Cf. the *Vita* by Symeon Metaphrastes in Philostorgius, pp. 192.16, 196.16, ed. Bidez.

[99] In the *Syriac Martyrology* (ed. F. Nau, *PO*, vol. 10, pt. 1, p. 12, line 3 of translation) it is said that Glycerius was martyred at Nicomedia on 14 January. In the so-called *Martyrologium Hieronymianum* it is recorded under 7, 14, and 15 January that he suffered at Antioch: *Acta SS Novembris*, vol. 2, pt. 2 (Brussels 1931), pp. 29-30, 40, 41. Glycerius is also mentioned in the *Vita* of Lucian by Symeon Metaphrastes, in Philostorgius, p. 198.4 ed. Bidez.

[100] The lady pupils are mentioned in the *Vita* of Lucian, p. 192.19-26 in Philostorgius, ed. Bidez. See Bardy, *Lucien d'Antioche* 72-73, 200, and Delehaye, *Origines du culte*[2] 204.

to make the account more edifying.[101] Pelagia's martyrdom which has already been mentioned is well known from other sources that do not connect her with Lucian.[102]

Lucian's influence will appear again in the period of the beginning of the Arian controversy at Antioch (described below).

7. Constantine as Sole Emperor, a.d. 324-337; The Octagonal Church and Other Buildings at Antioch

The thirteen years during which Constantine was sole ruler marked a turning point in the history of the Roman Empire and indeed in the history of Europe. The triumph of the Christian Church, and the foundation of the new capital of the empire at Constantinople (begun in A.D. 324, dedicated A.D. 330), both inaugurated a new era, and the completion of the military and administrative reforms begun by Diocletian placed the government of the empire on a new basis.

During these years the history of Antioch, as we know it, reflects the larger events in the Empire; and there begins here, as well, a period during which the history of the city is somewhat better known, thanks to an increase in the amount and the variety of the sources that have been preserved.

The principal monument of Constantine at Antioch was the octagonal Great Church, the *Domus Aurea*, which was begun by Constantine and completed by his son Constantius.[103] This is described as having been of unusual size and beauty, as befitted the principal city of the eastern provinces, which was, in addition, an ancient center of Christianity.[104] The work was begun in A.D. 327,[105] and the building was

---

[101] See Bardy, *Lucien d'Antioche* 200-201. The name of Eustolion recalls the young woman with whom Leontius, the bishop of Antioch, was accused of living; see Athanasius *Apol. de fuga sua* 26 = *PG* 25.677 B, and *Hist. arianor. ad monachos* 28 = *PG* 25.725 A.

[102] On Pelagia, see above, n. 60.

[103] Malalas errs in stating that Constantine inaugurated his building activities at Antioch when he visited the city on his return from a victorious campaign against the Persians. On the sources and the significance of these errors, see below, Excursus 15.

[104] See the description of Eusebius, cited below, nn. 107-108.

[105] The beginning of the work is placed in A.D. 327 by Jerome *Chronicle*, Olymp. 276, 3, p. 231-232 ed. Helm, and in the year A.D. 326/7 by Theophanes a. 5819, p. 28.16-17 ed. De Boor. The year A.D. 326/7 is also indicated by a lost Arian church history which states that the church was completed in A.D. 341 fifteen years after it had been begun; see Philostorgius *Hist. eccl.* ed. Bidez (Leipzig 1913) p. 212. This account is followed by the Syriac *Chronicon miscellaneum ad A.D. 724 pertinens*, ed. and transl. by E. W. Brooks and J.-B. Chabot, *CSCO, Scriptores Syri* (*versio*) ser. 3, vol. 4, p. 102. The construction of the church is also mentioned briefly in the anonymous *Life of Constantine* ed. by M. Guidi, *Rendiconti della R. Accad. dei Lincei, cl. di scienze morali, storiche e filologiche*, ser. 5, vol. 16 (1907) 338.9-11; see also the *Vita Pauli* arch. C/pl. in PG 116.886 A.

dedicated in A.D. 341, on the occasion of the meeting of a church council which, from the event, took the name of the Council of the Dedication.[106] In plan, the church was an octagon surrounded with "chambers and exedras (*oikoi, exedrai*)"; the whole was enclosed within walls (*periboloi*).[107] The *oikoi* and *exedrai*, which are said in one description to have been two-storied,[108] appear to have been either recesses (possibly

[106] Jerome *Chronicle*, Olymp. 280, 2, p. 235 ed. Helm, puts the dedication in A.D. 342, but the date of the Council of the Dedication in A.D. 341 is certain; see Kidd, *Hist. of the Church* 2.75ff., and Eltester, "Kirchen Antiochias" 254-255. Malalas (325.4ff.) and Socrates (*Hist. eccl.* 3.5 = PG 67.1042) place the dedication at the time of the Council, and the lost Arian church history also indicates A.D. 341 (see preceding note). Theophanes puts the dedication in A.D. 341 (a. 5833, p. 36.29-31 ed. De Boor). He says in this passage that the building of the church had taken six years, but this disagrees both with his own earlier statement concerning the beginning of the work in A.D. 326/7 (see preceding note) and with the other evidence for the dedication. Either "six" is a mistake for "sixteen" here, or the work, begun in A.D. 326/7, quickly lapsed, and was not effectively resumed until six years before A.D. 341. Socrates, *Hist. eccl.* 2.8 = PG 67.196 A, states that the church was dedicated at the synod of A.D. 341, "in the tenth year after the foundations were laid." This again might be taken to suggest that although the construction was officially inaugurated in A.D. 327, the actual work of building was not begun until later. The differing dates given for the inauguration of the work on the church, and the length of time that seems to have been required to build it, may reflect the practical difficulties that seem to have been caused by Constantine's ambitious building program. There seem to have been delays connected with the construction of the new capital at Constantinople (see Th. Preger, "Das Gründungsdatum von Konstantinopel," *Hermes* 36 [1901] 336ff.), and some of the work there was done hastily, so that some of Constantine's buildings, not being well constructed, had to be rebuilt or strengthened under Constantius (Julian *Or.* 1.41 A; Zosimus 2.32). Much of this condition may be traced to a shortage of trained personnel. A decree of A.D. 334 mentions a serious shortage of *architecti* (*CTh* 13.4.1), and the same condition existed in A.D. 337 (*ibid.* 13.4.2) and 334 (*ibid.* 13.4.3). See C. Barbagallo, *Lo stato e l'istruzione pubblica nell'Impero romano* (Catania 1911) 220ff. O. Seeck mistakenly dates the dedication of the church in A.D. 338; see below, n. 174.

[107] Theophanes calls the church an octagon (a. 5819, p. 28.16 ed. De Boor). The building is described (Ch. 9, p. 221.8-14 ed. Heikel) in the panegyric (*Triakontaeterikos*) which Eusebius composed for Constantine's thirtieth anniversary as emperor (A.D. 335); on this oration, which was delivered in Constantinople, see Christ-Schmid-Stählin, *Gesch. d. griech. Lit.*[6] 2, pt. 2, 1369-1370. Since the work of building the church was (according to Theophanes) begun in the same year, the description must represent the church as it was planned. The church is also described in the *Vita Constantini* (3.50, p. 98.29ff. ed. Heikel) which is attributed to Eusebius (see the following note). On the meaning of *peribolos*, see A. Heisenberg, *Grabeskirche u. Apostelkirche* (Leipzig 1908) 1.215, n. 3. The word does not necessarily imply that the walls were colonnaded, though they may well have been.

[108] The description in the *Vita Constantini* (cited in the preceding note) is for the most part the same as that in the *Triakontaeterikos* (also cited above). However, the *Vita* contains details that do not appear in the other description. In the anniversary oration, it is said that the building was "surrounded by many *oikoi* and *exedrai*," while in the *Vita*, instead of these words, it is stated that the building was "surrounded round about with upper and ground level spaces (χωρήματα) on all sides." χωρήματα is a vague and general term, quite unlike *oikoi* and *exedrai*, which have specific architectural significance (see the following note). The substitution of the different phrase in the *Vita* might be taken to mean that Eusebius, having to describe the church twice,

including chapels) opening out of the central octagon,[109] or two-storied side aisles, in which the upper level would have been used as *catechumena*, for the accommodation of the women in the congregation.[110] Particularly impressive was the hemispherical dome,[111] which was raised to a great height,[112] and appears to have been made of wood.[113] The outer covering of the roof was gilded,[114] so that the church was sometimes called the *Dominicum Aureum*.[115] The floor of the church

---

sought to vary his accounts of it; or the statement that the *oikoi* and *exedrai* were two-storied may represent information on the plans for the building available when Eusebius wrote the passage in the *Vita* but was not yet available when he wrote the *Triakontaeterikos*. It must also be noted, however, that there is good evidence that certain parts of the *Vita Constantini* were edited and altered after Eusebius' death, or that Eusebius left the work unfinished and that it was completed by an editor; see Downey, "Original Church of the Apostles," with additional material cited by F. Halkin, *Anal. Boll.* 70 (1952) 349-350. In this case the passage about the "upper and ground level χωρήματα" might be by another hand than Eusebius'; this would be suggested, of course, by the substitution of the colorless term χωρήματα for the more precise *oikoi* and *exedrai*. Also the uncertainty as to the source of the statement that the χωρήματα were two-storied may cast some doubt on the authenticity of this detail (though of course an editor of Eusebius' work might well have written on the basis of accurate knowledge of the building). It is characteristic that both the *Vita* and the *Triakontaeterikos* give the distinct impression that the church was wholly the work of Constantine, whereas Malalas and Theophanes, who had no panegyrical purpose, record that it was completed by Constantius.

[109] Compare the description of the church at Tyre by Eusebius, *Hist. eccl.* 10.4.45. On the meaning of *exedra*, see D. Mallardo, "L'exedra nella basilica cristiana," *RAC* 22 (1946) 207-211; Eltester, "Kirchen Antiochias" 257; also an inscription of Sardis, *Sardis* 7, 1, no. 12. *Oikos* is used of the side-aisles of the church at Tyre in Eusebius' description, cited above. It should be noted that κατάγειος means "ground level," not (as has sometimes been supposed) "subterranean"; see Heisenberg, *op.cit.* (above n. 107) 1.33. On the plan and reconstruction of the church, see A. Birnbaum, "Die Oktogone von Antiochia, Nazianz u. Nyssa," *Repertorium für Kunstwiss.* 36 (1913) 181-209; and Smith, *The Dome* 29-30.

[110] Cf. Eltester, "Kirchen Antiochias" 257.

[111] Theophanes a. 5833, p. 36.29 ed. De Boor, calls the church σφαιροειδής. On the use of this term to describe a domical building, see G. Downey, "On Some Post-Classical Greek Architectural Terms," *TAPA* 77 (1946) 23, with n. 3.

[112] Chrysostom (*Si esurierit inimicus* 3 = *PG* 51.175) says that the roof of the church rose εἰς ὕψος ἄφατον. The unusual height of the roof is also mentioned by Eusebius, *Triakontaeterikos* 9, p. 221.11 ed. Heikel, and in the *Vita Constantini* 3.50, p. 99.2 ed. Heikel. Chrysostom likewise speaks of the "marvelous roof" in *In cap. 1 Genes. hom.* 6.2 = *PG* 53.56 and in *De mutatione nominum* 2.1 = *PG* 51.125.

[113] Malalas (419.22 Bonn ed., with Church Slavonic version 127-128, transl. Spinka) says that in the great earthquake of A.D. 526, the church remained standing for several days after the beginning of the shocks, but then caught fire and was demolished. The circumstance that the building survived the initial shocks and that the roof finally caught fire would appear to show that the roof was of wood; see Birnbaum *op.cit.* (above, n. 109) 188ff., and Smith, *The Dome* 29-30. That the church had a wooden roof also seems to be suggested by the language of Chrysostom *In epist. ad Ephes. cap. 4 hom.* 10.2 = *PG* 62.77-78.

[114] Chrysostom *loc.cit.*

[115] Jerome *Chronicle* ad an. 327, pp. 231-232 ed. Helm.

was paved with stone slabs,[116] and there seem to have been statues inside the building.[117] It also contained brilliant marbles and columns, and decorations of brass and gold.[118] In the early part of the fifth century the altar was at the west of the building.[119]

No remains of the church have as yet been found, but it seems beyond question that it served as the prototype for the central, octagonal, portion of the famous pilgrimage church of St. Symeon Stylites (Kalat Siman) east of Antioch, and an approximate idea of the appearance of the church at Antioch can be gained from the ruins at Kalat Siman.[120] There is also a conventionalized representation of Constantine's church in the Yakto mosaic of Antioch (see below).[121]

The church was called by several different names, for various reasons. Some writers refer to it as "the octagonal church," from its plan.[122] Others call it "the Great Church," possibly with reference to its size (as would be suggested by the remarks cited above on the unusual height of the dome), but possibly also because it was customary to refer thus to the principal church in a city.[123] It could also be known as "the Golden Church" because of the gilding of the roof.[124] In the years following its construction it was sometimes called "the new church," to distinguish it from the "old," apostolic, church in the city.[125] In the fifth century the church was called "Repentance" (*Poenitentia*, Μετάνοια) or "Harmony" (*Concordia*, Ὁμόνοια); sometimes the two names are used together.[126] There is no direct evidence as to the origin

[116] Chrysostom *Si esurierit inimicus* 2 = PG 51.176.

[117] Chrysostom *In epist. ad Ephes. cap. 4 hom.* 10.2 = PG 62.77-78.

[118] Chrysostom *loc.cit.*; Eusebius *locc.citt.* (above, n. 112).

[119] This orientation is mentioned by the church historian Socrates (*Hist. eccl.* 5.22 = PG 67.640 A). Socrates' history covered events up to the year A.D. 439, and he died soon after that; see Christ-Schmid-Stählin, *Gesch. d. gr. Lit.*[6] 2, pt. 2, 1434-1435. See H. Leclercq, "Orientation," *DACL* 12.2665-2666, and J. Lassus, *Sanctuaires chrét. de Syrie* (Paris 1947) 97.

[120] On Kalat Siman, see Smith, *The Dome* 34-35.

[121] There is a question whether the church depicted on an Egyptian textile illustrated by J. Strzygowski, *Orient oder Rom* (Leipzig 1901) pl. 4, is the church at Antioch or the church at Alexandria; see H. Leclercq, "Martyrium," *DACL* 10.2519.

[122] Theophanes a. 5819, p. 28.16 ed. De Boor; Michael the Syrian, *Chronicle* 7.3, p. 259 ed. Chabot.

[123] E.g., Philostorgius 7.8, p. 94.10 ed. Bidez; Theodoret *Hist. eccl.* 3.12.1, p. 188.22 ed. Parmentier and 5.35.4, p. 338.2; Malalas 318.4. Cf. Eltester, "Kirchen Antiochias" 258.

[124] See above, with nn. 114-115.

[125] Theodoret *Hist. eccl.* 4.24.4 (of the reign of Jovian); see above, n. 82.

[126] *Metanoia* appears in the life of St. Symeon Stylites the Elder by Antonius, ed. H. Lietzmann, *Texte u. Untersuchungen* 32, 4, p. 77.10, cf. pp. 207, 209. In a Latin life of St. Symeon the church is mentioned with the phrase *quae vocatur Concordia poenitentiae* (other MSS: *Concordia et Poenitentiae* or *Poenitentialis* or *Poenitentia*): *Acta SS Ian.* tom. 1 (1863), 5 Jan., col. 274, with note *n*. In one MS of the so-called

or the date of the first use of this name (or names). However, Grabar
has plausibly suggested that the appellation *Homonoia* is the name
originally given to the church by Constantine. One of the major political concepts of the time was the *concordia* (*homonoia*) that was supposed to characterize the emperor's functions and to pervade the imperial government as a result of his activities. At the time when the
church was built, this concept would have been of particular importance
because of the *concordia* that had recently been brought to the empire
by the triumph of the Christian Church, whose association now with
the imperial government was opening a new era, the Christian Roman
Empire.[127]

Although the location of the church is not specifically stated by any
literary source, and although no trace of it has as yet been found by
excavation, it seems reasonably certain that it stood on the island in
the Orontes, the "New City," and that it was placed in close association
with the imperial palace there. The evidence for this comes partly from
indications furnished by the topographical border of the Yakto mosaic,
partly from the analogy of the association of churches with the imperial
palaces at Constantinople, Salona, and Thessalonica.[128] The border of
the Yakto mosaic, which is evidently designed to illustrate a tour of
Antioch and Daphne, exhibits, in the section which appears to represent
the island, a polygonal domed building which is apparently the Church
of Constantine.[129] This church was the most famous polygonal and

---

Martyrologium Hieronymianum the description is *ecclesia que vocatur poenitentiae,*
with *concordia* written above *poenitentiae* by a second hand: *Martyr. Hieron.* ed.
Quentin and Delehaye, in *Acta SS Nov.* tom. 2, pt. 2 (1931), p. 26 (*Non. Ian.*).

[127] Grabar, *Martyrium* 1.222-227. Eltester, "Kirchen Antiochias" 258, n. 30, suggests
that the name *Homonoia* may have been given to the church on the occasion of the
healing of the Antiochene schism by Alexander, bishop of Antioch A.D. 413-421, when
the meeting that marked the end of the schism took place in the Great Church:
Theodoret *Hist. eccl.* 5.35.4, p. 338.2 ed. Parmentier; cf. Kidd, *Hist. of the Church* 3.174.

[128] The two principal studies of the location of the church, to which the reader
should refer for detailed discussions, are those of Eltester, "Kirchen Antiochias" 258-
267, and of Grabar, *Martyrium* 1.214-227 (followed by Smith, *The Dome* 29-30). Grabar
in particular brings out the close connection that existed between palace and church.
The question is also examined, in less detail, by Lassus, *Antioch-on-the-Orontes* 1.144-146.
Levi (*Antioch Mosaic Pavements* 1.332-333) is inclined to be skeptical as to the extent
to which the Yakto mosaic can be used as a topographical document. In essentials, the
present writer agrees with Eltester and Grabar, and the present discussion adduces the
basic evidence. The present interpretation of the itinerary in the mosaic, outside the
island, differs from theirs, and offers a new restoration of the damaged mosaic inscription, which, however, supports their hypotheses; see Excursus 18.

[129] Lassus in *Antioch-on-the-Orontes* 1, p. 145, fig. 22, in the section of the mosaic to
which he assigns the number 41; Levi, *Antioch Mosaic Pavements* pl. 8oc; Eltester,
"Kirchen Antiochias" pl. 1, facing p. 264; Smith, *The Dome* fig. 29 (restoring the lost
portion of the mosaic). On the itinerary represented in the mosaic, see Excursus 18.

domical building in the city, and we should expect it to be represented in a mosaic border of this kind, no matter whether the border was intended to show all the principal monuments of the city, or only a selection of typical monuments. Moreover, the figure of a man facing the building, with his hands clasped in the gesture of prayer, seems clearly intended to identify the structure as a church.[130] In front of the building is an arcade which could correspond with the *peribolos* about the church mentioned in Eusebius' description, or might represent a colonnade about the square on which, we know from another source, the church stood.[131] Next to the polygonal building in the mosaic there is represented, apparently, such an open square, containing a column surmounted by a statue. On the other side of this square with its statue there is another colonnade, then an arcaded building (which might be a part of the palace), then a race course enclosed by trees, which might be a race track or private exercise ground in the grounds of the palace.

Over the colonnade which apparently faced the square, there is a fragmentary inscription, [. . .] PIANA, which provides one of the principal clues to the identification of this part of the mosaic. A biography of St. Symeon Stylites the Elder speaks of the octagonal church as Μετάνοια εἰς τὸν Μόσχον "(The Church of) Repentance 'at the Calf.' "[132] Antiochus IV Epiphanes (175-163 B.C.) received from the people of Cilicia a bronze statue of himself taming a bull, symbolizing the king's suppression of a band of robbers in the Taurus mountains, the bull (*tauros*) being a punning personification of the mountains.[133] This statue seems to have stood at a gate, to which it gave the name Ταυριανὴ πύλη. This gate was connected with a bridge,[134] and there is some reason to believe that the gate and bridge stood on the outer (western) side of the island,[135] at the terminus of the road from

[130] Lassus' no. 40.
[131] Theodoret *Hist. eccl.* 5.35.4, p. 338.2 ed. Parmentier, speaks of an *agora* in front of the church. This is not elsewhere mentioned, but one would expect that a church such as this would have an open square in front of it. Theodoret's account suggests that the church stood on the eastern side of the square.
[132] P. 77.10 in Lietzmann's publication (cited above, n. 126), cf. p. 207. This reference appears in the account of the burial of St. Symeon in the church (see below, Ch. 17, n. 28).
[133] See Ch. 5, n. 87.
[134] Theophanes a. 5878, p. 10.10-11 ed. De Boor.
[135] This is indicated by an allusion of Libanius (*Or.* 20.44) to hoped-for building operations of Theodosius I which apparently resulted in the actual work at the Ταυριανὴ πύλη and its bridge, recorded by Theophanes (cited in preceding note). See Eltester, "Kirchen Antiochias" 259, and Grabar, *Martyrium* 1.215.

Cilicia and the Taurus mountains. The region about this statue (in addition to the Ταυριανὴ πύλη) might very likely have come to be known as τὰ Ταυριανά,[136] and this in fact seems to be a plausible restoration of the damaged inscription in the mosaic, viz. [τὰ Ταυ]-ριανά.[137] All these indications, though they are by no means explicit, seem to show as reasonably as can be expected from such evidence as we possess, that the octagonal church stood near, or was a part of, the palace on the island. The use of the phrase "at the Calf" in the biography of St. Symeon may be a rather quizzical reference to the well-known statue of the bull.

The church itself, we are told, stood on the site of "the public bath of King Philip." The bath, it is said, was old and ruinous and was no longer in use, and so was demolished when the church was to be built. According to one report, Plutarchus, who is described as the first Christian "*archon* of Antioch" (i.e. governor of Syria?), was put in charge of the construction of the church.[138] According to another source, Constantius, Constantine's son, who was in Antioch after about A.D. 333,

---

[136] Cf. similar names for regions at Constantinople listed by R. Janin, *Constantinople byzantine* (Paris 1950), e.g. τὰ Γαστρία (328-329), τὰ Καλύβια (339), τὰ Καμίνια (340), τὰ Μάγγανα (355), τὰ Πιττάκια (379), τὰ Πρασινά (382), ὁ Ταῦρος (397), τὰ Πεύκια (458).

[137] Lassus, *Antioch-on-the-Orontes* 1.146, suggested the restoration [ἡ στήλη τιβη]ριανά, referring to the statue of Tiberius (mentioned above, Ch. 8, n. 90), but the ending in alpha would be unusual. Τιβηριανή would of course be more likely as a modifier of πύλη or πόρτα (see Eltester, "Kirchen Antiochias" 261-263, and Levi, *Antioch Mosaic Pavements* 1.332, n. 47). Eltester, *loc.cit.* (followed by Grabar, *Martyrium* 1.216) suggests [πόρτα Ταυ]ριανά as a Greek transcription of the Latin name, which, he thinks, would have been inscribed in Latin on the gate itself. The restoration [τὰ Ταυ]ριανά has the merit of being correct Greek and of being of a length which might be more suitable for the mosaic, on which it might have been arranged thus:

[TATAY]
PIANA.

The form Ταυριανός, as Eltester points out (*op.cit.* 259, n. 33), is listed by Stephanus of Byzantium, *s.v.* Ταῦρος, as the ethnic of the dwellers in the Taurus mountains, and it is so employed by Basil, *Hom. in Hexaem.* 6.6 = PG 29.129C.

[138] Malalas 318.3ff. The bath is not elsewhere mentioned. The king might be either Philip I Philadelphus (93-84 B.C.) or Philip II Barypous (67-66 B.C.). Plutarchus is not otherwise known. Since there is no other evidence for the office of "*archon* of Antioch," W. Ensslin plausibly suggests that he was governor of Syria: "Plutarchos," no. 5, RE 21 (1951) 975. Malalas states (317.17ff.) that Constantine inaugurated the construction of the church when he visited Antioch on his return from a victorious campaign against the Persians. However, Constantine, though he was preparing for war with Persia toward the end of his reign (see below), never actually conducted such a campaign, and so far as we know he never visited Antioch after his victory over Licinius made him sole emperor (cf. Benjamin, "Constantinus," no. 2, RE 4 [1901] 1013-1026). Malalas' statement evidently represents a motif which appears elsewhere in his chronicle: imperial buildings were properly, in his view, inaugurated by the ruler in person, and the return from a victorious campaign was an especially appropriate occasion for important building undertakings. On these errors, see Ch. 2, §4.

acted as his father's representative in the construction of the building.[139] Presumably Constantius had the over-all supervision of the undertaking, while Plutarchus was in charge of the actual operations.[140] Near the church was built a *xenon* or guest-house, the construction of which was also supervised by Plutarchus.[141] At a later period, at least, there were also dining rooms, close (*contigua*) to the church, for feeding the poor; these were very likely built when the church was, though there is no record of their original construction.[142] There was also presumably a baptistry attached to the church, though there happens to be no record of this. It would seem likely that there were schools of various kinds attached to the church, e.g. for the training of singers and the instruction of converts, but again we have no record of these.

In the course of the work of construction there was found a bronze statue of Poseidon that had originally been set up as a talisman against earthquakes.[143] Evidently this figure had been buried (possibly in an earthquake) and forgotten. Plutarchus had it melted and employed the metal to make a statue of Constantine which he set up outside his praetorium.[144]

Finally, there is a report that a *praefectus praetorio* named Rufinus built a basilica in Antioch during the reign of Constantine, which was called the Basilica of Rufinus. This is said to have stood on the site of the Temple of Hermes, which was demolished in order to make

[139] Sozomen *Hist. eccl.* 3.5 = *PG* 67.1041 A.

[140] On the various degrees of responsibility among officials connected with public building operations, see the study of W. K. Prentice, "Officials charged with the Conduct of Public Works in Roman and Byzantine Syria," *TAPA* 43 (1912) 113-123.

[141] Malalas 318.6ff.

[142] The dining rooms are mentioned only in the account of the rebuilding of the church by the Patriarch Ephraemius after the earthquakes of 526 and 528: Zacharias Rhetor *Hist. eccl.*, ed. and transl. by E. W. Brooks in *CSCO, Scr. Syri*, ser. 3, vol. 6, *Versio* pp. 128.24ff. In Chrysostom's time the Great Church fed 3,000 widows and virgins plus a number of other needy and sick persons and travelers: *Homil. in Matt.* 66 [67].3 = *PG* 58.630. On the significance of this information in connection with the size of the population of Antioch, see Excursus 2.

[143] On Poseidon as the god of earthquakes, see E. H. Meyer, "Poseidon," Roscher, *Lexikon* 3.2813-2816.

[144] Malalas (318.20-21) states that the statue bore the inscription BONO CONSTANTINO (given by Malalas in Greek letters). It seems quite impossible to believe that the words that Malalas gives can have been either a whole honorific inscription or even the beginning of one, since the honorific inscriptions of the emperors of this period are long and fulsome. The words which the chronicler quotes here are much more characteristic of the folk literature of his time. The chronicler also states that the statue was still standing in his own time. It should be noted that Malalas appears to have taken many of his ostensible texts of inscriptions from literary sources, and that some of his statements that monuments "still existed" (including monuments that he certainly cannot have seen) come from literary sources. On the chronicler's procedures in this respect, see Ch. 2, §4.

room for the basilica. Plutarchus again is said to have been in charge of this work. This report may be inaccurate since we have no other knowledge of a *praefectus praetorio Orientis* named Rufinus at this period, while we do know, on good evidence, of a Basilica of Rufinus at Antioch which was built during the reign of Theodosius I.[145]

Antioch not only received these buildings from Constantine, but in turn, like all the other great cities of the eastern part of the Empire, it furnished statues for the adornment of the emperor's new capital, Constantinople. These statues are not individually identified, save that one is said to have been of a hyena. All the statues brought from Antioch were placed in the hippodrome at Constantinople.[146]

8. THE CHRISTIAN COMMUNITY AT ANTIOCH UNDER CONSTANTINE

The history of the Christian community at Antioch in the time of Constantine is largely concerned with the course of the Arian controversy over the nature of the divinity of Christ, which had divided the church in the eastern part of the Empire into two camps.[147] This controversy, which came to play a major part in the history of the church at Antioch under Constantine's son Constantius, came to have a political significance of the first importance in that it developed into an effort on the part of the Arians to create a state church under the control of the emperor dominated by the political ideas of Constantine. At first, however, this significance did not appear. When he became sole emperor in A.D. 324, Constantine, who was chiefly anxious to

[145] Malalas 318.7ff. On the basilica of the time of Theodosius I, see Ch. 15, n. 130. A person named Vettius Rufinus was *ppo.* or *ppo. Galliarum* A.D. 318-320 (J.-R. Palanque, *Essai sur la préfecture du prétoire du bas-empire* [Paris 1933] 127-130; Seeck, *Regesten* 473-475), but it is difficult to see how he could have built the basilica. There were other officials named Rufinus who were active under Constantine (Lietzmann, "Rufinus," nos. 9-15, *RE* 1A, 1186-1188); although they are not known to have been *praefecti praetorio*, they might (if we can believe that Malalas' use of the title is incorrect) have built the basilica. It is also of course not impossible that Malalas refers to a *ppo. Orientis* who is otherwise unknown. However, the evidence for a basilica of Rufinus built under Theodosius I, which comes from a source that is not suspect, suggests that Malalas' information on the one built under Constantine is confused and inaccurate, especially since Malalas does not mention the basilica of the time of Theodosius. See the discussion of this problem below, Ch. 15, n. 130.

[146] *Patria Constantinoupoleos* 2.73 and 79 in *Scriptores originum Constantinopolitanarum* ed. T. Preger (Leipzig 1901-1907) pp. 189.13, 191.4-5.

[147] On the origin and history of this controversy, which had begun ca. A.D. 319, see Gwatkin, *Studies of Arianism*[2] and (more briefly) Kidd, *Hist. of the Church* 2.14ff. Only a brief account of the events in the controversy which affected Antioch will be given here; for more detailed treatment, the reader should refer to Kidd's history and to the works cited by him.

secure peace and unity within the Church, charged his counsellor Hosius (Ossius) with the mission of reconciling the quarrel. Hosius failed; but toward the end of the year an opportunity offered for an attempt to settle the differences. Philogonius, Bishop of Antioch since A.D. 319,[148] died in December 324, and a meeting of bishops was called (A.D. 325) for the election of a successor. Eustathius (Bishop A.D. 325-326) was elected; and the meeting took the opportunity to condemn the heresy of Arius.[149] At this meeting a great council to deal with the whole problem was proposed, and in an effort to forestall any chance of a mishap at the projected council, the synod of Antioch drew up and published a long and complicated anti-Arian creed, which is of great importance as an early example of synodal creed-making.[150]

The council planned at Antioch was the Council of Nicaea (A.D. 325), at which a solution was adopted by which the *homoousion* or consubstantiality of the Father and the Son was inserted in the Creed. The Council also, among its other acts, settled the status of the dissident group called Paulianists, some of whom remained in Antioch as followers of Paul of Samosata, who had been Bishop of Antioch in the middle of the third century; the Paulianists were to be rebaptized, and their clergy were to be reordained.[151] In its sixth canon the Council recognized the preeminent rights and privileges of the churches of Antioch and Alexandria, which, by virtue of the apostolic foundation that they could claim, were to be allowed to exercise greater rights than other churches.[152]

[148] Cf. Ensslin, "Philogonios," *RE* 19 (1938) 2483.

[149] There has been some doubt whether there was actually a council at Antioch in A.D. 325, but the evidence seems to show that there was; see G. Bardy in Fliche-Martin, *Hist. de l'église* 3.79-80; F. L. Cross, "The Council of Antioch in 325 A.D.," *Church Quarterly Review* 128 (1939) 49-76; E. Seeberg, *Die Synode von Antiochen im Jahre 324/25* (Berlin 1913); Loofs, *Paulus von Samosata* 174, n. 1; 193; Sellers, *Eustathius of Antioch* 22, n. 2. For bibliography, and a summary of the proceedings, see M. V. Anastos, *Dumbarton Oaks Papers* 6 (1951) 141ff.

[150] On this creed and its significance, see Kelly, *Early Christian Creeds* 208-211 (with an English version).

[151] See Kidd, *Hist. of the Church* 2.45; Loofs, *Paulus von Samosata* 172-180, 186-187; Bardy, *Paul de Samosate²* 385ff. Jerome *Chron.* p. 232 ed. Helm, records a certain Paulinus as bishop of Antioch between Philogonius and Eustathius, and it has been supposed that he might have been the leader of the Paulianists. No other source mentions such a bishop, and most scholars have concluded that Jerome made a chronological error and that he meant to speak of Paulinus of Tyre, who succeeded Eustathius; Loofs, however, suggested that this Paulinus was a heretical bishop. See Bardy, *op.cit.* 387-390.

[152] Hefele-Leclercq, *Hist. des Conciles* 1.552, 559ff. This decision was altered by the Council of Constantinople in 381: see below, Ch. 15, n. 30. On the history of the see of Antioch at this period and the functions and activities of its bishops, see G. Bardy, "Alexandrie, Antioche, Constantinople (325-451)," in *1054-1954, L'Église et les églises, études . . . offerts à Dom Lambert Beauduin* 1 (Chevetogne 1954) 183ff., and F.

Eustathius was not to enjoy his bishopric for long. In A.D. 326 the
Empress Helena made a pilgrimage to Jerusalem, and a sarcastic remark that Eustathius had the misfortune to make concerning her gave
a fatal opportunity to the Eusebians whom he had opposed at Nicaea.[153]
With the emperor's approval, a council was called at Antioch under
the presidency of Eusebius, bishop of Caesarea, the historian and imperial adviser.[154] The council deposed Eustathius and Asclepas of Gaza,
one of his chief supporters, and sent them into exile along with a number of their adherents. This action, and the conflicting opinions over
the election of Eustathius' successor, provoked disorders among the
Christians which soon involved the whole city, and Constantine had to
dispatch troops under Strategius Musonianus (one of his advisers in
theological matters) to restore order.[155]

There were various candidates for the succession; Eusebius of Caesarea seems to have had the most support. However, he did not wish
to be translated from Caesarea, and in this wish he had the support
of the emperor.[156] The sources do not agree entirely on who was elected;
but it appears that Paulinus of Tyre was chosen, that he died after six
months in office, and that he was succeeded by Eulalius, who likewise
held office for only a short time; and that finally Euphronius, who
had been one of the original candidates favored by the emperor, was
appointed.[157] The date of Euphronius' appointment is not certain, but

Dvornik, *The Idea of Apostolicity in Byzantium and the Legend of the Apostle Andrew*
(Cambridge, Mass., 1958) 8-23.

[153] Athanasius *Hist. Arianorum* 4 = *PG* 25.697ff.

[154] The council is described, and letters written by the emperor in connection with it
are quoted, in the *Vita Constantini* attributed to Eusebius 3.59-61. Certain parts of this
Vita cannot have been written by Eusebius, but must represent the work of a later
editor, who altered and interpolated the work, the core of which was originally by
Eusebius, for political purposes; see Downey, "Original Church of the Apostles," with
references to previous studies, also the further observations of F. Halkin, *Anal. Boll.*
70 (1952) 349-350. There seems no reason, however, to doubt the account of this
episode at Antioch, and scholarly opinion tends to accept the quoted letters of Constantine as genuine.

[155] This is plain from the *Vita Constantini* attributed to Eusebius 3.59 and 62; cf.
Socrates *Hist. eccl.* 1.24 = *PG* 67.144-145. On Strategius and his career, see O. Seeck,
"Strategius," no. 1, *RE* 4A (1932) 181-182. The account given here of Eustathius' deposition follows the study of H. Chadwick, "The Fall of Eustathius of Antioch," *JTS* 49
(1948) 27-35; cf. also Stevenson, *Studies in Eusebius* 108-116. Most historians in the
past have believed that Eustathius was deposed in A.D. 330; cf. e.g. Kidd, *Hist. of the
Church* 2.54-55; G. Bardy in Fliche-Martin, *Hist. de l'église* 3.102; Cavallera, *Schisme
d'Antioche* 57-58.

[156] The *Vita Constantini* attributed to Eusebius 3.60-62.

[157] Eusebius *Contra Marcellinum* 1.4.2-3; *Vita Constantini* attributed to Eusebius,
3.62; Socrates *loc.cit.* (see above, n. 155); Philostorgius *Hist. eccl.* 3.15; Theodoret
Hist. eccl. 1.21; cf. Devreesse, *Patriarcat d'Antioche* 115-116. I follow the sequence

it presumably took place about A.D. 327 or 328. Such were the events that began the Antiochene schism, which was to last until A.D. 414.[158] During this period, in A.D. 327 (as has already been noted), there took place the inauguration of the construction of the Great Church, which would typify the importance of the position of Antioch among the cities of the Christian East.

About A.D. 333 Antioch again appears in the Arian controversy, this time in connection with the attacks on Athanasius, who had become the principal champion of the Nicene cause and enemy of the Arians. Athanasius, in Egypt, was accused of magical practices, a serious crime, independent of the theological question; and the government was bound to take cognizance of the charges. Constantine ordered his half-brother (or nephew) Delmatius, the consul for A.D. 333, to take charge of the investigation. Delmatius was at this time in Antioch, with the title of *censor*. He summoned Athanasius to appear before him at Antioch, but Athanasius was able to clear himself without coming to the city, and the emperor put a stop to the proceedings.[159]

9. The Last Years of Constantine and the Preparations for the Persian War

In the latter years of Constantine's reign the growing expectation of war with Persia brought to Antioch the prominence as a military center that it was to retain until the reign of Julian the Apostate. Rome and Persia had been at peace since the treaty of A.D. 297, but when Sapor II came to the Persian throne in A.D. 310, he determined to win back the portions of his empire lost to the Romans thirteen years before. The Romans on their side resented Sapor's persecution of the Christians, whom the Persian king looked upon as enemy agents.

Tension increased, and as the Romans pushed forward their military preparations, Antioch must have felt the economic and social

---

adopted by Chadwick in his study (cited above, n. 155), with which Devereesse would agree; and Chadwick's chronology, worked out by him for the first time, seems to give the only plausible explanation of the events.

[158] On the history of this, see Cavallera, *Schisme d'Antioche*.

[159] Athanasius *Apologia contra Arianos* 65 = PG 25.365; Socrates *Hist. eccl.* 1.27 = PG 67.157; cf. Kidd, *Hist. of the Church* 2.58-59, and G. Bardy in Fliche-Martin, *Hist. de l'église* 3.106-107. The chronology of this episode is obscure, and it has been dated at various times between A.D. 332 and 334. There appears to be no other evidence for the office of *censor* at this time, and it is not certain why Delmatius had this title, or what he was doing in Antioch. In any case he would appear to have been occupying an important position; see O. Seeck, "Delmatius," no. 2, *RE* 4 (1901) 2455. The title presumably represents a revival by Constantine of the ancient Roman title, but the function need not have been exactly the same.

strains produced by the growing number of troops for which the city served as headquarters. Then, in the summer and autumn of A.D. 333, the city was visited with real distress when the whole of the eastern part of the Roman Empire suffered a severe famine, which is said to have been especially bad in Antioch and Cyrrhus and their vicinity. The presence of the troops may have been in part responsible for the shortage of food, as it was in the case of the famine and economic crisis that occurred at Antioch in the time of Julian the Apostate when a crop failure ruined the city's food supply just as preparations for a Persian campaign were in progress. In any event, the mobilization of the forces must have aggravated the shortage of food, and one can believe that in any competition for food between soldiers and civilians, the soldiers would secure what they considered to be their share. There are said to have been many deaths, and there may have been an epidemic of disease such as sometimes accompanied a famine. Constantine made the churches in the various cities serve as centers for the distribution of wheat; the church at Antioch was allotted 36,000 *modii*.[160]

It was just about this time (probably about the year A.D. 333) that Constantine, judging the situation serious enough to call for the presence of a member of the imperial house, sent his second son, the Caesar Constantius, to Antioch.[161] Constantius, who had been born in A.D. 317,[162] was still of course too young to take the active direction of the military preparations, which were in charge of the *praefectus praetorio per Orientem*, and, probably, of one of the *magistri militum praesentales*. However, the caesar's presence would be valuable for the morale of the troops and as an indication of the importance that the government attached to the military preparations centered in Antioch. The Persians began their operations with the occupation of Armenia in A.D. 334. On this, the Romans began preparations in earnest for war.

One of the special measures taken at this time was the creation of the office of *comes Orientis*. This official, who was unique in the administrative hierarchy, was a civilian administrator in charge of the

---

[160] The famine is described by Theophanes a. 5824, p. 29.13-23 ed. De Boor, and is mentioned in Jerome's *Chronicle* ad an. 333, p. 233 ed. Helm. Jerome states that "an innumerable multitude in Syria and Cilicia perished." On the famine under Julian, see below, Ch. 13, §1. Chapot, *Frontière de l'Euphrate* 213, by mistake gives the date of the famine as A.D. 324, so that he does not perceive its possible connection with the military preparations. He cites only the passage in Theophanes, and fails to calculate the date of the indiction, which makes Theophanes' date, in conjunction with that of Jerome, quite certain.

[161] On the date and circumstances, see Stein, *Gesch.* 1.199, with n. 5, also Parker, *Hist. of the Roman World A.D. 138-337* 308, and Piganiol, *Empire chrétien* 56-57.

[162] Seeck, "Constantius," no. 4, *RE* 4 (1901) 1044.

diocese of the Orient, which embraced the provinces from Mesopotamia and Syria on the north to Egypt on the south. The *comes Orientis* resembled the *vicarii* who were in charge of the other dioceses of the Empire, in that he supervised the governors of the provinces that made up his diocese, and had the same administrative and judicial functions as the *vicarii*. Like them, he occupied a position in the hierarchy between the provincial governors and the praetorian prefect. However, as the activities of the holders of the office show, the *comes Orientis* had special powers and duties in connection with military matters (probably concerning the organization of supplies and the quartering of troops), which were evidently given to him in order to facilitate the preparations for the Persian war.[163]

The first *comes Orientis* was a Christian named Felicianus, appointed in A.D. 335; he was given as a praetorium the Temple of the Muses in Antioch.[164]

In the following year hostility increased and Constantine sent his nephew Hannibalianus to drive the Persians out of Armenia, and to govern the country as king. Constantine then declared war, and was engaged in preparations for a campaign when he died at Nicomedia on 22 May A.D. 337. Constantius, who was at Antioch when the news came of the Emperor's illness, set out for Nicomedia at once, and arrived while his father was still living.[165]

10. Constantius (A.D. 337-361) at Antioch and the Persian War

Constantius was not yet twenty years old when his father died,[166] but for four years he had been, as caesar at Antioch, at least nominally in charge of the preparations for war against Persia; he had received a careful education and became an excellent soldier and military organizer.[167] Over a year after Constantine's death, a new partition of

---

[163] For a further discussion of the office and its history, which until recently has not been completely known, see Downey, *Comites Orientis* 7-11, also A. H. M. Jones, "The Roman Civil Service (Clerical and Sub-Clerical Grades)," *JRS* 39 (1949) 48, nn. 112, 116, and Ensslin, "Religionspolitik des Kaisers Theodosius d. Gr.," 60, with n. 1. The title *comes* here very likely represents a survival of Constantine's characteristic practice of appointing special commissioners, called *comites*, as his personal representatives, to deal with particular problems. See Piganiol, *Empire chrétien* 64-65.

[164] Malalas 318.23ff. In saying that previously a *delegator* had been stationed at Antioch in time of war, Malalas evidently means a *delegatus*; and he probably uses the title incorrectly anyway; see Downey, *Comites Orientis* 10.

[165] Zonaras 13.4.28.

[166] He was born 7 August A.D. 317; see above, n. 162.

[167] See the characterization of him by Ammianus Marcellinus 21.16, and the estimates of his character by Kidd, *Hist. of the Church* 2.69-70, and by Piganiol, *Empire chrétien*

the Empire took place (September A.D. 338), by which Constantius retained the East, where his capital would be Antioch.[168] Immediately after this settlement with his brothers, Constantius returned to Antioch, where he spent the winter of A.D. 338/9 busy with military preparations.[169] Special taxes were imposed to provide funds for the army.[170] The collecting of troops and of their supplies and equipment in and around Antioch, together with the presence in the city of the imperial court, must have had a marked effect upon the city's daily life and its business activities, and on the whole, although there were some strains on the economy, Antioch prospered under Constantius.[171] Since he made Antioch his headquarters and ordinary residence for a number of years during the Persian war, Constantius naturally took some interest in the city, and the future emperor Julian, in his panegyric of Constantius, written at the end of A.D. 355, speaks of stoas, fountains, and other buildings which the emperor caused his governors to present to the city. In gratitude, Julian says, Antioch even called itself by the name of Constantius.[172]

90-91. For an evaluation of Ammianus as a source, and detailed discussions of his accounts of events at Antioch, see Thompson, *Ammianus Marcellinus*.

[168] Piganiol, *Empire chrétien* 74-75; Seeck in *RE* 4.1047; Gwatkin, *Studies of Arianism*[2] 112, n. 4.

[169] *CTh* 12.1.23 shows that he was in Antioch on 11 October. He was in Emesa, a military center, on 28 October (*CTh* 12.1.25), and again in Antioch on 27 December (*CTh* 2.6.4). See P. Peeters, "L'Intervention politique de Constance II dans la Grande Arménie, en 338," *Bull. de l'Acad. r. de Belgique, Cl. des lettres* 17 (1931) 10-47 = *Recherches d'histoire et de philologie orientales* 1 (Brussels 1951; *Subsid. hagiogr.* 27) 222-250.

[170] Julian *Or.* 1.21 D; *CTh* 11.1.5 (9 Feb. A.D. 339).

[171] Constantius' activities in preparing the army and its equipment are described (presumably with a certain amount of adulation) by Julian *Or.* 1.20 D ff. and Libanius *Or.* 18.166-169, 205-207; *Or.* 69.69-72, 89-92. On the economic life of Antioch under Constantius, see further below. Beginning with the reign of Constantius, we have a new and exceptionally rich source for the history of Antioch in the voluminous works of Libanius, which have recently been exhaustively studied by P. Petit in his two monographs, *Libanius et la vie municipale à Antioche au IV*[e] *siècle après J.-C.* (Paris 1955) and *Les étudiants de Libanius* (Paris 1956). The amount of detailed information about the city that Libanius gives could not be reproduced in the present study. Readers who are concerned with further details should consult the works of Petit.

[172] Julian *Or.* 1.40 D-41 A. On the date of the oration, see Christ-Schmid-Stählin, *Gesch. der gr. Lit.*[6] 2, pt. 2, 1016. The public buildings which Julian mentions in general terms are not otherwise known. Due allowance must of course be made for the fact that Julian was writing a panegyric of Constantius. There is no other evidence that Antioch called itself by the name of Constantius (e.g. *Antiochia Constantia*), but there is no reason to doubt Julian's statement. It is on the other hand remarkable that we have no more evidence in the case of Antioch for the adoption of imperial cognomina, a custom which was widely followed elsewhere. See E. Spanheim's note on this passage (pp. 265-267) in his edition of the works of Julian (Leipzig 1696).

While Constantius was engaged in the recruitment and training of his army, and later while he was conducting his almost annual campaigns against the Persians, he was also continually involved in the ecclesiastical quarrels concerning the Arian dogma and the creed of Nicaea which continued to split the Church. Constantius himself, though he was apparently not actually an Arian, both disliked and distrusted those who adhered to the Nicene point of view,[173] and encouraged and favored the Arians, whose purpose it was to build up a state church dominated by the emperor. Constantius' steady occupation with both military and ecclesiastical problems gives a special character to the first fifteen years or so of his reign at Antioch.

The first of these episodes in which Antioch was concerned took place in December of A.D. 338. Athanasius, the champion of the Nicene cause, was attacked by a meeting of the supporters of Eusebius of Nicomedia, the leader of the Arian party. The Eusebians, meeting in Antioch, brought further accusations against Athanasius, and in an effort to thwart him, Constantius appointed as prefect of Egypt a personal enemy of Athanasius.[174]

In the following summer (A.D. 339) Constantius led an expedition as far as the Persian border, but encountered no resistance; and not being prepared to advance further into Persia, he returned to Antioch where he spent the winter.[175]

Early in A.D. 340 another council of the Eusebians met at Antioch,

---

[173] See Kidd, *Hist. of the Church* 2.69ff. For an account of the fundamental significance of the Arian controversy, see Cochrane, *Christianity and Classical Culture*[2] 232-260.

[174] On this council of A.D. 338 at Antioch, see Gwatkin, *Studies of Arianism*[2] 115-116; Hefele-Leclercq, *Conciles* 1.702-703; Kidd, *Hist. of the Church* 2.72-73; Piganiol, *Empire chrétien* 82. This might have been the council at which a canon was adopted confirming the limitations of the powers of the country bishops (*chorepiskopoi*), who were not allowed to ordain deacons or priests without the consent of their superiors in the cities: Mansi 2.1312 (cf. Bardy, *Paul de Samosate*[2] 275). O. Seeck, "Constantius," no. 4, *RE* 4 (1901) 1049, and *Gesch. d. Untergangs* 4, 54, with n. on p. 405, has attempted to show that this was a part of the Council of the Dedication, at which Constantine's octagonal church was dedicated, and that this council was in session continuously from A.D. 338 to 341; the dedication of the church took place, Seeck believed, at Christmas of A.D. 338. Seeck's view is adopted by Schwabe, *Analecta Libaniana* 49ff. However, Seeck took into account only a portion of the evidence; and sources that he does not mention in this connection show clearly that the councils of 338 and 341 were quite distinct (see especially Gwatkin, *op.cit.* 116, n. 1). Seeck seems not to have given sufficient consideration to the specific statement of Athanasius (*De synodis* 25 = *PG* 26.275) that the Council of the Dedication assembled in the 14th indiction, in the consulship of Marcellinus and Probinus (A.D. 341). He likewise does not seem to have taken into account other testimony on the date of the dedication of the church, e.g. that of Theophanes, cited above, n. 106.

[175] Libanius *Or.* 76-78; cf. Seeck, "Constantius," no. 4, *RE* 4 (1901) 1053.

at which, with the assent of the Emperor, Athanasius was once more deposed from his see in Egypt.[176]

In the summer of the same year Constantius conducted another campaign against the Persians, after which he returned to Antioch in the late summer.[177]

During the whole of this winter, apparently, Constantius was in Antioch;[178] and on the feast of the Epiphany, 6 January A.D. 341, Constantine's octagonal Great Church was dedicated.[179] The building, begun in A.D. 327, had still been unfinished when Constantine died (22 May A.D. 337);[180] and when it was at last completed, a dedication ceremony of great magnificence, suitable to the importance of the building, was planned, with over ninety bishops present.[181] On the church there is said to have been placed a metrical inscription of four lines:

Χρίστῳ Κωνσταντῖνος ἐπήρατα οἰκί ἔτευξεν,
οὐρανίαις ἀψῖσι πανείκελα παμφανόωντα
Κωνσταντείου ἄνακτος ὑποδρήσσοντος ἐφετμαῖς·
Γοργόνιος δὲ κόμης θαλαμηπόλον ἔργον ὕφανε.[182]

[176] For a discussion of the chronology and the sources, see Hefele-Leclercq, *Conciles* 1.695-696. Seeck is mistaken in regarding this council as a continuation of the one that had assembled at Antioch at the end of A.D. 338 (see above, n. 174).

[177] On the campaign, see Libanius *Or.* 18.207. The emperor was in Edessa on 12 August (*CTh* 12.1.30) and in Antioch on 9 September (*CTh* 6.4.5-6).

[178] He was in the city on 12 February (*CTh* 5.13.1-2), as well as in January when the church was dedicated (see below).

[179] The year of the council is fixed by Athanasius *De synodis* 25 = *PG* 26.725 A; Socrates *Hist. eccl.* 2.8 = *PG* 67.196-197; and Sozomen *Hist. eccl.* 3.5 = *PG* 67.1041. The day of the dedication is supplied by the Arian historian Philostorgius *Hist. eccl.*, p. 212.21 ed. Bidez. Seeck endeavored to show that this council first met in A.D. 338, and that the dedication took place in that year, but he did not take into account evidence which shows that A.D. 341 is the true date; see above, nn. 106, 174.

[180] Malalas 324.5ff. On the date when the church was begun, see above, n. 105.

[181] See Hefele-Leclercq, *Conciles* 1.702, and Kidd, *Hist. of the Church* 2.78.

[182] Malalas 326.1-4. The text as given in the MS of Malalas is obviously corrupt in several places (notably in bearing the name of Constantius in line 1, which does not suit the sense of line 3), and I follow the corrections of Müller, *Antiq. Antioch.* 104, n. 18, which are accepted by T. Preger, *Inscriptiones graecae metricae ex scriptoribus praeter Anthologiam collectae* (Leipzig 1891) no. 111. The text of the MS of Malalas is followed in *IGLS* no. 832 by Jalabert and Mouterde, who do not seem to have utilized Müller's corrections or Preger's text. Jalabert and Mouterde point out that the rather high-flown style, with its characteristic Homeric reminiscences, suggests a date later than the fourth century. Malalas could well have seen the inscription himself, though in other cases he is known to have taken his texts of inscriptions from literary sources; see Downey, "Inscriptions in Malalas," and above, Ch. 2, §4. It is characteristic that Malalas states (326.5ff.) that Constantius dedicated the church on his return from concluding a treaty of peace with the Persians. No such treaty at this time is known, but the chronicler evidently considered that it was fitting that such a notable building should be dedicated on such an occasion. Malalas' very brief account of Constantius' reign is highly distorted.

"For Christ Constantine made this lovely dwelling, like in all respects to the vaults of heaven, bright-shining, with Constantius obeying the commands of the ruler; the *comes* Gorgonius carried out the work of *cubicularius*."

Apparently the *comes* Gorgonius was a court chamberlain (*cubicularius*) who was put in charge of the work, replacing Plutarchus who had supervised operations in the time of Constantine.[183] Gorgonius later appears as the head chamberlain of the Caesar Gallus.[184] Constantius presented costly liturgical vessels to the church, in addition to those his father Constantine had already provided for it.[185]

The presence of the bishops provided an appropriate occasion for the holding of a council,[186] just as had been done at Jerusalem in A.D. 335 on the occasion of the dedication of Constantine's new Church of the Resurrection there.[187] As his father had done at Nicaea, Constantius presided at the council, at which, in addition to repeated condemnation of Athanasius and Arianism, efforts were made to find a new formula. Four creeds were drawn up and put into circulation, though only one, which was probably that of Lucian of Antioch, was regarded as official.[188]

After the council was over, Antioch suffered from an earthquake; the damage is not recorded, although the quake is said to have been severe.[189]

[183] See above, n. 140.

[184] Ammianus Marcellinus 15.2.10.

[185] Theodoret *Hist. eccl.* 3.12.4. These vessels were confiscated during the persecution of the Christians under Julian the Apostate; see Ch. 13, n. 48.

[186] Athanasius *De synodis* 22 = PG 26.720 C; Socrates and Sozomen *locc.citt.* (above, n. 179). On this council, see Hefele-Leclercq, *Conciles* 1.702ff., and Kidd, *Hist. of the Church* 2.77ff. Socrates and Sozomen write as though the council assembled in the fifth year following the death of Constantine, which would date the convening of the council after 22 May A.D. 341. This date might be difficult to reconcile with the statement of the lost Arian historian (which we have no reason to doubt) that the dedication took place on 6 January, for it might seem unusual for the council to convene only several months after the dedication. However, it might well be that Socrates and Sozomen were reckoning roughly by calendar years, and counted the fifth year after Constantine's death from 1 January A.D. 341. It should be noted that Athanasius, who was much better informed, dates the meeting of the council only by the consuls and the indiction (*De synodis, loc.cit.*). Eltester, "Kirchen Antiochias" 254-256, shows that the synod must have begun its sessions immediately after 6 January.

[187] Kidd, *Hist. of the Church* 2.63.

[188] On the creeds of the Council of 341, see Kelly, *Early Christian Creeds* 263-274. On the so-called Second Creed as the work of Lucian of Antioch, see Bardy, *Lucien d'Antioche* 9-10, 91-92, 119.131.

[189] Theophanes a. 5833, p. 36.28-29 ed. De Boor, says that the earthquake lasted for three days, while Socrates *Hist. eccl.* 2.10 = PG 67.204 C, and Sozomen *Hist. eccl.* 3.6 =

The winter of A.D. 341/2 Constantius spent in Antioch, with the exception of a brief and hurried journey to Constantinople, where he had to deal with serious disorders that followed the election of rival bishops to succeed Eusebius of Constantinople, who had died during the Council of Antioch in A.D. 341.[190] The emperor had returned to Antioch by 31 March and remained there at least until 11 May,[191] after which he carried out a summer campaign against the Persians.[192]

The next winter (A.D. 342/3) the emperor was again in Antioch.[193] In the summer he led a successful expedition against the Persians in Adiabene.[194]

Constantius presumably spent the following winter in Antioch. In the spring (A.D. 344), about Easter, he was in the city and witnessed the remarkable effort made by the bishop of Antioch, Stephen, to discredit the two bishops who had come to Antioch with a report on the Council that had been held at Serdica the previous year. Stephen, assisted by his nephew, one night introduced a prostitute into the bedroom of one of the bishops in order to provoke a scandal, but the trick and its authorship were soon found out, and Stephen was deposed by a council which met at Antioch in the summer of the same year.[195]

In this same summer of A.D. 344, presumably while the council was sitting at Antioch, the Persians crossed the Tigris and met Constantius with his army at Singara, near the border. The Romans were defeated,

PG 67.1048 B, say that the shocks lasted for a whole year. In the *Consularia Constantinopolitana* (Mommsen, *Chron. min.* 1.236) it is stated that the earthquake affected the East with the exception of Antioch; this appears to represent a misunderstanding of a statement in a source. Cedrenus, 1.522.7-8 Bonn ed., ascribes the earthquake to "the fourth and fifth year" of Constantius; since his reign began 9 September A.D. 337, the earthquake would have occurred between 9 September 340 and 8 September 342; presumably Cedrenus meant that the shocks lasted for a year, which overlapped the two regnal years. Capelle, "Erdbebenforschung," *RE* Suppl. 4 (1924) 356, by mistake gives the date as A.D. 334. There is evidence that the theater at Daphne was damaged or destroyed in the earthquake of A.D. 341: see D. N. Wilber in *Antioch* 2.59.

[190] Libanius *Or.* 59.96-97; Socrates *Hist. eccl.* 2.13 = *PG* 67.208-209; Sozomen *Hist. eccl.* 3.7 = *PG* 67.1049-1052. Cf. Seeck, "Constantius," no. 4, *RE* 4 (1901) 1056; Piganiol, *Empire chrétien* 83; Hefele-Leclercq, *Conciles* 1.733-734.

[191] *CTh* 3.12.1, 12.1.33-34, 11.36.6.

[192] Libanius *Or.* 18.207.

[193] *CTh* 9.21.5, 9.22.1 (19 February A.D. 343).

[194] Athanasius *Hist. Arianorum ad monachos* 16 = *PG* 25.712 B; Libanius *Or.* 59.82ff. See Stein, *Gesch.* 1.213. Socrates and Sozomen speak as if there had been a council at Antioch in the summer of A.D. 343, before the meeting of the Council of Serdica in the same year; but they apparently refer actually to the council at Antioch of A.D. 344; see Hefele-Leclercq, *Conciles* 1.735-736, 829. There were so many councils at Antioch at this period that the later historians could easily have confused them.

[195] Athanasius *Hist. Arianorum ad monachos* 20 = *PG* 25.716-717; Theodoret *Hist. eccl.* 2.8.56ff. See Kidd, *Hist. of the Church* 2.93-94, 97-98, and Hefele-Leclercq, *Conciles* 1.827-829.

but the Persians, who suffered heavy losses, also retired and brought the campaign to a close.[196]

In May of the following year (A.D. 345) Constantius had advanced to Nisibis, apparently to relieve a siege of the city by the Persians.[197]

The following year (A.D. 346) saw the completion of a new harbor at Seleucia Pieria, the port of Antioch, which improved the facilities there and greatly assisted the movement of military supplies.[198] Aside from its military importance, this new harbor also contributed materially to the economic prosperity of the city, by providing improved opportunities for travel and communications and for the movement of goods.[199] Presumably the work of constructing the new port was carried out by the army.[200]

In March or April of the same year Athanasius, on the invitation of Constantius, came to Antioch for a personal interview with the emperor.[201] Constantius destroyed all the past charges against Athanasius, and gave him assurance of protection from false attacks in the future; and Athanasius, presumably having spent some time in Antioch, proceeded to Alexandria, where he was allowed to resume his rightful place.

In the summer Constantius once more relieved a siege of Nisibis by the Persians.[202] We hear nothing of his activities at Antioch in the next few years. The campaign of A.D. 350 was the final one of the war for the time being. The Persians in this year again besieged Nisibis, and were again repulsed, with great losses. At the same time, barbarians

[196] On the sources and the date (which has been disputed), see Stein, *Gesch.* 1.213-214.
[197] *CTh* 11.7.5; see Stein, *Gesch.* 1.214, with n. 2.
[198] Jerome *Chronicle* 2361, p. 236 ed. Helm; Theophanes a. 5838, p. 38.6-7 ed. De Boor; *Expositio totius mundi* 28, p. 110 ed. Riese, *Geographi Latini minores*, and p. 140 ed. G. Lumbroso, *Atti della R. Accad. dei Lincei, Memorie, Cl. di sci. mor., stor. e filol.,* ser. 5, vol. 6 (1898). See also A. A. Vasiliev, "*Expositio Totius Mundi,*" *Seminarium Kondakovianum* 8 (1936), pp. 3 and 35, with n. 124 (with a translation). On the harbor, see Honigmann, "Seleukeia" 1192; he suggests that this represents the completion of work begun by Diocletian, with which the revolt of Eugenius in A.D. 303 was connected (see above, §4). Seeck, "Constantius," no. 4, *RE* 4 (1901) 1059, by mistake dates the completion of the work in A.D. 345.
[199] Libanius *Or.* 11.263-264; Julian *Or.* 1.40 D.
[200] The similar work in the time of Diocletian was done by five hundred soldiers; see above, §4.
[201] Athanasius *Apologia ad Constantium* 5 = *PG* 25.601; *Hist. Arianorum ad monachos* 22 and 43-44 = *PG* 25.717 and 744f.; Socrates *Hist. eccl.* 2.23 = *PG* 67.256; Sozomen *Hist. eccl.* 3.20 = *PG* 67.1100; Rufinus *Hist. eccl.* 10.19-20. Constantius was in Antioch on 21 March (*CTh* 10.14.1; on the date of the decree, see Seeck, *Regesten* 38.20). The chronology is also indicated by the movements of Athanasius at this time; see Gwatkin, *Studies of Arianism*² 131, n. 4, and Hefele-Leclercq, *Conciles* 1.855, n. 8 (though in both these studies the evidence of the *Code of Theodosius* for Constantius' presence in Antioch is not taken into account).
[202] Stein, *Gesch.* 1.214.

from the Caspian Sea invaded the northern provinces of Persia; and this new threat, coupled with the losses at Nisibis, made it impossible for the time being for Sapor to renew his attacks on the Roman Empire. The Romans were thus left in peace for a few years.

The respite was welcome to Constantius, for his presence was needed in the West. Early in A.D. 350 Magnentius, a pagan who was a high officer on the staff of Constantius' brother Constans, had proclaimed himself emperor. Constans fled and soon after was killed. Constantius, after some negotiations and final arrangements in the East, appointed his nephew Gallus caesar (15 March A.D. 351) and placed him in charge of the East, so that he himself might be free to deal with Magnentius in Europe.[203]

Gallus, the younger son of Julius Constantius, half-brother of Constantine the Great, was twenty-five or twenty-six years old when he became caesar.[204] He enjoyed great prestige, not only by virtue of his own descent, but because he was married to Constantia, the daughter of Constantine the Great and Fausta. However, he soon showed himself to be a brute, with a veritable Fury for a wife,[205] and the four years that he spent at Antioch were a time of trouble for the city, ending in disaster for the prince.

On his appointment as caesar, Gallus at once went to Antioch.[206] Here his naturally cruel disposition soon turned him into a tyrant; his wife's equally unpleasant character aided the process, and the court chamberlains, seeing opportunities for gain or personal revenge, took care to supply reports, often falsified or exaggerated, which brought prominent or wealthy persons under suspicion and usually led to their downfall.[207] One of the chief figures here was the chamberlain Gorgonius, who had some time before been placed by Constantius in charge

---

[203] Stein, *Gesch.* 1.215-217; Piganiol, *Empire chrétien* 85-87. Although a pagan, Magnentius employed Christian symbolism on his coins in order to attract the support of Christians: Piganiol, *op.cit.* 86; A. Solari, *L'Impero romano,* 4: *Impero provinciale; Restaurazione, 193-363* (Genova 1947) 210.

[204] He was born in A.D. 325 or 326; cf. Seeck, "Constantius Gallus," no. 5, *RE* 4 (1901) 1094. On his character and his career at Antioch, see Thompson, *Ammianus Marcellinus* 56-71; certain historical errors and exaggerations are corrected here, but in the present writer's estimation Thompson sometimes errs on the side of leniency toward Gallus.

[205] See Ammianus Marcellinus 14.1.

[206] Julian *Epist. ad Athen.* 272; Socrates *Hist. eccl.* 2.28 = *PG* 67.276; Zonaras 13.8.4-5; *Chronicon Paschale* 540.8-12 Bonn ed. (cf. Mommsen, *Chron. min.* 1.238). On the vision of the cross in the sky, which according to Socrates appeared at the time when Gallus was going to Antioch, see J. Vogt, "Berichte über Kreuzeserscheinungen aus dem 4. Jh. n. Chr.," *Annuaire de l'Inst. de philol. et d'hist. orient. et slaves* 9 (1949) 593-606 (*Mélanges H. Grégoire*).

[207] Ammianus Marcellinus 14.1.1ff., 14.11.3; Julian *loc.cit.*; John of Antioch, frag. 174 in *FHG* 4.604 = frag. 71, *Excerpta de insidiis,* p. 115 ed. De Boor; Zonaras 13.9.9ff.

of the construction work on the octagonal Great Church at Antioch.[208] Not only were informers encouraged, but a regular spy system was organized in the city and men disguised as travelers went everywhere in Antioch, picking up remarks which they carried to the Caesar.[209] Gallus himself, with a few attendants, would roam about the streets at night, asking people what they thought of the caesar; but he eventually had to give this up because, the streets being lit by night, he was often recognized.[210] People were put to death on mere suspicion, and without trial, or had their property confiscated and were driven into exile or beggary; and, as Ammianus writes, "wealthy and distinguished houses were being closed."[211] Accusations of magic and of plots to overthrow the government were common.[212] The Caesar was fond of horse racing; he also took particular pleasure in bloody spectacles in the circus, and accused persons were savagely tortured.[213]

At the same time, Gallus was a fervent Christian, and eagerly sought the company of holy men.[214] One of his favorite companions in Antioch was the well-known ultra-Arian apologist Aetius, whom Athanasius and his supporters called "the godless" because of his doctrines. After trying various callings as a young man, Aetius became distinguished as a theological disputant, and was ordained a deacon in Antioch in A.D. 350 and licensed to teach in the churches. Gallus was at first persuaded to order his execution because of his teaching, but Aetius' protector, the bishop of Antioch Leontius, induced Gallus to rescind his order, and Aetius and the caesar became close friends. Eventually, however, Leontius was compelled to dismiss his deacon through the efforts of the orthodox champions Diodorus and Carterus, who were the heads of a religious school or monastery at Antioch, and Flavian, who later became bishop of Antioch.[215]

[208] Ammianus Marcellinus 15.2.10; for his work in connection with the church, see above, n. 183.

[209] Ammianus Marcellinus 14.1.2, 14.1.5ff.

[210] Ammianus Marcellinus 14.1.9. Thompson, *Ammianus Marcellinus* 59, considers that this report "may well be a myth"; the same story is told of other monarchs, and Thompson believes that such stories could be invented because the streets of Antioch were as dark at night as those of other ancient cities, in spite of what Ammianus says. However, there is good evidence (apparently not known to Thompson) that the streets of Antioch were illuminated at night, and thus one of the reasons for suspecting the report is removed; see Libanius *Or.* 11.267, *Or.* 16.41, *Or.* 22.6, *Or.* 33.36-37; cf. Jones, *Greek City* 214.

[211] Ammianus Marcellinus 14.1.4, 14.9.3 and 6.

[212] Ammianus Marcellinus 14.1.2, 14.7.7.

[213] Julian *Misopogon* 340 A; Ammianus Marcellinus 14.7.3.

[214] Sozomen *Hist. eccl.* 3.15 = PG 67.1084-1085.

[215] Sozomen *loc.cit.;* Philostorgius *Hist. eccl.* 3.15-17 and 27. See Hefele-Leclercq, *Conciles* 1.887-888, and Kidd, *Hist. of the Church* 2.152, 193-4.

In his religious zeal, Gallus was moved (perhaps by the advice of his counsellors) to adopt a striking device in an effort to combat paganism at Antioch. One of the most celebrated pagan spots in the locality was the Temple of Apollo at Daphne, with which there was associated an oracle at the spring of Castalia, one of the famous springs of Daphne. The temple and the oracle must still have possessed great influence; and Daphne itself was widely known as a place of pleasure. Gallus determined to counteract the influence of Apollo, and to give a holy atmosphere to Daphne, by transporting thither the relics of St. Babylas, one of the most celebrated martyrs of Antioch, who, as bishop of the city, had suffered under Decius in A.D. 250, just over one hundred years previously.[216] A martyrium was built near the Temple of Apollo and the spring of Castalia, which seem to have been near one another, and the saint's body was taken there from its original resting place in the Christian cemetery at Antioch.[217] The oracle of Apollo was silenced. This event is notable as being the first translation of a martyr's relics recorded in our extant sources.[218]

In A.D. 352 Magnentius, in an effort to cause trouble for Constantius and force him to come to a settlement, sent an agent to Antioch to assassinate Gallus. The agent enlisted the help of some of the troops stationed in the city, but he talked indiscreetly in the hearing of his hostess, an old woman who lived in a hut on the bank of the Orontes,

---

[216] See above, Ch. 11, nn. 144-145.

[217] Socrates *Hist. eccl.* 3.18 = *PG* 67.425; Sozomen *Hist. eccl.* 5.19 = *PG* 67.1273-1275; Rufinus *Hist. eccl.* 10.36; Chrysostom *De S. Babyla* 2-3 = *PG* 50.530ff.; Pseudo-Chrysostom *De S. Babyla contra Iulianum et gentiles* 12, 17, 23 = *PG* 50.551, 560, 570; Libanius *Or.* 60.5-6; Evagrius 1.16; Theodoret *Hist. eccl.* 3.10.1-2; Zonaras 13.12.39-40; cf. Ammianus Marcellinus 22.12.8. See G. Downey, "The Shrines of St. Babylas at Antioch and Daphne," *Antioch-on-the-Orontes* 2.45-48. The date of the translation of the relics to Daphne is nowhere given. The relics were later returned to Antioch by order of Julian the Apostate; see Ch. 13, nn. 42-43. The location of the Temple of Apollo and its physical relation to the spring of Castalia are nowhere explicitly stated. Some writers (Ammianus, Rufinus, Chrysostom in *PG* 50.531, Evagrius, Theodoret, all cited above) say that the body of Babylas was buried near the spring, while others (Socrates, Sozomen, cited above) indicate that it was near the temple. Unless these statements are inaccurate, it would appear (as one might naturally suppose in any case) that the temple was placed close to the spring. Ammianus writes that the bodies of several martyrs had been buried near the spring and were removed. All the other sources, however, speak only of the body of Babylas, and Ammianus' statement must be an inference from the response that many visitors say was given by the oracle to Julian, to the effect that the oracle was impeded by the presence of "bodies," this response being an allusion, in true oracular fashion, to the presence of the body of Babylas.

[218] H. Delehaye, *Origines du Culte*[2] 54. The reports of the taking of relics of the Apostles Andrew, Luke, and Timothy to Constantinople by Constantine the Great are not trustworthy; see Downey, "Original Church of the Apostles," with the further comments of F. Halkin, *Anal. Boll.* 70 (1952) 349-350.

and the plot was revealed to the caesar; and Magnentius' agent was taken and executed.[219]

The tyrannical behavior of Gallus reached a climax in the spring and early summer of A.D. 354. When he was about to set out for Hierapolis to take part in a campaign against the Persians, who were plotting a raid into Mesopotamia at about this time,[220] the people of Antioch appealed to him to take measures to deal with a famine that was believed to be imminent.[221] The reason for this expected scarcity is not stated in our sources; it may have been due to a failure of the local crops caused by bad weather, or to the unusual demand for food created by the presence at Antioch of the army (which ordinarily used only local sources of supplies), or possibly to both causes as was true at Antioch a few years later in the time of Julian the Apostate. In Syria, wheat and other cereal crops were planted after the November rains had fallen, and in the region of Antioch the harvest took place in May and June, before the dry summer set in.[222] Thus if the crops were to be deficient, the fact would be known by early spring, at about the time when Gallus would be preparing for a summer campaign. On the expectation of a scarcity of food, prices would have risen, and land-owners and merchants (including no doubt some of the prominent men in the city) would have begun to hoard their stocks in anticipation of a further rise in prices. When the people appealed to Gallus for relief, he ordered a reduction in prices. This was opposed, naturally, by the leaders of the local senate, who were interested, either directly or on behalf of their colleagues, in the rise of prices; and when the senators protested too vigorously against the caesar's order, he ordered them all executed.[223] The men were cast into prison, and expected to

[219] Zonaras 13.8.25-31; Ammianus Marcellinus 14.7.4.

[220] Ammianus Marcellinus 14.7.5; cf. 14.3.

[221] Ammianus speaks of a threatened famine in two passages, as though there were two separate episodes (14.7.2, 14.7.5ff.). However, it seems clear from the testimony of Libanius (Or. 1.96-103, Ep. 394a W. = 391 F., cf. Sievers, Leben des Libanius 63-65) that Ammianus' two notices refer to the same threat of famine; Ammianus evidently described the incidents separately for literary purposes; see Thompson, Ammianus Marcellinus 60-62. There had been a famine in Antioch (as well as in the whole eastern part of the Empire) in A.D. 333, which may have been caused (or aggravated) by the concentration of troops in preparation for the Persian War; see above, n. 160.

[222] Normally, no rain falls in northern Syria between April and November, while the winter months are rainy; see Ammianus Marcellinus 22.13.4, Liban. Or. 11.31, and Ch. Combier, "La climatologie de la Syrie et du Liban," Revue de géographie physique et de géologie dynamique 6 (1933) 319-346.

[223] Gallus' measures for dealing with the crisis may be compared with those adopted a few years later by Julian the Apostate in a similar situation. The causes and effects of the famine under Julian are much better known, as the sources are more abundant. It is safe to assume that the famine in the time of Gallus was accompanied by the hoarding,

lose their lives, but they were saved by the firm attitude of Honoratus, the *comes Orientis*, who opposed the caesar's decree,[224] and the senators were released on the day following their imprisonment. Evidently price control, if it was introduced at all, was unsuccessful, and popular demands for assistance continued. Gallus did not order a distribution of food or import supplies, as he might have done, but put the blame for the situation on Theophilus, the *consularis Syriae*, saying that there would be no scarcity of food if the governor did not wish it. By this time actual hunger had set in, and the populace first set fire to the house of a wealthy citizen named Eubulus (who may have been a wealthy merchant or landowner suspected of having something to do with the scarcity), and then seized the governor Theophilus and dragged and beat him to death. The people were later punished for this lynching by Constantius.[225]

It was at this juncture that Libanius, the celebrated sophist, returned to Antioch. He had been pursuing a highly successful career as a teacher and orator at Constantinople, but he was anxious to return to his native city and establish himself there; and after some difficulty he secured the consent of Constantius to the change, and so began the career that was to make him one of the most distinguished citizens of Antioch.[226] Libanius happened to arrive at Antioch just at the time when Gallus had condemned the recalcitrant members of the senate to death, and he visited the senators in the prison where they were awaiting execution.[227] On the next day they were released (through the efforts of the *comes Orientis* Honoratus, as we have seen), and on the day following that, Libanius appeared before Gallus, by command, and delivered a discourse. In a short while, however, Libanius fell into disfavor with the caesar, who had received false accusations against the sophist, and

---

manipulation, and speculation that we know accompanied the crisis under Julian. See below, Ch. 13, §1. On Ammianus' account of the famine under Gallus, see Thompson, *Ammianus Marcellinus* 60-63. Thompson appears to go too far in trying to justify Gallus' conduct in this episode.

[224] On the career of Honoratus, see G. Downey, *Comites Orientis* 12.

[225] Julian *Misopogon* 363 C, 370 C; Libanius *Or.* 19.47-49; see further below, n. 236. On the career of Theophilus, see Ensslin, "Theophilus," no. 22, *RE* 5A (1934) 2166.

[226] Förster and Münscher, "Libanios," *RE* 12 (1925) 2491, date Libanius' return to Antioch in A.D. 353, but it is certain that A.D. 354 is the correct date, especially because Libanius became involved in the events connected with the famine; see Sievers, *Leben des Libanius* 63-65, 215-217, and O. Seeck, "Zur Chronologie u. Quellenkritik des Ammianus Marcellinus," *Hermes* 41 (1906) 496-497. Libanius first came to Antioch on a four months' leave of absence from Constantinople; but he had to return to the capital and obtain permission for the permanent change. On Libanius' life and writings, see further in the chapter on the sources for the history of Antioch, Ch. 2, §5.

[227] Libanius *Or.* 1.96-97.

Gallus rather menacingly advised Libanius to leave Antioch. However, Libanius' old teacher Zenobius interceded for him, and he was allowed to remain.[228]

The career of Gallus was now rapidly drawing to a close. His conduct had been reported to Constantius unfavorably, and sometimes with exaggeration, by Thalassius, who had been appointed *praefectus praetorio Orientis* when Gallus was made caesar, and so had served as the chief officer of the administration at Gallus' court.[229] It was rumored that Gallus was plotting to make himself emperor; and in any case Constantius feared that his many victims might join forces and start a revolution.[230] Thalassius died early in 254. Constantius then deprived Gallus of his command over all troops save his palace guards, and sent Domitianus to Antioch as praetorian prefect, to replace Thalassius, with instructions to induce Gallus to leave Antioch and travel to the court of Constantius.[231] Domitianus when he reached Antioch behaved arrogantly and ordered Gallus to leave the city, threatening to cut off the supplies of his palace if he delayed. Gallus ordered the prefect arrested. On this, Montius, Gallus' quaestor, intervened with the palace troops in an effort to prevent the prefect's arrest, which would have serious consequences. Gallus then assembled the troops and accused Montius of insubordination, whereupon the troops, urged on by Luscus, the *curator* of the city, seized both Domitianus and Montius and dragged them through the streets until they were dead; the mutilated bodies were thrown into the Orontes.

There followed all kinds of rumors and investigations.[232] It was said that some of the tribunes in charge of the imperial arms factories at Antioch had promised weapons if a revolution were attempted. Domitianus' son-in-law was found to have made seditious remarks among the troops in Mesopotamia; and an imperial purple robe, made secretly, was discovered in a weaving establishment at Tyre. Ursicinus, the *magister militum*, who had been reporting on events to Constantius, was summoned from Nisibis to Antioch to take charge of the investigations, but he served only as a figurehead and the trials were actually

[228] Libanius *Or.* 1.99-100.

[229] Ammianus Marcellinus 14.1.10; cf. Seeck, *Regesten* 146.4ff.

[230] Zonaras 13.9.11ff.; Ammianus Marcellinus 14.7.9; John of Antioch frag. 74, p. 115, *Excerpta de insidiis* ed. De Boor; Socrates *Hist. eccl.* 2.34 = PG 67.296; Sozomen *Hist. eccl.* 4.7 = PG 67.1125; Zosimus 2.55; Jerome *Chronicle* 2370, p. 239 ed. Helm.

[231] Ammianus Marcellinus 14.7.9ff. gives the only detailed account of the following events. See also Libanius *Or.* 19.6, 42.24; Philostorgius *Hist. eccl.* 3.28.

[232] Ammianus Marcellinus 14.7.18-21, 14.9.1-9; Gregory of Nyssa *Contra Eunomium* 1 = PG 45.257 A.

directed by Gallus with the utmost savagery and disregard for legal procedure.

Constantius was by now thoroughly alarmed, and began once more to try to induce Gallus to come to him.[233] One of the emperor's envoys sent to Antioch for this purpose was Theophilus the Indian, who was at that time a favorite of Constantius.[234] The emperor finally succeeded in persuading Gallus' wife Constantia to set out, and she did so, hoping that she might be successful in interceding with the emperor, her brother, on behalf of her husband. On the way, however, she died in Bithynia of a sudden attack of fever. Gallus himself hesitated for a long while, but finally yielded to the arguments of an officer named Scudilo who was specially sent to persuade him. He at last set out for Constantius' court, in the autumn of A.D. 354, and was summarily tried and executed on the journey.[235]

After the death of Gallus, Constantius proceeded to the punishment of the caesar's friends and accomplices. The investigations did not take place in Antioch itself, where the proceedings might have stirred up popular feeling, but the prisoners were taken to Aquileia and tried and punished there.[236] Punishment was also imposed upon the people of Antioch in general, though the precise details of this are not known.[237]

For the next few years Constantius remained in the West, occupied first with operations against the German tribes and with the revolt of Silvanus in Gaul (A.D. 355), later with campaigns in the Danube region (A.D. 357-359).[238] During these years three episodes, almost concurrent, form the history of Antioch, namely the events that led finally, in A.D. 359, to the renewal of the Persian war; the persecution of paganism which began in A.D. 357; and the developments in 357 and 358 which

---

[233] Ammianus Marcellinus 14.11.1ff.; Philostorgius *Hist. eccl.* 4.1; Julian *Epist. ad Athen.* 272.

[234] Philostorgius *loc.cit.*; cf. Ensslin, "Theophilos," no. 35, *RE* 5A (1934) 2167.

[235] Ammianus Marcellinus 14.11.23; on the date, see O. Seeck, "Zur Chronologie u. Quellenkritik des Ammianus Marcellinus," *Hermes* 41 (1906) 498-499, and "Constantius Gallus," no. 5, *RE* 4 (1901) 1099.

[236] Ammianus Marcellinus 15.3.1ff. It may have been at this time that Luscus, the *curator* of Antioch, was burned to death for his part in the deaths of Domitianus and Montius (Amm. Marc. 14.7.17). Thompson, *Ammianus Marcellinus* 64, suggests that Luscus was executed shortly after the deaths of Domitianus and Montius, possibly by Gallus himself. In support of this he quotes the words of Philostorgius *Hist. eccl.* 3.28, συνεπιψηφίζοντος καὶ τοῦ Γάλλου. This passage in Philostorgius refers, however, not to the death of Luscus, but to those of Domitianus and Montius. It seems unlikely that Gallus would have punished Luscus if he had approved of his deed, or that he would have allowed himself to be persuaded to execute Luscus.

[237] See above, n. 225.

[238] See Piganiol, *Empire chrétien* 92-100.

made Antioch the stronghold of Arianism. The difficulties within the church may be described first.

As long as Constans lived, Constantius was forced to abstain at least to some extent from the attack on Athanasius and the orthodox Christians; for Constans supported Athanasius and was instrumental in having him reinstated in Alexandria in A.D. 346.[239] However, when the death of Constans in A.D. 350 and the defeat of Magnentius in A.D. 351 left Constantius sole emperor, with more time to devote to ecclesiastical affairs, the position of the Arian party became more favorable.[240] So long as Constantius remained in the West, the principal events in the struggle took part there. Athanasius was again condemned, and in A.D. 356 was driven from Alexandria into exile, by imperial troops; and it appeared that there would be no further trouble in the church. In the same year, evidently thinking that the theological difficulties were finally solved, Constantius began a systematic attack on paganism; sacrifices, magic, and divination were all forbidden.[241]

At about this time we have evidence in connection with Antioch of the way in which the government was endeavoring to protect the immunities from compulsory municipal services which had been granted to the Christian clergy by Constantine the Great. Constantine's grant had been abused by decurions who had themselves ordained in order to escape their civic obligations, and there was no doubt an effort on the part of the local administrations to restrict the claims to immunity. In the case of Antioch we have a decree of Constantius and Julian—to be dated some time after A.D. 355, when Constantius made Julian his colleague—reaffirming the exemption of the clergy from compulsory public services.[242]

In the year following the exile of Athanasius, the disputes on the relationship between the Father and the Son were renewed; and the turn of events in this year (A.D. 357) once more brought Antioch into prominence in the question. The second Council of Sirmium had just adopted a formula concerning the Father and the Son which was basically Arian; and soon after this the Arians enjoyed a major success at Antioch. The bishop of the city, Leontius, who had been a crypto-Arian, died in A.D. 357, and the election of Eudoxius as his successor

[239] See Kidd, *Hist. of the Church* 2.93-101.

[240] See Kidd, *Hist. of the Church* 2.117ff.

[241] See Piganiol, *Empire chrétien* 96ff., also Downey, "Original Church of the Apostles" 72ff.

[242] *CTh* 16.2.16. On the exemptions of the clergy and the various modifications introduced in their immunities at different times see Jones, *Greek City* 198, with n. 83 on p. 346.

in the following year turned the city into a stronghold of Arianism. Eudoxius was the leader of the extreme Arians, called Anomoeans because they denied even a resemblance between the Father and the Son; and in the year of his election he presided at a council of the Anomoeans at Antioch at which the ultra-Arian position was reaffirmed.[243] Eudoxius maintained this cause at Antioch while it was failing elsewhere, but his translation from Antioch to the see of Constantinople in A.D. 360 posed a new problem when it became necessary to find a successor at Antioch, where the orthodox had always maintained themselves in the face of the occupation of the bishopric by Arians or crypto-Arians. Meletius, bishop of Beroea, was chosen, as a man who, it was thought, could reconcile the parties. However, he astonished his supporters by betraying orthodox sentiments, and was banished.[244] In his place, in A.D. 361, there was appointed the Arian Euzoius, who was to remain bishop of the city until 378. He called a council at Antioch in 361 which issued one final Arian creed, the most extreme of such statements.[245] Soon after this, Constantius died (3 November A.D. 361); and under his successor Julian the Apostate the problems of the Church were to be of a different nature, as the Christians united in the effort to counter the new emperor's pagan revival.

Such was the history of the Church at Antioch during Constantius' last years. At the same time the more prominent pagans in the city suddenly found themselves in great danger. The campaign against paganism which Constantius had begun in A.D. 356 had lapsed when, in the spring of the following year, the emperor visited Rome for the first time and saw the full majesty of the pagan faith in the ancient capital.[246] However, on 3 July A.D. 357, Constantius issued a decree that was designed to put an end to the consultation, by members of the court, of oracles, augurs, interpreters of dreams, and other diviners; the decree provided, contrary to all precedent, that the officials could be questioned under torture if they were accused of such practices.[247] This measure was adopted, largely because many high officials had been consulting the oracle of Bes at Abydos in Egypt, but it could be put

[243] Socrates *Hist. eccl.* 2.37 = *PG* 67.304; Sozomen *Hist. eccl.* 4.12 = *PG* 67.1141-1144; Philostorgius *Hist. eccl.* 4.4; see Kidd, *Hist. of the Church* 2.154, 157-158; Piganiol, *Empire chrétien* 103.
[244] Sozomen *Hist. eccl.* 4.28 = *PG* 67.1201-1204; Theodoret *Hist. eccl.* 2.31; see Kidd, *Hist. of the Church* 2.179-180.
[245] Socrates *Hist. eccl.* 2.45 = *PG* 67.360-361; Sozomen *Hist. eccl.* 4.28-29 = *PG* 67.1204-1205; see Kidd, *Hist. of the Church* 2.181.
[246] Piganiol, *Empire chrétien* 97-98.
[247] *CTh* 9.16.6. On the date, see Seeck, *Regesten* 83.38.

into operation against anyone suspected of superstitious practices, and could be a powerful weapon where there was any suspicion of treason. The imperial *notarius* Paulus, a man famous for cruelty, and the *comes Orientis* Domitianus Modestus were put in charge of carrying out the law.[248] They established their headquarters at Scythopolis in Palestine, because it was secluded and was midway between Antioch and Alexandria, where most of the accused persons were to be found. Many prominent men were tortured and executed, and anyone who gave any sign of magical practice, such as the wearing of an amulet to guard against disease, became a victim. The alarm and anxiety in Antioch were great,[249] and a terrifying portent appeared at Daphne, in the birth of a monstrous infant, reported to have been born with two heads, two sets of teeth, a beard, four eyes, and two very small ears.[250] This was regarded as an omen that the state was destined for deformity.

All this was happening while events were leading up to the renewal of the Persian war. In A.D. 355, the year following the death of Gallus, Strategius Musonianus, the *praefectus praetorio*, undertook diplomatic overtures designed to turn the truce with Persia into a permanent peace. Antioch was the headquarters of the negotiations, and Themistius speaks of seeing envoys from Susa and Ecbatana in the city.[251] Sapor, however, was falsely given to understand that the Romans were weak and were being constrained to sue for peace. On this basis he made excessive territorial demands that were quite unacceptable, and he threatened war if his conditions were not met (A.D. 358).[252] Alarm spread in Antioch.[253] In the next year Sapor followed up his threats by invading Mesopotamia. On learning of this, Constantius left Sirmium, where he had been making his headquarters, and went to Constantinople (autumn 359), where he spent the winter in order to be ready for another invasion if it came.[254] He doubtless chose Constantinople as his headquarters on this occasion not only because he wished to show favor to the new capital[255] but because Antioch was in a state

---

[248] The investigation is described by Ammianus 19.12.
[249] See Sievers, *Leben des Libanius* 79-81. Libanius describes a scene of torture in *Ep.* 112 W. = 112 F.
[250] Ammianus Marcellinus 19.12.19.
[251] Ammianus Marcellinus 16.9; Themistius *Or.* 4.57 B. Allusions to the negotiations, and to the activities of the envoys in Antioch, appear in several letters of Libanius: *Ep.* 1196 W. = 468 F.; *Ep.* 1261 W. = 463 F.; *Ep.* 419 W. = 505 F.; *Ep.* 475 W. = 561 F. See Stein, *Gesch.* 1.239; Piganiol, *Empire chrétien* 100.
[252] Ammianus Marcellinus 17.5.
[253] Libanius *Ep.* 47 W. = 49 F.; Ammianus Marcellinus 18.4.2.
[254] Ammianus Marcellinus 20.8.1.
[255] Cf. Piganiol, *Empire chrétien* 104-105.

of unrest as a result of the inquisitions of Paulus and Domitianus Modestus, begun the previous summer. Moreover, memories of the tyranny of Gallus and of the disorders and punishments that had accompanied and followed his regime would not have made Antioch a comfortable place of residence for the emperor at this time.

At this period the career of the Caesar Julian in Gaul was drawing toward a climax. The son of the half-brother of Constantine the Great, he was a half-brother of Gallus and a cousin of Constantius. Educated in seclusion, he had secretly become a pagan.[256] After the execution of Gallus in A.D. 355, Constantius, in need of assistance in Gaul, appointed Julian caesar; and the young man quickly showed himself a capable soldier and administrator. In time, however, he came into conflict with the advisers and officers with whom he was surrounded by Constantius, and it seemed possible that he might eventually meet the same fate as Gallus. Late in A.D. 359 Constantius took away Julian's best troops, ostensibly (and perhaps actually) because they were needed for the Persian war. Julian began to fear for his life; and in February A.D. 360 his troops, who were loyal to him and hostile to Constantius, proclaimed him emperor.

This news was brought to Constantius in March A.D. 360 at Caesarea in Cappadocia, while he was en route for a campaign against the Persians.[257] An attempt was made at negotiation; Constantius continued with his Persian campaign, Julian carried on his duties in Gaul. At the end of the year, having suffered severe losses in his operations against the Persians, Constantius went to Antioch and spent the winter there.[258] While in the city he celebrated his marriage with Faustina, his third wife, his second wife Eusebia having died some time previously.[259] In May A.D. 361 Constantius went out against the Persians, but learned that they did not intend to take the field that year, their omens having declared that a campaign should not be undertaken. In the mean time Julian, having discovered that Constantius was inciting a barbarian prince to attack him, saw that he must come to a settlement with the emperor. He set out from Gaul with his army, and marched toward Illyricum. When this news reached Constantius in the field, he returned to Antioch by forced marches,[260] made his preparations as

---

[256] On the sources for the life of Julian, and the modern studies of it, see below in the next chapter.

[257] Ammianus Marcellinus 20.9.1.

[258] Ammianus Marcellinus 20.11.32, 21.6.1; *CTh* 12.2.16.

[259] Ammianus Marcellinus 21.6.4.

[260] Ammianus Marcellinus 21.13.8, 21.15.1.

quickly as possible, and set out in the autumn to march toward Julian and his forces. En route he fell ill with a fever, and died at Mopsucrene (just beyond Tarsus), aged forty, on 3 November A.D. 361, after having, for the sake of the empire and the dynasty, designated Julian as his successor.[261]

11. Municipal Life at Antioch in the Middle of the Fourth Century: Libanius

The municipal life of Antioch during the middle and latter part of the century is one of the subjects in the history of the city about which we know most. Our abundant material on the political, economic, and social life of this time is provided primarily by the voluminous preserved writings of Libanius, whose orations, pamphlets, and letters fill six volumes in the Teubner edition of his works.[262] Additional evidence for this period comes from the writings of St. John Chrysostom, the Emperor Julian, and Ammianus Marcellinus; but Libanius constitutes our principal source. Born in Antioch in A.D. 314 into a prominent senatorial family, Libanius grew up in his native city, and after studying in Athens and beginning his highly successful teaching career in Constantinople, he settled in Antioch in A.D. 354. Having already established his reputation as a teacher of rhetoric in the imperial capital, Libanius soon became a leading public figure in his own city, and his school attracted students from all over the Greek East. His public activity continued for almost forty years, until A.D. 393 (or later), and the keen interest he took in everything that happened in Antioch, and his passionate concern for the welfare of the city, can be seen in all his writings, which became famous in his own day and were carefully preserved and studied in succeeding generations. Thanks to Libanius' special attachment to the city that he considered surpassed all others, we know more about Antioch at this time than during any other period of its existence.

The notable phase of Libanius' political activity began in the reign of Theodosius I (A.D. 379-395), and this will be treated in Chapter 15. However, Libanius begins to supply us with a detailed picture of all phases of life in Antioch from the latter years of the reign of Constantius. Since this material has recently been collected and exhaustively studied by Paul Petit in his monumental work *Libanius et la vie munici-*

[261] Ammianus Marcellinus 21.15.1-3.
[262] For the bibliography of the modern studies of Libanius, see the chapter describing the literary sources for the history of Antioch, above, Ch. 2, §5, with n. 60.

pale à Antioche au IVe siècle après J.-C. (1955), accompanied by his detailed study of Libanius' teaching activities, *Les étudiants de Libanius* (1956),[263] it will be sufficient here and in Chapter 15 to present the general outlines of the knowledge we gain from Libanius.

We should realize first of all that Libanius' career, both as a teacher and as a leading spokesman for his fellow-citizens, is significant testimony to the importance that attached at that time to rhetoric in education. Antioch at this period was a major center of education in the Greek tradition, and Libanius was the successor of famous teachers, the sophist Ulpian, the leading representative of his discipline in Antioch under Constantine the Great; his pupil Prohaeresius; and Zenobius, who had been Libanius' teacher.[264] The prestige of a successful teacher of rhetoric was great; and when Libanius to this added the effect of his own remarkable personality (and perhaps the influence of his family connections), he easily became, and remained, the most prominent private citizen, and the most prominent pagan, in the Antioch of his day. We shall see in the account of the reign of Theodosius I that Libanius was on occasion more powerful, and more respected, than some of the *comites Orientis* and the *consulares Syriae* who had their headquarters in Antioch and governed the city.

While some modern critics, on the basis of an incomplete knowledge of his work and its context, have thought of Libanius simply as a *laudator temporis acti*, a careful study of his writings shows that he was in fact a devoted and highly articulate representative of the political, social, and cultural tradition of the ancient Greek *polis*, which, as he shows us, still survived very strongly in the cities of the eastern Roman provinces. Antioch was able, as the metropolis of Syria and the capital of the Diocese of the Orient, to preserve both its economic well-being and its intellectual and cultural activity; and thanks to Libanius we are in a position to know more about the daily life and the interests and activities of Antioch in the middle and latter part of the fourth century than we do about any other Graeco-Roman city at that period.

Libanius enables us to see, first, what the traditions and the existing institutions were, and then how they were affected by the development of the Roman economic and political system, and we can follow the way in which the traditions survived, modified by the contemporary developments outside Antioch. We see all this in terms both of per-

---

[263] Petit's two volumes together comprise 652 pages.
[264] Eunapius, *Lives of the Philosophers* 486-487. See Christ-Schmid-Stählin, *Gesch. d. gr. Lit.*⁶ 986, and Petit, *Les étudiants de Libanius* 85-86, 92-94, 97, 99, 111.

sons—altogether 731 individuals are known from the works of Libanius[265]—and of institutions. The interests and activities of a number of families and of classes and groups, such as the leading senators and landowners, the professional men, and the imperial officials resident in Antioch, can all be traced in some detail.

One of the most important services of Libanius is to allow us to see the cultural life of the *polis* as this had maintained itself at Antioch. We get a very strong sense of the vigorous educational and cultural activity of the city, supported as they were by the economic prosperity and political prestige which Antioch enjoyed. This cultural life is vividly attested by the mosaics discovered in the excavations, with their classical motifs and their scenes from Greek mythology and literature. Libanius, always conscious of the past out of which the present grew, looked back to the Greek origin of Antioch, with its Athenian colonists, and to him the city of his own day was above all the natural heir of this past. In his encomium of Antioch, the *Antiochikos* (*Or.* 11) we see what six and a half centuries of such history meant to Libanius and his fellow citizens. If the city appears from Libanius' writings to be often preoccupied with public festivals and athletic contests, and with the local Olympic Games, celebrated in each Julian leap-year, this was because such activities and enjoyments represented an essential part of the life of the Greek city. In this framework there was no room for Christianity, which, to Libanius and his friends, not only played no part in the traditional life of the *polis*, but was an avowed enemy of the tradition itself. It was the Greek heritage, not the new religion, that was the living reality. As the recognized custodian and exponent of the Greek tradition, Libanius thought of himself, and was thought of by the people of the city, as a key figure, and his career shows us the way in which the educational system was regarded as the proved and accepted means by which the tradition was preserved.[266]

Nevertheless Libanius was very much aware that changes had taken place in public life and that some of the constituent elements and the activities of the *polis* had been fundamentally affected. He recognized clearly the alterations that had been brought about by Roman rule and by the development of society in the Empire as a whole, and he had an accurate understanding of what had happened and what this meant for the traditional culture. He opposed any threat to the culture

[265] Petit, *Libanius et la vie municipale à Antioche au IVe siècle après J.-C.* 359.
[266] On the political and social significance of the educational system in this respect, see J. W. H. Walden, *The Universities of Ancient Greece* (New York 1909), and G. Downey, "Ancient Education," *Classical Journal* 52 (1956-57) 337-345.

whenever he could, though he also tried to accept the changes as gracefully as possible when this was necessary.

Antioch in Libanius' time was beginning to show the effects of the reorganization of the government and the controls of social and economic life which had been introduced by Diocletian and Constantine the Great in an effort to save the state from the grave dangers that had begun to threaten it in the third century. The growth of the army and the bureaucracy, the increasing need for money for the expanded activities of the government, and the inflation resulting from Constantine's military plans and his elaborate building program, had all had the effect of depressing the economic condition of all classes except the wealthy. On all these developments Libanius gives us information that is not available elsewhere. Basically, he shows us, the problem was a financial one. The revenues of the city came, in principle, from the municipal lands the city owned, but much of the income from these was now being paid into the imperial *res privata* for the use of the government. This meant that the money for the upkeep of the city must now come largely from other sources. This created a new burden. With the disappearance of elected municipal officials in the third century, the responsibility for the municipal administration of Antioch and for the maintenance of the public services had now fallen on the local senators, who were forced not only to discharge routine public duties such as the regulation of the markets and provision for public order, but to meet the cost of the upkeep of the streets and aqueducts, to provide for the heating of the public baths, and to defray the expenses of the public games and festivals (including the Olympic Games) and hippodrome races, and to furnish transportation for grain, which was the basic element in the city's food supply. This burden was a heavy one, since the fiscal policies of Constantine the Great and Constantius had had the effect of reducing the number of wealthy senators and landowners. The farmers and working people of the city who had to supply labor and animals for the corvées also found themselves heavily burdened. Libanius lets us see how these developments worked not only to place a major responsibility on a small group of senatorial families—the *protoi*—which still retained their fortunes to some extent, but gave them an increasing amount of influence and power—a power which was sometimes used in favor of the propertied classes rather than for the benefit of the city as a whole.[267] To offset

[267] One example of this may be seen in the way in which the wealthy landowners hoarded grain during the famine which occurred during the reign of Julian; see below, Ch. 13, §1.

this power, we learn of the institution of new imperial functionary, the *defensor civitatis*, a law officer whose duty it was to protect the poor against the exactions of the wealthy and of unscrupulous imperial officials. Libanius himself had a deep and sincere interest in the reform of the social order and in the improvement of the administration of justice, matters with which he seems to have been much more concerned than many of his contemporaries, and his writings on these subjects, which are remarkable for that time, provide us with information we would not otherwise have had.[268]

While it had to take on new tasks and responsibilities, the local senate did retain some of its deliberative functions.[269] It continued to meet in the *bouleuterion* built by Antiochus Epiphanes.[270] Some of the meetings were presided over by imperial officials, sometimes the senate met alone. The deliberations dealt with questions of public order; with the educational facilities of the city; with the use of the public lands (Libanius and the other publicly appointed teachers were paid from some of the remaining revenues of the municipal lands); with the organization of festivals and shows; and with the collection of taxes imposed by the state. On occasion the senate offered advice to the imperial governors on matters of legislation.

One of the matters of major public interest with which the senators and their families had an intimate connection was the food supply, and Libanius gives us a detailed and valuable picture of the problems that could arise in this area. The wealthy families supplied themselves and their households with food from their properties near Antioch and elsewhere in northern Syria, but it was also necessary to assure a supply of provisions for the remainder of the population of the city, especially the poor. Because of the high cost and slowness of transportation, most of this food had to come from the neighborhood of the city, and it was distributed through the markets and small shops. When a local famine occurred as a result of unfavorable weather, plague, or insect pests, not only the supplies but the distribution and prices were dislocated, and extreme suffering might follow. During Libanius' career at Antioch there were three local famines, in A.D. 354, 362-363, and 382-384, and the detailed evidence that can be collected for these from his works gives us one of our most valuable insights into the special

---

[268] On this area of Libanius' interests, see especially Pack, *Studies in Libanius*, which includes a translation, with commentary, of *Or.* 45, *On the Prisoners*.

[269] Libanius *Or.* 35, gives us a picture of the duties of the *curia*.

[270] Libanius makes a number of allusions to the *bouleuterion* which give us useful information on its construction. See Petit, *Libanius et la vie municipale à Antioche au IVᵉ siècle après J.-C.* 64.

problems and difficulties connected with food supplies in the Roman Empire at that time.[271]

Except for the periods of the famines, Libanius shows us that the commercial life of the city was usually brisk, although it was organized in such a way that the best part of the profits went to the landowners. It is evident from what Libanius says that Antioch was able to maintain a satisfactory level of economic activity even while some of the smaller cities of Syria were suffering difficulties. In this connection one feature of Libanius' testimony that has attracted special interest is the way in which he refers to what has been taken to be unusual building activity in Antioch during his lifetime. He mentions a number of new buildings and tells how old ones were being replaced.[272] It may well be that there was an unusual amount of such activity in Antioch in the middle and latter part of the fourth century; but it must be remembered that Libanius was above all a patriot, always interested in emphasizing the superiority and the prosperity of his own city. We must also bear in mind that our extant sources do not provide us with comparable information for other periods in the history of Antioch,[273] so that the activity Libanius describes so enthusiastically may in reality be only the normal construction work that one would expect to find in a city like Antioch.

One special feature of city life to which Libanius often refers is the effect on Antioch of its being a great military center as the headquarters of the *comes Orientis* and the base for the vital operations on the Euphrates frontier. The neighborhood of Antioch was filled with permanent camps and training grounds, so that there were soldiers and military officials constantly in the city, and when a major campaign was being prepared, the city was uncomfortably crowded. There resulted, as might be expected, a number of problems, social, economic, and administrative;[274] and here again Libanius' writings give us much more information on this important subject than we possess for any other city of the Roman Empire at this period.

[271] The famines are studied in detail by Petit, *op.cit.* 107-122. For accounts of these episodes, see above, nn. 221-224, and below, Ch. 13, §1; Ch. 15, §2.

[272] A list of the buildings mentioned by Libanius is drawn up by Petit, *op.cit.* 315-316. These are mentioned in the appropriate places in the present study; see the entries for them in the Index.

[273] Except in the special case of Procopius' accounts of the rebuilding of Antioch after the severe earthquakes and the devastation by the Persians in the reign of Justinian; see below, Ch. 18, §§5-8.

[274] A characteristic part of the problem is illustrated by Libanius' *Or.* 47, *De patrociniis* (edited and translated by L. Harmand [Paris 1955]). See Petit, *op.cit.* 188-190.

Finally, Libanius (along with his friend the Emperor Julian) provides valuable insight into the relationships between Christianity and paganism in Antioch, insight which is of special interest to us because of the importance of Antioch both as a center of Hellenism and as a stronghold of Christianity. As one of the principal pagan spokesmen of the day, Libanius shows us a reaction against Christianity which was significantly different from those of the other great pagan leaders, the orator Themistius of Constantinople and the Emperor Julian. Libanius never had any real understanding of the nature of Christianity, and could see only some of the less attractive features of the new religion, as they were embodied for example in the sometimes disreputable behavior of the monks in and around Antioch.[275] A number of Libanius' friends and pupils were Christians, and for them as individuals he seems to have felt respect and esteem; but Christianity itself he regarded as a subversive and un-Hellenic force, and on the whole he ignored it. The contrast of his attitude with that of Themistius, who set out to compete with Christianity, or that of the Emperor Julian, who finally attempted to destroy it, is instructive.[276] Libanius' most important contribution in this matter is to give us welcome evidence concerning the strength of Christianity at Antioch, a topic on which, for the Empire as a whole at this time, we do not have much reliable information. We are enabled to see which officials and which members of the senatorial class were Christians, and what the proportion of Christians was among Libanius' students, who would in time become leaders in the professions and the imperial administration.[277] Christianity, it appears, was especially strong among the lower classes, less so (if we are to trust Libanius) among the middle classes.

[275] Libanius' *Or.* 30, *Pro Templis*, shows how high passions could become on these matters.

[276] On the attitudes of Themistius and Julian, see the studies by the present writer, "Education in the Christian Roman Empire: Christian and Pagan Theories under Constantine and his Successors," *Speculum* 32 (1957) 48-61; "Themistius and the Defense of Hellenism in the Fourth Century," *HTR* 50 (1957) 259-274; "The Emperor Julian and the Schools," *Classical Journal* 53 (1957-58) 97-103.

[277] The study of this subject by Petit, *op.cit.* 200-203, is very interesting.

CHAPTER 13

JULIAN THE PHILOSOPHER, A.D. 361-363

Thanks to the abundance of the sources, notably Julian's own writings and the works of Libanius, the events of Julian's reign at Antioch are known in some detail. The emperor's residence in the city (18 July A.D. 362—5 March A.D. 363) formed the middle part of his reign, and in many ways the most important portion of his brief career.[1]

1. JULIAN AT ANTIOCH

After the death of Constantius on 3 November A.D. 361, Julian proceeded to Constantinople, where he made a triumphal entry on 11 December. While spending the winter at the capital, he set in motion a purge of the advisers and close associates of Constantius, and began a series of measures for the reorganization of the government, the first of which was a substantial reduction in the number of the servants and officials of the court, notably the secret service. Julian's legislation at this period was primarily concerned with the establishment of freedom of worship and the restoration of their rights and property to pagans. He also recalled from exile all the bishops who had been banished under Constantius. Julian's ultimate plans envisaged not only the revival of Hellenism for its own sake and the elimination of Christianity as an unworthy cult, but the substitution of Hellenism as a "religion of good citizenship"[2] for the Christian faith, which in the view of Julian and others had been discredited by the attempt to set up an Arian state church dominated by the political ideas of Constantine and Constantius. The resulting tensions within the church had shown that Arianism was an impossible system, and the reaction

---

[1] For accounts of Julian's life and reign, see Allard, *Julien²*; Geffcken, *Julianus*; E. von Borries, "Iulianus," no. 26, *RE* 10 (1919) 26-91; A. Rostagni, *Giuliano l'Apostata* (Turin 1920); J. Bidez, *La Vie de l'empereur Julien* (Paris 1930), with a revised edition in German, *Julian der Abtrünnige*, transl. by H. Rinn (Munich 1940); also Piganiol, *Empire chrétien* 127ff. Libanius' relations with Julian are fully described by Sievers, *Leben des Libanius* 91-124, and by Petit, *Libanius et la vie municipale à Antioche*. Special studies are cited below. The principal bibliography on Julian is listed by Piganiol, *Empire chrétien* 110-111, note, and elsewhere in his account of Julian. For an excellent brief analysis of Julian's political ideas and political program, see Jeanne Croissant, "Un nouveau Discours de Thémistius," *Serta Leodiensia* (Liége 1930) 22ff. On Ammianus' picture of Julian, see Thompson, *Ammianus Marcellinus* 72ff. On Julian's writings as a source for the history of Antioch, see Ch. 2, §5. Details concerning the life of Antioch at this period which it seems unnecessary to reproduce here may be found in Petit's monograph cited above.

[2] The phrase is that of Cochrane, *Christianity and Classical Culture²* 285.

against the Arians and their aims paved the way for Julian's reforms. However, it was not until he went to Antioch in the summer of A.D. 362 that Julian's plans were fully put into motion.[3]

Julian left Constantinople for Antioch at some time after the middle of May A.D. 362, and after traveling through Asia Minor he reached the Syrian capital on 18 July.[4] He was eager to reach the city,[5] and one indication of the importance he attached to his coming residence there was his appointment early in his reign of his uncle Julian (his mother's brother) to the influential post of *comes Orientis*.[6] This appointment would ensure important support for the emperor's program, and it is plain from the promptness with which the appointment was made, and from the elder Julian's having been sent to Antioch at once in advance of the emperor's coming, that Antioch was looked upon by the new regime as an important center for its activities.

There were evidently several motives in Julian's mind when he made his plans to go to Antioch.[7] One practical consideration was that Julian planned to carry on the war against Persia. After the death of Constantius, Sapor had tried to make peace, but Julian was determined to administer a decisive check to the Persians and to reestablish the prestige of the Roman Empire; and although the Persians, wishing peace, would not invade Mesopotamia in the summer of A.D. 362, Julian evidently wished to spend some time at Antioch, the best headquarters for campaigns against the Persians, in order to make unusually careful preparations.[8]

It also seems likely that Julian looked upon Antioch as a more suitable headquarters for his religious program than Constantinople. Antioch, it was true, was an important center of Christianity, perhaps

[3] No attempt can be made in this place to treat in detail Julian's program for the revival of Hellenism, which has formed the subject of a number of studies, notably the biography of Bidez (cited above, n. 1) and the study of Cochrane, *Christianity and Classical Culture*[2] 261-291. In general, only those aspects of the program which directly concern Julian's sojourn at Antioch will be discussed here. On Julian's educational program, see G. Downey, "The Emperor Julian and the Schools," *Classical Journal* 53 (1957) 97-103.

[4] The emperor was in Constantinople on 12 May (*CTh* 13.3.4). He reached Antioch on the day of the lamentations in the festival of Adonis (Ammianus Marcellinus 22.9.14), which took place on 18 July (see Bidez, *Vie de Julien* 400, n. 1; *Julian der Abtrünnige* 419, n. 1; F. Cumont in *Syria* 8 [1927] 339).

[5] Ammianus Marcellinus 22.9.14; Julian *Misopogon* 367 C.

[6] On the career of Julian's uncle, see Seeck, "Iulianos," no. 39, *RE* 10 (1919) 94-95, and J. Bidez in *Mélanges P. Thomas* (Bruges 1930) 57-63.

[7] For a special study of Julian's reasons for making his headquarters at Antioch, see Downey, "Julian at Antioch," the principal results of which are reproduced here.

[8] Stein, *Gesch.* 1.261; Bidez, *Vie de Julien* 315-316, *Julian der Abtrünnige* 332-333; cf. Ammianus Marcellinus 22.9.2.

even more important, in this respect, than Constantinople; most of its population, especially the common people, seem to have been Christians, at least nominally.[9] However, the Syrian capital was also an ancient center of Hellenism, with its famous temples, including the celebrated shrines at Daphne, and the local Olympic Games, which drew visitors and competitors from all over the Roman world; moreover, Julian's friend, the famous pagan teacher Libanius, was now established at Antioch. All these factors were potentially of great importance for Julian's program; and while the frivolous and unstable character of the population of Antioch may eventually have deceived his hopes for a Hellenic revival, the city at least seemed to offer attractions that Constantinople did not possess.

A third, although less important, motive may have influenced Julian in establishing himself at Antioch. His program included an effort to win the support of the Jews, in return for which he undertook— unsuccessfully, as it proved—the rebuilding of the Temple at Jerusalem.[10] Antioch possessed an important Jewish community, and it may well have been that Julian, in going to the city, counted upon gaining the support of its leaders.[11] Libanius, one of Julian's principal supporters, was a friend of Gamaliel, son of the Jewish Patriarch Hillel II, who himself was later to become patriarch as Gamaliel V.[12]

Before Julian arrived at Antioch, there had developed in the city a difficult and disagreeable economic situation, which, as it proved, was to dominate the whole of his sojourn there.[13] Constantius' war with Magnentius, and the preparations for the Persian war, had produced an inflation that must have affected most of the people at Antioch.[14]

[9] This seems to be the meaning of Julian's allusion in the *Misopogon*, 357 D. On the size of the population in Julian's time, see below, Excursus 2.

[10] Chrysostom *Adversus Judaeos* 5.11 = *PG* 48.900-901; Socrates *Hist. eccl.* 3.20 = *PG* 67.428-432. The authenticity of Julian's letter to the Jews (*Ep.* 204 ed. Bidez-Cumont) is disputed; see the introduction to the letter in the edition of Bidez and Cumont, and Piganiol, *Empire chrétien* 138, n. 74. On Julian's relations with the Jews, see Bidez, *Vie de Julien* 305-309, *Julian der Abtrünnige* 321-326; Piganiol, *Empire chrétien* 138; J. Vogt, *Kaiser Julian u. das Judentum* (Leipzig 1939; *Morgenland*, Heft 30); Simon, *Verus Israel* 139-144.

[11] See Kraeling, "Jewish Community at Antioch" 156-158.

[12] Piganiol, *Empire chrétien* 138; Seeck, *Briefe des Libanius* 162; W. Bacher, "Gamaliel V," *Jewish Encyclopedia* 5.562-563.

[13] This account of the city's economic condition is based on Downey, "Economic Crisis under Julian." A study of the same subject has been written by P. de Jonge, "Scarcity of Corn and Cornprices in Ammianus Marcellinus," *Mnemosyne*, ser. 4, vol. 1 (1948) 238-245, in which the material is treated somewhat differently, although the results are substantially the same.

[14] Piganiol, *Empire chrétien* 80, 297; A. H. M. Jones, "Inflation under the Roman Empire," *Economic History Review*, ser. 2, vol. 5 (1953) 304.

In addition, the presence at Antioch of the soldiers and officials assembled there in connection with the Persian campaigns must have had the inevitable effect of raising prices, especially since the importation of goods was difficult and costly because of the cumbersome means of transportation.[15] There had been a famine in the time of Gallus,[16] and the city was once more crowded with troops in the summer of A.D. 360,[17] so that the economic situation must have been difficult by that time.[18] The troops themselves no doubt did little to mitigate the economic difficulties their presence caused; Libanius describes the way in which a soldier could bully a market vendor.[19] When Julian became emperor late in A.D. 361, Antioch sent the customary delegation to offer congratulations, and the occasion was doubtless taken to describe the city's troubles to the new emperor. Julian responded by remitting the arrears of the tribute, which had accumulated, and by increasing membership in the local senate by two hundred.[20] The seriousness of the situation may be gauged by the fact that Julian forgave the arrears of tribute in spite of his pressing need for funds in connection with his military preparations.

However, when Julian reached Antioch, on 18 July A.D. 362, he found that the situation had become even worse; and the day of his arrival was ill-omened (at least for Julian and the pagans) because it happened to be the second day of the annual festival of Adonis, when the death of the god was being lamented.[21] By particular bad luck, a drought at the beginning of the winter of A.D. 361/2 had caused the failure of the local wheat crop, which normally would have been harvested in May and June A.D. 362.[22] Although it must have been

[15] See Jones, *Greek City* 261.   [16] See above, Ch. 12, nn. 221-224.
[17] Libanius *Or.* 11.177-178 (written in the summer of A.D. 360). Julian (*Misop.* 370 B) and Socrates (*Hist. eccl.* 3.17 = *PG* 67.424 B) both comment upon the effect on prices of the presence of troops and of visitors and officials.
[18] On the effects on a local economy of the presence of an army, see E. Gren, *Kleinasien u. der Ostbalkan in der wirtschaftliche Entwicklung der röm. Kaiserzeit* (Uppsala 1941) 89ff.
[19] Libanius *Or.* 47.33; see Pack, *Studies in Libanius* 16.
[20] Julian *Misop.* 367 D. Here Julian writes that he remitted all the tribute; but 365 B shows that it was only the arrears which were canceled at this time.
[21] See above, n. 4.
[22] Ammianus Marcellinus 22.13.4; Libanius *Or.* 18.195; Julian *Misop.* 369 A. The drought is mentioned by Chrysostom *De S. hieromartyre Babyla* 1 — *PG* 50.531, and in the pseudo-Chrysostom *De S. Babyla contra Iulianum et gentiles* 22 = *PG* 50.567 it is said to have been of unparalleled severity. There may have been a famine in the province of Phoenice at the same time, for Libanius (*Ep.* 710 W. = 800 F.) speaks of the price of grain being regulated by Gaïnas, who was *consularis* of that province (cf. Seeck, *Briefe des Libanius* 160-161). On the times of planting and harvest, see above, in the account of the famine in the time of Gallus, Ch. 12, nn. 221-224. Again in A.D. 382 a local famine was brought on by drought; see below, Ch. 15, §2.

known for some time that there would be a scarcity, nothing seems to
have been done before Julian's arrival to relieve the shortage of wheat;
and prices, of course, had risen. Thus when Julian came to Antioch
the people at once greeted him in the hippodrome with the cry "Everything plentiful, everything dear!"[23] As a first step (in which he may
not actually have had much confidence) Julian on the following day
called a conference of the leading citizens, farmers, retailers, and
artisans, at which he attempted to persuade them to lower prices. They
promised (and we can imagine their sincerity) to correct the situation
themselves,[24] and Julian proceeded to his other concerns.

One of his principal interests, as was well known, was the revival
of Hellenism and the restoration of the full observances of the pagan
festivals and sacrifices. Julian had already sent to Antioch as *comes
Orientis* his uncle Julian. The *comes Orientis* had been a Christian,
and had held important posts in the civil administration. However,
he had been converted to Hellenism by his nephew, and showed great
zeal for Hellenism; and when he went to Antioch to take up his new
post he was charged not only with his regular duties (which at this
time included a part in the military preparations) but with the supervision of the maintenance and observance of the pagan cults and
sacrifices.[25] During the whole of the emperor's stay at Antioch his
uncle appears as the chief official responsible for these matters, and
when ultimately an actual persecution of the Christians was undertaken, the *comes Orientis* was in charge of that.

The emperor also relied upon his old friend Libanius for support
in his revival of Hellenism, and this was rendered in many ways.
Libanius was now one of the most distinguished teachers and important citizens in Antioch, and his influence both in the city and
beyond it, by means of his extensive correspondence, was of major
importance.[26]

Julian himself, when he reached Antioch, at once began to visit the
pagan temples and shrines on all the proper occasions, and to perform
the fitting sacrifices; he frequented especially the shrines of Zeus, Zeus
Philios, Tyche, Demeter, Hermes, Pan, Ares, Calliope and Apollo,
and also sacrificed under the trees in the garden of the palace.[27] He

---

[23] Julian *Misop.* 368 C; Liban. *loc.cit.* (above, n. 22).
[24] Julian *Misop.* 368 D; Liban. *loc.cit.* (above, n. 22).
[25] Libanius *Ep.* 624 W. = 712 F.
[26] Libanius' orations 12-18 and 24 are concerned with Julian.
[27] Julian *Misop.* 346 B-D; Libanius *Or.* 1.121-122, 15.79. Julian also ascended to Mount
Casius to sacrifice to Zeus (Ammianus Marcellinus 22.14.4). This sacrifice is dated by

had already, before his arrival at Antioch, ordered the repair of the famous Temple of Apollo in Daphne, from which the columns had been removed under Constantine and Constantius when it was permissible to pillage marbles from pagan temples.[28] Julian was, however, severely disappointed when he visited the restored temple. Soon after his arrival there occurred, in August, the annual festival of Apollo, and Julian went to the temple in Daphne expecting to find a rich procession provided by the municipal authorities. Instead, he found no one present but the chief priest, with a goose which he had brought from his own home as a sacrifice.[29] This proof of public indifference to the old cults must have been a serious shock to the emperor.

By way of setting an example, Julian saw to it that the sacrifices to the gods throughout the city were performed with great splendor and with a generous provision of victims, which seems hardly to have been appropriate in a time of high prices and shortage of wheat. These spectacles made a bad impression also because Julian's soldiers flocked to them and gorged themselves on the sacrificial meat; and when they had become stupefied by eating and drinking, they were carried back to their quarters by the passers-by. A particularly disagreeable impression was made by the Celts and the Petulantes whom Julian had brought with him from Gaul.[30]

Julian in fact was not received favorably by the people of Antioch. He was small in stature, undignified and personally unkempt, and addicted to philosophical study and conversation; and, with his ascetic and remote personality, he did not know how to make himself popular with, or at least acceptable to, the masses. To the people of Antioch, one of his most remarkable peculiarities was that he hated horse-racing, which was one of the city's favorite forms of entertainment, and never attended races unless they were connected with festivals of the gods.[31]

---

a letter of Libanius, 651 W. = 739 F., in the summer of 362; cf. O. Seeck in *Hermes* 41 (1906) 515. It is not clear why Seeck later, in his *Regesten*, dated the sacrifice in November.

[28] In a letter (*Epist.* 29 ed. W. C. Wright, Loeb Classical Library = *Epist.* 80 ed. Bidez-Cumont) written from Constantinople in April of 362, before he had gone to Antioch, Julian instructed his uncle Julian, the *comes Orientis*, who was then in Antioch, to restore the columns of the Temple of Daphne, removing them both from the public buildings and the Christian churches to which they had been taken. On the background of the letter, see the introduction to it in the edition of Bidez and Cumont.

[29] Julian *Misop.* 361 Dff.

[30] Ammianus Marcellinus 22.12.6-7.

[31] All this is seen clearly everywhere in the *Misopogon*, the extraordinary satire upon himself which Julian wrote just before leaving Antioch in March A.D. 363. See also Zosimus 3.11. For an example of Julian's appearance at the time when he was in

As to the early course of Julian's initial efforts to deal with the famine and the price situation in Antioch, we have no detailed evidence; the emperor apparently continued to hope that the problem could be solved by the municipal authorities without intervention on his own part. A month after his arrival in the city he did, however, take a step which would help the situation, by issuing, on 18 August, a decree to the effect that rations were to be drawn only by those of the *domestici* (subaltern officers of the imperial guard) who were actually ordered to be on duty at the court. Formerly officers in excess of the authorized strength had been allowed to be present at the court, presumably drawing rations, but officers in this status were now to leave and return to their homes.[32] How much of a saving in food and fodder this effected we do not know; however, it was a gesture of economy that ought to have improved the spirits of the people.

Ten days later (28 August) there was issued another decree that should have had a more pronounced effect on the economic crisis. Julian's original order increasing the size of the local senate, issued when he became emperor,[33] had not had the desired effect of helping to restore the city's financial situation. The senators had not elected those men who ought to have served but had hitherto succeeded in escaping the burden of membership.[34] Instead, the existing senators chose other men who were not qualified by birth but had been engaging in speculation, with the result that the new members were able to use their membership in the senate to further their own and their colleagues' gains.[35] Julian now (28 August) issued a decree that shows that the requirements for membership in the local senate were being more strictly enforced and that everyone liable to service as a decurion was being forced to undertake it.[36]

Antioch, see R. Jonas, "A Newly Discovered Portrait of the Emperor Julian," *AJA* 50 (1946) 277-282.

[32] *CTh* 6.24.1. On the interpretation of this decree, see Stein, *Gesch.* 1.188-189, with n. 1 on p. 189. In Downey, "Economic Crisis under Julian" 316, the number of the decree is by mistake given as 6.21.4.

[33] *Misop.* 367 D; see above, n. 20.

[34] On the heavy services and obligations of local senators at this time, and their efforts to escape their burdens, see Jones, *Greek City* 193-196, and R. Pack, "Ammianus Marcellinus and the Curia of Antioch," *CP* 48 (1953) 80-85.

[35] Julian *Misop.* 368 A-B. On the role of the wealthy landowners in resisting Julian's effort to control prices, see A. Segré, "The Byzantine Colonate" *Traditio* 5 (1947) 106, with notes 16-17.

[36] *C Th* 12.1.51 = *C J* 10.32.22, cf. *C Th* 10.32.61; Zosimus 3.11.5; Liban. *Or.* 48.15. Ammianus, himself a member of the curial class at Antioch, disapproved Julian's measures (25.4.21). Cf. W. Ensslin, "Kaiser Julians Gesetzgebungswerk u. Reichsverwaltung," *Klio* 18 (1922-1923) 145.

More time passed, and the situation still was not improved. As autumn approached, the hardships of the people increased; and about this time there occurred a most untoward event, the burning of the Temple of Apollo at Daphne.

This incident was typical of the difficulties Julian encountered at Antioch. There had been a famous oracle of Apollo at the spring of Castalia in Daphne, near which, apparently, stood the celebrated Temple of Apollo.[37] The spring had been closed, presumably because it had ceased to flow, during the reorganization of the water supply at Daphne by Hadrian.[38] However, the oracle apparently continued to operate, and the Caesar Gallus, in order to nullify its influence and that of the cult of Apollo in general, had moved the remains of the famous local martyr Babylas from the Christian cemetery at Antioch to a martyrium which he built near the spring and the temple, and this silenced the oracle.[39] When Julian, on coming to Antioch, tried to consult the oracle at the spring of Castalia, he was informed, presumably by the officials of the Temple of Apollo, acting *vice* the oracle,[40] that the god was silent because of the presence of "bodies" in the neighborhood.[41] This was interpreted as a reference to the relics of St. Babylas, and Julian accordingly, with the due ceremonies of purification, removed the relics to their original resting place at Antioch.[42] The stone coffin of the saint, when it was taken back to the city, was escorted by a large crowd of Christians singing.[43]

[37] On the location of the spring and the temple, see above, Ch. 12, n. 217.

[38] See above, Ch. 9, §7.

[39] The sources are cited above, Ch. 12, n. 217.

[40] This point is nowhere explicitly stated, but it may be inferred.

[41] P. R. Coleman-Norton points out in his study, "St. Chrysostom's Use of the Greek Poets," *CP* 27 (1932) 216, that the oracle which is said in pseudo-Chrysostom, *De S. Babyla contra Iul. et gent.* 15 = *PG* 50.555, to have been given to Julian in Daphne is an adaptation of the reply of the Pythian oracle to Croesus quoted by Herodotus 1.47.

[42] See the sources cited above, Ch. 12, n. 217; also Philostorgius, *Hist. eccl.* 7.8, p. 92 ed. Bidez and Theophanes a. 5854, p. 49.28ff. ed. De Boor. Ammianus speaks of the removal of "bodies" from Daphne to Antioch, but this must be an inference from the wording of the response given to Julian (see above, Ch. 12, n. 217). Ammianus notes that Julian in taking the body of Babylas from Daphne observed the rites of purification which were carried out when the Athenians purified Delos (cf. Herodotus 1.64, Thucydides 3.104.1-2). A different report, preserved in Ammianus Marcellinus 22.12.8 and in Sozomen *Hist. eccl.* 5.19 = *PG* 67.1273, had it that the spring of Castalia was closed by Hadrian because the oracle had given him a prophecy that he would become emperor, and he wished to make sure that such oracles would not be given to others. Moreover, according to Ammianus, it was Julian who decided (without prompting from the oracle) that the "bodies" buried about the spring should be moved. This story, which is at variance with all the other reports, sounds as though it had been invented at the time of Julian's removal of the body of Babylas, in a rather confused effort to account for his doing so. It seems much more likely, as has been observed, that the spring was closed in Hadrian's time because it was not active.

Soon after this, on 22 October, the Temple of Apollo caught fire, and the roof and the great chryselephantine statue of Apollo, which reached to the roof, were burned.[44] The Christians were accused of setting the fire in retaliation for the removal of the body of St. Babylas; the Christians themselves maintained that the building had been struck by lightning; and there was one report that the fire was started, through the negligence of the attendants, by candles lighted by the philosopher Asclepiades, who had visited the temple to worship and make an offering.[45] Although Julian himself later stated that the cause of the fire was not certain,[46] a persecution of the Christians was begun, directed by Julian the *comes Orientis*, Felix the *comes sacrarum largitionum*, Sallustius the *praefectus praetorio*, and Helpidius.[47] The octagonal Great Church was closed, and the liturgical vessels presented to it by Constantine and Constantius were confiscated.[48]

At about this same time, further troubles developed as the shortage of grain and the inflation of prices became critical. The prominent citizens had done nothing to correct the situation, but were making handsome profits from speculation.[49] Julian now, in the latter part of

---

The oracle was working in the time of Gallus, and the closing of the spring as a source of water supply need not have inhibited the operation of the oracle itself. Evagrius, writing in the latter part of the sixth century, states that the shrine of Babylas was still intact, outside the city, in his own day (*Hist. eccl.* 1.16). A trial excavation in 1932 showed that the cemetery lay beneath the modern barracks just outside the city walls, on the left of the road to Daphne (Elderkin in *Antioch* 1.106). On the Christian cemetery, see P. Franchi de' Cavalieri, "Il *koimeterion* di Antiochia," *Note agiografiche* 7 (Vatican City 1928) 146-153 (Studi e Testi 49).

[43] Philostorgius *loc.cit.* (above, n. 42); Socrates *Hist. eccl.* 3.18 = *PG* 67.425; Sozomen *Hist. eccl.* 5.19 = *PG* 67.1276; pseudo-Chrysostom, *De S. Babyla contra Iul. et gent.* 16 = *PG* 50.558.

[44] Ammianus Marcellinus 22.13.1-5 (with the date); Libanius *Monody on the Temple, Or.* 60 (fragments only); Julian *Misop.* 361 B; pseudo-Chrysostom *De S. Babyla contra Iul. et gent.* 17-23 = *PG* 50.559-572; Joh. mon., *Vita Artemii* 52, 56, in Philostorgius *Hist. eccl.* pp. 87-88, 93-94 ed. Bidez; Theophanes a. 5854, p. 50.2ff. ed. De Boor; Sozomen *Hist. eccl.* 5.20 = *PG* 67.1277; Theodoret *Hist. eccl.* 3.11.4ff.; Zonaras 13.12.42. Ammianus and some others state that the building was wholly destroyed, but in the pseudo-Chrysostom it is said expressly that the walls and columns were still standing twenty years later, and this seems much more likely (cf. Müller, *Antiq. Antioch.* 47). Sozomen and the *Vita Artemii* (*locc.citt.*) say only that the walls and columns were left standing after the fire.

[45] Ammianus Marcellinus *loc.cit.* (above, n. 44).   [46] *Loc.cit.* (above, n. 44).

[47] Philostorgius *Hist. eccl.* 7.10; Theodoret *Hist. eccl.* 3.12; Theophanes a. 5854, p. 50. 16ff. ed. De Boor; Socrates *Hist. eccl.* 3.19 = *PG* 67.428; Sozomen *Hist. eccl.* 5.19-20 = *PG* 67.1277ff.; pseudo-Chrysostom *De S. Babyla contra Iul. et gent.* 22 = *PG* 50.568.

[48] Theophanes a. 5854, p. 50.14ff. ed. De Boor; Theodoret *Hist. eccl.* 3.12.4. The report in Philostorgius *Hist. eccl.* 7.10 and Sozomen *Hist. eccl.* 5.8 = *PG* 67.1236, of the defiling of the church and the sacred vessels seems to be exaggerated, though it would have been easy for untoward incidents to occur on such an occasion.

[49] Julian *Misop.* 350 A.

October, found it necessary to issue an edict of maximum prices and to begin to import grain;[50] these were both measures which he had evidently hoped at first to avoid. He first imported 400,000 *modii* of grain from the region of Chalcis and Hierapolis.[51] This must have been an expensive undertaking, attempted only as a last resort, for we hear that during a severe famine at Caesarea in Cappadocia grain could not be brought in because of the prohibitive cost of transportation.[52] When this supply was used, Julian contributed grain from his own estates, in three lots, first 5,000 *modii*, then 7,000, finally 10,000; and when this was not enough he sent to Egypt for wheat. The grain was sold at a reduced price (15 *modii* at the price formerly charged for 10), and the price of bread was controlled.[53]

A further measure which appears to have been taken at this time was a reduction of the taxes by one fifth, apparently in an effort to lighten the burden of the cost of living; evidently the controlled prices were still high as compared with former prices.[54]

Another step was the distribution of 3,000 *cleri* of municipal land that had ceased to be cultivated.[55] This land was made available, at popular request, in an effort to assist the small landowners and farmers, and to increase the food supply.[56]

The special economic difficulties of Antioch must have been very serious indeed, but they were in part, so far as the inflation was concerned, shared with the rest of the Empire. Constantius' war with Magnentius and the preparations for the Persian war had inflated prices, and the effects of the currency reform of Constantius and Constans (A.D. 342) had been offset when their coins were later devalued.[57] Julian when he came to the throne found the resources of the government very straitened,[58] and he had in addition need of large

[50] Julian *Misop.* 368 Dff.   [51] Julian *Misop.* 369 A.
[52] Gregory of Nazianzus *Or. in laudem Basilii Magni* 34-35 = *PG* 36.541-544; cf. Jones, *Greek City* 261.
[53] Julian *Misop.* 369 D-370 A. For a discussion of the prices, see the study of inflation by Jones cited above, n. 14.
[54] Julian *Misop.* 365 D, 367 A. The arrears of taxes had been remitted before Julian reached Antioch (see above, n. 20).
[55] Julian *Misop.* 370 Dff.
[56] This was evidently, for Antioch, a quite substantial amount of land. Julian elsewhere (*Misop.* 362 C) speaks of 10,000 *cleri*, presumably municipal property, which were already in the hands of private citizens; and his allusion suggests that these 10,000 *cleri* played an important role in the city's economy. See Rostovtzeff, *Stor. econ. soc. imp. rom.* 312-314, and Jones, *Greek City* 257, with n. on p. 362.
[57] Piganiol, *Empire chrétien* 133, 297-298.
[58] Piganiol, *Empire chrétien* 128; R. Andreotti, "L'opera legislativa ed amministrativa dell'Imperatore Giuliano," *Nuova rivista storica* 14 (1930) 342-383.

sums for his military preparations. An additional source of financial difficulty was that gold and silver for coins were scarce because the metals were being used for the manufacture of jewelry and silverware.[59] Consequently Julian at some time in the autumn of A.D. 362 introduced a reform of the copper currency,[60] and this ought to have done something to alleviate the situation in Antioch, although the people of the city objected to the new coins.[61]

Julian's best efforts, however, were unsuccessful. All classes in the city failed to cooperate.[62] The imported wheat, sold at a fixed price, was bought by speculators and landowners who either held it against a further advance in prices, or sold it in the country where the price control could not be enforced.[63] Some of the merchants in the city, blaming the landowners for the high prices, simply ceased to do business,[64] either because they could no longer make a profit, or because they hoped that Julian's program would collapse and that a "free economy" would be restored. It was argued that the presence of the troops made hardship inevitable and that Julian had no right to try to reduce prices, but was only trying to gain popularity; the attempt to lower prices, it was claimed, would itself cause further scarcity.[65] Famine, it was pointed out, was caused by the weather, over which the authorities had no control; nature must be allowed to take its course and the market must be allowed to regulate itself.[66] Moreover, the distribution of municipal land was a failure, for the lots which were made available were promptly occupied by persons who did not need them.[67] Finally, the control of the price of bread failed in its purpose

[59] This is indicated by Themistius' address to Julian, which is extant only in an Arabic translation made from a lost Syriac version, which was in turn made from the lost Greek original; see lines 131-134 in the Latin paraphrase of M. Bouyges, *Archives de philosophie*, tome 2, cahier 3 (1924) 22. The authenticity of this document is doubted by J. Bidez, *La tradition manuscrit et les éditions des discours de Julien* (Gand 1929) 146-147, but it has been successfully defended by J. Croissant, "Un nouveau discours de Thémistius," *Serta Leodiensia* (Liége 1930) 7-30. The mining of precious metals is encouraged by a decree of 10 December A.D. 365 (*Cod. Theod.* 10.19.3).

[60] G. Elmer, "Die Kupfergeldreform unter Julianus Philosophus," *Num. Ztschr.* 70 (N.F. 30) (1937) 25-42; cf. Andreotti, *op.cit.* (above, n. 58) 347-348.

[61] Julian *Misop.* 355 D; cf. Elmer, *op.cit.* (above, n. 60) 30.

[62] Libanius *Or.* 15.23.

[63] Julian *Misop.* 369 Cff.; Libanius *Or.* 18.195.

[64] Julian *Misop.* 350 A; Socrates *Hist. eccl.* 3.17 = *PG* 67.424 B; Sozomen *Hist. eccl.* 5.19 = *PG* 67.1272 B.

[65] Ammianus Marcellinus 22.14.1-2; Libanius *Or.* 1.126; Socrates *loc.cit.* (above, n. 64).

[66] Libanius *Or.* 1.205 (of the famine in 382; see below, Ch. 15, §2), Libanius *Ep.* 1439 W. = 1379 F. (of the famine in 363).

[67] Julian *Misop.* 370 D.

of giving relief to the urban populace, for the country people flocked to town to buy it.[68] The shortage of food was to continue even after Julian left Antioch. At least, however, Julian had not resorted to violent measures, as Gallus had done in a similar situation.[69]

The preparations for the Persian war continued. Toward the end of A.D. 362 Sapor sent Julian a letter asking for a conference to settle their differences, but this overture was rejected,[70] for Julian, confident of success, planned to put on the throne of Persia the prince Hormisdas,[71] the younger brother of Sapor, who had fled from Persia in the time of Constantine and, after serving as a cavalry officer under Constantius, was now in Antioch with Julian, waiting to accompany him on the campaign.[72] Julian did, however, accept an offer of assistance from Arsaces, king of Armenia.[73]

On 1 January A.D. 363 Julian entered upon the consulship at Antioch, taking as his colleague a private individual (an unusual thing at this time), namely Sallustius, the former *praefectus praetorio Galliarum*.[74] Libanius wrote an address to the emperor for the occasion (*Or.* 12);

---

[68] Julian *Misop.* 369 D.
[69] Libanius *Or.* 18.195; see above, Ch. 12, nn. 221-224.
[70] Libanius *Or.* 18.164, cf. *Or.* 17.19.
[71] See Seeck, "Hormisdas," no. 3, *RE* 8 (1913) 2410.
[72] Libanius *Epist.* 1457 W. = 1402 F.; cf. *Or.* 18.258, also the *Passio* of SS. Bonosus and Maximilianus, *Acta SS*, 21 Aug., tom. 4.431 (Paris 1867). A house found in the excavations at Daphne contains a large mosaic floor consisting of a representation of the Phoenix, surrounded by a border of heraldic rams' heads: R. Stillwell in *Antioch-on-the-Orontes* 2.187, no. 56, and Levi, *Antioch Mosaic Pavements* 1.350-355, 478-480. The Phoenix is a well-known symbol of the eternity of Rome, and the rams' heads are equally prominent as a Persian symbol of royal power; see the literature cited by Doro Levi, also the passage in Ammianus Marcellinus 19.1.3 in which is described the headdress worn by Sapor in battle, consisting of a golden image of a ram's head set with precious stones. In the original publication of the mosaic in *Antioch-on-the-Orontes* 2 it was noted that two coins of the fourth century were found below the floor, the latest being one of Julian, A.D. 363 (353, given in *Antioch-on-the-Orontes* 2, is a typographical error). H. von Schoenebeck, in an explanatory note (on pp. 438-439) accompanying illustrations of the floor (facing p. 257) published in Bidez, *Julian der Abtrünnige*, suggested that the building in which the floor was found was a summer palace of Constantius and that the juxtaposition of the Roman and the Persian symbols was a premature representation of a coming Roman victory over Sapor, which might be ascribed to Julian rather than to Constantius. This attractive hypothesis is unfortunately deprived of its basis by the fact that in Levi's publication (which appeared after von Schoenebeck wrote) it was announced (351-352) that a much later coin, of Theodosius II or possibly even later, was found under the floor. The floor could still of course be an allusion to Roman hope of conquest of Persia. Levi (353, n. 12) believes that the rams' heads had at the time when the floor was made "a purely ornamental value," and he considers that even if they retained their royal significance it would be impossible to combine Roman and Persian symbolism of this kind in the same monument. This scruple does not seem cogent.
[73] Ammianus Marcellinus 23.2.1-2.
[74] Ammianus Marcellinus 23.1.1.

and during the ceremonies the consuls visited the Temple of the Genius of the Roman people.[75]

In the final stages of the preparations for the coming campaign there developed serious disaffection in the army, partly because of the measures taken against Christians in the service, partly (and perhaps principally) because the campaign itself was unpopular and the emperor's plans were thought to be too sanguine. Julian knew of the latter complaints and criticisms, but was unmoved by them.[76] One incident occurred in late December or early January, when two Christian soldiers named Bonosus and Maximilianus, who were standard-bearers of the Joviani and the Herculiani, refused to remove the Christian labarum from their standards, and likewise refused to perform the ritual sacrifices to the pagan gods. They were examined by Julianus the *comes Orientis* and were condemned to death, and a large crowd, including the orthodox Bishop Meletius, accompanied them to the military *campus* across the river, where they were beheaded.[77]

Even more serious were ideas circulating in the imperial guard itself.[78] Two officers, Romanus and Vincentius, were convicted of "making plans beyond their station" and were punished by exile.[79] Then, late in January, two other officers of the guard, Juventinus and Maximinus, were reported to the emperor for seditious talk, and it was said that there was a plot to assassinate Julian.[80] The emperor examined

[75] Ammianus Marcellinus 23.1.4.   [76] Ammianus Marcellinus 22.12.3-4.

[77] *Acta SS*, 21 Aug., tom. 4.430-432 (Paris 1867). It is certain that the executions took place in late December or early January, and that the traditional date in August is incorrect; see T. Ruinart, *Acta . . . martyrum sincera*[2] (Amsterdam 1713) 592-593. One of the hearings (*Acta SS* 431) took place "in the old bath" (*in balneo veteri*), evidently a bath which had been converted into a military praetorium. Bidez, *Vie de Julien* 405, n. 2, *Julian der Abtrünnige* 424, n. 2, doubts that Bonosus and Maximilianus can have kept the labarum on the standards of their units as late as the end of 362. However, it seems possible that Julian might have been forced to tolerate the labarum if these and other units were still predominantly Christian. The emperor evidently was not able to eliminate Christians completely even from his immediate entourage. The *comes* Hormisdas, brother of Sapor, whom Julian hoped to set on the Persian throne (see above, nn. 71-72), was a Christian and visited Bonosus and Maximilianus in prison when they were undergoing examination: *Acta SS* (cited above) 431. Moreover, there is actually no evidence that the labarum had been maintained continually on the standards. Bonosus and Maximilianus might have restored it to the standards when disaffection began to grow in the army, and it might have been their restoration of the symbol which seemed so alarming.

[78] See Allard, *Julien*[2] 3.154ff.   [79] Ammianus Marcellinus 22.11.2.

[80] Theodoret *Hist. eccl.* 3.15.4-9 (who indicates, but does not say explicitly, that they were officers); Chrysostom, *In Juventinum et Maximinum martyres* = PG 50.571-578; Malalas 327.15-21 (who calls them *candidati*; the name of the second is given as Maximianus); Libanius *Or.* 15.43, 18.199, cf. 12.84-90. On the accounts of the martyrdoms, see B. de Gaiffier, "'Sub Iuliano Apostata' dans le martyrologe romain," *Anal. Boll.* 74 (1956) 9-10.

the men himself, and they were condemned and executed, probably on 29 January;[81] according to one report, the execution took place secretly, in the middle of the night.[82]

All this while, shortage of food continued,[83] and this must have added to the unpopularity of the emperor. Julian on his part was saddened and discouraged by the deaths of two of his principal assistants, Felix and Julian the *comes Orientis*, the latter after a long and painful illness.[84] Scurrilous verses about the emperor were posted in the city.[85] Some time after the middle of February, when he had only a short time to remain in Antioch, Julian brought his efforts in the city to a fitting close by publishing the *Antiochikos* or *Misopogon* ("Beard-Hater"), the famous satire in which, by pretending to mock himself and his philosopher's beard, he gave final expression to his feelings about Antioch and its people.[86] Julian, as a bookish person, had already, in addition to his letters, written a number of satires and treatises, many of which were designed to play a part in his campaign for the revival of Hellenism.[87] This new satire, which was published outside the palace at Antioch, at the Tetrapylon of the Elephants,[88] near the Royal Street

[81] P. Peeters, "La date de la fête de SS. Juventin et Maximin," *Anal. Boll.* 42 (1924) 77-82.

[82] Chrysostom, *In Juvent. et Max. mart.* 3 = PG 50.576. There is a record of another officer, Eusignius, executed at Antioch under Julian, but it has been shown that the tradition of his martyrdom is legendary; see Gaiffier *op.cit.* 22-23.

[83] The scarcity is mentioned in a letter (695 W. = 785 F.) in which Libanius speaks of his oration to Julian on the latter's assumption of the consulship (1 January A.D. 363) as though the discourse either was just about to be delivered, or had just been delivered. Libanius *Ep.* 712 W. = 802 F. shows that the scarcity continued after Julian left Antioch in March.

[84] Felix died of a hemorrhage late in A.D. 362 or in the first part of A.D. 363; the *comes Orientis* died of a mysterious and unpleasant disease, some time after 23 February A.D. 363: Ammianus Marcellinus 23.1.4-5; Philostorgius *Hist. eccl.* 7.10 and 12; Sozomen *Hist. eccl.* 5.8 = PG 67.1236ff.; cf. Seeck, *Regesten* 97.5-11. Their deaths were thought by the Christians to have been punishment for their impious deeds.

[85] Libanius *Or.* 16.30.

[86] The date is indicated by Julian's statement in the work (344 A) that he had been in Antioch for seven months when he wrote the *Misopogon*. Since he had arrived on 18 July (see above, n. 4), the satire was written between 18 February and 5 March, when the emperor left the city (see below). On the sources and the literary form of the piece, see Geffcken, *Julianus* 116, 166, and R. Asmus, "Kaiser Julians Misopogon u. seine Quelle," *Philologus* 76 (1920) 266-292, 77 (1921) 109-141. In addition to the translation by W. C. Wright in the Loeb Classical Library edition of Julian's works, there is a translation, with an excellent commentary, in A. Rostagni, *Giuliano l'Apostata* (Turin 1920) 237-292. On the purpose of the work, see, in addition to the other studies of Julian's life and literary activity, Downey, "Julian at Antioch."

[87] On his literary activity, see Christ-Schmid-Stählin, *Gesch. d. gr. Lit.*⁶ 2, pt. 2, 1014-1027. On the question whether Julian's satire *The Caesars* was written at Antioch, see R. A. Pack in *TAPA* 77 (1946) 152, n. 4.

[88] Malalas 328.2-4. In this instance "publication" (Malalas writes προέθηκε) presumably means that a copy was officially displayed at the Tetrapylon in such a way

A History of Antioch

which served as an entrance to the Palace,[89] was an extraordinary document in which the emperor, by reviewing and commenting upon the criticisms and jokes that were circulating concerning himself, actually satirized the people of Antioch, attempting in the process to show them how they appeared to others. In doing this, Julian not only gave expression to his anger and disappointment with the people of the city, but contrived at the same time to set forth his own ideas and program. While designed ostensibly for local consumption, the piece was apparently intended as general propaganda in support of Julian's efforts, deliberately couched in undignified and sometimes coarse terms.

What success the *Misopogon* may have had, and how well it may have been understood, we do not know. Julian continued to be angry with the people of Antioch up to the time when he left the city, and before his departure he gave evidence of his displeasure by appointing to the post of *consularis Syriae* Alexander of Heliopolis, a man known for his bad temper and cruelty. Alexander, Julian said, was not worthy

that anyone who wished could read it aloud to the bystanders. The Tetrapylon of the Elephants seems not to be mentioned elsewhere. Apparently it was a triumphal arch surmounted by a quadriga of elephants drawing a chariot, such as were sometimes used in triumphal processions (the elephant being *par excellence* a royal beast); see Pliny *Nat. hist.* 8.4; *SHA Elagabalus* 23.1; cf. Müller, *Antiq. Antioch.* 99; M. Wellmann, "Elefant," *RE* 5 (1905) 2248-2257; and H. Leclercq, "Eléphant," *DACL* 4.2665-2666. Coins showing quadrigas of elephants are illustrated by Imhoof-Blumer and O. Keller, *Tier- und Pflanzenbilder auf Münzen u. Gemmen des klassischen Altertums* (Leipzig 1889) pl. 4, no. 5, cf. pl. 19, nos. 39 and 41.

[89] Malalas writes (328.3-4) that the *Misopogon was published* ἔξω τοῦ παλατίου . . . εἰς τὸ λεγόμενον Τετράπυλον τῶν ἐλεφάντων πλησίον τῆς 'Ρηγίας. *Regia* here appears to mean the short colonnaded street ('Ρηγία sc. e.g. ὁδός), mentioned by Libanius (*Or.* 11.205) which led to the palace, and, as Libanius says, formed a sort of propylaea for it. Malalas uses the word *Regia* in the same sense to describe a similar colonnaded street which led to the palace at Constantinople (321.8; cf. *Chronicon Paschale* 528. 19-21). It should be noted that in Latin, *regia* would be used to denote the palace itself, as for example by Ammianus Marcellinus 25.10.2, who speaks of a statue in the palace at Antioch as being *in vestibulo regiae*. The use of the Greek word *Regia* to describe a street or a portion of a street is illustrated by a number of references to the main street at Constantinople, which is sometimes called *Regia*, sometimes *Mese*; see R. Guilland, "Autour du Livre des Cérémonies de Constantin VII Porphyrogénète," *Actes du VIᵉ Congrès international d'études byzantines, Paris, 1948* (Paris 1951) 2.171-182. Müller, not being familiar with this usage, was unable to determine what the *Regia* in Malalas was (*Antiq. Antioch.* 99). The Tetrapylon of the Elephants is not mentioned elsewhere and it is not clear from this passage whether or not it stood at the crossing of the four main streets of the island, one of which would have been the *Regia* leading to the palace. One would expect that such a tetrapylon would stand at the crossing of the streets, and so at the beginning of the *Regia*, and this would be indicated if Malalas is here using πλησίον in the sense of "at" or "hard by," a sense in which it is used in late Greek (see D. Tabachovitz, *Études sur le grec de la basse époque* [Uppsala 1943] 62). However, if Malalas uses πλησίον to mean simply "near," we should have to understand that the tetrapylon stood on one of the other streets, near the *Regia* but not at its entrance. This view seems, architecturally, less likely.

of the post, but was the kind of man fit to govern the rebellious and avaricious people of Antioch. When Julian left the city, on 5 March, he announced that when the summer campaign was completed, he would not return to Antioch, but would make his winter headquarters at Tarsus in Cilicia. A large crowd accompanied the emperor as he left the city, wishing him success and attempting to placate his anger.[90] After Julian's departure, Libanius sent an address to the emperor (*Or.* 15) in an attempt to mollify him, and also delivered an address to the people of Antioch (*Or.* 16) upbraiding them for their behavior. After this the people of the city passed through an uncomfortable period. The shortage of food continued, and the new *consularis Syriae*, a zealous pagan,[91] performed his duties with the utmost rigor and harshness, so that the administration of the city was quite transformed, and the surprised and terrified people paid their taxes even before they were due.[92] Among other things, Alexander saw to it that as many young men as possible from all over Syria enrolled as students of Libanius, the foremost pagan teacher of the day.[93]

Julian never returned from his campaign. He was killed in Persia in June, and with him there came to an end the dynasty of Constantine. The news of his death was greeted with rejoicing by the people of Antioch,[94] as a whole, though the pagans mourned him, and Libanius wrote a Monody (*Or.* 17) and an Epitaphios (*Or.* 18) on the emperor.

No record is preserved of any public buildings constructed by Julian at Antioch, and what we know of the financial condition of both the imperial government and the municipality during his reign suggests that funds would not be readily available for such purposes. Julian did, however, found a new library at Antioch. George, bishop of Alexandria from A.D. 357 to A.D. 361, had formed an excellent collection of books including philosophy of every school, history and Christian writings, with which Julian had been familiar before he became emperor. Having been installed as bishop in Alexandria by the government, George was unpopular with many of the people of the city, and when the news

---

[90] Ammianus Marcellinus 23.2.3-6. Libanius (*Orat.* 15.79) records that before leaving Antioch, Julian offered sacrifices to Hermes, Pan, Demeter, Ares, Calliope, Apollo, and to Zeus. This could be taken to imply that there were still temples of these deities in Antioch at which sacrifices could be offered.

[91] Libanius *Ep.* 1375 W. = 1294 F.; *Ep.* 1084 W. = 1361 F.

[92] Libanius *Or.* 15.74; *Epist.* 722 W. = 811 F.; *Epist.* 1053 W. = 1351 F.; *Epist.* 1450 W. = 1392 F.; *Epist.* 1057 W. = 1411 F.

[93] Libanius *Epist.* 758 W. = 838 F. After Julian's death Alexander was removed from office and charges were brought against him, but he escaped punishment: Libanius *Epist.* 1492 W. = 1456 F.

[94] Theodoret *Hist. eccl.* 3.28; Libanius *Epist.* 1186 W. = 1220 F.

came of the death of Constantius, the bishop was lynched by a mob, on Christmas Eve A.D. 361.[95] Julian, when he was at Antioch (or shortly before he went there), secured the dead bishop's library and had it brought to Antioch and installed in the "small and graceful" temple which had been built by Hadrian in honor of the deified Trajan.[96] The temple and all the books were burned by a mob a short time later during the reign of Jovian.[97]

2. THE CHURCH AT ANTIOCH UNDER JULIAN

When Julian became emperor, the Christian community at Antioch was divided into three groups, (1) the Arians composing the "official" church under Euzoius, who was bishop from A.D. 361 to 378, and the orthodox or followers of Nicaea, divided into two groups, (2) the Eustathians, led by Paulinus, who later became bishop, and (3) the Meletians, whose leader Meletius soon returned from exile. Euzoius, as the official incumbent, occupied the octagonal Great Church.[98] The Meletians worshiped at different times, according to their status at the moment, either in the old "apostolic" church in the old part of the city,[99] or in a church outside the city, while Euzoius (no doubt glad to keep his opponents divided) allowed the Eustathians to use one of the smaller churches in the city.[100]

In allowing the exiled bishops to return, Julian probably hoped that they would resume their quarrels and thus weaken the opposition to his projected revival of Hellenism.[101] In reality, the Christians closed up their ranks in the face of the common foe and attempted to settle their differences, a process which was made easier by the decline in the strength of Arianism which took place at this time.[102] In the case of Antioch, however, the effort at consolidation failed. Soon after

---

[95] Athanasius *Hist. aceph.* 8 = *PG* 26.1445; cf. Kidd, *Hist. of the Church* 2.136-138.

[96] Julian *Epistt.* 106-107 ed. Bidez-Cumont; Suidas *s.v.* ʼΙοβιανός; Joh. Antioch. frag. 181, in *Excerpta de virtut. et vit.* 1.201 ed. Büttner-Wobst. See C. Callmer, "Die antiken Bibliotheken," *Opusc. arch.* 3 (1944) 184. On the building of the temple by Hadrian, see above, Ch. 9, §7.

[97] See below, Ch. 14, §1.

[98] Euzoius occupied the church when it was closed after the burning of the Temple of Apollo at Daphne; see Eltester, "Kirchen Antiochias" 274-275.

[99] The Arian church historian in Philostorgius, ed. Bidez, p. 230.14; Theodoret *Hist. eccl.* 3.4.3; cf. Eltester, "Kirchen Antiochias" 274-275.

[100] Theodoret *Hist. eccl.* 2.31.11; Socrates *Hist. eccl.* 3.9 = *PG* 67.404; cf. Eltester, "Kirchen Antiochias" 274.

[101] Ammianus Marcellinus 22.5.3-4.

[102] For these developments, see Gwatkin, *Studies of Arianism*² 202-216, and Kidd, *Hist. of the Church* 2.208-218. Only the major events, as they affected the church at Antioch, are described here.

Athanasius returned from exile, early in A.D. 362, a council was held at Alexandria which dealt, among other things, with the situation at Antioch.[103] An effort was made to unite Paulinus and Meletius and their followers. This plan, however, failed, for Lucifer of Calaris, who had not waited for the council of Alexandria to propose the reconciliation, had himself gone to Antioch, and had there seen fit to consecrate Paulinus, who had been a priest, as bishop.[104] This action, creating two "Nicene" bishops in Antioch, put an end to all hope of healing the local dissension, and created a schism which lasted for fifty years.

A new subject of dispute in Antioch at this time was the Christological debate that arose out of the differing doctrines concerning the nature of Christ which were taught by Diodorus, head of the catechetical school of Antioch, and Apollinaris, bishop of Laodicea in Syria. The council at Alexandria attempted, without success, to reconcile these differences, which may have been, even unconsciously, heightened by the traditional jealousy between Laodicea and Antioch.[105] Diodorus, as one of the leading Christian apologists in Antioch, drew a particularly strong attack from Julian.[106]

As might be expected from Julian's vigorous campaign against the Christians, a number of martyrs were executed at Antioch and elsewhere during his reign, in addition to the military martyrs at Antioch who have been mentioned above. In Antioch we hear of the martyrdom of the abbess Publia[107] and of the priest Theodore, who is reported to have endured severe tortures without feeling any pain.[108] Artemius, a high official who had been *dux Aegypti*, was listed as a martyr, though Ammianus Marcellinus wrote only that he was executed as a criminal.[109]

---

[103] See the synodal letter, *Tomus ad Antiochenos*, in *PG* 26.796-809. On the synod, see C. B. Armstrong, "The Synod of Alexandria and the Schism of Antioch in A.D. 362," *JTS* 22 (1920-21) 206-221, 347-365.

[104] Jerome *Chron*. Olymp. 285, p. 242 ed. Helm; Socrates *loc.cit*. (above, n. 100); Sozomen *Hist. eccl.* 5.13 = *PG* 67.1252-1253; Theodoret *Hist. eccl.* 3.5.1.

[105] On the debate, see Kidd, *Hist. of the Church* 2.212-215, and H. Lietzmann, *Apollinaris von Laodicea* (Tübingen 1904).

[106] Julian *Epist.* 55 ed. W. C. Wright (Loeb Classical Library) = *Ep.* 90 [79] ed. Bidez-Cumont. See Kidd, *Hist. of the Church* 3.193-194.

[107] B. de Gaiffier, "'Sub Iuliano Apostata' dans le martyrologe romain," *Anal. Boll.* 74 (1956) 14-15.

[108] Rufinus *Hist. eccl.* 10.37. See P. Franchi de' Cavalieri *Note agiografiche* 9 (Vatican City 1953) 110, n. 1 (*Studi e Testi* 175), and Gaiffier, *op.cit.* 16.

[109] Ammianus Marcellinus 22.11.2-3; see Gaiffier, *op.cit.* 15-16.

CHAPTER 14

JOVIAN AND VALENS, A.D. 363-378

1. Jovian

ON 27 JUNE A.D. 363, the day following Julian's death, a Christian officer of the imperial guard named Jovian was chosen emperor. He was a compromise candidate, after Salutius Secundus, the *praefectus praetorio Orientis*, had declined election.[1] The army at once began to retreat, and Jovian, anxious to terminate the Persian war in order to be free to make his own position secure, hastily concluded a disgraceful peace, in which unnecessary concessions were made to the Persians. While the army escorted the body of Julian to Tarsus for burial there, Jovian went to Antioch, where he arrived at some time before 22 October.[2] His stay in the city was not pleasant. The people made known their disapproval of Jovian and of the peace with their customary freedom of expression. Scurrilous lampoons, including apt quotations from Homer, appeared on handbills strewn on the streets or posted on walls. Rude remarks were shouted in the hippodrome, provoking universal laughter, and serious disorder was only averted with difficulty. Jovian himself added to the disorder when, at the instigation of his wife, he allowed a mob to burn the temple of the deified Trajan, along with the fine library that had been installed there by Julian.[3] Moreover, there were portents of coming disaster. The statue of the Caesar Maximianus in the vestibule of the palace dropped the bronze globe, symbol of imperial power, which it was holding, the beams of the roof of the *consistorium* creaked dreadfully, and comets were seen in broad daylight.[4] Jovian was extremely anxious to get away from the city but was detained by affairs that urgently needed attention.[5] His position in religious matters was moderate, and while the privileges of the Christians were reestablished, tolerance was shown

[1] Seeck, "Iovianus," *RE* 9.2006-2011; Piganiol, *Empire chrétien* 145-148.
[2] *Cod. Theod.* 10.19.2; Ammianus Marcellinus 25.10.1; Zosimus 3.34. The reader is reminded again that in this chapter as in Chapters 12, 13, and 15, the extensive writings of Libanius provide a detailed documentation of all aspects of the life of Antioch at this period, and that this material has recently been carefully studied and presented by P. Petit, *Libanius et la vie municipale* and *Les étudiants de Libanius* (1956).
[3] Suidas *s.v.* Ἰοβιανός; Joh. Antioch. frag. 181, in *Excerpta de virtut. et vit.* 1.201 ed. Büttner-Wobst. See C. A. Forbes, "Books for the Burning," *TAPA* 67 (1936) 121.
[4] Ammianus Marcellinus 25.10.1-2.
[5] Ammianus Marcellinus 25.10.4.

toward the pagans.[6] The various parties among the Christians sought to gain the emperor's favor, but he remained neutral, though he personally inclined toward the orthodox doctrine.[7] At Antioch, Meletius and his followers, as a sign of this favor, were allowed to occupy the Great Church.[8] The Acacians in the city, seeing the emperor's preference, made overtures to Meletius; and a synod was held at Antioch toward the end of A.D. 363 at which the Acacians and Meletius acknowledged the Nicene creed.[9] Athanasius, on the emperor's invitation, visited Antioch and tried to heal the schism there, but was not successful, for Meletius and Paulinus could not be brought together, and Meletius and Athanasius continued on terms of mutual disapproval.[10]

Jovian finally concluded his business at Antioch and set out for Constantinople, traveling rapidly, in the first part of November.[11] En route, he died suddenly, at Dadastana, on 17 February.[12]

2. VALENS

Jovian's successor was Valentinian,[13] a Christian army officer who had served at Antioch under Julian.[14] The Empire was threatened with attack on many of its frontiers,[15] and Valentinian soon chose as colleague, to share his labors, his brother Valens.[16] Freedom of worship was proclaimed.[17] The two emperors determined to divide the empire, Valens taking the east, Valentinian the west, where the danger from the barbarians was greater. Having settled the details of the division in a conference at Naissus, the brothers parted at Sirmium in August A.D. 364, Valens going to Constantinople.[18] After spending the winter

[6] See Piganiol, *Empire chrétien* 147-148, and Kidd, *Hist. of the Church* 2.220.

[7] Socrates *Hist. eccl.* 3.24-25 = *PG* 67.449.

[8] Theodoret *Hist. eccl.* 4.24.4; cf. Eltester, "Kirchen Antiochias" 275.

[9] Socrates *Hist. eccl.* 3.25 = *PG* 67.452ff.; Sozomen *Hist. eccl.* 6.4 = *PG* 67.1300ff.; Kidd, *Hist. of the Church* 2.221.

[10] Sozomen *Hist. eccl.* 6.5 = *PG* 67.1304-1305; Kidd, *Hist. of the Church* 2.222-223, 260-261.

[11] Ammianus Marcellinus 25.10.4. *CTh* 11.20.1 shows that he was in Mopsuestia on 12 November (cf. Seeck, *Regesten* 106.19).

[12] Seeck in *RE* 9.2010.

[13] A. Nagl, "Valentinianus I," no. 1, *RE* 7A (1948) 2158-2204; W. Heering, *Kaiser Valentinian I* (Diss., Jena 1927).

[14] Theophanes a. 5855, p. 51.7-11 ed. De Boor; Philostorgius, *Hist. eccl.* 7.7; Socrates, *Hist. eccl.* 4.1 = *PG* 67.464-465; Sozomen, *Hist. eccl.* 6.6 = *PG* 67.1308-1309; Theodoret, *Hist. eccl.* 3.16; Zonaras 13.15.4-5; cf. Nagl, *op.cit.* (above, n. 13) 2160.

[15] Ammianus Marcellinus 26.4.5-6.

[16] A. Nagl, "Valens," no. 3, *RE* 7A (1948) 2097-2137.

[17] *Cod. Theod.* 9.16.9; Theodoret, *Hist. eccl.* 4.24; Michael the Syrian, *Chronicle* 8.7, vol. 1, p. 294 tr. Chabot.

[18] Ammianus Marcellinus 26.5.1-4.

of A.D. 364/5 in the capital he set out for Syria,[19] apparently with the intention of making Antioch his headquarters.[20] While he was en route, however, there began the rebellion of Procopius, a relative of Julian's mother Basilina, who, having served under Julian and having the support of a number of elements within the Empire, undertook to make himself emperor. Valens was occupied during the winter and spring with operations against the usurper, who was defeated and killed on 27 May A.D. 366.

During the revolt of Procopius, on 21 July A.D. 365, Antioch suffered from an earthquake, which affected many other cities of the East.[21] No specific record of the damage has been preserved, but the shocks seem to have been moderately severe, and the damage done at this time may have furnished the occasion for the building operations that Valens carried out at Antioch later in his reign.

After the defeat of Procopius, an invasion of the Goths in the spring of A.D. 367 called Valens to Thrace, where he made his headquarters at Marcianopolis until a peace was concluded in A.D. 369. While Valens was in Thrace, Sapor was engaged in hostile operations in Armenia and Iberia, which became increasingly menacing.[22] Valens went to Constantinople in the late winter of A.D. 370, and after the dedication of the Church of the Apostles on 9 April[23] he set out on a hurried journey to Antioch,[24] which he reached on or before 30 April.[25] After spending the summer at Hierapolis engaged on military affairs, he returned to Antioch, before 30 October,[26] then went to Constantinople to spend the winter of A.D. 370/71.[27] A decree issued on 30 October,

[19] Ammianus Marcellinus 26.6.11.
[20] An embassy from Antioch had invited the emperor to visit the city: Libanius *Ep.* 1499 F. = 1526 b W.; *Ep.* 1505 F. = 1531 W.
[21] The date is given by Ammianus Marcellinus 26.10.15-19. Other records are preserved in Libanius *Or.* 18.292 (who speaks of Antioch as ἡ κάλλει μεγίστη [sc. πόλις]); Socrates *Hist. eccl.* 4.3. = *PG* 67.468; *Consularia Const.*, p. 240 ed. Mommsen *Chron. min.* 1; *Consularia Italica*, pp. 294-295 *ibid.*; *Chron. Pasch.* 556.15-16 Bonn ed.; Ephrem, *Hymn*, transl. G. Bickell, "Gedichte des h. Ephräm gegen Julian den Apostaten," *ZKT* 2 (1878) 354; *Chron. syr.* in Land *Anec. syr.* 1.106. This earthquake seems to be referred to by Chrysostom *Homil. ad pop. Antioch.* 2.2 = *PG* 49.35. The year 366 is indicated, wrongly, by Theophanes a. 5859, p. 56.10ff. ed De Boor, and Jerome *Chron.* Olymp. 286, p. 244 ed. Helm.
[22] Ammianus Marcellinus 27.12.
[23] *Chronica Constantinopolitana*, a. 370, p. 242 ed. Mommsen, *Chronica minora* 1; Jerome *Chron.* Olymp. 287, p. 245 ed. Helm; *Chronicon Paschale* p. 559.13-15 Bonn ed.; cf. Downey, "Original Church of the Apostles" 57, 76.
[24] Socrates *Hist. eccl.* 4.14 = *PG* 67.497; Sozomen *Hist. eccl.* 6.13 = *PG* 67.1328; Zosimus 4.13.
[25] *CTh* 10.19.5; cf. Seeck, *Regesten* 239 and 71.41ff.
[26] Zosimus 4.13; *CTh* 15.2.2; cf. Seeck, *Regesten* 241 and 71.42ff.
[27] Seeck, *Regesten* 241.

before Valens left Antioch, indicates that the emperor intended to return to the city and make his headquarters there. It had been found that during the preceding years, when Antioch had not been used as an imperial residence, private individuals had illegally tapped the aqueduct that supplied the palace at Daphne, thus reducing the palace's own supply of water; and Valens now issued a rescript which would put an end to this abuse,[28] thus indicating that he intended to occupy the palace.

In the summer of A.D. 371 Valens was busy with the Persian war, and at the end of the summer a truce was made, after which the emperor went to Antioch, arriving there on 10 November.[29] In the course of the winter[30] Valens' fear of magic, the practice of which he had recently made a capital offence,[31] was realized in spectacular fashion. It was discovered that various persons had been engaging in efforts to discover the name of the emperor who would succeed Valens. A wooden tripod, like that used by the oracle at Delphi, was marked with the letters of the alphabet, and a ring suspended on a thread above the tripod, when set in motion, swung toward the letters THEOD. The same result was reached by Libanius and a friend through *alektromanteia*: On each letter of an alphabet scratched on the ground a grain of wheat was dropped, and a message was formed by arranging the letters in the sequence in which a fowl pecked the grains from them. These discoveries resulted in a veritable reign of terror in Antioch, which eventually spread to Asia Minor. It developed that one of the imperial secretaries, named Theodorus, had been privy to the consultations. He and many others whose names also happened to begin with the fatal letters were executed. The investigations were carried on with the utmost ferocity, and the tortures and executions, as Ammianius writes, resembled the slaughtering of animals. Valens himself had a morbid love of torture, and was only sorry that the pain could not be continued after the death of the victim. It appeared that Valens had been in real danger; proper judicial procedures were suspended and many innocent persons perished or were exiled, and the confiscation of their estates, which brought a large increase of wealth to the emperor, came to be

---

[28] *CTh* 15.2.2.

[29] Ammianus Marcellinus 29.1.1-5, cf. 29.2.21; Malalas 338.10-19. On the chronology, see A. Nagl, "Valens," no. 3, *RE* 7A (1948) 2111-2112.

[30] On the chronology, see O. Seeck, "Zur Chronologie u. Quellenkritik des Ammianus Marcellinus," *Hermes* 41 (1906) 523-524, and Nagl *op.cit.* (above, n. 29) 2111.

[31] *CTh* 9.16.8 of 12 December A.D. 370; on the date, see Seeck, *Regesten* 34.21. See J. Maurice, "La terreur de la magie au IVe siècle," *Rev. hist. de Droit franç. et étr.*, ser. 4, vol. 6 (1927) 108-120.

regarded as one of the major factors in the persecution. Ultimately the investigation was extended to all persons who could be accused or suspected of any magical practice, and a number of philosophers lost their lives. Books dealing with magic were seized and burned, and many people as a precaution burned their entire libraries even though the books were innocent. The persecution continued until Valens left Antioch in A.D. 378.[32]

The truce made with Persia at the end of A.D. 371 lasted for only a short time. In A.D. 373 hostilities broke out again and the Persians were defeated. Indecisive diplomatic moves and negotiations for peace followed until finally the serious danger presented by the invasion of Thrace by the Goths called Valens away from Antioch in the spring of A.D. 378 and the Persian question had to be left unsettled.[33] During this time Valens had remained at Antioch except for summer expeditions during which the court was moved to Hierapolis.[34] During all this period Antioch must have been constantly busy with military preparations and the production of equipment. We have one glimpse of this activity in a decree of the Code of Theodosius, dated A.D. 374, which gives the comparative rates of the production of helmets in the arms factories at Antioch and Constantinople.[35]

On 28 March A.D. 373 Valens celebrated his *decennalia* in Antioch and heard a congratulatory address (*Or.* 11) from Themistius.[36] On 17 November A.D. 375 Valentinian died at Brigetio and his young son Gratianus became emperor in the West, with, as colleague, another son of the dead emperor, Valentinian II.[37]

[32] The principal account is given by Ammianus Marcellinus 29.1.5ff. Other details are furnished by Libanius *Or.* 1.171-175, 179 (cf. Sievers, *Leben des Libanius* 144-148); Eunapius *Lives of the Philosophers* pp. 479-480 ed. Boissonade, and frag. 38, p. 84 in *Excerpta de sententiis*, ed. Boissevain; Chrysostom *Ad vid. iun., PG* 48.604; Socrates *Hist. eccl.* 4.19 = *PG* 67. 504-505; Sozomen *Hist. eccl.* 6.35 = *PG* 67.1397ff.; Zosimus 4.13-15; Philostorgius *Hist. eccl.* 9.15; Theophanes a. 5867, p. 62.14-16 ed. De Boor; Zonaras 13.16.37ff.; Cedrenus 1.545.1-4 Bonn ed.; Victor *Epit.* 48. On the burning of the books, see Ammianus Marcellinus 29.1.41 and 29.2.4, and cf. C. A. Forbes, "Books for the Burning," *TAPA* 67 (1936) 125.

[33] On the sources and the chronology of these events, which present special problems, see Stein, *Gesch.* 1.288-289, and Nagl, *op.cit.* (above, n. 9) 2116-2117.

[34] For the emperor's movements, see Seeck, *Regesten* 243-251.   [35] *CTh* 10.22.1.

[36] I follow H. Scholze, *De temporibus librorum Themistii* (Diss. Göttingen 1911) 40-41, in believing that Themistius' address was delivered in Antioch in A.D. 373; Seeck believes that it was delivered in the following year, and Harduin that it was delivered in Constantinople; see Stegemann, "Themistios," *RE* 5A (1934) 1660. Themistius' brief *Or.* 25 may also have been presented to Valens on this occasion, though this has been disputed; see Stegemann, *op.cit.* 1664. For another address made by Themistius before the emperor in Antioch, in connection with Valens' persecution of the orthodox Christians, see below, nn. 87-88.

[37] Piganiol, *Empire chrétien* 176, 197, 201-203.

A.D. 363-378

Valens' stay at Antioch ended in the spring of 378, when he left the city hurriedly to deal with the Goths in Thrace.[38] After a brief visit to Constantinople he took the field and was killed in the disastrous battle of Adrianople on 9 August A.D. 378.[39]

3. Buildings at Antioch; The Forum of Valens

Valens was fond of building,[40] and from the beginning of his reign he took care that the cities in his part of the empire should have the use, for public building purposes, of specified portions, according to their needs, of what they had paid in taxes, a measure that was made especially necessary because of the damage done throughout the East by the earthquake of 21 July A.D. 365,[41] and at Nicaea by an earthquake in A.D. 368.[42]

In Antioch—which, Malalas says,[43] the emperor liked because of its site, its air, and its water—Valens carried out important building operations, the most notable of which was the construction of a new forum called the Forum of Valens.[44] This was probably built at some time

[38] Jerome *Chron.* Olymp. 289, p. 249 ed. Helm; Ammianus Marcellinus 31.7.1, 31.11.1; Philostorgius *Hist. eccl.* 9.17; Socrates *Hist. eccl.* 4.35 = *PG* 67.556; Sozomen *Hist. eccl.* 6.37 = *PG* 67.1408 B.

[39] Piganiol, *Empire chrétien* 167-168.

[40] Ammianus Marcellinus 31.14.4, cf. 30.9.1. Malalas (342.9) calls him φιλοκτίστης. On his building activities in general, see Nagl, *op.cit.* (above, n. 29) 2130-2132.

[41] See A. Schulten, "Zwei Erlasse des Kaisers Valens über die Provinz Asia," *Jahreshefte des Oesterr. Archäol. Inst.* 9 (1906) 40-70, and R. Heberdey, "Zum Erlass des Kaisers Valens an Eutropius," *ibid.* 182-192, also Nagl, *op.cit.* (above, n. 29) 2128. Heberdey's interpretation of the inscription is followed here. On the earthquake of A.D. 365, see above n. 21.

[42] *Chron. Pasch.* 557.13-15 Bonn ed.

[43] 338.19-20.

[44] The forum is described by Malalas 338.19-339.19. Below (Excursus 12), will be found translations of the texts relating to the buildings on and near the forum, together with detailed discussions of certain topographical questions that are too lengthy to be included in the present description. Only the results of these discussions are presented here. Hypothetical reconstructions of the forum have been offered by Müller (*Antiq. Antioch.*, Plate A, reproduced below, Fig. 9) and by Stauffenberg (*Malalas* 474-478); the reconstruction attempted here (which is based upon a somewhat more extended study of the texts) differs in some details from theirs. K. Lange, *Haus u. Halle* (Leipzig 1885) 190, plausibly suggests that in its general features the Forum of Valens resembled the Forum of Trajan at Rome (see Platner-Ashby, *Rome* 237-245). Malalas also states (338.7-8) that Valentinian built "many things" in Antioch, without specifying what they were. This statement almost certainly refers to the operations under the patronage of Valens which Malalas describes in 338.19ff., for public buildings erected in both parts of the Empire could be described in inscriptions as having been put up by the imperial colleagues (see Nagl, *op.cit.* [above, n. 29] 2132, and Platner-Ashby, *Rome* 322). Malalas' statement that Valentinian built public buildings in Antioch independently of Valens presumably means only that the chronicler, not understanding that buildings erected by one emperor would also bear the name of the other, misinterpreted the statement of a source and wrongly supposed that buildings put up at

before the death of Valentinian in November, A.D. 375, for it contained three statues of Valentinian, and it seemed unlikely that these statues of the senior Augustus would have been placed in the forum if it had been built after his death. The new forum was located at the eastern end of the short colonnaded street that ran between the mountain and the river, crossing the principal colonnaded street of the city; it also stood on the winter-torrent Parmenius, which flowed from the mountain to the Orontes, near or alongside the transverse street (Fig. 11). There already existed in this part of the city a number of notable public buildings. The oldest of which we know was the Temple of Ares, which existed in the time of Julius Caesar and was probably of Hellenistic date.[45] This presumably consisted of a large enclosure, for the assembly of troops at the rites, with a temple within it. Opposite this temple Caesar had built his basilica called the Kaisarion, which contained an open court and a vaulted apse, in front of which stood statues of Caesar and of the Tyche of Rome.[46] At the eastern end of the street, near the Temple of Ares, Trajan had built the Middle Gate, a monumental arch.[47] In the same neighborhood Commodus had built the Xystos for use in the Olympic Games, with a temple to Olympian Zeus; the same emperor had also erected here a public bath named for himself, and had restored the Temple of Athene, which was probably of the Seleucid period.[48] At the same time, or a little later, the Plethrion, another structure for use in the Olympic Games, was built near the Xystos and the Bath of Commodus.[49] In the same neighborhood stood the Horologion, which may be identical with the Tower of the Winds built by Vespasian.[50]

Antioch by "Valentinian and Valens" were built separately by the two emperors. That this is what happened is indicated of course by the circumstance that Malalas does not enumerate the buildings that he says Valentinian built.

[45] Malalas 216.19-21.

[46] Malalas *loc.cit.* (above, n. 45). On the plan of the Kaisarion, see above, Ch. 7, nn. 54-57.

[47] Malalas 275.14-17; see Excursus 10, §B.

[48] Malalas 283.4-9.

[49] Malalas 290.14-20; see Ch. 9, §10. The Plethrion is described by Libanius in *Or.* 10, a translation of which is printed below; see Appendices, Translation of Documents, 2.

[50] Malalas 338.22, 262.3-4; for Vespasian's work, see Ch. 9, n. 30. Müller supposed that the Horologion, like the Tower of the Winds, was built by Andronicus at Athens (*Antiq. Antioch.* 110, n. 5), but he strangely neglected to mention the shrine of the Winds built under Vespasian at Antioch (cf. his account of the work of Titus and Vespasian at Antioch, pp. 85-87), so that he had no occasion to express an opinion as to the identity of the buildings. His remark on the Horologion implies, however, that he would have identified it with Vespasian's monument. Stauffenberg (*Malalas* 483) mentions both buildings but expresses no opinion as to their identity, believing (for reasons which are not clear) that we do not know whether the structure of Vespasian was

This region, already prominent in the civic life of Antioch, was made still more important by the construction of Valens' new forum. Enough literary evidence is preserved to enable us to determine the main features of the forum, though it is not possible to fix the exact locations of all of the buildings connected with it.

Space for the open part of the forum was obtained by demolishing part of the Kaisarion, and by building heavy stone vaults over the Parmenius, with marble paving laid on top of them. Some of these vaults, and a part of what was apparently the paving of the forum itself, were found in the excavations.[51] The excavations show that the main street, which ran west of the forum, had always been carried over Parmenius on vaults. Apparently the course of the stream east of the main street, toward the mountain, had been left uncovered until the time of Valens, and when the forum was built, the existing vaults at the crossing of the main street were continued upstream along the site of the forum.[52] The vaulted apse ($\kappa\acute{o}\gamma\chi\eta$) of the Kaisarion was rebuilt or restored, and became a prominent feature of the new forum. The open part of the forum was surrounded by four porticoes, decorated with coffered ceilings,[53] paintings, variegated marbles, and mosaic work; the columns were of marble of Salona,[54] and the porticoes contained statues. Around the forum stood various buildings. The Plethrion had adjoined the demolished part of the Kaisarion[55] and so presumably stood on one side of the forum. The apse of the Kaisarion, which has been mentioned, must have stood on another side. On still another side was the Bath of Commodus, which later became the praetorium

---

actually a temple or was a horologion. On the Tower of the Winds at Athens, see Rehm, "Horologium," *RE* 8 (1913) 2426-2427, and E. Ardaillon, "Horologium," Daremberg-Saglio, *Dict. des antiq.* 3.259-260.

[51] See the report on the trial excavations in this area in *Antioch-on-the-Orontes* 2.4 and *Antioch-on-the-Orontes* 3.17-18. See also the report in *AJA* 44 (1940) 418.

[52] Malalas says that the Kaisarion was demolished "as far as the Plethrion" (338.19-339.1). This might be taken to imply that whatever part of the Kaisarion could be said to be "beyond the Plethrion" was allowed to remain standing; but since there is no other evidence for the positions of the two structures with relation to each other, the significance of the phrase is not certain. Malalas' words may mean only that the Plethrion adjoined the Kaisarion, and that the demolition of the Kaisarion cleared the space as far as the Plethrion.

[53] The context indicates that $\kappa\alpha\lambda\acute{a}\theta\omega\sigma\iota\varsigma$ here means coffering, not (as it sometimes does) basket-work capitals on columns. The word is used in the sense of coffering by Sophronius, *PG* 87, pt. 3, 3813, line 38, and in *Theophanes Continuatus* 147.10 Bonn ed. (see DuCange, *Lexicon s.v.*).

[54] There appears to be no other evidence for marble "of Salona." However, as Müller suggests (*Antiq. Antioch.* 110, n. 6), this name might naturally be applied to the well-known marble of Tragurium (Pliny *Nat. hist.* 3.141), which was on the Dalmatian coast not far from Salona.

[55] See above, n. 52.

A History of Antioch

of the consularis Syriae.[56] This bath was probably flanked by the Xystos. Opposite the bath and the Xystos, on the other side of the forum, Valens erected a new basilica.[57] The position of the Horologion is not certain, but its importance for the public was such that it is safe to assume that it was placed in a position in which it could be seen easily by the people who used the forum.[58]

Near the forum, but apparently not on it, was a new *macellum*, or provisions market, which Valens installed on the site of the former Temple of Ares.[59] This is said to have been "very close" or "closest"

[56] The date at which the bath became a praetorium is not known. The change had occurred by the time of the Emperor Zeno (A.D. 474-491), when the praetorium is mentioned in connection with a riot (see below, Ch. 17, §4).

[57] Some difficulty has been caused by the circumstance that Malalas in describing the forum uses βασιλική to mean both (1) a covered colonnade such as would be built along the side of a forum, and (2) a larger columnar structure such as would commonly be called a basilica. On this generic usage, which is followed by other ancient writers as well, see Downey, "Architectural Significance of *stoa* and *basilike*" 194-211; Malalas' description of the forum is studied there on pp. 201-202. Müller (*Antiq. Antioch.* 109-110), who was unaware of this usage, took Malalas' "four *basilikai*" to be four of the buildings which surrounded the forum, viz. the ἄλλη βασιλική which Valens built opposite the Bath of Commodus (339.4), the Conch of the Kaisarion, the Plethrion, and the Macellum. However, Malalas' description of the "four *basilikai*" seems to refer so plainly to colonnades such as would naturally be built about the forum that it is difficult to accept Müller's explanation. It therefore seems likely that the ἄλλη βασιλική was a new basilical building, not a colonnade.

[58] On the importance of the location of a horologion, see H. S. Robinson's study of that at Athens, "The Tower of the Winds and the Roman Market Place," *AJA* 47 (1943) 291-305.

[59] The Temple of Ares still existed, as such, in the time of the Emperor Julian, who visited it (Libanius *Or.* 15.79). There is no reference to the *Macellum* in Malalas' account of the forum, but it seems reasonably certain, as Müller recognizes (*Antiq. Antioch.* 110), that the *Macellum* stood on the forum, and that it was created at this time. Malalas mentions the *Macellum* (1) in his account (216.19-21) of the construction of the Kaisarion, saying that the Kaisarion was "opposite the Temple of Ares, which was later called the *Macellum*"; (2) in his account of the Middle Gate of Trajan (275.14-17), in which he writes that the gate was near the Temple of Ares, "which is now [i.e. in Malalas' time] called *Macellum*"; and (3) in another reference to the Kaisarion (287.3-7), which is described as opposite the Temple of Ares, "where there is the so-called *Macellum*." Either a reference to the *Macellum* in the account of the forum dropped out in the abridgement of our present text of Malalas, or the chronicler, who often worked mechanically and unintelligently, forgot to mention it. Müller suggests that Malalas in his account of the forum speaks of the *Macellum* as a "basilica," but this does not seem likely (see further in n. 57). One would naturally expect that on the occasion of the construction of a forum such as that of Valens, arrangements would be made, if possible, for a suitable *macellum*; and if an excellent site, such as that of the Temple of Ares, were available, it seems beyond question that Valens would have used it, especially since the change would do away with a pagan temple. Stauffenberg (*Malalas* 475-476) thinks that the *Macellum* was Hellenistic, that it was always distinct from the Temple of Ares, and that the Temple of Ares continued to exist after the time of Julian. It would, in Stauffenberg's estimation, be impossible to convert a Temple of Ares into a *Macellum*. Stauffenberg cites no evidence for the existence of the temple

[406]

(ἔγγιστα) to the Middle Gate of Trajan, and it seems likely that it stood behind the Conch of the Kaisarion and extended up the slope of the mountain to the Middle Gate.[60] Since this temple presumably had been surrounded by a large open space for the accommodation of troops at the rites in honor of the god, it would have been easy to transform the temple and its court into a *macellum*, which normally consisted of an open area surrounded by porticoes and shops, with a fountain, either hypaethral or covered by a tholus, in the center of the open space.[61] The transformation of the temple into a *macellum* had the merit not only of providing a new market, but of eliminating a pagan shrine.[62]

Three statues of Valentinian I were set up in and about the forum. One was placed on a column in the middle of the open space of the forum. Two others were placed in the so-called Conch, that is, the vaulted apse of the Kaisarion which had been retained and restored or rebuilt when the remainder of the Kaisarion was demolished. One of these statues was placed "in the *Senaton* of the Conch," which was presumably a part of the Conch in which the senators of Antioch assembled. The other statue, which was seated, and was made of "costly stone" (porphyry?), was placed "in the middle of the *basilike* which is in the Conch," that is, apparently, in the middle of a colonnade which formed a part of the Conch.[63]

In addition to the construction of the forum, Valens carried out other building operations in Antioch. One of his undertakings, the *kynegion*, reflects the changes which were being brought about through the influence of Christianity. Gladiatorial shows had been forbidden, as repugnant to the new religion, by Constantine the Great in A.D. 325,[64] and this form of entertainment, though it continued to be followed in

---

after the time of Julian, and I have been able to find none. The texts themselves, and the other considerations offered here, seem sufficient to refute Stauffenberg's beliefs.

[60] Malalas 275.16; see below, Excursus 12, the discussion of the locations of the buildings.

[61] On the construction and use of *macella*, see K. Schneider, "Macellum," *RE* 14 (1930) 129-130. On the history of the word, see A. Cameron, "Latin Words in the Greek Inscriptions of Asia Minor," *AJP* 52 (1931) 249-250. On temples of Ares and Mars, see Marbach, "Mars," *RE* 14 (1930) 1926-1928.

[62] It is of interest to note, as a possible parallel to the work at Antioch, that the *Macellum Liviae* on the Esquiline at Rome was restored under the auspices of Valentinian, Valens and Gratian; see Platner-Ashby, *Rome* 322-323. There is also evidence that a new forum was built at Rome on the Palatine at the same time (*ibid.* 229).

[63] The statues are described by Malalas 339.10-15; see Müller, *Antiq. Antioch.* 78, 110, and Downey, "Architectural Significance of *stoa* and *basilike*" 202, n. 1. For the use of *basilike* to mean a colonnade, see above, n. 57.

[64] *CTh* 15.12.1.

the West, must have declined at Antioch and elsewhere in the East,[65] although Libanius, in his autobiography written at the end of his life, in the latter part of the fourth century, says that both as a youth and as an old man he enjoyed gladiatorial combats.[66] Valens, however, transformed what had been a *monomacheion*, making it a *kynegion* in which hunts and combats of animals could be held.[67] The conversion was effected by the construction of two curved ends containing rows of seats carried on arches. Since the original *monomacheion* had presumably been square, with seats on all four sides, the addition of two curved ends would have enlarged the seating capacity, and if the curved ends were added outside the lines of the original straight sides, the size of the arena would also have been enlarged by the removal of the original seats. The conversion of the structure would also (though we hear nothing of this) have entailed the introduction of arrangements for the safe-keeping of the animals and their passage into the arena; also provision would presumably have been made for the scenery and stage-machinery required for the scenic effects that accompanied animal shows. The *kynegion* at Antioch may have resembled those in other cities in which both the animals and the scenic apparatus were kept in underground chambers below the arena.[68] This provision of a regular *kynegion* afforded better facilities for the shows of animals which formerly had been held elsewhere, probably in the hippodromes and scenic theaters at Antioch and Daphne.[69] Thus better use was made of a building that presumably was no longer in much demand for gladiatorial entertainments, and by the improvement of the animal shows the public was given some compensation for the loss of the gladiators.

The location of Valens' *kynegion* is nowhere specified, and it is not easy to identify it. There has been found in the excavations, not far

[65] See K. Schneider, "Gladiatores," *RE*, Suppl. 3 (1918) 771-772, and L. Roberts, *Les gladiateurs dans l'Orient grec* (Paris 1940) 330.

[66] *Or.* 1.5. Jones, *Greek City* 361, n. 87, thinks that Libanius here speaks of gladiatorial shows "as a thing of the past," but this does not seem to me to be certain.

[67] Malalas 339.15-17. The names which the chronicler gives to the building in its two phases, *monomacheion* and *kynegion*, are not, apparently, found elsewhere applied to buildings, though they are used of the spectacles which were presented in them. It would be natural to apply these terms also to the buildings, as Malalas does. On the use of σφενδόνη to describe the curved end of such a building, see Malalas 307.15 and 340.3 (of the *sphendonai* of hippodromes); cf. Stephanus, *Lexicon s.v.* The term also appears in the form of σφενδών; see *Scriptores originum Constantinopolitanarum* 137.3, 145.17, 191.11, 224.12, 276.15 ed. Th. Preger.

[68] On underground accommodations for machinery and animals, see Friedländer, *Sittengeschichte*[10] 2.90-91.

[69] Commodus had established a fund for the maintenance of animal shows and hunts (see Ch. 9, §10).

from the site of the Forum of Valens, a rebuilt structure intended for
shows and spectacles, with arena, podium, and cavea with curved rows
of seats, but no stage building. This is dated by the excavators possibly
in the fifth century, but more likely in the sixth, after the earthquake
of A.D. 526; and when found it was provisionally identified as a stadium.[70] It is not clear, however, whether enough of the building was
uncovered to make it certain that it was a stadium, and from the information now available it seems possible that it is the *kynegion* of
Valens, or a successor to it.[71] If this is the case, the *monomacheion*
which Valens converted to a *kynegion* would have been different from
the *monomacheion* built by Julius Caesar on the acropolis.[72] If, however, the *monomacheion* which Valens transformed was Caesar's, then
the building found in the excavations might be the successor to some
other building designed for spectacles. Caesar's *monomacheion* was
ultimately abandoned, and was demolished to provide stones for the
extension of the city wall under Theodosius II.[73] This suggests that
Caesar's structure, being difficult of access by reason of its location, was
replaced, even before its demolition, by a *monomacheion* more conveniently located in the city itself, which might have been the *monomacheion* which Valens rebuilt. This might have been a predecessor
of the structure found in the excavations; and the location of this near
the Forum of Valens might be taken as an indication that it is the one
altered by Valens. This hypothesis is supported by a remark of Libanius in his oration in praise of Antioch written in A.D. 360,[74] in which
the orator cites, as one of the many advantages of Antioch, the fact
that the *theatra* designed for *venationes* and those designed for gladiatorial shows are all in the central part of the city, and that the pleasure
of the spectacles is not spoiled beforehand by the length of the journey
to reach them.[75] The principal implication of course is that in other
cities these *theatra* are sometimes not readily accessible. Another implication might be that Caesar's *monomacheion* on the acropolis, being

[70] See the preliminary reports on the excavations in *Antioch-on-the-Orontes* 2.3 and
AJA 42 (1938) 208.
[71] Libanius (*Or.* 10.33) mentions an "oblong theatron" (πρόμηκες θέατρον) which
was not far from the Plethrion (cf. Müller, *Antiq. Antioch.* 79, n. 10). This would
certainly seem to be identical with the building found in the excavations. Unfortunately
Libanius' reference to the structure does not make it clear whether it was the *kynegion*
of Valens.
[72] Malalas 217.2-3; see above, Ch. 7, nn. 64-65.
[73] See below, Ch. 16, n. 13.   [74] *Or.* 11.219.
[75] Müller (*Antiq. Antioch.* 79) supposes that it was the *monomacheion* of Caesar
which Valens rebuilt. Müller was of course not acquainted with the evidence for the
structure found in the excavations.

A History of Antioch

A History of Antioch

difficult of access, had been abandoned and replaced by another before A.D. 360. However, there may well have been, in a city as large and as luxurious as Antioch, many "theaters" in which such spectacles could be presented, and it is perhaps unwise, without more evidence, to attempt specific identifications.

Valens also built a public bath, named for himself, near the hippodrome on the island; it is said that he took a particular interest in its construction.[76] The chronicler Malalas writes that the emperor also erected "many other marvelous works in the city," but does not name them.[77]

4. THE CHURCH AT ANTIOCH UNDER VALENS

Although Valentinian was disposed to be tolerant, and adhered to the orthodox belief, Valens favored Arianism, and his naturally cruel nature made him oppressive.[78] He decided that for the sake of order, it was desirable to support the Arians, who were in control at Constantinople and at Antioch through the bishops Eudoxius and Euzoius; and in the spring of A.D. 365 he began a veritable persecution of the orthodox, which opened with a decree ordering the expulsion of all the bishops exiled by Constantius and recalled by Julian.[79] In Antioch, at the opening of Valens' reign, the Christian community was still divided among the followers of Euzoius, Meletius, and Paulinus.[80] Meletius, expelled under Constantius, had returned from exile under Julian, and under the orthodox Jovian had even succeeded in occupying the Great Church, while the Arian bishop Euzoius was temporarily displaced and Paulinus continued to lead his separate orthodox flock, which could not be brought into communion with the Meletians.[81] The effect of Valens' decree was to restore the situation to what it had been at the end of the reign of Constantius. Meletius went into exile once more, and Euzoius again became the "official" bishop of the city. The followers of Meletius who refused communion with Euzoius were driven out of the churches of the city and were severely persecuted;

[76] Ammianus Marcellinus 31.1.2; Malalas 339.17-18. This bath was later burned, and was restored by Theodosius II; see below, Ch. 16, n. 14.
[77] Malalas 339.18-19.
[78] Socrates *Hist. eccl.* 4.1 = *PG* 67.464-465; Sozomen *Hist. eccl.* 6.10 = *PG* 67.1317f. On Valens' character and the influences to which he was subjected, see G. Bardy in Fliche-Martin, *Hist. de l'église* 3.248. On the history of the church under Valens, see Gwatkin, *Studies of Arianism*[2] 231-263, and Kidd, *Hist. of the Church* 2.224-266. A summary of ecclesiastical affairs during this period may be found in Piganiol, *Empire chrétien* 161-165.
[79] Athanasius *Hist. aceph.* 15 = *PG* 26.1447; cf. Kidd, *Hist. of the Church* 2.228.
[80] Socrates *Hist. eccl.* 4.1 = *PG* 67.465.
[81] See above, n. 10.

[410]

many indeed were executed, some by drowning in the Orontes.[82] The followers of Paulinus, however, were spared since he was not subject to Valens' decree. The Meletians held their services in the open air, first on the slopes of the mountain, then, when they were driven thence, on the banks of the river, and finally in the military area (*campus*) across the river.[83] The Arians in fact were now the majority of the Christian population of the city.[84] The Meletians, however, managed to maintain themselves, under the leadership of Flavian (later bishop of Antioch, A.D. 381-404) and of Diodorus and the ascetics Aphraates and Julian who came to the city from their retreats to help support the flock.[85] Aphraates had a celebrated conversation with Valens himself as the holy man passed beneath the portico of the palace on which the emperor happened to be standing.[86]

The persecution continued with such severity that late in A.D. 375 or early in A.D. 376 the pagan court orator Themistius thought it necessary to deliver before Valens, in Antioch, an oration in which he advised the emperor to cease the persecution.[87] This advice had some effect, and the persecution was made less rigorous.[88]

[82] Socrates *Hist. eccl.* 4.2 and 4.17 = *PG* 67.465f., 501; Sozomen *Hist. eccl.* 6.7 and 6.18 = *PG* 67.1313, 1336, cf. Bardy in Fliche-Martin, *Hist. de l'église* 3.248, n. 3.

[83] Theodoret *Hist. eccl.* 4.24-25; *Relig. hist.* 2 = *PG* 82.1317 C. From their use of the *campus* for their services, the Meletians came to be known as *campenses*: Jerome *Ep.* 15 = *CSEL* 54, pp. 64.14, 67.10. See Eltester, "Kirchen Antiochias" 276; on the *campus*, see Müller, *Antiq. Antioch.* 113, n. 21. The *campus* was reached by the Rhomanesia Gate; see the *Petitio Arianorum ad Jovianum* 1 = *PG* 26.820 A.

[84] Sozomen *Hist. eccl.* 6.21 = *PG* 67.1344.

[85] Theodoret *Hist. eccl.* 2.24.6 (activities of Flavian and Diodorus as laymen under Constantius) and 4.24-27, and *Relig. hist.* 2 and 8 = *PG* 82.1305-1324, 1369-1376; Theophanes a. 5867, p. 62.26-32 ed. De Boor. See Kidd, *Hist. of the Church* 2.244. The tombs and caves on the slope of Mount Silpius above Antioch formed a favorite retreat for holy men and women who wished to practice asceticism; see Theodoret *Religiosa historia* 12 (*PG* 82, 1397) for the well-known example of Zeno, the former officer.

[86] Theodoret, *Hist. eccl.* 4.26.

[87] Socrates *Hist. eccl.* 4.32 = *PG* 67.552 and Sozomen *Hist. eccl.* 6.36-37 = *PG* 67.1401-1404, mention the oration and give a summary of its contents; the date is indicated by the position of the references immediately after the notice of the death of Valentinian, which occurred on 17 November A.D. 375. There exists what purports to be a Latin translation of this oration made from a Greek MS that is now lost (Themistius *Or.* 12 ed. Dindorf), but this is considered to be a forgery by the sixteenth century humanist A. Dudith; see Stegemann, "Themistios," *RE* 5A (1934) 1660. Themistius had sent a letter to Julian advising him to cease the persecution of the Christians; see Jeanne Croissant, "Un nouveau discours de Thémistius," *Serta Leodiensia* (Liége 1930) 27, n. 4.

[88] On the career and influence of Themistius, see G. Downey, "Themistius and the Defense of Hellenism in the Fourth Century," *HTR* 50 (1957) 259-274. Themistius speaks of the gratifying way in which the people of Antioch showed their interest in him when he visited the city (*Or.* 23, 299a, p. 360.14 ed. Dindorf).

Meanwhile another attempt was made to heal the schism that still persisted between the two groups of the orthodox, the Meletians and the Eustathians led by Paulinus. Efforts in this direction under Julian and again under Jovian had failed.[89] Now Basil of Caesarea, in A.D. 371, tried to enlist the services of Athanasius, as the natural mediator; but it was impossible still, as in the past, for Athanasius either to desert Paulinus or to approve the views of Meletius.[90]

A further element of discord was introduced into the community by the rising influence of the teaching of Apollinaris, who had developed in Antioch the doctrine that Christ had the body but not the spirit of a man.[91] Although he was bishop of Laodicea (A.D. 361-377), Apollinaris was teaching in Antioch in A.D. 373, one of his pupils being Jerome, who had come to the city to learn Greek and study Biblical exegesis.[92] In 375 or 376 what had been a heresy became a schism when Apollinaris consecrated one of his followers, Vitalis, as bishop of Antioch.[93] This meant that there were now four rival bishops of the city, Euzoius (the official incumbent), Meletius, Paulinus, and Vitalis. Peace in the church at Antioch was, as we shall see, achieved after the death of Valens; but the years A.D. 360 to 378 had been especially grave ones in the history of the Christian community at Antioch since the city had played such a major role in the controversy over Arianism.[94]

Jerome's visit to Antioch in A.D. 374-375 is known in some detail thanks to his letters.[95] His host, the wealthy priest Evagrius, provided him with admirable facilities for work.[96] Many religious visitors and pilgrims on their way to and from Jerusalem passed through Antioch,

[89] See above, Ch. 13, §2; Ch. 14, §1.
[90] See the six letters of Basil on this subject to Athanasius and Meletius (*Epistt.* 61, 66, 67, 69, 80, 82). Cf. Kidd, *Hist. of the Church* 2.260-261, and Cavallera, *Schisme d'Antioche* 136ff.
[91] See above, Ch. 13, §2.
[92] Jerome *Ep.* 84.3 = *CSEL* 55, p. 122.24ff.
[93] Theodoret *Hist. eccl.* 5.4.1; cf. Basil *Epistt.* 258, 265. See Kidd, *Hist. of the Church* 2.254-255, 321; H. Lietzmann, *Apollinaris von Laodicea* (Tübingen 1904) 15ff.; Cavallera, *Schisme d'Antioche* 162ff., 194, with n. 2.
[94] See the summary of this period in the ecclesiastical history of Antioch by G. Bardy, "Alexandrie, Rome, Constantinople (325-451)," *1054-1954, L'Église et les églises. Travaux offerts à Dom Lambert Beauduin* 1 (Chevetogne 1954) 190ff. On the relationships between the church of Antioch and those of Rome, Alexandria, and Caesarea in Cappadocia in the years A.D. 370-379, see the study of D. Amand de Mendiéta, "Damase, Athanase, Pierre, Mélèce et Basile," in the same volume, 261-277.
[95] For a detailed study of Jerome's sojourn in Antioch and its vicinity, see F. Cavallera, *Saint Jérôme, sa vie et son œuvre* (Louvain-Paris, 1922) 1.26ff., with the Regesta Hieronymiana in the second volume, 153ff., giving the chronology of Jerome's activities, with references to his own writings which were associated with them. See also Kidd, *Hist. of the Church* 2.321-323.
[96] Jerome *Vita Malchi* 2; cf. Cavallera, *Saint Jérôme* 1.21, with n. 1 (on Evagrius).

and we hear much of their visits and their discussions.[97] In A.D. 375 Jerome decided to retire to the desert of Chalcis, east of Antioch, and there he passed the next years in study and literary work.[98] Finding himself forced to take part in the quarrels within the church at Antioch, he returned there in A.D. 379 and (as has been mentioned) was in touch with Apollinaris of Laodicea. At this time also Jerome was ordained to the priesthood by Paulinus, the Eustathian bishop.[99] In the same year Jerome left Antioch for further study at Constantinople. He was to visit Antioch again in A.D. 385, during his journey to Jerusalem.[100]

This was the time when many future leaders of the church were studying in Antioch, some of them being pupils of Libanius. One chapter in the *Ecclesiastical History* of Socrates tells us how "John of Antioch," later to be called St. John Chrysostom, studied under Libanius and heard the lectures of Andragathius, "the philosopher."[101] John had originally intended to study law, but following the example of his friend Evagrius, decided to follow the religious life. He persuaded Theodorus and Maximus to make this change with him. Theodorus later became bishop of Mopsuestia and Maximus bishop of Seleucia in Isauria. John and his companions then studied under Diodorus (later bishop of Tarsus) and Carterus, who were then heads of a school or monastery at Antioch. Basil, later bishop of Caesarea, was then a deacon under Bishop Meletius of Antioch. John himself was ordained to the diaconate by Meletius, and thus began his preaching career.

[97] Jerome *Epistt.* 3, 4, 8; cf. Cavallera, *Saint Jérôme* 1.33, 2.153-154.
[98] Cavallera, *Saint Jérôme* 1.39ff.; 2.154.
[99] *Contra Ioann. Hierosol.* 41 (*PL* 23.410-411); cf. Cavallera, *Saint Jérôme* 1.55-56.
[100] Jerome *Apol.* 3.22 (*PL* 23.495); Cavallera, *Saint Jérôme* 1.123.
[101] Socrates, *Hist. eccl.* 6.3. On the question of the date of the birth of Chrysostom (variously placed in A.D. 344, 347 or 354), see P. Franchi de' Cavalieri, *Note agiografiche* 9 (Vatican City 1953) 169 (*Studi e Testi* 175).

CHAPTER 15

THEODOSIUS I AND ARCADIUS, A.D. 379-408

THEODOSIUS' reign (A.D. 379-395), marking out important new directions in the history of the Empire, brought corresponding changes and developments in the history of Antioch. Moreover, thanks to the volume of the preserved writings of Libanius and St. John Chrysostom, the reign of Theodosius I is one of the periods in the history of Antioch about which we are relatively well informed. The reigns of Theodosius and of his son Arcadius (A.D. 395-408) are best treated here as one, since only a few events that occurred at Antioch in Arcadius' reign are known, and many of these had their beginnings in the reign of Theodosius.

When Valens was killed at the battle of Adrianople (9 August A.D. 378), the Empire was left in the hands of Gratianus, the son of Valentinian I, who had become senior Augustus on the death of his father in A.D. 375. Gratianus had chosen as colleague his younger brother Valentinian II, who was four years old at the time of their father's death; but when Valens was killed, it became necessary to find a ruler for the East, and Gratianus chose Theodosius, an officer of Spanish Christian family, whose father, also named Theodosius, may have been thought of, by the enemies of the regime, as a successor to Valens.[1]

1. PEACE IN THE CHURCH OF ANTIOCH

Since the exile of the orthodox bishop Eustathius, ca. A.D. 330, the church of Antioch, as we have seen, had been under the control of a whole series of bishops of Arian tendencies, many of whom aggravated their heterodoxy by violent and sometimes unscrupulous actions.[2] This period of troubles was now to come to an end, just as the Arian controversy was gradually dying out elsewhere as well. After the death of Valens, Gratianus, seeking peace in the church, issued a rescript of toleration, at the end of A.D. 378, which permitted the Catholic bishops to return from exile. The *magister militum* Sapor was put in charge of carrying out the mandate, and the exiled Bishop Meletius returned to

---

[1] See Piganiol, *Empire Chrétien* 200-201, 208-209. On the rumors which had pointed to an emperor whose name began with THEOD, see above, Ch. 14, n. 32.

[2] See the characterization of this period by G. Bardy, "Alexandrie, Rome, Constantinople (325-451)," *1054-1954. L'Église et les églises. Travaux offerts à Dom Lambert Beauduin*, 1 (Chevetogne 1954) 190-191.

Antioch, where he was warmly greeted by his supporters.[3] Meletius
and Paulinus came to an understanding by which each was to function
at the head of his own followers, and the foundation was laid for the
complete restoration of peace in Antioch which was to come later.[4]
Meletius was able to signalize the restoration of orthodoxy in two impressive undertakings. Arrangements were made for the meeting of a
synod of one hundred and fifty-three bishops, who assembled in Antioch
in September A.D. 379 and confirmed the reestablishment of orthodoxy
and studied the questions raised by the restoration of the Catholic
bishops.[5] Then, either at the same time or in the summer of A.D. 380,
Meletius began the construction of the cruciform church, designed as a
martyrium of St. Babylas, the foundations of which have been excavated opposite the city, on the right bank of the Orontes.[6] The construction of this fine church was very likely intended to celebrate the
return of orthodoxy by providing a worthy resting place for one of the
great martyrs of Antioch.[7] Also it is possible that it may have served
to provide a place of worship for Meletius in the period before the
settlement of the questions concerning the occupancy of the church
which had been raised by the recall of the Catholic bishops from exile.[8]
The relics of St. Babylas, which had been taken to Daphne by the
Caesar Gallus,[9] were brought back to Antioch and buried temporarily
in the *koimeterion* outside the city and then buried in the cruciform
church.[10] The date at which the final burial took place is not indicated
in the sources but the relics must have been placed in the church by
A.D. 381, for Meletius, who died in Constantinople in that year while

[3] Theodoret *Hist. eccl.* 5.2; Chrysostom *De Sancto Meletio* 2 = *PG* 50.517; see Kidd, *Hist. of the Church* 2.270, and Seeck, "Sapor," No. 4, *RE* 1A.2356. Cavallera, *Schisme d'Antioche* 211, n. 1, points out that Theodoret has mistakenly advanced to A.D. 378 the restoration of the churches to the Catholic bishops, which more probably took place in A.D. 381 (see further below).

[4] Theodoret *Hist. eccl.* 5.3-4; cf. Cavallera, *Schisme d'Antioche* 211ff.

[5] The acts of the synod have not been completely preserved and some of its actions must be reconstructed by inference or from allusive testimony; see Cavallera, *Schisme d'Antioche* 213, n. 2. As Cavallera points out, it is not clear that this synod was concerned specifically with the restoration of peace within the church at Antioch, which was actually accomplished only in 381 (see further below). On the council of 379, see Kelly, *Early Christian Creeds* 306, 320, 335.

[6] J. Lassus, "L'Église cruciforme," *Antioch-on-the-Orontes* 2.5-44; G. Downey, "The Shrines of St. Babylas at Antioch and Daphne," *ibid.* 45-48; Eltester, "Kirchen Antiochias" 282-283; Lassus, "Syrie," *DACL* 15 (1951) 1898-1899.

[7] On St. Babylas, see above, Ch. 11, nn. 138-143, 145.

[8] This suggestion is put forward by Eltester, "Kirchen Antiochias" 282; it seems plausible though we cannot be certain. The suggestion of the present writer that questions of occupancy might have been settled soon after Meletius' return (made in *Antioch-on-the-Orontes* 2.47, n. 13) has no more force than Eltester's.

[9] See above, Ch. 12, nn. 216-218.   [10] Downey, *op.cit.*

attending the great synod there, was brought back to Antioch and buried with the martyr Babylas in the church that he had built.[11] The crossing of the church, when excavated, revealed a monolithic sarcophagus designed for the reception of two bodies, one placed above the other,[12] and this can only have been designed for the reception of the relics of Babylas and the body of Meletius which, the contemporary sources relate, were buried in the same receptacle.[13]

Local developments were now further affected by the religious program of Theodosius, who was associated with Gratianus as emperor on 19 January A.D. 379. The famous decree *Cunctos populos*, issued 27 February A.D. 380,[14] established orthodoxy as the religion of the Empire and condemned heretics to both divine and earthly penalities. Less than a year later (10 January A.D. 381) another decree[15] deprived heretics of the right to meet in churches. Thus the Arian disorders were brought to an end, and at Antioch, as elsewhere, the final measures could be taken for the full restoration of the orthodox faith. The *magister militum* Sapor came to Antioch to put the decree concerning churches into effect, and after hearing the rival claims of Meletius and Paulinus, he expelled the Arians and awarded the custody of the churches, including the Great Church, to Meletius. Paulinus was allowed to continue in his own church.[16] Since they both claimed to profess the orthodox faith, Meletius offered to make an agreement with Paulinus by which the survivor of the two would be recognized by all the congregations as the orthodox bishop of Antioch.[17] Paulinus rejected the offer; but when Meletius died in Constantinople in A.D. 381, Paulinus attempted to have himself made bishop. The opposition against him was strong, however, and Flavian was chosen bishop and continued in office until his death at an advanced age in A.D. 404.[18]

---

[11] Downey, *op.cit.* Professor Eltester writes (*op.cit.* 283) that the completion of the church is dated by a mosaic in A.D. 387, but this is not exact. The inscribed mosaic in question (published by Lassus, *op.cit.* 39, cf. 40-41 = *IGLS* 774, cf. 776, 777) merely records the completion in A.D. 387 of the mosaic pavement in one of the exedras, and while this may have represented the completion of the construction of the whole church, it is not necessary to suppose that it did so. Another mosaic inscription (Lassus, *op.cit.* 42 = *IGLS* 778) records the completion of mosaic work in the church in the episcopate of Theodotus (A.D. 420-429), but this text need not be taken to mark the completion of the building.

[12] See Lassus' report on the excavations, *Antioch-on-the-Orontes* 2.11, with photograph of the sarcophagus (fig. 7), with his further discussion, *ibid.* 37-38.

[13] Downey, *op.cit.* 45-46.   [14] *CTh* 16.1.2.   [15] *CTh* 16.5.6.

[16] Theodoret *Hist. eccl.* 5.3; Cavallera, *Schisme d'Antioche* 215.

[17] Theodoret *Hist. eccl. loc.cit.* On this pact, see Cavallera's note *Schisme d'Antioche* 232-243.

[18] Theodoret *Hist. eccl.* 5.23; Cavallera, *Schisme d'Antioche* 245ff.

During his episcopate, in A.D. 387, the cruciform church of St. Babylas, constructed by Meletius, was further embellished with several mosaic pavements.[19] Paulinus continued to lead his own section of the local church, and just before he died in A.D. 388/9, he consecrated Evagrius (the friend of St. Jerome) as his successor, in an illegal ceremony.[20] Evagrius was acknowledged as bishop of Antioch by Egypt and the West, while Flavian was supported by the East. A few years later the rival claims of Evagrius and Flavian were laid before a council that met for the purpose at Caesarea in Palestine, and Evagrius' consecration was declared invalid. Flavian remained the officially recognized bishop of Antioch, and Evagrius died not long after his condemnation.[21] The Eustathian episcopate thus came to an end, and the schism of Antioch was nearly closed, though the final step would not be taken until the reign of Theodosius II.

About A.D. 390 we hear of a small synod convoked at Antioch by Flavian in order to make a renewed condemnation of the Messalian heresy, which had been gaining ground at that time with its teaching concerning the inborn sinfulness of man and the means for eradicating this through extreme ascetic practices. A heresy of this type would have had a special appeal to the numerous recluses reported as living in the neighborhood of Antioch, including the slopes of Mount Silpius above the city.[22]

In A.D. 398 John Chrysostom gave up his brilliant preaching career and left Antioch to succeed Nectarius as archbishop of Constantinople.[23] There Chrysostom became involved in troubles that caused him to be sent into exile in June of A.D. 404.[24] He had left behind many friends in Antioch, and when he was sent into exile a split was produced between those in Antioch who repudiated him and his supporters, who continued to look to him as their spiritual leader. When Bishop Flavian died at about the same time that Chrysostom went into exile, the two

---

[19] The work is recorded in inscriptions in the mosaics, published by Lassus, *Antioch-on-the-Orontes* 2.39-41 = *IGLS* 774, 776-777. On the inscriptions, see in addition to the comments of Lassus and of P. Mouterde in the *IGLS*, D. Mallardo, "L'exedra nella basilica cristiana," *Rivista di archeologia cristiana* 22 (1946) 208-211.

[20] Theodoret *Hist. eccl. loc.cit.*; Sozomen *Hist. eccl.* 7.15; see Kidd, *Hist. of the Church* 2.374-376.

[21] Cf. Sozomen, *Hist. eccl.* 7.15, and the quotation of the synodal letter in E. W. Brooks, *The Sixth Book of the Letters of Severus* 2, pt. 1, pp. 223-224; and see Cavallera, *Schisme d'Antioche* 285-286 (who translates the letter) and Kidd, *Hist. of the Church* 2.376.

[22] This synod is known chiefly from Photius, *Bibl.* cod. 52, *PG* 103.88-92; see E. Honigmann, *Patristic Studies* (Città del Vaticano 1953; Studi e Testi 173) 43-46.

[23] Socrates *Hist. eccl.* 6.2; Sozomen *Hist. eccl.* 8.2; Theodoret *Hist. eccl.* 5.27.

[24] See Kidd, *Hist. of the Church* 2.448ff.

parties in Antioch, representing the friends and the enemies of Chrysostom, each put forward a candidate for the bishopric.[25] Chrysostom's friends supported a presbyter named Constantius, an experienced and well-known local figure. The opposing candidate, a presbyter named Porphyrius, forced Constantius to flee the city by threatening to procure his banishment, and had some of Constantius' friends arrested. Then, waiting for a time when the people of the city had all gone to Daphne to attend the Olympic games, Porphyrius had himself hastily consecrated in Antioch. Porphyrius served as bishop of Antioch until his death in A.D. 413. Chrysostom's biographer Palladius describes Porphyrius in highly unfavorable terms, mentioning among other things that he was fond of horse races and theatrical shows,[26] but this characterization is perhaps not to be accepted literally. A neutral historian describes Porphyrius as a man of intellectual attainments and says that he left many examples of his munificence behind him in Antioch.[27] Chrysostom in exile continued in touch with his friends in Antioch, and his influence was felt in the church there until his death in A.D. 407.[28]

At the same time that it was freed from Arianism, the church at Antioch found its status altered in the hierarchy of the churches of the

[25] The principal source for the death of Flavian and the election of his successor Porphyrius is Palladius' *Dialogus de vita S. Ioannis Chrysostomi* 16.53ff., pp. 93ff. ed. Coleman-Norton. This is supplemented by the accounts of Socrates *Hist. eccl.* 7.9; Sozomen *Hist. eccl.* 8.24; Theodoret *Hist. eccl.* 5.35. See Cavallera, *Schisme d'Antioche* 292-293; Kidd, *Hist. of the Church* 2.449-450; Baur, *Der hl. Joh. Chrysostomus* 2.272ff. A detailed study of the election of Porphyrius, with the best collection of the sources that concern him (or possibly concern him), has been made by E. Honigmann, "The Lost End of Menander's *Epitrepontes*," *Acad. r. de Belgique, cl. des lettres et des sciences morales et politiques, Mémoires, coll. in 8°,* tome 46, fasc. 2 (1950) 32ff. Many scholars state that Flavian died on 26 September (e.g. Duchesne, *Hist. anc. de l'église,* tome 3, éd. 5 [Paris 1929] 99; Kidd, *Hist. of the Church* 2.450; Devreesse, *Patriarcat d'Antioche* 42, cf. 116), following an early conjecture of the Bollandist editors of the *Acta Sanctorum* (*Acta SS* 9 March [Paris reprint, 1865], p. 9 C) which gained circulation through a notation in Tillemont, *Mémoires pour servir à l'hist. eccl.* 10 [Paris 1705] 541 (where the suggested date is given as 26 September). It now seems clear, however, that Flavian was not canonized, and that the festival of Flavian on 27 September which appears in a Paris Synaxarium, which has been adopted by many scholars, is in reality based on a confusion with the Flavian who was patriarch of Antioch early in the sixth century; see the discussion of the problem in the *Acta SS,* 27 Sept. (Paris reprint 1867), p. 353 C-D. Palladius (16.53-54) puts Flavian's death at about the same time as Chrysostom's exile from Constantinople, and this would appear to be correct, since Palladius also relates (16.54-55) that Porphyrius' election took place during the celebration of the Olympic games of Antioch, which were celebrated during forty-five days in July and August.

[26] Palladius *Dialogus de vita S. Ioann. Chrys.* 16.53, p. 93 ed. P. R. Coleman-Norton (Cambridge, Eng., 1928).

[27] Theodoret *Hist. eccl.* 5.35.2. What forms Porphyrius' *philanthropia* took, we are not told.

[28] Palladius *Dial.* 11.37-38, p. 66 Coleman-Norton.

great cities of the Empire. Since the Council of Nicaea in A.D. 325, Antioch and Alexandria had been recognized as preeminent in the East, and as having the status of what would later be called patriarchal churches.[29] In the meantime, of course, the political authority of the new capital at Constantinople had grown to such an extent that its prestige in ecclesiastical matters demanded to be recognized along with its political status, and at the Council of A.D. 381, the church of Constantinople was given the first place of honor after that of Rome.[30] This pronouncement was primarily designed to put down the pretensions of Alexandria, but it also had the effect of reducing the prestige of Antioch, which had certainly not been enhanced by the role that it had played in the Arian troubles.

Theodosius' measures for the destruction of the pagan temples, and the story of the Jewish community at Antioch at this time, and its relations with the Christians, will be recorded later in the chapter.

2. Famine, a.d. 382-384; The Administration of the City and the Movement for Reform; The Insurrection of a.d. 387

The opening of Theodosius' reign was not an easy time for the Empire. It was urgently necessary to enlarge and improve the army, and the barbarians continued their attacks.[31] Themistius in an address to the emperor delivered early in A.D. 381 alludes tactfully but clearly to general economic distress and discontent within the Empire.[32] The historian Zosimus relates that the prevailing distress made it difficult to collect taxes, and says that people suffered so from the harshness of the collectors that they spoke of life as being pleasanter under the barbarians.[33]

In addition, Antioch suffered from a famine when bad weather during the winter of A.D. 381/2 damaged the crops due to be harvested in the spring.[34] Grain became scarce, and the local officials sent for

[29] See Ch. 12, n. 152.
[30] Canon 3, in Mansi 3, 560; Hefele-Leclercq, *Conciles* 2.24; see Kidd, *Hist. of the Church* 2.287ff., Lietzmann, *Era of the Church Fathers*² 43-47; E. Schwartz, "Das Nicaenum und das Constantinopolitanum auf der Synode von Chalkedon," *ZNTW* 25 (1926) 38-88.
[31] For the background, see Piganiol, *Empire chrétien* 208ff.
[32] *Or.* 15. For some modern interpretations of the occasion of the oration, see Piganiol, *Empire chrétien* 213, with n. 82.
[33] Zosimus 4.32.
[34] Libanius describes this period in his autobiography (*Or.* 1.205-211). On the season of the harvest, which in the region of Antioch takes place in the spring, see above, Ch. 13, n. 22. The famine and the measures taken to deal with it are described in detail

what supplies they could obtain from other places, but the price of bread increased, no doubt owing to the manipulations of speculators. The *comes Orientis* Philagrius[35] hesitated to coerce the bakers remembering that on a similar occasion in the past, the bakers had simply fled the city.[36] When Philagrius' exhortations produced no bread there was general public criticism, and it was said that the *comes Orientis* had been bribed by the bakers.[37] Philagrius became angry and ordered floggings for the bakers, in order to show that none of them could be compelled to confess that they had been bribed; and the punishment of the bakers would also give some satisfaction to the public.[38] When the seventh man was being beaten, Libanius intervened and succeeded in stopping the flogging.[39]

A famine and bread shortage is heard of again in A.D. 384, when Eumolpius was *consularis Syriae* and Icarius (Theodorus) was *comes Orientis*.[40] This very likely was a continuation of the general famine of A.D. 383, for Libanius says that in A.D. 384 the inhabitants of other cities traveled to Antioch hoping to find food there, only to be disappointed.[41] The farmers from the region of Antioch whose crops had failed also crowded into the city looking for help.[42] A limited supply of bread was available, but it was difficult to control its distribution. Guards were posted at the gates of the city to prevent travelers from carrying out more than two loaves of bread at once.[43] Eumolpius the

---

by Petit, *Libanius et la vie municipale à Antioche* 118-122. For the reign of Theodosius I (as for the preceding reigns) we possess abundant evidence for the history of Antioch from the works of Libanius, who furnishes an amount of detail which it would be impossible to include in the present volume. Since this material has been definitively presented by Petit in the study cited above, as well as in his companion monograph *Les étudiants de Libanius* (Paris 1956), it will be sufficient to refer the reader to these works for further material that cannot be accommodated here.

[35] On his career see Petit, *Libanius et la vie municipale à Antioche* 118-120, 211, 228, 273.

[36] Libanius *Or.* 1.206. On past experiences of shortage of bread, see above, Ch. 12, nn. 221-225. It is interesting to compare the decree concerning disturbances connected with the bakers' union at Ephesus in A.D. 200: W. H. Buckler, "Labor Disputes in the Province of Asia," *Anatolian Studies presented to Sir W. M. Ramsay* (Manchester 1923) 29-33.

[37] Libanius *Or.* 1.207-208.

[38] Libanius *Or.* 1.208; *Or.* 34.4.　　　[39] Libanius *Or.* 1.208.

[40] Libanius *Or.* 27.6. On the careers of Eumolpius and Icarius, see Downey, *Comites Orientis* 13, 17. A thesis of J. Léonard, *Icarius, comte d'Orient d'après quatre discours de Libanius* (Louvain) is reviewed in *Revue belge de philologie* 1942, 537. Icarius was probably a *signum* or second name in general use; his original name was probably Theodorus (Downey, *op.cit.* 13).

[41] Libanius *ibid.* A general famine in other parts of the Roman Empire is attested in A.D. 383 (G. Rauschen *Jahrbücher der christlichen Kirche unter dem Kaiser Theodosius dem Grossen* [Freiburg i.B. 1897] 484-485).

[42] Libanius *ibid.*　　　　　　　　　　　　　[43] Libanius *Or.* 27.14.

consularis Syriae made attempts to alleviate the scarcity, but his superior the *comes Orientis* Icarius gave no assistance.[44] Indeed Icarius made things worse by issuing a decree fixing the price of bread at a moderate figure. As a consequence bread disappeared from the shops and the bakers fled from the city.[45] The situation rapidly grew worse and deaths from starvation began to be reported. Libanius then went to the governor and persuaded him to rescind his price-fixing decree, and bread once again became available.[46]

The shortages of food and the attendant difficulties and disorders are only a part of the picture of life at Antioch as described in the writings of Libanius and St. John Chrysostom. Libanius, who was born in A.D. 314, was reaching the summit of his public career during the reign of Theodosius, and has left a number of pamphlets and addresses on a variety of public and private subjects.[47] His writings are supplemented by those of his pupil St. John Chrysostom, who was born in A.D. 354, ordained deacon in Antioch in A.D. 381 and priest in A.D. 386, and who as a priest delivered the notable series of discourses from which we learn much concerning the government and the social and economic life of the city at this period.[48] Chrysostom had an intimate acquaintance with public affairs in Antioch, since his father had been a civil servant of high rank in the office of the *magister militum per Orientem* at Antioch,[49] so that even though his father died when he was a child, Chrysostom and his mother must have been acquainted with the prominent people of the city. In their writings at this time

[44] Libanius *Or.* 27.6.   [45] Libanius *Or.* 1.226.

[46] Libanius *Or.* 29.3-7. Libanius' statement that when price controls were removed, bread became plentiful, suggests that there had been hoarding of grain by speculators who wished to force up the price.

[47] For the bibliography of Libanius' works, and the modern studies of them, see the chapter on the sources for the history of Antioch, above, Ch. 2, §5. It should be borne in mind that a number of Libanius' orations and letters have been lost, and are known (in the case of the orations) only from references to them in the extant texts (cf. Förster and Münscher, "Libanios," *RE* 12.2526-2528). Especially for the period of Libanius' political activity during the reign of Theodosius, his orations furnish us with much detail that would be impossible to accommodate in the present work. The essential information is presented here, and for further details the reader may consult the exhaustive study by P. Petit, *Libanius et la vie municipale à Antioche.*

[48] For accounts of Chrysostom's life and works, see H. Lietzmann, "Ioannes Chrysostomus," *RE* 9 (1916) 1811-1828 (on his birth and ordinations, see cols. 1812-1813) and Baur, *Der hl. Joh. Chrysostomus* (Munich 1929-1930; volume 1 deals with Chrysostom's life and work in Antioch). A French translation of Chrysostom's works in 21 volumes has been published by J. Bareille (Paris 1864-1878). One of the important sources for Chrysostom's life is the biography by Palladius (*Palladii Dialogus de vita S. Joannis Chrysostomi*, ed. by P. R. Coleman-Norton [Cambridge, Eng., 1928]).

[49] See the important study by A. H. M. Jones, "St. John Chrysostom's Parentage and Education," *HTR* 46 (1953) 171-173.

both Libanius and Chrysostom present a somewhat depressing account of the conduct of the local officials and of their fellow citizens; but while much of the information that they give is of great value, detailed study of it indicates that allowance must be made for the zeal of the reformer,[50] and in the case of Libanius, it is plain that personal enmity, disappointment, and chronic regret for bygone times render part of his testimony unreliable.[51]

Nevertheless we can recover an instructive picture of the problems and difficulties that both the imperial officials and the citizens encountered at Antioch at this period. The policies that had been followed for some years by the imperial government were tending to weaken the local municipal governments and to discourage and impoverish the middle classes; and the farmers and the lower classes, who had never found life easy under the prevailing economic system, continued to suffer from their usual troubles. We hear of all this from Libanius, who gives us, in addition, special information on certain problems in the "reform speeches" which begin in A.D. 381.[52] The orator was concerned with these matters not only because of his own personal interest in reform, but because the emperor rewarded him with the title of honorary *praefectus praetorio*, about the winter of A.D. 383/4,[53] and by virtue of this dignity, Libanius was close to the official life and the public problems of Antioch.

Libanius, himself a member of the curial class, was continually concerned with the way in which both the property and the energy of the decurions was being used up in the public services they were required to perform. Eligible men were avoiding service in every way, and Libanius advised the emperor that it was urgently necessary to increase the membership in the local senate in order to distribute the burden more equitably.[54] There was also an almost chronic state of warfare between the imperial governors and the decurions, as the governors sought to realize the financial profits that were a perquisite of their office.[55]

---

[50] See for example R. Stillwell's observations on the picture of Antiochene morals presented by Chrysostom and others, in his review of G. Haddad, *Aspects of Social Life in Antioch in the Hellenistic-Roman Period* (Diss. Chicago 1949) in *AJP* 73 (1952) 109-110.

[51] See Pack, *Studies in Libanius* 2, 6, 56ff., 68.

[52] Pack, *Studies in Libanius* 3; see the list of Libanius' speeches in Förster and Münscher, "Libanios," *RE* 12 (1925) 2498ff.

[53] P. Petit, "Sur la date du 'Pro Templis' de Libanius," *Byzantion* 21 (1951) 293.

[54] *Or.* 48-49.

[55] See *Or.* 28, of A.D. 385, complaining to the emperor of the severe and illegal cruelty

The farmers, who, along with the decurions, formed one of the important elements in the local economy, were also suffering, not only from the natural hazards to which their calling was subject (the famine in Theodosius' time has been mentioned), but from other evils. The governors compelled them to perform public services to which they should not have been subject, and their farms were damaged by swarms of wandering monks. They were also, as a result of the imperial policies of the time, liable to fall under the control of the large landowners who used their capital and their political influence to absorb or dominate the small farmers.[56] The monks who robbed the farmers and damaged their crops also attacked the pagan shrines, not only those in the country, but those in the city as well.[57]

It was not only the farmers and the bakers whose lives were made difficult. Libanius describes the way in which the small tradesmen in general suffered from official oppression.[58]

Finally, it was not only economic life and the conduct of the government that Libanius saw declining, but the intellectual life of the city as well. His own profession as teacher he had found to be in poor condition soon after he took up his career in Antioch in A.D. 354, and the same was true thirty years later, when Libanius had become a distinguished elder citizen.[59] Moreover, Libanius' own pupils were unwilling to take their proper part in local governmental and judicial proceedings, but sat in silence.[60] It is an interesting commentary on the contemporary attitude toward education that Libanius saw the decline of the world as deriving largely from the decay of his own profession.[61]

All these conditions, as Libanius portrays them, are inevitably associated with his own long series of personal quarrels with the successive *comites Orientis* and *consulares Syriae*. These enmities, which usually seem to have arisen from real or fancied personal slights suffered by Libanius, form the theme of something like eleven of his extant

with which Icarius, *comes Orientis* A.D. 384-385, had been treating the decurions, and especially one of their number named Lamachus.

[56] The picture of the farmers' troubles can be made up from *Or.* 30, 47 and 50, as well as from passages in other writings; see Pack, *Studies in Libanius* 26-29, and Petit, *Libanius et la vie municipale à Antioche* 188-190, 375-380. *Or.* 47 has been edited and translated by L. Harmand, *Libanius, Discours sur les patronages* (Paris 1955).

[57] *Or.* 30, *Pro Templis.* There is a translation by R. Van Loy, "Le Pro Templis de Libanius," *Byzantion* 8 (1933) 1-39, 384-404. See also Petit, *Libanius et la vie municipale à Antioche* 200, 212.

[58] See *Or.* 29.   [59] *Or.* 31 (A.D. 355); *Or.* 3 (A.D. 387).   [60] *Or.* 35 (A.D. 388).

[61] See Downey, "Education and Public Problems as Seen by Themistius," *Transactions of the American Philological Association* 86 (1955) 291-307.

orations. The charges that Libanius brings against the officials are freighted with personal animus and wounded vanity, but they do contain valuable information both on the characters of the officials who carried out the provincial administration of the Empire at this period, and on the local problems they encountered. Among the *comites Orientis,* Proculus (A.D. 383-384) was attacked because of his cruelty and maladministration, though he honored Libanius. His attempt to enlarge the Plethrion, one of the buildings at Antioch used for the local Olympic Games, is commemorated in a special pamphlet.[62] Proculus' successor Icarius (A.D. 384-385) was greeted with an open letter (*Or.* 26) warning him not to follow in his predecessor's footsteps; but Libanius later had to write three pieces (*Or.* 27-29) reproaching Icarius for his lack of friendship for Libanius and for his cruelty and misgovernment.

Of the *consulares Syriae,* practically all of those who held office between A.D. 384 and 393 were attacked by Libanius. Eumolpius (*cons. Syr.* A.D. 384), a relative of Libanius, earned the orator's praise for his mildness during the famine, but was eventually condemned for advising his pupils to go to Rome to study Latin.[63] Tisamenus (*cons. Syr.* A.D. 386) drew upon himself a variety of accusations of oppression and neglect.[64] Timocrates, who held office after A.D. 382, possibly in A.D. 387, is criticized for being influenced by the manifestations of approval or disapproval of his actions that came from the claque in the theater.[65] Celsus, who held office in A.D. 387, is noteworthy in that his conduct is praised and never blamed.[66] Lucianus, who was *consularis Syriae* in A.D. 388, was bitterly criticized for his severity toward the decurions and was removed from office as a result of the complaints that were made about him (he returned to Antioch as *comes Orientis* later in the reign of Theodosius, and the story of his execution while in office will be told below).[67] Eustathius, who came to Antioch in A.D. 388, ap-

[62] *Or.* 10. On Proculus' career, see Petit, *Libanius et la vie municipale à Antioche* (passages cited in index, p. 437, *s.n.*), also an inscription of Nahr-el-Kelb (*Suppl. epigr. gr.* 7 [1934], no. 195).

[63] *Or.* 27.6, 18; *Or.* 40; Downey, *Comites Orientis* 17.

[64] *Or.* 33. Tisamenus is accused of putting people in prison and then forgetting them; of burdening the decurions and the poor; of collecting taxes ahead of the time when they were due; and so on.

[65] *Or.* 41. On Timocrates' career, see Downey, *Comites Orientis* 17-19, and Petit, *Libanius et la vie municipale à Antioche* 222, 226, 255, 273.

[66] Downey, *Comites Orientis* 19-20 (clarifying some previous uncertainties and confusions concerning his career).

[67] Libanius' *Or.* 56 was an open letter against Lucianus. See the valuable study of this by O. Seeck, "Libanius gegen Lucianus," *Rh. Mus.* 73 (1924) 84-101.

parently as an official of the imperial treasury, was at first on excellent terms with Libanius, but after he became *consularis Syriae*, some time in the same year, Libanius quarreled with him and he caused an accusation of divination to be lodged against the orator.[68] Eustathius' successor was Eutropius, who held office in A.D. 389. He was accused of piling up money in all sorts of ways. One of his unpleasant practices was to put a mask representing an ass's head on men who were being flogged, as an insult to the Christians who were currently libeled as worshiping a god with an ass's head;[69] the spectators could amuse themselves by likening the cries of the victim to an ass's braying. Florentius, who served in A.D. 392, was accused, like many of his colleagues, of savage excesses in the use of flogging.[70] Finally, Severus, who was *consularis Syriae* at some time in the last decade of the century, during Libanius' old age,[71] incurred the orator's wrath for flogging to death an accused functionary for whom Libanius had intervened.[72]

It is not always easy to know the rights and wrongs involved in all of the difficulties between Libanius and these governors. It does, however, seem true that the administration of justice at Antioch at this time often left much to be desired; and Libanius wrote an address to the emperor on this subject (*Or. 45, On the Prisoners*) in A.D. 386 or soon after, in which we get what appears to be a not too distorted view of the problem.[73] Owing to a venal and inefficient judiciary, many men were committed to prison, but few left it. The judges often forgot or neglected the accused, and the decurions did not dare interfere; and the deplorable living conditions in the prisons made incarceration even for a short time a harsh experience. Libanius petitioned the emperor to compel the unwilling judges to observe the provisions of an existing law (*C.Th.* 9.3.6), which forbade the holding in prison either of convicted persons who had not yet been punished, or of guiltless persons who ought to be freed.

[68] *Orations* 44 and 54. On Eustathius' career see Downey, *Comites Orientis* 20 and R. Pack, "An Interpretation of Libanius Epistle 915," *Class. Weekly* 45 (1951/2) 38-40, as well as Petit *Libanius et la vie municipale à Antioche* (passages cited in index, p. 435, *s.n.*).

[69] *Or.* 4; Downey, *Comites Orientis* 20; R. Pack, "An Onocephalic Mask," *HTR* 48 (1955) 93-96.

[70] *Or.* 46; Downey, *Comites Orientis* 20, Seeck in *Rh. Mus.* 73 (1924) 96-101.

[71] C. Lacombrade, "Retouche à la biographie de Libanios," *Annuaire de l'Institut de philologie et d'histoire orientales et slaves* 10 (1950) 361-366 (*Mélanges Grégoire* 2), cites evidence which shows that Libanius was still alive in A.D. 404, at the age of ninety.

[72] *Or.* 58; Downey, *loc.cit.*

[73] A translation, commentary and study of this oration, with an essay on the contemporary interest in penal reform, forms an important part of Pack's *Studies in Libanius*.

It is against this background that we come to the insurrection of
A.D. 387, one of the best known episodes in the history of Antioch.[74]
Our sources make it plain that there was general economic discontent
not only at Antioch but throughout at least the eastern part of the
Empire, coupled with dissatisfaction with Theodosius' policy toward the
barbarians.[75] Taxation had to be increased to pay for the rebuilding of
the army after the disaster of Adrianople in A.D. 378, for Theodosius'
defensive operations against the barbarians, and to compensate for the
loss of income from land ruined by the wars.[76] Thus, when an imperial
edict calling for heavier taxation (evidently increased levies of the
collatio lustralis and the *aurum coronarium*) arrived at Antioch in the
early part of A.D. 387 (perhaps in the first days of February),[77] there
was immediate resistance to what was considered to be an unbearable

[74] On this insurrection see A. Hug, *Antiochia und der Aufstand im Jahre 387 n. Chr.*
(Winterthur 1863), reprinted with some revisions in the same author's *Studien über
das klass. Altertum*, 2. Ausgabe (Freiburg i.B. 1886) 1.133-200; Sievers, *Leben des
Libanius* 172-187; Rauschen, *Jahrbücher* 259-266, 512-520; R. Goebel, *De Ioannis
Chrysostomi et Libanii orationibus quae sunt de seditione Antiochensium* (Diss.
Göttingen 1910); Pack, *Studies in Libanius* 81-83; R. Browning, "The Riot of A.D. 387
in Antioch: The Role of the Theatrical Claques in the Later Empire," *Journal of Roman Studies* 42 (1952) 13-20; Petit, *Libanius et la vie municipale à Antioche* 238-244.
The principal sources are Libanius' five speeches concerned with the insurrection (*Or.*
19-23) plus allusions in other orations (1, 34) and Chrysostom's twenty-one "Homilies
on the Statues" (*P.G.* 49), translated by J. Bareille in volume 3 of his *Oeuvres complètes
de S. Jean Chrysostome* (Paris 1864). Other sources are Sozomen *Hist. eccl.* 7.23;
Theodoret *Hist. eccl.* 5.20; Zosimus 4.41.

[75] Piganiol, *Empire chrétien* 213 rightly points out the significance of Themistius'
Oration 15, delivered before the Emperor Theodosius at the beginning of A.D. 381, in
which the orator speaks with impressive frankness of the general discontent and anxiety
within the Empire. See also Zosimus 4.32. The amount of distress that is indicated by
Themistius and Zosimus could not be repaired within a few years. R. Browning (*op.cit.*
[above n. 74] 13) assembles evidence for disorders in Constantinople in A.D. 388, in
Alexandria in A.D. 389, and in A.D. 390 at Thessalonica (the famous massacre), as well
as disorders at Berytus just before those at Antioch (on these see further below).

[76] Piganiol, *Empire chrétien* 211, 213.

[77] The date is nowhere given exactly in the sources, and must be calculated from a
few rather vague references to the sequence of events following the riot itself. The best
discussion of the problem is that of Rauschen *Jahrbücher* 512-520, cf. 260 with n. 4.
Easter was probably celebrated in Antioch in A.D. 387 on 21 March: E. Schwartz,
"Christliche und jüdische Ostertafeln," *Abhandlungen d. K. Gesellschaft d. Wiss. zu
Göttingen, Philol. histor. Kl.*, N. F. VII, No. 6, p. 71; and the uprising appears to have
occurred in the week before the beginning of Lent, i.e. some time in the first week or
ten days of February (Rauschen 518-519). According to the view of Tillemont, Easter
was celebrated in Antioch in this year on 25 April, according to the usage of Alexandria; on the basis of this chronology, the insurrection would have taken place at the
end of February or in the first days of March. This chronology is adopted, with individual variations, by H. F. Clinton, *Fasti Romani* (Oxford 1845-1850) 1.512-515; T.
Hodgkin, *Italy and her Invaders*, ed. 2 (Oxford 1892-1916) 1.473; Hug, *op.cit.* (above
n. 74) in the edition of 1863, p. 28, n. 107, draws up a table of events but refrains from
assigning dates.

burden.[78] A part of the purpose of the levy may have been to meet
the heavy expenses of the tenth anniversary of Theodosius as emperor,
which would fall in January A.D. 388.[79] The fifth anniversary of his son
Arcadius (16 or 19 January A.D. 387) had in fact been celebrated just
before the arrival of the announcement of the increased taxation. Whatever the official reason may have been for the increase, there were so
many extra burdens to be paid for—past and future wars, imperial
anniversaries, the rehabilitation of the army—that all classes at Antioch,
traditionally an independent and explosive city, found the prospect un-
endurable,[80] and apparently reacted more violently than the other cities
of the East, where we hear of no other similar outbreaks of violence.[81]

When the edict was read at the *dikasterion* to the assembled curiales,
who filled the building, there was immediate complaint, and the
curiales, along with other prominent citizens, went to complain to
the *archon* (presumably the *consularis Syriae* Celsus) and to ask him
to have the tax reduced.[82] Getting no satisfaction from the governor,

[78] The sources do not make it clear what the taxation was. Libanius and Chrysostom,
the contemporaries, seem to speak of it as a regular levy, but of insupportable size
(Libanius *Or.* 19.25, 22.4; Chrysostom *Hom. de stat.* 3.7 = *PG* 49.58; *Hom.* 5.3 = *ibid.*
73; *Hom.* 8.4 = *ibid.* 102), as does Zosimus, writing later (4.41). The church historians
Theodoret and Sozomen, writing well after the event, speak of some kind of new tax
(Theodoret *Hist. eccl.* 5.20; Sozomen *Hist. eccl.* 7.23). Thus it has been debated whether
the tax was the *lustralis collatio*, which fell on the merchant class and was collected
at imperial anniversaries, or the *aurum coronarium*, which was imposed on the senatorial class on imperial anniversaries and in order to meet extraordinary demands
(Kubitschek, "Aurum coronarium," *RE* 2 [1896] 2552-2553; Seeck, "Collatio lustralis,"
ibid. 4 [1901] 370-376). Since all classes at Antioch seem to have been affected (see below), it may be that both taxes were imposed at this time, in increased proportions
(see Browning, *op.cit.* [above, n. 74] 14, 19).
[79] This is the suggestion of Piganiol, *Empire chrétien* 249. Some writers (e.g. Kidd,
Hist. of the Church 2.351) by mistake put Theodosius' *decennalia* in A.D. 387.
[80] Libanius, Chrysostom, and Zosimus (cited above, n. 78) do not connect the taxation specifically with Theodosius' wars, though Theodoret and Sozomen (cited *ibid.*)
do. It may well be that the latter authors, writing well after the events, were rationaliz-
ing from their general knowledge of Theodosius' reign. R. Browning (*op.cit.* [above,
n. 74] 19), suggests that Theodosius needed extra funds because the final campaign
against the usurper Maximus was in prospect. However, what we know of the relations
of Theodosius and Maximus at the beginning of A.D. 387 indicates that Theodosius was
still hoping that a conflict could be averted; and when war did come, Theodosius was
in part surprised and unprepared (Ensslin, "Maximus (Usurpator)," *RE* 14 [1930]
2552-2553).
[81] Libanius (*Or.* 19.14) speaks of disorders in the theater in Alexandria which appear
to have been, in part at least, manifestations of favor toward Maximus. It is by no
means certain, as Sievers (*Leben des Libanius* 173) and Kidd (*Hist. of the Church*
2.351) think, that these disorders were provoked by the increased taxation. It may be,
indeed, that the violence of the reaction at Antioch means that special taxation was imposed on that city, though in this case we should perhaps expect to hear something to
this effect in the local sources, Libanius and Chrysostom.
[82] Libanius *Or.* 19.25-26. On the career of Celsus, see Petit, *Libanius et la vie municipale à Antioche* (passages cited in index, p. 434, *s.n.*). Hug, *op.cit.* (above, n. 74) 158,

they then went to the residence of the Bishop Flavianus; but not finding him, they returned to the *dikasterion*.[83] At this point the crowd was taken in charge by the theatrical claque, an organized and paid body which is encountered elsewhere in the history of Antioch.[84] This claque, originally a group of dubious characters paid to applaud the dancers and actors in the theater, had come to take on a political role as well, by offering applause or censure of the measures of the local governor, the demonstrations taking place when the governor paid his quasi-official visits to the theater. Skilled in stirring up the crowd, these claques had come to be powerful leaders of mobs, and could be hired for political purposes. At Antioch and elsewhere they were feared by the governors.[85] On the present occasion, the mob was led by a man who was known to have been responsible for creating disorders in Berytus.[86] Gathering reinforcements from the crowd that had collected outside the *dikasterion*, the mob went to the headquarters of the *archon* (that is, presumably, the *consularis Syriae* Celsus) and fell upon the balustrade and the door behind it with such violence that the governors' servants feared that he would be killed, just as another mob had killed the *consularis Syriae* Theophilus thirty-four years previously, in A.D. 353. Fortunately the crowd could not break into the residence, and had to be content with shouting abuse.[87] Next the mob rushed along the portico which stood in front of the *dikasterion*, and came to a public bath, where the rioters cut the ropes by which the hanging lamps of the bath were suspended.[88]

After this the attack on the imperial images and statues brought the riot to a climax. The mob first stoned the wooden panels bearing painted portraits of the imperial family, and jeered at them as they

n. 1, identifies the *dikasterion* with the *praetorium* of the *comes Orientis*, but this is a conjecture.

[83] Libanius *Or.* 19.28.

[84] It is the merit of R. Browning, in the study cited above (n. 74), to have called attention to the importance of the part played in the uprising by this claque, and to have assembled valuable comparative material on the activities of such claques elsewhere in the Empire. His study should be consulted for these details.

[85] Browning, *op.cit.* (above, n. 74) 16. Libanius devoted his *Oration* 41 to warning the *consularis Syriae* Timocrates not to be influenced by this claque; see above, n. 65. On the part taken by the claque in the uprising of A.D. 387 see Libanius *Or.* 19.28, 20.3; Chrysostom *Hom. de Stat.* 2.3 = *PG* 49.38; *Hom.* 3.1 = *ibid.* 48; *Hom.* 5.3 = *ibid.* 73; *Hom.* 6.1 = *ibid.* 81; and especially, *Hom.* 17.2 = *ibid.* 175-176. As Browning points out (p. 18), there is a question, which it is not yet possible to settle for lack of evidence, whether these theatrical claques had any connection with the circus factions.

[86] Libanius *Or.* 19.28.

[87] Libanius *Or.* 20.3. On Theophilus' death, see above, Ch. 12, n. 225.

[88] Libanius *Or.* 22.6.

broke into pieces.[89] This was *laesa maiestas*, since these official portraits, made at Constantinople at the accession of a new emperor and distributed to the cities of the empire, had a constitutional and legal significance, being embodiments of the imperial dignity; the power of the emperor was thought of as residing in his portrait, so that the emperor was present, in the form of an image, everywhere in the empire.[90] To damage such an image was to offer violence to the emperor himself; and so the mob's action now passed from disorder into revolution. From the wooden portraits, the mob turned to the bronze statues of the emperor, his wife, and Arcadius. The statues were pulled down from their pedestals with ropes and dragged about; some were broken up, some were not.[91] At this point, messengers set out to take the news of the rebellion to Constantinople.[92] Leaving the remains of the statues to the children to play with, the mob now set fire to the house of a prominent citizen who had spoken in favor of paying the tax.[93] There was also talk of setting fire to the palace; but the commander of the *toxotai* or archers who acted as police now appeared with his men to put out the fire, and the *comes Orientis*, who apparently had not yet taken any action, now came up with his military guard and arrested the rioters, who were sent off to the *dikasterion*.[94] Order was restored by midday.[95] The authorities at once set about to separate the prisoners according to their crimes. Apparently the trials were conducted with the utmost dispatch. Some of the prisoners were beheaded, others burned alive, still others executed by being thrown to wild animals in the arena. Children were not spared on account of their age.[96]

Libanius gives us a vivid description of the spread of rumor as to the punishments that the emperor might be expected to inflict on the city. The city was to be devastated and plundered by soldiers; the curiales

[89] Libanius *Or.* 22.7. Browning, *op.cit.* (above, n. 74) 15, no. 40, supposes that all this took place in front of the imperial palace on the island, where the portraits on wood would be displayed.
[90] On the contemporary understanding of the nature of the images, see H. Kruse, *Studien zur offiziellen Geltung des Kaiserbildes im röm. Reiche* (Paderborn 1934); A. Grabar, *L'Empereur dans l'art byzantin* (Paris 1936) 4-10; the chapter "Imperial Images" in K. M. Setton *Christian Attitude towards the Emperor in the Fourth Century* (New York 1941) 196-211; E. Kitzinger, "The Cult of Images before Iconoclasm," *Dumbarton Oaks Papers* 8 (1954) 90ff., 122ff.
[91] Libanius *Or.* 19.44, 20.4, 22.8; Chrysostom *Hom. de stat.* 5.3 — PG 49.73.
[92] Libanius *Or.* 20.4.
[93] Libanius *Or.* 22.9.
[94] Libanius *Or.* 19.34-36, 22.9. The name of the *comes Orientis*, who is mentioned in *Or.* 19.36, is not known. There have been several unsuccessful attempts to identify him; see Downey, *Comites Orientis* 19-20.
[95] Libanius *Or.* 22.9.
[96] Libanius *Or.* 19.37.

were to be executed; property was to be confiscated; and so on.[97] Many people fled the city and took refuge in the mountains or the fields, and the *consularis Syriae* had to order the curiales to remain in Antioch.[98] The city was quiet and filled with apprehension.[99] John Chrysostom, beginning his career as a preacher, took this opportunity to deliver a series of twenty-one homilies (*On the Statues*) which were designed to bolster the spirits of the people and at the same time to show them how they could take advantage of the occasion for spiritual self-examination and renovation.[100]

Bishop Flavianus had carried out his duty as leader of the Christian community, and a few days after the riot had undertaken the journey to Constantinople, in spite of his advanced age, in order to intercede with the emperor.[101] Meanwhile the original report of the uprising had reached the capital and the emperor had despatched two commissioners to make an investigation, Caesarius, who was *magister officiorum*, and Hellebichus, who was *magister utriusque militiae per Orientem* and had already been living in Antioch, where he had made himself popular by his generosity to the city.[102] The commissioners were to conduct an inquiry; but a preliminary and comprehensive punishment of the whole city was conveyed in an imperial decree. The city was deprived of its rank of *metropolis* and made subordinate to its ancient rival Laodicea, a punishment reminiscent of that inflicted by the Emperor Septimius Severus nearly 200 years before; it was deprived of its military status; the hippodrome, the theaters, and the baths were all closed; and the free distribution of bread to poor persons was suspended.[103] Also it was made known that the emperor held the *curiales* responsible

---

[97] Libanius *Or.* 19.38ff., 20.5, 23.12.

[98] Libanius *Or.* 19.56-57, 21.20, 22.11. *Or.* 23 was written as a complaint against those who had fled the city and had in this way abandoned Libanius and brought his teaching activities to a stop.

[99] Libanius *Or.* 19.56ff.; Chrysostom *Hom. in stat.* 2.2 = *PG* 49.35.

[100] For the text and a translation of the sermons, see above, n. 74. The sequence in which the discourses were delivered is established by Goebel in the study cited there. For an excellent brief account of their contents, see Kidd, *Hist. of the Church* 2.356-358. A detailed study has been made by Sister Mary Albania Burns, *St. John Chrysostom's Homilies on the Statues: A Study of their Rhetorical Qualities and Form* (Washington, 1930).

[101] Chrysostom in the third homily (*PG* 49.47-60) describes the bishop's departure.

[102] See Petit, *Libanius et la vie municipale à Antioche*, passages cited in index, p. 434, *ss.nn.* Caesarius, Ellebichus.

[103] Libanius *Or.* 20.6-7, 23.25-26; Chrysostom *Hom. de stat.* 17.2 = *PG* 49.176; Theodoret *Hist. eccl.* 5.20.2. On the punishment of Antioch by Septimius Severus, see Ch. 10, §3. I take the phrase μετείληφε σχῆμα φρουρίου (Libanius *Or.* 23.26) to be a periphrastic reference to removal of military rank and function; the city was normally the headquarters of the *magister utriusque militiae per Orientem*, and presumably this headquarters was now transferred elsewhere, e.g. to Chalcis or Emesa.

for what had happened.[104] This was a relatively mild sentence, but the subordination of the city to Laodicea was a very thorough humiliation, and the closing of the baths, the hippodrome, and the theaters was a measure that would be especially irksome to the pleasure-loving population. It was recalled that when a mob had killed the *consularis Syriae* Theophilus in A.D. 353, the Emperor Constantius had not imposed any punishment upon the city.[105]

During the investigation that Caesarius and Hellebichus conducted, Libanius sat with the commissioners by virtue of the dignity of honorary *praefectus praetorio* which had been given to him several years earlier.[106] John Chrysostom stood first with the silent crowd outside the meeting place, then entered the courtyard, from which he could hear the proceedings.[107] The meetings were held in Hellebichus' regular military headquarters.[108] The first day was devoted to questioning the members of the local senate and other persons of prominence, and people were surprised and relieved by the mildness of the commissioners' deportment.[109] On the next day began the trials of accused persons. Again the commissioners were inclined to be moderate, but they were also firm.[110] In the end, no one was condemned to death, but it was announced that all the members of the senate were to be imprisoned until the emperor's decision, based on the commissioners' report, was made known.[111] Chrysostom saw the senators in chains being led to prison through the market place.[112]

The senators were at first confined in an unroofed building next to the bouleuterion itself. The confinement was rigorous and visitors were not allowed. Permission was finally obtained to break through the wall between this prison and the bouleuterion. This gave the senators more space, and also proper shelter, for they could use the auditorium of the bouleuterion, as well as the colonnaded courtyard, in the middle of which was a garden containing vines, figs, trees, and vegetables. Even so the confinement was a hardship.[113]

---

[104] Libanius *Or.* 23.25.   [105] Libanius *Or.* 19.48-49.

[106] *Or.* 22.23. The honorary dignity is mentioned at the beginning of the *Pro Templis* (*Or.* 30.1) and in the speech *On the Prisoners* (*Or.* 45.1). P. Petit shows that the honor was conferred, probably in A.D. 383-84, earlier than scholars had at one time supposed: "Sur la date du 'Pro Templis' de Libanius," *Byzantion* 21 (1951) 285-310.

[107] *Hom. de stat.* 13.1ff. = *PG* 49.137ff.

[108] Libanius *Or.* 21.7.   [109] Libanius *Or.* 1.12, 21.7, 22.20.

[110] Libanius *Or.* 22.21ff., *Ep.* 787 Wolf = 868 Förster; Chrysostom *Hom. de stat.* 13.1 = *PG* 49.138, 17.1 = *ibid.* 172.

[111] Libanius *Or.* 22.29.

[112] Chrysostom *Hom. de stat.* 17.2 = *PG* 49.139.

[113] Libanius *Or.* 22.29ff.

During the trials, many ascetics who lived in the caves in the mountain side above Antioch, left their dwellings and came down into the city to intercede with the commissioners, advising them to urge the emperor to put aside his anger and pardon the city. One of these holy men, named Macedonius, is reported to have made a particularly eloquent appeal to Hellebichus.[114] Whether moved wholly by these appeals (as the Christian writers say) or by other factors as well, the commissioners decided to recommend clemency to the emperor, and Caesarius set out for Constantinople, traveling at top speed, so that he reached the city on the sixth day after leaving Antioch.[115] He found the emperor inclined to listen to the official recommendations, for Bishop Flavianus had been in Constantinople for some time, interceding with the emperor,[116] and the senate and people of the capital had expressed a hope that Theodosius would pardon their sister city.[117] The emperor decided to grant clemency to Antioch, and wrote a detailed letter in which the existing penalties and restrictions were rescinded, privileges were restored, and poor relief was reinstated.[118] This message was given to a courier who could travel at top speed,[119] and when it reached Antioch there was great rejoicing, with illuminations and banquets in the streets, and all the other pleasures to which the city was devoted.[120] The news reached Antioch about Palm Sunday, and by Easter (probably celebrated in this year on 21 March) Bishop Flavianus was back in the city and could officiate at the festal service.[121] The people of the city in gratitude set up numerous portraits and statues of Hellebichus,[122] and Libanius presented laudatory addresses to him (*Or.* 22) and Caesarius (*Or.* 21). Probably by way of return for these honors, Hellebichus built a fine house in Antioch, and a bath in the central part of the city.[123] One result of the episode as a whole

---

[114] Chrysostom *Hom. de stat.* 17.1-2 = *PG* 49.139. Theodoret *Hist. eccl.* 5.20.4-10.
[115] Libanius *Or.* 21.15.
[116] Chrysostom *Hom. de stat.* 21.1-2 = *PG* 49.211-215.
[117] Libanius *Or.* 20.37.
[118] Libanius *Or.* 20.7, 37ff.; 21.21.
[119] Libanius *Or.* 21.23.
[120] Libanius *Or.* 22.37; Chrysostom *Hom. de stat.* 21.4 = *PG* 49.219-220.
[121] On Flavianus' return, see Chrysostom *Hom. de stat.* 21.1 = *PG* 49.211. The arrival of the imperial message at Antioch can be dated from Chrysostom's homilies; see the chronological tables of the homilies in Rauschen, *Jahrbücher* 519 and in Goebel's study (cited above n. 74), 55. On the date of Easter see Rauschen, *Jahrbücher* 518. Libanius mentions (*Or.* 34.6) that the period of anxiety at Antioch had been 34 days, which corresponds approximately with the evidence of the sequence of Chrysostom's homilies, which show that the uprising took place a few days before the beginning of Lent and that the news of the emperor's clemency reached the city on or about Palm Sunday.
[122] Libanius *Or.* 22.39-40.   [123] Libanius *Ep.* 816 Wolf = 898 Förster.

was that a number of pagans were so impressed by the part played by Bishop Flavianus, and by his discourses addressed to the public at large, that they were converted to Christianity.[124]

3. THE LATTER YEARS OF THEODOSIUS' REIGN; PUBLIC BUILDINGS; THE REIGN OF ARCADIUS

After the uprising of A.D. 387, there were few events of major importance in the public history of the city during Theodosius' reign.[125] The most striking episode is the end of the career of Lucianus, the one-time *consularis Syriae*, who returned to Antioch as *comes Orientis* (his whole career may conveniently be treated here, although it extended beyond the death of Theodosius on 17 January A.D. 395).

Lucianus, it will be recalled, had been *consularis Syriae* in A.D. 388 and had been removed from office because of complaints which were made about his administration.[126] Some time after the fall of the praetorian prefect Tatianus in A.D. 392,[127] Lucianus induced the new prefect Rufinus—by a massive bribe, it was said—to appoint him *comes Orientis*.[128] Lucianus' conduct in office is described by different sources as being correct and popular, or (perhaps more accurately) as being bumptious.[129] In any case, he made the mistake of refusing a favor to Eucherius, the maternal uncle of the new emperor Arcadius (who succeeded his father in January A.D. 395). Eucherius complained to Arcadius, who put the blame on Rufinus; and the prefect, in order to preserve his credit, set out posthaste for Antioch with a small suite to deal with Lucianus. Reaching the city at night, he summoned the *comes Orientis* to appear before him at once, went through the motions of a summary trial, condemned him to death, and had him executed at once by being flogged to death with lead-studded lashes. Rufinus attempted to conceal the execution, at least temporarily, by having the body carried away in a closed litter, giving it out that Lucianus was not dead, and

---

[124] Chrysostom *De Anna sermo* 1.1 = *PG* 54.634.

[125] For the history of Libanius himself at this time, and the numerous minor events in the city with which he was concerned, see Petit, *Libanius et la vie municipale à Antioche.*

[126] See above, n. 67.

[127] E. Demougeot, *De l'unité à la division de l'Empire romain* (Paris 1951) 122.

[128] Zosimus 5.2 is the principal source for the incident, which is also mentioned by Johannes Lydus *De mag.* 3.23, and alluded to by Claudianus *In Rufinum* 1.241ff. On the date of the incident, which has been disputed, see below, n. 130.

[129] Zosimus, a friendly source (see Demougeot, *op.cit.* [above, n. 127] 126, n. 45), describes Lucianus' behavior in glowing terms. Lydus writes that he was insubordinate, a report which is more in keeping with what is known of his conduct as *consularis Syriae* (see above, n. 67).

would be cared for. When the truth became known, the people of the city demonstrated their anger so plainly that Rufinus presented them with a new basilica in an effort to placate them.[130]

As to the physical history of the city, various records suggest that there was some expansion of the occupied area during Theodosius' reign. The construction of the large church of St. Babylas on what was previously open ground, on the far side of the Orontes, has already been mentioned.[131] Libanius, in an oration written soon after the insurrection of A.D. 387, invited Theodosius to make the city a present of a building either on the island in the Orontes or on the land beyond the river.[132] Libanius' invitation suggests that the territory beyond the river was being built up, or that people were anxious to see an expansion there. Evidence pointing in the same direction is found in the record[133] that in A.D. 386/7 the bridge that led from the Porta Tauriana on the island to the plain across the Orontes was widened and covered with a roof.[134] The widening of this bridge would certainly seem to indicate increasing occupancy of the land across the river. There is also recorded in the same year an addition to the Great Church of the city, in the form of a "small basilica" built near it. The date suggests that this work represented a thank-offering following the insurrection and the imperial pardon of the city,[135] after which, as we have seen, there were many new converts to Christianity.[136]

[130] The basilica is mentioned again in the reign of Theodosius II (see below, Ch. 16, n. 18). Malalas records the construction of a basilica by a praetorian prefect named Rufinus under Constantine the Great, but the details he gives do not win confidence and it seems likely that the chronicler mistakenly attributed to Constantine's reign an event that took place under Theodosius (see above, Ch. 12, n. 145). The execution of Rufinus was dated in A.D. 393 by O. Seeck ("Libanius gegen Lucianus," *Rh. Mus.* 73 [1924] 84-101; article "Lucianus," no. 6, *RE* 13 [1937] 1614-5), and this date is adopted by Downey, *Comites Orientis* 13. However, the traditional view, that the execution took place in A.D. 395, after Theodosius' death (cf. e.g. Rauschen, *Jahrbücher* 440-441; Stein, *Gesch.* 1.351-352) has recently been restated in conclusive fashion by Demougeot, *op.cit.* (above, n. 127) 126-128. The date of Lucianus' tenure in Downey, *Comites Orientis* 13, should be corrected accordingly.

[131] Above, nn. 6-13.

[132] Libanius *Or.* 20.44. A passage in another oration (48.38), written after A.D. 388, may refer to lively building activity in the city at this period (cf. Pack, *Studies in Libanius* 120), but the orator here is striving to make a point, and his words are perhaps not to be taken too seriously.

[133] Theophanes a. 5878, p. 70.10-11 ed. De Boor.

[134] See Eltester, "Kirchen Antiochias" 259.

[135] Theophanes a. 5878, p. 70.11-12 ed. De Boor. Chrysostom preached a sermon in the "old" apostolic church at Antioch at a time when, it seems, the Great Church was undergoing alterations: *Hom. In inscriptionem Actorum* 2.1 = *PG* 51.77; cf. Baur, *Der hl. Joh. Chrysostomus* 1.22, and Lietzmann in *RE* 9.1811ff.

[136] See above, n. 124.

Several secular buildings were constructed or enlarged.[137] We have already had occasion to mention the new basilica built by Rufinus, though this was constructed after the death of Theodosius.[138] Tisamenus, whose career as an unpopular *consularis Syriae* in A.D. 386 has been mentioned, seems to have built some porticoes which Libanius criticizes as showy and useless.[139]

The building at Antioch about which we hear most during Theodosius' reign is the Plethrion, which had been built in the reign of Commodus, or a little later, to accommodate the wrestling matches in the local Olympic Games,[140] and was used in Libanius' time for the try-outs and preliminary contest of the athletes who came to Antioch hoping to enter the Olympic Games. The Plethrion stood near the Xystos and the Bath of Commodus in the group of buildings that surrounded the Forum of Valens.[141] It was a quadrangular structure fitted with rows of stone seats around an open space in which the athletes performed.[142] The seating capacity, Libanius says, had been enlarged in A.D. 332 and 336 when Argyrius and Phasganius were in charge of

[137] Local building activities in Antioch are reflected in *Cod. Theod.* 15.1.36 (1 Nov. A.D. 397), addressed to Asterius, *comes Orientis*, in which it is said that material taken from demolished temples may be used for bridges, aqueducts, roads, and city walls: see also 15.2.7, another part of the same constitution. There is a very vague allusion in Chrysostom's *Homily on the Statues* 2.2 = *PG* 49.35 to an earthquake that might have affected the city during Theodosius' reign, before the outbreak of A.D. 387, or might have taken place before Theodosius' time. Our information about this is so meager that we cannot say how much of the building activity of Theodosius' reign might represent repair or replacement following such an earthquake. In the sixth sermon *De Lazaro* 1ff. (*PG* 48.1027ff.), Chrysostom mentions an earthquake that apparently lasted for three days and affected "the whole earth." This sermon is one of a group delivered in 388 or 393, more probably 388 (Lietzmann, "Ioannes Chrysostomos," *RE* 9.1816). In the *De S. Babyla contra Iulianum* 21 (*PG* 50.567), Chrysostom speaks of *seismoi* (which might mean either one earthquake, i.e. "shocks," or several) which had affected at least Daphne between the time when the Temple of Apollo there was burned (27 Oct. A.D. 362; see Ch. 13, n. 44) and the time when the sermon was delivered, probably 388, possibly 393 (Lietzmann, *loc.cit.*). In the third *Homily on the Statues*, delivered early in 387 (Lietzmann, *op.cit.* 1815), Chrysostom speaks in more general terms of earthquakes at Antioch (§7, *PG* 49.57), which, according to the context, might have occurred fairly recently; at least they are mentioned in such a way that they seem to have occurred within the memory of those who heard the sermon. There is no indication of how great the damage done may have been, but Chrysostom does not say in any of the passages that the disasters were catastrophic. The probable dates of all these texts make it unlikely that the references are to the earthquakes that occurred at Antioch in the 390's (see below n. 152).

[138] Above, n. 130. The location of this basilica is not known.

[139] Libanius *Contra Tisamenum, Or.* 33.14 and 34; cf. Pack, *Studies in Libanius* 105, n. 5, and 120. On Tisamenus' career, see above, n. 64.

[140] See above, Ch. 10, n. 5.

[141] See Excursus 12.

[142] See the description of the building in Libanius' tenth oration, *On the Plethrion*, in Appendices, Translation of Documents, 2. The oration is summarized by Pack, *Studies in Libanius* 62.

giving the local Olympic Games.[143] Now the *comes Orientis* Proculus, who held office in A.D. 383-384, was planning to enlarge the building, presumably in expectation of the celebration of the Olympic Games that would take place in July and August A.D. 384.[144] Libanius felt that such an enlargement would be most undesirable since it would make it possible for unworthy spectators to attend the trials, which would be desecrated by their unruly behavior; and the trials would no longer be properly carried out because the judges would be influenced by the applause and comments of the crowd. Libanius felt so strongly on the matter that he wrote an open letter to Proculus advising him not to carry out the enlargement, but we do not know whether this advice was followed.[145]

This is what we hear of Antioch itself. The emperor beautified Daphne by rebuilding the imperial palace there—Libanius writes that he "hid the old palace by means of the new"[146]—and by putting a stop to the cutting of trees in the famous cypress grove,[147] which by this time was imperial property.[148]

---

[143] *Or.* 10.9 and 12; *Or.* 53.4. See Downey, *Olympic Games* 429.

[144] On the career of Proculus, see above, n. 62. The Olympic Games were held during forty-five days in July and August (Malalas 284.16-17) in Julian leap-years (Sievers, *Leben des Libanius* 43, n. 2; 158, 207-208; Stauffenberg, *Malalas* 417, n. 11; 438). Libanius speaks of the games as a summer festival in *Or.* 1.185 and *Or.* 53.26.

[145] Libanius in three passages (*Or.* 10.1, 3, 23) speaks of the work of Proculus as though it were accomplished, but he may have done this for rhetorical effect, for there are other passages (*Or.* 10.17, 22, 36) in which Libanius speaks of the disorders that could be expected to result from the change as something that would happen in the future. Seeck, *Briefe des Libanius* 249, believed that the enlargement was made before Libanius wrote, but his opinion was a hasty one (he believed, for example, that the building enlarged by Proculus was the theater). Müller, *Antiq. Antioch.* 94-95, likewise believed that the enlargement was accomplished before Libanius wrote. Förster and Münscher ("Libanios," *RE* 12.2500) and Pack (*Studies in Libanius* 62) are noncommittal.

[146] Libanius *Or.* 20.44. The work was done before the composition of this oration, which was written just after the uprising of A.D. 387. In the same passage (as has been noted above) Libanius invited the emperor to beautify the palace on the island at Antioch, but there is nothing to show that this was done.

[147] Libanius (*Or.* 1.255, 262) writes of a governor in office about A.D. 388 (*Or.* 4.12), whom he does not name, who attempted to cut cypresses in the grove at Daphne but was prevented by the orator's protests. Cypress wood was valuable because of its durability, and a governor who was so inclined could have made a handsome sum from the sale of wood from this grove, which was a part of the *res privata* at this time (see the following note). There had doubtless been earlier attempts on the grove, as is suggested by a decree in the Code of Theodosius (10.1.12) dated 17 June A.D. 379, just five months after the accession of Theodosius, addressed to the *comes rerum privatarum*, which commands that the official known as the alytarch, who was in charge of the quadriennial Olympic Games, was to have the right to cut down one cypress tree in the grove at Daphne provided he planted more trees-implying that others as well had been cutting the trees—and by later decrees (*CJ* 11.78.1 and 2) limiting, and then finally forbidding the cutting of the trees. The alytarch's single tree was probably used

We have no exact information as to how the pagan temples of Antioch and its immediate vicinity were affected by the systematic campaign instituted by Theodosius I for the demolition of pagan shrines. Libanius' oration *Pro Templis* (*Oration* 30), written between the summer of A.D. 386 and the beginning of A.D. 387, does not specifically mention any of the buildings of Antioch that were torn down.[149] However, it would seem likely that there were some demolitions, and an imperial decree of A.D. 397 authorizes the *comes Orientis* to use the material of demolished temples for the repair of roads, bridges, and aqueducts.[150] This permission covered the whole of the *Oriens*, but in the specific case of Antioch it seems likely that the walls at least were an object of special care following the threat to the city in the invasion of Syria by the Huns in A.D. 395 or 396, which will be described in detail below. There is a report in Malalas that the city wall of Antioch was extended under Theodosius I, but it appears that this represents a confusion of names, and that the extension took place in the reign of Theodosius II.

For the reign of Arcadius, our knowledge of the history of Antioch is not extensive beyond events already noted—the death of Bishop Flavian, the election of his successor, and the execution of the *comes Orientis* Lucianus. We likewise hear of the sudden and unopposed invasion of Syria by the Huns in A.D. 395 or 396, in which Antioch seems to have been seriously threatened, though the available evidence does not make it certain that the city was actually besieged, as some modern writers have believed on the basis of ancient sources that can-

---

for some ceremonial purpose connected with the Olympic Games (see below). On the trees of Syria in general and the cypress grove at Daphne in particular, see Honigmann, "Syria" 1559-1560; A. Seidensticker, *Waldgeschichte des Altertums* (Frankfurt a. O. 1886) 1.116-117; Benzinger, "Daphne," *RE* 4.2136-2138; Jessen, "Daphnaios," *ibid.* 2135-2136.

[148] Cf. the decree of A.D. 370 cited above (Ch. 14, n. 28), addressed to the *comes rerum privatarum*, which regulates the use by private persons of the aqueduct which supplied water to the palace of Daphne (*Cod. Theod.* 15.2.2), the *comes rer. privat.* being in charge of the imperial private property (Seeck, "Comites," *RE* 4.668). Two decrees of the year 364 (*CTh* 10.1.8 and 6.13.3) show that temple property which had been confiscated, given away, or sold by earlier emperors (cf. Libanius *Pro Templis, Or.* 30.38; Sozomen *Hist. eccl.* 3.17), and then had been restored to the temples by Julian (cf. W. Ensslin, "Kaiser Julians Gesetzgebungswerk und Reichsverwaltung," *Klio* 18 [1923] 105-111), was to be confiscated again for the emperor; and the property of the Temple of Apollo must have come within this category since Julian had attempted to restore the oracle and the cult there (see above Ch. 13, nn. 28-29). Libanius in the oration *Pro Templis*, written between the summer of A.D. 386 and the beginning of A.D. 387 (see above, n. 106) says (*Or.* 30.43) that "the temples are imperial property, like other things [i.e. other monuments]."

[149] See the study of P. Petit cited above, n. 106.

[150] *CTh* 15.1.36.

not be considered reliable in such matters.[151] In A.D. 396, also, Antioch apparently was visited by the earthquake that seems to have affected most of the eastern part of the Empire, and we have a sermon preached by St. John Chrysostom after the earthquake,[152] though no evidence has been preserved about the damage done.

[151] The belief that Antioch was besieged, which was held for example by Rauschen, *Jahrbücher* 438; Bouchier, *Antioch* 176; and F. H. Dudden, *The Life and Times of St. Ambrose* (Oxford 1935) 2.481, rests upon (1) two allusions in letters of St. Jerome (*Epistt.* 60.16, 77.8), one containing the phrase *obsessa Antiochia*, the latter a reference to the strengthening of the walls of the city, supported by (2) the statement of Claudian *In Eutropium* 2.569-571 that the invaders "threatened the walls of Antioch and all but set fire" to the capital (see also the more general allusion in Claudian *In Rufinum* 2.33-35). The invasion of Syria and other eastern provinces is mentioned by a number of other sources, but they have nothing to say about any siege of Antioch: Socrates *Hist. eccl.* 6.1; Sozomen *Hist. eccl.* 8.1; Philostorgius *Hist. eccl.* 11.8; Claudian *In Rufinum* 2.33-35; Joshua the Stylite *Chronicle* 9, p. 8 ed. Wright; *Chronicon Edessenum* ed. I. Guidi in *CSCO*, Scr. Syri, versio, ser. 3, tom. 4, p. 6.20-21; *Liber Chalifarum* in Land, *Anecd. Syriaca* 1, 8.2 (also in L. Hallier, *Untersuchungen über die edessenische Chronik* [*Texte u. Untersuchungen* 9, pt. 1] 104). Jerome and Claudian are not reliable sources in such a matter. Read in the context of the letters, Jerome's statements about Antioch seem hyperbolical, and sound more like a rhetorical account of the alarm that was felt in Palestine, where Jerome was living when the invasion occurred. Also it is clear that Claudian was not able to obtain accurate information about events in the East, and that he tended to exaggerate for his own purposes; see J. C. Rolfe, "Claudian," *TAPA* 50 (1919) 141. Thus it seems better to conclude, with Stein, *Gesch.* 1.349-350; L. Halphen, *Les barbares,*[5] (Paris 1948) 28; E. A. Thompson, *A History of Attila and the Huns* (Oxford 1948) 27-28; and F. Cavallera, *Saint Jérôme, sa vie et son œuvre* (Paris 1922) 1.179, that Jerome's words really mean only that the Huns approached Antioch and threatened it. The date of the invasion is not certain, some sources indicating A.D. 395, some A.D. 396; as between the two years, A.D. 396 seems somewhat more probable (see Honigmann "The Lost End of Menander's *Epitrepontes*" [cited above, n. 25], p. 31, n. 2).

[152] We have two sermons of St. John Chrysostom which were preached in order to comfort and strengthen the people of Antioch after earthquakes: *In terrae motum, et in divitem et Lazarum* (*De Lazaro concio* VII), *PG* 48.1027-1043, and *Hom. post terrae motum*, *PG* 50.713-716. P. Chrysostomus Baur (*Der hl. Joh. Chrysostomus* 1.328-329) dates these two sermons in A.D. 394 and 396, without stating specifically what the evidence may be for the dates (the sermons themselves contain no indication of date). In this P. Baur was apparently following the commentary printed in the *Patrologia graeca*, in which reference is made to entries in the chronicle of Marcellinus Comes (ed. Mommsen, *Chronica minora* 3, p. 64) recording earthquakes for the years A.D. 394 and 396. The quake of A.D. 394, however, is specifically said to have been confined to the European provinces near Constantinople (cf. Rauschen, *Jahrbücher* 415), and one cannot safely suppose on this basis that such an earthquake affected Antioch. The quake of A.D. 396, however, is described as though it had a general effect everywhere (such a general earthquake is also mentioned by Glycas, p. 478.20ff. Bonn ed.; see G. Downey, "Earthquakes at Constantinople and Vicinity, A.D. 342-1454," *Speculum* 30 [1955] 597), and so we may suppose, in the absence of more satisfactory testimony, that Chrysostom's two sermons were preached on this occasion. Chrysostom does not say what the damage may have been, though he does mention in one sermon that the shocks lasted three days (*PG* 48.1027) and in another (*PG* 50.713) that he is preaching outside the city. This suggests that the people, as they often did on such occasions, were spending their time in the open air in fear of renewed shocks.

Presumably the threatened attack of the Huns, and the earthquake, made necessary the work on the walls, roads, bridges, and aqueducts for which the *comes Orientis* had to request help in A.D. 397, as we have seen in the decree of the Code of Theodosius, already mentioned, in which the *comes Orientis* is empowered to employ material from demolished pagan temples for such repairs of public works and defences.[153]

We are reminded again of the military importance of Antioch by several texts of the late fourth and early fifth centuries concerned with the imperial arms factories at Antioch which had been established by Diocletian, and with the use of public pasturage at Antioch for army horses.[154] It is, however, a curious commentary on the state of security in the Empire at this time to learn that a band of wild Isaurian mountaineers, who were much addicted to banditry, were able to make an extensive raid in Cilicia and Syria in A.D. 404 or 405, during which they occupied the fortifications on the mountain above Antioch during the night, and descended into the city at dawn to carry out what robberies they could. It is recorded that in overrunning the mountain-side they killed a number of the ascetics, both men and women, who lived in the tombs and caves on the slope of the mountain.[155]

4. THE OLYMPIC GAMES AND THE THEATER

During the reigns of Theodosius I and Arcadius we have rather more evidence concerning the Olympic Games and the theater than is available for the years immediately preceding. In the period A.D. 379-400 information on these two popular forms of entertainment is due in part to the evidence for the administrative and financial changes that were taking place, in part to the interest of Libanius and Chrysostom in the subject. Chrysostom is, in fact, one of our chief sources of knowledge concerning the theater in the fourth century, thanks to his efforts to steer his people in Antioch away from this unsuitable form of en-

[153] *CTh* 15.1.36. As to the responsibility of the *comes Orientis* for such matters at Antioch, see *CTh* 15.2.7.

[154] *CTh* 7.7.3, A.D. 398, on the use of public lands for grazing military horses at Apamea and Antioch; *CTh* 7.8.8, A.D. 400, 405, on the immunities of the armorers at Antioch; *Notitia Dignitatum, Or.* 11.21-22, compiled ca. A.D. 430, on the *clibanaria (fabrica)* and *fabrica scutaria et armorum* at Antioch, both under the control of the *magister officiorum*.

[155] Theodoret (*Religiosa historia* 12, PG 82, 1397) tells of this raid in describing the ascetic career of a man named Zeno who had resigned his commission as an army officer to become a hermit and live in a tomb on Mount Silpius. On the repeated plundering raids of the Isaurians, see the valuable collection of material on Isauria and its history in G. R. Sievers, *Studien zur Geschichte der römischen Kaiser* (Berlin 1870) 489-502 (for the raid on Antioch, see 494).

joyment. Chrysostom, however, apparently had no more success than the Emperor Julian, who had also been anxious to purify the theater at Antioch, but had found it impossible.[156]

The Olympic Games, as an official festival of ancient date and great prestige, had been allowed by the Christian emperors to continue, doubtless because of their popularity even with Christians, partly also, no doubt, because they attracted visitors from all parts of the Roman world, and the money they spent must have represented an important factor in the city's economy. The games continued to be celebrated in Julian leap-years, and we have evidence for celebrations in A.D. 380, 384, 388 and 404.[157]

How far the ancient pagan rites connected with the games may have been retained, or what changes may have been introduced, we do not know; but it is possibly significant, for example, that Palladius, Chrysostom's biographer, speaks of the games as being "observed every four years in honor of the labors of Hercules, called Olympia," which might be taken to show that the emphasis now had been shifted from the cult of Zeus to the cult of Herakles, which was much less offensive to Christianity.[158] The same tendency may be seen in the avoidance of any title or name of the games in the decrees of the Code of Theodosius issued in the years following A.D. 379 which are in reality concerned with various aspects of the games, called simply *ludi*.[159] Also the festival must now have lost the elements of the pagan imperial cult which it formerly had,[160] if, as seems likely, the games had come to be identified with those of the *Koinon* of Syria, which in pagan times were

[156] Julian *Epist.* 89, p. 172 ed. Bidez (304b-c).

[157] For further details concerning the actual productions of the festivals in the last two decades of the century, which need not be repeated here, see the study of Downey, *Olympic Games*. On the festival of A.D. 380, see Libanius' autobiography, *Or.* 1.184. That of A.D. 384 is mentioned in connection with the tenure of office of Proculus, the *comes Orientis*; see Libanius *Or.* 1.222, and Sievers, *Leben des Libanius* 158 (cf. Downey, *Olympic games* 438, and *Comites Orientis* 13). Libanius wrote an oration, now lost, for these games (frag. 40, volume 11.632 in Förster's edition). The festival of A.D. 388 is mentioned in connection with the career of the *consularis Syriae* Eustathius: Libanius *Or.* 54.56, cf. Downey, *Olympic Games* 438 and *Comites Orientis* 20. Palladius' reference (*Dialogus de vita S. Ioann. Chrysostomi* 16.54, p. 96.8 ed. Coleman-Norton) to the celebration in A.D. 404 has already been mentioned (above, n. 25). The study of W. Liebeschuetz, "The Syriarch in the Fourth Century," *Historia* 8 (1959) 113-126, appeared too late to be used here.

[158] Palladius *loc.cit.* (above, n. 157).

[159] *CTh* 6.3.1; 10.1.12; 12.1.103; *CJ* 11.78.1.

[160] On the connection between the Olympic Games and those of the *Koinon*, see above, Ch. 9, nn. 38, 151, and Stauffenberg, *Malalas* 427-437. While we have no direct testimony, it is to be presumed that the *Koinon* of Syria continued to survive in the fourth century; cf. J. A. O. Larsen, "The Position of Provincial Assemblies in the Government and Society of the Late Roman Empire," *CP* 29 (1934) 209-220.

connected with the imperial cult. It may have been in connection with the changes in the character of the games that a question arose in A.D. 379 as to the traditional right of the Alytarch, the presiding official of the games, to cut down one cypress tree in the sacred grove of Daphne. The fact that only one tree was involved suggests that it was used for cult purposes, rather than for commercial sale; and the fact that the Alytarch's right was questioned, and had to be confirmed by imperial decree, suggests that Christian interests were attempting to curtail the activities of this official.[161]

Along with the changes which were made necessary by the Christianization of the state, the public and the officials connected with the games began to lose interest in keeping up some of the traditional details of the festival. The *comes Orientis* Proculus, as we have already seen in another connection, attempted to enlarge the Plethrion in which were held the trial contests of the athletes who hoped to enter the games.[162] This enlargement, Libanius felt, would result in loss of decorum, by allowing an increased number of spectators whose applause or shouted disapproval would both rob the occasion of its solemn character and exert improper influence on the judges. Proculus was, Libanius believed, merely trying to gain popularity for himself by enlarging the building and by permitting the public to witness contests that they had formerly not been allowed to see. Another change for the worse, of which we hear from Libanius, was the custom of inviting young boys to the feasts held in honor of Olympian Zeus during the games.[163] Formerly only mature men had attended these festivals, but now fathers were bringing their sons of ten years of age and even younger, and it was obviously undesirable for these children to see their elders in their cups. The presence of the boys also, of course, entailed added expense for the decurions whose duties required them to provide the banquets.

As might be expected, we hear a good bit about the financial difficulties that arose at this time in connection with the giving of the games, difficulties which were typical of the general decline in munici-

---

[161] This decree, *CTh* 10.1.12, has already been mentioned (above, n. 147) in connection with the evidence which it provides concerning the palace and imperial property at Daphne. F. Cumont, "L'autel palmyrénien du Musée du Capitole," *Syria* 9 (1928) 105-108, on the basis of this decree, has advanced the hypothesis that the Alytarch used the tree in the local festival of Adonis. However, all that we know of the Alytarch, at least at present, indicates only that he was a priest of Zeus and presided at the Olympic Games, and there is nothing to connect him with the cult of Adonis.

[162] On Proculus and his career, see above, n. 62. Libanius' *Or.* 10, *On the Plethrion*, is translated below in Appendices, Translation of Documents, 2.

[163] Libanius *Or.* 53. On the place of the oration in Libanius' social thought, see Pack, *Studies in Libanius* 62-63.

pal life at this period and the increasing burden felt by the members
of the local senatorial orders in meeting the public obligations for which
they were traditionally responsible. A decree[164] issued to Proculus on
27 July A.D. 383 (just one year before the celebration which was due
to occur in A.D. 384) declares that the compulsory public service of the
Syriarchate must remain "voluntary," showing that (as one might expect) it had had to be forcibly imposed when no volunteers had come
forward. Proculus would doubtless be familiar with the means of dis-
covering suitable volunteers. Two letters of Libanius show that in A.D.
388 the giving of the games was still a liturgy, undertaken in this case
by a father on behalf of his son.[165] However, a change was introduced
by Flavius Tatianus when he held office as *praefectus praetorio*, from
A.D. 388 to the late summer of A.D. 392.[166] Tatianus had been *consularis
Syriae*, and then *comes Orientis*, between A.D. 370 and 374, and was
familiar with Antioch, and apparently in an effort to lighten the financial burden of giving the Olympic Games, he seems to have instituted
an arrangement by which all or part of the necessary money was raised
by an annual *collatio* levied on the property of the *decuriones* of Antioch.[167] This arrangement was abolished, as were all of Tatianus' measures, after his removal from office in A.D. 392,[168] but it may represent
one reason for the popularity of Tatianus at Antioch.[169]

After this, we hear nothing more concerning the Olympic Games
during the reign of Arcadius, with the exception of an imperial decree
issued some time between A.D. 395 and 400, a decree that suggests that
(as happened later) officials connected with the games were taking the
opportunity to recoup some of their expenses by cutting and selling
cypress trees from the sacred grove at Daphne.[170] This would reflect the

[164] *CTh* 12.1.103.
[165] Libanius *Epistt.* 763 Wolf = 843 Förster, and 937 Wolf = 1017 Förster.
[166] On the career of Tatianus as *praefectus praetorio*, see Ensslin, "Tatianus," no. 3, *RE* 4A (1932) 2465.
[167] On Tatianus' career at Antioch, see Downey, *Comites Orientis* 12. His arrange-
ment for the financing of the games is to be deduced from *CTh* 6.3.1, in which it is
abolished.
[168] *CTh* 6.3.1.
[169] See Libanius *Epistt.* 760 Wolf = 840 Förster, written A.D. 388, 860 Wolf = 941
Förster, written A.D. 390, also a fragment of a panegyric of Tatianus by Libanius, delivered in A.D. 391, Libanius frag. 45, vol. 11, p. 634 Förster.
[170] *CJ* 11.78.1; on the date, see Seeck, *Regesten* 136.8. This decree, it should be noted,
does not prohibit cutting trees, but is directed against their illegal cutting and sale,
implying that there were persons who were allowed to cut and sell them, presumably
in specified quantities. On the grove of Daphne, and on the question about cutting
trees which had arisen early in Theodosius' reign, see above, nn. 147, 161. On the
question of cutting trees in the time of Theodosius II, see below, Ch. 16, n. 25. Libanius' effort to prevent a *comes Orientis* from cutting the trees in A.D. 387 has been
mentioned above.

chronic financial difficulties connected with the games which appear again in the reign of Theodosius II.

The theatrical entertainments, a perennial form of enjoyment for which Antioch was famous—and in which the people of the city took great pride—do not seem to have presented serious financial problems such as those connected with the Olympic Games. The stage shows were, however, a major cause of distress to Christian moralists on account of their popularity even among Christians. These shows were completely unreformed, and their licentious character offended Christian teachers, whereas the Olympic Games, containing no similar subject matter, were apparently not considered offensive.

Our evidence for the theater at Antioch at this period—and indeed much of our evidence for the stage in the eastern part of the Empire—comes from Libanius and Chrysostom, both of whom made frequent references to matters connected with the stage.[171] There were a number of different types of entertainment—classical tragedy and comedy, pantomime, mime, and dancing, some of which seems to have been somewhat on the order of ballet. The stage shows were presented in two buildings—in the theater of classical type on the slope of Mount Silpius which we first hear of in the time of Julius Caesar,[172] and in the similar building at Daphne which is associated with the name of Vespasian.[173] There were other buildings, such as the *kynegion* near the Forum of Valens which had originally been a *monomacheion*—used for animal hunts and possibly for gladiatorial shows—as well as, of course, the hippodromes at Antioch and Daphne.[174]

[171] The material provided by Libanius and Chrysostom is so extensive that a complete review of it here would be out of proportion to the evidence that we have for other subjects. For a careful collection of the material, with good bibliography, see G. J. Theocharidis *Beiträge zur Geschichte des byzantinischen Profantheaters im IV. und V. Jahrhundert, hauptsächlich auf Grund der Predigten des Iohannes Chrysostomus, Patriarchen von Konstantinopel* (Diss., Munich; Thessalonica, 1940. *Laographia, Parartema* 3). Reference should also be made to the study of G. La Piana, "The Byzantine Theater," *Speculum* 11 (1936) 171-211, and to B. H. Vandenberghe, "Saint Jean Chrysostome et les spectacles," *Ztschr. für Religions- und Geistesgeschichte* 7 (1955) 34-46.

[172] On the history of this building, see Ch. 7, §2; Ch. 8, nn. 81-83; Ch. 9, n. 70.

[173] On this theater, which has been excavated, see Ch. 9, nn. 28-29.

[174] On the *kynegion*, see above, Ch. 14, nn. 64-75, where the evidence is discussed for a building found in the excavations which may or may not be identical with this structure. On the hippodromes of Antioch and Daphne, see Excursus 14. Theocharidis, in the study cited above (n. 171), 46-47 states that Antioch possessed four "Haupttheater," but this claim rests upon misunderstanding of some of the evidence. He is right in listing the "theater of Dionysus" as that at Antioch and the "theater of Olympian Zeus" as that at Daphne, which was the chief scene of the Olympic games. But the Plethrion, though called a *theatron* (as was any Greek building in which any kind of spectacle was held; see Liddell-Scott-Jones, *s.v.*), was not a (scenic) theater as Theocharidis be-

To Libanius and his peers, all this was a natural and desirable part of the Hellenic culture, which was, in their eyes, still being so brilliantly maintained in Antioch.[175] Libanius' prime concern was to keep the theater prosperous and protect it from attacks by Christian interests, though he did, as we shall see later, recognize the political dangers that arose from the activities of some of the theatrical companies and from the political employment of the applause and acclamations of the organized theatrical claques.

Chrysostom on the other hand attacked the stage shows vehemently on account of the licentiousness of the subject matter, the acting and the costumes, all of which, in his eyes, were calculated to appeal to the gross instincts; attendance at these shows could only corrupt the individual and, directing men's thoughts constantly to these subjects, would make them discontented with their family life.[176] In this respect the stage did not differ greatly from the wild pagan festivals such as the orgiastic Maiuma, a nocturnal "scenic" festival, which still survived.[177]

lieves, but an athletic building. Again, the building mentioned by Libanius in his *Oration on the Plethrion* (*Or.* 10.33) is not a scenic theater, as Theocharidis supposes, but is very likely the building found in the excavations which was apparently used for animal hunts; see above, Ch. 14, n. 71. The theater built by Vespasian, which Theocharidis mentions in the middle of p. 47, is identical with the theater of Olympian Zeus at Daphne which he mentions on the first line of the same page; and the theater "under the mountain" mentioned by Libanius (*Or.* 10.34) is identical with the "theater of Dionysus" which he has already listed on p. 46. We know, e.g. from the account of the enlargement of it by Tiberius, that this main scenic theater was on the mountain side (see above, Ch. 8, nn. 79-83). Elsewhere Libanius speaks of the crowd in "the *theatron*" overflowing on to the sides of the mountain; there is no evidence in the passage itself what this *theatron* was, although the fact that Libanius calls it simply "the *theatron*" implies that it was the dramatic theater (*Or.* 15.48). In a number of passages he speaks of people "going up" to "the *theatron*": (*Or.* 41.3 and 8); cf. Ep. 1380 Wolf = 1301 Förster. Julian is said to have commanded a martyr to be put into a rock "near the *theatron*" (Philostorgius, p. 172, app., line 8, ed. Parmentier). Ammianus Marcellinus (23.5.3), Eunapius (*Lives*, 465), and Libanius (*Or.* 24.387) tell the story of the way in which, when the Persians captured Antioch by surprise in the middle of the third century, the invaders at the top of the mountain were first perceived by actors on the stage of the theater.

[175] Libanius' principal oration on theatrical matters is the *De saltatoribus* (*Or.* 64), written in A.D. 361, but he has many allusions to the subjects in other orations, which are collected by Theocharidis *op.cit.* (above, n. 171). See Pack, *Studies in Libanius* 63, and G. Haddad, *Aspects of Social Life in Antioch in the Hellenistic-Roman Period* (Diss., Chicago; New York 1949) 167ff.

[176] Chrysostom's oration which is specifically devoted to an attack on theatrical entertainments is the *Contra ludos et theatra*, PG 56.263-270. This was written one year after he had moved to Constantinople (*op.cit.* col. 268) but it is typical of the utterances scattered through his sermons at Antioch, which are well utilized by Theocharidis *op.cit.* (above, n. 171). See also Haddad *loc.cit.* (above, n. 175).

[177] The principal source for the Maiuma, an orgiastic festival recurring every three

There was undoubtedly good reason for Chrysostom's alarm, and it was his duty to do everything possible to shield his congregations from these influences. It must, however, be remembered that Chrysostom was speaking with all the zeal of the reformer and moralist;[178] that Antioch seems to have been no worse in this respect than other cities such as Alexandria and Constantinople; and in particular that the gross sculptures and mosaics discovered in the excavations seem, if anything, relatively few in number and restricted in location, in comparison with the total of the archaeological finds of all descriptions. Also it has proved that the improper creations discovered at Antioch are of fairly common types such as are found not infrequently throughout the rest of the Graeco-Roman world.[179]

It is not surprising to find that not all the clergy of Antioch were as hostile to the stage as Chrysostom was. Palladius, the biographer of Chrysostom, relates that one of the criticisms brought against Porphyrius, who became bishop of Antioch in A.D. 404, was that he was fond of theatrical shows and horse races, and not only attended the performances, but associated with the actors and jockeys.[180] Palladius himself, while expressing disapproval of such behavior, quotes a phrase from Menander just before the passage in which he condemns Porphyrius' tastes.[181] Menander in fact is the only Greek author whom Palladius quotes, though there are unacknowledged citations of other writers, and it is plain that Palladius was acquainted with the principal classical writers.[182] Given the intellectual atmosphere of Antioch, such an interest in classical tragedy and comedy—as distinguished from the mimes and lower forms of entertainment—was quite natural, and it seems reasonable to suppose that the fourth century had the same fondness

years, is the description of Malalas 284.21-285.11; see also Preisendanz, "Maïumas," *RE* 14 (1930) 610-612, and Theocharidis *op.cit.* (above, n. 171) 72.

[178] See for example the observations by R. Stillwell in his review of Haddad's monograph in *AJP* 73 (1952) 109-110.

[179] The theater of Daphne contained several statues of satyrs and hermaphrodites (*Antioch* 2, p. 173, no. 161) of a fairly common type (Levi, *Antioch Mosaic Pavements* 1.183-185). These statues correspond to mosaics of satyrs of the same type found in a house in Daphne (Levi. *loc.cit.*, with plate 40 in volume 2) dated between A.D. 235 and 312 (Levi, *op.cit.* 625). There are many characteristic scenes of conviviality in the mosaics but these are all of the type found throughout the Empire.

[180] Palladius *Dialogus de vita S. Ioann. Chrysostomi* 16.53-54, p. 94 ed. Coleman-Norton. On Palladius' theatrical interests see the study of E. Honigmann cited above, n. 25, especially 35-38.

[181] *Dial. de vita S. Ioann. Chrys.* 16.53, p. 94.12 ed. Coleman-Norton. See Coleman-Norton's commentary on p. 183 of his edition.

[182] See Coleman-Norton's observations in the Introduction to his edition of Palladius' *Dialogus*, p. lxx.

for such matters as is shown by earlier mosaics showing dramatic scenes which have been found in the excavations.[183]

It was not solely in the cultural and religious life of the times that the theater played a part. A recent study by R. Browning[184] has shown that both the actors and the organized claques connected with the theatres exerted important political influence, comparable to that of the organized circus factions, whose political role has been known for some time. The leading part taken by actors and the claque in the revolt of A.D. 387 has been mentioned, and it is worth recalling that both Libanius and Chrysostom were quite aware of the role played by theatrical people in fomenting civil disorders.[185] Libanius devoted an oration (*Or.* 41) to advising Timocrates (*consularis Syriae* some time after A.D. 382) not to be influenced by the theatrical claque, which was notoriously venal.[186] This form of political intimidation was not confined to Antioch, but may be traced in other cities of the eastern part of the Empire at the same period.[187]

Gladiatorial shows were probably no longer presented at Antioch in Theodosius' reign. These exhibitions had been forbidden by Constantine the Great on religious grounds, and there was a noticeable decline in such presentations during the fourth century, though it was not possible, on account of their popularity, to put an end to them at once.[188] Libanius in his autobiography, written in A.D. 374, declares that he had enjoyed seeing gladiatorial combats both as a youth and in old age;[189] but the combats probably did not continue after this period, for the *monomacheion* built by Julius Caesar for gladiatorial fights was changed into a *kynegion* in the reign of Valens, which indicates that it was no longer used for gladiatorial exhibitions.[190]

---

[183] See the studies of K. Weitzmann, "Illustrations of Euripides and Homer in the Mosaics of Antioch," *Antioch* 3.233-247, and of A. M. Friend, Jr., "Menander and Glykera in the Mosaics of Antioch," *ibid.* 248-251. Weitzmann discusses mosaics with scenes of the *Hippolytus*, the *Meleager*, the *Stheneboea*, the *Troiades*, the *Medea*, the *Iphigeneia in Aulis*, and *Helen*, all dating in the third century after Christ, or perhaps in the late second century. Friend studies two mosaics of Menander with the hetaira Glykera, one from Daphne, dated later than the third century after Christ, the other from Antioch, dated in the third century (see also Levi, *Antioch Mosaic Pavements* 1.625).

[184] Cited above, n. 74.

[185] Libanius *Or.* 19.28; Chrysostom *Hom. in Matt.* 37.6-7 = *PG* 57.427.

[186] On the career of Timocrates, see above, n. 65.

[187] See the opening paragraph of Browning's study, cited above, n. 74.

[188] See above, Ch. 14, nn. 64-65.

[189] Libanius *Or.* 1.5.

[190] See above, Ch. 14, n. 67.

5. The Jewish Community and the
Judaizing Christians

The history of the Jewish community at Antioch under Theodosius I, and of the relations between Christians and Jews, forms a passage of unusual interest in the history of the city, which has recently been illuminated by the discovery of the important synagogue inscriptions at Apamea dated A.D. 391.

There had been a flourishing Jewish community at Antioch since Hellenistic times, and we have seen that the attraction of Judaism for some Gentiles was one of the factors which prepared Antioch to be an especially fruitful center of early Christian missions among the Gentiles.[191] There had been an outbreak of anti-Semitism in the time of Vespasian and Titus,[192] but the Jewish colony continued to exist, and sometimes to prosper. Libanius, in an oration written in A.D. 388 or later, mentions that he had very orthodox Jewish tenants who had worked on his lands near Antioch for four generations.[193] There was an affinity between Arians, pagans, and Jews,[194] and in the time of the Arian troubles, Judaism, with its emphasis on monotheism, attracted the interest of some Arians. Several distinguished rabbis were connected with Antioch in the fourth century.[195]

Under Theodosius, the Jewish community was evidently in flourishing condition. There were two synagogues, one at Antioch, one at Daphne, and perhaps others.[196] The *archisynagogos*, or chief of the community at Antioch, named Ilasios, was sufficiently well-to-do to make important financial contributions to the synagogue built by the community at Apamea in A.D. 391.[197] The tomb of Aidesios, *gerousiarch*

---

[191] See Ch. 11, §1.

[192] See above, Ch. 9, n. 20; and below, Excursus 4.

[193] *Or.* 47.13. On the interpretation of the passage (which does not refer to Libanius' property in Palestine, as some earlier scholars supposed) see Pack, *Studies in Libanius* 48-51.

[194] See the study of G. H. Williams, "Christology and Church—State Relations in the Fourth Century," *Church History* 20 (1951) 26.

[195] See Kraeling, *Jewish Community at Antioch* 155-156.

[196] Chrysostom *Adv. Jud.* 1.6 = PG 48.852 mentions one synagogue at Antioch and one at Daphne (the latter being the one in which Christians used to practice incubation). In another passage (*Adv. Jud.* 6.12 = PG 48.904) he speaks of "synagogues in the city, synagogues in the suburb [Daphne]." It is not clear whether the plural is rhetorical, or whether it is to be taken literally. On these synagogues, see Krauss, "Synagoge," *RE* 4A.1298.

[197] See the important series of mosaic inscriptions found by the Belgian excavators, published in *IGLS* 1319-1339, and cf. E. L. Sukenik in *Hebrew Union College Annual* 23, 2 (1951-1952) 541-551, and L. Robert in *REG* 67 (1954) 81-82.

of the Jewish community at Antioch, has been found at Beth Shearim.[198]
The Christian church itself, emphasizing as it did continuity between
the Old and the New Testaments, contributed to a Christian interest
in Judaism which some Christians found alarming. In Antioch, the
tomb of the Maccabean martyrs, Jews who had suffered under Antiochus Epiphanes, began to attract Christians because of the supposed
powers of these martyrs to effect miraculous cures, and the local Christian authorities, not liking the interest that their people felt in the
Jewish saints, solved the problem by taking over the synagogue where
the Maccabees were buried and turning it into a Christian shrine.[199]
A real cult of the Maccabees grew up and they were accepted on a
par with Christian saints since they had suffered and given their lives
for a (Jewish) Law that was a forerunner or early form of the Christian law. Chrysostom preached several eloquent sermons on these saints,
pointing out their courage and exhorting his hearers to imitate their
virtues; he also used the Maccabees as examples of the essential connection between the Old and New Testaments, and compared Eleazer
to St. Peter.[200]

The cult of the Maccabees was not the only aspect of Judaism to
which Antiochene Christians were attracted. Jewish ritual, the solemnity of the festivals, fasting, miraculous cures reputedly performed by
the rabbis, and the Jewish tribunals, which were supposed to be fairer
than secular courts, all tended to draw Christians away from their
proper religious observances, and Chrysostom in A.D. 386 and 387, that
is, in the first year of his ordination, preached a series of sermons in

[198] The text is published by M. Schwabe, *Israel Exploration Journal* 4 (1951) p. 252,
No. 207, pl. 23 B. I owe this reference to the kindness of R. P. René Mouterde, S.J.
[199] The literature on the Maccabees is cited above, Ch. 5, n. 121. See also M. Maas,
"Die Maccabäer als christliche Heilige," *Monatsschrift für Geschichte und Wissenschaft
des Judentums* 44 (1900) 145-156; J. Obermann, "The Sepulchre of the Maccabean
Martyrs," *JBL* 50 (1931) 250-265; E. Bikerman, "Les Maccabées de Malalas," *Byzantion* 21 (1951) 73ff. Bikerman dates the transformation of the Maccabean synagogue
ca. A.D. 380. Obermann, *op.cit.* 253 n. 12 points out that it was not infrequent for
Christians to take over synagogues.
[200] Chrysostom *In sanctos Maccabaeos* 1-3 = *PG* 50.617-628. There appears to be no
internal evidence for the date of these discourses, but the context and the reference to
Bishop Flavian, who was to speak on the subject after Chrysostom (*PG* 50.626) makes
it plain that the sermons were delivered in Antioch. M. Simon, "La polémique anti-
juive de S. Jean Chrysostome et le mouvement judaisant d'Antioche," *Annuaire de
l'Institut de philologie et d'histoire orientales et slaves* 4 (1936) 415 (*Mélanges Franz
Cumont* 1) suggests that the sermon on the Maccabees of Gregory of Nazianzus (*Or.*
15, *PG* 35.912ff.) was preached in Antioch in A.D. 375, but the evidence indicates
rather that this was a rhetorical piece delivered at Nazianzus in A.D. 365; see T.
Sinko, "De Gregorii Nazianzeni laudibus Macchabaeorum," *Eos* 13 (1907) 1-29, and
cf. Christ-Schmid-Stählin, *Gesch. d. gr. Lit.*[6] 1415 with n. 4.

which he warned Christians on Jewish practices.[201] Christian women, he says, were especially prone to be attracted.[202] Chrysostom points out that Jewish and Christian practices are not really so similar as some of the Judaizing Christians suppose, and that people can be attracted to Judaism chiefly if they have neglected, and do not understand, their own Christian belief and worship. There is no real evidence to show how many Christians were involved in the practices that Chrysostom described; in any case we do not hear of any further Judaizing tendencies after Chrysostom's time. Of the other side of the picture, namely the effect which Christianity must have had on Jewish practices, we unfortunately hear nothing in our extant sources.

[201] The eight sermons *Adversus Judaeos* are printed in *PG* 48.843-942. There is also a similar discourse, *Contra Judaeos et Gentiles, quod Christus sit Deus, ibid.* 813-838. For modern studies of the subject, see Simon, *op.cit.* (above, n. 200) and the same scholar's *Verus Israel* (Paris 1948) 175, 249, 379-380, 385, 415, 418; A. L. Williams, *Adversus Judaeos* (Cambridge, Eng., 1935) 132-139; Kraeling, *Jewish Community at Antioch* 156-157; J. E. Seaver, *Persecution of the Jews in the Roman Empire 300-438* (Lawrence, Kansas 1952) 40-41. On the chronology of the sermons *Adversus Judaeos*, see Rauschen, *Jahrbücher* 496ff.

[202] *Adv. Jud.* 2.3 = *PG* 48.860; *Adv. Jud.* 4.7 = *PG* 48.881. It is noteworthy that according to the mosaic inscriptions, the majority of the donors to the construction of the synagogue at Apamea were women (cf. *IGLS* 1322-1327, 1332, 1335, 1336). The same phenomenon was observed at Damascus by Josephus (*Bell. Jud.* 2.20.2).

CHAPTER 16

THEODOSIUS II (A.D. 408-450) AND
MARCIANUS (A.D. 450-457)

THEODOSIUS II, when he became emperor on the death of Arcadius, was seven years old, and the government was conducted for some years by regents, first the praetorian prefect Anthemius, then by the emperor's older sister Pulcheria.[1] By contrast with the history of the reign of the first Theodosius, our extant sources tell us comparatively little of the secular history of Antioch at this period. On the other hand, the ecclesiastical history of the city is filled with events, notably those connected with the Nestorian controversy.

1. SECULAR AFFAIRS

The best known event in the life of the city at this time is the visit of the Empress Eudocia in A.D. 438.[2] The empress was travelling to Jerusalem in fulfillment of a vow, accompanied by the Patriarch Cyril of Alexandria as spiritual adviser.[3] When she came to Antioch, Eudocia, who was the daughter of a pagan professor at Athens and was skilled in literary composition, delivered an encomium of the city before the local senate in the senate-chamber, where she was seated on

[1] On the reign of Theodosius II, see Bury, *Later Roman Empire* 1.212ff., and Stein, *Gesch.* 1.424ff.

[2] The principal sources are Malalas, Tusculan fragments, in *Spicilegium romanum* ed. A. Mai, vol. 2, pt. 2 (Rome 1839), frag. 2, p. 15 (the passage is missing from the Oxford MS of Malalas); *Chronicon Paschale* 584-5 Bonn ed.; Evagrius *Hist. eccl.* 1.20; cf. Socrates *Hist. eccl.* 7.47, Theophanes A.M. 5927, p. 92.25-29 ed. De Boor. The visit is securely dated in A.D. 438 by its relation to other events in Eudocia's life, and this date is adopted by most scholars, e.g. Bury, *op.cit.* 1.226-227, Stein, *op.cit.* 1.444; Seeck, art. "Eudocia," *RE* 6 (1909) 907; E. Honigmann, "Juvenal of Jerusalem," *Dumbarton Oaks Papers* 5 (1950) 225. In the *Chronicon Paschale loc.cit.* this visit to Antioch is mistakenly dated in A.D. 444 by confusion with the empress' second journey to Jerusalem, and this date is accepted by Bouchier, *Antioch* 177, by Christ-Schmid-Stählin, *Gesch. d. griech. Lit.*⁶ vol. 2, pt. 2, p. 170, and by A. Ludwich in his edition of the fragments of Eudocia's writings, *Eudociae Augustae Procli Lycii Claudiani . . . reliquiae* (Leipzig 1897) 11.

[3] The presence of Cyril of Alexandria is mentioned by John of Nikiu, 87.20, p. 106 ed. Charles. Honigmann, *loc.cit.* (above, n. 2) writes that "Cyril of Alexandria went to Antioch to salute [the empress] and accompanied her to Jerusalem." I have been unable to determine what is the basis of Honigmann's reference to this detail. The account of John of Nikiu could be taken to imply that the patriarch had accompanied the empress from Constantinople, and this is perhaps what we might expect from the position of influence which he occupied at the imperial court. See the description of the journey by F.-M. Abel, "Saint Cyrille d'Alexandrie dans ses rapports avec la Palestine," *Kyrilliana* (Cairo 1947) 223-224, who supposes that Cyril accompanied the empress during the whole journey.

a golden chair set with precious stones.[4] At the close of the piece she complimented the audience by paraphrasing a line of Homer, "Of your lineage and race I declare myself to be," alluding to the fact that her own Athenian origin united her in kinship with the people of Antioch, who were proud of the legend that their city had been colonized in part by settlers from Athens.[5] No courtesy could have been more warmly appreciated, and the senate in gratitude voted a gilded bronze statue of the empress to be set up in the *bouleuterion* in which she had delivered her encomium, and a bronze statue outside the Museum.[6] As was proper on such an occasion, the empress added material benefits to her literary praises, by giving funds for a distribution of grain and towards the restoration of the Bath of Valens, which had been partly burned.[7] The empress returned from Jerusalem to Constantinople the following year, and then, as a result of discord at the impe-

[4] The chair is mentioned in the Tusculan Fragments of Malalas and by the *Chronicon Paschale* (cited above, n. 2). This was very likely a portable throne that the empress took with her on her journey. If it had been an ordinary piece of the furniture of the *bouleuterion*, it might have been taken for granted and not mentioned in an account of the scene.

[5] Eudocia's phrase ὑμετέρης γενεῆς τε καὶ αἵματος εὔχομαι εἶναι, preserved by Evagrius *loc.cit.* (above, n. 2) is based upon the verse ταύτης τοι γενεῆς τε καὶ αἵματος εὔχομαι εἶναι which appears twice in the Iliad, at 6.211, where it is spoken by Glaucus, and at 20.241, where it is spoken by Aeneas. This is the only fragment of the empress' encomium which is preserved; see Ludwich's edition (cited above, n. 2) 10-13. Ludwich suggests that the whole of the empress' composition was in heroic verse. On the legend of the settlement of Athenian colonists at Antioch, see above, Ch. 4, n. 116.

[6] The Tusculan fragments of Malalas and the *Chronicon Paschale* (cited above, n. 2) mention a "gilded statue" (εἰκὼν ἔγχρυσος, which must have been gilt on bronze) inside the *bouleuterion*, and a bronze statue outside the Museum. Evagrius (cited above, n. 2) mentions only a bronze statue, and says that it was still to be seen in his own day, in the latter part of the sixth century. The *Chronicon Paschale* (585.14) adds that "the statues are standing to this day," a characteristic phrase that is presumably taken from the fuller form of the account of Malalas (lost in the Oxford MS and abridged in the Tusculan fragments), upon which the account in the *Chronicon Paschale* is presumably based. The statement that the statues "still existed" need not be taken literally, for it is known that such phrases were often taken over from his literary sources by Malalas (see above, Ch. 2, §4). The difference between the accounts might indicate that the gilt bronze statue had disappeared by Evagrius' time, while the bronze statue at the Museum still existed. Evagrius refers to the people of Antioch with the phrase παῖδες 'Αντιοχέων, a phrase which he often uses: 3.10, p. 109.9; 4.6, p. 156.18; 4.35, p. 185.14 ed. Bidez-Parmentier; cf. L. Thurmayr, *Sprachliche Studien zu dem Kirchenhistoriker Euagrios* (Diss., Eichstätt, 1910) 14; cf. παῖδες 'Απαμέων, 4.26, p. 173.2, and the *Chronicle of Edessa*, ch. 97, p. 132 ed. Hallier (*Texte und Untersuchungen*, 9 [1892]), of the earthquake of 526 at Antioch, "durch welches der grössere Theil von Antiochien zusammenstürtzte, seine Einwohner (wörtlich: Kinder) verschüttete und seine Bewohner erstickte."

[7] A gift λόγῳ σιτονικοῦ is mentioned by the *Chronicon Paschale* (cited above, n. 2), while Evagrius (above, n. 2) records that the empress gave a sum in gold for the restoration of the bath. On other building operations which are associated by some sources with the empress' visit, see below.

rial court, made a second, and final, journey to Jerusalem in A.D. 433,[8] but there is no record that she visited Antioch again and the circumstances of her second journey (which amounted to an exile) were such that she might not have wished to make a public appearance at Antioch. The empress' writings included an epic poem on the martyrdom of St. Cyprian of Antioch in the persecution under Diocletian.

One major event in the history of the city, which is also associated with Eudocia's visit, is the enlargement of the city wall.[9] According to the tradition, the empress requested Theodosius to make this enlargement, and the work was carried out under the supervision of Antiochus Chuzon, who had been *praefectus praetorio* in A.D. 430 and 431. It is not clear whether this extension of the wall had become necessary because of contemporary growth in the size of the city, reflecting an increase in its prosperity at this time, or whether the extension was made in order to accommodate an expansion outside the city that had already taken place; Malalas indicates the latter reason but his statement may represent an effort to assign a suitable explanation to the undertaking. As has been seen, the city walls had been repaired (but not, apparently, enlarged) ca. A.D. 397,[10] and if any growth in the city had taken place, it is presumably to be dated in the period following this repair.

The wall was extended, it is said, for one Roman mile at the south of the city, along the road which led to Daphne, and a new "Daphne gate" was built, which was gilded and named the Golden Gate, the gilding being carried out by the *consularis* Nymphidianus.[11] The new

[8] New evidence for dating the empress' second visit to Jerusalem in A.D. 443 is brought forward by Aline A. Boyce, "Eudoxia, Eudocia, Eudoxia," *American Numismatic Society Museum Notes* 6 (1954) 136-138.

[9] For a detailed study of the evidence, which is conflicting, see Downey, "Wall of Theodosius at Antioch." Malalas (346.5-347.5) states that the extension was made under Theodosius I because the city had grown beyond its old walls. Evagrius (1.20) knows the tradition that the wall was extended under Theodosius I, but rejects this report, and states that the extension took place, on the initiative of the empress, under Theodosius II. Evidently Malalas confused the two emperors named Theodosius, and also confused two *praefecti praetorio* named Antiochus Chuzon, just as in other cases it can be shown that he confused both emperors and private persons who had the same or similar names.

[10] See above, Ch. 15, nn. 151, 153.

[11] This description reproduces the accounts of Malalas and Evagrius (*locc. citt.*), which supplement each other. Malalas (360.15-20) describes the gilding of the Daphnetic Gate in another context, bringing it into relation with the gilding of the Golden Gate at Constantinople under Theodosius II. It seems reasonable to suppose that the gilding of the gate at Antioch would have been connected with the extension of the wall, and we can believe that Malalas preferred to record it in connection with the work at Constantinople, rather than to describe it in connection with the ex-

wall started from the Philonauta Gate (which from its name would appear to have stood on the Orontes) and ascended the mountain, joining the old wall of Tiberius at the source of the mountain stream called Phyrminus, at a place known as Rhodion ("The Roses"), which, as Müller suggests,[12] probably was a rose garden on the side of the mountain. Traces of the old wall, which Theodosius' work replaced, were still visible in Evagrius' day, in the latter part of the sixth century.

For the new construction, it is recorded, stones were taken from the old *monomacheion* on the acropolis, and from the aqueduct that supplied the acropolis with water brought from the road to Laodicea. This aqueduct had been built by Julius Caesar and was now demolished because it was, apparently, no longer needed.[13] Evidently no real settlement existed at this time on the acropolis, the people who lived there doubtless having found it more convenient to live in the city proper.

A number of other building operations are recorded during this period. The emperor granted two hundred gold pounds for the repair of the Bath of Valens, which had been partly burned.[14] Beginning in A.D. 437 or 438, Theodosius sent to Antioch three officials, named Memnonius, Zoilus, and Callistus, who are described as "governors," meaning, apparently that they were not sent all at once, but served in turn as *consulares Syriae* or *comites Orientis*. Each of them presented to the city a building that was known by his name.[15] Memnonius built a structure called the Psephion, which contained a hypaethral inner court; the purpose of the building is not stated, but its name (evidently

---

tension of the wall. On the gilding of the gate at Constantinople, see B. Meyer, "Das Goldene Tor in Konstantinopel," *Mnemosynon Th. Weigand* (Munich 1938) 87-99.

[12] Müller, *Antiq. Antioch.* 114. It should be noted that Müller, who was not aware of the confusion in Malalas, accepts the chronicler's statement that the wall was extended by Theodosius I. On the other hand, Bury, *Later Roman Empire* 1.227, knowing only Evagrius' account, attributes the work to Theodosius II.

[13] On the original construction of the *monomacheion* and the aqueduct, see above, Ch. 7, §2.

[14] Evagrius 1.20. On the Bath of Valens, see above, Ch. 14, §3. The excerpts from Malalas preserved in the *Excerpta de Insidiis* (§30, p. 160.21-24 ed. De Boor) mention that Theodosius put up buildings at Antioch, but do not give any details concerning them.

[15] Evagrius 1.18. Record of these buildings is not preserved in our extant texts of Malalas. These officials are not otherwise known except that Zoilus might be identical with the person of that name who was *praefectus praetorio* in A.D. 444 (Seeck, *Regesten* 373). The date of the activity of these officials at Antioch is indicated by the circumstance that Evagrius describes it in the chapter following his account (1.17) of the great earthquake of A.D. 437 (on the date and literary sources of that disaster, see Downey, "Earthquakes at Constantinople" 597), and that he states that they were followed at Antioch by Anatolius, who, as we know (see below, n. 20), was appointed *mag. mil. per Or.* in A.D. 438.

connected with ψηφίς or ψῆφος, vote) indicates that it served some judicial purpose, presumably being a law court.[16] This building may have been in or near the neighborhoods called Ostrakine and Bursia.[17]

Zoilus built a "basilica" south of the Stoa of Rufinus, which retained its name down to the time of Evagrius, though the structure itself had been altered as a result of damage that it suffered at various times.[18]

The third governor, Callistus, built a handsome stoa, called by his name, which stood before the law courts, opposite the forum on which was the praetorium of the *magistri militum*.[19]

Then, in A.D. 439, Theodosius ordered Anatolius, who was sent to Antioch as *magister militum per Orientem* in A.D. 438, to construct a "basilica" in the city, and provided the money for the work.[20] This is described as a "large illuminated basilica," splendidly adorned, bearing an inscription in gold mosaic giving the emperor's name; it also contained representations (whether in sculpture or mosaic is not made clear) of Theodosius II and Valentinian III, who ruled in the West. The building stood opposite "the Athla," the nature and location of which is not known.[21]

[16] This is the interpretation of Müller, *Antiq. Antioch.* 115, and of the Stephanus, *Thesaurus Graece Linguae, s.v.* ψηφεῖον. Müller notes (115 n. 2) that Du Cange (*Glossarium ad scriptores mediae et infimae graecitatis, s.v.* ψηφίον) makes the much less plausible suggestion that the building was named with reference to mosaics that it contained (ψηφίς being used to mean the mosaic cube). Evagrius employs the colloquial spelling current in his day, and since this represents contemporary usage, it should be retained, and need not be corrected to the classical form.

[17] Evagrius 6.8.

[18] On the Stoa of Rufinus, see above, Ch. 15, n. 130.

[19] By saying that the stoa was "directly opposite" (εὐθύ) the forum, Evagrius evidently means that it ran along one side of the forum. Which forum this was, we cannot be sure, as a praetorium of the *magistri militum* is not specifically mentioned elsewhere except in a description (Theophanes A.M. 6018, p. 172, 5 ed. De Boor) of the fire of A.D. 525, in which the building is mentioned as one of the terminal points of the fire, with no other indication of its location.

[20] Malalas 360.7-15; Evagrius 1.18. For Anatolius' date, see O. Seeck, "Anatolius," no. 9, *RE* 1.2072.

[21] Malalas describes the building (360.7-8) as βασιλικὴν διάφωτον μεγάλην, the epithet *diaphotos* perhaps meaning that it had a hypaethral court, like the Kaisarion; see further Downey, "Architectural Significance of *stoa* and *basilike*" 199. Evagrius (*loc.-cit.*) calls the building a *stoa*. It was rebuilt by the Empress Theodora after the earthquake of A.D. 526 (Malalas 423.7-9; see below, Ch. 18, n. 99). Malalas' statement (360.14) that the two emperors were ἐπάνω could apparently mean either that the representations of them were placed above the mosaic building inscription, or that statues of them were placed on the roof. Malalas quotes the building inscription as Ἔργον Θεοδοσίου βασιλέως, which can hardly represent the real text, but simply gives the chronicler's idea of what such an inscription should be. Malalas' ostensible quotations of inscriptions (which were often in reality cited from literary texts) are examined by Downey, "Inscriptions in Malalas." Malalas (360.8) describes the basilica

Alongside these records of secular buildings, we have two notices of ecclesiastical building activities. The remains of Ignatius, bishop of Antioch, who had been martyred in Rome under Trajan, had been brought back to Antioch and buried in the *koimeterion* outside the Daphnetic Gate. Theodosius determined to do greater honor to this famous saint of Antioch, and the Tychaion—the ancient shrine of the Tyche of Antioch—was converted into a church of St. Ignatius, to which the bones of the saint were taken.[22]

We hear also of the addition of two rooms to the cruciform church of St. Babylas which has been excavated at Kaoussie. A mosaic inscription found in one of the chambers records that the room was built, and the mosaic floor laid, during the episcopate of Theodotus (who was bishop of Antioch from A.D. 420 or 421 to 429), under the supervision of Athanasius, priest and *oikonomos* (administrator of the church) and of Akkiba, deacon and *paramonarius* (superintendent of the edifice). The room is called the *pistikon*, evidently meaning that it was designed for use in connection with the baptismal rites, specifically with the profession of faith, or recitation of the creed ($\dot{\eta}$ $\pi i \sigma \tau \iota s$).[23]

The Olympic Games of Antioch seem to have continued to suffer from the financial difficulties which, as we have seen, affected them in the time of Theodosius I.[24] Again, as in the time of Theodosius I,

---

as being located κατέναντι τῶν λεγομένων Ἄθλων. Müller (*Antiq. Antioch.* 115-116) conjectures that "the Athla" was a building named for its connection with the prizes in the Olympic Games, and located near the Xystos. This is a plausible explanation, but we have no real evidence in support of it.

[22] Evagrius *Hist. eccl.* 1.16; Nicephorus Callistus Xanthopulos *Hist. eccl.* 14.44 (*PG* 146.212); *Acta SS* Febr. tom. 1.34. The Patriarch Severus preached in this church: Wright, *Catalogue of the Syriac MSS in the British Museum*, pp. 536, 540. Evagrius mentions that the festival of St. Ignatius was still observed in the church in his own day, in the latter part of the sixth century, and that the Patriarch Gregory had made additions to the festival so as to make it more magnificent. There appears to be no evidence for the location of the church. For the return of St. Ignatius' bones to Antioch, see above, Ch. 11, n. 86. For the construction of the Tychaion, see above, Ch. 4, n. 93.

[23] J. Lassus, "L'Église cruciforme," *Antioch* 2.33, with Plan 4 on pp. 218-219, on which the rooms are nos. 2 and 3 on the plan, in the northeast angle of the crossing of the arms of the church. On the interpretation of their construction, in addition to Lassus' study, see Levi, *Antioch Mosaic Pavements* 1.425 n. 60. The inscription is published and commented upon by Lassus, *Antioch-on-the-Orontes* 2, pp. 41-43, no. 5, and by Jalabert and Mouterde *IGLS* 778. On the meaning of *pistikon* see also H. Grégoire in *Byzantion* 13 (1938) 180-182. I follow the interpretation of the term offered tentatively by Lassus and approved by Jalabert and Mouterde, rather than Grégoire's hypothesis (involving the supposition that the spelling in the inscription is an error for ποστικόν) that the term means "vestibule," "dependencies," "latrine."

[24] See above, Ch. 15, §4. A decree of A.D. 409 referring to a gift of 600 solidi for the restoration of the finances of the municipality of Antioch may have some refer-

A History of Antioch

an imperial decree had to be issued, in A.D. 427-429, putting an end to the right of the Alytarch to cut cypress trees in the grove at Daphne, which apparently had been a perquisite of office by which this official was able to reimburse himself for expenses connected with the games. This time, however, it is provided that the Alytarch is to be compensated for the loss of the privilege.[25] In the same decree, all officials (*omnes iudices*) are forbidden to cut down trees in the grove at Daphne, or to carry off trees that had fallen; but no provision is made for compensating them for the loss of the privilege. A little later, the financial burden of giving the Olympic Games must have been somewhat eased when Antiochus Chuzon of Antioch, who was *praefectus praetorio* in A.D. 430-431, gave an endowment for the support of the hippodrome spectacles, the Olympic Games and the Maiouma.[26] This relief seems to have been only temporary, for thirty-five years later, as we shall see, the leading offices of the games had to be turned into regular functions of the *comes Orientis* and the *consularis Syriae*.[27]

The general economic difficulties that are suggested by the history of the Olympic Games at this period were also accompanied by one sudden crisis. Heavy unseasonable rains in the late spring and early summer of A.D. 431 ruined the crops ready for harvest after the winter growing season. The resulting famine produced daily disorders in the city, and the rains themselves, swelling the streams that ran down the mountain side into the city, produced floods that caused serious damage. The emergency was so great that Bishop John, who was supposed to set out for the synod that had been convened to meet at Ephesus at this time, considered that his presence in the city was necessary, and so delayed his departure for some time—with serious consequences, as will be seen, at the Council.[28]

2. THE CHURCH AT ANTIOCH
IN THE FIRST PART OF THEODOSIUS' REIGN

The popular religious interest in Antioch, in the early part of the reign of Theodosius II, centered about two famous local figures, St. John Chrysostom and St. Symeon Stylites the Elder, and about the

ence to special financing of the Olympic Games, though the real significance of the edict is not clear; see *CTh* 12.1.169, with Gothofredus' commentary.
[25] *CJ* 11.78.2. [26] Malalas 362.18-21.
[27] See below, Ch. 17, nn. 35-36.
[28] Our knowledge of this episode comes from a letter which John of Antioch wrote to the emperor to explain the lateness of his arrival at the Council of Ephesus: Schwartz, *Acta Conciliorum* 1.1, pt. 5, p. 125.14-21.

final healing of the Antiochene schism. The bishop of Antioch Por- phyrius (A.D. 404-413), who was elected bishop as the leader of the group of Chrysostom's enemies in Antioch,[29] continued in office for several years after Theodosius' accession, and during these years the memory of Chrysostom was dishonored by being omitted from the list of departed bishops whose names were recited at the Eucharist; and for this reason the Patriarchate of Antioch, along with the other Eastern patriarchates, was out of communion with Rome,[30] while a large num- ber of Chrysostom's supporters, not only in Antioch but throughout Syria, felt so strongly that they separated themselves from the Church, and, on occasion, conducted their own synods.[31] However, the local party, which was loyal to Chrysostom's memory, found favor again when Porphyrius died and was succeeded by Alexander (A.D. 413-421), who restored the name of Chrysostom to commemoration, brought peace to Chrysostom's supporters in Antioch and the remainder of Syria, and restored the patriarchate to communion with Rome.[32] Alexander also was able, through his unusual gifts as a leader and peacemaker, to bring the Antiochene schism finally to an end. The reunion was symbolized when Alexander took his own congregation to the church occupied by the followers of Eustathius and combined the two congregations into one procession which then returned, singing psalms and hymns, to the Great Church.[33]

Having restored peace within the Church at Antioch itself, Alexander was naturally anxious to rebuild the prestige of Antioch, which had been greatly diminished during the long period of its internal troubles. To this end, he set out to make sure that the authority of the see of Antioch was properly acknowledged in the various provinces which were, as he understood it, subject to the ecclesiastical control of Antioch. Apparently he encountered difficulty in the case of Cyprus, for we find that he appealed to Pope Innocent I (A.D. 402-417) for a pronouncement on the status of Cyprus, and so we have for the first time a specific statement of the question of the ecclesiastical supremacy of Antioch over Cyprus.[34] The bishops of Cyprus, alarmed (they said) by the continua-

---

[29] See above, Ch. 15, n. 25.   [30] See Kidd, *Hist. of the Church* 3.53.
[31] Sozomen, *Hist. eccl.* 8.24.
[32] Theodoret *Hist. eccl.* 5.35.3; see Kidd, *Hist. of the Church* 3.174. On the career of Alexander, see P. Peeters, *Recherches d'histoire et de philologie orientales* 1 (Brussels) 146-150 (*Subsidia Hagiographica* 27).
[33] Theodoret *Hist. eccl.* 5.35.1-5; see Kidd, *loc.cit.*
[34] For a detailed study of this question, the results of which are summarized here, see G. Downey, "The Claim of Antioch to Ecclesiastical Jurisdiction over Cyprus," *Proceedings of the American Philosophical Society* 102 (1958) 224-228.

tion of Arian views at Antioch, had been filling episcopal vacancies on their own authority, in disregard (Antioch claimed) of the decision of the Council of Nicaea as to the authority of Antioch over dioceses beyond that of Syria. This problem raised again, in another form, the question of the Petrine tradition at Antioch, i.e. whether the ecclesiastical rank of Antioch was to be determined on the basis of Peter's having been bishop, first of Antioch and then of Rome, or whether Antioch could only claim that he founded the church there.[35] On this occasion, Pope Innocent, when appealed to by Alexander, followed the view that Peter had been bishop of Antioch, and so upheld the decision of Nicaea. In Antioch itself, the claims of jurisdiction over the bishops of the island could find support in the fact that the *comes Orientis* was the immediate superior of the *consularis* who governed Cyprus. However, when the matter came before the Council of Ephesus, as we shall see presently, a decree was issued supporting the independence of Cyprus.[36]

Alexander of Antioch was succeeded by Theodotus, who was bishop from A.D. 421 to 428. He brought back into communion with the local church the remnant of the followers of Apollinaris.[37] While he was in office, a council was held at Antioch, in A.D. 424, which pronounced the condemnation of Pelagius, whose views were being rejected throughout the East.[38] It was during his episcopate that one of the well-known episodes in the struggle between Antioch and Cyprus over episcopal supremacy occurred. Troilus, the metropolitan of Constantia (Salamis) on Cyprus, had occasion to visit Antioch, on business not connected with the hierarchical dispute, and while he was in the city, the clergy and bishop of Antioch attempted to convince him of their views. Though their efforts were unsuccessful in the end, they carried them to the point of beating the metropolitan, a procedure which hardly disposed the Cypriotes to be friendly when the hierarchical question came up at the Council of Ephesus (A.D. 431) following the death of Troilus.[39]

[35] On the contemporary views as to the Petrine tradition at Antioch, see the detailed account by Kidd, *Hist. of the Church* 3.175-178.

[36] On the Council of Ephesus, see below, §4.

[37] Theodoret *Hist. eccl.* 5.38.1-2; Kidd, *Hist. of the Church* 3.179.

[38] Of this Council, we know only that it met; no further details are preserved (see Mansi, 5.474-5 and cf. Hefele-Leclercq, *Conciles* 2, pt. 1, p. 214.

[39] For further detail, see the study cited above, n. 34.

3. SYMEON STYLITES

It was during this time that Symeon, the first and most famous of the pillar saints, was winning the veneration for his extreme self-mortification which gave him such enormous influence not only in Antioch itself, the city which always claimed him as its own, but throughout the Empire, and made him a familiar figure in later times.[40] Monasticism had become an important and well-developed movement within the church, and its power was increased and extended by the remarkable examples of men like Symeon.

Born about A.D. 389 or 390 in a village on the border between Syria and Cilicia, Symeon went as a young man, in A.D. 410 or 412, to Telanissos, about thirty miles or twelve hours' ride east of Antioch, in the mountains bordering the road to Beroea. There he began his ascetic training and commenced his stylite existence about A.D. 417, living on a series of pillars, each higher than the last, until about A.D. 429 he ascended his tallest column, about sixty feet high, on which he spent the remainder of his life until his death in A.D. 459.[41]

Symeon throughout his life was connected with Antioch in many ways, and when he died, his body was buried in the city. As his fame grew, numerous pilgrims came from all over the Christian world to see Symeon, and many of these must have passed through Antioch. Likewise many citizens of Antioch, both officials and private persons of all ranks, made the journey to the saint's column to consult him, or ask for his prayers, or receive his blessing. The *magister militum per Orientem* Dionysius, when stationed in Antioch, was cured by the saint after having suffered what sounds in Symeon's biography like a heart attack.[42] When an evil "senator" (not named) was sent as ruler to Antioch, and caused much suffering by his oppression, the people of the city invoked Symeon's aid. The saint reproved the wicked official, who was stricken with a dreadful illness and died.[43] On another occa-

---

[40] The principal Greek biographies of Symeon, and a German translation of the important Syriac biography are edited by H. Lietzmann and H. Hilgenfeld, "Das Leben des heiligen Symeon Stylites," *Texte und Untersuchungen* 32, 4 (Leipzig 1908). There is an English translation of the Syriac biography by F. Lent, *Journal of the American Oriental Society* 35 (1915-1917) 103-198, made from Bedjan's text. Information, largely drawn from the Syriac biography, is also given by Evagrius. See also Honigmann, "Syria," 1708-1709.

[41] See Lietzmann, *op.cit.* 238-241.

[42] The episode is described in the Syriac *Life* edited by Lietzmann and Hilgenfeld (see above, n. 40) pp. 117-118. Dionysius was consul in A.D. 429 (Lietzmann, *op.cit.*, p. 246; O. Seeck, "Dionysios," no. 89, *RE* 1.915), but we do not know when he was *magister militum*.

[43] Syriac *Life*, p. 135.

sion, an oppressive *comes Orientis*, likewise not named,[44] was attempting to force two young men of Antioch to serve in the senate of the
city—a severe financial burden to which they considered that they were
not obligated. The young men asked Symeon's aid and the *comes
Orientis* was denounced to the emperor, arrested in Antioch and beaten,
had his property confiscated and was exiled.[45] One of the saint's well-
known deeds was the conversion of a famous robber, Antiochus Gona-
tus, a man so powerful, it is said, that he entered Antioch boldly to
carry out his thefts. Finally a military force was sent to capture him.
He was to be condemned to execution by being made to fight with wild
beasts in the arena; bears and other animals were collected, and, as
Symeon's Greek biographer Antonius writes, the whole city was ex-
cited by the prospect. The soldiers sent to arrest him found Antiochus
drinking at a village inn. He escaped and sought sanctuary at Symeon's
pillar, where the saint converted him, and he died at the foot of the
column.[46]

On one notable occasion, Symeon played an important part in imperial affairs, in a matter that also concerned Antioch. In A.D. 414 Jews
in Immestar, a town between Antioch and Chalcis, murdered a Christian boy whom they had mockingly tied upon a cross.[47] Apparently
the Jews were not only punished locally but their synagogues in Antioch
were confiscated. Then, in A.D. 423, Asclepiodotus, who was *praefectus
praetorio* (A.D. 423-425),[48] persuaded Theodosius II to issue decrees
that would compensate the Jews for confiscated synagogues and allow
such synagogues to be replaced, and would also protect the Jews against
some kinds of attacks.[49] When the Christians in Antioch heard this
(Symeon's biographer reflects the characteristic exaggeration of the
news by writing that the synagogues were to be given back to the
Jews), they appealed to Symeon in great distress. The holy man, it is
said, dispatched a very bold letter to the emperor threatening him with
divine punishment for his action. The emperor was so frightened by

---

[44] These names would be known to contemporaries, and the biographer might
feel it more tactful to omit them since the families of the officials in question might
still be living in Antioch.

[45] Syriac *Life*, pp. 137-139.

[46] Life of Symeon by Antonius, in Lietzmann, *op.cit.*, pp. 48-54.

[47] Socrates *Hist. eccl.* 7.16; cf. Kraeling, "Jewish Community at Antioch" 159;
Kidd, *Hist. of the Church* 3.182. On the general background of the status of the
Jews under Theodosius II, see Simon, *Verus Israel* 160.

[48] On his career see Lietzmann, *op.cit.* 246. He was consul in A.D. 423. The Syriac
biography of Symeon (pp. 174-175) mistakenly gives his name as Asclepiades.
Evagrius (1.13) in describing the incident does not mention his name.

[49] *CTh* 16.8.25-27.

this that he rescinded his order and dismissed the *praefectus praetorio*. Although it is not clear how literally this story is to be accepted,[50] it does suggest the influence which Symeon had both at court and with the people. When the council of A.D. 432 met at Antioch, as will be described below, it is recorded that the emperor wrote to Symeon to ask for his prayers for the peace of the church and the success of the council.[51]

4. THE THEOLOGY OF ANTIOCH AND NESTORIANISM

The teaching of Nestorius, as a natural outcome of the theology characteristic of the School of Antioch, illustrates the results of the Antiochene insistence on the literal and exact interpretation of Scripture, as opposed to the allegorical method pursued at Alexandria.[52]

Nestorius' views had their ultimate origin in the teaching of Diodorus, Bishop of Tarsus A.D. 378-394. Diodorus, member of a distinguished family in Antioch and friend of Flavian, who became bishop of Antioch, became (with Carterius as colleague) head of a monastic establishment in or near the city, before becoming bishop of Tarsus.[53] In an effort to strengthen the orthodox teaching concerning the Person of Christ against heretical ideas, Diodorus sought to emphasize the completeness of the human nature of Christ. In doing this, he had to distinguish between the two natures in Christ, human and divine, to such an extent that they almost became two persons.

The successor to Diodorus' views was Theodore, who became bishop of Mopsuestia in Cilicia, A.D. 392-428, and had an important influence on Nestorius. Theodore studied under Libanius in Antioch and had John Chrysostom as a fellow pupil, and then entered the monastery headed by Diodorus and Carterius. He was ordained priest in A.D. 383 by Flavian of Antioch, and lived in the city until he became Bishop of

---

[50] The decrees in question were issued in A.D. 423 and Asclepiodotus remained in office until 425, so that it would seem that at least he was not dismissed immediately. Lietzmann in his discussion of the question points out (*op.cit.* pp. 247-248) that the inclusion of the decrees in the Code of Theodosius shows that they were considered to be in force in A.D. 439, when the Code was published.

[51] Schwartz, *Acta Conciliorum* I.I, pt. 4, pp. 5-6.

[52] See the account of the origin and development of Nestorianism in Kidd, *Hist. of the Church* 3.192-217, which is to be supplemented and corrected, on the basis of the subsequent discovery of a number of writings of Theodore of Mopsuestia, by the studies of R. Devreesse *Essai sur Théodore de Mopsueste* (Vatican City 1948) and M. V. Anastos, "The Immutability of Christ and Justinian's Condemnation of Theodore of Mopsuestia," *Dumbarton Oaks Papers* 6 (1951) 123-160.

[53] Socrates *Hist. eccl.* 6.3, Sozomen *Hist. eccl.* 8.2, Theodoret *Hist. eccl.* 4.25.3-5; cf. Kidd, *Hist. of the Church* 3.193-196, where the reference to Theodoret should be to Book 4, not Book 5 (193.6).

Mopsuestia. His exegetical works, some of which have only recently been recovered, show how he carried the literal method of expounding Scripture to its limit. Theodore's Christology carried that of Diodorus further, in an effort to establish the true character of our Lord's human nature and to show the significance of this for Christian doctrine. Theodore insisted that the manhood of Christ was complete, and that he was troubled by passions, and was peccable, that is, that Christ was human not only in nature but in person.

Two of the younger men in Antioch who were influenced by Theodore's teaching were Nestorius and his friend John, who became patriarch of Antioch (A.D. 428-441) on the death of Theodotus. Nestorius in Antioch had come to be known as an eloquent preacher, with a fine voice; and when a vacancy in the see of Constantinople produced such rivalries that it seemed expedient to find a new incumbent outside the city, Nestorius was chosen, in April A.D. 428.[54]

Nestorius took up his duties at Constantinople with vigor, and he and the companions whom he brought from Antioch began to extend the Antiochene views as to the human element in Christ's nature by showing that, as a consequence of these views, the traditional title given to the Virgin (Theotokos, Mother of God) was in reality not fitting. By seeming to attack traditional and popular beliefs, Nestorius' arguments soon precipitated a major controversy in which Antioch, as the ultimate place of origin of Nestorius' doctrine, inevitably became seriously involved. Also, of course, the traditional rivalry between Antioch and Alexandria in theological matters was revived when the patriarch of Alexandria, Cyril, became Nestorius' chief opponent and so also a potential enemy of Nestorius' friend, John the new patriarch of Antioch (A.D. 428-441).

While the controversy was growing, the church at Antioch and in Syria made what effort it could to avert a major outbreak, and a council which met at Antioch toward the end of A.D. 430, under the auspices of John of Antioch, warned Nestorius to avoid excess, and not to depart from the traditional orthodox teaching.[55] At the same time, the church at Antioch defended itself against the theological attacks of Cyril, the chief Antiochene apologist being the famous theologian and preacher, Theodoret, Bishop of Cyrrhus in Syria Euphratensis (A.D. 423-458),

---

[54] Socrates *Hist. eccl.* 7.29.

[55] The letter sent by John of Antioch to Nestorius, conveying the council's advice, is printed in Mansi, 4.1061-1068 (the council itself is mentioned at col. 1068 B-C); cf. Devreesse, *Patriarcat d'Antioche* 48, and the same scholar's *Essai sur Théodore de Mopsueste* (cited above, n. 52) 128, with n. 5.

who, having been born in Antioch (A.D. 393), had received his early training in the monastic establishments near the city. After becoming bishop in eastern Syria, Theodoret returned to Antioch annually for a preaching visit,[56] and when the Nestorian troubles became serious, Theodoret, at the initiative of John of Antioch, began to make weighty contributions to the refutation of Cyril and the maintenance of the Antiochene views.[57] Cyril had an agent of his own in Antioch, the deacon and archimandrite Maximus, a zealous opponent of Nestorius and of John. His energy and devotion to the cause seemed, in fact excessive even to Cyril. This Maximus is probably identical with the person of the same name who became patriarch of Antioch as successor to John's nephew Domnus, when he was deposed by the Council of Ephesus in A.D. 449.[58]

The opposition provoked by Nestorius' views soon became so serious that the imperial government thought it necessary to convoke a council, which met at Ephesus in the summer of A.D. 431. The complicated history of this meeting need not be repeated here.[59] John of Antioch and his party of Syrian bishops, delayed by unseasonable rains, famine, and floods at Antioch,[60] arrived late, and when they reached Ephesus, they found that Cyril had already convened the council without them and had deposed Nestorius. John proceeded to hold a synod consisting of his own party, at which Cyril was deposed. While efforts were being made to obtain a settlement from the emperor, the majority of the council continued to meet, under the leadership of Cyril.

The affairs of Antioch came before this section of the synod twice, although Antioch was not represented among the members of the session. The most important manoeuvre was the petition of the Cypriote delegates for a pronouncement on the question of the ecclesiastical supremacy of Antioch over Cyprus—a petition which, in view of the composition of the session, and of the absence of John of Antioch and

---

[56] Theodoret *Ep.* 83 (*PG* 83.1268). The first general study of Theodoret's city, Cyrrhus, has been published by E. Frézouls, "Recherches sur le ville de Cyrrhus," *Annales archéologiques de Syrie* tomes 4/5 (1954-1955) 89-128 (on Theodoret, pp. 109ff.). For a recent account of Theodoret's life and work, see the introduction in the first volume of the edition of his letters, edited by Y. Azéma, in the series *Sources chrétiennes* (vol. 40).

[57] See Kidd, *Hist. of the Church* 3.232 234.

[58] See the two letters of Cyril to Maximus, *Epp.* 57-58 (*PG* 77.320-321) and the letter, *Ep.* 69 (*ibid.* 337-340), in which Cyril speaks of Maximus. The identification is suggested by L. Duchesne, *Histoire ancienne de l'église,*[5] tome 3 (Paris 1911) 423, cf. 382, 399.

[59] For an account of the Council, see the chapter in Kidd, *Hist. of the Church* 3.218-253.

[60] See above, n. 28.

his party, came in the most favorable possible circumstances for the Cypriotes. In the spring of A.D. 431, a few months before the council met at Ephesus, Troilus, the metropolitan of Cyprus, died. John of Antioch hoped to be able to take advantage of this coincidence to obtain from the council at Ephesus a pronouncement favorable to the Antiochene claims to consecrate the metropolitans of Cyprus.[61] Accordingly he procured an order from the *comes Orientis* Flavius Dionysius (who may or may not have had legal jurisdiction in the matter) forbidding the election of a successor to Troilus until the council which had been called to meet at Ephesus should have considered the matter; or, if a successor should have been elected before the arrival of the order, the Cypriote bishops concerned were to appear at Ephesus and explain themselves.

When he made this move, John of Antioch did not foresee that he himself would be prevented from taking part in the synod. Whether he would have been successful in asserting the supremacy of Antioch, we cannot now say. The result proved to be the opposite of what John had hoped for. The Cypriote bishops, appearing before the synod under the presidency of Cyril of Alexandria, John's enemy, described their grievances and asked the synod to prevent Antioch from introducing an "innovation" and gaining ecclesiastical control of their island, asserting that their own local bishops and metropolitans had always been elected and consecrated locally, without outside approval or participation. In reply to a question, the Cypriotes maintained that their last three metropolitans (whose incumbency went back beyond the pronouncement of Innocent I) had all been consecrated independently of Antioch.

The Council made no investigation of these statements, but decided (though in conditional terms) in favor of Cyprus. The decision was embodied, not in a regular canon, but in a vote or resolution, which provided that "if, as it is asserted in memorials and orally by the religious men who have come before the Council—it has *not* been a continuous ancient custom for the bishop of Antioch to hold ordinations in Cyprus—the prelates of Cyprus shall enjoy, free from molestation and violence, their right to perform by themselves the ordinations of bishops [for their island]" (transl. of W. Bright).

This definition, though conditional on the truth of the Cypriote assertions, was not challenged by Antioch at any future synod, and Cyprus presumably continued to consecrate its own bishops. Antioch made

---

[61] For further details, see the study cited above, n. 34.

another effort, in the reign of Zeno (A.D. 474-491), to assert control over Cyprus, but, as we shall see, this met with no success.[62]

The other attack on Antioch at the Council of Ephesus came from Juvenal, the bishop of Jerusalem. Early in the meeting, when Cyril of Alexandria presented a memorial directed against Nestorius, and the council was discussing Nestorius' recalcitrance, Juvenal took the opportunity to declare, in the course of the discussion, that it had been the custom for the see of Antioch, following apostolic usage, to be "ruled and judged" by the "apostolic see of Jerusalem."[63] Apparently nothing developed out of this claim at the time, and the synod took no action with respect to it, but Juvenal had at least laid the basis for the more vigorous and successful attack on the territory of Antioch which he made later.[64]

At the end of the council, in September A.D. 431, the condemned and deposed Nestorius was sent back by imperial order to the monastery of Euprepius, two stadia outside of Antioch, where he had lived before going to Constantinople. Nestorius spent four years in his old monastery before being sent into exile in Egypt.[65]

When John of Antioch returned from the council, he summoned a local synod which promulgated the deposition of Cyril of Alexandria.[66] However, both the Alexandrian and the Antiochene parties soon decided to seek a basis for reconciliation and union, rather than to prolong the quarrel. In April A.D. 432 the Emperor Theodosius sent letters to John of Antioch, to Acacius, Bishop of Beroea, and to Symeon Stylites, who was a powerful influence, urging them all to work for

[62] See below, §4.

[63] Schwartz, *Acta Conciliorum* 1.1, pt. 3, pp. 18.30-19.7; see E. Honigmann, "Juvenal of Jerusalem," *Dumbarton Oaks Papers* 5 (1950) 214-215. Kidd, *Hist. of the Church* 3.331, writes that on this occasion Juvenal presented documents in support of his claim that the bishop of Antioch ought to be subject to Jerusalem, but this appears to be a lapse on Kidd's part, since I have not found evidence that such documents were presented.

[64] The old view (found e.g. in Kidd, *loc.cit.*) was that Juvenal, ambitious for his own see, had begun an attack on Antioch before A.D. 431, by consecrating bishops in Arabia and in Phoenicia I and II, which had always been recognized as parts of the diocese of the Orient, and as such subject to Antioch. However, as Honigmann shows (*op.cit.* 220-221), a previously unknown manuscript, published in 1920, shows that Juvenal had not consecrated bishops in these provinces, but instead had, as certain bishops of the diocese of the Orient complained in a letter to the emperor, made "attacks" upon the Oriental bishops.

[65] Mansi, 5.794, cf. Schwartz, *Acta Conciliorum* 1.1, pt. 7, nos. 55-56. Evagrius (1.7), who describes Nestorius' return to his monastery, tells how he lived there, honored and respected, for four years, after which it was decided that he should have a more distant exile, and he was sent to the Oasis. The monastery of Euprepius seems to be not otherwise known.

[66] Socrates *Hist. eccl.* 7.34.

peace within the church.[67] In September of the same year a council met at Antioch, on the invitation of John. Later the session was moved to Beroea, perhaps because the atmosphere there was less charged with local feeling.[68] The basis for peace was laid, and the reunion of Antioch and Alexandria was soon accomplished.[69]

5. THE EPISCOPATE OF DOMNUS;
THE "ROBBER-COUNCIL" OF EPHESUS

When John of Antioch died, he was succeeded by his nephew Domnus (A.D. 441/2-August 449).[70] Born in Antioch, Domnus had entered the monastery of Euthymius in Palestine, where he became a deacon; and when he heard of the difficulties that beset his uncle after the Council of Ephesus, Domnus returned to Antioch to give what aid he could to John, and eventually became his successor.[71] It was said later by his enemies that Domnus' consecration as bishop had been irregular, and that he had had the backing of undesirable elements in the city, including the "pagan" Isocasius, a disreputable figure who appears again in the history of Antioch during the reign of Leo I (A.D. 457-474).[72]

[67] The letter to John of Antioch is printed in Schwartz, *Acta Conciliorum* 1.1, pt. 4, pp. 3-5, that to Acacius in the same collection, 1.1, pt. 7, p. 146, no. 103. The letter to Symeon is printed in the same collection, 1.1, pt. 4, pp. 5-6. On the career of Symeon and his influence at this time, see above, §3.

[68] Mansi, 5.1055ff.; Schwartz, *Acta Conciliorum* 1.1, pt. 7, p. 146, nos. 103, 105; Hefele, *Hist. des Conciles* 2.387, 421; Kidd, *Hist. of the Church* 3.256-258.

[69] Kidd, *Hist. of the Church* 3.256-262.

[70] On the dates of Domnus' incumbency, see E. Honigmann, "The Patriarchate of Antioch," *Traditio* 5 (1947) 138.

[71] Cyril of Scythopolis, *Vita Euthymii*, ed. E. Schwartz (*Texte u. Untersuch.* 49, 2 [1939]) pp. 26.5ff., 33.10ff. Cyril relates that Euthymius attempted to persuade Domnus not to return to Antioch and become involved in the theological disputes there, and that he predicted that Domnus would become patriarch and would be attacked by evil men and deposed. Perhaps Euthymius recognized that Domnus had not his uncle's ability, or was not fitted for ecclesiastical politics. Domnus' career is described here in some detail because no adequate treatment of it has been available and because the sources are widely scattered. The lack of information about Domnus is reflected in the widely different conceptions of his activities that scholars have held. The Abbé Paulin Martin, *Le pseudo-synode connu dans l'histoire sous le nom de Brigandage d'Éphèse* (Paris 1875) 65-66, concludes that Domnus was of a weak disposition and incapable of freeing himself from the influence of his friends, while G. Bardy, writing in Fliche-Martin, *Hist. de l'église* 4.208, states that Domnus, inheriting his uncle's ideas, possessed a resolute intelligence with which to put them into effect. As Martin points out, the position in which Domnus found himself, on becoming patriarch, was very difficult.

[72] The accusation concerning Domnus' ordination was made at the "Robber-Council" of Ephesus in A.D. 449, at which he was deposed: *Akten der Ephesinischen Synode vom Jahre 449, syrisch, mit Georg Hoffmanns deutscher Uebersetzung, hrsg. von Johannes Flemming*, p. 115, lines 17ff. (*Abhandlungen der k. Gesellschaft der Wissenschaften zu Göttingen, philol.-histor. Kl.*, N.F. 15, 1 [1917]). On the career of Isocasius, see below, Ch. 17, §2.

In addition to John of Antioch, the patriarchs of Constantinople and Alexandria died at about this time, meaning that the great sees were all occupied by new men, and that of the major figures who had taken part in the Council of Ephesus in A.D. 431, only Theodoret of Cyrrhus remained. Theodoret, as the greatest theologian of the day, would be inevitably involved in any further controversy. He continued to make preaching visits to Antioch and to advise Domnus, the nephew and successor of his old friend.[73]

The see of Antioch at this period was still engaged in attempting to keep down the pretensions of the Patriarchate of Alexandria, and to some degree at least was able to make an alliance with Constantinople toward this end.[74] Domnus was also kept busy with local difficulties within his own jurisdiction, some of which were destined to grow large and eventually to play a part in his own fall.

One of these was the case of Athanasius, Bishop of Perre, near Samosata, who was accused by his own clergy of appropriating church property, including, it was said, some "silver columns" in the church. Domnus summoned a council of twenty-eight bishops to meet in Antioch in A.D. 444, to hear the charges.[75] The council met at the Great Church, "in the little colonnade of the summer secretariat," and Athanasius was condemned and deposed.[76]

There was also a disputed succession at Emesa, in which one of the claimants to the bishopric, Uranius, was adjudged to be a Nestorian because he had had the support of Domnus and of Theodoret of Cyrrhus.[77] The partisan feelings called forth by this question served to keep alive the question of the survival of Nestorianism, and with it the doubts as to Domnus' orthodoxy.

[73] Theodoret *Epist.* 83 (*PG* 83.1268). On the situation in Antioch, see, with further detail, Kidd, *Hist. of the Church* 3.281-282.

[74] Theodoret *Epist.* 86 (*PG* 83.1277-1281).

[75] The accusation of Athanasius (though without the memorials themselves) and the action of the synod are preserved in *Actio* 17 of the Council of Chalcedon in A.D. 451; see Mansi, 6.465 and 7.325-357; Schwartz, *Acta Conciliorum* 2.1, pt. 3, pp. 77-83, and cf. Hefele, *Hist. des Conciles* 2.479 and Devreesse, *Patriarcat d'Antioche* 55. On the silver columns, see Mansi, 7.341. On the date of the synod of A.D. 444, see E. Honigmann, "The Patriarchate of Antioch," *Traditio* 5 (1947) 136, correcting Devreesse's date of 445. The episode of the "columns," taken in conjunction with the alleged peculation of Ibas, described below, is of interest as suggesting the widespread use of silver in the churches of Syria at this time.

[76] The opening of the record of the synod describes the place of meeting as ἐν τῷ στοϊδίῳ τοῦ θερινοῦ σηκρήτου (Mansi, 7.341), presumably a colonnade suitable for gatherings in warm weather. The phrase implies that there was a "winter secretariat," presumably indoors, but this does not appear to be mentioned in the preserved sources.

[77] This case is preserved in the Syriac Acts of the "Robber-Council" of Ephesus (cited above, n. 72) 125-126.

Another case, in which Domnus was also concerned, represented a major attack from Constantinople on the Nestorian party in Syria. This was the accusation brought against Ibas, Bishop of Edessa, a well-known Nestorian theologian,[78] in the autumn of A.D. 447.[79] His own clergy charged that Ibas had diverted to his own use an important part of the funds obtained by melting down silver liturgical vessels, the property of his own church and others, which had been sacrificed by their congregations in order to pay the ransom of some monks and nuns who had been kidnaped by "the barbarian Arabs." There were also accusations of heresy. The charges were brought before Domnus in Antioch early in A.D. 448 and he collected a small synod of nine bishops.[80] Domnus found that he could not try the case because the charges against Ibas carried the death penalty,[81] and in February A.D. 448,[82] the investigation was moved to Tyre and Berytus. In the end Ibas was not condemned.

The attack on Ibas was in part at least connected with the emergence in Constantinople of a new theological party, powerful at the court, which set out to eliminate the Nestorians who remained influential in Syria. This party had come into being as a result of the new doctrines of Eutyches concerning the nature of Christ; these represented the beginning of the monophysite heresy,[83] which was to dominate the ecclesiastical history of Antioch for many years to come. Eutyches, putting forth the formula "Two natures before the Union; but after it, One," gained the favor of the imperial family, and he and his party determined to suppress Domnus and Theodoret (who had immediately attacked Eutyches' teaching) along with their supporters in Syria. The attack was made both by indirect means—such as the trial of Ibas—and by direct methods. The open announcement of this program came with an imperial rescript of 16 February A.D. 448,[84] condemning the

[78] On his career see Kidd, *Hist. of the Church* 3.270ff., 289ff.

[79] On the date, see Seeck, *Regesten* p. 379.

[80] The accusations against Ibas are preserved in *Actio* 11 of the Council of Chalcedon in A.D. 451, published in Mansi, 7.213-221; and in Schwartz, *Acta Conciliorum* 2.1, pt. 3, pp. 20-23; and his alleged peculation is also described in detail in the Syriac Acts of the "Robber-Council" of Ephesus (cited above, n. 72) p. 59. Cf. Hefele, *Hist. des Conciles* 2.490ff. The episode gives us valuable evidence both concerning the large quantity of liturgical silver in use in Syria, even in small rural churches, at this time, and the possible fate of much of this silver. Kidnaping for ransom was doubtless a favorite occupation of some of the Arab tribes.

[81] See the Syriac Acts of Ephesus (cited above, n. 72) 41.9ff.

[82] Seeck, *loc.cit.* (above n. 79).

[83] On this subject as a whole see Kidd, *Hist. of the Church* 3.277ff.

[84] *CJ* 1.1.3, preserved in a fuller form in Mansi, 5.417-420; see Kidd, *Hist. of the Church* 3.288.

works of Nestorius; and Theodoret was ordered to cease stirring up trouble, especially at the synods at Antioch, and to remain at home in Cyrrhus.[85] When these orders were published in Antioch, at about the time when the affair of Ibas was being investigated there, they caused a commotion and Domnus and Theodoret led the protestations of the people of the city, who did not like to see their local beliefs, and their popular leaders, proscribed by commands issuing from Constantinople.[86] Domnus and Theodoret preached against the imperial orders, and it was said later, by their enemies, that they stirred up their supporters, who represented the lowest classes in the city. The conduct of the two bishops on this occasion counted strongly among the grounds for their condemnation at the synod of Ephesus in the following year.

This synod, in fact, while ostensibly convened to investigate the orthodoxy of Eutyches, turned in effect into a carefully planned operation for the elimination of the Nestorians in Syria, and the conduct of the meeting became so openly partisan that it came to be known as the *Latrocinium* or "Robber-Synod" of Ephesus.[87] This council brought the close of Domnus' career. Theodoret of Cyrrhus looked forward to the meeting with the greatest foreboding,[88] and he himself was forbidden by imperial order to attend the synod unless he was expressly invited

[85] Theodoret *Epistt.* 79, 80 (*PG* 83.1256-1260).
[86] The reaction in Antioch is described in the Syriac Acts of the "Robber-Council" at Ephesus (cited above, n. 72) 57.49ff.
[87] Our principal source for this council is an account written in Syriac and dated A.D. 535, for the use of the Syriac-speaking communities in eastern Syria, edited and published by G. Hoffmann and J. Flemming: *Akten der ephesinischen Synode vom Jahre 449, syrisch, mit Georg Hoffmanns deutscher Uebersetzung hrsg. von Johannes Flemming (Abhandlungen der k. Gesellschaft d. Wissenschaften zu Göttingen, philol.-histor. Kl.*, N.F. 15, 1 [1917]). Hoffmann's earlier publication contained only the translation and commentary: *Verhandlungen der Kirchenversammlung zu Ephesus am 22 August 449 aus einer syrischen Handschrift vom Jahre 535 übersetzt von Dr. Georg Hoffmann (Festschrift, Herrn Dr. Justus Olshausen zu seinem 50 jährigen Doctorjubiläum am 29. Nov. 1873 gewidmet von der Universität Kiel*, published in: *Schriften der Universität Kiel*, vol. 20 [1873], pt. 6, no. 7). There is also an English translation of the Syriac Acts: *The Second Synod of Ephesus, Together with Certain Extracts Relating to it, from Syriac MSS Preserved in the British Museum, and Now First Edited by . . . S. G. F. Perry. English Version.* Dartford, Orient Press, 1881. On the council, see the Abbé Paulin Martin, *Le Pseudo-Synode connu dans l'histoire sous le nom de Brigandage d'Éphèse, étudié d'après ses Actes retrouvés en Syriaque* (Paris 1875); Hefele, *Hist. des Conciles* 2.555-621; Kidd, *Hist. of the Church* 3.301-310; E. Honigmann, "Juvenal of Jerusalem," *Dumbarton Oaks Papers* 5 (1950) 233-237. As Hefele points out (592, n. 3) the Syriac Acts do not constitute a complete and impartial account, but were written for the use of the Syriac-speaking Christians of eastern Syria, with the object of presenting the history of the Syrian bishops at the council in the most favorable light. The Syriac Acts do not, for example, mention the first session of the council at all. For further criticism of the Acts, see Martin's study cited above.
[88] Theodoret *Epist.* 112 (*PG* 83.1309-1312).

to do so by the synod itself;[89] and it was a foregone conclusion that he would not be asked. Moreover, Theodoret must have had misgivings as to Domnus' ability to uphold his own cause at the synod, for Theodoret wrote his superior a letter in which he urged him to use the greatest care in choosing the bishops and clergy who would accompany him to Ephesus.[90]

The synod met on 8 August A.D. 449, and concluded its business in a few meetings. Its main purpose, the rehabilitation of Eutyches and the deposition of his opponent Flavian, the Patriarch of Constantinople, was quickly finished. Domnus attempted to secure his own position and appease his powerful enemies by voting in the interest of Eutyches,[91] but this did him no good. Theodoret of Cyrrhus was deposed from his bishopric, one of the complaints against him being his association with Domnus.[92] Then a number of charges were laid against Domnus.[93] Many were trivial, but some of them would have made it impossible for him to continue in office, and his deposition—which had been assured since the opening of the synod, if not earlier—was voted.[94]

The proceedings of the council were so obviously partisan that a reaction, led by Pope Leo, set in at once.[95] Domnus, however, did not find further support. At the Council of Chalcedon, in A.D. 451, those who had been unjustly condemned at Ephesus two years earlier were rehabilitated, but Domnus' absence from the list of those who were vindicated suggests that he was not considered guiltless.[96]

By way of a complete change of ecclesiastical power in Antioch following the downfall of Domnus, the new bishop (consecrated some time between April and July A.D. 450) was Maximus, a protégé of Domnus' enemy, Dioscorus of Alexandria;[97] this Maximus was, in fact, very likely the same person as the deacon of the same name who

---

[89] Syriac Acts of the synod (cited above, n. 87) 5.1ff.

[90] Theodoret *loc.cit.* (above, n. 88).

[91] Syriac Acts (cited above, n. 87) 113.24ff.

[92] *Ibid.*, 85.22ff.

[93] These charges, which are preserved in various sources, are listed by Hefele, *Hist. des Conciles* 2.604, no. 2 (printed on p. 608).

[94] Syriac Acts (cited above, n. 87) 115-151.

[95] Kidd, *Hist. of the Church* 3.307.

[96] See Hefele, *Hist. des Conciles* 2.604, n. 2 (printed on p. 607). On the Council of Chalcedon, see below, §6.

[97] Leo *Epistt.* 104, 106, 119 (PL 54.995-997, 1003, 1046-1055), also edited by Schwartz, *Acta Conciliorum* 2.4, pp. 57.7, 60.6, 72.30. See Honigmann, "Juvenal of Jerusalem" (cited above, n. 87) 237-238. On the date and circumstances of the consecration of Maximus, see H. Chadwick, "The Exile and Death of Flavian of Constantinople: A Prologue to the Council of Chalcedon," *JTS*, N.S. 6 (1955) 17-34.

had been an active opponent of the Patriarch John in Antioch some years previously.[98]

The advent of Maximus and the accidental death of Theodosius II, who was killed on 28 July A.D. 450, by a fall from his horse, mark a new direction in the ecclesiastical affairs of Antioch, which next come into prominence as a result of the Council of Chalcedon, in A.D. 451, in the reign of Theodosius' successor Marcianus.

6. THE REIGN OF MARCIANUS, A.D. 450-457

Theodosius II left no male heir; and on his death his sister Pulcheria, already past fifty, chose the experienced military officer Marcianus, a man almost sixty, to become emperor as her nominal husband. Marcianus proved to be a good ruler, and he was later looked upon as an emperor to be imitated by those who followed him.[99] During his reign the eastern part of the Empire enjoyed peace, and he made a serious effort to relieve the financial burdens of the people.

What has come down to us of the history of Antioch during Marcianus' reign of seven years is concerned almost exclusively with ecclesiastical affairs in the city and in Syria, reflecting the vitally important consequences of the Council held at Chalcedon in A.D. 451. There is, however, one glimpse remaining of the everyday secular life of the city which helps to counteract the impression, resulting from the loss of the secular sources for this period, that life at Antioch at this time was predominantly concerned with church matters.

On the civilian side, we hear of the career of the *magister militum per Orientem* Ardaburius, who was commander of the forces in the *Oriens* and had his headquarters at Antioch. Son and grandson of powerful figures in the imperial government, Ardaburius was born probably not much later than A.D. 425. As a young man he distinguished himself by his military successes against the barbarian invaders of Thrace, and was appointed consul for the year A.D. 447.[100] As a reward for his work in Thrace, Marcianus, who before becoming emperor had served under Ardaburius' father and grandfather, appointed the young man *magister militum per Orientem*. In this capacity he was called upon to repel an invasion of some Arab tribes near Damascus, where

[98] L. Duchesne, *Histoire ancienne de l'église*, tome 3, éd. 5 (Paris 1911) 423. On Maximus' earlier activities, see above, n. 58.

[99] On the reign of Marcianus, see W. Ensslin, "Marcianus," no. 34, *RE* 14 (1930) 1514-1529.

[100] O. Seeck, "Ardabur," no. 3, *RE* 2 (1898) 610.

he met the historian Priscus during the ensuing peace negotiations.[101] The remainder of his term of office being peaceful, the young man gave himself up to the pleasures of life in Antioch and Daphne, indulging himself in "woman-like luxuriousness," and devoted to "mimes and magicians and all the delights of the stage."[102] Apparently in the course of these activities, he built himself in Daphne a private bath, *privatum,* which was sufficiently notable to be included among the buildings of Antioch and Daphne shown on the topographical border of a mosaic that was placed, at about this same time, in a large and luxurious building in Daphne designed for entertainment and social gatherings.[103] The position on this topographical border of Ardaburius' private bath, which is shown between the Olympic stadium and the famous springs of Daphne, suggests that it was one of the notable features of the suburb. The building in which the mosaic was found, dating as it does from about the time of Ardaburius' sojourn at Antioch, shows that substantial amounts of money could be devoted to the mundane pleasures in Antioch and Daphne at this period.[104]

The ecclesiastical history of Antioch at this time is, as has been indicated, of special interest because it marks the beginning of a long era of troubles in the church both in Antioch and in Syria as a whole. When Marcianus came to the throne, the Patriarch Maximus, already in power, represented a reaction against the theological views of Nestorius and of the Patriarchs John and Domnus, all of whom had had considerable local support in Antioch. Maximus, on the other hand, was a protégé of Alexandria, the traditional theological enemy of Antioch.[105] Early in his administration, Maximus apparently had to deal with a renewed effort of Juvenal, the bishop of Jerusalem, who was still bent on erecting his bishopric into a patriarchate at the territorial expense of Antioch.[106] On this occasion, when the experienced bishop of Jerusalem would have been able to count on harassing a new incumbent in Antioch, it appears that Maximus and Juvenal came to

---

[101] Priscus, frag. 20, in *FHG* 4.100, preserved in part in Suidas *s.v.* 'Αρδαβούριος. He became a *patricius* soon after A.D. 450: Mansi, 7.516 C.

[102] Priscus *loc.cit.*

[103] The mosaic was first published by J. Lassus in *Antioch-on-the-Orontes* 1.114-156, where the *privatum* is illustrated on p. 131 and discussed on the following page. See also the publication and discussion of the same mosaic by Doro Levi, *Antioch Mosaic Pavements* 1.323ff. On the topographical border as a whole, see below, Excursus 18.

[104] See Lassus' description of the building, *Antioch-on-the-Orontes* 1.116. Ardaburius' private bath must have been similar.

[105] Kidd, *Hist. of the Church* 3.309.

[106] For a summary of the history of the bishopric of Jerusalem, and of the efforts to turn it into a patriarchate, see Kidd, *Hist. of the Church* 3.330ff.

an agreement on their respective territorial jurisdictions, according to which Juvenal's see was to control the provinces of Phoenicia I and II and Arabia,[107] though this arrangement was to be changed later at the Council of Chalcedon.

The Council was called, at the instance of Pulcheria, in order to undo the injustices of the *Latrocinium* of Ephesus, as well as to make another effort to find a definition of the faith which would put an end to the recurrent troubles over the formulating of a description of the "two natures" in Christ, especially, of course, with a view to countering the doctrines of Eutyches recently of great influence at Constantinople.[108]

The meeting convened in October A.D. 451, and proceeded to rehabilitate most of the victims of the *Latrocinium*. Theodoret of Cyrrhus was recalled from exile and restored, and Ibas was also restored. Eutyches and Dioscorus, who had controlled the Council at Ephesus, were now sent into exile. Only Domnus, the deposed Bishop of Antioch, was not vindicated, a circumstance that indicates that the meeting could not excuse his former actions or his beliefs. His successor Maximus was able to get the council to authorize the payment of a pension to Domnus out of the income of the church at Antioch, but this would not necessarily mean that Domnus was looked upon with any general favor by the Council.[109] It may be that the granting of the pension was a way of making sure that Domnus would not in future claim the throne of Antioch;[110] in any case, Domnus' apparent acceptance of the pension

[107] See E. Honigmann, "Juvenal of Jerusalem," *Dumbarton Oaks Papers* 5 (1950) 238; and see further below.

[108] On the purpose and proceedings of the Council, reference may be made to Kidd, *Hist. of the Church* 3.311-339. The reader must bear in mind that the interest of the present work is primarily in the results of the synod as they affected the ecclesiastical and political history of Antioch, and that of a subject of such great importance—and in parts, of such difficulty—as this synod, it is not possible, in the present study, to give either a completely adequate account or an authoritative bibliography.

[109] *Actio de Domno Antiocheno*: Mansi, 7.269-271, published from better sources by E. Schwartz, "Aus den Akten des Konzils von Chalkedon," *Abhandlungen d. Bayer. Akad. d. Wiss., philosoph.-philolog.u. histor. Kl.*, 32, 3 (1925) 41-42.

[110] Cf. Schwartz' introduction, *op.cit.*, 8. There is no evidence to show that after his deposition at Ephesus in A.D. 449, Domnus tried to claim the throne of Antioch. If he had done this, one would expect to find him deposed again at Chalcedon. Pope Leo claimed that Maximus' consecration as bishop of Antioch was invalid because Domnus was (Leo asserted) still bishop when Maximus was consecrated in Constantinople (Leo *Epist.* 104, PL 54.991, also edited by Schwartz, *Acta Conciliorum* 2.4, p. 57). However, Leo had a very strong interest in discrediting or unseating Maximus. If Leo's claim were correct, we would expect to find evidence of some further action to secure for Maximus the appointment which, obviously, he continued to hold for a number of years.

may serve as an indication of his own conception of what his pretensions might or might not be.[111]

More important, for Antioch, was the agreement reached at the council by Maximus and Juvenal of Jerusalem, on the territory that was to be ceded by Antioch to Jerusalem. Apparently the agreement, which seems to have been made when Maximus became Patriarch of Antioch, was now reviewed, and after "a good deal of contention" (as Maximus expressed it) the two bishops decided by mutual consent—and the Council approved their decision—that Jerusalem was henceforth to have ecclesiastical control over the three Palestines (Palestina Prima, Secunda, Tertia), while Antioch was to govern Phoenicia I and II and Arabia.[112] Jerusalem was to be a patriarchate, and both parties agreed not to make any more territorial claims in the future.

The most important result of Chalcedon, of course, was the promulgation of the famous definition of the faith, the essential point of which was that Christ was declared to be "One Person in two Natures," i.e. that Christ existed not only as "One Person, resulting from two Natures," but "*in* two Natures."[113] This was a western definition, imposed on the synod by the will of Pope Leo and the Emperor Marcianus, in an effort to obtain precision, and thus, it was hoped, to put an end to disunion. The result, as will be seen, was further disunion. Syria, Egypt, and Armenia became Monophysite, claiming that there could be only *one* nature. This was not only because there was objection to the definition of Chalcedon itself, but because the definition was being imposed by the court in Constantinople. Nationalism in Syria, as in

---

[111] The *Vita Euthymii* of Cyril of Scythopolis (cited above, n. 71), p. 33.27 Schwartz, states that after his deposition at Ephesus in A.D. 449, Domnus returned to the *lavra* of St. Euthymius in Palestine. Schwartz in the commentary in his edition (p. 262, *s.v.* Domnos) doubts this, without making clear the reason for his hesitation. The granting of the pension to Domnus in A.D. 451 may be an indication that he did not return to Palestine, for we might suppose that he would be in no need of an income if he had re-entered his monastery, whereas he would need a pension if he were living in Antioch as an ex-patriarch, who would have to live with a certain amount of dignity. It would sound as though Cyril of Scythopolis, in having Domnus return immediately to his monastery, were trying to provide a dignified and peaceful close to his career. Theophanes (A.M. 5945, p. 107.21ff. ed. de Boor) preserves a report that on the outbreak of the disorders which began in Palestine as a consequence of the promulgation of the definition of Chalcedon, Domnus and Juvenal of Jerusalem "fled to the desert." Honigmann points out (*op.cit.* 249 n. 11) that this is obviously a mistake so far as Juvenal is concerned, and it is difficult to understand the reason for such action on Domnus' part.

[112] Mansi, 7.180 C-D; also edited by Schwartz, *Abh. d. Bayer. Akad.* 1925 (cited above, n. 109) 29-40, 43-46. The agreement is also mentioned by Evagrius *Hist. eccl.* 2.4, p. 50.22; 2.18, p. 92.10-14 ed. Bidez-Parmentier. See Kidd, *Hist. of the Church* 3.331 and Honigmann, "Juvenal of Jerusalem" (cited above, n. 107) 244-245.

[113] Kidd, *Hist. of the Church* 3.326-327.

Egypt, thus found its final and strongest expression in a religious cause.[114] To devout people in Syria, Monophysitism—as the opposite of the Chalcedonian belief—alone seemed to assure the divinity of Christ; and of course Monophysitism gained the strength that comes to a persecuted belief.[115] Starting with the reign of Leo I, this dispute began to assume serious proportions in Antioch.

[114] For an over-all study, see E. L. Woodward, *Christianity and Nationalism in the Later Roman Empire* (London 1916).

[115] For an account of the beginning of Monophysitism, see Kidd, *Hist. of the Church* 3.408ff. Further studies of the subject will be cited below.

CHAPTER 17

LEO I (A.D. 457-474), LEO II (A.D. 474), AND ZENO (A.D. 474-491)

1. Antioch under Leo I; Earthquake of a.d. 458; Death of Symeon Stylites, a.d. 459; Isocasius of Antioch

THE PRINCIPAL EVENT in the life of the city at this period was the severe earthquake, one of the most serious in the city's history, which is apparently to be dated in mid-September A.D. 458.[1] The damage must have been considerable, though the sources vary somewhat in their statements as to its extent. In the latter part of the sixth century Evagrius,[2] whose account, drawn from Malalas,[3] is the fullest preserved, states that the damage occurred primarily in the "new" quarter of the city, on the island, where "nearly all" the buildings were thrown down, and in the quarter called Ostrakine in the main part of the city, while Theophanes,[4] writing much later, in the latter half of the eighth century, records that "nearly the whole city fell." While Evagrius' account is circumstantial, and might seem to be preferable to the later and brief record in Theophanes, we may suspect that Evagrius does not describe the full extent of the damage, for it is stated in the Syriac biography of Symeon Stylites,[5] written by a disciple

---

[1] On the reign of Leo, see Ensslin, "Leo," no. 3, *RE* 12.1947-1961. The date of the earthquake is not certain, since the chronological data concerning it which the various sources give do not entirely agree; for a detailed discussion of the problem, see Excursus 7. There is a possibility, depending on the significance of the confusion in the sources which has been mentioned, that there were two earthquakes, in A.D. 457 and 459, the records of which were confused and consolidated into one, but in the present state of our knowledge it seems more likely that there was only one disaster; in any case, only one earthquake is described in detail by the sources.

[2] *H.E.* 2.12, pp. 63-64 ed. Bidez-Parmentier. The account of Nicephorus Callistus Xanthopulos, *H.E.* 15.20 (*P.G.* 147.60-61), is based upon that of Evagrius, but with certain alterations which are characteristic of this late compiler. Nicephorus states that the shocks threw down nearly all the buildings in the city, taking part of the phrase from Evagrius but omitting to say, as Evagrius does, that it was nearly all the buildings of the "new city" on the island that fell. Nicephorus adds that almost the whole of Antioch was destroyed, a detail that he invented or borrowed from Theophanes (see below), for it does not appear in Evagrius.

[3] In the Greek text, as preserved in the Codex Baroccianus, which is known to be an abridgement, the account of the earthquake is much abbreviated (369.5-9). The Church Slavonic version is even briefer, and contains some obvious corruptions of meaning (p. 89).

[4] a. 5950, p. 110.22-23 ed. De Boor.

[5] See the Syriac biography of Symeon edited by H. Lietzmann with a German translation by H. Hilgenfeld, "Das Leben des heiligen Symeon Stylites" (*Texte u. Untersuchungen* 32, 4 [1908]), ch. 133, p. 177.19-20; ch. 136, p. 179.22-24. There is also an

of Symeon who was a contemporary of the earthquake, that the walls of the city were thrown down by the shocks, and this detail is given in such a context that it would not seem to have been manufactured. Probably the truth lies somewhere between the accounts of Evagrius and Theophanes.[6]

The earthquake seems to have occurred on the night of 13 September, beginning (according to different accounts) either late Saturday night, the 13th, or just before dawn on Sunday. According to Evagrius, it was considered locally to be the most severe since the major earthquake in the reign of Trajan, in A.D. 115.[7] The damage in the earthquake under Leo is said to have been greatest on the island, which was still called the "new city" because it was the last to be settled of the original Seleucid quarters of Antioch.[8] This sector, Evagrius writes, "had become thickly populated, and had no vacant . . . spot, but had been greatly adorned by the prodigality of the emperors, who had emulated one another" in beautifying it. Of the palace, which was built in four quarters on the *castrum* plan, like Diocletian's palace at Spalato,[9] the "first and second buildings" (i.e. presumably the quarters on either side of the entrance) were thrown down, while the other two stood, along with the bath which lay beside them. The tetrapylon, which stood before the palace, at the crossing of the main streets of the island, was destroyed, along with the colonnades that flanked the approach

---

English translation of the Syriac biography by F. Lent, *Journal of the American Oriental Society* 35 (1915-1917) 103-198. As will be described below, Symeon died on 2 Sept. A.D. 459, almost exactly a year after the earthquake, if the date of the disaster here adopted is correct; and the people of Antioch, after the saint's death, were extremely eager to have his body buried in their city, to serve as a supernatural protection for them, their city walls having been thrown down in the earthquake.

[6] In fact Evagrius himself, in his account of the death of Symeon (1.13) quotes the petition of the people of Antioch to be allowed to keep Symeon's body, since the city walls had fallen in the earthquake. It would look as though Evagrius copied Malalas' account of the earthquake so faithfully that he did not add this detail which came to him from another source.

[7] Evagrius calculates that the earthquake under Leo I occurred 347 years after that which visited Antioch under Trajan, since (he writes) the earlier disaster occurred in the year 159 of the era of the city (A.D. 110/1), that under Leo I in the year 506 of the era (A.D. 457/8). The date which is thus given for the earlier disaster is mistaken, for other evidence shows that it occurred on 13 December 115 (see above, Ch. 9, n. 59). Evagrius evidently follows a tradition that placed the earthquake two years after a visit of Trajan to the East, and also, mistakenly, placed this visit in A.D. 108; see Longden, "Parthian Campaigns" 4-8, 29-35; idem, *CAH* 11 (1936) 241, n. 2, and 858; Stauffenberg, *Malalas* 277, n. 41; Lepper, *Trajan's Parthian War* 54-83.

[8] On the settlement of the island, see above, Ch. 5, §§3-4. Libanius in his encomium of Antioch (*Or.* 11.203) speaks of the island as "the new city" and of the remainder of Antioch, built on the mainland, as "the old city."

[9] On the plan of the palace, see above, Ch. 12, §2.

to the palace from this tetrapylon.[10] In the same neighborhood, the twin towers that flanked the entrance to the hippodrome were destroyed,[11] as well as some of the colonnades that adjoined this entrance.

The bath, which remained standing alongside the two uninjured sections of the palace, had previously, Evagrius says, fallen into disuse. Since it was the only bath on the island which had not suffered damage, it was put back into use and must have rendered important service for the health and comfort of the local survivors of the catastrophe, who must have sorely needed an opportunity to rid themselves of the dust and dirt produced by the earthquake.

In the "old city," on the mainland, Evagrius goes on, "there was no harm at all to the colonnades or the buildings, but the baths of Trajan, Severus, and Hadrian were somewhat damaged."[12] In the quarter called Ostrakine, the earthquake threw down certain buildings along with the Nymphaeum and "the colonnades," presumably those along the streets, which would be peculiarly liable to damage in an earthquake. The location of Ostrakine—presumably, from its name, the potters' quarter—we do not know. The Nymphaeum damaged in the earthquake apparently cannot have been the famous one described by Libanius on the main colonnaded street of the city, near the column and statue of Tiberius, for this region can scarcely have been known as the potters' quarter.[13]

[10] The tetrapylon and the colonnaded street are described by Libanius in his encomium of Antioch, *Or.* 11.204-205.

[11] The topographical border of the Yakto mosaic shows a tower at the entrance to the Olympic stadium at Daphne, which might, by artistic convention, represent twin towers. In any case the representation of this stadium in the mosaic presumably gives an idea of what the appearance of the hippodrome on the island would have been. See the original publication of this mosaic by J. Lassus *Antioch-on-the-Orontes* 1.131, fig. 11, no. 8, with description on p. 132, and (for a better plate) Doro Levi, *Antioch Mosaic Pavements* 2, pl. 79, *a*. The hippodrome on the island was partially excavated in 1932 (see the report by W. A. Campbell in *Antioch-on-the-Orontes* 1.34-41) but no clear traces of towers were found at that time and the excavation of the monument could not be completed.

[12] On these baths, see above, Ch. 9, n. 87; Ch. 10, nn. 39-40.

[13] Ostrakine seems to be known otherwise only from another passage in Evagrius (6.8, p. 227.19 ed. Bidez-Parmentier), in which it is said that this part of the city was again damaged in the earthquake under Maurice, in A.D. 588 (see below, Ch. 19, §3). Müller, *Antiq. Antioch.* 59, n. 18, suggests that the Nymphaeum mentioned by Evagrius in the present passage is identical with that on the main colonnaded street described by Libanius, since the name Ostrakine would come from the shells (*ostraka*) with which, Libanius says, the Nymphaeum was decorated. With all due respect, it seems a little difficult to believe that the name of a quarter of the city can have arisen in this fashion, especially when most ancient cities had potters' quarters that ordinarily had characteristic names. M. Schwabe in his dissertation *Analecta Libaniana* (Berlin 1918) 5-8 makes a far-fetched and unconvincing effort to show that the Nymphaea of Libanius and Evagrius are the same building, and to determine its

A late account of the earthquake adds that it was followed by a fire, as often happened on such occasions. The same source relates that the bishop of Antioch, Acacius, rendered notable service in rescuing and caring for the survivors.[14] The people of Antioch, fearing the successive shocks that often followed the initial earthquake, made a pilgrimage to the column of Symeon Stylites and remained there for fifty-one days (see below). Isaac of Antioch, a theologian and poet who wrote in Syriac, composed a monody on the city, lamenting its destruction in the disaster.[15]

---

location. Evagrius' description of the earthquake, Schwabe believes, is divided into two parts, one dealing with the heavy damage in the "new city," the other with the lighter losses in the "old city"; Ostrakine is plainly placed, Schwabe believes, by the position in which it is mentioned, in the old city. Taking γειτονία to mean "neighboring place," "neighboring region" (*vicinia*), he reasons that Ostrakine, being in the old city, must have been so called because it was near the new city. Thus it must have stood near the river; and the description of the damage to the Nymphaeum in Ostrakine would agree well with the natural course of an earthquake, which would lose its force gradually: after inflicting severe damage in the new city, it would begin to lose its power in Ostrakine, and then, proceeding from there into the old city, would do only slight damage there, just as Evagrius says. Schwabe also sees an indication of such a course of events in the grammatical construction of Evagrius' sentences. Evagrius begins by saying, of the new city, ὁ σεισμὸς . . . τὰς οἰκίας ἁπάσας σχεδὸν καταβέβληκε; then the transition to the second part of the account is made with κατὰ δὲ τὴν παλαιάν . . . After describing the slight damage in the new city, Evagrius goes on, καὶ τῆς γε 'Οστρακίνης . . . Here the verb is συγκατέλαβε—not simply κατέβαλε. No subject to the verb is expressed in this sentence, so that the verb must refer back to the subject of the opening sentence, Οὗτος τοίνυν ὁ σεισμὸς . . . καταβέβληκε; and of course the συν- in συγκατέλαβε is intended to effect a relationship with καταβέβληκε in the opening sentence. This shows, in Schwabe's opinion, that the description of the damage in the new city and in Ostrakine are closely connected. Schwabe's whole argument is vitiated by his misinterpretation of γειτονία. This word was commonly used, at the time when Evagrius wrote, of a quarter or ward of a city (Sophocles, *Lexicon*, *s.v.* Cf. the term γειτονάρχης). It means "neighboring place" in Plotinus and is used of "neighborship" by Plato, but no examples of this usage seem to occur in later writers. The word more often and more naturally used to mean "neighboring place" is γειτόνημα. Evagrius means that certain damage was done in Ostrakine, and it is evident that he mentions this separately simply because the Nymphaeum was completely destroyed, unlike the baths elsewhere in the old city, which were only slightly damaged. The common character of the damage in the two regions does not by any means imply that there was a topographical relationship between the new city and Ostrakine. As for Schwabe's analysis of the grammatical construction of the account, it is perfectly true that this indicates that Evagrius sought to indicate that there was a similarity in the kind of damage done in Ostrakine and in the new city, but this does not by itself indicate that there was a topographical connection between the two regions, and, as has been seen, there is no other evidence to that effect.

[14] This is the *Chronicon miscellaneum ad annum Domini 724 pertinens*, published in *CSCO, Scriptores Syri*, series tertia, tomus IV, *Chronica minora*, pars secunda, ed. E. W. Brooks, tr. J. B. Chabot (1904). The account of the earthquake is found on pp. 108-110 of the translation.

[15] Marcellinus *chron.* ad ann. 459 (Mommsen, *Chron. min.* II p. 87): Isaac Antiochenae ecclesiae presbyter . . . ruinam . . . Antiochiae elego carmine planxit. . . . The presence of this notice in the chronicle under the year A.D. 459 does not necessarily

As had been done elsewhere in similar catastrophes, the imperial government granted relief from taxation in order to facilitate the rebuilding of the city. On this occasion, Evagrius says at the end of his account of the earthquake, the emperor remitted from the tribute paid by the city "a thousand talents of gold,"[16] evidently a sizeable sum, though we cannot be sure what "talents" means here. It is also said that the citizens were excused from the payment of taxes on buildings that were destroyed.[17] The imperial government in addition took the responsibility for the restoration of the public buildings. How much rebuilding was accomplished, the sources do not indicate; but this earthquake may have been the beginning of what was apparently a decline in the importance and prosperity of the island, culminating in its definitive abandonment, as a part of the city, after the earthquakes and the Persian invasion in the reign of Justinian.[18]

While the city was still recovering from the earthquake, it suffered another calamity, the death of Symeon Stylites, on 2 September A.D. 459.[19] This must have seemed to the people of Antioch in those days nearly as great an affliction as any earthquake could be, for Symeon was regarded as the special patron and protector of the city.[20] After the recent earthquake, the people of Antioch, led by their clergy, had made a pilgrimage *en masse* to the saint's establishment and had remained camped around his column for fifty-one days, seeking guidance and comfort, and fearing to return to the city since further movements

indicate that the earthquake took place in this year, but might mean only that Isaac's poem was written in this year. On Isaac's career and writings, see O. Bardenhewer, *Gesch. der altkirchlichen Literatur* 4 (1st and 2nd ed., Freiburg i.B. 1924) 404-406.

[16] "Talents" in the ancient sense, in keeping with Evagrius' classical usage, can hardly be meant literally here, but it does not appear what unit of money is meant. The difficulty is partly that we do not know what sum the city paid, and so cannot judge how much relief thirty (whatever unit is meant) would be.

[17] As will be seen in Excursus 7 on the problem of the date of the earthquake, the chronological confusion in the sources appears to be connected with a change in the calendar of Antioch which took place at about this time, by which the beginning of the year in the era of Antioch was advanced from October first to September first, bringing it into conformity with the beginning of the indiction year. At the close of his study of the chronological problem (cited in the Excursus) E. Honigmann suggests that this change in the calendar was made when the taxes were remitted after the earthquake, and that the change was introduced in order to protect the people from the illegal collection of more taxes than were due. It is difficult to accept this suggestion since the indiction year was the tax year, and this was not changed.

[18] See below, n. 117, and Ch. 18, §8.

[19] I follow Lietzmann ("Das Leben des heiligen Symeon Stylites" [cited above, n. 5] 230-234) in accepting the date given by the Syriac biography of Symeon for his death (ch. 126, p. 171.8; ch. 137, p. 179.34 tr. Hilgenfeld), rather than H. Delehaye (*Les Saints stylites* [Brussels 1923] pp. x-xv) who works out 24 July as the date.

[20] For the account of the saint's connections with Antioch, see Ch. 16, §3.

of the earth might be expected.[21] Symeon's death, coming when the earthquake was still such a recent blow, would seem to leave Antioch deprived of its most precious source of counsel and spiritual strength.

After the saint's death, everyone, among his immediate followers and the people of that part of Syria, would think at once of the question of where the saint's relics should be placed, for Symeon had been a powerful wonder-worker and especially a healer; and his body, or any part of it, might be expected to continue his miracles.[22] As soon as Symeon's death became known, the *magister militum per Orientem,* Ardaburius, went to the saint's *mandra* accompanied by members of his staff and by a considerable body of troops,[23] both in order to do honor to the saint and to prevent disorder in connection with the disposition of his relics. The people of Antioch made a special request to be allowed to receive the body so that it might serve as a protection for their city, which had lost its walls in the earthquake.[24] How or by whom the question was decided, we are not told. Ardaburius was the imperial representative on the ground, with a strong military force. He was fond of Antioch and its pleasures; and no doubt Antioch had promised that Symeon's body would be buried with exceptional honor. It was decided that the remains should be given to Antioch, and the festal procession escorting the coffin took five days on the journey, reaching Antioch on Friday, 25 September.[25]

After passing the suburb Meroë, five miles from the city, the procession was greeted by a great crowd who came out on the road to meet the body.[26] The coffin was taken first to the Church of Cassianus.[27] Thirty days later it was taken to the Great Church of Constantine— the first time, it was said, that a body had rested there—and finally a

---

[21] See the Syriac biography (cited above, n. 5) ch. 123-124, pp. 168-169 tr. Hilgenfeld.

[22] *Ibid.,* ch. 127, p. 171 tr. Hilgenfeld.

[23] *Ibid.,* ch. 133, p. 177 tr. Hilgenfeld. It is not clear whether Ardaburius was in Antioch when he learned of Symeon's death. Antioch was his headquarters, and he would be there unless his duties took him elsewhere.

[24] Syriac biography (cited above, n. 5), ch. 133, p. 177.17-21 tr. Hilgenfeld.

[25] *Ibid.,* ch. 137, p. 180 tr. Hilgenfeld. Symeon's death, and the taking of the body to Antioch, are described by Malalas 369.10-16, the *Chronicon Paschale* 1.593.17—594.3, and Evagrius 1.13. The *Chronicon Paschale* states that Ardaburius was *comes Orientis,* but no other source has this information.

[26] Syriac biography (cited above, n. 5), ch. 134-135, p. 178 tr. Hilgenfeld; Greek biography by Antonius, ed. Lietzmann, *op.cit.,* ch. 34, p. 74.2. Here the MSS have Meroë or Meron or Merope, the two last obviously being errors.

[27] The temporary sojourn of the body at the Church of Cassianus is mentioned only in the *Life* by Antonius, ch. 32, p. 76.7 ed. Lietzmann. The Syriac biography says that the body was taken directly to the Great Church, and adds that it was the first time that a body had rested there, ch. 134, p. 178 tr. Hilgenfeld.

special church was built for the permanent reception of the remains.[28]
The Emperor Leo wrote and requested that the body be sent to Constantinople, so that it might lend its spiritual strength to the whole
Empire, but the people of Antioch begged to keep their saint, as a
protection for their city, and they were successful in their petition.[29]
The saint's remains were treated with the greatest honor, and Martyrius,
the bishop of Antioch, and his clergy held services before the coffin
every day.[30] As had been hoped, the relics were reputed to have worked
many miracles, and the corpse was still well preserved when Evagrius
saw it at the end of the sixth century.[31]

As to other details in the secular history of Antioch during Leo's
reign, our available sources are meager and we possess only a few details, which do, however, give us characteristic glimpses of economic
and intellectual affairs in the city.

Like his predecessor Marcianus, Leo found it necessary to deal with
economic difficulties throughout his empire, and we possess laws of
his designed to enforce economy and to keep the revenue from taxes
up to its former levels. At the same time, Leo was anxious to lighten
the fiscal burdens of his subjects.[32] In the case of Antioch, the assistance
provided by the imperial government toward recovery from the earthquake has already been described. After the earthquake, the senatorial
class, which had been responsible, through the performance of liturgies,
for many public services, apparently continued to find difficulty meeting
its public obligations, at least so far as the presentation of the local
Olympic Games was concerned. These games, celebrated every four
years, entailed a considerable outlay, and we have already seen that
beginning in the latter part of the fourth century, various measures
were enacted, in successive reigns, in an effort to assure the financing
of the spectacles.[33] In the middle of the reign of Theodosius II, An-

[28] Antonius in his biography (ch. 32, p. 76.9-10) records the deposition of the body
in the Great Church, followed by its transfer to the shrine especially built for Symeon.
The church built for Symeon is also mentioned by Malalas, followed by the *Chronicon
Paschale* (see above, n. 25). The Syriac *Life* (*loc.cit.*) does not mention the building
of the special church, and Evagrius (1.13) does not specify where he was buried.
[29] Syriac biography (cited above, n. 5), ch. 136, p. 179.14-27 tr. Hilgenfeld.
[30] *Ibid.*, ch. 134, p. 178.15-22 tr. Hilgenfeld; Evagrius 1.13.
[31] Evagrius 1.13. The great church at Symeon's *mandra*, the construction of which
must have been started as soon as possible after his death, was almost certainly built
by workmen from Antioch, and may originally have been an octagon, like Constantine's
Great Church at Antioch (Honigmann, "Symeonos temenos," *RE* 4A.1099-1102; E. B.
Smith, *The Dome* [Princeton 1950] 34, 79). The people of Antioch doubtless contributed toward the construction.
[32] See W. Ensslin, "Leo," no. 3, *RE* 12 (1924) 1959.
[33] See above, Ch. 15, §4.

tiochus Chuzon attempted to ease the situation by presenting the city
with an endowment, the income of which was to be used toward the
cost of the games.[34] The problem seems to have become acute again
in the reign of Leo, for in A.D. 465 an imperial decree was issued providing that in future the function of the Alytarch in presenting the
games should be borne by the *comes Orientis*, and the function of the
Syriarch by the governor of Syria; and it was further provided that
the members of the local curial order should not be allowed to assume
these burdens even if they wished to do so.[35] It is not made clear
whether the imperial government was to provide some or all of the
funds for the presentation of the games, so that the *comes Orientis* and
the *consularis Syriae* would function in this case *ex officio*, as representatives of the imperial government, or whether these officials were now
required to pay for the games as a regular part of the burden of office,
as, for example, was the case with the consulship.[36]

In the field of cultural history, we get a valuable insight into the
survival of paganism at this period from the reports of the trial of
the pagan sophist Isocasius of Antioch, which occurred at this time.
This trial seems to have made a considerable impression, and is recorded in a number of sources. We first hear of Isocasius in the time
of Domnus, bishop of Antioch A.D. 441/2—August 449, in connection
with the claim, made by the bishop's enemies at the Council of Ephesus
in A.D. 449, that Domnus had been ordained bishop in an irregular way,
and that he had had the support of the "pagan" Isocasius and of other
"disreputable" persons.[37] Isocasius was a friend and correspondent of
Bishop Theodoret of Cyrrhus, and from the bishop's letters we learn
that Isocasius kept a school in Antioch, and that he was also concerned in some way with the law.[38] Isocasius remained a pagan, and
became a man of wealth and property in Antioch, holding many public
offices, it is recorded. In the reign of Leo I, when Isocasius was a
quaestor, an accusation against him for various offences, including

---

[34] See above, Ch. 16, n. 26.
[35] *CJ* 1.36.1; cf. Downey, *Olympic Games* 437.
[36] See Stein, *Hist.* 2.69.
[37] "Akten des Ephesinischen Synode vom Jahre 449, Syrisch, mit G. Hoffmann's
Deutscher Uebersetzung, hrsg. von Johannes Flemming," *Abhandlungen der k. Gesellschaft der Wiss. zu Göttingen*, philol.-histor. Kl., N.F. 15, 1 (1917), p. 127.16; on the
career of Domnus, see above, Ch. 16 §5.
[38] Theodoret *Epistt.* 27, 28, 38, 44, 52 in *Théodoret de Cyr, Correspondance*, ed. Y.
Azéma, 1 (1955), in the series *Sources chrétiennes*. On the career of Isocasius, see
Azéma's introduction to his edition, p. 45. Only one of the letters can be dated; this
(no. 44) was written before A.D. 446.

paganism, was laid before the emperor. His property was confiscated and he was arrested and brought to trial in Constantinople, in the year A.D. 468, according to the chronology of Theophanes.[39] Isocasius defended himself with a philosophical speech which seems to have made a great impression, and the trial was brought to an end, it appears, when he agreed to receive Christian baptism.[40] The episode is instructive as an example of the survival of paganism among the highly placed and wealthy persons at Antioch at this time.[41]

2. ZENO IN ANTIOCH; BISHOP MARTYRIUS, PETER THE FULLER, AND THE RISE OF MONOPHYSITISM

The Emperor Leo, in order to offset the rising influence of the Germans at the court and in the army, which had become one of his chief problems, had sought the support of the Isaurian mountaineers who lived in the wild regions of the Taurus mountains at no great distance from Antioch. In order to consolidate this support, he had married his elder daughter Ariadne to an Isaurian chieftain named Tarasicodissa, who took the Greek name of Zeno, under which he later became emperor.[42] Zeno was named consul for A.D. 469, three or four years after his marriage, and toward the end of that year he was also appointed *magister militum per Orientem*, an office which he held until at least the first of June A.D. 471.[43] After his appointment he took with

[39] Theophanes a. 5960, p. 115.9-18 ed. De Boor.

[40] The most detailed preserved account is that of Malalas 369.17-371.4, which is reproduced faithfully, with some further details, in the *Chronicon Paschale* 595.6-596.12. The account in the Slavonic Malalas (pp. 89-91) is garbled; and a similarly garbled version, reproduced from Malalas, but with some additions of a pious and didactic character, appears in John of Nikiu, ch. 88.7-11, pp. 109-110 ed. Charles. Manasses vv. 2864-2892 puts an impressive speech into the mouth of Isocasius. Shorter versions of the episode appear in Cedrenus 1.612.21-613.7; in Zonaras 14.1.9-11; J. A. Cramer, *Anec. Graeca e codd. MSS. Bibl. Reg. Paris* (Oxford 1839-1841) 2.313.24-30. On the trial of Isocasius, see W. Ensslin, "Leo," no. 3, *RE* 12.1961.

[41] Neoplatonism seems to have been notably strong during the reign of Leo I; see Stein, *Gesch.* 1.524-525; J. Geffcken, *Der Ausgang des griech.-röm. Heidentums,*[2] (Heidelberg 1929) 211-212. On the anecdotal level, we have the story of a cultivated gentleman of Antioch named Hilarius who, about this time, took a most philosophical view of his wife's unfaithfulness; see the biography of the philosopher Isidoros by Damascius of Damascus, edited by R. Asmus (*Das Leben des Philosophen Isidoros von Damaskios aus Damaskos* [Leipzig 1911]) 82-83.

[42] On Leo's relations with the Isaurians, and the career of Zeno, see E. W. Brooks, "The Emperor Zenon and the Isaurians," *English Historical Review* 8 (1893) 209-238, also, more briefly, Stein, *Gesch.* 1.526-532, and Bury, *Later Roman Empire* 1.316-319.

[43] Theodore Lector *Hist. eccl.* 1.20 (*P.G.* 86, 1, col. 176); Theophanes a. 5956, p. 113.17-18 ed. De Boor; *CJ* 1.3.29; cf. Bury, *op.cit.* 1.318, n. 6 (Bury by a slip cites the Code of Justinian as 10.3.29). The date A.D. 464 which Devreesse, *Patriarcat d'Antioche* 65, gives for the appointment of Zeno as *magister militum per Orientem* follows the

him to his headquarters, in Antioch, a priest named Peter the Fuller, who had won Zeno's favor and was congenial to his monophysite views. When Zeno and Peter arrived at Antioch, the bishop was Martyrius, a Chalcedonian, or, as his enemies said, a Nestorian, who had been bishop of Antioch when Symeon Stylites died.[44] Apparently Peter found in Antioch conditions that suggested to him that he could make himself bishop of the city, with Zeno's support, and he started to work toward that end.[45] Probably he found that there were in the city monophysite elements that thus far had lacked leadership, though with proper guidance they would, Peter thought, be strong enough to over-throw the orthodox regime. He brought monks into Antioch to go about among the common people and spread his doctrines, and he is also said to have gained the support of the local "followers of Apollinaris" (i.e., actually, anti-Chalcedonians) by bribing them.[46]

Understanding very well the way in which popular support might be created, Peter provided a slogan, which had instant success, in the form of the phrase "Who was crucified for us," which was to be added to the Trisagion which formed an important part of the liturgy of the church—"Holy God, Holy and Strong, Holy and Immortal, have mercy upon us." If Peter's phrase, added between the third invocation and the refrain, was taken to be added to an address to Our Lord, there could be no objection to it. But some people—and we know that this

---

chronology indicated by Theophanes, but the chronicler's reckonings appear to be in disorder at this point; see Bury *loc.cit.* As a result of this, Devreesse, *Patriarcat* 117, no. 44, is led to conclude that Martyrius was bishop of Antioch on two occasions, though all of our extant sources indicate that he was bishop only once. See E. Honigmann in *Traditio* 5 (1947) 138.

[44] Theophanes a. 5956, p. 113.19-114.4 ed. De Boor; Zachariah of Mitylene *Chronicle* 4.11, p. 80 transl. Hamilton and Brooks; Ensslin, "Martyrius," no. 16, *RE* 14.2040-2041; cf. Devreesse, *Patriarcat d'Antioche* 65. The account given by Theophanes reappears in abbreviated form in Cedrenus 1.611-612 Bonn ed. On Martyrius and the death of Symeon, see Evagrius 1.13, and see above, §1. A panegyric published by A. Mai under the name of Martyrius (*P.G.* 47, pp. xliii-liv) was actually written at another date and cannot be by him; see O. Bardenhewer, *Gesch. der altkirchl. Lit.* 3 (Freiburg i.B. 1912) 329.

[45] Theodore Lector *loc.cit.*

[46] *Ibid.* An imperial decree of A.D. 471 (*CJ* 1.3.29) forbids monks to leave their monasteries and live in Antioch, or other cities, with the exception of *apocrisiarii* (who had to visit the cities on business); and these were forbidden to discuss worship or doctrine with the citizens. It seems evident that this decree was made necessary by Peter the Fuller's use of monks as propagandists in Antioch. There is a report (Mansi, 7.872B) that Peter convoked a synod in Antioch which decreed the addition of the Trisagion, but the evidence for the meeting of such a synod is rather slender. On Peter's early activities in Antioch, see E. Schwartz, "Publizistische Sammlungen zum Acacianischen Schisma," *Abhandlungen d. Bayer. Akad. d. Wiss.*, Philosoph.-histor. Abteilung, N.F. 10 (1934) 182.

A History of Antioch

was true at Constantinople[47]—considered that the Trisagion was addressed to the Trinity; and in this case Peter's phrase expressed the patripassian or theopaschite heresy, by stating that God had been crucified.[48] As Peter intended it should, the slogan split the population of Antioch, and every religious service now became an occasion for a demonstration by the monophysite party. Not only was the authority of the bishop threatened, but the monophysites had gained a powerful rallying point.[49] Martyrius was so alarmed by this consolidation of the local monophysite feeling that he went to Constantinople to appeal to the emperor. By the good offices of Gennadius, the patriarch of Constantinople, Martyrius was received with great honor by the emperor, who was strongly orthodox;[50] but while Martyrius was away from Antioch, Peter the Fuller, with the support of Zeno—and it was said, by the use of force—got himself consecrated as bishop of Antioch by some bishops at Seleucia Pieria,[51] and exercised the office for a time while Martyrius was in Constantinople. This was the first of the four occasions (A.D. 469-470, 470-471, 475-476, 484-491 (?)) on which Peter was bishop of Antioch.[52] When Martyrius returned from Constantinople and found Peter acting as bishop, with the support of Zeno, and

[47] Evagrius 3.44.
[48] Theophanes a. 5956, p. 113.27-28 ed. De Boor; Kidd, *Hist. of the Church* 3.409, n. 3.
[49] Cf. Stein, *Gesch.* 1.526. On the epigraphical evidence for the local popularity in Syria of Peter's formula, see W. K. Prentice, "Fragments of an Early Christian Liturgy in Syrian Inscriptions," *TAPA* 33 (1902) 81-86, and *IGLS* 1726, commentary. In the present study it is not possible to go into all the details of the development of Monophysitism, on which there is a large and growing literature. On the subject as a whole, consult *Das Konzil von Chalkedon*, ed. by A. Grillmeier and H. Bacht, 3 vols. (Würzburg 1951-1954). Studies in this collection which are of special interest for Antioch and Syria are: J. Lebon, "La christologie du monophysisme syrien" 1.425-580; P. Mouterde, "Le concile de Chalcédoine d'après les historiens monophysites de langue syriaque" 1.581-602; W. de Vries, "Die syrisch-nestorianische Haltung zu Chalkedon" 1.603-635; C. Moeller, "Le chalcédonisme et le néochalcédonisme en Orient de 451 à la fin du VIe siècle" 1.637-720; H. Bacht, "Die Rolle des orientalischen Mönchtums in den kirchenpolitischen Auseinandersetzungen um Chalkedon (431-519)" 2.193-314.
[50] Theophanes a. 5956, p. 113.28-29 ed. De Boor; on Leo's religious views, see Ensslin, "Leo," no. 3, *RE* 12.1948. The account of Nicephorus Callistus Xanthopoulos *Hist. eccl.* 15.28 (*PG* 147, 81) is that Peter stirred up his troubles in Antioch while Martyrius was absent in Constantinople on business, but this does not agree with the versions of Theodore Lector and Theophanes, and has the sound of a rationalization. Ensslin, *loc.cit.* (above, n. 44) and Kidd, *Hist. of the Church* 3.409 follow the accounts of Theodore Lector and Theophanes.
[51] John Aegeates, in E. Miller, *Mélanges de philologie et d'épigraphie* (Paris 1876) 66, cited by Devreesse, *Patriarcat d'Antioche* 65, n. 5.
[52] The chronology of Devreesse (*Patriarcat d'Antioche* 117-118) is inexact because he did not have occasion to work out the sequence of the historical events connected with Peter's career. Some of Devreesse's dates are corrected by Honigmann, *Tradito* 5 (1947) 138.

severe disorders in progress, he concluded that opposition was hopeless, and resigned his episcopate.[53] This placed Peter in power, for a time, as nominal bishop, but a synod was called at Antioch, presumably on the emperor's orders, which deposed Peter the Fuller and elected Julian in his place; and at the instance of the Patriarch Gennadius, the emperor on 1 June A.D. 471 ordered Peter into exile.[54] The exile was, however, commuted to internment with the Acoemetae, the Sleepless Monks, in Constantinople,[55] so that Peter remained in a position to take advantage of any future opportunities. So ended the first two of Peter's four occupancies of the bishopric of Antioch. Julian occupied the see (A.D. 471-475) during the remainder of Leo's reign and that of Leo II, and we do not hear of further disorders at Antioch, though the monophysite doctrine continued to be strong there.

3. Leo II and Zeno; Peter the Fuller and the Monophysites; Antioch and the Rebellion of Illus and Leontius

When the Emperor Leo I died (3 February A.D. 474), he left, as Augustus, his grandson Leo the Younger, son of Zeno. Since the younger Leo was a child of six years, his father naturally became regent. It was decided that the child should confer the imperial dignity on his father, and when Leo II died, later in the same year, Zeno became sole emperor (17 November A.D. 474).[56] Zeno's reign was to be a troubled one, with the Empire beset by external troubles and the emperor surrounded by a court that was bitterly hostile to him and to his advisers and supporters, because they were Isaurians. At Antioch, after what seems to have been an extended period of peace, the new reign was a troubled one, and the city served as the headquarters of the various

[53] Theodore Lector *Hist. eccl.* 1.21 (*PG* 86, 1, col. 176); Theophanes a. 5956, p. 113.30-34 ed. De Boor.

[54] Mansi, 7.999-1000, 1175; Hefele-Leclercq, *Conciles* 2.907; Theodore Lector 1.22 (*PG* 86, 1, cols. 176-177); Theophanes a. 5956, p. 114, 1-4 ed. De Boor; *Cod. Just.* 1.3.29. Zacharias of Mitylene, who was hostile to Martyrius, writes that he was deposed (*loc.cit.*, above, n. 44), and this version is accepted by E. Honigmann in *Traditio* 5 (1947) 138, no. 44, who dates the deposition in the autumn of A.D. 471.

[55] Mansi, 7.872 B, cf. Theodore Lector 1.22 (*PG* 86, 1 col. 177 A). See Kidd, *Hist. of the Church* 3.409-410.

[56] For the reign of Zeno, the basic study continues to be that of E. W. Brooks, "The Emperor Zenon and the Isaurians," *English Historical Review* 8 (1893) 209-238. A briefer and less accurate account may be found in Bury, *Later Roman Empire* 1.388-404. Stein's account, *Gesch.* 1.535-539, *Hist.* 2.7-76, is inclusive and utilizes sources which Bury did not use or did not have available. See also the study of this period by E. Schwartz, "Publizistische Sammlungen zum Acacianischen Schisma," *Abhandlungen der Bayerischen Akad. d. Wiss.*, Philosoph.-histor. Abt., N.F. 10 (1934) 171-218.

rebels who set themselves up against Zeno. Religious strife continued at the same time, as Peter the Fuller returned to the city and the disorders connected with the monophysite movement continued.

The first of the plots against Zeno was formed by his mother-in-law the Augusta Verina, widow of Leo I, with the cooperation of her brother Basiliscus. She persuaded Zeno that his position was insecure and that he was in such danger that he ought to leave Constantinople (January A.D. 475). Zeno, realizing his unpopularity as an Isaurian, believed her and took refuge in Isauria. Verina's plan was not, however, wholly successful, for after Zeno's flight, Basiliscus succeeded in putting Verina aside and in having himself crowned as Augustus.

Basiliscus favored the monophysite party and sought to strengthen his position by appointing monophysite patriarchs in Alexandria and Antioch, Timothy Aelurus and Peter the Fuller respectively,[57] so as to secure the support of the monophysite elements in Syria and Egypt and in their capitals. When Peter the Fuller arrived at Antioch to take over the throne of the city for the third time (A.D. 475-476), the orthodox patriarch Julian, who had been elected to succeed Peter when the latter had been deposed in A.D. 471,[58] was so strongly affected that he died, it was said, "of vexation."[59] Peter proceeded to take strong measures against the orthodox in Antioch and his insistence on the monophysite addition to the Trisagion[60] caused riots in which people were killed.[61]

After Zeno fled to Isauria, Basiliscus sent two military officers, the Isaurian brothers Illus and Trocundus, with a force of troops, to keep Zeno shut up in the stronghold in which he had taken refuge.[62] However, Basiliscus failed to keep his promises to Illus and Trocundus, and in the summer of A.D. 476, after Basiliscus had reigned as emperor for two years, they decided to join forces with Zeno and restore him to the throne. Zeno and Illus, with a strong force of Isaurian troops, set out for Constantinople, where Zeno reestablished himself, while another

---

[57] Theodore Lector 1.31, *PG* 86, pt. 1, col. 181.

[58] See §2 of this chapter.

[59] Theodore Lector 1.31, *PG* 86, pt. 1, col. 181; Theophanes a. 5967, p. 121.1-23 ed. De Boor; Liberatus *Breviarium*, *PL.* 68.1027 C. The text of Malalas in both the Greek (377.2-5 Bonn ed.) and the Church Slavonic (p. 91) states that it was Zeno who made the appointment of Peter the Fuller, but this can scarcely be true. Perhaps this statement reflects Malalas' use of two conflicting sources for the career of Peter the Fuller, which appears later in his narrative (see further below, n. 64). Liberatus (*loc.cit.*) writes that Peter was appointed by Timothy.

[60] See §2 of this chapter.

[61] Theophanes a. 5967, p. 121.22-26 ed. De Boor.

[62] *Ibid.*, 5969, p. 124.10-11. On the careers of the brothers, see, in addition to Brooks' article cited above, n. 56, Nagl, "Illos," *RE* 9.2532-2541, and Ensslin, "Trocundus," no. 2, *RE* 7A.590-591.

Isaurian force, commanded by Trocundus, was sent to Antioch to depose Peter the Fuller.[63] An imperial order was issued (A.D. 476) exiling Peter to Pityus in the Caucasus, but he managed to escape and took refuge in the monastery of St. Theodore in Euchaita in Heleno-pontus.[64] The diocesan synod met and elected John Codonatus to succeed Peter, but this appointment was not acceptable to the government, since John was a monophysite and a protégé of Peter's and attempted to carry on his policies. John was removed from office after three months and was replaced by Stephen, a supporter of Chalcedonian orthodoxy.[65] The supporters of Peter the Fuller, as might be expected, attacked Stephen on the ground that he was a Nestorian and laid an accusation before Zeno, but a synod which the emperor summoned to meet at Laodicea vindicated the patriarch and restored him to his throne.[66] However, in the first part of A.D. 479, Stephen was murdered by the monophysites, who found a convenient occasion when the patriarch had gone outside the city to the church of the local martyr Barlaam, to celebrate the festival of the Forty Martyrs of Sebaste, which occurred on 9 March.[67] Stephen was attacked by some monophysite clergy in the baptistry of the church, and was stabbed to death with sharpened reeds; his body was thrown into the Orontes.[68] This brutal

[63] Theophanes a. 5969, pp. 124.10-125.19; Malalas 378.17-379.3 Bonn ed.; Mansi, 7.1018.

[64] Theophanes a. 5969, p. 125.17-19; Malalas 380.21ff. Bonn ed. This account and that given on p. 378.17-379.3 (cited in the preceding note) apparently represent two different and conflicting sources concerning the career of Peter the Fuller which Malalas used without troubling to discriminate between them or combine them. Theophanes' version (cited in the preceding note) represents only one of these sources, and he does not mention the sending of Trocundus and the Isaurian troops to Antioch. The highly orthodox Evagrius (*Hist. eccl.* 3.8) mentions the expulsion of Peter very briefly but does not describe the circumstances (he had not, in fact, mentioned Peter's appointment by Basiliscus).

[65] Theodore Lector 1.22, *PG* 86, pt. 1, 176-177; Theophanes a. 5969, p. 125.15-16 ed. De Boor; Malalas 380.24 ed. De Boor; Liberatus *Breviarium, PL* 68.1027 B-C; Mansi, 7.1018, 1175, cf. Hefele-Leclercq, *Conciles* 2, pt. 2, pp. 913-914, and E. Schwartz, "Publizistische Sammlungen zum Acacianischen Schisma," *Abhandlungen d. Bayer. Akad. d. Wiss.*, Philosoph.-histor. Abteilung, N.F. 10 (1934) 192. Again (see the preceding note) Evagrius *Hist. eccl.* 3.10 shows his orthodox feelings by passing over the election of John Codonatus in silence and mentions only the appointment of his successor Stephen.

[66] Theophanes a. 5970, p. 126.5-9 ed. De Boor.

[67] On Barlaam, who had been martyred at Antioch, see the *Laudatio* by St. John Chrysostom *PG* 50, 675-682. The festival of the Forty Martyrs of Sebaste was celebrated on 9 March; cf. *Bibliotheca Hagiographica Graeca*² (Brussels 1909) p. 168.

[68] Theophanes a. 5973, p. 128.17-22 ed. De Boor, cf. Evag. *Hist. eccl.* 3.10; Malalas 381.2-6 Bonn ed.; John of Nikiu *Chronicle* 88.44, p. 114 transl. Charles; Mansi, 7.1175. The location of the church of St. Barlaam is not known; it may be conjectured, from the fate of the patriarch's body, that the church was somewhere convenient to the Orontes. I follow the accounts of Malalas and Evagrius, who mention only one bishop

murder must have touched off serious disorders in the city,[69] and from the strength of the local feelings which such episodes indicated, the emperor concluded that it was not practical to hope for the orderly election of a patriarch at Antioch itself. An unusual measure seemed necessary, and so he instructed Acacius, the patriarch of Constantinople, to fill the vacancy. Acacius appointed Calandio, an outspoken Chalcedonian, and doubtless urged him to do what he could to restore peace; but at Antioch, where the fact that an appointment was being made by Acacius was not yet known, John Codonatus had been elected. When Calandio reached Antioch, he reassigned John to be bishop of Tyre.[70]

At about this time, a rupture occurred at Constantinople between Zeno and Illus, and two attempts were made to assassinate Illus. He then asked the emperor to be given an assignment outside of Constantinople, and he was made *magister militum per Orientem*, with the right to choose the *duces* or commanders who were to serve under him.[71] Thus, at the end of A.D. 481 or the beginning of 482,[72] Illus arrived at Antioch, his headquarters, accompanied by several dignitaries whom he had chosen to assist him in his new post, and a substantial military escort. Among his suite were Leontius, the patricius Pamprepius, the ex-consul Marsus, the ex-consul Justinian, the ex-prefect Aelianus, two officials named Matronianus and Kouttoules and "many others."[73]

---

named Stephen at this period. Honigmann in *Traditio* 5 (1947) 138 prefers the sources which mention two Stephens, and supposes that it is only "by incident" (i.e., presumably, "by coincidence") that Malalas and Evagrius speak of one bishop of this name. It seems to me that Malalas and Evagrius, as local authors, are to be preferred here. The accounts of two Stephens very likely reflect confusion caused by the comings and goings of Peter the Fuller, which have confused modern scholars as well as ancient historians; and if there were two Stephens, we must suppose that not only Malalas and Evagrius, but other sources as well, are in error.

[69] See E. Schwartz, "Publizistische Sammlungen zum Acacianischen Schisma," *Abhandlungen d. Bayer. Akad. d. Wiss.*, Philosoph.-histor. Abteilung, N.F. 10 (1934) 192.

[70] Theophanes a. 5973, p. 128.22-26 ed. De Boor; Malalas 381.7-9 Bonn ed.

[71] Malalas in *Excerpta de insidiis*, pp. 164-165 ed. De Boor; cf. the version reproduced in the Bonn ed., 388.15-16; Theophanes a. 5972, pp. 127.13—128.12 ed. De Boor; Evagrius *Hist. eccl.* 3.27; Joshua the Stylite *Chronicle* 13; Marcellinus comes *Chron.* ad ann. 484, 1.

[72] On the date see Stein, *Hist.* 2.19, n. 1, and Brooks in *English Historical Review* 8 (1893) 222.

[73] Illus' arrival at Antioch is described in several sources: the fragment of Malalas preserved in the *Excerpta de insidiis*, p. 165 ed. De Boor; Evagrius *Hist. eccl.* 3.27 (cf. Eustathius Epiphan. frag. 4, *FHG* 4, p. 140); Theophanes a. 5972, p. 128.5-12 ed. De Boor; Joshua the Stylite *Chronicle* 13; Marcellinus comes *Chron.* ad ann. 484, 1. All of the sources that give the names of Illus' chief companions mention Leontius as one of the group. Brooks *op.cit.* (above, n. 72) 223, 225-226, followed by Bury, *Later Roman Empire* 1.396 and by Stein, *Hist.* 2.19, n. 1, supposed that Leontius could not have accompanied Illus to Antioch on this occasion, since we hear that Zeno later sent Leontius from Constantinople, on a mission to Illus in Antioch. However, Brooks did not allow

Some or all of these companions had very likely been chosen on the basis of their potential support of Illus' ambitions. Leontius was probably a Syrian, distinguished both for his education and his military experience, whom Illus had attached to himself.[74] The Neo-Platonist Pamprepius of Panopolis was a prominent pagan, born in Egypt, who after serving as quaestor in Constantinople had found a protector in Illus.[75] Marsus was an Isaurian military officer,[76] Justinian may have been an ex-prefect of Constantinople.[77] Matronianus, a military officer, was Illus' brother-in-law,[78] Aelianus had recently been *praefectus praetorio per Orientem.*[79] "Kouttoules" is otherwise unknown; perhaps this is a garbled form of the name of Kottomanes, the Isaurian who was later *magister militum.*[80]

Illus spent the next two years in Antioch (i.e. until the end of A.D. 483 or the beginning of 484) making careful plans for the rebellion that would be the natural outcome of recent events.[81] He adopted a favorite means to make himself popular in Antioch and presented the city with a number of buildings (which the preserved sources mention only briefly and do not list by name).[82] Some, if not all, of the companions whom Illus had brought with him must have been engaged in the preparations for the revolt. One of the plans that was launched appears to have been an effort to bring together the forces of orthodox Christianity (which was now on the defensive in the eastern part of the Empire) and of paganism, in an effort to combat the monophysite party which Zeno had supported before he came to the throne,

---

for the possibility that Leontius returned to Constantinople after journeying to Antioch with Illus. Our sources concerning these events are so very meager that we could not be sure that a record of a trip by Leontius from Antioch to Constantinople would appear in the preserved accounts, and it seems unnecessary to suppose with Brooks that all the sources that record the names of Illus' original companions must be wrong on this point. See further below, note 96.

[74] On Leontius' career see W. Ensslin, "Leontius," no. 28, RE Suppl. 8.939-941; Stein, *Hist.* 2.28-31.

[75] On Pamprepius, see R. Keydell, "Pamprepios," no. 1, RE 18, 2. Heft (part 3) 409-415, and Stein, *Hist.* 2.9.

[76] See Stein, *Gesch.* 1.577 and *Hist.* 2.9.

[77] O. Seeck, "Iustinianus," no. 5, RE 10.1313. In the fragment of Malalas cited above (n. 73) Justinian is called "ex-consul," but no consul of this name appears to be recorded at this period.

[78] See W. Ensslin, "Matronianus," no. 3, RE 14.2310; and Stein, *Hist.* 2.13, n. 1.

[79] See Stein, *Hist.* 2.19, n. 1.

[80] The name Kouttoulos appears only in the fragment of Malalas in the *Excerpta de insidiis* p. 165, cited above, n. 73. On Cottomenes, see Stein, *Hist.* 2.30.

[81] See the discussion of Illus' plans by Stein, *Hist.* 2.19ff.

[82] Malalas in *Excerpta de insidiis* p. 165 ed. De Boor (more briefly in the text printed in the Bonn ed., 388.15-16).

and was apparently not too eager to persecute after he became emperor.[83] It had not been very long since the pagan sophist Isocasius had been a prominent figure in Antioch,[84] and Illus' plans suggest that he and his advisers considered that there was enough pagan sentiment remaining in Antioch and Asia Minor to justify an attempt to find support in that quarter.[85] Some of the large private houses of Antioch of this period which were explored during the excavations were found to contain a number of mosaic floors illustrating pagan literary and mythological themes, and this would suggest that the authors were well acquainted with, and interested in, classical literature. Such scenes may, however, only be natural reflections of the "culture" that was the normal educational heritage of cultivated Christians at that time, and the presence of such mosaics in private houses does not necessarily indicate that the owners were themselves pagans.[86] It would be easy, in any case, to appeal to the Hellenic heritage as a means of rallying pagans and classically-educated Christians, on a patriotic and cultural basis, against the monophysites. We hear of a trip by Pamprepius to his native Egypt, and it seems safe to suppose that he went there in an effort to win support for Zeno among the Greeks in Egypt.[87]

When Calandio was bishop (A.D. 479-484), he arranged to have brought back to Antioch the relics of Eustathius "the Great," the famous orthodox bishop of the city in the fourth century who defended the Nicene cause against the Arians and was finally deprived of office and exiled in A.D. 330 to Philippi in Thrace, where he died and was buried ca. A.D. 356-360.[88] When Calandio brought the relics back, more than one hundred years after Eustathius' death, the people went ten miles outside the city and met the procession with great signs of honor. Those who were, through loyalty to Eustathius' principles, still separated from the local church, were now reunited.[89] Calandio's undertaking thus not only restored peace among the local orthodox Christians, but also served to give them a stronger front against the Mono-

---

[83] See Stein, *Hist.* 2.21.   [84] See above, §1.

[85] On this aspect of Illus' plans see Stein, *Hist.* 2.23.

[86] For a list of figured mosaics found at Antioch which may be dated in this period, see Levi *Antioch Mosaic Pavements* 1.626.

[87] R. Keydell, "Pamprepios," no. 1, *RE* 18, 2. Heft (part 3) 412-413; Stein, *Hist.* 2.19, n. 1.

[88] Kidd, *Hist. of the Church* 2.54-55, and see above, Ch. 12, nn. 154-155.

[89] Theodore Lector 2.1, *PG* 86, pt. 1, 184; Theophanes a. 5981, p. 133.3-7 ed. De Boor. Theophanes places the event in the year which ought to correspond to A.D. 489, while Fravitta was patriarch of Constantinople, but we know that Calandio's tenure of office did not extend to this date. On the translation of the relics of Eustathius, see Delehaye, *Origines du culte*² 59, and cf. 94, 96, 200, 203, 245.

physites. Whether Calandio was acting in concert with Illus, we do not know. More likely he was simply attempting to restore peace at Antioch, in conformity with the desires of the Patriarch Acacius and of the Emperor who, though he had once been openly friendly toward the Monophysites and was now secretly sympathetic with their beliefs, had now evidently become alarmed by their excesses at Antioch.

At about the same time, in A.D. 482, Zeno attempted to furnish a general basis for reunion in the Christological dispute, by addressing to the bishops of Egypt the Henoticon, or Instrument of Union, in which there was set forth a statement of the faith which, it was hoped, might be acceptable to both the supporters and the opponents of the Chalcedonian definition.[90] The phraseology did, however, show that the government was not prepared to make an express condemnation of the monophysite teaching,[91] and to this extent the separatist theological tendency which had been developing in Antioch, as well as in Egypt, could continue to grow. In Antioch, Bishop Calandio protested against the terms of the Henoticon, but was allowed to remain in office, presumably because Zeno either was timid, or was anxious to avoid trouble in this quarter if possible.[92]

Late in A.D. 483 or early in 484, after Illus had been in Antioch for two years,[93] both Zeno and Illus took measures that could only lead to war between them.[94] Knowing that as an Isaurian he would suffer from the same popular enmity that had been directed against the Isaurian Zeno, Illus did not attempt to make himself emperor, but instead chose to put forward Leontius, not an Isaurian but probably a

[90] Text in Evagrius *H.E.* 3.14; translation in *Documents Illustrative of the History of the Church*, ed. B. J. Kidd 2 (London 1932) 330-332.

[91] On the background of the document and its significance, see Kidd, *Hist. of the Church* 3.413; Stein, *Hist.* 2.25.

[92] Evagrius *H.E.* 3.16; Zachariah of Mitylene, *Chron.* 5.9; see Schwartz, *op.cit.* (above, n. 69) 209.

[93] On the date of Illus' arrival, see above, n. 72.

[94] The sources for the rebellion of Illus at Antioch are to some extent fragmentary, and also contradictory in several respects: Eustathius *apud* Evag. *H.E.* 3.27; Malalas 388.15ff., with additional information, representing the more complete form of the text of Malalas, in *Excerpta de insidiis* pp. 165-166 ed. De Boor, and in the Church Slavonic version of Malalas pp. 106-107; John of Antioch, frag. 214, 2 (*FHG* IV, p. 620 = frag. 98 in *Excerpta de insidiis*, p. 136); Theodore Lector 2.3, *P.G.* 86, pt. 1, 185; Joshua the Stylite 14; Theophanes a. 5973, pp. 128.30ff. ed. De Boor. The most detailed studies of this episode are those of Brooks in the *English Historical Review* 8 (1893) 223-228, and of Stein, *Hist.* 2.28-31. In some details the present account differs from the conclusions reached by these scholars, since neither of them, in view of the nature of their works, had occasion to adduce all of the considerations which may be suggested here.

Syrian by birth,[95] who had been one of Illus' companions when he
went to Antioch.[96] In order to provide a legal basis for his action, Illus
released the Augusta Verina from the fortress in Isauria in which she
had been imprisoned, and he had no difficulty in enlisting her services
against her son-in-law Zeno, through whom she had suffered so much.
As Augusta, Verina crowned Leontius emperor, on 19 July A.D. 484,
in the Church of St. Peter outside Tarsus, and on this occasion she
issued an edict in which she pointed out that it was she who had
crowned Zeno emperor; she then went on to say that since Zeno's rule
was ruining the commonwealth, she had now crowned the pious and
just Leontius.[97] When it was read in Antioch at the *praetorium* of the

[95] Leontius was a Syrian, according to Theophanes, a. 5972, p. 128.8-9 ed. De Boor.
According to John of Antioch *loc.cit.* (above, n. 94), Leontius came from Dalisandos.
There was a Dalisandos in Pamphylia, which was at an earlier period included in
Isauria, and Brooks (*English Historical Review* 8 [1893] 225, n. 101) and Ensslin (art.
"Leontius," *RE* Suppl. 8.939) conclude that Leontius came from this Dalisandos,
though, as Brooks points out, it is clear from Joshua the Stylite 14 that Leontius would
not have been considered an Isaurian in the same sense that Illus was. However, there
were at least two places named Dalisandos in Asia Minor (W. M. Ramsay, *Historical
Geography of Asia Minor* [London 1890] 366, 379, 395, cited by Brooks *loc.cit.*), and
if there were two such places in Asia Minor, it is possible that there was another of the
same name in Syria, from which Leontius might have come. A writer like John of
Antioch, to whom Syria was a familiar subject, would not think it necessary, in mentioning Dalisandos, to add that it was in Syria; and it is to be noted that he does not
seem to have stated that it was in Pamphylia or Isauria. In the Church Slavonic version
of Malalas (p. 106), it is stated that Leontius was by birth a Thracian, but as Stein
points out (*Hist.* 2.28, n. 2) this probably represents a misunderstanding of the fact
that he had previously been *magister militum* in Thrace (Theophanes *loc.cit.*).

[96] There is considerable disagreement in the sources as to Leontius' activities during
the time that Illus was in Antioch. Eustathius, quoted by Evagrius *HE* 3.27; Malalas,
in the Church Slavonic version, pp. 106-107; and Theophanes, a. 5972, p. 128.7-8 ed.
De Boor, all state that Leontius was one of the suite whom Illus took to Antioch with
him when he left Constantinople to take up his duties as *magister militum* of the
Oriens in Antioch at the end of A.D. 481 or the beginning of 482, while Jordanes (*Rom.*
352) states that Zeno sent Leontius to Antioch to bring Illus to Constantinople, or kill
him if necessary, when he began his rebellion. As has been noted above (n. 73), Brooks
(*English Historical Review* 8 [1893] 223, 225) rejects the testimony of Eustathius,
Malalas and Theophanes, and supposes that Leontius did not accompany Illus on his
original journey to Antioch. It seems hazardous to reject authors such as Eustathius
and Malalas, who had access to local sources, in favor of a writer like Jordanes; and
Stein (*Hist.* 2.28, n. 2) believes that Leontius first went to Antioch at the time that
Illus did, but not as a member of his party. We know so little of the details of Illus'
rebellion that we cannot be sure of what happened. It is worth while to remark that
on Brooks' hypothesis, we should have to believe that Illus put forward Leontius as
emperor immediately after having won him over from Zeno. It may seem more likely
that Illus would have taken this step only after having had a longer opportunity to
know Leontius. Leontius could have gone to Antioch with Illus, and then could have
returned to Constantinople, from which (as in Jordanes' account) he set out a second
time for Antioch on orders from Zeno. It is not impossible that Leontius was trying to
keep up connections with both Zeno and Illus until he saw which man was more
likely to win.

[97] The version of Verina's proclamation is reproduced, with variations, in both

magister militum, this proclamation appears to have been well received,[98] and Leontius entered the city on 27 July and made it his headquarters.[99]

Leontius seems to have maintained his regime in Antioch for about sixty or seventy days.[100] Whether he struck coins at Antioch is not certain;[101] but we know that he set up a government, with Aelian as *praefectus praetorio*, Pamprepius as *magister officiorum* and Justinian as *comes largitionum*, while Illus remained the guiding spirit of the whole enterprise.[102] Verina seems to have remained with the court of the new Augustus.[103] Bishop Calandio, who had disapproved of Zeno's issuing the Henoticon, joined the rebels.[104] The only opposition in Syria seems to have been at Edessa and Chalcis, which refused to receive the imperial images, used for official purposes, which each new emperor sent out at his accession.

Zeno, when the news of the rebellion reached him, sent a strong force of troops under John the Scythian, which defeated Leontius' soldiers.[105]

Malalas (*Excerpta de insidiis*, pp. 165-166 ed. De Boor; Church Slavonic version pp. 107-108) and Theophanes a. 5974, p. 129.10-20 ed. De Boor. Brooks (*op.cit.* 226-227) prints a translation that combines the versions of Malalas and Theophanes. He points out that the original was probably in Latin, and that the "baldness" of the Greek is to be explained on this ground; but in Antioch, where knowledge of Latin was at this date extremely limited, there would have had to be an official Greek version.

[98] Since Leontius would have entered Antioch and set up his headquarters there only if the people of the city approved his coronation, one may, with Brooks (*op.cit.* 227), accept the statement of Theophanes that the Antiochenes acclaimed Leontius. This is also the interpretation placed by the Church Slavonic translator of Malalas (p. 108) upon the words preserved in the fragment of Malalas in the *Excerpta*, following "Great is God. Lord have mercy." τὸ καλὸν καὶ τὸ συμφέρον παράσχου. Brooks translates the phrase "give us what is good and beneficial," taking this as "a token of dissent," while the Church Slavonic translator took the phrase to mean "may God the Lord grant you [i.e. Verina, or Leontius] things good and useful." This seems a much more natural interpretation.

[99] Some sources give the date as 27 June, but it is certainly 27 July; see Ensslin, art. "Leontius," *RE* Suppl. 8.940; Stein, *Hist.* 2.29, n. 1.

[100] John of Antioch, fr. 214, pt. 5 (*FHG* 4.620-621 = fr. 98, p. 136 *Excerpta de insidiis*); Church Slavonic version of Malalas, p. 108. On the details of what follows, see Brooks in *English Historical Review* 8 (1893) 227-231; cf. also Stein, *Hist.* 2.29-31.

[101] J. Sabatier, *Description générale des monnaies byzantines* (Paris 1862, reprinted Leipzig 1930) 1.146-148, publishes four coins alleged to have been issued by Leontius, but three of these are forgeries: see I. I. Tolstoi, *Monnaies byzantines* (1912-1914) 1.168-169. Tolstoi will not commit himself as to the fourth (which is in Paris), but is inclined to think it genuine.

[102] Malalas in *Excerpta de insidiis* p. 165 ed. De Boor; Theophanes a. 5976, p. 129.29-31 ed. De Boor; Evagrius *HE* 3.27.

[103] John of Antioch *loc.cit.* (see above, n. 100); and see below, n. 105.

[104] Zachariah of Mitylene *Chron.* 5.9; see Schwartz, *op.cit.* (above, n. 69) 209.

[105] Malalas in *Excerpta, loc.cit.* (above, n. 102). The location of the battle is not specified, but the accounts seem to indicate that it did not take place in or near Antioch. According to Malalas, Leontius and Pamprepius were in Antioch when Leontius'

Leontius, Illus, Verina and their supporters fled from Antioch to the
stronghold of Papyrion in Isauria (late summer, A.D. 484), where they
withstood a siege for four years, and in the end were captured through
treachery and executed in A.D. 488.[106]

4. THE LAST YEARS OF ZENO'S REIGN; THE ECCLESIASTICAL
INDEPENDENCE OF CYPRUS; FACTIONAL DISORDERS;
BUILDINGS IN ANTIOCH AND DAPHNE

After the suppression of the regime of Illus and Leontius in Antioch
in A.D. 484, Bishop Calandio was removed from office and exiled, on
the emperor's orders, because of his adherence to the rebels.[107] Zeno
then sent Peter the Fuller back to Antioch to be bishop for the fourth
time A.D. 484-491 (?).[108] A synod met and recognized Peter, who proceeded to acknowledge his recognition of the changed state of affairs
by subscribing to the Henoticon.[109]

We do not hear any details of the persecution of Peter's theological
opponents which followed his return to power; a friendly source declares that he restored peace at Antioch, while hostile writers describe
the "many evil things" that he did and the trouble that he stirred up.[110]
In A.D. 488, Peter apparently decided to gain special distinction for
his career by re-asserting, and this time enforcing, the ecclesiastical
supremacy of Antioch over the island of Cyprus.[111] The question had

---

troops were defeated; John of Antioch *loc.cit.* (above, n. 100), adds that Verina was
with them. Joshua the Stylite 16 relates that when the people of Antioch heard of the
imperial force that had been dispatched against them, they "tumultuously" called upon
Illus and Leontius to leave the city.

[106] Malalas p. 389.5-14 Bonn ed. and in *Excerpta loc.cit.* (above, n. 102); Theophanes
a. 5976, p. 130.1-8 ed. De Boor; John of Antioch fr. 214, pt. 6 (see above, n. 100);
Theodore Lector 2.4 = *PG* 86, pt. 1, 185.

[107] Theophanes a. 5982, p. 133.30-32 ed. De Boor; Zachariah of Mitylene *Chron.* 5.9.

[108] Theophanes and Zachariah *locc.citt.* Zeno would not wait until the siege of Illus
and Leontius and their followers, in the castle in Isauria, had been completed, but
would replace Calandio as soon as the rebels had been forced to leave Antioch. Since
the rebels left Antioch probably in the summer of A.D. 484 (see above), the exile of
Calandio and the appointment of Peter the Fuller are presumably to be placed in this
year, and not in A.D. 483, as Devreesse, *Patriarcat d'Antioche* 118, writes. On the
chronology of the last days of Peter the Fuller see below, Ch. 18, nn. 18-19.

[109] The synod is described, and the synodal letter quoted, by Zachariah of Mitylene
Chron. 5.9-10; see also Theophanes a. 5982, p. 133.32ff. ed. De Boor. Cf. Mansi, 7.1165-
1166, and Schwartz, *op.cit.* (above, n. 69) 209-210.

[110] Zachariah and Theophanes *locc.citt.* (above, n. 109); Cyril of Scythopolis *Life of
Sabas,* in E. Schwartz, *Kyrillos von Skythopolis,* in *Texte u. Untersuchungen* 49.2
(1939) p. 118.7ff.; Alexander the Monk *Encomium of St. Barnabas, PG* 87, pt. 3,
4099ff.

[111] For the previous history of this question, and the details of the episode in the
time of Peter the Fuller, see G. Downey, "The Claim of Antioch to Ecclesiastical

been passed upon at the Council of Ephesus in A.D. 431 in such terms that the see of Antioch must have been made to realize that its claim was looked upon as weak, and we do not hear of any attempt on the part of Antioch, between A.D. 431 and 488, to renew the question. The extant evidence does not tell us whether there may have been any special circumstances at Cyprus that may have given Peter the Fuller reason to hope for success. All our evidence about this episode comes from a Cypriote source, the encomium of St. Barnabas by Alexander the Monk, and while the outcome is clear, we may not know the true details.

We are told that Peter first attempted to assert the supremacy of Antioch and that his assertion was rejected. Then he is said to have put forward a new argument, based on the fact that Christianity had been carried to Cyprus from Antioch, as related in Acts;[112] and since Antioch was an apostolic foundation, Cyprus, which was not (Peter claimed) an apostolic foundation, must be subject to it. Cyprus was saved from this argument by the timely intervention of its principal saint, Barnabas, who, according to the bishop of Salamis, visited him in a dream and revealed to him the location of his tomb, which had not previously been known. When opened, the tomb proved to contain the perfectly preserved body of St. Barnabas, holding on his chest a copy of the Gospel of Matthew written in Barnabas' own hand. This exceedingly precious book was presented to the Emperor Zeno, who placed it in one of the churches in the Great Palace at Constantinople, and the independence of Cyprus was held to be vindicated by this convincing demonstration of St. Barnabas' opinion that Cyprus ranked among the apostolic foundations, and therefore deserved to be, as it had always claimed to be, autocephalous; and it so remained.

About this same time, in the last years of the reign of Zeno,[113] we have fairly detailed reports of factional disorders at Antioch, coupled with an anti-Jewish outbreak. Coming after a long period in which nothing is preserved concerning the internal political affairs of the city, the evidence for the episodes under Zeno serves to illustrate how much evidence concerning the history of Antioch at this period has been lost, for the democratic power which is shown by these occur-

---

Jurisdiction over Cyprus," *Proceedings of the American Philosophical Society* 102 (1958) 224-228.

[112] Acts 11:19; 13:4-12; 15:39.

[113] The only indication of the date of these episodes is provided by the position in which they are recorded in the chronicle of Malalas, toward the end of the account of Zeno's reign, and following the suppression of the revolt of Illus and Leontius.

rences must have made itself felt in Antioch on other occasions of which we now know nothing, just as in the history of Constantinople we hear of the political power exercised by the circus factions on a number of occasions.[114]

At Antioch, the first incident recorded was a clash in the hippodrome between the Greens and the Blues, the two principal circus factions originally formed to support rival charioteers but which came to have the additional function of political and religious parties. In Antioch at this time the Greens represented the Monophysites and the local Syrian elements in the population, while the Blues, traditionally the conservative and aristocratic party, supported orthodoxy and thus represented the interests of the central government.[115] In the hippodromes at Constantinople and elsewhere, the two factions occupied fixed locations, and their cheering and applause (or the contrary) were regulated by their leaders, as were the ceremonial acclamations with which the emperor and other officials were on occasion greeted. In this first outbreak at Antioch,[116] the Greens began to attack the Blues in the hippodrome by throwing stones at them. One stone hit the *consularis Syriae* Thalassius on the head and he left the hippodrome. Thalassius had identified the thrower of the stone as one Olympius, an attendant in one of the baths[117]—he must have been a well-known ringleader for Thalassius to have recognized him—and when he reached the safety of his praetorium, which was on or near the Forum of Valens, he sent *commentarienses* to arrest Olympius and bring him to the headquarters. When Olympius was brought, Thalassius began to conduct the customary examination in which the prisoner was flogged in order to elicit reliable testimony.

[114] On the circus factions at Constantinople and elsewhere in the Empire, and their political and religious significance, see G. Manojlović, "Le peuple de Constantinople," *Byzantion* II (1936) 617-716 (on the episodes at Antioch, 636-637, 639-640, 644, 675), and F. Dvornik, "The Circus Parties in Byzantium, Their Evolution and their Suppression," *Byzantina-Metabyzantina* I, pt. I (1946) 119-133, with bibliography.

[115] Cf. Dvornik, *op.cit.* 126.

[116] In the Oxford MS of Malalas (pp. 389.15-390.3 Bonn ed.) the account of the disorders is much abbreviated. A longer account is preserved in the fragments of Malalas in the *Excerpta de insidiis*, pp. 166-167 ed. De Boor. The fullest account, based on an older Greek text, which adds details not preserved in the *Excerpta*, appears (unfortunately marred in places by the translator's misunderstanding of the Greek) in the Church Slavonic version of Malalas, pp. 109-112. The following account combines the versions of the Church Slavonic version and the *Excerpta*, indicating the differences between them only when these are significant.

[117] According to a garbled passage in the Church Slavonic version of Malalas, the bath may have been called the Bath of Urbicius; cf. C. E. Gleye, *B.Z.* 3 (1894) 626, and the note on the passage in the English translation of the Church Slavonic version by Spinka and Downey, p. 110, n. 148. This would be the only preserved evidence for the existence of such a bath.

When the Greens heard of Olympius' arrest and examination, they attacked the praetorium and set it on fire and rescued the prisoner. The fire spread into the colonnade with which the Forum of Valens was surrounded, and reached the Xystus, which stood on one side of the Forum, and burned it.[118] Thalassius fled to Hippocephalus, a place several miles outside the city.[119] He resigned his office and was replaced by Quadratus, and the disorder was brought to an end.

Six months later there was a new outbreak of fighting between the factions, this time involving the Jews, who had made common cause with the Blue party. The Greens attacked the Blues and their Jewish allies in the hippodrome and killed a number of them, and then plundered and burned the synagogue named for Asabinus.[120] Theodorus the *comes Orientis* was relieved of his office,[121] presumably because he had failed to keep order, and the disorders ceased.

The third episode that is reported is a further outbreak of anti-Semitism, which may have been connected with the violence under Theodorus. It is related that a monk walled himself up in one of the towers of the southern wall of the city, leaving a small opening through which he harangued the people. Apparently he preached an attack on the Jews, who had one of their principal synagogues near by, in the southern quarter of the city.[122] The Greens attacked the synagogue and burned it, and dug up and burned on a pyre the bodies of the Jews who were buried there. They also burned other buildings in this area, which was called the Distadion because it occupied the interval of two stadia between the older wall of Tiberius and the new wall enclosing an enlarged area built by Theodosius II.[123] Malalas reports that when Zeno, who was favorable to the Greens, was told of this incident, he was angry with the Greens because they had burned only dead Jews and had not thrown living ones on the fire.[124]

[118] On the topography of the Forum of Valens, see Excursus 12.

[119] On Hippocephalus, see above, Ch. 4, n. 108.

[120] Asabinus was the name of a Jewish property owner at Antioch whose land was purchased as the site for the Plethrion built under Didius Julianus; see above, Ch. 10, §1.

[121] Aside from the passage in Malalas, nothing seems to be known about Theodorus (see Ensslin, art. "Theodorus," no. 87, *RE* 5A.1904). A *comes* Theodorus, who might be identical with the *comes Orientis*, is mentioned in a Greek inscription of Cyprus published by T. B. Mitford, *Byzantion* 20 (1950) 157-158.

[122] On this synagogue, see above, Ch. 5, n. 121; Ch. 15, nn. 196, 199.

[123] On the enlargement of the wall, see above, Ch. 16, nn. 10-12. For the courses of the two walls, see Fig. 11.

[124] It is to be noted that at least in the preserved accounts there is no record of any action on the part of the Blues. Stein points out (*Hist.* 2.32) that one could conclude from these episodes that the pagans, the Jews, and the Blue faction had combined to support the rebel Illus.

During the reign of Zeno we hear of new public buildings put up at Antioch and Daphne by Mammianus, who, having started life as an artisan, became a senator.[125] In Daphne, he built the Antiphorus,[126] on a site formerly planted with vines, opposite a public bath; and the citizens in gratitude set up a bronze statue of "Mammianus the benefactor of the city."[127] In Antioch he built two *basileioi stoai*—that is, according to the context, colonnades rather than basilicas—described

[125] Whether Mammianus became a senator at Constantinople or at Antioch is not clear. He does not seem to be otherwise known, and there is no indication of the date of his activity, save that both Malalas and Evagrius place it in their accounts of the latter part of the reign of Zeno. Malalas' account of the buildings has disappeared entirely from the Oxford MS and has left only a brief trace in the Church Slavonic version (p. 103), but Evagrius (*Hist. eccl.* 3.28) quotes Malalas' account in some detail.

[126] Etymologically, this term could be taken to mean either that the place or building so designated served "instead of a forum," i.e., perhaps, was "a little forum," or that it stood "opposite a forum." The former interpretation seems more natural, and is perhaps supported by the other texts in which the word occurs. Malalas says that in the course of factional rioting at Antioch under Anastasius the corpse of the *nykter-parchos* Menas, who had been murdered by the crowd, was hung up "on the bronze statue called Kolonisios in the middle of the antiphoros" (397.22-23). Joshua the Stylite, who often uses Greek words in transliteration in his Syriac chronicle, says that during a festival at Edessa in A.D. 495/6 the people hung up lighted lamps (*kandelai*) on the bank of the river, "in the porticoes (*stoai*), in the town hall (*antiphoros*), in the upper streets, and in many (other) places" (ch. 27, p. 18-19, Wright's translation). The same building may be mentioned in Procopius's account of the restoration of the city by Justinian after it had been damaged by a flood of the river Scirtus; Justinian rebuilt all the ruined structures, "among which were the Christian church and the so-called antiphoros" (*De aedificiis* 2.7-6). The word has been variously interpreted. Sophocles *Lexicon*, *s.v.*, cites only the passages in Evagrius and Malalas and believes that "Antiphorus" was "a place at Antioch." Wright, in his note on the passage in Joshua, cites only the passage in Procopius, and does not explain why he translates "town-hall," although the choice of this interpretation is not difficult to understand. Müller, in connection with the antiphoros at Daphne, notes only (*Antiq. Antioch.* 118, n. 8), "Quid eo vocabulo significetur, ex ipso vocabulo tantum divinari potest." In noticing the reference to the antiphoros at Antioch, he suggests in general terms that it was identical with the forum of Valens (p. 109, n. 4). Du Cange, *s.v.*, although he cites only the passage in Evagrius, points out, more critically, that the word might be used either because the building was opposite a public forum or because it was used as a forum: he does not attempt to decide between these interpretations.

[127] The way in which Evagrius describes the statue makes it seem likely that Malalas quoted an inscription placed upon it; certainly the words "Mammianus the friend of the city" resemble some of the ostensible quotations of inscriptions which Malalas gives, e.g. that on the statue of the Syriarch Artabanes at Daphne (290.2; cf. *Chronicon Paschale* 490.15); for other examples, see Downey, "Inscriptions in Malalas." The word order of Evagrius' description might at first be thought ambiguous, in that it is not immediately clear whether the statue stood in the antiphorus or in the public bath, but it would seem more fitting to suppose that it was placed in the antiphorus. The topographical mosaic from Yakto shows (in the section which represents scenes at Daphne) a building labelled TO ΔHMOCIN, with a figure which might be a statue standing under the pediment (*Antioch-on-the-Orontes* I, p. 135, fig. 13, no. 14). Δημόσιον (spelled δημόσιν in the Byzantine fashion on the mosaics) is a common locution for δημόσιον (λουτρόν); its counterpart, πριβάτον (sc. λουτρόν) appears elsewhere on the same mosaic.

as being "very seemly in their construction and adorned with striking and brilliant stone work," and paved with stone from Proconnesus. These colonnades were named for Mammianus. Between them he erected a tetrapylon, "very finely adorned with columns and bronze work." In which part of the city the colonnades and the tetrapylon stood, is not clear, though they may have been on the island.[128] The colonnades, rebuilt after suffering damage on various occasions, were still visible in the time of Evagrius, in the latter part of the sixth century, but the tetrapylon had by that time disappeared.[129]

Our texts, which are meager for this period, would have given us no hint of the growing prosperity of Antioch and its neighborhood in the reigns of Zeno and Anastasius which has recently been revealed by the archaeological researches of G. Tchalenko in the mountain region of the Belus, east of Antioch. A new examination of the remains of the farms and agricultural communities in this region, and in particular the evidence for the greatly increased building activity at this

[128] Förster ("Antiochia" 130) suggests that the two *basileioi stoai* and the tetrapylon were a partial replacement of the colonnades of the four main streets of the island, and the tetrapylon at their intersection, all of which, Evagrius records (*Hist. eccl.* 2.12), had been destroyed in the severe earthquake in the time of Leo I (see above, §1 in this chapter). According to Evagrius' account the island must have suffered heavy damage in that disaster, and while nothing is said specifically about the four main colonnaded streets and the tetrapylon, it is tempting to think, as Förster does, that Mammianus, as a private benefactor, was repairing some of the damage done a generation before—though it must always be kept in mind, of course, that in a city of the size of Antioch there could be other places in which two colonnades came together at a tetrapylon. Förster's suggestion is interesting in connection with the history of the island. When Antioch was rebuilt after the sack by the Persians in A.D. 540, the island seems to have been abandoned as a part of the city, and seems to have lain outside the new city wall which Justinian built (see below, Ch. 18, §8). We might conclude that Mammianus' work reflected the diminished state of the public buildings on the island, in that his two colonnades and tetrapylon replaced the earlier four colonnaded streets and tetrapylon; and then a further impoverishment would be indicated by Evagrius' comment that at the end of the sixth century the tetrapylon had disappeared and only the colonnades, rebuilt, remained. This of course is hypothesis, depending upon the location of Mammianus' work; but the suggestion of the diminishing prosperity of Antioch is characteristic of what we know of its history at this time.

[129] As Förster pointed out ("Antiochia," 130, n. 120), Müller (*Antiq. Antioch.* 118) happened to overlook the description of the buildings of Mammianus in Evagrius, and derived his information concerning them wholly from the much later and briefer account of Nicephorus (*Hist. eccl.* 16.23 = PG 147.160) which was based on that of Evagrius. Nicephorus' description, however, abbreviates the information given by Evagrius, and is so short and vague that Müller was led into error, believing that the two *basileioi stoai* joined by a tetrapylon, which Evagrius says Mammianus built at Antioch, were in the antiphoros at Daphne. It is worth noting that this illustrates what may very well have happened on occasion in the extant sources for the buildings and topography of Antioch. Much of what is extant was derived from earlier sources which have been lost, and these earlier sources may be represented only incompletely and carelessly in the extant material, just as the text of Malalas, lost in the original, is quoted by Evagrius and then is inaccurately reproduced by Nicephorus.

period, show that there was a major expansion in the production of olive oil. Much or most of this olive oil must have been exported through Antioch, and it is safe to conclude that some of the olive-producing property in the Belus region was owned by persons living in Antioch. It is certain that there must have been a real increase in the wealth of the city at this time, which has hitherto been thought to have been a period of obscurity and decline.[130]

[130] See Tchalenko 1.422.

CHAPTER 18

ANASTASIUS (A.D. 491-518), JUSTIN I
(A.D. 518-527), AND JUSTINIAN (A.D. 527-565)

1. Special Characteristics of Anastasius' Reign; Economic Prosperity of the Region around Antioch; Factional Disorders in the City

THE LITERARY SOURCES for the history of Antioch during the reign of Anastasius are limited both in quantity and in the kind of information that they preserve, and we are told specifically about only a few episodes in the history of the city which happened to be of a somewhat sensational character, in keeping with both the rather explosive characteristics of the people of Antioch and the special problems created by the religious tensions of the period.

We know, however, that this is not a complete or trustworthy picture of life in Antioch at this time, for the study of the agricultural area in in the Belus region, east of Antioch, which was closely connected with the metropolis by economic interests, shows a continuation of the prosperity that had been exhibited beginning with the reign of Zeno. The very marked increase in the building activity in the Belus region during the reigns of both Zeno and Anastasius attests a rise in the production and export of olive oil, which indicates among other things a growing consumption of oil at Antioch itself; and in the economic circumstances of the time, this is a reliable index of an increase in the prosperity of the city, which was to continue down to the reign of Justinian.[1] This well attested development must be borne in mind during the rehearsal of the record of disorders that, from the literary sources alone, seem to form the most prominent feature in the life of Antioch at this time.

The history of Anastasius' rule everywhere in the Empire was colored, first, by his position in the religious situation, and, later, by his financial policy in rebuilding the resources of the state which Zeno's reign had seriously depleted. Both Anastasius' support of the Monophysites, and his energetic measures for financial reform and recoupment, made him highly unpopular in many quarters. The emperor possessed admirable personal qualities, and his long experience as an official in the imperial administration gave him qualifications

---

[1] Tchalenko, *Villages antiques de la Syrie du Nord* 1.422.

for his office which were not always found in the emperors of those times; but at the same time, the unpopularity of some of his measures actually produced an increase in the public disorders and clashes between the circus factions throughout his reign.[2] We happen to possess relatively detailed information concerning events of this kind at Antioch, which were typical of what went on elsewhere in the Empire. Our sources do not inform us specifically of all of the immediate causes of these episodes at Antioch, but it is easy enough to see in them the working of the various reasons for public discontent which have been mentioned, with, as an added local factor at Antioch, the anti-Semitic feeling that had appeared during the reign of Zeno.

The first episode known at Antioch, which is described only briefly in the extant sources, is said to have consisted of an attack by the Greens (the popular and monophysite party) on a new *comes Orientis,* Calliopius, who had been appointed by his father Hierius, the *praefectus praetorio,* in the year A.D. 494/5.[3] What the immediate cause of the outbreak may have been, is not clear. The Greens attacked Calliopius in his *praetorium* and he fled the city. When this was reported to the emperor, he took such a serious view of the revolutionary character of the Greens' behavior that he sent to Antioch a new *comes Orientis,* Constantius of Tarsus, with power of life and death; and Constantius is said to have restored order,[4] presumably by measures that rendered the Monophysites powerless at least for the time being.

The second series of riots, which occurred in A.D. 507, we know in considerable detail, and the account incidentally provides valuable information concerning the topography of Antioch.[5] The trouble began after the arrival at Antioch of Porphyrius Calliopas, the most celebrated charioteer of the fifth and sixth centuries, who in the year A.D. 507 was about forty years old and at the height of his career.[6] He had

---

[2] On the characteristics of Anastasius and the beginnings of his reign, see Stein, *Hist.* 2.77ff. On the factional disorders, see Stein, *op.cit.* 81-82, and (for a detailed study of their political significance) G. Manojlović, "Le peuple de Constantinople," *Byzantion* 11 (1936) 617-716. For a summary of the evidence, see Dvornik, "Circus Parties" 127. It has been thought that a personal preference for Monophysitism on the part of the chronicler begins to appear in Malalas' work in his account of the reign of Anastasius; see E. Černousov, "Études sur Malalas: Époque d'Anastase Dicoros," *Byzantion* 3 (1926) 65-72.

[3] Malalas 392.12-393.8; Downey, *Comites Orientis* 14.

[4] For other similar occasions on which strong measures were adopted, see Manojlović, *op.cit.* (above, n. 2) 709-710.

[5] Malalas 395.20-398.4, and *Excerpta de insidiis,* p. 168, fr. 40; cf. John of Nikiu, *Chronicle* 89.23-30. This passage in Malalas is so valuable for its topographical information that it is translated in full in Excursus 11.

[6] See the detailed study of the career of Porphyrius, based on both the archaeo-

been a popular and powerful figure among the factions at Constantinople, where he had been acclaimed in a number of epigrams (preserved in the *Greek Anthology*), and had been honored by a monument, still partly preserved, erected in the Hippodrome about the year A.D. 500. What the circumstances were of his transfer of his activities from Constantinople to Antioch is not explicitly stated, but the chronicler Malalas writes[7] that he took over the "stable of the Greens, which had been abandoned," and this allusion might be taken to suggest that the Green party, after a period during which it had been suppressed (as it had been after the riot of A.D. 494/5), was now in a position to resume its activities, and was able to secure the services of Porphyrius (doubtless with the consent of the Greens of Constantinople) in order to make a major attempt to regain control in Antioch. There is reason to believe that about the year A.D. 507 the Emperor Anastasius changed his policy toward the Monophysites, as a result of the war of A.D. 502-505 with Persia. In such a case, there might be some connection between the outbreaks at Antioch and Constantinople and the emperor's apparent decision to lend some support to the Monophysites; but of this we cannot be sure (see further later in this chapter). At any rate, Porphyrius' presence in Antioch as leader of the Greens had spectacular results. After some victories of the new charioteer in the hippodrome,[8] violence broke out during the celebration of the Olympic Games in July and August of A.D. 507,[9] beginning with an assault on the Jews, who had already been attacked, as associates of the Blue party, during

---

logical and the literary evidence, by A. A. Vasiliev, "The Monument of Porphyrius in the Hippodrome at Constantinople," *Dumbarton Oaks Papers* 4 (1948) 29-49, with plates illustrating the monument. Porphyrius is heard of again as being involved in factional disorders at Constantinople during the reign of Justin, when he returned to an active career at the age of sixty (see Vasiliev's study, 40). He died at about the end of Justin's reign.

[7] 396.1-3.   [8] Malalas 396.3-4.

[9] The games were regularly celebrated during the summer, when it was most convenient for visitors to come to Antioch, and there would not be interruptions caused by rain. All other celebrations of the festival that can be dated occurred in Julian leap-years (see the list of dated celebrations in the Index, below, *s.v.* Olympic Games). The celebration in A.D. 507, which is not a Julian leap-year, presumably reflects a dislocation caused by the war with Persia which broke out in A.D. 502 and lasted until A.D. 505 (see further below). The last celebration before the outbreak of the war would have been that of A.D. 500, and another would have been scheduled for A.D. 504, but conditions in Antioch, which was the military headquarters and staging area, may well have made this impossible, and it is also quite likely that the government was unable to provide the funds necessary. When the war ended in A.D. 505, the next scheduled celebration would have been that of A.D. 508. Evidently the government, in order to satisfy the demand for this popular festival, permitted the celebration to be advanced for one year before the normal schedule was resumed.

the reign of Zeno.[10] Our sources do not give any clue as to whether this outbreak in Antioch was planned to synchronize with the rioting that took place at Constantinople in the same year, but a connection is of course quite possible. The outbreak at Constantinople was serious enough to call for the intervention of troops,[11] and the rioting at Antioch seems to have been exceptionally serious and protracted. When most of the people in Antioch were in Daphne for the Olympic Games, Calliopas and the Greens attacked the Jewish synagogue there and plundered and burned it, and killed many people. This occurred on 9 July. The cross was planted on the site of the synagogue, and it was later made into a *martyrion* of St. Leontius.[12]

When this outbreak was reported to the emperor, he removed the *comes Orientis*, Basilius of Edessa, from office, and appointed in his stead Procopius of Antioch, a former *commerciarius*. The emperor also sent to Antioch, along with Procopius, a new chief of police (*nykteparchos*), Menas of Byzantium. When the next outbreak of violence occured, Menas set about seizing some of the rioters. Having had advance notice of his intention, they fled to the Church of St. John, outside the city, to seek sanctuary there.[13] The chief of police discovered where they had gone, and went to St. John's with a force of Gothic troops, choosing as the time of his expedition the noon hour when the rioters might be expected to be off their guard. One of the rioters, Eleutherios by name, was found hiding under the holy table, and was killed and beheaded on the spot, and Menas took the head back to Antioch and threw it into the Orontes from the principal bridge. In the afternoon the Greens went to the church and found the body of their comrade. They bore the body on a stretcher back to the city. When they came opposite the "basilica" of Rufinus, at the Bath of Olbia, they encountered the guards of the chief of police, and the Blues, in the street called the Street of the Thalassioi.[14] In the fight that followed, the

[10] See above, Ch. 17, §4.

[11] Marcellinus comes *ad ann.* 507, 1 (*Chronica Minora* ed. Mommsen, 2, p. 96); cf. Stein, *Hist.* 2.81.

[12] A reference to a church of the martyr Leontius in Athanasius, *The Conflict of Severus*, Ethiopic text with transl. by E. J. Goodspeed (*PO* 4.596-598), appears to be to the shrine at Daphne. A building labelled TO ΛEONTIOY is shown in the topographical border of the Yakto mosaic (*Antioch-on-the-Orontes* 1, p. 137, fig. 14; Levi, *Antioch Mosaic Pavements,* pl. 79, b), but according to the context of the mosaic this is probably a private house, and in any case the mosaic was probably made before A.D. 507.

[13] For other references to this church, see the list of churches in Excursus 17.

[14] On the other evidence for the "basilica" of Rufinus and the Bath of Olbia, see below, Excursus 11, on the Hellenistic Agora in Epiphania. The street of the Thalassioi does not seem to be mentioned elsewhere.

Greens won. They then seized the "basilicas" of Rufinus and Zenodotus and set them afire. The fire destroyed the whole "basilica" of Rufinus, with the two *tetrapyla* on either side of it, and the praetorium of the *comes Orientis*. The *comes Orientis* Procopius fled the city; and the Greens then seized Menas, cut off his head, mutilated the body, and dragged it to the *antiphoros*, where they hung it on a bronze statue.[15] Later they took down the body, dragged it outside the city, and burned it. The emperor appointed as *comes Orientis* Irenaeus Pentadiastes, who as a citizen of Antioch was well acquainted with local conditions. Irenaeus held an investigation, and, as Malalas writes, "caused terror in the city." Irenaeus restored order, and the emperor rebuilt the structures that had been burned.[16]

2. THE MONOPHYSITES AND THE ACCESSION OF THE PATRIARCH SEVERUS

The religious situation in Syria presented Anastasius with a special problem, since feeling between the orthodox and the Monophysites was becoming very bitter, and the monophysite cause was becoming associated with the nationalist feelings, which were strong in Syria and were associated with the use of the Syriac language.[17] Anastasius must have been familiar with these things, since he had been living in Antioch at the time of the death of the Patriarch Peter the Fuller in A.D. 488, and, evidently because of his own monophysite leanings, had been one of the candidates for the vacancy.[18] At the opening of Anastasius' reign, the patriarch of Antioch was Palladius, who was apparently a Syrian, and before becoming patriarch had been a priest of the great *martyrion* of St. Thecla at Seleucia Pieria; like other bishops in northern Syria, he accepted the Henotikon of Leo and attempted to make it work.[19] Of ecclesiastical events in Antioch during Palladius'

[15] On the antiphoros, see above, Ch. 17, n. 126. There was also an *antiphoros* at Daphne.

[16] See Malalas 398.9-10, supplemented by John of Nikiu, *Chronicle* 89.29-30.

[17] On the religious situation at the opening of Anastasius' reign, see L. Duchesne, *L'Église au VIᵉ siècle* (Paris 1925) 1ff., and P. Charanis, *Church and State in the Later Roman Empire; The Religious Policy of Anastasius the First, 491-518* (Madison 1939) 10ff. For the evidence for the monophysite bishops, showing the diffusion and strength of the party, see E. Honigmann, *Évêques et évêchés monophysites d'Asie antérieure au VIᵉ siècle* (Louvain 1951; *CSCO* 127, *Subsidia* 2). On Monophysitism and the nationalist feelings in Syria and Egypt, see the study of E. L. Woodward, *Christianity and Nationalism in the Later Roman Empire* (London 1916) 41ff.

[18] Theophanes a. 5983, p. 135.23-24 ed. De Boor; cf. Duchesne, *op.cit.* (above, n. 17) 5.

[19] On Palladius' religious views, see Zachariah of Mitylene *Chronicle* 6.6; cf. Duchesne, *op.cit.* (above, n. 17) 8-9, 31. His connection with the *martyrion* at Seleucia is mentioned by Theophanes a. 5983, p. 135.22-23 ed. De Boor. On the excavation of

tenure of office we have no specific record. It is clear, however, that monophysite sentiment was gathering strength in the city under the powerful influence of Philoxenus (or Xenaias), bishop of Hierapolis (Mabboug), a protégé of Peter the Fuller, who was becoming the spokesman of the extreme Monophysites in Syria and exerted great influence through his writings.[20]

Palladius died in A.D. 498 and was succeeded by another patriarch of moderate views, Flavian II (A.D. 498-512), who had been a priest and *apocrisiarius* or delegate representing the church of Antioch at Constantinople.[21] He adhered to the Henotikon, and could be expected to try to keep peace in Antioch. However, Flavian would have to contend with the rising influence of Philoxenus; and this inevitable friction made the whole of his regime uneasy. The religious troubles in Syria, and in particular the hostilities between Philoxenus and Flavian, were somewhat abated when war broke out between the Roman Empire and Persia in A.D. 502. Philoxenus' energies were diverted to the troubles of his own people at Hierapolis, who suffered severely from the Persian inroads in their territory;[22] and Antioch, as the permanent headquarters

---

this *martyrion*, whose plan and decorations have been recovered, see W. A. Campbell, "The Martyrion at Seleucia Pieria," *Antioch-on-the-Orontes* 3.35-54, and K. Weitzmann, "The Iconography of the Reliefs from the Martyrion," *ibid*. 135-149. There is conflicting testimony as to the date of Palladius' accession and the identity of his predecessor. Theophanes apparently followed different traditions. He first records that during Zeno's reign Peter the Fuller died and was succeeded by Palladius, one of the other candidates having been Anastasius the future emperor (a. 5983, p. 135.21-25 ed. De Boor). This entry is apparently contradicted by the fact that in the table of bishops at the head of this year in his chronicle, Theophanes lists Palladius as being in his second year at patriarch of Antioch. Then, in his entry for the following year, Theophanes writes that after the accession of Anastasius, the emperor recalled Peter the Fuller from exile, but did not permit him to resume his patriarchate, and had Palladius elected in Antioch (a. 5984, p. 137.7-11). Some modern scholars have preferred one account or the other and so have dated Palladius' accession in either A.D. 488 or 491 (cf. W. Ensslin, "Palladios," no. 69, *RE* 18.2., 225). The explanation is perhaps to be found in the chronicle of Victor Tonnennensis, in which there is a rather obscure passage that suggests that when Peter the Fuller died, he was succeeded by Calandio, who had been patriarch under Zeno and had been exiled in A.D. 484, and was succeeded by Peter the Fuller: Vict. Tonn. *ad ann.* 491, 2, in *Chronica minora* ed. Mommsen, 2.192. It may be that Calandio returned from exile and was allowed to resume office after the death of Peter; and the orthodox in Antioch would in any case have regarded Peter as an interloper and would have considered that Calandio was the lawful patriarch even though exiled.

[20] See Duchesne, *op.cit.* (above, n. 17) 17; Honigmann, *op.cit.* (above, n. 17) 7; Charanis, *op.cit.* (above, n. 17) 17.

[21] Theophanes a. 5991, p. 142.9-11 ed. De Boor; Victor Tonn. *ad ann.* 497, 3 (*Chron. min.* ed. Mommsen 2.193).

[22] On the religious situation during the war, see J. Lebon, *Le Monophysisme sévérien. Étude historique, littéraire et théologique sur la résistance monophysite au Concile de Chalcédoine jusqu'à la constitution de l'église jacobite* (Louvain 1909. Universitas

of the *comes Orientis* and the *magister militum per Orientem*, had to take up the role of a center of military supplies and communications which always devolved on it during hostilities with Persia. However, we do hear that all this time there were still more manifestations of the doctrinal dispute between Flavian and Philoxenus.[23] The war also affected the situation by bringing reinforcements to the Monophysites, when numbers of monophysite refugees fled from Persia, where the government favored Nestorianism, the original form of Christianity in Persia.[24]

The conclusion of the war in A.D. 505 gave Anastasius more freedom to deal with domestic problems, and it is noticeable that at this time he began to take measures—not always openly, of course—to strengthen the Monophysites. He had always favored the doctrine, and in the case of Syria, this development of the emperor's policy may in addition have represented an effort to strengthen the Monophysites as the anti-Persian party, and give them greater solidity against the Nestorians with whom the Persian government was in sympathy.[25] The evidence (discussed above) that the Green circus faction in Antioch, which also represented the monophysite element in the population, was being revived, and was receiving support from Constantinople in A.D. 507, may be thought to suggest that the emperor may have initiated, or given his approval to, this means of extending the monophysite power and activities.

It was about this time that Severus, the future patriarch of Antioch, who was to be the most important figure in the history of Monophysitism, was beginning his career in Constantinople.[26] In A.D. 508 Severus went to the capital, accompanied by two hundred monks, to try to win the imperial favor; and he remained at the court for three years. The emperor would have liked to see Severus become patriarch of Constantinople, but the orthodox party in the capital was too strong. In the mean while Flavian was being strongly attacked by Philoxenus and the Monophysites in Antioch.[27] In A.D. 508 or 509, Flavian, in order to defend himself, called a synod in Antioch, in

---

Catholica Lovanensis, Dissertationes, ser. 2, tom. 4) 41; also Honigmann, *op.cit.* (above, n. 17) 7, and Charanis *op.cit.* (above, n. 17) 30-31.

[23] Evagrius *Hist. eccl.* 3.31-32.

[24] Honigmann and Charanis, *locc.citt.*

[25] Charanis, *loc.cit.*

[26] On the career of Severus, see Lebon, *op.cit.* (above, n. 22) 43ff. and, more briefly, Honigmann, *op.cit.* (above, n. 17) 19-60. Duchesne, *op.cit.* (above, n. 17) 18ff.; Stein, *Hist.* 2.158ff., 168ff.

[27] See Lebon, *op.cit.* (above, n. 22) 47.

which he once more subscribed to the Henotikon and condemned the Antiochene theologians who were supposed to have supported Nestorian doctrine.[28] The emperor, however, desired a more explicit statement and toward the end of A.D. 511 called a synod at Sidon, at which Philoxenus and Severus were present, as well as Flavian.[29] The extremist monophysite monks of Antioch, led by the learned monk Cosmas of Chalcis, who had come to live in Antioch, presented a long accusation of Flavian.[30] However, Flavian was able to show that his position was not inconsistent with that of the patriarchate of Alexandria, which was certainly monophysite, and the synod was brought to an end without conclusive result.

However, Flavian's enemies turned to other ways of forcing him out of Antioch; and on his return to the city, bands of the monophysite monks who lived in the vicinity, invaded Antioch under the leadership of Bishop Philoxenus of Hierapolis himself, and staged organized demonstrations against the patriarch.[31] The citizens resisted the invaders by force and killed a number of them, and threw their bodies into the Orontes. Further disorders then occurred when the orthodox monks of Syria Secunda, among whom Flavian had lived before becoming patriarch, came to the city *en masse* to defend him. In order to give an opportunity for the disorders to quiet down, Flavian left Antioch (perhaps at the suggestion of imperial officials), and stayed at the suburb Platanon (modern Beilan), on the road from Antioch north to Tarsus and Asia Minor. The emperor, when the disorders at Antioch were reported to him, on top of the accusations that were being made against Flavian at Constantinople, had decided to depose him; and the Monophysites, taking advantage of Flavian's withdrawal from the city, had seized the opportunity to establish themselves in

[28] Theophanes a. 6001, p. 151.11-31 ed. De Boor; cf. a. 6002, p. 153.7-10; Mansi, 8.347; Hefele-Leclercq, *Conciles* 2.1004; Honigmann, *op.cit.* (above, n. 17) 11.

[29] The accounts of the synod differ, according to the sympathies of the writers, and some of the proceedings are not altogether clear, although the main result so far as Flavian is concerned is fairly certain. The principal account is that of Theophanes, a. 6003, p. 153.12-154.2 ed. De Boor. On his version, and the other less detailed sources, see Mansi, 8.371-374; Hefele-Leclercq, *Conciles* 2.1016; Duchesne, *op.cit.* (above, n. 17) 27ff.; Honigmann, *op.cit.* (above, n. 17) 12-14; Charanis, *op.cit.* (above, n. 17) 44ff.; Stein, *Hist.* 2.172; E. Schwartz, "Publizistische Sammlungen zum Acacianischen Schisma," *Abh. d. Bayerischen Akad. d. Wiss., Philosoph.-histor. Abt.* N.F. 10 (1934) 245, and the same scholar's commentary to the *Life of Sabas* by Cyril of Scythopolis, published in *Texte u. Untersuchungen* 49.2 (1939) 141ff.

[30] Zachariah of Mitylene *Chronicle* 7.10.

[31] Zachariah of Mitylene *Chronicle* 7.10; Evagrius *Hist. eccl.* 3.32; Theophanes a. 6003, p. 153.29.154.2 ed. De Boor. Theophanes reports that the monks were instigated by the emperor himself.

power.[32] Flavian was formally deposed by a synod which met at Laodicea (A.D. 512), and was exiled by imperial order to Petra.[33] Other bishops, clergy and monks were likewise driven into exile,[34] and the Monophysites came into full control of Antioch, and were in a stronger position even than they had been during the days of Peter the Fuller.

Apparently immediately after the departure of Flavian, a synod was held in Antioch, under the presidency of Bishop Philoxenus of Hierapolis, at which Severus was elected patriarch.[35] He was consecrated by twelve bishops in the Great Church at Antioch, on 16 November A.D. 512.[36] Immediately after his consecration, Severus mounted the *ambon* of the Great Church and delivered a brief address in which he condemned the Council of Chalcedon and the Tome of Leo, though it was said that he had given the emperor written assurance that if he became patriarch of Antioch, he would not condemn the doctrine of Chalcedon.[37] After the address, Severus' statement was signed by the

[32] On the deposition of Flavian, see Evagrius *Hist. eccl.* 3.32, and Theophanes a. 6004, p. 156.15 ed. De Boor; cf. Lebon, *op.cit.* (above, n. 22) 55. Severus could not have been elected as soon as Flavian left the city, as Theophanes' account might be taken to imply. On Platanon, see Procopius *De aed.* 5.5.1.

[33] Severus of Antioch *Select Letters* 5.3, p. 284 ed. Brooks; Malalas 400.5-6; Evagrius *Hist. eccl.* 3.32; cf. Duchesne, *op.cit.* (above, n. 17) 30.

[34] Theophanes a. 6004, p. 156.17-19 ed. De Boor.

[35] Theophanes a. 6004, p. 156.16-17 ed. De Boor; Mansi, 8.373-376. The place at which this synod met is not stated, but the circumstances having been what they were, it seems reasonably certain that it would have been at Antioch. The encomiastic *Life of Severus* by Zachariah claims that after the monks had made him their choice, Severus was also elected by the whole population of Antioch (*PO* 2.110-111), but there is no good evidence that such a procedure was followed at this time. Naturally he was acclaimed by his supporters (cf. John of Beith-Apthonia *Life of Severus*, *PO* 2.241-242), but subsequent events suggest that the city was by no means solidly monophysite. E. Schwartz, "Publizistische Sammlungen" (cited above, n. 29) writes (247), of the synodical letter, that it called for a protest from Asterius, the "city prefect" of Antioch. As E. W. Brooks points out (*PO* 12.321, n. 3), Asterius is actually called ex-prefect of Constantinople, and so could not have had an appointment of lesser rank at Antioch. As E. Stein observes (*Hist.* 2.173, n. 1), we never hear of a "prefect of the city" of Antioch.

[36] Malalas 400.7-10; Evagrius *Hist. eccl.* 3.33; cf. Charanis, *op.cit.* (above, n. 17) 47ff.; Stein, *Hist.* 2.173. On the date, see below, n. 38. On the bishops present at the consecration, see Honigmann *op.cit.* (above, n. 17) 15.

[37] Theodore Lector *Hist. eccl.* 2.31 (*PG* 86, 1, 200-201). A Syriac translation of this allocution (*prosphonêsis*), preserved in the British Museum, has been edited and translated by M.-A. Kugener, "Allocution prononcée par Sévère après son élévation sur le trône patriarcal d'Antioche," *OC* 2 (1902) 266-282, and by the same scholar in *PO* 2 (1907) 322-325. In the manuscript tradition, the text of this allocution is followed by a statement that the declaration was signed by Severus and the patriarchs who had consecrated him; and at the end of the signatures there is a declaration that the bishops signed this document inside the sanctuary of the Great Church and that they had each pronounced the anathemas before the altar. A Coptic version of Severus' initial discourse (containing a note on the circumstances in which it was delivered) is published by E. Porcher, "Sévère d'Antioche dans la littérature copte," *Revue de l'Orient chrétien* 12 (1907) 119-124.

bishops present. Severus' election was hardly a welcome one to many people in Antioch, and there was so much disorder and noise in the church while the new patriarch was speaking that many people could not hear his statement. Being anxious to have his position known as widely as possible, Severus decided to repeat his statement, and since the festival of St. Romanus, the famous martyr of Antioch, happened to occur on 18 November, two days after the consecration, Severus took the occasion to repeat his declaration at a service held in the Church of St. Romanus.[38] Apparently even this was not enough—there may well have been further disorder at the Church of St. Romanus—and Severus had to pronounce his declaration a third time in the Martyrion of St. Euphemia in Daphne.[39]

Concerning Severus' ecclesiastical activities while he was patriarch, we have a considerable amount of information in his preserved writings, notably his letters, and these illustrate the difficulties that he encountered in controlling bishops and clergy who were often hostile to him. Given the intensity of the feelings that had been aroused, the other accounts of Severus' work are either highly laudatory, or extremely bitter in their denunciation of his wicked deeds. There seems to be good reason to believe that Severus and his followers employed physical violence against their opponents,[40] though not all of the things

[38] The second delivery of the statement at the Church of St. Romanus, two days after the patriarch's consecration, is recorded in the Coptic translation of Severus' address, published by Porcher, *op.cit.* (above, n. 36) 120. Some of the ancient sources are uncertain about the day of the consecration itself, perhaps because the original discourse had to be repeated twice, and the dates of these repetitions may have been confused with the date of the consecration. P. Hieronymus Engberding points out in his study "Wann wurde Severus zum Patriarchen von Antiochien geweiht," *OC* 37 (1953) 132-134 that the date of the festival of St. Romanus, which is well established (18 Nov.), gives a valuable clue to the date of Severus' consecration, which has been overlooked by previous scholars who have tried to determine which of the various dates given in the sources is correct. Unfortunately P. Engberding overlooked the explicit statement attached to the Syriac translation of Severus' allocution (cited above, n. 37) to the effect that the consecration took place in the Great Church of Antioch (as one would expect) and that the public declaration of the new patriarch's position was made immediately after the consecration (again as one would expect). Instead, P. Engberding supposed that the occasion on which Severus spoke at the Church of St. Romanus was the consecration (here again P. Engberding overlooked the explicit statement in the Coptic text that the allocution in the Church of St. Romanus was delivered two days after the consecration service). Thus we are led to see that Elias of Nisibis is right in putting the consecration on 16 November (*PO* 2.308); P. Engberding is mistaken in stating that Elias of Nisibis dated it on the 18th.

[39] The record of this occasion is preserved in two Greek extracts of the document, one of which was quoted at the Lateran council, A.D. 649 (Mansi, 10.1116C), the other in *Actio* IV of the Council at Constantinople in A.D. 680 (Mansi, 11.273A); see Kugener's notes in *OC* 2 (1902) 269, n. 2, and in *PO* 2.323, n. 5.

[40] Evagrius *Hist. eccl.* 3.33.

said about the Monophysites can be true.[41] Antioch can hardly have been a peaceful place during Severus' patriarchate, and there was such intense activity that Severus found it necessary to keep a permanent synod of bishops regularly resident in Antioch,[42] apparently on the model of the similar synod which was maintained by the patriarch of Constantinople. We also hear of a large oriental synod that met at Antioch early in A.D. 513, which seems to have been convoked in order to present an official statement of the views of Severus and his supporters.[43] There is likewise evidence for a special synod convoked in A.D. 515 in order to deal with the bishops of Syria Secunda who had joined in opposing both Severus and the metropolitan of Syria Secunda, Peter of Apamea, whom Severus had appointed. Peter attended the synod but his bishops refused to do so, and were excommunicated.[44] We hear nothing specifically of the orthodox party in Antioch at this time, and we do not know what kind of an existence it was able to maintain, but the opposition to Severus which continued outside Antioch implies that he was not able to suppress his enemies in the city completely. Certainly he had not enough local support to keep him in office after the death of Anastasius, aged nearly eighty-eight years, on the night of 9 July, A.D. 518.[45] The new emperor, Justin I, who was orthodox, regarded Severus as one of the most dangerous men in the Empire, and he soon issued an order to Irenaeus, the *magister militum per Orientem* at Antioch, for Severus' arrest; some even said that the emperor ordered the patriarch's tongue cut out. Severus, however, got word of the order and fled on the night of 29 September to Seleucia Pieria; from there he took a boat to Alexandria, where he was welcomed by the monophysite patriarch, Timothy.[46]

[41] For some of the accusations made agains Severus, see Honigmann *op.cit* (above, n. 17) 22-24. Honigmann (20-21) endeavors to present a moderate view of Severus' character and methods, which disposes of some of the childish accusations, such as the charge of performing magical rites at the springs of Daphne (*PO* 2.342). Perhaps Honigmann does not do entire justice to the unquestioned evidence that the monophysites inaugurated a real reign of terror in northern Syria (Stein, *Hist.* 2.173-174).

[42] Severus *Select Letters* 1.11, p. 48 transl. Brooks; 1.21, p. 73; cf. Schwartz, "Publizistische Sammlungen" (cited above, n. 29) 256 and Honigmann, *op.cit.* (above, n. 17) 22.

[43] Honigmann, *op.cit.* (above, n. 17) 15-16.

[44] Severus *Select Letters* 1.20-21, pp. 70-75 transl. Brooks; cf. Honigmann, *op.cit.* (above, n. 17) 57-58.

[45] Stein, *Hist.* 2.216-217.

[46] Malalas 411.17-18 Theophanes a. 6011, p. 165.9-12 ed. De Boor; Liberatus *Brev.* PL 68.1033; Evag. *Hist. eccl.* 4.4; cf. Vasiliev, *Justin the First* 226-227. The date of Severus' departure from Antioch is given by a fragment which probably comes from John of Ephesus (Land, *Anecdota Syriaca* I, p. 113). On the date, see J. Maspero, *Histoire des patriarches d'Alexandrie* (Paris 1923) 70, n. 3. It is worth noting that

3. Other Events at Antioch under Anastasius

Of other happenings at Antioch in the reign of Anastasius, we possess only a few brief notices. In A.D. 500/1 there was a famine that extended over the whole area between Antioch and Nisibis.[47] The chroniclers record the visit to Antioch in A.D. 507 of the famous alchemist John Isthmeus of Amida, who made money by selling the silversmiths of Antioch fragments of statues made of counterfeit gold, telling them that he had found a treasure. After having gone the rounds in Antioch he proceeded to Constantinople, where he was also successful for a time before he was discovered.[48]

There was a portent of coming disaster when a violent windstorm struck Daphne and uprooted some of the famous cypress trees in the sacred grove, which it was forbidden by law to cut down. This omen was later regarded as being fulfilled when the Persians captured and sacked Antioch in A.D. 540.[49]

Among the details of administration, we hear that in A.D. 498, John the Paphlagonian, later the famous finance minister, served in Antioch as *tractator* of the province of Syria Prima—that is, as a special official whose function was to assure the regular payment of taxes. John was promoted to be *comes sacrarum largitionum* and was succeeded at Antioch by Marinus.[50]

As a final bit of information we have a passage in the *Plerophoriai* of John Rufus, bishop of Maiouma (written apparently while Severus was patriarch, A.D. 512-518), in which the bishop reports that while in Antioch he saw a hermit living, winter and summer, in a little tent which he had built in the doorway of the imperial palace on the island, which was closed and empty.[51]

there is a homily attributed to Severus of Antioch, preserved in Coptic, which purports to have been delivered by Severus in the shrine of the martyr Claudius at Antioch: J. Drescher, "An Encomium Attributed to Severus of Antioch," *Bulletin de la Société d'Archéologie copte* 10 (1945) 43-68 (on the shrine of Claudius, see p. 56). As its editor points out, however, this work is certainly spurious, and was written by an Egyptian for Egyptians.

[47] Joshua the Stylite *Chronicle* 44, p. 34 transl. Wright. No details are given.
[48] Malalas 395.6-19; Theophanes a. 5999, p. 150.12-22 ed. De Boor.
[49] Procopius *Wars* 2.14.5.
[50] Malalas 400.11-14; cf. Stein in *Gnomon* 6 (1930) 411-412, on the function of the tractator, and in *Hist.* 2.204.
[51] John Rufus *Plerophoriai*, transl. from the Syriac by F. Nau, *Revue de l'Orient chrétien* 3 (1898), ch. 88, p. 385. The topographical and historical information found in this work is discussed by Ch. Clermont-Ganneau, *Recueil d'archéologie orientale* 3 (Paris, 1900) 223-242; for date, cf. p. 224.

4. Accession of Justin I; Change of Religious Policy and Factional Disorders

When Justin I became emperor (9 July A.D. 518), the advent of a new and exceptionally able dynasty opened an important era in the history of the later Roman Empire, which was to bring many changes to Antioch as well as to the other great cities of the Empire.[52] During the reign of Justin, his nephew and heir Justinian (sole emperor A.D. 527-565) exerted a powerful influence both in the determination of policy and in the administration of the government, so that the two reigns form in reality a single unit, which is one of special interest in the development of the Roman Empire and the formation of the Byzantine state.

The period is also one of more than ordinary interest in the history of Antioch. Beginning with the time of Justin, which was also the lifetime of the chronicler, Malalas' chronicle, at least in its preserved form, becomes much more detailed than it had been for previous reigns. Malalas himself lived at Antioch during at least part of this period and was an eye witness of some of the events; and after he settled in Constantinople (possibly after A.D. 526), he and his continuator show a special interest in events connected with Antioch.[53] Further literary material of special value, such as is not available for previous periods, comes from the work of Procopius, who devotes two major passages to the sack of Antioch by the Persians in A.D. 540, and its rebuilding following that disaster. The capture of the city by the Persians, coming soon after the fire of A.D. 525 and the earthquakes of A.D. 526 and 528, marked the beginning of the end of the prosperity and importance of ancient Antioch, and the history of the city as a Graeco-Roman metropolis comes to an end not long after, with the invasion of Syria in the seventh century first by the Persians and then by the Moslems.

The accession of Justin had an immediate importance for Antioch, as a center of the monophysite party under Anastasius, for the new emperor was orthodox and it was certain that he would reverse his predecessor's policy of imperial favor toward the Monophysites. This also entailed, of course, a change in the standing of the circus factions, for it would now be the Blue party—the party of the orthodox—which

[52] On the reign of Justin, see the detailed monograph of A. A. Vasiliev, *Justin the First* (Cambridge 1950), and the relevant part of E. Stein's *Histoire du Bas-Empire* 2 (Paris 1949), which was published almost simultaneously.

[53] On the career and work of Malalas, see the chapter on the sources for the history of Antioch, above, Ch. 2, §4.

would represent the interests of the government, rather than the Green faction, which in Antioch, at least, had been the party of the Monophysites.[54] It was inevitable, in these circumstances, that disorders would occur, and Antioch, as a center of vigorous monophysite action, could be expected to see serious fighting. The new emperor made gifts of money to the major cities in an effort to forestall factional disorders, and presented Antioch with a thousand pounds of gold.[55] This generosity was not, however, enough to pacify long-suppressed enmities, and we hear of disorders throughout the Empire as the Blues won the upper hand. The clashes were particularly severe in Antioch, which is described as a center from which the disorders spread to other cities.[56] The Patriarch Severus evidently realized that the monophysite party in Antioch would not be strong enough to warrant an attempt on his part to retain his office, and, as has been noted, he fled from the city secretly, on 29 November, and took a ship from Seleucia Pieria to Alexandria.[57]

The finding of a successor to the Patriarch Severus was a problem of the utmost importance, especially since Justin and Justinian were eager to heal the breach with the church in Rome which had kept Constantinople out of communion with Rome during the "Acacian schism," which had lasted since A.D. 484. It would be most important to fill the vacany at Antioch with a patriarch who could be acceptable to Pope Hormisdas in Rome.[58] After several months of consideration, the choice had settled, by the early part of A.D. 519, on Paul, the head

[54] On the change in policy introduced by Justin, see further Vasiliev, *Justin the First* 102ff.; and Stein, *Hist.* 2.223ff.

[55] Theophanes a. 6011, p. 165.18-21 ed. De Boor.

[56] Theophanes a. 6012, p. 166.26-33 ed. De Boor. The Oxford MS of Malalas (416.3ff.) has been shortened, and more detail concerning Antioch has been preserved in the Church Slavonic version, p. 91. On the political significance of the events at Antioch, see G. Manojlović, "Le peuple de Constantinople," *Byzantion* 11 (1936) 640, 659-661; and Dvornik, "Circus Parties" 127.

[57] See above, n. 46.

[58] For an account of the resumption of relations with Rome, see Vasiliev, *Justin the First* 160. If it could be dated accurately, interesting material on the relations between Antioch and Rome at this general period could be found in the list in the *Liber Pontificalis* (1.177 ed. Duchesne) of a number of income-producing properties in and near Antioch which were the property of St. Peter's in Rome. However, we have no way of being sure how and when these properties passed into the possession of St. Peter's, and how long they were owned by the Roman church. The properties in Antioch are listed as *domus Datiani, dumuncula in Caene* (i.e. in the New City, on the Island), *cellae in Afrodisia, balneum in Cerateas, pistrinum ubi supra, propina ubi supra, hortum Maronis, hortum ubi supra*. There is also listed, *sub civitatem Antiochiam*, a *possessio Sybilles, donata Augusto*, which seems to have produced *charta, aromata, nardinum*, and *balsamum*. *Cerateas* is evidently the Kerateion at the southern end of the city. The location of *Afrodisia* is not known.

of the hospices which the church maintained in Constantinople for
the accommodation of strangers visiting the capital.[59] Paul seemed to
have excellent personal qualifications for the post, and in addition
he had valuable knowledge of the situation since he had been stationed in Antioch for two years during the patriarchate of Severus,
and had been a stubborn opponent of the Monophysites.[60] Inevitably
he had enemies, and his monophysite opponents called him "the Jew."
On his appointment, Paul immediately organized a vigorous persecution of the Monophysites all through the *Oriens*.[61] According to monophysite sources, Paul's campaign was brutal in the extreme. Some
of the stories can perhaps be discounted, but it does seem certain that
Paul's discharge of his difficult duties eventually caused real dissatisfaction in Constantinople, and by A.D. 521 he realized that it would be
better for him to resign before grave charges were brought against
him.[62]

Of Paul's activities in Antioch itself we have no specific information,
but it is safe to suppose that the Monophysites there were identified
and dealt with no less vigorously than they were elsewhere in Syria;
and no doubt those of the leaders who had not already fled were sent
into exile. This was the beginning of a period during which adherents
of the monophysite doctrine must have been forced by continuing
persecution to leave Antioch. Some of them doubtless returned when
conditions seemed favorable, while others remained in exile or carried
on their work elsewhere; we hear, for example, of convents founded
at Constantinople by women of monophysite views who had been forced
to flee from Antioch, and took their exile as an occasion to enter the
religious life.[63]

[59] Malalas 411.19-20, with additions in the Church Slavonic version, p. 121; Theophanes a. 6011, p. 165.17-18 ed. De Boor. It seems to have been not uncommon for a
xenodochos to achieve a high post; see *La géographie ecclésiastique de l'empire byzantin.
Iere partie, Le siège de Constantinople et le patriarcat oecuménique. Tome 3, Les églises
et les monastères*, par R. Janin (Paris 1953) 564.
[60] Zachariah of Mitylene *Chronicle* 8.1 and 6; Evagrius *Hist. eccl.* 4.4; John of Nikiu
Chronicle 90.14, p. 134 transl. Charles. Paul's qualifications for the appointment are
described in laudatory terms in two reports sent to Rome by the papal envoys to Constantinople (*Collectio Avellana*, Nos. 216-217). Cf. L. Duchesne, *L'église au VIe siècle*
(Paris 1925) 66-67.
[61] This is described by Vasiliev, *Justin the First* 235-236; cf. Michael the Syrian 2.173-
174 transl. Chabot.
[62] Paul's unsatisfactory conduct, and his decision to resign, are described in letters
of the Emperor Justin and of the Patriarch Epiphanius addressed to Pope Hormisdas
in May A.D. 521 (*Collectio Avellana*, Nos. 241-242).
[63] John of Ephesus 3.19, p. 198 transl. Payne Smith.

The hunting out of the Monophysites was accompanied by continued hostilities between the circus factions. The Olympic Games of
Antioch were discontinued in A.D. 520, and the ancient report (whether
expressly or by chance) connects the suppression of the games with
the fighting between the Blues and the Greens in Antioch.[64] There
had been financial difficulties in the past, and the government had had
to take over the support of the games, through the official participation
of the *comes Orientis* and the *consularis Syriae*, when it became impossible for private persons in Antioch to bear the expense;[65] at the
same time, however, the festival was of great economic importance
because of the throngs of visitors that it attracted to the city, and it also
carried great prestige because of its antiquity. It would seem as though
only very serious reasons would cause the abandonment of such a
famous and characteristic festival. There was, however, a great increase
in the factional disorders at this time, and the authorities in both
Antioch and Constantinople could not fail to be apprehensive about
the opportunity for further rioting provided by the Olympic Games
of A.D. 520—which would be the first regularly scheduled celebration
of the festival following the accession of Justin. The memory of the
great riot of A.D. 507 at Antioch, which had started at an Olympic
festival, was still fresh, and Calliopas, the famous charioteer who had
led that riot, had now come out of retirement and resumed his career
at Constantinople.[66] There was a very serious riot in the hippodrome
at Constantinople in A.D. 520,[67] and if this did not have a direct connection with the suppression of the Olympic festival at Antioch, it
certainly shows how widespread such disorders were. Against such a
background it would seem that the ending of the Olympic Games at
Antioch was decided upon primarily as a measure of public order.[68]
The suppression of the games must have been highly unpopular with
the people at Antioch, and it seems clear that only some very grave
reason could have caused the government to take this step.

The termination of the Olympic festival did not put an end to the
factional disorders, and riots continued in Antioch as they did in all
the other large cities of the Empire. On occasion, however, officials
could be found who were capable of dealing effectively with the situation. One such was the *comes Orientis* Theodotus, who had such success

---

[64] Malalas 417.5-8, cf. the Church Slavonic version, pp. 123-124.
[65] See above, Ch. 17, nn. 35-36.
[66] Vasiliev, *Justin the First* 120.   [67] *Ibid.*, 110-111.
[68] On the considerations which affected the suppression of the games, see Vasiliev,
Justin the First 119.

in dealing with the rioters in Antioch that in A.D. 522/3 he was promoted to be prefect of the city at Constantinople, where he continued to deal successfully with the factions.[69] He was succeeded at Antioch by Ephraemius of Amida (later to become Patriarch of Antioch), who opposed the Blues with such vigor that they subsided temporarily; and the cessation of the disorders in both Constantinople and Antioch brought peace in the other cities. As a precaution against further disorders, the government forbade theatrical shows and performances by dancers, since experience had shown that such occasions could be the beginnings of riots.[70]

The Patriarch Paul died, apparently, soon after his resignation in A.D. 521.[71] He was succeeded by Euphrasius of Jerusalem, who continued the vigorous campaign for the suppression of the Monophysites, and the five years of his tenure (A.D. 521-526) were, as we have seen, a continued period of unrest and disorder for the people of Antioch. During this time, in A.D. 523, there was also an alarm in Antioch when the Saracen chief al-Mundhir, in the service of Persia, made a devastating raid as far as the territories of Apamea and Antioch and carried off many captives.[72]

5. The Fire of a.d. 525 and the Earthquake of a.d. 526

The closing years of Justin's reign brought the two major catastrophes that marked the beginning of the physical decline of Antioch—a decline that continued throughout the sixth century and paved the way for the Persian and Moslem occupations of Syria in the seventh century. The earthquakes that occurred at Antioch were apparently a part of a series of seismic disturbances that were especially frequent in this part of the

[69] Malalas 416.3ff.; cf. Downey, *Comites Orientis* 14.
[70] Malalas 416.20—417.4; cf. Stein, *Hist.* 2.240-241. On the theaters as centers for political demonstrations, see the account of the riot of A.D. 387 at Antioch, above, Ch. 15, §2. On the career of Ephraemius, see J. Lebon, "Ephrem d'Amid patriarche d'Antioche, 526-544," *Mélanges d'histoire offerts à Charles Moeller* (Louvain—Paris 1914) 1.197-214 (Université de Louvain, Recueil de Travaux publiés par les Membres des Conférences d'Histoire et de Philologie, fas. 40); G. Downey, "Ephraemius, Patriarch of Antioch," *Church History* 7 (1938) 364-370, with a correction concerning his *cursus honorum* by Stein, *Hist.* 2.241, n. 1; Jülicher, "Ephraemios," *RE* 6.17; Karalevskij, "Antioche," 577; Fliche-Martin, *Hist. de l'église* 4.431. A record of work performed by Ephraemius in repairing bridges and maintaining the important road between Antioch and Seleucia Pieria is preserved in an inscription dated in November A.D. 524 (*IGLS* 1142).
[71] Evagrius *Hist. eccl.* 4.4 Malalas (415.22) and John of Nikiu (*Chronicle* 90.14, p. 134 transl. Charles) are mistaken in saying that Paul died in office (for the evidence for his resignation, see above, n. 62), and their accounts are evidently to be taken to mean that Paul died soon after his resignation.
[72] Zachariah of Mitylene *Chronicle* 8.5; cf. Vasiliev, *Justin the First* 277.

world at this period. Both Antioch and Constantinople seem to have
been located in "earthquake belts," which were subject from time to
time to special disorders;[73] and in addition, several of the other great
cities in the eastern part of the Empire were visited by floods or famines.[74]
In the case of Antioch, the disasters under Justin, a fire in A.D. 525 and
an earthquake in A.D. 526, were quickly followed in Justinian's reign
by another earthquake in A.D. 528 and the capture and sack of the city
by the Persians in A.D. 540; and after A.D. 540 it is evident that the city
was smaller than previously and had lost much of its former importance.

The first of these disasters, the great fire of October A.D. 525, was
taken (especially in later times) to be an omen of the coming wrath
of God against the city.[75] The fire burned the area from the Martyrion
of St. Stephen to the *praetorium* of the *magister militum*, which seems
to have been near the Forum of Valens.[76] According to one account,
the fire was started by lightning; there was also a report that it was

[73] See O. Weismantel, *Die Erdbeben des vorderen Kleinasiens in geschichtlicher
Zeit* (Diss., Marburg 1891) and B. Willis, "Earthquakes in the Holy Land," *Bulletin
of the Seismological Society of America* 18 (1928) 73-103. Among the published catalogues of recorded earthquakes in this part of the world one may consult A. Perrey,
"Mémoire sur les tremblements de terre ressentis dans la péninsule turco-hellénique
et en Syrie," *Acad. roy. de Belgique, Mémoires couronnés et mémoires des savants
étrangers* 23 (1848-1850) 1-73; R. and J. W. Mallet, *The Earthquake Catalogue of the
British Association* (London 1858); F. W. Unger, *Quellen der byz. Kunstgeschichte*
(Vienna 1878) 92-100; Joh. Fried. Jul. Schmidt, *Studien über Vulkane und Erdbeben*
(Leipzig 1881) 2.143-157; E. Oberhummer, list of earthquakes and fires in "Constan-
tinoplis," *RE* 4.1000; J. Dück, "Die Erdbeben von Konstantinopel," *Die Erdbeben-
warte* 3 (1903-04) 121-139, 177-196; W. Capelle, "Erdbebenforschung," *RE* Suppl. 4.356;
G. Downey, "Earthquakes at Constantinople and Vicinity, A.D. 342-1454," *Speculum*
30 (1955) 596-600. For the bibliography of earthquakes, see F. Montessus de Ballore,
Bibliografía general de temblores y terremotos (Santiago de Chile 1915-1919).

[74] The earthquakes and other disasters elsewhere in the Empire at this period are
listed by Stein, *Hist.* 2.241-243 and by Vasiliev, *Justin the First* 349-353.

[75] Accounts of the fire are preserved by Malalas (the version in the Oxford MS,
417.9-19, is supplemented by additional material in the Church Slavonic version, p. 124,
and in the *Chronicle* of John of Nikiu 90.24-25, p. 135 transl. Charles); Evagrius
Hist. eccl. 4.5; Theophanes a. 6018, p. 172.1-11 ed. De Boor. The date is given by
Theophanes. Müller, *Antiq. Antioch.* 118, n. 5, by a miscalculation places the fire in
October A.D. 526, after the earthquake, which took place in May of the same year; but
the date in Theophanes is clear and all the sources indicate that the earthquake preceded the fire. Cf. Stein, *Hist.* 2.242, n. 3. The famous writer Procopius of Gaza composed a monody on Antioch which was a lamentation for the destruction of the city
in either the earthquake of A.D. 526 or that of A.D. 528; see Bekker, *Anecdota graeca*,
I, pp. 125.26, 153, 21, 24, and K. Seitz, *Die Schule von Gaza* (Diss. Heidelberg 1892)
10, 20.

[76] On the location of the *praetorium* of the *magister militum*, see Excursus 11. The
location of the Martyrion of St. Stephen is not known. The *Chronicle* of John of Nikiu
(cited in the preceding note), which appears to be based on a fuller text of Malalas
than is preserved elsewhere, states that the fire also extended "as far as the bath called
Tainâdônhûs and the bath of the Syrian nation." These two baths cannot be identified
from other evidence. The first name suggests something like Adonis.

set by members of the warring factions.[77] Following the great fire, a series of fires broke out in other parts of the city for a period of six months. Some of these were said to have started in the roofs of the buildings. Many buildings were destroyed and there was considerable loss of life; and the magnitude of the damage is indicated by the fact that at the representations of the Patriarch Euphrasius, the emperor granted the city two *centenaria* of gold for the reconstruction of the burned areas.[78]

The earthquake of A.D. 526 happened to occur on the evening of 29 May, the day before Ascension Day, when the city was crowded with visitors who had come to Antioch for the festival.[79] The shocks began at a time when people were for the most part indoors, eating their evening meal, and this coincidence, combined with the influx of strangers, made the loss of life much greater than it otherwise might have been. The figure of 250,000 dead which is given in the sources is by no means impossible.[80] The most distinguished victim was the Patriarch Euphrasius;[81] Bishop Asclepius of Edessa also lost his life.

[77] John of Nikiu *Chronicle* 90.24, p. 135 transl. Charles; Church Slavonic Malalas p. 124.

[78] In the Oxford MS of Malalas it is stated that Ephraemius was patriarch at the time of the fire (417.17), although Malalas later says (423.19) that he was elected patriarch about the time of the death of Justinus on 1 Aug. A.D. 527 (see also Evagrius 4.6, Theophanes a. 6019, p. 173, 20 ed. De Boor). The Church Slavonic version states that Euphrasius was patriarch at the time of the fire (*loc.cit.*), proving that the reference to Ephraemius in the Greek text is the mistake of a scribe or an editor; the names would be liable to confusion because of their similarity, also because it was known that Ephraemius later became patriarch. The *comes Orientis* at the time of the fire was Anatolius, son of Carinus (Malalas 417.9), Ephraemius having apparently retired from this office some time between November A.D. 524 (see above, n. 70) and the time of the fire.

[79] The earthquake is described in detail by Malalas (who was probably present), the long account given in the Oxford MS (419.5—422.8) being supplemented by a number of additional details preserved in the Church Slavonic version, pp. 125-131. The complete date, part of which has been lost from the Oxford MS, is given in the first lines of the Church Slavonic version. Briefer accounts are preserved in Evagrius *Hist. eccl.* 4.5 (with the date), Theophanes a. 6018-6019, pp. 172.11—173.13 ed. De Boor (where part of the date has disappeared), John of Nikiu *Chronicle* 90.26-34, pp. 135-137 transl. Charles. See also, for allusions to the disaster, Procopius *Wars* 2.14.6-7 and *Anec.* 18.41; John Lydus *De mag.* 3.54; Cedrenus 1.640.10-22 Bonn ed. (where the date is given as 3 Oct., probably by confusion with the fire of A.D. 525). For a detailed discussion of the date, cf. L. Hallier, *Texte und Untersuchungen*, 9, pt. 1 (1892) 43-45, 132-135, and F. Haase, "Die Abfassungszeit der Edessenischen Chronik," *O.C.* 7/8 (1918) 93-96. The most detailed modern description of the earthquake is that of Vasiliev, *Justin the First* 345-350.

[80] Malalas gives the figure 250,000 (420.6, cf. Church Slavonic version, 128), while Procopius, who was in Syria on a number of occasions, and must certainly have visited Antioch not very long after the event, gives the number as 300,000 (*Wars* 2.14.6). Stein (*Hist.* 2.242) writes that the disaster "coûta la vie à cinquante mille personnes ou même davantage." I am unable to determine what the basis for this figure might be.

[81] According to Evagrius 4.5 and Theophanes a. 6019, p. 172.30-31 ed. De Boor, the

The magnitude of the earthquake is indicated by the fact that it was reckoned among the major disasters that had visited the city, and was, in the local records, numbered fifth among the great catastrophes, the second, third and fourth having been the earthquakes which occurred in A.D. 37, 115 and in the reign of Leo I, while that of A.D. 528 was to be counted as the sixth.[82]

According to the accounts, the disaster destroyed practically the whole city, leaving standing only the buildings along the slope of Mount Silpius.[83] As often happened on such occasions, the earth shocks started fires, and people buried beneath the ruins were burned to death, while sparks of fire filled the air. The foundations of buildings, weakened by both the earthquake and the fire, collapsed, and walls which had been left standing, later fell and killed people. Rain followed the earthquake and it was said that burning rain fell.

The Great Church built by Constantine the Great stood alone for several days[84] when everything else had fallen, and then caught fire and burned to the ground. The Church of the Archangel Michael built by the Emperor Zeno, as well as the Church of the Virgin Mary, likewise remained undamaged by the earthquake, but later burned. The Church of the Holy Prophets and the Church of St. Zacharias collapsed after remaining standing for some time.

On Ascension Day, the day following the initial shocks, the survivors gathered in the Church of the Kerateion for a service of intercession.[85]

---

patriarch was buried under debris. Marcellinus comes *ad ann.* 526 (Mommsen, *Chron. min.* 2.102) relates more specifically that Euphrasius was struck by the obelisk in the circus when it fell, and was buried under it. This is plausible since during an earthquake people naturally took refuge in open spaces such as the circus. Zachariah of Mitylene *Chronicle* 8.4 relates that the patriarch was killed when he fell into a boiling cauldron of wax (cf. Vasiliev *Justin the First* 240, n. 190). The death of Asclepius is recorded by Michael the Syrian 2.181-182 transl. Chabot.

[82] Malalas 243.12 (earthquake of A.D. 37), 275.4 (A.D. 115), 369.6 (reign of Leo I), 442.19 (A.D. 528). Because of the paucity of Malalas' information concerning the Seleucid period, it is not clear which earthquake was regarded as number one in this series (see Downey, "Seleucid Chronology" 107, n. 1). The other earthquakes at Antioch, such as that of A.D. 341, evidently were not considered sufficiently severe to be reckoned in the numbered series of major disasters (see the list of earthquakes below in the Index). In Malalas' chronicle we find numbered series of earthquakes at other cities in the imperial period (see Downey, *loc.cit.*, and the Chronology below, 735-738).

[83] Most of the description of the damage reproduced here is taken from the account of Malalas, who was (as has been mentioned) probably an eye-witness. While Malalas' description included a certain amount of picturesque detail, it also seems quite accurate on certain characteristic features of earthquakes.

[84] The Oxford MS gives the figure seven days (according to Bury's collation of the MS printed in *B.Z.* 6 [1897] 229; the figure "two days" printed in the Bonn text is an error of transcription), while in the Church Slavonic version (p. 127) the number is five.

[85] This detail is preserved only in the account of John of Nikiu *Chronicle* 90.30,

This church may have been used for the service because it probably stood in the southern outskirts of the city, and may have survived when the churches in the city proper were destroyed or damaged.

Some of the survivors of the earthquake, when they fled from the city, carrying what they could of their goods, were robbed by country people, who killed any who refused to surrender their possessions. The robbers also entered the city and pillaged the ruins, finding chests of silver plate and gold and silver coins scattered about.[86] They also robbed the corpses, especially those of women who had been wearing jewelry. However, it was observed that the thieves later received divine punishment for their acts, in the form of death and sickness. One man whose example was recorded was a *silentiarius* named Thomas the Hebrew. He had escaped the earthquake without harm, and then with his servants stationed himself three miles outside the city, at the place called the Gate of St. Julian,[87] where he and his people despoiled everyone who passed by. He did this for four days and accumulated a great deal of loot; and then, although healthy, he suddenly collapsed, by divine retribution, and died, and everything that he had collected was dispersed.

There were the usual stories of miraculous escapes. Pregnant women were buried under the ruins for twenty-one days and survived. Some of them gave birth underneath the debris and both mothers and children lived.

Three days after the disaster, on Sunday, a vision of the Holy Cross appeared over the northern part of the city, and remained visible for an hour, while the people wept and prayed. It was apparently as a result of this appearance that the northern part of Mount Silpius, over which the vision had been seen, was renamed Mount Staurin (Greek *staurin* being the colloquial form of the word for "cross").[88]

---

p. 136 transl. Charles, but his description is so plainly drawn from that of Malalas that it seems reasonably clear that this information existed in Malalas' account and was lost in the process of abbreviation.

[86] It is a curious commentary on this part of Malalas' description that the archaeological excavations produced very large numbers of the coins of Justin I and Justinian, and that the coins of Justin I were especially plentiful. Many of these coins of Justin were presumably lost in the earthquake, while those of Justinian were probably lost when the Persians sacked the city in A.D. 540 (see below). On the quantity of the coins found see the observation of Dorothy B. Waagé in her catalogue of coins, *Antioch-on-the-Orontes* 4, pt. 2, p. 153, note on No. 2112.

[87] This is very likely associated with the Church of St. Julian outside of Antioch which is mentioned in connection with the burial of the relics of St. Marinus in A.D. 529 or 530; see below, Excursus 17.

[88] The change in the name of part of the mountain is not mentioned in the preserved

Both Seleucia Pieria and Daphne, and a considerable area around Daphne, were completely ruined by the earthquake.[89]

When he heard of the disaster, the emperor was deeply grieved because he was familiar with Antioch, having been stationed there during his military career, before becoming emperor. The emperor and the court put on mourning and public entertainments in Constantinople were suspended. On Pentecost the emperor walked on foot to St. Sophia dressed in mourning.

As was done whenever possible on such an occasion, the imperial government sent financial aid for the relief of the victims and the rebuilding of the city.[90] Justin's first measure was to order the *comes* Carinus to proceed to the city, with five *centenaria* of gold, and begin excavating in a search for possible survivors, and clearing the site; and Carinus was to report on what further assistance was needed. Justin also sent, with Carinus, the *patricius* Phocas, son of Craterus, and the *patricius* Asterius, a former *referendiarius* and city prefect of Constantinople, putting them in charge of the care of the survivors and of the rebuilding of the city; the bridges, the water system, and the baths were to be restored as soon as possible, the baths being regarded as of special importance for hygienic reasons. It was reported, ultimately, that thirty *centenaria* were given for restoring the city, and ten *centenaria* for rebuilding the churches.[91] The chief local official in charge of the work of restoration was the *comes Orientis* Ephraemius, who was holding this office for the second time when the earthquake occurred.[92] The work of rebuilding was naturally not all carried out immediately, but

account of the vision, but it seems safe to conclude that this was the reason for the adoption of the name, which first appears shortly after this time in Procopius' account of the topography of the city in *Buildings* 2.10.16. Honigmann in his entry "Staurin oros," *RE* 3A.2236, did not know the account of the vision, and so was unable to suggest the origin of the name.

[89] In the Oxford ms of Malalas (421.14-15) it is stated that an area of twenty miles around Daphne was damaged. This would of course include both Seleucia Pieria and Seleucia itself. The Church Slavonic version is more probably correct in saying that the damage extended over an area twenty stadia in length and width around Daphne.

[90] The account of this in the Church Slavonic version (pp. 131-132) preserves a number of details that do not appear in the Oxford ms (422.1-8). For a list of the other cities to which Justinus sent assistance after natural disasters, see Vasiliev, *Justin the First* 376.

[91] Malalas 424.10-13, cf. Church Slavonic version, p. 133.

[92] Malalas 423.19-20 and Theophanes a. 6019, p. 173.20-21 state that Ephraemius was *comes Orientis* at the time of the earthquake and the death of the Patriarch Euphrasius. It is not known how long Ephraemius had been in office when the earthquake occurred. Anatolius was *comes Orientis* at the time of the fire in October A.D. 525 (see above, n. 78). Perhaps Ephraemius had been put back in office because of his notable success in dealing with the factional disorders during his first incumbency.

(as will be seen) some of it extended into the reign of Justinian, and some of the restoration work which followed the earthquake of A.D. 528 (to be described below) was very likely occasioned originally by the earthquake of A.D. 526.[93] However, the city never really recovered from the disaster of A.D. 526, which did grave damage not only to the commercial prosperity of Antioch itself, but (through the inevitable decrease in the activity of Antioch) to the trade of Syria in general.[94] Also this was the beginning of the period when people began to leave Antioch and its vicinity to settle elsewhere in less troubled places. This process continued after the disasters of A.D. 528 and 540, and there was as we shall see a notable exodus from Antioch and Syria after the Arab occupation of Syria in the seventh century. A number of the refugees went to the western part of the Empire, where their presence is clearly attested. At Milan, for example, one finds the cults of St. Babylas and St. Romanus, who were specifically Antiochene saints, and the plan of San Lorenzo clearly reflects that of the great *martyrion* at Seleucia Pieria which was recovered in the excavations. Since St. Babylas and St. Romanus were not commemorated elsewhere in Italy, it seems plain that it must have been refugees from Antioch and Seleucia who introduced these memorials of their homeland in Milan.[95]

One year after the earthquake, on 1 April A.D. 527, Justin conferred the dignity of Augustus on Justinian and so made him co-emperor.[96] Justinian and Theodora, to mark this occasion, made gifts to various cities; and in the case of Antioch it is recorded[97] that they undertook to supply the funds for various buildings, in partial replacement of structures destroyed in the earthquake. Justinian built the Church of the Virgin Mary, opposite the Basilica of Rufinus,[98] and also constructed a Church of SS. Cosmas and Damian near by. He also built a hospice, baths, and cisterns. The Augusta Theodora made a number of gifts in her own name, building the very handsome Church of the Archangel

[93] The archaeological excavations revealed the remains of two important buildings in which the evidence of coins makes it possible to see how these structures were damaged in the earthquake of A.D. 526 and rebuilt; see Levi, *Antioch Mosaic Pavements* 1.257, 311. In the case of another large building, a dated mosaic suggests that a public bath damaged in the earthquakes of A.D. 526 or 528 was not repaired until A.D. 537/8; see Levi, *op.cit.* 1.366-368 (the inscription is published in an improved text in *IGLS* 786).

[94] Cf. Vasiliev, *Justin the First* 360.

[95] See U. Monneret de Villard, "Antiochia e Milano nel VI° secolo," *Orientalia Christiana Periodica* 12 (1946) 374-380.

[96] Malalas 422.9-12; cf. Stein, *Hist.* 2.240.

[97] Malalas 423.1-12.

[98] On this Basilica, see above, Ch. 15, n. 130.

Michael, as well as the Basilica of Anatolius, for which the columns were sent from Constantinople.[99]

Another result of Justinian's advancement affected the position of the circus factions at Antioch, for the two emperors now issued an edict on factional disorders which really put an end to the hostilities, at least for a time, in the major cities, including Antioch.[100]

The death of Euphrasius in the earthquake had brought up once more the problem of the choice of a Patriarch of Antioch, always a difficult one in these years and especially troublesome at the time when it was still necessary to pursue with full vigor the orthodox drive against the Monophysites. Apparently almost a year passed after the death of Euphrasius with no successor chosen, and finally, some time after the promotion of Justinian in April A.D. 527, and before the death of Justin in August, it was at length determined that the best candidate was Ephraemius the *comes Orientis*. He was a layman, but he had evidently shown conspicuous ability in his civil post, and presumably he had the confidence of the orthodox party at Antioch. It is recorded that he was at first unwilling to accept the office, which is not surprising; but he was duly elected and presumably went through the successive necessary ordinations as promptly as possible, in a process that was not unparalleled on similar occasions.[101] His successor as *comes Orientis* was Zachariah of Tyre. After Zachariah's appointment, he went to Constantinople, taking with him the bishop of Amida, to ask Justin and Justinian for further help for the city, which was granted.[102]

Later in the summer, on 1 August, Justin died, and Justinian became sole emperor.[103] The history of Antioch during the reign of Justin had not been a tranquil or prosperous one. Yet the city at this period did not lose consciousness of its ancient dignity and prestige. It may even have made a special effort to recall its ancient history by the issuing of coins showing the famous Tyche of Antioch in a distyle shrine, which appear in Justin's reign.[104]

[99] On the Basilica of Anatolius and its history, see above, Ch. 16, n. 21.
[100] Malalas 422.15-21; Stein, "Iustinus," *RE* 10.1319; idem, *Hist.* 2.240.
[101] Malalas 423.19ff.; Evagrius *Hist. eccl.* 4.6; cf. Stein, *Hist.* 2.242 and 638, n. 1, who puts Ephraemius' ordination in April or May. For examples of the appointment to high ecclesiastical offices of men who had previously been laymen, see J. Maspero, *Histoire des patriarches d'Alexandrie* (Paris 1923) 256-257. It is not clear whether there may have been any connection between the advancement of Justinian to Augustus and the choice of Ephraemius as patriarch.
[102] Malalas 424.2-13.
[103] Stein, *Hist.* 2.272-273.
[104] See the catalogue of coins by Dorothy B. Waagé *Antioch-on-the-Orontes* 4, pt. 2, pp. 149-150. One detail of the history of Antioch during the reign of Justin, which it

6. The Beginning of the Reign of Justinian; Ephraemius and the Campaign against the Monophysites; The Earthquake of A.D. 528; Local Events and the Resumption of the Persian War

The opening of the reign of Justinian meant for the history of Antioch a continuation of the momentous events of the reign of Justin, culminating, after a few years, in the sack of the city by the Persians in A.D. 540, which brought the real greatness of Antioch to a close.

Ephraemius inaugurated his patriarchate (A.D. 527-545) by continuing the campaign to stamp out the Monophysites, a task which was now complicated by the fact that the Empress Theodora favored and protected the Monophysites, in spite of Justinian's orthodoxy.[105] Ephraemius carried out his duties with vigor, and, according to his theological enemies, with cruelty.[106] In A.D. 531 the Monophysites in Antioch still had sufficient strength and leadership to riot and attack the *patriarcheion*, throwing stones and shouting insults, when a particularly strong imperial edict, prescribing exile for heretics, reached Antioch. The guards of the *patriarcheion*, led by the *comes Orientis* (who had perhaps been expecting trouble) made a sortie and drove off the mob and killed many of them.[107] It is a question whether the popular reaction to the edict may not have been motivated in part by the rigor with which Ephraemius had been carrying out his duties.[108] In the

---

is difficult to fit into the narrative, is the record of the visit to the city of a female giant from Cilicia, taller by a cubit than the average man, who went from city to city collecting contributions from the shops (Malalas 412.4-9).

[105] On the history of Monophysitism at this period, see J. Lebon, *Le Monophysisme sévérien. Étude historique, littéraire et théologique sur la résistance monophysite au Concile de Chalcedoine jusqu'à la constitution de l'église jacobite* (Louvain 1909. Universitas Catholica Louvanensis, Dissertationes, ser. 2, tome 4) 73ff. The career of Ephraemius as patriarch of Antioch is described by the same scholar, "Ephrem d'Amid patriarche d'Antioche, 526-544," *Mélanges d'histoire offerts à Charles Moeller* (Louvain—Paris 1914) 1.197-214 (Université de Louvain, Recueil de Travaux publiés par les membres des Conférences d'Histoire et de Philologie, fasc. 40). See also Downey, "Ephraemius, Patriarch of Antioch," *Church History* 7 (1938) 364-370, and Vasiliev *Justin the First* 123-124, 240-241. Information concerning Ephraemius' literary activity is preserved by Photius, *Bibl.*, codd. 228-229, *PG* 103.957-1024.

[106] Theophanes a. 6019, p. 173.22-23 ed. De Boor speaks of Ephraemius' "holy zeal." John of Ephesus calls him "a worse persecutor than either Paul or Euphrasius" (1.41, p. 79 transl. Payne Smith). Zachariah of Mitylene, who praises Ephraemius (*Chron.* 8.4), also describes the severity of his dealings with the Monophysites (10.1).

[107] Malalas 468.1-9. The name of the *comes Orientis* is not preserved, at least in the Oxford MS of Malalas. It is not clear whether it was Patricius the Armenian, who had been made *comes Orientis* in October, A.D. 527, soon after Justinian became sole emperor (Malalas 425.10ff., Theophanes a. 6020, p. 174.11-14 ed. De Boor). There appears to be no record preserved of any of Patricius' activities at Antioch.

[108] This is the interpretation of Stein, *Hist.* 2.377.

winter of A.D. 536/7 Ephraemius made a special tour of Syria (especially the region east of Beroea) in a final effort to stamp out Monophysitism; and the severity with which he carried out his duties on this visitation made a great impression, though the results that he seems to have achieved appear to be somewhat doubtful.[109]

The seismic disturbance which had caused the great earthquake of May A.D. 526 had not come to its end. The original earthquake was followed by a series of earth shocks that lasted for a year and a half,[110] and these culminated in a second major earthquake—the sixth in the numbered series of disasters which had visited Antioch—which occurred on 29 November A.D. 528, early in the day.[111] The shocks lasted for an hour, and were said to be accompanied by supernatural noises from the upper air (probably thunder). The preserved accounts do not mention any buildings specifically, but they state that all the buildings in the city, and the walls, fell and that structures which had survived the previous earthquake now fell. Any rebuilding undertaken after A.D. 526 was also presumably destroyed. Damage extended beyond the city itself, and Laodicea and Seleucia Pieria must have been affected since they later received government grants when assistance for rebuilding such as was also given to Antioch. It was recorded that 4,870

[109] Zachariah of Mitylene *Chronicle* 10.1; Michael the Syrian 2.185-189, 206; cf. Lebon, "Ephrem d'Amid" (cited above, n. 105) 200-201.

[110] Malalas 421.12-14.

[111] The principal account of this earthquake is that of Theophanes a. 6021, p. 177.22—178.7 ed. De Boor. The account preserved in the Oxford MS of Malalas (442.18—443.7; the Church Slavonic version is not available at this point) is much less detailed and is strikingly different from the full and vivid description of the earthquake of A.D. 526. Malalas had evidently left Antioch and gone to live at Constantinople after the earthquake of A.D. 526, and so no longer had direct access to local records. The edition of Malalas' chronicle which Evagrius used ended with the earthquake of A.D. 526 (Evag. *Hist. eccl.* 4.5); on the composition of this portion of the chronicle, see J. B. Bury in *Classical Review* 11 (1897) 209-212, and Wolf, "Ioannes Malalas," *RE* 9.1796-1797. There are several verbal resemblances between Malalas' account and Theophanes' which might be taken to mean that Theophanes knew the passage in Malalas, and used another source or sources in addition. The event is mentioned very briefly by Evagrius *Hist. eccl.* 4.6. The disaster is dated by Theophanes, p. 177.22-24, on 29 November in the seventh indiction (1 September A.D. 528—31 August A.D. 529); cf. the accounts of Georgius Monachus 2.643.4ff. ed. De Boor; Cedrenus 1.646.5-21 Bonn; Leo Grammaticus 126.1-5 Bonn; and Nicephorus 17.3 = *PG* 147.225. The date is discussed by L. Hallier in *Texte und Untersuchungen* 9, pt. 1 (1892) 43-45, 133-135, and by F. Haase, "Die Abfassungszeit der Edessenischen Chronik," *O.C.* 7/8 (1918) 93-96. F. Martroye attempted to show that the disaster occurred in A.D. 529, instead of in A.D. 528, the date accepted by all other scholars (*Bull. de la Soc. nat. des antiquaires de France*, 1910, p. 292-295). His attempt was unsuccessful because he seems to have misunderstood the system of reckoning the indictions and thus placed the seventh indiction in the current cycle in A.D. 529/30 instead of in A.D. 528/9. He also overlooked Hallier's discussion of the date.

people were killed.[112] Even allowing for the fact that the earlier earthquake, with its much greater loss of life, had occurred when the city
was crowded for Ascension Day, the number of the dead in A.D. 528
suggests that the population of the city had diminished since the earlier
disaster.

The leader of the people on this occasion was again Ephraemius,
who made the report of the disaster to the emperor. It seemed as
though Antioch really were being visited by the wrath of God in the
form of these two overwhelming earthquakes, and it is not surprising
to read that some of the survivors fled to other cities, or went to live
in huts on the mountains around Antioch. To add to the distress, the
winter that followed the earthquake was exceptionally severe and the
people who remained in Antioch made constant supplication to God
for pardon, weeping and throwing themselves headlong in the snow.
Apparently the shocks continued, as they had after the earthquake of
A.D. 526, until a certain pious man had a dream that commanded him
to tell the survivors to inscribe over their doors the phrase "Christ is
with us; stand."[113] This was done, and the earthquake tremors stopped.

Justinian and Theodora again sent gifts for the rebuilding of the
city, as well as for the relief of Laodicea and Seleucia Pieria, and as a
measure of special assistance Antioch was freed from the payment
of taxes for three years.[114] As a propitiatory gesture the name of Antioch was changed to Theoupolis, "City of God."[115] It was said locally
that the change was made by command of a holy man named Symeon
(probably not St. Symeon Stylites the Younger, who was a child at
this time, though the command may later have been associated with
his name),[116] and also as the result of the discovery, in Antioch itself,

[112] This is the figure given by Theophanes a. 6021, p. 177.31-32 ed. De Boor. In the
chronicle of Malalas it is stated that "nearly five thousand died" (443.2-3). Michael the
Syrian states that 4,770 were killed, 2.194 transl. Chabot. With such a loss of life it
would be possible to make a more or less specific count, whereas any exact estimate
would have been impossible in the greater disaster of A.D. 526.

[113] On the use of such phrases, especially over doors and windows of houses, see L.
Jalabert and R. Mouterde, "Inscriptions grecques chrétiennes," *DACL* 7.687-688. The
phrase is not literally scriptural, but it is an expression of a thought which is common
in the New Testament, e.g. in Matt. 28:20.

[114] Malalas 443.22ff.

[115] The name is used on coins of Antioch (W. Wroth, *Catalogue of the Imperial
Byzantine Coins in the British Museum* [London 1908] 1.53ff.; *Antioch* 4, pt. 2, pp.
151-153, with the note on no. 2112 in Mrs. Waagé's catalogue) and occasionally in
literature, but it does not wholly supplant the original name in literary use. It could
have been suggested by such passages as LXX Psalms 45.5, 47,1 and 9, 86.3. On the
change of name, see Honigmann, "Syria," 1713-1714, and the same scholar's article,
"Theoupolis," *RE* 6A.257.

[116] In the Oxford MS of Malalas it is stated that the change was made at the com-

of a written "oracle" which said, "And thou, wretched city, shalt not be called by the name of Antiochus." The people welcomed the change and it was hoped that the new name would place the city under the protection of the deity in a special way.[117]

Life in Antioch in these years was also very much concerned with the resumption of hostilities in the Persian war, for Antioch was a military headquarters and communications center of great importance when campaigns were in progress on the eastern frontier. The Persian war of Anastasius had been terminated by a truce in A.D. 505, to last for seven years. The truce had never been renewed, so that after it ended a state of war continued in theory, though hostilities were not renewed for some time, and it was not until A.D. 528, the year of the second great earthquake at Antioch, that fighting broke out again.[118] We hear of a *comes Orientis* named Cerycus who was engaged in the fighting at about this time and was miraculously preserved in battle by a hair shirt that had been given to him by the famous St. Theodosius when he made a pilgrimage to Jerusalem.[119] In March of A.D. 529 the Arabs of al-Mundhir, the famous chief who was in the Persian service, made a swift raid that took them as far as the territory of Antioch. They burned property and killed numbers of people, and retreated with their captives and loot before the Roman troops could reach them.[120] The general Belisarius was appointed *magister militum*, with headquarters in Antioch, to succeed Hypatius, who had not been able to deal with the raid; and in the middle of May the emperor's special envoy Hermogenes reached Antioch, en route to attempt negotiations (which eventually proved fruitless) with the Persians.[121]

mand of "St. Symeon the Thaumatourgos," but as J. B. Bury points out in his collation of the Oxford MS (*B.Z.* 6 [1897] 229), the word Symeon alone is original in the MS, the epithets being written by a second hand and over an erasure. On the connection of St. Symeon Stylites with Antioch, see further below. The name Symeon was a very common one at this time because of the fame of the elder Symeon Stylites.

[117] Malalas 443.16-22. This passage contains a reference to *acta urbis* which suggests that Malalas was not in Antioch at the time of this earthquake, but derived his knowledge of it from the written records.

[118] See Bury, *Later Roman Empire* 2.79-81; Stein, *Hist.* 2.283.

[119] See Theodorus *Life of St. Theodosius* 83.9, in H. Usener, *Der hl. Theodosius* (Leipzig 1890), with Usener's commentary 179-181; *Synaxarium eccl. Const.* (*Propylaeum ad Acta SS Novembris*, ed. H. Delehaye, Brussels 1902) 385.40; J. Haury, *Zur Beurteilung des Geschichtsschreibers Procopius von Caesarea* (Progr., Munich 1896) 29.

[120] Malalas 445.1-7; John of Nikiu *Chronicle* 90.79, pp. 142-143 transl. Charles; Theoph. a. 6021, p. 178.7-15 ed. De Boor; Zachariah of Mitylene *Chronicle* 8.5; cf. Stein, *Hist.* 2.284.

[121] Theophanes a. 6021, p. 178.15-22 ed. De Boor. A decree of Justinian (*Nov.* 155), dated 1 Feb. A.D. 533, which is addressed to the General Belisarius shows that the gen-

In the same year, A.D. 529, there was a renewal in Antioch of factional troubles, which it had not been possible to suppress completely by the severe measures of A.D. 527.[122] The outbreak in the theater at Antioch at this time was so severe that the emperor issued a decree forbidding permanently the performance of any theatrical spectacles at Antioch.[123] (This decree was eventually relaxed, for we hear that performances were again held in A.D. 531.) The disorders in Antioch occurred at about the same time as the revolt of the Samaritans in Palestine, which proved extremely difficult to put down. After an initial failure on the part of the imperial forces, a new general, Irenaeus of Antioch, was sent and he succeeded in defeating the rebels.[124]

About this time, in A.D. 529 or 530, Justinian presented to the people of Antioch one of his own robes, ornamented with precious stones. It is recorded that this was spread out in the Church of Cassianus, and its presentation suggests that the garment had acquired healing powers, and so was put in a place where it would be accessible to the people.[125] Apparently at about the same time the emperor presented an annual income of 40,000 *nomismata* to the hospice at Antioch,[126] which was maintained by the church as a safe and respectable place in which poor visitors to the city could find lodging. Also at this period the remains of St. Marinus, who had been martyred at Anazarbus in the time of Justinian, were discovered outside Gindarus and were brought to Antioch, where they were buried outside the city in the Church of St. Julian.[127]

---

eral and the patriarch of Antioch, Ephraemius, were instructed to see that justice was done to a female minor in the city, who had sent to the emperor a complaint that her mother was not discharging properly her duties as guardian, and was not rendering satisfactory accountings of her financial responsibilities. This document suggests that during the troubled period of the Persian wars the routine administration of justice had ceased to function normally in Antioch, and that it was necessary for the emperor to call upon such officials as the general and the patriarch for the redress of what seems to have been a serious wrong.

[122] See above, n. 100.
[123] Malalas 448.20—449.2; cf. Stein, *Hist.* 2.449, with n. 3.
[124] Malalas 447.19-20; on the rebellion see Stein, *Hist.* 2.287-288.
[125] Malalas 450.16-18. This church does not appear to be known otherwise, and the origin of its name is not certain. There were a number of saints named Cassianus for whom it might have been named, but it does not appear that any of them had a particular connection with Antioch. Procopius (*Buildings* 1.7.15-16) describes a tunic of the emperor preserved in the Great Palace at Constantinople which had acquired healing powers through having been saturated with holy oil through the miraculous action of the relics of the Forty Martyrs of Melitene.
[126] Malalas 452.1-3.
[127] Malalas 452.4-12. This is very likely associated with the Gate of St. Julian which is mentioned in the account of the robberies of the *silentiarius* following the earthquake of A.D. 526; see Excursus 17.

Hostilities in the Persian war had continued, with annual campaigns, and in A.D. 531 a group of Christians who had been captured by the Arabs sent a message to the Patriarch Ephraemius begging him to raise money for their ransom. The captors allowed sixty days for the money to be raised. When the petition was read in Antioch, the people, led by the patriarch, the clergy, and the civil officials, took what they could of their own belongings to the treasuries of the various churches. Later there was a general public meeting and the people of the city placed their contributions on a carpet which had been spread on the ground. The ransom was dispatched and the captives were freed.[128]

In the spring of the same year there was a raid into Syria by the Persians which reached Gabboula and seemed to threaten Antioch. The defenses of the city must have been very weak, for at the news of the Persians' approach the people of Antioch fled to the coast of the Mediterranean.[129] Later in the year the emperor's special commissioner Constantiniolus passed through Antioch on his way to make an investigation of the defeats which the Roman troops had been suffering.[130] Another official, Demosthenes, visited Antioch en route to Osrhoene, where he was to build store-houses for grain for the use of the army.[131] In December of the same year a raiding party of Huns, who were in alliance with the Persians, made a raid through the Caspian Gates and penetrated deep into Roman territory, getting as far as Cilicia Secunda and Cyrrhestica, and seeming to threaten Antioch. They were pursued by the Roman general Dorotheus who succeeded in recovering some of the booty which they were carrying off.[132]

The theaters in Antioch, which had been closed "permanently" in A.D. 529, must have been allowed to re-open, for in A.D. 531 a fire in the theater is recorded.[133] There was also, in A.D. 531, a riot, already described,[134] caused by the publication of a stringent law concerning heretics. Two other episodes at about this time are mentioned in Malalas' chronicle. One is the publication in Antioch, where they were inscribed in Greek on wooden tablets, of laws restricting the amount

[128] Malalas 460.10—461.7.
[129] Malalas 462.21—463.1. On the episode see Stein, *Hist.* 2.292.
[130] Malalas 465.14-16. On the circumstances see Stein, *Hist.* 2.292-293.
[131] Malalas 467.19-22.
[132] Malalas 472.15ff.; cf. Stein, *Hist.* 2.293.
[133] Malalas 467.15-18, 471.1-3. It is worth noting that Chilmead in his Latin translation reprinted in the Bonn edition of Malalas failed to understand the latter passage because of his unfamiliarity with the various meanings of χρηματίζω. Cf. Müller *Antiq. Antioch.* 131, n. 24.
[134] Above, §4.

of money which could be spent in litigation.[135] The other is an earthquake, which apparently occurred between A.D. 531 and 534, which is
described as "terrible but harmless," meaning presumably that it was
one of the occasional tremors which are not uncommon in that part
of the world, which actually do no damage.[136]

During all of this period there was activity in the rebuilding of the
city. The Patriarch Ephraemius rebuilt the great octagonal church of
Constantine the Great, with the four *triclinia* which were attached to
it, and when the church was ready to be dedicated, in A.D. 537/8 (the
year following his famous tour of Syria for the suppression of the
Monophysites[137]), he held a synod of 132 bishops, all of whom in writing reaffirmed the faith of the Council of Chalcedon and anathematized
Severus of Antioch.[138] The excavations have recovered evidence of
other rebuilding operations which were carried out at the same time,[139]
and it is not surprising to find that rebuilding was going on as long
as this after the earthquake. One of the structures that was not restored
until A.D. 537/8 was the large and important bath, designated as Bath F,
which stood on the main street.[140]

7. THE PERSIAN INVASION AND THE CAPTURE AND SACK OF ANTIOCH IN A.D. 540

One of the last major events in the history of ancient Antioch is also,
thanks to Procopius' detailed and vivid account of it, one of the best
known episodes in the city's life. The capture and sack of Antioch by
the Persians in June A.D. 540,[141] was not only an almost unbelievable
disaster in itself, but also one of the famous events in a reign that was
notable for both its successes and its reverses. The capture and destruction of one of the three great cities of the eastern part of the Empire,
and the principal city of Syria, matched in a sense the siege and recovery

[135] Malalas 470.19—471.1. This law was promulgated in June, A.D. 530; see Stein,
Hist. 2.438.
[136] Malalas 478.16-17. The date is indicated by the reference at 473.5 to the tenth
indiction (A.D. 531/2) and at 478.22 to the twelfth indiction (A.D. 533/4). A "harmless
but terrible" earthquake at Constantinople is mentioned, 488.18-19.
[137] See above, nn. 105-109.
[138] Zachariah of Mitylene *Chronicle* 10.5; Michael the Syrian 2.207 transl. Chabot.
See Lebon, "Ephrem d'Amid" (cited above, n. 105), 201.
[139] See above, n. 93, for the evidence, which includes a building inscription dated
in A.D. 537/8, published in *IGLS* 786. This includes the name of the *comes Orientis*
which has not been completely preserved but may plausibly be restored as Flavius. . .
[140] See *Antioch-on-the-Orontes* 3.8-9, with the inscription cited in the preceding note.
[141] The date is given by Malalas 479.23. This passage is the next to the last reference
to Antioch in the *Chronicle* of Malalas, the final record (485.8-11) being a very brief
notice of the earthquake of A.D. 550/1.

of Naples and Rome, which Procopius also had to describe. Coming
as it did at a time when the Persians were inflicting severe losses on
the inhabitants of Syria and on the Roman forces there, which had
been weakened in order to furnish troops for the campaigns in the
West (the fall of Antioch occurred a few weeks after Belisarius' capture of Ravenna),[142] the sack of Antioch was a resounding calamity in
the career of an emperor many of whose ambitious undertakings were
criticized by a number of his subjects, including Procopius. Following
the two great earthquakes of A.D. 526 and 528, the sack of A.D. 540
could only be regarded—by some at least—as a further and very impressive omen of divine disfavor.[143]

In the case of Antioch and Syria there was also a special local significance, in that this was just the time when the Monophysites, under
the energetic leadership of Jacob Baradaeus—and with the support of
the Empress Theodora—were gathering renewed strength and were
organizing themselves into what amounted to an independent church,
totally detached from official orthodoxy.[144] The separatist movement
in religion which was thus gathering strength was aided by the local
oriental patriotism centered about the Syriac language—the principal
or only tongue of many people in Syria, including Antioch itself—and
Syriac literature, as these were consciously set in opposition to the
Greek language associated with the central imperial government and
the orthodox hierarchy. At what precise point in the development of
this religious and political movement the Persian march through Syria
came, it is not possible to say. It does seem plain, in any case, that the
shocking defeat of the Roman army, and the disappearance, in its
ancient form, of the great city of Antioch, could only increase the
local feelings throughout Syria of resentment against the central government. The magnitude of the calamity was emphasized when (as we
shall see) the city had to be rebuilt on a much smaller scale than it
had formerly been. It is here that one can see some of the reasons for
the growth of the sentiment that in the succeeding century caused the
people of Syria—like those of Egypt whose experience had been similar
—to welcome first the Persian and then the Moslem invaders as better
masters than the hated and distrusted Constantinople government.[145]

[142] See Stein, *Hist.* 2.310, 368.
[143] Cf. Procopius *Wars* 2.14.5-7.
[144] See Stein, *Hist.* 2.622-628.
[145] See E. L. Woodward, *Christianity and Nationalism in the Later Roman Empire*
(London 1916) 41-66, and Stein, *Hist.* 2.161-163, 389.

How much of all this may have been in Procopius' mind, we cannot in the circumstances be sure; but some of it must have been quite plain to students of contemporary affairs, and Procopius himself, when he came to describe the sack of the city, must certainly have looked upon this task as more than simply an unusual opportunity for writing a brilliant passage on a complex and tragic episode that involved the military, the civil, and the ecclesiastical authorities. At the same time it is curious—but not at all surprising—to find that in writing this account Procopius considered it desirable to minimize certain short-comings on the Roman side, failures which it has been possible to detect both by study of Procopius' account itself and by comparison of it with other preserved records.

Invading Syria in the spring of A.D. 540, the Persians under Chosroes seem to have had a force large enough to overcome the very limited Roman defense forces that had been left when troops were withdrawn for service elsewhere. The Persian expedition, it was plain from its activities, was directed, not at the occupation of Syria or any part of it, but at doing the maximum damage and collecting the maximum loot.[146] After by-passing the first fortified cities that they met, Circesium and Zenobia, the Persians burned Sura and sent one of the local Roman officials to announce the disaster to Justinian.[147] The emperor seems to have realized that the Roman troops in Syria would not be able to stand against a force such as the Persians seemed to have, and in the expectation that the invaders might reach Antioch, Justinian sent Germanus, his cousin or nephew (the relationship is not certain), to inspect the fortifications of the city and make sure that they were in order after the recent earthquakes.[148] Procopius states that Justinian promised to send Germanus in time "a numerous army."[149]

---

[146] The principal source for this campaign is Procopius' account, *Wars* 2.5-8. A detailed study of the military operations and negotiations, and of the light that Pro-copius' account throws on his use of his sources, has been made by G. Downey, "The Persian Campaign in Syria in A.D. 540," *Speculum* 28 (1953) 340-348. The present account condenses parts of this study, and also adds some new considerations. More general descriptions of the campaign, which do not have occasion to deal with all the questions investigated here, may be found in Bury, *Later Roman Empire* 2.93-100, and in Stein, *Hist.* 2.485-492.

[147] Procopius *Wars* 2.5.1-27.

[148] *Ibid.* 2.6.9ff.

[149] *Ibid.* 2.6.9. Whether this refers to the reinforcements that went to Antioch from the Lebanon region, arriving just before the Persians (see below), is not clear. Prob-ably, as will be seen below, the troops from the southern border would not be removed from their garrisons before the line of the Persian march became certain. In any case, no troops seem to have been dispatched from Constantinople or Asia Minor; presumably none were available.

When Germanus reached Antioch, with his personal bodyguard of 300 men, he inspected the fortifications and found them for the most part secure; presumably they had been repaired as promptly as possible after the earthquakes. There was, however, one vulnerable point above the city on Mount Silpius. Here, Procopius says, there was a rock which spread out "to a very considerable width" and rose "to a height only a little less than the fortifications."[150] According to Procopius' account, Germanus wished to have the wall altered so as to bring the rock within the fortifications, or, if this was not possible, to have the rock cut off from the wall by means of a ditch. However, the engineers objected that there was not time for such operations before the Persians could be expected to arrive, and pointed out that if the enemy did reach Antioch and find the work in progress, they would discover the weak point at once. As a consequence, nothing was done. Reports kept coming of the Persians' continued advance, and no Roman reinforcements arrived; evidently it seemed impossible to find them. The people of Antioch believing that the Persians would be able to capture the city if they tried to, decided to attempt to save the city by offering the Persians a ransom in money—a device which could be expected to appeal to the Persians. It is not clear from the sources just how this decision was reached, but we know that the Patriarch Ephraemius was in favor of the offer of a ransom (if he was not in fact a leader in the plan), and the popular support of the idea must have been great, for we do not hear that it was opposed by Germanus. It is possible, indeed, that Germanus approved the plan, at least tacitly, since there seemed no safe prospect of the arrival of reinforcements.[151]

Bishop Megas of Beroea happened to be in Antioch, presumably having come there to seek aid and counsel since his city was in the

---

[150] Procopius *Wars* 2.6.11.

[151] Procopius (perhaps for a reason) does not say by whom the decision to ransom the city was made (*Wars* 2.6.16). Evagrius' rather brief account of the capture of the city (*Hist. eccl.* 4.25) makes it clear that he at least understood that Ephraemius favored the plan to ransom the city, and a later passage in Procopius (2.7.16), which will be discussed below, indicates that Ephraemius remained committed to the ransom even after it was officially disapproved. In the circumstances of the moment, there might very well have been a general public meeting, even a spontaneous gathering. A public meeting in the hippodrome, led by the officers of the circus factions, was quite possible, for in similar conditions the factions were often the mouthpieces of public sentiment. The civil authorities in the city very likely felt that they would have to pay some attention to such an expression of popular feeling, especially when it was based on the evident inability of the government to provide an adequate garrison. Bury (*Later Roman Empire* 2.96) and J. Haury (*B.Z.* 9 [1900] 346) believe that Germanus proposed the plan to ransom the city. This is possible; and if he did not make the proposal, he would hardly have been able to resist the overwhelming feeling of the populace.

path of the Persians.[152] He was chosen to go to Chosroes to negotiate the ransom, and set out. After four days of travel he found the Persian king and his troops not far from Hierapolis. Chosroes agreed to accept ten *centenaria* of gold as ransom for Antioch, and Megas started to return to the city with the news, while Chosroes and his army began to move on Beroea.

Reaching Antioch ten days, or perhaps a little more, after he had left it,[153] Megas found that the situation had changed. While he had been away, there had arrived at Antioch two envoys, John, son of Rufinus, and Julian, *a secretis*, who had been dispatched by Justinian to negotiate with Chosroes. Apparently the emperor had realized that it would not be possible to find a force capable of stopping the Persians, and that it might be possible to save the people of Syria and their cities, to at least some extent, by the offer of a money settlement. As was proper in the circumstances, the ambassadors were instructed to forbid the negotiation by the cities of individual ransoms, a process which would be in the end much more costly and would hamper future diplomatic dealings. In order to obtain the latest news of the situation, the ambassadors first visited Antioch, the military headquarters; they arrived, apparently, soon after Megas had set out to make the ransom offer to Chosroes.

At the same time that the ambassadors were prepared to negotiate a general ransom with Chosroes, it was hoped that it would be possible to defend at least Antioch if that should prove necessary. Now that the direction and purpose of the Persian march was known, it would be possible to detach some of the Roman troops who had been stationed along the southern part of the border; and probably about the time that the ambassadors were dispatched from Constantinople (or possibly somewhat later), an order was issued from Constantinople summoning six thousand troops stationed in the Lebanon region to reinforce the garrison at Antioch.[154] This was a relatively sizeable force for the time,

---

[152] Procopius *Wars* 2.6.17. To judge from the amount of high speed traveling which he did, with very little intermission, in the course of the negotiations with Chosroes, Megas may have been chosen as emissary because he was relatively young and active.

[153] The journey from Antioch to Hierapolis and return took eight days of traveling (Procopius *Wars* 2.7.2-4). The negotiations with Chosroes (2.6.17-25) may be supposed to have taken at least two days, if not more.

[154] As will be seen below, these troops reached Antioch just before the Persians did (Procopius *Wars* 2.8.2). The distance which these troops would have had to cover, combined with the timetable of events in Antioch, shows that an order summoning the forces from the Lebanon region was very likely issued at the time when Justinian's ambassadors left Constantinople, or, at the very latest, at about the time when the ambassadors reached Antioch; see *Speculum* 28 (1953) 345.

and one that presumably could have been expected to put up a real resistance within the fortifications of Antioch.[155] These troops, then, either were en route at about the time the ambassadors arrived at Antioch, or started a little later. Knowing that the troops would come, and learning that Chosroes was already at Beroea, so that they could do nothing now to prevent the ransoming of that city, the imperial ambassadors decided to remain at Antioch, so as to be able to confer with Chosroes in a place that would also be possible to defend.

As we would expect in the circumstances, Procopius' account[156] indicates that the imperial commissioners' plan to negotiate with the Persians with Antioch as a base, and to defend the city if necessary, produced mixed reactions. When the imperial envoys arrived, the Persians were known to be at Beroea, or drawing near it; and while the emperor's representatives were able to say that reinforcements were en route, or soon would be, these reinforcements would have to cover a considerably greater distance than the Persians would in order to reach Antioch. Also it was remembered that when Germanus arrived to take command at Antioch, he had brought with him a promise that reinforcements would soon be sent, and that these had not appeared. There seems to have been a substantial body of opinion, represented by the Patriarch Ephraemius, which thought it would be better in the long run to purchase the city's immunity, and escape the horrors of a siege, by payment of a ransom. People had begun to flee from the city.[157] Thus when Megas returned to Antioch from his mission to Chosroes he found that the ransom that he had arranged had now been forbidden, and that there were differences among the various leading figures in the city. A conference was held at which Megas was unable to persuade the men in command to go through with payment of the ransom. Procopius' narrative suggests that the patriarch held out for payment of a ransom, and was as a consequence charged with treason by the envoy Julian, who could with good ground argue that

---

[155] Agathias (5.13) states that the whole Roman army in Justinian's time totaled 150,000 men. When the Persians invaded Armenia in A.D. 530, they had 30,000 men, the Romans less than 15,000 (Procopius *Wars* 1.15.11). At the battle of Daras in the same year 25,000 Romans opposed 40,000 Persians (*ibid.* 1.13.23). In the following year, the Persians invaded Syria with 15,000 men as against 20,000 Roman troops (*ibid.* 1.18.5); see *Speculum* 28 (1953) 343.

[156] *Wars* 2.7.14-18.

[157] See below. When the Persians invaded Syria in A.D. 531, the people of Antioch fled to the coast (Malalas 462.1), evidently not expecting that the city would be adequately defended. On the discrepancy between the accounts of Procopius and Evagrius of the conduct of Ephraemius, see also A. Tricca, "Evagrio e la sua fonte più importante Procopio," *Roma e l'Oriente* 9 (1915) 286-287.

payment of a ransom would simply amount to turning over the city to the Persians, who on other occasions had accepted the ransom of a city and then had pillaged it and killed or enslaved the inhabitants. This had already been done, during the present campaign, at Sura,[158] and the temptation to do the same at a rich and populous city like Antioch would be all the greater. Whether a formal charge was made against the Patriarch Ephraemius we do not know. In any case, he seems to have found it either necessary or prudent to leave Antioch and go to Cilicia; and as Procopius tells the story, he did this soon after the conference which was held after Bishop Megas returned from his mission to Chosroes.[159]

It is puzzling to know just what the conduct was, at this time, of Germanus, who by virtue of his military responsibility for the defense of Antioch and his kinship with the emperor, ought to have been the leading figure in the city. In the sources, appearances are all against him. Procopius relates[160] that after the conference that was held on Bishop Megas' return from Chosroes, at which the imperial commissioners made it plain that the ransom would not be paid, first the Patriarch Ephraemius and then Germanus left Antioch for Cilicia. Germanus, Procopius adds, took with him only a few of his personal bodyguards, and left most of them in Antioch. Procopius assigns no reason for Germanus' departure, and one is allowed to conclude that he was simply deserting the city.

Another hostile account of his conduct comes from Malalas' chronicle, in which it is stated that Germanus had accomplished nothing during his stay in Antioch, but bought silver from the people of the city.[161] Malalas does not say so, but our evidence suggests that Germanus was buying it at a discount.[162]

A third consideration that puts Germanus in an unfavorable light is Procopius' account of the rock on the top of the mountain which made the fortifications vulnerable. Procopius, as we have seen, relates that because of the impossibility, in the time available, of remedying this defect, Germanus was unable to take any measures to put the defences in order. This story is difficult to believe for a number of reasons. It seems incredible that the city wall can have been built in

---

[158] Procopius *Wars* 2.5.8-33.
[159] Procopius *Wars* 2.7.14-17.
[160] *Wars* 2.7.18.
[161] Malalas 480.1-5.
[162] On the evidence for the value of silver, see below. The question of discount is important because it would throw light on Germanus' motives.

the first place in such a way as to leave it so obviously vulnerable. There is no other ancient evidence for the existence of such a rock, and there is no trace of one today.[163] One is tempted to think that a detail of this kind (possibly exaggerating some natural feature of less prominence) was included in Germanus' official report in order to explain his lack of activity, and that Procopius in his account simply followed the report, to which he had access at Constantinople.[164] If Procopius was not under the necessity of shielding the shortcomings of a member of the imperial family, he would certainly have been glad to mention a factor which could help to explain the defeat of the Romans.

Certainly everything that we are told appears to be to Germanus' discredit. But it should be remembered that our sources are very limited and that they do not undertake to treat such matters at length. It would be quite possible, for example, to believe that Germanus was buying silver for official purposes, both in order to accommodate people fleeing the city, who would wish to convert their silver into gold, which was more portable, and in order to accumulate a supply of silver for use of the imperial ambassadors if they paid a ransom. The Persians seem to have had a preference for silver, in that at this time, they coined only silver, and not gold;[165] and in the present campaign they had received the ransoms of Hierapolis and Beroea in silver rather than in gold.[166] Malicious gossip could easily misinterpret such purchasing of silver, and turn it into an operation for Germanus' personal profit.[167] A great deal happened in Antioch just before the Persians

[163] Förster, who was very skeptical about this detail of Procopius' account, reported that he had been unable to find the rock during his own visit to Antioch ("Antiochia" 134). The significance of Procopius' claims about the rock will be discussed more fully below, in the course of the present examination of Procopius' narrative. For the general background of Procopius' reliability in such matters, see the detailed study of his account by G. Downey, "Procopius on Antioch: A Study of Method in the *De aedificiis*," *Byzantion* 14 (1939) 361-378.

[164] B. Rubin, *Prokopios von Kaisareia* (Stuttgart, 1954) 109, believes that the story about the rock is based on Germanus' official report, but he also believes (306) that the rock existed, since, in his opinion, such a detail sounds natural, and could not be invented.

[165] Procopius *Wars* 7.33.6.

[166] Procopius *Wars* 2.6.24 (ransom of Hierapolis); 2.7.6 (ransom of Beroea). The Persians' apparent preference for silver is pointed out by Stein, *Hist.* 2.489.

[167] Stein (*Hist.* 2.489) believes that Germanus was purchasing silver for the government, and suggests that people were getting rid of their silver because of the Persians' apparent preference for it, and because gold could be more easily carried away from the city or hidden. According to this hypothesis, Germanus would be shipping the silver out of Antioch, presumably sending it to Seleucia Pieria and thence by sea to Constantinople. Stein believed that the official ratio of gold to silver at this time was 1:18 (*Hist.* 2.426, n. 1), so that the proper price of a pound of silver would be 4 *nomismata* or *solidi*. Malalas' statement (Mal. 480.4-5) that Germanus was buying silver

took the city, and we cannot be aware of all the factors involved, though we can also be sure that there were all kinds of rumors and reports going about. The one certain thing is that what happened was caused by the weakness of the Roman defenses in Syria, and also by what seems to have been a certain lack of coordination in the imperial government; and it is evident that Procopius is trying to make plain, within the limitations of discretion, his opinion of the behavior of the authorities.[168]

After he learned that the ransom he had negotiated would not be paid, Bishop Megas set out in haste to take this news to Chosroes, an action which required a good bit of courage, since the king might choose to make the bishop suffer for his disappointment.[169] It was known in Antioch that Chosroes was now at Beroea; and when Germanus and the Patriarch Ephraemius left Antioch soon after the conference with Bishop Megas (and presumably after the bishop's own departure), more of the people of Antioch began to leave the city.[170] There would have been a general exodus, Procopius writes, if the six

---

for 2 or 3 *nomismata* a pound would mean that he was buying it at less than the official price. Whether the government would approve such a transaction is not clear. People anxious to leave the city with their funds might be willing to take a loss in order to obtain gold; and Germanus himself might conceivably have arranged to re-sell the silver to the imperial treasury at the official rate, thus making a handsome profit for himself. There is reason to believe that Stein's understanding of the ratio of gold to silver (which is the ratio attested for A.D. 422) is not correct, and that silver by Justinian's time had risen in value, so that the gold:silver ratio was now 1:6± (see *Speculum* 28 [1953] 346, with n. 16). If this is true, Germanus was buying silver at one-quarter or one-sixth of the mint ratio.

[168] On Procopius' estimate of the proceedings, see B. Rubin *Prokopios von Kaisareia* (Stuttgart, 1954) 110. Two earlier studies by Downey in which the conduct of Ephraemius and Germanus was discussed (cited above, notes 105, 146) did not take into account all of the considerations examined here, and the conclusions formerly reached are subject to revision to that extent. It is clear in any case that Procopius does not always tell all of the truth. For example it has been shown in the author's study in *Speculum* 28 (1953) 345ff. that it must have been known, at the time of the conference held at Antioch when Megas returned from his mission to Chosroes, that reinforcements had been summoned from the Lebanon territory, but Procopius does not mention this in his account of the conference, though his narrative does permit an investigator to reconstruct the timetable of the troop movements. Procopius as a military man, and a member of Belisarius' staff, must have been very keenly aware of the factors involved in the movements of the reinforcements from Lebanon and the departure of Germanus from Antioch. We know, then, that Ephraemius and Germanus left the city knowing that reinforcements were on the way. Whether their motives were really independent of this knowledge, we do not know; but in the case of Germanus we are tempted to conclude that his action was not soldierly. Procopius' discretion concerning Germanus is of a piece with his rather marked efforts elsewhere to present Germanus in a favorable light; cf. *Wars* 7.40.9, *Anecdota* 5.8ff., and see J. Haury in *B.Z.* 9 (1900) 346. Germanus was replaced by Belisarius as commander in the East in A.D. 541, and for some years after that he was not in favor at court (Benjamin, "Germanus," *RE* 7.1259).

[169] Procopius *Wars* 2.7.19.   [170] *Ibid.* 2.8.2.

thousand troops from the Lebanon territory, under the command of
Theoctistus and Molatzes, had not arrived, providentially reaching the
city only a short time (perhaps a few days) before the Persians did.[171]

The Persians arrived and camped along the Orontes.[172] Chosroes
sent his interpreter, the renegade Paulos, up the walls, to announce
the Persian demand for the ransom of ten *centenaria*, though it seemed
plain, Procopius says, that Chosroes would have accepted less. Paulos'
appearance must have been especially distasteful to the people of
Antioch, since he had been brought up in the city and had gone to
school there, and it was said that he was of Roman extraction.[173]
Nothing resulted from Paulos' message, and on the same day the
emperor's ambassadors went to Chosroes and conferred with him, trying to arrange terms, but without result. On the following day, the
people of Antioch mounted the battlements and shouted insults at
Chosroes; and when the despised Paulos appeared again and began
to urge the people to pay a ransom they shot at him with their bows
and nearly killed him. Upon this Chosroes decided to assault the wall.

On the next day the attack was begun at several places along the
river, and also on the top of the mountain. Whether or not we accept
Procopius' description of the vulnerability of the wall at this point, the
top of the mountain offered a good opportunity for attack, since the
ground outside the wall there sloped away gently (not precipitously,
as it did inside the city), and so made it possible for troops and siege
engines to be brought into place fairly easily; and once a part of the
wall could be occupied, the attackers were in a commanding position
and could shoot down into the city with ease. It was on the top of the
mountain that the Persians made their successful entrance when they
captured Antioch in the middle of the third century,[174] and Chosroes
doubtless knew of, and hoped to repeat, this operation.

[171] *Ibid.* 2.8.2.
[172] The account that follows is based upon the narrative of Procopius, which is very
full, and was intended to be a *chef d'œuvre* (*Wars* 2.8.5—2.11.13). Specific references
to passages in the text will be given only for special reasons. The capture of the city is
described much more briefly, in the form of a prophetic vision of the younger Symeon
Stylites (who lived ca. A.D. 521 or 523—596 or 598; cf. Honigmann, "Syria," 1710)
which is related in the *Vita* published by H. Delehaye, *Les Saints stylites* (Brussels
1923), 248-249, ch. 57 (paraphrased by Nicephorus in *Acta* SS, Maii, tom. 5.331ff.).
Another text of a part of this vision is published by P. Van den Ven, "Encore Romanos
le Mélode," *B.Z.* 12 (1903) 159-160.
[173] Procopius mentions Paulos' antecedents in his account of the Persian negotiations
at Hierapolis (*Wars* 2.6.23).
[174] On the Persian capture of the city in the third century, see above, Ch. 10, §8. The
enemy's entry into the city at the top of the mountain is described by Ammianus
Marcellinus 23.5.3.

At first the Romans met the Persians with equal strength, and the young men of the circus factions, who were trained and armed as a citizen militia,[175] fought effectively alongside the soldiers. The Romans had brought a larger number of troops into action, and increased their fire power substantially, by constructing platforms of timbers and suspending them between the towers of the wall, so that an additional line of fighting men could go into action standing on the platforms that hung over the heads of the troops stationed on the battlements.[176] The fighting continued, it seems on equal terms, with the Persians, urged on by Chosroes, exerting all their strength, when a sudden accident put an end to the Roman resistance. The ropes binding together the timbers of one of the platforms proved unable to bear the weight imposed on them, and broke, so that both the troops and the heavy timbers fell to the ground with a great crash. The other Roman troops, not knowing what had happened, supposed that the noise meant that the wall itself had been breached, and so they fled down the side of the mountain into the city. In the streets of the city, the young men of the circus factions stayed together and prepared to continue fighting. The regular soldiers, however, seized what horses were available and rode off toward the city gates (which the Persians had not been attacking). They claimed that the Roman general Bouzes, with the mobile defense force which thus far had avoided an engagement with the Persians, had now arrived and was ready to join forces with the garrison of the city. Seeing the soldiers in flight, the citizens began to rush toward the gates, where many of them were thrown to the ground in the crush and trampled by the mounted soldiers.

Meanwhile the Persians had been mounting the walls with ladders. They did not at first advance into the city, whether because they feared an ambush, or because Chosroes wished to give the Roman troops a chance to get out of the city so that he could capture and pillage it more easily. Most of the Romans, with their commanders, were thus able to get away through the gate that led to Daphne, for the Persians left this gate open while they seized the others. When the troops, and some of the populace had left, the Persians descended into the city, but then they encountered the young men of the factions who were determined to continue resistance. Some of them, Procopius says, were

[175] On the bearing of arms by the *demos*, see G. Manojlović, "Le peuple de Constantinople," *Byzantion* 11 (1936) 621-625 (especially, on the siege of Antioch, 624, 637, n. 1).

[176] Procopius implies (*Wars* 2.8.14) that it would have been possible for the Romans to send a force outside the wall and occupy the rock, from which they could have had a special advantage against the Persians. It seems difficult to believe this.

in heavy armor, though the majority were unarmed and could only use stones as missiles. The young men at first seemed to have the upper hand, and once even drove the Persians back. However, Chosroes sent reinforcements and the Roman resistance was brought to an end, whereupon the Persians began to kill everyone whom they encountered.

Chosroes then ordered his men to begin rounding up the survivors and holding them as captives, to be taken back to Persia as slaves. The pillaging of the city was begun,[177] and Chosroes, accompanied by the imperial ambassadors, descended into the city and went to the Great Church. Here he found the great treasure of the church's gold and silver fittings and offerings, which had been left in place and not hidden or carried away. These made wonderful booty for the Persians, and Chosroes also had many of the ornamental marbles removed from the church and carried outside the city so that they could be taken back to Persia. Chosroes then directed that after it had been pillaged, the whole city was to be burned. The Great Church was spared, at the request of the Roman ambassadors, who pointed out that this church had furnished the Persians with an abundance of loot.[178]

The city (except for the church) was burned systematically, though the southern quarter called the Kerateion escaped because there was an open space between it and the remainder of the city.[179] The Persians also burned the suburbs, except for the sanctuary of St. Julian and the dwellings attached to it, about three miles outside the city, where the

[177] As has been already noted, the unusually large number of the bronze coins of Justin and Justinian found in the excavations suggests that these coins were lost either in the earthquakes or in the capture of the city by the Persians or in all three disasters; see the catalogue of coins by Dorothy B. Waagé *Antioch-on-the-Orontes* 4, pt. 2, p. 153, with note on no. 2112.

[178] The account given above is that of Procopius (*Wars* 2.9.14-18). Evagrius (*Hist. eccl.* 4.25) adds that it was the Patriarch Ephraemius who had ordered the church to be adorned with all its treasures, in the hope that the Persians, in return for obtaining all of the church's valuables, would spare the building. The alternative, of course, would have been to carry away or bury the treasures and let the building be destroyed. It may be a sign of what seems to have been an anti-clerical feeling on Procopius' part (G. Downey, "Paganism and Christianity in Procopius," *Church History* 18 [1949] 89-102) that he does not mention Ephraemius' part in saving the church building. On the descriptions of Ephraemius' action, see also A. Tricca, "Evagrio e la sua fonte più importante Procopio," *Roma e l'Oriente* 9 (1915) 286-287, and Stein, *Hist.* 2.488, n. 3 (on 489).

[179] The Kerateion seems to have been the Jewish quarter (see below, §9). It may have become isolated from the remainder of the city because the population of Antioch had been declining, as a result of the earthquakes of A.D. 526 and 528, so that there would have been vacant spaces appearing in the city. The Kerateion, being traditionally the Jewish quarter, would have continued to be occupied even if vacant spaces had come to exist between it and the remainder of the city.

Roman ambassadors had taken up their lodgings.[180] The fortifications were left untouched, presumably because it would have taken the Persians too long to wreck them.

After this, the imperial ambassadors conferred again with Chosroes, who consented to leave Roman territory, and do no further damage, in consideration of a promise of fifty *centenaria* and a perpetual tribute of five *centenaria*.[181] Chosroes then visited Seleucia Pieria, which he found completely deserted.[182] After returning to his camp at Antioch, he visited Daphne, where he admired the grove and the springs and left without doing any other damage than burning the Church of the Archangel Michael and some other buildings, in retaliation for the killing of a Persian nobleman by a young Roman whom he was pursuing.[183]

The Persians then left Antioch, to visit Apamea (and extract more tribute) on the way back to Persia. When he came to Edessa, Chosroes received a letter from Justinian promising to carry out the terms of peace which the imperial ambassadors had agreed upon. On this Chosroes released the hostages which he had held pending ratification of the peace, and also wished to sell the captives whom he had taken at Antioch. The people of Edessa, with great personal sacrifices, raised the sum demanded, but the Roman general Bouzes, it was said, forbade the payment of this ransom and the captives were taken to Persia.[184] There Chosroes built them a city which he named "Chosroes'-Better-than-Antioch," provided with a bath and a hippodrome and other amenities, and here there were settled captives from other Roman cities as well.[185]

[180] St. Julian's was three miles outside the city, but it is not known in which direction it lay (see Excursus 17). There were accommodations for visitors connected with the church and on at least one occasion a small local synod met there; see the *Life of St. Pelagia* by Symeon Metaphrastes, *PG* 116.909 C. According to Theodoret (*Religiosa historia* 10 and 13, *PG* 82.1393 A, 1412 A), the Church of St. Julian contained the tombs of three holy men of Antioch, Theodosius, Macedonius, and Aphraates. All these burials must have been made before the *Religiosa historia* was written, ca. A.D. 444.

[181] On the conditions laid down by the Persians, see Stein, *Hist.* 2.490-491.

[182] For an emendation of a passage in Procopius' account of Chosroes' visit to Seleucia Pieria, see D. S. Robertson in *Classical Review* 55 (1941) 82-83.

[183] There were, as Procopius relates (*Wars* 2.11.6-13), two shrines of the Archangel Michael. One, near the Tretum, had been built by Evaris. It was near this that the Persian noble was slain. There was another Church of the Archangel Michael at Daphne; and when Chosroes commanded the burning of the church near which the Persian had been killed, his soldiers misunderstood and burned the wrong church.

[184] Procopius *Wars* 2.13.1-6; cf. Stein, *Hist.* 2.492.

[185] Procopius *Wars* 2.14.1-2; Cramer, *Anec. gr. Paris.* 2.111.1-4; C. Huart and L. Delaporte, *L'Iran antique* (Paris 1943) 354-355.

The consequences of the catastrophe at Antioch were many.[186] In addition to being one of the greatest possible blows to Roman prestige, it added to the hostility toward the central government which many people in Syria already felt in connection with the separatist movement growing out of the monophysite controversy. The material loss was very severe, for in addition to the waste of all the money that had been spent on the reconstruction of the city after the earthquakes of A.D. 526 and 528, Justinian felt obliged to spend a further large sum rebuilding the city; and the temporary cessation of the city's commercial activities, coupled with what must have been a marked drop in the population, meant that there would be a distinct loss to the government in current revenue.

8. THE REBUILDING OF ANTIOCH

For an account of the rebuilding of Antioch we are again indebted to Procopius. His description of this operation, which forms one of the major passages in his panegyrical description of the building activities of the Emperor Justinian, published in A.D. 560 or soon thereafter, is a passage of unusual interest for several reasons.[187] The topographical information which it gives is valuable, though it is not as extensive as we might have hoped. Further, the account is of interest as an example of the characteristic topographical details that would be chosen by Procopius, and expected by his readers, as illustrations of what was involved in the rebuilding of a great city like Antioch after it had been sacked and burned by the Persians. The panegyrical purpose of Procopius' treatise naturally affects the passage strongly, and there are the same exaggerations, or suppressions of the truth, which were found in the account of the capture of the city. As a consequence, the passage is of unusual value as a commentary on Procopius' method and an illustration of his manipulation of his material; and it is necessary to make the character of the account plain since Procopius was in

---

[186] The most realistic ancient assessment of the significance of the capture and burning of Antioch is that written by John Lydus *De mag.* 3.54.

[187] The account of the reconstruction of the city appears in Procopius' *Buildings* 2.10.2-25. A detailed study of this account will be found in G. Downey, "Procopius on Antioch: A Study of Method in the *De aedificiis*," *Byzantion* 14 (1939) 361-378, which will be drawn upon in the present description. On the writing of the *Buildings*, and its sources, see G. Downey, "The Composition of Procopius, *De aedificiis*," *TAPA* 78 (1947) 171-183, and "Notes on Procopius, *De aedificiis*, Book I," *Studies Presented to David Moore Robinson on his Seventieth Birthday* 2 (St. Louis 1953) 719-725. A few details of Justinian's rebuilding of the city are by mistake put by Michael the Syrian in his description of the earthquake of A.D. 528 (2.194 transl. Chabot).

a position to be unusually well informed on such subjects, and a passage of this kind written by him could be expected to carry great authority.

From the literary point of view, it must be kept in mind that the account of the rebuilding of Antioch must be viewed, not as a description of the city and its reconstruction, but primarily as one of a number of passages in a panegyric, in which accuracy and fullness of detail were necessarily sacrificed to considerations of literary technique—a technique which, in such a work, made it desirable to introduce as much variety and novelty as possible into a number of passages on the rebuilding or adornment of cities in which the material was of an unavoidable sameness and monotony. The description of the rebuilding of Antioch is by no means the most elaborate and detailed account of the rebuilding of a city which Procopius included in his work. Before the passage on Antioch he placed the much more detailed account of the reconstruction of Dara,[188] which is three times as long as the account of the work done at Antioch. Thus, when he reached the passage on Antioch, the reader would already have been given a quite elaborate picture of what happened when the wise and powerful Emperor Justinian rebuilt a city. Accordingly, certain details that would be important for us, with our interest in historical topography, are not present in the passage on Antioch.

The passage is divided into four sections of almost equal length. The first three describe particular operations that can be used as examples of the emperor's unusual wisdom and munificence, while the last portrays the rebuilding of the city as a whole in more general terms. It is plain that Procopius picked out certain details because of their value for the purposes of his panegyric. In this passage, as elsewhere throughout the work, Procopius attributes directly to Justinian the initiative and the supervision of the work which in reality, of course, was carried out by subordinates.

One can easily discover the exaggeration that one would naturally expect. Certainly the city cannot have been, as Procopius says it was, made "fairer . . . by far than it had been formerly," for the straitened finances of both the government[189] and the inhabitants at this time would undoubtedly have confined the work to the most necessary repairs. Also it must be remembered that there is good evidence that after A.D. 540 the population of Antioch was considerably smaller than

[188] *Buildings* 2.1.4—2.3.26.
[189] On the financial difficulties of Justinian's regime at this period see Stein, *Hist.* 2.419-422.

it had been before the earthquake of A.D. 526. In addition to the losses
of the victims of the earthquakes of A.D. 526 and 528, and those who
were killed or carried off by the Persians, a certain number of the
survivors must have left Antioch permanently after each of the three
disasters. The results of the archaeological excavations have shown very
clearly the reduced scale on which the city was rebuilt. The main
colonnaded street, for example, was now reconstructed at just about
one half of its original width.[190]

The opening of Procopius' account does in fact betray the shrinkage
that had occurred in the inhabited area of the city. Procopius devotes
the first quarter of his description to a recital of the Emperor Justinian's
wisdom and skill in rearranging the lower parts of the city walls in
order to make them more efficient. The lower part of the circuit,
Procopius says, had been dangerously spread out so that it enclosed
areas that did not need to be defended, and its excessive length, caused
both by its unnecessary extent and by too many turnings, also meant
that it required more troops to defend it than were really needed. Accordingly, Procopius writes, Justinian reduced the length of the wall
and also straightened it, and in addition made better use of the Orontes
river as a defense by diverting the course of the river, through an
artificial channel, so that it ran as near the wall as possible. The necessary new bridges, Procopius adds, were built.

The reader who was familiar with the situation could readily deduce
something that Procopius does not say, namely that with the city's
loss of population there had come to be uninhabited areas within
the wall, so that a consolidation of the population would make possible
a reduction in the circuit wall which would be highly desirable for
defense purposes; and the traces and preserved remains of the ancient
walls do confirm a reduction in the circuit at the northern part of the
city (Fig. 11).

An equally important development that might be betrayed by Procopius' account—and it is not surprising that he should try to minimize
this—is that the account suggests that the quarter of the city located
on the island in the Orontes may have been abandoned at this time,
at least as a regular walled part of the city. The island quarter, it will
be recalled, seems to have suffered particularly severely in the earth-

[190] See Fig. 10, based on the drawing by J. Lassus showing the successive stages in
the history of the main street. For the archaeological evidence for the reconstruction of
the street on a reduced scale in Justinian's time, see *Antioch-on-the-Orontes* 3.13-14, 16.

quake which occurred in the reign of Leo I, eighty years previously;[191] and while we hear of some public buildings on the island in the latter part of the sixth century, these seem to have been rebuilt on a much reduced scale.[192] Procopius' account, it should be observed, seems to indicate a change both in the line of the wall and in the course of the Orontes, a combination of changes that suggests a major rearrangement, such as would be necessary if the island were being left outside the fortifications, and not simply a rectification of the city wall alone.[193] The evidence of the excavations indicates that in Justinian's time the wall of the city ran along the present line of the Orontes river in the neighborhood of the present bridge,[194] and while it was not possible to trace Justinian's wall for any length along the river, this circumstance would suggest that the change described by Procopius might have been made primarily in connection with the island.

Finally, it should be noted that Procopius does not in his account of the rebuilding of the city mention one detail that he had included in his description of the sack by the Persians, namely that the Persians had left the walls untouched (presumably because they did not have the time and the means to wreck them).[195] Thus Justinian's operation did not have to include a complete rebuilding of the walls.

Improvements were also made in the wall on the mountain above the city.[196] Procopius describes the famous rock which he says rose outside the fortifications and rendered them vulnerable, and he also comments on the broken and difficult character of the terrain inside the wall at this point. He states that the course of the wall was now changed by Justinian, and made to run as far away from the threatening rock as possible, and that the region within the wall was, so far as possible, leveled and provided with better communications with the

---

[191] According to the account of Evagrius (*Hist. eccl.* 2.12), "nearly all" the buildings on the island were thrown down by the earthquake under Leo; see above, Ch. 17, §1.

[192] See above, Ch. 17, nn. 128-129.

[193] This is the opinion of Förster, "Antiochia" 132.

[194] See *Antioch-on-the-Orontes* 3.19.   [195] Procopius *Wars* 2.10.9.

[196] It must be pointed out that Procopius does not, either here or in his account of the capture of the city, employ Silpius, the name ordinarily given to the mountain above Antioch, but speaks of the mountain as being composed of two parts, one of which he calls Orocassias (*Wars* 2.6.10, *Buildings* 2.10.9, 16), with reference to the Casius range which comes to an end at Antioch, the other Staurin (*Buildings* 2.10.16), a new name which was evidently given to the northern part of Mount Silpius after the vision of the Holy Cross which appeared over it following the earthquake of A.D. 526 (see above, n. 88). Procopius also applies to the mountain-torrent Parmenius the colloquial name Onopnictes, "Donkey-Drowner" (*Buildings* 2.10.16). The use of these distinctive names may be taken to indicate—what we should expect in any case—that Procopius had some personal knowledge of the topography of Antioch.

city. Also baths and reservoirs were built inside the wall, and a cistern for the storage of rain water was provided at each tower in the wall. This account seems quite acceptable, with the proviso, already noted, that it is difficult to believe that the rock outside the wall on which Procopius lays so much stress can really have been as dangerous in the first place as he says it was.

These details have occupied the first half of Procopius' account. The next section, comprising the third quarter of the passage, introduces a topic of special importance at Antioch, namely the problem of the drainage of the water which ran down the mountain into the city during the winter rainy season, which lasted from October to April. The climate being what it was, this was a continual source of difficulty at Antioch and from some points of view the site of the city could be regarded as undesirable for this reason. A description of the effects of a heavy rainstorm which occurred in May 1938 shows the problem of flooding and the extent of the damage which could be done, on just one occasion, by the wash of stone, gravel, and silt down the mountain side when there is no adequate provision for channeling and carrying off the water.[197] It is recorded that when Seleucus Nicator founded Antioch he built his original settlement on the flat ground near the river, away from the mountain, in order to avoid the wash down the slopes, and the excavations have uncovered two large masonry vaults constructed to carry the torrent Parmenius under the course of the main street; these possibly date from the Hellenistic period and were in use at least until the time of Justinian.[198] Further arrangements for drainage were made under the auspices of Tiberius, in connection with the construction of the main colonnaded street of the city, a very important measure since the colonnades would have been exposed to serious damage from uncontrolled drainage down the side of the mountain.[199] The problem must have been a constant one at Antioch (as well as at other ancient cities which were similarly situated), and Procopius takes the opportunity to make what he can of some measures that were carried out in connection with the general reconstruction operations.

Procopius lets it be quite clearly understood that until A.D. 540 there had never existed any device for controlling the winter torrent Onopnictes (Parmenius) which flowed out of the ravine between the

[197] See the account of the rainstorm by W. A. Campbell in *Antioch-on-the-Orontes* 3.5-6, with a photograph showing some of the flooding.
[198] Seleucus' avoidance of the mountain is recorded by Malalas 200.10-11.
[199] Malalas 233.10-18.

two parts of Mount Silpius. The torrent, Procopius says, on occasion swept over the circuit wall of the city and spread into the streets, doing ruinous damage. But Justinian, Procopius goes on, found a remedy for this. He confined the stream by building a dam containing sluice gates by means of which the flow of water could be regulated. Procopius' closing words convey as clearly as possible that no such device had previously existed, when he tells how the water could now "proceed through the channel wherever the inhabitants of former times would have wished to conduct it if it had been so manageable."[200]

Of course it is impossible to believe that there had never existed any adequate means of controlling Parmenius, and that no one before Justinian had thought of such an obvious device as Procopius describes.[201] Work of some kind must have been done in Justinian's time, for the present wall across the ravine, the famous Bab el-Hadid or Iron Gate, contains masonry characteristic of Justinian's time (Fig. 17), but it also reveals work that plainly belongs to another, and presumably earlier period. We may conclude that Justinian repaired or improved an existing structure, and also diverted part of the flow of Parmenius. The main bed of the torrent ran to the river in a fairly straight course, passing under the Forum of Valens and the main colonnaded street through masonry vaults that were discovered in the excavations.[202] However, the excavators also found a large masonry drain, datable in the time of Justinian, well to the north of the main bed of the torrent, and this suggests that a part of Justinian's contribu-

---

[200] Förster in his study of this passage ("Antiochia" 135-138) finds a difficulty in that (as he thinks) Procopius does not make it clear how the water got over the old *peribolos* (§16) after passing through the new *toichos* fitted with sluice gates which Justinian built (§17). Förster concluded that the passage is confused and that Procopius was in reality describing only one wall, *toichos* and *peribolos* being synonymous. Förster's difficulty seems to arise from his misunderstanding of Procopius' description of the relationships of the old wall and the new one, though this seems really to be clear. Procopius says that Justinian built his new wall πρὸ τοῦ περιβόλου, "before the circuit wall," "in front of" being used from the point of view of the city, to mean that Justinian's wall with sluice gates looked toward the city, and stood on the city side of the *peribolos* so as to discharge through the sluices the water that came in over the old *peribolos*. On the other hand, Förster took "in front of" to be used with reference to the outer side of the *peribolos*, in the sense that the new wall was built outside the old wall, i.e. in front of it from the point of view of one looking out from the circuit wall. In either case the *peribolos* would not play much of a part in the new scheme since, according to Procopius, it was already inadequate, and was being overflowed. On Förster's difficulty, see also Downey, "Procopius on Antioch," *Byzantion* 14 (1939) 372-373. As a consequence, Förster's criticism of E. G. Rey (*Étude sur les monuments de l'architecture militaire des Croisés en Syrie* [Paris 1871] 190-191) for misinterpreting the passage is not justified.

[201] This is pointed out by Förster, "Antiochia" 137.

[202] *Antioch-on-the-Orontes* 3.13.

tion was a diversion of part of the torrent in another direction so that it would be more manageable.[203]

The final section of Procopius' account has to do with the reconstruction of the buildings in the city. According to Procopius, the city had been so thoroughly burned and wrecked that nothing was left but mounds of ruins, and people were not even able to recognize the sites of their own houses; forums, main streets, and side streets no longer existed. Accordingly, Procopius says, Justinian first had the whole city cleared of debris and then laid out once more the streets, colonnades and forums. He restored the water supply and the sewers, and built the necessary public buildings, including theaters and baths. He also brought into Antioch a number of laborers and craftsmen to help build the houses.

This gives a typical picture of the rebuilding of a great city, resembling several other passages in Procopius' treatise in which large-scale reconstruction of this kind is described.[204] We can be sure that Justinian, for the sake of the prestige of the Empire and his own prestige, would have done everything possible to restore Antioch as quickly as he could. There may be only two questions, first as to how thoroughly the city had been wrecked, and second as to how quickly it was rebuilt. We do not of course know how long the Persians stayed at Antioch after they captured the city, but it would not have been prudent for them to stay too long, and aside from the burning, the amount of damage that they could have done would have been limited by the time available and also the means at their disposal. Procopius himself notes in his account of the capture of the city that the houses in the Kerateion, at the southern end of the city, remained standing because this district was isolated from the remainder of the city and the fire did not reach it.[205] We must also recall that rebuilding of this kind necessarily proceeded slowly; for example, when the Great Church, probably the most important single structure in the city, was rebuilt after having been destroyed in the earthquake of A.D. 526, it was not ready to be dedicated until A.D. 537/8.[206]

Procopius closes his account by mentioning specifically certain of the buildings that were reconstructed. First in order is the large Church of the Theotokos, which was not only rebuilt but endowed with a large income. There was also a large Church of the Archangel Michael.

[203] *Antioch-on-the-Orontes* 3.5-6.
[204] E.g. *Buildings* 2.3.24-26; 3.4.18; 4.2.23; 5.2.4-5.
[205] *Wars* 2.10.7.
[206] See above, n. 93.

The emperor likewise constructed hospitals for the sick poor, for men and women separately, and built guest-houses for strangers who were visiting the city.[207] In another passage Procopius records that Justinian restored "the church at Daphne," which may be the Church of the Archangel Michael at Daphne which had been burned by the Persians.[208]

9. THE PLAGUE OF A.D. 542.

Two years after the sack by the Persians, when the rebuilding of the city was still in progress, Antioch, along with the rest of the Empire, suffered from a devastating visitation of the bubonic plague.[209] Originating in Abyssinia, the plague spread through the Empire from Egypt, reaching Antioch in A.D. 542,[210] and Constantinople in the same year. In the capital it caused the death of two out of every four or five persons, and the normal activities of the city were completely disorganized. We have no statistics of the losses at Antioch, but they must have been severe (in some other cities, we are told, nearly all the inhabitants died), and the blow to the city's prosperity, following all the other misfortunes that it had suffered, must have been a very great one.

The effect of the arrival of the plague at Antioch and the symptoms it produced are described in a passage in the *Ecclesiastical History* of Evagrius, who had the plague himself as a boy in Antioch, but survived it.[211] There is also a curious reference to it in the biography of St. Symeon Stylites the Younger, who had taken the place as protector of Antioch which the elder Symeon had filled in the fifth century. The younger Symeon had been born at Antioch about A.D. 521, and had been named for the elder Stylite.[212] When he was a child, he lived in

---

[207] Malalas in his list of the benefactions of Justinian and Theodora to Antioch following the earthquake of A.D. 526 (423.1-9) lists the Church of the Theotokos and the Church of the Archangel Michael, as well as a guest-house. If these structures had been rebuilt after A.D. 526, only to be destroyed again in A.D. 540, the emperor would presumably make a point of restoring them again as quickly as possible. Procopius notes early in his treatise that Justinian had a special interest in churches of the Virgin and built a number of them in all parts of the Empire (*Buildings* 1.3.1-2), and the frequency with which Procopius lists churches of the Archangel Michael built by Justinian indicates that the Archangel was another special object of the emperor's devotion (cf. *Buildings* 1.3.14; 1.8.2, 19; 1.9.14; 5.3.20).

[208] *Buildings* 2.9.29; see *Wars* 2.11.6-13.

[209] For the history of this plague, see Stein, *Hist.* 2.758-761.

[210] Evagrius *Hist. eccl.* 4.29.

[211] Evagrius *loc.cit.*

[212] On the saint's career and the literary sources for his life, see H. Delehaye, *Les Saints stylites* (Brussels 1923) pp. LVIIIff., and P. Van den Ven, "A propos de la vie de Saint Syméon Stylite le jeune," *Anal. Boll.* 67 (1949) 425-443 (*Mélanges Paul Peeters*,

the quarter at the southern part of the city called the Cherubim, where the old city gate stood on top of which Titus had placed some representations of cherubim as part of the spoils of the fall of Jerusalem.[213] When the southern wall of the city was enlarged, probably by Theodosius the Younger,[214] the Gate of the Cherubim, as it had come to be known, was replaced by a new one called the Daphne Gate, but the old gate, or part of it, may have remained standing, for we are told that in Symeon's childhood there were still traces of the old wall. The Kerateion at this period was regarded as having special religious associations. It possessed an image of Christ—whether a statue or other representation is not clear from the Greek term *eikon* that is used to describe it—which was an object of particular veneration, and on one occasion a local holy man dreamed that Christ emerged from the image and spoke to him.[215] Here, while he was a child, Symeon had a vision of Christ on the old city wall, accompanied by the multitude of the just.[216]

Symeon first mounted a column at the age of seven years; and in time, when he had become definitively established on his pillar on the Miraculous Mountain near the Orontes between Antioch and Seleucia Pieria,[217] he came, through his holiness and his miracles, to exert a wide influence, especially at Antioch, and he was frequently consulted by the people of the city, and rendered aid in local crises. Pictures and

---

1). Delehaye published (pp. 238ff.) *capitula selecta* of the biography which appears to have been written not long after the saint's death and is attributed to Bishop Arcadius of Cyprus. This was the source of the more elaborate and better known biography by Nicephorus Ouranos, published in *Acta SS Maii* tome 5 (24 May) 307-401 = *PG* 86, pt. 2, 2987-3216. Nicephorus' biography contains details that do not appear in the published text of the older Life, but it does not have independent value. On the topographical value of these texts, see for the present Honigmann, "Syria" 1710-1711. Professor Van den Ven has edited the complete text of the *Vita* of Symeon the Younger for publication in the *Subsidia Hagiographica*. It is expected that this text will appear during 1961.

[213] See above, Ch. 9, nn. 24-27.   [214] See above, Ch. 16, §1.

[215] The reference to the region of the Cherubim and the *eikon* of Christ occurs in an anecdote in the *Pratum spirituale* of John Moschus (published by T. Nissen, "Unbekannte Erzählungen aus dem Pratum spirituale," *BZ* 38 [1938] 367-368) concerning a man who was the head of one of the numerous *diakoniai*, or centers for charitable relief, in Antioch. It was the chief of a *diakonia* (whose name John Moschus does not mention) who saw Christ come down (κατελθόντα) out of the *eikon* and speak to him.

[216] *Vita*, ch. 9, p. 238 ed. Delehaye. In his paraphrase of the passage (*Acta SS Maii* tome 5.310ff.) Nicephorus Ouranos explains the origin of the name of the Cherubim Gate.

[217] Excavations have been carried out at the Miraculous Mountain; see the preliminary report by the R. P. Jean Mécérian in *Comptes rendus, Acad. des Inscr. et Belles Lettres* 1948, 323-328. The cruciform church of Symeon the Younger had an octagonal center, like that of the elder Symeon; see E. B. Smith, *The Dome* (Princeton 1950) 35.

medallions of Symeon were manufactured[218] and people at Antioch, grateful for healing, set up images of the saint in their houses; there is a report of one of these, which possessed miraculous powers.[219]

Symeon's biographer relates that when the plague was brought to Antioch by the devil, a throng of the people went to the Miraculous Mountain, as they would always do on such an occasion, to tell the saint of this new and great misfortune which had come to the "Gate of Syria," as one of the gates of the city is called here (presumably, from what follows, the gate at the northern end of the city which led to Beroea and the greater part of Syria).[220] The saint's mother, the blessed Martha, who dwelt at the foot of his pillar, bade her son pray that the place of his birth might be delivered from this manifestation of the divine anger. When Sunday dawned, the saint began to pray, and he then seemed to be caught up by the Holy Spirit and borne to Antioch by a multitude of angels. When he reached the "Gate of Syria" he stood facing the east and prayed. It was granted to him to have his petition fulfilled, for that part of the city only, and the mourning ceased in the region around that gate. The devil then took the plague to the gate at the southern end of the city, which led to Daphne,[221] and there now arose a wailing in the Kerateion,[222] which lay in that quarter, and the mourning extended from the Cherubim

[218] For a study of one of these medallions, see P. Lesley, "An Echo of Early Christianity," *Art Quarterly* 1939, 215-232.

[219] For the miraculous image, see a passage from an unpublished life of Symeon printed by K. Holl, *Gesammelte Aufsätze zur Kirchengeschichte, 2: Der Osten* (Tübingen 1928) 390. Another passage in a biography of Symeon, which was read into the acts of the second council of Nicaea (A.D. 787), and is printed in Mansi, 13.76 and by Holl, *op.cit.* 391, tells of a workman who put up an image of Symeon over the door of his shop in Antioch, and thereby provoked the opposition of some of the local pagans, who tried to have it taken down. It is apparently this episode which lies behind the statement of C. Diehl, *Manuel d'art byzantin*, ed. 2 (Paris 1925-1926) 1.361 (followed by A. A. Vasiliev, *History of the Byzantine Empire* [Madison 1952] 255) that in the sixth century in Antioch there was a serious outbreak of iconoclasm. Neither Diehl nor Vasiliev cites a source for his statement, but no other episode at Antioch which might be interpreted in this fashion is known. The objection of some pagans to public display of an image of a Christian saint does not appear to be iconoclasm. See E. Kitzinger in *Dumbarton Oaks Papers* 8 (1954) 132, n. 212.

[220] This is the subject of ch. 126 and of the *Vita* published by Delehaye (pp. 257-258). See the version by Nicephorus, *Acta SS Maii* tome 5.359 Bff.

[221] Nicephorus does not mention the Daphne Gate or the Kerateion, but says that Symeon in his vision seemed to go to "the gate toward Seleucia." This would be the gate at the bridge which formed the beginning of the road to Seleucia, on the other side of the river from Antioch. The reason for this change is not clear. Perhaps there was a local variant in the legend.

[222] The text has Κρεαταίων, corrected by Delehaye, on the basis of the more common usage, to Κερατέων. This, it will be recalled, was the quarter which had escaped destruction when the Persians burned the city (see above, n. 179).

to the Rhodion.[223] When day came, Symeon described this vision to his mother Martha; and a multitude of people came to the saint and described to him their affliction.

As the plague continued, one of Symeon's disciples, named Conon, died of it, and was brought back to life through the prayers of the saint.[224] The plague in Antioch came to an end, at least so far as the original outbreak was concerned, in a miraculous manner.[225] A certain monk named Thomas, who was *apocrisiarius* of a monastery in the region of Apamea (or Emesa, according to another version), came to Antioch on business of his monastery. While in Antioch he became ill of the plague, and died in Daphne—in the public hospital or in the Church of St. Euphemia, according to different accounts which have been preserved. His body was placed in the common grave outside Daphne, at the place called Elephantôn,[226] in which it was the custom to bury strangers who died in Daphne. When other burials in the common grave were made, it was noticed that Thomas' body always showed signs of supernatural power. This portentous phenomenon was reported to the patriarch at Antioch and Thomas' remains were taken to Antioch in a festal procession and given suitable burial in the famous cemetery outside the Daphne Gate, where other distinguished religious figures had been buried. The presence of his body put an end to the plague in Antioch, and a small oratory was built over Thomas' tomb,

[223] The precise location of this area, and the significance of its name ("Rose Garden"?) are not known.

[224] *Vita*, ch. 129, pp. 258-261 ed. Delehaye.

[225] The story of St. Thomas at Antioch is preserved, in two versions that differ in some details—though not in essentials—by Evagrius *Hist. eccl.* 4.35, and by John Moschus in his *Pratum spirituale*, PG 87, pt. 3, 2945. A few details are added by the biography of St. Martha, the mother of St. Symeon Stylites the Younger, published in the *Acta SS Maii*, tome 5, 402-431. See W. Ensslin, "Thomas," no. 43, *RE* 6A.328-329. On the relationships of the sources, see the detailed study by P. Peeters, "Saint Thomas d'Émèse et la vie de Sainte Marthe," *Anal. Boll.* 45 (1947) 262-296. The account given here combines the information provided by the various sources, where there is no question as to a serious variation of tradition. Evagrius' account is on the whole to be preferred since he lived in Antioch and was an educated and intelligent writer, taking care over his sources, while John Moschus, who heard the story while visiting Antioch about ten years after Evagrius wrote, was primarily a collector of edifying tales. According to Evagrius, Thomas died during the epidemic of A.D. 543. The accounts of Moschus and of the *Vita* of St. Martha seem to Père Peeters to suggest that Thomas died in A.D. 551, but it does not seem necessary to accept this hypothesis.

[226] We know the name of the place because St. Martha wished to be buried there, in order to be associated with St. Thomas: *Acta SS Maii*, tome 5, 412-413; cf. Peeters, *op.cit.* (in the preceding note) 270-271, 281-282. Père Peeters points out that Elephantôn would have had to be outside Daphne and away from the houses; but it appears to the present writer that he places it too near Symeon's monastery, which was at some distance from Daphne.

and it became the custom for the people of Antioch to celebrate an annual festival in his honor.

Although the plague was stopped for the time being, minor outbreaks of it kept recurring at Antioch throughout the remainder of the sixth century. The historian Evagrius, who was born in Epiphania about A.D. 536, and (as has been noted) had the plague while a school boy but lived, tells us that after the original outbreak, the plague reappeared four times in Antioch, and caused the death of various members of his own household and his family.[227]

10. The Remaining Years of Justinian's Reign

During the remainder of Justinian's life, the sources for the history of Antioch grow scanty and little is known about events in the city. We hear of a synod held at Antioch in A.D. 542, the year of the plague, at which the teachings of Origen, which were then being revived in Palestine, were anathematized.[228] A few years later, in A.D. 545,[229] the Patriarch Ephraemius died and was succeeded by Domninus.[230] Domninus, who came from Thrace and had been director of a poorhouse at Lychnidus, was appointed to the patriarchate, it was said, because he happened to visit Constantinople on business of the poorhouse at the time when candidates for the vacancy at Antioch were being considered; and when he was taken by some palace officials to see the emperor, Justinian liked him immediately and had him appointed.[231] A monophysite chronicler speaks disparagingly of his personal habits,[232] but another source writes of him as "most holy."[233]

[227] Evagrius Hist. eccl. 4.29.

[228] The acts of the synod have not been preserved and we know it only from scattered references; see Cyril of Scythopolis Life of St. Sabas, ch. 85-86, p. 191 ed. E. Schwartz, Kyrillos von Skythopolis, in Texte u. Untersuchungen 49, 2 (1939), and Mansi, 9.23, 707, also Hefele-Leclercq, Conciles 2, pt. 2, 1178 (where the date 592 is a typographical error for 542).

[229] According to the sources, Ephraemius was patriarch for eighteen years, beginning in A.D. 527; see Stein, Hist. 2.638, n. 1. St. Symeon Stylites the Younger had had a prophetic vision of his death: Vita, ch. 71 pp. 252-253 in Delehaye's edition, cited above (n. 212).

[230] Cf. Stein, Hist. 2.656, n. 4.

[231] The manner of Domninus' appointment is described by the biographer of St. Symeon Stylites the Younger, ch. 72, pp. 253-255 in Delehaye's edition cited above (n. 212). The biographer goes on to say that when the new patriarch arrived at Antioch, he saw the beggars at St. Job's outside the city gate, and finding their presence there unseemly, threatened to move them elsewhere. The beggars appealed to St. Symeon, who promised that the patriarch would be punished; and shortly thereafter Domninus lost the use of his hands and feet, "wherefore [Symeon's biographer concludes] he lived in much contempt."

[232] Michael the Syrian 2.267 transl. Chabot.

[233] Life of St. Symeon Stylites the Younger, ch. 204, p. 266 ed. Delehaye, in the edi-

In July A.D. 551, Antioch was visited by a severe earthquake that also caused damage in many other parts of the east.[234] The sources do not describe what happened at Antioch, but the walls of the city must have collapsed, either in this disaster or in that of A.D. 557, for when, in the reign of Justin II, a Persian raid got as far as Antioch (A.D. 573), the people of the city fled because the walls were ruinous and the city could not be defended.

For two years beginning about A.D. 553, the region of Antioch, along with the rest of the diocese of the *Oriens*, suffered from a cattle plague which had serious economic consequences, since a considerable amount of land went out of cultivation because of the loss of the animals used for ploughing.[235]

In A.D. 557 there was another earthquake,[236] and in A.D. 560/1 the bubonic plague broke out once more in Cilicia, Anazarbus, and Antioch, accompanied by earthquakes.[237] In the same year there was an especially serious outbreak of hostilities between the orthodox and the followers of Severus of Antioch, which was put down by Zemarchus, the *comes Orientis*, on special orders from the emperor.[238]

We have a record of a prosecution in Constantinople, in A.D. 562, of a group of pagan priests, one of whom came from Athens, two

---

tion cited above, n. 212. Domninus is mentioned in an inscription dated A.D. 554 found in the region of Antioch (*IGLS* 618), which gives the spelling of his name as Domninus, rather than Domnus, which is sometimes found.

[234] Malalas 485.8-23, with the more complete text preserved in the Tusculan fragments published by Mai, *Spicilegium Romanum* 2, pt. 2 (Rome 1839), frag. 4, pp. 27-28, where the event is dated in July of the fourteenth indiction (1 Sept. 550—31 Aug. 551). Essentially the same account of the earthquake is given by Theophanes a. 6043, pp. 227.21-228.4 ed. De Boor, who dates it on 9 July. Leclercq, "Antioche," *DACL* 2378, with n. 5, accepts the date A.D. 543 which is given in the Latin translation of Theophanes in *PG* 108.499, and accordingly states that the sources are in disagreement in dating the event in both 543 and 551; it is certain, however, that the entry in Theophanes represents the year 551, for in his entry for the following year (a. 6044) an event is dated in September of the fifteenth indiction (= Sept. A.D. 552). The earthquake recorded by Cedrenus 1.674, which he dates in A.D. 553, may in reality be the one which occurred in A.D. 551. On other sources, not connected with Antioch, and the problem of the date, see Stein, *Hist.* 2.757, with n. 5.

[235] James of Edessa, in *CSCO*, Scr. Syri, ser. 3, tome 4, p. 243; Agapius of Menbidj, in *PO* 8.432; cf. Stein, *Hist.* 2.758.

[236] Cedrenus 1.676; cf. Stein, *Hist.* 2.758, and G. Downey, "Earthquakes at Constantinople and Vicinity, A.D. 342-1454," *Speculum* 30 (1955) 598.

[237] Theophanes a. 6053, p. 235.10-11 ed. De Boor; cf. Stein, *Hist.* 2.759, n. 1.

[238] Theophanes a. 6053, p. 235.11-15 ed. De Boor. The tentative date for Zemarchus' tenure of office, A.D. 565, suggested in Downey *Comites Orientis* 15, needs to be corrected. A similar expedition, in which the *dux Audono* (? Evodian) was assisted by Basiliscus, a presbyter of Antioch, is described by Zachariah of Mitylene, who dates the proceedings in A.D. 553 (*Chronicle* 12.7).

from Antioch, and two from Hierapolis (Baalbek).[239] This was a late episode in the vigorous persecution of pagans and other non-Christians (in addition to heretics) which Justinian carried on throughout his reign,[240] and the circumstance that two pagans from Antioch happen to be named in connection with this trial must be taken as a reminder that there were many other such prosecutions earlier in Justinian's reign, the records of which have been lost. It seems significant to find the name of Antioch linked in this connection with those of Athens and Hierapolis, which were known to be strong centers of paganism. We also hear of pagan sacrifices being performed in Daphne in A.D. 578.[241]

The Patriarch Domninus died in A.D. 559 and was succeeded by Anastasius, who is praised by Evagrius for his learning and his manner of life.[242] He led the widespread resistance against the aging Emperor Justinian's edict on the incorruptibility of Christ, which, to the emperor's surprise, had been almost universally rejected as heretical. In the last year of Justinian's life, A.D. 565, Anastasius assembled a large synod at Antioch which addressed to the emperor a very firm statement of faith.[243] Anastasius knew that the emperor would depose him for this action, and composed a farewell address to the people of Antioch, but the emperor died before Anastasius could be ordered into exile.[244] It is curious that while the reign of Justinian is remembered for the magnificence of its undertakings and its real achievements, the history of Antioch during this period is principally a record of calamities and physical decline. From the end of Justinian's reign to the Moslem occupation of Syria, seventy or eighty years later, less and less is known about Antioch; and the real greatness of the city must have come to an end in A.D. 540.

[239] Michael the Syrian 2.271 transl. Chabot.
[240] On Justinian's measures against paganism, including the trial of A.D. 562, see Stein, *Hist.* 2.373.
[241] See below, Ch. 19, n. 12.
[242] Evagrius *Hist. eccl.* 4.39-41. According to the *Chronicon Paschale* (699.18 Bonn ed.), Anastasius was ἀπὸ σχολαστικῶν.
[243] Quoted by Michael the Syrian in his account of the synod 2.272ff. transl. Chabot. See Duchesne, *L'Église au VIe siècle* 272-273.
[244] Evagrius *Hist. eccl.* 4.40-41; cf. Stein, *Hist.* 2.689.

CHAPTER 19

FROM JUSTIN II TO HERACLIUS, A.D. 565-641

1. Justin II, A.D. 565-578

THE REIGN OF Justinian's nephew Justin II opens what has been called "one of the most cheerless periods in Byzantine history,"[1] during which the state, weakened by Justinian's ambitious undertakings, suffered from both political disorder and poverty. This epoch, which lasted until the accession of Heraclius in A.D. 610, is a singularly obscure one in the history of Antioch since the preserved sources are meager and have little to say about the city, which, as we have seen, had already begun to decline in size and importance.

The sudden death of Justinian occurred, as has been said, just when it was expected that the emperor would depose the Patriarch Anastasius of Antioch for his firm opposition to the emperor's edict on the incorruptibility of Christ, which Anastasius and the bishops of his patriarchate regarded as heretical. The new emperor, however, deemed it prudent to allow this theological enterprise of his uncle's to die, and the Patriarch Anastasius remained in office.[2] In time, however, he became embroiled with Justin II and was expelled in A.D. 570. One tradition had it that when he was accused of spending his patriarchal revenues with unseemly lavishness, he replied that he did this in order to keep the money from falling into the hands of the emperor, who had the name of being avaricious. According to another account, Anastasius was critical of the appointment of the Patriarch John of Alexandria.[3] Probably these two traditions are reflections of a growing

---

[1] A. A. Vasiliev, *History of the Byzantine Empire* (Madison 1952) 169. On the reigns of Justin II and Tiberius II, see E. Stein, *Studien zur Geschichte des byzantinischen Reiches, vornehmlich unter den Kaisern Justinus II u. Tiberius Constantinus* (Stuttgart 1919).

[2] Evagrius *Hist. eccl.* 5.1; see Stein, *Hist.* 2.689 and Duchesne, *L'Église au VIᵉ siècle* 273. No attempt can be made here to record the careers of the monophysite patriarchs of Antioch during this period; not being resident in the city, they did not take a direct part in its activities. For an example of the complicated affairs of these patriarchs "in exile," see E. W. Brooks, "The Patriarch Paul of Antioch and the Alexandrian Schism of 575," *BZ* 30 (1929/30) 468-476. Paul was consecrated in A.D. 564 and died in Constantinople in A.D. 581.

[3] The first account is that given by Evagrius (5.5), who as a friend and admirer of Anastasius' successor Gregory might have felt disposed to be critical of Anastasius, especially when he was returned to office as successor to Gregory, who had originally replaced him. The second account of his deposition is that of Theophanes (a. 6062, p. 243.24-29 ed. De Boor), who elewhere, in his account of Anastasius' violent death in a riot (a. 6101, p. 296.18-19) speaks of him as "the great patriarch of Antioch."

antipathy between Justin II and Anastasius which was developed by a number of other factors. Anastasius was kept in forced residence in Constantinople until in the reign of Maurice, after twenty-three years, he was reappointed to his patriarchate (A.D. 593).

Anastasius' successor was Gregory (A.D. 570-593),[4] who had distinguished himself as *apocrisiarius* of a "monastery of the Byzantines" (which was probably in Syria rather than in Constantinople) and then as *higoumenos* of a monastery at Pharan in the Sinai peninsula.[5] Gregory was a man of saintly character and of real distinction and ability, as is shown by his career at Antioch, about which we hear in some detail because the historian Evagrius served under him in a legal capacity and greatly admired him.

About the year A.D. 570 the pilgrim Antoninus visited Antioch and saw the churches of St. Babylas *"et tres parvuli,"* of St. Justina, of St. Julian, and of the Maccabean brothers.[6]

Hostilities with Persia, which had come to an end in A.D. 561, broke out again in A.D. 572, when Justin II refused to pay the annual tribute that the Roman Empire had been engaged to pay to Persia.[7] The resumption of the war brought with it all the military activities that centered in Antioch during hostilities with Persia. In A.D. 573 the Persian commander Adharmahan, with a force of mailed cavalry and Arab auxiliaries, made a raid into Syria, where the Roman forces were so weak that it seemed plain that the Persians would get to Antioch, as they had done in A.D. 540. We are told that the news of the Persians' approach provoked disorders in the city. The walls were in ruins,

---

Anastasius' name appears in the building inscription of the baptistery of the Church of St. Sergius at Dar Qita (*IGLS* 546).

[4] The principal sources for Gregory's biography are the numerous references to him in Book 5 of Evagrius' *Ecclesiastical History* (which will be noted below); two chapters devoted to Gregory in the *Pratum spirituale* of John Moschus (*PG* 87, pt. 3, col. 3001-3004, ch. 139-140); and the notice of his appointment as patriarch in Theophanes a. 6062, p. 243.28-29 ed. De Boor. Several of his discourses are preserved (*PG* 88.1845-1886); cf. K. Krumbacher, *Gesch. der byzantinischen Litteratur*,[2] (Munich 1897) 163-164. One of these homilies (*PG* 88.1865-1872) was delivered in a church decorated with scenes of the baptism of Christ, to which Gregory alludes.

[5] See G. Hölscher, "Pharan," no. 2, *RE* 19.1811-1812.

[6] Antoninus *Itinerarium* 47, in *Itinera Hierosolymitania saec. IIII-VIIII* ed. P. Geyer (*CSEL* 39) p. 190.18-21. Who the *tres parvuli* buried with Babylas were, is not clear. This is the last reference in an ancient source to St. Julian's. The place kept its name, and was still used as a lodging for distinguished visitors in the time of the Crusades; see the continuation of the chronicle of William of Tyre in *Recueil des historiens des Croisades, Historiens occidentaux* 2.208.

[7] Goubert, *Byzance avant l'Islam* 1.69. On Roman relations with Persia during the period A.D. 572-591, see M. J. Higgins, "International Relations at the Close of the Sixth Century," *Catholic Historical Review* 27 (1941) 279-315.

evidently not having been repaired after the earthquakes of A.D. 551 and 557, and there was presumably only a weak garrison, if any, in the city. The populace must have been bitter against the government and the local authorities for leaving the city so badly protected. What the outcome of the disorders was, we do not know; but as the Persians continued to approach, many of the people fled, as did the Patriarch Gregory, taking with him the sacred treasures. The Persians, when they came, did not in fact take the city, but burned the suburbs, including the famous Church of St. Julian.[8] The Persians then went on to capture Seleucia Pieria.

In the following year the emperor's mind gave way under the pressure of the Roman reverses in Syria and elsewhere, and he became violently insane, though with intervals of lucidity. In one of his sane periods Justin appointed as caesar the able military commander (and future emperor) Tiberius, who thus became in effect regent, though the Empress Sophia continued to exert a considerable influence. Tiberius saw the pressing need of gaining a respite from the Persian war, and in A.D. 575 a truce for three years was negotiated, on the condition of an annual payment of tribute by the Romans.[9] During this truce the Roman army was reorganized and strengthened, the new commander of the army in the East being Maurice, who was in time to succeed Tiberius as emperor.[10] Here again Antioch must have played an important part as a center of the recruiting and other military preparations.

During this period, in A.D. 577, there was a severe earthquake at Antioch and Daphne, in which it is recorded that the whole of Daphne was destroyed, though the damage at Antioch itself was not serious, buildings being shaken and cracked but not thrown down. There was an earthquake at the time at Constantinople.[11]

---

[8] The Persian expedition is described by Evagrius *Hist. eccl.* 5.9; Theophanes a. 6066, p. 247.8-10 ed. De Boor; John of Epiphania frag. 4, in *FHG* 4.275; cf. Theophylactus Simocatta 3.10, p. 135.4-7 Bonn ed. John of Epiphania remarks on the defenceless state of Syria. The burning of the Church of St. Julian is mentioned in the *Chronicon ad annum 724 pertinens* (the so-called *Liber Chalifarum*): CSCO Scr. Syri, versio, ser. 3, tom. 4, *Chronica minora*, tr. Chabot, p. 112, and by Gregory of Tours in his brief notice of the Persian raid into Syria, *Hist. Francorum*, 4.40, p. 174 ed. Arndt (*MGH, Scr. rerum Merov.* 1 [1885]). Gregory by mistake writes of "Antioch of Egypt." For a commentary on this chapter of Gregory's work, and a discussion of his interest in the events in the East which he records, see A. Carrière, "Sur un chapitre de Grégoire de Tours relatif à l'histoire d'Orient," *École pratique des Hautes Études, Annuaire* 1898, 5-23.

[9] Goubert, *Byzance avant l'Islam* 1.71.

[10] Evagrius *Hist. eccl.* 5.19.

[11] Evagrius *Hist. eccl.* 5.17. Evagrius dates the earthquake in Tiberius' third year

About this same time, and before the death of Justin II in A.D. 578, we have a record of an accusation of paganism in Antioch which not only furnishes another reminder of the persistence of paganism in the city, but shows what bitter feelings could be stirred up, and what false charges could be put about, when there was any suspicion of pagan practice. The story is told by two sources in some detail, since it concerned both Gregory, the patriarch of Antioch, and Anatolius, the *vicarius* of the *praefectus praetorio* in Edessa.[12] It is related that serious tension developed at Heliopolis, a strong center of paganism, between the pagans, who were in the majority in the city, and the Christians. When the pagans threatened to destroy them, the Christians appealed to the emperor, who dispatched a special commissioner, Theophilus, to deal with the unbelievers. Under torture, they named associates "in every district and city in their land, but especially at Antioch the Great." One Rufinus was named as high priest in Antioch. Theophilus sent an officer to arrest him, but it was found that Rufinus had left Antioch to make a visit to Edessa. There the imperial officials came upon him while he was performing a sacrifice to Zeus, but he succeeded in committing suicide on the spot. Some of the people present, on being questioned, named Anatolius, the *vicarius* of the *praefectus praetorio* in Edessa, as an associate. Taken to Antioch for examination, Anatolius and his secretary Theodore were tortured, and made con-

---

as caesar, i.e. A.D. 577, which, as Valesius points out in his commentary on Evagrius, should not be taken to mean Tiberius' third year as sole emperor, since Evagrius describes the earthquake (5.17) before he records the death of Justin II and the accession of Tiberius as sole emperor (5.19). The much later historian Nicephorus Callistus Xanthopoulos (*Hist. eccl.* 18.3 = PG 147.332) understood Evagrius to mean that the earthquake occurred during Tiberius' third year as sole emperor, i.e. A.D. 581, but Nicephorus seems to have overlooked the position of the description of the earthquake, in Evagrius' narrative, with respect to the notice of Justin's death. It should, however, be noted that the coins issued at the mint of Antioch during Tiberius' rule show a curious usage in giving his regnal years by two systems, one of which reckons a full series of regnal years beginning with Tiberius' appointment as Caesar, while the other counts the regnal years from his accession as sole emperor in A.D. 578 (see W. Wroth, *British Museum, Catalogue of Imperial Byzantine Coins* [London 1908] 1.125-126). The explanation of this curious phenomenon is not apparent. The date A.D. 587 which Müller (*Antiq. Antioch.* 17) gives for this earthquake is a typographical error for A.D. 577 (Müller follows Valesius' dating of the disaster in that year, rather than in A.D. 581). This typographical error reappears in the list of earthquakes at Antioch in Leclercq, "Antioche," *DACL* 1.2359, n. 4.

[12] Evagrius *Hist. eccl.* 5.18; John of Ephesus 3.26-34, pp. 209-227 trans. R. Payne Smith. Evagrius, as might be expected, shortens the narrative and presents it in such a way as to minimize the charges made against his friend and protector the patriarch. On the other hand, John of Ephesus, as a Monophysite, includes a number of details designed to embarrass the memory of the patriarch. On Anatolius' title, see Stein, *Studien zur Geschichte des byzantinischen Reiches* (cited above, n. 1) 87.

fessions in which they accused Gregory, the patriarch of Antioch, and a priest named Eulogius, who later became Patriarch of Alexandria, of having been present with them at the sacrifice of a boy, performed at Daphne. This report caused a commotion in the whole city and it was said that Gregory did not dare to leave his residence. It was reported that Anatolius bribed the *comes Orientis*, and was nearly acquitted, but that a mob prevented his release. Suspicion was aroused to such a point that Tiberius ordered Anatolius and his companions to be brought to Constantinople and made to tell the truth about the patriarch. At this point, Anatolius' wickedness in accusing the patriarch was plainly demonstrated when an ikon of the Theotokos, to which he appealed in his prison, turned its face away from him. When this became known to the guards it was taken as a sure sign of Anatolius' fraud; and in addition the Theotokos appeared in a vision to some of the faithful and declared Anatolius' guilt.

When Anatolius was taken to Constantinople, the trial aroused great excitement, and when some of Anatolius' associates were condemned to exile, and not to death, a crowd seized and killed them, and began to accuse the emperor and the patriarch of betraying the faith. Anatolius and Theodore were executed with barbarous cruelty. The Patriarch Gregory was acquitted after he had gone to Constantinople himself. The reports of this episode evidently contain a certain amount of exaggeration in the accounts of the disorders provoked at Constantinople, but it is plain that paganism was still strong, and that charges of this kind could still stir up the bitterest passions; and the experience of the Patriarch Gregory shows what kind of attacks could be made upon a man in his position by his religious enemies.

There is a report of one further event of great interest at Antioch during Tiberius' reign, namely the receipt in the city of a piece of the true cross which had been preserved at Apamea. At the time of an earthquake at Constantinople, the emperor had been advised to send for this piece of the cross from Apamea, in the hope that this would serve to protect the imperial city. The fragment was removed from Apamea, with some difficulty, and taken to Antioch where it was sawn in two lengthwise, so that one of the halves could be sent to the capital and the other returned to Apamea.[13]

[13] This story is preserved by Michael the Syrian 2.285 transl. Chabot. Presumably Antioch was chosen for the partition of the relic because of the disorder that had been provoked at Apamea and also because Antioch, as an apostolic foundation would be a suitable place for such an operation.

2. TIBERIUS II, A.D. 578-582

Tiberius became emperor in September A.D. 578, a short time before the death of the mad Justin (October A.D. 578), when he became sole emperor; and it was hoped that he would be able to save the Empire from the losses and reverses that it had been suffering under Justin. The rebuilding of the army by Maurice had progressed to the point at which, at the end of the truce in A.D. 578, the Romans were able to take the field again, in an operation based on Armenia.[14] Tiberius, however, was anxious to put an end to hostilities, in order to gain more time for building up the Roman strength, and negotiations for peace were begun, but the sudden death of Chosroes in the spring of A.D. 579 put an end to these efforts since his successor wished to continue fighting.

The sources for this whole period are so meager that we hear little about the history of Antioch during the brief reign of Tiberius. A well-known episode, which attracted much attention, was the visit to the city in A.D. 580 of the Arab prince Mundir, who was a powerful ally of the Romans at this period. Mundir, a monophysite Christian, had visited Constantinople in order to assist the general Maurice in making plans for a campaign in the Mesopotamian and Syrian desert, in which Mundir's followers would be of great importance. While he was in the capital, Mundir undertook, as a means of preparing the way for Roman military success, to heal the breach that had divided the Monophysites into two groups, the Jacobites and the Paulites. A council was summoned in Constantinople, and Mundir succeeded in bringing about a union between the two parties. In addition, Mundir was able to persuade the emperor to issue an order that the official persecution of the Monophysites should cease. On his way home, Mundir visited Antioch, bringing with him the news of the cessation of the persecution. In Antioch, this was an event of the first importance so far as the local Monophysites were concerned. However, the Patriarch Gregory objected so strongly to this edict of toleration that he succeeded in having it revoked.[15]

[14] Goubert, *Byzance avant l'Islam* 1.74.

[15] The most detailed account of Mundir's efforts toward union and toleration is that of the Monophysite John of Ephesus 4.39-42, pp. 296-305 transl. R. Payne Smith. For the opposition of the Patriarch Gregory and the revocation of the edict (which John of Ephesus neglects to mention), see Michael the Syrian 2.344 transl. Chabot. In the same passage John of Ephesus describes in detail the contemporary hierarchical operations of the Monophysites, who were determined to have a Patriarch of Antioch, and diocesan bishops, of their own.

3. Maurice, a.d. 582-602

The general Maurice's advancement to the imperial throne, on the death of Tiberius, had been foretold, at Antioch, by impressive portents. Late one night, when Maurice was worshiping privately in the great church of the Virgin Mary which Justinian had built at Antioch, the *parapetasma* or curtain that surrounded the holy table caught fire, and the Patriarch Gregory, who was present, declared that this was a divine portent, and that it signified that the greatest and most exalted things would come to Maurice. Maurice himself also saw a vision of Christ, asking that he be revenged. Also Symeon Stylites the Younger died at this time, after having said and done many things which predicted that Maurice would rule.[16]

Maurice was one of the great emperors of his epoch. His reign, though troubled for ten years by the Persian war, brought the empire closer to the Byzantine form of the state which inevitably had to replace the old Roman system.[17] At the same time that this development was taking place, Antioch was continuing to live in the twilight of its own history.

We do not have a connected history of the city during Maurice's reign. On the other hand we happen to possess a considerable amount of information about events in the years a.d. 588-589. The Patriarch Gregory once more is prominent. First we hear of a quarrel between the patriarch and the *comes Orientis* Asterius. Our source is Evagrius, the patriarch's assistant and admirer, and he does not mention the cause of the unpleasantness.[18] Given the religious and political circumstances of the time, this kind of dissension between the chief civil and religious dignitaries in the city must have been not uncommon, and there must have been a number of similar episodes, involving other patriarchs, of which we do not hear; and so Evagrius' accounts of Gregory's involvements are valuable since they suggest a state of local feeling, and its developments, which must have been fairly typical.

On this occasion, Evagrius tells us, the whole city took the part of the *comes Orientis*, and all kinds of insults against the patriarch were going about in the streets and in the theater, where the actors saw a good opportunity and joined with the townspeople. The clamor grew to such proportions that Asterius, as the official responsible for public

[16] Evagrius *Hist. eccl.* 5.21, 6.23.
[17] See M. J. Higgins, *The Persian War of the Emperor Maurice (582-602): Part I, The Chronology with a Brief History of the Persian Calendar* (Washington 1939).
[18] Evagrius *Hist. eccl.* 6.7. On the *comites Orientis* in question, see Downey, *Comites Orientis* 15.

order in Antioch, was removed from office and his successor, John, was ordered to conduct an investigation of the disorders, though, Evagrius says, he was not in the least capable of carrying out such a commission.[19]

When the investigation began, the whole city continued to be filled with uproar; and a local money changer filed a written charge that the patriarch had had incestuous relations with his own sister, a married woman. From other similar sources there were received accusations that Gregory had caused disturbances of the public peace. The patriarch declared himself ready to answer all these charges, and on the accusation of incest he asked to be judged by the emperor and a civil and religious court. Taking Evagrius with him as his legal adviser, Gregory went to Constantinople, where he was acquitted by a court composed of the other patriarchs (or their representatives), a number of metropolitan bishops, and the Senate of Constantinople. His accuser was whipped and paraded through the city and then sent into exile. Gregory and Evagrius returned to Antioch at about the time of the mutiny of the imperial troops near Edessa.

This mutiny occurred when the new commander of the eastern front, Priscus, took command of his troops at Monokarton in Mesopotamia. Priscus, whose appointment had created considerable interest and some dissatisfaction, had passed through Antioch en route to his new command.[20] He had the bad luck to be the bearer of an order that had the effect of reducing the troops' pay, and when he reached the camp, his arrogant behavior, combined with the reduction in pay, provoked a mutiny, on 21 April A.D. 588.[21] The emperor was in time forced to remove Priscus and reappoint the former commander, Philippicus, but this still did not satisfy the troops, and the mutiny was continuing when Gregory returned to Antioch from Constantinople, in June A.D. 588.[22]

[19] How long John remained in office, we do not know. A building inscription at Kasr il-Benat (*AAES* No. 75) containing a date corresponding to A.D. 588/89 mentions a *comes Orientis* whose name appears to be Paulos (the first three letters of the name are not certain). This official, who could (according to the date given in the inscription) have been appointed as early as 1 Sept. A.D. 588, might have been the successor of John. See Downey, *Comites Orientis* 15.

[20] Theophanes a. 6079, p. 260.5 ed. De Boor; Theophylactus Simocatta 3.1, p. 112.13 Bonn ed.

[21] The mutiny is described by Evagrius *Hist. eccl.* 6.4-6, 9-13; Theophylactus Simocatta 3.1-3; Theophanes a. 6079, pp. 259.25—261.2 ed. De Boor; cf. Michael the Syrian 2.359 transl. Chabot. On the chronology, see Higgins, *The Persian War of the Emperor Maurice* (cited above, n. 17) 31-33.

[22] Evagrius (*Hist. eccl.* 6.8) places the patriarch's return four months before the earthquake that (as we shall see below) occurred in October of the same year.

The troops in the meantime had chosen a leader of their own, named Germanus, and were carrying on operations against the Persians during the summer; but they still refused to accept Philippicus as general.

When the autumn came, and the mutiny still continued, Antioch suffered from another severe earthquake.[23] This occurred at nine o'clock in the evening of the last day of October. The whole city was shaken and many buildings were destroyed when their foundations were thrown up out of the ground. The whole of the Great Church was destroyed, except for the dome, which the Patriarch Ephraemius had rebuilt with cypress wood from the grove at Daphne after the earthquake of A.D. 526.[24] The dome had been tilted toward the north, Evagrius says, by the subsequent earthquakes (i.e. those of A.D. 551, 557, and 587). It had remained in this position, braced with timbers, and then the shocks of A.D. 588 set it back in place.

Most of the quarters called Ostrakine and the Psephion, and the whole of the quarter called Byrsia, were destroyed.[25] All the dependencies that surrounded the Church of the Virgin were thrown down, while, paradoxically, the colonnade of the courtyard around the church was preserved. All the towers of the city wall surrounding the level part of the city were destroyed, though the walls themselves remained unharmed except for the battlements, which were in places tilted inward but did not fall. Other churches were destroyed, as well as the two public baths that were specially designed for use in the summer and in the winter.[26] It was estimated, from the decline in the consumption of bread (the baking of which was officially supervised) that sixty thousand persons were killed.

The Patriarch Gregory was saved, beyond all expectation. His residence was totally destroyed, but the patriarch and those who happened to be with him were unhurt; and when another earth shock made an opening in the ruins, Gregory was let down to safety by a

[23] The earthquake is described by Evagrius 6.8, and is mentioned by Agapius of Menbidj, *PO* 8.440. Evagrius dates it in the 637th year of Antioch, which began on 1 Oct. A.D. 588. On the dating, see Higgins, *The Persian War of the Emperor Maurice* (cited above, n. 17) 31, n. 56, and cf. P. Peeters in *Anal. Boll.* 65 (1947) 6.

[24] The church is reported to have been burned to the ground in the earthquake of A.D. 526 (Malalas 420.3-4), and we hear that it was rebuilt by the Patriarch Ephraemius and rededicated in A.D. 537/8 (see above, Ch. 18, n. 137).

[25] The quarter called Ostrakine is mentioned in the account of the earthquake under Leo I (see above, Ch. 17, n. 13). The Psephion was constructed under Theodosius II (see above, Ch. 16, nn. 16-17). The Byrsia is not otherwise mentioned; from its name, it might be the tanners' quarter, or a neighborhood occupied with leather-working.

[26] We hear elsewhere of baths specially designed for use in the summer and the winter; see Libanius Or. 11.220. Presumably the summer baths were designed with more open construction than the winter baths.

rope. The patriarch's enemy, the former *comes Orientis* Asterius, was killed. There was one divine dispensation, Evagrius notes, in that the earthquake produced no conflagration, although the city contained many fires in normal use, in hearths, public and private lamps, kitchens, ovens, baths, and many other places.

As was customary on such occasions, the emperor made a grant of money for relief work and restoration of the damage; but Evagrius does not add any details of the reconstruction.

The mutiny of the Roman troops in Syria already mentioned continued during the winter,[27] and while the soldiers obeyed Germanus, the leader whom they had chosen, they refused to receive the general Philippicus, whom the emperor had appointed to replace the unpopular Priscus as commander in the east. The Patriarch Gregory was now called upon by the authorities to try to bring the troops back to obedience.[28] He could not only bring to bear upon the soldiers the great prestige of his office, but he enjoyed great personal popularity because he often distributed gifts of money among the troops, and had also been accustomed to supply recruits with money and food when they were on their way to join the service. Gregory undertook this mission, and sent out messengers summoning two thousand of the officers and most influential private soldiers to meet with him at Litarba, a road junction on the road between Antioch and Beroea. When the soldiers were assembled, during Holy Week, early in April, A.D. 589, Gregory made a speech in which—according to the preserved report—he skillfully employed praise and flattery, and also made an official promise of full pardon for the mutiny. The soldiers were won over, and agreed to accept Philippicus as their commander; and to seal the reconciliation, the patriarch thereupon celebrated the holy communion in the open air. Gregory returned to Antioch the following day, and a messenger was sent for Philippicus, who was then at Tarsus on his way to Constantinople. He returned to Antioch and there met the soldiers, who had followed Gregory, and there was a ceremony at which the troops pledged their obedience and the general confirmed the amnesty.

At just about this time, the Persians captured Martyropolis; and as soon as Philippicus had taken command of the army at Antioch, he

---

[27] Theophylactus Simocatta 3.4, p. 119.18 Bonn ed.

[28] Evagrius describes the patriarch's mission, and its result, in detail, and gives the text of the address that he made to the soldiers (6.11-13). Gregory's successful intervention is mentioned very briefly by Theophylactus Simocatta 3.5, p. 122.5-8 Bonn ed. On the chronology see Higgins, *The Persian War of the Emperor Maurice* (cited above, n. 17) 33-34.

set out to recapture the city from the Persians. After they arrived, however, the Romans despaired of taking the city immediately. Once more the Patriarch Gregory was called upon by the emperor, and he proceeded to the camp before Martyropolis to convey the imperial orders that the assault was to be continued. The fighting was resumed, and the Romans, though at first unsuccessful, eventually recaptured the city.[29]

Early in the following year, A.D. 590, the unpopular Persian king Hormisdas was deposed by one of his generals, Bahram, and there followed a contest between Bahram and the lawful heir Chosroes II. Chosroes fled to Circesium, in Roman territory, and asked the Emperor Maurice for assistance in regaining his throne.[30] The emperor was at first inclined to accept this appeal, and as a compliment to his guest, he sent his kinsman, Domitianus, bishop of Melitene, and the Patriarch Gregory to visit Chosroes.[31]

When Chosroes regained his throne, at the end of A.D. 591, he sent Gregory a cross ornamented with gold and precious stones which the Empress Theodora had once dedicated to St. Sergius in the church at Sergiopolis. The elder Chosroes had carried this off when he plundered the city in the reign of Justinian, and the new Persian king now returned it, along with another gold cross, made in Persia. Under the influence of his Christian wife Sirin, Chosroes had prayed to St. Sergius for assistance in regaining his throne, and had made a vow to the saint; and his effort having been successful, he now fulfilled his pledge by returning Theodora's cross and adding another to it. The Patriarch Gregory dedicated these crosses with great pomp in the Church of Sergius at Sergiopolis, and Chosroes later sent other gifts for the altar of the church.[32]

Following the dedication of Chosroes' gifts (probably in A.D. 592), the Patriarch Gregory, with the emperor's permission, made a tour of the eastern parts of Syria, preaching the true doctrine to the followers of Severus, and (Evagrius reports) converting many of them.[33]

---

[29] Evagrius *Hist. eccl.* 6.14.

[30] Evagrius *Hist. eccl.* 6.16. Other writers give various cities as the refuge of Chosroes. Tabari (transl. by T. Nöldeke, *Geschichte der Perser u. Araber zur Zeit der Sasaniden* [Leyden 1879] 282-283) states that Chosroes went to Antioch and sent his message to the emperor from that city, but this late report does not seem credible; see Goubert, *Byzance avant l'Islam* 1.133.

[31] Evagrius *Hist. eccl.* 6.18.

[32] Evagrius *Hist. eccl.* 6.21; Theophylactus Simocatta 5.13; cf. Goubert, *Byzance avant l'Islam* 1.149, 176-178; P. Peeters, "Les ex-voto de Khosrau Aparwez à Sergiopolis," *Anal. Boll.* 65 (1947) 5-56.

[33] Evagrius *Hist. eccl.* 6.22.

In A.D. 592/3 we hear once more of the Jewish community, about which not much is recorded in the sixth century. In this year, in punishment for a sacrilege committed by a Jew of the Antioch group, the whole community had their heads shorn in the center and were expelled from the city.[34] They later returned, however, and we hear of them again during the reign of Phocas.

In A.D. 593 Gregory, after twenty-three years as patriarch, died of gout, and Anastasius, who had been his predecessor, was reappointed to office.[35]

In A.D. 599 a drought killed olive trees and other trees in Syria and Palestine, and in the following year an infestation of weevils throughout Syria ruined all the crops.[36]

4. Phocas, A.D. 602-610

In A.D. 602 Maurice was overthrown by a rebellion that began in the army, and the usurper Phocas got possession of the throne, murdering Maurice and his sons. Phocas' eight years in power were a reign of terror during which the Empire steadily grew weaker. The government lost ground both in military strength and in the authority that it exercised in its own cities and provinces. In addition, Syria and Egypt were weakened by the growing discontent of the Monophysites and their open opposition to the government, and there were continual factional disorders that were at least in part connected with the religious and political tensions. Naturally the Persians lost no opportunity to take advantage of what really amounted to a state of anarchy in Roman territory.

The literary sources for this period are not extensive, and they have so much to report in the way of intrigue and disorder throughout the Empire that Antioch, among so many cities that were in the throes of disorder, is only seldom mentioned. In two successive years—ca. A.D. 606 and 607—Syria is said to have been "overrun" by the Persians, with

---

[34] Agapius of Menbidj *PO* 8.439-440; cf. J. Starr, "Byzantine Jewry on the Eve of the Arab Conquest" *Journal of the Palestine Oriental Society* 15 (1935) 283. A mosaic inscription found in the excavations at Antioch shows that the Jewish community there in the sixth century possessed a *triklinion* or hall for social gatherings, like the similar hall mentioned in a mosaic inscription found at Apamea (*IGLS* 770 and 1344).

[35] Evagrius 6.24. It is at this point that Evagrius terminates his *Ecclesiastical History*. He tells us in this concluding chapter that he had written a companion volume containing the reports, letters, decrees, speeches, and minutes of conversations relating to the *Ecclesiastical History*. Included in this were the official reports of the Patriarch Gregory which Evagrius had drawn up. This volume seems not to have been preserved.

[36] Michael the Syrian 2.374 tr. Chabot. See Tchalenko, *Villages antiques de la Syrie du Nord* 428, n. 1.

large numbers of the people led into captivity. Antioch is not mentioned by name in the tradition concerning these raids, but the presumption is that it would have been captured, or at least assaulted, in such large scale operations as these raids seem to have been.[37]

In keeping with the history of the remainder of the Empire at this period, the only specific picture of events at Antioch under Phocas which we possess is a meager but sensational record of a riot—or series of disorders—followed by repression described as being of the utmost brutality.

This episode is dated in September A.D. 610, the last month of Phocas' reign.[38] Two sources—one contemporary, one written twenty years after the event—indicate that there were factional disorders, perhaps related to similar outbreaks elsewhere in the Empire, and that the Patriarch Anastasius, who must now have been a very old man, was killed by troops.[39] How he was involved is not stated, but the presump-

[37] On the literary sources see R. Spintler, *De Phoca imperatore Romanorum* (Diss., Jena 1905). The tradition of these raids is preserved in Theophanes, who places them in successive years. The first passage (a. 6098, p. 293.23-26 ed. De Boor) records the occupation of "all Mesopotamia and Syria," with countless captives carried away, in the fourth year of Phocas' reign. The second notice (a. 6099, p. 295.14-16) states that in the following year, the fifth of Phocas' reign, the Persians overran "all Syria and Palestine and Phoenicia." Theophanes' chronology may be one year out of order here, since he gives Phocas only seven regnal years, instead of eight. Thus if the raids really took place in Phocas' fourth and fifth years, they would have occurred in A.D. 605 and 606, but—depending on where the year is lost in Theophanes' reckoning of Phocas' reign—they might have taken place in A.D. 606 and 607. The latter chronology is adopted by N. H. Baynes in *Cambridge Mediaeval History* 2.285. The Armenian historian Sebeos (*Histoire d'Héraclius par l'évêque Sebéos* trad. de l'arménien par F. Macler [Paris 1904], ch. 23, p. 62) states that in one of these raids the people of Antioch submitted willingly to the Persians, hoping to escape the cruelties of Phocas. Sebeos' statement is accepted by Spintler, *op.cit.* 42, but it is not certain that this might not be an exaggeration on the part of the historian.

[38] The *Chronicon Paschale*, which is an almost contemporary source, gives the date (699.16-18 Bonn ed.) as September of the 14th indiction (which corresponded to 1 Sept. A.D. 610—31 Aug. A.D. 611), in the same year as the coronation of Heraclius, which took place in October A.D. 610 (*Chr. Pasch.* 701.11-13). Theophanes (a. 6101, p. 296.17-25 ed. De Boor) dates the episode in the last year of Phocas' reign, which, according to Theophanes' inaccurate chronology, was his seventh year. Theophanes puts the riot at Antioch two years after the second of the invasions of Syria mentioned above.

[39] The contemporary source is the Greek document called the *Doctrina Iacobi nuper baptizati*, ed. N. Bonwetsch *Abhandlungen d. k. Gesellsch. d. Wissenschaften zu Göttingen, philol.-histor. Kl.*, N.F. 12, no. 3 (1910). This is a discussion of the Christian teaching, written by one of the Jews who were forcibly converted at Phocas' orders, for the benefit of other newly baptized Jews. The author gives examples of his ignorance and hatred of Christianity before his conversion. In ch. 40, p. 39.7-9 he tells how, when Bonosus was punishing the Greens in Antioch, he himself went to Antioch and, in the guise of a Blue and a friend of the emperor, pretended to take part in the punishment of the Greens, and in this way was able to inflict many sufferings on the Christians—which was his real object. This document has been shown to

tion is that he lost his life either by accident, or because he was leading some action that had to be stopped by force. The *comes Orientis* Bonosus was given a force of soldiers and proceeded to punish the rioters in the most savage way. There is a report that the Jews took advantage of Bonosus' mission to attack the Christians under the pretext of helping to punish the offending circus faction.

Another, even more sensational, tradition, which appears in later sources and in somewhat greater detail, describes the original outbreak wholly in terms of fighting between Jews and Christians. The Jews, it is said, murdered the Patriarch Anastasius, mutilated his body and dragged it along the *Mesê* or main colonnaded street and burned it, along with the bodies of many other people whom they killed. The Emperor Phocas sent the *comes Orientis* and the general Kottanas (? Kotys) to punish the guilty persons, and these officials collected troops in Cilicia, went to Antioch and inflicted severe punishments, which put an end to the disorders.[40] A background for this report is supplied by the texts that describe hostilities between the Jews and the Christians elsewhere in the Empire under Phocas. It is said that the Jews in Syria and Mesopotamia had plotted to massacre the Christians and defile their churches; that the plot was discovered and that the Christians joined with the imperial authorities in punishing the Jews; and that the Emperor Phocas levied fines on the Jews in Antioch, Laodicea, and elsewhere.[41]

From the end of the century comes still another report—in a rather confused form—which describes an outbreak of the Monophysites in Antioch, which had to be put down by troops, with considerable loss of life. The disorder, it is said, spread to Palestine and Egypt. The death of the Patriarch is not mentioned. Here again—and this is really the only common ground of this report with the preceding ones—

---

be valuable in other connections for the information that it gives concerning the factional disorders under Phocas; cf. Y. Janssens, "Les Bleus et les Verts sous Maurice, Phocas et Héraclius" *Byzantion* 11 (1936) 520, 530. The other source of this period is the *Chronicon Paschale*, compiled soon after A.D. 629, by an author at Alexandria who might himself remember the events under Phocas. Here it is said that Anastasius was killed by troops, and that Bonosus inflicted the most severe punishment on the city (699.16-18, 700.4-6 Bonn ed.).

[40] This account appears in Theophanes a. 6101, p. 296.17-25 ed. De Boor, and is repeated in the later writers Cedrenus 1.712.9-15 Bonn ed. and Zonaras 14.14.31-32, p. 200.16—201.4 ed. Büttner-Wobst. Michael the Syrian 2.379 transl. Chabot mentions the murder of Anastasius by the Jews but not the punishment inflicted by Bonosus.

[41] This is the account of Agapius of Menbidj (*PO* 8.449). A detailed report of such a Jewish plot is preserved in the Chronicle of Eutychius of Alexandria, *PG* 111.1084-1085.

there is the punitive expedition of Bonosus and the brutality of his punishments.[42]

These three traditions could all refer to one outbreak, or series of related outbreaks, with some details transferred or emphasized, by different sources, while other details were omitted. Certainly the patriarch's being killed by troops sounds more plausible than the other account, especially since the mutilation and burning of the body has the appearance of a well-known atrocity story. It should be borne in mind that the report of the uprising of the Monophysites need not form a part of the other episodes described, though it might be a part of a series of incidents.[43] In any case, it is quite plain what conditions were like in Antioch under Phocas.

5. HERACLIUS, A.D. 610-641

The reign of Heraclius, which began (October A.D. 610) shortly after the disorders in Antioch just described, marked a turning point in the history of the Empire, and a beginning in the revival of its strength; but it was too late to save Syria from the Moslem invasion, and the history of Antioch as a city of the ancient world comes to an end at this time.[44]

[42] This is the report preserved in John of Nikiu 104-105, p. 166 transl. Charles.

[43] There have been various efforts to reconcile these accounts or explain their discrepancies. A. Pernice, *L'imperatore Eraclio* (Florence 1905) 22-24, followed by N. H. Baynes in *Cambridge Mediaeval History* 2.286, believed that the monophysite patriarchs of Alexandria and Antioch met in Antioch to try to reconcile their differences, that the local authorities interfered, and the Jews and Jacobites joined forces to resist the imperial troops. The orthodox Patriarch Anastasius was slain and the rioters were successful, but Phocas sent Bonosus and Kottanas to punish Antioch. From Antioch, Bonosus went to Jerusalem where the factional disorders had been severe. Starr, *op.cit.* (above, n. 34) 283-284, thinks that there was a great pogrom "throughout Asia Minor" [actually the sources seem to mention only Mesopotamia and Syria], which occurred when Antioch "was in the throes of a civil war between the Monophysites and the Orthodox," and that the Jews joined forces with the heretics. Spintler, *op.cit.* (above, n. 37) 46-47 accepts the accounts of Theophanes and John of Nikiu, and rejects that of the *Chronicon Paschale*. For the reasons stated in the text above, the present writer feels that it is hazardous to give so much weight to the account of John of Nikiu. Duchesne, *L'église au VIe siècle* 372, n. 1, believes that there is no reason to believe that the Monophysites had anything to do with the murder of the patriarch. J. Kulakovsky, "A Criticism of the Account of Theophanes of the Last Year of the Reign of Phocas," *Vizant. Vremmenik* 21 (1914) 1-14 (in Russian; summarized in *BZ* 23 [1914/19] 478) believes that Theophanes' account of the last year of Phocas is confused and represents the incorrect combination of different events that were not actually related. He believes that Bonosus was executed in A.D. 608 and that as a consequence he could not have taken part in the punishment of Antioch after the outbreak of A.D. 610. It is difficult to reconcile this interpretation of Theophanes with the testimony of the other sources. A general account of the happenings is given by A. Sharf, "Byzantine Jewry in the Seventh Century," *BZ* 48 (1955) 106-107.

[44] For the best study of the reign of Heraclius, see Pernice, *L'imperatore Eraclio* (cited above, n. 43).

The accession of Heraclius did not put an end to the Persian attacks on Syria, and in May of A.D. 611 a new invasion was launched in which Edessa, Apamea, and Antioch were captured, with great loss of life among the Romans.[45] This time the Persians remained in Antioch.[46] We hear no details of the history of the city during their occupation. However, it is said, of the Persian occupation of Syria in general, that Chosroes collected the treasures of all the churches in the territory occupied by the Persians, and that he forced all the Christians in the occupied territory to become Nestorians.[47] Presumably both these measures would have applied to Antioch, though it is not clear how much success the Persians would have had in forcing the whole population to become Nestorians.

The city remained in the hands of the Persians during all the campaigns through which Heraclius reestablished the Roman power and finally defeated the Persians. It is recorded that during Heraclius' campaign of A.D. 622, he fought a battle with the Persians "under the walls of Antioch," but the Romans were defeated.[48] When Chosroes was overthrown, in A.D. 628, and his son hastened to make peace with the Romans, Antioch and the other occupied cities were evacuated by the Persians, and the Roman captives in Persia were released.[49]

In A.D. 628, of course, it was expected that Antioch had returned to the Empire for good, and no one could foresee that in eight or nine years it would be occupied by the Arabs and would remain in their possession for a long time. However, the city must have been quite a different place from the prosperous and important Antioch of earlier times, and commercially and in all other ways its activity must now

[45] Theophanes a. 6102, p. 299.14-18 ed. De Boor; Michael the Syrian 2.400 transl. Chabot. Both sources place the event in the first year of Heraclius' reign, but N. H. Baynes, *Cambridge Mediaeval History* 2.289 and G. Ostrogorsky, *Geschichte des byzantinischen Staates*[2] (Munich 1952) 77 give the date as A.D. 613. John of Nikiu (109.21, p. 176 transl. Charles) records that the Persians took Antioch, but gives no date.

[46] The Persian occupation of Antioch is confirmed by the absence of any coins of Heraclius issued by the mint of Antioch. One coin type of Heraclius which has been assigned to Antioch, in the years A.D. 616/7, was in reality struck at Seleucia in Isauria; see P. Grierson, "The Isaurian Coins of Heraclius," *Num. Chron.* ser. 6, vol. 11 (1951) 56-57, 59. Grierson points out that the mint of Antioch does not seem to have been open at all during the reign of Heraclius and that there are no coins from this mint even during the period of Heraclius' reign (Oct. A.D. 610—summer A.D. 611) before the Persian invasion. There are likewise no coins of Heraclius from the mint of Antioch during the period between the Persian evacuation of the city (A.D. 628) and the Arab conquest a few years later.

[47] Theophanes a. 6116, p. 314.23-26 ed. De Boor.

[48] Sebeos, ch. 24, p. 67 transl. Macler.

[49] Theophanes a. 6118, p. 327.10-16 ed. De Boor.

have been very much reduced. It is significant of the city's loss of importance that the mint was not reopened after A.D. 628.[50]

During these last few years of its history under Heraclius, we hear of the city very little. It is mentioned in connection with the efforts that the emperor had been making for some time to find a means of reconciling the Monophysites and reuniting them with the orthodox element in the empire. Heraclius understood very well the political effects of the Monophysite position, which had always tended to alienate the indigenous elements in Syria and Egypt from the orthodox population and from the central government; and when Syria and Egypt were actually occupied by the Persians, whom the Monophysites would welcome as bringing relief from imperial persecution, Heraclius saw the pressing need for some formula that would supply a bond between the Monophysite Christians in the occupied lands and their orthodox brethren within the Empire. Such a reconciliation would lend powerful support to Heraclius' efforts to win back these Monophysite lands; and it was the patriarch of Constantinople, Sergius, who was himself of Syrian origin, who provided a formula that it was thought would be acceptable to both the Monophysites and the Orthodox. Sergius supposed that the Monophysites might accept the orthodox concept of Christ as composed of two natures, human and divine, if it was made clear that at the same time he had only a single, not a double, energy and will and operation.[51] Approaches had been made to representatives of the Monophysites in Syria and Egypt while these countries were still occupied, but there was no immediate success. When the occupied territories were freed in A.D. 628, the effort was renewed with increased vigor, and a special opportunity was provided by the fact that both Alexandria and Antioch happened to be without orthodox patriarchs, so that candidates who favored a reunion could be installed there. After Anastasius of Antioch had been killed in A.D. 610, no successor had been appointed before the Persians captured the city, and an appointment had not been possible while they occupied it. There was a Jacobite patriarch of Antioch, Athanasius, who had occupied this position, as a rival of the orthodox patriarchs, since A.D. 595, but since his position was illegal, he (like the other Jacobite patriarchs) did not live in Antioch.[52] In A.D. 610, he had renewed ties with the Monophysites in Egypt which had been broken by an internal dispute among the Monophysites there. Since Athanasius occupied a certain position of

[50] See above, n. 46.
[51] On the efforts of Heraclius and the Patriarch Sergius in this direction, see Duchesne, *L'église au VIe siècle* 384ff.
[52] On his career, see Devreesse, *Patriarcat d'Antioche* 102.

leadership, Heraclius made an overture to him, and the Jacobite patriarch seems to have made some concessions in the direction of reunion.[53]
Conversations were then held at Maboug, probably in A.D. 631, between the emperor and Athanasius, and it appears that the latter
agreed to a reunion, and probably Heraclius promised to make
Athanasius orthodox patriarch of Antioch if the reunion could be
effected.[54] Any such consent by Athanasius did not, however, mean
that all the Monophysites in Syria would agree at once to follow him,
and at least so far as Antioch was concerned, the undertaking came
to an end when Athanasius died in A.D. 631.[55] We hear nothing further
of what happened in the ecclesiastical affairs of Antioch.

The final loss of the city came very quickly. In the tremendous
expansion of the Arabs, when so many cities and strongholds in
Palestine and Syria were being occupied one after the other, we hear
relatively little of Antioch. When the Moslems began their attack on
this part of the Roman world, in A.D. 634, Heraclius made Antioch his
headquarters; but when the overwhelming Arab victory at the battle
of Yarmuk, in August A.D. 636, made it plain that it would not be
possible to save Syria, the emperor left Antioch and retired to Constantinople.[56] In 16 a.H. (= Feb. A.D. 637—Jan. A.D. 638) the Moslem
forces advanced on the main cities in northwestern Syria.[57] It was an
easy conquest and the Monophysites were not altogether sorry to find
themselves free from the orthodox government which persecuted them.
The Arabs offered the inhabitants the choice of leaving for Roman
territory, or remaining and paying tribute. Planning a prompt occupation of the key cities, the Arabs moved on Kinnesrin (Chalcis), which
was a military center. Here they met some resistance, though the city
soon surrendered. A force of Roman troops managed to escape from
Chalcis and got to Antioch, where they prepared to make a stand.
When the Arabs reached Antioch, however, the city made little re-

[53] Michael the Syrian 2.402-408 transl. Chabot, quoting documents exchanged by
Heraclius and Athanasius. See Duchesne, L'église au VIe siècle 397.

[54] Michael the Syrian 2.411-413 transl. Chabot, with the observations of Duchesne,
L'église au VIe siècle 397-398 (on the date, see 398, n. 1).

[55] Michael the Syrian 2.419 transl. Chabot; Elias of Nisibis, Chron., ad ann. 10, p.
63 transl. Brooks (CSCO, Scr. Syri, ser. 3, tom. 7).

[56] See the Arab historian al-Balâdhuri, pp. 175 176, 189, 210 transl. Hitti; Elias of
Nisibis Chron., ad ann. 15, p. 64 transl. Brooks (CSCO, Scr. Syri, ser. 3, tom. 7);
Theophanes a. 6125, p. 337.8-10 ed. De Boor. See P. K. Hitti, History of the Arabs,[6]
(London and New York 1956) 152-153. The sources for this part of the Arab advance,
and the capture of Antioch, are translated and evaluated by L. Caetani, Annali dell'
Islam 3 (Milan 1910) pp. 794-795, 800, 816-818; cf. the same scholar's Chronographia
Islamica 1 (Paris 1912) pp. 180, 191.

[57] The account of al-Balâdhuri (p. 211 transl. Hitti) of the way in which the Christians and Jews in Syria welcomed Moslem rule cannot be entirely an exaggeration.

sistance, and the city was soon surrendered on the terms that the Arabs were offering everywhere, so that some of the inhabitants now left Antioch.[58] The Arab sources make it plain that the conquerors regarded the possession of Antioch as a matter of the first importance, and a strong garrison was stationed in it.[59] We have a report that Antioch, like some others of the newly occupied cities, very soon rebelled against the new masters and had to be subdued by force, but the details of this tradition do not seem to be entirely trustworthy.[60] This brings to an end the history of Antioch as a city of the Graeco-Roman world.

EPILOGUE

The history of Antioch under the Arabs, the Crusaders, and the Turks, which lies beyond the scope of this book, has already been carefully studied by a number of scholars.[61] The appearance and activities of the city at this period are known, and we have an Arabic description of Antioch.[62] We also learn, from the intellectual history of both the Arab and the Byzantine states, something of the share of Antioch in the transmission of the intellectual legacy of the Greeks to Islam.

After more than three centuries of Arab rule, Antioch was recaptured by the Byzantine army of Nicephorus II Phocas in A.D. 969, and served as an outpost of the Byzantine Empire for more than a century, until in A.D. 1084 it was taken by the Seljuk Turks. In A.D. 1098, after a long and famous siege, the city was captured by the Crusaders under Bohemond and the Frankish Principality of Antioch was founded. This lasted until A.D. 1268, when the city was taken by the Mamelukes under Bibars. It then remained under the Egyptian Sultans until it passed into the control of the Ottoman Turks in A.D. 1517.

[58] Theophanes a. 6129, p. 340.12 ed. De Boor; Nicephorus Patr. *Historia syntomos* p. 23.3-4 ed. De Boor; Michael the Syrian 2.421 transl. Chabot; al-Balâdhuri p. 211 transl. Hitti; cf. Caetani, *locc.citt.* (above, n. 56), and M. J. De Goeje, *Mémoire sur la conquête de la Syrie* (Leyden 1900) 111. On refugees from Syria from the invasions of the Persians and the Arabs, and the places to which they went, see S. Borsari, "Le migrazioni dall'Oriente in Italia nel VII secolo," *Parola del Passato* 17 (1951) 133-138.
[59] See al-Balâdhuri p. 227 transl. Hitti.
[60] See al-Balâdhuri pp. 213-214, 227, 246 transl. Hitti. On the criticism of the sources, see Caetani, *Annali* (cited above, n. 56) 3.817-818.
[61] See for example Hitti, *History of the Arabs* (cited above, n. 56), and the monograph of C. Cahen, *La Syrie du Nord à l'époque des Croisades et la principauté franque d'Antioche* (Paris 1940: Institut Français de Damas, Bibl. Orientale, 1), also M. Gaudefroy-Demombynes, *La Syrie à l'époque des Mamelouks d'après les Auteurs Arabes* (Paris 1923; Haut-Commissariat de la République Française en Syrie et au Liban, Bibl. Archéologique et Historique, tome 3). Valuable details are collected by Förster, "Antiochia" 140-143.
[62] Guidi, "Descrizione araba."

APPENDICES

APPENDICES

HISTORICAL EXCURSUS

EXCURSUS 1

THE NAME OF ANTIOCH

THERE was disagreement in antiquity as to whether Antioch was named for Seleucus Nicator's father or for his son, both of whom were named Antiochus. Some writers say that the city was named for the founder's son: Malalas 29.1-3, 200.19, 204.2; Julian *Misopogon* 347 A; Sozomen *Hist. eccl.* 5.19 = *PG* 67.1273 C; John of Nikiu 61, p. 48 ed. Charles. The younger Antiochus, (the future Antiochus I Soter), was about twenty-four years old when Antioch was founded (Wilcken, "Antiochos," no. 21, *RE* 1 [1894] 2450). Other sources state that the city was named for the founder's father: Strabo 16.2.4, p. 749 C; Appian *Syr.* 57; Pausanias of Damascus, quoted by Malalas 204.2-6, and by Tzetzes *Chiliades* 7.118, v. 169; Justinus 15.4.8; Eustathius, commentary on Dionysius Periegetes 918. In the passage in the *Antiochikos* of Libanius in which the naming of the city is mentioned (*Or.* 11.93), some MSS state that the city was named for Seleucus' father, while others say that it was named for his son; the MSS that refer to Seleucus' father are the best, from the point of view of the literary tradition. Malalas expressly cites the opinion of Pausanias of Damascus, which differs from his own, and is emphatic in his refutation of it (204.206), saying that "no one, building a city, names it for a dead man; but he calls it by the name of a living and existing person." Nevertheless it seems clear that in the circumstances Seleucus would choose to honor his father rather than his son, for it would have been markedly disrespectful to his father to name so many of his new cities for his son, while neglecting to honor his father. This opinion follows Müller, *Antiq. Antioch.* 29; Beloch, *Griech. Gesch.²*, vol. 4, pt. 1, 255; Bouché-Leclercq, *Hist. des Séleucides* 32, with note on 255; and Hugi in his commentary on the passage in Libanius (*Der Antiochikos*, pp. 137-139). This was the original opinion of Förster, in his "Antiochia" 110, and in a later study, "De Libanio, Pausania . . ." 47-48, 50; later, however, he changed his mind, and supposed that the city was named for the younger Antiochus; see the introduction to vol. 3 of Förster's edition of Libanius, pp. xxxiv-xxxv. Like Hugi, *loc.cit.*, I feel that Förster's reasons for changing his opinion are not convincing and that they do not outweigh the undisputed superiority of the MSS that state that the city was named for the elder Antiochus.

The most convincing reason for supposing that Antioch was named for Seleucus' father is found in the way in which the other cities of the tetrapolis were named. If Seleucia Pieria was named for Seleucus, Apamea for his wife, and Laodicea for his mother, it seems logical to suppose that Antioch was named for Seleucus' father rather than for his son.

The name of Antioch occurs in several forms in the sources. In addition to the simple, and most common, form Ἀντιόχεια, various epithets are added to the name to distinguish the city from the other Antiochs. We find Ἀντιόχεια τῆς Συρίας (Josephus *Bell. Jud.* 3.2.4); Ἀντιόχεια ἡ ἐπὶ Δάφνῃ (Strabo 16.2.4, p. 749, cf. *Fouilles de Delphes* 3, pt. 1, No. 547, lines 15-16, cf. No. 551, line 25); Ἀντιόχεια ἡ πρὸς Δάφνην (*Fouilles de Delphes* 3, pt. 6, no. 143, line 5); ἡ Ἀντιόχου (sc. πόλις) (Evagrius 2.12); ἡ Σελεύκου παρὰ τῷ Ὀρόντῃ (Pausanias 8.33.3, certainly referring to Antioch rather than to Seleucia Pieria; cf. Libanius *Or.* 11.93). Tacitus in the well-known passage makes the epithet ἐπὶ Δάφνῃ into the name of Daphne: speaking of the death of Germanicus at Antioch, he writes (*Ann.* 2.83) *sepulchrum Antiochiae ubi crematus, tribunal Epidaphnae quo in loco vitam finierat.*

It is said that the city was at one time called by the name of the Emperor Constantius, the son of Constantine the Great. This usage was probably established by an honorific decree of the city, but it can only have been temporary, for it seems to be attested in only one literary text (Ch. 12, n. 172). In the sixth century, as a propitiatory measure, the name of the city was changed to Theoupolis, following an earthquake, and this appears on the coins and in some of the literary texts (Ch. 18, nn. 115, 117). However, the name Antioch continued in current use.

EXCURSUS 2

THE SIZE OF THE POPULATION OF ANTIOCH

THE evidence for the size of the population of Antioch between 301 B.C. and A.D. 588 has been collected and discussed in detail in an article entitled "The Size of the Population of Antioch," *TAPA* 89 (1958) 84-91. The testimonia are mentioned above in the appropriate places in the narrative, and are also, for convenience, collected here. The reader who is interested in the problems connected with the various texts should consult the article cited above.

1. Malalas (201.12-16) records that at the time of the foundation of Antioch in 301 B.C., the Athenians and Macedonians who were settled in the city numbered τοὺς πάντας ἄνδρας ,ετ΄. It is not clear whether this figure of 5,300 is intended to represent the grand total, or only the adult male citizens. The number suggests a comparison with the figure 5,040 which Plato (*Laws* 737E, 740 D-E) gives for the heads of households and landowners in the ideal city. There is no indication of the number of the native Syrians whom Seleucus Nicator settled in Antioch at the same time (above, Ch. 4, §4).

2. Strabo (16.2.5, p. 750C) states that Antioch in his time (the reign of Augustus and the early part of Tiberius' reign) Antioch was not much

smaller in size that Alexandria in Egypt and Seleucia on the Tigris. This estimate may be compared with the statement of Diodorus Siculus (17.52) that just before the middle of the first century before Christ Alexandria had more than 300,000 *eleutheroi* (free inhabitants). Half a century after Strabo, Pliny (*Nat. hist.* 6.122) wrote that Seleucia on the Tigris contained 600,000 people. When Avidius Cassius destroyed Seleucia on the Tigris in A.D. 165, its population was thought to be 300,000 or 400,000 (M. Streck, "Seleukeia," *RE* 2A.1158, 1183).

3. In the time of Bishop Ignatius, who was martyred at Rome under Trajan, the *dêmos* of Antioch, St. John Chrysostom says, amounted to 200,000 (*In S. Ignat.* 4, *PG* 50.591). Here *dêmos* might mean the whole free population, or only free adult men and women.

4. In the latter part of A.D. 363, Libanius writes (*Epist.* 1137 ed. Wolf = 1119 ed. Förster), Antioch contained 150,000 *anthropoi*.

5. In a homily delivered between A.D. 386 and 393, St. John Chrysostom (*In Matth. hom.* 85 [86], 4, *PG* 58.762f.) speaks of 100,000 Christians in Antioch. It is not clear whether he refers to orthodox Christians, as distinct from the members of other groups (Arians and followers of Apollinaris), or whether he refers to all the Christians in the city.

6. In the earthquake of A.D. 526, 250,000 persons were killed, according to Malalas (420.5ff.), while Procopius (*Wars* 2.14.6) gives the number of dead as 300,000. Malalas remarks that the earthquake occurred at the time of the festival of the Ascension, when the city was crowded with visitors.

7. Two years later, in the earthquake of A.D. 528, the casualties are given as "about 5,000" (Malalas 443.3), or 4,870 (Theophanes, *a.* 6021, p. 177.31 ed. De Boor).

8. After the earthquake of A.D. 588, it was estimated from the decline in the consumption of bread that 60,000 persons had been killed (Evagrius *Hist. eccl.* 6.8).

EXCURSUS 3

PETER IN ANTIOCH

IN APPROXIMATE chronological order of composition, so far as this can be determined, the principal *testimonia* for Peter's activities in Antioch are as follows:

1. *Gal.* 2.11 mentions a visit to Antioch by Peter, when the dispute with Paul occurred.

2. The *Pseudo-Clementine Romance*, dated in the early third century (before A.D. 230), mentions Peter in Antioch twice. In the *Recognitiones* 10.68-71 (*PG* 1.1452-1453) it is told how Peter went to Antioch after his defeat of Simon Magus, and how he healed the sick there. A house was converted into a church *in qua Petro apostolo constituta est ab omni populo*

cathedra (ch. 71, col. 1453). In *Homily* 20.23 (*PG* 2.468) it is reported briefly that after overcoming Simon Magus, Peter went to Antioch. This romance originated in the Orient, and though most of its details are of dubious authenticity, it doubtless embodied current tradition.

3. Origen (ca. A.D. 185-253/4) in his sixth homily on Luke speaks of Ignatius as "the second bishop of Antioch after Peter" (p. 37 ed. Rauer).

4. Eusebius in his *Ecclesiastical History*, begun before A.D. 303 and completed soon after A.D. 324, speaks (3.36.2) of Ignatius as "the second after Peter to succeed to the bishopric of Antioch." It is to be noted that Eusebius does not say that Peter was bishop of Antioch, and that he does not mention Evodius in this passage. In another passage in the history (3.22.1) Eusebius states, without mentioning Peter, that Evodius was first bishop of Antioch, and Ignatius second bishop.

In his *Chronicle*, published about A.D. 303, Eusebius stated that Peter "founded the first church in Antioch," then went to Rome and was the first head of the church there, remaining in this position until his death (Greek text preserved by Syncellus, *Chronographia*, 1.627.7-8 Bonn ed.). The Armenian translation adds that Peter founded the church of Antioch in the third year of Gaius (A.D. 39/40) and puts the appointment of his successor Evodius in the second year of Claudius (A.D. 42/3); it also states that Peter was head of the church at Rome for twenty years (*Eusebii Chronicorum libri II*, ed. A. Schoene [Berlin 1866-1875] 2.150, 156).

5. Jerome in his *Chronicle*, which was a free Latin translation of Eusebius', with a continuation to the year A.D. 378, writes under the year A.D. 42 that Peter, after having been the first to found the church at Antioch, was bishop of Rome for twenty-five years (ed. Helm, p. 179). Jerome here does not call Peter bishop of Antioch; and in a later entry in his *Chronicle* (ed. Helm, *ibid.*) he records that in A.D. 44 Evodius was ordained first bishop of Antioch. On the entries concerning Peter in the Chronicles of Eusebius and Jerome, see C. H. Turner, "The Early Episcopal Lists," *JTS* 18 (1916-1917) 110.

In the *De viris illustribus* 1, Jerome writes that after his episcopate at Antioch (*post episcopatum Antiochensis ecclesiae*) Peter went to Rome in the second year of Claudius (A.D. 42/3) and remained there for twenty-five years until the last year of Nero (A.D. 68/9). In ch. 16 of the same work Jerome writes of Ignatius as "the third bishop of Antioch after Peter the apostle."

6. Chrysostom in his homily on St. Ignatius, written in the last quarter of the fourth century (ch. 4, *PG* 50.591), speaks of Peter as head and ruler of the church at Antioch; Chrysostom does not use the term "bishop," but he does speak of Ignatius as Peter's successor in terms that suggest that they had the same office. Chrysostom does not mention Evodius but indicates that Ignatius was the immediate successor of Peter.

7. In the *Apostolic Constitutions* (7.26), composed ca. A.D. 380 in Syria or

Constantinople, Peter himself is represented as saying that he consecrated Evodius bishop of Antioch, while Paul chose Ignatius as bishop.

8. Theodoret of Cyrus, who died about A.D. 460, speaks of Ignatius as receiving his office from the hand of Peter (*Homil.* 1, *Immutabilis* = *PG* 83.81; *Ep.* 151 = *PG* 83.1440 A).

9. Leo I, the Great, who was Pope from A.D. 440 to 461, speaks of Peter at Antioch in two letters. In one he writes of Peter preaching in Antioch (*Ep.* 106, in *Acta concil. oec.*, ed. E. Schwartz, tom. 2, vol. 4, p. 61.28). In the other (*Ep.* 119), addressed to Maximus of Antioch, Leo speaks of Peter founding the churches in Antioch and Rome *speciali magisterio* (*ibid.* p. 73.14).

10. The first edition of the *Liber Pontificalis*, as restored by Duchesne, reflecting the Roman tradition of the early sixth century, states (p. 51 ed. Duchesne) that Peter was bishop of Antioch for seven years and bishop of Rome for twenty-five years. The same figures appear in the second edition, p. 118 ed. Duchesne. In the Felician abridgement (ca. A.D. 530), however, it is stated that Peter was bishop of Antioch for ten years and of Rome for twenty-five years.

11. At the end of the sixth century, Gregory the Great (*Ep.* 7.37 = *MGH Epist.* 1, p. 485.34) states that Peter occupied the see of Antioch, which he founded, for seven years. In this Gregory agrees with the first edition of the *Liber Pontificalis*.

12. The Antiochene chronicler Malalas, who wrote in the middle and latter part of the sixth century, has three references to the activity of Peter in Antioch:

a. 242.8-22. Four years after the resurrection and ascension of Christ, after Paul left Antioch (where he had been preaching) for Cilicia, Peter came to Antioch from Jerusalem and taught, and "enthroned himself" (αὐτὸν ἐν-θρονίσας). He was won over by the Jewish Christians and would not associate with the Gentile converts. Peter then left Antioch. When Paul returned to the city, he "abolished the scandal" and "received" everyone (i.e. both Jews and Gentiles, cf. Acts 28:30, in which it is said that in Rome Paul "received" all those who came to him). This information is quoted from Clement and Tatian, "the most wise chronographers." This quotation does not mean that Malalas himself derived the information from these writers; he often takes his information from an intermediary source, and gives the name of the ultimate source which the intermediary mentions (see above Ch. 2, §4d). Malalas dates the crucifixion in A.D. 31 (confusing the consuls of 33 with those of 31), so that he would put Peter's arrival in Antioch in A.D. 35.

b. 246.20ff. Ten years after the ascension (i.e., according to Malalas, in A.D. 41), at the beginning of the reign of Claudius (A.D. 41-54), Euodos became the first "patriarch" of Antioch after Peter. Euodos gave the faithful the name "Christians."

Appendices

c. 252.5-12. In the reign of Nero, Simon Magus went to Rome, and Peter, hearing of this, went to Rome himself. As he was passing through Antioch on his journey, it happened that Euodos, the "bishop and patriarch of Antioch," died, and Peter appointed Ignatius bishop.

13. The *Chronicon Paschale*, which was compiled soon after A.D. 629, has several references to Peter in Antioch, at least one of which is derived from Malalas:

a. 421.5-8 Bonn ed. A list of the "first bishops" is given: in Rome, Peter; in Alexandria, Mark: in Jerusalem, James the brother of the Lord; "in Antioch, the aforementioned Apostle Peter."

b. 431.4-9. An abbreviated version of Malalas 242.8-22 is given, with the same date, but with no reference to Paul.

c. 432.9-11. Under the year A.D. 39 it is reported that "Peter the Apostle first founded the church at Antioch." In the following entry, under the same year, is recorded Mark's foundation of the church at Alexandria.

It is worth noting that the Syriac *Doctrine of the Apostles*, published by W. Cureton, *Ancient Syriac Documents* (London 1864), from a manuscript of the fifth or sixth centuries after Christ, contains the statement (translation, p. 33) that "Antioch, and Syria, and Cilicia, and Galatia, even to Pontus, received the Apostles' Hand of Priesthood from Simon Cephas, who himself laid the foundation of the church there [one MS adds "and he built a church at Antioch"; cf. Cureton's note, p. 172], and was priest, and ministered there up to the time when he went up from thence to Rome, on account of Simon the Sorcerer. . . ." On this document, see A. Baumstark, *Gesch. der syrischen Literatur* (Bonn ed. 1922) 83-84.

EXCURSUS 4

THE ANTI-JEWISH OUTBREAK OF NOVEMBER, A.D. 70

CARL H. KRAELING ("Jewish Community at Antioch," 150-152) believes that Josephus' descriptions of the anti-Jewish outbreak at Antioch at the time of Vespasian's arrival (*Bell.* 7.46-52) and of the fire in November, A.D. 70 (*ibid.* 54-60) are "two different accounts of one and the same series of events." His reasons are (1) that the massacres reported in the earlier passage "hardly seem called for, if the attempt to fire the city had not actually been made," while as a sequel to the actual fire both they and the curtailment of the Jews' privileges can be understood, and (2) that "a two-fold denunciation of the individuals concerned in plots to fire the city by one and the same person hardly seems probable." Kraeling concludes that the truth behind Josephus' narrative is somewhat as follows: during Mucianus' regime (A.D. 67-69) the people of Antioch attempted to revoke certain rights of the Jews—Sabbath privileges and the refund of the oil-tax (Mucianus is known from another passage in Josephus, *Ant.* 12.120, to have confirmed the latter right). This attempt was partly due, Kraeling thinks, to current anti-Jewish sentiment, but in the main to "the suggestion of certain men of Jewish birth, like the Antiochus mentioned by Josephus, who probably saw in Jewish exclusiveness an obstacle to the achievement of a 'higher' type of religion." This attack upon the Jewish privileges, Kraeling thinks, failed; but when the fire occurred in A.D. 70, Antiochus, disgruntled by his previous failure, again accused the Jews and a pogrom followed, which was a violent one because Syria at that moment had no regular governor and no effective garrison. Although Kraeling's knowledge of the history of the Jewish community at Antioch commands such respect that it is very hazardous to differ from him, the present writer (following Dobiáš, *Hist.* 473-474, 509-510) prefers to accept Josephus' division of the story into two episodes, for the following reasons: (1) The state of anti-Jewish feeling at the time being what it was, it seems entirely possible to believe that the mere accusation of an incendiary plot could have produced massacres; compare Josephus' accounts of the massacres in Syria and Palestine in A.D. 66 (*Bell.* 2.461-478). (2) Antiochus did not denounce the same persons twice for plotting to fire the city; those whom he accused on the first occasion had been executed or massacred before the second outbreak (this point is stressed by Dobiáš, *Hist.* 510, n. 199). (3) It seems questionable whether Josephus' account shows that the attack on Jewish privileges came from men of Jewish birth who saw in Jewish exclusiveness an obstacle to a "high" type of religion. Josephus expressly says that Antiochus was a convert to paganism and was anxious to furnish proof of the genuineness of his conversion and of his hatred of Jewish customs. (4) There is no proof that Mucianus' upholding of the refund of the oil tax was connected with the episodes described by Josephus. (5) Kraeling, in dating the second episode between late A.D. 69 and early A.D. 70, seems to have overlooked the evidence cited above (Ch. 9, nn. 17-18) which places it in November of A.D. 70. The occurrence of the episode after, rather than before, the fall of Jerusalem, during the time when Titus in his triumphal progress was slaughtering Jewish captives wholesale, makes it much easier to understand how such an outbreak could have occurred at Antioch.

On the sources and literary composition of this section of Josephus' work, see Weber, *Josephus u. Vespasian* 246ff.

EXCURSUS 5

THE TAKING OF ANTIOCH BY SAPOR I

THE preserved sources that tell how Sapor captured Antioch are as follows. The thirteenth book of the *Sibylline Oracles* is one of the two contemporary sources that are still extant. This collection of purported prophecies is in reality based on contemporary knowledge of the events that are supposedly foretold.[1] Though difficult to interpret, the document has a certain value, especially when (as with the present problem) other literary sources are meager or lacking. Olmstead's study[2] of the Sibyl's account (13.89ff.) led him to believe that there was an invasion of Syria by Sapor I, during which Antioch was captured, in A.D. 251. Rostovtzeff, however, believed[3] that the date indicated by the same text was A.D. 253, and his conclusion is supported by numismatic evidence (not available to Olmstead) which shows that the mint of Antioch was moved to Emesa in A.D. 253, a change such as would be made necessary if Antioch were captured by the Persians in this year (see further below).

The other contemporary source, the text that has come to be called the *Res gestae divi Saporis*, is a trilingual inscription (in Parsik, Pehlevik, and Greek) set up by Sapor I on three walls of the first floor of the Kaabah of Zoroaster at Naksh i Rustem near Persepolis. Its discovery in 1936 and 1939 cast an entirely new light on the history of Sapor's times. The Greek text was not at first published in full, and scholars in the beginning of their studies had to use a re-transliteration into Greek characters of the transliteration into Latin characters which the discoverers first published. Publication of the Greek text, by Martin Sprengling, followed in 1953.[4]

The text includes accounts of two invasions of Syria by Sapor, for neither of which a date is given. The date to be assigned to the first invasion is not certain; that of the second is fixed by good evidence from other sources (discussed below) in A.D. 260, and scholars are in substantial agreement on this point. Antioch and Seleucia Pieria are listed among the cities captured during the first invasion.[5] They do not appear in the list of cities taken in the second invasion, in A.D. 260;[6] but since there is good evidence that these cities

---

[1] See Rzach, "Sibyllinische Orakel," *RE* 2A (1923) 2158-2162, also the description and evaluation of the work, with bibliography, by A. T. Olmstead, "The Mid-Third Century of the Christian Era," *CP* 37 (1942) 248ff.

[2] *Op.cit.* 398ff.

[3] "Res gestae divi Saporis and Dura," *Berytus* 8 (1943) 17-60.

[4] The original publication was made by Martin Sprengling, *American Journal of Semitic Languages and Literatures* 57 (1940) 197-228, 330-340, 341-420. A Greek text based on the Latin transliteration is printed by G. Pugliese Carratelli, "Res gestae divi Saporis," *La Parola del Passato* 2 (1947) 211-215, and "Ancora sulle Res gestae divi Saporis," *ibid.* 357-358, also by W. Ensslin, "Zu den Kriegen des Sassaniden Schapur I," *Sitzungsberichte d. Bayer Akad. d. Wiss., phil.-hist. Kl.*, 1947, No. 5 (published 1949) 92-94. See also W. B. Henning, "The Great Inscription of Sapur I," *Bulletin of the School of Oriental Studies* (University of London) 9 (1937-1939) 823-849 and R. N. Frye, "An Epigraphical Journey in Iran, 1948," *Archaeology* 2 (1949) 186-192, and the same scholar's review of Ensslin's study, in *Bibliotheca Orientalis* 4 (1951) 103-106. Since the work of the above-named scholars, the Greek text has been published by Martin Sprengling, *Third Century Iran: Sapor and Kartir* (Prepared and distributed at the Oriental Institute, University of Chicago, 1953). See also *Excavations at Dura-Europos, Final Report*, 8, pt. 1, C. H. Kraeling, *The Synagogue* (New Haven [1956] 336-337).

[5] Line 15.

[6] This list (lines 27-33) includes principally cities in Asia Minor. The Antioch and Seleucia which appear in this list (line 31) are thus thought not to be the Syrian cities; but see further below.

were captured on this occasion, it has been supposed that Sapor did not repeat, in the list of places captured during his second invasion, those which he had named in the account of his earlier campaign.[7] Olmstead, on the basis of the testimony of the *Sibylline Oracles*, concludes that the first invasion began in A.D. 251 and that the Persians occupied some of the captured cities (including Antioch) until A.D. 253, when they withdrew from Syria. Rostovtzeff, as has been noted, believes that the invasion took place in A.D. 253, and that Antioch was not occupied beyond that year. On this point, it will be observed, Olmstead was attempting to reconcile his mistaken interpretation of the *Sibylline Oracles* (according to which Syria was invaded in A.D. 251) with the evidence that points to the capture of Antioch in A.D. 253. The occupation of Antioch by the Persians during A.D. 251-253, which Olmstead was thus led to assume, is nowhere specifically mentioned or indicated by our sources. Olmstead's chronology also makes it necessary to suppose that when Valerian came to the East in A.D. 253/4 he had to recapture Antioch from the Persians—an event of which we hear nothing in our sources. Ensslin believes that Antioch was captured only once, in A.D. 260.[8]

Three other sources, Libanius, Ammianus Marcellinus, and Malalas, though not contemporary, would be expected to be of special value in that these writers lived in Antioch, and so could have had access to reliable records for the city's history at this period (if, indeed, such sources existed). Libanius mentions in two passages that the Persians captured Antioch. In one (*Or.* 24.38) he tells the story, which also appears in Ammianus, of how the Persians surprised the city while the people were sitting in the theater. It is evident that this was a celebrated episode in the city's history. In the other passage (*Or.* 60.2-3) Libanius says that Sapor took and burned the city, and then went to Daphne, to destroy it likewise, but was checked by Apollo, so that he paid worship to the god instead of burning his shrine. Libanius does not say that Antioch was captured more than once.

[7] This is the explanation adopted by Henning, *op.cit.* (above, n. 4) 836, Rostovtzeff, *op.cit.* (above, n. 3) 30, 40, n. 54, and Ensslin, *op.cit.* (above, n. 4) 106. H. Grégoire finds himself in agreement with this conclusion: "Les persécutions dans l'Empire romain," *Académie roy. de. Belgique, Classe des lettres et des sciences morales et politiques, Mémoires, Collection in-8°*, tome 46 (1950) 118-120, 137. While it is not possible to study the entire problem in this place, it may be suggested, for future consideration, that the Antioch and Seleucia mentioned in the account of the second invasion may actually be Antioch on the Orontes and Seleucia Pieria. The list of cities captured during the first invasion appears (as scholars have recognized) to represent the itinerary followed by the Persian forces, which after traveling for a time in one body split into two groups, which then operated simultaneously in different parts of Syria. However, there are parts of the list given for the second invasion which will not, in spite of the best efforts of Olmstead, Rostovtzeff, and Ensslin, yield any satisfactory itinerary, whether of one army or of two (or even more) separate forces. This suggests that while parts of this list may represent an itinerary, parts contain names of cities set down at random. Hence it is not necessary to suppose that all the cities listed are in Asia Minor; and if this is true, the Antioch and Seleucia mentioned could be those in Syria.

[8] On this point Ensslin, after having studied the *Res gestae divi Saporis*, continues (*op.cit.*, above, n. 4) to maintain the position which he adopted in the chapter describing these events in *CAH* 12.136 (published 1939), which was written before the inscription of Sapor became available.

Appendices

In the case of Ammianus we are disappointed because the section of his history that covered this period in detail has been lost. We do, however, possess in the preserved later books two references that mention events in connection with Sapor. In one of these (23.5.3) Ammianus tells how the Persians took Antioch by surprise; they were guided, he says, by a local traitor named Mareades. Ammianus places this event (*Gallieni temporibus*) in the reign of Valerian's successor. In another place (20.11.11) he mentions a great battering-ram (*aries*) which the Persians used for razing Antioch; on their withdrawal from Syria, they abandoned it at Carrhae. Ammianus speaks of only one Persian capture of Antioch, though there would have been no reason for him, in either of these passages, to speak of a second capture.

Malalas likewise fails to solve the question for us. He describes (295.20–297.20) the capture of Antioch by Sapor during the reign of Valerian, and gives some information on the remainder of the Persian campaign in Syria. The Persians were led to Antioch, he says, by the traitor Mareades. The greater part of his account, Malalas seems to imply, comes from his source Domninus. He notes, however, that Philostratus, another source, gave an account of the campaign which differed in some respects from Domninus'. The capture of Antioch is dated (in the section which was ostensibly based on Domninus) in the year 314 ($\tau\iota\delta'$) of the era of Antioch = A.D. 265/6. This date disagrees with all the other evidence for the capture (or captures) of Antioch, and attempts have been made to emend it. C. Müller (*FHG* 4, p. 192) emended it to $\delta\tau' = $ A.D. 255/6. The conjecture is accepted by Stauffenberg in the commentary of his edition of Malalas (*Malalas* 366, with n. 89), though in his text he prints the numeral as $\tau\iota\delta'$ (*ibid.* 65). Ensslin[9] suggested that the δ of the MS represents a misunderstanding of an original *L*, the sign for the word "year," so that the text would have originally contained the numeral $\tau\iota' = $ A.D. 261/2. Although this gives still another date for the capture of Antioch, Ensslin believes that it "at least agrees better with the account of Malalas, who also places the fall of Antioch after the capture of the Emperor."[10] Two considerations make us hesitate to accept Ensslin's conjecture. First, Malalas nowhere mentions that Valerian was captured by the Persians, writing instead (298.1) that Valerian was killed at Milan; evidently the chronicler (or his source) confused Valerian with Gallienus, who was killed at Milan in A.D. 268.[11] Malalas actually inserts his account of the taking of Antioch between his notice of the accession of

[9] *CAH* 12.133, n. 3 and *op.cit.* (above, n. 4) 33-35.
[10] Valerian was captured by the Persians in midsummer A.D. 260; see Ensslin in *CAH* 12.135-136. G. Lopuszanski puts the capture in June A.D. 259, though he recognizes that this is hypothetical: "La date de la capture de Valérien et la chronologie des empereurs gaulois," *Cahiers de l'Institut d'études polonaises en Belgique* 9 (1951) 37. See also G. Bersanetti, "Quando Valeriano fu fatto prigioniero dai Persiani," *Rivista Indo-greco-italica* 21 (1937) 157-161.
[11] Wickert, "Licinius (Egnatius)," *RE* 13 (1927) 361.

Valerian (295.17ff.) and the statement that the emperor wished to go to the East from Italy but could not (297.21ff.). The second objection to supposing that a sign for "year" was misread as a *delta* is that Malalas gives the date with the formula χρηματιζούσης τῆς μεγάλης 'Αντιοχείας (296.8-9), which suggests that the word or sign for "year" has not dropped out. The usual formula found in Malalas is ἔτους χρηματίζοντος κατὰ τοὺς 'Αντιοχεῖς (or sometimes κατὰ τὴν 'Αντιόχειαν),[12] and if the sign or word for "year" had, as Ensslin thinks, dropped out, we should expect χρηματίζοντος to have remained in the text, instead of χρηματιζούσης, which is actually written.[13] Rostovtzeff[14] suggests emending the date to ατ′ = A.D. 252/3, the year which, he thinks, Zosimus and the *Sibylline Oracles* indicate for Sapor's invasion; he adds, however, that neither this nor any other proposed emendation is convincing, and in this the present writer concurs. Malalas apparently believed that Antioch was taken only once by the Persians, but his knowledge and judgment in such matters could be quite faulty, and Rostovtzeff suggests,[15] with some plausibility, that Malalas' citation of two sources, Domninus and Philostratus, shows that the chronicler used two accounts which actually referred to two different invasions, though he mistakenly supposed that they referred to the same invasion.[16] However, it is plain that Malalas' account is defective, and that by itself it gives little help with the chronology.[17]

Peter Patricius described the capture of the city, but of his account we possess only one fragment (*FHG* 4, p. 192, fr. 1). Peter's source, the Continuator of Dio, was a contemporary and his account must have been excellent. Peter was used by Zonaras, whose account, though late in date, should have some authority. Zonaras (12.23) relates that Antioch was taken only once by the Persians, after the capture of Valerian.[18]

[12] See 227.5-6, 241.9-11, 243.13-14, 248.11-12, 275.5-6, 286.7-8, 319.6-7, 322.1-2, 369.7-8, 376.18-19, 393.7-8, 400.9-10, 401.24, 425.3-4. The numeral for the year is given at different points in the phrase.
[13] The phrase χρηματιζούσης τῆς μεγάλης 'Αντιοχείας (or τῆς πόλεως) appears, in Malalas, only in the passage under discussion. Evagrius (2.12, p. 63.15-16 ed. Bidez-Parmentier) once writes χρηματιζούσης τῆς πόλεως. It might be argued, in support of Ensslin's conjecture, that if the sign for "year," being misinterpreted as a *delta*, had dropped out of a formula with χρηματίζοντος, the resulting ungrammatical phrase might then have been "corrected" to the phrase that now stands in the MS. But if a scribe had felt the need of making a correction, why might he not have restored the word ἔτους (or the sign for that word)? It may be that the presence of the unique phrase χρηματιζούσης τῆς μεγάλης 'Αντιοχείας betrays the use of a source that Malalas did not usually employ; but it would be unsafe to place any weight upon so slight an indication.
[14] *Op.cit.* (above, n. 3) 38, n. 51; cf. Stauffenberg 374-376.
[15] *Op.cit.* (above, n. 3) 32, 34, 39.
[16] Ensslin *op.cit.* (above, n. 4) 54, 107, disagrees with Rostovtzeff and thinks that Malalas speaks of only one invasion.
[17] Malalas might have been particularly confused (or badly informed) on the wars between the Romans and the Persians. There is some reason, in fact, to think that his fantastic story of a Persian capture of Antioch in Trajan's time may have arisen out of a misunderstanding of the events of the time of Valerian; see R. P. Longden, "Notes on the Parthian Campaigns of Trajan," *Journal of Roman Studies* 21 (1931) 29-35.
[18] Olmstead, *op.cit.* (above, n. 1) 243.

Appendices

Zosimus (1.27, cf. 1.32) relates that Antioch was captured and destroyed only once, in the time of Valerian's predecessor Gallus, i.e. between A.D. 251 and 253. He describes Sapor's capture of Valerian in A.D. 260 (1.36) without mentioning the invasion of Syria which followed.[19]

Syncellus (715.16—716.3 Bonn ed.) seems to speak of two captures of Antioch by Sapor, once before and once after Valerian fell into the hands of the Persians.[20]

A brief biography of Cyriades (i.e. Mareades) appears as No. 2 in the collection called "The Thirty Pretenders" in the *Scriptores Historiae Augustae*, a compilation of uncertain date and on occasion of dubious value. Rostovtzeff[21] thinks that "the source of Cyriades' biography in *SHA* was of the same kind as the sources used by Domninus, that is to say a historical work compiled in Syria, probably by a native or resident of that country." Olmstead[22] points out that the confusion of *r* and *d* in a proper name, exemplified in the way in which Cyriades' biographer writes Odomastes for Oromastes (Hormizd) shows that he had a source that was written in Aramaic characters. The biography is brief and contains statements that must be legendary. It speaks of Cyriades as guiding the Persians on two invasions of the Roman dominions, but gives no indication of their dates.

Among the literary sources may be mentioned, finally, two oriental works. The Arabic chronicle of al-Tabari records, with a certain amount of obviously incorrect detail, that Antioch was captured from Valerian by Sapor, and that the Persians deported many of the inhabitants and settled them in Persia.[23] The Nestorian history called the *Chronicle of Seert*, written in Arabic soon after A.D. 1036, records that Antioch was captured twice at this period by the Persians, and that some of the inhabitants, including the bishop Demetrianus, were carried off and settled in Persia.[24] This chronicle, which

[19] On Zosimus' account see Rostovtzeff, *op.cit.* (above, n. 3) 37. Ensslin *op.cit.* (above, n. 4) 26-27, defending his thesis that Antioch was captured only once, in A.D. 260, maintains that Rostovtzeff is wrong in believing that Zosimus in 1.27 speaks of a capture of the city under Gallus, i.e. between A.D. 251 and 253. Zosimus is, however, explicit on the chronology here, and Ensslin does not mention or attempt to explain away the fact (pointed out by Rostovtzeff) that Zosimus mentions the capture of Valerian elsewhere (1.36), thus suggesting that in the earlier passage (1.27) he had in mind another occasion on which Antioch was captured. Ensslin strains the meaning of the text when he argues that when Zosimus mentions that capture of Antioch again (3.32.5), he connects the event with Valerian. Actually it is far from plain, from what he says, that Zosimus intended to suggest this.
[20] Ensslin, *op.cit.* (above, n. 4) 30, thinks that Syncellus' words (καταδραμὼν Συρίαν ἦλθεν εἰς Ἀντιόχειαν καὶ πᾶσαν Καππαδοκίαν ἐδῄωσε 715.16-17) show that in the first invasion Sapor merely progressed as far as Antioch without taking it. While this interpretation might be correct, there is nothing to show that Syncellus meant to mention Antioch exclusively rather than inclusively in listing the Persians' progress through Syria; and when there is other evidence that Antioch was taken twice, it seems more natural to suppose that Syncellus, who aimed at brevity, merely had the misfortune to choose a phrase which could be misunderstood.
[21] *Op.cit.* (above, n. 3) 42. [22] *Op.cit.* (above, n. 1) 242.
[23] Tabari, ed. Nöldeke 32-33, 40-41. See G. Bardy, *Paul de Samosate*² 240-241.
[24] *Histoire nestorienne inédit (Chronique de Séert)*, ed. by A. Scher, PO 4.221. See Bardy, *Paul de Samosate*² *loc.cit.* (above, n. 23); and P. Peeters, "Démétrianus, évêque d'Antioche?" *Anal. Boll.* 42 (1924) 288-314 (on the *Chronicle of Seert*, see 309-310). As F. Nau points out

can be shown to be based on valuable sources, is the only preserved text that speaks expressly of two captures of Antioch by the Persians.

The evidence of the coins remains to be described. Alföldi, on the basis of a hoard then lately discovered in Syria, thought it necessary to make certain important revisions in the chronology of the period.[25] Among other things there were, he noticed, certain interruptions in the activity of the mint of Antioch during the period A.D. 253-261, and also that there was a period during which a new mint, which Alföldi located at Samosata, was issuing coins for Valerian. In A.D. 258/9 the operation of the mint of Antioch ceased, and remained suspended for the rest of Valerian's rule. Alföldi concluded that the history of its mint showed that Antioch was captured not only in A.D. 253 and 260, but for a third time as well, in A.D. 258 or 259; and his study of the coins found at Dura led him to believe that that city was captured by the Persians in A.D. 255. Alföldi made his study before the *Res Gestae divi Saporis* became available, and his hypothesis that Antioch was captured three times has not been followed by the scholars who have studied the inscription of Sapor. The suspension of the mint of Antioch in A.D. 258/9, it is thought, need mean only that Valerian found it more practical to have his coins issued from a mint that was more conveniently located, for his military purposes, than Antioch; and the inscription of Sapor shows that this new mint cannot have been located at Samosata.[26] Moreover, it is now certain that Dura fell to the Persians not in A.D. 255, as Alföldi thought, but in A.D. 256.[27]

Since Alföldi wrote, a study by Bellinger[28] of coins found at Dura has shown that in the last year of Trebonianus Gallus (A.D. 253) the mint of Antioch was moved to Emesa. This evidence would seem to support Rostovtzeff's conclusion from the literary evidence that Antioch was captured in A.D. 253.

A final piece of numismatic evidence is furnished by a specimen of a Syrian provincial tetradrachm issued at Antioch in the reign of Trebonianus Gallus (A.D. 251-253), as a part of the last Roman provincial issue put out at Antioch before the city was lost to the Persians; this bears overstrikes which evidently were made when Antioch was under Sassanian control.[29]

On the other hand, the evidence which points to A.D. 256 as the year in

---

(PO 5.220), the *Chronicle of Seert* is the immediate or ultimate source of the late chroniclers Amr and Sliba, who describe the carrying off of Demetrius and other bishops by Chosroes when he captured Antioch; see the passage in *Maris Amri et Slibae De patriarchis Nestorianorum commentaria* ed. and transl. by E. Gismondi (Rome 1896-1899), pp. 8-9 of the Latin translation, reprinted and discussed by Delehaye, *op.cit.* 292ff.

[25] "Die Hauptereignisse der Jahre 253-261 n. Chr. im Orient im Spiegel der Münzprägung," *Berytus* 4 (1937) 41-68. The results of this study are summarized in Alföldi's chapter in *CAH* 12.170ff. See also D. B. Waagé, "Coins," pp. 101-103.

[26] See Rostovtzeff, *op.cit.* (above, n. 3) 47.

[27] A. R. Bellinger, "The Numismatic Evidence from Dura," *Berytus* 8 (1943) 61-71; idem in *Excavations at Dura-Europos, Final Report* VI, *The Coins* (New Haven 1949) 138, 209-210.

[28] In *Berytus*, cited above (n. 27).

[29] F. M. Heichelheim, "Numismatic Comments," *Hesperia* 16 (1947) 277-278.

which Antioch was taken has gained supporters. The evidence for the capture of Dura by the Persians indicates that the city was taken in A.D. 256, or possibly in a later year, and it is tempting to suppose that Antioch was captured in the campaign in which Dura fell. There is a letter of Dionysius of Alexandria addressed to Pope Stephen I (12 May A.D. 254—2 Aug. A.D. 257), preserved by Eusebius,[30] in which Demetrianus is mentioned as being still active in Antioch as bishop, and according to this, the city could not have been taken, and the bishop carried into captivity, in A.D. 253. R. N. Frye[31] and Honigmann and Maricq[32] have been led to conclude that the city was taken in 256. As Frye points out,[33] the Persians could have considered the operations of A.D. 253-256 as one campaign, to be recorded as one unit in the inscription, and it would have been quite possible for the Persians to appear before Antioch in A.D. 253 (causing the removal of the mint), though they did not capture it until A.D. 256.

Summary

Enough has been said to indicate that the problem has been made to seem unusually complicated by the very allusive character of the references to the capture of the city appearing in the literary sources that have come down to us. To the present writer it seems that the best interpretation of the evidence (though it is plain that there still remain questions which cannot be solved satisfactorily with our present material) is as follows: Sapor made two campaigns in Syria and captured Antioch twice. The second taking of the city is to be placed in A.D. 260, after the capture of Valerian. The date of the first is uncertain, but appears to be A.D. 256. The moving of the mint of Antioch to Emesa in A.D. 253, which has been taken to mean that Antioch was captured in that year, need only mean that Antioch was threatened and that the mint was moved to a more convenient location. It seems more satisfactory to suppose that Antioch was captured in A.D. 256 (or in one of the following years), when Dura-Europos was taken. It seems not at all impossible that, as Frye has suggested, there were annual invasions of Syria by the Persians from A.D. 253 to 256, and that this was regarded by Sapor, or at least described in his inscription, as one continuous operation. We could thus suppose that the Persians appeared before the city, or near it, in A.D. 253, but did not take it.

[30] Eusebius *Eccl. hist.* 7.5; cf. E. Honigmann and A. Maricq, "Recherches sur les *Res gestae divi Saporis*," *Académie roy. de Belgique, Classe des lettres et des sciences morales et politiques, Mémoires, Collection in-8°*, tome 47 (1953) 140.

[31] *Bibliotheca Orientalis* 8 (1951) 104-105.

[32] Honigmann and Maricq, *op.cit.* (above, n. 30) 132-140. This opinion is shared by Henning, *op.cit.* (above, n. 4) 826. Maricq claims to have been the first to utilize the testimony of the *Chronicle of Seert* for the question of the date of the first capture of Antioch, but this information had been generally available since it was cited by P. Peeters in his article on Demetrianus in the *Analecta Bollandiana* in 1924 (see above, n. 24), and the same evidence had been utilized by Frye in the *Bibliotheca Orientalis* in 1951 (see above, n. 31).

[33] *Op.cit.* (above, n. 31).

Historical Excursus

That so many of the literary sources seem to imply that the city was captured only once seems to the present writer to be explicable by a general confusion on this matter which came to prevail (exemplified by Malalas) or by the fact that in the texts that we happen to have, the writers had occasion to mention only one capture and did not have occasion to speak explicitly of two captures. That there was a considerable amount of ignorance concerning the Persian episodes at this period in the history of Syria and in the history of Antioch, and a considerable amount of misinformation in circulation, is shown not only by the condition of the literary sources which we have examined, but by the tradition which appears in *SHA Gordian* that the city was also taken in A.D. 241, for which there is no other evidence whatever (see above, Ch. 10, n. 94). It is not without significance that, as Rostovtzeff points out,[34] the short epitomes of Roman history (Eutropius, Orosius, Victor, Rufius Festus) do not mention the first invasion of Syria at all, and mention the second only briefly. Syria must have been in a state of turmoil and alarm from A.D. 253 to A.D. 260, and to some writers the events of this period might well have seemed to be one long invasion, especially on account of the attack on Dura in A.D. 256 (or one of the following years); the various invasions of Syria, indeed, seem to have been looked upon merely as episodes in a continuous war with Persia.[35]

It may be suggested that if Sapor himself visited Antioch on only one of the two occasions when the city was taken (that mentioned by Libanius in *Or.* 60.2-3), the story of the Persian monarch's one visit might have given rise eventually to the tradition that the city was taken only once by the Persians.

EXCURSUS 6

AMMIANUS MARCELLINUS (22.13.1) ON THE STATUE IN THE TEMPLE OF APOLLO AT DAPHNE

In Ammianus' account (22.13.1) of the burning of the temple of Apollo at Daphne in the reign of Julian the Apostate, on 22 Oct. A.D. 362 (on the incident, see above, Ch. 13, nn. 44-46), the manuscript tradition is as follows: *Eodem tempore diem undecimum kalendarum Nouembrium, amplissimum Dafnei Apollinis fanum, quod Epifanes Antiochus rex ille condidit iracundus et saeuus, et simulacrum in eo Olympiaci Iouis semitamenti aequiperans magnitudinem, subita ui flammarum exustum est.* The meaningless *semitamenti,* which occurs in the principal MSS, has generally been corrected by the editors of Ammianus (including V. Gardthausen in his Teubner text and C. U. Clark in his edition, Berlin 1910-1915) to *imitamenti (simulacrum in eo Olympiaci Iouis imitamenti aequiperans magnitudinem).* This would

---

[34] *Op.cit.* (above, n. 3) 42.
[35] This point is well brought out by Pugliese Carratelli *op.cit.* (above, n. 4) 223.

mean that the fire destroyed the statue in the temple, which equaled the size of the image of Olympian Zeus, *imitamentum* being used in this case as the equivalent of *imago*. This interpretation, which seems perfectly clear and simple (the only peculiarity of the sentence, if indeed it be a peculiarity, being the use of the rather unusual word *imitamentum*), has been discussed most recently by Lacroix, "Copies de statues sur les monnaies des Séleucides," 164-165. However, certain scholars have been unable to accept it. Müller (*Antiq. Antioch* 63) considered Ammianus' words somewhat obscure and capable of being interpreted in different ways. They might, he thought, be explained on the basis of coins of Antiochus IV which show a statue of Zeus which is a close imitation of the statue of Olympian Zeus of Phidias (Newell, *Seleucid Mint of Antioch* 23-24; Lacroix, *op.cit.* 165). Thus Antiochus IV would have set up in the temple of Apollo a statue of Zeus that was a copy of that of Phidias. This same explanation led Mommsen to propose an emendation of the text of Ammianus according to which the name of Phidias would actually be mentioned: *simulacrum in eo Olympiaci Iouis imitamenti Phidiaci eiusque aequiperans magnitudinem*. This emendation, which amounts to a rewriting of Ammianus to fit a hypothesis, seems of course to be unnecessarily violent, as P. H. Damsté points out, *Mnemosyne* N.S. 58 (1930) 4, and it has been accepted by no editor of Ammianus. Damsté proposed another emendation, by which the text would be made to read *simulacrum in eo Olympiaci Iouis imitamentum, eiusque aequiperans magnitudinem*, thus yielding the same sense, namely that Antiochus IV set up a statue that was an imitation of the Zeus at Olympia. *Eiusque*, Damsté thinks, was omitted by haplography because of its similarity to the following word, and then *imitamentum*, which was rendered meaningless by the omission, was "corrected" to *imitamenti*. Damsté's emendation was accepted by J. C. Rolfe in his edition of Ammianus in the Loeb Classical Library.

Arguing strongly against this emendation (as well as against Mommsen's) is the fact (pointed out by Lacroix, *op.cit.* 166) that Libanius, in his account of the burning of the temple (*Or.* 60), mentions the destruction of the statue of Apollo but says nothing about the destruction of a statue of Zeus. Moreover, Libanius' remark (*Or.* 60.12) that the statue reached almost to the roof of the temple shows that the comparison of the image with that of the Olympian Zeus was justified, and suggests, of course, that the true sense of the text of Ammianus is that indicated by the manuscript reading (*imitamenti*), according to which the statue of Zeus is mentioned merely by way of comparison in point of size. Thus, when the manuscript reading yields a satisfactory sense without being emended, it seems improper to emend; and so we must conclude that Ammianus' text does not mean that the temple of Apollo contained a statue of Olympian Zeus.

TOPOGRAPHICAL EXCURSUS

EXCURSUS 7

THE DATE OF THE EARTHQUAKE AT ANTIOCH
IN THE REIGN OF LEO I

A NUMBER of sources record an earthquake at Antioch during the reign of Leo I which they date by various chronological indications and synchronisms. These are at times not only inconsistent with the data given by other sources, but show internal disagreements within the same source. One late chronicle mentions two earthquakes, which it dates in two successive years. The problem of when the earthquake actually occurred (or whether, indeed, there really were two earthquakes) has presented a difficult puzzle. In recent years, as more evidence bearing on the question has come to be generally available, the difficulty has been made the subject of detailed studies, by the present writer,[1] by E. Honigmann,[2] by the R. P. Paul Peeters,[3] and by the R. P. V. Grumel.[4] These investigations have made it plain that it is impossible, with the evidence at present available, to find a complete and definitive solution to the problem, but they have made clear the nature of the difficulties involved (which had not, in the past, always been understood), and have suggested what seems to be a reasonable conclusion, namely that there was one earthquake and that it occurred in the night of the 13th to the 14th September A.D. 458.

The most detailed, and ostensibly the most authoritative chronological data are furnished by Malalas and Evagrius, whose accounts ought, it would seem, to command respect since they were both closely concerned with the history of Antioch and could have had access to local official records.

Malalas (369.5-8) describes an earthquake at Antioch which he dates "in the reign of Leo, on 13 September, as Sunday was dawning, in the year 506 of the era of Antioch, in the consulship of Patricius" (a passage corresponding to this is preserved in the Church Slavonic edition of Malalas,

---

[1] G. Downey, "The Calendar Reform at Antioch in the Fifth Century," *Byzantion* 15 (1940-41) 39-48.

[2] E. Honigmann, "The Calendar Change at Antioch and the Earthquake of 458 A.D.," *Byzantion* 17 (1944-45) 336-339.

[3] P. Peeters, *Orient et Byzance: Le tréfonds oriental de l'hagiographie byzantine* (Brussels 1950; *Subsidia Hagiographica* 26) 127-133. The study in which this discussion of the date of the earthquake appears is a revision of an earlier article, "S. Syméon Stylite et ses premiers biographes," *Anal. Boll.* 61 (1943) 29-71.

[4] In his valuable handbook *La Chronologie* (*Traité d'études byzantines*, ed. by P. Lemerle, vol. 1; Paris 1958) 194-195. The reader must bear in mind that P. Grumel in his discussion omits the testimony of Malalas and utilizes that of Evagrius as being more precise. I gladly acknowledge P. Grumel's correction of my interpretation of Evagrius' ἐπικαταλαβούσης, which means (as P. Grumel points out) that Sunday had already arrived. However, it is still necessary to consider this datum in connection with the testimony of Malalas. It may be noted that P. Grumel does not mention the study of P. Peeters.

but this has become hopelessly corrupt). Evagrius, describing the same event, gives greater detail concerning the date (*Hist. eccl.* 2.12, p. 63 ed. Bidez-Parmentier): ". . . in the second year of the reign of Leo, in the year 506 of the era of the city, about the fourth hour of the night, on the 14th of the month Gorpiaios, which is called September, when Sunday had commenced, in the eleventh indiction, the sixth [earthquake] which is recorded, 347 years having passed since that which occurred under Trajan; for that occurred in the 159th year of the autonomy of the city, while that under Leo occurred in the 506th. . . ." Evagrius then goes on to describe the damage done in the disaster, and quotes his account of it from Malalas.

Various chronicles mention an earthquake which they date in A.D. 457 (Theophanes, a. 5950, p. 110.22 ed. De Boor; Cedrenus 1.608.3; Bar Hebraeus, *Hist. dynast.* tr. E. Pococke [Oxford 1663] p. 92), or in A.D. 459 (Marcellin. *Chron. ad ann.* 459, in Mommsen, *Chron. min.*, II, p. 87), or during the episcopate of Acacius (Nicephorus patriar., *Chronographikon syntomon*, p. 131.21 ed. De Boor), or merely during the reign of Leo (John of Nikiu, ch. 88.1, transl. Charles, presumably based on Malalas; Nicephorus Callistus, *Hist. eccl.* 15.20, presumably based on Evagrius; Zonaras 14.1.20).

The only contemporary reference to such an earthquake which is preserved is that in the Syriac *Life* of Symeon Stylites published by Lietzmann and Hilgenfeld,[5] in which there are three references to an earthquake at Antioch which preceded the death of Symeon (ch. 123, p. 168; ch. 133, p. 177.19-20; ch. 136, p. 179.22-24). The date of this earthquake is not stated, and the event can be dated only with reference to the death of Symeon, which occurred on 2 September A.D. 459, according to the Syriac *Life* (ch. 137, p. 179.34), though it has been argued that his death actually occurred on 24 July of that year;[6] in any case, the Syriac *Life* indicates A.D. 459 as the year.

Finally, one late Syriac source, the so-called *Liber Chalifarum*, or *Chronicon Miscellaneun ad annum Domini 724 pertinens*, mentions two earthquakes at Antioch, one of which it dates in the year 506 of the era of the city, on 14 September (with details which show that this corresponds to the earthquake mentioned by Evagrius), the other in the year 507 of the era, on 19 June.[7] There is, however, a confusion in the author's synchronisms. He puts the first disaster in the year 506 of the era of Antioch and in the year 767 of the "era of Alexander," i.e. the Seleucid era, while he dates the second earthquake in the year 507 of Antioch and in the year 771 of the

---

[5] "Das Leben des heiligen Symeon Stylites," *Texte und Untersuchungen*, 32, 4 (1908), including a German translation of the Syriac biography by H. Hilgenfeld. The biography of Symeon by Antonius, which dates from the sixth century and has little value as a source (Peeters, *op.cit.* 107, 112), does not mention an earthquake in connection with the death of Symeon, or, indeed, in any other connection.

[6] Delehaye, *Saints stylites* pp. x-xv.

[7] *CSCO, Scriptores Syri, Versio*, ser. III, tomus IV, *Chronica minora*, pars secunda, ed. E. W. Brooks, interpretatus est J. B. Chabot (1904), pp. 108.27ff. (earthquake in the year 506, in connection with which Bishop Acacius is mentioned), 110.6ff. (earthquake in the year 507).

Seleucid era. The year 767 Seleucid (A.D. 455/6) cannot correspond to the year 506 of Antioch (A.D. 457/8), although 771 Seleucid (A.D. 459/60) might correspond with 507 of Antioch (A.D. 458/9) if the years of the two eras began at different periods and overlapped by one month, at the end of one and the beginning of the other.

There are obviously many discrepancies in the chronological data. The year 506 of Antioch corresponds to A.D. 457/58, beginning in the autumn; Patricius was consul in A.D. 459; the eleventh indiction = 1 Sept. A.D. 457—31 Aug. A.D. 458; the Emperor Leo came to the throne on 7 Feb. A.D. 457. It would look at first glance as though some sources dated the earthquake in A.D. 457, some in 458, some in 459. The statements concerning the day of the week also indicate confusion. Malalas places it on Sunday, 13 September, and the 13th was a Sunday in A.D. 459. Evagrius appears to mean that the event occurred on the 14th of the month, after Sunday had arrived; and the 14th of September was a Saturday in A.D. 457. This divergence, taken by itself, would seem to reflect the variations in some of the later chronicles, mentioned above, between A.D. 457 and 459.

In the past, scholars have reached various conclusions about the date of the earthquake (or earthquakes), sometimes without having access to all the material listed above, sometimes without knowing of the existence of all of it.

The first study of the evidence known to the present writer, which long remained the most intelligent account of the problem although the author did not possess important material which was not yet published in his time, was that of the scholar Enrico Noris (Henricus Norisius), in a study of the Syro-Macedonian calendar published in 1696.[8] Noris knew from the synchronisms given in a passage in Evagrius (4.4) that in the year A.D. 518, the year of the era of Antioch began on 1 September, instead of on 1 October, as it had originally done.[9] This change in the beginning of the year suggested, to Noris, that since the earthquake in question was said to have occurred in September, the discrepancies between the accounts of Malalas and Evagrius might have been caused by a misunderstanding, on their part (or on the part of their sources), of dates reckoned by the "old style" (with the year of Antioch beginning on October first) or the "new style" (with the year beginning on September first). For example, a writer who did not know of the change of the beginning of the year, and adopted, or worked out for himself, a synchronism with another mode of reckoning, might very well make an error of a year in dating events which occurred in September. Looking at the problem from this point of view, Noris saw that the data of

---

[8] *Annus et epochae Syromacedonum* (Leipzig 1696) 208-217.

[9] Here Evagrius records that Severus, bishop of Antioch, was deposed and exiled in the first year of the Emperor Justinus (who came to the throne on 9 April A.D. 518), in the month of Gorpiaios or September, in the year 567 of the era of Antioch. Since 567 Antioch corresponds to A.D. 518/9, the year of the era must have begun on 1 September in the year A.D. 518. On the evidence for the original beginning of the year on October first, see further below.

Evagrius would indicate September of A.D. 457, if Evagrius supposed that the year 506 of Antioch began on September first, as it did in his own time, and as it had done (he knew) as early as A.D. 518. If the earthquake did occur in September A.D. 457, Malalas, for example, might not have known of the change in the calendar, or might have supposed that his source was mistaken, and so might have altered or added to the evidence in such a way that the event would be placed in A.D. 459. Noris also saw that one could suppose that the earthquake was originally dated in September A.D. 458, by reference to the year 506 of Antioch, and that the dates of Malalas and Evagrius represent two different misunderstandings of the same original date.

Noris' study, unfortunately, was not always understood or appreciated. H. F. Clinton[10] supposed that Evagrius named the wrong indiction, Malalas the wrong consul, and that the earthquake was to be dated on Saturday, 13 September A.D. 458. This would indicate that the year 506 of Antioch began on 1 October A.D. 457. However, Clinton seems not to have understood Noris' exposition, for he is at pains to refute the earlier scholar's opinion that the earthquake occurred in September A.D. 457, while C. O. Müller[11] believed that Noris had adopted September A.D. 458, as the date. Ideler[12] observed that Evagrius' synchronisms are really harmonious if one supposes that Leo's second regnal year was counted from 1 September A.D. 457, the beginning of the indiction which followed his accession, rather than from the anniversary of his accession (a method of counting regnal years found in other Byzantine writers[13]). Thus Ideler dated the event on Saturday, 14 September A.D. 457, and concluded that the year 506 of Antioch began on 1 September A.D. 457. Ideler dismissed the testimony of Malalas, on the ground that Evagrius' seemed so much more accurate.

Lietzmann, having no comment on the passages in the Syriac *Life* of Symeon in which the earthquake was mentioned, was apparently the first scholar who knew and used the passages in the *Liber Chalifarum* according to which two earthquakes occurred.[14] Lietzmann concluded that, as between Malalas and Evagrius, Malalas was right, since his material was based on the official chronicle of Antioch, and that, putting aside the error of the consulship, Malalas' date indicated 14 September A.D. 457.[15] This corresponds to the first of the earthquakes mentioned in the *Liber Chalifarum*. As to the second of the disasters recorded in that chronicle, which is, as Lietzmann observes, mentioned in no other chronicle, Lietzmann concludes that this

[10] *Fasti Romani* (Oxford 1845-1850) 1.658-660, 2.213-214.
[11] *Antiq. Antioch.* 15. n. 10.
[12] L. Ideler, *Handbuch der mathematischen und technischen Chronologie* (Berlin 1825-1826) 1.453-457, 463-465.
[13] See Clinton, *op.cit.* 2.1, and N. Lewis, "On the Chronology of the Emperor Maurice," *AJP* 60 (1939) 414-421.
[14] Lietzmann, *op.cit.* (above, n. 5) 228-233.
[15] In Lietzmann's discussion, p. 231, line 16, the year given for the era of Antioch, 806, is a typographical error for 506.

earthquake is the one mentioned in the Syriac *Life* of Symeon, and dates it in June A.D. 459.

Apparently Lietzmann worked without knowing Noris' study, and without realizing himself that the difficulty might be connected with the calendar change. Lietzmann did, however, know several Greek inscriptions of Syria, published in 1870, which indicated by their synchronisms that at about this time there had been a change in the beginning of the year of Antioch from October first to September first; the text that Lietzmann cites indicates that the year began on 1 September in A.D. 479 (see further below). Previously all that had been known, from Evagrius, was that the change took place some time before A.D. 518 (see above). To Lietzmann, this meant that the change to the beginning of the year on 1 September had taken place by the time of the earthquake; and so, Lietzmann supposed, the obvious existence of error in Malalas' synchronisms meant that he had falsified some of the data in order to make them agree, for it is Evagrius' date which is correct if the year of the era of Antioch began, in the year of the earthquake, on 1 September. Lietzmann thus came to the conclusion that the earthquake occurred on 14 September A.D. 457.

What Lietzmann did not realize was that the inscriptions which he knew, but apparently did not fully understand, contain synchronisms from which it can be demonstrated that there was a change in the beginning of the year of Antioch from 1 October to 1 September, made at some time between A.D. 449 (the last inscription known in which the year begins on 1 October) and 483 (the earliest known inscription in which the year begins on 1 September).[16] It was on the basis of this evidence that the present writer took up the problem, in an article which was designed primarily as a study in ancient literary technique, showing the way in which ancient difficulties in synchronising different calendars could produce errors in dates; from this point of view, the dating of the earthquake (or earthquakes) was of secondary interest.[17] All the sources, with the exception of the *Liber Chalifarum*, mention only one earthquake at Antioch at this period. Nevertheless, the chronological data in Malalas, cited above, could be taken to mean that there were two earthquakes which occurred a year or two years apart. The reckonings of Evagrius could refer, as has been seen, only to A.D. 457 or 458. Malalas' reckoning by the year of Antioch would refer to A.D. 457 or 458 (depending on the beginning of the year), while his dating by the consul corresponds to A.D. 459. Abstractly, it would seem that there might have been two disasters, which Malalas confused and consolidated into one. Evagrius, verifying

<hr/>

[16] The inscriptions, originally published by Waddington, *Inscriptions grecques et latines de la Syrie*, nos. 2667, 2689, were republished, with new evidence and with a commentary in which their significance was pointed out, by W. K. Prentice in *PAES*, III B, see commentary on no. 1108. See now *IGLS* nos. 524, and 1876, commentary. Lietzmann, who published his book on Symeon in 1908, did not have the advantage of being able to use Prentice's commentary, published in 1914.

[17] It seems worth while to recall this fact, in view of the criticisms which Honigmann makes of my study.

Malalas' account, would reject the parts of his date that indicated A.D. 459, without realizing (perhaps because he had no other source) that there had been two earthquakes, and that Malalas confused them.

It is, in fact, possible to see how Malalas might have blundered through ignorance of the calendar change, or of the date at which it occurred, or through using different sets of sources in which the beginning of the new year was reckoned from different times (i.e. from 1 September or 1 October), without the difference being made plain. If the year 506 of the local era began on 1 October A.D. 457, the earthquake would be dated (by reference to the year 506 Ant.) in A.D. 458; but if 506 Ant. began on 1 September A.D. 457, the date of the earthquake would be A.D. 457. The 13th of September (Malalas' day for the event) fell on a Friday in A.D. 457, a Saturday in 458, a Sunday in 459. If we suppose that Malalas found in his source (or in two sources) records of two earthquakes which were dated in September, year 506 of Antioch (A.D. 457/58) and in the consulship of Patricius (A.D. 459), it would be possible to think that Malalas confused the dates by faulty arithmetic. A disaster occurring in A.D. 458 could immediately be confused with one dated in the following year. Or if, as the notices in some of the other chroniclers could be taken to mean, there were two earthquakes, in A.D. 457 and 459, Malalas might through misunderstanding suppose that the one which occurred in A.D. 457 actually occurred in A.D. 458, which was closer to Patricius' consulship (A.D. 459). In such circumstances he would doubtless feel no hesitation in adjusting the day of the week recorded for the earlier disaster to the day required for the later event. This would be especially easy to do, of course, if the earthquake occurred during the night, as it seems to have done.

Evagrius obviously was not wholly easy about the date. The number of reckonings that he employs indicates that he was anxious to fix the date as accurately as possible. It is notable, also, that Evagrius does not reproduce Malalas' reference to the consul, which, as we have seen, would disagree with all the other data given by Evagrius. The indiction that he gives could only indicate A.D. 457. However, the year 506 of Antioch and the regnal year could also indicate A.D. 458, if Leo's second regnal year were reckoned from 7 February A.D. 458, the anniversary of his accession, rather than from the indiction following his accession, and if the year 506 of Antioch began on 1 October A.D. 457. It would be possible then, if Evagrius found a synchronism which placed the earthquake in A.D. 458 by reference to Leo's second regnal year, reckoned from the anniversary of his accession, for him to think that this regnal year was calculated from the indiction which followed his accession, and so place the earthquake in September A.D. 457. The reference to the regnal year would in this case be a trace of an original date in A.D. 458. Evagrius would then conclude that 506 Antioch began on 1 September (A.D. 457), as it did in his own time, and would add the indiction

Topographical Excursus

to make the date certain. On the other hand, he may have assumed, wrongly, that 506 Ant. began on 1 September (i.e. A.D. 457), as it did in his own day, and so may have concluded that Leo's second regnal year began on the same day, and then added the indiction. Or both regnal year and indiction could have been added, for the sake of greater certainty, to what was originally only a reference to the year of the era. It would be as easy for Evagrius as for Malalas to adjust the date of the month and day of the week to what he thought was the right date, i.e. he could very well adjust the original date, Saturday, 13 September A.D. 458, to the date required for A.D. 457, namely 14 September. If Malalas had already confused two earthquakes and consolidated them into one, Evagrius may have had no way of knowing that there had originally been two.

If one starts from the point of view of the possibilities involved in the calendar change, it is equally easy to see how errors could occur. If the year 506 of Antioch began on 1 September (i.e. 1 September A.D. 457) and an earthquake occurred in that month, Malalas, not knowing of, or misunderstanding the calendar change, could confuse the disaster with that dated in September A.D. 459. Evagrius would then have only to omit the consular dating and adjust the days of the month and week. Or Malalas may have supposed, wrongly, that 506 Antioch began on 1 October, and so may have assigned the earthquake to the equivalent of September A.D. 458, at the same time confusing it with that which actually occurred in the following year. If it seems difficult to suppose that Malalas and Evagrius, both natives of Antioch and accustomed to using local sources, were not aware of the time when the change in the local new year had taken place, and could not deal with dates of the period involved, we have only to recall the difficulties which some modern historians, even those with reputable training, find in dealing with Old Style and New Style dates in the eighteenth century. In a given instance, Malalas and Evagrius (like modern researchers) may have been unable to determine whether a given source used the old calendar or the new one.

This study seemed to Honigmann to be defective, so that he published his own investigation, in which he made an important addition by calling attention to the reference, in Nicephorus' *Chronicon*, to the fact that Acacius was bishop at the time of the earthquake (see above). Since Acacius was in office for only a few months, during A.D. 458, this would constitute, in Honigmann's view, additional reason to believe that the disaster is to be dated in that year. Père Peeters' study, following Honigmann's, is concerned largely with the reliability of the Syriac *Life* of Symeon, as an eye-witness account of the saint's life, written not more than fifteen years after his death. The biographer's references to the earthquake are vague as to chronology, since this is a detail that is not germane to the edifying purpose of his book; but it is important to note that only one earthquake is mentioned. P. Peeters dates it on 14 September A.D. 458.

Such is the present state of this problem. While the possibility exists that there were actually two earthquakes in A.D. 457 and 459, it still seems to the present writer, as it did to Noris, most likely that there was one earthquake, in September of A.D. 458, and that the confusions in the accounts of Malalas and Evagrius reflect difficulties caused by misunderstandings connected with the change in the beginning of the new year in the calendar of Antioch. The problem is one of singular interest, but also of singular complexity, and we apparently cannot look for its solution until new evidence is found.

At the end of his description of the disaster, Evagrius, quoting Malalas, says that "the emperor exempted the city from a thousand talents of gold from the tribute, and the citizens from the taxes on the property which had been destroyed in the disaster." Honigmann suggests, at the close of his study, that the change of the beginning of the year to 1 September was connected with this remission of taxes. "In such a case [Honigmann writes] it could have been important for the inhabitants that the years of exemption were equalized with the indictions, for a malevolent tax-collector could perhaps try to shorten the granted space by turning the peculiarity of the Antiochene year to account." It seems difficult to accept this suggestion, since the indiction year was already the tax year,[18] and the adjustment to it of the local calendar year would not have had any effect on the collection of taxes. It seems more likely that the change was made simply in order to put an end to possible confusions in records of all kinds (including business documents), and that the local calendar year was brought into line with the indiction year because the latter was, doubtless, the one year which was most used in reckoning dates throughout the Roman world.

EXCURSUS 8

MAPS OF ANTIOCH

(See also Excursus 9, "The Points of the Compass at Antioch in Antiquity and the Orientation of the Maps of the City.")

A. Modern Maps

(listed in chronological order of publication)

1. Rey, E. G. *Étude sur les monuments de l'architecture militaire des Croisés en Syrie et dans l'île de Chypre* (Paris 1871) pl. 17.

   Reproduced on a smaller scale in the same author's *Les colonies franques de Syrie au XIIe et XIIIe siècles* (Paris 1883) 326. This is apparently the earliest map based on a topographical survey. It is incorrectly oriented.

[18] Seeck, "Indictio," *RE* 9.1330, 1332.

2. Baedeker, K. *Palestine and Syria* (Leipzig 1876), facing p. 578.
   Repeated with minor alterations down to the fifth English edition of
   1912, and always incorrectly oriented. See below, Excursus 9, n. 23.
3. Chauvet and Isambert. *Syrie, Palestine* (Guides-Joanne) (Paris 1882) 727.
   Based on Rey's map.
4. Förster, R. "Antiochia am Orontes," *JDAI* 12 (1897), pl. 6.
   Based, with modifications, on the Baedeker map; incorrectly oriented.
   See below, Excursus 9, n. 22.
5. Antioche, 1:20,000. Reproduit par le B. T. de l'A. F. L. 1920.
   Incorrectly oriented.
6. Antioche, Régie du cadastre. Map of the city at 1:2000, based on surveys
   in 1928-1929. Correctly oriented.
7. Jacquot, Lt.Col. Paul. *Antioche, centre de tourisme* (Antioch 1931), vol. 2,
   facing p. 344. Correctly oriented.
8. Les Guides bleus. *Syrie, Palestine, Iraq, Transjordanie* (Paris 1932),
   facing p. 194.
   Based, with modifications, on Rey's map. The incorrect orientation
   resembles that of the map of 1920 (No. 5 above).
9. Bazantay, P. "Contribution à l'étude géographique de la Syrie: Un petit
   pays alaouite, le plateau de Daphne," *Haut-commissariat de la Rép. franç.
   en Syrie et au Liban, Bulletin de l'enseignement* 11 (1933/34):
   a. Topographic map of plateau of Daphne, showing springs, p. 336.
   b. Detail map of springs, p. 340.
   c. Modern distribution of water on Daphne plateau, p. 354.
   All correctly oriented.
10. Sauvaget, J. "Le plan de Laodicée-sur-mer," *Bull. d'études orientales
    (Institut franç. de Damas)* 4 (1934) 108.
    Plan showing survival of ancient plan of Antioch in the modern city;
    correctly oriented.
11. Weulersse, J. "Antioche: essai de géographie urbaine," *Bull. d'études
    orientales (Institut franç. de Damas)* 4 (1934):
    a. Contour map showing site of modern city in relation to mountain
       and river, p. 28.
    b. Schematic map of vicinity of Antioch, p. 32.
    c. Air photograph of part of the city, with overlay indicating survival
       of ancient city plan in modern streets, pl. 5, facing p. 36.
    d. Ethnographic map of modern city, p. 39.
    e. Plan of a section of the city showing survival of ancient plan, p. 47.
    All correctly oriented.
12. *Antioch-on-the-Orontes* 2 (1938):
    a. Antioch, map of the excavations, plan 1, p. 215.
    b. Daphne, map of the excavations, plan 2, p. 216.

Appendices

c. Contour map of Antioch and Daphne showing course of aqueducts, plan 8, p. 222.

All correctly oriented.

13. See also the air photograph of the city reproduced below, Fig. 6.

B. Restored Plans of the City

(listed in chronological order)

1. Poujoulat, J. J. *Correspondance d'Orient, 1830-1831* (Brussels 1841 and other editions). At end of vol. 8, a map of Antioch during the Frankish period, reproduced (with certain omissions) by Jacquot, *Antioche* 2.362.
2. Müller, C. O. *Antiq. Antioch.* (Göttingen 1839). Pl. A, at end of volume, gives a hypothetical restoration of the ancient city plan, based on travelers' descriptions and sketch maps and ancient texts. Reproduced by Jacquot, *Antioche* 2.242.
3. Le Camus, E. *Notre voyage aux pays bibliques* (Paris 1890). Vol. 3, facing p. 32, a restoration of the ancient plan, reproduced by Jacquot, *Antioche* 2.224. The restoration is of very limited value; see Förster, "Antiochia" 104.
4. Morey, C. R. "The Excavation of Antioch-on-the-Orontes," *Proceedings of the American Philosophical Society* 76 (1936) 638, reproduced in the same author's *The Mosaics of Antioch* (New York 1938) 17.

   A restored plan based on literary and archaeological evidence, drawn by D. N. Wilber with the assistance of G. Downey, A. M. Friend, Jr., and R. Stillwell.
5. Restored plan, based on No. 4 above, with modifications and additions indicated by the present study, below, Fig. 11.

C. Medieval Maps and Travelers' Sketch Maps

Medieval Maps

1. A small schematic map of Antioch, which is without topographical value, is found, in differing renditions, in three fourteenth-century manuscripts of the *Chronologia magna* of Paulinus the Minorite of Venice (died 1344). These are as follows:

   a. Venice, Cod. Marc. lat. 399, fol. 74 verso: G. Valentinelli, *Bibliotheca manuscripta ad S. Marci Venetiarum* 6 (Venice 1873), p. 80. This is reproduced in facsimile by G. M. Thomas, *De passagiis in Terram Sanctam. Excerpta ex Chronologia magna cod. lat. 399 Bibl. ad D. Marci Venetiarum* (Venice 1879).

   b. Paris, Bibl. nat. lat. 4939, fol. 98 recto, reproduced by E. G. Rey, *Étude sur les monuments de l'architecture militaire des Croisés en Syrie et dans l'île de Chypre* (Paris 1871) pl. 18.

   c. Rome, Cod. Vatic. lat. 1960, fol. 268 verso; cf. *Codices Vaticani Latini*, tom. 3, rec. B. Nogara (Rome 1912) pp. 373-374.

Topographical Excursus

On these maps, see Förster, "Antiochia" 121 and G. Golubovich, *Biblioteca Bio-Bibliografica della Terra Santa e dell'Oriente Francescano*, tom. 2 (Florence 1913) pp. 75-77, 81-83, 86, 90.

Travelers' Sketch Maps

1. Valle, Pietro della. *Viaggi di Pietro della Valle il pellegrino* (Bologna 1672) 3.521-523.

   This is the earliest printed map of Antioch. The author, who visited the city in 1625, apparently either drew the map later from memory, or drew it on the spot without taking measurements.

2. Pococke, Richard. *A Description of the East, and some other countries. Vol. II, part I. Observations on Palestine or the Holy Land, Syria, Mesopotamia, Cyprus and Candia* (London 1745) pl. 26.

   The author, who visited Antioch in 1738 (cf. pp. 2, 194, 228), made approximate measurements but not an actual survey, so that the map, while it resembles the site in general, is not accurate.

3. Niebuhr, Carsten. *C. Niebuhr's Reisebeschreibung nach Arabien und andern umliegenden Laendern. Dritter Band. Reisen durch Syrien und Palaestina, nach Cypern und durch Kleinasien und die Turkey . . . hrsg. von J. N. Gloyer und J. Olshausen* (Hamburg 1837) pl. 2, facing p. 16.

   Niebuhr visited the site in 1766. His map was evidently made in the same manner as Pococke's, but with somewhat more accurate measurements.

D. Maps of the Vicinity of Antioch (a selection)

1. Hydrographic Office, U.S. Navy, No. 3972, Mediterranean Sea, Syria and Turkey, Karatas to Markhab. From a British Survey in 1858. First ed. 1914, 4th ed. 1947. 1:236,660.
2. Antakya (Antioche), Levant 1:200,000, NJ-36-VI, NJ-37-I. Dessiné et imprimé par le Service géographique des F. F. L. Second ed. 1944.
3. Eastern Turkey in Asia: Alexandretta. 1:250,000. I. D. W. O. No. 1522, May 1902, corrected to Nov. 1915.
4. A. A. F. Aeronautical chart, 1:1,000,000. Iskenderun Gulf (341).
5. Geographical Section, General Staff, No. 2555. Asia 1:1,000,000: Erzerum. First ed. 1916, 4th ed. 1942.
6. Dussaud, R. *Topographie historique de la Syrie antique et médiévale* (Paris 1927):

   Map 14: Ancient and medieval roads in Syria.
   Map 9: Antioch and vicinity.
7. Mouterde, R., and A. Poidebard. *Le limes de Chalcis* (Paris 1945):

   a. "Le limes de Chalcis," 1:500,000, in pocket at end of volume of plates, showing Roman roads in N. Syria.

[607]

Appendices

b. Frontispiece of text volume, showing Roman roads in N. Syria.
8. Braidwood, R. J. *Mounds in the Plain of Antioch* (Chicago 1937):
    a. Frontispiece: "The Plain of Antioch and its Environs. Key Map,"
      1:400,000.
    b. Map 9, p. 39: "Ancient Roads Serving the Plain of Antioch,"
      1:600,000.
9. Sauvaget, J. *Alep* (Paris 1941):
    a. Northern Syria, relief and natural resources, p. 15.
    b. Northern Syria, geological sketch, p. 15.

EXCURSUS 9

THE POINTS OF THE COMPASS AT ANTIOCH IN ANTIQUITY AND THE ORIENTATION OF THE MAPS OF THE CITY

It is a remarkable feature of the study of the history of Antioch that the first correctly oriented map of the city was that published in 1931 by Lt.-Col. P. Jacquot, who had extensive personal knowledge of the site and presumably based his map on an independent survey (*Antioche*, 2, facing p. 344). The maps that have been published since Jacquot's, such as those of the excavators (1934 ff.),[1] of J. Weulersse (1934),[2] and of C. R. Morey (1936),[3] were likewise based on independent surveys (an exception is the map in the *Guide Bleu* of 1932; see below). The long axis of the city, in conformity with the contours of the site, follows a northeast and southwest direction, and the main colonnaded street, which ran straight through the city, followed this axis (Fig. 11).

In antiquity there was a curious diversity in this matter. Some authors, e.g. Evagrius,[4] Procopius,[5] and the anonymous biographer of St. Symeon Stylites the Younger,[6] knew the true points of the compass, and speak in correct terms of the southern wall of the city and of the gate in the southern wall which led to Daphne. On the other hand Libanius, in his oration in praise of Antioch, which is one of the best known sources for the topography of the city, speaks of the orientation of Antioch, on its long axis, as east-west, and of the streets as running east-west and north-south; the main street, he says, ran east and west, and Daphne was west of the

---

[1] In the excavation reports the correct orientation first appears in *Antioch-on-the-Orontes* 1 (1934), pl. 2, facing p. viii. See also the maps in subsequent volumes, e.g. *Antioch-on-the-Orontes* 2, plan 1, p. 215.
[2] "Antioche," 39.
[3] *Proceedings of the Amer. Philosophical Society* 76 (1936) 638, reprinted in his *Mosaics of Antioch* 17. This map was drawn by D. N. Wilber with the collaboration of A. M. Friend, Jr., R. Stillwell, and G. Downey. It is the basis of Fig. 11 in the present volume.
[4] See above, Ch. 16, n. 11.   [5] *Wars* 2.8.25.   [6] See above, Excursus 10, §A.

city (*Or.* 11.196, 198, 204, 233, 250). It seems plain that this usage must have been familiar to Libanius' audience, for it is difficult to understand how he could have employed it if it had not been well known. There seem to be various possible explanations for such an error. In antiquity, only engineers and architects could, as a rule, determine the true compass points, and then not always accurately. The general public, not possessing compasses or accurate printed maps, must have been rather uncertain on such matters. If general knowledge of the subject were not precise, the fact that the main street ran northeast and southwest could easily give rise to loose usage in speaking of it, for one could, if one wished to use general rather than exact compass points, speak of the street as running east-west just as easily as one could speak of it as running north-south. Moreover, in the summer the sun would rise close to the northeast beginning of the street, and this might well contribute to the common impression that the street began at the east.

While it may seem difficult to understand how two different usages with respect to the points of the compass can have been current at Antioch, there is, curiously enough, in Malalas evidence that it was possible to employ the true and the inexact points of reference simultaneously. This becomes evident when several references to the points of the compass by Malalas are examined. After describing the new city wall that (he says) Tiberius built at Antioch (232.20ff.), Malalas writes (235.3-6) that the same emperor erected the Eastern Gate ('Ανατολικὴ πόρτα).[7] There is no evidence in this first reference to the monument to show whether it was eastern in the sense of the true point of the compass, or whether it was "eastern" according to the convention followed by Libanius, according to which it would have stood, actually, in the northeastern or northern part of the city. However, Malalas has another reference to the gate that shows its true position, and shows that it was named according to the usage found in Libanius. In his account of the visit to Antioch of the celebrated seer Apollonius of Tyana, in the reign of Domitian, Malalas says (264.7-10) that the people of the city requested Apollonius "to make . . . talismans against certain things. And he made one against the north wind, placing this talisman at the Eastern Gate." One can only assume that a talisman against a wind would be placed at the point at which the wind first struck the city; and if the talisman at Antioch were placed in the northern part of the city, at the Eastern Gate, it would seem clear that this gate was so named according to the usage reflected in Libanius, and that it actually stood at the northern end of the city. This is, in fact, one of the places at which we should expect to find a monumental gate built

---

[7] Malalas ascribes the work to Tiberius but it is not certain that the work was done by him; in any case the paving of the streets and the erection of the gate took place during the reign of Augustus; see above, Ch. 8, §2. On the symbolism and significance of the Eastern Gate, see Excursus 10, §13.

by Tiberius, for the main street of the city had recently been embellished with colonnades, and a monumental gate bearing a statue of the she-wolf with Romulus and Remus would be a fitting complement to the colonnades.

The only other reference to a point of the compass in Malalas reflects the true rather than the conventional usage. In his account of the earthquake of A.D. 526 the chronicler writes (421.9ff.) that "on the third day after the disaster there appeared in the sky the holy cross, in a cloud, in the northern part of the same city." This vision must have appeared over the northern part of Mount Silpius, for Procopius in his description of the rebuilding of Antioch after its capture by the Persians in A.D. 540 speaks (*De Aed.* 2.10.16) of the two sections of Mount Silpius, as they are divided by the torrent Parmenius or Onopnictes,[8] as Staurin and Orocassias, and it is evident that the name Staurin was given to the northern part of the mountain from the vision of the cross that appeared there.

The usage that appears in Libanius persisted, with a few notable exceptions, down to modern times. The travelers Cotovicus (1599), Pietro della Valle (1625), De la Roque (1688), Pococke (1738) and Drummond (1748) all speak of the orientation of the city as east-west, with the mountains to the south and the river to the north, and this orientation is shown on the printed maps of della Valle and Pococke.[9] In the middle of the eighteenth century, however, scientifically trained travelers began to visit the city. Apparently the earliest visitors who made accurate observations of the points of the compass were the Dutch travelers Egmond and Heyman, who visited the city at some time before 1759; they record that the mountain is to the east of the city.[10] Carsten Niebuhr in 1766 came closer to making a correct observation, but did not wholly succeed, for north, in his map, was toward what is actually northwest.[11] Parsons in 1772 was apparently the next traveler to make an accurate observation with a compass of the direction of the long axis of the city.[12] It is interesting to note that at the same time Parsons spoke of the gates on the roads leading to Beroea and to Daphne as the east gate and the west gate respectively. Corancez in 1809 and Kinneir in 1813 combined the true and the false directions.[13] Von Richter in 1816 returned to the usage of Libanius, while Buckingham in the same year has the points of the compass exactly right,[14] being apparently the next traveler after Parsons to make an accurate observation. The Pou-

8 Procopius calls the stream Onopnictes, rather than by its usual name Parmenius; see above, Ch. 18, §8, with n. 200.

9 Cotovicus 499; della Valle 521, 523; De la Roque 249, 253; Pococke pl. 26, facing p. 189; Drummond 221. In this and the following notes, references to the statements of travelers are to the works cited in the list of travelers' descriptions below, Excursus 19.

10 Egmond and Heyman 2.325. The year in which the journey was made is not specified in the account of it.

11 See his map, pl. 2, facing p. 16.   12 Parsons 70.

13 Corancez 116, Kinneir 147, 151, 152.

14 Von Richter 281, Buckingham 556, 562, 565.

joulat map of 1830-1831 shows the false orientation, with north at what is actually west.[15] Lt.-Col. Chesney in 1835 was the next visitor, after Buckingham, to state the directions correctly (his account was not published until 1850).[16]

When C. O. Müller made his study of Antioch, he was unable to visit the site, but he knew all the travelers' descriptions mentioned above (except Chesney's which appeared after Müller wrote, and those of Egmond and Heyman and of Parsons, which were apparently unknown to him) and he had the printed maps of della Valle, Pococke, Niebuhr, and Poujoulat.[17] Having no way of judging the accuracy of the various conflicting statements as to the points of the compass, Müller (pl. A, at end of *Antiq. Antioch.*) adopted a compromise, with a north somewhat to the west of Niebuhr's. This orientation was commonly followed for some time. The missionary Thomson in 1840 observed that the Orontes flowed south at the city, rather than west, as Müller and others stated.[18] However, the maps of E. G. Rey,[19] E. Le Camus,[20] and R. Förster,[21] who visited the city in 1859, 1888 and 1896 respectively, followed Müller's orientation (with very slight variations), as did the maps in the successive editions of Baedeker, beginning in 1876.[22]

One last variation appears in the French army map of Antioch at 1:20,000 dated 1920, in which the main street is shown running almost due north and south. This orientation is followed in the map of the city in the *Guide Bleu* of Palestine and Syria (1932).[23]

[15] Michaud and Poujoulat, *Corresp. d'Or.*, folding map at end of vol. 8. Poujoulat's map is reproduced, with the original orientation, by Jacquot, *Antioche*, 2.362.

[16] Chesney 424.

[17] Cf. Müller, *Antiq. Antioch.* 3, n. 2; and 5, n. 9.

[18] Thomson in *Missionary Herald* 37 (1841) 237, col. A. Thomson writes as though he were consciously correcting the prevailing misinformation.

[19] E. G. Rey, *Étude sur les monuments de l'architecture militaire des croisés en Syrie et dans l'île de Chypre* (Paris 1871) pl. 17, repeated on a smaller scale in his *Les colonies franques de Syrie au XII*^e *et XIII*^e *siècles* (Paris 1883) 326, and by Chauvet and Isambert, *Syrie, Palestine (Guides-Joanne)* (Paris 1882) 727. On the date of Rey's visit to Antioch (which is not indicated in his book), see C. Enlart, *Les monuments des croisés dans le royaume de Jérusalem* (Paris 1925-1928) 2.11 and 40.

[20] E. Le Camus, *Notre voyage aux pays bibliques* (Paris 1890) 3, folding map facing p. 32. This is reproduced, with the original orientation, by Jacquot, *Antioche* 2.224.

[21] Förster's map (pl. 6 accompanying his article "Antiochia") is based on the Baedeker map (see below), with alterations and corrections, but with the same orientation; see Förster's note on the subject, "Antiochia" 105, n. 8.

[22] The first Baedeker map is that in the English edition of the guide to Palestine and Syria (1876), facing p. 578 (the original German edition of this guide, in 1875, had no map of Antioch). According to Förster, "Antiochia" 105, n. 8, the Baedeker map was prepared by an engineer named Cernik. This map is repeated, with minor alterations but no correction of the orientation, in the various editions of Baedeker, down to the fifth English edition of 1912.

[23] *Guide Bleu*, facing p. 194. In the preface it is stated (p. vi) that the material on Antioch was supplied by V. Chapot. It is not clear whether this map was prepared before the accurate map of Jacquot was published in 1931.

Appendices

EXCURSUS 10

WALLS AND GATES

A. The Walls and Gates at the Southern End of the City
(Walls of Seleucus I, Tiberius, Theodosius II, and Justinian)

The Walls

While there is no specific statement as to the course of the original walls of Seleucus I (mentioned by Malalas 200.14-15 and by Strabo 16.2.4, p. 750C), it seems plain that Seleucus' city lay between the river and the line upon which the main colonnaded street of the city was later built.[1] Tiberius is said to have built a wall which brought a larger area within the city and joined the old wall of Seleucus (Malalas 232.22ff.).[2] Presumably the southern portion of Tiberius' wall ran in the same general east-west course as the southern part of Seleucus' wall. There is no evidence whether the walls were destroyed or damaged in the various earthquakes that occurred between the time of Tiberius and the time when Theodosius II built his wall,[3] and we can only suppose that if the walls were destroyed or damaged in these disasters, they would have been rebuilt in their original locations.

Malalas (346.8ff.) and Evagrius (1.20) describe an extension of the wall at the southern end of the city which was carried out by Theodosius II.[4] Malalas says that the wall was extended because there were many buildings for one mile outside the walls, and that the new wall went from the Philonauta Gate to the quarter called Rhodion.[5] It enclosed the mountain as far as the old wall of Tiberius, and extended as far as the stream called Phyrminus which ran down a ravine in the mountain. This ravine, with the remains of a wall along it, still exists at the southern end of the city.[6] Evagrius writes that Theodosius "extended the wall as far as the gate which leads to the suburb Daphne. Those who wish to do so can see this, since the old wall can be traced even in our own day, with the remains guiding the eye." Evagrius' "old wall," being that which preceded the wall of Theodosius, must be that of Tiberius, plus, perhaps, parts of the original Seleucid wall, which the wall of Tiberius joined. The most striking feature of Evagrius' description is the statement that the wall of Theodosius extended "as far as the gate which leads to Daphne." The reference seems certainly to be to the gate which led to Daphne in the time of Evagrius. This gate was presumably in the wall that had existed since the time when Justinian reorganized the fortifications

---

[1] See above, Ch. 4, §§3-4.
[2] See above, Ch. 8, §2.
[3] On Theodosius' wall, see above, Ch. 16, §1.
[4] Malalas wrongly attributes the work to Theodosius I; see Downey, "Wall of Theodosius."
[5] Förster is mistaken in stating ("Antiochia" 128) that the wall of Theodosius went as far as the πόρτα τοῦ Ῥοδίωνος. If Malalas had meant to say this, he would have written ἕως τῆς (sc. πόρτας) τοῦ λεγομένου Ῥοδίωνος. There appears to be no other evidence for such a gate.
[6] See the map showing the reconstruction of the topography of Antioch, Fig. 11.

of the city after its capture by the Persians in 540.[7] The reference to the gate at first seems puzzling and one might suppose that Evagrius mentioned it only in order to indicate that at least some part of the Theodosian wall extended as far as the Daphne gate of what was presumably a wall built by Justinian after 540. Immediately after this, however, Evagrius states that the remains of the old wall were still to be seen in his own time. This can refer only to one old wall, and the reference can only be to the wall of Tiberius; for if Evagrius had meant to say that the remains of the wall of Theodosius could still be seen in his own time, he would certainly have called it, in this context, "the wall" or "this wall [of Theodosius]" rather than "the old wall." From this text it seems certain, then, that the course of the wall of Theodosius must have corresponded, whether exactly or approximately, with that of the wall of Justinian; and we can believe that Evagrius mentions the gate leading to Daphne simply in order to indicate in which part of the city the wall was built. At least the passage shows that the wall of Theodosius did not extend beyond the course of Justinian's wall, for if it had, Evagrius would certainly not have said that Theodosius extended the wall "as far as the gate which leads to Daphne."

The walls of the city were destroyed, or at least extensively damaged, in the earthquake that occurred in the reign of Leo, probably in A.D. 458.[8] Our sources, which are very meager for this period, do not preserve a record of their being reconstructed, although it seems safe to assume that they would have been rebuilt as quickly as possible.

The walls were again destroyed in the earthquake of 528 (Malalas 422.22). There is no specific evidence to show what course the walls followed when they were rebuilt on this occasion, and we can assume only that they were rebuilt along the same lines. We know that they existed before the attack of the Persians in 540 (Procopius, *Wars* 2.6.10-14, 2.7.8) and that the Persians did not destroy the walls when they sacked the city (Procop. *De aed.* 2.10.9).

In his study of the walls Förster points out[9] that the only changes made by Justinian in the fortifications of the city after 540 (which Procopius de-

---

[7] Procopius describes the capture of the city in *Wars* 2.8.1—2.10.9 and gives an account of Justinian's measures for the restoration of the city in *De aed.* 2.10.2-25; see above Ch. 18, §8.

[8] For the evidence for the earthquake, and its date, see above, Ch. 17, §1. In his account of the earthquake (2.12), Evagrius says nothing about the walls; but in his account of the death of St. Symeon Stylites the Elder in 459 he writes (1.13) that the people of Antioch claimed the body, saying that "since the city has no wall, for it fell in the earthquake, we have brought the most holy body, so that it might be a wall and a defense for us." Evagrius is repeating verbatim the statement in the Syriac biography of Symeon written soon after his death (cf. the English translation by F. Lent, *Journal of the American Oriental Society* 35 [1915] 197, and the German translation by H. Hilgenfeld in H. Lietzmann, "Das Leben des hl. Symeon Stylites," *Texte u. Untersuchungen* 32, 4 |1908| 179). Having overlooked the statement of the Syriac biography, as repeated by Evagrius, Förster ("Antiochia" 139-140) concluded that the wall which existed in the southern part of the city in the time of Justinian must have been the Theodosian wall, since the preserved remains are different in construction from the wall on the river bank, which is certainly of the time of Justinian. If the passage on the death of Symeon is to be trusted, the wall at the south was built after 459, rather than during the reign of Theodosius II (408-450).

[9] "Antiochia" 131.

scribes in the *De aedificiis*) are in the eastern and western walls. Procopius'
statement (*De aed.* 2.10.9) that the Persians did not destroy the walls in
540 seems to indicate that the southern wall preserved until modern times
was that of Theodosius. If the walls were left intact by the Persians there
would be much less incentive to make extensive changes in them than if they
had been destroyed or damaged. Procopius' description (*De aed.* 2.10.2ff.) of
the changes effected by Justinian shows that alterations were made in the
walls only in places where serious weaknesses had been revealed by the siege,
and that the walls were contracted where shrinkage in the population of
the city made a shorter circuit desirable for military purposes. However, the
course of the southern wall along the ravine is admirably suited for defense
(as is illustrated by the fact that the Persians did not attack on this side),
so that if a wall existed there before the siege it seems reasonable to suppose
that it would be allowed to remain.

Further evidence for the walls at the southern end of the city is supplied
by the earliest biography of St. Symeon Stylites the Younger, who was born
in Antioch about 520 and spent most of his life on the mountain between
Antioch and Seleucia. This biography was written soon after the saint's death
in 592. In ch. 126 of this biography, extensive selections from which were
first published in 1923,[10] the biographer of the saint describes a visit of the
devil to Antioch for the purpose of making trial of the inhabitants. Symeon
succeeded, through prayer, in driving the devil out of one part of the city,
but was not able to banish him completely from the city. Then, we are told,
"the destroyer went toward the gate at the south, which issues towards
Daphne, and there rose from the so-called Cherubim, and as far as the Rhodion, in all of the quarter called the Kerateion, a great cry and mourning
and much lamentation." In another passage (ch. 9) it is said that when the
saint was still a child in Antioch, he saw, "in the place called Cherubim,"
a vision of Christ, who appeared to him "on the old wall of the Cherubim."
This "old wall" must be that of Tiberius, which had been replaced, at the
time when Symeon was born (ca. 520), by the wall of Theodosius.

The quarter called "the Cherubim" was evidently so called because it was
near the Gate of the Cherubim. This gate is mentioned in two passages by
Malalas. In the first he states (260.22ff.) that "Vespasian with the Jewish
spoils built in Antioch the so-called Cherubim before the gate of the city;
for there he fixed the bronze Cherubim which his son Titus found in the
Temple of Solomon. . . ."[11] In the second passage Malalas writes (280.20ff.)

[10] Excerpts were published by Delehaye, *Saints stylites.* Only the biography written at some
time after A.D. 1001 by Nicephorus of Antioch was available to Müller and Förster (*Acta SS.
Maii*, tom. 5.310ff.). Although Nicephorus used the earlier *Vita* (cf. Delehaye, *op.cit.* lixff.), he
did not always reproduce the details given by the earlier writer.

[11] The work would actually have been done by Titus rather than by Vespasian; see above,
Ch. 9, §1. While Müller (*Antiq. Antioch.* 86) and Förster ("Antiochia" 123, n. 90) locate the
Gate of the Cherubim in the southern wall of the city, they had no real evidence for this, since
the earliest biography of Symeon, the only text that makes the location certain, was not published in their time.

that Antoninus Pius "coming to Antioch executed the paving of the street of the great porticoes built by Tiberius and of the whole city, paving it with granite, granting from his own funds stone from the Thebaid and [granting] the other expenses from his own funds, inscribing the generosity on a stone tablet which he set in the gate called that of the Cherubim, for he had begun [the work] from that point. This *stele* is there now, a memorial of such great munificence."[12]

The description of the visitation of the devil in the earliest biography of Symeon suggests the reason for the extension of the wall by Theodosius II. Malalas says merely (346.10-11) that the wall was extended because the city had grown so that there were "many houses outside the walls for one mile." From the biography of Symeon it is known that the quarter called the Kerateion was in the southern part of the city. It is also known that this district, though within the walls, was separated from the remainder of the city, for Procopius says, in his description of the sack of the city by the Persians (*Wars* 2.10.7-8), that many houses about the Kerateion were left unharmed, not intentionally, but because, since they were situated at the extremity of the city, and not connected with it, the fire failed to reach them. It seems likely, then, since this isolated district was in the southern part of the city within the Theodosian wall, that the wall had been extended in order to enclose it.

The Gates

Though a gate at the south of the city must have existed, we have no specific evidence for such a gate before the time of Vespasian, when the Gate of the Cherubim is mentioned (see above). The Daphnetic Gate, also called the Golden Gate, is mentioned twice by Malalas. In the first reference to this gate the chronicler states (272.18-20) that after his victory over the Persians "Trajan came from Daphne and entered Antioch through the gate which is called Golden, that is, the Daphnetic Gate." In the second reference Malalas writes (360.12-20) that Theodosius II "gilded the two bronze doors of the Daphnetic Gate, in the same manner as the gate which he gilded in Constantinople, which is still called the Golden Gate; likewise in Antioch it is still called the Golden Gate, being gilded by the consularis Nymphidianus." The second passage shows that the earlier reference to gate as the Golden Gate is an anachronism, for the gate, whatever it may have been called in the time of Trajan, cannot have been called Golden until the time of Theodosius II. Malalas' account of the gilding is too circumstantial to be suspected; but his use of the name Golden Gate in writing of a period before it actually came into use is not unusual, for he often employs technical terms current in his own day, particularly official titles and

[12] There is a question whether the work that Malalas describes here was done by Antoninus Pius (as Malalas says) or by Caracalla; see above, Ch. 9, §8; Ch. 10, §4.

the names of provinces, in his accounts of periods in which these terms were not yet in use.

Evidently (as has been seen above in the discussion of the walls) the Gate of the Cherubim remained standing when the wall was extended by Theodosius II, and the gate in Theodosius' wall was called the Daphnetic Gate or the Golden Gate. However, it would have been natural for the gate at this end of the city to be called the Daphnetic Gate at all times.

This gate is mentioned in Procopius' account of the capture of the city by the Persians in 540, in which it is said (*Wars* 2.8.25-26, transl. of Dewing in the Loeb Classical Library) that "the soldiers of the Romans together with their commanders took a hasty departure, all of them, through the gate which leads to Daphne, the suburb of Antioch; for from this gate alone the Persians kept away while the others were seized; and of the populace some few escaped with the soldiers."

A slightly different account is given in the biographies of the younger St. Symeon Stylites, who was born ca. 520.[13] We are told that Symeon had a detailed vision of the way in which the Persians would capture the city in 540. Both of his biographers then describe the actual capture of the city, and they both state that when the Persians had scaled the walls some of the inhabitants cast themselves from the walls while others escaped through the two gates at the north and south of the city. The earlier biographer says, of the gates, ἄλλοι δὲ τῶν δύο πυλῶν ἀνεῳχθεισῶν τῶν κατὰ νότον καὶ μεσημβρίαν ἔφυγον.[14] Nicephorus, who based his work on the earlier *Vita*, uses the following words: ὡς . . . τοὺς δὲ διὰ τῆς πρὸς ἄρκτον τῆς τε πρὸς μεσημβρίαν πύλης ὑπεξελθόντες διαφυγεῖν. . . .[15] The disagreement of these two accounts with Procopius' statement that the soldiers fled through the southern gate alone need not trouble us, for the discrepancy is not vital, and Procopius' account gives indications in other respects of being more accurate. The account given in the biographies of Symeon is probably not completely accurate (e.g. the biographies both state that the walls were burned, while Procopius says specifically, *Wars* 2.10.9, that the Persians did not harm them), but it evidently reflects a local tradition and hence furnishes valuable supplementary evidence that there was only one gate in the southern wall, that is, on the side of the wall opening toward Daphne.

Nicephorus' account of Symeon's vision of the capture of the city agrees with his narrative of the actual event, in the statement[16] that Symeon saw the people escaping through the two gates at the north and the south (εἶτα καὶ δύο πύλας αὐτῆς κατά τε ἄρκτον καὶ μεσημβρίαν διανοιγείσας . . .); but in the earlier biography it is stated (p. 248.33-35 ed. Delehaye) that in the vision the two gates leading toward the sea and the south were opened

13 The biographies are cited above, n. 10.   14 Ch. 57, p. 249.5-6 ed. Delehaye.
15 *Acta SS, Maii*, tom. 5.332 D.   16 *Acta SS, Maii*, tom. 5.331 C.

Topographical Excursus

(εἶτα καὶ ὅτι αἱ δύο πύλαι τῆς πόλεως αἱ κατὰ θάλασσαν καὶ μεσημ-βρίαν ἀνεῴχθησαν). It is difficult to understand why the account of the vision does not agree in this respect with the account of the event; there is, however, no contradiction in the information about the gates in the two passages in the earlier biography, for in the description of the vision the two gates toward the south and toward the sea are specifically distinguished. It is certain that at this time the route toward the sea (i.e. toward Seleucia) followed its present course along the right bank of the river, beginning at the western end of the city, rather than the road to Daphne on the left bank of the river. Proof of this is found in Nicephorus' description already cited of the visit of the devil to Antioch. Here it is stated, as we have seen, that when the prayers of Symeon had released one part of the city from the visitation, the devil went toward the southern part of the city. On this Symeon again prayed and turned the devil away from that part of the city toward the gate which led to Seleucia (ἐπὶ τὴν κατὰ Σελεύκειαν πύλην).[17] We see, then, that the gate leading to Seleucia was not in the southern part of the city. The retention of this circumstantial statement is important because of the disappearance in Nicephorus' account of the statement of the earlier biography that the devil went toward the southern gate. Since Nicephorus says only that the devil went toward the south, his preservation of the statement that Symeon drove the devil thence to the gate leading toward Seleucia indicates that this statement is derived from the earlier biography and is not an addition by Nicephorus.

Another gate that seems to have been located in the southern part of the city is the Philonauta[18] Gate mentioned by Malalas (346.13) in his account of the extension of the wall by Theodosius as being one of the terminal points of the new wall. A gate of this name does not seem to be recorded elsewhere in the extant sources. As Müller points out,[19] the association with sailors which is indicated in the colloquial name given to the gate suggests that it was located in the wall along the Orontes. Presumably there was a landing area at this point, at which river traffic from Seleucia Pieria would first reach the city. It would have been at this point that the Egyptian flotilla is thought to have landed at Antioch in 246 B.C. when there was a dispute over the succession to the Seleucid throne on the death of Antiochus II.[20] The Philonauta Gate might be the gate leading toward the sea mentioned in a passage in the earlier biography of Symeon which has been quoted above.

[17] Acta SS, Maii, tom. 5.359 C, 360 D.
[18] The unique Greek MS of Malalas gives the name of the gate as φίλον αὐτοῦ. Chilmead's emendation to Φιλοναύτου has been accepted by all scholars. This passage does not appear in the Church Slavonic version of Malalas. Förster ("Antiochia" 128, n. 111) points out that the name Φιλοναύτης appears in inscriptions of Orchomenos.
[19] Antiq. Antioch. 114, cf. Förster "Antiochia" 127-128.
[20] See above, Ch. 5, nn. 13-14.

Appendices

Malalas' account of the extension of the wall under Theodosius states that the wall was extended ἕως τοῦ λεγομένου Ῥοδίωνος (346.13-14). This locality called "the Roses" or "the Rose-Garden" is not mentioned elsewhere in our sources. Förster[21] takes the passage in Malalas to mean that there was a πόρτα τοῦ Ῥοδίωνος. While this is possible, it does not seem certain that the words of Malalas must necessarily have this meaning.

B. The Eastern Gate of Tiberius and the Middle Gate of Trajan

There might appear to be some question as to whether the Eastern Gate (Ἀνατολικὴ Πόρτα) of Tiberius (Malalas 235.3-6, 264.7-10) and the Middle Gate (Μέση Πύλη) of Trajan (Malalas 275.14ff.) were identical. The Middle Gate, Malalas says, was built near the stream Parmenius and the Temple of Ares. Very likely it was a monumental arch, not a true city gate, and stood on the street which ran toward the mountain from the main colonnaded street, leaving the main street at the point where this thoroughfare altered its course slightly as it crossed Parmenius.[22] It was in this neighborhood that the Forum of Valens was later built.[23] That these two gates were identical is suggested (1) by the fact that the Middle Gate would have been on the eastern side of the city, and (2) by the circumstance that, according to Malalas, a statue of the she-wolf with Romulus and Remus stood on both the Eastern Gate and the Middle Gate. According to Malalas, Trajan built the Middle Gate after the earthquake of A.D. 115, and if Trajan were rebuilding Tiberius' gate, which had been damaged or destroyed in the earthquake, it would be quite in keeping with the chronicler's mechanical method of writing for him to record, as new work of Trajan, what was actually restoration or replacement of Tiberius' work.[24] The name of the original gate, it might be supposed, might well have been changed when Trajan's work was done, in order to make Trajan's monument seem more like a new work, so that instead of being called Eastern from the geographical point of view, the new gate might have been named Middle because it stood approximately in the middle of the long axis of the city. It would be quite consonant with Malalas' procedures for him to omit to mention that the Middle Gate had formerly been the Eastern Gate.

It is difficult to base any argument on whether it would be unusual for a city such as Antioch to possess two monumental representations of the she-wolf with Romulus and Remus, a symbol of great significance to the Romans; and hence it seems impossible to say that being ornamented with such a statue shows that the Eastern Gate and the Middle Gate must be identical. There is, however, good evidence for the locations of these gates,

[21] "Antiochia" 128.
[22] On Trajan's work, see above, Ch. 9, §5. On the main street, see above, Ch. 8, §2, and the restored plan of the city, Fig. 11.
[23] See above, Ch. 14, §3.
[24] On Malalas' procedures, see Downey, "Building Records in Malalas."

which shows that they were not identical. The position of the Middle Gate, as has been seen, is clearly fixed by Malalas' description of it. The evidence for the location of the Eastern Gate is connected with the curious situation that prevailed at Antioch with respect to the points of the compass, which has been discussed in Excursus 9. The main axis of the city, along which the principal colonnaded street ran, had a northeast and southwest direction, but Libanius speaks of the main street, and the principal axis of the city, as running from east to west. On the other hand, other writers use the points of the compass correctly, speaking of the monuments at the southern end of the city, which according to Libanius' usage would be western. Whatever the reason for this curious diversity of usage may have been, the location of the Eastern Gate is indicated in a passage that exhibits the simultaneous use of both the true and what may be termed the conventional compass points. Malalas writes (264.7-10) that Apollonius of Tyana, when he visited Antioch in the reign of Domitian, set up a talisman against the north wind at the Eastern Gate. One can only conclude that a talisman against a wind would be placed at the point where the wind would first strike the city. Hence it seems plain that the Eastern Gate, where the talisman against the north wind stood, was in the northern part of the city, and that this gate, presumably standing at the northeastern beginning of the colonnaded main street, was called Eastern according to the usage represented by Libanius. This conclusion seems inescapable; and it follows of course that the Eastern and the Middle Gates were different structures.

C. The Porta Tauriana

A gate called "the Bull Gate" or "the Gate of the Bull" stood at the head of a bridge. This is mentioned by Theophanes, who states, in his entry corresponding to the year A.D. 386 (A.M. 5878, p. 70.10-12 ed. De Boor) that "in this year in Antioch there was built, at the gate called *Tauriana* (ἐν τῇ Ταυριανῇ λεγομένῃ πύλῃ), an addition to the width of the bridge, and it [i.e. the bridge] was roofed over." Libanius, in a letter written in 363 to Datianus, also speaks of τὴν γέφυραν τὴν ἐπώνυμον Ταυρέου, by which, he says, Datianus had left the city.[25] Müller in one place suggests[26] that the bridge and the gate might have had this name because it was above this gate that Titus set up the "statue in honor of the moon with four bulls facing toward Jerusalem" mentioned by Malalas (261.16-7). Müller was able to make this suggestion because he did not take Malalas' reference to the statue of the moon to mean that it was set up over the gate before which were placed the Cherubim, representing the spoils of Jerusalem. This is, however, the evident implication of the passage in Malalas, and if we accept it we find a serious difficulty in the way of Müller's interpretation. It seems

[25] Libanius *Epist.* 1482 W. = 1446 F. For the occasion of the letter see Seeck *Briefe des Libanius* 115.
[26] *Antiq. Antioch.* 86-87.

certain from another passage in Malalas (281.5) that the Cherubim Gate stood at one end of the street of Tiberius, which certainly did not at any point go near the river; and it is also certain from ch. 126 of the earlier biography of St. Symeon Stylites the Younger which has been cited above that the Cherubim Gate was in the southern part of the city and was near the Kerateion, which we know from the Arabic description of Antioch preserved in Codex Vaticanus Arabicus 286 was "near the summit of the mountain,"[27] i.e. at least nearer the mountain than the river. The evidence that the Cherubim Gate was at least not on the river is thus just as clear as the evidence that the Porta Tauriana was on the river, so that it seems impossible to believe that they were identical.[28]

The Porta Tauriana may have been so called from some circumstance concerning which we have no evidence. We know, however, from Libanius of a statue that was set up to Antiochus Epiphanes by the Mysians in gratitude for his suppression of a band of robbers who infested the Taurus Mountain. In this statue the king was represented as having subdued a bull (*tauros*) which symbolized the mountain,[29] and while there is no evidence to show where in Antioch the statue would have been erected, it is possible, as Müller suggests, that the Porta Tauriana had this name from the statue, which may have stood near it.[30]

D. OTHER GATES

A gate that appears to be attested only once in the preserved sources is

[27] Guidi, "Descrizione araba" p. 26 of the translation.

[28] Further reason for doubting that the gates were identical is found in the epithets applied to them, for it may be difficult to see how the same gate could be called by some people the Porta Tauriana because of a statue which was placed above it, while at the same time it was called the Gate of the Cherubim by others because of statues which were placed in front of it. Förster, who accepts the implication of Malalas' account that the statue of the moon was set up over the gate before which the Cherubim were placed, rejects ("Antiochia" 126, n. 102) Müller's identification of the gates because the Porta Tauriana was on the river and the Gate of the Cherubim was "an der Westseite" (i.e., actually, the south). It is to be noted that Förster gives no evidence for his placing of the Gate of the Cherubim on the western (southern) side of the city ("Antiochia" 123, n. 90), although in this he presumably follows Müller (*Antiq. Antioch.* 86), who placed the gate in this wall merely because he believed that Titus would have entered the city from this direction. It is only from ch. 126 of the earlier biography of Symeon, as has been noted, that the Gate of the Cherubim can be proved to have been in the southern part of the city.

[29] Libanius mentions the statue in a passage in the *Antiochikos* (*Or.*11.123): "Since a band of robbers had formed itself in the Tauros and was making the property of the Mysians the spoil of the Cilicians and had ruined their intercourse with other men, he [Antiochus] went against them and expelled them more swiftly than Minos did the Carians from the Cyclades, and restored to the cities the power to communicate with each other, and casting out the fear which hung over them he opened up the roads to the traders. In return for this there was erected, by those who had benefited, a bronze statue [of the king] having subdued a bull, in which the name of the animal (*tauros*) represented the mountain of the same name." See Ch. 5, n. 87 and Ch. 8, n. 90, and cf. the commentary of Hugi in *Der Antiochikos* 157-158. Müller (*Antiq. Antioch.* 62, n. 2) notes that it can scarcely be doubted that the statue was set up in Antioch.

[30] *Antiq. Antioch.* 62, n. 2. Förster ("Antiochia" 126, n. 102) puts forward the suggestion that the bridge and the gate were so called after a person named Tauros or after the mountain of that name. At least in the present state of our evidence this does not seem as plausible as Müller's explanation.

mentioned in a passage in Theophanes (a. 5856, p. 54.12 ed. De Boor), who speaks of ἡ πύλη τῆς πόλεως ἐπὶ τὸ λεγόμενον Τρίπυλον. There is no indication of the location of this gate.

Müller in his list of the gates in the city walls[31] includes the Gate of St. Julian, but he was not acquainted with the evidence that indicates that this gate was associated with the Church of St. Julian, which was three miles outside the city.[32]

EXCURSUS 11

THE HELLENISTIC AGORA IN EPIPHANIA
(with Notes on Other Agoras and Forums)

In addition to the original agora of Seleucus Nicator, which lay along the Orontes river, there is considerable evidence for the location of buildings about an agora that appears to date from the Seleucid period, probably from the time of Antiochus Epiphanes (175-164 B.C.). About this we know more, in some respects, than about any other complex of buildings in Antioch, but in other respects the evidence is less precise than it is in the case of the forum of Valens.[1]

As to the location of the agora, the presumption is that it was in Epiphania. This rests upon the presence, on the agora, of the *bouleuterion* said to have been burned in A.D. 23/4, which is presumably that built by Antiochus Epiphanes (Malalas, 205.14, 234.2) and restored or rebuilt by Pompey after it had been damaged in some way (Malalas, 211.8). A *bouleuterion* built by Epiphanes would have been placed, it seems safe to assume, in Epiphania, the quarter of the city which he developed. This is said by Malalas (205.19-22, 233.22) to have been "outside the city" (i.e. outside the walls that existed when the quarter was founded) and on or beside the mountain (ἐπὶ τὸ ὄρος, 205.22; τὸ παρὰ τὸ ὄρος μέρος τῆς πόλεως, 234.1). Since Seleucus is said to have "avoided the mountain" because of the torrents that flowed down from it in the time of heavy rains, and to have built his city "opposite the mountain, near the river" (Malalas, 200.10, cf. 233.10), Epiphania must have lain between the original foundation and the mountain, perhaps extending up the first slopes.

---

[31] *Antiq. Antioch.* 130, n. 17.

[32] See the passages cited in the List of Churches (below, Excursus 17), under the name of the Church of St. Julian.

[1] The principal texts concerning this agora, which will be discussed below, are as follows:

Malalas 235	Fire under Tiberius, A.D. 23/4
Malalas 317-319	Work of Constantine the Great
Evagrius 1.18	Buildings of Memnonius, Zoilus, Callistus, Anatolius (reign of Theodosius II)
Malalas 395-398	riot of A.D. 507
Malalas 423	reference to *basilike* of Rufinus, after earthquake of A.D. 526

Appendices

Other buildings on this agora are mentioned by Malalas in his account of a fire that occurred there in A.D. 23/4, during the reign of Tiberius (235.15—236.1):

In the time of the same Tiberius there was a fire in Antioch of Syria, in the 72nd year of its autonomy [= A.D. 23/4], at night, secretly burning the greater part of the agora and the *bouleuterion* and the shrine of the Muses which had been built by Antiochus Philopator [111-95 B.C.] from the money left in a will by Maron of Antioch, who had removed to Athens and then ordered that from his money there should be built a shrine of the Muses and a library.

The conversion of the shrine of the Muses into the *praetorium* of the *comes Orientis* during the reign of Constantine the Great is described in another passage in Malalas (317.17—319.13):

And he [Constantine] made war on the Persians and conquered and made a treaty of peace with Sarabaros, king of the Persians, the Persian asking that he might have peace with the Romans. The same Emperor Constantine also made Euphratesia an *eparchia*, separating it from Syria and Osrhoene and giving the rank of metropolis to Hierapolis. And returning he went to Antioch the Great, and he built there the great church, an undertaking of the greatest magnitude, demolishing the so-called public bath of the emperor [or king?] Philip, for the bath was old and in ruins because of the passage of time, and no longer serviceable. He built also a guest-house nearby. Likewise he built the so-called *basilike* of Rufinus. This was the shrine of Hermes and Rufinus the prefect of the sacred praetorium demolished it. And going away with the emperor to the war he was commanded by him to remain in Antioch the Great; and he finished the same *basilike* as the emperor returned to Rome. As Constantine was about to leave the same Antioch he for the first time made governor of Antioch in Syria a man named Plutarchus, a Christian; and he was commanded to act as supervisor of the construction of the church and the *basilike*. This same Plutarchus, having found, while building the guest-house, a bronze statue of Poseidon which had been set up as a talisman so that the city should not suffer from earthquakes, took this and melted it and made it a statue to the same emperor Constantine, setting it up outside his praetorium, inscribing beneath it "To the good Constantine." This bronze statue is still standing. The same emperor, in the same great city of Antioch, appointed for the first time a *comes Orientis*, in the consulship of Illus and Albinus [A.D. 335], making the shrine of the Muses his *praetorium*, so that he filled the place in the *Oriens* of the *praefectus praetorio*, a man named Felicianus, a Christian, bestowing upon the same city of Antioch by his sacred edict the rights of the rank of a second *comitatus*, in the 383rd year of the era of Antioch the Great. For before this there was no *comes Orientis* stationed in the same city of Antioch the Great, but as war arose a *delegator* was stationed in Antioch in Syria, and when the war ceased the *delegator* was removed. The Emperor Constantine departed from Antioch, leaving the *praefectus* Rufinus; and this Rufinus zealously completed the *basilike*, and for this reason it was called that of Rufinus.

Further evidence for buildings that were on or near the Hellenistic agora in Epiphania appears in Malalas' account of a riot that took place in Antioch in A.D. 507. The description, with two brief allusions that follow it, is as follows (Malalas 395.20—398.4):

At the same period of his [Anastasius'] reign, in the consulship of the same emperor Anastasius for the third time [A.D. 507] there came to Antioch the Great a certain Calliopas, a racing driver, a member of one of the factions [p. 396] of Constantinople; and he was given to the Green faction of Antioch at the time when Basilius of Edessa was *comes Orientis*; and he took over the stable of the Green faction which had been abandoned, and won by his strength. And after a little there was celebrated in Daphne of Antioch, according to the custom, the usual celebration of the Olympics; and when the throng of the people of Antioch went up to Daphne, those of the faction rose up with the driver Calliopas and, attacking the synagogue of the Jews which was in the same Daphne, burned it, plundering everything that was in the synagogue; and they killed many people, on the 9th of July in the fifteenth indiction [9 July A.D. 507]; and planting the holy cross there they caused it to become a *martyrion* of St. Leontius. When these things became known to the same Emperor Anastasius, he appointed, as *comes Orientis*, the former *commerciarius*, Procopius of Antioch; and he brought with him, by divine decree, a *nykteparchos* [chief of police], Menas by name, of Byzantium. And when a disorder was created by the Green faction the same Menas wished to seize some of the rioters, and they, learning it, fled to St. John's outside the city. And the *nykteparchos* learning this, he went out at midday with a force of Goths to St. John's; and he entered the church suddenly and found there under the holy table of the altar one of the rioters, Eleutherios by name; and he slew him there with his sword, and dragging [p. 397] his corpse out of the altar, he beheaded it, so that the holy altar was filled with blood. And taking the head he went to the city of Antioch, and going to the bridge of the river Orontes he cast the head into the river. And he went to Procopius the *comes Orientis*, describing to him what had happened. And in the afternoon this became known to the Greens, and going to St. John's they found the corpse of Eleutherios. And taking his corpse up on a stretcher, they entered the city bearing it. And they came opposite the *basilike* of Rufinus, at the bath called that of Olbia; and beginning a fight in the street of the Thalassioi with the guards of the *nyk-*

Appendices

teparchos and the members of the Blue faction, the members of the Green faction won; and seizing the *basilike* of Rufinus and that called [the *basilike*] of Zenodotus, they started a fire and there was burned the whole of the [*basilike*] of Rufinus and the two *tetrapyla* on each side of it and the praetorium of the *comes Orientis*, and everything that was destroyed by the fire collapsed. And the *comes Orientis* fled to the Alexandria of Cambyses. And those of the Green faction seized the *nykteparchos* Menas and cutting off his head, they tore out his entrails. And after dragging the corpse they hung it up on the bronze statue called *Kolonisios* which stood in the middle of the *antiphoros*; and taking down the corpse, and dragging it outside the city Antioch, they burned it with faggots. And the Emperor Anastasius, informed of this, appointed as *comes Orientis* Irenaeus Pentadiastes, of Antioch; and he held an investigation and caused terror in the city.

398.5-8: The same emperor removed the perpetual liturgy called *chrysargyron* by divine decree, which is a great and marvellous munificence, giving to the *sacrae largitiones*, in place of it, an income from his own funds. 398.8-9: The same emperor built in Antioch also the so-called [*basilike*] of Rufinus and various buildings in the cities of *Romania*.

The identification of the scene of the riot with the Hellenistic agora in Epiphania is made certain by the reference (Malalas 397.17) to the *praetorium* of the *comes Orientis*, which was formerly the shrine of the Muses (Malalas 319.2); and this we know from the account of the fire under Tiberius (Malalas 235.15ff.) stood on the agora that contained the *bouleuterion*, which it seems quite certain was a part of the new agora built by Antiochus Epiphanes.

A final passage in Malalas, by means of its references to the basilica of Rufinus, brings two other buildings into association with the Hellenistic agora in Epiphania (423.1-4):

He [Justinian] built in the same Antioch a shrine of the Holy Mother of God and Ever-Virgin Mary, opposite the so-called *basilike* of Rufinus, building nearby another shrine of Saints Cosmas and Damian.

We learn, then, that the agora contained the *bouleuterion*, the *basilike* of Rufinus with two *tetrapyla*, and the shrine of the Muses, which later became the *praetorium* of the *comes Orientis*, and a church of the Virgin. Other buildings associated with these, though it is not clear whether they actually stood on the agora, are the Bath of Olbia and the *basilike* of Zenodotus.

THE HELLENISTIC AGORA AND OTHER FORUMS

It seems clear that the agora is not to be identified with various forums mentioned in the literary sources, namely: the Forum of Valens, built ca. A.D. 370/372; the forum confirmed by implication in Libanius's account of

Topographical Excursus

the riot of A.D. 387; that mentioned by Evagrius (1.18) in his account of various building activities at Antioch in the reign of Theodosius II (A.D. 408-450); the "tetragonal agora" said by Josephus to have been burned in A.D. 69/70; and the forum in which the body of Germanicus was cremated in A.D. 19.

The Forum of Valens was in Epiphania (see Excursus 12), but it seems certain that it is not identical with the Hellenistic agora in Epiphania, for we hear a good bit in Malalas about the buildings that stood about the Forum of Valens, and these do not include any of the buildings associated, in Malalas and other sources, with the Hellenistic agora in Epiphania; and conversely, the buildings that are (as we have seen) associated with the agora in Epiphania are nowhere mentioned in connection with the Forum of Valens.

The identification of the other forums with the Hellenistic agora or the Forum of Valens would depend upon the references to the official buildings which stood about them. The Forum of Valens had the *praetorium* of the *consularis Syriae*, formerly the Kommodion; the Hellenistic agora had the *praetorium* of the *comes Orientis*, formerly the Museum: the conversion was made, according to Malalas (319.2) when the office of *comes Orientis* was instituted in A.D. 335. It also had the *bouleuterion* built by Antiochus Epiphanes.

Of what appear to be other forums the one for which there is the most evidence is that mentioned by Evagrius in his account of the building activities of the reign of Theodosius II (1.18, pp. 27.18—28.3 ed. Bidez-Parmentier):

At this period Memnonius and Zoilus and Callistus were sent by Theodosius [the Younger] as rulers to Antioch, men who paid honor to our faith. And Memnonius fittingly and elaborately built from the ground what is called by us the *Psephion*,[2] leaving a hypaethral court in the middle. Zoilus [built or rebuilt][3] the *basileios stoa* at the southern side of that of Rufinus which has continued to bear his name until our times, although the structure itself has been changed as a result of the various calamities.[4] And Callistus raised a magnificent and conspicuous edifice, which both men of the past and we today call the *stoa* of Callistus, before the seats of justice, opposite the forum where is the splendid edifice, the head-

[2] The *Psephion* is said by Evagrius (6.8) to have been destroyed in the earthquake of A.D. 588. The building is mentioned in a letter of Severus, patriarch of Antioch at the beginning of the sixth century: *The Sixth Book of the Select Letters of Severus, Patriarch of Antioch, in the Syriac Version of Athanasius of Nisibis*, ed. and transl. by E. W. Brooks, 2, pt. 1 (London 1903), 1.38, p. 108.

[3] Since Evagrius does not use a verb here, "rebuilt" is presumably to be supplied from the preceding verb, but this does not necessarily make it certain that Zoilus rebuilt an existing building.

[4] The reference presumably is to rebuildings or restorations of the "basilica," which might have suffered in the various earthquakes that occurred between the time of Theodosius II and that of Evagrius, or in the burning of the city by the Persians in A.D. 540.

quarters of the *strategoi*. After these men Anatolius, sent as *strategos* of the eastern troops, built the so-called *stoa* of Anatolius, adorning it with materials of every kind. These things, even though they are outside the scope of this work, will not be without interest to the curious reader.

The terminology which Evagrius uses is, however, so vague that it is difficult to determine whether the buildings which he mentions are identical with any of those that are known to have stood on the Hellenistic agora or any other forum for which there is evidence. Evagrius says (p. 27.27) that Callistus built a *stoa πρὸ τῶν ἑδῶν ἃ τῇ δίκῃ ἱδρύεται, εὐθὺ τοῦ φόρου οὗ ἡ περικαλλὴς οἰκία, τῶν στρατηγῶν τὰ καταγώγια*. The first building, the description of which may be rendered "the seats of justice," would presumably be a *dikasterion*, but might be the praetorium of the *comes Orientis* or that of the *consularis Syriae*, both of whom had judicial powers. The *katagogia* of the *strategoi* is probably the headquarters (either a residence or a praetorium) designed for the use of the *magistri militum* when they were in Antioch.[5] If the "seats of justice" is the praetorium of the *consularis Syriae*, then the reference is to the Forum of Valens; if it is the praetorium of the *comes Orientis*, then the forum meant is the Hellenistic agora. A praetorium for the generals is not, however, known to have been on either of these forums, although Malalas mentions such a praetorium, in his account of the fire of October A.D. 525, as though it were on a forum.[6] This passage in

[5] The primary meaning of *καταγώγιον* (and of *καταγωγή* and *καταλυτήριον*) is *inn*, and the words could easily be used of official lodging-houses or inns maintained for the accommodation of officials on their journeys. It would be natural, then, to use the words to describe official residences. A distinction between the uses of the words would be the more difficult to maintain in antiquity because there could very easily be variation, in actual practice, in the uses to which any given building of this kind might be put at various times: it might be difficult, for example, to make a distinction between the terms applied to a building used by an official who visited a city more or less regularly but was not permanently stationed there, and those applied to a building used by an official who was stationed permanently in a city but was sometimes or frequently absent from it. Procopius speaks fairly often of *katagogia* and *katalyteria* designed for the use of officials, and while in the majority of the references to them it is not possible to determine whether lodgings, residences, or praetoria are meant (*Buildings* 3.4.18, p. 93.7 ed. Haury; 4.1.23, p. 105.16; 5.2.5, p. 152.24; 5.3.3, p. 154.12; 6.1.13, p. 172.23), in the two cases in which the context does give some evidence of the nature of the buildings, it is clear that *katagogion* is applied to a building in which an official regularly transacted business (*Anec.* 29.7; 30.29), and would thus be either a residence and praetorium (if the buildings were the same) or a praetorium (if he resided in another place). Accordingly it seems reasonable to conclude that in the present passage in Evagrius the *katagogia* of the *strategoi* is either the residence and *praetorium* combined, or at least the praetorium alone, of the *magistri militum*. Theodoret (*Hist. eccl.* 2.8.27, p. 119.11 ed. Parmentier) speaks of a *katagogē* of an official, but there is no indication in the context whether it was a lodging, an official residence, or a praetorium. Libanius three times speaks of the *katagogai* of officials, but in all of these passages likewise the precise meaning of the word is not clear (*Oratt.* 2.8; 22.17; 51.4).

[6] Malalas (417.12) says that in the fire of October A.D. 525 the city was burned "from the *martyrion* of St. Stephen as far as the praetorium of the *stratelates* [i.e., *strategos* or *magister militum*]." This certainly implies that the praetorium of the *stratelates* was on a forum, which might naturally be the place at which a fire would stop. Malalas does not mention the date scvof the fire, but it is dated in October of the fourth indiction by Theophanes, A.M. 6018, p. 172.1 ed. De Boor; for the chronology cf. L. Hallier, "Untersuchungen über die Edessenische Chronik," *Texte und Untersuchungen zur Geschichte der altchristlichen Literatur*, 9, 1 (1892), pp. 43-45, 132-134.

Evagrius might accordingly refer to either the Hellenistic agora, the Forum of Valens, or to still a third forum. Possible evidence that the Hellenistic agora is meant might be found in the circumstance that in the same passage Evagrius mentions the construction of the *basileios stoa* at the south of "that of Rufinus," which is presumably the *basilike* of Rufinus known from Malalas to have stood on the Hellenistic agora. That Evagrius refers to the *basileios stoa*, the "seats of justice," and the *katagogia* of the *strategoi* in the same passage might, but of course does not necessarily, indicate that he was describing work done in connection with a single complex of buildings, perhaps in the same way that Malalas, from whom Evagrius certainly took his information here,[7] describes the complex built under Commodus and Didius Julianus, or the construction of the Forum of Valens. The same conclusion might be favored by the possibility that the *Psephion*, the reconstruction of which Evagrius also mentions in this passage, might, from its name, be the bouleuterion, which is known from Malalas to have been located on the Hellenistic agora: the identification would be supported by Evagrius' reference to the hypaethral court in the middle of the building, for Libanius, in connection with the riot of A.D. 387, tells us that the bouleuterion contained an open court (*Orat.* 22.31).

The evidence accordingly indicates that the forum mentioned in this passage might be the Hellenistic agora, but this identification must remain hypothetical; if it is correct, it adds, to our knowledge of the agora, evidence that the bouleuterion was rebuilt in the time of Theodosius II, and the praetorium or praetorium and residence combined of the *magistri militum*.[8]

Not a great deal of topographical information is furnished by the allusions of Libanius and Chrysostom to various buildings in their references to the riot of A.D. 387 and the consequent judicial proceedings.[9] In this riot a mob destroyed statues of the imperial family and engaged in other disorders, which are described by Libanius and Chrysostom in orations and homilies written during and after the inquiries that followed. As one might expect from immediately contemporary writings of this kind, addressed to an audience only too familiar with the events, topographical references are scanty and vague. Libanius remarks that before the beginning of the disorders, a crowd filled the *dikasterion* (*Orat.* 19.26); that later the people rushed ἐπὶ τὴν πρὸ τοῦ δικαστηρίου στοάν, and then went to the nearby bath and cut

[7] Cf. E. Patzig, *Unerkannt und unbekannt gebliebene Malalas-Fragmente* (Progr. Leipzig 1891) 17-20, and C. E. Gleye, *BZ* 3 (1894) 627.

[8] If the whole of the passage is to be taken to be a description of building activities connected with the Hellenistic agora, then the stoa of Anatolius would be associated with this agora. Malalas describes the construction of this building in some detail, calling it an "illuminated *basilike*" (360.7-15); he says also that it was rebuilt after the earthquake of A.D. 526 (423.7; in this passage he calls it simply *basilike*). If Malalas gave some indication that all of these buildings were placed about the Hellenistic agora, Evagrius might well have neglected to reproduce this, just as, for example, he does not take over Malalas's careful note that the *basilike* named for Anatolius was constructed with funds given by the emperor.

[9] On the riot, see above, Ch. 15, §2.

down the lamps (*Orat.* 22.6).[10] In the course of the disorders, after destroying the imperial statues, the rioters set fire to the house of "one of the
prominent men" and were thinking of attacking the palace but were dispersed by archers and later by the *comes Orientis* (*Oratt.* 19.32ff.; 22.9).[11]
The only other topographical indication which we have is that one might
naturally suppose that the statues which were destroyed stood on a forum
(Libanius, *Oratt.* 19.44, 48; 22.7; Chrysostom, *Homil. ad pop. Antioch.* 5 =
PG 49.73). From the accounts of the judicial proceedings that followed the
riot we learn that the bouleuterion was next to the *desmoterion* and that it
contained a hypaethral court (Libanius, *Orat.* 22.30ff.). This bouleuterion is
presumably identical with that of Epiphanes, for all of the references to a
bouleuterion at Antioch imply that there was only one, and its hypaethral
court suggests that it is to be identified with the *Psephion*, said by Evagrius
(quoted above) to have been rebuilt by Memnonius in the reign of Theodosius II.[12] We learn from these passages, then, that one of the *dikasteria*
had a public bath near it,[13] and that a *desmoterion* was contiguous to the
bouleuterion. The latter passage is, at present, the more useful of the two,
because of the presumption that the bouleuterion is that which stood on the
Hellenistic agora, although there is no evidence whether the *desmoterion*
likewise faced on the agora.[14] Since it is not certain whether the *dikasterion*
which had a stoa in front of it and a bath near it was the praetorium of
the *consularis Syriae* or that of the *comes Orientis*, or even some other court-
building, the information concerning it is not helpful in the reconstruction
either of the Forum of Valens or the Hellenistic agora.

There is less evidence concerning the "tetragonal agora" said by Josephus
to have been burned late in A.D. 69 or early in A.D. 70, and the forum in which
the body of Germanicus was burned in A.D. 19 (see below, n. 17). These might

[10] For the bath near the *dikasterion*, see also Libanius *Or.* 20.3.

[11] Sievers (*Leben des Libanius* 174-5) takes the passage in Libanius, *Or.* 19.34-35, to mean
that, after setting fire to the house of a prominent citizen, the mob also threatened the house
of the commander of the archers, but it seems to me preferable to interpret the passage as
referring only to the attack on the house of a "prominent person." I am not sure what the
basis is for Pack's note on Libanius *Or.* 45.16 (*Studies in Libanius* 110), "xxii, 6, describing
the route which the rioters of 387 followed through the city, shows that the courthouse, with
its adjoining portico, must have stood between the governor's residence and one of the
important public baths." Presumably Pack takes the house that was threatened to be that of
the governor; this is possible, although not certain, but so far as I know there is no indication in either Libanius or Chrysostom of the relative location of the buildings.

[12] Libanius, praising the humanity of one of the imperial commissioners in allowing the
senators of Antioch, who were confined in the *desmoterion* during the investigation which
followed the riot, says (*Or.* 22.29) that the *desmoterion* was too small for them and had no
roof, and this official allowed them to use the bouleuterion as well, which had a common wall
with the *desmoterion* (30); the bouleuterion was more comfortable because it had "a roofed
theatron, and four stoas forming a court inside of them, a forced garden with vines, figs,
other trees, and various vegetables. . ." (31).

[13] On the bath see also Libanius, *Orat.* 20.3.

[14] There were at least two *desmoteria* at Antioch at this time, and perhaps more, for
Libanius speaks of the *desmoterion* of the *consularis Syriae* (*Or.*45.31), implying that there
was at least one other, probably for the use of the *comes Orientis*. Ammianus Marcellinus
(29.1.13) speaks of the *carceres publici* at Antioch.

or might not be identical with the Hellenistic agora burned in A.D. 23/24: in each case the evidence is so slight that it is not decisive in either direction.

Josephus describes the destruction of the tetragonal agora in his account of the persecution of the Jews at Antioch which was occasioned by their war against the Romans (on the episode see above, Excursus 4). The Jews were accused of setting the fire, but it was found to have had quite a different cause:

> (*Bell. Jud.* 7.55, transl. Thackeray, Loeb ed.): For a fire having broken out, which burnt down the market-square, the magistrates' quarters, the record-office and the basilicae, and the flames having with difficulty been prevented from spreading with raging violence over the whole city, Antiochus accused the Jews of the deed.[15]

> (*Ibid.* 60-61): By careful investigation Collega then discovered the truth. Not one of the Jews incriminated by Antiochus had any part in the affair, the whole being the work of some scoundrels, who, under the pressure of debts, imagined that if they burnt the market-place and the public records they would be rid of all demands.

The terminology of Josephus is so vague that the enumeration of the buildings about this agora does not indicate whether it is identical with that burned in A.D. 23/4: the *archeia* or the *grammatophylakion* might be the bouleuterion but this is not certain.

Josephus's use of "tetragonal" certainly seems to imply the existence of another agora (or of other agoras) which was not tetragonal (i.e., resembling that at Jerash).[16]

The reference in Tacitus is much less useful. As the purpose and literary style of his account would lead one to expect, he gives no topographical information in his reference to the forum in which the body of Germanicus was burned; he says simply (*Annales* 2.73.5):

> *Corpus antequam cremaretur nudatum in foro Antiochensium, qui locus sepulturae destinabatur, praetuleritne veneficii signa, parum constitit; nam et quis misericordia in Germanicum et praesumpta suspicione aut favore in Pisonem pronior, diversi interpretabantur.*

Presumably, in view of the important nature of the event, this would have been the chief agora or forum of the city.[17]

---

[15] *Bell. Jud.* 7.55: ἐπεὶ γὰρ συνέβη καταπρησθῆναι τὴν τετράγωνον ἀγορὰν ἀρχεῖά τε καὶ γραμματοφυλάκιον καὶ τὰς βασιλικάς . . . Zonaras reads χαρτοφελάκιον M. has τὸ γραμματοφυλάκιον.

[16] In his reference to the account of Josephus, Muller (*Antiq. Antioch.* 85, n. 3) seems to believe that this tetragonal agora was identical with that burned in the reign of Tiberius. Müller had not, however, had occasion to examine the evidence in detail.

[17] In his note on the passage in Tacitus quoted above, Furneaux points out that *sepulturae* = *cremationi.* Elsewhere Tacitus says that Germanicus died at Daphne (*Ann.* 2.83.3): Arcus additi Romae et apud ripam Rheni et in monte Suriae Amano, cum inscriptione rerum gestarum ac mortem ob rem publicam obisse, sepulchrum Antiochiae, ubi crematus, tribunal Epidaphnae, quo in loco vitam finierat. Furneaux notes, *ad loc.,* that the *sepulchrum* mentioned

Appendices

No topographical value attaches to the vague references in the *Antiochikos* of Libanius and the Arabic description of Antioch to numerous forums in the city. Libanius says (*Orat.* 11.251-252):

> But may none of the gods ever take away from us this rivalry which is caused by the fact that the advantage lies with each of us. What is more inexhaustible, more lasting, than the wealth of goods which we have for sale? These are so distributed through the whole city that no one part of the city can be called the market (*agora*); neither must those who wish to buy things come together in any one place, but the goods are right before everyone, before their very doors, and everywhere it is possible for one simply to stretch out his hand in order to take what he wishes. (252) One cannot find any street (*aguia*) so despised or so remote that it sends elsewhere, lacking anything of what they need, those who dwell in it, but the middle of the town and the furthest quarters are equally well supplied, and they are all as full of goods for sale as they are of people.

Probably Libanius uses *agora* here in the general sense in which he employs it in *Epist.* 771 W = XI, p. 11.12 F., where the reference plainly cannot be to large forums.[18]

The Arabic description of Antioch in Codex Vaticanus Arabicus 286 mentions (Guidi, "Descrizione araba," p. 23 of the offprint) seven "markets" running through the length of the city. It is said that three of these are covered, four uncovered, and that they are so wide that carts may pass in them. Whether these are colonnaded streets (including the main street with its covered colonnades?), or markets distributed throughout the city, is not clear.

Positions of Buildings about the Agora; Hypothetical Reconstruction of the Agora

The evidence for the positions and relative locations of the buildings about the agora may be summed up briefly. In the table below, the indications on the right, of the context of the evidence, refer to the episodes discussed above. Doubtful evidence is enclosed in parentheses.

---

here was a cenotaph; in *Ann.* 3.1-2 it is said that the ashes of Germanicus were taken to Rome by Agrippina. On the tribunal at Daphne, Furneaux says, "Probably, as Nipperdey thinks, this took the form of a scaffold or bier, to represent that on which the body was laid out; such an erection being sometimes part of an important funeral (*CIL* 9. 1783), or afterwards set up as a monument (*ibid.* 1729). It need not therefore (as Walther thinks) be commemorative of his imperium." I am unable to discover what basis there may be for the statement of Bouchier *Antioch* 100: "At Antioch a cenotaph was erected in the forum where the body had been burned, and in the suburb where the prince died a *tribunal*, probably a statue elevated on some kind of circular shrine surrounded by pilasters."

[18] Later in *Or.* 11, Libanius uses the word almost in the sense of "commerce": (254) "One may understand the superiority of our trade (agora) from the following circumstance. The cities which we know pride themselves especially on their wealth exhibit only one row of goods for sale, that which lies before the houses, but between the columns of the stoas no one works; with us, however, even these spaces are turned into shops. . . ."

Topographical Excursus

Buildings that were certainly contiguous to the agora:

bouleuterion	fire under Tiberius
basilike of Rufinus, with two tetra-pyla	buildings of Constantine the Great; riot of A.D. 507
shrine of Muses, later *praetorium* of *com. Or.*	fire under Tiberius; riot of A.D. 507
Church of the Virgin	reconstruction of Antioch after earthquake of A.D. 526
(stoa of Callistus)	Evagrius 1.18 (provided this passage
("seats of justice")	refers to the Hellenistic agora).
(headquarters of the *strategoi*)	

Buildings that were possibly or probably contiguous to the agora:

Bath of Olbia	riot of A.D. 507
basilike of Zenodotus	riot of A.D. 507
basileios stoa of Zoilus	Evag. 1.18 (see above)

Positions of the buildings:

basilike of Rufinus was opposite Bath of Olbia	riot of A.D. 507
basilike of Rufinus and that of Zenodotus were contiguous	riot of A.D. 507
basilike of Rufinus and praetorium of *com. Or.* were contiguous	riot of A.D. 507
basilike of Rufinus was opposite Church of the Virgin	rebuilding of Antioch after earthquake of A.D. 526
basilike of Rufinus had *basileios stoa* of Zoilus at its southern side	Evag. 1.18
(stoa of Callistus, before "seats of justice," opposite the forum where is the splendid edifice, the headquarters of the *strategoi*)	Evag. 1.18

The only attempt that has been made to reconstruct the agora is Müller's; in his plan (Fig. 9 below), he shows the *basilike* of Rufinus along one side of the agora, with the *bouleuterion* and the Museum, later the praetorium of the *comes Orientis*, facing it on the other side, with the "basilica" of Zoilus on one of the sides between them, and nothing on the other side facing the "basilica" of Zoilus. The Church of the Virgin he places at some distance from the agora.

[631]

Appendices

EXCURSUS 12

THE FORUM OF VALENS AND ITS VICINITY

THANKS to the material provided by Malalas and other sources, we know more about this forum, and the buildings on and near it, than we do about any similar group of buildings at Antioch. The principal features of the forum, as they emerge from the texts, have been presented above in the account of the reign of Valens (Ch. 14, §3); and trial excavations have confirmed the statements of the literary texts as to the location and paving of the forum, though they have not furnished new information concerning the buildings.

In a number of cases, Malalas indicates the relative positions of the buildings. On the basis of this information, it is possible to reconstruct certain details of the plan of the forum (see the restoration proposed by Müller in his Plate A, and Stauffenberg 475-478). The information is not, however, sufficiently clear or detailed to make a complete reconstruction possible at this time. The topographical problems will be discussed here, and such conclusions as it seems possible to reach will be offered. It must be borne in mind throughout that Malalas probably had no intention of giving a complete and systematic picture of the topography of the forum and of the buildings near it. His chief interest in most cases was in recording which buildings various emperors built, and in doing this he mentions, largely as a matter of interest, the existing buildings near which the new buildings were placed. In the case of the account of the building of the forum itself Malalas is, characteristically, interested primarily in the enumeration and description of the structures involved in Valens' operations, not in a description of the plan of the forum as such.

The principal features of the forum are described above (Ch. 14, §3). The conclusions embodied in that description are based in part on the discussion that is presented here; but the description given above contains certain material, not of a controversial character, which is not repeated here. Thus the description of the forum in the account of the reign of Valens should be read first, and the present excursus should be regarded, not as a complete description of the forum, but as a discussion of some of the texts which concern it.

The principal texts, in translation, are as follows:

Julius Caesar, ca. 48 B.C. Malalas 216.19-21.

"And he built a *basilike*, which he called the Kaisarion, opposite the Temple of Ares, which is re-named Macellum."[1]

Claudius, A.D. 41-54. Malalas 246.13-19 (account of an earthquake).

---

[1] For details concerning the plan of the Kaisarion, which contained a Conch or vaulted apse and an exaeron or hypaethral court, see the account of its construction, above, Ch. 7, §2.

"There was shaken then also the great city Antioch, and there was destroyed the Temple of Artemis and that of Ares and that of Herakles, and certain houses fell. The same Emperor Claudius [freed the people of Antioch from a liturgy or tax] for the restoration of the roofed colonnades which had been built by Tiberius Caesar."[2]

Vespasian, A.D. 69-79. Malalas 262.3-4.

"He built also in Antioch the Great near the theater a shrine which he called that of the Winds."[3]

Trajan, A.D. 98-117. Malalas 275.14-17.

". . . Trajan built in Antioch the Great, making a beginning with it as his first work, the so-called Middle Gate, near the Temple of Ares, where the winter-torrent Parmenius comes down, nearest (ἔγγιστα) to what is now called the Macellum. . ."[4]

Commodus, A.D. 180-192. Malalas 283.4-9.

"He built in Antioch the Great a public bath, which he called the Kommodion, and the Temple of Athene which was opposite it he restored, and between them (εἰς τὸ μέσον αὐτῶν) he made the so-called Xystos, building seats and the colonnades. And at the lower end (εἰς τὴν ἀρχὴν δὲ τὴν κάτω)[5] of the Xystos he built a temple to Olympian Zeus."

Malalas 287, 1-7 (account of reorganization of Olympic Games).

"He [the Alytarch] slept during those days [forty-five days in July and August during which the festival was held][6] in the *exaeron* of the *basilike* called the Kaisarion, which was built by Julius Caesar the dictator, that [which was] outside the Conch of the *basilike*. The same Kaisarion was opposite the Temple of Ares, where [is] what is called the Macellum because the pig's flesh is cut up there alone, near the Temple of Ares."

Didius Julianus, A.D. 193. Malalas 290.14-20.

"He built in Antioch the Great the so-called Plethrin,[7] (*sic*) since they performed the contests in the Olympics in the theater. And because of a petition of the land-owners of the city Antioch, who made the request, he granted to them funds for the building of the same Plethrin. And they built it near the Kaisarion, having purchased the house of the curialis Asabinos, of the Jewish faith, near the Xystos and the Bath of Commodus."[8]

Valens, A.D. 364-378. Malalas 338.19—339.15.

"And in Antioch, being pleased with the situation and the breezes and

[2] For the reign of Claudius, see above, Ch. 8, §5.

[3] See above, Ch. 9, §1. The Temple of the Winds, as will be seen below, may have been identical with the building elsewhere called the Horologion.

[4] For Trajan's work at Antioch see above, Ch. 9, §5.

[5] On the meaning of this phrase, see further below.

[6] See Ch. 9, §10.

[7] Malalas uses the colloquial diminutive instead of the correct technical name, Plethrion.

[8] Malalas ascribes this work to Didius Julianus but there may be reason to doubt that it could have been done during his brief reign. In any case the building of the Plethrion formed a part of the project which was planned in the time of Commodus. For further discussion of this question, see above, Ch. 10, §1.

the waters,[9] he built first[10] the forum, undertaking a great work,[11] demolishing the *basilike* formerly called the Kaisarion, which was near the Horologion and the Kommodion, which is now the praetorium of the consularis Syriae, as far as the so-called Plethrion, and restoring its Conch, and building vaults above the so-called Parmenius, the winter torrent which flows from the mountain through the middle of the city Antioch. And building another *basilike* opposite the Kommodion, and adorning the four *basilikai* with great columns from Salona, paneling the ceilings and adorning [them] with paintings and various marbles and mosaic, and paving with marble above the vaults of the mountain torrent the whole of the open space (*mesaulon*), he completed his forum, and giving various adornments to the four *basilikai* and setting up statues, in the middle erecting a very great column bearing a statue of the Emperor Valentinian, his brother; and he set up a marble statue in the *Senaton* of the Conch and in the middle of the *basilike* which is in the Conch another statue of costly stone, seated, to the same most divine Emperor Valentinian."[12]

Theodosius I, A.D. 379-395. Libanius, *On the Plethron, Or.* 10.33-34.[13]

". . . If one thinks it beneficial to the public that these things [the trial contests of the Olympic games, held in the Plethrion] should be seen by all, why should we have still more affairs piled upon others when it is possible to give over what is done in the afternoon [in the Plethrion] to the neighboring oblong *theatron*,[14] and when it is possible to make what is now done in three days the work of a month, and not to make any distinction, for anybody, in the matter of costume? For in this way there would be a greater number [of spectators]. (34) Indeed there is something even better than this for such things. What is this? The *theatron* under the mountain, especially since the mountain itself takes the place of a *theatron*. . . ."

Zeno, A.D. 474-491. Account by Malalas of factional disorders, from the codex Baroccianus (Greek) and the Church Slavonic version. Words which appear in the latter but not in the former are printed in italic.[15]

---

[9] Cf. the similar phrases used by Malalas 140.15f., 222.15f., 291.15f., and by Festus *Breviarium* 16.4 and Eutropius 6.14.2.

[10] Cf. the similar phrases used by Malalas 199.1f., 205.14f., 275.14f.; cf. also 173.3f.

[11] "Work," i.e. work of construction. *Ktisma* has this meaning elsewhere in Malalas: 235.5, 275.15, 299.23, 318.15, 360.10; it probably has the same meaning also in 318.4, 324.8, 360.5, 361.18, 369.8, 406.21. Cf. the use of the word in the same sense in an inscription of A.D. 635/6 at Baalbek, AAES 3, No. 342, pp. 272-273.

[12] The translation reproduces the loose construction of the last sentence; the meaning is, however, clear.

[13] The oration is translated, with introduction and commentary, below, 687-693. Libanius uses the classical word *plethron* instead of the technical term *plethrion*.

[14] A structure which could be that to which Libanius refers has been found in the excavations; see above, Ch. 14, n. 70.

[15] The account of the Baroccianus, the unique MS of the Greek text of Malalas, is shortened and garbled (cf. the Bonn edition 389.16ff.). The translation given here represents the fuller

Topographical Excursus

"In the reign of this Emperor Zeno, those of the Green faction of the same city Antioch, beginning a fight with stones in the hippodrome *with those of the Blue faction*, while Thalassius, the governor and consularis, was in attendance, they hit him on the head with a stone and drove him out of the hippodrome. And looking about for the man who had hit him, Thalassius recognized him, and sending for him as soon as he had reached his praetorium,[16] he secured him by means of his commentarienses, and had him brought to his praetorium; he was a bath-attendant *from the bath of Urbicius, named Olympius*.[17] And he began to examine him, and the people of the Green faction, learning this, made an attack on the *consul's* praetorium,[18] against the governor, and setting fire to it they burned the Xystos *and the whole portico as far as the consul's praetorium was burned*,[19] and they liberated the prisoner *Olympius*."[20]

The information concerning the relationships of the various buildings may be summarized as follows:

Building		Reign
1. Kaisarion	opposite Temple of Ares, "later called the Macellum"	Caesar
	opposite Temple of Ares, where the Macellum is,	
	near the Temple of Ares	Commodus
	near Plethrion, Xystos and Kommodion	Didius Julianus
	near Horologion and Kommodion; demolished	
	"as far as the Plethrion"; its Conch restored	Valens
2. Plethrion	near Kaisarion, Xystos and Kommodion	Didius Julianus
	(enlarged, perhaps only in interior,	
	332 and 336)[21]	
	Kaisarion demolished "as far as the Plethrion"	Valens

---

form of the Greek text as preserved in the Excerpta de Insidiis (§35, pp. 166.29-167.2 ed. De Boor), and the Church Slavonic version (p. 109 transl. M. Spinka), which adds words and phrases that no longer appear in the Greek.

[16] Formerly the Bath of Commodus.

[17] The Church Slavonic version, which is evidently corrupt in this place, reads, literally, "They were bath-keepers of the bath called Urbicius and Eupatius." The translation given above represents the emendation of C. E. Gleye, *Byz. Ztschr.* 3 (1894) 626. In the text, the word "bath-keepers" is in the plural and the name Urbicius modifies the noun "bath"; it is not clear, from the text, whether Eupatius is the name of the bath-keeper or of the bath. The relative pronoun after Eupatius is in the singular, so that it is not clear whether there were two bath-keepers or one. Possibly the Greek text which the Church Slavonic translator used was so corrupt that he did not understand it. This is suggested particularly by the plural verb in the present sentence, and it is not impossible that the omission of the proper names in the Excerpta indicates that the compiler of the Excerpta likewise did not understand his original. This might be indicated also by the fact that the text in the Excerpta states, a little later in the passage, only that the rioters "liberated the prisoner," while the Church Slavonic version also gives his name.

[18] I.e. the praetorium of the *consularis*, not of the consul.

[19] Instead of the phrase preserved in the Church Slavonic text, the text of the *Excerpta* has only "and other things." Possibly the compiler of the *Excerpta* did not understand a reference in his original to the portico.

[20] See above, n. 17.

[21] See the translation of Libanius *Or.* 10, below, 687-693.

near a "neighboring oblong *theatron*" (a further
enlargement made or planned at this time)   Theodosius I

3. Kommodion   opposite Temple of Athene; Xystos between
them, with Temple of Zeus at its lower end   Commodus
near Plethrion, Kaisarion and Xystos   Didius Julianus
near Kaisarion and Horologion; a *basilike*
built opposite it by Valens   Valens
(as praetorium of cons. Syr.) near Xystos, connected
by a colonnade   Zeno

4. Xystos   between Kommodion and Temple of Athene, with
Temple of Zeus at its lower end   Commodus
near Plethrion, Kaisarion, and Kommodion   Didius Julianus
burned; connected by colonnade with
Kommodion   Zeno

5. Temple of Ares,
Macellum   Kaisarion opposite the Temple of Ares, later called
Macellum   Caesar
Temple of Ares destroyed in earthquake   Claudius
Middle Gate close to Temple of Ares, where
Parmenius comes down, nearest the Macellum   Trajan
Kaisarion opposite Temple of Ares, where the
Macellum is, near the Temple of Ares   Commodus
Temple of Ares converted into Macellum[22]   Valens

6. Temple of
Athene   restored; opposite Kommodion, with
Xystos between them and Temple of Zeus at lower
side of Xystos   Commodus

7. Temple of Zeus at lower end of Xystos   Commodus

8. *basilike* of
Valens   opposite Kommodion   Valens

9. Horologion   near Kaisarion and Kommodion   Valens

Before the texts are examined, a word must be said on the way in which
Malalas indicates the relative locations of the buildings. Statements that
buildings are "opposite" one another may be taken at face value. The meaning of "near" (πλησίον, 262.4, 275.15, 287.6, 290.18-19, 338.22) seems less
easy to define. One would expect it to indicate general proximity, and to
indicate a less close situation than "very near," "closest to," "nearest"
(ἔγγιστα, used of the Temple of Ares and the Middle Gate of Trajan,

[22] Malalas does not mention that it was Valens who made the Temple of Ares into a
macellum, but it seems reasonably certain that it was Valens who made the change; See Ch.
14, §3.

275.16);[23] but the degree of closeness implied by πλησίον is not easy to determine, and doubtless it was not a matter of great moment to Malalas himself. It is curious to note, for example, that in writing of the Middle Gate, πλησίον and ἔγγιστα are both used in a redundant description: ". . . Trajan built the . . . Middle Gate, near (πλησίον) the Temple of Ares, where the winter-torrent Parmenius comes down, very close (ἔγγιστα) to what is now called Macellum . . . (275.14-17)." In another redundant description, "opposite" and "near" are used synonymously; here, in the reference to the Kaisarion in the reign of Commodus, it is said that "The Kaisarion was opposite (κατέναντι) the Temple of Ares, where [is] what is called the Macellum because the pig's flesh is cut up there alone, near (πλησίον) the Temple of Ares (287.4-7)."[24] It is evident that too much weight cannot be placed upon the literal interpretation of such terms as Malalas uses them. However, the meaning in most cases seems to be reasonably clear.

The structure selected as a point of reference for the location of another may or may not be the most important in the vicinity, and it may or may not be actually contiguous to the building described; but it seems reasonably certain that when Malalas gives the location of a building by reference to another that we should understand that the building used as a point of reference is not separated by any other important structure from the building whose location Malalas wishes to indicate. Commodus is said to have built the bath named for himself, restoring the Temple of Athene opposite it, and building the Xystos between them, as well as a Temple to Olympian Zeus at the lower end of the Xystos. According to Malalas these are the only buildings which Commodus built or restored in Antioch; apparently he does not give their location with reference to other buildings already in existence because they formed a group of some importance and extent and thus needed no further description. In his description of the Plethrion built in the time of Didius Julianus, however, Malalas gives the location of the new structure with reference to three existing buildings, the Kaisarion, the Xystos, and the Kommodion. Apparently these points of reference are used because the Plethrion was the only building constructed in the time of Didius Julianus. The first passage shows that the Xystos and the Kommodion were next to each other; thus it follows from the second passage that the Plethrion and the Kaisarion were the nearest important structures to the Xystos and the Kommodion. The way in which the Plethrion is located may indicate a desire to indicate the relationship of this structure to the group built by

---

[23] On the significance of ἔγγιστα see D. Tabachovitz, *Études sur le grec de la basse époque* (Uppsala-Leipzig 1943) 62-63.

[24] The two passages quoted here might, by themselves, be taken to mean that the Temple of Ares and the Macellum were different structures. However, it seems certain, from the account of Julius Caesar's work, that the temple was converted into a macellum. The passages quoted here are characteristic examples of Malalas' mechanical method of writing. The second passage, at least, might indicate that the chronicler had forgotten for the moment that the temple later became a macellum.

Commodus. It is also to be noted that the Kaisarion is introduced in the later passage, though it was not mentioned in the earlier one.

In studying the testimonia for the buildings, we may begin with those which are fairly certainly associated with the forum, and then proceed to the other buildings which are associated with those whose locations with respect to the forum can be seen reasonably clearly.

Since part of the space for the forum was obtained by demolishing part of the Kaisarion, the evidence for the Kaisarion and the buildings which are said to be related to it will form the best point of departure. The Kaisarion was demolished "as far as the Plethrion,"[25] but its Conch was retained and this became a prominent feature of the forum, with statues of Valentinian placed in it. The first clue to the plan of the forum is the statement that the Kaisarion was demolished "as far as the Plethrion." This statement could be interpreted in two ways. (1) The Plethrion, after the demolition, faced the Conch, so that Malalas used this phrase in order to indicate, in one phrase, that the whole of the Kaisarion was demolished save for the Conch, and that the Plethrion stood opposite the Conch, the two structures thus forming one of the axes of the forum, and, by their survival, furnishing the natural boundaries by which a contemporary or later observer would delimit two of the sides of the open space. (2) The Plethrion stood on one side of the Kaisarion, and the demolition of the Kaisarion proceeded only to the point abreast of the Plethrion, with a certain amount of the Kaisarion left standing after that point.

That the first interpretation mentioned above may be right is suggested by the less complicated implication of the statement that Valens built "another *basilike* opposite the Kommodion." The most natural interpretation of this is that the Kommodion and the new *basilike* faced each other across the forum; and this phrase, taken together with the reference to the Plethrion, might suggest that the phrases mean that the Conch and the Plethrion stood on one axis of the forum, the Kommodion and the new *basilike* on the other.

The other structure certainly associated with the forum is the Plethrion, which, as has been seen, seems certainly (from the account of the demolition of the Kaisarion) to have stood on the forum, possibly, as has been suggested, opposite the Conch of the Kaisarion. The buildings mentioned in connection with the Plethrion are the Xystos and the Kommodion, which must have been side by side since Commodus is said to have built the Xystos between the Kommodion and the Temple of Athene (that they were contiguous is also suggested by the account of the riot under Zeno). The Xystos is also said, in another passage (the account of the work under Didius Julianus) to have been near the Kaisarion. Thus, since the Xystos was near the Kaisarion

---

[25] Elsewhere (Malalas 290.14-20) it is said that when the Plethrion was built it was "near" the Kaisarion. This is of interest as suggesting that "near" could be used in the sense of "next to."

(whose site was partly converted into the forum) and the Plethrion, which fairly certainly stood on the forum, and was also next to the Kommodion, which was likewise near the Kaisarion and the Plethrion, there is further reason to think that the Kommodion stood on one side of the forum, with the new "basilica" of Valens opposite it across the forum. Such a location for the Kommodion would be in keeping with the circumstance that the Kommodion came to be used as the praetorium of the consularis Syriae, for it would be natural to have so important an office as this praetorium on a major forum.

Likewise near both the Kaisarion and the Kommodion was the Horologion, which is mentioned only in the account of the construction of the forum. If this was near both the Kaisarion and the Kommodion, it would seem to have been either on or very close to the forum; but since it is not mentioned in connection with the other buildings which are associated with the forum, there is no further clue to its location. The Horologion may be identical with the Tower of the Winds which Malalas says was built by Vespasian.[26] The Tower of the Winds, Malalas says, was near the theater, that is, presumably, the main scenic theater. The main theater is not mentioned in connection with any of the buildings associated with the forum, and we know only that it was located on the side of the mountain.[27]

Thus far, the texts have suggested that the buildings that stood about the forum are the Conch of the Kaisarion, the Plethrion, the Kommodion, the Xystos, the "basilica" of Valens, and possibly the Horologion. Among the major buildings that remain to be examined are the Temple of Ares or Macellum and the Temple of Athene.

While the Kaisarion is spoken of as opposite the Temple of Ares, later the Macellum, the other buildings which are said to be near the Kaisarion (Plethrion, Kommodion, Xystos, Horologion) are nowhere said to be near the Temple of Ares or Macellum. This would appear to mean that the Temple of Ares or Macellum stood on a different side of the Kaisarion from the Plethrion, Kommodion, Xystos, and Horologion. Its apparent lack of connection with other buildings which seem to have stood on the forum would thus suggest that the Temple of Ares or Macellum was not actually on the forum. Malalas says that the Temple of Ares was "very close" (ἔγγιστα, 275.16) to the Middle Gate of Trajan; and there is no other reference to the Middle Gate in connection with the forum. It seems likely, then, that the Temple of Ares or Macellum stood between the forum and the Middle Gate, which was further toward the mountain than the forum. Possibly the Temple of Ares or Macellum stood behind the Conch of the Kaisarion.

The same would be true, apparently, of the Temple of Athene. The only reference to this, which is in the account of Commodus' work, indicates that

---

[26] Malalas 262.3-4; see above, in the account of Vespasian's reign, Ch. 9, §1. On the possible identification of the Horologion and the Tower of the Winds, see above, Ch. 14, n. 50.

[27] See above, Ch. 7, n. 62.

it stood alongside the Xystos, which in turn was next to the Kommodion. Since this temple is not mentioned in connection with any other of the buildings which seem to have stood about the forum, it would appear that the Temple of Athene was on a side of the Xystos which was away from the forum.

The Temple of Olympian Zeus at the lower end or lower side (εἰς τὴν ἀρχὴν δὲ τὴν κάτω) of the Xystos likewise is not mentioned in connection with any other building which might have stood on the forum, and so would seem to have been placed on a side of the Xystos which was away from the forum. The meaning of "lower ἀρχή" is not entirely clear. Since the Xystos was an oblong building,[28] the "lower ἀρχή" would apparently be either (1) the end which was away from the main or "upper" end, or (2) the end at which the level of the ground was lower than the terrain on which the other end was built. Since the forum stood on the lower slope of the mountain, the latter interpretation would seem more plausible.[29]

Conclusion

The texts indicate that the forum was surrounded by the Conch of the Kaisarion, the Plethrion, the Kommodion, the Xystos, the "basilica" of Valens, and possibly the Horologion. The way in which Malalas speaks of the Conch and the Plethrion, and of the Kommodion and the "basilica" of Valens, suggests that the Conch and the Plethrion faced each other at the ends of one axis of the forum, and that the Kommodion and the "basilica" of Valens stood facing each other on the other two sides. The Kommodion was flanked by the Xystos, and possibly by the Horologion. It is tempting to suppose that the forum was an oblong rectangle, with the Conch and the Plethrion, as the smaller buildings, on the short sides, and the Kommodion (with the Xystos) and the "basilica" of Valens, as the larger buildings, on the long sides.

EXCURSUS 13

THE PALACES AT ANTIOCH AND DAPHNE

A. Antioch

Antioch became the Seleucid capital and residence early in the Seleucid

---

[28] See above, on the account of its construction, Ch. 9, nn. 155-156.

[29] Compare the passages in which Malalas uses κάτω to indicate the position of a building with relation to the mountain and the river. He says that under Caligula the Roman senators Pontius and Varius built a public bath, the Varium, κάτω παρὰ τὸ τεῖχος πλησίον τοῦ ποταμοῦ (244.7). An expression such as this reflects the same point of view, comparatively, as the more frequent παρὰ τὸ ὄρος (222.15, 233.22, 234.11, 263.11) or πρὸς τῷ ὄρει (234.17, 234.22) used of other buildings, as well as such phrases as ἄνω εἰς τὴν ἀκρόπολιν (216.21, 346.19, cf. 217.2) and ἄνω εἰς τὸ ὄρος (347.1); cf. also εἰς τὴν πεδιάδα τῆς πόλεως (294.19, 306.22). Seleucus Nicator is said to have invited the people who dwelt on the acropolis οἰκεῖν ἅμα αὐτῷ τὴν κάτω πόλιν Ἀντιόχειαν (347.4).

period.[1] At this time, however, there would have been at Antioch no building that could be called a palace in the generally accepted sense of the term
since the royal residence in the Hellenistic period was not a specific type of
building designed for the use of the king and his court, but merely an elaborate dwelling resembling the private house of the then usual type—enlarged and developed, presumably, to a size suitable for the purpose and appointed in an appropriate manner, but still essentially a private house.[2]

The first royal residence to be built at Antioch would presumably have
been placed in the original quarter of the city founded by Seleucus I, but
we have no specific evidence as to its location.[3]

The earliest trustworthy references to a royal residence at Antioch occur
in the description of the rioting that took place in 147 b.c., during the reign
of Demetrius II Nicator. Here it is said that the king was forced to barricade
himself "in the royal residence." The building, whatever it was, was strong
enough to withstand assault by an armed mob; and it is also said that there
were houses around it.[4]

We hear of a palace in Malalas' account of the visit to Antioch in 67 b.c.
of Q. Marcius Rex, the proconsul of Cilicia.[5] The chronicler says that Marcius
Rex built "the old circus and the old palace (*palation*)." Apparently this was
done in order to show that Philip, the Seleucid kinglet who was then on the
throne, enjoyed the support of Rome, and possibly also in an effort to introduce Roman culture and customs in Antioch. That the circus is the one of
which remains are preserved on the island is indicated by the archaeological
evidence found in the excavations, which shows that this structure was built
in the first century b.c.[6] In calling the palace and the hippodrome "old,"
Malalas is apparently writing from the point of view of his own day. In

[1] Seleucia Pieria was the original Seleucid capital. The change to Antioch seems to have
been made on the death of Seleucus I; see above, Ch. 5, n. 2.

[2] See A. von Gerkan, *Griech. Städteanlagen* (Berlin 1924) 108-109 and T. Fyfe, *Hellenistic
Architecture* (Cambridge University Press 1936) 154-55.

[3] Förster ("Antiochia" 140) adduces the testimony of the anonymous Arabic writer (whom
he calls "Zeineddini") who in his description of the foundation of Antioch states that the
"palazzo del re" was "nel centro della città" (Guidi, "Descrizione araba" p. 157, cited by
Förster as p. 23,21, from the special pagination of the offprint). This Arabic account contains
so many legendary features that although it may be a useful document (as Förster thinks, 110,
n. 34), it is difficult to know how far it is to be trusted; and the present statement, if true,
is not particularly helpful.

[4] On the episode, see above, Ch. 6, nn. 17-19, where the sources (1 Macc., Josephus,
Diodorus) are cited. The term used, *basileia*, really means only "the royal residence," and
cannot be taken to imply that the structure was a "palace" of the Roman type, since the sources,
in using this term, may have been employing it anachronistically, in the sense in which it was
current in their own day. Müller (*Antiq. Antioch.*, 65) thinks that this palace was located on
the island; cf. his description of the island, 52, to which he apparently refers when he writes
(65) *quam supra descripsi*. However, this is a conjecture, since we have no evidence for a
palace on the island before the Roman period. The reason adduced by Förster (117) for supposing that Antiochus III, the Great (222-187 b.c.) built a palace on the island is not convincing, as will be seen from an examination of the evidence for the palace of Diocletian on
the island (Ch. 12, §2; Excursus 13, §3). Förster's hypothesis is accepted by K. Lehmann-
Hartleben, "Städtebau," *RE* 3A (1929) 2124.

[5] Malalas 225.8.

[6] See Excursus 14.

Malalas' time there was a stadium on the island (called the "Byzantine stadium" by the excavators) whose construction is dated by archaeological evidence in the late fifth or early sixth centuries after Christ.[7] Thus the earlier circus, built by Marcius Rex, would have become "the old one" after the new structure was built. If (as seems reasonable) we are to suppose that Malalas was using the epithet "old" in the same sense in his allusion to the palace built by Marcius Rex, then it would follow that the palace built by the Roman proconsul was "the old one" in comparison with another, newer, one; and this would presumably be that built on the island by Diocletian (see further below).[8]

B. DAPHNE

That Daphne, so loved by the people of Antioch and by the Seleucid rulers, had a royal residence or villa, seems beyond question. It happens, however, that there is no reference to such a residence in our meager literary sources.

One episode in Seleucid history has been thought to be associated with a palace at Daphne. It is, however, by no means certain that a palace was involved; the incident might have occurred just as well in a temple or even in an ordinary house. Antiochus II (261-247/6 B.C.) first married Laodice, and had by her a son who in time became his successor as Seleucus II (246-226 B.C.). Much later Antiochus II married the Egyptian princess Berenice, and had by her another son. After the death of Antiochus II, Seleucus II, at the instigation of his mother Laodice, assassinated Berenice and her son. This is said by Justinus to have been done at Daphne, where Berenice had "shut herself up" (27.1.4-7): *Porro Beronice [sic], cum ad se interficiendam missos didicisset, Daphinae se claudit. Ubi cum obsideri eam cum parvulo filio nuntiatum Asiae civitatibus esset. . . . Sed Beronice ante adventum auxiliorum, cum vi expugnari non posset, dolo circumventa trucidatur.* The assassination is also mentioned by Appian, *Syr.* 65; Valerius Maximus 9.10, ext. I; Polyaenus 8.50; and Jerome, Commentar. in Danielem 11.5ff. = *PL* 25.585-586. All these sources merely mention the incident, and do not speak of Daphne at all. The sources are cited, and the incident discussed, by Stähelin, Seleukos II Kallinikos, *R.E.* 2.A.1235-6. Bouchier *Antioch* 28-29 relates the incident and says that "Berenice withdrew to the Seleucid palace at Daphne, protected by Galatian guards, until help from Egypt should arrive. . . . Laodice won over the queen's physician Aristarchus, assassins made an

[7] See Excursus 14.
[8] If we are to suppose that Malalas was in this case (as he often does elsewhere) using "built" to describe repair, reconstruction, or the like, instead of new building, then it would follow that the epithet "old" was used with reference to the time of Marcius Rex, and Malalas' notice would mean that Marcius Rex rebuilt or repaired a palace and a circus which had been in existence before his day, and so were "old" before he rebuilt them. However, since his use of "old" can be plausibly explained on the basis of the existence of the "Byzantine stadium" in addition to the great circus, it seems more reasonable to suppose that the same usage applied to the palace.

[642]

entry into the palace, and Berenice fell." The reference to the palace is purely an inference, presumably from the passage in Justinus, although Bouchier cites no sources for the incident. Elsewhere (46) Bouchier cites Justinus 15.4 as evidence for the existence of a Seleucid palace at Daphne, but there is nothing in this passage on a palace; it contains only a reference (very brief) to the foundation of Antioch and to the establishment of the temple of Apollo at Daphne. On the same page Bouchier cites Justinus 39.2 in another connection. Presumably this writer confused the passages in Justinus and cited one when he meant another, so that on p. 46 his reference to Justinus was supposed to be to the passage on Berenice cited above.

C. The Palace on the Island

The only certain evidence that we have for the location of the Roman palace (or indeed of any palace before the Arab conquest) is furnished by the passages in Libanius, Theodoret, and Evagrius in which a palace on the island is mentioned. The reference in Libanius shows that about A.D. 360 a palace stood upon the island, occupying one-fourth of it and extending from near the *tetrapylon*, which was presumably near the center of the island, as far as the outer wall along the river.[9] The passage in Theodoret corroborates this in somewhat less detail.[10] Evagrius says that in the earthquake which occurred during the reign of Leo, probably in A.D. 458,[11] the "first and second *oikos* of the palace were thrown down, but the others, with the bath which lay beside them, stood."[12] This passage occurs in the description of the damage done in the "new city," that is, the island, and it certainly must refer to the palace mentioned by Libanius and Theodoret. Evagrius goes on to say that the disaster "also threw down the stoas before the palace, and the *tetra-*

---

[9] Libanius, *Or.* 11.206: "This palace occupies so much of the island that it constitutes a fourth part of the whole. For it joins the middle, which we call the omphalos, and extends as far as the outer branch of the river, so that the wall, having columns instead of battlements, furnishes a view worthy of the emperor, with the river flowing below and the suburbs delighting the eye from all sides."

[10] Theodoret, *Eccl. Hist.*, 4.26.1-3, p. 264.22ff., ed. Parmentier: "From the north the river Orontes flows by the palace and from the south a two-storied *stoa* of the greatest size is built on the circuit wall of the city, having high towers at either side. Between the palace and the river is a highway which receives those who leave the city by the gate at this place and leads to the suburbs. The holy Aphraates was passing along this, going to the military *gymnasion* [i.e. the *Campus Martius* on the right bank of the Orontes] to care for his flock. Looking out from above, from the *basileios stoa*, the emperor perceived him hurrying along, though in advanced age, dressed in the hide of an animal; and someone having said that this was Aphraates, to whom most of the people in the city were devoted, the emperor said to him, 'Tell me, where are you going'?" Theodoret then proceeds to report an extended conversation between them. The incident is said to have occurred during the reign of Valens, A.D. 364-378, and the *History* was written at some time shortly before A.D. 450 (see Parmentier's introduction, pp. xcix-ci). Since Theodoret presumably followed the prevalent usage of placing north in what was actually northwest or west (see Excursus 9), the passage indicates that the palace stood on the western bank of the island. This is indicated also by Libanius's statement that it extended as far as the "outer" side of the island.

[11] See Excursus 7.

[12] Evagrius 2.12, p. 63.30ff. ed. Bidez-Parmentier: τῶν δὲ βασιλείων ὁ πρῶτος καὶ δεύτερος οἶκος κατεβλήθησαν, τῶν ἄλλων σὺν τῷ παρακειμένῳ βαλανείῳ μεινάντων . . .

pylon which stood at their ends; and of the hippodrome it threw down the towers at the gates, and some of the stoas which led to them. . . ."[13] The existence of a "first and second *oikos*" in the palace, in addition to "others," certainly means that there were several distinct parts of the palace, all of which might have been built at one time, or might represent additions made at different periods.[14] The phrase "first and second *oikos*" of course suggests even more strongly a palace built in four quarters, on the *castrum* plan familiar from Diocletian's palace at Spalato.

This passage might indicate, then, that several periods of building were represented in the palace on the island. One of these, at least, might date from the time of Gallienus (A.D. 253-260) and Diocletian (A.D. 284-305), for Malalas says (306.21) that Diocletian at Antioch "built . . . a great palace, finding the foundations already laid by Gallienus, who was also called Licinianus." There is no evidence for the location of this, but the colonnade on the wall described by Libanius and Theodoret might, from its resemblance to the similar arrangement in the palace of Diocletian at Spalato, indicate that this part of the palace, at least, was either built or rebuilt by Diocletian.[15]

The question is, accordingly, whether this palace on the island, begun by Gallienus and completed by Diocletian, was the first to be built on the island, or whether it was an extension or a rebuilding of an older (perhaps Seleucid) palace, or the palace built by Q. Marcius Rex. There is a reference in the *Scriptores Historiae Augustae* (*Sev. Alex.* 54.6) to a *Palatium* at Antioch during the reign of Severus Alexander (A.D. 222-235), but this source is so anecdotal in character that it cannot be taken as evidence of the existence of a monumental palace, and the term *Palatium*, used as it is in this passage, need mean nothing more than the imperial residence in any provincial city or town.

A somewhat similar text is provided by Dio's account of the earthquake of A.D. 115, in which he relates how Trajan "escaped through a window from the building (*oikēma*) in which he was staying" and lived for several days in the Hippodrome (68.25.5); the passage does not indicate clearly whether the emperor was staying in a palace, and it is not certain that the hippodrome meant is the one on the island. If the Seleucid palace was no longer in use at this time, Trajan might have been staying in some other place; furthermore, it does not necessarily follow from the passage that the hippodrome was near the building in which Trajan was staying. The hippodrome on the

[13] *Ibid.*, p. 64.2ff.: κατέρριψε καὶ τὰς στοὰς τὰς πρὸ τῶν βασιλείων καὶ τὸ ἐπ' αὐτὰς τετράπυλον, καὶ τοῦ ἱπποδρομίου δὲ τοὺς περὶ τὰς θύρας πύργους, καί τινας τῶν ἐπ' αὐταῖς στοῶν . . .

[14] In the *Chronicon Paschale* (622.8) it is said that in the Nika riot at Constantinople ἐκαύθησαν αἱ στέγαι τῶν δύο βασιλικῶν οἴκων. Cf. *IGRR* 4.293, p. 110, line 36 (Pergamum), εἰς τὴν στοὰν καθ' ὃν τόπον ἐστὶν ὁ πρῶτος οἶκος.

[15] Stauffenberg (*Malalas* 459) believes that the division of the island by four streets in the manner of a Roman camp goes back to Probus and Gallienus. Both Förster ("Antiochia" 117, 125) and Stauffenberg (458-459) place the palace of Diocletian on the island; Müller (*Antiq. Antioch.* 99) places it in the mainland part of the city (see Fig. 9; and see below, n. 18).

island, however, is the only one at Antioch at this period, for which we have certain evidence, and if it can be assumed that this is the one meant in the passage in Dio, and that the emperor would have sought refuge in it from a building which was near by, and if, in addition, it be supposed that the emperor would have been staying in a palace, then the passage would indicate that there was a palace on the island in A.D. 115.[16]

It is certain, then, that there was a palace on the island in A.D. 360, partly destroyed in A.D. 458, which had been built by Diocletian on foundations laid by Gallienus; whether it stood on the site of, or was an extension or a rebuilding of, a Seleucid palace, is still a matter of question. If the passage in Dio is taken to show that there was a palace on the island in A.D. 115, this might have been originally Seleucid although it might equally well be a Roman "palace" or *palatium* for which we have no other extensive evidence.

Förster ("Antiochia" 117) rightly concluded that the palace on the island mentioned by Libanius would be a Roman one at least; he also, however, supposed that near this was a building called the *Regia*, which would indicate, to him, that a Seleucid palace had been located on the island (presumably Förster believed, although he did not state it in this way, that the *Regia* was the Seleucid palace): this supposition was based upon a passage in Malalas's account of the reign of Julian, in which he says (328.4) that the emperor published his *Misopogon* at Antioch "outside the *palation* of the city at the *Tetrapylon* of the Elephants near the *Regia*."

Förster's interpretation of the passage does not take into account the way in which Malalas uses the word *Regia*. One might suppose, as Förster did, that *Regia* and *palation* could both be used to designate a palace; on the other hand it would seem possible that Malalas used the two terms in order to distinguish the buildings, perhaps in accordance with local custom. Examination of Malalas's usage indicates, however, that he employed *Regia* to designate the approach to a palace, or a place near it, for he says that at Constantinople Constantine ἔκτισε δὲ δύο ἐμβόλους ἀπὸ τῆς εἰσόδου τοῦ παλατίου ἕως τοῦ αὐτοῦ φόρου . . . καλέσας τὸν τόπον τῶν ἐμβόλων 'Ρηγίαν . . . (321.6).[17] This usage, which Förster did not take into consideration, indicates that the *Regia* near the palace on the island was an open

---

[16] Müller did not see that this passage may have value for the location of the palace. It apparently did not occur to him that Trajan might have been staying in a palace, and (being unaware of the existence of the hippodrome on the ancient island) he was somewhat uncertain as to the location of the hippodrome in which Trajan would have taken refuge: in *Antiq. Antioch.* 67, n. 8, he locates it "vel in nova urbe vel prope eam," and on p. 88 places it "in campo extra urbem"; on his plan he places it across the river from the city. The passage in Evagrius certainly implies that the hippodrome was on the island.

[17] A little later Malalas says (322.5) that the bath called the Zeuxippon was πλησίον . . . τοῦ Ἱππικοῦ καὶ τῆς 'Ρηγίας καὶ τοῦ παλατίου. The same distinction is reflected more clearly in the form in which the same statement appears in the *Chronicon Paschale* (530.1), πλησίον . . . τοῦ Ἱππικοῦ καὶ τῆς 'Ρηγίας τοῦ παλατίου (Malalas and the compiler of the *Chronicon Paschale* probably took their information at this point from a common source: cf. F. C. Conybeare, "The Relation of the Paschal Chronicle to Malalas," *BZ* 11 [1902] 395-405).

space or the monumental approach to the palace mentioned by Libanius, and not another building.[18]

The later history of the palace on the island is not well known. We are told in the *Plerophoriai* of John Rufus that when he visited Antioch, during the period (A.D. 512-518) when Severus was patriarch, he saw a hermit living in a little tent which he had built in front of the imperial palace on the island, which was closed.[19] The evidence indicates that when Antioch was rebuilt following the sack by the Persians in A.D. 540, the island was abandoned as a part of the city (it had been badly damaged in the earthquake which occurred during the reign of Leo I, probably in A.D. 458).[20] Whether a new palace was built in the mainland part of the city is not specifically stated in the preserved sources. Förster (140) concludes that the palace was transferred to the mainland, and in support of this he cites the statements of Hadji Chalifa and of the anonymous Arabic description of Antioch preserved in Codex Vaticanus Arabicus 286 that "the palace of the king" was in the

---

[18] An allusion in Libanius's description of the island would thus be to what Malalas calls the *Regia*. Describing the four pairs of colonnades which ran from the center of the island to "each quarter of the heaven," Libanius says (*Or.* 11.205), "Three of these pairs, running as far as the wall, are joined to its circuit, while the fourth is shorter but is the more beautiful just in proportion as it is shorter, since it runs toward the palace which begins hard by and serves as an approach to it (ἀντὶ προπυλαίων)." When Ammianus Marcellinus uses *regia* of the palace at Antioch, he clearly employs it in the regular Latin sense, of which the sense appearing in Malalas and the *Chronicon Paschale* is a later development; his understanding of the word is shown most clearly by a passage in the account of the activities of Gallus at Antioch (14.7.4): *accenderat super his incitatum propositum ad nocendum aliqua mulier vilis, quae ad palatium (ut poposcerat) intromissa, insidias ei latenter obtendi prodiderat a militibus obscurissimis. quam Constantina exultans, ut in tuto iam locato mariti salute, muneratam vehiculoque inpositam, per regiae ianuas emisit in publicum . . . ;* cf. also the reference in 14.1.6 to secret doors in the *regia*. Further examples of Ammianus' understanding of the word are furnished by two other passages: in 14.7.10 it is said that an official named Domitianus, on his arrival at Antioch, *"praestrictis palatii ianuis, contempto Caesare* [scil. Constantio] *quam videri decuerat . . . nec regiam introiit nec processit in publicum*; elsewhere there is a reference to a statue (25.10.2), *. . . Maximiani statua Caesaris, quae locata est in vestibulo regiae. . . ."* Förster ("Antiochia" 117, n. 62) quotes the last two passages as though to support the belief that Malalas uses *Regia* to mean a palace; he does not mention the first two. Müller (*Antiq. Antioch.* 99, with n. 2), expressed himself more guardedly with respect to the passage in Malalas, saying, *quae ea Regia fuerit, ubive sita, ignoratur*; he noted the passage in the *Chronicon Paschale* quoted in the preceding note, but, like Förster, did not take into consideration the two other passages in Malalas which illustrate his understanding of *Regia*: perhaps if Müller had known these he would have seen the meaning of the present passage. Müller (*ibid.*) placed the palace of Diocletian (which he supposed was identical with that mentioned by Malalas in the passage on Julian) in the mainland part of the city, suggesting that it was in the southern and western region, where there seems to have been a palace in the time of the Crusades. Förster is mistaken in his statement (117) that Müller concluded from Libanius' description of the palace on the island that Antiochus the Great built a palace there, which he is said by Libanius to have established as a part of the city (for the evidence, cf. Förster, 116). Müller nowhere expresses the belief that Antiochus the Great built a palace on the island, and Förster's remark presumably arose from a misreading of the passage in which Müller, immediately after discussing the tradition that Antiochus established the island (50-51), goes on to describe the plan and appearance of the island (51-53). Müller expressly says (51) that he will describe the features of the island mentioned by Libanius and Evagrius (among which he of course enumerates the palace).

[19] See above, Ch. 18, §3.

[20] See the discussions of the history of the island, above, Ch. 17, §1, Ch. 18, §8.

center of the city.[21] This is quite possible, though we must always bear in mind that the financial stringency of the period may have made it necessary to adapt an existing building, instead of constructing a new palace.[22]

EXCURSUS 14

THE STADIA OR CIRCUSES AT ANTIOCH AND DAPHNE

A. Antioch

There exist remains of two circuses or stadia at Antioch, both on the island (Fig. 11).[1] The larger, which is "one of the largest and most important circuses in the Roman Empire," is dated by its excavator, W. A. Campbell, on the basis of coins and of the characteristics of the preserved masonry, probably in the first century B.C.; certainly it must be later than the reign of Antiochus VI Dionysus (145-142 B.C.).[2] This circus was repaired and reconstructed on various occasions, most extensively in the fourth century A.D. There is no indication of when it fell into disuse.

The other structure, which is not greatly inferior in size, is called a "Byzantine stadium" by the excavators, who believe that it was "simply an exercising ground enclosed by a thin wall with an exterior arcade."[3] The type of construction and the pottery found in the excavation indicate that it was built in the late fifth or early sixth century A.D., and the excavators believe that it was probably not used after the disastrous earthquakes early in Justinian's reign. Either there was no permanent provision of seats, or there were only simple seating arrangements of light material, for no foundations for seats were discovered. That there were no seats is suggested by the circumstances that the stadium is oriented east and west, so that spectators

[21] Hadji Chalifa, *Gihan Numa*, II, p. 344: *media in urbe locus, Belat elmelek vocatus et marmore varii generis pavimentatus.* See above, n. 3

[22] Förster's suggestions in this matter seem to have misled Stauffenberg, who supposed (*Malalas* 457-458) that there were two palaces dating from the Seleucid period in addition to the palace on the island. There would have been, in his opinion, a palace built by Seleucus Nicator on the mainland because Seleucus must have built a palace when he founded the city; and there would have been another built by Antiochus the Great on the island because Antiochus established the island; the palace on the island mentioned by Libanius, finally, would date from the Roman period. Stauffenberg then suggests that the palace on the mainland was placed "an die Stelle des ehemaligen Seleukospalastes" (457, n. 17). The review of the evidence presented here shows how hypothetical this suggestion must be. Stauffenberg's belief that Seleucus Nicator built a palace on the mainland is perhaps based upon Förster's assumption (111) that Antioch was the royal residence from the time of its foundation. Stauffenberg (457) does not undertake to decide whether the work attributed to Marcius Rex is to be considered to be a reconstruction of the palace of Seleucus on the mainland or an improvement of the *Regia*, which, following Förster, he supposed was a Hellenistic palace on the island.

[1] See also the map in *Antioch-on-the-Orontes* 1, pl. 2, facing p. viii, and W. A. Campbell's excavation reports, *ibid.* 32-41, also the general map of the excavations in *Antioch-on-the-Orontes* 2, p. 215, plan 1, on which the location of the structures is indicated.

[2] *Antioch-on-the-Orontes* 1.40-41.   [3] *Antioch-on-the-Orontes* 1.33.

sitting on the northern side would have had the sun in their eyes constantly (the great circus is oriented north and south to prevent this inconvenience). It appears, then, that the structure was not designed to supplant the great circus, but was intended only to supplement it.

There are no known traces of any other similar structures in Antioch or its immediate vicinity, so that so far as we know at present, the great circus, which was built probably in the first century B.C., is the oldest in Antioch proper. It may seem difficult to believe that a city such as Antioch can have lacked a stadium from the time of its foundation in 300 B.C. to the first century B.C., and there may have been an earlier structure the remains of which have now disappeared completely. However, the preserved accounts of games that Antiochus IV presented at Daphne in 195 B.C. (before he succeeded his father on the throne) and ca. 167 B.C. indicate that a stadium existed at Daphne at this time (see further below), and it may be that this was the only one available to the people of Antioch until the construction of the great circus on the island in the first century B.C.

Malalas refers several times to what he regularly calls "the old circus," τὸ παλαιὸν ἱππικόν. According to him (225.7-11), this was originally built with his own money by Q. Marcius Rex, the proconsul of Cilicia who in 67 B.C. visited Philip II, the Seleucid kinglet then occupying the throne in Antioch. Whether Marcius Rex actually used his own money to build this circus is not clear.[4] There is a question also whether Malalas' statement that Marcius "built" the circus means that he actually was the first to construct it, or whether he only repaired an existing building.[5] The archaeological evidence indicating that the circus on the island was probably constructed during the first century B.C. could imply that Marcius Rex built this circus for the first time or that he repaired an existing one that had been damaged by an earthquake a short time before. What is known of the economic circumstances of the last Seleucid kings suggests, however, that they could not have found the means to construct a large stadium, and the design of the circus is, as W. A. Campbell points out, typically Roman, so that it would seem that Marcius Rex actually did build the circus. If there was no stadium at Antioch before Marcius Rex's time, the only such structure available for the use of the people of Antioch being that at Daphne, the Roman proconsul might well have built a new circus as a token of Roman support and in an effort to bolster Philip's prestige.

The next event in the history of this "old circus" of which we hear (again from Malalas, 225.4-7) is its rehabilitation by Agrippa, the son-in-law and lieutenant of Augustus, who removed from it the debris with which it had

[4] See above, Ch. 6, n. 104.
[5] In Malalas, the rubric ἔκτισε really refers to building operations in general, and may denote either new work or repair or reconstruction. On his usage in this respect, see above, Ch. 2, §4.

become filled as the result of an earthquake.[6] Agrippa presided at games that were given in the circus to celebrate its reopening.

What is apparently the same circus appears again in Malalas' record (307.1-2) that Diocletian built a public bath "in the plain [or: "flat part"] near the old circus." By the πεδιάς Malalas could mean either the oldest section of the city, along the left bank of the river, or the island, or the flat ground across the river from the city, which seems never to have been incorporated within the walls.

Taken together, the archaeological and literary evidence appears to have the following meaning. In speaking of an "old" circus, Malalas might simply have meant that it was old in point of time. However, his use of the epithet in connection with the ostensible construction of the circus by Q. Marcius Rex ought to mean (if it has any meaning at all) that this circus was the "old" one in comparison with another circus or circuses (even though the chronicler does not have occasion to mention the other "new" circus or circuses), and that this epithet had become attached to Marcius Rex's structure when another newer one was built. The existence, then, of the "Byzantine stadium" of the fifth or sixth centuries (which would have been relatively new when Malalas lived in Antioch, in the sixth century) suggests that Malalas used the epithet to distinguish the circus of Marcius Rex from the "Byzantine stadium." Thus it would follow that the great circus on the island, which according to the archaeological evidence was built probably in the first century B.C., is Malalas' "old circus," and that Diocletian built his public bath near it.[7]

A scene which might be a representation of the "Byzantine stadium" appears in the Yakto mosaic; see Excursus 18.

B. DAPHNE

When Hannibal visited Antioch in the summer of 195 B.C. during the reign of Antiochus III, the Great (223-187 B.C.), he found the king's son, the future Antiochus IV, celebrating games at Daphne, and the phraseology of Livy's allusion to these games implies that they were of sufficient magnitude to require a stadium.[8] Polybius' account of the famous games which Antiochus IV presented at Daphne ca. 167 B.C. makes it seem practically certain that there was one at Daphne at that time.[9]

When the Olympic games of Antioch were established under Augustus and Claudius, at least a part of the festival was held at Daphne, which possessed a temple of Olympian Zeus, and the sources indicate that there was

---

[6] On Agrippa's work at Antioch, see above, Ch. 8, §2.
[7] The remains of such a bath have not yet been found in the excavations.
[8] Livy 33.49; Hannibal arrived at Antioch to find that Antiochus III was in Asia, *filiumque eius sollemne ludorum ad Daphne celebrantem convenisset*. . . .
[9] Polybius 30.25-27 *apud* Athen. 5.194, 10.439. See above, Ch. 5, §6.

also a stadium.[10] Malalas states (307.5ff.) that Diocletian "built" a stadium (which the chronicler calls a στάδιον) at Daphne for the Olympic games, but it seems clear that the chronicler is confused on this point and that Diocletian merely repaired or renovated an existing stadium[11] as a part of his program for religious revival in which the cult of Jupiter played an important part.[12]

A stadium labeled τὸ Ὀλυμπιακόν appears in the section that seems to be devoted to Daphne in the topographical border of the Yakto mosaic; see Excursus 18.

EXCURSUS 15

MALALAS ON THE WORK OF CONSTANTINE
THE GREAT AT ANTIOCH

WITH the exception of the brief references in other sources to the construction of the emperor's Great Church there, the passage in Malalas constitutes the sole evidence for the building and administrative measures that Constantine took concerning Antioch. Malalas relates (317.17ff.) that the emperor conducted a campaign against the Persians and conquered them and made a treaty with them. When he was returning from this campaign he visited Antioch and built his church there, with a hospice (*xenon*) near it. He also built the *basilike* called that of Rufinus; this had been a temple of Hermes, which was demolished by Rufinus the *praefectus praetorio*. This Rufinus, when he was going with the emperor to the war, had been commanded to remain in Antioch, "and he completed the *basilike* as the emperor was returning to Rome." And as Constantine was about to leave Antioch, he appointed as the first *archon* of Antioch a certain Plutarchus, a Christian, whom he commanded to supervise (ἐργοδιωκτεῖν) the construction of the church and the *basilike*.[1] Rufinus completed the *basilike*, "and for this reason it was called that of Rufinus." Malalas also relates that Constantine appointed a certain Felicianus to be the first *comes Orientis*, with headquarters at Antioch.[2]

This passage contains several characteristic motifs that appear in other

---

[10] Malalas (289.15) mentions that the victors were crowned at Daphne; this ceremony would presumably have been performed in a stadium. See Stauffenberg, *Malalas* 420-421.

[11] See Downey, "Antioch under Severus and Caracalla," 141-152.

[12] On Diocletian's work, see above, Ch. 12, nn. 33-34.

[1] There is no other evidence that at this period Antioch had an *archon* properly so called; evidently Malalas here (as he sometimes does elsewhere) has substituted a vague term for a more precise title. Possibly Plutarchus was *consularis Syriae*, for the *consularis*, who had his headquarters at Antioch, was so much concerned with the administration of the city itself (in addition to that of the province) that he might well have been thought of as the *archon* of the city. This subject is discussed in Downey, *Comites Orientis*.

[2] This passage in Malalas is the only extant literary evidence for the origin of the office of *comes Orientis*: see Downey, *Comites Orientis* 7-11.

Topographical Excursus

similar passages in Malalas. Constantine never conducted a campaign in person against the Persians, and he never visited Antioch after he became emperor.[3] These two fictions are typical; there are several other instances in which Malalas declares that various Roman emperors visited Antioch (and other cities of the East) when there is either sure evidence or a strong probability that they made no such visits. These fictitious visits are uniformly said to have been made following victorious campaigns and to have included the inauguration of various public building activities. Evidently the invention of these visits is to be ascribed to Malalas' peculiar point of view in the recording of public building operations, according to which it would apparently seem appropriate to suppose that important buildings would naturally be planned and constructed under the personal supervision of the ruler; and the feeling seems to have been that the personal journeys that such operations should be taken to imply were occasions of such great moment that it would be natural to suppose that they were made following successful campaigns.[4] In the present instance the fictitious character of Constantine's tour is betrayed especially by the statement (318.11) that Rufinus completed his *basilike* "as the emperor was returning to Rome": Malalas would evidently take it for granted that Constantine would return to Rome simply because he was a "Roman Emperor."[5]

These features of the passage are easily accounted for. Less easy to solve is the problem raised by the account of the activities of the prefect Rufinus. No person of this name is known to have been praetorian prefect in the East during the reign of Constantine,[6] and there is no other evidence for a *basilike* at Antioch called that of Rufinus as early as this period.[7] On the contrary, Zosimus states that a praetorian prefect named Rufinus built at Antioch a *basilike stoa* (which could be the same as a *basilike*) in or soon after A.D. 393 in order to placate the popular anger aroused by his execution of the *comes Orientis* Lucianus in 393.[8]

[3] See Benjamin, "Constantinus," *RE* 4.1013-1028.
[4] On Malalas's methods, see above, Ch. 2, §4.
[5] A comparable inference appears in the chronicler's account of the visit paid to Antioch by Q. Marcius Rex, proconsul of Cilicia in 67 B.C. (Mal. 225.4). Malalas calls him Κόϊντος Μαρκιανὸς [*sic*] ῥὴξ Ῥωμαίων, with an easily comprehensible misunderstanding of the cognomen Rex, and in the same way it is said in the Church Slavonic version of Malalas (which sometimes, as in the present instance, preserves material now lost from the Greek text) that Marcius came to Antioch from Rome, though it is certain that the visit was made from Cilicia (see Downey, "Q. Marcius Rex at Antioch," *CP* 32 [1937] 144-151, esp. 146, n. 12).
[6] See the lists in J.-R. Palanque, *Essai sur la préfecture du prétoire du Bas-empire* (Paris 1933) 127-130, and in Seeck, *Regesten* 473-475.
[7] On the meaning of the term *basilike*, see Downey, "Architectural Significance of *stoa* and *basilike*" 194-211, also Ch. Picard, "La Stoa Basileios d'Athènes et les 'basiliques,'" *RA*, sér. 6, vol. 11 (1938) 332-333.
[8] Zosimus 5.2, p. 219 ed. Mendelssohn. On the career of this Rufinus, see above, Ch. 15, n. 130. Müller (*Antiq. Antioch.* 105, n. 1), making the assumption that the *basilike stoa* mentioned by Zosimus would have been known as that of Rufinus, and supposing that there could not have existed at Antioch two "basilicas" each named for Rufinus, was forced to conclude that either Malalas or Zosimus must be wrong. Since he believed that Malalas is more to be trusted in such matters, he concluded that Zosimus confused two persons named Rufinus, ascribing

[651]

Various explanations of Malalas's account can be suggested, but none of them seems satisfactory. Vettius Rufinus, who was *praefectus praetorio* or *praefectus praetorio Galliarum* from A.D. 318 to A.D. 320, might have built a *basilike* at Antioch, but this seems only a remote possibility.[9] There are several other officials named Rufinus who were active under Constantine who, though they are not known to have been praetorian prefects might (if one can believe that Malalas's use of the title may be incorrect) have built the *basilike*.[10] Vulcacius Rufinus was *comes Orientis* on 5 April, A.D. 342,[11] and he might have built a *basilike* at Antioch during his term of office, which was in the reign of Constantius. Constantius was much in Antioch during this time, and it was from the city that he set out on his annual summer campaigns against the Persians at this period.[12] Elsewhere (325.14) Malalas relates that Constantius completed the church at Antioch begun by Constantine, and then departed and made a treaty of peace with the Persians; and that on his return he celebrated the *encaenia* of the church. The church was dedicated by Constantius on the occasion of the meeting of the synod of Antioch in A.D. 341,[13] and the statement of Malalas that the church was completed by Constantius before he departed to make a treaty with the Persians and that it was dedicated by him on his return from this journey represents a typical combination of events on the part of Malalas: no treaty with the Persians was signed while the synod was in session (here again there is the characteristic combination of military activities with building operations), but Constantius was in Antioch on several occasions during the meeting. This connection between the dedication of the church and the Persian war suggests that the erroneous connection between the building of the church by Constantine and the Persian war may have been occasioned, at least in part, by a confusion of Constantine with Constantius, by which, according to a practice not uncommon on the part of Malalas, some of the work of the later emperor could have been ascribed, because of the similarity of their names, to the earlier emperor.[14] Malalas might thus have mistakenly supposed that work done by the *comes Orientis* during a visit of Constantius to Antioch was instead done by a praetorian prefect of the same name on an occasion when Constantine visited the city.[15]

This explanation is, however, decidedly tenuous, and it seems simpler to suppose that Malalas, knowing the evidence for the structure, said by Zosimus to have been built by the prefect Rufinus, for some reason mistak-

---

to the later one work done by the earlier. (Müller did not take into consideration that there is no evidence for a prefect Rufinus who could have been active at Antioch under Constantine.)

[9] E. Stein, *Byzantion* 9 (1934) 328-329.

[10] For these persons, see H. Lietzmann, "Rufinus," nos. 9-13, *RE* 1 A, 1186.

[11] *CTh* 12.1.33.

[12] Seeck, "Constantius," *RE* 4.1050-1057; idem, *Regesten* 186-190.

[13] See above, Ch. 12, nn. 179-185.

[14] For such errors in Malalas, see above, Ch. 2, §4.

[15] In this case it would be necessary to assume that Rufinus held office in A.D. 341 as well as in A.D. 342; this is possible, though there is no evidence to this effect.

enly transferred the event to the reign of Constantine.[16] Actually, of course, there is no necessity to suppose that a *basilike stoa* built by Rufinus in or after A.D. 393 would necessarily have been named for him, and so to think that there could not have been two such structures called by the same name in Antioch at the same time.[17] If there existed at Antioch a *basilike* named for a Rufinus before A.D. 393, it is not necessary to suppose that a *basilike stoa* built in A.D. 393 or later by an official named Rufinus would have been called by his name (Zosimus does not say that it was so named), and there is accordingly not necessarily any real contradiction between the accounts of Malalas and Zosimus.

EXCURSUS 16

PARMENIUS AND THE OTHER STREAMS FLOWING THROUGH ANTIOCH

PARMENIUS is the only one of the streams flowing through the city from the mountain which Malalas calls "winter-flowing river," χείμαρρος ποταμός: the others he characterizes as "mountain streams," "torrents," ῥύακες (Malalas 233.10-18; 339.2-4; 346.14-17). The presumption is that Parmenius was the largest of the streams that flowed through the city, and this makes the identification of the stream certain on the basis both of the literary evidence and of the fact that there is on the site only one place (namely, the ravine starting from the Bab el-Hadid) where such a stream could flow (Fig. 11). In his account of the restoration of Antioch by Justinian, Procopius describes the emperor's construction of a water-gate for the control of a torrent which flowed through the city.[1] From this description it is clear that the gate was identical with, or occupied the site of, the present Bab el-Hadid (Fig. 17).[2] The implication of the passage is that the torrent that flowed through this gate was the only one that was sufficiently large to damage the city regularly, and that it was the only one that could be controlled by the construction of a water-gate such as Procopius describes. All of this evidence agrees with the conclusion that would naturally be drawn from the conformation of the mountain above the city, which is such that, while there would undoubtedly be smaller streams flowing in the ravines after the winter rains, there is only one place, behind the present Bab el-Hadid, where water could collect in sufficient volume to form what could be called a winter-flowing river. There seems, then, reason to identify the stream that flowed

---

[16] Or Malalas (or his source), knowing that a *basilike stoa* was built at Antioch by the praefectus praetorio Rufinus in or after A.D. 393, mistakenly applied the title to an earlier official of the same name who built a *basilike* in the city.

[17] Cf. Müller's opinion cited above, n. 8; his conclusion is in reality only an effort to vindicate Malalas.

---

[1] *De aed.* 2.10.5ff.; for criticism of Procopius' account, see above, Ch. 18, §8.

[2] Photographs and old engravings of this water-gate are reproduced by Förster, *Antiochia* 113, 135-137.

from the Bab el-Hadid as Parmenius. If Parmenius were not to be identified with the stream flowing from the Bab el-Hadid, it would be necessary to suppose that a stream flowing from some other part of the mountain would be of sufficient magnitude to be called a "winter-flowing *potamos*" by Malalas, while the stream flowing from the Bab el-Hadid was so much smaller that it could be classed by him among the ῥύακες.

The evidence of Malalas and Procopius for these streams has been discussed by Müller, *Antiq. Antioch.* 8-9, and by Förster, "Antiochia," 128, n. 109, cf. 135, n. 145, both of whom identify Parmenius with the stream that flowed from the Bab el-Hadid; it will be necessary, however, to review the evidence in order to add certain considerations that these scholars overlooked.

Malalas mentions the streams and torrents that flowed down from the mountain in several passages. He says, first, that when Seleucus Nicator founded the city he placed it in the plain, near the river, and opposite the mountain, "fearing the streams of Mount Silpios and the winter torrents which came down from it" (200.11). The same statement is repeated in the account of the work of Tiberius at Antioch: ". . . Tiberius . . . learning that King Seleucus, fearing the streams of the waters coming down from the mountain in winter and forming lakes, avoiding the mountain founded the city in the plain, himself placed in his column a stone box, in which he made [i.e., put] a talisman of Ablakkon, the seer and priest, against the streams of the winter-flowing *potamos* Parmenius, and the streams which came down from the mountain, so that the same part of the city should not be harmed or the two great colonnades built by him be harmed" (233.10). Then, in his account of the building of the Middle Gate by Trajan, Malalas says that it was placed "near the temple of Ares, where the winter-torrent Parmenius flows down" (275.16).

In the first passage, then, none of the streams is named: they are simply called "the streams of the waters flowing from the mountain" and "the winter torrents that came down" from it, while in the second passage Malalas speaks more specifically of "the *potamos*, the winter torrent Parmenios," in addition to the ῥύακες which came down from the mountain. Parmenius is spoken of in exactly the same terms, but more precisely, in the account of the building of the forum of Valens: ". . . constructing arches above the so-called Parmenios, the winter-flowing *potamos*, which flows down from the mountain through the city Antioch" (339.2).

The only other reference that Malalas makes to the streams that flowed down from the mountain occurs in his account of the building of a wall which he attributes to Theodosius I (see above, Ch. 16, n. 9). Malalas says that "the new wall took in the mountain as far as the old wall built by Tiberius Caesar, and he [Theodosius] continued the new wall as far as the stream called Phyrminos which comes down from the gorge in the mountain" (346.14). Müller supposed that Phyrminos and Parmenios were identical, the former being a barbarian form and the latter the correct Greek form of the name (*Antiq. Antioch.* 8, cf. 114). This view is, however, untenable for two reasons. In the first place, as Förster asks ("Antiochia" 128, n. 109), why should Malalas use the form Phyrminos in 346.16 when shortly before this (339.2) he has used the form Parmenios, which he also uses elsewhere (233.15; 275.16)? More important than this is the way in which, as Förster points out, Malalas speaks of Parmenios and of Phyrminos: Phyrminos is only a ῥύαξ while Parmenios is twice called χείμαρρος ποταμός (233.15; 339.2) and once χείμαρρος (substantively, 275.16); in the only reference to it in which he speaks of the other streams as well, Malalas calls Parmenios χείμαρρος ποταμός and the others ῥύακες (233.15).[3] This distinction, not noticed by Müller, would alone be enough to show that Parmenios and Phyrminos are different streams, but other proof (likewise overlooked by Müller) exists, as Förster points out ("Antiochia" 127-128), in the evidence of Evagrius for the location of the extension made in the city wall by Theodosius. Evagrius (1.20) says that the wall was extended "as far as the gate that leads to Daphne," that is, presumably, as far as what was the Daphnetic gate in the time of Evagrius (ca. A.D. 530—600). The change in the wall is described by both Malalas and Evagrius as an extension, and the passage in Evagrius implies that it was confined to the southern part of the city. Therefore, since Phyrminos is given by Malalas as one of the limits of the new wall, the presumption is that it was in the southern part of the city, so that if Parmenios was, as both Müller and Förster supposed, the stream which flowed from the Bab el-Hadid, Parmenios and Phyrminos cannot have been identical, especially since Parmenios is said by Malalas to flow "through the middle of the city" (339.2). Accordingly Parmenios would be, as its description as a winter-flowing *potamos* indicates, the principal torrent coming from the present Bab el-Hadid, while Phyrminos would be a lesser stream (ῥύαξ) in the southern part of the city, evidently flowing in the ravine near the modern barracks and hospital.

The only other reference to a stream at Antioch in the literature of the period before the Arab conquest occurs in Procopius' account of the restoration of Antioch by Justinian, cited above. This too implies that the stream that flowed from the Bab el-Hadid was the only major stream, and the most important stream, which flowed from the mountain through the city. That Procopius, in his description of the water-gate which he says Justinian built to check and control the stream, fails to mention any other device for con-

---

[3] Malalas uses χείμαρρος as a substantive in the plural in 200.11, with reference in general to the streams which came down from the mountain; he uses it again as a substantive (in the singular), in apposition with Parmenios, in the account of Trajan's work (275.16); and elsewhere he uses it as an adjective in the singular modifying *potamos* (233.15; 339.2). In its adjectival sense it means "winter-flowing," "swollen by rain and melted snow" (from χεῖμα and ῥέω); when used as a substantive it, of course, means a stream or torrent of the same nature. When Parmenios is called χείμαρρος alone it is in the passage on Trajan's work, in which the other streams are not mentioned.

trolling a stream at Antioch, or the necessity for such control, might be taken to imply that such work was necessary in only one place (although it is possible, indeed, that he would mention only the construction of the Bab el-Hadid because of a desire to concentrate his account on the emperor's work). Of greater significance, however, is the fact that he calls this stream by the colloquial name Onopniktes, that is, "Donkey-Drowner."[4] This furnishes additional evidence that Parmenios is identical with this stream, since the name used by Procopius implies a volume and force of water corresponding with the description of Parmenios as "winter-flowing *potamos.*" Procopius' use of the name Onopniktes does not constitute an objection to the identification, since the name is obviously a colloquial one such as could readily be in use concurrently with the name Parmenios.

The only satisfactory interpretation of the whole of the evidence, then, is that Parmenios (also called Onopniktes) was the principal stream (and the only major stream) which flowed through the city, entering it through the gorge across which the Bab el-Hadid is built, while Phyrminos, a ῥύαξ, was at the other end of the city, and other ῥύακες, the names of which are not preserved, crossed the city at various places.

EXCURSUS 17

CHURCHES AND MONASTERIES IN AND NEAR ANTIOCH AND DAPHNE

This list is designed to enumerate both the churches and monasteries mentioned in the text and those not described in the text because the references to them are so meager that their history cannot be determined. Among the latter are several buildings of uncertain location, included because the texts suggest the possibility that they were in or near Antioch or Daphne, and evidence discovered in the future may throw further light on their location.

The buildings are listed in alphabetical order by the name or designation by which they are mentioned in the sources. The celebrated octagonal church built by Constantine the Great was called by several names. It is listed here under the term Great Church because this was the name commonly used in the cities of the Greek-speaking part of the Empire to designate the principal church in the city.

Churches in or near Daphne—those of St. Babylas, St. Euphemia and St. Leontius, and the two churches of the Archangel Michael—are included in the general list because there is sometimes a question of their identity or location. It is not known whether one of these is the church in which the mother of St. Symeon Stylites saw a vision (*Vita S. Marthae, Acta SS*, Maii,

[4] See Honigmann, *"Onopniktes potamos," RE* 18, pt. 1, 520-521. A river (*potamos*) in Cappadocia called Onopniktes is mentioned by Constantine Porphyrogenitus, *De Basilio Maced.* 48, p. 280.11, Bonn ed.

tom. 5.404 F; see above, Ch. 18, §9). Another unidentified church outside the city was used by the Meletians during the reign of Julian (see above, Ch. 13, n. 100).

In the present list, information is briefly summarized. For fuller details, consult the Index entries under the names of the buildings.

"Apostolic" Church, *see* "Old Church"
Babylas, St.
  1. martyrium at Daphne, built by Caesar Gallus
  2. cruciform church at Antioch, on right bank of Orontes, the burial place of Meletius, by whom construction was initiated A.D. 379 or 380
Barlaam, St., Church of: outside Antioch
Carterus (or Carterius): Monastery of Carterus and Diodorus
Cassianus, Church of: temporary resting place of body of St. Symeon Stylites the Elder; a robe of Justinian was preserved there
Cemetery: Christian cemetery at Antioch outside Daphne Gate
Concordia, see "Great Church"
Cosmas and Damian, SS., Church of: built by Justinian after earthquake of A.D. 526
Damian, St., *see* Cosmas and Damian, SS.
Diodorus: Monastery of Carterus and Diodorus
Dominicum aureum, see "Great Church"
Domus aurea, see "Great Church"
Euphemia, St., martyrium at Daphne
Euprepius, Monastery of, outside Antioch
"Golden Church" of Constantine, *see* "Great Church"
Great Church, begun by Constantine the Great, completed by Constantius, variously called Octagonal Church, New Church, *Domus aurea, Dominicum aureum, Concordia, Poenitentia*; burned after earthquake of A.D. 526 and rebuilt, plundered by Persians A.D. 540, damaged in earthquake of A.D. 588
House churches, in earliest Christian community at Antioch
Ἰάσων, Church of, near Antioch or Daphne: mentioned in the biography of St. Martha, mother of St. Symeon Stylites the Younger (*see above*, Ch. 18, §9): *Vita S. Marthae, Acta SS*, Maii, tom. 5.405 A, 409 C
Ignatius, St., Church of: the Tychaion was converted into a Church of St. Ignatius by Theodosius II
John, St., Church of: outside Antioch
John the Baptist, Church of: mentioned in the biography of St. Martha, mother of St. Symeon Stylites the Younger (*see above*, Ch. 18, §9) as being at τὸ λεγόμενον Τιβερίνον χωρίον, three miles from Daphne: *Vita S. Marthae, Acta SS, Maii*, tom. 5.408 D-E, cf. 404 F
Julian, St., Church of: outside Antioch
Justina, St., Church of: seen by a pilgrim about 570

Appendices

Leontius, St., Martyrium of, in Daphne: formerly a synagogue

Maccabean Martyrs, Synagogue (later Church) of

Μετάνοια: name applied to the Great Church

Μετάνοια εἰς τὸν Μόσχον, name applied to the Great Church

Michael, St., Church of: Severus, *Homily* 72 (*PO* 12, 1), on the deposition of the bodies of the martyrs Procopius and Phocas in the Church of St. Michael, may refer to a church at Antioch

Michael, Archangel, Churches of
  1. in Antioch: built by Emperor Zeno, burned in earthquake of A.D. 526; rebuilt by Theodora after earthquake of A.D. 526
  2. in Daphne: burned by the Persians in A.D. 540, and rebuilt
  3. in Daphne, at Tretum: one of two churches of the Archangel Michael in Daphne

"New Church," *see* Great Church

Octagonal Church of Constantine the Great, *see* Great Church

"Old Church," in the "old" part of the city on the site of a more ancient building which was reputed to date from the time of the apostles

Ὁμόνοια, name sometimes applied to Great Church

Poenitentia, name applied to the Great Church

Peter, St., Grotto of

Prophets, Holy, Church of the, destroyed in earthquake of A.D. 526

Romanesia, name of a martyrium or church outside Antioch, in which St. John Chrysostom delivered a sermon (*In Ascensionem D. N. Jesu Christi*, *PG* 50.441ff.)

Romanus, St., Church of: Severus delivers an address

Rufinus, Monastery of, the reference to *Beth Rufin* in the title of the *Plerophoriai* of John Rufus, Bishop of Maiouma (written in the time of Severus of Antioch, 512-518), may indicate that John had been attached to a monastery of this name in Antioch; *see* C. Clermont-Ganneau in *Recueil d'archéologie orientale* 3 (1900) 225 (for a translation of the *Plerophoriai* from the Syriac by F. Nau, *see Revue de l'Orient chrétien* 3 [1898] 232-259, 337-392)

Stephen, St., Martyrium of: Bishop Domnus, the suspected Nestorian, preached there: "Akten des Ephesinischen Synode vom Jahre 449, Syrisch, mit George Hoffmanns Deutscher Uebersetzung, hrsg. von Johannes Flemming," *Abhandlungen d. k. Gesellschaft der Wissenschaften zu Göttingen, Philol.-histor. Kl.*, N.F. 15, 1 (1917), p. 119, line 35; it is mentioned in the account of the fire of A.D. 525

Symeon Stylites the Elder, St., Church of: built to receive the saint's body after his death

Theodosius Monastery of: near Antioch; near it was a κώμη Μαρατὼ Συριστὶ καλουμένη, Theodoret *Hist. relig.* 10 (*PG* 82.1393 B); cf. Honigmann "Syria" 1708

Theophilus, house of: reputedly used as a church, in earliest Christian community

Theotokos, *see* Virgin Mary

Thomas, Mar, Church of: Agapius *PO* 8, 3, p. 421

Thomas, *apocrisiarius* of a monastery in Apamea (or Emesa): a chapel built over his tomb in the cemetery outside the Daphne Gate

Virgin Mary, Church of: burned in earthquake of A.D. 526, and rebuilt by Justinian; burned by Persians in A.D. 540 and rebuilt

Zacchaeus, Martyr, Church of: erected 434, Assemani, *Acta sanct. martyrum* 2.173

Zacharias, St., Church of: destroyed in earthquake of A.D. 526

EXCURSUS 18

THE TOPOGRAPHICAL BORDER OF THE MOSAIC FROM YAKTO

THE significance of this mosaic among our sources for the topography and monuments of Antioch about the middle of the fifth century after Christ has been discussed above (Ch. 2, §3). The present Excursus will summarize the interpretations of the border which have thus far been proposed, and will offer a new interpretation based on literary evidence that has not previously been utilized in this connection.

J. Lassus, who first published the mosaic ("La mosaïque de Yakto," *Antioch-on-the-Orontes* 1.114-156), assigned to the scenes shown in it a sequence of numbers from 1 to 56. In Lassus' view, the scenes, in the order in which he numbered them, depicted an itinerary from the springs of Daphne to a monumental gate on the island that indicated the point at which a visitor coming from Seleucia would enter the city. In the present writer's view, as will be seen, the itinerary proceeds in the opposite direction; but since a new series of numbers for the scenes would only introduce a complication, Lassus' numbers are employed here.

According to Lassus' reconstruction of the itinerary, the scenes shown and the route depicted are as follows (this list comprises the principal scenes, and those which may have topographical significance, but does not include all the minor scenes which are not of assistance in establishing the topography; for a full account of the scenes shown, the reader should refer to Lassus' detailed descriptions).

Lassus
No.

1-3   Beginning of the itinerary; the springs of Daphne.

5-6   The πρίβατον of Ardaburius.[1]

[1] The *pribaton* of Ardaburius was evidently a bath managed by private enterprise. On the

8–9 The Olympic stadium.

11 τὰ ἐργαστήρια τοῦ μαρτυρίου.[2]

12 ὁ περίπατος

14 τὸ δημόσιν (i.e. δημόσιον)

16 τὸ Λεοντίου

17 τὸ Ἡλιάδου

19 τὸ Μαειουρίνου

The buildings and scenes shown in Nos. 1–14, Lassus thinks, are in Daphne. With No. 14, the spectator leaves Daphne and follows the road from Daphne to Antioch, along which stand the three private houses, Nos. 16, 17, 19, while the rustic character of the route is indicated by the trees (not numbered) which follow No. 19 (see Lassus, p. 155). Lassus remarks that it is surprising that the entrance to the city is not more clearly indicated, e.g. by a gate.

20 This scene, located in a corner of the room, begins a new section of the itinerary, bringing the spectator to the stands of outdoor merchants who displayed their wares in the southern end of the city (No. 20, a vendor of fish; No. 21, a man selling oil; No. 22, butchers).

23–24 A building and a scene of entertainment.

25–28 This scene shows a public square containing three statues and a tree. The first statue (No. 25) seems to be that of an emperor or a high official; the second statue, differently clothed, holds a lance (No. 26), while the third statue (No. 28) resembles the first (No. 25). Lassus suggests (pp. 140-141) that these are honorific statues of local officials.

29 A building with colonnades, or two colonnaded streets forming a right angle, which might mark one of the corners of the main colonnaded street (cf. Lassus, pp. 141-142).

30–35 The remainder of the border along this side of the room has been so damaged that it is not possible to determine with any degree of satisfaction what the itinerary was at this point.

---

meaning of the word, see Campbell Bonner, "Note on the Mosaic of Daphne," *AJA* 38 (1934) 340; B. E. Perry, "Some Addenda to Liddell and Scott," *AJP* 60 (1939) 35. See also an inscription found at Ephesus (*Ephesos* 2, no. 78, p. 183), and a sign on a bath in a village in Syria (*IGLS* 1379), PUBLICVM, ΔΗΜΟCION. On πριβατάριοι (= παραβαλανεῖς) see H. Grégoire, "Sur le personnel hospitalier de l'église," *Byzantion* 13 (1938) 283-285.

[2] Lassus takes this to be a workshop belonging to a martyrion, and this is very possibly the famous martyrion of St. Babylas. For a χαλκευτικὸν ἐργαστήριον apparently attached to a church, see F. M. Heichelheim, "Ineditum Campioneum Nottinghamense," *Journal of Egyptian Archaeology* 30 (1945) 76-77. See also *Anal. Boll.* 73 (1955) 237.

At this point the border has reached a corner of the room, and the continuation, which ran at right angles along the adjacent wall, has not been preserved. The scenes continue, beginning with No. 36, along the next side of the room.

36 The first scene preserved on this side of the room, near the corner, is a bridge. Lassus does not suggest which bridge this might be (p. 143). Another bridge which is shown later (No. 45, below) he takes to indicate a transition from the old part of the city to the island.

40 A person standing in the attitude of prayer is shown.

41 A polygonal building presumably represents the celebrated Great Church built by Constantine the Great.

42 A column bearing a statue, identified by an inscription, now incomplete, of which only the letters PIANA remain. Lassus suggests (p. 146) that this may be a statue of Tiberius, and that the inscription is to be restored [ἡ στήλη Τιβε]ριανά.[3]

43 A circular race track, which is probably not a hippodrome, but may be a private exercise ground.

44-45 A woman and child are shown about to cross a bridge. Lassus believes (p. 148) that this indicates that the spectator is now passing from the old part of the city to the island.

47 A monumental façade, with a two-storied colonnade which, it is suggested, represents the palace on the island (Lassus, p. 149).

56 The final scene is a monumental gate, which, Lassus (p. 151) suggests, represents the gate at which a visitor coming from Seleucia would enter the city. This brings the spectator to the corner of the room adjacent to the point at which the itinerary started.

In his concluding remarks (pp. 155-156) Lassus points out that if it is to be supposed that the preserved parts of the border show two bridges (Nos. 36 and 45), it would be almost necessary to suppose that all the monuments shown between these two bridges were located on the island. However, he believes that this involves difficulties.

After Lassus' publication, the mosaic was studied by Eltester, "Kirchen Antiochias," 252-254. Being interested primarily in the churches of the city, Eltester confines his study to a few of the monuments shown in the mosaic. He follows Lassus in believing that the itinerary begins in Daphne. He takes the area between the two bridges (Nos. 36 and 45) to depict the

---

[3] One would rather expect the ending of the adjective to be Τιβερίνη or Τιβεριανή. The present writer takes this inscription to be a part of the name of the Porta Tauriana; see above, Excursus 10, §C.

island, and supposes that the following scenes (Nos. 47-55) show the suburb across the Orontes from the city, which opens on to the plain of Antioch at a gate (No. 56). According to this hypothesis, the Great Church (No. 41) would be located on the island.

Eltester's conclusion that the mosaic was intended to show an itinerary which would place the Great Church on the island was impressively confirmed by A. Grabar (*Martyrium* 1.214-227), who pointed to the evidence which shows that in other cities which had imperial palaces, the great church of the city was connected with the palace. Since it is certain from literary texts that the palace at Antioch stood on the island, Grabar demonstrated beyond doubt that the Octagonal Church of Constantine was associated with the palace on the island. Grabar's contribution thus made it certain that the mosaic, with its two bridges, was intended to indicate that the itinerary included two crossings of the Orontes, to and from the island.

The next scholar to study the mosaic, Doro Levi, concluded (*Antioch Mosaic Pavements* 1.326) that the border does not show an itinerary, and that it is not even certain that any of the buildings shown were outside Daphne itself.

In the present writer's view, the scenes in the border show the same route as the itinerary described in Libanius' oration in praise of Antioch (*Or.* 11, *Antiochikos*). Libanius begins his description of the beauties of the city at the gate by which one entered Antioch on the road which led from Beroea. He proceeds, in imagination, through the main part of the city, visits the island, returns to the main part of the city, and continues through the city to Daphne, finishing his account with the famous springs. In this itinerary, the scenes in the mosaic begin in the left-hand corner as one enters the room and succeed each other in order from left to right around the room. This seems, in itself, a more natural order than Lassus', in which the scenes would have to be read from right to left.

The reconstruction of the itinerary proposed here is as follows, the numbers of the paragraphs in Libanius' itinerary being indicated alongside the numbers of the scenes in the mosaic.

Las-sus No.	Liba-nius *Or.* 11	
56-55	196	Monumental gate on the road from Beroea, with travelers entering the city. It should be noted that the travelers are shown moving from left to right as they enter the city.
54-51	197-198	Street scenes, with mutilated buildings; the street is the main colonnaded street. The figures shown in 53 and 52 move from

left to right, like the travelers entering through the gate. Libanius at this point describes the main street.

50   198   Street scene, showing transverse street. Libanius describes the side streets which open off the main street.

49–48   Café and street scene

47   202   Monumental colonnaded building, perhaps representing a structure on the transverse street which led from the main street to the island. Libanius here describes the street that led to the island.

46–45   203   Bridge to island, with woman and child crossing it. Libanius at this point begins to describe the island.

44–43   Building and race track on the island.

42   206   Façade of palace and the Porta Tauriana, known to have been on the island.[4] Libanius describes the palace.

41-40   Octagonal Great Church of Constantine the Great, with a praying figure. The pagan Libanius would naturally not mention the church.

39–37   Street scenes, with figures moving from left to right.

36   208   Bridge indicating a return from the island to the main part of the city. Libanius' itinerary returns from the island to the main part of the city. The mosaic has reached the corner of the room. At this point the border of the mosaic, along the rear wall of the room, is lost. According to the present hypothesis, the lost section of the border depicted scenes in the main part of the city.

35–30   209–   Street scenes and mutilated buildings, in the main part of the
        213   city. Libanius describes the main part of the city in general terms.

29–24   Colonnaded streets forming an angle at a square adorned with a tree and three statues. It is known from other evidence that the Forum of Valens (not yet built in the time of Libanius, but built before the time when the mosaic was made) stood on the continuation of the colonnaded street which led from the island to the main street (see Excursus 12 and Fig. 11). The three statues shown could be those of Caesar, Valens, and Valentinian, which are known to have stood in this Forum, and the building (No. 24) in front of which two men are seated at a game could be the Bath of Commodus, which stood on this Forum. No. 23 could be another public building which stood on the Forum.

---

[4] On the Porta Tauriana, see Excursus 10, §C.

22–20	230	Street scenes showing vendors of food, suggesting that a market area near the entrance to the city is represented. Libanius mentions the abundant food supply of the city.
19–15	234–236	Road to Daphne, represented by private villas and trees, as described by Libanius.
14	236, 242	Public bath. Libanius describes the pleasures of bathing at Daphne.
12	236–237	Colonnaded promenade. Libanius describes the pleasures of social life at Daphne.
8	236	The Olympic stadium (mentioned by Libanius).
3–1	240–245	The springs of Daphne, described by Libanius as the chief of the beauties of Daphne.

It may be noted that two fragments of a mosaic containing a similar topographical border were found outside the northern wall of Antioch (Levi, *Antioch Mosaic Pavements* 1.345-346). Unfortunately the fragments are so meager that they give little indication of what the floor as a whole contained. H. Seyrig (*Berytus* 2 [1935] 46-47, with plate 18) suggests that the well-known textile in Berlin (also published by J. Strzygowski, *Orient oder Rom* [Leipzig 1901] plate 4), which shows Daniel in the lion's den and contains a topographical border, either comes from Antioch or is of Antiochene inspiration, and that it may be a hasty industrial reproduction of an original from which the Yakto mosaic was copied with greater care.

EXCURSUS 19

ARCHAEOLOGICAL TESTIMONIA OF TRAVELERS WHO VISITED ANTIOCH BETWEEN 1163 AND 1918

SOME of the accounts published by mediaeval and modern visitors to Antioch and Daphne are of special value for the information they give concerning monuments that have since deteriorated or disappeared, and for the views that they publish of single monuments, or of the city as a whole. In these accounts it is possible to trace the gradual decay of the ancient city and to observe how the city walls and buildings vanished as they were systematically pillaged for building stones.

The present list is divided into two sections. The first contains the accounts that provide specific evidence concerning archaeological monuments. In order to show the dates to which certain monuments survived, or the dates at which they began to disappear, these accounts are listed in the chronological order of the visits. The second section includes the accounts that are of a general character and do not provide specific archaeological evidence, though they describe the general condition of the city at the time when the visitors saw it. These accounts are listed here because of their intrinsic interest as showing the number of the travelers who visited Antioch, and what it was about the city that attracted their attention. For convenience of reference, these accounts are also listed in chronological order.

This list includes only persons who visited the city as travelers (though some of them stayed for several months). It does not include others (e.g., William of Tyre) who after visiting the city left accounts of it in historical texts. References to such works may be found in modern studies that are concerned with the later period in the history of Antioch, e.g., M. Gaudefroy-Demombynes, *La Syrie à l'époque des Mamelouks* (Paris 1923) and C. Cahen, *La Syrie du Nord à l'époque des Croisades et la Principauté franque d'Antioche* (Paris 1940).

The list does not include epigraphists who visited the city primarily in order to collect inscriptions, since these travelers are conveniently recorded in the collection of the inscriptions of Antioch and its vicinity in *IGLS* 750-1105. An exception is made in the case of Perdrizet and Fossey (1896), who published a valuable account of the Charonion.

On the maps published by the travelers, see Excursus 8, "List of the Maps of Antioch."

The dates of the visits can in some cases be determined only approximately. When no special note is made, it is to be understood that the date can be determined from the published account itself. Where the date is indicated by other evidence, a note is appended.

Books that are listed in the catalogues of travel books in the Gennadius Library in Athens are identified by the numbers assigned to them in these catalogues. The titles of the catalogues are abbreviated as follows:

Gennadius Cat. 1 = *Voyages and Travels in the Near East Made During the XIX Century . . . Compiled by Shirley Howard Weber.* Princeton, N.J., American School of Classical Studies at Athens, 1952. (Catalogues of the Gennadius Library, 1)

Gennadius Cat. 2 = *Voyages and Travels in Greece, the Near East and Adjacent Regions Made Previous to the Year 1801 . . . Compiled by Shirley Howard Weber.* Princeton, N.J., American School of Classical Studies at Athens, 1953. (Catalogues of the Gennadius Library, 2.)

A. Travel Books Containing Archaeological Evidence
(References to the monuments mentioned are listed in the Index)

1163 Benjamin of Tudela. *Early Travels in Palestine*, ed. by Thomas Wright (London 1848). *Viajes de Benjamin de Tudela, 1160-1173, por primera vez traducidos al Castellano con introducción, aparato crítico y anotaciones*

Appendices

por Ignacio González Llubera (Madrid 1918). Other eds., *Gennadius Cat.* 2, Nos. 67-73.

Describes (p. 78 Wright, p. 66 González Llubera) walls, aqueducts, and a colony of ten Jewish glass makers.

1211 Wilbrand of Oldenbourg. In: *Peregrinatores medii aevi quatuor*, ed. J. C. M. Laurent (Leipzig 1864) 171-173

Visit in November 1211, dated by reference to eclipse (171, n. 94). Mentions the walls and a number of churches, especially that of St. Peter and a round (*rotunda*) church. Quotes a Latin inscription in the palace of the Patriarch.

Between 1325 and 1349, Ibn Batuta. *Voyage d'Ibn Batuta, texte arabe accompagné d'une traduction par C. Defrémery et le Dr. B. R. Sanguinetti.* (Paris, Société asiatique, 1893). Other eds., *Gennadius Cat.* 2, Nos. 86-87.

A general description of the city (1.162-163), in which it is stated that the walls had been destroyed by Baibars.

1432 Bertrandon de la Brocquière. *Le Voyage d'outremer de Bertrandon de la Brocquière, premier écuyer tranchant et conseiller de Philippe le Bon, duc de Bourgogne. Publié et annoté par Ch. Schefer* (Paris 1892. *Recueil de voyages et de documents pour servir à l'histoire de la géographie,* 12). Other eds., *Gennadius Cat.* 2, Nos. 107-108.

Mentions that the walls are still intact; there are not more than three hundred houses in the city (pp. 83-85, 100-101, 150).

1548 Belon, Pierre. *Les observations de plusieurs singularitez et choses memorables trouvées en Grèce, etc.* (Paris 1588) 357-358. *Gennadius Cat.* 2, No. 156; other eds., Nos. 153-155, 157-161.

Describes the walls, which he says are not less in extent than those of Nicomedia or Constantinople, and "le palays d'Antiochus qui n'est pas du tout ruiné." "Les murailles qui sont du costé de l'occident sont de tel artifice qu'on peut mener les charettes et chevaux du bas de la ville au haut du chasteau touz chargez et monter à cheval par l'entre-deux des deux voûtes per le dedans de la muraille." See Förster 141, n. 159.

1568 Rauter, Ludwig von. In: R. Röhricht and H. Meisner, *Deutsche Pilgerreisen nach dem Heiligen Lande* (Berlin 1880) 434-435.

Visit 11-13 July 1568. The account of the city is primarily concerned with churches and legendary holy spots, and various marvels.

1594 Wrag, Richard. In: R. Hakluyt, *The Principal Navigations Voyages Traffiques and Discoveries of the English Nation* 6 (Glasgow and New York 1904) 108.

Visit late in 1594. The writer mentions that he passed by Antioch, "whose walles still stand with 360 turrets upon them."

1599 Cotovicus (Cootweyk), J. *Itinerarium Hierosolymitanum et Syri-acum . . . auctore Ioanne Cotovico Ultraiectino* (Antwerp 1619) 496-501. *Gennadius Cat.* 2, No. 224.

The author describes the extant ruins, including the gates of St. Paul and St. George, and gives an account of the history of the city and of its present population and government. This is the first detailed account of the city in which more than a few of the monuments are described.

1599 Sherley Brothers. *The Three Brothers; or, The travels and adventures of Sir Anthony, Sir Robert and Sir Thomas Sherley in Persia, Russia, Turkey, Spain, etc.* (London and Edinburgh 1825) 32-33. *Gennadius Cat.* 2, No. 227.

A brief account of the city, which "is very much decayed and ruinated, only the walls stand firm." The tomb of St. Lawrence is mentioned.

1625 Valle, Pietro della. *Viaggi de Pietro della Valle il pellegrino . . .* (Bologna 1672) 3.521-523.

The walls, a city gate, and the ancient main street are described; the city is said to be "un miglio" in length. This account has the distinction of being the first printed description that contains a map of the city. For other editions of this famous book, see *Gennadius Cat.* 2, Nos. 249-253.

1629 Philippe, Père. *Voyage d'Orient du R. P. Philippe de la tres-saincte Trinité carme deschaussé . . . traduit du Latin par un religieux du mesme ordre* (Lyons 1669) 15-16, 67.

Mentions the walls, which were intact and contained forty-seven square towers.

1667 Troilo, F. F. von. *Frantz Ferdinand von Troilo, Rittern des Heiligen Grabes, Orientalische Reise-Beschreibung* (Dresden and Leipzig 1734) 623-624. *Gennadius Cat.* 2, No. 351.

Mentions the walls.

1648 Monconys. *Les Voyages de Monsieur de Monconys en Syrie et en Natolie. Seconde partie* (Paris 1695) 129-131. Another ed., *Gennadius Cat.* 2, No. 258.

Visit on 10 March 1648. Mentions the walls and the remains of a temple.

1688 De la Roque. *Voyage de Syrie et du Mont-Liban . . . par Monsieur de la Roque* (Paris 1722) 246-263. *Gennadius Cat.* 2, No. 433.

Describes the walls, and ruins that purported to be the palace of Seleucus and the Great Church of Constantine.

1734 Leandro di S. Cecilia. *Persia ovvero secondo viaggio di F. Leandro di Santa Cecilia, Carmelitano scalzo, dell'Oriente, scritto dal medesimo* (Rome 1757) 6-7.

The city was "un mare di rovinati edifizii"; in the southern part there was "un edifizio di forma esagona così vasto, che forma un colle di rovine, e quì ergesi un lungo ordine di portici." In the center of the city were the remains of the "patriarchal church," where the inhabitants were accustomed to dig looking for treasure. Many coins, including gold ones, were found daily throughout the city.

1737 Otter, J. *Voyage en Turquie et en Perse . . . par M. Otter* (Paris 1748) 1.79-82. *Gennadius Cat.* 2, No. 512.

Visit 10-12 February 1737 (cf. p. 59). Mentions various ruins that were ostensibly temples and churches.

1738 Pococke, Richard. *A Description of the East, and some other countries.* Vol. 2, part 1: *Observations on Palestine or the Holy Land, Syria, Mesopotamia, Cyprus and Candia* (London 1745) 188-194. *Gennadius Cat.* 2, No. 513; other eds., Nos. 514-516.

The earliest careful and scholarly description of the site and the extant monuments, with a plan of the site (pl. 26) and views of the Iron Gate and of an aqueduct (pl. 27).

Between 1739 and 1742 Perry, Charles. *A View of the Levant, particularly of Constantinople, Syria, Egypt and Greece . . . by Charles Perry, M.D.* (London 1743) 142. *Gennadius Cat.* 2, No. 523.

Describes the walls.

1748 Drummond, Alexander. *Travels through different cities of Germany, Italy and Greece, and several parts of Asia . . . in a series of letters . . . by Alexander Drummond, Esq., H. M. Consul at Aleppo* (London 1754) 221-224. *Gennadius Cat.* 2, No. 524.

Describes the walls and illustrates (pl. facing p. 223) part of an aqueduct.

Before 1759 Egmond, J. Aegidius van. *Travels through part of Europe, Asia Minor, the Islands of the Archipelago, Syria, Palestine, Egypt, Mount Sinai, etc. . . . by the Honourable J. Aegidius van Egmont, Envoy Extraordinary from the United Provinces to the Court of Naples, and John Heyman, Professor of the Oriental Languages in the University of Leyden. Translated from the Low Dutch.* (London 1759) 2.322-327. *Gennadius Cat.* 2, No. 539.

Notable is the statement that the mountain is to the east of the city, this being one of the earliest correct observations of the compass points (see Excursus 9). Of interest also is the remark that "it is very surprising that scarce the least remains of the many stately and superb edifices, for which this city was so famous, are now to be seen."

1766 Niebuhr, Carsten. *C. Niebuhr's Reisebeschreibung nach Arabien und andern umliegenden Laendern. Dritter Band. Reisen durch Syrien und*

Palaestina, nach Cypern und durch Kleinasien und die Turkey . . . hrsg. von J. N. Gloyer und J. Olshausen (Hamburg 1837) 15-18.

Visit June 1766. A careful description of the walls and gates, with a plan (pl. 2, facing p. 16; on its orientation see Excursus 9).

1772 Parsons, Abraham. *Travels in Asia and Africa, including a journey from Scanderoon to Aleppo . . . by the late Abraham Parsons, Consul and Factor-Marine at Scanderoon* (London 1808) 70-73.

A useful account is given of the ancient walls, particularly those along the river, which are seldom mentioned by other travelers. There are also observations, not made by other travelers, on the ruins of ancient houses along the roads outside the city leading to Daphne and to Beroea (Aleppo). Parsons was apparently the first visitor to make an accurate compass observation of the direction of the long axis of the city (see Excursus 9). The view of the city drawn by the author, facing p. 70, is apparently the earliest modern panoramic picture of the site; it was evidently somewhat embellished in the interests of artistic composition. Parsons has interesting comments on Pococke's account of Seleucia Pieria (28-35).

Parsons writes in part (p. 71-72): "The walls on the banks of the river are in a very ruinous state; they reached, at the first building, from one end of the city to the other; now there are breaches of nearly half a mile in length in two places, and many others of considerable extent. It is probable that the floods have gradually undermined the foundations, and that they have fallen into the river. There are many of these fragments which are from twenty to twenty-two feet thick; others think (and that with great probability) that they have been thrown down by earthquakes into the river, which at the same time deepened its bed in such a manner, as entirely to swallow them up. . . . The old city extended nearly half way up the mountain (as still plainly appears from the old foundations) but that part of the city now built on the side of the mountain does not reach one sixth part ascent. . . . Without both gates there have been extensive suburbs, the foundations of which reach a great way from the eastern gate; not a house of these is at present standing. Without the western gate there is not an appearance of so large a suburb; there are, however, forty or fifty houses still remaining: from this a steep road leads to the site of the celebrated village, formerly called Daphne. . . ."

1784-1787 Cassas, Louis François. *Voyage pittoresque de la Syrie, de la Palestine, et de la Basse-Egypt, avec texte par Laporte-Dutheil et Langlès* (Paris 1799). Cf. *Gennadius Cat.* 2, No. 832.

Visit between 1784 and 1787 (Thieme-Becker, *Allg. Lex. d. bild. Künstler, s.n.*). Cassas' engravings, in folio, are the earliest accurate views of the city and of the major monuments then extant. They are reproduced by

Förster (as indicated here, F.) and some are reproduced by Bartlett (as noted by Förster). Pl. 3 (F. fig. 4, p. 115), general view of city. Pl. 5-6 (F. figs. 11-12, p. 138), gate on road from Aleppo (Beroea). Pl. 7 (F. fig. 5, p. 126), walls at southern end of city. Pl. 9 (F. fig. 3, p. 113), Iron Gate. Pl. 10 (F. fig. 2, p. 112), general view of city. The accompanying text has nothing to do with the city or its monuments. C. Enlart, *Les monuments des Croisés dans le royaume de Jérusalem* (Paris 1925-1928) 2.39, states that Cassas published ten plates of Antioch, but I have been unable to discover any trace of more than the six listed above. Enlart's statement may represent an inference from the fact that Cassas' last plate is numbered 10.

1799ff. Barker, John. *Syria and Egypt under the last five Sultans of Turkey, being experiences during fifty years of Mr. Consul-General Barker, chiefly from his letters and journals, edited by his son Edward B. B. Barker* (London 1876).

John Barker, born 1771, was sent to Aleppo in 1799. He visited Lady Hester Stanhope at Antioch in 1816 (1.278-279), describes the earthquake of 1822 (1.321-324), and tells how Ibrahim Pasha demolished the ancient walls and used the stones to build a palace and a barracks (2.204, 223-224).

1809 Corancez, Louis Alexandre Olivier de. *Itinéraire d'une partie peu connue de l'Asie Mineure, contenant la description des régions septentrionales de la Syrie, celle des côtes méridionales de l'Asie Mineure...* (Paris 1816) 116-136. *Gennadius Cat.* 1, No. 42.

Describes the gates and walls, and the present condition of the city.

1816 Buckingham, James Silk. *Travels among the Arab Tribes inhabiting the Countries East of Syria and Palestine ... and by the Valley of the Orontes to Seleucia, Antioch and Aleppo ... by James Silk Buckingham* (London 1825) 556-567.

The author describes the walls and gates with some care. The view of the city on p. 556 is borrowed from Cassas (cf. p. xi).

1827 Laborde, Alexandre de. *Voyage de la Syrie par Mrs Alexandre de Laborde, Becker, Hall et Léon de Laborde, rédigé et publié par Léon de Laborde* (Paris 1837) 2-4.

Visit on 8-9 Jan. 1827. Describes the walls and the re-use, in rebuilding the city, of the debris of the walls thrown down in the earthquake of 1822. There is a lithograph (pl. 1, 1) of the springs at Daphne.

1830-1831 Poujoulat, Jean-Joseph. *Correspondance d'Orient, 1830-1831, par M. Michaud et M. Poujoulat* (Brussels 1841) 8.96-149, 183. An exchange of letters between Poujoulat who traveled in Syria and Michaud who traveled in Egypt. (H. Bordeaux, *Voyageurs d'Orient* [Paris 1926] 2.135-195). Poujoulat describes the walls and gates, the history of the city under the Crusaders, and its modern state. At Daphne (183) he saw ruins, next to the deepest of the springs, which he took to be the temple of Apollo. He supplies a map (at end of volume) of Antioch during the Frankish period, which is reproduced (with certain omissions) by Jacquot, *Antioche* 2.362.

1835 Ainsworth, William Francis. *A personal narrative of the Euphrates expedition, by William Francis Ainsworth, surgeon and geologist to the expedition* (London 1888) 1.67-81, 2.395-399.

Supplements the account of R. F. Chesney (below). Mentions the Charonion, apparently for the first time. Ainsworth made a second visit in 1839 (see the following entry).

1835 Chesney, Francis Rawson. *The Expedition for the Survey of the Rivers Euphrates and Tigris, carried on by Order of the British Government, in the Years 1835, 1836 and 1837 . . . by Lieut.-Colonel Chesney* (London 1850) 1.424-428.

The expedition was at Seleucia and Antioch from May to October 1835, according to W. F. Ainsworth (above). Chesney's description of the city, particularly of the walls and towers, is more careful than any previous account. There is a small engraving of the gate on the road from Aleppo (425).

1836 Russegger, Joseph. *Reise in Griechenland, Unteregypten, im nördlichen Syrien und südöstlichen Kleinasien, mit besonderer Rücksicht auf die naturwissenschaftlichen Verhältnisse der betreffenden Länder, unternommen in dem Jahre 1836 von J. R.* (Stuttgart 1841; vol. 1 of his *Reisen in Europa, Asien und Afrika . . . unternommen in den Jahren 1835 bis 1841*) 365-369.

Visit on 26-30 May 1836. Describes chiefly the walls and aqueducts.

Before 1836 Bartlett, W. H. and John Carne. *Syria, the Holy Land, Asia Minor, etc., illustrated, in a series of views drawn from nature by W. H. Bartlett, William Purser, etc. With descriptions of the plates by John Carne* . . . (London 1836-1838).

There are ten plates of scenes in and near Antioch. One, vol. 1, facing p. 23 (general view), is taken from Cassas pl. 10. The others are original with Bartlett. Most of those of archaeological interest are reproduced by Förster (F.): vol. 1, facing p. 63, Iron Gate (F. fig. 8, p. 135); vol. 1, facing p. 19, general view (F. fig. 7, p. 129); v. 3, facing p. 11, walls at southern end of city (F. fig. 6, p. 128; not western side, as title states; see Excursus 9). The view of the walls on the island, v. 3, facing p. 54, is not reproduced by Förster. The remaining illustrations are "local color": vol. 1, facing pp. 21, 31, 56, and vol. 2, facing p. 70.

1838 Montfort, Antoine-Alphonse.

The painter Montfort visited Antioch in 1838 in the course of a sojourn in Syria. The visit to Antioch was made in company with Comte

Adolphe de Caraman, *q.v.* (R. Dussaud, "Le peintre Montfort en Syrie," *Syria* 2 [1921] 72). It has not been possible to trace the publication of views of Antioch which Montfort may have made.

1839 Ainsworth, William Francis. *Travels and researches in Asia Minor, Mesopotamia, Chaldea and Armenia, by William Francis Ainsworth ... in charge of the expedition sent by the Royal Geographical Society and the Society for Promoting Christian Knowledge, to the Christian Tribes in Chaldea* (London 1842) 2.93-95. *Gennadius Cat.* 1, No. 333.

The description is brief. There is an incomplete copy of a Greek inscription on a tower in the wall (*IGLS* 785), also, on p. 87, an engraving of a "Tower at Antioch."

1830's Taylor, Isidore-Justin-Séverin. *La Syrie, la Palestine et la Judée; pèlerinage à Jérusalem et aux lieux saints, par le Baron I. Taylor* (Paris 1860) 94-104.

The author, a Belgian of English descent, visited Antioch in the 1830's. He describes the walls and aqueducts, the history of the city, and its present condition. His five engravings show remarkable resemblances to those of Cassas.

1840 Thomson, W. M. Extracts of a journal of a trip in north Syria, in *Missionary Herald* (Boston, Mass.) 37 (1841) 236-238.

Thomson observed that there were granite columns and other debris that showed that nearly the whole distance from Daphne to Antioch was covered with buildings. The writer made a second visit in 1845, the account of which does not contain archaeological information (*Bibliotheca Sacra* [New York] 5 [1848] 454-458).

1847 Neale, Frederick Arthur. *Evenings at Antioch* (London 1854).

Describes the earthquake of 1822 and the damage it did to the ancient monuments (pp. xxiv-xxxv, 6), and mentions the use of ancient stones for the construction of the new barracks and palace of Ibrahim Pasha (pp. xlii, xliv).

Before 1853 Guys, Henry. *Statistique du Pachalik d'Alep, par M. Henry Guys, ancien consul . . .* (Marseilles 1853).

Material on the contemporary condition of Antioch will be found throughout this useful book, such as the size and analysis of the population, pp. 52-53.

1855 Petermann, Heinrich. *Reisen im Orient von H. Petermann. Zweite Ausgabe* (Leipzig 1865) 2.366-367.

Mentions an ancient gate and a Roman road.

1858 Morgan, Homer B. Extract of a letter, in: *Journal of the American Oriental Society* 6 (1860) 550-551.

The writer, an American missionary, in 1858 discovered and copied in Daphne the inscription of Antiochus III on the appointment of a chief priest of Apollo and Artemis (*IGLS* 992). He describes the place of discovery, and other traces of antiquity at Daphne.

1858-1859 Beaufort, Emily A. (Viscountess Strangford). *Egyptian Sepulchres and Syrian Shrines, including some stay in the Lebanon, at Palmyra and in Western Turkey, by Emily A. Beaufort. Second edition* (London 1862) 2.307-313. *Gennadius Cat.* 1, No. 581, first ed., 1861.

There is a general account of the modern town, with accurate observations on the walls and some of the principal ruins.

1859 Rey, Emmanuel Guillaume. *Étude sur les monuments de l'architecture militaire des Croisés en Syrie et dans l'île de Chypre, par G. Rey* (Paris 1871) 183-204.

Rey visited Antioch in 1859, according to C. Enlart, *Les monuments des Croisés dans le royaume de Jérusalem* (Paris 1925-1928) 2.40. He provides the first scholarly survey of the walls and fortifications, with five plans and drawings and a map of the city (pl. 17) which was the best thus far published, though not oriented accurately (see Excursus 9). He also reproduces (pl. 18) a schematic and stylized map, of the fourteenth century (Paris, Bibl. nat., MS lat. 4939, fol. 98r). Rey's fig. 47, p. 187, is borrowed from a part of Cassas (see above under 1784-87) pl. 7.

1860 or 1861 Renan, E. *Comptes-rendus, Académie des inscriptions et belles-lettres*, 1865, 308-310.

The first scholarly description of the Charonion (not illustrated).

1868 Lycklama à Nijeholt, T. M. *Voyage en Russie, au Caucase et en Perse, dans la Mésopotamie, le Kurdistan, la Syrie, la Palestine et la Turquie exécuté pendant les années 1866, 1867 et 1868 par T. M. Chevalier Lycklama à Nijeholt* (Paris 1872-1875) 4.287-332.

Contains a few observations on the more prominent antiquities.

1896 Perdrizet, P., and C. Fossey. "Voyage dans la Syrie du Nord," *Bulletin de Correspondance Hellénique* 21 (1897) 79-85.

Cited here as containing the best description and illustration (pl. 2) of the Charonion.

1896 Förster, Richard. "Antiochia am Orontes," *Jahrbuch des kaiserlich deutschen Archäologischen Instituts* 12 (1897) 103-149.

Förster's article, which was designed as a supplement to Müller's *Antiq. Antioch.*, embodies the results of the first scholarly study, on the ground, of the topography.

Between 1914 and 1918 Wiegand, T. "Denkmalschutz in Syrien," *Klio* 15 (1918) 422-424.

Appendices

As officer in charge of the preservation of monuments, Wiegand visited Antioch and Daphne and in the latter place determined the site of the theater.

B. Travel Books Containing Brief Incidental References

1177 Johannes Phocas. In *Recueil des Historiens des Croisades, Historiens grecs* 1 (Paris 1875) 528-530 (Greek text with Latin translation by E. Miller). English version by A. Stewart in the *Palestine Pilgrims' Text Society*, vol. 5, pt. 3 (London 1896) 6-8 (not entirely accurate).

Visit in 1177 (*Recueil*, preface, pp. viii ff.). The author was a Cretan monk who made a pilgrimage to Jerusalem and wrote a brief account of the fortresses and cities of Syria and Palestine, beginning with Antioch. The account of Antioch is an encomium rather than a description.

1255 William of Rubruck. *The Journey of William of Rubruck to the Eastern Parts of the World, 1253-55, as narrated by himself . . . transl. from the Latin, and ed. . . . by W. W. Rockhill.* London, Hakluyt Society, 1900, second ser., vol. 4, pp. 278-279.

A very brief mention; the place was "in a most dilapidated condition."

1436-1438 Tafur, Pero. *Pero Tafur, Travels and Adventures, 1435-1439. Transl. and ed. with an introd. by Malcolm Letts* (London 1926) 63. *Gennadius Cat.* 2, No. 111; other eds., Nos. 110, 112.

1465-1466 Basil the Merchant. *Pèlerinage du marchand Basile, 1465-1466,* in: *Itinéraires russes en Orient, traduits pour la Société de L'Orient latin par Mme B. de Khitrowo* (Geneva 1889) 255.

1477 Anonymous Arabic description of a journey of Sultan Qâït-bây. Arabic text ed. by R. V. Lanzone, *Viaggio in Palestine e Soria de Kaid Ba, XVIII sultano della II dinastia mamelucca, fatto nel 1477* (Turin 1878).

On the account of the city, which is brief, see Ch. Clermont-Ganneau, *Recueil d'archéologie orientale* 3 (1900) 254.

1587 Eldred, John. In: R. Hakluyt, *The Principal Voyages Traffiques and Discoveries of the English Nation* 6 (Glasgow and New York 1904) 8.

1598 Sanderson, John. *The Travels of John Sanderson in the Levant, 1584-1602, with his Autobiography and Selections from his Correspondence, ed. by Sir William Foster* (London, Hakluyt Society, 1931) 63. *Gennadius Cat.* 2, No. 205.

1600 Biddulph, William. In: *Hakluytus Posthumus or Purchas his Pilgrimes . . . by Samuel Purchas* 8 (Glasgow 1905) 258. Other eds., *Gennadius Cat.* 2, Nos. 232-234.

1605 Teixeira, Pedro. *The Travels of Pedro Teixeira . . . translated and annotated by William F. Sinclair . . . and Donald Ferguson* (London, Hakluyt Society, 1902) 127-128.

    The author passed near Antioch and saw it from a distance but did not visit the city.

Between 1651 and 1656 Quaresimus, F. *Historica theologica et moralis terrae sanctae elucidatio* (Venice 1880) 2.687-689.

1652 Macarius, Patriarch. *Voyage du Patriarche Macaire d'Antioche. Texte arabe et traduction française par Basile Radu. Patrologia Orientalis,* 22, fasc. 1 (1930) 70-72.

Before 1668 Goujon, J. *Histoire et voyage de la Terre-Sainte . . . par le R. P. Iaques Goujon* (Lyons 1671) 25-27. *Gennadius Cat.* 2, No. 718.

Before 1670 Tavernier, J. B. *The Six Voyages of John Baptista Tavernier, a noble man of France, now living, through Turky [sic] into Persia, and the East Indies, finished in the year 1670 . . . Made English by J. P(hillips)* (London 1678) 56. Other editions, *Gennadius Cat.* 2, Nos. 270-282.

1681 Dapper, Olfert. *Asia, oder Genaue und Gruendliche Beschreibung des gantzen Syrien und Palestins . . . von Doct. O. Dapper* (Amsterdam 1681) 118-127.

1707 Lucas, Paul. *Voyage du sieur Paul Lucas fait par ordre du roy dans la Grèce, l'Asie mineure, la Macédoine et l'Afrique* (Paris 1712) 1.366-368. *Gennadius Cat.* 2, No. 465; another ed., No. 466.

Between 1755 and 1776 Tott, Baron de. *Mémoires du Baron de Tott, sur les Turcs et les Tartares* (Paris 1785) 2.233.

Between 1783 and 1785 Volney, C.-F. *Voyage en Syrie et en Egypte, pendant les années 1783, 1784, et 1785 . . . par M. C.-F. Volney. Seconde édition revue et corrigée* (Paris 1787) 142-144.

1785 (or later) Griffiths, J. *Travels in Europe, Asia Minor, and Arabia, by J. Griffiths, M.D.* (London 1805) 317-323. *Gennadius Cat.* 2, No. 607.

1789 Taylor, John. *Travels from England to India in the Year 1789 by the way of the Tyrol, Venice, Scanderoon, Aleppo . . . by Major John Taylor . . .* (London 1799) 1.177-195.

Before 1791 Jenour, Matthew. *The Route to India through France, Germany, Hungary, Turkey, Natolia, Syria and the Desart [sic] of Arabia . . . by Captain Matthew Jenour* (London 1791) 23.

    The book is intended as a practical guide for travelers. Antioch is mentioned only as a stopping place on the journey.

Appendices

1797 Browne, W. G. *Travels in Africa, Egypt and Syria, from the year 1792 to 1798, by W. G. Browne* (London 1799) 390-391.

1807 Badia y Leblich, Domingo. *Travels of Ali Bey* [pseudonym of D. Badia y Leblich] *in Morocco, Tripoli, Cyprus, Egypt, Arabia, Syria and Turkey, between the Years 1803 and 1807, written by himself and illustrated by maps and numerous plates* (London 1816) 2.298-304.

1813 Kinneir, John MacDonald. *Journey through Asia Minor, Armenia and Koordistan, in the years 1813 and 1814, by John MacDonald Kinneir* (London 1818) 147-159.

1816 Richter, Otto Friedrich von. *Otto Friedrich von Richter, Wallfahrten im Morgenlande, aus seinen Tagebüchern und Briefen dargestellt von Johann Philipp Gustav Ewers* (Berlin 1822) 281-283.

1816 Stanhope, Lady Hester. Lady Hester Stanhope spent seventy days at Antioch in the autumn of 1816, in a secluded house outside the town. No archaeological information is mentioned in connection with her visit. See *Travels of Lady Hester Stanhope, being the completion of her memoirs, narrated by her physician* [Charles Lewis Meryon] (London 1846) 3.308-39, 333, 338-340 (*Gennadius Cat.* 1, No. 390); and *The Life and Letters of Lady Hester Stanhope, by her niece the Duchess of Cleveland* (London 1914) 129, 149, 195.

1817 Irby, Charles Leonard, and James Mangles. *Travels in Egypt and Nubia, Syria and Asia Minor, during the years 1817 and 1818, by . . . Charles Leonard Irby and James Mangles, Commanders in the Royal Navy. Printed for private distribution* (London 1823) 229-230. *Gennadius Cat.* 1, No. 123.

1820 [Fuller, John] *Narrative of a tour through some parts of the Turkish Empire. Not published.* (London, Printed by Richard Taylor 1829) 474-488. *Gennadius Cat.* 1, No. 179, also No. 188?.

1821 Berggren, Jakob. *Resor i Europa och Oesterlaenderne af J. Berggren* (Stockholm 1826-1828) 2.165-180.
The chapter in which this visit is described is omitted in the German translation, *Reisen in Europa und im Morgenlande von J. Berggren. Aus dem Schwedischen übersetzt von Dr. F. H. Ungewitter* (Leipzig—Darmstadt 1834).

1830 Wellsted, J. R. *Travels to the city of the Caliphs, along the shores of the Persian Gulf and the Mediterranean . . . by J. R. Wellsted* (London 1840) 2.60, 69-70. *Gennadius Cat.* 1, No. 320.

1831 Robinson, George. *Travels in Palestine and Syria, by George Robinson . . .* (London 1837) 2.273-300. *Gennadius Cat.* 1, No. 260.

1833 Monro, Vere. *A summer ramble in Syria, with a Tartar trip from Aleppo to Stamboul, by the Rev. Vere Monro* (London 1835) 2.138-143. *Gennadius Cat.* 1, No. 234.

Before 1835 Callier, C. "Voyage en Asie Mineure, en Syrie, en Palestine et en Arabie-Pétrée, par M. Camille Callier, Capitaine au corps royal d'état-major," *Bulletin de la Société de géographie* (Paris), ser. 2, vol. 3 (1835) 15. *Gennadius Cat.* 1, No. 228.

1836 Poujoulat, Baptistin. *Récits et souvenirs d'un voyage en Orient, par M. Baptistin Poujoulat. Huitième édition* (Tours 1866; *Bibliothèque de la jeunesse chrétienne*) 105-118.

1838 Salle, Eusèbe de. *Pérégrinations en Orient, ou voyage pittoresque, historique et politique en Egypte, Nubie, Syrie, Turquie, Grèce pendant les années 1837-38-39, par Eusèbe de Salle* . . . (Paris 1840) 1.172-181. *Gennadius Cat.* 1, No. 316.

1838 Caraman, Comte Adolphe de. "Aperçus généraux sur la Syrie," *Bulletin de la Société de géographie de Paris*, ser. 2, vol. 15 (1841), 13-15.
Report on a journey in company with the painter Montfort (R. Dussaud, "Le peintre Montfort en Syrie," *Syria* 2 [1921] 72).

1840 Beadle, The Rev. Mr. Extracts from his journal in *Missionary Herald* (Boston, Mass.) 37 (1841) 207-209.
Visit in company with W. M. Thomson (*q.v.*).

1841-1843 [Paton, A. A.] *The Modern Syrians, or, Native society in Damascus, Aleppo and the Mountain of the Druses, from notes made in those parts during the years 1841-2-3, by An Oriental Student* (London 1844) 219-222. *Gennadius Cat.* 1, No. 357.

1847 Neale, Frederick Arthur. *Eight years in Syria, Palestine and Asia Minor, from 1842 to 1850, by F. A. Neale . . . late attached to the consular service in Syria. Second edition* (London 1852) 2.9-54, 76-82. *Gennadius Cat.* 1, No. 438, first ed., 1851.

1850 Sandreczki, C. *Reise nach Mosul und durch Kurdistan nach Urmia, unternommen im Auftrage der Church Missionary Society in London, 1850, in brieflichen Mittheilungen aus dem Tagebuche von C. Sandreczki* (Stuttgart 1857), vol. 2, pt. 4, pp. 464-473.

1850-1851 Walpole, Frederick. *The Ansayrii, or Assassins, with travels in the further East, in 1850-1851, including a visit to Nineveh, by . . . F. Walpole* . . . (London 1851) 3.248-268. *Gennadius Cat.* 1, No. 443.

1852 Belgiojoso, Princess Barbiano di. *Asie Mineure et Syrie, souvenirs de voyages par Mme. la Princesse de Belgiojoso* (Paris 1858) 131-133. *Gennadius Cat.* 1, No. 550.

1880 Sachau, Eduard. *Reise in Syrien und Mesopotamien, von . . . Eduard Sachau* (Leipzig 1883) 462-463.

1881 Chantre, Ernest. "De Beyrouth à Tiflis . . . par M. Ernest Chantre, sous-directeur de Muséum de Lyon, chargé d'une mission scientifique par le Ministre de l'instruction publique, 1881," *Le Tour du Monde, nouveau journal de voyages* 58 (1889) 220-224.
A popular account, with a view of the city taken from Taylor (1830's).

1882 Hartmann, Martin. "Das Liwa Haleb (Aleppo) und ein Teil des Liwa Dschebel Bereket," *Ztschr. der Gesellschaft für Erdkunde zu Berlin* 29 (1894) 164.
Visit in the course of a geographical survey.

1888 Le Camus, E. *Notre voyage aux pays bibliques, par l'Abbé E. Le Camus* (Paris 1890) 3.30-81.
An account of the present city with an attempt (marred by errors) to restore its ancient plan, shown on a map facing facing p. 32 (reproduced by Jacquot, *Antioche* 2.224). On Le Camus' criticism of Müller (76), see Förster, "Antiochia" 104.

1895 Berchem, Max van, and Edmond Fatio. *Voyage en Syrie* (*Mém. publ. par les membres de L'Inst. franç. d'archéol. orient. du Caire*, nos. 37-38 [Cairo 1914-1915]) 1.238-241.

1898 [Saint-German, H. de]. *L'Orient à vol d'oiseau. Carnet d'un pélerin. Hellénisme, aramaïsme, sémitisme.* Paris, 1902. *Gennadius Cat.* 1, No. 1067.
A banal account of Antioch is given on pp. 209-312. The book is propaganda, in connection with European political aspirations in the Near East.

1899 Butler, Howard Crosby. *Architecture and other arts* (*Publications of an American Archaeological Expedition to Syria in 1899-1900*, pt. 2; New York 1903) 20, 51-52.
Butler's expedition visited Antioch but found no architectural material for its purpose.

1899 Garrett, Robert. *Topography and itinerary* (*Publications of an American Archaeological Expedition to Syria in 1899-1900*, pt. 1; New York 1914) 5-6.
Describes the visit of the expedition led by H. C. Butler (above).

1904 Lammens, H., S.J. "Promenades dans L'Amanus et dans la région d'Antioche," *Missions belges de la Compagnie de Jésus* 7 (1905) 409-421, 8 (1906) 41-49, 201-202.
A general description, mostly of the modern town, with numerous photographs.

Before 1907 Bell, Gertrude Lowthian. *Syria: the desert and the sown* (New York 1907) 318-327.

A general description, with photographs largely of the modern town.

1914 Barrès, Maurice. *Une enquête aux pays du Levant* (Paris 1923) 2.30-52.

Visit in company with G. Contenau, who was investigating possibilities of excavation. The account is largely concerned with the history of the Capucin missions at Antioch.

Before 1925 Baumann, Emile. *Saint Paul* (Paris 1925) 106.

Before 1927 Weber, Wilhelm. "Studien zur Chronik des Malalas," *Festgabe für Adolf Deissmann* (Tübingen 1927) 20-66.

The visit to Antioch of Weber and Deissmann (cf. 20) led to the publication of these studies.

TRANSLATIONS OF DOCUMENTS

LIBANIUS, *ORATION 5, ARTEMIS*

1. The very fact that I am now alive and speaking, and seeing you and being seen by you, gentlemen, is something that has, it is perfectly clear, come to me from Artemis, who rescued me and preserved me from the very gates of death.[1] One must not be ungrateful to the goddess who has granted these things, but it is proper to observe the custom which has been set before us concerning these matters. 2. The custom indeed is that when a man has enjoyed a benefit from one of the Mighty Ones, this man does honor to the one who has acted kindly toward him. One man offers this return by dedicating bowls of wine, another by presenting vessels of gold plate, another, some other kind of vessel, or another, a crown, while the shepherd dedicates his flute and the hunter, the head of a beast; and the poet offers a hymn in meter and the orator a hymn without meter. I believe that by the gods a hymn is preferred to gold; and if indeed it is a good man who shows his feeling concerning the gods in this way, he becomes more noble because of the hymn than because of the gold. 3. We bring in return for our salvation a discourse, and in giving, it is possible for me not to fail wholly in the discourse concerning the goddess who has granted it to me to exist; and it is possible for her to receive this discourse more easily than from her brother[2] the leader of the Muses.

4. Artemis was the daughter of Zeus and Leto, that is, of a father who was the greatest of the gods, and of a mother whom he had chosen for such a birth; and when Delos[3] gave support to Leto and made her stand and strengthened her, Artemis came forth before Apollo, and aided her mother in giving birth to Apollo. 5. It is indeed a fair action for one who has been born to make return for his rearing, at some later time, to those who bore him; but this goddess, as soon as she came into being, requited the one who bore her, at the time when she was especially in need of help. Thus, for the good things for which Apollo is responsible among men, one must give thanks to each of the two, to Apollo who granted these things as soon as he was born, and to her who acted as midwife at his birth.

6. And just as, in her first days, she immediately became more courageous than Apollo in facing Hera's terrors—whence their names were given to them, Artemis to her, Loxias to him[4]—so let me be excused from praising

---

[1] *Iliad* 15.290; 5.646. On the circumstances of the oration, see above, Ch. 3, n. 14.

[2] Apollo.

[3] Leto gave birth to Artemis and Apollo on the island of Delos. See further in the following note.

[4] Hera, the wife of Zeus, became jealous of Leto when she learned that Zeus had been paying attention to Leto; and when Leo was about to give birth to the children of which Zeus was the father, Hera pursued her and would not let her rest until she reached the island of Delos. The names of Leto's children were supposed to reflect the hostility which had been felt

them in the same fashion for other things.[5] 7. There came to her as gifts of Earth, when she was born, bows and arrows, and the power of understanding the art at once, and deer appeared at once—and this, too, I believe, came from Earth—and they were struck one after the other as practice in the art of shooting. And this, it seems, is what made Apollo an archer, namely imitation of Artemis, so that Apollo was the pupil of Artemis in the art of shooting.

8. As she grew, the goddess both shone with beauty and fled marriage, and swore by the head of her father that she would remain a maiden. To her beauty all the poets bore witness, including the very prudent Homer, sometimes honoring the daughter of Alcinous by comparing her with this goddess,[6] sometimes the daughter of Icarius,[7] adding Aphrodite to Artemis so as to bring the beauty of the two goddesses to equal terms. 9. And of the River Parthenios, in Paphlagonia, which was fair, there was a story that it was fair because it became the bath of Artemis.[8] And that she fled from association with men, a sufficient witness is the unhappy Orion, brought to the grave by a scorpion, great as he was, because he laid hold of things which it was not permitted to touch.[9] 10. It is in no way astonishing that Athena should have chosen to be a maiden, since she came forth from her father[10] alone; but she[11] who came into being through marriage nevertheless sought virginity. And while Aphrodite, because of her beauty, both joined herself to a man and set herself over marriages and bridal songs, beauty did not persuade the other to live in wedlock with a god and conceive and give birth; nor would she submit herself to the desires of a bridegroom.

11. Nor did she think fit to oversee the loom and wool and spinning, and the labors of women, judging these things to be inferior to her nature, but she gave herself over to the chase of wild animals, making her way through valleys and mountains and groves and thickets, counting hunting as her pleasure. Artemis needed no effort in order to shoot, but the skill that we employ against captive birds, she used against boars and deer and whatever wild beast she wished. 12. And she is more completely mistress of wild animals than we are of domestic ones. Of the animals, one or another gazed at her and was frightened when she spoke, and departed in flight, while

---

toward them. By a popular but probably incorrect etymology, Ἄρτεμις was connected with ἀρτεμής, "safe," "sound," while Λοξίας, the epithet of Apollo, was usually associated with his "slanting" (λόξος) daily course as the sun, or with his "ambiguous" oracles. It is not clear just what Libanius has in mind in the present allusion. It is possible that he means that Apollo, as "slanting" or "ambiguous," was less courageous against Hera than his sister was.

[5] Libanius means that this is only one example among many of the praises he would be able to enumerate; thus he gives this one specimen as typical.

[6] *Odyssey* 6.102.   [7] *Odyssey* 17.37; 19.54.   [8] *Iliad* 2.854.

[9] There were a number of different versions of the death of Orion, some of which related that he was killed by Artemis because he had attempted to force himself upon her while they were hunting together. According to another version, Orion was killed by Gaia with a scorpion while he was hunting with Artemis. See Kuentzle, "Orion," in *Ausführliches Lexikon der griechischen u. römischen Mythologie*, ed. W. H. Roscher (Leipzig, 1884-1937) 3.1043-1045.

[10] Zeus.   [11] Artemis.

others endure whatever she wishes and take pleasure in what comes from the goddess. 13. But she takes pleasure as she sees them running, takes pleasure in pursuing them, and takes pleasure in shooting them. By means of this pleasure she protects the human race, reducing to a smaller number the animals that are hostile to the race, I am sure, and bringing it about that they do not run to the cities or fall upon them and tear to pieces and empty the cities of human beings. 14. Who indeed could endure the tribes of animals all together coming upon us, when if even one of those unfortunate beasts kept in the menageries leaps over the barrier and runs through a city, he causes terror by his look alone and spreads consternation and causes each of us to look and see where he may save himself; and people shout to each other, and there is as much uproar as there would be from an attack of an enemy? 15. What then should we think would happen in assaults by wild beasts, with lions in the lead? What happens at present is indeed a gift of the goddess, namely that those animals which we could not withstand, if they came upon us, remain in the forests.

16. Some one may say that Ares and Athena are set over the great deeds of war.[12] No small part of the deeds of war belongs to Artemis, unless those who fight view as a small thing the bow and arrow through which it is possible to conquer the enemy from a distance without suffering any harm. 17. If some of the combatants possessed bowmen, and some did not, the infantry forces would be annihilated by the arrows with the utmost speed, before they came together, and these bowmen would go off with the victory, unmarked by wounds; and in a siege, the bowman can often bring down the soldier fighting on the wall, and from the wall the besieged fighter can often strike down the besieger. Think what the work of the foot soldier would be in such a case.

18. One may learn admirably from Herakles how great is the power of the bow, for he, setting out to cleanse the earth, did not put on a breast-plate or take a shield as he went to his work, but a bow and quiver, by means of which he accomplished most of his labors. 19. And the army which after his time went to Ilium enjoyed the benefits of his arrows for its victory. If Philoctetes had not come from Lemnos with the arrows of Herakles, the accomplishments of the foot-soldiers would have been small. 20. In a word, whoever is good at hunting, is good at fighting. Hunting is an effective teacher of war. The man comes home from it valiantly, knowing both how to save himself and to destroy his enemies, while he who has not hunted is cowardly and useless, and a joy to his adversaries.

21. The good Xenophon in his book on hunting[13] counts those who have been hunters as blessed and worthy of admiration and able to overcome dangers. And you, young men, know the men whom Xenophon enumer-

---

[12] The use of μέγα ἔργον to mean "battle" is Homeric; see for example *Iliad* 13.366.
[13] *Cynegetica* 13.17-18.

ates.[14] 22. Admirable here also are the women whom Artemis loved and kept at their exercises in hunting.[15] These women, capturing in war men who were without experience of hunting, seem to me to demonstrate beautifully what a counterfeit soldier it is who undertakes to fight before he has hunted. 23. The city of the Lacedaemonians shows this. The more it seems to have studied military matters, the more it shows that it has studied the art of hunting. They have a law in the festival of Artemis that the man who comes to the banquet without having hunted has plainly committed a crime and should pay a penalty. And the penalty is that a man brings a jar of water and pours it over the boy's head, if it is a boy, but if it is a man this is done to the finger on his hand; and in Lacedaemon this water is a disgrace. Being as we know eager to win with military weapons, they consider that this one thing is the greatest preparation for victory, namely to conquer wild animals.

24. One might say that it is not with Ares and Athena alone that Artemis should be compared, if one wished to do so, but with all the gods who, having presented skills to mankind, keep them at work at these and enjoy the honors which come from this fact. If there were no men, these skills would perish; indeed men would not suffer if the gods who brought their gifts also destroyed what they brought. In such a case there would be a common ruin for both, and this would be the state of affairs if the person who could bring help did not exist. 25. Who, indeed, if those who brought them to birth did not exist, would have sailed the sea or worked the soil or written discourses or healed bodies or forged bronze or built buildings or fought on ships or fought on foot or fought from horseback, if death had forestalled their coming into being? Or rather nothing would have come into existence, or at most only a very limited number of creatures, and these not unmaimed. 26. For all those things which either did not escape the flood, or came to the light in an imperfect condition, so that it was a loss when they failed to die—it was without the help of the goddess that these creatures in some cases did not travel over that path of life, or in other cases did not do it properly. It is to such a degree as this, in every respect, that the race of mankind which has possessed the earth, or possesses it, or will possess it, in all ages, is bestowed upon the earth by Artemis, both that which exists and that which does not exist and that which will exist. 27. And the praises which we are wont to sing to the god Gamos[16] at weddings, as being the father of mankind— both the work of this god and the work of Aphrodite would be in vain, if Artemis did not stretch forth her hand in the pangs of delivery. For whenever you hear Eilithyia spoken of, you hear of Artemis.[17] 28. Thus too the

---

[14] This is an allusion to the list of famous hunters which appears at the opening of the *Cynegetica* (1.2).

[15] Women hunters are mentioned by Xenophon, *Cynegetica* 13.18.

[16] Gamos was the god Marriage personified. Cf. Nonnus, *Dionysiaca* 40.402; Choricius, *Epithalam. Procop.* p. 19.

[17] Eilithyia was the epithet applied to Artemis in connection with her function as goddess of childbirth.

zeal of Aphrodite, which itself is devised for the sake of children, comes to its fulfilment through this goddess,[18] just as their goal comes to those who sail the sea, in the form of harbors. If all regions were without harbors, and there were nothing to receive them, it would be in vain to have made a voyage, if the vessels were wrecked on the headlands. 29. Wherefore she is honored everywhere and by all men, and possesses magnificent temples and altars and sacrifices and festivals. The Athenians also honor the goddess by naming a month for her, which is Elaphebolion. And in another month, I mean Munychion, they bring the maidens to her before marriage, so that, prepared beforehand by Artemis, they may proceed to the realm of Aphrodite. 30. Of the two places which are most honored among them, Peiraeus and the Acropolis, the one belongs to Athena, the other to Artemis. With the Ephesians, the coin bore the stag, in requital to the goddess for her great benefits.

31. That health comes to men from Artemis, her name itself proclaims, and we learn from Homer that Aeneas was healed in the great shrine by Leto and this goddess.[19] 32. That she cares for men in every way, the following is a great sign. For when men sacrificed to her, knowing that mortals need to pay honor in the greatest way, in return for the greatest gifts, she altered the law, because, when she was thus honored by men with a sacrifice of blood, it was living blood with which she was honored.[20] 33. She herself was a lover of mankind and a lover of Greeks. When she came to the Greeks, indeed, it was to leave the Scythians. And the good things which come from Selene, both for plants and for men, are the gift of Aphrodite, and the realm of Hekate, composed of those many divine beings, should be thought of as the realm of Artemis; for those goddesses are the same as Artemis.

34. Knowing how to benefit men, the goddess also knows how to punish men, doing the work of her father, I mean, from whom come both wealth and thunderbolts, the former for just men, and the fire for those who are not so. 35. See her brother also doing both things, as for example when the Greeks made war upon the Trojans over Helen, and he both sent the plague upon them and stopped it,[21] in each case granting a favor to the priest, sending the disease because he had been ill used, and the relief from it, because he had received his daughter back. 36. Of the same kind are the works of Artemis. She sent the colony to Ionia because of a dog,[22] and gave her approval to Alexander when he set forth for his campaign in Asia.[23] 37. That

---

[18] Artemis. [19] *Iliad* 5.445ff.
[20] Euripides, *Iph. Taur.* 1456ff. [21] *Iliad* 1.8ff.
[22] This seems to be a recondite allusion, the meaning of which is not wholly clear, to the founding of the cult of Artemis in Ephesus. See the apparatus criticus in Förster's text of the oration, *ad loc.*
[23] See the passage in Arrian's *Anabasis* of Alexander the Great (1.17.10-13) concerning Alexander's conduct in passing through Ephesus, where he paid special honor to the shrine of Artemis, and won great popularity among the citizens.

it is better to honor her than to despise her, Niobe has shown, the daughter of Tantalus, weeping for her six daughters slain by arrows, and Actaeon likewise has shown, he who saw what it was not right to see, and Oeneus the ruler of Aetolia has shown, who, when he had deprived her of a sacrifice, groaned for his trees which fell when their roots were destroyed by the attack of one boar. When the beast was overcome, with difficulty, and to the harm of those who captured him—for he destroyed many men—his skin and his head created another evil, a war, so that among the honors of the gods no one should either voluntarily neglect Artemis, or be forgetful of her.[24]

38. Moreover, she teaches men not to do or to say anything immoderate. When Agamemnon boasted that he shot her fairest hind, she forced him to bring his daughter to the sacrificial altar for the sake of his voyage, which the goddess held up, punishing his arrogance by detention in port, since the winds obeyed her no less than they did Aeolus, their own keeper; and here the goddess mingled her love of mankind, transferring the sword from the maiden to the deer, and the one vanished—the maiden—while the other was left in their hands, the deer. 39. Another thing was both like this and unlike it. A certain man, considering that an Italian boar was a thing of the greatest value, said to himself, "Now the head of the boar will not belong to Artemis but this will be my own possession, since I captured it." When he said this, he hung the head from a tree, and slept under it, when midday came; but the fastening broke and the head fell on his chest, and killed the hunter who considered himself greater than the goddess.

40. What she is like when she is honored, if on the other hand you wish to hear this—when the Athenians were about to hurry out against the barbarians who were landing in their country, the fleet of Darius, they promised to the Huntress to sacrifice to her as many he-goats as they slew barbarians. And they did slay the number that we hear of. Herakles too was among those tens of thousands, and Pan was also, putting himself forward as greater, I mean, than Artemis, who was the more powerful deity.[25] 41. And why must one speak of other examples? This great city would have belonged to the Scythians, and would have been captured in that campaign long ago, if this goddess, joining herself to her brother, had not by her shooting put them to flight when they already occupied Phlegrae here.[26] We had no army to await their attack when they came, but such was the power of those that smote them that they, the Scythians, went off bawling, not able to withstand these two archers.[27]

---

[24] When Oeneus, King of Calydon, forgot to perform a sacrifice to Artemis, she sent the "Calydonian Boar" to ravage his country. The boar destroyed the roots of the trees.

[25] This alludes to Pan as a hunting god.

[26] Phlegrae is probably the same as Pagrae, the locality between Antioch and Alexandretta. See Müller, *Antiq. Antioch.* 13, with note 3.

[27] The Scythians overran Mesopotamia and Syria ca. 650—620 B.C.

42. And this great temple here, toward the east, in the suburb,[28] was built at the cost of the wife of Cambyses, in return for her eyes, which were saved by the goddess. 43. I myself am aware of owing recompense, not for my eyes alone or indeed for my hands or feet or any other part, but for my whole self and my band of students. It was the month which is named for Artemis,[29] and the seventh day of the month was begun, on which it is the custom in this suburb of Meroë to celebrate the festival of the goddess, whose principal feature is the blood shed in boxing. The boxers are as many as there are tribes in the city, one from each, and there is amazing rivalry for the victory, not for the sake of the great sums spent for these men by the tribes, for this seems a mad way for men to give thanks to the goddess. 44. In ancient times everybody went out to the spectacle, and not to go was impious; but with time the festival became dull, and while the boxers boxed, the teachers of literature continued meeting with their classes, not seeming to most people to do wrong in acting thus, but merely giving way to the custom of the time.

45. And so, recently, some people went to Meroë, namely the boxers, while I summoned the young men to school. Some of them did not obey; there was something which created fear, one could not say what it was. When I said that it would be laziness, if they sought to act as they had on the previous day, which was not a day devoted to work, a certain fear troubled their souls, and they gave their word of honor not to absent themselves from the class meetings. 46. And so they came together. This was a favor of Artemis, who put a stop to the harm which had taken place. And when the students who had felt the fear of the goddess had gone away and I was alone in this council-house, there arrived, not much later, a young man, in response to an invitation which I had often given him, namely that if time allowed, he should come with his book; and we discussed the discourse. 47. So I rose and went to the door, and stood listening to him, as he stood also. More than two hundred lines were read, and I remembered the infirmity of my feet, and it occurred to me that it would be much better to listen seated. 48. I went and sat on my professorial chair and bade him do the same on the other side of the room; and before forty lines had been read, I saw dust coming out of the wall above the great door in the middle of the chamber. Then the great stone molding broke and fell and lay on the ground with most of the stones broken. 49. I was shaken by what I had seen, and I would have suffered more if my ears had received the whole of the crash. But I had had enough foresight so that my hands protected them.

50. The man whose task it was to admit the students[30] happened to be

---

[28] Meroë. The suburb was named for Cambyses' wife Meroë. On the visit of Cambyses and his queen, see above, Ch. 3, n. 13.

[29] In the Syro-Macedonian calendar, in use at Antioch, the month named Artemisios corresponded to May.

[30] I.e. the doorkeeper.

coming in and was saved by seeing the shadow of what was falling, when he happened to look up; he was rising on one foot and had the other already inside, so that the tip of his shoe was struck. 51. This architrave which shattered was placed above the door for the sake of ornament, and the gleaming stone had been set on top of the one which was not so large. They had hollowed this out for the reception of the larger piece, and had put the one in place, and had allowed the other to project, so as to be a pleasing sight to those who looked at it. So long as what held it was strong—this was a very small piece of wood—it remained in place; but when that wood, with the passage of time, became weakened, the portion which was fitted in, came out of its place, and there lay on the ground a great heap of stones which did not, I am sure, seem so many before the accident. These not only would have destroyed the young men as they came in and went out, but not even the heads of camels and elephants would have escaped if the stones had not remained in place. 52. But she saved us, as Homer would have said,[31] and she gave back the children to their parents and manifestly rescued me from such a near blow, by means of the thought concerning my feet; and her father Zeus preserved this sacred building unsullied by deaths. If she had not come to our aid, how many litters would have come here to lift up the flower of the city! 53. So I am now permitted to give thanks in the manner of Simonides. The Brothers[32] saved him also, who sprang from the same father as Artemis. These things came to Simonides from the Dioscuri in return for an ode, but in my case, what I have offered here may take the place of an ode.

But now we have made our return; it will rest with the goddess and Apollo the leader of the Muses to determine whether we have spoken not unworthily.

LIBANIUS, *ORATION* 10, *ON THE PLETHRON*[1]

1. Since I see that many people are grateful to Proculus for the addition that makes greater the *theatron* which has four sides, in the midst of which the Plethron receives the afternoon toil of the athletes who come for the Olympic games, I wish to show that he is at fault in making this addition, and that some have been induced to praise what should instead have been blamed. 2. One might bring the charge against the senators more fittingly than against Proculus, for it was possible for them to oppose him on the ground of public interest and to stop him when he was making his plans, for the man was accustomed to follow their wishes in many things; they preferred, however, to flatter him by admiring what had been undertaken rather

---

[31] *Iliad* 11.752; *Odyssey* 4.513.
[32] The Dioscuri.

[1] On the history of the building, and the circumstances of its enlargement, against which Libanius protests, see above, Ch. 10, p. 2, Ch. 15, p. 22. Libanius prefers to use the classical form *plethron*, rather than the form *plethrion* which had come to be the usual designation of this type of building (see above, Ch. 10, n. 5).

Libanius, Oration 10, On the Plethron

than to discuss what was fitting. 3. If I had had any friendship with the governor and any habit of association and discussion with him, as I did with those who held this office before him, I should have attempted to put a stop to this and to as many of the other things as were, in my opinion, not being done rightly; but since he came from Phoenice resolved to pay no attention at all to anything concerned with me, as though he might do much harm by an excess of friendship, I, having perceived this, make use, in order to present my respects, of the receptions which are held four times a month; and when I go I sit in silence, to show that I do not wish to meddle. Indeed, he heard about this, and he showed no anger to the person who told him. All that remained for me to do was to let him do what he wished, and to show, to such as were willing to pay heed to me, that the Olympic games would be worse because of his zeal in these matters.

4. Concerning what occurred in the games themselves, it was possible for everyone to serve, so to speak, as trumpeter and herald.[2] This building, however, with which the present speech is concerned, served to receive the athletes, at the eighth hour and the one following, and spectators, at a time when they were without food, which prevented any harm from the heat; these were the guards and the judges, and as many as wished of those who had performed the liturgy of giving the games. There might come also patrons and trainers. 5. There were two rows of seats of stone, and as much of the ground as was near the first row was used for seats. There was no need of more, for the attendance was not great; there were no slaves, no school-boys, no workingmen, no idlers. The sort of people who took special care of the locks on their heads were kept away by the strong guards at the doors, or, by Zeus, they did not even approach, knowing that they would be stopped. 6. The things which were done in the Plethron had the honor which is given to mysteries: such was the respect which those present felt for each other and for the athletes, such was the stillness and such the hush; and if any contest was worthy of admiration, it was admired in silence. The spectators were forced to repress their cries, for the staff kept them in fear. 7. This custom, of not having many people present, was far more severe, and better; and they were not many because the place that received them was not large. This part of the Olympics had no need of many people, for its natural excellence was that it should not be shared by many. Such, indeed, is the peculiar character of the mystic rites at initiations; and you would not be displeased by these if they actually made themselves smaller rather than larger. 8. Here,[3] then, nothing had greater power than the law, and the law was that there should be no shouting at either good or bad performances. It

---

[2] The meaning seems to be that in former times the public could hear of what went on in the Plethron (i.e. the results of the contests) from the trumpeter and the herald. This gives point to the reference in the words which follow to the admission to the Plethron itself of only a small number of persons who had an immediate interest in the contests.
[3] In the Plethron.

was possible to see and recognize each of these, and one was permitted to say what was proper to one's neighbor concerning the one or the other, and to say it quietly; but anything beyond this was contrary to the law.

9. What was it then that destroyed the excellence maintained in this respect, which was as full of moderation as it could have been? Argyrius presented the games, following the other of my two uncles, the older one.[4] He was a very worthy man in other respects, but he gave the Olympics a harmful gift, for he doubled the stone seats by adding to them as much as they had formerly consisted of. This of course doubled the number of those who came to see the spectacle. 10. There were some who went about praising Argyrius as though he had done a noble work, saying that with what he had done he had surpassed all of his predecessors; but this actually was fated to upset what was right in this matter, and there came in, along with the increased number of spectators, many things which had not existed before. He [Argyrius], coming angrily upon those who made disturbances, would put an end to some things, although he could not stop others; but it would have been much better had he maintained what was established, rather than created the need for a remedy. 11. However, he had some pleasure even from these things as he saw everything greater,[5] and he had no lack of people to praise what had been added, who could not perceive what it was that had been destroyed and who admired that which had destroyed it, saying that Zeus was his debtor because of this offering.

12. I thought that Phasganius, the younger of my uncles, would fall into no error in this respect, and that he would differ in his attitude toward such matters, and would consider that he [Argyrius] had done an evil instead of a good thing, and that he would laugh at those who praised it, as though they were devoid of right judgment in this matter. 13. But that prudent man was stung with the same desire and became jealous; he imitated his predecessor with that unseemly rivalry, and contributed another enlargement, as great as both the others, both the old accommodation and what had followed it, and so both the crowd and the disorder were greater. The personage who was powerful in inspiring fear was of some avail, but such things were of small account, and at each Olympiad the lawlessness could be seen to have increased. 14. When some of the work of the athletes was not finished before sunset, because the time for the beginning of their labors had been upset— for those who started later had to stop later—and when many dared to confess openly that they could not endure the heat, although in older times the spectators had prided themselves on being able to bear it without hesitation, the voices of the other spectators were all heard there, those of the Romans mingled with those of the Greeks, some clamoring that the competitor had been overstrained, others saying not. Thus those who knew what the customs

---

4 Panolbius.
5 I.e. the greater number of seats and the increase of spectators.

had formerly been could not but deplore these things, and they gave to them the name of that feast in which lack of restraint is supreme.

15. When the things carried out in the Plethron, which were the most honored and solemn part of the festival, had been outraged and scorned, other things were easily changed; some demanded that the *agonothetes* and the *hellanodikai* should make the evening banquets into luncheons, and they succeeded, so that those officials could be seen, as they left their tables and scattered to their homes, showing the wine in their faces beneath the laurel. 16. This, I maintain, had its origin there, in the disorder in the Plethron, for those who approved these things considered that it was not unseemly to do wrong in affairs of such importance. The cause of the offence in this matter was the crowd, and the cause of this in turn was that there was room where so many might sit. 17. Thus this fine fellow Proculus makes matters there worse, and when he rejoices that we shall have this larger *theatron*, he rejoices also because the licentiousness will be greater. In so rejoicing, he attacks the Olympic Games, and shows that he would not wish the real Olympic Games to be celebrated.

18. I supposed that Proculus would learn all of the traditions of the place and would support the old customs. This would have meant taking away the newer part and seating people in the older part alone, paying no heed to those who condemned such a change as this, since they would only be flatterers. A man who supports what is lawful is not unjust, neither does one who diminishes something always do wrong, nor are additions always an improvement; but it is possible for one who adds to something to harm it, and for one who takes away from it to help it. 19. One may perceive this especially in the case of bodies in which excessive growths call for people who will cut them off; and if the physician is able to do this with drugs or with the knife, he has his recompense for what he has removed. It was rather in this way, then, that the good and great Proculus ought to have shown his zeal for Zeus to all men. 20. Thus, at any rate, he would have induced, if not many, at least the worthy, to praise him. If he were ashamed to be seen doing this, this feeling of shame would not be reasonable, although there would be some justification for such a feeling of shame in this matter. What is it that has persuaded him to offer us stones piled upon stones and renewed labor and further expense, and an eagerness which strives to surpass all three?[6] 21. Who will be able to endure what will happen? Who will tolerate the crowd which will burst in? Who will not think the herald is mad when he calls for silence? Who will fear the staff? Who will feel respect before the laurel crown, or even before the administration itself? 22. They will know that if he does not make himself a slave to the spectators when they are so many, he will flee, stunned by their shouts as though by thunder, thinking it enough to save himself, and leaving to their wishes the decision

[6] I.e. the stones, the labor and the expense.

concerning the athletes. The very size of the *theatron* will draw to it those who are not worthy to take part in what goes on in it. Even now some such persons do take part, but not so many as will in the future; more of those who sit in the added section will take part, and the fault will be in the very increase in the number. 23. So what do you go about saying? "Proculus found the city a small one and made it large." I, however, belong to this other party, and the facts bear me out when I say that he has made the city smaller: for in building such things as this he destroys the chief part of the city's fair name, or rather he adds destruction by means of his stones to the damage which came from the first evils,[7] so that in the future there will be no difference between the *theatron* of Dionysus and that of Olympian Zeus. 24. These unseemly disturbances ought to have been cast out of all the places belonging to the festival, and in none of those three[8] ought there to be anything stronger than the law; but if all of these were weaker than the means of remedy which were available for each of them, this at least [the Plethron] should have been kept sound.[9]

25. But now it is considered a misfortune that a greater source of corruption does not take possession of it. The city, some say, has become more populous. I would have wished, in the first place, that the misfortunes of other cities should not have increased ours with their people, but that each should have kept its own, and that we should have had fewer people rather than so many; but since those whose misdeeds cast them out of their homes have flowed together here, I should have wished that we should not enlarge this *theatron* for this reason. 26. It is, indeed, not right that the flight of these people to us should become a source of harm to the Olympic Games. But even though the refugees from elsewhere settle here, let them not in addition to this destroy that part of the festival which possesses the greatest solemnity of any of the things which are done in it. 27. Those who sat upon those original seats were not the only people who inhabited the city, but when there were not a few inhabitants—for it is impossible that the city could ever have had a small population—not more than was fitting came to see these things. How, then, when those men observed what was ordained, shall we honor these people by an act which dishonors the proceedings? How shall these compel us to increase the size of the *theatron* when the crowd which existed in former times did not compel the rulers of that time to make it greater? 28. It is not, in fact, in the powers of Proculus to make it so large that it will receive everybody, not even if he thinks he can achieve everything. The people who are not spectators are not suffering an injustice merely because they can say that others are; neither should these latter pro-

---

[7] The allusion seems to be to the additions made to the seats by Argyrius and Phasganius.

[8] The Plethron, the Xystus at Antioch, and the Olympic Stadium at Daphne.

[9] I.e., if all of the three places in which the festival is celebrated were so corrupted that they could no longer be benefited by the means of cure which could be found in each one of them, the Plethron at least should be made sound.

test if they are not spectators themselves. In former times, Proculus, there were stones too, and the mountain was here to be hewn out, and there was the skill of builders too and other hands, and wagons and beams and ropes, but there was no reasoning which impelled the increase of the spectators. 29. You think that by means of the crowd you make the Plethron nobler, but your understanding is bad. For you see that when the Olympic Games begin we reduce the city's multitude of theatrical entertainments, driving out many, both courtesans and male and female prostitutes. But if improvement lay in increase in size, it would be necessary for us to consider how we might actually add to the number of these people from other sources. 30. Now that we reserve Daphne for men alone[10] and keep the women outside its boundaries, what do we do? Do we thus make Daphne more ignoble? No, we make it holier; for once, when they were offered violence by an impious man, we wept because we could not cast out all of them.[11] What then was done in Daphne was more important than the [loss of] the women, but nevertheless we cursed the drunkard, and not in vain, as the fashion of his end showed, for pressing his face against his toes for a long time he knew among what people he lay, and he called on death. 31. One may see this same thing among the athletes, when the herald calls some forth and by his silence does not bring forth others, after the test which they have undergone has determined both of these things. Indeed there would be more of them if no examination were made; but then the worse would be included among the better; the smaller number, however, is better than the greater. 32. It is because they know this that the Eleans are so proud of having scarcely seven athletes enter their contests. There is something similar at Delphi. With other peoples, indeed, the bands of athletes are so great that they need a second day for the contests, but their fame of course is not the same, and there is no one so reckless that in comparing the athletes he could think these worthy to be placed before those who have to do only with a few competitors. 33. In a word, if one thinks it beneficial to the public that these things should be seen by all, why should we have still more affairs piled upon others when it is possible to give over what is done in the afternoon [in the Plethron] to the neighboring elongated *theatron*,[12] and when it is possible to make what is now done in three days the work of a month and not to make any distinction, for anybody, in the matter of costume?[13] For in this way there would be a greater number. 34. Indeed there is something even superior to this for such things. What is this? The *theatron* under the mountain,[14] especially since the mountain itself takes

10 During the Olympic festival.
11 The episode to which Libanius refers seems not to be mentioned in other sources.
12 Presumably the amphitheater.
13 This may imply that there were different regulations concerning costume for the contests in the Plethron and those held elsewhere before the general public. Perhaps the athletes were nude in the Plethron, clothed elsewhere.
14 I.e. the scenic theater.

the place of a *theatron*. "But this is contrary to what is right." But tell me, is what we now have right? Or is it right to take to another place a practice which is now out of place and in this way to make seemly the *theatron* which is now incongruous?

35. Proculus does not suppose that he is loved by me, but he would not have had as many reproaches as he now has if he had not scorned my advice. He never, indeed, urged me to take counsel with him. And now some say that he will gain much and great praise in the matters concerned with the Plethron; but he would have profited if he had not restrained those who opposed him. 36. I know how great all this will be when the Plethron surges with disorder, and when the crowd, torn according to its passions, breaks all bounds according to the right which it believes exists on both sides, supporting some and being opposed by others, and when hands are lifted everywhere and the clamor spreads over the whole city, and some go so far as to hiss. Then not a few of the old men who see these things, and have seen what things were in the past, what will they not utter in their grief at this great change, old lovers of the true Olympic festival that they are? 37. These things, then, are the rewards of this fine enlargement. And they will pass over through the son to the father, who has done no wrong in this matter; and he will be afraid to take his seat,[15] knowing what sort of things he will hear from those who grieve at this and who reproach him with this astonishing Olympic festival.

[15] Tatianus.

LIST OF ABBREVIATIONS AND
BIBLIOGRAPHY

NOTE TO THE READER

The List of Abbreviations and the Bibliography are complementary. The items in the List of Abbreviations are not repeated in the Bibliography, but the Bibliography includes the names of the modern authors whose works are cited in the List of Abbreviations, so that the Bibliography contains a complete list of the authors whose names are cited.

The two lists are not intended to provide a complete listing of all the works on Antioch for such a listing would make a book by itself. The purpose has been to name (1) the chief works dealing with the history and antiquities of the city, (2) general historical studies that deal with the history of Antioch and its place in the larger history of the Hellenistic and Roman worlds, and (3) the special studies that have been consulted in the preparation of the present book. Other works, such as the older books and the studies dealing with the details of the abundant material available from the fourth century after Christ, may be found in the existing bibliographies, such as P. Thomsen's *Die Palästina-Literatur*, C. O. Müller's *Antiquitates Antiochenae*, Leclercq's article "Antioche" in the *Dictionnaire d'archéologie chrétienne et de liturgie*, Honigmann's "Syria" in the *Real-Encyclopädie*, and, most recently, Paul Petit's monumental *Libanius et la vie municipale d'Antioche au IVe siècle après J.-C.*, together with his *Les étudiants de Libanius*.

The individual chapters and archaeological studies published in the reports of the excavations of 1932-1939 are not listed here, but the periodic reports on the excavations and the preliminary studies that were published in journals during the excavations have been listed.

While the present monograph does not attempt to treat the church history and theology of Antioch in detail, some studies of these subjects, particularly recent ones, have been listed here in an effort to indicate the nature of the work that is being carried on in this field.

In the same way, although the book does not undertake to deal with Antiochene art, it has seemed useful to list some of the more significant modern works dealing with the mosaics and silver of Antioch. Here again the works cited are principally those of recent date.

Since the recent publication of the Greek and Latin inscriptions of Antioch and its vicinity in the third volume of the *Inscriptions grecques et latines de la Syrie*, edited by L. Jalabert and R. Mouterde, assembles the earlier literature on these inscriptions, the original publications and first studies of these texts are not included in the present bibliography, with a few exceptions in which older articles are utilized here for special purposes.

LIST OF ABBREVIATIONS

(these items are not repeated in the Bibliography)

AAES = W. K. Prentice, *Greek and Latin Inscriptions*, Part 3 of *Publications of an American Archaeological Expedition to Syria in 1899-1900*. New York 1908.

AJ = *The Antiquaries Journal*.

AJA = *American Journal of Archaeology*.

AJP = *American Journal of Philology*.

Acta SS = *Acta Sanctorum*, cited from the Paris edition.

Al-Balâdhuri, transl. Hitti = *The Origins of the Islamic State, being a Translation from the Arabic, Accompanied with Annotations, Geographic and Historic Notes of the Kitâb Futûh al-Buldân of al-Imâm abu-l 'Abbâs Ahmad ibn-Jâbir al-Balâdhuri by Philip K. Hitti* (New York 1916; Studies in History, Economics and Public Law edited by the Faculty of Political Science of Columbia University, vol. 68).

Alès, "Autour de Lucien d'Antioche" = Adhémar d'Alès, "Autour de Lucien d'Antioche," *MUSJ* 21 (1937-1938) 185-199.

Allard, *Dernières persécutions du 3ᵉ siècle⁴* = P. Allard, *Les dernières persécutions du troisième siècle (Gallus, Valérien, Aurélien)*, ed. 4. Paris 1924.

Allard, *Julien²* = P. Allard, *Julien l'Apostat*, ed. 2. Paris 1902-1903.

Allard, *Persécution de Dioclétien²* = P. Allard, *La persécution de Dioclétien et le triomphe de l'église*, ed. 2. Paris 1900.

Allard, *Persécutions pendant la 1ᵉʳᵉ moitié du 3ᵉ siècle²* = P. Allard, *Histoire des persécutions pendant la première moitié du troisième siècle (Septime Sévère, Maximin, Dèce)*, ed. 2. Paris 1894.

Allard, *Persécutions pendant les deux premiers siècles²* = P. Allard, *Histoire des persécutions pendant les deux premiers siècles*, ed. 2. Paris 1892.

Altaner, *Patrologie²* = B. Altaner, *Patrologie*, ed. 2. Freiburg 1950.

Anal. Boll. = *Analecta Bollandiana*.

Antioch-on-the-Orontes 1, 2, 3, 4 =

Antioch-on-the-Orontes (Publications of the Committee for the Excavation of Antioch and its Vicinity), 1: *The Excavations of 1932*, ed. by G. W. Elderkin. Princeton 1934.

Antioch-on-the-Orontes 2: The Excavations, 1933-1936, ed. by R. Stillwell. Princeton 1938.

Antioch-on-the-Orontes 3: The Excavations, 1937-1939, ed. by R. Stillwell. Princeton 1941.

Antioch-on-the-Orontes 4, pt. 1: Ceramics and Islamic Coins, ed. by F. O. Waagé. Princeton 1948.

Antioch-on-the-Orontes 4, pt. 2: Greek, Roman, Byzantine and Crusaders' Coins, by Dorothy B. Waagé. Princeton 1952.

For a list of the reviews of these volumes, see the Bibliography.

BCH = Bulletin de correspondance hellénique.

BHG² = Bibliotheca hagiographica graeca, ed. 2 *(Subsidia hagiographica,* 8). Brussels 1909.

BMC Galatia etc. = British Museum, Catalogue of the Greek Coins of Galatia, Cappadocia and Syria, by Warwick Wroth. London 1899.

BMC Rom. Emp. = Coins of the Roman Empire in the British Museum, by Harold Mattingly. vols. 1-5, London 1923-1950.

BMC Seleucid Kings of Syria = British Museum, Catalogue of Greek Coins, Seleucid Kings of Syria, by Percy Gardner. London 1878.

BZ = Byzantinische Zeitschrift.

Babelon, *Rois de Syrie = Catalogue des monnaies grecques de la Bibliothèque Nationale*: E. Babelon, *Les rois de Syrie, d'Arménie et de Commagène.* Paris 1890.

Bardy, *Lucien d'Antioche =* G. Bardy, *Recherches sur Saint Lucien d'Antioche et son école.* Paris 1936.

Bardy, *Paul de Samosate² =* G. Bardy, *Paul de Samosate, étude historique.* Nouv. éd. Louvain 1929.

Bauer, *Antiochia =* K. Bauer, *Antiochia in der ältesten Kirchengeschichte.* Tübingen 1919.

Bauer, *Rechtgläubigkeit u. Ketzerei =* W. Bauer, *Rechtgläubigkeit und Ketzerei im ältesten Christentum.* Tübingen 1934.

Baur, *Der hl. Joh. Chrysostomus =* P. Chrysostomus Baur, *Der heilige Johannes Chrysostomus und seine Zeit.* Munich 1929-1930.

Bazantay, *Le plateau de Daphné =* P. Bazantay, "Contribution à l'étude géographique de la Syrie: Un petit pays alaouite, le plateau de Daphné," *Haut-commissariat de la République française en Syrie at au Liban, Bulletin de l'enseignement (Publication du Service de l'instruction publique)* 11 (1933-1934) 335-366.

Beginnings of Christianity = F. J. F. Jackson and K. Lake, *The Beginnings of Christianity: The Acts of the Apostles.* London 1920-1933.

Bell, *Jews and Christians in Egypt =* H. I. Bell, *Jews and Christians in Egypt.* London 1924.

Bellinger, "Early Coinage of Roman Syria" = A. R. Bellinger, "The Early Coinage of Roman Syria," *Studies in Roman Economic and Social History in Honor of Allan Chester Johnson* (Princeton 1951) 58-67.

Bellinger², "End of the Seleucids" = A. R. Bellinger, "The End of the Seleucids," *Transactions of the Connecticut Academy of Arts and Sciences* 38 (1949) 51-102.

Bellinger, "Some Coins from Antioch" = A. R. Bellinger, "Notes on Some Coins from Antioch in Syria," *American Numismatic Society Museum Notes* 5 (1952) 53-63.

Bellinger, *Tetradrachms of Caracalla and Macrinus =* A. R. Bellinger, *The*

Syrian Tetradrachms of Caracalla and Macrinus (*American Numismatic Society, Numismatic Studies*, 3). New York 1940.

Beloch, *Bevölkerung* = K. J. Beloch, *Die Bevölkerung der griechisch römischen Welt*. Leipzig 1886.

Beloch, *Griech. Gesch.²* = K. J. Beloch, *Griechische Geschichte*. Ed. 2. Berlin 1912-1925.

Bengston, *Strategie* = H. Bengston, *Die Strategie in der hellenistischen Zeit*. Berlin 1937-1952.

Beurlier, "Koinon de Syrie" = E. Beurlier, "Le Koinon de Syrie," *Rev. num.* ser. 3, vol. 12 (1894) 286-300.

Bevan, *House of Seleucus* = E. R. Bevan, *The House of Seleucus*. London 1902.

Bidez, *Julian der Abtrünnige* = J. Bidez, *Julian der Abtrünnige,* transl. by H. Rinn. Munich 1940. Translation, with revisions and additions, of *La vie de l'empereur Julien* (see below).

Bidez, *Vie de Julien* = J. Bidez, *La vie de l'empereur Julien*. Paris 1930. Later translated into German, with revisions and additions (see above).

Bikerman, *Institutions des Séleucides* = E. Bikerman, *Institutions des Séleucides*. Paris 1938.

Bikerman, "Les Maccabées de Malalas" = E. Bikerman, "Les Maccabées de Malalas," *Byzantion* 21 (1951) 63-83.

Bosch, *Kleinasiatischen Münzen* = C. Bosch, *Die kleinasiatischen Münzen der römischen Kaiserzeit*. Stuttgart 1931.

Bouché-Leclercq, *Hist. des Séleucides* = A. Bouché-Leclercq, *Histoire des Séleucides*. Paris 1913-1914.

Bouchier, *Antioch* = E. S. Bouchier, *A Short History of Antioch*. Oxford 1921.

Bourne, *Public Works* = F. C. Bourne, *The Public Works of the Julio-Claudians and Flavians*. Diss. Princeton 1946.

Braidwood, *Mounds in the Plain of Antioch* = R. J. Braidwood, *Mounds in the Plain of Antioch, an Archaeological Survey* (*The University of Chicago, Oriental Institute Publications*, 18). Chicago 1937.

Bury, "Malalas: the Cod. Barocc." = J. B. Bury, "Johannes Malalas: the Text of the Codex Baroccianus," *BZ* 6 (1897) 219-230.

Bury, *Later Roman Empire* = J. B. Bury, *History of the Later Roman Empire*. London 1923; reprinted, New York, Dover Publications, 1958.

CAH = *Cambridge Ancient History.*

CJ = *Codex Justinianus.*

CP = *Classical Philology.*

CSCO = *Corpus scriptorum Christianorum orientalium.*

CSEL = *Corpus scriptorum ecclesiasticorum latinorum.*

CTh = *Codex Theodosianus.*

CW = *Classical Weekly.*

List of Abbreviations

Cavallera, *Schisme d'Antioche* = F. Cavallera, *Le schisme d'Antioche.* Paris 1905.

Chapot, *Frontière de l'Euphrate* = V. Chapot, *La frontière de l'Euphrate de Pompée à la conquête arabe.* (*Bibliothèque des écoles françaises d'Athènes et de Rome,* fasc. 99). Paris 1907.

Christ-Schmid-Stählin, *Gesch. d. gr. Lit.*[6] = W. von Christ, *Geschichte der griechischen Litteratur,* ed. 6, edited by W. Schmid and O. Stählin, Pt. 2, *Die nachklassische Periode der griechischen Litteratur,* in 2 vols. (*Handbuch der Altertumswissenschaft,* Bd. 7). Munich 1920-1924.

Church Slavonic Malalas = *Chronicle of John Malalas, Books 8-18, translated from the Church Slavonic by M. Spinka in collaboration with G. Downey.* Chicago 1940. References are to the pages of the translation.

Cook, *Zeus* = A. B. Cook, *Zeus.* Cambridge, Eng., 1914-1940.

Crowfoot-Kenyon-Sukenik, *Buildings at Samaria* = J. W. Crowfoot, K. M. Kenyon, E. L. Sukenik, *The Buildings at Samaria* (*Reports of the Work of the Joint Expedition in 1931-1933 and of the British Expedition in 1935,* no. 1). London 1942.

DACL = *Dictionnaire d'archéologie chrétienne et de liturgie,* ed. by Cabrol and Leclercq, Paris.

DTC = *Dictionnaire de théologie catholique.*

Daniel, *M. Vipsanius Agrippa* = R. Daniel, *M. Vipsanius Agrippa, eine Monographie.* Diss. Breslau 1933.

Debevoise, *Hist. of Parthia* = N. C. Debevoise, *A Political History of Parthia.* Chicago 1938.

Delehaye, *Légendes hagiographiques*[3] = H. Delehaye, *Les légendes hagiographiques,* ed. 3 (*Subsidia hagiographica,* 18). Brussels 1927.

Delehaye, *Origines du culte*[2] = H. Delehaye, *Les origines du culte des martyrs,* ed. 2 (*Subsidia hagiographica,* 20). Brussels 1933.

Delehaye, *Passions des martyrs* = H. Delehaye, *Les passions des martyrs et les genres littéraires.* Brussels 1921.

Delehaye, *Saints stylites* = H. Delehaye, *Les saints stylites.* Brussels 1923.

Devreesse, *Patriarcat d'Antioche* = R. Devreesse, *Le patriarcat d'Antioche.* Paris 1945.

Dieudonné, "Monnaies grecques de Syrie" = A. Dieudonné, "Les monnaies grecques de Syrie au Cabinet des médailles," *Rev. num.,* ser. 4, vol. 30 (1927) 1-50, 155-169.

Dobiáš, *Hist.* = J. Dobiáš, *Dějiny římské provincie Syrské* [*History of the Roman Province of Syria*]. Pt. 1, Prague 1924 (all published). In Czech, with summary in French.

Dobiáš, "Occupation de la Syrie" = J. Dobiáš, "Les premiers rapports des Romains avec les Parthes et l'occupation de la Syrie," *Archiv orientální* 3 (1931) 215-256.

Dobiáš, "Syrský prokonsulát M. Calpurnia Bibula" = J. Dobiáš, "Syrský prokonsulát M. Calpurnia Bibula v letech 51/50 př. Kr.," *Rozpravy České Akademie věd a Umění*, Třída I, Pro Vedy Filosoficke, Čís. 65 (1923).

Dobiáš, "Philippos Barypous" = J. Dobiáš, "Philippos Barypous," *Listy filologické* 51 (1924) 214-227, with summary in French, pp. vi-vii.

Domaszewski, "Personennamen bei den SHA" = A. von Domaszewski, "Die Personennamen bei den SHA," *Sitzungsberichte d. Heidelberger Akad. d. Wiss., phil.-hist. Kl.*, 1918, 13. Abh.

Downey, "Antioch under Severus and Caracalla" = G. Downey, "Malalas on the History of Antioch under Severus and Caracalla," *TAPA* 68 (1937) 141-156.

Downey, "Architectural Significance of *stoa* and *basilike*" = G. Downey, "The Architectural Significance of the Use of the Words *stoa* and *basilike* in Classical Literature," *AJA* 41 (1937) 194-211.

Downey, "Building Records in Malalas" = G. Downey, "Imperial Building Records in Malalas," *BZ* 38 (1938) 1-16, 299-311.

Downey, "Calendar Reform at Antioch" = G. Downey, "The Calendar Reform at Antioch in the Fifth Century," *Byzantion* 15 (1940-1941) 39-48.

Downey, *Comites Orientis* = G. Downey, *A Study of the Comites Orientis and the Consulares Syriae*. Diss. Princeton 1939.

Downey, "Economic Crisis under Julian" = G. Downey, "The Economic Crisis at Antioch under Julian the Apostate," *Studies in Roman Economic and Social History in Honor of Allan Chester Johnson* (Princeton 1951) 312-321.

Downey, "Gate of the Cherubim" = G. Downey, "The Gate of the Cherubim at Antioch," *Jewish Quarterly Review* 29 (1938) 167-177.

Downey, "Inscriptions in Malalas" = G. Downey, "References to Inscriptions in the Chronicle of Malalas," *TAPA* 66 (1935) 55-72.

Downey, "Megalopsychia" = G. Downey, "The Pagan Virtue of Megalopsychia in Byzantine Syria," *TAPA* 76 (1945) 279-286.

Downey, "Occupation of Syria" = G. Downey, "The Occupation of Syria by the Romans," *TAPA* 82 (1951) 149-163.

Downey, "Olympic Games" = G. Downey, "The Olympic Games of Antioch in the Fourth Century A.D.," *TAPA* 70 (1939) 428-438.

Downey, "Personifications of Abstract Ideas" = G. Downey, "Personifications of Abstract Ideas in the Antioch Mosaics," *TAPA* 69 (1938) 349-363.

Downey, "Political Status of Roman Antioch" = G. Downey, "The Political Status of Roman Antioch," *Berytus* 6 (1939-1940) 1-6.

Downey, "Seleucid Chronology" = G. Downey, "Seleucid Chronology in Malalas," *AJA* 42 (1938) 102-120.

Downey, "Strabo on Antioch" = G. Downey, "Strabo on Antioch: Notes on his Method," *TAPA* 72 (1941) 85-95.

Downey, "Wall of Theodosius" = G. Downey, "The Wall of Theodosius at Antioch," *AJP* 62 (1941) 207-213.

Downey, "Water Supply" = G. Downey, "The Water Supply of Antioch on the Orontes in Antiquity," *Annales archéologiques de Syrie* 1 (1951) 171-187.

Duchesne, *L'église au VI*ᵉ *siècle* = L. Duchesne, *L'église au VI*ᵉ *siècle*. Paris 1925.

Dudden, *St. Ambrose* = F. H. Dudden, *The Life and Times of St. Ambrose.* Oxford 1935.

Dura Final Rep. 6: Bellinger, *The Coins* = *Excavations at Dura-Europos, Final Report,* 6: A. R. Bellinger, *The Coins.* New Haven 1949.

Dura Prelim. Rep. 5th Season = *Excavations at Dura-Europos, Preliminary Report of Fifth Season of Work, October 1931—March 1932.* New Haven 1934.

Dura Prelim. Rep. 7th-8th Seasons = *Excavations at Dura-Europos, Preliminary Report, Seventh and Eighth Seasons.* New Haven 1939.

Dussaud, *Topographie* = R. Dussaud, *Topographie historique de la Syrie antique et médiévale.* Paris 1927.

Dvornik, "Circus Parties" = F. Dvornik, "The Circus Parties in Byzantium, their Evolution and their Suppression," *Byzantina Metabyzantina* 1, pt. 1 (1946) 119-133.

Eckhel, *Doct. num.* = J. H. von Eckhel, *Doctrina numorum veterum.* Vienna 1792-1828.

Eltester, "Kirchen Antiochias" = W. Eltester, "Die Kirchen Antiochias im iv. Jh.," *ZNTW* 36 (1937) 251-286 (published 1939).

Ensslin, "Zu den Kriegen des Schapur I" = W. Ensslin, "Zu den Kriegen des Sassaniden Schapur I," *Sitzungsberichte d. Bayer. Akad. d. Wiss., phil.-hist. Kl.* 147, no. 5 (published 1949).

FGrHist = *Fragmente der griechischen Historiker,* ed. F. Jacoby.

FHG = *Fragmenta historicorum graecorum,* ed. Müller.

Fliche-Martin, *Hist. de l'église* = *Histoire de l'église, depuis les origines jusqu'à nos jours, publiée sous la direction de A. Fliche et V. Martin.* Paris 1946ff.

Förster, "Antiochia" = R. Förster, "Antiochia am Orontes," *Jahrbuch des k. deutschen Archäologischen Instituts* 12 (1897) 103-149.

Förster, "De Libanio, Pausania . . ." = R. Förster, "De Libanio, Pausania, templo Apollinis Delphico," *Album gratulatorium in honorem H. van Herwerden* (Utrecht 1902) 45-54.

Förster, "Skulpturen von Antiochia" = R. Förster, "Skulpturen von Antiochia," *Jahrbuch d. k. deut. Archäol. Inst.* 13 (1893) 177-191.

Friedländer, *Sittengeschichte*¹⁰ = L. Friedländer, *Darstellungen aus der Sittengeschichte Roms,* ed. 10, ed. by G. Wissowa. Leipzig 1921-1923.

List of Abbreviations

Gagé, "Les Perses à Antioche" = J. Gagé, "Les Perses à Antioche et les courses de l'hippodrome au milieu du IIIᵉ siècle, à propos du 'transfuge' syrien Mariadès," *Bulletin de la Faculté des lettres de Strasbourg* 31 (1935) 301-324.

Geffcken, *Julianus* = J. Geffcken, *Kaiser Julianus*. Leipzig 1914.

Gerkan, *Griech. Städteanlagen* = A. von Gerkan, *Griechische Städteanlagen*. Berlin 1924.

Goubert, *Byzance avant l'Islam* = P. Goubert, *Byzance avant l'Islam*. Paris 1951—.

Grabar, *Martyrium* = A. Grabar, *Martyrium: Recherches sur le culte des reliques et l'art chrétien antique*. Paris 1946.

Grant, *Anniversary Issues* = M. Grant, *Roman Anniversary Issues*. Cambridge, Eng., 1950.

Grant, *Imperium to Auctoritas* = M. Grant, *From Imperium to Auctoritas*. Cambridge, Eng., 1946.

Grant, *Principate of Tiberius* = M. Grant, *Aspects of the Principate of Tiberius: Historical Comments on the Colonial Coinage Issued Outside Spain* (*Numismatic Notes and Monographs*, 116). New York 1950.

Grant, "Odes of Solomon" = R. M. Grant, "The Odes of Solomon and the Church of Antioch," *JBL* 63 (1944) 363-377.

Grant, "The Problem of Theophilus" = R. M. Grant, "The Problem of Theophilus," *HTR* 43 (1950) 179-196.

Greenslade, *Schism in the Early Church* = S. L. Greenslade, *Schism in the Early Church*. New York, no date (Edward Cadbury Lectures, 1949-1950).

Grégoire, "Les persécutions" = H. Grégoire, "Les persécutions dans l'empire romain," *Académie r. de Belgique, Cl. de lettres et des sciences morales et politiques, Mémoires, collection in-8°*, vol. 46, fasc. 1 (1951).

Groag, "Lurius Varius" = E. Groag, "Prosopographische Bemerkungen, 3: Lurius Varius," *Wiener Studien* 50 (1932) 202-205.

Guidi, "Descrizione araba" = I. Guidi, "Una descrizione araba di Antiochia," *Rendiconti della R. Accademia dei Lincei, Cl. di scienze morali, storiche e filologiche*, ser. 5, vol. 6 (1897), 137-161.

Gwatkin, *Studies of Arianism*² = H. M. Gwatkin, *Studies of Arianism*. Ed. 2. Cambridge, Eng., 1900.

HTR = *Harvard Theological Review*

Harnack, *Chronologie d. altchr. Lit.* = A. Harnack, *Gesch. der altchr. Lit. bis Eusebius*, Pt. 2: *Die chronologie der altchr. Lit.* Leipzig 1897-1904.

Harnack, *Mission u. Ausbreitung*⁴ = A. von Harnack, *Die Mission und Ausbreitung des Christentums*. Ed. 4. Leipzig 1924.

Harrer, *Studies* = G. A. Harrer, *Studies in the History of the Roman Province of Syria*. Diss. Princeton 1915.

List of Abbreviations

Hastings, *Enc. Rel. Eth.* = J. Hastings, *Encyclopaedia of Religion and Ethics.* New York 1928.

Hefele-Leclercq, *Conciles* = K. J. Hefele, *Histoire des conciles. Nouvelle traduction franç. par un religieux bénédictin* [H. Leclercq]. Paris 1907ff.

Heichelheim, *Roman Syria* = F. M. Heichelheim, *Roman Syria,* in: *An Economic Survey of Ancient Rome,* ed. by T. Frank, 4 (Baltimore 1938) 121-257.

Herzog-Hauser, "Tyche" = Gertrud Herzog-Hauser, "Tyche," *RE* 7 A (1948) 1643-1689.

Hitti, *History of Syria* = P. K. Hitti, *History of Syria including Lebanon and Palestine.* London 1951.

Holleaux, "Le papyrus de Gourob" = M. Holleaux, "Remarques sur le papyrus de Gourob," *BCH* 30 (1906) 330-348, republished in the same author's *Études d'épigraphie et d'histoire grecques,* ed. by L. Robert, 3 (Paris 1942) 281-310. References are given here to the publication in the *Études.*

Holmes, *Roman Republic* = T. Rice Holmes, *The Roman Republic and the Founder of the Empire.* Oxford 1923.

Honigmann, "Seleukeia" = E. Honigmann, "Seleukeia (Pieria)," *RE* 2 A (1923) 1184-1200.

Honigmann, "Syria" = E. Honigmann, "Syria," *RE* 4 A (1932) 1549-1727.

Honigmann, "Topographie, pt. 1, pt. 2" = E. Honigmann, "Historische Topographie von Nordsyrien im Altertum," *Zeitschrift des deutschen Palästina-Vereins,* pt. 1 = 46 (1923) 149-193; pt. 2 = 47 (1924) 1-64.

Hort, *Ecclesia* = F. J. A. Hort, *The Christian Ecclesia.* London 1914.

Hüttl, *Antoninus Pius* = W. Hüttl, *Antoninus Pius.* Prague 1933-1936.

Hugi, *Der Antiochikos* = L. Hugi, *Der Antiochikos des Libanius, eingeleitet, übersetzt und kommentiert.* Diss., Freiburg in der Schweiz; Solothurn 1919. Contains only §§1-131 of the oration.

IG = *Inscriptiones graecae.*

IGLS = *Inscriptions grecques et latines de la Syrie,* ed. L. Jalabert and R. Mouterde. Paris 1929ff.

IGRR = *Inscriptiones graecae ad res romanas pertinentes.*

JBL = *Journal of Biblical Literature.*

JHS = *Journal of Hellenic Studies.*

JR = *Journal of Religion.*

JTS = *Journal of Theological Studies.*

Jacquot, *Antioche* = Lt. col. P. Jacquot, *Antioche, centre de tourisme.* Antioch 1931.

Jansen, "Politik Antiochos' des IV" = H. L. Jansen, "Die Politik Antiochos des IV," *Skrifter utgitt av det Norske Videnskaps-Akademi i Oslo,* 2, *Hist.-filos. Kl.,* 1942, No. 3.

List of Abbreviations

John of Nikiu, *Chronicle* = *The Chronicle of John, Bishop of Nikiu, Translated from Zotenberg's Ethiopic Text by R. H. Charles.* London 1916 (Text and Translation Society).

Jones, *Cities of the East. Rom. Prov.* = A. H. M. Jones, *Cities of the Eastern Roman Provinces.* Oxford 1937.

Jones, "Civitates liberae et immunes" = A. H. M. Jones, "Civitates liberae et immunes in the East," *Anatolian Studies Presented to William Hepburn Buckler* (Manchester 1939) 103-117.

Jones, *Greek City* = A. H. M. Jones, *The Greek City from Alexander to Justinian.* Oxford 1940.

Karalevskij, "Antioche" = C. Karalevskij, "Antioche," Baudrillart, *Dict. d'histoire et de géographie ecclésiastiques* 3 (1924) 563-703.

Kelly, *Early Christian Creeds* = J. N. D. Kelly, *Early Christian Creeds.* London 1950.

Kidd, *Hist. of the Church* = B. J. Kidd, *A History of the Church to A.D. 461.* Oxford 1922.

Kirk (ed.), *The Apostolic Ministry* = *The Apostolic Ministry*, ed. by K. E. Kirk. London 1946.

Knox, *St. Paul and the Church of Jerusalem* = W. L. Knox, *St. Paul and the Church of Jerusalem.* Cambridge, Eng., 1951.

Kraeling, "Jewish Community at Antioch" = C. H. Kraeling, "The Jewish Community at Antioch," *JBL* 51 (1932) 130-160.

Lacroix, "Copies de statues sur les monnaies des Séleucides" = L. Lacroix, "Copies de statues sur les monnaies des Séleucides," *BCH* 73 (1949) 158-175.

Lassus, "Syrie," *DACL* = J. Lassus, "Syrie," *DACL* 15 (1951) 1855-1942.

Leclercq, "Antioche," *DACL* = H. Leclercq, "Antioche," *DACL* 1 (1907) 2359-2427.

Lepper, *Trajan's Parthian War* = F. A. Lepper, *Trajan's Parthian War.* Oxford 1948.

Levi, *Antioch Mosaic Pavements* = Doro Levi, *Antioch Mosaic Pavements.* Princeton 1947.

Lex. f. Theol. u. Kirche = *Lexikon für Theologie und Kirche.*

Libanius = *Libanii opera*, ed. R. Förster, 12 v., Leipzig, Teubner, 1903-1927. Letters are cited by the number according to the edition of J. C. Wolf (Amsterdam 1738) plus the number in Förster's edition.

Libanius, *Or.* 11 = Libanius, *Antiochikos*, translated, with commentary, by G. Downey, *Proceedings of the American Philosophical Society* 103 (1959) 652-686.

Liebenam, *Legaten* = W. Liebenam, *Forschungen zur römischen Verwaltungsgeschichte*, 1: *Die Legaten in den Provinzen.* Leipzig 1888.

Liebenam, *Städteverwaltung* = W. Liebenam, *Städteverwaltung im römischen Kaiserreiche.* Leipzig 1900.

Lietzmann, *Beginnings of the Christian Church* = H. Lietzmann, *The Beginnings of the Christian Church*, transl. by B. L. Woolf. London 1952.

Lietzmann, *Era of the Church Fathers*² = H. Lietzmann, *The Era of the Church Fathers*, transl. by B. L. Woolf, ed. 2. London 1953.

Lietzmann, *Founding of the Church Universal*² = H. Lietzmann, *The Founding of the Church Universal*, transl. by B. L. Woolf, ed. 2. London 1950.

Longden, "Parthian Campaigns" = R. P. Longden, "Notes on the Parthian Campaigns of Trajan," *JRS* 21 (1931) 1-35.

Loofs, *Paulus von Samosata* = F. Loofs, *Paulus von Samosata: eine Untersuchung zur altkirchlichen Literatur- und Dogmengeschichte.* Leipzig 1924. (*Texte und Untersuchungen*, Bd. 44, Heft 5 = 3. Reihe, Bd. 14, Heft 5).

MGH = *Monumenta Germaniae Historica.*

MUSJ = *Mélanges de l'Université Saint Joseph* (Beirut).

Maass, *Tagesgötter* = E. Maass, *Die Tagesgötter in Rom und den Provinzen.* Berlin 1902.

Macdonald, "Pseudo-Autonomous Coinage of Antioch" = G. Macdonald, "The Pseudo-Autonomous Coinage of Antioch," *Num. Chron.* ser. 4, vol. 4 (1904) 105-135.

Magie, *Asia Minor* = D. Magie, *Roman Rule in Asia Minor.* Princeton 1950.

Malalas = *Ioannis Malalae chronographia.* Books 1-8 and 13-18 are cited by page and line of the text published by L. Dindorf in the *Corpus scriptorum historiae Byzantinae* (Bonn 1831; anastatic reprint, Bonn 1926). Books 9-12 (pp. 214-315 in the Bonn ed.) are cited (according to page and line of the Bonn ed.) from the text of A. Schenk von Stauffenberg, *Die römische Kaisergeschichte bei Malalas, griech. Text der Bücher IX-XII und Untersuchungen* (Stuttgart 1931).

[Malalas] Church Slavonic Version, transl. Spinka = *Chronicle of John Malalas, Books 8-18, translated from the Church Slavonic by M. Spinka . . . in collaboration with G. Downey.* Chicago 1940. Cited by page.

Mansi = J. D. Mansi, *Sacorum conciliorum nova . . . collectio.* Florence 1759ff., reprinted Paris 1901ff.; the reprint is cited in the present work.

Marquardt, *Staatsverwaltung*² = J. Marquardt, *Römische Staatsverwaltung*, ed. 2. Leipzig 1881.

Mattingly-Sydenham, *Rom. Imp. Coinage* = H. Mattingly and E. A. Sydenham, *Roman Imperial Coinage.* London 1923ff. (in progress).

Meyer, *Ursprung und Anfänge* = E. Meyer, *Ursprung und Anfänge des Christentums.* Stuttgart 1921-1923.

Michel, *Recueil* = C. Michel, *Recueil d'inscriptions grecques.* Brussels 1900.

Mionnet, *Descr. de médailles* = T. E. Mionnet, *Description de médailles antiques grecques et romaines.* Paris 1807-1837.

Morey, *Mosaics of Antioch* = C. R. Morey, *The Mosaics of Antioch*. New York 1938.

Mouterde, "Pierides Musae" = R. Mouterde, "Pierides Musae," *MUSJ* 25 (1942-1943) 3-9.

Müller, *Antiq. Antioch.* = Carl Otfried Müller, *Antiquitates Antiochenae.* (Göttingen 1839), cited here by page. The work was also published in the *Commentationes societatis regiae scientiarum Gottingensis recentiores, classis historicae et philologicae* 8 (1832-1837, published 1841), pp. 205-340. Both publications were printed from the same type. In the publication in book form, the page following p. 120 is by mistake numbered 125 but the text is consecutive. Important "reviews" by the author himself were published in *Götting. gelehrte Anzeigen* 1834, St. 109-111; 1839, St. 101-104 = *Kleine deutsche Schriften* 1 (Breslau 1847) 90-102, 110-129.

Murphy, *The Reign of the Emperor L. Septimius Severus* = G. J. Murphy, *The Reign of the Emperor L. Septimius Severus from the Evidence of the Inscriptions.* Diss., University of Pennsylvania; Philadelphia 1945.

Newell, *Ake-Ptolemais and Damascus* = E. T. Newell, *Late Seleucid Mints in Ake-Ptolemais and Damascus.* New York 1939. (*Numismatic Notes and Monographs* No. 84.)

Newell, "Pre-Imperial Coinage of Rom. Antioch" = E. T. Newell, "The Pre-Imperial Coinage of Roman Antioch," *Num. Chron.* ser. 4, vol. 19 (1919) 69-113.

Newell, *Seleucid Mint of Antioch* = E. T. Newell, *The Seleucid Mint of Antioch.* New York 1918. (Reprinted from *American Journal of Numismatics* 51.)

Newell, *West. Sel. Mints* = E. T. Newell, *The Coinage of the Western Seleucid Mints from Seleucus I to Antiochus III.* New York 1941. (*Numismatic Studies* No. 4.)

Num. Chron. = *Numismatic Chronicle.*

OCD = *Oxford Classical Dictionary.*

OGIS = *Orientis graeci inscriptiones selectae,* ed. W. Dittenberger.

Obermann, "Sepulchre of the Maccabean Martyrs" = J. Obermann, "The Sepulchre of the Maccabean Martyrs," *JBL* 50 (1931) 250-265.

Olmstead, "Hellenistic Chronology" = A. T. Olmstead, "Cuneiform Texts and Hellenistic Chronology," *CP* 32 (1937) 1-14.

Olmstead, "The Mid-Third Century" = A. T. Olmstead, "The Mid-Third Century of the Christian Era," *CP* 37 (1942) 241-262, 398-420.

PAES = *Publications of the Princeton University Archaeological Expeditions to Syria in 1904-5 and 1909,* Part III B: W. K. Prentice, *Greek and Latin Inscriptions.* Leyden 1922.

PG = Migne, *Patrologia graeca.*

*PIR*² = *Prosopographia imperii romani*, ed. 2. Berlin 1933ff. (in progress).

PL = Migne, *Patrologia latina*.

PO = *Patrologia orientalis*.

*PRE*³ = *Realencyclopädie für protestantische Theologie und Kirche*, ed. by Herzog and Hauck, ed. 3. Leipzig 1896-1913.

Pack, *Studies in Libanius* = R. A. Pack, *Studies in Libanius and Antiochene Society under Theodosius*. Diss., University of Michigan 1935. Includes a translation, with commentary, of Libanius, *Or.* 45, *Concerning the Prisoners*.

Parker, *Hist. of the Roman World A.D. 138-337* = H. M. D. Parker, *A History of the Roman World from A.D. 138 to 337*. London 1935.

Parker, *Roman Legions* = H. M. D. Parker, *The Roman Legions*. Oxford 1928.

Petit, *Libanius et la vie municipale à Antioche* = P. Petit, *Libanius et la vie municipale à Antioche au IVᵉ siècle après J.-C.* (Paris 1955).

Pflaum, *Procurateurs équestres* = H. G. Pflaum, *Les procurateurs équestres sous le Haut-Empire romain*. Paris 1950.

PhW = *Philologische Wochenschrift*.

Piganiol, *Empire chrétien* = A. Piganiol, *L'Empire chrétien (325-395)* (Paris 1947).

Pirot, *Théodore de Mopsueste* = L. Pirot, *L'œuvre exégétique de Théodore de Mopsueste, 350-428 après J.-C.* Rome 1913.

Platner-Ashby, *Rome* = S. B. Platner and T. Ashby, *Topographical Dictionary of Ancient Rome*. Oxford 1929.

RA = *Revue archéologique*.

RAC = *Rivista di archeologia cristiana*.

RE = Pauly-Wissowa-Kroll *et al.*, *Realencyclopädie der classischen Altertumswissenschaft*.

REA = *Revue des études anciennes*.

REG = *Revue des études grecques*.

Rauschen, *Jahrbücher* = G. Rauschen, *Jahrbücher der christlichen Kirche unter dem Kaiser Theodosius dem Grossen*. Freiburg-i.-B. 1897.

Reinach, *Cultes, mythes et religions*² = S. Reinach, *Cultes, mythes et religions*, ed. 2. Paris 1908-1923.

Reinhold, *Marcus Agrippa* = M. Reinhold, *Marcus Agrippa, a Biography*. Diss., Columbia University; Geneva, N.Y. 1933.

Reusch, *Caracallavita* = W. Reusch, "Der historische Wert der Caracallavita in den *S.H.A.*," *Klio, Beiheft* 24 (1931).

Rev. bibl. = *Revue biblique*.

Rev. num. = *Revue numismatique*.

Rh. Mus. = *Rheinisches Museum*.

Richter, *Sculpture and Sculptors of the Greeks*³ = Gisela M. A. Richter, *The*

List of Abbreviations

Sculpture and Sculptors of the Greeks. New revised edition. New Haven 1950.

Riedmatten, *Procès de Paul de Samosate* = H. de Riedmatten, *Les Actes du procès de Paul de Samosate: étude sur la christologie du III⁰ au IV⁰ siècle.* Fribourg en Suisse 1952.

Robert, "Eutychides" = C. Robert, "Eutychides," no. 2, *RE* 6 (1909) 1532-1533.

Robertson, *Greek and Roman Architecture²* = D. S. Robertson, *A Handbook of Greek and Roman Architecture,* ed. 2. Cambridge, Eng., 1945.

Roscher, *Lexikon* = Roscher, *Lexikon der griech. und röm. Mythologie.*

Rostovtzeff, "Le Gad de Doura" = M. Rostovtzeff, "Le Gad de Doura et Seleucus Nicator," *Mélanges syriens offerts à M. René Dussaud* (Paris 1939) 1.281-295.

Rostovtzeff, "*Progonoi*" = M. Rostovtzeff, "*Progonoi*," *JHS* 55 (1935) 56-66.

Rostovtzeff, "Res gestae divi Saporis" = M. Rostovtzeff, "Res gestae divi Saporis and Dura," *Berytus* 8 (1943) 41-60.

Rostovtzeff, *Soc. Econ. Hist. Hellenistic World* = M. Rostovtzeff, *The Social and Economic History of the Hellenistic World.* Oxford, 1941.

Rostovtzeff, *Stor. econ. soc. imp. rom.* = M. Rostovtzeff, *Storia economica e sociale dell'Impero romano.* Florence, 1933, reprinted 1946. The second English edition, *The Social and Economic History of the Roman Empire,* prepared by P. M. Fraser (Oxford 1957), appeared after most of the present work was completed; it does not contain major additions to the Italian edition.

SHA = *Scriptores historiae augustae.*

Sauvaget, *Alep* = J. Sauvaget, *Alep.* Paris 1941.

Sauvaget, "Plan de Laodicée-sur-mer" = J. Sauvaget, "Le plan de Laodicée-sur-mer," *Bulletin d'études orientales (Institut français de Damas)* 4 (1934) 81-114.

Schürer, *Gesch. d. jüd. Volkes³⁻⁴* = E. Schürer, *Geschichte des jüdischen Volkes im Zeitalter Jesu Christi,* ed. 3 and 4. Leipzig 1901-1911.

Schultze, *Antiocheia* = V. Schultze, *Altchristliche Städte und Landschaften,* 3: *Antiocheia.* Gütersloh 1930.

Schwabe, *Libaniana* = M. Schwabe, *Analecta Libaniana.* Diss., Berlin 1918.

Schwartz, *Acta Conciliorum* = *Acta Conciliorum Oecumenicorum iussu atque mandato Societatis Scientiarum Argentoratensis edidit Eduardus Schwartz.* Berlin 1927 ff.

Seeck, *Briefe des Libanius* = O. Seeck, *Die Briefe des Libanius zeitlich geordnet.* Leipzig 1906. (Texte und Untersuchungen 30, 1-2).

Seeck, *Gesch. d. Untergangs* = O. Seeck, *Geschichte des Untergangs der Antiken Welt.* Berlin, 1⁴ (1921), 2² (1921), 3² (1921), 4-6 (1911-1921).

Seeck, *Regesten* = O. Seeck, *Regesten der Kaiser und Päpste.* Stuttgart 1919.

List of Abbreviations

Sellers, *Eustathius of Antioch* = R. V. Sellers, *Eustathius of Antioch and his Place in the Early History of Christian Doctrine*. Cambridge, Eng., 1928.

Sellers, *Two Ancient Christologies* = R. V. Sellers, *Two Ancient Christologies: A Study in the Christological Thought of the Schools of Alexandria and Antioch in the Early History of Christian Doctrine*. London 1940.

Seyrig, "Poids antiques de la Syrie" = H. Seyrig, "Poids antiques de la Syrie et de la Phénicie sous la domination grecques et romaine," *Bulletin du Musée de Beyrouth* 8 (1949) 37-79.

Seyrig, "Sur les ères de quelques villes de Syrie" = H. Seyrig, "Antiquités syriennes, 42: Sur les ères de quelques villes de Syrie," *Syria* 27 (1950) 5-15.

Sievers, *Leben des Libanius* = G. R. Sievers, *Das Leben des Libanius*. Berlin 1868.

Simon, *Verus Israel* = M. Simon, *Verus Israel*. Paris 1948.

Smith, *The Dome* = E. Baldwin Smith, *The Dome: A Study in the History of Ideas*. Princeton 1950.

Starcky, *Palmyre* = J. Starcky, *Palmyre*. Paris 1952. (*L'Orient ancien illustré* 7.)

Stauffenberg, *Malalas* = A. Schenk von Stauffenberg, *Die römische Kaisergeschichte bei Malalas, griech. Text der Bücher IX-XII und Untersuchungen*. Stuttgart 1931.

Stein, *Gesch.* 1 = E. Stein, *Geschichte des spätrömischen Reiches*, 1: *Vom römischen zum byzantinischen Staate (284-476 n. Chr.)*. Vienna 1928.

Stein, *Hist.* 2 = E. Stein, *Histoire du Bas-empire*, 2: *De la disparition de l'empire d'Occident à la mort de Justinien (476-565)*. Paris 1949.

Stevenson, *Studies in Eusebius* = J. Stevenson, *Studies in Eusebius*. Cambridge, Eng., 1929.

Streeter, *Four Gospels* = B. H. Streeter, *The Four Gospels, A Study of Origins*, 4th impression, revised. London 1930.

Streeter, *Primitive Church* = B. H. Streeter, *The Primitive Church*. New York 1929.

Studies in Honor of A. C. Johnson = *Studies in Roman and Economic and Social History in Honor of Allan Chester Johnson*. Princeton 1951.

Syme, "A Governor of Syria under Nerva" = R. Syme, "A Governor of Syria under Nerva," *Philologus* 91 (1936) 238-245.

TAPA = *Transactions of the American Philological Association*.

Tabari, ed. Nöldeke = *Geschichte der Perser und Araber zur Zeit der Sasaniden, aus der arabischen Chronik des Tabari übersetzt . . . von T. Nöldeke*. Leyden 1879.

Tarn-Griffith, *Hellenistic Civilization*[3] = W. W. Tarn and G. T. Griffith, *Hellenistic Civilization*, ed. 3. London 1952.

Tchalenko, *Villages antiques de la Syrie du Nord* = G. Tchalenko, *Villages antiques de la Syrie du Nord. La région du Bélus à l'époque romaine*. Paris 1953—.

Thompson, *Ammianus Marcellinus* = E. A. Thompson, *The Historical Work of Ammianus Marcellinus*. Cambridge, Eng., 1947.

Tondriau, "Comparisons and Identifications of Rulers with Deities" = J. L. Tondriau, "Comparisons and Identifications of Rulers with Deities in the Hellenistic World," *Review of Religion* 13 (1948-1949) 24-47.

Tondriau, "Souverains et souveraines Séleucides en divinités" = J. Tondriau, "Souverains et souveraines Séleucides en divinités," *Le Muséon* 61 (1948) 171-182.

Toynbee, *Hadrianic School* = J. M. C. Toynbee, *The Hadrianic School*. Cambridge, Eng., 1934.

Tscherikower, "Hellenistische Städtegründungen" = V. Tscherikower," "Die hellenistische Städtegründungen," *Philologus, Suppl.* 9, pt. 1 (1927).

Van Sickle, "Particularism in the Roman Empire" = C. E. Van Sickle, "Particularism in the Roman Empire during the Military Anarchy," *AJP* 51 (1930) 343-357.

Vasiliev, *Justin the First* = A. A. Vasiliev, *Justin the First. An Introduction to the Epoch of Justinian the Great*. Cambridge 1950.

Waagé, D. B., "Coins" = Dorothy B. Waagé, "Greek, Roman, Byzantine and Crusaders' Coins," *Antioch-on-the-Orontes*, vol. 4, pt. 2. Princeton 1952.

Waddington = H. W. Waddington, *Inscriptions grecques et latines de la Syrie* (Paris 1870) = P. Le Bas, *Voyage archéologique*, tome 3.

Weber, *Hadrianus* = W. Weber, *Untersuchungen zur Geschichte des Kaisers Hadrianus*. Leipzig 1907.

Weber, *Josephus u. Vespasian* = W. Weber, *Josephus und Vespasian*. Berlin 1921.

Weber, "Studien" = W. Weber "Studien zur Chronik des Malalas," *Festgabe für Adolf Deissmann* (Tübingen 1827) 20-66.

Welles, *Royal Correspondence* = C. B. Welles, *Royal Correspondence in the Hellenistic Period*. New Haven 1934.

West, "Commercial Syria" = L. C. West, "Commercial Syria under the Roman Empire," *TAPA* 55 (1924) 159-189.

Weulersse, "Antioche" = J. Weulersse, "Antioche, essai de géographie urbaine," *Bulletin d'études orientales (Institut français de Damas)* 4 (1934) 27-79.

Weulersse, *L'Oronte* = J. Weulersse, *L'Oronte: étude de fleuve*. Thèse complémentaire, Université de Paris; Tours 1940.

Woolley, "Al Mina" = L. Woolley, "Excavations at Al Mina, Suedia," *JHS* 58 (1938) 1-30.

Wruck, *Syrische Provinzialprägung* = W. Wruck, *Die syrische Provinzialprägung von Augustus bis Traian*. Stuttgart 1931.

List of Abbreviations

Wycherley, *How the Greeks Built Cities* = R. E. Wycherley, *How the Greeks Built Cities*. London 1949.

ZKT = *Zeitschrift für katholische Theologie.*

ZNTW = *Zeitschrift für die neutestamentliche Wissenschaft.*

BIBLIOGRAPHY

Anonymous, *La grotte de S. Pierre à Antioche. Étude par un missionaire Capucin.* Beirut 1934. See the review by M. van Cutsem, *Anal. Boll.* 54 (1936) 184.

Adler, "Kasios," No. 3, *RE* 10.2265-2267. Includes material on the cult of Zeus Kasios and its relation to Antioch.

Alès, Adhémar d'. See the List of Abbreviations.

Alexander, C., "A Mosaic from Antioch," *Bulletin of the Metropolitan Museum of Art*, New York 35 (1940) 244-247. On a mosaic showing a personification of a Season (Levi, *Antioch Mosaic Pavements* 1.60ff.).

Alföldi, A., "Die Hauptereignisse der Jahre 253-261 n. Chr. im Orient im Spiegel der Münzprägung," *Berytus* 4 (1937) 41-68. On the Persian invasions of Syria in which Antioch was captured.

———, "Die römische Münzprägung und die historischen Ereignisse im Osten zwischen 260 u. 270 n. Chr.," *Berytus* 5 (1938) 47-92. Continuation of the preceding article.

Allard, P. See the List of Abbrevations.

Altaner, B. See the List of Abbreviations.

Amand de Mendiéta, D., "Damase, Athanase, Pierre, Mélèce et Basile," *1054—1954: L'Église et les églises. Travaux offerts à Dom Lambert Beauduin* 1 (Chevetogne 1954) 261-277. On the relationship of the church of Antioch with those of Rome, Alexandria, and Caesarea in Cappadocia, A.D. 370-379.

Andreotti, R., "L'opera legislativa ed amministrativa dell'Imperatore Giuliano," *Nuova rivista storica* 14 (1930) 342-383.

Antioch-on-the-Orontes, volumes 1-4. For complete titles, see the List of Abbreviations. Reviews of these volumes are as follows:

   Reviews of *Antioch-on-the-Orontes* 1: Anonymous, *JHS* 54 (1934) 230; Anonymous, *Times Literary Supplement* (London) 1935, 229; C. Bonner, *AJA* 39 (1935) 158-159; S. Casson, *Antiquity* 9 (1935) 369; V. Chapot, *Journal des Savants* 1935, 11-17; H. Delehaye, *Anal. Boll.* 53 (1935) 382-383; Ch. Dugas, *REG* 48 (1935) 438-439; R. Dussaud, *Syria*, 17 (1936) 88-89; G. Lippold, *Deutsche Literaturzeitung* 56 (1935) 2048-2050; R. M(outerde), *MUSJ* 18 (1934) 216-217; W. Müller, *PhW.* 56 (1936) 455-458; H. Philipp, *Petermanns Geographische Mitteilungen* 1936, 291; Ch. P(icard), *RA*, ser. 6, vol. 6 (1935) 118-121; J. C. Sloane, Jr., *Jewish Quarterly Review* 27 (1936) 175-177; P. Thomsen, *Archiv für Orientforschung* 11 (1937) 249-250; L. H. Vincent, *Rev. Bibl.* 44 (1935) 316-317; E. Weigand, *BZ* 35 (1935) 424-429.

   Reviews of *Antioch-on-the-Orontes* 2: G. Bendinelli, *Rivista di filologia e d'istruzione classica* 1939, 207-209; J. Berchmans, *L'antiquité classique* 8 (1939) 482-487; A. Blanchet, *Journal des Savants* 1939, 88-90;

Bibliography

J. M. R. Cormack, *JHS* 58 (1938) 288-289; J. W. Crowfoot, *Antiquity* 13 (1939) 472-475; R. D(ussaud), *Syria* 20 (1939) 269; C. Hopkins, *AJA* 42 (1938) 605-607; R. Krautheimer, *Rivista di archeologia cristiana* 14 (1939) 355-358; R. M(outerde), *MUSJ* 22 (1939) 129-132; W. Müller, *PhW.* 59 (1939) 875-880; G. E. Mylonas, *Classical Weekly* 32 (1939) 282-283; Ch. Picard, *RA*, ser. 6. vol. 14 (1939) 112-116; P. Thomsen, *Archiv für Orientforschung* 13 (1941) 335-337.

Reviews of *Antioch-on-the-Orontes* 3: Anonymous, *Journal of the American Society of Architectural Historians* 1 (1941) 30; F. E. Brown, *AJA* 45 (1941) 644-646; M. Lawrence, *Art Bulletin* 24 (1942) 185-188; R. Mouterde, *MUSJ* 26 (1944-1946) 103-105.

Reviews of *Antioch-on-the-Orontes* 4, pt. 1: O. Broneer, *AJA* 54 (1950) 85-89; R. Mouterde, *MUSJ* 27 (1947-1948) 318-320; J. Walker, *Num. Chron.* ser. 6, vol. 9 (1949) 118.

Armstrong, C. B., "The Synod of Alexandria and the Schism of Antioch in A.D. 362," *JTS* 22 (1920-1921) 206-221, 347-365.

Arnason, H. H., "The History of the Chalice of Antioch," *Biblical Archaeologist* 4 (1941) 50-64; 5 (1942) 10-16. Summarizes the discussions of the authenticity of the Chalice, with bibliography.

Ausfeld, A., "Zur Topographie von Alexandria und Pseudokallisthenes," *Rh. Mus.* 55 (1900) 348-384. Discusses the legends of the founding of Antioch.

Babelon, E., "Sarcophage romain trouvé à Antioche," *Gazette archéologique* 10 (1885) 233.

———. See also the List of Abbreviations.

Babelon, J., "Dieux fleuves," *Aréthuse* 7 (1930) 109-115. Discusses the representations of the Orontes in the statues of the Tyche of Antioch.

Bacht, H., "Die Rolle des orientalischen Mönchtums in den kirchenpolitischen Auseinandersetzungen um Chalkedon (431-519)," *Das Konzil von Chalkedon,* ed. A. Grillmeier and H. Bacht (Würzburg 1951-1954) 2.193-314.

Bacon, B. W., "Peter's Triumph at Antioch," *JR* 9 (1929) 204-233.

Bardy, G., "L'église d'Antioche au temps de la crise arienne," *Bulletin d'ancienne littérature et d'archéologie chrétienne* 4 (1914) 243-261.

———, "Alexandrie, Antioche, Constantinople (325-451)," *1054-1954: L'Église et les églises. Travaux offerts à Dom Lambert Beauduin* 1 (Chevetogne 1954) 183-207. On the relative ranks and relationships of the churches of the principal eastern cities.

———. See also the List of Abbreviations.

Bate, D. M. A., "Note on an Animal Mosaic from Antioch-on-the-Orontes," *Honolulu Academy of Arts, Annual Bulletin* 1 (1939) 26-31. On a mosaic showing animals (Levi, *Antioch Mosaic Pavements* 1.365).

Bauer, K. See the List of Abbreviations.

Bibliography

Bauer, W. See the List of Abbreviations.

Baur, C. See the List of Abbreviations.

Bazantay, P. See the List of Abbreviations.

Bell, H. I. See the List of Abbreviations.

Bellinger, A. R., *The Syrian Tetradrachms of Caracalla and Macrinus*. New York 1940 (American Numismatic Society, Numismatic Studies, No. 3). Coins of Antioch, 21-29.

——, "Crassus and Cassius at Antioch," *Num. Chron.* ser. 6, vol. 4 (1944) 59-61.

——, "The Bronze Standards of Antiochus III, Seleucus IV, and Antiochus IV," *Numismatic Review* 2 (October 1944) 5-6.

——, "King Antiochus in 151/0 B.C.," *Hesperia* 14 (1945) 58-59. On a coin which has been wrongly attributed to the mint of Antioch.

——, *Excavations at Dura-Europos, Final Report*, 6: *The Coins*. New Haven 1949. Includes coins from the mint of Antioch.

——, "Notes on Some Coins from Antioch in Syria," *American Numismatic Society, Museum Notes* 5 (1952) 53-63.

——. See also the List of Abbreviations.

Beloch, K. J. See the List of Abbreviations.

Bengtson, H. See the List of Abbreviations.

Benzinger, I., "Antiochia," *RE* 1.2442-2445.

Bersanetti, G. M., "Sulla guerra fra Settimio Severo e Pescennio Nigro in Erodiano," *Rivista di filologia et d'istruzione classica* 66 (1938) 357-364. Includes discussion of Pescennius Niger's activities at Antioch.

Beurlier, E. See the List of Abbreviations.

Bevan, E. R. See the List of Abbreviations.

Bickerman, E. J., "Syria and Cilicia," *AJP* 68 (1947) 353-362.

——, "The Name of Christians," *HTR* 42 (1949) 109-124. On the origin and use of the term at Antioch.

——, "Notes on Seleucid and Parthian Chronology," *Berytus* 8 (1943-1944) 73-83. On the origin and initial date of the Seleucid era; correction of the dating of events connected with Antiochus Hierax and Attalus I.

——. See also under Bikerman.

Bidez, J. See the List of Abbreviations.

Bikerman, E., "La cité grecque dans les monarchies hellénistiques," *Revue de philologie* 65 (1939) 335-349.

——. See also the List of Abbreviations, under Bikerman.

Birnbaum, A. "Die Oktogone von Antiochia, Nazianz und Nyssa," *Repertorium für Kunstwissenschaft* 36 (1913) 181-209. Includes discussion of the octagonal Great Church at Antioch.

Bober, P. P., "The Mithraic Symbolism of Mercury Carrying the Infant Bacchus," *HTR* 39 (1946) 75-84. Of interest in connection with the mosaic of Hermes and Dionysus from Antioch (Levi, *Antioch Mosaic Pavements* 1.285-289).

Bonner, C., "Witchcraft in the Lecture Room of Libanius," *TAPA* 63 (1932) 34-44.

——, "Note on the Mosaic of Daphne," *AJA* 38 (1934) 340. On the "*pribaton* of Ardaburius" shown in the topographical border of the mosaic from Yakto (Levi, *Antioch Mosaic Pavements* 1.324).

Bosanquet, R. C., "Town Planning in Syria," *Town Planning Review (University of Liverpool)* 6 (1915) 101-113. Includes a study of Antioch in the fourth century after Christ.

Bosch, C. See the List of Abbreviations.

Bouché-Leclercq, A. See the List of Abbreviations.

Bouchier, E. S. See the List of Abbreviations.

Bourne, F. C. See the List of Abbreviations.

Braidwood, R. J. See the List of Abbreviations.

Bréhier, L., "Les trésors d'argenterie syrienne et l'école artistique d'Antioche," *Gazette des Beaux-Arts* 1920, 1, pp. 173-196.

Brett, G., "The Brooklyn Textiles and the Great Palace Mosaic," *Coptic Studies in Honor of Walter Ewing Crum*. Boston 1950 (*Bulletin of the Byzantine Institute* 2) 433-441. Includes observations on the Antioch mosaics.

Brooks, E. W., "The Patriarch Paul of Antioch and the Alexandrian Schism of 575," *BZ* 30 (1929-1930) 468-476.

Browning, R., "The Riot of A.D. 387 in Antioch: The Role of the Theatrical Claques in the Later Empire," *JRS* 42 (1952) 13-20.

Bury, J. B. See the List of Abbreviations.

Buttrey, T. V., Jr., "*Thea neotera* on Coins of Antony and Cleopatra," *American Numismatic Society, Museum Notes* 6 (1954) 95-109. Discusses a coin of Antony and Cleopatra which has mistakenly been attributed to Antioch.

Caley, E. R., "Analysis of the Body Material of Ancient Faience Found at Antioch-on-the-Orontes," *Technical Studies* 8 (1940) 151-154.

Campbell, W. A., "Excavations at Antioch-on-the-Orontes," *AJA* 38 (1934) 201-206. Report on work during 1932-1933.

——, "The Third Season of Excavations at Antioch-on-the-Orontes," *AJA* 40 (1936) 1-9. Report on the campaign of 1934.

——, "The Fourth and Fifth Seasons of Excavations at Antioch-on-the-Orontes, 1935-6," *AJA* 42 (1938) 205-217.

——, "The Sixth Season of Excavations at Antioch-on-the-Orontes, 1937," *AJA* 44 (1940) 412-427.

——, "The Seventh Campaign at Antioch-on-the-Orontes," *AJA* 43 (1939) 299. Abstract of a report on the season of 1938.

Bibliography

Carrington, P., "Peter in Antioch," *Anglican Theological Review* 15 (1933) 1-15.

Cavallera, F. See the List of Abbreviations.

Chadwick, H. "The Fall of Eustathius of Antioch," *JTS* 49 (1948) 27-35.

————, "The Exile and Death of Flavian of Constantinople: A Prologue to the Council of Chalcedon," *JTS* N.S. 6 (1955) 17-34. Discusses contemporary events in the church at Antioch.

Chapot, V., "Antiquités de la Syrie du Nord," *BCH* 26 (1902) 162-164. Publication of a sarcophagus found near the road between Antioch and Daphne and of two colossal statues of Roman emperors (Hadrian and Titus?) found at the site of the theater in Daphne; also fragments of two other statues.

————. See also the List of Abbreviations.

Charbonneaux, J., *Revue des Beaux-Arts de France*, 1 (Nov.-Dec. 1942) 9-15. Illustrates mosaics of Antioch recently acquired by the Louvre.

Charlesworth, M. P., "Roman Trade with India: A Resurvey," *Studies in Roman Economic and Social History in Honor of A. C. Johnson* (Princeton 1951) 131-143. Includes material on the trade of Antioch and Syria.

Chowen, R. S., "The Nature of Hadrian's *Theatron* at Daphne," *AJA* 60 (1956) 275-277.

Coche de la Ferté, E., *L'antiquité chrétienne au Musée du Louvre* (Paris 1948). Contains the first publication (Nos. 41-42) of three pieces of the silver "treasure of Antioch."

Cook, A. B. See the List of Abbreviations.

Cross, F. L., "The Council of Antioch in 325 A.D.," *Church Quarterly Review* 128 (1939) 49-76.

Crowfoot, J. W. See the List of Abbreviations.

Cumont, F., "The Population of Syria," *JRS* 24 (1934) 187-190.

Daniel, R. See the List of Abbreviations.

Debevoise, N. C. See the List of Abbreviations.

Deichmann, F. W., "Ein frühchristliches Kapitell in Antiochia," *Archäologischer Anzeiger* 1941, 81-84. On a sixth-century capital in the Museum at Antioch.

De Jonge, P., "Scarcity of Corn and Cornprices in Ammianus Marcellinus," *Mnemosyne*, ser. 4, vol. 1 (1948) 238-245. On the famine at Antioch under the Emperor Julian.

Delehaye, H., "S. Barlaam, martyr à Antioche," *Anal. Boll.* 22 (1903) 129-145.

————, "Cyprien d'Antioche et Cyprien de Carthage," *Anal. Boll.* 39 (1921) 314-332.

————, "S. Romain, martyr d'Antioche," *Anal. Boll.* 50 (1932) 241-283.

————. See also the List of Abbreviations.

Devambez, G., "Grands bronzes du Musée de Stamboul," *Mémoires de*

Bibliography

l'Institut Français d'archéologie à Stamboul 4 (1937) 87-90. On the
bronze group of Hermes (?) published by R. Förster, *Archäologischer
Anzeiger* 1898, 241; cf. *Jahrbuch d. k. deutschen Archäologischen Instituts* 16 (1901) 39-53.

Devreesse, R. See the List of Abbreviations.

De Vries, W., "Die syrische-nestorianische Haltung zu Chalkedon," *Das
Konzil von Chalkedon*, ed. by A. Grillmeier and H. Bacht (Würzburg 1951-1954) 1.603-635.

Dieckmann, H., *Antiochien, ein Mittelpunkt urchristlicher Missionstätig-
keit*. Aachen 1920.

Diehl, C., "L'école artistique d'Antioche et les trésors d'argenterie syrienne,"
Syria 2 (1921) 81-95.

————, "Un nouveau trésor d'argenterie syrienne," *Syria* 7 (1926) 105-122.

Dieudonné, A., "L'aigle d'Antioche et les ateliers de Tyr et d'Emèse," *Rev.
num.*, ser. 4, vol. 13 (1909) 458-480.

————, "Tyr ou Antioche? Tétradrachmes de Trajan à Caracalla," *Rev.
num.*, ser. 4, vol. 13 (1909) 164-174.

————, "Du droit de monnaie à Antioche à l'époque impériale," *Congrès
international numismatique* 1910, 577-596. Corrects the classification
given in "Les sigles littérales des monnaies d'Antioche," *Journal international Svoronos* 1907, 273-286.

————, "Les consulats de Philippe et de Trébone Galle à Antioche," *Bulletin de la Société des antiquaires de France* 1913, p. 308.

————, "De la manière de compter les années de règne des empereurs à
Antioche [Nero, Galba]," *Rev. num.* 1909, 174-181.

————, "Les dernières monnaies pseudo-autonomes d'Antioche," *Mémoires
de la Société des Antiquaires de France*, 1907, 246-267.

————. See also the List of Abbreviations.

Dobiáš, J. See the List of Abbreviations.

Dodd, C. H., "Chronology of the Eastern Campaigns of the Emperor Lucius
Verus," *Num. Chron.* ser. 4, vol. 11 (1911) 209-267. Deals with the emperor's sojourn at Antioch and Daphne.

Dölger, F., *Die frühbyzantinische und byzantinisch beeinflusste Stadt* (Spo-
leto 1958; Atti del 3° Congresso internazionale di studi sull'alto me-
dioevo, 1956).

Domaszewski, A. von. See the List of Abbreviations.

Downey, G., "Q. Marcius Rex at Antioch," *CP* 32 (1937) 144-151.

————, "Ephraemius, Patriarch of Antioch," *Church History* 7 (1938)
364-370.

————, "The Work of Antoninus Pius at Antioch," *CP* 34 (1939) 369-372.

————, "Procopius on Antioch: A Study of Method in the *De aedificiis*,"
Byzantion 14 (1939) 361-378.

————, "Julian the Apostate at Antioch," *Church History* 8 (1939) 305-315.

————, "Ethical Themes in the Antioch Mosaics," *Church History* 10 (1941) 367-376.

————, "Representations of Abstract Ideas in the Antioch Mosaics," *Journal of the History of Ideas* 1 (1940) 112-113.

————, "The Claim of Antioch to Ecclesiastical Jurisdiction over Cyprus," *Proceedings of the American Philosophical Society* 102 (1958) 224-228.

————. See also under Spinka, M.

————. See also the List of Abbreviations.

Duchesne, L. See the List of Abbreviations.

Dudden, F. H. See the List of Abbreviations.

Dumortier, J., "Le mariage dans les milieux chrétiens d'Antioche et de Byzance d'après Saint Jean Chrysostome," *Lettres d'humanité* 5 (1946) 102-166.

Dura Reports. See the List of Abbreviations.

Dussaud, R., P. Deschamps, H. Seyrig, *La Syrie antique et médiévale illustrée*. Paris 1931.

————. See also the List of Abbreviations.

Dvornik, F. See the List of Abbreviations.

Eckhel, J. H. von. See the List of Abbreviations.

Edson, C., "*Imperium Macedonicum*: The Seleucid Empire and the Literary Evidence," *CP* 53 (1958) 153-170.

Elderkin, G. W., "A Dionysiac Personification in Comedy and Art," *AJA* 40 (1936) 348-351. On the mosaic of Agros and Opora (Levi, *Antioch Mosaic Pavements* 1.186-190).

————, "Mosaics of the Seven Sages," *Römische Mitteilungen* 52 (1937) 223-226. Includes discussion of the mosaic of the Judgment of Paris (Levi, *Antioch Mosaic Pavements* 1.16-21).

Eltester, W., "Zum syrisch-makedonischen Kalender im IV. Jh.," *ZNTW* 37 (1938) 286-288. On the beginning of the year in the calendar used in Antioch.

————. See also the List of Abbreviations.

Enfrey, L. M., *Antioche*. Paris 1930.

Engberding, H., "Wann wurde Severus zum Patriarchen von Antiochien geweiht," *Oriens Christianus* 37 (1953) 132-134.

Ensslin, W., "Kaiser Julians Gesetzgebungswerk und Reichsverwaltung," *Klio* 18 (1922-1923) 104-199. Includes material on Julian's visit to Antioch and his activities there.

————, "La politica ecclesiastica dell'Imperatore Teodosio agli inizi del suo governo," *Nuovo Didaskaleion* 2 (1948) 5-35. Deals with measures of Theodosius I concerning Antioch.

————. See also the List of Abbreviations.

Ermoni, V., "Antioche, Conciles d'," *Dictionnaire de théologie catholique*

I, pt. 2 (1937) 1433-1435; "Antioche, École théologique d'," *ibid.* 1435-1439.

Festugière, A. J., "Le symbole du phénix et le mysticisme hermétique," *Monuments Piot* 38 (1941) 147-151. Includes discussion of the Phoenix mosaic (Levi, *Antioch Mosaic Pavements* 1.351-355).

Filsinger, C., "Mosaic from Daphne," *St. Louis Museum Bulletin* 27 (May 1942) 6-9. On a border from the "House of the Bird-Rinceau" (Levi, *Antioch Mosaic Pavements* 1.366).

Fliche, A., and V. Martin. See the List of Abbreviations.

Förster, R. See the List of Abbreviations.

Förster, R., and K. Münscher, "Libanios," *RE* 12.2485-2551.

Franchi de' Cavalieri, P., "Il ꝁoimeterion di Antiochia," *Note agiografiche*, 7 (Vatican City 1928) 146-153. (Studi e Testi 49.)

Freund, A., *Beiträge zur antiochenischen und zur konstantinopolitanischen Stadtchronik.* Diss. Jena 1882.

Friedländer, L. See the List of Abbreviations.

Friedländer, P., *Documents of Dying Paganism: Textiles of Late Antiquity in Washington, New York and Leningrad.* Berkeley 1945. Provides material for study of some of the Antioch mosaics.

Fyfe, T. [Note on the excavations], *Royal Institute of British Architects, Journal*, ser. 3, vol. 42 (1935) 362-363.

Gaechter, P., "Jerusalem und Antiochia: Ein Beitrag zur urkirchlichen Rechtsentwicklung," *Zeitschrift für ꝁatholische Theologie* 70 (1948) 1-48.

———, "Petrus in Antiochia (Gal. 2.11-14)," *Zeitschrift für ꝁatholische Theologie* 72 (1950) 177-212.

Gagé, J. See the List of Abbreviations.

Gaiffier, B. de, "'Sub Iuliano Apostata' dans le martyrologe romain," *Anal. Boll.* 74 (1956) 5-49.

Geffcken, J. See the List of Abbreviations.

Gerkan, A. von. See the List of Abbreviations.

Goebel, R., *De Ioannis Chrysostomi et Libanii orationibus quae sunt de seditione Antiochensium.* Diss. Göttingen 1910.

Goubert, P. See the List of Abbreviations.

Grabar, A. See the List of Abbreviations.

Grant, M., "Complex Symbolism and New Mints, *c.* 14 B.C.," *Num. Chron.* ser. 6, vol. 9 (1949) 22-35. Includes material on the mint of Antioch.

———. See also the List of Abbreviations.

Grant, R. M., "Theophilus of Antioch to Autolycus," *HTR* 40 (1947) 227-256.

———, "The Bible of Theophilus of Antioch," *JBL* 66 (1947) 173-196.

———, "The Early Antiochene Anaphora," *Anglican Theological Review* 30 (1948) 91-94.

————, "The Textual Tradition of Theophilus of Antioch," *Vigiliae Christianae* 6 (1952) 146-159.

————. See also the List of Abbreviations.

Gray, L. H., "The Armenian Acts of the Martyrdom of S. Ignatius of Antioch," *Armenian Quarterly* 1 (1946) 47-66.

Greenslade, S. L. See the List of Abbreviations.

Grégoire, H., "Le peuple de Constantinople ou les Bleus et les Verts," *Comptes-rendus, Académie des inscriptions et belles lettres,* 1946, pp. 568-578. Includes remarks on the circus factions at Antioch.

————, "Sur une inscription d'Antioche," *Byzantion* 13 (1938) 177-179.

————, "Qu'est-ce que le Peistikon?" *Byzantion* 13 (1938) 180-182. On the significance of the term as used in an inscription in the cruciform Church of St. Babylas.

————. See also the List of Abbreviations.

Grierson, P., "The Isaurian Coins of Heraclius," *Num. Chron.* ser. 6, vol. 11 (1951) 56-67. Assigns to the mint of Seleucia Isauriae certain coins which had been attributed to the mint of Antioch.

Griffin, R. P., Jr., "An Early Christian Ivory Plaque in Cyprus and Notes on the Asiatic Ampullae," *Art Bulletin* 20 (1938) 266-279. Includes discussion of an ampulla showing St. John found at Antioch, now in Princeton.

Groag, E. See the List of Abbreviations.

Grundmann, W., "Das Problem des hellenistischen Christentums innerhalb der Jerusalemer Urgemeinde," *ZNTW* 38 (1939) 45-73. Includes discussion of the early Christian community at Antioch.

————, "Die Apostel zwischen Jerusalem und Antiochia," *ZNTW* 39 (1940) 110-137.

Les Guides Bleus, *Syrie, Palestine, Iraq, Transjordanie.* Paris 1932. The best modern guide book of Antioch.

Guidi, I. See the List of Abbreviations.

Guillet, J., "Les exégèses d'Alexandrie et d'Antioche, conflit ou malentendu," *Recherches de science religieuse* 1947, 247-302. On the work and reciprocal relationships of the theological schools of the two cities.

Gwatkin, H. M. See the List of Abbreviations.

Haddad, G., *Aspects of Social Life in Antioch in the Hellenistic-Roman Period.* Diss. Chicago; New York 1949.

Hanfmann, G. M. A., "Notes on the Mosaics from Antioch," *AJA* 43 (1939) 229-246. On the mosaics of Hermes and Dionysus, Eros driving Psyches, and Metiochus and Parthenope (Levi, *Antioch Mosaic Pavements* 1.118-119, 176-178, 287-289).

————, "The Seasons in John of Gaza's *Tabula Mundi*," *Latomus* 3 (1939) 111-118. On the mosaic of Ge and Karpoi (Levi, *Antioch Mosaic Pavements* 1.263-269), with notes on other mosaics.

———, "Socrates and Christ," *Harvard Studies in Classical Philology* 60 (1951) 205-233. Includes discussion of several Antioch mosaics.

———, *The Season Sarcophagus in Dumbarton Oaks*. Cambridge 1951. Discusses a number of Antioch mosaics.

———, "A Masterpiece of Late Roman Glass Painting," *Archaeology* 9 (1956) 3-7. On a painted glass bowl showing the Judgment of Paris, thought to have been made in Antioch.

Hardy, E. R., *Christian Egypt: Church and People. Christianity and Nationalism in the Patriarchate of Alexandria*. New York 1952. Contains observations on the church of Antioch in relation to that of Alexandria.

Harmand, L., *Libanius, Discours sur les patronages [Or. 47], texte, traduit, annoté et commenté*. Paris 1955.

Harnack, A. See the List of Abbreviations.

Harrent, A., *Les écoles d'Antioche*. Paris 1898.

Harrer, G. A., "Was Arrian Governor of Syria," *CP* 11 (1916) 338-339.

———, "Inscriptions of Legati in Syria," *AJA* 36 (1932) 287-289.

———. See also the List of Abbreviations.

Hatay Müzesi kisa kilavuzu. Ankara 1948 (Eski Eserler ve Müzeler Genel Müdürlüğü Yayimlari). A brief guide to the Antioch Museum.

Hefele, K. J. See the List of Abbreviations.

Heichelheim, F. M., "Numismatic Comments, IV: A Sassanian Issue of Antioch at the Time of Trebonianus Gallus," *Hesperia* 16 (1947) 277-278.

———. See also the List of Abbreviations.

Henning, W. B., "The Great Inscription of Sapur I," *Bulletin of the School of Oriental Studies (University of London)* 9 (1937-1939) 823-849. Includes material on the capture of Antioch by Sapor.

Hermann, T., "Patriarch Paul von Antiochia und das alexandrinische Schisma vom Jahre 575," *ZNTW* 27 (1928) 263-304.

———, "Monophysitica," *ZNTW* 32 (1933) 277-293. On the doctrines of Paul of Antioch and his followers.

Herzog-Hauser. See the List of Abbreviations.

Higgins, M. J., *The Persian War of the Emperor Maurice, Part I: The Chronology*. Washington 1939. Includes material on chronology at Antioch.

Hirth, F., *China and the Roman Orient*. Leipzig 1885. Contains Chinese descriptions of Antioch, and accounts of commercial relations between Antioch and China.

Hitti, P. K., *History of the Arabs*. 6th ed. London 1956.

———. See also the List of Abbreviations.

Holleaux, M., "Un prétendu décret d'Antioche sur l'Oronte," *Études d'épigraphie et d'histoire grecques* 2 (Paris 1938) 127-147.

———, *Lagides et Séleucides (Études d'épigraphie et l'histoire grecques*, 3). Paris 1942.

———. See also the List of Abbreviations.

Holmes, T. R. See the List of Abbreviations.

Honigmann, E., "Studien zur Notitia Antiochena," *BZ* 25 (1925) 60-88.

———, "The Calendar Change at Antioch and the Earthquake of 458 A.D.," *Byzantion* 17 (1944-1945) 336-339.

———, "The Patriarchate of Antioch: A Revision of Le Quien and the *Notitia Antiochena,*" *Traditio* 5 (1947) 135-161.

———, "The Lost End of Menander's *Epitrepontes,*" *Académie royale de Belgique, Classe des lettres et des sciences morales et politiques, Mémoires,* 46, fasc. 2 (1950). Deals with events in the history of the church at Antioch in the time St. John Chrysostom and Porphyrius.

———, "Juvenal of Jerusalem," *Dumbarton Oaks Papers* 5 (1950) 209-279. Deals with the transfer of certain bishoprics from the jurisdiction of Antioch to that of Jerusalem.

———, *Le couvent de Barsauma et le patriarcat jacobite de Barsauma et de Syrie.* Louvain 1954 (Corpus Scriptorum Christianorum Orientalium, Subsidia, 7).

———, *Patristic Studies.* Vatican City 1953 (Studi e Testi 173). Cited especially for the chapter "The Monks Symeon, Jacobus and Baradatus," in which their relations with Antioch are described.

———. See also the List of Abbreviations.

Hopkins, C., "Antioch Mosaic Pavements," *Journal of Near Eastern Studies* 7 (1948) 91-97.

Hort, F. J. A. See the List of Abbreviations.

Hüttl, W. See the List of Abbreviations.

Hug, A., *Antiochia und der Aufstand im Jahre 387 n. Chr.* Winterthur 1863, reprinted with some revisions in his *Studien über das klassische Altertum,* 2d ed., 1 (Freiburg-i.-B. 1886) 133-200.

Hugi, L. See the List of Abbreviations.

Jacquot, P. See the List of Abbreviations.

Jalabert, L. See the List of Abbreviations, under *IGLS.*

Jansen, H. L. See the List of Abbreviations.

Jeremias, J., "Die Makkabäer-Kirche in Antiochia," *ZNTW* 40 (1941) 254-255.

Jessen, "Daphnaios," *RE* 4.2135-2136. Deals with the cult of Apollo at Daphne.

Johnson, J., *Dura Studies.* Diss. Pennsylvania; Rome 1931. Includes material on the Seleucid calendar.

Jones, A. H. M., "St. John Chrysostom's Parentage and Education," *HTR* 46 (1953) 171-173.

———. See also the List of Abbreviations.

Judeich, W., *Caesar im Orient.* Leipzig 1885. Includes material on Caesar's visit to Antioch.

Karalevskij, C. See the List of Abbreviations.

Kelly, J. N. D. See the List of Abbreviations.

Kidd, B. J. See the List of Abbreviations.

Kirk, K. E. See the List of Abbreviations.

Kitzinger, E., "The Horse and Lion Tapestry at Dumbarton Oaks," *Dumbarton Oaks Papers* 3 (1946) 1-72. Includes discussion of Antioch mosaics.

Knox, W. L. *The Acts of the Apostles.* Cambridge, Eng., 1948.

——. See also the List of Abbreviations.

Kollwitz, J. "Antiochia am Orontes," *Reallexikon für Antike und Christentum* 1.461-469.

Kraeling, C. H. See the List of Abbreviations.

Krauss, S., "Antioche," *Revue des études juives* 45 (1902) 27-49.

——, "Antioch," *Jewish Encyclopedia* 1.632-633.

Kunkel, W., "Der Process der Gohairiener vor Caracalla," *Festschrift Hans Lewald* (Basel 1953) 81-91. On the preserved minutes of a trial held before Caracalla at Antioch.

Lacroix, L. See the List of Abbreviations.

La Piana, G., "The Byzantine Theatre," *Speculum* 11 (1936) 171-211. Includes material bearing on the theater at Antioch.

Lassus, J., "Fouilles à Antioche," *Gazette des Beaux-Arts,* ser. 6, vol. 9 (1933) 257-272.

——, "Dans les rues d'Antioche," *Institut Français de Damas, Bulletin d'études orientales* 5 (1935) 121-124. Comparison of street scenes in modern Antioch with those shown in the topographical border of the Yakto mosaic.

——, "Les mosaïques d'Antioche," *Comptes-rendus, Académie des inscriptions et belles lettres* 1936, 33-42.

——, "La mosaïque du Phénix provenant des fouilles d'Antioche," *Monuments Piot* 36 (1938) 81-122.

——, *Sanctuaires chrétiens de Syrie: Essai sur la génèse, la forme et l'usage des édifices du culte chrétien en Syrie du III*e *siècle à la conquête musulmane.* Paris 1947. Discusses churches at Antioch.

——, "Le thème de la chasse dans les mosaïques d'Antioche," *Arte del primo millenio. Atti del II*o *Convegno per lo studio dell'arte dell'alto medio evo tenuto presso l'Università di Pavia nel Settembre 1950* (Turin 1953[?]) 141-146.

——. See also the List of Abbreviations.

Lassus, J., and G. Tchalenko, "Ambons syriens," *Cahiers archéologiques* 5 (1951) 75-122. Includes material on the bemas of martyriums at Antioch.

Laurent, V., "Le patriarcat d'Antioche du IV*e* au VII*e* siècle, à propos d'un livre récent," *Revue des études byzantines* 4 (1946) 239-256. Review of Devreesse, *Le patriarcat d'Antioche.*

———, "La Notitia d'Antioche, origine et transmission," *Revue des études byzantines* 5 (1947) 67-89.

Lebon, J., *Le monophysisme sévérien, étude historique, littéraire et théologique sur la résistance monophysite au Concile de Chalcédoine jusqu'à la constitution de l'église jacobite.* Louvain 1909 (Universitas Catholica Lovanensis, Dissertationes, ser. 2, tom. 4).

———, "Ephrem d'Amid, patriarche d'Antioche," *Mélanges Charles Moeller = Université de Louvain, Recueil des travaux*, 40, pt. 1 (1914) 197-214.

———, "La christologie du monophysisme syrien," *Das Konzil von Chalkedon*, ed. by A. Grillmeier and H. Bacht (Würzburg 1951-1954) 1.425-580.

Leclercq, H., "Macchabées," *DACL* 10.724-727. On the Maccabean martyrs at Antioch.

———. See also the List of Abbreviations.

Le Gentilhomme, P., "Le jeu des mutations de l'argent au IIIe siècle. Étude sur l'altération de la monnaie romaine de 215 à 273," *Métaux et civilisation* 1 (1946) 113-137. Includes material on the mint of Antioch.

Lemerle, P., "Aux origines de l'architecture chrétienne; découvertes et théories nouvelles," *RA* ser. 6, vol. 33 (1949) 167-194. Includes discussion of the cruciform church of St. Babylas.

Lepper, F. A. See the List of Abbreviations.

Lesley, P., "An Echo of Early Christianity," *Art Quarterly* 1939, 215-232. Includes discussion of a medallion of St. Symeon Stylites the Younger.

Levi, D., "The Allegories of the Months in Classical Art," *Art Bulletin* 23 (1941) 251-291. Discusses Antioch mosaics showing months.

———, "*Mors voluntaria*: Mystery Cults on Mosaics from Antioch," *Berytus* 7 (1942) 19-55.

———, "Aion," *Hesperia* 13 (1944) 269-314. On a mosaic allegorizing Time (Levi, *Antioch Mosaic Pavements* 1.195-198).

———, "The Novel of Ninus and Semiramis," *Proceedings of the American Philosophical Society* 87 (1944) 420-428. On a mosaic from Daphne illustrating the story of Ninus and Semiramis in a Hellenistic novel.

———, "I mosaici di Antiochia sull'Oronte," *La parola del passato* 2 (1946) 184-196.

———, "Antiochia," *Enciclopedia dell'arte antica* 1 (1958) 421-428.

———. See also the List of Abbreviations.

Liebenam, W. See the List of Abbreviations.

Liebeschuetz, W. "The Syriarch in the Fourth Century," *Historia* 8 (1959) 113-126.

Lietzmann, H., *Das Leben des heiligen Symeon Stylites, mit einer deutschen*

Uebersetzung der Syrischen Lebensbeschreibung und der Briefe von H. Hilgenfeld. Texte und Untersuchungen 32, 4 (1908).

——, "Ioannes Chrysostomus," *RE* 9.1811-1828.

——. See also the List of Abbreviations.

Longden, R. P. See the List of Abbreviations.

Loofs, F. See the List of Abbreviations.

Maas, M., "Die Maccabäer als christliche Heilige," *Monatsschrift für Geschichte und Wissenschaft des Judenthums* 44 (1900) 145-156. On the Maccabean martyrs at Antioch.

Maass, E. See the List of Abbreviations.

Macdonald, G. See the List of Abbreviations.

Macurdy, Grace H., *Hellenistic Queens*. Baltimore 1932.

Magie, D. See the List of Abbreviations.

Mallardo, D., "L'exedra nella basilica cristiana," *Rivista di archeologia cristiana* 22 (1946) 207-211. Includes material on the Great Church and the Church of St. Babylas.

Mansi, J. D. See the List of Abbreviations.

Maricq, A., "La durée du régime des partis populaires à Constantinople," *Bulletin de l'Académie royale de Belgique, Classe des lettres*, ser. 5, vol. 35 (1949) 63-74. Contains material on the factions at Antioch.

Marquardt, J. See the List of Abbreviations.

Mattern, J., *Villes mortes de Haute Syrie*. 2d ed. Beirut 1944. Deals with the relations between Antioch and the regions to the east of it.

Mattingly, H., "The Palmyrene Princes and the Mints of Antioch and Alexandria," *Num. Chron.* ser. 5, vol. 16 (1936) 89-114.

——. See also the List of Abbreviations.

Mattingly, H. B., "The Origin of the Name Christiani," *JTS* N.S. 9 (1958) 26-37.

Maurice, J. "Essai de classification chronologique des émissions monétaires de l'atelier d'Antioche pendant la période constantinienne," *Num. Chron.* ser. 3, vol. 19 (1899) 208-240.

Mazzarino, S. *Aspetti sociali del quarto secolo* (Rome 1951).

McKinney, R. J., and R. Wehrheim, "Restoration of the Mosaics," *Museum Quarterly of the Baltimore Museum of Art* 2 (1937-1938) 5-6. On the Antioch mosaics in the Baltimore Museum of Art.

Mécérian, J., "Monastère de Saint-Symeon-Stylite-le-Jeune: Exposé des fouilles," *Comptes-rendus, Académie des inscriptions et belles lettres*, 1948, 323-328. On the relationship of the two Sts. Symeon Stylites to Antioch; also information on the course of the Roman road between Antioch and Seleucia.

Merlat, P., "Nouvelles images de St. Symeon le Jeune," *Mélanges C. Picard* 2 (1949) = *RA* ser. 6, vol. 31-32 (1949) 720-731. On medallions and a lamp in the Antioch Museum.

Metzger, B. M., "Antioch-on-the-Orontes," *Biblical Archaeologist* 11 (1948) 69-88. An excellent brief account of the history and archaeology of the city.

Meyer, E. See the List of Abbreviations.

Michaelis, D. W., "Judaistische Heidenchristen," *ZNTW* 30 (1931) 83-89. On the question of circumcision in the early church at Antioch.

Michel, C. See the List of Abbreviations.

Michon, E., *Bulletin de la Société nationale des antiquaires de France*, 1899, 208-209. On the statue found at Antioch, identified as Libanius or the Emperor Julian.

Mionnet, T. E. See the List of Abbreviations.

Misson, J., *Recherches sur le paganisme de Libanios*. Louvain 1914.

———, "Libanios et le Christianisme," *Musée belge* 1920, 73-89.

Moeller, C., "Le chalcédonisme et le néochalcédonisme en Orient de 451 à la fin du VIᵉ siècle," *Das Konzil von Chalkedon*, ed. by A. Grillmeier and H. Bacht (Würzburg 1951-1954) 1.637-720.

Moffatt, J., "Ignatius of Antioch: A Study in Personal Religion," *JR* 10 (1930) 169-186.

Monneret de Villard, U., "Antiochia e Milano nel VI secolo," *Orientalia Christiana Periodica* 12 (1946) 374-380.

Monnier, E., *Histoire de Libanius. Première partie, Examen de ses Mémoires depuis sa naissance jusqu'à l'année 355 ap.* Paris 1866.

Moravcsik, G., *Die byzantinischen Quellen der Geschichte der Türkvölker*. Budapest 1942. The bibliography on Malalas (186-189) contains items relating to Antioch.

Moreau, J., "Le nom des Chrétiens," *Nouvelle Clio* 1-2 (1949-1950) 190-192.

Morey, C. R., "The Excavations of Antioch-on-the-Orontes," *Parnassus* 7 (1935) 9-12.

———, "The Excavation of Antioch-on-the-Orontes," *Proceedings of the American Philosophical Society* 76 (1936) 637-651.

———, "Art of the Dark Ages," *Art News*, vol. 35, no. 21 (Feb. 20, 1937) 9-16, 24.

———, "The Antioch Mosaics at Baltimore," *Museum Quarterly of the Baltimore Museum of Art* 2 (1937-1938) 3-5.

———, *Early Christian Art*. 2d ed. Princeton 1953. Includes studies of the Antioch mosaics.

———. See also the List of Abbreviations.

Mouterde, P., "Le Concile de Chalcédoine d'après les historiens monophysites de langue syriaque," *Das Konzil von Chalkedon*, ed. by A. Grillmeier and H. Bacht (Würzburg 1951-1954) 1.581-602.

Mouterde, R., "Reliquiae Antiochenae," *MUSJ* 26 (1944-1946) 39-44. On several sculptured monuments of Antioch.

———. See List of Abbreviations, under Mouterde and *IGLS*.

Mouterde, R., and A. Poidebard, *Le limes de Chalcis*. Paris 1945. Contains a study of the road-system radiating from Antioch.

Müller, C. O. See the List of Abbreviations.

Murphy, G. J. See the List of Abbreviations.

Neale, J. M., *The Patriarchate of Antioch*. London 1873.

Newell, E. T. See the List of Abbreviations.

Nock, A. D., "Early Gentile Christianity and its Hellenistic Background," in: *Essays on the Trinity and the Incarnation*, ed. by A. E. J. Rawlinson (London 1928) 51-156. Deals with the early community at Antioch.

——, "The Praises of Antioch," *Journal of Egyptian Archaeology* 40 (1954) 76-82. Notes on Libanius' encomium of Antioch (*Or.* 11).

Norman, A. F., "Notes on Some Consulares of Syria," *BZ* 51 (1958) 73-77.

Obermann, J. See the List of Abbreviations.

Olmstead, A. T. See the List of Abbreviations.

Pack, R. A., "Curiales in the Correspondence of Libanius," *TAPA* 82 (1951) 176-192.

——, "An Interpretation of Libanius *Epistle* 915," *Classical Weekly* 45 (1951-1952) 38-40. On the career and activities at Antioch of Eustathius, *consularis Syriae* 388-389.

——, "Ammianus Marcellinus and the 'curia' of Antioch," *CP* 48 (1953) 80-85.

——, "An onocephalic mask," *HTR* 48 (1955) 93-96. On the use of such a mask at Antioch as reflecting anti-Christian feeling.

——. See also the List of Abbreviations.

Papadopoulos, Chrysostom A. (Archbishop of Athens), Ἱστορία τῆς Ἐκκλησίας Ἀντιοχείας. Alexandria 1951. Published posthumously.

Paribeni, R., "Sul'origine del nome Cristiano," *Nuovo bullettino di archeologia cristiana* 19 (1913) 37-41.

Parker, H. M. D. See the List of Abbreviations.

Partsch, J., "Der Flächeninhalt von Antiochia," *Archäologischer Anzeiger* 1898, 223-224.

Peeters, P., "La date de la fête de SS. Juventin et Maximin," *Anal. Boll.* 42 (1924) 77-82. On their execution at Antioch in the reign of Julian.

——, "Démétrianus, évêque d'Antioche?" *Anal. Boll.* 42 (1924) 288-314.

——, "La passion de S. Basile d'Epiphanie," *Anal. Boll.* 48 (1930) 302-323. Includes study of the sources for Babylas, Bishop of Antioch.

——, "Un saint hellénisé par annexion: Syméon Stylite," in: *Orient et Byzance: Le tréfonds oriental de l'hagiographie byzantine* (Brussels 1950; Subsidia hagiographica 26) 93-136. Contains studies of the material concerning Antioch to be found in the biographies of Symeon: a revision of the author's earlier article "S. Syméon Stylite et ses premiers biographes," *Anal. Boll.* 61 (1943) 29-71.

Perdrizet, P., "Une inscription d'Antioche qui reproduit un oracle d'Alexandre d'Abonotichos," *Comptes-rendus, Académie des inscriptions et belles lettres* 1903, 62-66.

Perler, O., "Das vierte Makkabaeerbuch, Ignatius von Antiochien und die ältesten Martyrerberichte," *Rivista di archeologia cristiana* 25 (1949) 47-72.

Pervès, M., "La préhistoire de la Syrie et du Liban," *Syria* 25 (1946-1948) 109-129.

Peterson, E., "Christianus," *Miscellanea G. Mercati* 1 (Vatican City 1946; Studi e Testi 121) 355-372. On the origin of the term at Antioch.

Petit, L., *Essai sur la vie et la correspondance du sophiste Libanius.* Paris 1866.

Petit, P., "Sur la date du 'Pro Templis' de Libanius," *Byzantion* 21 (1951) 285-310. Deals with the history of Antioch under Theodosius I.

———, *Les étudiants de Libanius. Un professeur de faculté et ses élèves au Bas Empire.* Paris 1956.

———. See also the List of Abbreviations.

Picard, C., [Note on the mosaic of Megalopsychia], *RA* ser. 6, vol. 18 (1941) 159-163.

Picard, G.-C., "Autour des mosaïques d'Antioche," *RA* ser. 6, vol. 34 (1949) 145-150. A review of Levi, *Antioch Mosaic Pavements.*

Pieper, K., "Antiochien am Orontes im apostolischen Zeitalter," *Theologie und Glaube* 22 (1930) 710-728.

Piganiol, A. See the List of Abbreviations.

Pink, K., "Antioch or Viminacium? A Contribution to the History of Gordian III and Philip I," *Num. Chron.* ser. 5, vol. 15 (1935) 94-113. On the capture of Antioch by the Persians in 241 and the history of the mint during this period.

———, "XI, IA und XII auf Antoninianen," *Numismatische Zeitschrift* 74 (1951) 46-49. On the mint of Antioch under the Emperor Tacitus.

Pirot, L. See the List of Abbreviations.

Platner, S. B. and T. Ashby. See the List of Abbreviations.

Poulsen, F., "Portrait hellénistique du Musée d'Antioche," *Syria* 19 (1938) 355-361. On a male head found in a private house in Antioch in 1936.

Puech, A., *Saint Jean Chrysostome et les moeurs de son temps.* Paris 1891.

Pugliese Carratelli, G., "Res gestae divi Saporis," *La parola del passato* 2 (1947) 209-239; "Ancora sulle Res gestae divi Saporis," *ibid.* 356-362. Contains material on the capture of Antioch by Sapor I.

Rampolla, Cardinal, "Del luogo del martirio e del sepolcro dei Maccabei," *Bessarione* 1 (1896-1897) 655-662, 751-763, 853-866; 2 (1897-1898) 9-22. Reprinted under the same title as a pamphlet (Rome 1917), and published also in French translation, "Martyre et sépulture des Machabées," *Revue de l'art chrétien* 48 (1899) 290-305, 377-392, 457-465.

Reinach, S. See the List of Abbreviations.

Reinhold, M. See the List of Abbreviations.

Reusch, W. See the List of Abbreviations.

Richardson, C. C., *The Christianity of Ignatius of Antioch*. New York 1935.

——, "The Church in Ignatius of Antioch," *JR* 17 (1937) 428-443.

Richter, G. M. A. See the List of Abbreviations.

Riddle, D. W., "Environment as a Factor in the Achievement of Self-Consciousness in Early Christianity," *JR* 7 (1927) 46-63. Includes study of the community at Antioch.

Riedmatten, H. de. See the List of Abbreviations.

Robert, C. See the List of Abbreviations.

Robert, L., "Contribution à la topographie de villes de l'Asie Mineure méridionale," *Comptes-rendus, Académie des inscriptions et belles lettres* 1951, 255-256. On a newly discovered inscription recording the construction of a canal at Antioch in A.D. 73-74.

Robertson, D. S. See the List of Abbreviations.

Rorimer, J., "The Authenticity of the Chalice of Antioch," *Studies in Art and Literature for Belle Da Costa Greene* (Princeton 1954) 161-168.

Ross, Marvin C., "A Small Byzantine Treasure Found at Antioch-on-the-Orontes," *Archaeology* 5 (1952) 30-32. First publication of a silver candlestick and three gold ornaments found in the excavations in 1938.

——, "A Silver Treasure from Daphne-Harbie," *Archaeology* 6 (1953) 39-41.

——. See also Walters Art Gallery.

Rostovtzeff, M., *"Karpoi,"* *Mélanges d'études anciennes offerts à G. Radet* = *REA* 42 (1940) 508-514. Includes discussion of the mosaic of Ge and Karpoi (Levi, *Antioch Mosaic Pavements* 1.263-269).

——. See also the List of Abbreviations.

Roussel, P., and F. de Visscher, "Les inscriptions du temple de Dmeir," *Syria* 23 (1942-1943) 173-200. Includes an inscription recording a hearing held before Caracalla at Antioch in a dispute over a priesthood at Dmeir.

Rubin, B., *Prokopios von Kaisareia*. Stuttgart, n.d. (1954?). A reprint with additions of the article "Prokopios" in *RE*. Contains commentary on Procopius' references to Antioch.

Rüsch, T., *Die Entstehung der Lehre vom Heiligen Geist bei Ignatius von Antiochia, Theophilus von Antiochia und Irenäus von Lyon*. Zürich 1952.

Sauvaget, J. See the List of Abbreviations.

Schemmel, F., "Der Sophist Libanius als Schüler und Lehrer," *Neue Jahrbücher für das klassische Altertum und für Pädagogik* 20 (1907) 52-69.

——, "Die Schule von Karthago," *PhW* 1927, 1342-1344. Contains material on Antioch.

Schenck, E. C., "The Hermes Mosaic from Antioch," *AJA* 41 (1937) 388-396.

————, "Mosaic from Daphne," *Honolulu Academy of Arts Bulletin* 6 (1938) 35-44. On a mosaic showing animals (Levi, *Antioch Mosaic Pavements* 1.365).

Schmidt, J., and E. Honigmann, "Orontes," *RE* 18, pt. 1, 1160-1164.

Schürer, E. See the List of Abbreviations.

Schultze, V. See the List of Abbreviations.

Schwabe, M. See the List of Abbreviations.

Schwartz, E., "Zur Kirchengeschichte des vierten Jahrhunderts," *ZNTW* 34 (1935) 129-213. Includes material on the schism of Antioch.

Seeberg, E., *Die Synode von Antiochien im Jahre 324/25.* Berlin 1913.

Seeck, O., "Libanius gegen Lucianus," *Rh. Mus.* 73 (1924) 84-101. A commentary on Libanius *Or.* 56, having to do with the career of the *comes Orientis* Lucianus (A.D. 392).

————. See also the List of Abbreviations.

Seippel, G., *Der Tryphonmythus.* Greifswald 1939. Includes material on Tryphon at Antioch.

Sellers, R. V. See the List of Abbreviations.

Seyrig, H., "Monuments syriens du culte de Némésis (Antiquités syriennes, 1)," *Syria* 13 (1932) 50-64. Discusses cult of Nemesis at Daphne.

————, "Notes archéologiques, 1: Megalopsychia; 2, Sur le style de la mosaïque de Yakto," *Berytus* 2 (1935) 42-47.

————, "Note sur Hérodien, prince de Palmyre," *Syria* 18 (1937) 1-4. On lead tokens of Herodian and Zenobia struck at Antioch.

————, [A funerary inscription of Antioch], *Syria* 20 (1939) 314.

————, "Les rois Séleucides et la concession de l'asylie," *Syria* 20 (1939) 35-39.

————, "Scène historique sur un chapiteau du Musée de Beyrouth," *Mélanges d'études anciennes offerts à G. Radet = REA* 42 (1940) 340-344. A scene of figures grouped about an altar is interpreted as the sacrifice to Zeus which preceded the foundation of Antioch.

————, "Le casque d'Emèse," *Annales archéologiques de Syrie* 2 (1952) 101-108. The author suggests that the helmet was made in Antioch.

————. See also the List of Abbreviations.

Sievers, G. R. See the List of Abbreviations.

Simon, M., "La politique anti-juive de S. Jean Chrysostome et le mouvement judaïsant d'Antioche," *Mélanges F. Cumont = Université libre de Bruxelles, Annuaire de l'Institut de philologie et d'histoire orientales et slaves* 4 (1936) 403-421.

————. See also the List of Abbreviations.

Sjöqvist, E., "Kaisareion. A Study in Architectural Iconography," *Opuscula Romana, 1, edidit Institutum Romanum Regni Sueciae; Acta Instituti Romani Regni Sueciae,* series in 4°, 18 (1954) 86-108. Includes a study of the Kaisareion at Antioch.

Smith, E. B. See the List of Abbreviations.

Spinka, M., *The Chronicle of John Malalas, Books 8-18, translated from the Church Slavonic by M. Spinka in collaboration with G. Downey*. Chicago 1940.

Sprengling, M., *Third Century Iran, Sapor and Kartir*. Prepared and distributed at the Oriental Institute, University of Chicago, 1953. Text volume and separate plates. The text of the *Res gestae divi Saporis*. Specially distributed, not available through booksellers.

Srawley, J. H., "Antiochene Theology," Hastings, *Enc. Rel. Eth.* 1.584-593.

Starcky, J. See the List of Abbreviations.

Starr, J., "Byzantine Jewry on the Eve of the Arab Conquest (565-638)," *Journal of the Palestine Oriental Society* 15 (1935) 280-293. Includes notes on the Jewish community at Antioch.

Stauffenberg, A. Schenk von. See the List of Abbreviations.

Stein, E. See the List of Abbreviations.

Stevenson, J. See the List of Abbreviations.

Stinespring, W. F., *The Description of Antioch in Codex Vaticanus Arabicus 286*. Diss., Yale University 1932, unpublished.

Strauss, P., "Un sou d'or inédit de Constantin II Auguste," *Rev. num.* ser. 5, vol. 10 (1947-1948) 127-131. On a coin struck at Antioch.

Streck, "Antakiya," *Encyclopaedia of Islam* 1.359-361.

Streeter, B. H. See the List of Abbreviations.

Strong, E., "Terra Mater or Italia?" *JRS* 27 (1937) 114-126. Includes discussion of the mosaic of Ge and Karpoi (Levi, *Antioch Mosaic Pavements* 1.263-269).

Strzygowski, J., "Antiochenische Kunst," *Oriens Christianus* 2 (1902) 421-433.

Syme, R. See the List of Abbreviations.

Tarn, W. W., and G. T. Griffith. See the List of Abbreviations.

Taylor, F. H., "Antioch: Its Significance for Worcester," *Worcester Art Museum Annual* 2 (1936-1937) 13-24.

Tchalenko, G. See the List of Abbreviations.

Telfer, W., "The *Didache* and the Apostolic Synod of Antioch," *JTS* 40 (1939) 133-146, 258-271.

Tenney, M. C., "The Influence of Antioch on Apostolic Christianity," *Bibliotheca Sacra* 107 (1950) 298-310.

Ternant, P., "La *theoria* d'Antioche dans le cadre des sens de l'Écriture," *Biblica* 34 (1953) 135-158, 354-383, 456-486.

Theocharides, G. J., *Beiträge zur Geschichte des byzantinischen Profantheaters im 4. u. 5. Jh. hauptsächlich auf Grund der Predigten des Johannes Chrysostomus (Laographia, Parartema 3)*. Diss. Munich 1940.

Thompson, E. A. See the List of Abbreviations.

Tondriau, J. See the List of Abbreviations.

Bibliography

Toynbee, J. M. C., "Some Notes on Artists in the Roman World, 3: Painters," *Latomus* 9 (1950) 175-182. Includes notes on landscape painters at Antioch.

——. See also the List of Abbreviations.

Tscherikower, V. See the List of Abbreviations.

Vacca, V., G. Levi della Vida, C. Korolevskij, C. Cecchelli, "Antiochia," *Enciclopedia italiana* 3.507-513.

Vailhé, S., "Antioche, patriarcat grec," *Dictionnaire de théologie catholique* 1, pt. 2, 1399-1416; "Antioche, patriarcat grec-melkite," *ibid.* 1416-1420; "Antioche, patriarcat latin," *ibid.* 1420-1425; "Antioche, patriarcat jacobite," *ibid.* 1425-1430; "Antioche, patriarcat syrien-catholique," *ibid.* 1430-1433.

Vandenberghe, B. H., "Saint Jean Chrysostome et les spectacles," *Zeitschrift für Religions- und Geitesgeschichte* 7 (1955) 34-46.

Van den Ven, P., "A propos de la Vie de S. Syméon Stylite le jeune," *Mélanges P. Peeters* 1 = *Anal. Boll.* 67 (1949) 425-443.

Van Sickle, C. E. See the List of Abbreviations.

Vasiliev, A. A., "The Monument of Porphyrius in the Hippodrome at Constantinople," *Dumbarton Oaks Papers* 4 (1948) 27-49. Includes material on Calliopas the charioteer of Antioch, and on anti-Jewish disorders in the city.

——. See also the List of Abbreviations.

Voetter, O., "Die Münzen des Kaisers Gallienus und seiner Familie," *Numismatische Zeitschrift* 33 (1901) 84-85. On coins of Macrianus the Younger and Quietus issued at Antioch.

Volbach, W. F., "Ein antiochenischer Silberfund," *Germania* 2 (1918) 23.

——, "Spätantike syrische Silberarbeiten," *Archäologischer Anzeiger* 1920, 94.

——, "Der Silberschatz von Antiochia," *Zeitschrift für bildende Kunst* 56 (1921) 110-113.

Volkmann, H., "Zur Münzprägung des Demetrios I. und Alexander I. von Syrien," *Zeitschrift für Numismatik* 34 (1924) 51-66.

Walden, J. W. H., *The Universities of Ancient Greece.* New York 1909. Includes an account of Libanius' school at Antioch, with translations of passages in Libanius illustrating the conduct of the school.

Walters Art Gallery, *Early Christian and Byzantine Art, an Exhibition Held at the Baltimore Museum of Art April 25—June 22.* Baltimore 1947. Edited by M. C. Ross. Includes mosaics and sculpture from Antioch.

Watson, J., "Tigris Personified, a Mosaic at the Detroit Institute," *Magazine of Art* 34 (1941) 41. Brief notice of mosaic showing personification of Tigris (Levi, *Antioch Mosaic Pavements* 1.57-59).

Weber, W. See the List of Abbreviations.

Bibliography

Welles, C. B., "The Greek City," *Studi in Onore di Aristide Calderini e Roberto Paribeni* (Milan 1956) 81-99.

———. See also the List of Abbreviations.

Wenger, L., "Ein Prozess vor Caracalla in Syrien," *Université libre de Bruxelles, Annuaire de l'Institut de philologie et d'histoire orientales et slaves* 11 (1951) 469-504. On an inscription recording a hearing before Caracalla in Antioch.

West, L. C. See the List of Abbreviations.

Weulersse, J. See the List of Abbreviations.

Wilber, D. N., "Iranian Motifs in Syrian Art," *Bulletin of the American Institute for Iranian Art and Archaeology* 5 (1937) 22-26. Discusses Iranian motifs in Antioch mosaics.

Wolf, K., "Ioannes Malalas," *RE* 9.1795-1799.

Wolf, P., *Vom Schulwesen der Spätantike. Studien zu Libanius.* Baden-Baden 1952.

Woolley, L., *A Forgotten Kingdom, being a Record of the Results Obtained from the Excavation of Two Mounds, Atchana and al Mina, in the Turkish Hatay.* London, Penguin Books, 1953. A general account of the plain of Antioch in pre-Macedonian times.

———. See also the List of Abbreviations.

Worcester Art Museum, *The Dark Ages: Catalogue of the Loan Exhibition of Pagan and Christian Art in the Latin West and Byzantine East, 20 February—21 March 1937.* Worcester 1937. Includes mosaics and sculpture from Antioch.

Wruck, W. See the List of Abbreviations.

Wycherley, R. E. See the List of Abbreviations.

Zahn, T., *Cyprian von Antiochien und die deutsche Faustsage.* Erlangen 1882.

CHRONOLOGY

Since Antioch, in addition to being besieged and captured several times, suffered from a number of earthquakes, it has seemed useful to provide a list of the disasters that were significant in the city's physical history. References in the text to these disasters may be found in the Index under Earthquakes; Fires; Sieges. The list of rulers (Seleucid kings and Roman emperors) is provided for convenience. The epithets of the Seleucid rulers are omitted in order to save space, and it is to be noted that the chronology of the last Seleucid kings is sometimes uncertain (for details see Ch. 6). This list includes usurpers during the Roman period only if they played a part in the city's history. Lists of Roman governors of Syria, of the *comites Orientis* and *consulares Syriae*, and of the bishops and patriarchs may be found in the Index under Bishops; Comites Orientis; Consulares Syriae; Syria, Governors.

B.C.		B.C.	
300 (April)	Foundation of Seleucia Pieria		
(May)	Foundation of Antioch		
281/0	Death of Seleucus I		
281/0—261	Antiochus I		
261—247/6	Antiochus II		
246—226	Seleucus II		
246—244	Occupation of Antioch by the Egyptians		
226—223	Seleucus III		
223—187	Antiochus III		
187—175	Seleucus IV		
175—163	Antiochus IV		
163—162	Antiochus V		
162—150	Demetrius I		
150—145	Alexander I	148 (?)	Earthquake
145—139	Demetrius II	145	City burned and plundered in warfare of Seleucid rivals
145—142/1	Antiochus VI		
142/1—138	Tryphon		
138—129	Antiochus VII	130 (?)	Earthquake
128—127/6	Demetrius II (second reign)		
128—123	Alexander II		
125—121	Cleopatra and Antiochus VIII		
121—96	Antiochus VIII	112	Siege of city by Antiochus VIII
114—95	Antiochus IX		
96/5—88	Demetrius III		

Chronology

B.C.   B.C.

96—95	Seleucus VI	
95—92	Antiochus X	
94—93	Antiochus XI	
88—84/3	Philip I	
87—84	Antiochus XII	
	Philip II	
	Antiochus XIII	
83—69	Occupation of Syria by Tigranes	Between 83 and 69 Earthquake
69/8	Antiochus XIII	
67/6 and 66/5	Philip II	
65/4	Antiochus XIII	
64	Beginning of Roman occupation under Pompey	
		51 Siege of Antioch by the Parthians
47—41	Cassius and Antony in Syria	
40—39	Occupation of Antioch by the Parthians	
31 B.C.—A.D. 14	Augustus	
A.D. 14—37	Tiberius	A.D. 23/24 Fire
37—41	Gaius (Caligula)	37 Earthquake
41—54	Claudius	Between 41 and 54 Earthquake
54—68	Nero	
68—69	Galba, Otho, Vitellius	
69—79	Vespasian	70 Fire
79—81	Titus	
81—96	Domitian	
96—98	Nerva	
98—117	Trajan	115 Earthquake
117—138	Hadrian	
138—161	Antoninus Pius	Between 138 and 161 Fire
161—180	Marcus Aurelius	
	161—169 Lucius Verus	
180—192	Commodus	
193—194	Pertinax, Didius Julianus, Pescennius Niger	
193—211	Septimius Severus	
211—217	Caracalla	
217—218	Macrinus	
218—222	Elagabalus	
222—235	Severus Alexander	
235—238	Maximinus	

Chronology

Chronology

Index

Arcadius, emperor, 427, 429, 437ff
Archias, poet, 129
archives, 204, 629
Ardaburius, *mag. mil. per Or.*, 471f, 481. *See also* baths
Ares, temple, 384, 395 n. 90; in Seleucid period, 196; position, 154, 215f, 618; on Forum of Valens, 404; converted into *macellum*, 406, 632f; Ares and Artemis, festival, 196 n. 144
Argives, settled on Mt. Silpius, 50
Argyrius, senator, 435, 690
Arianism, 457f; Paul of Samosata, 312; Lucian of Antioch and his pupils, 338-41; under Constantius, 350ff, 357ff, 369ff; under Julian, 380f, 396; under Valens, 410f; restoration of orthodoxy, 414f; affinity of Arians, pagans and Jews, 447
Aristarchus, physician, 642
army, size of, 538 n. 155; forces in Syria, A.D. 540, 535ff; horses, pasturage, 439; troops: Celts, 385; Christians, 330f; *Herculiani*, 392; *Joviani*, 392; *Petulantes*, 385; Seleucid army, 118, 125f. *See also* military affairs
Arsane, Persian queen, 318
Artabanios, Syriarch and Alytarch, 232f
Artemidorus, philosopher, 210
Artemis, temple, 196; temple and cult in Meroë, 632ff, 681-88; temple built by Queen Meroë, 687; temple in Daphne, 86, 131, 218; statue, 88, 131; called Eleusinia, 88. *See also* Apollo, Ares
Artemius, martyr, 397
Asabinos, Jewish curialis, 237, 633; synagogue named for him, 499
Asclepas of Gaza, 352
Asclepiades, bishop, 303, 305
Asclepiades, philosopher, 388
Asclepiodotus, *ppo.* 460f
Asclepius, bishop of Edessa, 521
Asclepius, temple, 208
Assyrians at future site of Antioch, 48f
Asterius, 511 n. 35
Asterius, *com. Or.*, 435 n. 137; 566f, 569
Asterius, *patricius*, 524
Asterius the Sophist, 340
Athanasius, bishop of Perre, 467
Athanasius, St., 353; at Antioch, 361, 399
Athanasius, *oikonomos*, 455
Athanasius, Jacobite patriarch, 576f
Athanasius of Anazarbus, 340
Athena: temple, 233, 404, 633ff; statue, 76, 151; on coins, 77
Athenian settlers in Antioch, 79f, 451
Athens: Antiochene merchant in, 132; paganism in, 558f
Athla, locality or building, 454
Attaeus, and foundation of Antioch, 35
Augustus, emperor, 158f, 161, 163ff; cult of, at Antioch, 167
Aurelian, emperor, 261, 265ff
aurum coronarium, 426f
Avidius Cassius, 226ff

Babylas, St., bishop, 253, 271 n. 178; 305ff; martyrium at Daphne, 364, 387; church at Antioch, 415ff, 434, 455; cult at Milan, 525
Badia y Leblich, D., traveler, 676
Ballista, *see* Callistus
balsam, produced near Antioch, 516 n. 58
Barker, J., traveler, 670
Barlaam, martyr, 332. *See also* churches
Barnabas, St., 274ff, 296; and ecclesiastical status of Cyprus, 497
Barrès, M., traveler, 679
Bartlett, W. H., traveler, 671
Basil, bishop of Caesarea, 413
Basil the Merchant, traveler, 674
basilica: of Anatolius, 454, 526, 626, 627 n. 8; of Julius Caesar, *see* Kaisarion; of Rufinus, 349f, 434, 506f, 525, 622f, 625, 627, 631, 650-53; of Valens, 406; of Zenodotus, 507, 624, 631; of Zoilus, 625, 631; meaning of term, 406 n. 57
Basilides, Gnostic teacher, 291
Basiliscus, presbyter, 558 n. 238
Basiliscus, usurper, 488ff
Basilius of Edessa, *com. Or.*, 506, 623
baths, 155, 325; of Adonis (?), 520 n. 76; of Agrippa, 171; Centenarium, 229; of Commodus, 233, 237, 404f, 435, 633f, 663; of Diocletian, 324; of Domitian, 208; of Hadrian, 221, 478; of Hellebichus, 432; of Justinian, 525; Livianum, 242; of Medea, 208; of Olbia, 506, 623, 631; of Philip, 135 n. 78; 141 n. 108; 348, 622; "Senatorial," 325; of Septimius Severus, 242, 478; "of the Syrian nation," 520 n. 76; of Tiberius, 182; of Trajan, 212, 223, 478; of Urbicius, 635; of Valens, 410, 451, 453; Variae, Varium, 167 n. 25; 192; bath near palace, 478; "Bath F" restored A.D. 537/8, 533; private bath of Ardaburius, 472, 659; designed for use in summer and winter, 568; cost of heating, 243
Baumann, E., traveler, 679
Beadle, traveler, 677
Beaufort, Emily A., traveler, 673
Belgiojoso, Princess Barbiano di, traveler, 677
Belisarius, *mag. mil. per Or.*, 530
Bell, Gertrude L., traveler, 679
Belon, P., traveler, 666
Berchem, M. van, visit to Antioch, 678
Berenice, wife of Antiochus II, 87ff, 642f
Berggren, J., traveler, 676
Bernice, martyr, 332
Bertrandon de la Brocquière, traveler, 666
Bible, Lucian's recension, 338
Biddulph, W., traveler, 674
bishops and patriarchs, *see* Acacius, Alexander, Anastasius, Asclepiades, Babylas, Calandio, Cornelius, Cyril, Demetrianus, Domninus, Domnus I and II, Ephraemius, Eros, Eudoxius, Eulalius, Euphrasius, Euphronius, Eustathius, Euzoius, Evagrius, Evodius, Fabius, Flavian I and II, Gregory, Heron, Ignatius, John I and II, Julian, Leontius, Martyrius, Maximinus, Palladius, Paulinus I and II,

Index

[741]

Index

Index

Euphemia, St., *see* churches
Euphorion of Chalcis, 37, 94
Euphrasius, patriarch, 519, 521, 526
Euphrates of Tyre, 210
Euphronius, bishop, 352f
Euprepius, *see* monastery
Eusebius of Caesarea, 352
Eusebius of Nicomedia, 340
Eusignius, martyr (?), 393
Eustathius, bishop, 351f, 414, 492; his followers, 396, 412, 457
Eustathius, *cons. Syr.*, 424f, 440 n. 157
Eustolion, martyr, 341
Eutolmius Tatianus, Fl., *cons. Syr.* and *com. Or.*, 329 n. 51; 442
Eutropius, *cons. Syr.*, 425
Eutychides of Sicyon, sculptor, 73
Euzoius, bishop, 370, 396, 410
Evagrius, bishop, 417
Evagrius, historian, 43f, 557, 566f
Evagrius, presbyter, 413
Evaris, built Church of Archangel Michael, 545 n. 183
Evodius, bishop, 200, 283ff, 296, 584ff
exaeron, meaning, 154 n. 57
exedrai of a church, 343f

Fabius, bishop, 308
Fabius Agrippinus, governor of Syria, 250
famines: under Claudius, 195f; A.D. 313, 334; A.D. 324, 336f; A.D. 333, 354; A.D. 362, 383ff, 386ff; A.D. 381/2, 419ff; A.D. 384, 420; A.D. 431, 456; A.D. 500/1, 514; threatened famine, A.D. 354, 365ff
Fatio, E., visit to Antioch, 678
Faustina, wife of Constantius, 372
Felicianus, *com. Or.*, 355, 622, 650
Felix, *com. sacr. larg.*, 388, 393
festivals: games of Antiochus IV, 97f; of Antiochus VIII, 128; of Eucrates, 168; in honor of Hadrian, 222f; in honor of Commodus, 223 n. 104; 235; others, names unknown, 168f, 225, 226 n. 122. *See also* Maiuma, Olympic Games
fires: 145 B.C., 123; A.D. 23/4, 133, 175, 185f, 622; A.D. 70, 204; between A.D. 138 and 161, 224; reign of Zeno, 499; A.D. 507, 506f; A.D. 525, 520
Flavian I, bishop, 363, 411, 416f, 428, 430, 432f
Flavian II, bishop, 508ff
Flavius . . . , *com. Or.*, 533 n. 139
Florentius, *cons. Syr.*, 425
Förster, R., visit to Antioch, 605, 611, 673
food supply, 21-23, 365, 376ff, 389ff; grain storage, 72, 324; prices, 336f; crops ruined by weevils, 571
forums, 624ff; Forum of Valens, 29, 154, 215, 403ff, 435, 443, 498f, 520, 551, 618, 626ff, 632-40, 654; shown in mosaic, 663
Fossey, C., visit to Antioch, 673
foundation of Antioch, 54ff; ancient accounts,

35ff, 56ff; depicted on column capital, 67 n. 55
Fuller, J., traveler, 676

Gaius, emperor, 187, 190ff
Galba, emperor, 202f
Galerius, emperor, 318, 329, 331ff; serves as Alytarch, 326; arch of, at Thessalonica, 318, 321
Gallienus, emperor, 262
Gallus, Caesar, 359, 362ff
Gamaliel V, Jewish patriarch, 382
Garrett, R., visit to Antioch, 678
GATES, 16-17
Beroea, on road to, 610; shown in mosaic, 662
Bull Gate, Porta Tauriana, 347f, 434, 619f; shown in mosaic, 663
Cherubim Gate, 224, 554, 614f, 616, 620
Daphnetic Gate, 90, 206, 293, 543, 554f, 608, 610, 612-13; also called Golden Gate, 452f, 615f
Eastern Gate, 181f, 208, 609, 618f
"Gate of Syria," 555
Julian, St., Gate of, in suburbs, 523, 621
Middle Gate, 215, 404, 407, 618f, 633f
Philonauta Gate, 453, 612, 617
Romanesian Gate, 76, 411 n. 83
Seleucia Pieria, gate leading to, 617
Tripylon, gate at the, 621
Gaza, literary school, 8
Geminus, presbyter, 306
Genius of the Roman people, temple, 392
George, bishop of Alexandria, 395f
Germanicus, 175, 190, 197; death, 186ff; monument, 629 n. 17
Germanus, relative of Justinian, 535ff
gerousia, 82
Geta, emperor, 243
gladiators, 97, 161, 226 n. 122; 407f, 443, 446
glass, 84 n. 140
Glycerius, martyr, 341
Gnosticism, 288ff
gold, supply of, 390
goldsmith work, 22, 98
Gordian III, emperor, 253
Gorgonius, chamberlain, 358f, 362f
Goujon, J., traveler, 675
grammateia, 128
grammatophylakion, 101, 204, 629
Granius, Lucius, 135f
Gratianus, emperor, 414ff
Greek settlers on future site of Antioch, 49-53
Gregory, patriarch, 43, 455 n. 22; 561ff, 566ff, 570f
Griffiths, J., traveler, 675
guest-houses, 349, 525; built by Constantine, 622, 650; built by Justinian, 553; maintained by church, 531
guilds, 196 n. 45
Guys, H., traveler, 672
gymnasia, 128; students of, 90

Index

Index

Julian, *a secretis*, 537ff
Julian, bishop, 487f
Julian, *com. Or.*, 381, 385 n. 28; 388, 392f
Julius Caesar, C., at Antioch, 151ff; statue, 154, 404, 663. *See also* Kaisarion
Julius Caesar, Sextus, 158
Julius Saturninus, 270 n. 175; 271
Jupiter Capitolinus, temple, 100, 103ff, 179
Justin I, emperor, 513ff
Justin II, emperor, 560ff
Justina, St., *see* churches
Justinian the Great, emperor, 526ff; gifts to Antioch, 525, 531
Justinian, supporter of Illus and Leontius, 490f, 495
Juvenal, bishop of Jerusalem, 465, 472ff
Juventinus, officer under Julian, 392f

Kaineus, 90
Kaisarion, 231, 632-40; location, 29, 196, 215, 237; construction, 154; on Forum of Valens, 404f, 407
Kasiotis, on Mt. Silpius, 50
Kasos of Crete, legend, 50
Kerateion, 516 n. 58; 554f; location, 544, 552, 555, 614f, 620; Jewish quarter, 544 n. 179. *See also* churches
Kinneir, J. M., traveler, 610, 676
Koinon of Syria, 218; games, 214 n. 60; amalgamated with Olympic Games, 168 n. 31; 209, 440f; Syriarch, 232
Kolonisios, statue called, 624
Kottanas (Kotys?), general, 573
Kottomanes, *see* Kouttoules
Kotys, *see* Kottanas
Kouttoules (Kottomanes?), supporter of Illus, 490f
Kronos, temple, 51
kynegion, 407ff, 443, 446
Kyriades, *see* Mariades

Laborde, A. de, traveler, 670
Ladon, father of Daphne, 84
Lammens, H., visit to Antioch, 678
Laodice, wife of Antiochus II, 87f, 90
Laodicea-on-the-Sea, 54, 79; rivalry with Antioch, 238ff, 397; Antioch made a *kome* of Laodicea, 241, 430f
Lasthenes, mercenary leader, 122
law-courts, 427, 454, 625-28, 631
Leandro di S. Cecilia, traveler, 667
Le Camus, E., traveler, 606, 611, 678
Leios, seer, 104
Leo I, emperor, 476ff, 482
Leo II, emperor, 487
Leontius, bishop, 340, 363, 369
Leontius, house of, 660
Leontius, St., *see* churches
Leontius, usurper, 490ff
Libanius, 382, 384, 408f; as source for history of Antioch, 40-42; account of foundation, 57ff; relations with Gallus, 366f; his picture of Antioch, 373-79; role under Julian, 391, 395; *alektromanteia*, 401; taught John

Chrysostom and Theodore of Mopsuestia, 413, 421, 461; in reign of Theodosius I, 420-31, 434; and enlargement of Plethrion, 435f
libertas, of Antioch, 145, 152f
libraries: in Seleucid period, 94, 132f; library founded by Julian, 395f, 398
Licinius, 332, 334ff
Licinius Crassus, M., governor of Syria, 149
Licinius Mucianus, C., governor of Syria, 200, 203, 205
liturgical vessels, 359, 388, 468
Lucas, P., traveler, 675
Lucian of Antioch, 315f, 327f, 334, 337
Lucianus, *cons. Syr.* and *com. Or.*, 424, 433f, 651
Lucifer of Calaris, 397
Lucilla, wife of Ti. Claudius Pompeianus, 228
Lucius Verus, emperor, 225ff
Luke, St., 277
Lurius Varius, 191ff
Luscus, *curator*, 367, 368 n. 236
Lycklama à Nijeholt, T. M., traveler, 673
Lysias, minister of Antiochus IV, 119

Macarius, patriarch, visit to Antioch (1652), 675
Maccabees: martyrs, 109-11; tomb and Christian cult, 448. *See also* churches
Macedonian political institutions, 112f
Macedonian settlers in Antioch, 79f
Macedonius, holy man, 432, 545 n. 180
macellum, 215f, 406f, 632f
Macrianus, emperor, 262ff
Macrinus, emperor, 247ff
Magadates, viceroy of Tigranes, 137f
magister militum, praetorium, 431, 454, 494f, 520, 625-27, 631. *See also* army
Magnentius, revolt of, 362
Maiuma, 234, 444, 456
Majorinus, house of, 660
Malalas, Ioannes, chronicler, as source for history of Antioch, 37-40; account of foundation, 56ff
Malchion, presbyter, 264 n. 152; 314
Mammianus, senator, 501f
Mangles, J., traveler, 676
Μαρατώ, κώμη, 658
Marcianus, 471ff
Marcion, heretic, 291
Marcius Philippus, L., governor of Syria, 147
Marcius Rex, Q., 73, 140f, 641, 648ff
Marcus Aurelius, emperor, 225ff
Mariades, traitor, 254ff, 261, 311, 590, 592
Marinus, *tractator*, 514
Maris of Chalcedon, 340
Mark, companion of St. Paul, 281
Maron, merchant, 132f, 622
Maronis hortum, 516 n. 58
Marsus, supporter of Illus, 490f
Martha, mother of St. Symeon Stylites the Younger, 555
Martius Verus, 226, 228
Martyrius, bishop, 482, 485ff

Index

Matronianus, supporter of Illus, 490f
Matthew, Gospel according to St., 282f
Maurice, emperor, 562, 566ff
Maxentius, emperor, 334
Maximian, emperor, statue, 319 n. 11; 398
Maximilianus, Christian soldier, 392
Maximinus, bishop, 301, 303
Maximinus, governor of Syria, 269
Maximinus, officer under Julian, 392f
Maximinus Daia, emperor, 331ff
Maximus, bishop, 463, 470ff, 585
Maximus, bishop of Seleucia in Isauria, 413
Medea, statue, 208
Medusa head, 50 n. 18
Megas, bishop of Beroea, 536ff
Meletius, bishop, 370, 392, 396, 399, 410, 413ff; his followers, 411f
Memnonius, *cons. Syr.* or *com. Or.*, 453, 625
Menaen, "companion" of Herod, 279
Menander, Gnostic teacher, 290f
Menander, poet, 445
Menas of Byzantium, *nykteparchos*, 506, 623f
Meroë, wife of Cambyses, 49, 687
Meroë, suburb, 481; Temple of Artemis, 48f, 687f
Messalian heresy, 417
metropolis, title of Antioch, 145, 153, 159
Michael, Archangel, *see* churches
military affairs, Antioch as military center, 353-56, 378, 383, and headquarters of *magister militum per Orientem*, 430f, 454, 472, 484f, 490, 508f, 530, 626; arms factories at Antioch, 204, 324, 367, 402, 439; disaffection under Julian, 392; mutiny under Maurice, 567-69; Seleucia Pieria as military port, 361; revolt of Eugenius, 330f. *See also* army
militia, in Seleucid period, 114, 116, 118; A.D. 540, 543f
al-Mina, 47f, 52f, 66
ministry, Christian, 294ff
mint, Seleucid, 58, 87, 113, 130, 134f, 138; under Tigranes, 138f; under Roman Republic, 143ff, 147ff, 153, 160; under Roman Empire, 165ff, 188, 190, 201; moved to Emesa, 257f, 588, 593f; work suspended, 260; report of rebellion of mint workers, 266 n. 158; reorganized under Diocletian, 324; inactive under Heraclius, 575 n. 46
Molatzes, general, 542
Molon, revolt of, 117
monastery, of Diodorus and Carterus, 363; of Euprepius, 465; of Rufinus, 658; of Theodosius, 658
Monconys, traveler, 667
monomacheion, 156, 408ff, 443, 446, 453
Monophysitism, origin, 474f; under Peter the Fuller, 485ff; Monophysitism and factional disorders, 498, 504ff, 515ff, 571; accession of Severus, 507ff; decline in power, 515ff; suppression, 527ff, 565; separatist movement, 534, 546, 571; outbreak under Phocas, 573f; under Heraclius, 576f
Monro, V., traveler, 677

Montfort, A.-A., traveler and artist, 671f
Montius, *quaestor*, 367, 368 n. 236
Moon, statue, 206, 619
Morgan, H. B., traveler, 672f
mosaics, 32-35; pagan subjects, 492; topographical mosaic, 659-64
al-Mundhir, Saracen chief, 519; raid, 530; visit to Antioch, 565
municipality: public land, 377, 389f, 439; public services, 196 n. 145; 369, 376ff, 422f, 441f, 483
Muses, cult, 132 n. 60; temple (Museum), 270, 355, 451, 622, 631; bequest of Maron, 132f, 185; Museum built by Marcus Aurelius, 229
music, church, 298, 313, 349
Musonius Rufus, C., 210

nardinum, 516 n. 58
nationalism, in Syria, 474f, 534, 546
Neale, F. A. traveler, 672, 677
Nemesis, temple, 326
Nero, emperor, 198ff
Nerva, 210f
Nestorius, teaching, 461, 575
Nicolaitan heresy, 288ff
Nicolaus of Antioch, deacon, 273, 289
Nicolaus of Damascus, 37, 164
Niebuhr, C., traveler, 607, 610f, 668f
numerals, acrophonic, 201 n. 161
nymphaeum, 176, 217, 478; sigma-shaped *nymphaeum*, later called "Ocean," 229, 270
nymphagogia, 216 n. 71; 217 n. 76
Nymphidianus, *consularis*, 452, 615
Nymphidius Lupus, 210
Nymphs, temple, 222

Octavian, *see* Augustus
Octavius Tidius Tossianus L. Iavolenus Priscus, C., governor of Syria, 211 n. 47
Odenath, 262ff
olive industry: oil shipped through Antioch, 502f; trees killed by drought, 571
Olympias, spring, 54, 182
Olympic Games, 209, 217 n. 73; 418, 424, 506, 623, 649; called Heraklian, 83 n. 132; 440; founded under Augustus and Claudius, 168f, 197; abolished as punishment, 228; restored by Commodus, 230ff, 633; construction of Plethrion, 237, 435f, 688-94; removed to Issus, 241; restored, 243ff; under Diocletian, 325ff; liturgy, 376; buildings, 404; under Theodosius I, 439ff; under Theodosius II, 455ff; under Leo I, 482f; discontinued, A.D. 520, 518; women excluded, 693; known celebrations, A.D. 181, 231; A.D. 212, 245; A.D. 296 (?), 326 n. 38; A.D. 300, 326; A.D. 332, 435; A.D. 336, 435; A.D. 384, 436; A.D. 380, 440; A.D. 384, 436, 440; A.D. 388, 440; A.D. 404, 418, 440; A.D. 507, 505, 623
Olympius, factionist, 498f, 635
Onias III, Jewish high priest, 109f
Onopnictes, *see* Parmenius

[747]

Index

Ophites, early name of Orontes, 184
oracle of Apollo, *see* Daphne
Orentes, *see* Orontes
Origen, 252, 305f
Orocassias, *see* Silpius
Orontes river, 73; navigability, 18, 52f; other names, 184
Ostrakine, locality, 454, 476, 478, 568
Otho, emperor, 202
Otter, J., traveler, 668
Οὐαλαθά, region near Antioch, 189

paganism, relation with Christianity, 379; revival under Maximinus, 333; revival under Julian, 380ff; suppression, 364, 369f, 437; survival, 483f, 491f, 555 n. 219; 558f, 563f
Pagrae, 686
palace, 640-47; built by Marcius Rex, 140f; on island, built by Diocletian, 318ff; foundations, 259; near Great Church, 346; garden, 384; entrance, 393f; statue of Maximian, 398; consistorium, 398; damaged in earthquake, 477; closed in time of Patriarch Severus, 514; shown in mosaic, 661ff. *See also* Daphne
Palladius, bishop, 507f
Pallas, spring at Daphne, 222
Palmyra, in control of Antioch, 262ff
Palût, bishop of Edessa, 304
Pamprepius of Panopolis, 490-94, 495
Pan, temple, 180, 384, 395 n. 90
Pantheon, 155, 275
papyrus, produced near Antioch, 516 n. 58
Paris, dancer, 208 n. 35
Paris, Judgment of, 84
Paris, landowner, 208 n. 35
Parmenius, stream, 17, 154, 196, 215f, 610, 618, 653-56; excavations, 29, 178, 550; flooding, 63, 550ff; Forum of Valens, 404f, 632-40; called Onopnictes, 103, 549 n. 196; 656. *See also* Iron Gate
Parsons, A., traveler, 610f, 669
Parthians, invade Syria, 150; capture Antioch, 159
Paton, A. A., traveler, 677
patriarcheion, 527, 568
Patricius the Armenian, *com. Or.*, 527 n. 107
Paul, bishop, 516f
Paul, St., in Antioch, 275ff, 288f, 296, 585; house of, 284 n. 47
Paul, Chosroes' interpreter, 542
Paul, *com. Or.* (?), 567 n. 19
Paul, *notarius*, 370, 372
Paul of Samosata, 263ff, 302, 309ff, 351
Paulianists, 351
Paulinus I, bishop, 351 n. 151; 352
Paulinus II, bishop, 396f, 399, 410-12, 415ff
Pausanias, history of Antioch, 36f; cited by Malalas, 37, 39
Pedo Vergilianus, M., 214
Peisander, history of Antioch, 43
Pelagia, courtesan, martyr, 332 n. 60
Pelagia, martyr, 332, 341f

Pelagius, 458
peliganes, 112f
Perdrizet, P., visit to Antioch, 673
Perittas, and foundation of Antioch, 35
Perry, C., traveler, 668
persecutions of Christians, under Marcus Aurelius, 300; A.D. 235-238, 306; A.D. 249-251, 308; A.D. 257-260, 310; A.D. 303, 328ff, 341; A.D. 311-313, 341
Perseus, legend, 50, 75
Persia, influence of at Antioch, 34f, 49, 213, 232f, 254, 391 n. 72; wars with, 253ff, 353ff, 371, 381, 391, 402, 505, 508, 530, 532ff, 561ff; Antioch taken by in third century, 253 n. 94; 255-61, 587-94; captives deported to, 258f, 309, 545, 572 n. 37; 592f; captives released by, 575; raid, 519; Antioch taken A.D. 540, 533-46; invasions in reign of Phocas, 571ff; Antioch taken A.D. 611, 575
Pertinax, emperor, 236
Pescennius Niger, emperor, 236ff
Peter the Fuller, bishop, 485ff, 496ff, 507
Peter, St., as "founder" of church at Antioch, 200, 277f, 281ff, 288, 296, 458, 583-86; *cathedra*, 284; grotto, 284 n. 47
Petermann, H., traveler, 672
Petronius, P., governor of Syria, 193
Pharnakes, gymnasiarch, 207
Phasganius, senator, 435, 690
Philagrius, *com. Or.*, 420
Philetus, bishop, 305
Philip I, 133ff, 148
Philip II, 136, 139ff, 641
Philip, minister of Antiochus IV, 119
Philip the Arabian, emperor, 253, 306ff
Philippe, Père, traveler, 667
Philippicus, general, 569
Philogonius, bishop, 336, 351
Philonides, philosopher, 95, 120
Philoxenus, bishop of Hierapolis, 508ff
Phineas, Jewish high priest, 193
Phlegon, on early history of Antioch, 43
Phlegrae, *see* Pagrae
Phocas, emperor, 571ff
Phocas, Ioannes, visit to Antioch (1177), 674
Phocas, *patricius*, 524
Phoenix, mosaic of, 391 n. 72
Phyrminus, stream, 453, 612, 654f
Piso, Cn., governor of Syria, 186f
pistikon, room in church, 455
plague, A.D. 251, 254; A.D. 313, 334; A.D. 542, 553ff; A.D. 560/1, 558; effect on cattle, A.D. 553, 558
Platanon, suburb, 510, 511 n. 32
Plato, on population of ideal city, 82
Plethrion, 633-40, 688-94; construction, 237; location, 404f; enlargement, 424, 435f, 441
plintheia, 207 n. 31
Pliny the Younger, 210
Plutarchus, governor of Syria (?), 348f, 359, 622, 650
Pococke, R., traveler, 607, 610, 668

Index

Index

Index

Tiberius II, emperor, 565
Tiberius, bath or village of, 182 n. 89
Tigranes of Armenia, 136ff
Timaeus, bishop, 316, 340
Timocrates, *cons. Syr.*, 424, 446
Timotheus, cited by Malalas, 37, 39
Tisamenus, *cons. Syr.*, 424, 435
Titus, emperor, 204ff
tokens, lead, 265 n. 153
topographical mosaic, 30-32, 478 n. 11; 500
n. 127; 506 n. 12
Tott, Baron von, traveler, 675
Tower of the Winds, 207, 404, 633ff, 639
Trajan, emperor, 211ff; temple, 220, 396, 398
travel, length of journeys: between Antioch
and Constantinople, 432; between Antioch
and Hierapolis, 537
travelers visiting Antioch, *see* Ainsworth, Badia
y Leblich, Barker, Barrès, Bartlett, Basil the
Merchant, Baumann, Beadle, Beaufort,
Belgiojoso, Bell, Belon, Berchem, Berggren,
Bertrandon, Biddulph, Browne, Bucking-
ham, Butler, Callier, Caraman, Carne,
Cassas, Chantre, Chesney, Corancez, Coto-
vicus, Dapper, De la Roque, Drummond,
Egmond, Eldred, Fatio, Förster, Fossey,
Fuller, Garrett, Goujon, Griffiths, Guys,
Hartmann, Heyman, Ibn Battuta, Irby, Jen-
our, Kinneir, Laborde, Lammens, Leandro,
Le Camus, Lucas, Lycklama, Mangles, Mon-
ro, Montfort, Morgan, Neale, Niebuhr,
Otter, Parsons, Paton, Perdrizet, Perry, Peter-
mann, Philippe, Phocas, Pococke, Poujoulat,
Qâit-bây, Quaresimus, Rauter, Renan, Rey,
Richter, Robinson, Russegger, Sachau, Saint-
Germain, Salle, Sanderson, Sandreczki,
Sherley, Stanhope, Tafur, Tavernier, Taylor,
Teixeira, Thomson, Tott, Troilo, Valle,
Volney, Walpole, Weber, Wellsted, Wieg-
and, Wilbrand, William, Wrag
Tretum, locality in Daphne, 545 n. 183
tribes, 115
tribute, paid by Antioch, 245 n. 51
Trinymphon, 192
Triptolemus, 50f
Tripylon, locality, 621
Trisagion, 485f, 488
Trocundus, Isaurian, 489
Troilo, F. F. von, traveler, 667
Troilus, metropolitan of Constantia, 458, 464
Tryphon, *see* Diodotus
Tyche of Antigonia, 74-76, 180
Tyche of Antioch, statue by Lysippus, 73-75;
on coins, 73 n. 88; 119 n. 3; 138, 166,
220 n. 93; 526; on column capital, 67 n.
55; shrine, 384; statue of Calliope as Tyche,
217f
Tyche of Rome, 154, 404
Typhon, early name of Orontes, 184
Typhon, legend, 53
Tyrannio, bishop of Tyre, martyr, 332
Tyrannus, bishop, 329

Ulpian, sophist, 43, 374
Ulpius Traianus, M., governor of Syria, 207 n.
30; 211
Urbicius, *see* baths
Ursicinus, *mag. mil.*, 367

Valens, emperor, 399ff, 643 n. 10; statue, 663
Valentinian I, emperor, 399ff; statues, 404,
407, 634, 663
Valentinian III, emperor, portrait, 454
Valeria, wife of Maximinus Daia, 335
Valerian, emperor, 259ff, 321, 589ff
Valle, P. della, traveler, 607, 610f, 667
Veiento, governor of Syria, 151
venationes, 234, 407ff
Verina, Augusta, 488ff, 494
Vespasian, emperor, 202ff
Vettius Rufinus, 652
Vettius Valens, 225
Victory, image of, 128, 131
Vincentius, officer under Julian, 392
Virgin Mary, *see* churches
Vitalis, bishop, 336, 412
Vitellius, emperor, 202f
Volney, C.-F., traveler, 675
Vonones, king of Armenia, 188f
Vulcacius Rufinus, *com. Or.*, 652

Wabalath, 263ff
wall, city, 612-20; Seleucid period, 71, 78, 91,
102, 178f, 612; extended by Tiberius, 176f,
182, 453, 499, 612, 614; extended by Theodosius II, 409, 452f, 499, 554, 612ff; repaired by *comes Orientis*, 437; damaged in
earthquake, A.D. 458, 477, 613; damaged in
earthquake, A.D. 528, 613; spared by Persians, A.D. 540, 545; altered under Justinian,
548, 612f; damaged in earthquake, A.D. 551
or 557, 561f, 558; towers destroyed, A.D.
588, 568
Walpole, F., traveler, 677
water supply, 20, 62, 84, 155, 212, 221, 524,
552. See also aqueducts
Weber, W., visit to Antioch, 679
weights, 201 n. 161
Wellsted, J. R., traveler, 676
Wiegand, T., visit to Antioch, 673
Wilbrand of Oldenbourg, traveler, 666
William of Rubruck, traveler, 674
Wrag, R., traveler, 666

Xenarius, architect, 70
xenon, see guest-houses
Xystos, construction, 233; location, 404, 406,
435, 633ff; burned, 499

Zabdas, Palmyrene general, 266ff
Zachariah of Tyre, *com. Or.*, 526
Zacharias, St., *see* churches
Zamaris, Jewish emir, 189
Zebennus, bishop, 305
Zemarchus, *com. Or.*, 558
Zeno, emperor, 484f, 487ff

Index

Zeno, hermit, 439 n. 155
Zenobia, 263ff, 312
Zenobius, martyr, 332
Zenobius, sophist, 374
Zenodotus, basilica of, 507, 624
Zethos, son of Antiope, 180
Zeus: protector of Seleucid dynasty, 68, 75, 217; statues, 85, 128, 130f; shown on coins, 596; temple, 128, 384, 395 n. 90; represented at Olympic Games, 231f
Zeus Bottiaios, temple, 54, 68, 72
Zeus Epikarpios, temple, 51

Zeus Kasios, 213
Zeus Keraunios, temple, 50f, 67, 75; statue, 75f, 151
Zeus, Nemean, temple, 51
Zeus Nikephoros, statue, 105
Zeus, Olympian, 100; temple in Antioch, 233, 404, 633-40; in Daphne, 326; statue (?), 595f
Zeus Philios, temple, 384; statue, 333f
Zeus Soter, temple in Daphne, 214
Zoilus, *cons. Syr.* or *com. Or.*, 453, 625

PLATES

1. PANORAMA OF ANTIOCH, LOOKING TOWARD MT. SILPIUS. View of the modern city (1934), looking east toward Mt. Silpius from across the Orontes river (1). The Frankish citadel (2) may be seen on the top of the mountain. The ancient walls and towers may be traced along the top of the mountain, and the remains of the southern wall of the city (3) may be seen descending the mountain to the right of the citadel. The road to Daphne (4) runs south, to the right of the picture. The "Iron Gate" (Bab el-Hadid) appears (5) in the cleft in the mountain. (Photograph courtesy of the Committee for the Excavation of Antioch and its Vicinity.)

2. PANORAMA OF ANTIOCH, LOOKING FROM MT. SILPIUS. View of the modern city (1934) taken from the top of Mt. Silpius, looking west. The Orontes river appears in the middle ground, flowing south, towards the left of the photograph. The modern city occupies only the southern portion of the ancient site; the remainder of the ancient city lay in the area at the right now covered with orchards and fields. The dotted line indicates the position of the ancient island, although the island may not have extended as far to the right as the dotted lines indicate. The arm of the river, which in antiquity separated the island from the mainland part of the city, was gradually filled in during the Middle Ages and is now represented by a depression in the ground; the ancient left bank of the river along the mainland, opposite the island, is shown by a dotted line.

At the left, the road to Daphne (1) follows the line of the ancient road at this point. At the left of the road is the rectangular enclosure containing the modern barracks (2). Trial excavations have indicated that the Christian cemetery lies beneath this area. The barracks area stands just outside the ancient southern wall of the city, which extended along the nearer side of the watercourse seen between the barracks and the modern city (3). The Daphne Gate (4) stood at the southern end of the main colonnaded street.

The original Seleucid settlement lay in the southern part of the site, between the main street and the river (5). In the pre-Roman period, the street that later became the main colonnaded street ran along the outer side of the wall of the Seleucid city (6). Later in the Seleucid period the island was settled, and the city also expanded up the slope of the mountain.

Near the center of the panorama the bridge across the Orontes (7) leads to the road to Seleucia Pieria, which runs south along the right bank of the river (8), and to the road to Alexandretta and Cilicia, which runs west across the plain (9). In antiquity, the plain across the river from the city served as a Campus Martius.

The gridiron plan of the ancient streets has been preserved in many places in the modern city (see Figs. 6-8, 11).

The remains of the Hippodrome may be seen on the outer side of the island (10). The palace probably lay near this. (Photograph courtesy of the Committee for the Excavation of Antioch and its Vicinity.)

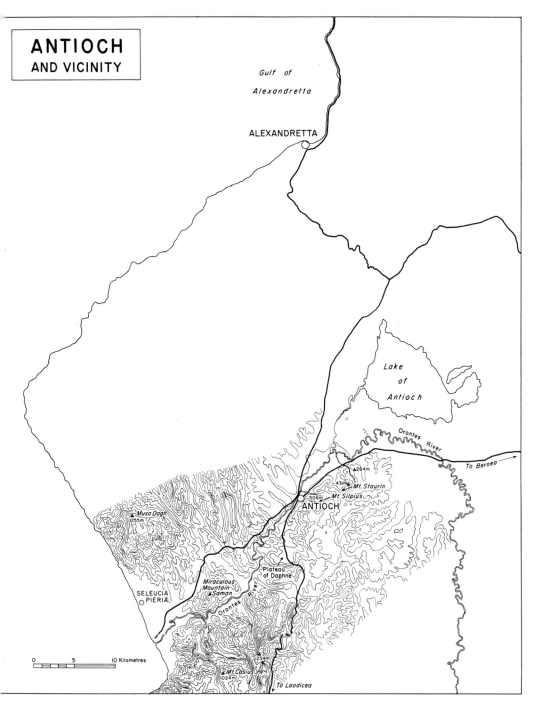

ANTIOCH
AND VICINITY

Gulf of
Alexandretta

ALEXANDRETTA

Lake
of
Antioch

Orontes River

To Beroea

▲264m

431m ▲Mt. Staurin
506m ▲ Mt. Silpius
ANTIOCH

▲Musa Dagh
1255m

Plateau
of Daphne

Miraculous
Mountain
▲Saman

Orontes River

SELEUCIA
PIERIA

254m

▲Mt. Casius
1024m

To Laodicea

0   5   10 Kilometres

3. TOPOGRAPHICAL MAP OF THE REGION OF ANTIOCH
Based on details from several maps (see Excursus 9).
Contours are at intervals of 100 meters;
heights are in meters above sea level.

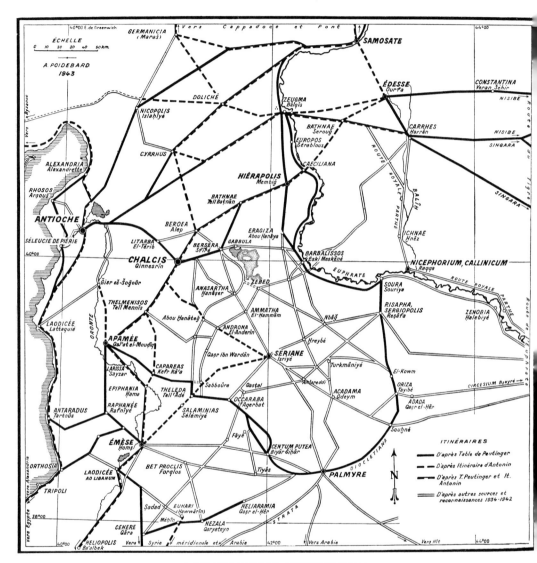

4. ROMAN ROADS IN NORTHERN SYRIA
Reproduced, by permission, from R. Mouterde and A. Poidebard,
Le limes de Chalcis (Paris, Geuthner, 1945) Map 1.

5. TOPOGRAPHICAL MAP OF ANTIOCH AND
DAPHNE. The locations of the excavations through the
season of 1934 are shown. (Reproduced, by permission,
from *Antioch-on-the-Orontes* [Princeton University Press,
1938], 2.222, pl. 8.)

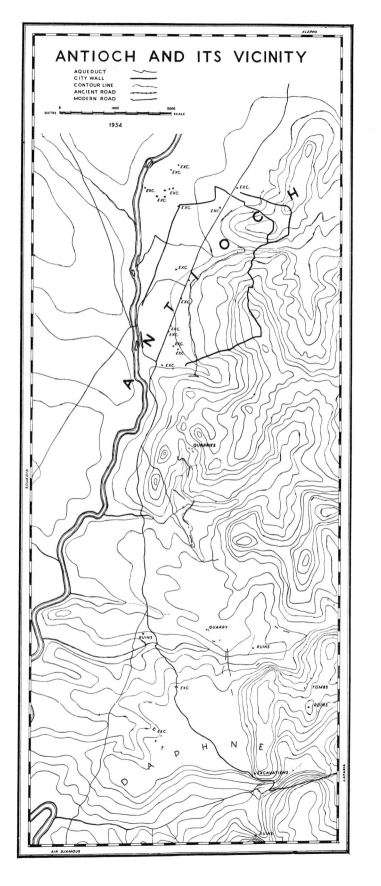

ANTIOCH AND ITS VICINITY

AQUEDUCT
CITY WALL
CONTOUR LINE
ANCIENT ROAD
MODERN ROAD

METRE ___ 1000 ___ 2000 SCALE

1934

6. MOSAIC AIR PHOTOGRAPH OF MODERN
ANTIOCH. Taken before the beginning of the
excavations (1932). The line of the ancient main
street, preserved in the modern straight street,
can be traced in the center of the photograph.
(Photograph assembled by C. K. Agle; courtesy
of the Committee for the Excavation of Antioch
and its Vicinity.)

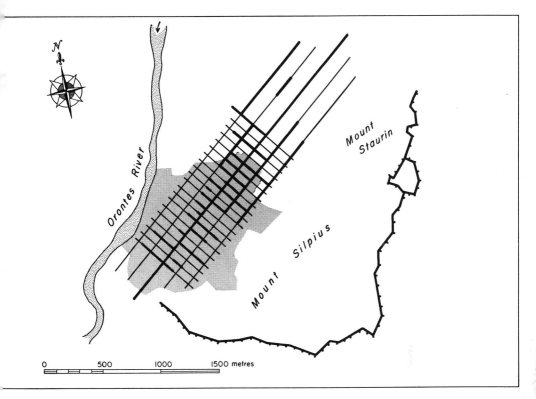

7. SKETCH MAP SHOWING THE MODERN CITY AND THE ANCIENT STREETS. The shaded area represents the modern city, with the plan of the ancient streets superimposed. The streets shown in heavy lines have been preserved in the modern plan; those shown in light lines are restored hypothetically. The long axis of the streets indicates approximately the extent of the ancient city, and the traces of the ancient walls on Mt. Silpius are indicated. (Based, by permission, on J. Sauvaget, "Le plan de Laodicée-sur-mer," *Bulletin d'études orientales* 4 [1934], fig. 11 on p. 108.)

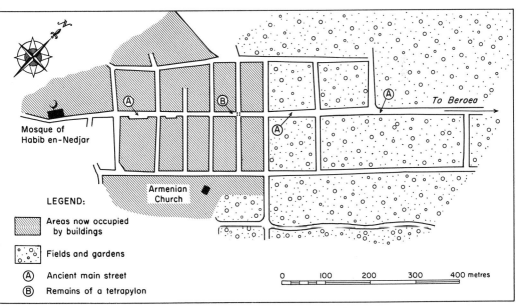

8. SURVIVAL OF THE ANCIENT STREETS IN THE MODERN CITY. Detail of the plan of modern Antioch, showing the course of the modern straight street following the line of the main colonnaded thoroughfare of antiquity, with other modern streets preserving the ancient plan. The Mosque stands at the point at which the ancient main street altered its course slightly. At this point the ancient street opened to form a plaza containing a column bearing a statue of Tiberius. (Based, by permission, on J. Weulersse, "Antioche, essai de géographie urbaine," *Bulletin d'études orientales* 4 [1934], fig. 5 on p. 47.)

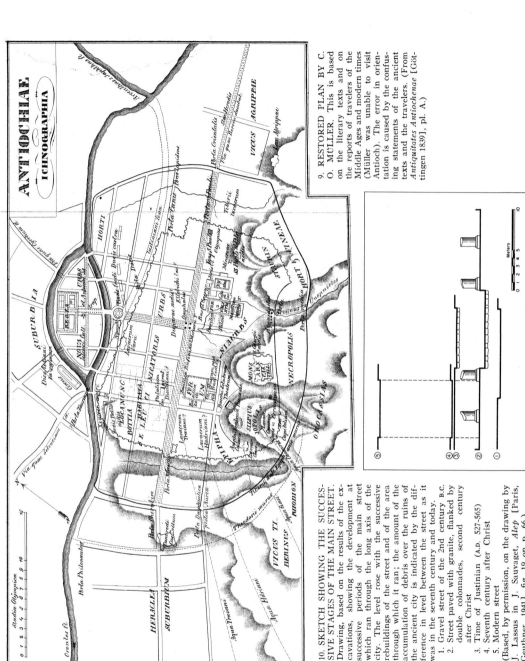

9. RESTORED PLAN BY C. O. MÜLLER. This is based on the literary texts and on the reports of travelers of the Middle Ages and modern times (Müller was unable to visit Antioch). The error in orientation is caused by the confusing statements of the ancient texts and the travelers. (From *Antiquitates Antiochenae* [Göttingen 1839], pl. A.)

10. SKETCH SHOWING THE SUCCESSIVE STAGES OF THE MAIN STREET. Drawing, based on the results of the excavations, showing the development at successive periods of the main street which ran through the long axis of the city. The level rose with the successive rebuildings of the street and of the area through which it ran; the amount of the accumulation of debris over the ruins of the ancient city is indicated by the difference in level between the street as it was in the seventh century and today.

1. Gravel street of the 2nd century B.C.
2. Street paved with granite, flanked by double colonnades, second century after Christ
3. Time of Justinian (A.D. 527-565)
4. Seventh century after Christ
5. Modern street

(Based, by permission, on the drawing by J. Lassus in J. Sauvaget, *Alep* [Paris, Geuthner, 1941], fig. 19 on p. 66.)

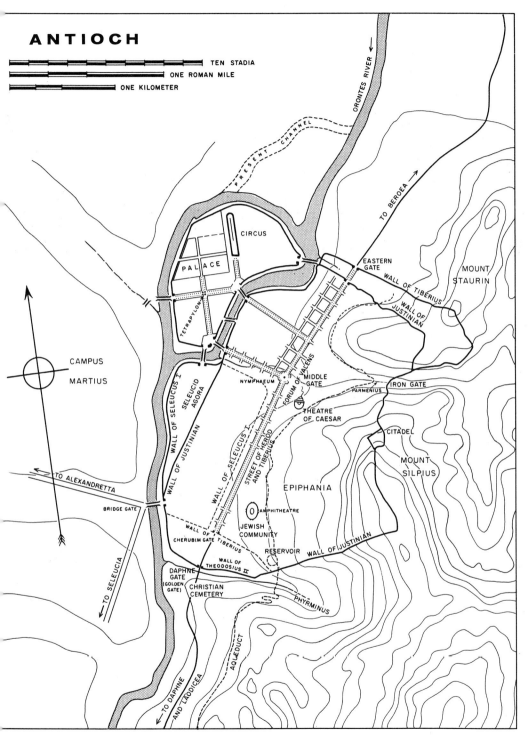

ANTIOCH

TEN STADIA
ONE ROMAN MILE
ONE KILOMETER

ORONTES RIVER

PRESENT CHANNEL

TO BEROEA

CIRCUS

PALACE

EASTERN GATE

WALL OF TIBERIUS

MOUNT STAURIN

WALL OF JUSTINIAN

TETRAPYLON

CAMPUS MARTIUS

WALL OF SELEUCIS I

SELEUCID AGORA

WALL OF JUSTINIAN

NYMPHAEUM

FORUM OF VALENS

MIDDLE GATE

PARMENIUS

IRON GATE

THEATRE OF CAESAR

CITADEL

WALL OF SELEUCIS I

STREET OF HEROD AND TIBERIUS

MOUNT SILPIUS

TO ALEXANDRETTA

EPIPHANIA

BRIDGE GATE

AMPHITHEATRE

WALL OF TIBERIUS

JEWISH COMMUNITY

RESERVOIR

WALL OF JUSTINIAN

CHERUBIM GATE

TO SELEUCIA

WALL OF THEODOSIUS II

DAPHNE GATE (GOLDEN GATE)

CHRISTIAN CEMETERY

PHYRMINUS

AQUEDUCT

TO DAPHNE AND LAODICEA

11. RESTORED PLAN OF ANTIOCH BASED ON THE LITERARY TEXTS AND THE EXCAVATIONS. This plan shows monuments and topographical features that actually exist or can be traced on the terrain, and indicates the principal buildings and topographical data known from literary texts and from the excavations. It does not include buildings of uncertain location known from literary texts. The drawing is based on the restored plan prepared by D. N. Wilber and published by C. R. Morey, *The Mosaics of Antioch* (New York and London, Longmans Green, 1938), p. 17.

12. MEDIAEVAL CITADEL ON THE TOP OF MT. SILPIUS. View of the citadel (1932), looking north. The wall running toward the citadel, at the spectator's right, follows the line of the ancient wall. (Photograph courtesy of the Committee for the Excavation of Antioch and its Vicinity.)

13. REMAINS OF AQUEDUCTS BETWEEN DAPHNE AND ANTIOCH. View from southeast (1934) near the road between Antioch and Daphne of the remains of the two Roman aqueducts that carried water to Antioch. The road is out of the picture, at the spectator's right. At the left lies the mountain range that terminates in Mt. Silpius. (Photograph courtesy of the Committee for the Excavation of Antioch and its Vicinity.)

14. VIEW FROM THE PLATEAU OF DAPHNE ACROSS THE ORONTES
The plateau (1933), looking west.
(Photograph courtesy of the Committee for the Excavation of Antioch and its Vicinity.)

15. MAP OF DAPHNE. Plan of modern Daphne, showing the road to Antioch, the plateau of Daphne, and the location of the ancient springs (indicated by stars), which are still active. The three springs that stand together (marked Beit el-Ma) are the three principal ancient springs. Literary sources indicate that the Temple of Apollo stood just below these. (Reproduced, by permission, from P. Bazantay, "Contribution à l'étude géographique de la Syrie: Un petit pays alaouite, le plateau de Daphné," *Haut-commissariat de la République française en Syrie et au Liban, Bulletin de l'enseignement* [*Publication du Service de l'instruction publique*], 11 [1933-34], 336.)

16. THE CHARONION. The rock-carved bust known as the Charonion, with a smaller figure at its right shoulder. View looking east, taken after the excavation of the area below the figures in 1932. (Photograph courtesy of the Committee for the Excavation of Antioch and its Vicinity.)

17. "IRON GATE" (BAB EL-HADID), 1934, looking east, from within the city. The masonry is of the time of Justinian. The structure, described by Procopius, was designed to control the torrent that entered the city here. The city wall, in which the Gate stood, has disappeared at this point. (Photograph courtesy of the Committee for the Excavation of Antioch and its Vicinity.)

18. ANTIOCH, SEEN FROM ACROSS THE ORONTES
RIVER, engraving by Louis François Cassas (1756-
1827), who visited Antioch between 1784 and 1787. (From
his *Voyage pittoresque de la Syrie, de la Palestine, et de
la Basse-Egypt* [sic], *avec texte par La porte-Dutheil et
Langlois* [Paris 1799], pl. 3.)

19. REMAINS OF THE WALLS AT THE SOUTHERN END OF THE CITY,
engraving by Cassas. (*Voyage pittoresque*, pl. 7.)

20. EXTERIOR OF THE GATE ON THE ROAD TO BEROEA,
engraving by Cassas. (*Voyage pittoresque*, pl. 5.)

21. INTERIOR OF THE GATE ON THE ROAD TO BEROEA,
engraving by Cassas. (*Voyage pittoresque*, pl. 6.)

11839